THE OXFORD
DICTIONARY
OF
QUOTATIONS

THE OXFORD
DICTIONARY
OF
QUOTATIONS

SECOND EDITION

UNIV.
OXONIENSIS

DOM MINA
INUS· TIO·
ILLU MEA

OXFORD UNIVERSITY PRESS

Oxford University Press, Amen House, London E.C.4

GLASGOW NEW YORK TORONTO MELBOURNE WELLINGTON
BOMBAY CALCUTTA MADRAS KARACHI CAPE TOWN IBADAN

Geoffrey Cumberlege, Publisher to the University

FIRST EDITION	1941
SECOND IMPRESSION, REVISED	1942
THIRD IMPRESSION, REVISED	1943
FOURTH IMPRESSION	1944
FIFTH IMPRESSION	1948
SIXTH IMPRESSION	1949
SEVENTH IMPRESSION, REVISED	1950
SECOND EDITION	1955

PRINTED IN THE UNITED STATES OF AMERICA BY
KINGSPORT PRESS, INC., KINGSPORT, TENNESSEE

NOTE TO THE SECOND EDITION

(1953)

DURING the twelve years that have passed since the publication of the first edition the compilers have received a great many suggestions for quotations to be added to the *Dictionary*. These have now been considered in committee, *familiarity* being the criterion as in the first edition, and some 1,300 of them now appear. About 250 quotations originally included seemed no longer familiar and have been omitted. A number of errors have been corrected during the resetting of the type, and it has been possible to give many sources more precisely. The compilers wish to thank, among many others, Dr. R. W. Chapman for innumerable suggestions; Mr. S. H. Moore, who has enlarged the French, German, and Spanish entries; and Sir Humphrey Milford, who, before his death, read the proofs.

The arrangement has also been modified; foreign quotations and those under the headings Anonymous, Ballads, Holy Bible, Nursery Rhymes, Prayer Book, Scottish Psalter, and *Punch*, which in the first edition were to be found in separate sections at the end of the main body of the book, are now incorporated in the general alphabetical scheme. Under every author the arrangement of the quotations remains alphabetical according to the title of the poem or work from which the extract is taken, but where authors have written both poetry and prose, that medium is now given first in which the bulk of the quoted work appears. It is hoped that these alterations will assist quicker reference, toward which end also we have numbered each quotation, the first quotation on each page appearing as 1. An index reference therefore reads 163:15 (page number: quotation number).

The Oxford Dictionary of Nursery Rhymes (1951), edited by Iona and Peter Opie, has made it possible to give earlier sources than hitherto for many rhymes. While the text given below (pp. 366–369) represents the most generally familiar version of each rhyme, the source quoted indicates the place of its earliest known written appearance, often in a form greatly different from that now current.

The index has been entirely remade and is somewhat fuller than that to the first edition. Greek quotations are indexed separately.

THE COMPILERS TO THE READER

(1941)

CLASSICAL quotation', said Johnson, 'is the *parole* of literary men all over the world.' Although this is no longer strictly true the habit of quoting, both in speech and writing, has steadily increased since his day, and Johnson would undoubtedly be surprised to find here eight and a half pages of his own work that have become part of the *parole* of the reading public. Small dictionaries of quotations have been published for many years—in 1799 D. E. Macdonnel brought out a *Dictionary of Quotations chiefly from Latin and French translated into English*—and during comparatively recent years several large works of American editorship have been produced. In this book the Oxford Press publishes what it is hoped will be a valuable addition to the Oxford Books of Reference already in existence.

The work remained in contemplation for some time before it first began to take shape under the general editorship of Miss Alice Mary Smyth, who worked, for purposes of selection, with a small committee formed of members of the Press itself. The existing dictionaries were taken as a foundation and the entries, pasted on separate cards, considered individually for rejection or inclusion. With these as a basis the most important authors were again dealt with either by the expert, or in committee, or by both. The Press is indebted for a great deal of work to the late Charles Fletcher, who among others made the original selections from Shakespeare, Milton, Pope, Tennyson, and Dryden: among those who dealt with single authors were Lady Charnwood and Mr. Bernard Darwin, who did the Dickens entries, Professor Dewar the Burns, Professor Ernest de Selincourt the Wordsworth: Mr. Colin Ellis did the Surtees, Sterne, and Whyte-Melville, Mr. E. Latham contributed the French quotations, and Mr. Harold Child made many valuable suggestions. A great many people, whom it is impossible to name individually, sent in one or more quotations.

During the whole work of selection a great effort was made to restrict the entries to actual current quotations and not to include phrases which the various editors or contributors believed to be quotable or wanted to be quoted: the work is primarily intended to be a dictionary of *familiar* quotations and not an anthology of every author good and bad; popularity and not merit being the password to inclusion. The selections from the Bible and Shakespeare were the most difficult because a great part of both are familiar to most people; but as concordances of both the Bible and Shakespeare are in print the quotations here included are meant to be the most well known where all is well known.

It has been found very difficult to put into precise words the standard of familiarity that has been aimed at or to imagine one man who might be asked whether or not the particular words were known to him. But it is believed that any of the quotations here printed might be found at some time in one or other of the leading articles of the daily

[vii]

and weekly papers with their wide range of matter—political, literary, descriptive, humorous, &c. So much for the very elastic standard to which the quotations conform. No one person having been imagined to whom everything included in this book would be familiar, the committee have tried to keep in mind that a number of different kinds of readers would be likely to use the book: these are the 'professionals', such as journalists, writers, public speakers, &c.; the cross-word devotee, since this form of intellectual amusement appears to have come to stay; the man who has in his mind either a few or many half-completed or unidentified quotations which he would like to complete or verify; and (since, as Emerson wrote—'By necessity, by proclivity—and by delight, we all quote') everyone who has found joy and beauty in the words of the writers and wishes to renew that pleasure by using the words again—he whom perhaps Johnson meant by 'the literary man'. The book is not intended as a substitute for the complete works nor as an excuse to anyone not to drink deep of the Pierian spring. But it *is* hoped that the lover of Dickens, for instance, may find pleasure in reading through his entries and that even his detractors will have to admit how good he is in quotation: that the man who has always regarded Milton as a heavy and dull poet may here come across some lovely line and be inclined to read *Paradise Lost*. If the book serves to start people reading the poets it will have accomplished a great deal besides being a work of reference.

It is interesting to observe that the following are the most quoted writers (arranged in the order in which they appear here): Browning, Byron, Cowper, Dickens, Johnson, Kipling, Milton, Shakespeare, Shelley, Tennyson, Wordsworth, the Bible, and the Book of Common Prayer. On the other hand, certain authors of accepted merit or favour such as Trollope, Henry James, Jane Austen, and P. G. Wodehouse have none of them as much as one page to their credit: it would seem that their charm depends on character and atmosphere and that quotability is no real criterion of either popularity or merit in a writer.

The arrangement of authors is alphabetical and not chronological. Under each author the arrangement of the extracts is alphabetical according to the title of the poem or work from which the quotation is taken. The text is, wherever possible, the acknowledged authoritative text and the source of the quotation is always given as fully as possible. Some quotations have had to be omitted because every effort to trace their source has failed—e.g. 'Home, James, and don't spare the horses'. Proverbs and phrases are not included, since these have been dealt with fully in the *Oxford Dictionary of English Proverbs*.

It is to be expected that almost every reader will be shocked by what he considers obvious omissions. Should the reader's indignation be strong enough to prompt him to write pointing these out it is to be hoped that he will give the source of all his suggestions. It is not possible to give all the quotations familiar to every reader; almost all households have favourite books and authors from whom they frequently quote: to one family Stevenson is known and quoted by heart, to another the whole of the *Beggar's Opera* is as familiar as the extracts given here. Nor must the user expect to find here every quotation given in cross-word puzzles: compilers of these often seek to be obscure rather than familiar.

Latin is no longer a normal part of the language of educated people as it was in the eighteenth century; but from that age certain classical phrases have survived to become part of contemporary speech and writing. It is these 'survivals' that have been included here together with a few of the sayings or writings of the Schoolmen and early theologians. In many places more of the context of the actual familiar phrase has been given than is strictly necessary; but this has been a practice throughout the book, and one which it was thought would add to its value and charm. The translations are usually taken from the works of the better-known translators. Some one or two of the Greek quotations may be known to the general reader in their English versions—e.g. 'The half is better than the whole' or 'Call no man happy till he dies'; but no apology is needed for the inclusion of two pages of matter most of which cannot pretend to be familiar to any but classical scholars.

The foreign quotations are not intended to satisfy the foreigner: they include such things as have become part of the speech and writings of English-speaking people either in their own language, such as 'les enfants terribles', or in an English translation, such as 'We will not go to Canossa'. As hardly any Spanish and no Russian or Swedish quotations are familiar to English readers most of these have been given only in translation.

The index occupies approximately one-third of the total bulk of the book. A separate note will be found at the beginning of the index explaining the arrangement that has been adopted. Of the Latin quotations only those phrases that are familiar to the reader have been indexed; the unfamiliar context has not. In the English translations much the same principle has been followed: where the quotation is known to the reader in its English equivalent it has been indexed; where only the Latin is familiar and a translation is merely supplied to assist the reader it is left unindexed. A great deal of care has been spent on the index and the compilers look at it with some pride, believing that unless the searcher has to say 'Iddy tiddity' for every important word in the quotation he is looking for he will be able to find it; if, like Pig-wig (in Beatrix Potter's *Pigling Bland*), he has only forgotten some of the words, the index is full enough for him to trace it.

CONTENTS

CONTENTS

INTRODUCTION

By BERNARD DARWIN

QUOTATION brings to many people one of the intensest joys of living. If they need any encouragement they have lately received it from the most distinguished quarters. Mr. Roosevelt quoted Longfellow to Mr. Churchill; Mr. Churchill passed on the quotation to us and subsequently quoted Clough on his own account. Thousands of listeners to that broadcast speech must have experienced the same series of emotions. When the Prime Minister said that there were some lines that he deemed appropriate we sat up rigid, waiting in mingled pleasure and apprehension. How agreeable it would be if we were acquainted with them and approved the choice! How flat and disappointing should they be unknown to us! A moment later we heard 'For while the tired waves, vainly breaking' and sank back in a pleasant agony of relief. We whispered the lines affectionately to ourselves, following the speaker, or even kept a word or two ahead of him in order to show our familiarity with the text. We were if possible more sure than ever that Mr. Churchill was the man for our money. He had given his ultimate proofs by flattering our vanity. He had chosen what we knew and what, if we had thought of it, we could have quoted ourselves. This innocent vanity often helps us over the hard places in life; it gives us a warm little glow against the coldness of the world and keeps us snug and happy. It certainly does its full share in the matter of quotations. We are puffed up with pride over those that we know and, a little illogically, we think that everyone else must know them too. As to those which lie outside our line of country we say, with Jowett as pictured by some anonymous genius[1] at Balliol, 'What I don't know isn't knowledge.' Yet here again we are illogical and unreasonable, for we allow ourselves to be annoyed by those who quote from outside our own small preserves. We accuse them in our hearts, as we do other people's children at a party, of 'showing off'. There are some departments of life in which we are ready to strike a bargain of mutual accommodation. The golfer is prepared to listen to his friend's story of missed putts, in which he takes no faintest interest, on the understanding that he may in turn impart his own heart-rending tale, and the bargain is honourably kept by both parties. The same rule does not apply to other people's quotations, which are not merely tedious but wound us in our tenderest spot. And the part played by vanity is perhaps worth pointing out because everybody, when he first plunges adventurously into this great work, ought in justice to the compilers to bear it in mind.

It is safe to say that there is no single reader who will not have a mild grievance or two, both as to what has been put in and what has been left out. In particular he will 'murmur a little sadly' over some favourite that is not there. I, for instance, have a

[1] Since identified as H. C. Beeching.

small grievance. William Hepworth Thompson, sometime Master of Trinity, the author of many famous and mordant sayings on which I have been brought up, is represented by but a single one. Can it be, I ask myself, that this is due to the fact that an Oxford Scholar put several of the Master's sayings into his Greek exercise book but attributed them to one Talirantes? Down, base thought! I only mention this momentary and most unworthy suspicion to show other readers the sort of thing they should avoid as they would the very devil. It is not that of which any one of us is fondest that is entitled as of right to a place. As often as he feels ever so slightly aggrieved, the reader should say to himself, if need be over and over again, that this is not a private anthology, but a collection of the quotations which the public knows best. In this fact, moreover, if properly appreciated, there ought to be much comfort. 'My head', said Charles Lamb, 'has not many mansions nor spacious',[1] and is that not true of most of us? If in this book there are a great many quotations that we do not know, there are also a great many that we do. There is that example of Clough with which I began. We may have to admit under cross-examination that we have only a rather vague acquaintance with Clough's poems, but we do know 'Say not the struggle'; and there on page so-and-so it is. Both we and the dictionary's compilers are thereupon seen to be persons of taste and discrimination.

If I may be allowed to harp a little longer on this string of vanity, it is rather amusing to fancy the varied reception given to the book by those who are quoted in it. They will consist largely of more or less illustrious shades, and we may picture them looking over one another's pale shoulders at the first copy of the dictionary to reach the asphodel. What jealousies there will be as they compare the number of pages respectively allotted to them! What indignation at finding themselves in such mixed company! Alphabetical order makes strange bedfellows. Dickens and Dibdin must get on capitally and convivially together, but what an ill-assorted couple are Mrs. Humphry Ward and the beloved Artemus of the same name! George Borrow may ask, 'Pray, who is this John Collins Bossidy?' Many readers may incidentally echo his question, and yet no man better merits his niche, for Mr. Bossidy wrote the lines ending 'And the Cabots talk only to God', which have told the whole world of the blue blood of Boston. John Hookham Frere, singing of the mailed lobster clapping his broad wings, must feel his frivolity uncomfortably hushed for a moment by his next-door neighbour, Charles Frohman, on the point of going down with the *Lusitania*. And apropos of Frere, there rises before me the portentous figure of my great-great-grandfather, Erasmus Darwin. He was thought a vastly fine poet in his day and there is a family legend that he was paid a guinea a line for his too fluent verses. And yet he is deservedly forgotten, while those who parodied him in the *Anti-Jacobin* attain an equally well-deserved immortality. He was a formidable old gentleman, with something of the Johnson touch, but not without a sense of humour, and I do not think he will be greatly hurt.

The most famous poets must be presumed to be above these petty vanities, though

[1] *Elia*, 'The Old and the New Schoolmaster'.

it would be agreeable to think of Horace contemplating his array of columns and saying, 'I told you so—Exegi monumentum'. In any case the number of columns or pages does not constitute the only test. Another is the number of words in each line by which any particular quotation can be identified, and this gives me a chance of making my compliments to the ingenuity and fullness of the index. The searcher need never despair and should he draw blank under 'swings' he is pretty sure to find what he wants under 'roundabouts'. There is a little game to be played (one of the many fascinating games which the reader can devise for himself) by counting the number of 'key words' in each line and working out the average of fame to which any passage is entitled. Even a short time so spent shows unexpected results, likely to spread envy and malice among the shades. It might be imagined that Shakespeare would be an easy winner. It has been said that every drop of the Thames is liquid history and almost every line of certain passages in Shakespeare is solid quotation. Let us fancy that his pre-eminence is challenged, that a sweepstake is suggested, and that he agrees to be judged by 'To be or not to be'. It seems a sufficiently sound choice and is found to produce fifty-five key words in thirty-three lines. All the other poets are ready to give in at once; they cannot stand against such scoring as that and Shakespeare is about to pocket the money when up sidles Mr. Alexander Pope. What, he asks, about that bitter little thing of his which he sent to Mr. Addison? And he proves to be right, for in those two and twenty lines to Atticus there are fifty-two key words. I have not played this game nearly long enough to pronounce Pope the winner. Very likely Shakespeare or someone else can produce a passage with a still higher average, but here at any rate is enough to show that it is a good game and as full of uncertainties as cricket itself.

Though the great poets may wrangle a little amongst themselves, they do not stand in need of anything that the dictionary can do for them. Very different is the case of the small ones, whose whole fame depends upon a single happy line or even a single absurd one. To them exclusion from these pages may virtually mean annihilation, while inclusion makes them only a little lower than the angels. Their anxiety therefore must be pitiful and their joy when they find themselves safe in the haven proportionately great. Sometimes that joy may be short-lived. Think of Mr. Robert Montgomery, who was highly esteemed till the ruthless Macaulay fell upon him. With trembling hand he turns the pages and finds no less than four extracts from 'The Omnipresence of the Deity'. Alas! under his own letter M the traducer is waiting for him, and by a peculiar refinement of cruelty there are quoted no less than five of Lord Macaulay's criticisms on that very poem. This is a sad case; let us take a more cheerful one and still among the M's. Thomas Osbert Mordaunt has full recognition as the author of 'Sound, sound the clarion, fill the fife', after having for years had to endure the attribution of his lines to Sir Walter Scott, who in pure innocency put them at the head of a chapter. This to be sure was known already, but whoever heard before the name of the author of 'We don't want to fight', the man who gave the word 'Jingo' to the world? We know that the Great McDermott sang it, but even he may not have known who wrote it, just as Miss Fotheringay did not know who wrote 'The Stranger'. Now G. W. Hunt comes into his kingdom and with him another who helped many thousands of soldiers on their way during the last war. Mr. George H. Powell[1] is fortunately still alive to enjoy the celebrity of 'Pack up your troubles in your old kit bag'. How many thousands, too, have sung 'Wrap me up in my tarpaulin jacket' without realizing that it was by Whyte-Melville? To him, however, recognition is of less account. His place was already secure.

Among the utterers of famous sayings some seem to have been more fortunate than others. Lord Westbury, for instance, has always had the rather brutal credit of telling some wretched little attorney to turn the matter over 'in what you are pleased to call your mind'; but how many of us knew who first spoke of a 'blazing indiscretion' or called the parks 'the lungs of London'? We may rejoice with all these who, having for years been wronged, have come into their rights at last, but there are others with whom we can only sympathize. They must be contented with the fact that their sayings or their verses have been deemed worth recording, even though their names 'shall be lost for evermoe'. The Rugby boy who called his headmaster 'a beast but a just beast' sleeps unknown, while through him Temple lives. He can only enjoy what the dynamiter Zero called 'an anonymous infernal glory'. So do the authors of many admirable limericks, though some of the best are attributed to a living divine of great distinction, who has not disclaimed such juvenile frolics. So again do those who have given us many household words from the advertisement hoardings, the beloved old jingle of 'the Pickwick, the Owl, and the Waverley pen', the alluring alliteration of 'Pink Pills for Pale People'. Let us hope that it is enough for them that they did their duty and sent the sales leaping upward.

So much for the authors without whom this book could never have been. Now for the readers and some of the happy uses to which they will put it. 'Hand me over the Burton's *Anatomy*', said Captain Shandon, 'and leave me to my abominable devices.' It was Greek and Latin quotations that he sought for his article, but fashion has changed and today it would rather be English ones. Here is one of the most obvious purposes for which the dictionary will be used. It cannot accomplish impossibilities. It will not prevent many an honest journalist from referring to 'fresh fields and pastures new' nor from describing a cup-tie as an example of 'Greek meeting Greek'. There is a fine old crusted tradition of misquoting not lightly to be broken and it might almost seem pedantry to deck these ancient friends in their true but unfamiliar colours. Misquoting may even be deemed an amiable weakness, since Dickens in one of his letters misquoted Sam Weller; but here at least is a good chance of avoiding it. There is likewise a chance of replenishing a stock grown somewhat threadbare. 'Well, you're a boss word', exclaimed Jim Pinkerton,[2] when he lighted on 'hebdomadary' in a dictionary. 'Before you're very much older I'll have you in type as long as yourself.' So the hard-pressed writer in turning over these pages may find and note many excellent phrases against future contingencies, whether to give a

---

[1] George Asaf.　　　　[2] *The Wrecker*, ch. vii.

pleasing touch of erudition or to save the trouble of thinking for himself. These, how-ever, are sordid considerations, and the mind loves rather to dwell on fireside quoting-matches between two friends, each of whom thinks his own visual memory the more accurate. There are certain writers well adapted to this form of contest and among the moderns Conan Doyle must, with all respect to Mr. Wodehouse, be assigned the first place. Sherlock Holmes scholars are both numerous and formidable; they set them-selves and demand of others a high standard. It is one very difficult to attain since there often seems no reason why any particular remark should have been made on any particular occasion. This is especially true of Dr. Watson. He was constantly saying that his practice was not very absorbing or that he had an accommodating neighbour, but when did he say which? Even the most learned might by a momentary blunder confuse 'A Case of Identity' with 'The Final Problem'. It would be dry work to plough through all the stories, even though the supreme satisfaction of being right should reward the search. Now a glance at the dictionary will dispose of an argument which would otherwise 'end only with the visit'.

It is incidentally curious and interesting to observe that two authors may each have the same power of inspiring devotion and the competitive spirit, and yet one may be, from the dictionary point of view, infinitely more quotable than the other. Hardly any prose writer, for instance, produces a more fanatical adoration than Miss Austen, and there are doubtless those who can recite pages of her with scarce a slip; but it is perhaps pages rather than sentences that they quote. Mr. Bennet provides an excep-tion, but generally speaking she is not very amenable to the treatment by scissors and paste. George Eliot, if we leave out Mrs. Poyser, a professed wit and coiner of aphor-isms, is in much poorer case. Another and a very different writer, Borrow, can rouse us to a frantic pitch of romantic excitement, but it is the whole scene and atmosphere that possess this magic and we cannot take atmosphere to pieces. These are but three examples of writers who do not seem to lend themselves to brief and familiar quota-tions. They have jewels in plenty, but these form part of a piece of elaborate ornament from which they cannot be detached without irreparable damage. The works of some other writers may by contrast be said to consist of separate stones, each of which needs no setting and can sparkle on its own account. Dickens is an obvious and unique instance. Stevenson, too, has the gift of producing characters such as Prince Florizel and Alan Breck, John Silver and Michael Finsbury, whose words can stand memorable by themselves, apart from context or atmosphere. Those who share my love for Florizel will rejoice to observe that he has had some faithful friend among the compilers. As for Michael I cannot help feeling that he has been rather scurvily used, for *The Wrong Box* is admirably suited to competition and even learned Judges of the Court of Appeal have been known, all unsuspected by their ignorant auditors, to bandy quotations from it on the Bench. Here, however, I take leave to give any indignant reader a hint. Let him not cry too loudly before he is hurt! It is true that 'nothing like a little judicious levity' is not in the main body of the dictionary, but someone awoke just in time and it is among the addenda.

To return to those friends by the fireside whom I pictured indulging in a heated quoting-match, it may be that they will presently become allies and unite to use the dictionary over a cross-word puzzle. It is hardly too much to say that the setters of these problems should not use a quotation unless it is to be found in the dictionary. A cross-word quotation should not be too simple, but it should be such that that hypothetical personage, the reasonable man, might have heard of it. The solver demands fair play, and the setter who takes a volume of verse at haphazard, finds a word that fits, and substitutes a blank for it, is not playing the game. There are solvers whose standard of sportsmanship is so high that they would as soon allow themselves to cheat at patience as have recourse to a book. We may admire though we cannot emulate this fine austere arrogance. It is the best fun to win unaided, but there is good fun too in ferreting out a quotation. It well repays the ardours of the chase. Moreover a setter of puzzles who oversteps honourable limits should be fought with his own weapons. He has palpably used books and this is an epoch of reprisals. Then let us use books too and hoist him with his own petard.

It is difficult today not to deal in warlike metaphors, but perhaps the truest and most perfect use of the dictionary is essentially peaceful. Reviewers are apt to say of a detective story that it is 'impossible to lay it down till the last page is reached'. It is rather for books of reference that such praise should be reserved. No others are comparable with them for the purposes of eternal browsing. They suggest all manner of lovely, lazy things, in particular the watching of a cricket match on a sunshiny day. We have only dropped in for half an hour, but the temptation to see just one more over before we go is irresistible. Evening draws on, the shadows of the fielders lengthen on the grass, nothing much is happening, a draw becomes every minute more inevitable, and still we cannot tear ourselves away. So it is with works of reference, even with the most arid, even with Bradshaw, whose vocabulary, as Sherlock Holmes remarked, is 'nervous and terse but limited'. Over the very next page of Bradshaw there may be hidden a Framlingham Admiral; adventure may always be in wait a little farther down the line. So, but a thousand times more so, is some exciting treasure-trove awaiting us over the next page of this dictionary. What it is we cannot guess, but it is for ever calling in our ears to turn over just one more. We have only taken down the book to look up one special passage, but it is likely enough that we shall never get so far. Long before we have reached the appropriate letter we shall have been waylaid by an earlier one, and shall have clean forgotten our original quest. Nor is this all, for, if our mood changes as we browse, it is so fatally, beautifully easy to change our pasture. We can play a game akin to that 'dabbing' cricket, so popular in private-school days, in which the batsman's destiny depended or was supposed to depend—for we were not always honest—on a pencil delivered with eyes tightly shut. We can close the book and open it again at random, sure of something that shall set us off again on a fresh and enchanting voyage of not too strenuous discovery.

Under this enchantment I have fallen deep. I have pored over the proofs so that only by a supreme effort of will could I lay them down and embark on the impertinent task of trying to write about them. I now send them back to their home with a sense of privation and loneliness. Here seems to me a great book. Then

> Deem it not all a too presumptuous folly,

this humble tribute to Oxford from another establishment over the way.

B. D.

May 1941

DICTIONARY OF QUOTATIONS

PETER ABELARD
1079–1142

1 O quanta qualia sunt illa sabbata,
  Quae semper celebrat superna curia.

  O what their joy and their glory must be,
  Those endless sabbaths the blessed ones see!
  Hymnus Paraclitensis. Trans. by Neale in *Hymnal Noted*, 1858

SIR J. E. E. DALBERG,
FIRST BARON ACTON
1834–1902

2 Power tends to corrupt and absolute power corrupts absolutely.
  Letter in Life of Mandell Creighton (1904), i. 372

CHARLES FOLLEN ADAMS
1842–1918

3 But ven he vash asleep in ped,
    So quiet as a mouse,
  I prays der Lord, 'Dake anyding,
    But leaf dot Yawcob Strauss.'
                          Yawcob Strauss

CHARLES FRANCIS ADAMS
1807–1886

4 It would be superfluous in me to point out to your lordship that this is war.
  Dispatch to Earl Russell, 5 Sept. 1863. C. F. Adams's Charles Francis Adams, p. 342

JOHN QUINCY ADAMS
1767–1848

5 Think of your forefathers! Think of your posterity!
                          Speech, 22 Dec. 1802

SAMUEL ADAMS
1722–1803

6 A Nation of shop-keepers are very seldom so disinterested.
  Oration said to have been delivered at Philadelphia, 1776, p. 10. (*See also* 360:22, 503:11)

JOSEPH ADDISON
1672–1719

7 Pray consider what a figure a man would make in the republic of letters. *Ancient Medals*, 1

8 There is nothing more requisite in business than dispatch. *Ib.* 5

9 'Twas then great Marlbro's mighty soul was prov'd.
                          The Campaign, l. 279

10 In peaceful thought the field of death survey'd,
  To fainting squadrons sent the timely aid,
  Inspir'd repuls'd Battalions to engage,
  And taught the doubtful battle where to rage.
                          Ib. l. 283

11 And, pleas'd th' Almighty's orders to perform,
  Rides in the whirl-wind, and directs the storm.
                          The Campaign, l. 291

12 And those who paint 'em truest praise 'em most.
                          Ib. l. 476

13 The dawn is overcast, the morning lowers,
  And heavily in clouds brings on the day,
  The great, the important day, big with the fate
  Of Cato and of Rome. *Cato,* I. i. 1

14 'Tis not in mortals to command success,
  But we'll do more, Sempronius; we'll deserve it.
                          Ib. ii. 43

15 Blesses his stars, and thinks it luxury. *Ib.* iv. 70

16 'Tis pride, rank pride, and haughtiness of soul;
  I think the Romans call it stoicism. *Ib.* 82

17 Were you with these, my prince, you'd soon forget
  The pale, unripened beauties of the north. *Ib.* 134

18 Am I distinguished from you but by toils,
  Superior toils, and heavier weight of cares?
  Painful pre-eminence! *Ib.* III. v. 23

19 The woman that deliberates is lost. *Ib.* IV. i. 31

20 Curse on his virtues! they've undone his country.
  Such popular humanity is treason. *Ib.* iv. 35

21 Content thyself to be obscurely good.
  When vice prevails, and impious men bear sway,
  The post of honour is a private station. *Ib.* 139

22 It must be so—Plato, thou reason'st well!—
  Else whence this pleasing hope, this fond desire,
  This longing after immortality?
  Or whence this secret dread, and inward horror,
  Of falling into naught? Why shrinks the soul
  Back on herself, and startles at destruction?
  'Tis the divinity that stirs within us;
  'Tis heaven itself, that points out an hereafter,
  And intimates eternity to man.
  Eternity! thou pleasing, dreadful thought! *Ib.* v. i. 1

23 If there's a power above us,
  (And that there is all nature cries aloud
  Through all her works) he must delight in virtue.
                          Ib. 15

24 But thou shalt flourish in immortal youth,
  Unhurt amidst the wars of elements,
  The wrecks of matter, and the crash of worlds.
                          Ib. 28

25 From hence, let fierce contending nations know
  What dire effects from civil discord flow.
                          Ib. iv. 111

26 Music, the greatest good that mortals know,
    And all of heaven we have below.
                          Song for St. Cecilia's Day, st. 3

27 Round-heads and Wooden-shoes are standing jokes.
                          Prologue to The Drummer

28 I should think my self a very bad woman, if I had done what I do, for a farthing less.
                          The Drummer, Act I

1 He more had pleas'd us, had he pleas'd us less.
   English Poets (referring to Cowley)

2 For wheresoe'er I turn my ravished eyes,
   Gay gilded scenes and shining prospects rise,
   Poetic fields encompass me around,
   And still I seem to tread on classic ground.
   Letter from Italy

3 A painted meadow, or a purling stream. *Ib.*

4 A reader seldom peruses a book with pleasure until
   he knows whether the writer of it be a black man
   or a fair man, of a mild or choleric disposition,
   married or a bachelor. *The Spectator*, No. 1

5 Thus I live in the world rather as a spectator of mankind than as one of the species. *Ib.*

6 When I am in a serious humour, I very often walk
   by myself in Westminster Abbey. *Ib.* No. 26

7 A perfect tragedy is the noblest production of human
   nature. *Ib.* No. 39

8 In all thy humours, whether grave or mellow,
   Thou'rt such a touchy, testy, pleasant fellow;
   Hast so much wit, and mirth, and spleen about thee,
   There is no living with thee, nor without thee.
   Ib. No. 68

9 There is no place in the town which I so much love to
   frequent as the Royal Exchange. *Ib.* No. 69

10 The infusion of a China plant sweetened with the pith
   of an Indian cane. *Ib.*

11 Sir Roger . . . will suffer nobody to sleep in it [the
   church] besides himself; . . . if he sees anybody else
   nodding, either wakes them himself, or sends his
   servants to them. *Ib.* No. 112

12 Sir Roger told them, with the air of a man who would
   not give his judgment rashly, that much might be
   said on both sides. *Ib.* No. 122

13 My friends Sir Roger de Coverley and Sir Andrew
   Freeport are of different principles, the first of them
   inclined to the *landed* and the other to the *monied*
   interest. *Ib.* No. 126

14 It was a saying of an ancient philosopher, which I
   find some of our writers have ascribed to Queen
   Elizabeth, who perhaps might have taken occasion
   to repeat it, that a good face is a letter of recom-
   mendation. *Ib.* No. 221

15 I have often thought, says Sir Roger, it happens very
   well that Christmas should fall out in the Middle
   of Winter. *Ib.* No. 269

16 . . . launched out into the praise of the late act of
   parliament for securing the Church of England,
   and told me with great satisfaction, that he believed
   it already began to take effect; for that a rigid dis-
   senter, who chanced to dine at his house on Christmas day, had been observed to eat very plentifully
   of his plum-porridge. *Ib.*

17 Dr. Busby, a great man! he whipped my grandfather;
   a very great man! I should have gone to him myself,
   if I had not been a blockhead; a very great man!
   Ib. No. 329

18 These widows, Sir, are the most perverse creatures
   in the world. *Ib.* No. 335

19 The Knight in the triumph of his heart made
   several reflections on the greatness of the *British
   Nation*; as, that one *Englishman* could beat three

Frenchmen; that we cou'd never be in danger of
Popery so long as we took care of our fleet; that
the *Thames* was the noblest river in *Europe*; that
London Bridge was a greater piece of work than any
of the Seven Wonders of the World; with many
other honest prejudices which naturally cleave to
the heart of a true *Englishman*.
   The Spectator, No. 383

20 This Mr. Dryden calls 'the fairy way of writing'.
   Ib. No. 419

21 The Lord my Pasture shall prepare,
   And feed me with a Shepherd's Care;
   His Presence shall my wants supply,
   And guard me with a watchful Eye.
   Ib. No. 441

22 When all thy Mercies, O my God,
   My rising Soul surveys;
   Transported with the View, I'm lost
   In Wonder, Love, and Praise.
   Ib. No. 453

23 Through all Eternity to Thee
   A joyful Song I'll raise,
   For oh! Eternity's too short
   To utter all thy Praise. *Ib.*

24 We have in England a particular bashfulness in every
   thing that regards religion. *Ib.* No. 458

25 The spacious firmament on high,
   With all the blue ethereal sky.
   Ib. No. 465. *Ode*

26 Soon as the evening shades prevail,
   The moon takes up the wondrous tale,
   And nightly to the listening Earth
   Repeats the story of her birth. *Ib.*

27 Whilst all the stars that round her burn,
   And all the planets, in their turn,
   Confirm the tidings as they roll,
   And spread the truth from pole to pole. *Ib.*

28 In Reason's ear they all rejoice,
   And utter forth a glorious Voice,
   For ever singing as they shine,
   'The Hand that made us is Divine.' *Ib.*

29 A woman seldom asks advice before she has bought
   her wedding clothes. *Ib.* No. 475

30 Our disputants put me in mind of the skuttle fish,
   that when he is unable to extricate himself, blackens
   all the water about him, till he becomes invisible.
   Ib. No. 476

31 I value my garden more for being full of blackbirds
   than of cherries, and very frankly give them fruit
   for their songs. *Ib.* No. 477

32 If we may believe our logicians, man is distinguished
   from all other creatures by the faculty of laughter.
   Ib. No. 494

33 'We are always doing', says he, 'something for Posterity, but I would fain see Posterity do something
   for us.' *Ib.* No. 583

34 I remember when our whole island was shaken with
   an earthquake some years ago, there was an impudent mountebank who sold pills which (as he told
   the country people) were very good against an
   earthquake. *The Tatler*, No. 240

35 I have but ninepence in ready money, but I can draw
   for a thousand pounds. [On his deficiency in conversation.] Boswell's *Life of Johnson*, 7 May 1773

1 See in what peace a christian can die.
Dying words to his stepson Lord Warwick.
Young's *Conjectures on Original Composition*, 1759

2 Should the whole frame of nature round him break,
In ruin and confusion hurled,
He, unconcerned, would hear the mighty crack,
And stand secure amidst a falling world.
Translation of Horace, Odes, bk. III. iii

THOMAS ADY
c. 1655

3 Matthew, Mark, Luke, and John,
The Bed be blest that I lie on.
Four angels to my bed,
Four angels round my head,
One to watch, and one to pray,
And two to bear my soul away.
Quoted in part by Ady in *A Candle in the Dark*
(1656)

AESCHYLUS
525–456 B.C.

ποντίων τε κυμάτων ἀνήριθμον γέλασμα.

4 Multitudinous laughter of the waves of ocean.
Prometheus Bound, 88. Trans. by Herbert Weir
Smith (Loeb edition).

AGATHON
447 ?–401 B.C.

5 Even God cannot change the past.
Attributed by Aristotle *in* The Nicomachean
Ethics, vi.

CHARLES HAMILTON AÏDÉ
1830–1906

6 I sit beside my lonely fire,
And pray for wisdom yet—
For calmness to remember
Or courage to forget.   *Remember or Forget*

ALFRED AINGER
1837–1904

7 No flowers, by request.
At a dinner given to the contributors to the Dict.
*of Nat. Biog., 8 July 1897: his summary of their
editor's instructions*

ARTHUR CAMPBELL AINGER
1841–1919

8 God is working His purpose out as year succeeds to
year,
God is working His purpose out and the time is drawing near;
Nearer and nearer draws the time, the time that shall
surely be,
When the earth shall be fill'd with the glory of God
as the waters cover the sea.
God is Working His Purpose Out (1894)

MARK AKENSIDE
1721–1770

9 Such and so various are the tastes of men.
Pleasures of Imagination, bk. iii, l. 567

ALCUIN
735–804

10 Vox populi, vox dei.
The voice of the people is the voice of God.
Letter to Charlemagne, A.D. 800. *Works, Epis.* **127**

HENRY ALDRICH
1648–1710

11 If all be true that I do think,
There are five reasons we should drink;
Good wine—a friend—or being dry—
Or lest we should be by and by—
Or any other reason why.   *Reasons for Drinking*

THOMAS BAILEY ALDRICH
1836–1907

12 The fair, frail palaces,
The fading alps and archipelagoes,
And great cloud-continents of sunset-seas.
Sonnet: Miracles

ALEXANDER
356–323 B.C.

13 εἰ μὴ Ἀλέξανδρος ἤμην, Διογένης ἂν ἤμην.
If I were not Alexander, I would be Diogenes.
Plutarch, *Life of Alexander*, xiv. 3

CECIL FRANCES ALEXANDER
1818–1895

14 All things bright and beautiful,
All creatures great and small,
All things wise and wonderful,
The Lord God made them all.
All Things Bright and Beautiful (1848)

15 The rich man in his castle,
The poor man at his gate,
God made them, high or lowly,
And order'd their estate.   *Ib.*

16 By Nebo's lonely mountain,
On this side Jordan's wave,
In a vale in the land of Moab
There lies a lonely grave. *The Burial of Moses* (1854)

17 Do no sinful action,
Speak no angry word;
Ye belong to Jesus,
Children of the Lord. *Do No Sinful Action* (1848)

18 There's a wicked spirit
Watching round you still,
And he tries to tempt you
To all harm and ill.

But ye must not hear him,
Though 'tis hard for you
To resist the evil,
And the good to do.   *Ib.*

19 Jesus calls us; o'er the tumult
Of our life's wild restless sea. *Jesus Calls Us* (1852)

20 Once in royal David's city
Stood a lowly cattle shed,
Where a Mother laid her Baby
In a manger for His bed:
Mary was that Mother mild.
Jesus Christ her little Child.
Once in Royal David's City (1848)

1 With the poor, and mean, and lowly,
Lived on earth our Saviour Holy.
Once in Royal David's City (1848)

2 Christian children all must be
Mild, obedient, good as He.   *Ib.*

3 For He is our childhood's pattern,
Day by day like us He grew,
He was little, weak, and helpless,
Tears and smiles like us He knew;
And He feeleth for our sadness,
And He shareth in our gladness.   *Ib.*

4 There is a green hill far away,
Without a city wall,
Where the dear Lord was crucified,
Who died to save us all.
There is a Green Hill (1848)

5 He only could unlock the gate
Of Heav'n, and let us in.   *Ib.*

6 The roseate hues of early dawn,
The brightness of the day,
The crimson of the sunset sky,
How fast they fade away!
The Roseate Hues of Early Dawn (1852)

7 We are but little children weak
Nor born in any high estate.
We are but Little Children Weak (1850)

8 There's not a child so small and weak
But has his little cross to take,
His little work of love and praise
That he may do for Jesus' sake.   *Ib.*

SIR WILLIAM ALEXANDER, EARL OF STIRLING
1567?–1640

9 The weaker sex, to piety more prone.
Doomsday, Hour v, lv

10 Yet with great toil all that I can attain
By long experience, and in learned schools,
Is for to know my knowledge is but vain,
And those that think them wise, are greatest fools.
The Tragedy of Crœsus, II. i

HENRY ALFORD
1810–1871

11 Come, ye thankful people, come,
Raise the song of Harvest-home:
All is safely gathered in,
Ere the winter storms begin.
Come, Ye Thankful People, Come (1844)

12 Ten thousand times ten thousand,
In sparkling raiment bright.
Ten Thousand Times Ten Thousand (1867)

CYRIL ARGENTINE ALINGTON
1872–

13 As swift to scent the sophist as to praise
The honest worker or the well turned phrase.
Bishop Henson. The Times, 4 Oct. 1947

RICHARD ALISON
fl. c. 1606

14 There cherries grow, that none can buy
Till cherry ripe themselves do cry.
An Hour's Recreation in Music

ABBÉ D'ALLAINVAL
1700–1753

15 L'embarras des richesses.
The more alternatives, the more difficult the choice.
Title of Comedy, 1726

ELIZABETH AKERS ALLEN
1832–1911

16 Backward, turn backward, O Time, in your flight,
Make me a child again, just for to-night!
Rock Me To Sleep, Mother

GRANT ALLEN
1848–1899

17 The Woman who Did.   *Title of Novel, 1895*

WILLIAM ALLINGHAM
1828–1889

18 Up the airy mountain,
Down the rushy glen,
We daren't go a-hunting,
For fear of little men.   *The Fairies*

19 Four ducks on a pond,
A grass-bank beyond,
A blue sky of spring,
White clouds on the wing:
What a little thing
To remember for years—
To remember with tears!   *A Memory*

ST. AMBROSE
c. 340–397

20 Si fueris Romae, Romano vivito more;
Si fueris alibi, vivito sicut ibi.
If you are at Rome live in the Roman style; if you
are elsewhere live as they live elsewhere.
Quoted by Jeremy Taylor, Ductor Dubitantium,
I. i. 5

FISHER AMES
1758–1808

21 A monarchy is a merchantman which sails well, but
will sometimes strike on a rock, and go to the bottom; a republic is a raft which will never sink, but
then your feet are always in the water.
Speech in the House of Representatives, 1795

MAXWELL ANDERSON
1888–

22 What Price Glory.   *Title of Play, 1924*

BISHOP LANCELOT ANDREWES
1555–1626

23 The nearer the Church the further from God.
Sermon on the Nativity before James I (1622)

NORMAN ANGELL
1874–

24 The Great Illusion.
Title of book on the futility of war

ARCHIBALD DOUGLAS, FIFTH EARL OF ANGUS

1449?–1514

1 **I** shall bell the cat.
Attr. by J. Man in Buchanan's Rerum Scoticarum *Historia, 1762, bk. xii, § 41, note*

ANONYMOUS

English

2 A beast, but a just beast.
Of Dr. Temple, Headmaster of Rugby, 1857–69

3 Absence makes the heart grow fonder.
Davison, Poetical Rhapsody, *1602 (see 36:28)*

4 Adam
Had 'em.
On the Antiquity of Microbes. (Said to be the shortest poem.)

5 All present and correct.
King's Regulations (Army). Report of the Orderly Sergeant to the Officer of the Day

6 An abomination unto the Lord, but a very present help in time of trouble. [A lie.]
(Cf. Proverbs xii. 22; *the second half is from* Psalms *xlvi. 1)*

7 An Austrian army, awfully arrayed,
Boldly by battery besieged Belgrade;
Cossack commanders cannonading come,
Dealing destruction's devastating doom.
Siege of Belgrade. The Trifler, 1817

8 And when with envy Time, transported,
Shall think to rob us of our joys;
You'll in your girls again be courted,
And I'll go wooing in my boys.
Winifreda. D. Lewis, Miscellaneous Poems, *1726*

9 An old Soldier of the Queen's,
And the Queen's old Soldier.
Merry Drollery, 1661–9. An Old Soldier of The Queen's. Oxford Book of 17th Cent. Verse

10 An old song made by an aged old pate,
Of an old worshipful gentleman who had a great estate.
The Old Courtier

11 A place within the meaning of the Act.
The Betting Act

12 Appeal from Philip drunk to Philip sober.
See Valerius Maximus, Facta et Dicta Memorabilia *(c. A.D. 15), bk. vi, ch. ii*

13 Are we downhearted? No!
Expression much used by British soldiers in War of 1914–18, probably based on remark of Joseph Chamberlain, q.v.

14 As I sat on a sunny bank,
On Christmas Day in the morning,
I spied three ships come sailing by.
Carol: As I Sat on a Sunny Bank. Oxford Book of Carols

15 As Joseph was a-walking,
He heard an angel sing:
'This night shall be born
Our heavenly king.'
As Joseph was a-walking. Oxford Book of Carols

16 He neither shall be clothed
In purple nor in pall,
But all in fair linen.
As were babies all.

He neither shall be rock'd
In silver nor in gold,
But in a wooden cradle
That rocks on the mould. *As Joseph was a-walking*

17 A swarm of bees in May
Is worth a load of hay;
A swarm of bees in June
Is worth a silver spoon;
A swarm of bees in July
Is not worth a fly. *Old Rhyme*

18 A willing foe and sea room.
Naval toast in the time of Nelson. Beckett, A Few Naval Customs, Expressions, Traditions, and Superstitions (1931)

19 Begone, dull care! I prithee begone from me!
Begone, dull care, you and I shall never agree.
Begone Dull Care

20 Be happy while y'er leevin,
For y'er a lang time deid.
Scottish Motto for a house. Notes and Queries, 7 Dec. 1901, p. 469

21 Born 1820, still going strong.
Advertisement for Johnnie Walker Whisky

22 Bovril prevents that sinking feeling. *Advertisement*

23 Christmas is coming, the geese are getting fat,
Please to put a penny in the old man's hat;
If you haven't got a penny, a ha'penny will do,
If you haven't got a ha'penny, God bless you!
Beggar's Rhyme

24 Come, landlord, fill the flowing bowl
Until it doth run over. . . .
For to-night we'll merry be,
To-morrow we'll be sober.
Come, Landlord, Fill the Flowing Bowl. Oxford Song Book

25 Come lasses and lads, get leave of your dads,
And away to the Maypole hie,
For every he has got him a she,
And the fiddler's standing by.
For Willie shall dance with Jane,
And Johnny has got his Joan,
To trip it, trip it, trip it, trip it, trip it up and down.
Come Lasses and Lads (c. 1670). Oxford Song Book

26 Conduct . . . to the prejudice of good order and military discipline. *Army Act, § 40*

27 Dear Sir, Your astonishment's odd:
I am always about in the Quad.
And that's why the tree
Will continue to be,
Since observed by Yours faithfully, God.
Reply to limerick on Idealism, 'There was once a man who said "God . . ."' (see 305:10)

28 Defence, not defiance.
Motto of the Volunteers Movement, in 1859

29 Dollar Diplomacy.
Term applied to Secretary Knox's activities in securing opportunities for the investment of American capital abroad, particularly in Latin America and China. See Harper's Weekly, 23 Apr. 1910, p. 8

1 Dr. Williams' pink pills for pale people.
Advertisement

2 Early one morning, just as the sun was rising,
I heard a maid sing in the valley below:
'Oh, don't deceive me; Oh, never leave me!
How could you use a poor maiden so?'
Early One Morning. Oxford Song Book

3 Earned a precarious living by taking in one another's
washing.
In *The Commonweal, 6 Aug. 1887, William
Morris suggested that this was an invention of
Mark Twain's*

4 Esau selleth his birthright for a mess of potage.
Genevan Bible: chapter heading to Genesis, ch. 25

5 An intelligent Russian once remarked to us, 'Every
country has its own constitution; ours is absolutism
moderated by assassination.'
Georg Herbert, Count Münster, *Political
Sketches of the State of Europe, 1814–1867*, ed.
1868, p. 19

6 Every minute dies a man,
And one and one-sixteenth is born.
*Parody by a Statistician of Tennyson's Vision of
Sin, pt. iv, st. 9. (See 541:13)*

7 Father of his Country [George Washington].
Francis Bailey, *Nord Americanische Kalender,*
1779

8 Frankie and Johnny were lovers, my gawd, how they
could love,
Swore to be true to each other, true as the stars above;
He was her man, but he done her wrong.
Frankie and Johnny, st. 1

9 From ghoulies and ghosties and long-leggety beasties
And things that go bump in the night,
Good Lord, deliver us! *Scottish*

10 God be in my head,
And in my understanding;

God be in my eyes,
And in my looking;

God be in my mouth,
And in my speaking;

God be in my heart,
And in my thinking;

God be at my end,
And at my departing. *Sarum Missal*

11 God rest you merry, gentlemen,
Let nothing you dismay.
*Carol: God Rest You Merry. Oxford Book of
Carols*

12 O tidings of comfort and joy. *Ib.*

13 God save great *George* our King.
Harmonia Anglicana. The Gentleman's Magazine,
Oct. 1745. *But see 125:15, 250:14, and Corri-
genda, p. 587*

14 God's own country.
*Sir St. V. Troubridge (Notes and Queries, 26 Sept.
1942) quotes from Sir W. Craigie's Dictionary of
American English:*
'A special part of the U.S. or the country as a
whole, viewed nostalgically as almost a paradise.'
*The earliest example without 'own' given is 1865, the
earliest with 'own' is 1921*

15 Good-morning! Have you used Pears' Soap?
Advertisement

16 Great Chatham with his sabre drawn
Stood waiting for Sir Richard Strachan;
Sir Richard, longing to be at 'em,
Stood waiting for the Earl of Chatham.
At Walcheren, 1809

17 Great God, what do I see and hear?
The end of things created.
Great God, What do I see. Collyer's *Hymns:
Partly Collected and Partly Original, 1812*

18 Greensleeves was all my joy,
Greensleeves was my delight,
Greensleeves was my heart of gold,
And who but Lady Greensleeves?
*A new Courtly Sonnet of the Lady Greensleeves,
to the new tune of 'Greensleeves'. From A Hand-
ful of Pleasant Delites (1584)*

19 Ha-ha-ha, you and me,
Little brown jug, don't I love thee.
The Little Brown Jug. Oxford Song Book

20 Here lies Fred,
Who was alive and is dead:
Had it been his father,
I had much rather;
Had it been his brother,
Still better than another;
Had it been his sister,
No one would have missed her;
Had it been the whole generation,
Still better for the nation:
But since 'tis only Fred,
Who was alive and is dead,—
There's no more to be said.
Horace Walpole, *Memoirs of George II (1847),*
vol. i, p. 436

21 Here's a health to all those that we love,
Here's a health to all those that love us,
Here's a health to all those that love them that love
those
That love them that love those that love us.
Old Toast

22 Here we come a-wassailing. *Old Song*

23 Here we come gathering nuts in May
Nuts in May,
On a cold and frosty morning. *Children's Song*

24 He talked shop like a tenth muse.
Of Gladstone's Budget speeches. G. W. E.
Russell's *Collections and Recollections*, ch. 12

25 He that fights and runs away
May live to fight another day.
*Musarum Deliciae, collected by Sir John Mennes
and Dr. James Smith, 1656*

26 He was a wight of high renown,
And thou's but of low degree.
It's pride that puts this country down:
Man, put thy old cloak about thee!
The Old Cloak. Oxford Book of 16th Cent. Verse

27 He won't be happy till he gets it.
Advertisement for Pears' Soap

28 Hierusalem, my happy home,
When shall I come to thee?
When shall my sorrows have an end,
Thy joys when shall I see?
Hierusalem. See *Songs of Praise Discussed*

1 Homocea touches the spot.   *Advertisement*

2 'How different, how very different from the home life
of our own dear Queen!'
                Irvin S. Cobb, *A Laugh a Day*
*As Cleopatra, Sarah Bernhardt stabbed the slave who
bore to her the tidings of Mark Antony's defeat at
Actium; she stormed, raved, wrecked some of the
scenery in her frenzy and finally, as the curtain
fell, dropped in a shuddering, convulsive heap.*
    *As the applause died, a middle-aged British
matron was heard to say to her neighbour: 'How
different, how very different from the home life of
our own dear Queen!' (Victoria).*

3 I feel no pain dear mother now
But oh, I am so dry!
O take me to a brewery
And leave me there to die.
            C. Fox-Smith's *Book of Shanties*, 1927

4 If he only knew a little of law, he would know a little
of everything.
Of Lord Brougham. Emerson, *Quotation and
Originality*, 1877

5 If you your lips would keep from slips
Of five things have a care:
To whom you speak, of whom you speak,
And how, and when, and where.
        Quoted in Augustus Hare, *Story of My Life*

6 I know two things about the horse,
And one of them is rather coarse.
                    The Week-End Book

7 I'm arm'd with more than complete steel—The justice
of my quarrel.
        Lust's Dominion (1657), IV. iii (*See 331:9*)

8 In Dublin s fair city, where girls are so pretty,
I first set my eyes on sweet Molly Malone,
As she wheeled her wheelbarrow through streets
broad and narrow,
Crying, Cockles and mussels! alive, alive, oh!
        Cockles and Mussels. Oxford Song Book

9 In good King Charles's golden days,
When loyalty no harm meant;
A furious High-Churchman I was,
And so I gain'd preferment.
Unto my flock I daily preach'd,
Kings are by God appointed,
And damned are those who dare resist,
Or touch the Lord's Anointed.
And this is law, I will maintain,
Unto my dying day, Sir,
That whatsoever King shall reign,
I will be the Vicar of Bray, Sir!
    The Vicar of Bray. Brit. Musical Miscellany
    (1734), i

10 The Church of Rome I found would suit
Full well my constitution.   *Ib.*

11 I turned the cat in pan again,
And swore to him allegiance.   *Ib.*

12 When George in pudding time came o'er,
And moderate men look'd big, Sir.   *Ib.*

13   I saw my lady weep,
And Sorrow proud to be exalted so
In those fair eyes where all perfections keep.
    Her face was full of woe;

But such a woe, believe me, as wins more hearts,
Than Mirth can do with her enticing parts.
        Songs set by John Dowland, iii. Oxford Book of
        16th Cent. Verse

14 I saw three ships a-sailing there,
    —A-sailing there, a-sailing there,
Jesu, Mary and Joseph they bare
    On Christ's Sunday at morn.
Joseph did whistle and Mary did sing,
    —Mary did sing, Mary did sing,
And all the bells on earth did ring
    For joy Our Lord was born.
O they sail'd in to Bethlehem!
    —To Bethlehem, to Bethlehem;
Saint Michael was the steresman,
    Saint John sate in the horn.
        I saw three ships. Oxford Book of Carols

15 I sing of a maiden
    That is makeless;
King of all kings
    To her son she ches.
        Carol: I Sing of a Maiden (15th cent.). *Oxford*
        Book of Carols

16 He came all so still
    Where His mother was,
As dew in April
    That falleth on the grass.   *Ib.*

17 Mother and maiden
    Was never none but she!
Well may such a lady
    God's mother be.   *Ib.*

18 I slept and dreamed that life was beauty;
I woke and found that life was duty.
        Duty, c. 1850. *But see* Corrigenda, *p.* 587

19 Is that Mr. Reilly, can anyone tell?
Is that Mr. Reilly that owns the hotel?
Well, if that's Mr. Reilly, they speak of so highly,
Upon me soul, Reilly, you're doin' quite well.
                Is that Mr. Reilly? (1882). *Chorus*

20 The children of Lord Lytton organized a charade.
The scene displayed a Crusader knight returning
from the wars. At his gate he was welcomed by his
wife to whom he recounted his triumphs and the
number of heathen he had slain. His wife, pointing
to a row of dolls of various sizes, replied with pride,
'And I too, my lord, have not been idle'.
        G. W. E. Russell's *Collections and Recollections*,
        ch. 31

21 It's a long time between drinks.
        *The Governor of South Carolina required the
        return of a fugitive slave. The Governor of North
        Carolina hesitated because of powerful friends of the
        fugitive. He gave a banquet to his official brother.
        The Governor of South Carolina in a speech de-
        manded the return of the slave and ended with 'What
        do you say?' The Governor of North Carolina
        replied as above*

22 It is good to be merry and wise,
It is good to be honest and true,
It is best to be off with the old love,
Before you are on with the new.
        Songs of England and Scotland. London, 1835,
        vol. ii, p. 73

23 It's love, it's love that makes the world go round.
        Chansons Nationales et Populaires de France,
        vol. ii, p. 180

1 I wish I were single again.
> *I Married a Wife* (19th century)

2 Jesus Christ is risen to-day,
Our triumphant holy day;
Who did once upon the cross
Suffer to redeem our loss.
    Hallelujah!
> *Jesus Christ is Risen To-day. From a Latin Hymn of the 15th cent. Translator unknown*

3 King Charles the First walked and talked
Half an hour after his head was cut off.
> *See* Peter Puzzlewell, *A Choice Collection of Riddles, Charades and Rebusses* (1792)

4 Know all men by these presents, that I John Griffin make the aforementioned my last will and testament.
> Cruise, *Digest*, 1752

5 Like a fine old English gentleman,
All of the olden time.
> *The Fine Old English Gentleman. Oxford Song Book*

6 The newly-elected mayor who . . . said that during his year of office he should lay aside all his political prepossessions and be, 'like Caesar's wife, all things to all men'.
> G. W. E. Russell's *Collections and Recollections*, ch. 29

7 Lizzie Borden took an axe
And gave her mother forty whacks;
When she saw what she had done
She gave her father forty-one!
> *After an American murder trial of the 1890's in which Miss Borden was acquitted of murdering her father and stepmother*

8 Love me little, love me long,
Is the burden of my song.
> *Love me Little, Love me Long* (1569–70)

9 March winds and April showers
Bringeth vo'th May flowers.
> *West Somerset Word-Book*, ed. Frederick Thomas Elworthy (1886), March

10 Miss Buss and Miss Beale
Cupid's darts do not feel.
How different from us,
Miss Beale and Miss Buss.
> *Of the Headmistress of the North London Collegiate School and the Principal of the Ladies' College, Cheltenham. 19th cent.*

11 Most Gracious Queen, we thee implore
To go away and sin no more,
But if that effort be too great,
To go away at any rate.
> *Epigram on Queen Caroline, 1820. Quoted in Lord Colchester's Diary, 15 Nov. 1820; sent to him by Francis Burton*

12 Multiplication is vexation,
Division is as bad;
The Rule of three doth puzzle me,
And Practice drives me mad.
> *Elizabethan MS. dated 1570*

13 My anvil and hammer lies declined,
My bellows have quite lost their wind,
My fire's extinct, my forge decay'd,
My vice is in the dust all laid.
My coals is spent, my iron gone,
My nails are drove, my work is done,

My mortal part rests nigh this stone,
My soul to heaven I hope is gone.
> *Epitaph on John Hunter, a blacksmith, d. 10 Apr. 1792. Found in St. Andrew's Chapel, Shotley, and on other blacksmiths elsewhere*

14 My Love in her attire doth show her wit,
    It doth so well become her:
For every season she hath dressings fit,
    For winter, spring, and summer.
No beauty she doth miss,
    When all her robes are on;
But beauty's self she is,
    When all her robes are gone.   *Madrigal*

15 My name is George Nathaniel Curzon,
I am a most superior person.
> *The Masque of Balliol, composed by and current among members of Balliol College in the late 1870's (see also 39:5, 511:5 and 6)*

16 My face is pink, my hair is sleek,
I dine at Blenheim once a week.
> *Ib. (a later addition)*

17 I am rather tall and stately,
And I care not very greatly
What you say, or what you do.
I'm Mackail,—and who are you?   *Ib.*

18 Now I lay me down to sleep;
I pray the Lord my soul to keep.
If I should die before I wake,
I pray the Lord my soul to take.
> *First printed in a late edition of the New England Primer, 1781*

19 O Death, where is thy sting-a-ling-a-ling,
O Grave, thy victoree?
The bells of Hell go ting-a-ling-a-ling
For you but not for me.
> *Song popular in the British Army, 1914–18*

20 O God, if there be a God, save my soul, if I have a soul!
> *Prayer of a common soldier before the battle of Blenheim (see Notes and Queries, clxxiii. 264). Quoted in Newman's Apologia*

21 Oh, Shenandoah, I long to hear you.
Away, you rolling river,
Oh Shenandoah, I long to hear you.
Away, I'm bound to go
'Cross the wide Missouri.   *Oxford Song Book*

22 Oh! the oak, and the ash, and the bonny ivy-tree,
They flourish at home in my own country.
> *O The Oak and The Ash (c. 1650). Oxford Song Book*

23 Oh, 'tis my delight on a shining night, in the season of the year.
> *The Lincolnshire Poacher. Oxford Song Book*

24 Oh, 'twas in the broad Atlantic,
    'Mid the equinoctial gales,
That a young fellow fell overboard
    Among the sharks and whales.
And down he went like a streak of light,
    So quickly down went he,
Until he came to a mer-ma-id
    At the bottom of the deep blue sea.
Singing, Rule Britannia, Britannia, rule the waves!
Britons never, never, never shall be mar-ri-ed to a
    mer-ma-id
At the bottom of the deep blue sea.
> *Oh! 'Twas in the Broad Atlantic. Oxford Song Book*

1 Oh! where is my wandering boy to-night?
  The boy who was bravest of all.
                    Oh! Where is My Boy To-night?

2 Old soldiers never die;
  They only fade away!
        War Song of the British Soldiers, 1914–18

3 One Friday morn when we set sail,
  And our ship not far from land,
  We there did espy a fair pretty maid,
  With a comb and a glass in her hand.
  While the raging seas did roar,
  And the stormy winds did blow,
  And we jolly sailor-boys were all up aloft
  And the land-lubbers lying down below.
              The Mermaid. Oxford Song Book

4 O No John! No John! No John! No!
                O No, John. Oxford Song Book

5 On Waterloo's ensanguined plain
  Full many a gallant man was slain,
  But none, by sabre or by shot,
  Fell half so flat as Walter Scott.
            On Scott's Field of Waterloo. *1815*

6 O Paddy dear, an' did ye hear the news that's goin'
    round?
  The shamrock is by law forbid to grow on Irish
    ground!
  No more St. Patrick's Day we'll keep, his colour can't
    be seen,
  For there's a cruel law agin the wearin' o' the Green!
  I met wid Napper Tandy, and he took me by the
    hand,
  And he said, 'How's poor ould Ireland, and how does
    she stand?'
  She's the most disthressful country that iver yet was
    seen,
  For they're hangin' men an' women there for the
    wearin' o' the Green.
      *The Wearin' o' the Green. (Famous street ballad,
      later added to by Boucicault.)*

7 O ye'll tak' the high road, and I'll tak' the low road,
  And I'll be in Scotland afore ye,
  But me and my true love will never meet again,
  On the bonnie, bonnie banks o' Loch Lomon'.
  The Bonnie Banks o' Loch Lomon'. Oxford Song Book

8 But the broken heart it kens nae second spring again,
  Tho' the waefu' may cease frae their greeting.   *Ib.*

9 Please her the best you may,
  She looks another way.
  Alas and well a day!
      Phillida flouts me.
    *The Disdainful Shepherdess. Oxford Book of 16th
    Cent. Verse*

10 But she did all disdain,
  And threw them back again;
  Therefore it's flat and plain
      Phillida flouts me.   *Ib.*

11 Please to remember the Fifth of November,
  Gunpowder Treason and Plot.
      Traditional since 17th cent.   (See also 368:13)

12 Raise the stone, and there thou shalt find me, cleave
    the wood and there am I.
    *Oxyrhynchus Sayings of Christ. Sayings of Our
    Lord,* Logion 5, l. 23 (*1897*), p. 12

13 Remember the Maine!
      Slogan of the Spanish-American War

14 See the happy moron,
  He doesn't give a damn,
  I wish I were a moron,
  My God! perhaps I am!
              Eugenics Review, July 1929, 86/2

15 Seven wealthy Towns contend for HOMER Dead
  Through which the Living HOMER begged his Bread.
      *Epilogue to Aesop at Tunbridge; or, a Few
      Selected Fables in Verse. By No Person of
      Quality, 1698*

16 She has kilted her coats o' green satin,
    She has kilted them up to the knee,
    And she's aff wi' Lord Ronald Macdonald,
    His bride and his darling to be.   *Lizzy Lindsay*

17 Will ye gang wi' me, Lizzy Lindsay,
    Will ye gang to the Highlands wi' me?
  Will ye gang wi' me, Lizzy Lindsay,
    My bride and my darling to be?   *Ib.*

18 She was poor but she was honest,
  And her parents was the same,
  Till she met a city feller,
  And she lost her honest name.
      1914–18 War Song. There are many versions

19 In a village in the country,
  There her people now do live,
  Drinking port wine that she sends 'em,
  But they never can forgive.   *Ib.*

20 Its the same the whole world over,
  Its the poor wot gets the blame,
  Its the rich wot gets the pleasure,
  Ain't it all a blooming shame.   *Ib.*

21 Since first I saw your face, I resolved to honour and
    renown ye;
  If now I be disdained, I wish my heart had never
    known ye.
  What? I that loved and you that liked, shall we begin
    to wrangle?
  No, no, no, my heart is fast, and cannot disentangle.
      Songs set by Thomas Ford, ii. *Oxford Book of
      16th Cent. Verse (Music of Sundry Kinds, 1607).*

22 Since wars begin in the minds of men, it is in the
    minds of men that the defences of peace must be
    constructed.
      *Constitution of the United Nations Educational,
      Scientific and Cultural Organisation (1946)*

23 So I wish him joy where'er he dwell,
  That first found out the leather bottel.
                          The Leather Bottel

24 Some talk of Alexander, and some of Hercules;
  Of Hector and Lysander, and such great names as
    these;
  But of all the world's brave heroes, there's none that
    can compare
  With a tow, row, row, row, row, row, for the British
    Grenadier.   *The British Grenadiers*

25 Spheres of influence.
      *'Spheres of action', found in Earl Granville's
      letter to Count Münster, 29 Apr. 1885. Hertslet's
      Map of Africa by Treaty, 3rd edn., p. 868. (See
      313:21)*

26 Sumer is icumen in,
    Lhude sing cuccu!
  Groweth sed, and bloweth med,
    And springth the wude nu.
                  Cuckoo Song, c. 1250

1 Cuccu, cuccu, well singes thu, cuccu:
  Ne swike thu never nu;
  Sing cuccu, nu, sing cuccu,
  Sing cuccu, sing cuccu, nu! *Cuckoo Song, c. 1250*

2 Swing low, sweet chariot—
  Comin' for to carry me home;
  I looked over Jordan and what did I see?
  A band of angels comin' after me—
  Comin' for to carry me home.
    American Negro Spiritual, c. 1850

3 That Kruschen feeling.
    Advertisement for Kruschen Salts

4 That schoolgirl complexion.
    Advertisement for Palmolive Soap

5 That we spent, we had:
  That we gave, we have:
  That we left, we lost.
    *Epitaph of the Earl of Devonshire, as quoted by
    Spenser in* The Shepherd's Calendar, May, l. 70
    (see 11:17)

6 The almighty dollar is the only object of worship.
    Philadelphia Public Ledger, 2 Dec. 1836

7 The animals went in one by one,
  There's one more river to cross.
    One More River. Oxford Song Book

8 The animals went in four by four,
  The big hippopotamus stuck in the door. *Ib.*

9 The Campbells are comin', oho, oho.
    The Campbells are Comin' (c. 1715). *Oxford
    Song Book*

10 The children in Holland take pleasure in making
   What the children in England take pleasure in breaking.   *Nursery Rhyme*

11 The eternal triangle.
    Book review in The Daily Chronicle, 5 Dec. 1907

12 The fault is great in man or woman
   Who steals a goose from off a common;
   But what can plead that man's excuse
   Who steals a common from a goose?
    The Tickler Magazine, 1 Feb. 1821

13 The girl I left behind me.
    Title of song, c. 1759. Oxford Song Book

14 The holly and the ivy,
   When they are both full grown,
   Of all the trees that are in the wood,
   The holly bears the crown:
   The rising of the sun
   And the running of the deer,
   The playing of the merry organ,
   Sweet singing in the choir.
    The Holly and the Ivy. Oxford Book of Carols

15 The King over the Water. *Jacobite Toast, 18th cent.*

16 The ministry of all the talents.
    *A name given ironically to Grenville's coalition of
    1806; also applied to later coalitions*

17 The nature of God is a circle of which the centre is
   everywhere and the circumference is nowhere.
    *Origin unknown; said to have been traced to a lost
    treatise of Empedocles. Quoted in the Roman de
    la Rose, and by S. Bonaventura in Itinerarius
    Mentis in Deum, cap. v. ad fin.*

18 Then he kissed her cold corpus
   A thousand times o'er,
   He called her his Dinah—
   Though she was no more!
   He swallowed the pison
   Like a true lovier brave,
   And Vilikins and his Dinah
   Lie a-buried in one grave.
    In Henry Mayhew's *The Wandering Minstrels,
    1834*

19 The noble Duke of York,
   He had ten thousand men,
   He marched them up to the top of the hill,
   And he marched them down again.
   And when they were up, they were up,
   And when they were down, they were down,
   And when they were only half way up,
   They were neither up nor down.
    The Noble Duke of York, first printed in
    A. Rackham, *Mother Goose* (1913)

20 There is a lady sweet and kind,
   Was never face so pleased my mind;
   I did but see her passing by,
   And yet I love her till I die.
    *Found on back of leaf 53 of 'Popish Kingdome or
    reigne of Antichrist', in Latin verse by Thomas
    Naogeorgus, and Englished by Barnabe Googe.
    Printed 1570. See Notes and Queries, 9th series,
    x. 427*

21 There is a tavern in the town,
   And there my dear love sits him down,
   And drinks his wine 'mid laughter free,
   And never, never thinks of me.
   Fare thee well, for I must leave thee,
   Do not let this parting grieve thee,
   And remember that the best of friends must part.

   Adieu, adieu, kind friends, adieu, adieu, adieu,
   I can no longer stay with you.
   I'll hang my harp on a weeping willow-tree,
   And may the world go well with thee.
    *There is a Tavern in the Town. Oxford Song
    Book*

22 There's nae luck about the house,
   There's nae luck at a',
   There's nae luck about the house
   When our gudeman's awa'.
    The Mariner's Wife

23 There was an old Fellow of Trinity,
   A Doctor well versed in Divinity;
   But he took to free-thinking,
   And then to deep drinking,
   And so had to leave the vicinity.
    A. C. Hilton, in The Light Green, No. II, 1872

24 There was an old man of Boulogne,
   Who sang a most topical song.
   It wasn't the words
   Which frightened the birds,
   But the horrible double entendre.
    Langford Reed, The Limerick Book, p. 51

25 There was a young lady of Kent,
   Who said that she knew what it meant
   When men asked her to dine,
   Gave her cocktails and wine,
   She knew what it meant—but she went! *Ib. p. 49*

ANONYMOUS

1 There was a young lady of Lynn
Who was so uncommonly thin
 That when she essayed
 To drink lemonade,
She slipped through the straw and fell in.
   Langford Reed, The Limerick Book, p. 150

2 There was a young lady of Riga,
Who rode with a smile on a tiger;
 They returned from the ride
 With the lady inside,
And the smile on the face of the tiger. *Ib. p. 103*

3 The Sun himself cannot forget
His fellow traveller.
  On Sir Francis Drake. Wit's Recreations (1640),
  Epigrams, No. 146

4 They come as a boon and a blessing to men,
The Pickwick, the Owl, and the Waverley pen.
         Advertisement

5 They that wash on Monday
Have all the week to dry;
They that wash on Tuesday
Are not so much awry;
They that wash on Wednesday
Are not so much to blame;
They that wash on Thursday
Wash for shame;
They that wash on Friday
Wash in need;
And they that wash on Saturday,
Oh! they're sluts indeed.
  See Robert Hunt, Popular Romances of the West
  of England (1865), p. 430

6 To change the name, and not the letter,
Is a change for the worse, and not for the better.
  Book of Days (ed. Robert Chambers, 1802–71),
  vol. i, June, p. 723

7 Two men wrote a lexicon, Liddell and Scott;
Some parts were clever, but some parts were not.
Hear, all ye learned, and read me this riddle,
How the wrong part wrote Scott, and the right part
 wrote Liddell.
  On Henry Liddell (1811–98) and Robert Scott
  (1811–87), co-authors of the Greek Lexicon, 1843

8 Wash me in the water
That you washed the colonel's daughter
And I shall be whiter
Than the whitewash on the wall.
  Song popular among the British troops in France,
  1914–18

9 We don't want to fight; but, by Jingo, if we do,
We won't go to the front ourselves, but we'll send the
 mild Hindoo.
  1878 parody, on hearing that Indian troops were
  being sent to Malta to help the English. G. W. E.
  Russell's Collections and Recollections, ch. 28

10 Weep you no more, sad fountains;
What need you flow so fast?
  Songs set by John Dowland, viii. Oxford Book of
  16th Cent. Verse

11 We hold these truths to be self-evident, that all men
are created equal, that they are endowed by their
Creator with certain unalienable rights, that among
these are life, liberty, and the pursuit of happiness.
  The American Declaration of Independence,
  4 July 1776. (See 268:19)

12 'Well, what sort of sport has Lord — had?'
'Oh, the young Sahib shot divinely, but God was very
merciful to the birds.'
  G. W. E. Russell's Collections and Recollections,
  ch. 30

13 We're here because we're here because we're here
because we're here.
  Refrain of an American folk-song, popular in the
  British Army, 1914–18

14 Western wind, when wilt thou blow,
The small rain down can rain?
Christ, if my love were in my arms
And I in my bed again!
  Oxford Book of 16th Cent. Verse

15 What did you do in the Great War, daddy?
  Recruiting placard, 1914–18 war

16 What shall we do with the drunken sailor?
Early in the morning?
Hoo-ray and up she rises
Early in the morning.
  What shall we do with the Drunken Sailor? Oxford
  Song Book

17 What wee gave, we have;
What wee spent, wee had;
What wee kept, wee lost.
  Epitaph on Edward Courtenay, Earl of Devon
  (d. 1419) and his wife, at Tiverton. (See 10:5)

18 When Adam delved, and Eve span,
Who was then a gentleman?
  Text of Ball's revolutionary sermon at Blackheath
  in Wat Tyler's Rebellion, 1381. See J. R. Green,
  Short Hist. (1893), ii. 484. (See 235:7)

19 When Johnny Comes Marching Home Again.
  Title of Song. Oxford Song Book

20 When Molly smiles beneath her cow,
I feel my heart—I can't tell how.
    When Molly smiles, 1732

21 When the wind is in the east,
'Tis neither good for man nor beast;
When the wind is in the north,
The skilful fisher goes not forth;
When the wind is in the south,
It blows the bait in the fishes' mouth;
When the wind is in the west,
Then 'tis at the very best.
  See J. O. Halliwell, Popular Rhymes (1849)

22 Where is the man who has the power and skill
To stem the torrent of a woman's will?
For if she will, she will, you may depend on't;
And if she won't, she won't; so there's an end on't.
  From the Pillar Erected on the Mount in the Dane
  John Field, Canterbury. Examiner, 31 May 1829

23 Whilst Adam slept, Eve from his side arose:
Strange his first sleep should be his last repose.
      The Consequence

24 Who passes by this road so late?
 Compagnon de la Majolaine!
Who passes by this road so late?
 Always gay!
Of all the king's knights 'tis the flower,
 Compagnon de la Majolaine,
Of all the king's knights 'tis the flower,
 Always gay!
  Old French Song quoted by Dickens, Little Dorrit,
  ch. 1

1 Will yóu hěar a Spanish lady
　How she woo'd an Englishman?
Garments gay and rich as may be,
Decked with jewels had she on.
　　　　　　　　The Spanish Lady's Love

2 With a heart of furious fancies,
　Whereof I am commander;
With a burning spear,
　And a horse of air,
To the wilderness I wander.　　*Tom o' Bedlam*

3 Woo'd and married and a',
　Woo'd and married and a'
Was she nae very weel aff,
　Was woo'd and married and a'.
　　　　　　　　Woo'd and Married and a'

4 Workers of the world, unite!
　Common form of 'Working men of all countries,
　unite!' *This is the English Translation* (1888)
　by Samuel Moore, revised by Engels, of 'Prole-
　tarier aller Länder, vereinigt euch!' *which con-
　cludes* The Communist Manifesto (1848), *by
　Marx and Engels, and is quoted as the final words
　of the programme of the Communist International
　(1928). Another common form is* 'Proletarians of
　the world, unite!'

5 Worth a guinea a box.
　　　　　Advertisement for Beecham's Pills

6 Yet, if his majesty our sovereign lord
Should of his own accord
Friendly himself invite,
And say 'I'll be your guest tomorrow night',
How should we stir ourselves, call and command
All hands to work!
　　　　　　　From Christ Church MS.

7 'tis a duteous thing
To show all honour to an earthly king,
And after all our travail and our cost,
So he be pleased, to think no labour lost.
But at the coming of the King of Heaven
All's set at six and seven:
We wallow in our sin.
Christ cannot find a chamber in the inn.
We entertain Him always like a stranger,
And as at first still lodge Him in the manger.　　*Ib.*

8 You should see me on Sunday.
　　Advertisement for Knight's Family Health Soap

9 You press the button, and we'll do the rest.
　　Advertisement for the first Kodak cameras, c. 1888

French

10 An army marches on its stomach.
　*Attrib. to Napoleon in, e.g., Windsor Magazine,
　1904, p. 268*
　*Probably condensed from a long passage in Las
　Cases, Mémorial de Ste-Hélène (Nov.* 1816)

11 Ça ira.
　Untranslatable phrase, meaning 'That will certainly
　happen'.　*Refrain of French Revolutionary Song*

12 Cet animal est très méchant,
　Quand on l'attaque il se défend.

　This animal is very mischievous; when it is attacked
　it defends itself.
　　　　La Ménagerie, by Théodore P. K., 1868

13 Chevalier sans peur et sans reproche.
　Knight without fear and without blemish.
　*Description in contemporary chronicles of Pierre
　Bayard, 1476-1524*

14 Il ne faut pas être plus royaliste que le roi.
　One must not be more royalist than the king.
　*Phrase originated under Louis XVI. Chateau-
　briand, La Monarchie selon la Charte, ed. 1876,
　p. 94*

15 Le monde est plein de fous, et qui n'en veut pas voir
Doit se tenir tout seul, et casser son miroir.
　The world is full of fools, and he who would not
　see it
　Should live alone and smash his mirror.
　*An adaptation from an original form attributed to
　Claude Le Petit (1640-1665) in Discours Sati-
　riques, 1686*

16 Liberté! Égalité! Fraternité!
　Liberty! Equality! Fraternity!
　*Phrase of unknown origin dating from before the
　French Revolution. Aulard in Études et Leçons
　sur la Révolution Française (6e série) gives the
　first official use of the phrase in the motion
　passed by the Club des Cordeliers (30 June
　1793):* 'que les propriétaires seront invités, . . .
　de faire peindre sur la façade de leurs maisons,
　en gros caractères, ces mots: Unité, indivi-
　sibilité de la République, Liberté, Égalité,
　Fraternité ou la mort.'
　　　　　　(Journal de Paris, No. 182)

17 L'ordre règne à Varsovie.
　Order reigns in Warsaw.
　*On 16 Sept. 1831, the Comte Horace Sebastiani,
　minister of foreign affairs, said that* 'La tran-
　quillité règne à Varsovie'. *The newspaper* Moni-
　teur *took it up*

18 Retournons à nos moutons.
　Let us return to our sheep. (Let us get back to the
　subject.)　*Maistre Pierre Pathelin (line* 1191)

19 Taisez-vous! Méfiez-vous! Les oreilles ennemies
vous écoutent.
　Be quiet! Be on your guard! Enemy ears are listen-
　ing to you.　*Official Notice in France in 1915*

20 Toujours perdrix!
　Always partridge!
　*Said to originate in a story of Henri IV's having
　ordered that nothing but partridge should be served
　to his confessor, who had rebuked the king for his
　liaisons*

21 Tout passe, tout casse, tout lasse.
　Everything passes, everything perishes, everything
　palls.　　*Cahier, Quelques six mille proverbes*

Greek

22 μηδὲν ἄγαν.
　Nothing in excess.
　*Written up in the temple at Delphi by Cleobulus,
　according to some accounts. Quoted by Plato in
　Protagoras, 343 b*

23 γνῶθι σεαυτόν.
　From the gods comes the saying 'Know thyself'.
　Juvenal, *Satires, xi. 27. The saying was written
　up in the temple of Delphi*

Italian

1 Se non è vero, è molto ben trovato.

If it is not true, it is a happy invention.
Apparently a common saying in the sixteenth century. Found in Giordano Bruno (1585) in the above form, and in Antonio Doni (1552) as 'Se non è vero, egli è stato un bel trovato'

Latin

2 Adeste, fideles,
Laeti triumphantes;
Venite, venite in Bethlehem.

O come, all ye faithful,
Joyful and triumphant,
O come, ye, O come ye to Bethlehem.
French or German hymn of 18th Cent. Trans. by Oakeley in Murray's Hymnal, 1852. See Songs of Praise Discussed

3 Ad majorem Dei gloriam.

To the greater glory of God.
Motto of the Society of Jesus

4 Ave Caesar, morituri te salutant.

Hail Caesar; those who are about to die salute you.
Salutation of Roman gladiators on entering the arena

5 Cras amet qui nunquam amavit, quique amavit cras amet!

Let those love now, who never lov'd before:
Let those who always lov'd, now love the more.
Pervigilium Veneris, 1. Trans. by Parnell

6 De non apparentibus et de non existentibus eadem est ratio.

It is presumed that what does not appear does not exist.
Law Maxim

7 Et in Arcadia ego.
Inscription on a tomb, frequently reproduced in paintings, e.g. by Guercino, Poussin, and Reynolds

Usually translated : 'And I too [the occupant of the tomb] was in Arcadia.' But perhaps rather, 'I too [the tomb itself] am in Arcadia': even in Arcadia there am I (Death). (See E. Panofsky in *Philosophy and History*: essays presented to E. Cassirer, 1936.)

8 Gaudeamus igitur,
Juvenes dum sumus
Post jucundam juventutem,
Post molestam senectutem,
Nos habebit humus.

Let us live then and be glad
While young life's before us
After youthful pastime had,
After old age hard and sad,
Earth will slumber o'er us.
Medieval students' song, traced to 1267, but revised in the 18th cent.

9 Meum est propositum in taberna mori,
Uinum sit appositum sitienti ori:
Ut dicant cum uenerint angelorum chori
'Deus sit propitius isti potatori.'

I desire to end my days in a tavern drinking,
May some Christian hold for me the glass when I am shrinking,
That the Cherubim may cry, when they see me sinking,
'God be merciful to a soul of this gentleman's way of thinking.'
The 'Archipoeta'. Trans. by Leigh Hunt

10 Nemo me impune lacessit.

No one provokes me with impunity.
Motto of the Crown of Scotland and of all Scottish regiments

11 Orare est laborare, laborare est orare.

To pray is to work, to work is to pray.
See Notes and Queries, 6th series, vol. xi, p. 477

12 Quidquid agas, prudenter agas, et respice finem.

Whatever you do, do cautiously, and look to the end.
Gesta Romanorum, cap. 103. init.

13 Surrexit Christus hodie
Humano pro solamine:
Alleluia.

Jesus Christ is risen to-day,
Alleluia!
Our triumphant holy day!
Alleluia!
German Easter Carol of 14th cent. Translation in Lyra Davidica, 1708. See Songs of Praise Discussed

14 Te Deum laudamus.

We praise thee, O God.
First words and title of Canticle attr. to S. Ambrose

15 Tempora mutantur, et nos mutamur in illis.

Times change, and we change with them.
Harrison, Description of Britain (1577), Pt. III, ch. iii, p. 99

CHRISTOPHER ANSTEY
1724-1805

16 If ever I ate a good supper at night,
I dream'd of the devil, and wak'd in a fright.
The New Bath Guide. Letter 4. A Consultation of the Physicians

17 You may go to Carlisle's, and to Almack's too;
And I'll give you my head if you find such a host,
For coffee, tea, chocolate, butter, and toast:
How he welcomes at once all the world and his wife,
And how civil to folk he ne'er saw in his life.
Ib. (1766), letter 13, A Public Breakfast

18 Hearken, Lady Betty, hearken,
To the dismal news I tell,
How your friends are all embarking
For the fiery gulf of hell.
Ib. letter 14

CHARLES JAMES APPERLEY
see
NIMROD

THOMAS APPLETON
1812-1884

19 A Boston man is the east wind made flesh.
Attr.

1 Good Americans, when they die, go to Paris.
O. W. Holmes, *Autocrat of the Breakfast Table*,
ch. 6

ARABIAN NIGHTS

2 Who will change old lamps for new ones? . . . new
lamps for old ones? *The History of Aladdin*

3 Open Sesame! *The History of Ali Baba*

WILLIAM ARABIN

1773–1841

4 Prisoner, God has given you good abilities, instead
of which you go about the country stealing ducks.
Attributed. See Notes and Queries, clxx. 310

JOHN ARBUTHNOT

1667–1735

5 He warns the heads of parties against believing their
own lies. *The Art of Political Lying*, 1712

6 Law is a bottomless pit.
The History of John Bull (1712), ch. xxiv

7 Hame's hame, be it never so hamely.
Law is a Bottomless Pit

8 One of the new terrors of death.
Of Edmund Curll's biographies. R. Carru-
thers's *Life of Pope* (1857), p. 199

ARCHIMEDES

287–212 B.C.

9 εὕρηκα.

Eureka! (I have found!)
Vitruvius Pollio, *De Architectura*, ix. 215

10 δός μοι ποῦ στῶ καὶ κινῶ τὴν γῆν..

Give me but one firm spot on which to stand, and
I will move the earth.
Pappus Alexandr., Collectio, lib. viii, prop. 10,
§ xi (ed. Hultsch, Berlin 1878)

COMTE D'ARGENSON

1652–1721

11 L'ABBÉ GUYOT DESFONTAINES: Il faut que je vive.
D'ARGENSON: Je n'en vois pas la nécessité.

DESFONTAINES: I must live.
D'ARGENSON: I do not see the necessity.
Voltaire, *Alzire, Discours Préliminaire.* (*See* 412:3)

GEORGE DOUGLAS CAMPBELL, EIGHTH DUKE OF ARGYLL

1823–1900

12 The Reign of Law. *Title of a book*, 1867

ARISTOPHANES

c. 444–c. 380 B.C.

13 ὁ δ' εὔκολος μὲν ἐνθάδ', εὔκολος δ' ἐκεῖ.

'But he was easy there, is easy here' (Sophocles)
Frogs, 82. Trans. by Rogers

ARISTOTLE

384–322 B.C.

14 ἄνθρωπος φύσει πολιτικὸν ζῷον.

Man is by nature a political animal.
Politics, i. 2. 9. 1253 *a* (ed. W. L. Newman)

15 ἢ θηρίον ἢ θεός.

Either a beast or a god. *Politics*, i. 14. 1253 *a*

16 ἔστιν οὖν τραγῳδία μίμησις πράξεως σπουδαίας καὶ τελείας
μέγεθος ἐχούσης . . . δι' ἐλέου καὶ φόβου περαίνουσα
τὴν τῶν τοιούτων παθημάτων κάθαρσιν.

A tragedy is the imitation of an action that is
serious and also, as having magnitude, complete
in itself . . . with incidents arousing pity and fear,
wherewith to accomplish its purgation of such
emotions. *Poetics*, 6. 1449 *b*. Trans. by Bywater

17 διὸ καὶ φιλοσοφώτερον καὶ σπουδαιότερον ποίησις ἱστορίας
ἐστίν.

Poetry is something more philosophic and of graver
import than history. *Ib.* 9. 1451 *b*

18 προαιρεῖσθαί τε δεῖ ἀδύνατα εἰκότα μᾶλλον ἢ δυνατὰ ἀπίθανα.

A likely impossibility is always preferable to an
unconvincing possibility. *Ib.* 24. 1460 *a*

19 Amicus Plato, sed magis amica veritas.

Plato is dear to me, but dearer still is truth.
Original ascribed to Aristotle

SIR JOHN ARKWRIGHT

1872–

20 O valiant hearts who to your glory came. *Hymn*

ROBERT ARMIN

fl. 1610

21 A flea in his ear. *Foole upon Foole*, 1605, c. 3

LEWIS ADDISON ARMISTEAD

1817–1863

22 Give them the cold steel, boys!
Attr. remark during Amer. Civil War, 1863

JOHN ARMSTRONG

1709–1779

23 Virtuous and wise he was, but not severe;
He still remember'd that he once was young.
Art of Preserving Health, 1744, bk. iv, l. 226

24 Much had he read,
Much more had seen; he studied from the life,
And in th' original perus'd mankind. *Ib.* l. 231

25 'Tis not for mortals always to be blest. *Ib.* l. 260

26 Of right and wrong he taught
Truths as refin'd as ever Athens heard;
And (strange to tell!) he practis'd what he preach'd.
Ib. l. 303

27 'Tis not too late to-morrow to be brave. *Ib.* l. 460

SIR EDWIN ARNOLD

1832–1904

28 Veil after veil will lift—but there must be
Veil upon veil behind. *The Light of Asia*, bk. viii

29 Lord! make us just, that we may be
A little justified with Thee.
Pearls of the Faith, No. 47

30 Nor ever once ashamed
So we be named
Press-men; Slaves of the Lamp; Servants of Light.
The Tenth Muse, st. 18

GEORGE ARNOLD

1834–1865

1 The living need charity more than the dead.

The Jolly Old Pedagogue

MATTHEW ARNOLD

1822–1888

2 And we forget because we must
And not because we will. *Absence*

3 Their ineffectual feuds and feeble hates,
Shadows of hates, but they distress them still.

Balder Dead, iii. 466

4 Hath man no second life?—Pitch this one high!

. . . . .

Was Christ a man like us?—Ah! let us try
If we then, too, can be such men as he!

The Better Part

5 The same heart beats in every human breast.

The Buried Life, l. 23

6 A bolt is shot back somewhere in our breast,
And a lost pulse of feeling stirs again.

. . . . .

A man becomes aware of his life's flow . . .
And there arrives a lull in the hot race

. . . . .

And then he thinks he knows
The hills where his life rose,
And the sea where it goes. *Ib. l. 84*

7 The Sea of Faith
Was once, too, at the full, and round earth's shore
Lay like the folds of a bright girdle furl'd.
But now I only hear
Its melancholy, long, withdrawing roar,
Retreating, to the breath
Of the night-wind, down the vast edges drear
And naked shingles of the world. *Dover Beach, l. 21*

8 And we are here as on a darkling plain
Swept with confused alarms of struggle and flight,
Where ignorant armies clash by night. *Ib. l. 35*

9 The will is free;
Strong is the soul, and wise, and beautiful;
The seeds of godlike power are in us still;
Gods are we, bards, saints, heroes, if we will!

Written in a copy of Emerson's Essays

10 Be neither saint nor sophist-led, but be a man.

Empedocles on Etna, i. ii. 136

11 We do not what we ought;
What we ought not, we do;
And lean upon the thought
That chance will bring us through;
But our own acts, for good or ill, are mightier powers.

Ib. 237

12 Nature, with equal mind,
Sees all her sons at play,
Sees man control the wind,
The wind sweep man away. *Ib. 257*

13 Is it so small a thing
To have enjoy'd the sun,
To have lived light in the spring,
To have loved, to have thought, to have done;
To have advanced true friends, and beat down baffling
foes? *Ib. 397*

14 Far, far from here,
The Adriatic breaks in a warm bay
Among the green Illyrian hills;

And there, they say, two bright and aged snakes,
Who once were Cadmus and Harmonia,
Bask in the glens or on the warm sea-shore,
In breathless quiet, after all their ills.

Empedocles on Etna, i. ii. 427

15 Not here, O Apollo!
Are haunts meet for thee.
But, where Helicon breaks down
In cliff to the sea. *Ib. ii. 421*

16 'Tis Apollo comes leading
His choir, the Nine.
—The leader is fairest,
But all are divine. *Ib. 445*

17 The day in his hotness,
The strife with the palm;
The night in her silence,
The stars in their calm. *Ib. 465*

18 I must not say that thou wast true,
Yet let me say that thou wast fair;
And they, that lovely face who view,
Why should they ask if truth be there?

Euphrosyne, 1

19 Eyes too expressive to be blue,
Too lovely to be grey. *Faded Leaves, 4. On the Rhine*

20 This heart, I know,
To be long lov'd was never framed;
For something in its depths doth glow
Too strange, too restless, too untamed.

A Farewell, st. 5

21 I too have long'd for trenchant force,
And will like a dividing spear;
Have prais'd the keen, unscrupulous course,
Which knows no doubt, which feels no fear.

Ib. st. 9

22 Come, dear children, let us away;
Down and away below. *The Forsaken Merman, l. 1*

23 Now the great winds shoreward blow;
Now the salt tides seaward flow;
Now the wild white horses play,
Champ and chafe and toss in the spray. *Ib. l. 4*

24 Sand-strewn caverns, cool and deep,
Where the winds are all asleep;
Where the spent lights quiver and gleam;
Where the salt weed sways in the stream;
Where the sea-beasts rang'd all round
Feed in the ooze of their pasture-ground;

. . . . .

Where great whales come sailing by,
Sail and sail, with unshut eye,
Round the world for ever and aye. *Ib. l. 35*

25 Children dear, was it yesterday
(Call yet once) that she went away? *Ib. l. 48*

26 Children dear, were we long alone?
'The sea grows stormy, the little ones moan.
Long prayers', I said, 'in the world they say.'

Ib. l. 64

27 But, ah, she gave me never a look,
For her eyes were seal'd to the holy book.
Loud prays the priest; shut stands the door.
Come away, children, call no more.
Come away, come down, call no more. *Ib. l. 80*

1 She will start from her slumber
When gusts shake the door;
She will hear the winds howling,
Will hear the waves roar.
We shall see, while above us
The waves roar and whirl,
A ceiling of amber,
A pavement of pearl.
Singing, 'Here came a mortal,
But faithless was she!
And alone dwell for ever
The kings of the sea.' *The Forsaken Merman*, l. 112

2 Who saw life steadily, and saw it whole:
The mellow glory of the Attic stage;
Singer of sweet Colonus, and its child.
Sonnet to a Friend: 'Who prop, thou ask'st.'

3 A wanderer is man from his birth.
He was born in a ship
On the breast of the river of Time. *The Future*, l. 1

4 And the width of the waters, the hush
Of the grey expanse where he floats,
Freshening its current and spotted with foam
As it draws to the Ocean, may strike
Peace to the soul of the man on its breast:
As the pale waste widens around him—
As the banks fade dimmer away—
As the stars come out, and the night-wind
Brings up the stream
Murmurs and scents of the infinite Sea. *Ib.* l. 78

5 Ah! not the nectarous poppy lovers use,
Not daily labour's dull, Lethaean spring,
Oblivion in lost angels can infuse
Of the soil'd glory, and the trailing wing.
To a Gipsy Child by the Sea-shore

6 Not as their friend or child I speak!
But as on some far northern strand,
Thinking of his own Gods, a Greek
In pity and mournful awe might stand
Before some fallen Runic stone—
For both were faiths, and both are gone.
The Grande Chartreuse, l. 79

7 Wandering between two worlds, one dead,
The other powerless to be born. *Ib.* l. 85

8 What helps it now, that Byron bore,
With haughty scorn which mock'd the smart,
Through Europe to the Aetolian shore
The pageant of his bleeding heart?
That thousands counted every groan,
And Europe made his woe her own? *Ib.* l. 133

9 Years hence, perhaps, may dawn an age,
More fortunate, alas! than we,
Which without hardness will be sage,
And gay without frivolity. *Ib.* l. 157

10 It is—last stage of all—
When we are frozen up within, and quite
The phantom of ourselves,
To hear the world applaud the hollow ghost
Which blamed the living man. *Growing Old*

11 So thou arraign'st her, her foe;
So we arraign her, her sons.
Yes, we arraign her! but she,
The weary Titan! with deaf
Ears, and labour-dimmed eyes,
. . . goes passively by,
Staggering on to her goal;

Bearing on shoulders immense,
Atlanteän, the load . . .
Of the too vast orb of her fate. *Heine's Grave*, l. 85

12 Who, Goethe said,
'Had every other gift, but wanted love.' *Ib.* l. 99

13 Only he,
His soul well-knit, and all his battles won,
Mounts, and that hardly, to eternal life. *Immortality*

14 The solemn peaks but to the stars are known,
But to the stars, and the cold lunar beams:
Alone the sun arises, and alone
Spring the great streams. *In Utrumque Paratus*

15 This truth—to prove, and make thine own:
'Thou hast been, shalt be, art, alone.'
Isolation. To Marguerite, l. 29

16 The unplumb'd, salt, estranging sea.
To Marguerite (contd.), l. 24

17 Calm soul of all things! make it mine
To feel, amid the city's jar,
That there abides a peace of thine,
Man did not make, and cannot mar!
Lines written in Kensington Gardens, l. 37

18 Calm, calm me more! nor let me die
Before I have begun to live. *Ib.* l. 43

19 Let the long contention cease!
Geese are swans, and swans are geese.
The Last Word, l. 5

20 Let the victors, when they come,
When the forts of folly fall,
Find thy body by the wall. *Ib.* l. 14

21 When Byron's eyes were shut in death,
We bow'd our head and held our breath.
He taught us little: but our soul
Had *felt* him like the thunder's roll.

.

We watch'd the fount of fiery life
Which serv'd for that Titanic strife.
Memorial Verses, l. 6

22 He spoke, and loos'd our heart in tears.
He laid us as we lay at birth
On the cool flowery lap of earth. [Wordsworth]
Ib. l. 47

23 Time may restore us in his course
Goethe's sage mind and Byron's force:
But where will Europe's latter hour
Again find Wordsworth's healing power? *Ib.* l. 60

24 Ere the parting hour go by,
Quick, thy tablets, Memory! *A Memory Picture*

25 All this I bear, for, what I seek, I know:
Peace, peace is what I seek, and public calm:
Endless extinction of unhappy hates. *Merope*, l. 100

26 With women the heart argues, not the mind.
Ib. l. 341

27 He bears the seed of ruin in himself. *Ib.* l. 856

28 For this is the true strength of guilty kings,
When they corrupt the souls of those they rule.
Ib. l. 1436

29 We cannot kindle when we will
The fire which in the heart resides,
The spirit bloweth and is still,
In mystery our soul abides:
But tasks in hours of insight will'd
Can be through hours of gloom fulfill'd.
Morality, st. 1

1 With aching hands and bleeding feet
   We dig and heap, lay stone on stone;
We bear the burden and the heat
Of the long day, and wish 'twere done.
Not till the hours of light return,
All we have built do we discern.   *Morality*, st. 2

2 Strew no more red roses, maidens,
Leave the lilies in their dew:
Pluck, pluck cypress, O pale maidens:
Dusk, O dusk the hall with yew!
          The New Sirens, l. 267

3 But Wordsworth's eyes avert their ken
From half of human fate.
   In Memory of the Author of Obermann, l. 53

4 What shelter to grow ripe is ours?
What leisure to grow wise?   *Ib.* l. 71

5 Too fast we live, too much are tried,
Too harass'd, to attain
Wordsworth's sweet calm, or Goethe's wide
And luminous view to gain.   *Ib.* l. 77

6 We, in some unknown Power's employ,
Move on a rigorous line:
Can neither, when we will, enjoy;
Nor, when we will, resign.   *Ib.* l. 133

7 On that hard Pagan world disgust
And secret loathing fell.
Deep weariness and sated lust
Made human life a hell.   *Obermann Once More*, l. 93

8 The East bow'd low before the blast,
In patient, deep disdain.
She let the legions thunder past,
And plunged in thought again.   *Ib.* l. 109

9 That gracious Child, that thorn-crown'd Man!
He lived while we believed.

Now he is dead. Far hence he lies
In the lorn Syrian town,
And on his grave, with shining eyes,
The Syrian stars look down.   *Ib.* l. 167

10 Say, has some wet bird-haunted English lawn
Lent it the music of its trees at dawn?   *Parting*, l. 19

11 Hark! ah, the Nightingale!
The tawny-throated!
Hark! from that moonlit cedar what a burst!
What triumph! hark—what pain!   *Philomela*, l. 1

12 Listen, Eugenia—
How thick the bursts come crowding through the
   leaves!
Again—thou hearest!
Eternal Passion!
Eternal Pain!   *Ib.* l. 28

13 Cruel, but composed and bland,
Dumb, inscrutable and grand,
So Tiberius might have sat,
Had Tiberius been a cat.   *Poor Matthias*, l. 40

14 Nature's great law, and law of all men's minds?
To its own impulse every creature stirs:
Live by thy light, and Earth will live by hers.
          Religious Isolation, l. 12

15 Strew on her roses, roses,
   And never a spray of yew.
In quiet she reposes:
   Ah! would that I did too.

Her cabin'd ample Spirit,
   It flutter'd and fail'd for breath.
To-night it doth inherit
   The vasty hall of death.   *Requiescat*

16 Coldly, sadly descends
The autumn evening. The Field
Strewn with its dank yellow drifts
Of wither'd leaves, and the elms,
Fade into dimness apace,
Silent.   *Rugby Chapel*, l. 1

17 Somewhere, surely, afar,
In the sounding labour-house vast
Of being, is practised that strength,
Zealous, beneficent, firm.   *Ib.* l. 40

18 Friends who set forth at our side,
Falter, are lost in the storm.
We, we only, are left!   *Ib.* l. 102

19 Therefore to thee it was given
Many to save with thyself;
And, at the end of thy day,
O faithful shepherd! to come,
Bringing thy sheep in thy hand.   *Ib.* l. 140

20 Then, in such hour of need
Of your fainting, dispirited race,
Ye, like angels, appear,
Radiant with ardour divine!
Beacons of hope, ye appear!
Languor is not in your heart,
Weakness is not in your word,
Weariness not on your brow.   *Ib.* l. 188

21 Ye fill up the gaps in our files,
Strengthen the wavering line,
Stablish, continue our march,
On, to the bound of the waste,
On, to the City of God.   *Ib.* l. 204

22 But so many books thou readest,
But so many schemes thou breedest,
But so many wishes feedest,
   That thy poor head almost turns.   *The Second Best*

23 Others abide our question. Thou art free.
We ask and ask: Thou smilest and art still,
Out-topping knowledge.   *Shakespeare*

24 And thou, who didst the stars and sunbeams know,
Self-school'd, self-scann'd, self-honour'd, self-secure,
Didst tread on Earth unguess'd at.—Better so!
All pains the immortal spirit must endure,
All weakness which impairs, all griefs which bow,
Find their sole speech in that victorious brow.   *Ib.*

25 Curl'd minion, dancer, coiner of sweet words!
          Sohrab and Rustum, l. 458

26   and Ruksh, the horse,
Who stood at hand, utter'd a dreadful cry:
No horse's cry was that, most like the roar
Of some pain'd desert lion, who all day
Hath trail'd the hunter's javelin in his side,
And comes at night to die upon the sand.   *Ib.* l. 501

27 Truth sits upon the lips of dying men.   *Ib.* l. 656

28 But the majestic River floated on,
Out of the mist and hum of that low land,
Into the frosty starlight, and there mov'd,
Rejoicing, through the hush'd Chorasmian waste,
Under the solitary moon: he flow'd
Right for the Polar Star, past Orgunjè,
Brimming, and bright, and large: then sands begin

To hem his watery march, and dam his streams,
And split his currents; that for many a league
The shorn and parcell'd Oxus strains along
Through beds of sand and matted rushy isles—
Oxus, forgetting the bright speed he had
In his high mountain cradle in Pamere,
A foil'd circuitous wanderer—till at last
The long'd-for dash of waves is heard, and wide
His luminous home of waters opens, bright
And tranquil, from whose floor the new-bathed stars
Emerge, and shine upon the Aral Sea.
Sohrab and Rustum, l. 875

1 France, fam'd in all great arts, in none supreme.
To a Republican Friend (contd.)

2   The high
Uno'erleap'd Mountains of Necessity.   *Ib.*

3 Not deep the Poet sees, but wide. *Resignation*, l. 214

4 Yet they, believe me, who await
No gifts from Chance, have conquer'd Fate.
Ib. l. 247

5 Go, for they call you, Shepherd, from the hill.
The Scholar-Gipsy, l. 1

6 All the live murmur of a summer's day.   *Ib.* l. 20

7 Tired of knocking at Preferment's door.   *Ib.* l. 35

8 In hat of antique shape, and cloak of grey,
The same the Gipsies wore.   *Ib.* l. 55

9 Crossing the stripling Thames at Bab-lock-hithe,
Trailing in the cool stream thy fingers wet,
As the slow punt swings round.   *Ib.* l. 74

10 Rapt, twirling in thy hand a wither'd spray,
And waiting for the spark from heaven to fall.
Ib. l. 119

11 The line of festal light in Christ-Church hall.
Ib. l. 129

12 Thou waitest for the spark from heaven! and we,
Light half-believers in our casual creeds

Who hesitate and falter life away,
And lose to-morrow the ground won to-day—
Ah, do not we, Wanderer, await it too? *Ib.* l. 171

13 With close-lipp'd Patience for our only friend,
Sad Patience, too near neighbour to Despair.
Ib. l. 194

14 This strange disease of modern life.   *Ib.* l. 203

15 Still nursing the unconquerable hope,
Still clutching the inviolable shade.   *Ib.* l. 211

16 As some grave Tyrian trader, from the sea,
Descried at sunrise an emerging prow
Lifting the cool-hair'd creepers stealthily,
The fringes of a southward-facing brow
Among the Aegean isles;
And saw the merry Grecian coaster come,
Freighted with amber grapes, and Chian wine,
Green bursting figs, and tunnies steep'd in brine;
And knew the intruders on his ancient home,

The young light-hearted Masters of the waves;
And snatch'd his rudder, and shook out more sail,
And day and night held on indignantly
O'er the blue Midland waters with the gale,
Betwixt the Syrtes and soft Sicily,
To where the Atlantic raves
Outside the Western Straits, and unbent sails

There, where down cloudy cliffs, through sheets
of foam,
Shy traffickers, the dark Iberians come;
And on the beach undid his corded bales.
The Scholar-Gipsy, l. 232

17 Resolve to be thyself: and know, that he
Who finds himself, loses his misery.
Self-Dependence, l. 31

18 And see all sights from pole to pole,
And glance, and nod, and bustle by;
And never once possess our soul
Before we die.   *A Southern Night*, l. 69

19 Mild o'er her grave, ye mountains, shine!
Gently by his, ye waters, glide!
To that in you which is divine
They were allied.   *Ib.* l. 137

20 Still bent to make some port he knows not where,
Still standing for some false impossible shore.
A Summer Night, l. 68

21 The signal-elm, that looks on Ilsley downs,
The Vale, the three lone weirs, the youthful
Thames.   *Thyrsis*, l. 14

22 And that sweet City with her dreaming spires,
She needs not June for beauty's heightening.
Ib. l. 19

23 But Thyrsis of his own will went away. *Ib.* l. 40

24 It irk'd him to be here, he could not rest.

He went; his piping took a troubled sound
Of storms that rage outside our happy ground;
He could not wait their passing, he is dead! *Ib.* l. 41

25 So have I heard the cuckoo's parting cry,
From the wet field, through the vext garden-trees,
Come with the volleying rain and tossing breeze:
'The bloom is gone, and with the bloom go I.'
Ib. l. 57

26 Too quick despairer, wherefore wilt thou go?
Soon will the high Midsummer pomps come on,
Soon will the musk carnations break and swell,
Soon shall we have gold-dusted snapdragon,
Sweet-William with his homely cottage-smell,
And stocks in fragrant blow.   *Ib.* l. 61

27 For Time, not Corydon, hath conquer'd thee.
Ib. l. 80

28 She loved the Dorian pipe, the Dorian strain.
But ah, of our poor Thames she never heard!
Her foot the Cumner cowslips never stirr'd;
And we should tease her with our plaint in vain.
Ib. l. 97

29 I know what white, what purple fritillaries
The grassy harvest of the river-fields,
Above by Ensham, down by Sandford, yields,
And what sedg'd brooks are Thames's tributaries.
Ib. l. 107

30 The foot less prompt to meet the morning dew,
The heart less bounding at emotion new,
And hope, once crushed, less quick to spring again.
Ib. l. 138

31 Hear it, O Thyrsis, still our Tree is there!—
Ah, vain! These English fields, this upland dim,
These brambles pale with mist engarlanded,
That lone, sky-pointing tree, are not for him.

To a boon southern country he is fled,
    And now in happier air,
Wandering with the great Mother's train divine

. . . . .

Within a folding of the Apennine.   *Thyrsis*, l. 171

1 Why faintest thou? I wander'd till I died,
    Roam on! the light we sought is shining still.
    Dost thou ask proof? Our Tree yet crowns the hill,
Our Scholar travels yet the loved hill-side.   *Ib.* l. 237

2 Know, man hath all which Nature hath, but more,
    And in that *more* lie all his hopes of good.
                                    To an Independent Preacher

3   Philip's peerless son,
Who carried the great war from Macedon
Into the Soudan's realm, and thunder'd on
To die at thirty-five in Babylon.
                            Tristram and Iseult, iii. 147

4   For this and that way swings
        The flux of mortal things,
    Though moving inly to one far-set goal.—
    After light's term, a term of cecity.
                            Westminster Abbey, l. 151

5 Nor bring, to see me cease to live,
    Some doctor full of phrase and fame,
    To shake his sapient head and give
    The ill he cannot cure a name.   *A Wish*

6 Calm's not life's crown, though calm is well.
    'Tis all perhaps which man acquires,
    But 'tis not what our youth desires.   *Youth and Calm*

7 And sigh that one thing only has been lent
    To youth and age in common—discontent.
                                    Youth's Agitations

8 The magnificent roaring of the young lions of the
    Daily Telegraph.
                    Essays in Criticism, First Series, preface.

9 Passionate, absorbing, almost blood-thirsty clinging to
    life.   *Ib.*

10 [Oxford] Beautiful city! so venerable, so lovely, so
    unravaged by the fierce intellectual life of our cen-
    tury, so serene! . . . whispering from her towers the
    last enchantments of the Middle Age. . . . Home of
    lost causes, and forsaken beliefs, and unpopular
    names, and impossible loyalties!   *Ib.*

11 Wragg is in custody.
        Ib. Functions of Criticism at the Present Time

12 I am bound by my own definition of criticism: a dis-
    interested endeavour to learn and propagate the
    best that is known and thought in the world.   *Ib.*

13 It always seems to me that the right sphere for
    Shelley's genius was the sphere of music, not of
    poetry.   *Ib. Maurice de Guérin*, footnote

14 Philistine must have originally meant, in the mind of
    those who invented the nickname, a strong, dogged,
    unenlightened opponent of the chosen people, of
    the children of the light.   *Ib. Heinrich Heine*

15 Philistinism!—We have not the expression in English.
    Perhaps we have not the word because we have so
    much of the thing.   *Ib.*

16 The absence, in this country, of any force of educated
    literary and scientific opinion.
                    Ib. Literary Influence of Academies

17 The great apostle of the Philistines, Lord Macaulay.
                                    Ib. Joubert

18 His expression may often be called bald . . . but it is
    bald as the bare mountain tops are bald, with a
    baldness full of grandeur.
        Ib. Second Series, preface to *Poems of Words-
        worth*

19 Nature herself seems, I say, to take the pen out of his
    hand, and to write for him with her own bare,
    sheer, penetrating power.   *Ib.*

20 The difference between genuine poetry and the poetry
    of Dryden, Pope, and all their school, is briefly
    this: their poetry is conceived and composed in
    their wits, genuine poetry is conceived and com-
    posed in the soul.   *Ib. Thomas Gray*

21 In poetry, no less than in life, he is 'a beautiful and
    ineffectual angel, beating in the void his luminous
    wings in vain'.   *Ib. Shelley*
    [Quoting his own sentence in his essay on Byron,
    Essays on Criticism, Second Series]

22 [Poetry] a criticism of life under the conditions fixed
    for such a criticism by the laws of poetic truth and
    poetic beauty.   *Ib. The Study of Poetry*

23 Our society distributes itself into Barbarians, Philis-
    tines, and Populace; and America is just ourselves,
    with the Barbarians quite left out, and the Populace
    nearly.   *Culture and Anarchy*, preface

24 The great aim of culture [is] the aim of setting our-
    selves to ascertain what perfection is and to make
    it prevail.   *Ib. p.* 12

25 The pursuit of perfection, then, is the pursuit of
    sweetness and light . . . He who works for sweet-
    ness and light united, works to make reason and the
    will of God prevail.   *Ib. p.* 47

26 The men of culture are the true apostles of equality.
                                    Ib. p. 49

27 One has often wondered whether upon the whole
    earth there is anything so unintelligent, so unapt to
    perceive how the world is really going, as an ordi-
    nary young Englishman of our upper class.
                                    Ib. pp. 70-1

28 For this [Middle] class we have a designation which
    now has become pretty well known, and which we
    may as well still keep for them, the designation of
    Philistines.   *Ib. p.* 97

29 But that vast portion, lastly, of the working-class
    which . . . is now issuing from its hiding-place to
    assert an Englishman's heaven-born privilege of
    doing as he likes, and is beginning to perplex us by
    marching where it likes, meeting where it likes,
    bawling what it likes, breaking what it likes—to this
    vast residuum we may with great propriety give the
    name of Populace.
        Thus we have got three distinct terms, Barbarians,
    Philistines, Populace, to denote roughly the three
    great classes into which our society is divided.
                                    Ib. pp. 104-5

30 Hebraism and Hellenism—between these two points
    of influence moves our World. . . . Hebraism and
    Hellenism are, neither of them, the law of human
    development . . .; they are, each of them, contribu-
    tions to human development.   *Ib. pp.* 143, 157

31 'He knows', says Hebraism, 'his Bible!'—whenever
    we hear this said, we may, without any elaborate
    defence of culture, content ourselves with answering
    simply: 'No man, who knows nothing else, knows
    even his Bible.'   *Ib. pp.* 181-2

1 The grand, old, fortifying, classical curriculum.
Friendship's Garland

2 The translator of Homer should above all be penetrated by a sense of four qualities of his author:— that he is eminently rapid; that he is eminently plain and direct both in the evolution of his thought and in the expression of it, that is, both in his syntax and in his words; that he is eminently plain and direct in the substance of his thought, that is, in his matter and ideas; and, finally, that he is eminently noble. *On Translating Homer*, i

3 Wordsworth says somewhere that wherever Virgil seems to have composed 'with his eye on the object', Dryden fails to render him. Homer invariably composes 'with his eye on the object', whether the object be a moral or a material one: Pope composes with his eye on his style, into which he translates his object, whatever it is. *Ib.*

4 He [the Translator] will find one English book and one only, where, as in the *Iliad* itself, perfect plainness of speech is allied with perfect nobleness; and that book is the Bible. *Ib.* iii

5 Nothing has raised more questioning among my critics than these words—noble, the grand style. . . . I think it will be found that the grand style arises in poetry, when a noble nature, poetically gifted, treats with simplicity or with severity a serious subject. *Ib.* Last words

6 The theatre is irresistible; organise the theatre!
Irish Essays. The French Play in London

7 Miracles do not happen.
Literature and Dogma, preface to 1883 edition, last words

8 Culture, the acquainting ourselves with the best that has been known and said in the world, and thus with the history of the human spirit.
Ib. preface to 1873 edition

9 Terms like grace, new birth, justification . . . : terms, in short, which with St. Paul are literary terms, theologians have employed as if they were scientific terms. *Ib.* ch. i, § 1

10 When we are asked further, what is conduct?—let us answer: Three-fourths of life. *Ib.*

11 The true meaning of religion is thus not simply morality, but morality touched by emotion.
Ib. § 2

12 Conduct is three-fourths of our life and its largest concern. *Ib.* § 3

13 For science, God is simply *the stream of tendency by which all things seek to fulfil the law of their being*.
Ib. § 4. (*See 524:27*)

14 Let us put into their 'Eternal' and 'God' no more science than they [the Hebrew writers] did:—the enduring power, not ourselves, which makes for righteousness. *Ib.* § 5

15 For it is what we call the Time-Spirit that is sapping the proof from miracles. . . . The human mind, as its experience widens, is turning away from them.
Ib. ch. v, § 3

16 What is called 'orthodox divinity' is, in fact, an immense literary misapprehension. *Ib.* ch. vi, § 3

17 The eternal not ourselves which makes for righteousness. *Ib.* ch. viii, § 1

18 But there remains the question: what righteousness really is. The method and secret and sweet reasonableness of Jesus. *Literature and Dogma*, ch. xii, § 2

19 So we have the Philistine of genius in religion— Luther; the Philistine of genius in politics— Cromwell; the Philistine of genius in literature— Bunyan. *Mixed Essays, Lord Falkland*

SAMUEL JAMES ARNOLD
1774–1852

20 Our ships were British oak,
And hearts of oak our men. *Death of Nelson*

THOMAS ARNOLD
1795–1842

21 What we must look for here is, 1st, religious and moral principles: 2ndly, gentlemanly conduct: 3rdly, intellectual ability.
Arnold of Rugby (ed. J. J. Findlay), p. 65

22 My object will be, if possible, to form Christian men, for Christian boys I can scarcely hope to make.
Letter, in 1828, on appointment to Headmastership of Rugby

GEORGE ASAF
[GEORGE H. POWELL]
1880–1951

23 What's the use of worrying?
It never was worth while,
So, pack up your troubles in your old kit-bag,
And smile, smile, smile.
Pack Up Your Troubles In Your Old Kit-Bag

JOHN DUNNING, BARON ASHBURTON
1731–1783

24 The power of the Crown has increased, is increasing, and ought to be diminished.
Motion passed in the House of Commons, 1780

THOMAS ASHE
1836–1889

25 Meet we no angels, Pansie? *At Altenahr*, ii. *Poems*

DAISY ASHFORD
contemporary

26 Mr. Salteena was an elderly man of 42 and was fond of asking peaple to stay with him.
The Young Visiters (1919), ch. i

27 I do hope I shall enjoy myself with you . . . I am parshial to ladies if they are nice I suppose it is my nature. I am not quite a gentleman but you would hardly notice it. *Ib.*

28 You look rather rash my dear your colors dont quite match your face. *Ib.* ch. 2

29 Bernard always had a few prayers in the hall and some whiskey afterwards as he was rarther pious
Ib. ch. 3

30 Oh this is most kind said Mr. Salteena.
Minnit closed his eyes with a tired smile.
Not kind sir he muttered quite usual. *Ib.* ch. 5

31 It was a sumpshous spot all done up in gold with plenty of looking glasses. *Ib.*

1 Oh I see said the Earl but my own idear is that these things are as piffle before the wind.
The Young Visiters, ch. 5

2 Ethel patted her hair and looked very sneery.
Ib. ch. 8

3 My life will be sour grapes and ashes without you.
Ib.

4 Take me back to the Gaierty hotel. *Ib.* ch. 9

HERBERT HENRY ASQUITH,
EARL OF OXFORD
1852–1928

5 Wait and see.
Phrase used repeatedly in speeches in 1910.
Spender and Cyril Asquith's *Life of Lord Oxford and Asquith*, vol. i, p. 275

6 We shall never sheathe the sword which we have not lightly drawn until Belgium receives in full measure all and more than all that she has sacrificed, until France is adequately secured against the menace of aggression, until the rights of the smaller nationalities of Europe are placed upon an unassailable foundation, and until the military domination of Prussia is wholly and finally destroyed. *Speech at the Guildhall, 9 Nov. 1914*

SIR JACOB ASTLEY
1579–1652

7 O Lord! thou knowest how busy I must be this day: if I forget thee, do not thou forget me.
Prayer before the Battle of Edgehill (Sir Philip Warwick, *Memoires*, 1701, p. 229)

EDWARD L. ATKINSON
and
APSLEY CHERRY-GARRARD

8 A very gallant gentleman.
Inscription on the burial place of Capt. L. E. G. Oates *in the Antarctic*, *Nov. 1912. Being almost crippled, he walked to his death in a blizzard to enable his companions to proceed on their journey more quickly.*

HARRIET AUBER
1773–1862

9 And His that gentle voice we hear,
Soft as the breath of even,
That checks each fault, that calms each fear,
And speaks of heaven.
Spirit of the Psalms (1829), *Our Blest Redeemer, ere He breathed*

JOHN AUBREY
1626–1697

10 He was so fair that they called him *the lady of* Christ's College. *Brief Lives. John Milton*

11 Sir Walter, being strangely surprised and put out of his countenance at so great a table, gives his son a damned blow over the face. His son, as rude as he was, would not strike his father, but strikes over the face the gentleman that sat next to him and said 'Box about: 'twill come to my father anon'.
Ib. Sir Walter Raleigh

12 When he killed a calf he would do it in a high style, and make a speech. *Ib. William Shakespeare*

13 He was a handsome, well-shaped man: very good company, and of a very ready and pleasant smooth wit. *Brief Lives. William Shakespeare*

ALEXANDER BOSWELL,
LORD AUCHINLECK
1706–1782

14 He [Cromwell] gart kings ken they had a *lith* in their neck.
gart ken = made to know; lith = joint.
Boswell, v. 382, n. 2

ÉMILE AUGIER
1820–1889

15 La nostalgie de la boue.
Homesickness for the gutter.
Le Mariage d'Olympe, I. i

ST. AUGUSTINE
354–430

16 Fecisti nos ad te et inquietum est cor nostrum, donec requiescat in te.
Thou hast created us for thyself, and our heart cannot be quieted till it may find repose in thee.
Confessions, bk. i, ch. 1. Trans. by Watts

17 Nondum amabam, et amare amabam . . . quaerebam quid amarem, amans amare.
I loved not yet, yet I loved to love . . . I sought what I might love, in love with loving.
Ib. bk. iii, ch. 1

18 Et illa erant fercula, in quibus mihi esurienti te inferebatur sol et luna.
And these were the dishes wherein to me, hunger-starven for thee, they served up the sun and moon. *Ib.* ch. 6

19 Fieri non potest, ut filius istarum lacrimarum pereat.
It is not possible that the son of these tears should be lost. *Ib.* ch. 12

20 Da mihi castitatem et continentiam, sed noli modo.
Give me chastity and continency, but do not give it yet. *Ib.* bk. viii, ch. 7

21 Tolle lege, tolle lege.
Take up and read, take up and read. *Ib.* ch. 12

22 Sero te amavi, pulchritudo tam antiqua et tam nova, sero te amavi! et ecce intus eras et ego foris, et ibi te quaerebam.
Too late came I to love thee, O thou Beauty both so ancient and so fresh, yea too late came I to love thee. And behold, thou wert within me, and I out of myself, where I made search for thee. *Ib.* bk. x, ch. 27

23 Da quod iubes et iube quod vis. Imperas nobis continentiam.
Give what thou commandest, and command what thou wilt.
Thou imposest continency upon us. *Ib.* ch. 29

24 Securus iudicat orbis terrarum.
The verdict of the world is conclusive.
Contra Epist. Parmen. iii. 24

1 Salus extra ecclesiam non est.

No salvation exists outside the church.
De Bapt. IV, c. xvii. 24, referring back to St. Cyprian's 'Habere non potest Deum patrem qui ecclesiam non habet matrem' (He cannot have God for his Father who has not the church for his mother), *De Cath. Eccl. Unitate.* vi

2 Audi partem alteram.

Hear the other side. *De Duabus Animabus,* xiv. ii

3 Ama et fac quod vis.

Love and do what you will.
Popular version of St. Augustine's 'Dilige et quod vis fac' (Love and do what you will), *In Joann.* vii. 8

4 Multi quidem facilius se abstinent ut non utantur, quam temperent ut bene utantur.

To many, total abstinence is easier than perfect moderation. *On the Good of Marriage,* xxi.

5 Roma locuta est; causa finita est.

Rome has spoken; the case is concluded.
Sermons, bk. i

6 De vitiis nostris scalam nobis facimus, si vitia ipsa calcamus.

We make a ladder of our vices, if we trample those same vices underfoot. *Ib.* iii. *De Ascensione*

JANE AUSTEN
1775–1817

7 An egg boiled very soft is not unwholesome. [*Mr. Woodhouse.*] *Emma,* ch. 3

8 One half of the world cannot understand the pleasures of the other. [*Emma.*] *Ib.* ch. 9

9 A basin of nice smooth gruel, thin, but not too thin. *Ib.* ch. 12

10 With men he can be rational and unaffected, but when he has ladies to please, every feature works. [*Mr. Knightley of Mr. Elton.*] *Ib.* ch. 13

11 She believed he had been drinking too much of Mr. Weston's good wine. *Ib.* ch. 15

12 My mother's deafness is very trifling, you see, just nothing at all. By only raising my voice, and saying anything two or three times over, she is sure to hear. [*Miss Bates.*] *Ib.* ch. 19

13 'But, my dear sir,' cried Mr. Weston, 'if Emma comes away early, it will be breaking up the party.' 'And no great harm if it does,' said Mr. Woodhouse. 'The sooner every party breaks up the better.' *Ib.* ch. 25

14 That young man . . . is very thoughtless. Do not tell his father, but that young man is not quite the thing. He has been opening the doors very often this evening and keeping them open very inconsiderately. He does not think of the draught. I do not mean to set you against him, but indeed he is not quite the thing. [*Mr. Woodhouse.*] *Ib.* ch. 29

15 Open the windows! But, surely Mr. Churchill, nobody would think of opening the windows at Randalls. Nobody could be so imprudent. [*Mr. Woodhouse.*] *Ib.*

16 So extremely like Maple Grove. [*Mrs. Elton.*] *Emma,* ch. 32

17 They will have their barouche-landau, of course. [*Mrs. Elton.*] *Ib.*

18 Young ladies should take care of themselves. Young ladies are delicate plants. They should take care of their health and their complexion. My dear, did you change your stockings? [*Mr. Woodhouse.*] *Ib.* ch. 34

19 One has no great hopes from Birmingham. I always say there is something direful in the sound. [*Mrs. Elton.*] *Ib.* ch. 36

20 How shall we ever recollect half the dishes for grandmamma? [*Miss Bates.*] *Ib.* ch. 38

21 Let other pens dwell on guilt and misery. *Mansfield Park,* ch. 48

22 'And what are you reading, Miss —?' 'Oh! it is only a novel!' replies the young lady: while she lays down her book with affected indifference, or momentary shame.—'It is only Cecilia, or Camilla, or Belinda:' or, in short, only some work in which the most thorough knowledge of human nature, the happiest delineation of its varieties, the liveliest effusions of wit and humour are conveyed to the world in the best chosen language.
Northanger Abbey, ch. 5

23 But are they all horrid, are you sure they are all horrid? [*Catherine.*] *Ib.* ch. 6

24 Oh, Lord! not I; I never read much; I have something else to do. [*John Thorpe.*] *Ib.* ch. 7

25 Sir Walter Elliot, of Kellynch-hall, in Somersetshire, was a man who, for his own amusement, never took up any book but the Baronetage; there he found occupation for an idle hour, and consolation in a distressed one; . . . this was the page at which the favourite volume always opened: ELLIOT OF KELLYNCH-HALL. *Persuasion,* ch. 1

26 My sore throats are always worse than anyone's. [*Mary Musgrove.*] *Ib.* ch. 18

27 All the privilege I claim for my own sex . . . is that of loving longest, when existence or when hope is gone. [*Anne.*] *Ib.* ch. 23

28 It is a truth universally acknowledged, that a single man in possession of a good fortune, must be in want of a wife. *Pride and Prejudice,* ch. 1

29 'Kitty has no discretion in her coughs,' said her father: 'she times them ill.' 'I do not cough for my own amusement,' replied Kitty fretfully. *Ib.* ch. 2

30 How can you contrive to write so even? [*Miss Bingley.*] *Ib.* ch. 10

31 Mr. Collins had only to change from Jane to Elizabeth —and it was soon done—done while Mrs. Bennet was stirring the fire. *Ib.* ch. 15

32 You have delighted us long enough. [*Mr. Bennet.*] *Ib.* ch. 18

33 An unhappy alternative is before you, Elizabeth. From this day you must be a stranger to one of your parents.—Your mother will never see you again if you do *not* marry Mr. Collins, and I will never see you again if you *do.* [*Mr. Bennet.*] *Ib.* ch. 20

1 Nobody is on my side, nobody takes part with me: I am cruelly used, nobody feels for my poor nerves. [*Mrs. Bennet.*]   *Pride and Prejudice*, ch. 20

2 '. . . It is very hard to think that Charlotte Lucas should ever be mistress of this house, that *I* should be forced to make way for *her*, and live to see her take my place in it.'
'My dear, do not give way to such gloomy thoughts. Let us hope for better things. Let us flatter ourselves that *I* may be the survivor.'   *Ib.* ch. 23

3 No arguments shall be wanting on my part, that can alleviate so severe a misfortune: or that may comfort you, under a circumstance that must be of all others most afflicting to a parent's mind. The death of your daughter would have been a blessing in comparison of this. [*Mr. Collins.*]   *Ib.* ch. 48

4 You ought certainly to forgive them as a christian, but never to admit them in your sight, or allow their names to be mentioned in your hearing. [*Mr. Collins.*]   *Ib.* ch. 57

5 For what do we live, but to make sport for our neighbours, and laugh at them in our turn? [*Mr. Bennet.*]   *Ib.*

6 I have been a selfish being all my life, in practice, though not in principle. [*Mr. Darcy.*]   *Ib.* ch. 58

7 If any young men come for Mary or Kitty, send them in, for I am quite at leisure. [*Mr. Bennet.*]   *Ib.* ch. 59

8 An annuity is a very serious business. [*Mrs. Dashwood.*]   *Sense and Sensibility*, ch. 2

9 Only conceive how comfortable they will be. Five hundred a year! I am sure I cannot imagine how they will spend half of it. [*Mrs. J. Dashwood.*] *Ib.*

10 'I am afraid,' replied Elinor, 'that the pleasantness of an employment does not always evince its propriety.'   *Ib.* ch. 13

11 Lady Middleton . . . exerted herself to ask Mr. Palmer if there was any news in the paper.
'No, none at all,' he replied, and read on. *Ib.* ch. 19

12 'The little bit (two inches wide) of ivory on which I work with so fine a brush as produces little effect after much labour.'   *Letter, 16 Dec. 1816*

ALFRED AUSTIN
1835–1913

13 An earl by right, by courtesy a man.   *The Season*

14 Across the wires the electric message came:
'He is no better, he is much the same.'
On the Illness of the Prince of Wales, afterwards Edward VII. Attr. to Austin, but probably not his. *See* J. Lewis May in the *Dublin Review*, July 1937

SIR ROBERT AYTOUN
1570–1638

15 I loved thee once, I'll love no more,
   Thine be the grief, as is the blame;
Thou art not what thou wast before,
   What reason I should be the same?
     To an Inconstant Mistress

WILLIAM EDMONDSTOUNE AYTOUN
1813–1865

16 Take away that star and garter—
   Hide them from my aching sight!
Neither king nor prince shall tempt me
   From my lonely room this night.
     Charles Edward at Versailles on the Anniversary of Culloden

17 Nowhere beats the heart so kindly
   As beneath the tartan plaid!   *Ib. l. 219*

18 Sound the fife, and cry the slogan—
   Let the pibroch shake the air.
     The Burial-march of Dundee, l. 1

19 On the heights of Killiecrankie
   Yester-morn our army lay.   *Ib. l. 49*

20 Like a tempest down the ridges
   Swept the hurricane of steel,
Rose the slogan of Macdonald—
   Flashed the broadsword of Lochiell!   *Ib. l. 137*

21 So, amidst the battle's thunder,
   Shot and steel, and scorching flame,
In the glory of his manhood
   Passed the spirit of the Graeme!   *Ib. l. 165*

22 News of battle!—news of battle!
   Hark! 'tis ringing down the street:
And the archways and the pavement
   Bear the clang of hurrying feet.
     Edinburgh after Flodden, st. 1

23 Warder—warder! open quickly!
   Man—is this a time to wait?   *Ib. st. 2*

24 Do not lift him from the bracken,
   Leave him lying where he fell—
Better bier ye cannot fashion:
   None beseems him half so well
As the bare and broken heather,
   And the hard and trampled sod,
Whence his angry soul ascended
   To the judgement-seat of God!
     The Widow of Glencoe, st. 1

25 They bore within their breasts the grief
   That fame can never heal—
The deep, unutterable woe
   Which none save exiles feel.
     The Island of the Scots, xii

26 Fhairshon swore a feud
      Against the clan M'Tavish;
   Marched into their land
      To murder and to rafish;
For he did resolve
   To extirpate the vipers,
With four-and-twenty men
   And five-and-thirty pipers.
     The Massacre of the Macpherson, i

27 Fharshon had a son,
      Who married Noah's daughter,
   And nearly spoiled ta Flood,
      By trinking up ta water:

28 Which he would have done,
      I at least pelieve it,
   Had the mixture peen
      Only half Glenlivet.   *Ib. vii, viii*

29 Come hither, Evan Cameron!
   Come, stand beside my knee.
     The Execution of Montrose, i

1 And some that came to scoff at him
Now turned aside and wept.
The Execution of Montrose, vi

2 But onwards—always onwards,
In silence and in gloom,
The dreary pageant laboured,
Till it reached the house of doom. *Ib.* vii

3 The master-fiend Argyle! *Ib.*

4 The Marquis gazed a moment,
And nothing did he say. *Ib.* viii

5 Then nail my head on yonder tower—
Give every town a limb—
And God who made shall gather them:
I go from you to Him! *Ib.* xii

6 'He is coming! he is coming!'
Like a bridegroom from his room,
Came the hero from his prison
To the scaffold and the doom. *Ib.* xiv

7 The grim Geneva ministers
With anxious scowl drew near,
As you have seen the ravens flock
Around the dying deer. *Ib.* xvii

8 Like a brave old Scottish Cavalier,
All of the olden time! *The Old Scottish Cavalier*

9 Have you heard of Philip Slingsby,
Slingsby of the manly chest;
How he slew the Snapping Turtle
In the regions of the West?
The Fight with the Snapping Turtle

10 The earth is all the home I have,
The heavens my wide roof-tree.
The Wandering Jew, l. 49

FRANCIS BACON
1561–1626

11 For all knowledge and wonder (which is the seed
of knowledge) is an impression of pleasure in itself.
Advancement of Learning, bk. I. i. 3 (ed. 1605)

12 Time, which is the author of authors. *Ib.* iv. 12

13 If a man will begin with certainties, he shall end in
doubts; but if he will be content to begin with
doubts, he shall end in certainties. *Ib.* v. 8

14 [Knowledge is] a rich storehouse for the glory of the
Creator and the relief of man's estate. *Ib.* 11

15 Antiquities are history defaced, or some remnants of
history which have casually escaped the shipwreck
of time. *Ib.* bk. II. ii. 1

16 Poesy was ever thought to have some participation of
divineness, because it doth raise and erect the mind,
by submitting the shows of things to the desires of
the mind; whereas reason doth buckle and bow the
mind unto the nature of things. *Ib.* iv. 2

17 The knowledge of man is as the waters, some descending from above, and some springing from beneath;
the one informed by the light of nature, the other
inspired by divine revelation. *Ib.* v. 1

18 There was never miracle wrought by God to convert
an atheist, because the light of nature might have
led him to confess a God. *Ib.* vi. 1

19 They are ill discoverers that think there is no land,
when they can see nothing but sea. *Ib.* vii. 5

20 Words are the tokens current and accepted for conceits, as moneys are for values. *Ib.* xvi. 3

21 A dance is a measured pace, as a verse is a measured
speech. *Advancement of Learning*, II. xvi. 5

22 But men must know, that in this theatre of man's life
it is reserved only for God and angels to be lookers
on. *Ib.* xx. 8

23 We are much beholden to Machiavel and others, that
write what men do, and not what they ought to do.
Ib. xxi. 9

24 Men must pursue things which are just in present,
and leave the future to the divine Providence.
Ib. 11

25 Did not one of the fathers in great indignation call
poesy *vinum dæmonum*? *Ib.* xxii. 13

26 All good moral philosophy is but an handmaid to
religion. *Ib.* 14

27 Man seeketh in society comfort, use, and protection.
Ib. xxiii. 2

28 A man must make his opportunity, as oft as find it.
Ib. 3

29 Caesar, when he went first into Gaul, made no scruple
to profess 'That he had rather be first in a village
than second at Rome'. *Ib.* 36

30 Fortunes . . . come tumbling into some men's laps.
Ib. 43

31 That other principle of Lysander, 'That children are
to be deceived with comfits, and men with oaths.'
Ib. 45

32 It is in life as it is in ways, the shortest way is commonly the foulest, and surely the fairer way is not
much about. *Ib.*

33 There are in nature certain fountains of justice,
whence all civil laws are derived but as streams.
Ib. 49

34 The inseparable propriety of time, which is ever more
and more to disclose truth. *Ib.* xxiv

35 Books must follow sciences, and not sciences books.
Proposition touching Amendment of Laws

36 Anger makes dull men witty, but it keeps them poor.
Related as a remark of Queen Elizabeth.
Apothegms, 5

37 A beautiful face is a silent commendation. *Ib.* 12

38 Wise nature did never put her precious jewels into
a garret four stories high: and therefore . . .
exceeding tall men had ever very empty heads.
Ib. 17

39 Hope is a good breakfast, but it is a bad supper.
Ib. 36

40 Like strawberry wives, that laid two or three great
strawberries at the mouth of their pot, and all the
rest were little ones.
A saying of Queen Elizabeth. Ib. 54

41 Sir Henry Wotton used to say, 'That critics are like
brushers of noblemen's clothes.' *Ib.* 64

42 Mr. Savill was asked by my lord of Essex his opinion
touching poets; who answered my lord; 'He thought
them the best writers, next to those that write
prose.' *Ib.* 66

43 Demosthenes when he fled from the battle, and that
it was reproached to him, said; 'That he that flies
mought fight again.' *Ib.* 169

1 One of the Seven was wont to say; 'That laws were like cobwebs; where the small flies were caught, and the great brake through.' *Apothegms*, 181

2 Pyrrhus, when his friends congratulated to him his victory over the Romans, under the conduct of Fabricius, but with great slaughter of his own side, said to them again; 'Yes, but if we have such another victory, we are undone.' *Ib.* 193

3 Cosmus duke of Florence was wont to say of perfidious friends; 'That we read that we ought to forgive our enemies; but we do not read that we ought to forgive our friends.' *Ib.* 206

4 One of the fathers saith . . . that old men go to death, and death comes to young men. *Ib.* 270

5 Diogenes said of a young man that danced daintily, and was much commended: 'The better, the worse.' *Ib.* 266

6 Riches are a good handmaid, but the worst mistress.
De Dignitate et Augmentis Scientiarium, pt. 1, bk. vi, ch. 3. *Antitheta*, 6 (ed. 1640, trans. Gilbert Watts)

7 Antiquitas saeculi juventus mundi.
The age of the centuries is the youth of the world.
Ib. bk. vii, ch. 81

8 The voice of the people hath some divineness in it, else how should so many men agree to be of one mind? *Ib.* 9

9 Envy never makes holiday. *Ib.* 16

10 No terms of moderation takes place with the vulgar. *Ib.* 30

11 Silence is the virtue of fools. *Ib.* 31

12 The worst solitude is to be destitute of sincere friendship. *Ib.* 37

13 Omnia mutari, et nil vere interire, ac summam materiae prorsus eandem manere, satis constat.
That all things are changed, and that nothing really perishes, and that the sum of matter remains exactly the same, is sufficiently certain.
Cogitationes de Natura Rerum, v. Trans. Spedding

14 I hold every man a debtor to his profession.
The Elements of the Common Law, preface

15 My essays . . . come home, to men's business, and bosoms. *Essays*. Dedication of 1625 edition

16 It was a high speech of Seneca (after the manner of the Stoics) that, 'the good things which belong to prosperity are to be wished, but the good things that belong to adversity are to be admired.'
Ib. 5 *Of Adversity*

17 It is yet a higher speech of his than the other, . . . 'It is true greatness to have in one the frailty of a man, and the security of a God.' *Ib.*

18 Prosperity is the blessing of the Old Testament, adversity is the blessing of the New. *Ib.*

19 The pencil of the Holy Ghost hath laboured more in describing the afflictions of Job than the felicities of Solomon. *Ib.*

20 Prosperity is not without many fears and distastes; and adversity is not without comforts and hopes. *Ib.*

21 Prosperity doth best discover vice, but adversity doth best discover virtue. *Ib.*

22 He that plots to be the only figure among ciphers, is the decay of the whole age.
Essays, 36. *Of Ambition*

23 I had rather believe all the fables in the legend, and the Talmud, and the Alcoran, than that this universal frame is without a mind. *Ib.* 16. *Atheism*

24 God never wrought miracle to convince atheism, because his ordinary works convince it. *Ib.*

25 A little philosophy inclineth man's mind to atheism, but depth in philosophy bringeth men's minds about to religion. *Ib.*

26 They that deny a God destroy man's nobility; for certainly man is of kin to the beasts by his body; and, if he be not of kin to God by his spirit, he is a base and ignoble creature. *Ib.*

27 Virtue is like a rich stone, best plain set.
Ib. 43. *Of Beauty*

28 That is the best part of beauty, which a picture cannot express. *Ib.*

29 There is no excellent beauty that hath not some strangeness in the proportion. *Ib.*

30 There is in human nature generally more of the fool than of the wise. *Ib.* 12. *Boldness*

31 He said it that knew it best. *Ib.*

32 In civil business; what first? boldness; what second and third? boldness: and yet boldness is a child of ignorance and baseness. *Ib.*

33 Boldness is an ill keeper of promise. *Ib.*

34 Mahomet made the people believe that he would call a hill to him, and from the top of it offer up his prayers for the observers of his law. The people assembled: Mahomet called the hill to come to him again and again; and when the hill stood still, he was never a whit abashed, but said, 'If the hill will not come to Mahomet, Mahomet will go to the hill.' *Ib.*

35 Houses are built to live in and not to look on; therefore let use be preferred before uniformity, except where both may be had. *Ib.* 45. *Of Building*

36 Light gains make heavy purses.
Ib. 52. *Of Ceremonies and Respects*

37 Small matters win great commendation. *Ib.*

38 He that . . . giveth another occasion of satiety, maketh himself cheap. *Ib.*

39 A wise man will make more opportunities than he finds. *Ib.*

40 Books will speak plain when counsellors blanch.
Ib. 20. *Of Counsel*

41 There be that can pack the cards and yet cannot play well; so there are some that are good in canvasses and factions, that are otherwise weak men.
Ib. 22. *Of Cunning*

42 In things that are tender and unpleasing, it is good to break the ice by some whose words are of less weight, and to reserve the more weighty voice to come in as by chance. *Ib.*

43 I knew one that when he wrote a letter he would put that which was most material in the postscript, as if it had been a bymatter. *Ib.*

44 Nothing doth more hurt in a state than that cunning men pass for wise. *Ib.*

1 Men fear death as children fear to go in the dark; and as that natural fear in children is increased with tales, so is the other. *Essays, 2. Of Death*

2 There is no passion in the mind of man so weak, but it mates and masters the fear of death . . . Revenge triumphs over death; love slights it; honour aspireth to it; grief flieth to it. *Ib.*

3 It is as natural to die as to be born; and to a little infant, perhaps, the one is as painful as the other. *Ib.*

4 Above all, believe it, the sweetest canticle is *Nunc dimittis*, when a man hath obtained worthy ends and expectations. Death hath this also, that it openeth the gate to good fame, and extinguisheth envy. *Ib.*

5 Intermingle . . . jest with earnest. *Ib. 32. Of Discourse*

6 If you dissemble sometimes your knowledge of that you are thought to know, you shall be thought, another time, to know that you know not. *Ib.*

7 I knew a wise man that had it for a by-word, when he saw men hasten to a conclusion, 'Stay a little, that we may make an end the sooner.' *Ib. 25. Of Dispatch*

8 To choose time is to save time. *Ib.*

9 It is a miserable state of mind to have few things to desire and many things to fear. *Ib. 19. Of Empire*

10 Riches are for spending. *Ib. 28. Of Expense*

11 A man ought warily to begin charges which once begun will continue. *Ib.*

12 Lookers-on many times see more than gamesters. *Ib. 48. Of Followers and Friends*

13 There is little friendship in the world, and least of all between equals. *Ib.*

14 Chiefly the mould of a man's fortune is in his own hands. *Ib. 40. Of Fortune*

15 It had been hard for him that spake it to have put more truth and untruth together, in a few words, than in that speech: 'Whosoever is delighted in solitude is either a wild beast, or a god.' *Ib. 27. Of Friendship. (See 14:15)*

16 A crowd is not company, and faces are but a gallery of pictures, and talk but a tinkling cymbal, where there is no love. *Ib.*

17 It [friendship] redoubleth joys, and cutteth griefs in halves. *Ib.*

18 Cure the disease and kill the patient. *Ib.*

19 God Almighty first planted a garden; and, indeed, it is the purest of human pleasures. *Ib. 46. Of Gardens*

20 The inclination to goodness is imprinted deeply in the nature of man: insomuch, that if it issue not towards men, it will take unto other living creatures. *Ib. 13. Goodness, and Goodness of Nature*

21 If a man be gracious and courteous to strangers, it shows he is a citizen of the world. *Ib.*

22 Men in great place are thrice servants: servants of the sovereign or state, servants of fame, and servants of business. *Ib. 11. Of Great Place*

23 It is a strange desire to seek power and to lose liberty. *Ib.*

24 The rising unto place is laborious, and by pains men come to greater pains; and it is sometimes base, and by indignities men come to dignities. The standing is slippery, and the regress is either a downfall, or at least an eclipse. *Essays, 11. Of Great Place*

25 Set it down to thyself, as well to create good precedents as to follow them. *Ib.*

26 Severity breedeth fear, but roughness breedeth hate. Even reproofs from authority ought to be grave, and not taunting. *Ib.*

27 As in nature things move violently to their place and calmly in their place, so virtue in ambition is violent, in authority settled and calm. *Ib.*

28 All rising to great place is by a winding stair. *Ib.*

29 As the births of living creatures at first are ill-shapen, so are all innovations, which are the births of time. *Ib. 24. Of Innovations*

30 He that will not apply new remedies must expect new evils; for time is the greatest innovator. *Ib.*

31 The place of justice is a hallowed place. *Ib. 56. Of Judicature*

32 The speaking in a perpetual hyperbole is comely in nothing but in love. *Ib. 10. Of Love*

33 It has been well said that 'the arch-flatterer with whom all the petty flatterers have intelligence is a man's self.' *Ib.*

34 He that hath wife and children hath given hostages to fortune; for they are impediments to great enterprises, either of virtue or mischief. *Ib. 8. Of Marriage and Single Life*

35 There are some other that account wife and children but as bills of charges. *Ib.*

36 A single life doth well with churchmen, for charity will hardly water the ground where it must first fill a pool. *Ib.*

37 Wives are young men's mistresses, companions for middle age, and old men's nurses. *Ib.*

38 He was reputed one of the wise men that made answer to the question when a man should marry? 'A young man not yet, an elder man not at all.' *Ib.*

39 Nature is often hidden, sometimes overcome, seldom extinguished. *Ib. 38. Of Nature in Men*

40 It is generally better to deal by speech than by letter. *Ib. 47. Of Negotiating*

41 It is a reverend thing to see an ancient castle or building not in decay. *Ib. 14. Of Nobility*

42 New nobility is but the act of power, but ancient nobility is the act of time. *Ib.*

43 Nobility of birth commonly abateth industry. *Ib.*

44 The joys of parents are secret, and so are their griefs and fears. *Ib. 7. Of Parents and Children*

45 Children sweeten labours, but they make misfortunes more bitter. *Ib.*

46 The noblest works and foundations have proceeded from childless men, which have sought to express the images of their minds where those of their bodies have failed. *Ib.*

1 Fame is like a river, that beareth up things light and swollen, and drowns things weighty and solid.
Essays, 53. *Of Praise*

2 [Dreams and predictions] ought to serve but for winter talk by the fireside. *Ib*. 35. *Of Prophecies*

3 Age will not be defied. *Ib*. 30. *Of Regimen of Health*

4 Revenge is a kind of wild justice, which the more man's nature runs to, the more ought law to weed it out. *Ib*. 4. *Of Revenge*

5 Why should I be angry with a man for loving himself better than me? *Ib*.

6 A man that studieth revenge keeps his own wounds green. *Ib*.

7 Defer not charities till death; for certainly, if a man weigh it rightly, he that doth so is rather liberal of another man's than of his own. *Ib*. 34. *Of Riches*

8 The four pillars of government . . . (which are religion, justice, counsel, and treasure).
Ib. 15. *Of Seditions and Troubles*

9 The surest way to prevent seditions (if the times do bear it) is to take away the matter of them. *Ib*.

10 Money is like muck, not good except it be spread. *Ib*.

11 The remedy is worse than the disease. *Ib*.

12 The French are wiser than they seem, and the Spaniards seem wiser than they are.
Ib. 26. *Of Seeming Wise*

13 Studies serve for delight, for ornament, and for ability. *Ib*. 50. *Of Studies*

14 To spend too much time in studies is sloth. *Ib*.

15 They perfect nature and are perfected by experience. *Ib*.

16 Read not to contradict and confute, nor to believe and take for granted, nor to find talk and discourse, but to weigh and consider. *Ib*.

17 Some books are to be tasted, others to be swallowed, and some few to be chewed and digested; that is, some books are to be read only in parts; others to be read but not curiously; and some few to be read wholly, and with diligence and attention. Some books also may be read by deputy, and extracts made of them by others. *Ib*.

18 Reading maketh a full man; conference a ready man and writing an exact man. *Ib*.

19 Histories make men wise; poets, witty; the mathematics, subtile; natural philosophy, deep; moral, grave; logic and rhetoric, able to contend. *Ib*.

20 It were better to have no opinion of God at all than such an opinion as is unworthy of him; for the one is unbelief, the other is contumely.
Ib. 17. *Of Superstition*

21 There is a superstition in avoiding superstition. *Ib*.

22 Suspicions amongst thoughts are like bats amongst birds, they ever fly by twilight. *Ib*. 31. *Of Suspicion*

23 There is nothing makes a man suspect much, more than to know little. *Ib*.

24 Neither is money the sinews of war (as it is trivially said). *Ib*. 29. *Of The True Greatness of Kingdoms*

25 Neither will it be, that a people overlaid with taxes should ever become valiant and martial. *Ib*.

26 Thus much is certain; that he that commands the sea is at great liberty, and may take as much and as little of the war as he will.
Essays, 29. *Of The True Greatness of Kingdoms*

27 Travel, in the younger sort, is a part of education; in the elder, a part of experience. He that travelleth into a country before he hath some entrance into the language, goeth to school, and not to travel.
Ib. 18. *Of Travel*

28 Let diaries, therefore, be brought in use. *Ib*.

29 What is truth? said jesting Pilate; and would not stay for an answer. *Ib*. 1. *Of Truth*

30 A mixture of a lie doth ever add pleasure. *Ib*.

31 It is not the lie that passeth through the mind, but the lie that sinketh in, and settleth in it, that doth the hurt. *Ib*.

32 The inquiry of truth, which is the love-making, or wooing of it, the knowledge of truth, which is the presence of it, and the belief of truth, which is the enjoying of it, is the sovereign good of human nature. *Ib*.

33 Certainly, it is heaven upon earth, to have a man's mind . . . turn upon the poles of truth. *Ib*.

34 All colours will agree in the dark.
Ib. 3. *Of Unity in Religion*

35 It was prettily devised of Aesop, 'The fly sat upon the axletree of the chariot-wheel and said, what a dust do I raise.' *Ib*. 54. *Of Vain-Glory*

36 In the youth of a state arms do flourish; in the middle age of a state, learning; and then both of them together for a time; in the declining age of a state, mechanical arts and merchandise.
Ib. 58. *Of Vicissitude of Things*

37 Be so true to thyself as thou be not false to others.
Ib. 23. *Of Wisdom for a Man's Self*

38 It is a poor centre of a man's actions, himself. *Ib*.

39 It is the nature of extreme self-lovers, as they will set a house on fire, and it were but to roast their eggs. *Ib*.

40 It is the wisdom of the crocodiles, that shed tears when they would devour. *Ib*.

41 Young men are fitter to invent than to judge, fitter for execution than for counsel, and fitter for new projects than for settled business.
Ib. 42. *Of Youth and Age*

42 I have often thought upon death, and I find it the least of all evils. *An Essay on Death*. § 1

43 I do not believe that any man fears to be dead, but only the stroke of death. *Ib*. 3

44 Why should a man be in love with his fetters, though of gold? *Ib*. 4

45 He is the fountain of honour. *Essay of a King*

46 Lucid intervals and happy pauses.
History of King Henry VII, par. 3

47 Quare videmus araneam aut muscam aut formicam, in electro, monumento plus quam regio, sepultas, aeternizari.

Whence we see spiders, flies, or ants, entombed and preserved for ever in amber, a more than royal tomb.
Historia Vitae et Mortis, Provisional Rules Concerning the Duration of Life and the Form of Death, rule 1, Explanation. Trans. Spedding

1 I have taken all knowledge to be my province.
Letter to Lord Burleigh, 1592

2 Opportunity makes a thief.
Letter to the Earl of Essex, 1598

3 I am too old, and the seas are too long, for me to double the Cape of Good Hope.
Memorial of Access

4 I would live to study, and not study to live. *Ib.*

5 God's first Creature, which was Light. *New Atlantis*

6 Quatuor sunt genera Idolorum quae mentes humanas obsident. Iis (docendi gratia) nomina imposuimus; ut primum genus, Idola Tribus; secundum, Idola Specus; tertium, Idola Fori; quartum, Idola Theatri vocentur.

There are four classes of Idols which beset men's minds. To these for distinction's sake I have assigned names—calling the first class, Idols of the Tribe; the second, Idols of the Cave; the third, Idols of the Market-place; the fourth, Idols of the Theatre.
Novum Organon, Aphor. xxxix. Trans. Spedding

7 Quod enim mavult homo verum esse, id potius credit.

For what a man had rather were true he more readily believes. *Ib.* xlix. Trans. Spedding

8 Magna ista scientiarum mater.

This great mother of the sciences [natural philosophy]. *Ib.* lxxx. Trans. Spedding

9 Naturae enim non imperatur, nisi parendo.

We cannot command nature except by obeying her. *Ib.* cxxix. Trans. Spedding

10 Nam et ipsa scientia potestas est.

Knowledge itself is power.
Religious Meditations. Of Heresies

11 De Sapientia Veterum.

The wisdom of the ancients.
Title of Work. Tr. Sir Arthur Gorges, 1619

12 Praecipue autem lignum, sive virga, versus superiorem partem curva est.

Every rod or staff of empire is truly crooked at the top. *Ib.* 6, *Pan, sive Natura*

13 Universities incline wits to sophistry and affectation.
Valerius Terminus of the Interpretation of Nature, ch. 26

14 I have rather studied books than men.
Advice to Sir Geo. Villiers, Works, ed. 1765, vol. ii, p. 258

15 For my name and memory, I leave it to men's charitable speeches, and to foreign nations, and the next ages. *Last Will* (19 Dec. 1625). *Ib.* vol. iii, p. 677

16 The world's a bubble; and the life of man
Less than a span. *The World*

17 Who then to frail mortality shall trust,
But limns the water, or but writes in dust. *Ib.*

18 What is it then to have or have no wife,
But single thraldom, or a double strife? *Ib.*

19 What then remains, but that we still should cry,
Not to be born, or being born, to die? *Ib.*

CARL BAEDEKER

1801–1859

20 Oxford is on the whole more attractive than Cambridge to the ordinary visitor; and the traveller is therefore recommended to visit Cambridge first, or to omit it altogether if he cannot visit both.
Baedeker's Great Britain (1887), 30. *From London to Oxford*

WALTER BAGEHOT

1826–1877

21 The mystic reverence, the religious allegiance, which are essential to a true monarchy, are imaginative sentiments that no legislature can manufacture in any people.
The English Constitution, ch. 1. *The Cabinet*

22 The Crown is, according to the saying, the 'fountain of honour'; but the Treasury is the spring of business. *Ib.* (See 27: 45)

23 It has been said that England invented the phrase, 'Her Majesty's Opposition'; that it was the first government which made a criticism of adminstration as much a part of the polity as administration itself. This critical opposition is the consequence of cabinet government. *Ib.*

24 The *Times* has made many ministries. *Ib.*

25 We turned out the Quaker (Lord Aberdeen), and put in the pugilist (Lord Palmerston). (Change of Ministry, 1855). *Ib.*

26 The best reason why Monarchy is a strong government is, that it is an intelligible government. The mass of mankind understand it, and they hardly anywhere in the world understand any other.
Ib. ch. 2. *The Monarchy*

27 The characteristic of the English Monarchy is that it retains the feelings by which the heroic kings governed their rude age, and has added the feelings by which the constitutions of later Greece ruled in more refined ages. *Ib.*

28 Women—one half the human race at least—care fifty times more for a marriage than a ministry. *Ib.*

29 Royalty is a government in which the attention of the nation is concentrated on one person doing interesting actions. A Republic is a government in which that attention is divided between many, who are all doing uninteresting actions. Accordingly, so long as the human heart is strong and the human reason weak, Royalty will be strong because it appeals to diffused feeling, and Republics weak because they appeal to the understanding. *Ib.*

30 An Englishman whose heart is in a matter is not easily baffled. *Ib.*

31 Throughout the greater part of his life George III was a kind of 'consecrated obstruction'. *Ib.*

32 But of all nations in the world the English are perhaps the least a nation of pure philosophers. *Ib.*

33 The order of nobility is of great use, too, not only in what it creates, but in what it prevents. It prevents the rule of wealth—the religion of gold. This is the obvious and natural idol of the Anglo-Saxon.
Ib. ch. 4. *The House of Lords*

34 The House of Peers has never been a House where the most important peers were most important. *Ib.*

1 A severe though not unfriendly critic of our institutions said that 'the *cure* for admiring the House of Lords was to go and look at it.'
The English Constitution, ch. 4. *The House of Lords*

2 Nations touch at their summits. *Ib.*

3 Years ago Mr. Disraeli called Sir Robert Peel's Ministry—the last Conservative Ministry that had real power—'an organized hypocrisy', so much did the ideas of its 'head' differ from the sensations of its 'tail'. *Ib.*

4 It has been said, not truly, but with a possible approximation to truth, 'that in 1802 every hereditary monarch was insane'. *Ib.*

5 Queen Anne was one of the smallest people ever set in a great place. *Ib.* ch. 7. *Checks and Balances*

6 The soldier—that is, the great soldier—of to-day is not a romantic animal, dashing at forlorn hopes, animated by frantic sentiment, full of fancies as to a love-lady or a sovereign; but a quiet, grave man, busied in charts, exact in sums, master of the art of tactics, occupied in trivial detail; thinking, as the Duke of Wellington was said to do, *most* of the shoes of his soldiers; despising all manner of *éclat* and eloquence; perhaps, like Count Moltke, 'silent in seven languages'. *Ib.*

7 The most melancholy of human reflections, perhaps, is that, on the whole, it is a question whether the benevolence of mankind does most good or harm.
Physics and Politics, No. v

8 Wordsworth, Tennyson, and Browning; or, Pure, Ornate, and Grotesque Art in English Poetry.
Title of Essay, National Review, Nov. 1864

PHILIP JAMES BAILEY
1816–1902

9 We live in deeds, not years; in thoughts, not breaths;
In feelings, not in figures on a dial.
We should count time by heart-throbs. He most lives
Who thinks most—feels the noblest—acts the best.
Festus, v

10 America, thou half-brother of the world;
With something good and bad of every land. *Ib.* x

CHARLES BRUCE BAIRNSFATHER
1887–

11 Well, if you knows of a better 'ole, go to it.
Fragments from France, No. 1 (1915)

HENRY WILLIAMS BAKER
1821–1877

12 The King of Love my Shepherd is,
Whose goodness faileth never.
Hymns Ancient and Modern. The King of Love my Shepherd is (1868)

13 There is a blessed home
Beyond this land of woe.
Ib. There is a Blessed Home (1861)

MICHAEL BAKUNINE
d. 1876

14 We wish, in a word, equality—equality in fact as corollary, or, rather, as primordial condition of liberty. From each according to his faculties, to each according to his needs; that is what we wish sincerely and energetically.
Declaration signed by forty-seven anarchists on trial after the failure of their uprising at Lyons in 1870. See J. Morrison Davidson, The Old Order and the New, 1890. *(See 333:12)*

STANLEY BALDWIN, EARL BALDWIN
1867–1947

15 When you think about the defence of England you no longer think of the chalk cliffs of Dover. You think of the Rhine. That is where our frontier lies to-day. *Speech, House of Commons, 30 July 1934*

BISHOP JOHN BALE
1495–1563

16 Though it be a foul great lie: Set upon it a good face.
King John, l. 1978

ARTHUR JAMES BALFOUR
1848–1930

17 Defence of philosophic doubt. *Article in Mind*, 1878

18 Do not hesitate to shoot.
Attrib. to Balfour, actually part of a telegram sent by the Divisional Magistrate for Cork district in 1888: 'Deal very summarily with any organized resistance to lawful authority. If necessary do not hesitate to shoot. Plunkett.'

19 The energies of our system will decay, the glory of the sun will be dimmed, and the earth, tideless and inert, will no longer tolerate the race which has for a moment disturbed its solitude. Man will go down into the pit, and all his thoughts will perish.
The Foundations of Belief, pt. i, ch. 1

20 It is unfortunate, considering that enthusiasm moves the world, that so few enthusiasts can be trusted to speak the truth. *Letter to Mrs. Drew*, 1918

21 Frank Harris . . . said . . .: 'The fact is, Mr. Balfour, all the faults of the age come from Christianity and journalism.' 'Christianity, of course, but why journalism?'
Autobiography of Margot Asquith, vol. i, ch. 10

BALLADS

22 There was a youth, and a well-beloved youth,
And he was an esquire's son,
He loved the bailiff's daughter dear,
That lived in Islington.
The Oxford Book of Ballads. The Bailiff's Daughter of Islington

23 But when his friends did understand
His fond and foolish mind,
They sent him up to fair London,
An apprentice for to bind. *Ib.*

24 She stept to him, as red as any rose,
And took him by the bridle-ring:
'I pray you, kind sir, give me one penny,
To ease my weary limb.'

'I prithee, sweetheart, canst thou tell me,
Where that thou wast born?'
'At Islington, kind sir,' said she,
'Where I have had many a scorn.'

'I prithee, sweetheart, canst thou tell me
  Whether thou dost know
The bailiff's daughter of Islington?'
  'She's dead, sir, long ago.'

'Then will I sell my goodly steed,
  My saddle and my bow;
I will into some far countrey,
  Where no man doth me know.'

'O stay, O stay, thou goodly youth!
  She's alive, she is not dead;
Here she standeth by thy side,
  And is ready to be thy bride.'
    The Oxford Book of Ballads. The Bailiff's Daughter of Islington

1 In Scarlet town, where I was born,
    There was a fair maid dwellin',
  Made every youth cry *Well-a-way!*
    Her name was Barbara Allen.

  All in the merry month of May,
    When green buds they were swellin',
  Young Jemmy Grove on his death-bed lay,
    For love of Barbara Allen. *Ib. Barbara Allen's Cruelty*

2 So slowly, slowly rase she up,
    And slowly she came nigh him,
  And when she drew the curtain by—
    'Young man, I think you're dyin'!'. *Ib.*

3 'O mother, mother, make my bed,
    O make it saft and narrow;
  My love has died for me to-day,
    I'll die for him to-morrow.' *Ib.*

4 'Farewell,' she said, 'ye virgins all,
    And shun the fault I fell in:
  Henceforth take warning by the fall
    Of cruel Barbara Allen.' *Ib.*

5 It fell about the Lammas tide
    When husbands win their hay,
  The doughty Douglas bound him to ride
    In England to take a prey.
      Ib. The Battle of Otterburn, i

6 My wound is deep: I am fayn to sleep,
    Take thou the vaward of me,
  And hide me by the bracken bush
    Grows on yonder lilye-lee. *Ib. lvii*

7 There were twa sisters sat in a bour;
    Binnorie, O Binnorie!
  There came a knight to be their wooer,
    By the bonnie milldams o' Binnorie. Ib. Binnorie

8 Ye Highlands and ye Lawlands,
    O where hae ye been?
  They hae slain the Earl of Murray,
    And hae laid him on the green.
      Ib. The Bonny Earl of Murray

9 He was a braw gallant,
    And he rid at the ring;
  And the bonny Earl of Murray,
    O he might hae been a king! *Ib.*

10 He was a braw gallant,
    And he play'd at the gluve;
  And the bonny Earl of Murray,
    O he was the Queen's luve!

  O lang will his Lady
    Look owre the Castle Downe,
  Ere she see the Earl of Murray
    Come sounding through the town! *Ib.*

11 The Percy out of Northumberland,
    An avow to God made he
  That he would hunt in the mountains
    Of Cheviot within days three,
  In the maugre of doughty Douglas,
    And all that e'er with him be.
      The Oxford Book of Ballads. Chevy Chase, I. i

12 This began on a Monday at morn,
    In Cheviot the hills so hye;
  The child may rue that is unborn,
    It was the more pitye. *Ib. iv*

13 'But I hae dream'd a dreary dream,
    Beyond the Isle of Sky;
  I saw a dead man win a fight,
    And I think that man was I.'
      Ib. (xix in the Scottish version, but not included in the Oxford Book version)

14 For Witherington my heart was woe
    That ever his sons should be:
  For when both his legs were hewn in two
    Yet he kneel'd and fought on his knee. *Ib.* II. i

15 Clerk Saunders and may Margaret
    Walk'd owre yon garden green;
  And deep and heavy was the love
    That fell thir twa between.

  'A bed, a bed,' Clerk Saunders said,
    'A bed for you and me!'
  'Fye na, fye na,' said may Margaret,
    'Till anes we married be!' *Ib. Clerk Saunders*

16 There's nae room at my head, Marg'ret,
    There's nae room at my feet;
  My bed it is fu' lowly now,
    Among the hungry worms I sleep. *Ib.*

17 He turn'd him round and round about,
    And the tear blinded his e'e:
  'I wad never hae trodden on Irish ground
    If it hadna been for thee'. *Ib. The Daemon Lover*

18 She hadna sail'd a league, a league,
    A league but barely three,
  Till grim, grim grew his countenance
    And gurly grew the sea.

  'What hills are yon, yon pleasant hills,
    The sun shines sweetly on?'—
  'O yon are the hills o' Heaven,' he said,
    'Where you will never won.' *Ib.*

19 He strack the top-mast wi' his hand,
    The fore-mast wi' his knee;
  And he brake that gallant ship in twain,
    And sank her in the sea. *Ib.*

20 O well's me o' my gay goss-hawk,
    That he can speak and flee!
  He'll carry a letter to my love,
    Bring another back to me. *Ib. The Gay Gosshawk*

21 But ne'er a word wad ane o' them speak,
    For barring of the door.
      Ib. Get Up and Bar the Door

22 Goodman, you've spoken the foremost word!
    Get up and bar the door. *Ib.*

23 A ship I have got in the North Country
    And she goes by the name of the *Golden Vanity*,
  O I fear she will be taken by a Spanish Ga-la-lee,
    As she sails by the Low-lands low.
      Ib. The Golden Vanity

1 He bored with his augur, he bored once and twice,
   And some were playing cards, and some were playing dice,
   When the water flowed in it dazzled their eyes,
   And she sank by the Low-lands low.

   So the Cabin-boy did swim all to the larboard side,
   Saying 'Captain! take me in, I am drifting with the tide!'
   'I will shoot you! I will kill you!' the cruel Captain cried,
   'You may sink by the Low-lands low.'
   The Oxford Book of Ballads. The Golden Vanity

2 Then they laid him on the deck, and he closed his eyes and died,
   As they sailed by the Low-lands low. *Ib.*

3 I wish I were where Helen lies,
   Night and day on me she cries;
   O that I were where Helen lies,
   On fair Kirkconnell lea!

   Curst be the heart that thought the thought,
   And curst the hand that fired the shot,
   When in my arms burd Helen dropt,
   And died to succour me! *Ib. Helen of Kirkconnell*

4 And when we came through Glasgow toun,
   We were a comely sight to see;
   My gude lord in the black velvet,
   And I mysel' in cramasie. *Ib. Jamie Douglas*

5 O come ye here to fight, young lord,
   Or come ye here to play?
   Or come ye here to drink good wine
   Upon the weddin'-day? *Ib. Katharine Johnstone*

6 O is my basnet a widow's curch?
   Or my lance a wand of the willow-tree?
   Or my arm a ladye's lilye hand,
   That an English lord should lightly me!
   Ib. Kinmont Willie, x

7 He is either himself a devil frae hell,
   Or else his mother a witch maun be;
   I wadna have ridden that wan water
   For a' the gowd in Christentie. *Ib. xlvi*

8 O he's gart build a bonny ship,
   To sail on the salt sea;
   The mast was o' the beaten gold,
   The sails o' cramoisie. *Ib. The Lass of Lochroyan*

9 Lady Nancy she died out of pure, pure grief,
   Lord Lovel he died out of sorrow. *Ib. Lord Lovel*

10 'What gat ye to your dinner, Lord Randal, my Son?
   What gat ye to your dinner, my handsome young man?'
   'I gat eels boil'd in broo'; mother, make my bed soon,
   For I'm weary wi' hunting, and fain wald lie down.'
   Ib. Lord Randal

11 And the Lowlands o' Holland has twin'd my love and me. *Ib. The Lowlands o' Holland*

12 This ae nighte, this ae nighte,
   —*Every nighte and alle,*
   Fire and fleet[1] and candle-lighte,
   And Christe receive thy saule. Ib. Lyke-Wake Dirge

13 From Brig o' Dread when thou may'st pass,
   —*Every nighte and alle,*
   To Purgatory fire thou com'st at last;
   And Christe receive thy saule.

   ¹ =floor. Other readings are 'sleet' and 'salt'.

If ever thou gavest meat or drink,
   —*Every nighte and alle,*
   The fire sall never make thee shrink;
   And Christe receive thy saule.
   The Oxford Book of Ballads. Lyke-Wake Dirge

14 When captains courageous, whom death could not daunt,
   Did march to the siege of the city of Gaunt,
   They mustered their soldiers by two and by three,
   And the foremost in battle was Mary Ambree.
   Mary Ambree

15 For in my mind, of all mankind
   I love but you alone. *Ib. The Nut Brown Maid*

16 For I must to the greenwood go
   Alone, a banished man. *Ib.*

17 Marie Hamilton's to the kirk gane
   Wi' ribbons on her breast;
   The King thought mair o' Marie Hamilton
   Than he listen'd to the priest.
   Ib. The Queen's Maries

18 Yestreen the Queen had four Maries,
   The night she'll hae but three;
   There was Marie Seaton, and Marie Beaton,
   And Marie Carmichael, and me. *Ib.*

19 O little did my mother ken,
   The day she cradled me,
   The lands I was to travel in
   Or the death I was to die! *Ib.*

20 'O pardon, O pardon', said the Bishop,
   'O pardon, I thee pray!
   For if I had known it had been you,
   I'd have gone some other way.'
   Ib. Robin Hood and the Bishop of Hereford

21 There are twelve months in all the year,
   As I hear many men say,
   But the merriest month in all the year
   Is the merry month of May.
   Ib. Robin Hood and the Widow's Three Sons

22 'Let me have length and breadth enough,
   And under my head a sod;
   That they may say when I am dead,
   —*Here lies bold Robin Hood!*'
   Ib. The Death of Robin Hood

23 The king sits in Dunfermline town
   Drinking the blude-red wine.
   Ib. Sir Patrick Spens

24 Our king has written a braid letter,
   And seal'd it with his hand,
   And sent it to Sir Patrick Spens,
   Was walking on the strand.

   'To Noroway, to Noroway,
   To Noroway o'er the faem;
   The king's daughter o' Noroway,
   'Tis thou must bring her hame.'

   The first word that Sir Patrick read
   So loud, loud laughed he;
   The neist word that Sir Patrick read
   The tear blinded his e'e. *Ib.*

25 I saw the new moon late yestreen
   Wi' the auld moon in her arm;
   And if we gang to sea, master,
   I fear we'll come to harm.'

Go fetch a web o' the silken claith,
  Another o' the twine,
And wap[1] them into our ship's side,
  And let nae the sea come in.
     The Oxford Book of Ballads. Sir Patrick Spens

1 O laith, laith were our gude Scots lords
  To wat their cork-heel'd shoon;
But lang or a' the play was play'd
  They wat their hats aboon.   *Ib.*

2 O lang, lang may the ladies sit,
  Wi' their fans into their hand,
Before they see Sir Patrick Spens
  Come sailing to the strand!

And lang, lang may the maidens sit
  Wi' their gowd kames in their hair,
A-waiting for their ain dear loves!
  For them they'll see nae mair.

Half-owre, half-owre to Aberdour,
  'Tis fifty fathoms deep;
And there lies gude Sir Patrick Spens,
  Wi' the Scots lords at his feet!   *Ib.*

3 And she has kilted her green kirtle
  A little abune her knee;
And she has braided her yellow hair
  A little abune her bree.   *Ib. Tam Lin.* v

4 About the dead hour of the night
  She heard the bridles ring;
And Janet was as glad at that
  As any earthly thing.   *Ib.* xli

5 'But what I ken this night, Tam Lin,
  Gin I had kent yestreen,
I wad ta'en out thy heart o' flesh,
  And put in a heart o' stane.'   *Ib.* l

6 True Thomas lay on Huntlie bank;
  A ferlie he spied wi' his e'e;
And there he saw a ladye bright
  Come riding down by the Eildon Tree.
     Ib. Thomas the Rhymer, i.

7 True Thomas he pu'd aff his cap,
  And louted low down on his knee.   *Ib.* iii

8 She's mounted on her milk-white steed,
  She's ta'en true Thomas up behind.   *Ib.* viii

9 'And see ye not yon braid, braid road,
  That lies across the lily leven?
That is the Path of Wickedness,
  Though some call it the Road to Heaven.' *Ib.* xii

10 That is the Road to fair Elfland,
  Where thou and I this night maun gae.   *Ib.* xiii

11 It was mirk, mirk night, there was nae starlight,
  They waded thro' red blude to the knee;
For a' the blude that's shed on the earth
  Rins through the springs o' that countrie. *Ib.* xvi

12 And till seven years were gane and past,
  True Thomas on earth was never seen.   *Ib.* xx

13 There were three ravens sat on a tree,
  They were as black as they might be.
The one of them said to his make,
  'Where shall we our breakfast take?'
     Ib. The Three Ravens

14 All the trees they are so high,
  The leaves they are so green,
The day is past and gone, sweet-heart,

     [1] wap = wrap.

That you and I have seen.
It is cold winter's night,
You and I must bide alone:
Whilst my pretty lad is young
And is growing.
     The Oxford Book of Ballads. The Trees so High

15 As I was walking all alane,
I heard twa corbies[2] making a mane:
The tane unto the tither did say,
'Where sall we gang and dine the day?'

'—In behint yon auld fail[3] dyke
I wot there lies a new-slain knight;
And naebody kens that he lies there
But his hawk, his hound, and his lady fair.

'His hound is to the hunting gane,
His hawk to fetch the wild-fowl hame,
His lady's ta'en anither mate,
So we may make our dinner sweet.

'Ye'll sit on his white hause-bane,[4]
And I'll pike out his bonny blue e'en:
Wi' ae lock o' his gowden hair
We'll theek[5] our nest when it grows bare.
     Ib. The Twa Corbies

  [2] corbies = ravens.   [3] fail = turf.
  [4] hause = neck.   [5] theek = thatch.

16 'The wind doth blow to-day, my love,
  And a few small drops of rain;
I never had but one true love;
  In cold grave she was lain.

'I'll do as much for my true-love
  As any young man may;
I'll sit and mourn all at her grave
  For a twelvemonth and a day.'
     Ib. The Unquiet Grave

17 ''Tis down in yonder garden green,
  Love, where we used to walk,
The finest flower that ere was seen
  Is wither'd to a stalk.

'The stalk is wither'd dry, my love,
  So will our hearts decay;
So make yourself content my love,
  Till God calls you away.'   *Ib.*

18 O waly, waly, up the bank,
  And waly, waly, doun the brae,
And waly, waly, yon burn-side,
  Where I and my Love wont to gae!

I lean'd my back unto an aik,
  I thocht it was a trustie tree;
But first it bow'd and syne it brake—
  Sae my true love did lichtlie me.

O waly, waly, gin love be bonnie
  A little time while it is new!
But when 'tis auld it waxeth cauld,
  And fades awa' like morning dew.

O wherefore should I busk my heid,
  Or wherefore should I kame my hair?
For my true Love has me forsook,
  And says he'll never lo'e me mair.
     Ib. Waly, Waly

19 But had I wist, before I kist,
  That love had been sae ill to win,
I had lock'd my heart in a case o' gowd,
  And pinn'd it wi' a siller pin.

And O! if my young babe were born,
And set upon the nurse's knee;
And I mysel' were dead and gane,
And the green grass growing over me!
The Oxford Book of Ballads. Waly, Waly

1 'Tom Pearse, Tom Pearse, lend me your grey mare,
All along, down along, out along, lee.
For I want for to go to Widdicombe Fair,
Wi' Bill Brewer, Jan Stewer, Peter Gurney, Peter
Davey, Dan'l Whiddon, Harry Hawk,
Old Uncle Tom Cobbleigh and all.
Old Uncle Tom Cobbleigh and all.'
Ib. Widdicombe Fair

2 It fell about the Martinmass,
When nights are lang and mirk,
The carline wife's three sons came hame,
And their hats were o' the birk.

It neither grew in dike nor ditch,
Nor yet in any sheugh;
But at the gates o' Paradise
That birk grew fair eneugh.
Ib. The Wife of Usher's Well

JOHN CODRINGTON BAMPFYLDE
1754–1796
3 Rugged the breast that beauty cannot tame.
Sonnet in Praise of Delia

GEORGE BANCROFT
fl. 1548
4 Where Christ erecteth his church, the devil in the
same churchyard will have his chapel.
Sermon preached at Paul's Cross, 9 Feb. 1588

GEORGE BANCROFT
1800–1891
5 It [Calvinism in Switzerland] established a religion
without a prelate, a government without a king.
History of the United States, vol. iii, ch. 6

EDWARD BANGS
fl. 1775
6 Yankee Doodle, keep it up,
Yankee Doodle dandy;
Mind the music and the step,
And with the girls be handy.
*Yankee Doodle; or Father's Return to Camp. See
Nicholas Smith, Stories of Great National Songs*

Yankee Doodle came to town
Riding on a pony;
Stuck a feather in his cap
And called it Macaroni. *Ib.*

GEORGE LINNÆUS BANKS
1821–1881
For the cause that lacks assistance,
For the wrong that needs resistance,
For the future in the distance,
And the good that I can do.
Daisies in the Grass. What I Live For

THÉODORE DE BANVILLE
1823–1891
Nous n'irons plus aux bois, les lauriers sont coupés.
We will go no more to the woods, the laurel-trees
are cut. *Les Cariatides, Les Stalactites*
(Nursery rhyme, earlier than Banville)

ANNA LETITIA BARBAULD
1743–1825
10 So fades a summer cloud away;
So sinks the gale when storms are o'er;
So gently shuts the eye of day;
So dies a wave along the shore.
The Death of the Virtuous

11 The world has little to bestow
Where two fond hearts in equal love are joined.
Delia

12 And when midst fallen London, they survey
The stone where Alexander's ashes lay,
Shall own with humbled pride the lesson just
By Time's slow finger written in the dust.
Eighteen Hundred and Eleven

13 Of her scorn the maid repented,
And the shepherd—of his love.
Leave Me, Simple Shepherd

14 Life! we've been long together,
Through pleasant and through cloudy weather;
'Tis hard to part when friends are dear,
Perhaps 'twill cost a sigh, a tear;
Then steal away, give little warning;
Choose thine own time;
Say not 'Good-night'; but in some brighter clime
Bid me 'Good-morning'. *Ode to Life*

15 Society than solitude is worse,
And man to man is still the greatest curse.
Ovid to His Wife

JOHN BARBOUR
1316?–1395
16 Storys to rede ar delitabill,
Suppos that thai be nocht bot fabill.
The Bruce, bk. i, l. 1

17 A! fredome is a noble thing!
Fredome mayse man to haiff liking. *Ib. l. 225*

REV. RICHARD HARRIS BARHAM
1788–1845
18 Like a blue-bottle fly on a rather large scale,
With a rather large corking-pin stuck through his tail.
The Ingoldsby Legends. The Auto-da-Fé

19 Be kind to those dear little folks
When our toes are turned up to the daisies!
Ib. The Babes in the Wood

20 She help'd him to lean, and she help'd him to fat,
And it look'd like hare—but it might have been cat.
Ib. The Bagman's Dog

21 There was cakes and apples in all the Chapels,
With fine polonies, and rich mellow pears.
Ib. Barney Maguire's Account of the Coronation

22 Take a suck at the lemon, and at him again!
Ib. The Black Mousquetaire

23 Though I've always considered Sir Christopher
Wren,
As an architect, one of the greatest of men;
And, talking of Epitaphs,—much I admire his,
'Circumspice, si Monumentum requiris';
Which an erudite Verger translated to me,
'If you ask for his Monument, Sir-come-spy-see!'
Ib. The Cynotaph

1 What Horace says is,
Eheu fugaces
Anni labuntur, Postume, Postume!
Years glide away, and are lost to me, lost to me!
The Ingoldsby Legends. Epigram: Eheu fugaces

2 There, too, full many an Aldermanic nose
Roll'd its loud diapason after dinner.
Ib. The Ghost

3 'He won't—won't he? Then bring me my boots!' said
the Baron. *Ib. Grey Dolphin*

4 Tallest of boys, or shortest of men,
He stood in his stockings, just four foot ten.
Ib. Hon. Mr. Sucklethumbkin's Story

5 Tiger Tim, come tell me true,
What may a Nobleman find to do? *Ib.*

6 What *was* to be done?—'twas perfectly plain
That they could not well hang the man over again;
What *was* to be done?—The man was dead!
Nought *could* be done—nought could be said;
So—my Lord Tomnoddy went home to bed! *Ib.*

7 A servant's too often a negligent elf;
—If it's business of consequence, *do it yourself!*
Ib. The Ingoldsby Penance. Moral

8 The Jackdaw sat on the Cardinal's chair!
Bishop, and abbot, and prior were there;
Many a monk, and many a friar,
Many a knight, and many a squire,
With a great many more of lesser degree,—
In sooth a goodly company;
And they served the Lord Primate on bended knee.
Never, I ween,
Was a prouder seen,
Read of in books, or dreamt of in dreams,
Than the Cardinal Lord Archbishop of Rheims!
Ib. The Jackdaw of Rheims

9 And six little Singing-boys,—dear little souls!
In nice clean faces, and nice white stoles. *Ib.*

10 He cursed him in sleeping, that every night
He should dream of the devil, and wake in a fright.
Ib.

11 Never was heard such a terrible curse!
But what gave rise to no little surprise,
Nobody seem'd one penny the worse! *Ib.*

12 Heedless of grammar, they all cried, 'That's him!' *Ib.*

13 The Lady Jane was tall and slim,
The Lady Jane was fair.
Ib. The Knight and the Lady

14 He would pore by the hour, o'er a weed or a flower,
Or the slugs that come crawling out after a shower.
Ib.

15 Or great ugly things, all legs and wings,
With nasty long tails arm'd with nasty long stings.
Ib.

16 Go—pop Sir Thomas again in the pond—
Poor dear!—he'll catch us some more!! *Ib.*

17 Though his cassock was swarming
With all sorts of vermin,
He'd not take the life of a flea!
Ib. The Lay of St. Aloys

18 Ah, ha! my good friend!—Don't you wish you may
get it? *Ib.*

19 Here's a corpse in the case with a sad swell'd face,
And a Medical Crowner's a queer sort of thing!
The Ingoldsby Legends. A Lay of St. Gengulphus

20 And her bosom went in, and her tail came out.
Ib. A Lay of St. Nicholas

21 A German,
Who smoked like a chimney. *Ib. Lay of St. Odille*

22 So put that in your pipe, my Lord Otto, and smoke
it! *Ib.*

23 'Twas in Margate last July, I walk'd upon the pier,
I saw a little vulgar Boy—I said, 'What make you
here?' *Ib. Misadventures at Margate*

24 He had no little handkerchief to wipe his little nose!
Ib.

25 And now I'm here, from this here pier it is my fixed
intent
To jump, as Mr. Levi did from off the Monu-ment!
Ib.

26 I could not see my little friend—because he was not
there! *Ib.*

27 But when the Crier cried, 'O Yes!' the people cried.
'O No!' *Ib.*

28 It's very odd that Sailor-men should talk so very
queer—
And then he hitch'd his trousers up, as is, I'm told,
their use,
It's very odd that Sailor-men should wear those things
so loose. *Ib.*

29 He smiled and said, 'Sir, does your mother know that
you are out?' *Ib.*

30 You intoxified brute!—you insensible block!—
Look at the clock!—Do!—Look at the clock!
Ib. Patty Morgan. Fytte i.

31 They were a little less than 'kin', and rather more than
'kind'. *Ib. Nell Cook*

32 She drank Prussic acid without any water,
And died like a Duke-and-a-Duchess's daughter!
Ib. The Tragedy

33 *Cob* was the strongest, *Mob* was the wrongest,
Chittabob's tail was the finest and longest!
Ib. The Truant

34 Though port should have age,
Yet I don't think it sage
To entomb it, as some of your *connoisseurs* do,
Till it's losing its flavour, and body, and hue;
—I question if keeping it does it much good
After ten years in bottle and three in the wood.
Ib. The Wedding-Day. More

SABINE BARING-GOULD
1834-1924

35 Now the day is over,
Night is drawing nigh,
Shadows of the evening
Steal across the sky.
Hymns Ancient and Modern. Now the Day is Ov

36 Birds and beasts and flowers
Soon will be asleep.

37 Guard the sailors tossing
On the deep blue sea.

1 Onward, Christian soldiers,
  Marching as to war,
With the Cross of Jesus
  Going on before.
      *Hymns Ancient and Modern. Onward, Christian
      Soldiers*

2 Hell's foundations quiver
    At the shout of praise;
Brothers, lift your voices,
  Loud your anthems raise.   *Ib.*

3 Gates of hell can never
    'Gainst that Church prevail;
We have Christ's own promise,
  And that cannot fail.   *Ib.*

4 Through the night of doubt and sorrow
Onward goes the pilgrim band,
Singing songs of expectation,
Marching to the Promised Land.
  Ib. Tr. from the Danish of B. S. Ingemann,
  1789–1862. *Through the Night of Doubt and
  Sorrow*

5 Brother clasps the hand of brother,
Stepping fearless through the night.   *Ib.*

6 Soon shall come the great awaking,
  Soon the rending of the tomb,
Then, the scattering of all shadows
And the end of toil and gloom.   *Ib.*

LADY ANNE BARNARD
1750–1825

7 When the sheep are in the fauld, when the cows come
      hame,
When a' the weary world to quiet rest are gane.
                              Auld Robin Gray

8 My mither she fell sick—my Jamie was at sea—
And Auld Robin Gray, oh! he came a-courting me.
                              Ib.

9 My father argued sair—my mother didna speak,
But she look'd in my face till my heart was like to
      break.   *Ib.*

0 I hadna been his wife, a week but only four,
When mournfu' as I sat on the stane at my door,
I saw my Jamie's ghaist—I cou'dna think it he,
Till he said, 'I'm come hame, my love, to marry thee!'
                              Ib.

CHARLOTTE ALINGTON BARNARD
1840–1869

I cannot sing the old songs
I sang long years ago,
For heart and voice would fail me,
And foolish tears would flow.
      Fireside Thoughts. I Cannot Sing the Old Songs

BARNABE BARNES
1569?–1609

Ah, sweet Content! where doth thine harbour hold?
      Parthenophil and Parthenophe, Sonnet lxvi

WILLIAM BARNES
1801–1886

An' there vor me the apple tree
Do leän down low in Linden Lea.
      My Orcha'd in Linden Lea

14 But still the neäme do bide the seäme—
'Tis Pentridge—Pentridge by the river.
                        Pentridge by the River

15 My love is the maïd ov all maïdens,
Though all mid be comely.   *In the Spring*

16 Since I noo mwore do zee your feäce.
                        The Wife A-Lost

RICHARD BARNFIELD
1574–1627

17 As it fell upon a day,
In the merry month of May,
Sitting in a pleasant shade,
Which a grove of myrtles made.
Beasts did leap and birds did sing,
Trees did grow and plants did spring,
Everything did banish moan,
Save the nightingale alone.
She, poor bird, as all forlorn,
Lean'd her breast up-till a thorn,
And there sung the dolefull'st ditty
That to hear it was great pity.
Fie, fie, fie, now would she cry;
Tereu, Tereu, by and by.
            Poems: in Divers Humors, An Ode

18 King Pandion, he is dead,
All thy friends are lapp'd in lead.   *Ib.*

19 If Music and sweet Poetry agree,
As they must needs (the Sister and the Brother)
Then must the love be great, 'twixt thee and me,
Because thou lov'st the one, and I the other.
                        Ib. Sonnet 1

20 Nothing more certain than incertainties;
Fortune is full of fresh variety:
Constant in nothing but inconstancy.
                        The Shepherd's Content, xi

21 My flocks feed not,
My ewes breed not,
My rams speed not,
    All is amiss.
Love is dying,
Faith's defying,
Heart's denying,
    Causer of this.   *A Shepherd's Complaint*

22 She [Pecunia] is the sovereign queen, of all delights:
For her the lawyer pleads; the soldier fights.
                        Encomion of Lady Pecunia, xvi

23 The waters were his winding sheet, the sea was made
      his tomb;
Yet for his fame the ocean sea, was not sufficient
      room.
      Ib. To the Gentlemen Readers. (On the death of
      Hawkins.)

PHINEAS T. BARNUM
1810–1891

24 There's a sucker born every minute.   *Attrib.*

EATON STANNARD BARRETT
1786–1820

25 She, while Apostles shrank, could dangers brave,
Last at His cross and earliest at His grave.
                        Woman, pt. i, l. 143

SIR JAMES MATTHEW BARRIE

1860–1937

1 His lordship may compel us to be equal upstairs, but there will never be equality in the servants' hall.
The Admirable Crichton, Act I

2 I'm a second eleven sort of chap. *Ib.* Act III

3 Never ascribe to an opponent motives meaner than your own.
'*Courage*', *Rectorial Address, St. Andrews, 3 May 1922*

4 Courage is the thing. All goes if courage goes. *Ib.*

5 Facts were never pleasing to him. He acquired them with reluctance and got rid of them with relief. He was never on terms with them until he had stood them on their heads.
Love Me Never or For Ever

6 I do loathe explanations.
My Lady Nicotine, ch. 16

7 When the first baby laughed for the first time, the laugh broke into a thousand pieces and they all went skipping about, and that was the beginning of fairies. *Peter Pan*, Act I

8 Every time a child says 'I don't believe in fairies' there is a little fairy somewhere that falls down dead. *Ib.*

9 To die will be an awfully big adventure. *Ib.* Act III

10 Do you believe in fairies? ... If you believe, clap your hands! *Ib.* Act IV

11 That is ever the way. 'Tis all jealousy to the bride and good wishes to the corpse. *Quality Street*, Act I

12 Oh the gladness of her gladness when she's glad,
And the sadness of her sadness when she's sad,
But the gladness of her gladness
And the sadness of her sadness
Are as nothing, Charles,
To the badness of her badness when she's bad.
Rosalind

13 The Twelve-pound Look. *Title of Play*

14 Have you ever noticed, Harry, that many jewels make women either incredibly fat or incredibly thin?
The Twelve-pound Look

15 It's a sort of bloom on a woman. If you have it [charm], you don't need to have anything else; and if you don't have it, it doesn't much matter what else you have. *What Every Woman Knows*, Act I

16 A young Scotsman of your ability let loose upon the world with £300, what could he not do? It's almost appalling to think of; especially if he went among the English. *Ib.*

17 You've forgotten the grandest moral attribute of a Scotsman, Maggie, that he'll do nothing which might damage his career. *Ib.* Act II

18 There are few more impressive sights in the world than a Scotsman on the make. *Ib.*

19 Every man who is high up loves to think that he has done it all himself; and the wife smiles, and lets it go at that. It's our only joke. Every woman knows that. *Ib.* Act IV

GEORGE BARRINGTON

b. 1755

20 True patriots we; for be it understood,
We left our country for our country's good.
Prologue for the opening of the Playhouse, Sydney, New South Wales, 16 Jan. 1796. The company was composed of convicts.

WILLIAM BASSE

d. 1653?

21 Renowned Spenser, lie a thought more nigh
To learned Chaucer, and rare Beaumont lie,
A little nearer Spenser, to make room
For Shakespeare, in your threefold, fourfold tomb.
Poetical Works. On Shakespeare

EDGAR BATEMAN

nineteenth century

22 Wiv a ladder and some glasses,
You could see to 'Ackney Marshes,
If it wasn't for the 'ouses in between.
If it wasn't for the 'Ouses in between

KATHERINE LEE BATES

1859–1929

23 America! America!
God shed His grace on thee
And crown thy good with brotherhood
From sea to shining sea! *America the Beautiful*

RICHARD BAXTER

1615–1691

24 I preach'd as never sure to preach again,
And as a dying man to dying men!
Love Breathing Thanks and Praise, pt. ii

25 In necessary things, unity; in doubtful things, liberty; in all things, charity. *Motto*

THOMAS HAYNES BAYLY

1797–1839

26 I'd be a butterfly born in a bower,
Where roses and lilies and violets meet.
I'd be a Butterfl

27 I'm saddest when I sing. *Title of poem*

28 Absence makes the heart grow fonder,
Isle of Beauty, Fare thee well!
Isle of Beauty (see 5:5

29 It was a dream of perfect bliss,
Too beautiful to last.
It was a Dream

30 The mistletoe hung in the castle hall,
The holly branch shone on the old oak wall.
The Mistletoe Boug

31 Oh! no! we never mention her,
Her name is never heard;
My lips are now forbid to speak
That once familiar word.
Oh! No! We Never Mention H

32 Oh, Pilot! 'tis a fearful night,
There's danger on the deep. *The Pil*

33 Fear not, but trust in Providence
Wherever thou may'st be.

1 She wore a wreath of roses,
The night that first we met.
She Wore a Wreath of Roses

2 Gaily the Troubadour
Touch'd his guitar. *Welcome Me Home*

3 We met, 'twas in a crowd, And I thought he would
shun me. *We Met, 'twas in a Crowd*

4 Why don't the men propose, mamma,
Why don't the men propose?
Why Don't the Men Propose?

JAMES BEATTIE
1735–1803

5 His harp, the sole companion of his way.
The Minstrel, bk. I. iii

6 In truth, he was a strange and wayward wight,
Fond of each gentle and each dreadful scene.
In darkness and in storm he found delight. *Ib.* xxii

DAVID BEATTY, EARL BEATTY
1871–1936

7 There's something wrong with our bloody ships
to-day, Chatfield.
Remark during the Battle of Jutland, 1916: Winston Churchill, The World Crisis (1927), Pt. I,
p. 129. The additional words commonly attributed:
*'Steer two points nearer the enemy' are denied by
Lord Chatfield*

TOPHAM BEAUCLERK
1739–1780

8 [On Boswell saying that a certain man had good
principles.] Then he does not wear them out in
practice. Boswell's *Life of Johnson, 14 Apr. 1778*

PIERRE-AUGUSTIN DE BEAUMARCHAIS
1732–1799

9 Je me presse de rire de tout, de peur d'être obligé
d'en pleurer.
I make myself laugh at everything, for fear of
having to weep. *Le Barbier de Séville*, I. ii

10 (Figaro, to the Count Almaviva)
Est-ce qu'un homme comme vous ignore quelque
chose?
Can anything be beyond the knowledge of a man
like you? *Ib.* vi.

11 Parce que vous êtes un grand seigneur, vous vous
croyez un grand génie!... Vous vous êtes donné
la peine de naître, et rien de plus.
Because you are a great lord, you believe yourself
to be a great genius!... You took the trouble to
be born, but no more. *Mariage de Figaro*, v. iii

FRANCIS BEAUMONT
1584–1616

12 What things have we seen,
Done at the Mermaid! heard words that have been
So nimble, and so full of subtil flame,
As if that every one from whence they came,
Had meant to put his whole wit in a jest,
And had resolv'd to live a fool, the rest
Of his dull life. *Letter to Ben Jonson*

13 Here are sands, ignoble things,
Dropt from the ruin'd sides of Kings;
Here's a world of pomp and state,
Buried in dust, once dead by fate.
On the Tombs in Westminster Abbey

FRANCIS BEAUMONT
1584–1616
and
JOHN FLETCHER
1579–1625

14 There is no drinking after death.
The Bloody Brother, II. ii

15 And he that will to bed go sober,
Falls with the leaf still in October. *Ib.*

16 Three merry boys, and three merry boys,
And three merry boys are we,
As ever did sing in a hempen string
Under the gallows-tree. *Ib.* III. ii

17 Bad's the best of us. *Ib.* IV. ii

18 You are no better than you should be.
The Coxcomb, IV. iii

19 I care not two-pence. *Ib.* v. i

20 Death hath so many doors to let out life.
The Custom of the Country, II. ii

21 But what is past my help, is past my care.
The Double Marriage, I. i

22 It is always good
When a man has two irons in the fire.
The Faithful Friends, I. ii

23 Our acts our angels are, or good or ill,
Our fatal shadows that walk by us still.
Upon an Honest Man's Fortune, v

24 Let's meet, and either do, or die.
The Island Princess, II. ii

25 Nose, nose, jolly red nose,
And who gave thee this jolly red nose?...
Nutmegs and ginger, cinamon and cloves,
And they gave me this jolly red nose.
Knight of the Burning Pestle, I. iii

26 This is a pretty flim-flam. *Ib.* II. iii

27 Go to grass. *Ib.* IV. vi

28 Something given that way.
The Lovers' Progress, I. i

29 Deeds, not words shall speak me. *Ib.* III. vi

30 Thou wilt scarce be a man before thy mother. *Ib.* ii

31 I find the medicine worse than the malady. *Ib.*

32 Faith, Sir, he went away with a flea in 's ear. *Ib.* IV. iii

33 I'll put on my considering cap.
The Loyal Subject, II. i

34 I'll put a spoke among your wheels.
The Mad Lover, III. vi

35 Upon my buried body lie
Lightly, gentle earth. *The Maid's Tragedy*, II. i

36 Those have most power to hurt us that we love.
Ib. v. iv

37 Fountain heads, and pathless groves,
Places which pale passion loves.
The Nice Valour, Song, III. iii

1 Nothing's so dainty sweet, as lovely melancholy.
The Nice Valour, Song, III. iii

2 　　　All your better deeds
Shall be in water writ, but this in marble. *Ib.* v. iii

3 'Tis virtue, and not birth that makes us noble:
Great actions speak great minds, and such should
govern. 　　　*The Prophetess*, II. iii

4 I'll have a fling.
Rule a Wife and have a Wife, III. v

5 Kiss till the cow comes home. *Scornful Lady*, II. ii

6 There is no other purgatory but a woman. *Ib.* III. i

7 It would talk:
Lord how it talk't! 　　　*Ib.* IV. i

8 Daisies smell-less, yet most quaint,
　　　And sweet thyme true,
Primrose first born child of Ver,
Merry Spring-time's Harbinger.
Two Noble Kinsmen, I. i

9 Care-charming Sleep, thou easer of all woes,
Brother to Death. 　　*Valentinian*, v. ii

10 God Lyæus ever young,
Ever honour'd, ever sung. 　　*Ib.* viii

11 Come sing now, sing; for I know ye sing well,
I see ye have a singing face.
The Wild Goose Chase, II. ii

12 Though I say't, that should not say't.
Wit at Several Weapons, II. ii

13 Whistle and she'll come to you.
Wit Without Money, IV. iv

14 Let the world slide. 　　　*Ib.* v. ii

15 Have not you maggots in your brains?
Women Pleased, III. iv

CARL BECKER
1873-1945

16 Twice tricked by the British into a European war in
order to pull their chestnuts out of the fire.
Progress and Power (1935)

PETER BECKFORD
1740-1811

17 The colour I think of little moment; and am of
opinion with our friend Foote, respecting his negro
friend, that a good dog, like a good candidate,
cannot be of a bad colour.
Thoughts upon Hare and Fox Hunting, letter 3

WILLIAM BECKFORD
1759-1844

18 When he was angry, one of his eyes became so terrible,
that no person could bear to behold it; and the
wretch upon whom it was fixed instantly fell backward, and sometimes expired. For fear, however,
of depopulating his dominions, and making his
palace desolate, he but rarely gave way to his anger.
Vathek (1893), p. 1

19 He did not think, with the Caliph Omar Ben Adalaziz,
that it was necessary to make a hell of this world to
enjoy paradise in the next. 　　*Ib.* p. 2

20 Your presence I condescend to accept and beg you
will let me be quiet, for I am not over-fond of resisting temptation. 　　*Ib.* p. 134

THOMAS BECON
1512-1567

21 For when the wine is in, the wit is out.
Catechism, 375

THOMAS LOVELL BEDDOES
1798-1851

22 If thou wilt ease thine heart
Of love and all its smart,
Then sleep, dear, sleep. 　*Death's Jest Book*, II. ii

23 But wilt thou cure thine heart
Of love and all its smart,
Then die, dear, die. 　　　*Ib.*

24 　　If man could see
The perils and diseases that he elbows,
Each day he walks a mile; which catch at him,
Which fall behind and graze him as he passes;
Then would he know that Life's a single pilgrim,
Fighting unarmed amongst a thousand soldiers.
Ib. IV. i. (MS. III)

25 I have a bit of FIAT in my soul,
And can myself create my little world. 　*Ib.* v. i

26 Old Adam, the carrion crow. 　　*Ib.* IV

27 King Death hath asses' ears. 　　*Ib.*

28 If there were dreams to sell,
　　What would you buy?
Some cost a passing bell;
　　Some a light sigh,
That shakes from Life's fresh crown
Only a roseleaf down.
If there were dreams to sell,
Merry and sad to tell,
And the crier rung the bell,
　　What would you buy? 　　*Dream-Pedlary*

29 　　　Him
Who was the planet's tyrant, dotard Death.
Letter from Göttingen

30 How many times do I love thee, dear?
Tell me how many thoughts there be
　　In the atmosphere
　　Of a new-fal'n year,
Whose white and sable hours appear
The latest flakes of Eternity:
So many times do I love thee, dear.
Torrismond, I. iii

BEDE
673-735

31 Talis, inquiens, mihi videtur, rex, vita hominum
praesens in terris, ad conparationem eius, quod
nobis incertum est, temporis, quale cum te resi-
dente ad caenam cum ducibus ac ministris tuis
tempore brumali, . . . adveniens unus passerum domum citissime pervolaverit; qui cum per unum
ostium ingrediens, mox per aliud exierit. Ipso quidem tempore, quo intus est, hiemis tempestate non
tangitur, sed tamen parvissimo spatio serenitatis ad
momentum excurso, mox de hieme in hiemem re-
grediens, tuis oculis elabitur. Ita haec vita hominum ad modicum apparet; quid autem sequatur,
quidve praecesserit, prorsus ignoramus.

'Such,' he said, 'O King, seems to me the present life of men on earth, in comparison with
that time which to us is uncertain, as if when

on a winter's night you sit feasting with your ealdormen and thegns,—a single sparrow should fly swiftly into the hall, and coming in at one door, instantly fly out through another. In that time in which it is indoors it is indeed not touched by the fury of the winter, but yet, this smallest space of calmness being passed almost in a flash, from winter going into winter again, it is lost to your eyes. Somewhat like this appears the life of man; but of what follows or what went before, we are utterly ignorant.'
Ecclesiastical History, bk. ii, ch. 13

1 Scio, inquiens, quia ubi navem ascenderitis, tempestas vobis et ventus contrarius superveniet: sed tu memento ut hoc oleum quod tibi do, mittas in mare; et statim quiescentibus ventis, serenitas maris vos læta prosequetur.

I know, he said, that when you go on board ship, a storm and contrary wind will come upon you: but remember to pour this oil that I give you, on the water; and immediately with the winds dropping happy calm of ocean will ensue.
Ib. bk. iii, ch. 15

BERNARD ELLIOTT BEE
1823–1861

2 Let us determine to die here, and we will conquer. There is Jackson standing like a stone wall. Rally behind the Virginians.
First Battle of Bull Run, 1861. Poore, *Reminiscences of Metropolis*, ii. 85

HENRY CHARLES BEECHING
1859–1919

3 With lifted feet, hands still,
I am poised, and down the hill
Dart, with heedful mind;
The air goes by in a wind.
Going Down Hill on a Bicycle

4 Alas, that the longest hill
Must end in a vale; but still,
Who climbs with toil, wheresoe'er
Shall find wings waiting there.
Ib.

5 First come I; my name is Jowett.
There's no knowledge but I know it.
I am Master of this college:
What I don't know isn't knowledge.
The Masque of Balliol, composed by and current among members of Balliol College in the late 1870's (see also 8:15, 511:5 and 6)

6 Not when the sense is dim,
But now from the heart of joy,
I would remember Him:
Take the thanks of a boy.
Prayers

SIR MAX BEERBOHM
1872–

7 Most women are not so young as they are painted.
A Defence of Cosmetics

8 I belong to the Beardsley period.
Diminuendo

9 There is always something rather absurd about the past.
1880

10 To give an accurate and exhaustive account of that period would need a far less brilliant pen than mine.
Ib.

11 She swam to the bell-rope and grasped it for a tinkle.
(Parody of Meredith.)
Euphemia Clashthought

12 A swear-word in a rustic slum
A simple swear-word is to some,
To Masefield something more.
(Caption to a cartoon.)
Fifty Caricatures, 1913

13 Not that I had any special reason for hating school. Strange as it may seem to my readers, I was not unpopular there. I was a modest, good-humoured boy. It is Oxford that has made me insufferable.
Going Back to School

14 None, it is said, of all who revelled with the Regent, was half so wicked as Lord George Hell.
The Happy Hypocrite, ch. 1

15 Mankind is divisible into two great classes: hosts and guests.
Hosts and Guests

16 I maintain that though you would often in the fifteenth century have heard the snobbish Roman say, in a would-be off-hand tone, 'I am dining with the Borgias to-night,' no Roman ever was able to say, 'I dined last night with the Borgias.'
Ib.

17 The Nonconformist Conscience makes cowards of us all.
King George the Fourth

18 Fate wrote her [Queen Caroline] a most tremendous tragedy, and she played it in tights.
Ib.

19 They so very indubitably *are*, you know! *(Parody of Henry James.)*
Mote in the Middle Distance

20 'After all,' as a pretty girl once said to me, 'women are a sex by themselves, so to speak.'
The Pervasion of Rouge

21 Savonarola love-sick! Ha, ha, ha!
Love-sick? He, love-sick? 'Tis a goodly jest!
The confirm'd misogyn a ladies' man!
Savonarola Brown, Act I

22 Had Sav'narola spoken less than thus,
Methinks me, the less Sav'narola he.
Ib.

23 LUCREZIA BORGIA. And what name gave he?
PORTER. Something-arola—
LUC. Savon?—show him up.
Ib. Act II

24 Enter Michael Angelo. Andrea del Sarto appears for a moment at a window. Pippa passes.
Ib. Act III

25 O the disgrace of it!—
The scandal, the incredible come-down! *Ib.* Act IV

26 A pretty sort of prison I have come to,
In which a self-respecting lady's cell
Is treated as a lounge.
Ib.

27 Zuleika, on a desert island, would have spent most of her time in looking for a man's foot-print.
Zuleika Dobson, ch. 2

28 Your mentality, too, is bully, as we all predicate.
Ib. ch. 8

29 Deeply regret inform your grace last night two black owls came and perched on battlements remained there through night hooting at dawn flew away none knows whither awaiting instructions Jellings.
Ib. ch. 14

30 Prepare vault for funeral Monday Dorset.
Ib.

31 The Socratic manner is not a game at which two can play.
Ib. ch. 15

1 'Ah, say that again,' she murmured. 'Your voice is music.'

He repeated his question.

'Music!' she said dreamily; and such is the force of habit that 'I don't', she added, 'know anything about music, really. But I know what I like.'
Zuleika Dobson, ch. 16

ETHEL LYNN BEERS
1827-1879

2 All quiet along the Potomac to-night,
No sound save the rush of the river,
While soft falls the dew on the face of the dead—
The picket's off duty forever.
All Quiet along the Potomac

APHRA BEHN
1640-1689

3 Oh, what a dear ravishing thing is the beginning of an Amour! *The Emperor of the Moon*, I. i

4 Of all that writ, he was the wisest bard, who spoke this mighty truth—
He that knew all that ever learning writ,
Knew only this—that he knew nothing yet. *Ib.* iii

5 Love ceases to be a pleasure, when it ceases to be a secret. *The Lover's Watch, Four o'clock*

6 Faith, Sir, we are here to-day, and gone to-morrow.
The Lucky Chance, IV

7 I owe a duty, where I cannot love.
The Moor's Revenge, III. iii

8 A brave world, Sir, full of religion, knavery, and change: we shall shortly see better days.
The Roundheads, I. i

9 Variety is the soul of pleasure.
The Rover, Part II, Act I

10 Come away; poverty's catching. *Ib.*

11 Money speaks sense in a language all nations understand. *Ib.* III. i

12 Beauty unadorn'd. *Ib.* IV. ii

13 'Sure, I rose the wrong way to-day, I have had such damn'd ill luck every way.' *The Town Fop*, V. i

14 The soft, unhappy sex. *The Wandering Beauty*

W. H. BELLAMY
nineteenth century

15 Old Simon the Cellarer keeps a rare store
Of Malmsey and Malvoisie.
Song: Simon the Cellarer

JOACHIM DU BELLAY
1515-1560

16 France, mère des arts, des armes et des loix.

France, mother of arts, of warriors, and of laws.
Sonnets

17 Heureux qui comme Ulysse a fait un beau voyage.

Happy the wanderer, like Ulysses, who has come happily home at last. *Ib.*

HILAIRE BELLOC
1870-1953

18 The road went up, the road went down,
And there the matter ended it.
He broke his heart in Clermont town,
At Pontgibaud they mended it. *Auvergnat*

19 Child! do not throw this book about;
Refrain from the unholy pleasure
Of cutting all the pictures out!
Preserve it as your chiefest treasure.
Bad Child's Book of Beasts, dedication

20 Your little hands were made to take
The better things and leave the worse ones:
They also may be used to shake
The massive paws of elder persons. *Ib.*

21 A manner rude and wild
Is common at your age. *Ib.* introduction

22 Who take their manners from the Ape,
Their habits from the Bear,
Indulge the loud unseemly jape,
And never brush their hair. *Ib.*

23 Yet may you see his bones and beak
All in the Mu-se-um. *Ib. The Dodo*

24 The Dromedary is a cheerful bird:
I cannot say the same about the Kurd.
Ib. The Dromedary

25 When people call this beast to mind,
They marvel more and more
At such a little tail behind,
So large a trunk before. *Ib. The Elephant*

26 The Frog is justly sensitive
To epithets like these. *Ib. The Frog*

27 I shoot the Hippopotamus
With bullets made of platinum,
Because if I use leaden ones
His hide is sure to flatten 'em.
Ib. The Hippopotamus

28 You have a horn where other brutes have none:
Rhinoceros, you are an ugly beast.
Ib. The Rhinoceros

29 Mothers of large families, who claim to common sense,
Will find a Tiger well repay the trouble and expense.
Ib. The Tiger

30 The Whale that wanders round the Pole
Is not a table fish.
You cannot bake or boil him whole
Nor serve him in a dish. *Ib. The Whale*

31 Here is a House that armours a man
With the eyes of a boy and the heart of a ranger.
To the Balliol Men still in Africa

32 Balliol made me, Balliol fed me,
Whatever I had she gave me again;
And the best of Balliol loved and led me,
God be with you, Balliol men. *Ib.*

33 The nicest child I ever knew
Was Charles Augustus Fortescue.
Cautionary Tales. Charles Augustus Fortescue

34 Children in ordinary dress
May always play with sand. *Ib. Franklin Hyde*

35 Godolphin Horne was nobly born;
He held the human race in scorn.
Ib. Godolphin Horne

1 The chief defect of Henry King
Was chewing little bits of string.
Cautionary Tales. Henry King

2 Physicians of the utmost fame
Were called at once; but when they came
They answered, as they took their fees,
'There is no cure for this disease.'   *Ib.*

3 'Oh, my friends, be warned by me,
That breakfast, dinner, lunch, and tea
Are all the human frame requires . . .'
With that, the wretched child expires.   *Ib.*

4 'Ponto!' he cried, with angry frown,
'Let go, Sir! Down, Sir! Put it down!'   *Ib. Jim*

5 Lord Lundy from his earliest years
Was far too freely moved to tears.   *Ib. Lord Lundy*

6 In my opinion Butlers ought
To know their place, and not to play
The Old Retainer night and day.   *Ib.*

7 Towards the age of twenty-six,
They shoved him into politics.   *Ib.*

8 We had intended you to be
The next Prime Minister but three:
The stocks were sold; the Press was squared;
The Middle Class was quite prepared.
But as it is! . . . My language fails!
Go out and govern New South Wales!   *Ib.*

9 Matilda told such Dreadful Lies,
It made one Gasp and Stretch one's Eyes;
Her Aunt, who, from her Earliest Youth,
Had kept a Strict Regard for Truth,
Attempted to Believe Matilda:
The effort very nearly killed her.   *Ib. Matilda*

10 Summoned the Immediate Aid
Of London's Noble Fire Brigade.   *Ib.*

11 Until Matilda's Aunt succeeded
In showing them they were not needed;
And even then she had to pay
To get the Men to go away!   *Ib.*

12 For every time she shouted 'Fire!'
They only answered 'Little liar!'   *Ib.*

13 It happened that a few Weeks later
Her Aunt was off to the Theatre
To see that Interesting Play
The Second Mrs. Tanqueray.   *Ib.*

14 She was not really bad at heart,
But only rather rude and wild;
She was an aggravating child.   *Ib. Rebecca*

15 Her funeral sermon (which was long
And followed by a sacred song)
Mentioned her virtues, it is true,
But dwelt upon her vices too.   *Ib.*

16 Of Courtesy—it is much less
Than courage of heart or holiness;
Yet in my walks it seems to me
That the Grace of God is in Courtesy.   *Courtesy*

17 From quiet homes and first beginning,
  Out to the undiscovered ends,
There's nothing worth the wear of winning,
  But laughter and the love of friends.
Dedicatory Ode

18 But I will sit beside the fire,
  And put my hand before my eyes,
And trace, to fill my heart's desire,
  The last of all our Odysseys.   *Ib.*

19 We were? Why then, by God, we *are*—
Order! I call the Club to session!   *Dedicatory Ode*

20 The moon on the one hand, the dawn on the other:
The moon is my sister, the dawn is my brother.
The moon on my left and the dawn on my right.
My brother, good morning: my sister, good night.
The Early Morning

21 The hundred little lands within one little land that lie
Where Severn seeks the sunset isles or Sussex scales
  the sky.   *The English Graves*

22 They died to save their country and they only saved
  the world.   *Ib.*

23 When I am dead, I hope it may be said:
'His sins were scarlet, but his books were read.'
Epigrams. On his Books

24 Of this bad world the loveliest and the best
Has smiled and said 'Good Night,' and gone to rest.
Ib. On a Dead Hostess

25 I said to Heart, 'How goes it?' Heart replied:
'Right as a Ribstone Pippin!' But it lied.
Ib. The False Heart

26 The accursed power which stands on Privilege
(And goes with Women, and Champagne, and Bridge)
Broke—and Democracy resumed her reign:
(Which goes with Bridge, and Women and Cham-
  pagne).   *Ib. On a Great Election*

27 The Devil, having nothing else to do,
Went off to tempt my Lady Poltagrue.
My Lady, tempted by a private whim,
To his extreme annoyance, tempted him.
Ib. On Lady Poltagrue, a Public Peril

28 Dear Mr. Noman, does it ever strike you,
The more we see of you, the less we like you?
Ib. On Noman, A Guest

29 Sally is gone that was so kindly,
Sally is gone from Ha'nacker Hill.   *Ha'nacker Mill*

30 But Catholic men that live upon wine
Are deep in the water, and frank, and fine;
Wherever I travel I find it so,
Benedicamus Domino.   *Heretics All*

31 Remote and ineffectual Don
That dared attack my Chesterton.   *Lines to a Don*

32 Don different from those regal Dons!
With hearts of gold and lungs of bronze,
Who shout and bang and roar and bawl
The Absolute across the hall,
Or sail in amply billowing gown.
Enormous through the Sacred Town.   *Ib.*

33 The Llama is a woolly sort of fleecy hairy goat,
With an indolent expression and an undulating throat
Like an unsuccessful literary man.
More Beasts for Worse Children. The Llama

34 I had an aunt in Yucatan
Who bought a Python from a man
And kept it for a pet.
She died, because she never knew
These simple little rules and few;—
The Snake is living yet.   *Ib. The Python*

35 Birds in their little nests agree
With Chinamen, but not with me.
New Cautionary Tales. On Food

36 A smell of burning fills the startled air—
The Electrician is no longer there!   *Newdigate Poem*

1 To praise, revere, establish and defend;
  To welcome home mankind's mysterious friend
  Wine, true begetter of all arts that be;
  Wine, privilege of the completely free;
  Wine, the foundation, wine the sagely strong;
  Wine, bright avenger of sly-dealing wrong.
      *Short Talks With The Dead. The Good Poet and
      the Bad Poet. Heroic Poem on Wine.* (An adapta-
      tion from the *Heroic Poem in Praise of Wine.*)

2 Strong Brother in God, and last Companion: Wine.
      Ib.

3 When I am living in the Midlands
    That are sodden and unkind
         .   .   .   .
  the great hills of the South Country
  Come back into my mind.   *The South Country*

4 The faith in their happy eyes
  Comes surely from our Sister the Spring
    When over the sea she flies;
  The violets suddenly bloom at her feet,
    She blesses us with surprise.   *Ib.*

5 I never get between the pines
    But I smell the Sussex air.   *Ib.*

6 A lost thing could I never find,
    Nor a broken thing mend.   *Ib.*

7 If I ever become a rich man,
    Or if ever I grow to be old,
  I will build a house with deep thatch
    To shelter me from the cold,
  And there shall the Sussex songs be sung
    And the story of Sussex told.
  I will hold my house in the high wood
    Within a walk of the sea,
  And the men that were boys when I was a boy
    Shall sit and drink with me.   *Ib.*

8 Do you remember an Inn,
  Miranda?   *Tarantella*

9 The fleas that tease in the high Pyrenees.   *Ib.*

10 We also know the sacred height
     Up on Tugela side,
   Where those three hundred fought with Beit
   And fair young Wernher died.
       *Verses to a Lord who said that those who opposed
       the South African adventure confused soldiers with
       money-grubbers*

11 Tall Goltman, silent on his horse,
     Superb against the dawn.
   The little mound where Eckstein stood
     And gallant Albu fell,
   And Oppenheim, half blind with blood
   Went fording through the rising flood—
     My Lord, we know them well.   *Ib.*

12 They sell good beer at Haslemere
     And under Guildford Hill.
   At Little Cowfold as I've been told
     A beggar may drink his fill:
   There is a good brew in Amberley too,
     And by the bridge also;
   But the swipes they take in at Washington Inn
     Is the very best Beer I know.
       West Sussex Drinking Song

13 It is the best of all trades, to make songs, and the
   second best to sing them.
       On Everything. On Song

14 From the towns all Inns have been driven: from the
   villages most. . . . Change your hearts or you will
   lose your Inns and you will deserve to have lost
   them. But when you have lost your Inns drown
   your empty selves, for you will have lost the last of
   England.   *This and That. On Inns*

JULIEN BENDA
1868–

15 La trahison des clercs.
   The treason of the educated classes.   *Attrib.*

ENOCH ARNOLD BENNETT
1867–1931

16 'Ye can call it influenza if ye like,' said Mrs. Machin.
   'There was no influenza in my young days. We called
   a cold a cold.'   *The Card*, ch. 8

17 Being a husband is a whole-time job.   *The Title*, Act I

18 Journalists say a thing that they know isn't true, in
   the hope that if they keep on saying it long enough
   it *will* be true.   *Ib.* Act II

HENRY BENNETT
1785–?

19 Oh, St. Patrick was a gentleman,
     Who came of decent people;
   He built a church in Dublin town,
     And on it put a steeple.
       St. Patrick was a Gentleman (Oxford Song Book)

ARTHUR CHRISTOPHER BENSON
1862–1925

20 Land of Hope and Glory, Mother of the Free,
   How shall we extol thee, who are born of thee?
   Wider still and wider shall thy bounds be set;
   God who made thee mighty, make thee mightier yet.
       Song from Pomp and Circumstance *by* Elgar, op.
       39, No. 1

JEREMY BENTHAM
1748–1832

21 The greatest happiness of the greatest number is the
   foundation of morals and legislation. (*See* 266:11)
       The Commonplace Book (Works, vol. x. 142)

22 All punishment is mischief: all punishment in itself is
   evil. *Principles of Morals and Legislation,* ch. 13, § 2

EDMUND CLERIHEW BENTLEY
1875–

23 The art of Biography
   Is different from Geography.
   Geography is about maps,
   But Biography is about chaps.
       Biography for Beginners

24 Chapman and Hall
   Swore not at all.
   Mr. Chapman's yea was yea,
   And Mr. Hall's nay was nay.
       Ib. Mr. Chapman and Mr. Hall

25 What I like about Clive
   Is that he is no longer alive.
   There is a great deal to be said
   For being dead.   *Ib. Clive*

1 Edward the Confessor
Slept under the dresser.
When that began to pall
He slept in the hall.
Biography for Beginners. Edward the Confessor

2 John Stuart Mill
By a mighty effort of will
Overcame his natural bonhomie
And wrote 'Principles of Political Economy'.
Ib. John Stuart Mill

3 Sir Christopher Wren
Said, 'I am going to dine with some men.
If anybody calls
Say I am designing St. Paul's.'
Ib. Sir Christopher Wren

4 George the Third
Ought never to have occurred.
One can only wonder
At so grotesque a blunder.
More Biographies. George the Third

RICHARD BENTLEY
1662–1742

5 He is believed to have liked port, but to have said of
claret that 'it would be port if it could'.
R. C. Jebb, *Bentley*, p. 200

6 It is a pretty poem, Mr. Pope, but you must not call
it Homer. *In* Johnson's *Life of Pope*

7 I hold it as certain, that no man was ever written out
of reputation but by himself.
William Warburton, *The Works of Alexander
Pope*, iv. 159

THOMAS BENTLEY
1693?–1742

8 No man is demolished but by himself.
A Letter to Mr. Pope, 1735

PIERRE-JEAN DE BÉRANGER
1780–1857

9 Il était un roi d'Yvetot
Peu connu dans l'histoire.
There was a king of Yvetot
Little known to history.
Œuvres, i, *Le Roi d'Yvetot*

10 Nos amis, les ennemis.
Our friends, the enemy.
L'Opinion de ces demoiselles

LORD CHARLES BERESFORD
1846–1919

11 The idea of a Commercial Alliance with England
based on the integrity of China and the open door
for all nations' trade.
*The Break-Up of China, a Report to the British
Associated Chambers of Commerce, from Shanghai,
20 Nov.* 1898

BISHOP GEORGE BERKELEY
1685–1753

12 All the choir of heaven and furniture of earth—in a
word, all those bodies which compose the mighty
frame of the world—have not any subsistence without a mind. *Principles of Human Knowledge*

13 Westward the course of empire takes its way;
The four first acts already past,
A fifth shall close the drama with the day:
Time's noblest offspring is the last.
*On the Prospect of Planting Arts and Learning
in America*

14 [Tar water] is of a nature so mild and benign and
proportioned to the human constitution, as to warm
without heating, to cheer but not inebriate.
Siris, par. 217

15 Truth is the cry of all, but the game of the few.
Ib. par. 368

IRVING BERLIN
1888–

16 Come on and hear, come on and hear, Alexander's
Ragtime Band. *Alexander's Ragtime Band*

ST. BERNARD
1091–1153

17 Liberavi animam meam.
I have freed my soul. *Epistle 371*

WILLIAM BAYLE BERNARD
1807–1875

18 A Storm in a Teacup. *Title of farce,* 1854

SIR WALTER BESANT
1836–1901

19 The World went very well then. *Title*

RICHARD BETHELL, BARON WESTBURY
1800–1873

20 Deprive mankind of their hope of eternal damnation.
Attrib.

21 His Lordship says he will turn it over in what he is
pleased to call his mind.
Nash, *Life of Westbury*, i. 158

THEOBALD VON BETHMANN HOLLWEG
1856–1921

22 Just for a word—'neutrality', a word which in war-
time has so often been disregarded, just for a scrap
of paper—Great Britain is going to make war.
*To Sir Edward Goschen, 4 Aug. 1914. Dispatch
by Sir Edward Goschen to the British Foreign
Office*

JACOB BEULER
nineteenth century

23 If I had a donkey wot wouldn't go,
D'ye think I'd wollop him? no, no, no.
Music Hall Song (c. 1822)

HOLY BIBLE
Old Testament

24 Upon the setting of that bright *Occidental Star,*
Queen *Elizabeth* of most happy memory.
Holy Bible, Authorized Version, Epistle Dedicatory

25 The appearance of Your Majesty, as of the *Sun* in his
strength. *Ib.*

1 In the beginning God created the heaven and the earth.
And the earth was without form, and void; and darkness was upon the face of the deep. And the Spirit of God moved upon the face of the waters.
And God said, Let there be light: and there was light.
Genesis i. 1

2 Fiat lux.
Let there be light. *Ib.* 3 (Vulgate)

3 And the evening and the morning were the first day.
Ib. 5

4 And God saw that it was good. *Ib.* 10

5 And God made two great lights; the greater light to rule the day, and the lesser light to rule the night: he made the stars also. *Ib.* 16

6 And God said, Let us make man in our image, after our likeness. *Ib.* 26

7 Dominion ... over every creeping thing that creepeth upon the earth. *Ib.*

8 Male and female created he them. *Ib.* 27

9 Be fruitful, and multiply, and replenish the earth, and subdue it: and have dominion over the fish of the sea, and over the fowl of the air, and over every living thing that moveth upon the earth. *Ib.* 28

10 But there went up a mist from the earth, and watered the whole face of the ground. *Ib.* ii. 6

11 And the Lord God formed man of the dust of the ground, and breathed into his nostrils the breath of life; and man became a living soul.
And the Lord God planted a garden eastward in Eden. *Ib.* 7

12 The tree of life also in the midst of the garden. *Ib.* 9

13 But of the tree of the knowledge of good and evil, thou shalt not eat of it: for in the day that thou eatest thereof thou shalt surely die. *Ib.* 17

14 It is not good that the man should be alone; I will make him an help meet for him. *Ib.* 18

15 The Lord God ... brought them unto Adam to see what he would call them. *Ib.* 19

16 And the Lord God caused a deep sleep to fall upon Adam, and he slept: and he took one of his ribs, and closed up the flesh instead thereof;
And the rib, which the Lord God had taken from man, made he a woman. *Ib.* 21

17 Bone of my bones, and flesh of my flesh. *Ib.* 23

18 Therefore shall a man leave his father and his mother, and shall cleave unto his wife: and they shall be one flesh. *Ib.* 24

19 Now the serpent was more subtil than any beast of the field. *Ib.* iii. 1

20 Ye shall be as gods, knowing good and evil. *Ib.* 5

21 And they sewed fig leaves together, and made themselves aprons [breeches *in Genevan Bible*, 1560].
And they heard the voice of the Lord God walking in the garden in the cool of the day. *Ib.* 7

22 The woman whom thou gavest to be with me, she gave me of the tree, and I did eat. *Ib.* 12

23 What is this that thou hast done? *Ib.* 13

24 The serpent beguiled me, and I did eat. *Ib.*

25 It shall bruise thy head, and thou shalt bruise his heel.
Genesis iii. 15

26 In sorrow thou shalt bring forth children. *Ib.* 16

27 In the sweat of thy face shalt thou eat bread. *Ib.* 19

28 For dust thou art, and unto dust shalt thou return.
Ib.

29 The mother of all living. *Ib.* 20

30 Am I my brother's keeper? *Ib.* iv. 9

31 The voice of thy brother's blood crieth unto me from the ground. *Ib.* 10

32 My punishment is greater than I can bear. *Ib.* 13

33 Dwelt in the land of Nod. *Ib.* 16

34 The father of such as dwell in tents. *Ib.* 20

35 And Enoch walked with God: and he was not; for God took him. *Ib.* v. 24

36 And Noah begat Shem, Ham, and Japheth. *Ib.* 32

37 There were giants in the earth in those days.
Ib. vi. 4

38 Mighty men which were of old, men of renown. *Ib.*

39 But the dove found no rest for the sole of her foot.
Ib. viii. 9

40 For the imagination of man's heart is evil from his youth. *Ib.* 21

41 While the earth remaineth, seedtime and harvest, and cold and heat, and summer and winter, and day and night shall not cease. *Ib.* 22

42 At the hand of every man's brother will I require the life of man. *Ib.* ix. 5

43 Whoso sheddeth man's blood, by man shall his blood be shed. *Ib.* 6

44 I do set my bow in the cloud. *Ib.* 13

45 Even as Nimrod the mighty hunter before the Lord.
Ib. x. 9

46 Let there be no strife, I pray thee, between thee and me ... for we be brethren. *Ib.* xiii. 8

47 An horror of great darkness fell upon him. *Ib.* xv. 12

48 In a good old age. *Ib.* 15

49 His hand will be against every man, and every man's hand against him. *Ib.* xvi. 12

50 Old and well stricken in age. *Ib.* xviii. 11

51 And the Lord said unto Abraham, Wherefore did Sarah laugh? *Ib.* 13

52 Shall not the Judge of all the earth do right? *Ib.* 25

53 But his wife looked back from behind him, and she became a pillar of salt. *Ib.* xix. 26

54 Take now thy son, thine only son Isaac, whom thou lovest. *Ib.* xxii. 2

55 My son, God will provide himself a lamb. *Ib.* 8

56 Behold behind him a ram caught in a thicket by his horns. *Ib.* 13

57 Esau was a cunning hunter, a man of the field; and Jacob was a plain man, dwelling in tents.
Ib. xxv. 27

58 And he sold his birthright unto Jacob. *Ib.* 33

59 Behold, Esau my brother is a hairy man, and I am a smooth man. *Ib.* xxvii. 11

1 The voice is Jacob's voice, but the hands are the hands of Esau. *Genesis* xxvii. 22

2 Thy brother came with subtilty, and hath taken away thy blessing. *Ib.* 35

3 And he dreamed, and behold a ladder set up on the earth, and the top of it reached to heaven: and behold the angels of God ascending and descending on it. *Ib.* xxviii. 12

4 Surely the Lord is in this place; and I knew it not. *Ib.* 16

5 This is none other but the house of God, and this is the gate of heaven. *Ib.* 17

6 And Jacob served seven years for Rachel; and they seemed unto him but a few days, for the love he had to her. *Ib.* xxix. 20

7 A troop cometh: and she called his name Gad. *Ib.* xxx. 11

8 Mizpah; for he said, The Lord watch between me and thee, when we are absent one from another. *Ib.* xxxi. 49

9 There wrestled a man with him until the breaking of the day.
And when he saw that he prevailed not against him, he touched the hollow of his thigh; and the hollow of Jacob's thigh was out of joint, as he wrestled with him. *Ib.* xxxii. 24

10 I will not let thee go, except thou bless me. *Ib.* 26

11 For I have seen God face to face, and my life is preserved. *Ib.* 30

12 Now Israel loved Joseph more than all his children, because he was the son of his old age; and he made him a coat of many colours. *Ib.* xxxvii. 3

13 Behold, your sheaves stood round about, and made obeisance to my sheaf. *Ib.* 7

14 Behold, this dreamer cometh. *Ib.* 19

15 Some evil beast hath devoured him. *Ib.* 20

16 And she caught him by his garment, saying, Lie with me; and he left his garment in her hand, and fled. *Ib.* xxxix. 12

17 And the lean and the ill favoured kine did eat up the first seven fat kine. *Ib.* xli. 20

18 And the thin ears devoured the seven good ears. *Ib.* 24

19 Jacob saw that there was corn in Egypt. *Ib.* xlii. 1

20 Ye are spies; to see the nakedness of the land ye are come. *Ib.* 9

21 Bring down my gray hairs with sorrow to the grave. *Ib.* 38

22 Benjamin's mess was five times so much as any of their's. *Ib.* xliii. 34

23 Ye shall eat the fat of the land. *Ib.* xlv. 18

24 See that ye fall not out by the way. *Ib.* 24

25 Few and evil have the days of the years of my life been. *Ib.* xlvii. 9

26 Unstable as water, thou shalt not excel. *Ib.* xlix. 4

27 Issachar is a strong ass couching down between two burdens. *Ib.* 14

28 Unto the utmost bound of the everlasting hills. *Ib.* 26

29 Now there arose up a new king over Egypt, which knew not Joseph. *Exodus* i. 8

30 She took for him an ark of bulrushes, and daubed it with slime. *Ib.* ii. 3

31 Who made thee a prince and a judge over us? *Ib.* 14

32 I have been a stranger in a strange land. *Ib.* 22

33 Behold, the bush burned with fire, and the bush was not consumed. *Ib.* iii. 2

34 Put off thy shoes from off thy feet, for the place whereon thou standest is holy ground. *Ib.* 5

35 And Moses hid his face; for he was afraid to look upon God. *Ib.* 6

36 A land flowing with milk and honey; unto the place of the Canaanites, and the Hittites, and the Amorites, and the Perizzites, and the Hivites, and the Jebusites. *Ib.* 8

37 I AM THAT I AM. *Ib.* 14

38 The Lord God of your fathers, the God of Abraham, the God of Isaac, and the God of Jacob. *Ib.* 15

39 But I am slow of speech, and of a slow tongue. *Ib.* iv. 10

40 I know not the Lord, neither will I let Israel go. *Ib.* v. 2

41 My signs and my wonders in the land of Egypt. *Ib.* vii. 3

42 Aaron's rod swallowed up their rods.
And he hardened Pharaoh's heart, that he hearkened not. *Ib.* 12

43 A boil breaking forth with blains. *Ib.* ix. 10

44 Darkness which may be felt. *Ib.* x. 21

45 Your lamb shall be without blemish. *Ib.* xii. 5

46 Roast with fire, and unleavened bread; and with bitter herbs they shall eat it.
Eat not of it raw, nor sodden at all with water, but roast with fire; his head with his legs, and with the purtenance thereof. *Ib.* 8

47 With your loins girded, your shoes on your feet, and your staff in your hand; and ye shall eat it in haste; it is the Lord's passover.
For I will pass through the land of Egypt this night, and will smite all the firstborn in the land of Egypt, both man and beast. *Ib.* 11

48 And there was a great cry in Egypt. *Ib.* 30

49 And they spoiled the Egyptians. *Ib.* 36

50 And the Lord went before them by day in a pillar of a cloud, to lead them the way; and by night in a pillar of fire, to give them light. *Ib.* xiii. 21

51 The Lord is a man of war. *Ib.* xv. 3

52 Would to God we had died by the hand of the Lord in the land of Egypt, when we sat by the flesh pots, and when we did eat bread to the full. *Ib.* xvi. 3

53 But let not God speak with us, lest we die. *Ib.* xx. 19

54 Life for life,
Eye for eye, tooth for tooth, hand for hand, foot for foot,
Burning for burning, wound for wound, stripe for stripe. *Ib.* xxi. 23

55 Thou shalt not suffer a witch to live. *Ib.* xxii. 18

1 Thou shalt not seethe a kid in his mother's milk.
Exodus xxiii. 19

2 The Urim and the Thummim. *Ib.* xxviii. 30

3 And the people sat down to eat and to drink, and rose up to play. *Ib.* xxxii. 6

4 If not, blot me, I pray thee, out of thy book which thou hast written. *Ib.* 32

5 A stiffnecked people. *Ib.* xxxiii. 3

6 Joshua the son of Nun. *Ib.* 11

7 There shall no man see me, and live. *Ib.* 20

8 Let him go for a scapegoat into the wilderness.
Leviticus xvi. 10

9 Thou shalt love thy neighbour as thyself.
Ib. xix. 18; *St. Matthew* xix. 19

10 The Lord bless thee, and keep thee:
The Lord make his face shine upon thee, and be gracious unto thee:
The Lord lift up his countenance upon thee, and give thee peace. *Numbers* vi. 24

11 Would God that all the Lord's people were prophets.
Ib. xi. 29

12 Now the man Moses was very meek, above all the men which were upon the face of the earth.
Ib. xii. 3

13 Sent to spy out the land. *Ib.* xiii. 16

14 The giants, the sons of Anak. *Ib.* 33

15 Hear now, ye rebels; must we fetch you water out of this rock? *Ib.* xx. 10

16 Smote him with the edge of the sword. *Ib.* xxi. 24

17 He whom thou blessest is blessed, and he whom thou cursest is cursed. *Ib.* xxii. 6

18 Let me die the death of the righteous, and let my last end be like his! *Ib.* xxiii. 10

19 God is not a man, that he should lie. *Ib.* 19

20 I called thee to curse mine enemies, and, behold, thou hast altogether blessed them these three times.
Ib. xxiv. 10

21 Be sure your sin will find you out. *Ib.* xxxii. 23

22 I call heaven and earth to witness against you this day. *Deuteronomy* iv. 26

23 Man doth not live by bread only, but by every word that proceedeth out of the mouth of the Lord doth man live. *Ib.* viii. 3

24 A dreamer of dreams. *Ib.* xiii. 1

25 The wife of thy bosom. *Ib.* 6

26 Thou shalt not muzzle the ox when he treadeth out the corn. *Ib.* xxv. 4

27 Cursed be he that removeth his neighbour's landmark.
Ib. xxvii. 17

28 In the morning thou shalt say, Would God it were even! and at even thou shalt say, Would God it were morning! *Ib.* xxviii. 67

29 The secret things belong unto the Lord our God.
Ib. xxix. 29

30 I have set before you life and death, blessing and cursing: therefore choose life, that both thou and thy seed may live. *Ib.* xxx. 19

31 In the waste howling wilderness.
Deuteronomy xxxii. 10

32 Jeshurun waxed fat, and kicked. *Ib.* 15

33 As thy days, so shall thy strength be. *Ib.* xxxiii. 25

34 The eternal God is thy refuge, and underneath are the everlasting arms. *Ib.* 27

35 No man knoweth of his sepulchre unto this day.
Ib. xxxiv. 6

36 As I was with Moses, so I will be with thee: I will not fail thee, nor forsake thee. *Joshua* i. 5

37 Be strong and of a good courage; be not afraid, neither be thou dismayed: for the Lord thy God is with thee, whithersoever thou goest. *Ib.* 9

38 This line of scarlet thread. *Ib.* ii. 18

39 All the Israelites passed over on dry ground.
Ib. iii. 17

40 When the people heard the sound of the trumpet, and the people shouted with a great shout, that the wall fell down flat, so that the people went up into the city. *Ib.* vi. 20

41 Hewers of wood and drawers of water. *Ib.* ix. 21

42 Sun, stand thou still upon Gibeon; and thou, Moon, in the valley of Ajalon. *Ib.* x. 12

43 Is not this written in the book of Jasher? *Ib.* 13

44 I am going the way of all the earth. *Ib.* xxiii. 14

45 He delivered them into the hands of spoilers.
Judges ii. 14

46 Then Jael Heber's wife took a nail of the tent, and took an hammer in her hand, and went softly unto him, and smote the nail into his temples, and fastened it into the ground: for he was fast asleep and weary. *Ib.* iv. 21

47 I arose a mother in Israel. *Ib.* v. 7

48 The stars in their courses fought against Sisera.
Ib. 20

49 She brought forth butter in a lordly dish. *Ib.* 25

50 At her feet he bowed, he fell, he lay down. *Ib.* 27

51 The mother of Sisera looked out at a window, and cried through the lattice, Why is his chariot so long in coming? why tarry the wheels of his chariots?
Ib. 28

52 Have they not divided the prey; to every man a damsel or two? *Ib.* 30

53 Is not the gleaning of the grapes of Ephraim better than the vintage of Abi-ezer? *Ib.* viii. 2

54 Faint, yet pursuing. *Ib.* 4

55 Out of the eater came forth meat, and out of the strong came forth sweetness. *Ib.* xiv. 14

56 If ye had not plowed with my heifer, ye had not found out my riddle. *Ib.* 18

57 He smote them hip and thigh. *Ib.* xv. 8

58 The Philistines be upon thee, Samson. *Ib.* xvi. 9

59 He wist not that the Lord was departed from him.
Ib. 20

60 He did grind in the prison house. *Ib.* 21

61 From Dan even to Beer-sheba. *Ib.* xx. 1

62 The people arose as one man. *Ib.* 8

1 Intreat me not to leave thee, or to return from following after thee: for whither thou goest, I will go; and where thou lodgest, I will lodge: thy people shall be my people, and thy God my God:

Where thou diest, will I die, and there will I be buried: the Lord do so to me, and more also, if ought but death part thee and me. *Ruth* i. 16

2 Girded with a linen ephod. *I Samuel* ii. 18

3 The flower of their age. *Ib.* 33

4 The Lord called Samuel: and he answered, Here am I. *Ib.* iii. 4

5 Here am I; for thou calledst me. And he said, I called not; lie down again. *Ib.* 5

6 Speak, Lord; for thy servant heareth. *Ib.* 9

7 The ears of every one that heareth it shall tingle. *Ib.* 11

8 Quit yourselves like men. *Ib.* iv. 9

9 He fell from off the seat backward by the side of the gate, and his neck brake. *Ib.* 18

10 I-chabod, saying, The glory is departed from Israel. *Ib.* 21

11 Is Saul also among the prophets? *Ib.* x. 11

12 God save the king. *Ib.* 24

13 A man after his own heart. *Ib.* xiii. 14

14 I did but taste a little honey with the end of the rod that was in mine hand, and, lo, I must die. *Ib.* xiv. 43

15 What meaneth then this bleating of the sheep in mine ears, and the lowing of the oxen which I hear? *Ib.* xv. 14

16 To obey is better than sacrifice, and to hearken than the fat of rams.

For rebellion is as the sin of witchcraft. *Ib.* 22

17 Agag came unto him delicately. And Agag said, Surely the bitterness of death is past. *Ib.* 32

18 For the Lord seeth not as man seeth: for man looketh on the outward appearance, but the Lord looketh on the heart. *Ib.* xvi. 7

19 Now he was ruddy, and withal of a beautiful countenance, and goodly to look to. *Ib.* 12

20 I know thy pride, and the naughtiness of thine heart. *Ib.* xvii. 28

21 Let no man's heart fail because of him [Goliath]. *Ib.* 32

22 Go, and the Lord be with thee. *Ib.* 37

23 Five smooth stones out of the brook. *Ib.* 40

24 Am I a dog, that thou comest to me with staves? *Ib.* 43

25 Saul hath slain his thousands, and David his ten thousands. *Ib.* xviii. 7

26 And Jonathan gave his artillery unto his lad. *Ib.* xx. 40

27 As saith the proverb of the ancients, Wickedness proceedeth from the wicked. *Ib.* xxiv. 13

28 I have played the fool. *Ib.* xxvi. 21

29 The beauty of Israel is slain upon thy high places: how are the mighty fallen!

Tell it not in Gath, publish it not in the streets of Askelon; lest the daughters of the Philistines rejoice, lest the daughters of the uncircumcised triumph.

Ye mountains of Gilboa, let there be no dew, neither let there be rain, upon you, nor fields of offerings: for there the shield of the mighty is vilely cast away. *2 Samuel* i. 19

30 Saul and Jonathan were lovely and pleasant in their lives, and in their death they were not divided: they were swifter than eagles, they were stronger than lions.

Ye daughters of Israel, weep over Saul, who clothed you in scarlet, with other delights, who put on ornaments of gold upon your apparel.

How are the mighty fallen in the midst of the battle! O Jonathan, thou wast slain in thine high places.

I am distressed for thee, my brother Jonathan: very pleasant hast thou been unto me: thy love to me was wonderful, passing the love of women.

How are the mighty fallen, and the weapons of war perished! *Ib.* 23

31 Smote him under the fifth rib. *Ib.* ii. 23

32 Set ye Uriah in the forefront of the hottest battle. *Ib.* xi. 15

33 The poor man had nothing, save one little ewe lamb. *Ib.* xii. 3

34 Thou art the man. *Ib.* 7

35 As water spilt on the ground, which cannot be gathered up again. *Ib.* xiv. 14

36 Come out, come out, thou bloody man, thou son of Belial. *Ib.* xvi. 7

37 Would God I had died for thee, O Absalom, my son, my son! *Ib.* xviii. 33

38 The sweet psalmist of Israel. *Ib.* xxiii. 1

39 Went in jeopardy of their lives. *Ib.* 17

40 I have somewhat to say unto thee. And she said, Say on. *I Kings* ii. 14

41 A proverb and a byword among all people. *Ib.* ix. 7

42 And when the queen of Sheba had seen all Solomon's wisdom . . . there was no more spirit in her. *Ib.* x. 4

43 Behold, the half was not told me. *Ib.* 7

44 Ivory, and apes, and peacocks. *Ib.* 22

45 But king Solomon loved many strange women. *Ib.* xi. 1

46 My little finger shall be thicker than my father's loins. *Ib.* xii. 10

47 My father hath chastised you with whips, but I will chastise you with scorpions. *Ib.* 11

48 To your tents, O Israel: now see to thine own house, David. *Ib.* 16

49 He slept with his fathers. *Ib.* xiv. 20

50 Nevertheless in the time of his old age he was diseased in his feet. *Ib.* xv. 23

51 He went and dwelt by the brook Cherith, that is before Jordan.

And the ravens brought him bread and flesh in the morning, and bread and flesh in the evening; and he drank of the brook. *Ib.* xvii. 5

1 An handful of meal in a barrel, and a little oil in a cruse. *1 Kings* xvii. 12

2 How long halt ye between two opinions? *Ib.* xviii. 21

3 He is talking, or he is pursuing, or he is in a journey, or peradventure he sleepeth, and must be awaked. *Ib.* 27

4 There is a sound of abundance of rain. *Ib.* 41

5 There ariseth a little cloud out of the sea, like a man's hand. *Ib.* 44

6 He girded up his loins, and ran before Ahab. *Ib.* 46

7 Sat down under a juniper tree. *Ib.* xix. 4

8 But the Lord was not in the wind: and after the wind an earthquake; but the Lord was not in the earthquake:
And after the earthquake a fire: but the Lord was not in the fire: and after the fire a still small voice. *Ib.* 11

9 And it shall come to pass, that him that escapeth the sword of Hazael shall Jehu slay: and him that escapeth from the sword of Jehu shall Elisha slay. *Ib.* 17

10 Elijah passed by him, and cast his mantle upon him. *Ib.* 19

11 Let not him that girdeth on his harness boast himself as he that putteth it off. *Ib.* xx. 11

12 Hast thou found me, O mine enemy? *Ib.* xxi. 20

13 I saw all Israel scattered upon the hills, as sheep that have not a shepherd. *Ib.* xxii. 17

14 Feed him with bread of affliction and with water of affliction, until I come in peace.
And Micaiah said, If thou return at all in peace, the Lord hath not spoken by me. *Ib.* 27

15 And a certain man drew a bow at a venture, and smote the king of Israel between the joints of the harness. *Ib.* 34

16 The chariot of Israel, and the horsemen thereof. *2 Kings* ii. 12

17 The spirit of Elijah doth rest on Elisha. *Ib.* 15

18 Go up, thou bald head. *Ib.* 23

19 Is it well with the child? And she answered, It is well. *Ib.* iv. 26

20 There is death in the pot. *Ib.* 40

21 He shall know that there is a prophet in Israel. *Ib.* v. 8

22 Are not Abana and Pharpar, rivers of Damascus, better than all the waters of Israel? *Ib.* 12

23 I bow myself in the house of Rimmon. *Ib.* 18

24 Whence comest thou, Gehazi? *Ib.* 25

25 Is thy servant a dog, that he should do this great thing? *Ib.* viii. 13

26 Is it peace? And Jehu said, What hast thou to do with peace? turn thee behind me. *Ib.* ix. 18

27 The driving is like the driving of Jehu, the son of Nimshi; for he driveth furiously. *Ib.* 20

28 She painted her face, and tired her head, and looked out at a window. *Ib.* 30

29 Had Zimri peace, who slew his master? *Ib.* 31

30 Who is on my side? who? *Ib.* 32

31 And he said, Throw her down. So they threw her down. *2 Kings* ix. 33

32 They found no more of her than the skull, and the feet, and the palms of her hands. *Ib.* 35

33 Thou trustest upon the staff of this bruised reed, even upon Egypt, on which if a man lean, it will go into his hand, and pierce it. *Ib.* xviii. 21

34 He died in a good old age, full of days, riches, and honour. *1 Chronicles* xxix. 28

35 Every one with one of his hands wrought in the work, and with the other hand held a weapon. *Nehemiah* iv. 17

36 The man whom the king delighteth to honour. *Esther* vi. 9

37 Behold also, the gallows fifty cubits high. *Ib.* vii. 9

38 The sons of God came to present themselves before the Lord, and Satan came also among them.
And the Lord said unto Satan, Whence comest thou? Then Satan answered the Lord, and said, From going to and fro in the earth, and from walking up and down in it. *Job* i. 6

39 Doth Job fear God for naught? *Ib.* 9

40 The Lord gave, and the Lord hath taken away; blessed be the name of the Lord. *Ib.* 21

41 All that a man hath will he give for his life. *Ib.* ii. 4

42 And he took him a potsherd to scrape himself withal. *Ib.* 8

43 Curse God, and die. *Ib.* 9

44 Let the day perish wherein I was born, and the night in which it was said, There is a man child conceived. *Ib.* iii. 3

45 For now should I have lain still and been quiet, I should have slept: then had I been at rest,
With kings and counsellors of the earth, which built desolate places for themselves. *Ib.* 13

46 There the wicked cease from troubling, and there the weary be at rest. *Ib.* 17

47 Wherefore is light given to him that is in misery, and life unto the bitter in soul? *Ib.* 20

48 Then a spirit passed before my face; the hair of my flesh stood up. *Ib.* iv. 15

49 Shall mortal man be more just than God? shall a man be more pure than his maker? *Ib.* 17

50 Man is born unto trouble, as the sparks fly upward. *Ib.* v. 7

51 He taketh the wise in their own craftiness. *Ib.* 13

52 My days are swifter than a weaver's shuttle. *Ib.* vii. 6

53 He shall return no more to his house, neither shall his place know him any more. *Ib.* 10

54 The land of darkness and the shadow of death. *Ib.* x. 21

55 A land . . . where the light is as darkness. *Ib.* 22

56 Canst thou by searching find out God? *Ib.* xi. 7

57 No doubt but ye are the people, and wisdom shall die with you. *Ib.* xii. 2

58 With the ancient is wisdom; and in length of days understanding. *Ib.* 12

1 Man that is born of a woman is of few days, and full of trouble. *Job* xiv. 1

2 Miserable comforters are ye all. *Ib.* xvi. 2

3 The king of terrors. *Ib.* xviii. 14

4 I am escaped with the skin of my teeth. *Ib.* xix. 20

5 Oh that my words were now written! oh that they were printed in a book! *Ib.* 23

6 I know that my redeemer liveth, and that he shall stand at the latter day upon the earth:
And though after my skin worms destroy this body, yet in my flesh shall I see God. *Ib.* 25

7 Seeing the root of the matter is found in me. *Ib.* 28

8 The price of wisdom is above rubies. *Ib.* xxviii. 18

9 I was eyes to the blind, and feet was I to the lame. *Ib.* xxix. 15

10 The house appointed for all living. *Ib.* xxx. 23

11 My desire is . . . that mine adversary had written a book. *Ib.* xxxi. 35

12 Great men are not always wise. *Ib.* xxxii. 9

13 For I am full of matter, the spirit within me constraineth me. *Ib.* 18

14 One among a thousand. *Ib.* xxxiii. 23

15 Far be it from God, that he should do wickedness. *Ib.* xxxiv. 10

16 He multiplieth words without knowledge. *Ib.* xxxv. 16

17 Who is this that darkeneth counsel by words without knowledge? *Ib.* xxxviii. 2

18 Gird up now thy loins like a man. *Ib.* 3

19 Where wast thou when I laid the foundations of the earth? declare, if thou hast understanding. *Ib.* 4

20 When the morning stars sang together, and all the sons of God shouted for joy. *Ib.* 7

21 Hitherto shalt thou come, but no further: and here shall thy proud waves be stayed. *Ib.* 11

22 Hast thou entered into the springs of the sea? or hast thou walked in the search of the depth? *Ib.* 16

23 Hath the rain a father? or who hath begotten the drops of dew? *Ib.* 28

24 Canst thou bind the sweet influences of Pleiades, or loose the bands of Orion? *Ib.* 31

25 Canst thou guide Arcturus with his sons? *Ib.* 32

26 He paweth in the valley, and rejoiceth in his strength: he goeth on to meet the armed men. *Ib.* xxxix. 21

27 He swalloweth the ground with fierceness and rage: neither believeth he that it is the sound of the trumpet.
He saith among the trumpets, Ha, ha; and he smelleth the battle afar off, the thunder of the captains, and the shouting. *Ib.* 24

28 Behold now behemoth, which I made with thee; he eateth grass as an ox. *Ib.* xl. 15

29 Canst thou draw out leviathan with an hook? *Ib.* xli. 1

30 Wilt thou play with him as with a bird? or wilt thou bind him for thy maidens? *Ib.* 5

31 Hard as a piece of the nether millstone. *Ib.* 24

32 He maketh the deep to boil like a pot. *Ib.* 31

33 I have heard of thee by the hearing of the ear: but now mine eye seeth thee. *Job* xlii. 5

34 So the Lord blessed the latter end of Job more than his beginning. *Ib.* 12

35 Dominus illuminatio mea.
The Lord is my light. *Psalms* xxvii. 1 (Vulgate)

36 Nisi dominus frustra.

Except the Lord keep the city the watchman waketh but in vain. *Ib.* cxxvii. 1 (Vulgate) abridged
(*Motto of the City of Edinburgh*)

For psalms in the Book of Common Prayer see Prayer Book

37 My son, if sinners entice thee, consent thou not. *Proverbs* i. 10

38 Surely in vain the net is spread in the sight of any bird. *Ib.* 17

39 Wisdom crieth without; she uttereth her voice in the streets. *Ib.* 20

40 Length of days is in her right hand; and in her left hand riches and honour. *Ib.* iii. 16

41 Her ways are ways of pleasantness, and all her paths are peace. *Ib.* 17

42 Wisdom is the principal thing; therefore get wisdom: and with all thy getting get understanding. *Ib.* iv. 7

43 The path of the just is as the shining light, that shineth more and more unto the perfect day. *Ib.* 18

44 For the lips of a strange woman drop as an honeycomb, and her mouth is smoother than oil:
But her end is bitter as wormwood, sharp as a twoedged sword. *Ib.* v. 3

45 Go to the ant, thou sluggard; consider her ways, and be wise. *Ib.* vi. 6

46 Yet a little sleep, a little slumber, a little folding of the hands to sleep. *Ib.* 10

47 So shall thy poverty come as one that travelleth, and thy want as an armed man. *Ib.* 11

48 Neither let her take thee with her eyelids. *Ib.* 25

49 Can a man take fire in his bosom, and his clothes not be burned? *Ib.* 27

50 Come, let us take our fill of love until the morning: let us solace ourselves with loves.
For the goodman is not at home, he is gone a long journey. *Ib.* vii. 18

51 As an ox goeth to the slaughter. *Ib.* 22

52 Wisdom is better than rubies. *Ib.* viii. 11

53 Stolen waters are sweet, and bread eaten in secret is pleasant. *Ib.* ix. 17

54 A wise son maketh a glad father: but a foolish son is the heaviness of his mother. *Ib.* x. 1

55 The destruction of the poor is their poverty. *Ib.* 15

56 In the multitude of counsellors there is safety. *Ib.* xi. 14

57 He that is surety for a stranger shall smart for it. *Ib.* 15

58 As a jewel of gold in a swine's snout, so is a fair woman which is without discretion. *Ib.* 22

1 **A** virtuous woman is a crown to her husband.
Proverbs xii. 4

2 **A** righteous man regardeth the life of his beast: but the tender mercies of the wicked are cruel. *Ib.* 10

3 Hope deferred maketh the heart sick. *Ib.* xiii. 12

4 The way of transgressors is hard. *Ib.* 15

5 The desire accomplished is sweet to the soul. *Ib.* 19

6 He that spareth his rod hateth his son. *Ib.* 24

7 The heart knoweth his own bitterness; and a stranger doth not intermeddle with his joy. *Ib.* xiv. 10

8 In all labour there is profit. *Ib.* 23

9 Righteousness exalteth a nation. *Ib.* 34

10 A soft answer turneth away wrath. *Ib.* xv. 1

11 A merry heart maketh a cheerful countenance.
Ib. 13

12 Better is a dinner of herbs where love is, than a stalled ox and hatred therewith. *Ib.* 17

13 Better is a mess of pottage with love, than a fat ox with evil will. *Ib.* (Matthew's Bible, 1535)

14 A word spoken in due season, how good is it! *Ib.* 23

15 Pride goeth before destruction, and an haughty spirit before a fall. *Ib.* xvi. 18

16 The hoary head is a crown of glory. *Ib.* 31

17 He that is slow to anger is better than the mighty; and he that ruleth his spirit than he that taketh a city. *Ib.* 32

18 He that repeateth a matter separateth very friends.
Ib. xvii. 9

19 He that begetteth a fool doeth it to his sorrow. *Ib.* 21

20 A merry heart doeth good like a medicine. *Ib.* 22

21 A wounded spirit who can bear? *Ib.* xviii. 14

22 There is a friend that sticketh closer than a brother.
Ib. 24

23 Wine is a mocker, strong drink is raging. *Ib.* xx. 1

24 Every fool will be meddling. *Ib.* 3

25 Even a child is known by his doings. *Ib.* 11

26 The hearing ear, and the seeing eye. *Ib.* 12

27 It is naught, it is naught, saith the buyer: but when he is gone his way, then he boasteth. *Ib.* 14

28 It is better to dwell in a corner of the housetop, than with a brawling woman in a wide house.
Ib. xxi. 9

29 A good name is rather to be chosen than great riches.
Ib. xxii. 1

30 Train up a child in the way he should go: and when he is old, he will not depart from it. *Ib.* 6

31 Riches certainly make themselves wings. *Ib.* xxiii. 5

32 Look not thou upon the wine when it is red, when it giveth his colour in the cup, . . .
At the last it biteth like a serpent, and stingeth like an adder. *Ib.* 31

33 The heart of kings is unsearchable. *Ib.* xxv. 3

34 A word fitly spoken is like apples of gold in pictures of silver. *Ib.* 11

35 Heap coals of fire upon his head. *Ib.* 22

36 As cold waters to a thirsty soul, so is good news from a far country. *Ib.* 25

37 As the bird by wandering, as the swallow by flying, so the curse causeless shall not come.
Proverbs xxvi. 2

38 Answer a fool according to his folly. *Ib.* 5

39 As a dog returneth to his vomit, so a fool returneth to his folly. *Ib.* 11

40 Seest thou a man wise in his own conceit? There is more hope of a fool than of him. *Ib.* 12

41 The slothful man saith, There is a lion in the way: a lion is in the streets. *Ib.* 13

42 The sluggard is wiser in his own conceit than seven men that can render a reason. *Ib.* 16

43 Boast not thyself of to morrow; for thou knowest not what a day may bring forth. *Ib.* xxvii. 1

44 Open rebuke is better than secret love. *Ib.* 5

45 Faithful are the wounds of a friend. *Ib.* 6

46 A continual dropping in a very rainy day and a contentious woman are alike. *Ib.* 15

47 Iron sharpeneth iron; so a man sharpeneth the countenance of his friend. *Ib.* 17

48 Though thou shouldest bray a fool in a mortar among wheat with a pestle, yet will not his foolishness depart from him. *Ib.* 22

49 The wicked flee when no man pursueth: but the righteous are bold as a lion. *Ib.* xxviii. 1

50 He that maketh haste to be rich shall not be innocent.
Ib. 20

51 A fool uttereth all his mind. *Ib.* xxix. 11

52 Where there is no vision, the people perish. *Ib.* 18

53 Give me neither poverty nor riches. *Ib.* xxx. 8

54 The horseleach hath two daughters, crying, Give, give. *Ib.* 15

55 There are three things that are never satisfied, yea, four things say not, It is enough:
The grave; and the barren womb; the earth that is not filled with water; and the fire that saith not, It is enough. *Ib.*

56 The way of an eagle in the air; the way of a serpent upon a rock; the way of a ship in the midst of the sea; and the way of a man with a maid. *Ib.* 19

57 Who can find a virtuous woman? for her price is far above rubies. *Ib.* xxxi. 10

58 Her children arise up, and call her blessed. *Ib.* 28

59 Vanity of vanities, saith the Preacher, vanity of vanities; all is vanity.
What profit hath a man of all his labour which he taketh under the sun?
One generation passeth away, and another generation cometh. *Ecclesiastes* i. 2

60 All the rivers run into the sea; yet the sea is not full.
Ib. 7

61 All things are full of labour; man cannot utter it: the eye is not satisfied with seeing, nor the ear filled with hearing.
The thing that hath been, it is that which shall be; and that which is done is that which shall be done: and there is no new thing under the sun. *Ib.* 8

62 All is vanity and vexation of spirit. *Ib.* 14

63 He that increaseth knowledge increaseth sorrow.
Ib. 18

1 Wisdom excelleth folly, as far as light excelleth darkness. *Ecclesiastes* ii. 13

2 One event happeneth to them all. *Ib.* 14

3 To every thing there is a season, and a time to every purpose under the heaven:
A time to be born, and a time to die. *Ib.* iii. 1

4 Wherefore I praised the dead which are already dead more than the living which are yet alive. *Ib.* iv. 2

5 A threefold cord is not quickly broken. *Ib.* 12

6 God is in heaven, and thou upon earth: therefore let thy words be few. *Ib.* v. 2

7 Better is it that thou shouldest not vow, than that thou shouldest vow and not pay. *Ib.* 5

8 The sleep of a labouring man is sweet. *Ib.* 12

9 A good name is better than precious ointment; and the day of death than the day of one's birth.
It is better to go to the house of mourning, than to go to the house of feasting. *Ib.* vii. 1

10 As the crackling of thorns under a pot, so is the laughter of a fool. *Ib.* 6

11 Better is the end of a thing than the beginning thereof. *Ib.* 8

12 Say not thou, What is the cause that the former days were better than these? for thou dost not enquire wisely concerning this. *Ib.* 10

13 In the day of prosperity be joyful, but in the day of adversity consider. *Ib.* 14

14 Be not righteous over much. *Ib.* 16

15 One man among a thousand have I found; but a woman among all those have I not found. *Ib.* 28

16 God hath made man upright; but they have sought out many inventions. *Ib.* 29

17 There is no discharge in that war. *Ib.* viii. 8

18 A man hath no better thing under the sun, than to eat, and to drink, and to be merry. *Ib.* 15

19 A living dog is better than a dead lion. *Ib.* ix. 4

20 Go thy way, eat thy bread with joy, and drink thy wine with a merry heart; for God now accepteth thy works. *Ib.* 7

21 Whatsoever thy hand findeth to do, do it with thy might; for there is no work, nor device, nor knowledge, nor wisdom, in the grave, whither thou goest. *Ib.* 10

22 The race is not to the swift, nor the battle to the strong. *Ib.* 11

23 Dead flies cause the ointment of the apothecary to send forth a stinking savour. *Ib.* x. 1

24 He that diggeth a pit shall fall into it. *Ib.* 8

25 Wine maketh merry: but money answereth all things. *Ib.* 19

26 For a bird of the air shall carry the voice, and that which hath wings shall tell the matter. *Ib.* 20

27 Cast thy bread upon the waters: for thou shalt find it after many days. *Ib.* xi. 1

28 In the place where the tree falleth, there it shall be. *Ib.* 3

29 He that observeth the wind shall not sow; and he that regardeth the clouds shall not reap. *Ib.* 4

30 In the morning sow thy seed, and in the evening withhold not thine hand. *Ecclesiastes* xi. 6

31 Truly the light is sweet, and a pleasant thing it is for the eyes to behold the sun. *Ib.* 7

32 Rejoice, O young man, in thy youth; and let thy heart cheer thee in the days of thy youth. *Ib.* 9

33 Remember now thy Creator in the days of thy youth, while the evil days come not, nor the years draw nigh, when thou shalt say, I have no pleasure in them;
While the sun, or the light, or the moon, or the stars, be not darkened, nor the clouds return after the rain:
In the day when the keepers of the house shall tremble, and the strong men shall bow themselves, and the grinders cease because they are few, and those that look out of the windows be darkened,
And the doors shall be shut in the streets, when the sound of the grinding is low, and he shall rise up at the voice of the bird, and all the daughters of musick shall be brought low;
Also when they shall be afraid of that which is high, and fears shall be in the way, and the almond tree shall flourish, and the grasshopper shall be a burden, and desire shall fail: because man goeth to his long home, and the mourners go about the streets:
Or ever the silver cord be loosed, or the golden bowl be broken, or the pitcher be broken at the fountain, or the wheel broken at the cistern.
Then shall the dust return to the earth as it was: and the spirit shall return unto God who gave it. *Ib.* xii. 1

34 The words of the wise are as goads. *Ib.* 11

35 Of making many books there is no end; and much study is a weariness of the flesh. *Ib.* 12

36 Fear God, and keep his commandments: for this is the whole duty of man.
For God shall bring every work into judgment, with every secret thing, whether it be good, or whether it be evil. *Ib.* 13

37 The song of songs, which is Solomon's.
Let him kiss me with the kisses of his mouth: for thy love is better than wine. *The Song of Solomon* i. 1

38 Thy name is an ointment poured forth, therefore do the virgins love thee. *Ib.* 3

39 I am black, but comely, O ye daughters of Jerusalem, as the tents of Kedar, as the curtains of Solomon. *Ib.* 5

40 Tell me, O thou whom my soul loveth, where thou feedest, where thou makest thy flock to rest at noon. *Ib.* 7

41 O thou fairest among women. *Ib.* 8

42 A bundle of myrrh is my wellbeloved unto me; he shall lie all night betwixt my breasts. *Ib.* 13

43 I am the rose of Sharon, and the lily of the valleys. *Ib.* ii. 1

44 His banner over me was love. *Ib.* 4

45 Stay me with flagons, comfort me with apples: for I am sick of love.
His left hand is under my head, and his right hand doth embrace me. *Ib.* 5

1 Rise up, my love, my fair one, and come away.
For, lo, the winter is past, the rain is over and gone;
The flowers appear on the earth; the time of the singing of birds is come, and the voice of the turtle is heard in our land.   *The Song of Solomon* ii. 10

2 Take us the foxes, the little foxes, that spoil the vines.   *Ib.* 15

3 My beloved is mine, and I am his: he feedeth among the lilies.
Until the day break, and the shadows flee away.   *Ib.* 16

4 By night on my bed I sought him whom my soul loveth.   *Ib.* iii. 1

5 Behold, thou art fair, my love; behold, thou art fair; thou hast doves' eyes within thy locks: thy hair is as a flock of goats, that appear from mount Gilead.
Thy teeth are like a flock of sheep that are even shorn, which came up from the washing; whereof every one bear twins, and none is barren among them.
Thy lips are like a thread of scarlet, and thy speech is comely: thy temples are like a piece of a pomegranate within thy locks.
Thy neck is like the tower of David builded for an armoury, whereon there hang a thousand bucklers, all shields of mighty men.
Thy breasts are like two young roes that are twins, which feed among the lilies.   *Ib.* iv. 1

6 Thou art all fair, my love; there is no spot in thee.   *Ib.* 7

7 A garden inclosed is my sister, my spouse; a spring shut up, a fountain sealed.   *Ib.* 12

8 Awake, O north wind; and come, thou south; blow upon my garden, that the spices thereof may flow out. Let my beloved come into his garden, and eat his pleasant fruits.   *Ib.* 16

9 I sleep, but my heart waketh: it is the voice of my beloved that knocketh, saying, Open to me, my sister, my love, my dove, my undefiled.   *Ib.* v. 2

10 My beloved put in his hand by the hole of the door, and my bowels were moved for him.   *Ib.* 4

11 I opened to my beloved; but my beloved had withdrawn himself.   *Ib.* 6

12 The watchmen that went about the city found me, they smote me, they wounded me; the keepers of the walls took away my veil from me.
I charge you, O daughters of Jerusalem, if ye find my beloved, that ye tell him, that I am sick of love. What is thy beloved more than another beloved, O thou fairest among women?   *Ib.* 7

13 My beloved is white and ruddy, the chiefest among ten thousand.   *Ib.* 10

14 His hands are as gold rings set with the beryl: his belly is as bright ivory overlaid with sapphires.
His legs are as pillars of marble, set upon sockets of fine gold: his countenance is as Lebanon, excellent as the cedars.
His mouth is most sweet: yea, he is altogether lovely. This is my beloved, and this is my friend, O daughters of Jerusalem.   *Ib.* 14

15 Who is she that looketh forth as the morning, fair as the moon, clear as the sun, and terrible as an army with banners?   *Ib.* vi. 10

16 Return, return, O Shulamite; return, return, that we may look upon thee.   *The Song of Solomon* vi. 13

17 How beautiful are thy feet with shoes, O prince's daughter!   *Ib.* vii. 1

18 Thy navel is like a round goblet, which wanteth not liquor: thy belly is like an heap of wheat set about with lilies.   *Ib.* 2

19 Thy neck is as a tower of ivory; thine eyes like the fishpools in Heshbon, by the gate of Bath-rabbim: thy nose is as the tower of Lebanon which looketh toward Damascus.   *Ib.* 4

20 Like the best wine, for my beloved, that goeth down sweetly, causing the lips of those that are asleep to speak.   *Ib.* 9

21 O that thou wert as my brother, that sucked the breasts of my mother! when I should find thee without, I would kiss thee; yea, I should not be despised.
I would lead thee, and bring thee into my mother's house.   *Ib.* viii. 1

22 Who is this that cometh up from the wilderness, leaning upon her beloved? I raised thee up under the apple tree: there thy mother brought thee forth: there she brought thee forth that bare thee.
Set me as a seal upon thine heart, as a seal upon thine arm: for love is strong as death; jealousy is cruel as the grave.   *Ib.* 5

23 Many waters cannot quench love, neither can the floods drown it: if a man would give all the substance of his house for love, it would utterly be contemned.   *Ib.* 7

24 We have a little sister, and she hath no breasts.   *Ib.* 8

25 Make haste, my beloved, and be thou like to a roe or to a young hart upon the mountain of spices.   *Ib.* 14

26 The ox knoweth his owner, and the ass his master's crib.   *Isaiah* i. 3

27 The whole head is sick, and the whole heart faint.   *Ib.* 5

28 As a lodge in a garden of cucumbers.   *Ib.* 8

29 Bring no more vain oblations; incense is an abomination unto me; the new moons and sabbaths, the calling of assemblies, I cannot away with.   *Ib.* 13

30 Though your sins be as scarlet, they shall be as white as snow.   *Ib.* 18

31 They shall beat their swords into plowshares, and their spears into pruninghooks: nation shall not lift up sword against nation, neither shall they learn war any more.   *Ib.* ii. 4

32 Cease ye from man, whose breath is in his nostrils.   *Ib.* 22

33 The stay and the staff, the whole stay of bread, and the whole stay of water.   *Ib.* iii. 1

34 Grind the faces of the poor.   *Ib.* 15

35 Walk with stretched forth necks and wanton eyes, walking and mincing as they go, and making a tinkling with their feet.   *Ib.* 16

36 In that day seven women shall take hold of one man.   *Ib.* iv. 1

37 My wellbeloved hath a vineyard in a very fruitful hill.   *Ib.* v. 1

1 And he looked that it should bring forth grapes, and it brought forth wild grapes. *Isaiah* v. 2

2 And he looked for judgment, but behold oppression; for righteousness, but behold a cry. *Ib.* 7

3 Woe unto them that join house to house, that lay field to field, till there be no place. *Ib.* 8

4 Woe unto them that rise up early in the morning, that they may follow strong drink. *Ib.* 11

5 Woe, woe unto them that draw iniquity with cords of vanity, and sin as it were with a cart rope. *Ib.* 18

6 Woe unto them that call evil good, and good evil. *Ib.* 20

7 For all this his anger is not turned away, but his hand is stretched out still. *Ib.* 25

8 In the year that king Uzziah died I saw also the Lord sitting upon a throne, high and lifted up, and his train filled the temple.

Above it stood the seraphims: each one had six wings; with twain he covered his face, and with twain he covered his feet, and with twain he did fly.

And one cried unto another, and said, Holy, holy, holy, is the Lord of hosts: the whole earth is full of his glory.

And the posts of the door moved at the voice of him that cried, and the house was filled with smoke.

Then said I, Woe is me! for I am undone; because I am a man of unclean lips, and I dwell in the midst of a people of unclean lips. *Ib.* vi. 1

9 Whom shall I send, and who will go for us? Then said I, Here am I; send me. *Ib.* 8

10 Make the heart of this people fat, and make their ears heavy, and shut their eyes; lest they see with their eyes, and hear with their ears, and understand with their heart, and convert, and be healed. *Ib.* 10

11 Then said I, Lord, how long? *Ib.* 11

12 Behold, a virgin shall conceive, and bear a son, and shall call his name Immanuel.

Butter and honey shall he eat, that he may know to refuse the evil, and choose the good. *Ib.* vii. 14

13 For a stone of stumbling and for a rock of offence. *Ib.* viii. 14

14 The people that walked in darkness have seen a great light: they that dwell in the land of the shadow of death, upon them hath the light shined.

Thou hast multiplied the nation, and not increased the joy: they joy before thee according to the joy in harvest, and as men rejoice when they divide the spoil. *Ib.* ix. 2

15 For unto us a child is born, unto us a son is given: and the government shall be upon his shoulder: and his name shall be called Wonderful, Counsellor, The mighty God, The everlasting Father, The Prince of Peace.

Of the increase of his government and peace there shall be no end. *Ib.* 6

16 The zeal of the Lord of hosts will perform this. *Ib.* 7

17 And there shall come forth a rod out of the stem of Jesse, and a Branch shall grow out of his roots:

And the spirit of the Lord shall rest upon him, the spirit of wisdom and understanding, the spirit of counsel and might, the spirit of knowledge and of the fear of the Lord. *Isaiah* xi. 1

18 The wolf also shall dwell with the lamb, and the leopard shall lie down with the kid; and the calf and the young lion and the fatling together; and a little child shall lead them. *Ib.* 6

19 And the lion shall eat straw like the ox.

And the sucking child shall play on the hole of the asp, and the weaned child shall put his hand on the cockatrice' den.

They shall not hurt nor destroy in all my holy mountain: for the earth shall be full of the knowledge of the Lord, as the waters cover the sea. *Ib.* 7

20 Dragons in their pleasant palaces. *Ib.* xiii. 22

21 Hell from beneath is moved for thee to meet thee at thy coming. *Ib.* xiv. 9

22 How art thou fallen from heaven, O Lucifer, son of the morning! *Ib.* 12

23 I will also make it a possession for the bittern, and pools of water: and I will sweep it with the besom of destruction. *Ib.* 23

24 And in mercy shall the throne be established. *Ib.* xvi. 5

25 The burden of the desert of the sea. *Ib.* xxi. 1

26 Watchman, what of the night? Watchman, what of the night?

The watchman said, The morning cometh, and also the night. *Ib.* 11

27 Let us eat and drink; for to morrow we shall die. *Ib.* xxii. 13

28 Fasten him as a nail in a sure place. *Ib.* 23

29 Whose merchants are princes. *Ib.* xxiii. 8

30 Howl, ye ships of Tarshish. *Ib.* 14

31 A feast of fat things, a feast of wines on the lees. *Ib.* xxv. 6

32 We have as it were brought forth wind. *Ib.* xxvi. 18

33 For precept must be upon precept, precept upon precept; line upon line, line upon line; here a little, and there a little. *Ib.* xxviii. 10

34 We have made a covenant with death, and with hell are we at agreement. *Ib.* 15

35 They are drunken, but not with wine. *Ib.* xxix. 9

36 Their strength is to sit still. *Ib.* xxx. 7

37 Now go, write it before them in a table, and note it in a book. *Ib.* 8

38 Speak unto us smooth things, prophesy deceits. *Ib.* 10

39 In quietness and in confidence shall be your strength. *Ib.* 15

40 One thousand shall flee at the rebuke of one. *Ib.* 17

41 The bread of adversity. *Ib.* 20

42 This is the way, walk ye in it. *Ib.* 21

43 And a man shall be as an hiding place from the wind, and a covert from the tempest; as rivers of water in a dry place, as the shadow of a great rock in a weary land. *Ib.* xxxii. 2

44 The liberal deviseth liberal things. *Ib.* 8

45 An habitation of dragons, and a court for owls. *Ib.* xxxiv. 13

1 The wilderness and the solitary place shall be glad for them; and the desert shall rejoice, and blossom as the rose. *Isaiah* xxxv. 1

2 Strengthen ye the weak hands, and confirm the feeble knees. *Ib.* 3

3 Then shall the lame man leap as an hart, and the tongue of the dumb sing: for in the wilderness shall waters break out, and streams in the desert. *Ib.* 6

4 The wayfaring men, though fools, shall not err therein. *Ib.* 8

5 Sorrow and sighing shall flee away. *Ib.* 10

6 Set thine house in order. *Ib.* xxxviii. 1

7 I shall go softly all my years in the bitterness of my soul. *Ib.* 15

8 Comfort ye, comfort ye my people, saith your God. Speak ye comfortably to Jerusalem, and cry unto her, that her warfare is accomplished. *Ib.* xl. 1

9 The voice of him that crieth in the wilderness, Prepare ye the way of the Lord, make straight in the desert a highway for our God.
Every valley shall be exalted, and every mountain and hill shall be made low: and the crooked shall be made straight, and the rough places plain:
And the glory of the Lord shall be revealed, and all flesh shall see it together: for the mouth of the Lord hath spoken it. *Ib.* 3

10 The voice said, Cry. And he said, What shall I cry? All flesh is grass, and all the goodliness thereof is as the flower of the field:
The grass withereth, the flower fadeth: because the spirit of the Lord bloweth upon it: surely the people is grass. *Ib.* 6

11 He shall feed his flock like a shepherd: he shall gather the lambs with his arm, and carry them in his bosom, and shall gently lead those that are with young. *Ib.* 11

12 The nations are as a drop of a bucket, and are counted as the small dust of the balance: behold, he taketh up the isles as a very little thing. *Ib.* 15

13 Have ye not known? have ye not heard? hath it not been told you from the beginning? *Ib.* 21

14 But they that wait upon the Lord shall renew their strength: they shall mount up with wings as eagles; they shall run, and not be weary; and they shall walk, and not faint. *Ib.* 31

15 A bruised reed shall he not break, and the smoking flax shall he not quench. *Ib.* xlii. 3

16 He warmeth himself, and saith, Aha, I am warm, I have seen the fire. *Ib.* xliv. 16

17 Shall the clay say to him that fashioneth it, What makest thou? *Ib.* xlv. 9

18 Verily thou art a God that hidest thyself. *Ib.* 15

19 I have chosen thee in the furnace of affliction. *Ib.* xlviii. 10

20 O that thou hadst hearkened to my commandments! then had thy peace been as a river, and thy righteousness as the waves of the sea. *Ib.* 18

21 There is no peace, saith the Lord, unto the wicked. *Ib.* 22

22 How beautiful upon the mountains are the feet of him that bringeth good tidings, that publisheth peace; that bringeth good tidings of good, that publisheth salvation; that saith unto Zion, Thy God reigneth! *Isaiah* lii. 7

23 For they shall see eye to eye, when the Lord shall bring again Zion.
Break forth into joy, sing together, ye waste places of Jerusalem: for the Lord hath comforted his people, he hath redeemed Jerusalem. *Ib.* 8

24 Who hath believed our report? and to whom is the arm of the Lord revealed? *Ib.* liii. 1

25 He hath no form nor comeliness; and when we shall see him, there is no beauty that we should desire him.
He is despised and rejected of men; a man of sorrows, and acquainted with grief: and we hid as it were our faces from him; he was despised, and we esteemed him not.
Surely he hath borne our griefs, and carried our sorrows. *Ib.* 2

26 But he was wounded for our transgressions, he was bruised for our iniquities: the chastisement of our peace was upon him; and with his stripes we are healed.
All we like sheep have gone astray; we have turned every one to his own way; and the Lord hath laid on him the iniquity of us all.
He was oppressed, and he was afflicted, yet he opened not his mouth: he is brought as a lamb to the slaughter, and as a sheep before her shearers is dumb, so he openeth not his mouth. *Ib.* 5

27 He was cut off out of the land of the living. *Ib.* 8

28 He was numbered with the transgressors; and he bare the sin of many, and made intercession for the transgressors. *Ib.* 12

29 Ho, every one that thirsteth, come ye to the waters, and he that hath no money; come ye, buy, and eat; yea, come, buy wine and milk without money and without price.
Wherefore do ye spend money for that which is not bread? and your labour for that which satisfieth not? *Ib.* lv. 1

30 Seek ye the Lord while he may be found, call ye upon him while he is near. *Ib.* 6

31 For my thoughts are not your thoughts, neither are your ways my ways, saith the Lord. *Ib.* 8

32 Instead of the thorn shall come up the fir tree, and instead of the brier shall come up the myrtle tree. *Ib.* 13

33 I will give them an everlasting name, that shall not be cut off. *Ib.* lvi. 5

34 Peace to him that is far off, and to him that is near. *Ib.* lvii. 19

35 Is it such a fast that I have chosen? a day for a man to afflict his soul? *Ib.* lviii. 5

36 Is not this the fast that I have chosen? to loose the bands of wickedness, to undo the heavy burdens, and to let the oppressed go free, and that ye break every yoke? *Ib.* 6

37 Then shall thy light break forth as the morning, and thine health shall spring forth speedily. *Ib.* 8

38 They make haste to shed innocent blood. *Ib.* lix. 7

39 Arise, shine; for thy light is come, and the glory of the Lord is risen upon thee. *Ib.* lx. 1

[54]

1 A little one shall become a thousand, and a small one a strong nation. *Isaiah* lx. 22

2 The Spirit of the Lord God is upon me. *Ib.* lxi. 1

3 To bind up the brokenhearted, to proclaim liberty to the captives, and the opening of the prison to them that are bound;
To proclaim the acceptable year of the Lord, and the day of vengeance of our God; to comfort all that mourn. *Ib.* 1

4 To give unto them beauty for ashes, the oil of joy for mourning, the garment of praise for the spirit of heaviness. *Ib.* 3

5 Who is this that cometh from Edom, with dyed garments from Bozrah? *Ib.* lxiii. 1

6 I have trodden the winepress alone. *Ib.* 3

7 In all their affliction he was afflicted. *Ib.* 9

8 All our righteousnesses are as filthy rags; and we all do fade as a leaf. *Ib.* lxiv. 6

9 For, behold, I create new heavens and a new earth. *Ib.* lxv. 17

10 As one whom his mother comforteth, so will I comfort you. *Ib.* lxvi. 13

11 They were as fed horses in the morning: every one neighed after his neighbour's wife. *Jeremiah* v. 8

12 This people hath a revolting and a rebellious heart. *Ib.* 23

13 The prophets prophesy falsely, and the priests bear rule by their means; and my people love to have it so: and what will ye do in the end thereof? *Ib.* 31

14 Saying, Peace, peace; when there is no peace. *Ib.* vi. 14

15 Do they provoke me to anger? saith the Lord: do they not provoke themselves to the confusion of their own faces? *Ib.* vii. 19

16 The harvest is past, the summer is ended, and we are not saved. *Ib.* viii. 20

17 Is there no balm in Gilead? *Ib.* 22

18 Can the Ethiopian change his skin, or the leopard his spots? *Ib.* xiii. 23

19 A man of strife and a man of contention. *Ib.* xv. 10

20 The heart is deceitful above all things, and desperately wicked. *Ib.* xvii. 9

21 As the partridge sitteth on eggs, and hatcheth them not. *Ib.* 11

22 And seekest thou great things for thyself? seek them not. *Ib.* xlv. 5

23 Is it nothing to you, all ye that pass by? behold, and see if there be any sorrow like unto my sorrow. *Lamentations* i. 12

24 The wormwood and the gall. *Ib.* iii. 19

25 It is good for a man that he bear the yoke in his youth. *Ib.* 27

26 He giveth his cheek to him that smiteth him. *Ib.* 30

27 As if a wheel had been in the midst of a wheel. *Ezekiel* x. 10

28 As is the mother, so is her daughter. *Ib.* xvi. 44

29 The fathers have eaten sour grapes, and the children's teeth are set on edge. *Ib.* xviii. 2

30 When the wicked man turneth away from his wickedness that he hath committed, and doeth that which is lawful and right, he shall save his soul alive. *Ezekiel* xviii. 27

31 The king of Babylon stood at the parting of the way. *Ib.* xxi. 21

32 She doted upon the Assyrians her neighbours, captains and rulers clothed most gorgeously, horsemen riding upon horses, all of them desirable young men. *Ib.* xxiii. 12

33 The valley which was full of bones. *Ib.* xxxvii. 1

34 Can these bones live? *Ib.* 3

35 The image that Nebuchadnezzar the king had set up. *Daniel* iii. 3

36 The sound of the cornet, flute, harp, sackbut, psaltery, dulcimer, and all kinds of musick. *Ib.* 5

37 Cast into the midst of a burning fiery furnace. *Ib.* 6

38 We are not careful to answer thee in this matter. *Ib.* 16

39 Commanded that they should heat the furnace one seven times more than it was wont to be heated. *Ib.* 19

40 Then these men were bound in their coats, their hosen, and their hats, and their other garments, and were cast into the midst of the burning fiery furnace. *Ib.* 21

41 Shadrach, Meshach, and Abed-nego, ye servants of the most high God, come forth, and come hither. *Ib.* 26

42 MENE, MENE, TEKEL, UPHARSIN.
This is the interpretation of the thing: MENE; God hath numbered thy kingdom, and finished it.
TEKEL; Thou art weighed in the balances, and art found wanting.
PERES; Thy kingdom is divided, and given to the Medes and Persians. *Ib.* v. 25

43 The Ancient of days. *Ib.* vii. 9

44 O Daniel, a man greatly beloved. *Ib.* x. 11

45 Many shall run to and fro, and knowledge shall be increased. *Ib.* xii. 4

46 They have sown the wind, and they shall reap the whirlwind. *Hosea* viii. 7

47 Ye have plowed wickedness, ye have reaped iniquity. *Ib.* x. 13

48 I drew them . . . with bands of love. *Ib.* xi. 4

49 I have multiplied visions, and used similitudes. *Ib.* xii. 10

50 That which the palmerworm hath left hath the locust eaten. *Joel* i. 4

51 I will restore to you the years that the locust hath eaten. *Ib.* ii. 25

52 And it shall come to pass afterward, that I will pour out my spirit upon all flesh; and your sons and your daughters shall prophesy, your old men shall dream dreams, your young men shall see visions. *Ib.* 28

53 Multitudes in the valley of decision. *Ib.* iii. 14

54 Can two walk together, except they be agreed? *Amos* iii. 3

55 Shall there be evil in a city, and the Lord hath not done it? *Ib.* 6

1 A firebrand plucked out of the burning. *Amos* iv. 11

2 Woe to them that are at ease in Zion. *Ib.* vi. 1

3 The Lord stood upon a wall made by a plumbline, with a plumbline in his hand.
And the Lord said unto me, Amos, what seest thou? And I said, A plumbline. *Ib.* vii. 7

4 Come, and let us cast lots, that we may know for whose cause this evil is upon us. So they cast lots, and the lot fell upon Jonah. *Jonah* i. 7

5 Jonah was in the belly of the fish three days and three nights. *Ib.* 17

6 They shall sit every man under his vine and under his fig tree. *Micah* iv. 4

7 But thou, Beth-lehem Ephratah, though thou be little among the thousands of Judah, yet out of thee shall he come forth unto me that is to be ruler in Israel. *Ib.* v. 2

8 What doth the Lord require of thee, but to do justly, and to love mercy, and to walk humbly with thy God? *Ib.* vi. 8

9 Write the vision, and make it plain upon tables, that he may run that readeth it. *Habakkuk* ii. 2

10 Your fathers, where are they? And the prophets, do they live for ever? *Zechariah* i. 5

11 For who hath despised the day of small things? *Ib.* iv. 10

12 Turn you to the strong hold, ye prisoners of hope. *Ib.* ix. 12

13 I was wounded in the house of my friends. *Ib.* xiii. 6

14 Have we not all one father? hath not one God created us? *Malachi* ii. 10

15 But unto you that fear my name shall the Sun of righteousness arise with healing in his wings. *Ib.* iv. 2

Apocrypha

16 The first wrote, Wine is the strongest.
The second wrote, The king is strongest.
The third wrote, Women are strongest: but above all things Truth beareth away the victory.
1 Esdras iii. 10

17 Great is Truth, and mighty above all things. *Ib.* iv. 41

18 I shall light a candle of understanding in thine heart, which shall not be put out. *2 Esdras* xiv. 25

19 Magna est veritas et praevalet.
Great is truth and it prevails.
3 Esdras iv. 41 (Vulgate)

20 The holy spirit of discipline. *The Wisdom of Solomon* i. 5

21 The ear of jealousy heareth all things. *Ib.* 10

22 Through envy of the devil came death into the world. *Ib.* ii. 24

23 But the souls of the righteous are in the hand of God, and there shall no torment touch them.
In the sight of the unwise they seemed to die: and their departure is taken for misery,
And their going from us to be utter destruction: but they are in peace.

For though they be punished in the sight of men, yet is their hope full of immortality.
And having been a little chastised, they shall be greatly rewarded: for God proved them, and found them worthy for himself.
The Wisdom of Solomon iii. 1

24 And in the time of their visitation they shall shine, and run to and fro like sparks among the stubble. *Ib.* 7

25 Even so we in like manner, as soon as we were born, began to draw to our end. *Ib.* v. 13

26 Passeth away as the remembrance of a guest that tarrieth but a day. *Ib.* 14

27 O Lord, thou lover of souls. *Ib.* xi. 26

28 For men, serving either calamity or tyranny, did ascribe unto stones and stocks the incommunicable name. *Ib.* xiv. 21

29 My son, if thou come to serve the Lord, prepare thy soul for temptation. *Ecclesiasticus* ii. 1

30 For the Lord is full of compassion and mercy, long-suffering, and very pitiful, and forgiveth sins, and saveth in time of affliction. *Ib.* 11

31 We will fall into the hands of the Lord, and not into the hands of men: for as his majesty is, so is his mercy. *Ib.* 18

32 Be not curious in unnecessary matters: for more things are shewed unto thee than men understand. *Ib.* iii. 23

33 For if he curse thee in the bitterness of his soul, his prayer shall be heard of him that made him. *Ib.* iv. 6

34 Woe to him that is alone when he falleth, for he hath not another to help him up. *Ib.* 10

35 Be not ignorant of any thing in a great matter or a small. *Ib.* v. 15

36 A faithful friend is the medicine of life. *Ib.* vi. 16

37 Miss not the discourse of the elders. *Ib.* viii. 9

38 Open not thine heart to every man. *Ib.* 19

39 Give not thy soul unto a woman. *Ib.* ix. 2

40 Forsake not an old friend; for the new is not comparable to him; a new friend is as new wine; when it is old, thou shalt drink it with pleasure. *Ib.* 10

41 Many kings have sat down upon the ground; and one that was never thought of hath worn the crown. *Ib.* xi. 5

42 Judge none blessed before his death. *Ib.* 28

43 He that toucheth pitch shall be defiled therewith. *Ib.* xiii. 1

44 For how agree the kettle and the earthen pot together? *Ib.* 2

45 They received the use of the five operations of the Lord, and in the sixth place he imparted them understanding, and in the seventh speech, an interpreter of the cogitations thereof. *Ib.* xvii. 5

46 Be not made a beggar by banqueting upon borrowing. *Ib.* xviii. 33

47 He that contemneth small things shall fall by little and little. *Ib.* xix. 1

48 If thou hast heard a word, let it die with thee; and be bold, it will not burst thee. *Ib.* 10

1 All wickedness is but little to the wickedness of a woman. *Ecclesiasticus* xxv. 19

2 Neither [give] a wicked woman liberty to gad abroad. *Ib.* 25

3 The stroke of the tongue breaketh the bones.
Many have fallen by the edge of the sword: but not so many as have fallen by the tongue. *Ib.* xxviii. 17

4 And weigh thy words in a balance, and make a door and bar for thy mouth. *Ib.* 25

5 Envy and wrath shorten the life. *Ib.* xxx. 24

6 Leave off first for manners' sake. *Ib.* xxxi. 17

7 Let thy speech be short, comprehending much in few words. *Ib.* xxxii. 8

8 Leave not a stain in thine honour. *Ib.* xxxiii. 22

9 Honour a physician with the honour due unto him for the uses which ye may have of him: for the Lord hath created him. *Ib.* xxxviii. 1

10 For of the most High cometh healing. *Ib.* 2

11 The wisdom of a learned man cometh by opportunity of leisure: and he that hath little business shall become wise. *Ib.* 24

12 How can he get wisdom . . . whose talk is of bullocks. *Ib.* 25

13 They will maintain the state of the world, and all their desire is in the work of their craft. *Ib.* 34

14 Let us now praise famous men, and our fathers that begat us. *Ib.* xliv. 1

15 Such as did bear rule in their kingdoms. *Ib.* 3

16 Such as found out musical tunes, and recited verses in writing:
Rich men furnished with ability, living peaceably in their habitations. *Ib.* 5

17 There be of them, that have left a name behind them. *Ib.* 8

18 And some there be, which have no memorial. *Ib.* 9

19 Their bodies are buried in peace; but their name liveth for evermore. *Ib.* 14

20 It is a foolish thing to make a long prologue, and to be short in the story itself. *2 Maccabees* ii. 32

21 When he was at the last gasp. *Ib.* vii. 9

22 It was an holy and good thought. *Ib.* xii. 45

New Testament

23 There came wise men from the east to Jerusalem, Saying, Where is he that is born King of the Jews? for we have seen his star in the east, and are come to worship him. *St. Matthew* ii. 1

24 They presented unto him gifts; gold, and frankincense, and myrrh. *Ib.* 11

25 They departed into their own country another way. *Ib.* 12

26 Rachel weeping for her children, and would not be comforted, because they are not. *Ib.* 18

27 Repent ye: for the kingdom of heaven is at hand. *Ib.* iii. 2

28 The voice of one crying in the wilderness, Prepare ye the way of the Lord, make his paths straight. *Ib.* 3

29 Raiment of camel's hair, and a leathern girdle about his loins; and his meat was locusts and wild honey. *St. Matthew* iii. 4

30 O generation of vipers, who hath warned you to flee from the wrath to come? *Ib.* 7

31 And now also the axe is laid unto the root of the trees. *Ib.* 10

32 Suffer it to be so now: for thus it becometh us to fulfil all righteousness. *Ib.* 15

33 This is my beloved Son, in whom I am well pleased. *Ib.* 17

34 Man shall not live by bread alone, but by every word that proceedeth out of the mouth of God. *Ib.* iv. 4

35 Thou shalt not tempt the Lord thy God. *Ib.* 7

36 The devil taketh him up into an exceeding high mountain, and sheweth him all the kingdoms of the world, and the glory of them. *Ib.* 8

37 Angels came and ministered unto him. *Ib.* 11

38 Fishers of men. *Ib.* 19

39 Blessed are the poor in spirit: for their's is the kingdom of heaven.
Blessed are they that mourn: for they shall be comforted.
Blessed are the meek: for they shall inherit the earth.
Blessed are they which do hunger and thirst after righteousness: for they shall be filled.
Blessed are the merciful: for they shall obtain mercy.
Blessed are the pure in heart: for they shall see God.
Blessed are the peacemakers: for they shall be called the children of God. *Ib.* v. 3

40 Ye are the salt of the earth: but if the salt have lost his savour, wherewith shall it be salted? *Ib.* 13

41 Ye are the light of the world. A city that is set on an hill cannot be hid. *Ib.* 14

42 Let your light so shine before men, that they may see your good works. *Ib.* 16

43 Think not that I am come to destroy the law, or the prophets: I am come not to destroy, but to fulfil. *Ib.* 17

44 Except your righteousness shall exceed the righteousness of the scribes and Pharisees. *Ib.* 20

45 Whosoever shall say, Thou fool, shall be in danger of hell fire. *Ib.* 22

46 Agree with thine adversary quickly, whiles thou art in the way with him. *Ib.* 25

47 Till thou hast paid the uttermost farthing. *Ib.* 26

48 Swear not at all; neither by heaven; for it is God's throne:
Nor by the earth; for it is his footstool. *Ib.* 34

49 Let your communication be, Yea, yea; Nay, nay. *Ib.* 37

50 Resist not evil: but whosoever shall smite thee on thy right cheek, turn to him the other also. *Ib.* 39

51 Whosoever shall compel thee to go a mile, go with him twain. *Ib.* 41

52 He maketh his sun to rise on the evil and on the good, and sendeth rain on the just and on the unjust. *Ib.* 45

53 Do not even the publicans the same? *Ib.* 46

1 Be ye therefore perfect. *St. Matthew* v. 48

2 When thou doest alms, let not thy left hand know what thy right hand doeth. *Ib.* vi. 3

3 Use not vain repetitions, as the heathen do: for they think that they shall be heard for their much speaking. *Ib.* 7

4 After this manner therefore pray ye: Our Father which art in heaven, Hallowed be thy name.
Thy kingdom come. Thy will be done in earth, as it is in heaven.
Give us this day our daily bread.
And forgive us our debts, as we forgive our debtors.
And lead us not into temptation, but deliver us from evil: For thine is the kingdom, and the power, and the glory, for ever. Amen. *Ib.* 9

5 Lay not up for yourselves treasures upon earth, where moth and rust doth corrupt, and where thieves break through and steal. *Ib.* 19

6 Lay up for yourselves treasures in heaven. *Ib.* 20

7 Where your treasure is, there will your heart be also. *Ib.* 21

8 If therefore the light that is in thee be darkness, how great is that darkness! *Ib.* 23

9 No man can serve two masters. *Ib.* 24

10 Ye cannot serve God and mammon. *Ib.*

11 Is not the life more than meat, and the body than raiment?
Behold the fowls of the air: for they sow not, neither do they reap, nor gather into barns. *Ib.* 25

12 Which of you by taking thought can add one cubit unto his stature? *Ib.* 27

13 Consider the lilies of the field, how they grow; they toil not, neither do they spin:
And yet I say unto you, That even Solomon in all his glory was not arrayed like one of these. *Ib.* 28

14 Seek ye first the kingdom of God, and his righteousness; and all these things shall be added unto you. *Ib.* 33

15 Take therefore no thought for the morrow: for the morrow shall take thought for the things of itself. Sufficient unto the day is the evil thereof. *Ib.* 34

16 Judge not, that ye be not judged. *Ib.* vii. 1

17 Why beholdest thou the mote that is in thy brother's eye, but considerest not the beam that is in thine own eye? *Ib.* 3

18 Neither cast ye your pearls before swine. *Ib.* 6

19 Ask, and it shall be given you; seek, and ye shall find; knock, and it shall be opened unto you. *Ib.* 7

20 Every one that asketh receiveth; and he that seeketh findeth. *Ib.* 8

21 Or what man is there of you, whom if his son ask bread, will he give him a stone? *Ib.* 9

22 Therefore all things whatsoever ye would that men should do to you, do ye even so to them: for this is the law and the prophets. *Ib.* 12

23 Wide is the gate, and broad is the way, that leadeth to destruction, and many there be that go in thereat. *Ib.* 13

24 Strait is the gate, and narrow is the way, which leadeth unto life, and few there be that find it. *Ib.* 14

25 Beware of false prophets, which come to you in sheep's clothing, but inwardly they are ravening wolves. *St. Matthew* vii. 15

26 Do men gather grapes of thorns, or figs of thistles? *Ib.* 16

27 By their fruits ye shall know them. *Ib.* 20

28 And great was the fall of it. *Ib.* 27

29 For he taught them as one having authority, and not as the scribes. *Ib.* 29

30 Lord, I am not worthy that thou shouldest come under my roof. *Ib.* viii. 8

31 I am a man under authority, having soldiers under me: and I say to this man, Go, and he goeth; and to another, Come, and he cometh; and to my servant, Do this, and he doeth it. *Ib.* 9

32 I have not found so great faith, no, not in Israel. *Ib.* 10

33 But the children of the kingdom shall be cast out into outer darkness: there shall be weeping and gnashing of teeth. *Ib.* 12

34 The foxes have holes, and the birds of the air have nests; but the Son of man hath not where to lay his head. *Ib.* 20

35 Let the dead bury their dead. *Ib.* 22

36 The whole herd of swine ran violently down a steep place into the sea, and perished in the waters. *Ib.* 32

37 Sitting at the receipt of custom. *Ib.* ix. 9

38 Why eateth your Master with publicans and sinners? *Ib.* 11

39 They that be whole need not a physician, but they that are sick. *Ib.* 12

40 I am not come to call the righteous, but sinners to repentance. *Ib.* 13

41 Can the children of the bridechamber mourn, as long as the bridegroom is with them? *Ib.* 15

42 Neither do men put new wine into old bottles. *Ib.* 17

43 The maid is not dead, but sleepeth. *Ib.* 24

44 He casteth out devils through the prince of the devils. *Ib.* 34

45 The harvest truly is plenteous, but the labourers are few. *Ib.* 37

46 Go rather to the lost sheep of the house of Israel. *Ib.* x. 6

47 Freely ye have received, freely give. *Ib.* 8

48 When ye depart out of that house or city, shake off the dust of your feet. *Ib.* 14

49 Be ye therefore wise as serpents, and harmless as doves. *Ib.* 16

50 He that endureth to the end shall be saved. *Ib.* 22

51 The disciple is not above his master, nor the servant above his lord. *Ib.* 24

52 Are not two sparrows sold for a farthing? and one of them shall not fall on the ground without your Father. *Ib.* 29

53 The very hairs of your head are all numbered. *Ib.* 30

54 Fear ye not therefore, ye are of more value than many sparrows. *Ib.* 31

1 I came not to send peace, but a sword.
St. Matthew x. 34

2 A man's foes shall be they of his own household.
Ib. 36

3 He that findeth his life shall lose it: and he that loseth his life for my sake shall find it. *Ib.* 39

4 Whosoever shall give to drink unto one of these little ones a cup of cold water only in the name of a disciple, verily I say unto you, he shall in no wise lose his reward. *Ib.* 42

5 Art thou he that should come, or do we look for another? *Ib.* xi. 3

6 What went ye out into the wilderness to see? A reed shaken with the wind?
But what went ye out for to see? A man clothed in soft raiment? . . .
But what went ye out for to see? A prophet? yea, I say unto you, and more than a prophet. *Ib.* 7

7 The kingdom of heaven suffereth violence, and the violent take it by force. *Ib.* 12

8 We have piped unto you, and ye have not danced; we have mourned unto you, and ye have not lamented. *Ib.* 17

9 Wisdom is justified of her children. *Ib.* 19

10 Come unto me, all ye that labour and are heavy laden, and I will give you rest.
Take my yoke upon you, and learn of me; for I am meek and lowly in heart: and ye shall find rest unto your souls.
For my yoke is easy, and my burden is light. *Ib.* 28

11 He that is not with me is against me. Ib. xii. 30

12 The blasphemy against the Holy Ghost shall not be forgiven unto men. *Ib.* 31

13 The tree is known by his fruit. *Ib.* 33

14 Out of the abundance of the heart the mouth speaketh.
Ib. 34

15 Every idle word that men shall speak, they shall give account thereof in the day of judgment. *Ib.* 36

16 An evil and adulterous generation seeketh after a sign. *Ib.* 39

17 Behold, a greater than Solomon is here. *Ib.* 42

18 Empty, swept, and garnished. *Ib.* 44

19 Then goeth he, and taketh with himself seven other spirits more wicked than himself, and they enter in and dwell there: and the last state of that man is worse than the first. *Ib.* 45

20 Behold my mother and my brethren! *Ib.* 49

21 Some seeds fell by the wayside. *Ib.* xiii. 4

22 Because they had no root, they withered away. *Ib.* 6

23 But other fell into good ground, and brought forth fruit, some an hundredfold, some sixtyfold, some thirtyfold. *Ib.* 8

24 The care of this world, and the deceitfulness of riches.
Ib. 22

25 His enemy came and sowed tares. *Ib.* 25

26 An enemy hath done this. *Ib.* 28

27 Let both grow together until the harvest. *Ib.* 30

28 The kingdom of heaven is like to a grain of mustard seed. *Ib.* 31

29 So that the birds of the air come and lodge in the branches thereof. *St. Matthew* xiii. 32

30 One pearl of great price. *Ib.* 46

31 An householder, which bringeth forth out of his treasure things new and old. *Ib.* 52

32 Is not this the carpenter's son? *Ib.* 55

33 A prophet is not without honour, save in his own country, and in his own house. *Ib.* 57

34 They took up of the fragments that remained twelve baskets full. *Ib.* xiv. 20

35 In the fourth watch of the night Jesus went unto them, walking on the sea. *Ib.* 25

36 Be of good cheer; it is I; be not afraid. *Ib.* 27

37 O thou of little faith, wherefore didst thou doubt?
Ib. 31

38 Not that which goeth into the mouth defileth a man; but that which cometh out of the mouth, this defileth a man. *Ib.* xv. 11

39 They be blind leaders of the blind. And if the blind lead the blind, both shall fall into the ditch.
Ib. 14

40 The dogs eat of the crumbs which fall from their masters' table. *Ib.* 27

41 When it is evening, ye say, It will be fair weather: for the sky is red. *Ib.* xvi. 2

42 The signs of the times. *Ib.* 3

43 Thou art Peter, and upon this rock I will build my church; and the gates of hell shall not prevail against it. *Ib.* 18

44 Get thee behind me, Satan. *Ib.* 23

45 What is a man profited, if he shall gain the whole world, and lose his own soul? *Ib.* 26

46 It is good for us to be here. *Ib.* xvii. 4

47 If ye have faith as a grain of mustard seed, ye shall say unto this mountain, Remove hence to yonder place; and it shall remove. *Ib.* 20

48 Except ye be converted, and become as little children, ye shall not enter into the kingdom of heaven.
Ib. xviii. 3

49 But whoso shall offend one of these little ones which believe in me, it were better for him that a millstone were hanged about his neck, and that he were drowned in the depth of the sea. *Ib.* 6

50 It must needs be that offences come; but woe to that man by whom the offence cometh! *Ib.* 7

51 If thine eye offend thee, pluck it out, and cast it from thee: it is better for thee to enter into life with one eye, rather than having two eyes to be cast into hell fire. *Ib.* 9

52 For where two or three are gathered together in my name, there am I in the midst of them. *Ib.* 20

53 Until seventy times seven. *Ib.* 22

54 Lord, have patience with me, and I will pay thee all.
Ib. 26

55 Pay me that thou owest. *Ib.* 28

56 What therefore God hath joined together, let not man put asunder. *Ib.* xix. 6

57 Thou shalt love thy neighbour as thyself. *Ib.* 19

1 If thou wilt be perfect, go and sell that thou hast, and give to the poor, and thou shalt have treasure in heaven.
St. Matthew xix. 21

2 He went away sorrowful: for he had great possessions.
Ib. 22

3 It is easier for a camel to go through the eye of a needle, than for a rich man to enter into the kingdom of God.
Ib. 24

4 With men this is impossible; but with God all things are possible.
Ib. 26

5 But many that are first shall be last; and the last shall be first.
Ib. 30

6 Why stand ye here all the day idle?
Ib. xx. 6

7 Borne the burden and heat of the day.
Ib. 12

8 I will give unto this last, even as unto thee.
Is it not lawful for me to do what I will with mine own?
Ib. 14

9 It is written, My house shall be called the house of prayer; but ye have made it a den of thieves.
Ib. xxi. 13

10 For many are called, but few are chosen. *Ib.* xxii. 14

11 Whose is this image and superscription?
Ib. 20

12 Render therefore unto Cæsar the things which are Cæsar's.
Ib. 21

13 Last of all the woman died also.
Ib. 27

14 For in the resurrection they neither marry, nor are given in marriage.
Ib. 30

15 They make broad their phylacteries, and enlarge the borders of their garments,
And love the uppermost rooms at feasts, and the chief seats in the synagogues.
Ib. xxiii. 5

16 Whosoever shall exalt himself shall be abased; and he that shall humble himself shall be exalted. *Ib.* 12

17 Woe unto you, . . . for ye pay tithe of mint and anise and cummin.
Ib. 23

18 Blind guides, which strain at a gnat, and swallow a camel.
Ib. 24

19 Whited sepulchres, which indeed appear beautiful outward, but are within full of dead men's bones.
Ib. 27

20 O Jerusalem, Jerusalem, thou that killest the prophets, and stonest them which are sent unto thee, how often would I have gathered thy children together, even as a hen gathereth her chickens under her wings, and ye would not!
Ib. 37

21 Wars and rumours of wars.
Ib. xxiv. 6

22 But the end is not yet.
Ib.

23 For nation shall rise against nation, and kingdom against kingdom.
Ib. 7

24 Abomination of desolation.
Ib. 15

25 Wheresoever the carcase is, there will the eagles be gathered together.
Ib. 28

26 Eating and drinking, marrying and giving in marriage.
Ib. 38

27 One shall be taken, and the other left.
Ib. 40

28 Unto one he gave five talents, to another two, and to another one; to every man according to his several ability.
Ib. xxv. 15

29 Well done, thou good and faithful servant. *Ib.* 21

30 Enter thou into the joy of thy lord.
St. Matthew xxv. 21

31 Lord, I knew thee that thou art an hard man, reaping where thou hast not sown, and gathering where thou hast not strawed.
Ib. 24

32 Unto every one that hath shall be given, and he shall have abundance: but from him that hath not shall be taken away even that which he hath.
Ib. 29

33 I was a stranger, and ye took me in:
Naked, and ye clothed me: I was sick, and ye visited me: I was in prison, and ye came unto me.
Ib. 35

34 Inasmuch as ye have done it unto one of the least of these my brethren, ye have done it unto me.
Ib. 40

35 A woman having an alabaster box of very precious ointment.
Ib. xxvi. 7

36 To what purpose is this waste?
Ib. 8

37 What will ye give me, and I will deliver him unto you? And they covenanted with him for thirty pieces of silver.
Ib. 15

38 It had been good for that man if he had not been born.
Ib. 24

39 This night, before the cock crow, thou shalt deny me thrice.
Ib. 34

40 Though I should die with thee, yet will I not deny thee.
Ib. 35

41 If it be possible, let this cup pass from me. *Ib.* 39

42 What, could ye not watch with me one hour? *Ib.* 40

43 The spirit indeed is willing, but the flesh is weak.
Ib. 41

44 Hail, master; and kissed him.
Ib. 49

45 Friend, wherefore art thou come?
Ib. 50

46 All they that take the sword shall perish with the sword.
Ib. 52

47 Thy speech bewrayeth thee.
Then began he to curse and to swear, saying, I know not the man. And immediately the cock crew.
Ib. 73

48 Have thou nothing to do with that just man.
Ib. xxvii. 19

49 He took water, and washed his hands before the multitude, saying, I am innocent of the blood of this just person: see ye to it.
Ib. 24

50 His blood be on us, and on our children.
Ib. 25

51 He saved others; himself he cannot save.
Ib. 42

52 Eli, Eli, lama sabachthani? . . . My God, my God, why hast thou forsaken me?
Ib. 46

53 The sabbath was made for man, and not man for the sabbath.
St. Mark ii. 27

54 If a house be divided against itself, that house cannot stand.
Ib. iii. 25

55 He that hath ears to hear, let him hear.
Ib. iv. 9

56 With what measure ye mete, it shall be measured to you.
Ib. 24

57 My name is Legion: for we are many.
Ib. v. 9

58 Clothed, and in his right mind.
Ib. 15

59 My little daughter lieth at the point of death. *Ib.* 23

60 Had suffered many things of many physicians, and had spent all that she had, and was nothing bettered, but rather grew worse.
Ib. 26

1 Knowing in himself that virtue had gone out of him.
St. Mark v. 30

2 I see men as trees, walking. *Ib.* viii. 24

3 For what shall it profit a man, if he shall gain the whole world, and lose his own soul? *Ib.* 36

4 Lord, I believe; help thou mine unbelief. *Ib.* ix. 24

5 Where their worm dieth not, and the fire is not quenched. *Ib.* 44

6 Suffer the little children to come unto me, and forbid them not: for of such is the kingdom of God.
Ib. x. 14

7 Which devour widows' houses, and for a pretence make long prayers. *Ib.* xii. 40

8 And there came a certain poor widow, and she threw in two mites. *Ib.* 42

9 Go ye into all the world, and preach the gospel to every creature. *Ib.* xvi. 15

10 It seemed good to me also . . . to write unto thee . . . most excellent Theophilus. *St. Luke* i. 3

11 To turn the hearts of . . . the disobedient to the wisdom of the just. *Ib.* 17

12 Hail, thou that art highly favoured, the Lord is with thee: blessed art thou among women. *Ib.* 28

13 My soul doth magnify the Lord,
And my spirit hath rejoiced in God my Saviour.
For he hath regarded the low estate of his hand-maiden: for, behold, from henceforth all genera-tions shall call me blessed. *Ib.* 46

14 He hath shewed strength with his arm; he hath scat-tered the proud in the imagination of their hearts.
He hath put down the mighty from their seats, and exalted them of low degree.
He hath filled the hungry with good things; and the rich he hath sent empty away. *Ib.* 51

15 To give light to them that sit in darkness and in the shadow of death, to guide our feet into the way of peace. *Ib.* 79

16 And it came to pass in those days, that there went out a decree from Cæsar Augustus, that all the world should be taxed. *Ib.* ii. 1

17 Because there was no room for them in the inn.
Ib. 7

18 And, lo, the angel of the Lord came upon them, and the glory of the Lord shone round about them: and they were sore afraid. *Ib.* 9

19 Glory to God in the highest, and on earth peace, good will toward men. *Ib.* 14

20 Lord, now lettest thou thy servant depart in peace, according to thy word. *Ib.* 29

21 Wist ye not that I must be about my Father's busi-ness? *Ib.* 49

22 Jesus increased in wisdom and stature, and in favour with God and man. *Ib.* 52

23 Be content with your wages. *Ib.* iii. 14

24 Shewed unto him all the kingdoms of the world in a moment of time. *Ib.* iv. 5

25 Physician, heal thyself. *Ib.* 23

26 Many widows were in Israel in the days of Elias . . .
But unto none of them was Elias sent. *Ib.* 25

27 Master, we have toiled all the night, and have taken nothing: nevertheless at thy word I will let down the net. *St. Luke* v. 5

28 No man . . . having drunk old wine straightway desireth new: for he saith, The old is better.
Ib. 39

29 Woe unto you, when all men shall speak well of you!
Ib. vi. 26

30 Judge not, and ye shall not be judged. *Ib.* 37

31 Give, and it shall be given unto you; good measure, pressed down, and shaken together, and running over, shall men give into your bosom. *Ib.* 38

32 The only son of his mother, and she was a widow.
Ib. vii. 12

33 Simon, I have somewhat to say unto thee. And he saith, Master, say on. *Ib.* 40

34 Peace be to this house. *Ib.* x. 5

35 For the labourer is worthy of his hire. *Ib.* 7

36 I beheld Satan as lightning fall from heaven. *Ib.* 18

37 I thank thee, O Father, Lord of heaven and earth, that thou hast hid these things from the wise and prudent, and hast revealed them unto babes: even so, Father; for so it seemed good in thy sight.
Ib. 21

38 For I tell you, that many prophets and kings have desired to see those things which ye see, and have not seen them; and to hear those things which ye hear, and have not heard them. *Ib.* 24

39 Fell among thieves. *Ib.* 30

40 He passed by on the other side. *Ib.* 31

41 He took out two pence, and gave them to the host.
Ib. 35

42 Whatsoever thou spendest more, when I come again, I will repay thee. *Ib.*

43 Go, and do thou likewise. *Ib.* 37

44 But Martha was cumbered about much serving.
Ib. 40

45 But one thing is needful: and Mary hath chosen that good part, which shall not be taken away from her.
Ib. 42

46 When a strong man armed keepeth his palace, his goods are in peace. *Ib.* xi. 21

47 All his armour wherein he trusted. *Ib.* 22

48 He that is not with me is against me. *Ib.* 23

49 Take heed therefore that the light which is in thee be not darkness. *Ib.* 35

50 Woe unto you, lawyers! for ye have taken away the key of knowledge. *Ib.* 52

51 Are not five sparrows sold for two farthings, and not one of them is forgotten before God? *Ib.* xii. 6

52 Soul, thou hast much goods laid up for many years; take thine ease, eat, drink, and be merry. *Ib.* 19

53 Thou fool, this night thy soul shall be required of thee. *Ib.* 20

54 Let your loins be girded about, and your lights burning. *Ib.* 35

55 But he that knew not, and did commit things worthy of stripes, shall be beaten with few stripes. *Ib.* 48

1 Cut it down; why cumbereth it the ground?
St. Luke xiii. 7

2 Begin with shame to take the lowest room. *Ib.* xiv. 9

3 Friend, go up higher. *Ib.* 10

4 For whosoever exalteth himself shall be abased; and he that humbleth himself shall be exalted. *Ib.* 11

5 They all with one consent began to make excuse.
Ib. 18

6 I pray thee have me excused. *Ib.*

7 I have married a wife, and therefore I cannot come.
Ib. 20

8 The poor, and the maimed, and the halt, and the blind. *Ib.* 21

9 Go out into the highways and hedges, and compel them to come in. *Ib.* 23

10 Leave the ninety and nine in the wilderness.
Ib. xv. 4

11 Rejoice with me; for I have found my sheep which was lost. *Ib.* 6

12 Joy shall be in heaven over one sinner that repenteth, more than over ninety and nine just persons, which need no repentance. *Ib.* 7

13 Wasted his substance with riotous living. *Ib.* 13

14 He would fain have filled his belly with the husks that the swine did eat: and no man gave unto him.
And when he came to himself, he said, How many hired servants of my father's have bread enough and to spare, and I perish with hunger!
I will arise and go to my father, and will say unto him, Father, I have sinned against heaven, and before thee,
And am no more worthy to be called thy son: make me as one of thy hired servants. *Ib.* 16

15 Bring hither the fatted calf, and kill it. *Ib.* 23

16 This my son was dead, and is alive again; he was lost, and is found. *Ib.* 24

17 Which hath devoured thy living with harlots. *Ib.* 30

18 I cannot dig; to beg I am ashamed. *Ib.* xvi. 3

19 Take thy bill, and sit down quickly, and write fifty.
Ib. 6

20 And the Lord commended the unjust steward, because he had done wisely: for the children of this world are in their generation wiser than the children of light. *Ib.* 8

21 Make to yourselves friends of the mammon of unrighteousness. *Ib.* 9

22 He that is faithful in that which is least is faithful also in much. *Ib.* 10

23 There was a certain rich man, which was clothed in purple and fine linen, and fared sumptuously every day. *Ib.* 19

24 The crumbs which fell from the rich man's table.
Ib. 21

25 Carried by the angels into Abraham's bosom. *Ib.* 22

26 Between us and you there is a great gulf fixed. *Ib.* 26

27 It were better for him that a millstone were hanged about his neck, and he cast into the sea.
Ib. xvii. 2

28 Say, We are unprofitable servants: we have done that which was our duty to do. *Ib.* 10

29 Were there not ten cleansed? but where are the nine?
St. Luke xvii. 17

30 The kingdom of God is within you. *Ib.* 21

31 Remember Lot's wife. *Ib.* 32

32 Men ought always to pray, and not to faint.
Ib. xviii. 1

33 God, I thank thee, that I am not as other men are.
Ib. 11

34 God be merciful to me a sinner. *Ib.* 13

35 How hardly shall they that have riches enter into the kingdom of God! *Ib.* 24

36 Have thou authority over ten cities. *Ib.* xix. 17

37 Out of thine own mouth will I judge thee. *Ib.* 22

38 Thou knewest that I was an austere man. *Ib.*

39 If these should hold their peace, the stones would immediately cry out. *Ib.* 40

40 The things which belong unto thy peace. *Ib.* 42

41 And when they heard it, they said, God forbid.
Ib. xx. 16

42 In your patience possess ye your souls. *Ib.* xxi. 19

43 He shall shew you a large upper room furnished.
Ib. xxii. 12

44 I am among you as he that serveth. *Ib.* 27

45 Nevertheless, not my will, but thine, be done. *Ib.* 42

46 And the Lord turned, and looked upon Peter. *Ib.* 61

47 For if they do these things in a green tree, what shall be done in the dry? *Ib.* xxiii. 31

48 Father, forgive them; for they know not what they do. *Ib.* 34

49 Lord, remember me when thou comest into thy kingdom. *Ib.* 42

50 To day shalt thou be with me in paradise. *Ib.* 43

51 Father, into thy hands I commend my spirit. *Ib.* 46

52 He was a good man, and a just. *Ib.* 50

53 Why seek ye the living among the dead? *Ib.* xxiv. 5

54 Their words seemed to them as idle tales. *Ib.* 11

55 Did not our heart burn within us, while he talked with us by the way? *Ib.* 32

56 He was known of them in breaking of bread. *Ib.* 35

57 A piece of a broiled fish, and of an honeycomb. *Ib.* 42

58 In the beginning was the Word, and the Word was with God, and the Word was God. *St. John* i. 1

59 All things were made by him; and without him was not any thing made that was made. *Ib.* 3

60 And the light shineth in darkness; and the darkness comprehended it not. *Ib.* 5

61 There was a man sent from God, whose name was John. *Ib.* 6

62 The true Light, which lighteth every man that cometh into the world. *Ib.* 9

63 He came unto his own, and his own received him not.
Ib. 11

64 And the Word was made flesh, and dwelt among us, (and we beheld his glory, the glory as of the only begotten of the Father,) full of grace and truth.
Ib. 14

1 No man hath seen God at any time.   *St. John* i. 18

2 Who coming after me is preferred before me, whose shoe's latchet I am not worthy to unloose.   *Ib.* 27

3 Can there any good thing come out of Nazareth?   *Ib.* 46

4 Behold an Israelite indeed, in whom is no guile!   *Ib.* 47

5 Woman, what have I to do with thee? mine hour is not yet come.   *Ib.* ii. 4

6 When he had made a scourge of small cords, he drove them all out of the temple.   *Ib.* 15

7 The wind bloweth where it listeth, and thou hearest the sound thereof, but canst not tell whence it cometh, and whither it goeth.   *Ib.* iii. 8

8 How can these things be?   *Ib.* 9

9 God so loved the world, that he gave his only begotten Son, that whosoever believeth in him should not perish, but have everlasting life.   *Ib.* 16

10 Men loved darkness rather than light, because their deeds were evil.   *Ib.* 19

11 The friend of the bridegroom . . . rejoiceth greatly because of the bridegroom's voice.   *Ib.* 29

12 He must increase, but I must decrease.   *Ib.* 30

13 God is a Spirit: and they that worship him must worship him in spirit and in truth.   *Ib.* iv. 24

14 They are white already to harvest.   *Ib.* 35

15 Other men laboured, and ye are entered into their labours.   *Ib.* 38

16 Rise, take up thy bed, and walk.   *Ib.* v. 8

17 Passed from death unto life.   *Ib.* 24

18 He was a burning and a shining light.   *Ib.* 35

19 Search the scriptures.   *Ib.* 39

20 What are they among so many?   *Ib.* vi. 9

21 Gather up the fragments that remain, that nothing be lost.   *Ib.* 12

22 Him that cometh to me I will in no wise cast out.   *Ib.* 37

23 It is the spirit that quickeneth.   *Ib.* 63

24 Never man spake like this man.   *Ib.* vii. 46

25 Are ye also deceived?   *Ib.* 47

26 He that is without sin among you, let him first cast a stone at her.   *Ib.* viii. 7

27 Neither do I condemn thee: go, and sin no more.   *Ib.* 11

28 The truth shall make you free.   *Ib.* 32

29 Ye are of your father the devil.   *Ib.* 44

30 There is no truth in him.   *Ib.*

31 He is a liar, and the father of it.   *Ib.*

32 Which of you convinceth me of sin?   *Ib.* 46

33 The night cometh, when no man can work.   *Ib.* ix. 4

34 He is of age; ask him: he shall speak for himself.   *Ib.* 21

35 One thing I know, that, whereas I was blind, now I see.   *Ib.* 25

36 I am the door.   *Ib.* x. 9

37 The good shepherd giveth his life for the sheep.   *St. John* x. 11

38 The hireling fleeth, because he is an hireling, and careth not for the sheep.   *Ib.* 13

39 Other sheep I have, which are not of this fold.   *Ib.* 16

40 I am the resurrection, and the life.   *Ib.* xi. 25

41 Jesus wept.   *Ib.* 35

42 It is expedient for us, that one man should die for the people.   *Ib.* 50

43 Why was not this ointment sold for three hundred pence, and given to the poor?   *Ib.* xii. 5

44 The poor always ye have with you.   *Ib.* 8

45 Sir, we would see Jesus.   *Ib.* 21

46 Walk while ye have the light, lest darkness come upon you.   *Ib.* 35

47 Lord, dost thou wash my feet?   *Ib.* xiii. 6

48 Now there was leaning on Jesus' bosom one of his disciples, whom Jesus loved.   *Ib.* 23

49 That thou doest, do quickly.   *Ib.* 27

50 Let not your heart be troubled: ye believe in God, believe also in me.   *Ib.* xiv. 1

51 In my Father's house are many mansions.   *Ib.* 2

52 I go to prepare a place for you.   *Ib.*

53 I am the way, the truth, and the life: no man cometh unto the Father, but by me.   *Ib.* 6

54 Lord, shew us the Father, and it sufficeth us.   *Ib.* 8

55 Have I been so long time with you, and yet hast thou not known me, Philip?   *Ib.* 9

56 Judas saith unto him, not Iscariot.   *Ib.* 22

57 Greater love hath no man than this, that a man lay down his life for his friends.   *Ib.* xv. 13

58 Ye have not chosen me, but I have chosen you.   *Ib.* 16

59 Quo vadis? Whither goest thou?   *Ib.* xvi. 5 (Vulgate) and the Apocryphal *Acts of Peter*

60 It is expedient for you that I go away: for if I go not away, the Comforter will not come unto you.   *Ib.* 7

61 I have yet many many things to say unto you, but ye cannot bear them now.   *Ib.* 12

62 A little while, and ye shall not see me: and again, a little while, and ye shall see me, because I go to the Father.   *Ib.* 16

63 Do ye now believe?   *Ib.* 31

64 In the world ye shall have tribulation: but be of good cheer; I have overcome the world.   *Ib.* 33

65 The son of perdition.   *Ib.* xvii. 12

66 Put up thy sword into the sheath.   *Ib.* xviii. 11

67 Answerest thou the high priest so?   *Ib.* 22

68 Pilate saith unto him, What is truth?   *Ib.* 38

69 Now Barabbas was a robber.   *Ib.* 40

70 Ecce homo.
Behold the man.   *Ib.* xix. 5 (Vulgate)

71 What I have written I have written.   *Ib.* 22

72 Woman, behold thy son! . . .
Behold thy mother!   *Ib.* 26

1 I thirst. *St. John* xix. 28

2 It is finished. *Ib.* 30

3 A new sepulchre, wherein was never man yet laid. *Ib.* 41

4 The first day of the week cometh Mary Magdalene early, when it was yet dark, unto the sepulchre, and seeth the stone taken away from the sepulchre. *Ib.* xx. 1

5 So they ran both together: and the other disciple did outrun Peter, and came first to the sepulchre. *Ib.* 4

6 She, supposing him to be the gardener. *Ib.* 15

7 She turned herself and saith unto him, Rabboni. *Ib.* 16

8 Touch me not. *Ib.* 17

9 Except I shall see in his hands the print of the nails, and put my finger into the print of the nails, and thrust my hand into his side, I will not believe. *Ib.* 25

10 Be not faithless, but believing. *Ib.* 27

11 Thomas, because thou hast seen me, thou hast believed: blessed are they that have not seen, and yet have believed. *Ib.* 29

12 Simon Peter saith unto them, I go a fishing. *Ib.* xxi. 3

13 Children, have ye any meat? *Ib.* 5

14 Simon, son of Jonas, lovest thou me more than these? *Ib.* 15

15 Feed my lambs. *Ib.*

16 Feed my sheep. *Ib.* 16

17 Lord, thou knowest all things; thou knowest that I love thee. *Ib.* 17

18 When thou wast young, thou girdedst thyself, and walkedst whither thou wouldest: but when thou shalt be old, thou shalt stretch forth thy hands, and another shall gird thee, and carry thee whither thou wouldest not. *Ib.* 18

19 The disciple whom Jesus loved. *Ib.* 20

20 What shall this man do?
Jesus saith unto him, If I will that he tarry till I come, what is that to thee? *Ib.* 21

21 The former treatise have I made, O Theophilus. *The Acts of the Apostles* i. 1

22 Ye men of Galilee, why stand ye gazing up into heaven? *Ib.* 11

23 His bishoprick let another take. *Ib.* 20

24 A rushing mighty wind. *Ib.* ii. 2

25 Cloven tongues like as of fire. *Ib.* 3

26 Parthians, and Medes, and Elamites, and the dwellers in Mesopotamia, and in Judæa, and Cappadocia, in Pontus, and Asia.
Phrygia, and Pamphylia, in Egypt, and in the parts of Libya about Cyrene, and strangers of Rome, Jews and proselytes,
Cretes and Arabians, we do hear them speak in our tongues the wonderful works of God. *Ib.* 9

27 Silver and gold have I none; but such as I have give I thee. *Ib.* iii. 6

28 I wot that through ignorance ye did it. *Ib.* 17

29 They took knowledge of them, that they had been with Jesus. *The Acts of the Apostles* iv. 13

30 Barnabas, . . . The son of consolation. *Ib.* 36

31 We ought to obey God rather than men. *Ib.* v. 29

32 If this counsel or this work be of men, it will come to nought:
But if it be of God, ye cannot overthrow it; lest haply ye be found even to fight against God. *Ib.* 38

33 It is not reason that we should leave the word of God, and serve tables. *Ib.* vi. 2

34 The witnesses laid down their clothes at a young man's feet, whose name was Saul. *Ib.* vii. 58

35 Saul was consenting unto his death. *Ib.* viii. 1

36 Thy money perish with thee. *Ib.* 20

37 Thou hast neither part nor lot in this matter. *Ib.* 21

38 In the gall of bitterness, and in the bond of iniquity. *Ib.* 23

39 Understandest thou what thou readest? . . .
How can I, except some man should guide me? *Ib.* 30

40 Breathing out threatenings and slaughter. *Ib.* ix. 1

41 Saul, Saul, why persecutest thou me? *Ib.* 4

42 It is hard for thee to kick against the pricks. *Ib.* 5

43 The street which is called Straight. *Ib.* 11

44 Full of good works. *Ib.* 36

45 One Simon a tanner. *Ib.* 43

46 As it had been a great sheet knit at the four corners, and let down to the earth. *Ib.* x. 11

47 What God hath cleansed, that call not thou common. *Ib.* 15

48 God is no respecter of persons. *Ib.* 34

49 It is the voice of a god, and not of a man. *Ib.* xii. 22

50 He was eaten of worms, and gave up the ghost. *Ib.* 23

51 The gods are come down to us in the likeness of men. *Ib.* xiv. 11

52 We also are men of like passions with you. *Ib.* 15

53 Come over into Macedonia, and help us. *Ib.* xvi. 9

54 Lydia, a seller of purple, of the city of Thyatira. *Ib.* 14

55 A certain damsel possessed with a spirit of divination. *Ib.* 16

56 Certain lewd fellows of the baser sort. *Ib.* xvii. 5

57 These that have turned the world upside down. *Ib.* 6

58 What will this babbler say? *Ib.* 18

59 For all the Athenians and strangers which were there spent their time in nothing else, but either to tell, or to hear some new thing. *Ib.* 21

60 Ye men of Athens, I perceive that in all things ye are too superstitious.
For as I passed by, and beheld your devotions, I found an altar with this inscription, TO THE UNKNOWN GOD. Whom therefore ye ignorantly worship, him declare I unto you. *Ib.* 22

1 For in him we live, and move, and have our being.
The Acts of the Apostles xvii. 28

2 As certain also of your own poets have said. *Ib.*

3 Gallio cared for none of those things. *Ib.* xviii. 17

4 Mighty in the scriptures. *Ib.* 24

5 We have not so much as heard whether there be any Holy Ghost. *Ib.* xix. 2

6 Demetrius, a silversmith. *Ib.* 24

7 Some therefore cried one thing, and some another: for the assembly was confused; and the more part knew not wherefore they were come together.
Ib. 32

8 All with one voice about the space of two hours cried out, Great is Diana of the Ephesians. *Ib.* 34

9 For we are in danger to be called in question for this day's uproar. *Ib.* 40

10 I go bound in the spirit unto Jerusalem. *Ib.* xx. 22

11 It is more blessed to give than to receive. *Ib.* 35

12 A citizen of no mean city. *Ib.* xxi. 39

13 Brought up in this city at the feet of Gamaliel.
Ib. xxii. 3

14 And the chief captain answered, With a great sum obtained I this freedom. And Paul said, But I was free born. *Ib.* 28

15 God shall smite thee, thou whited wall. *Ib.* xxiii. 3

16 Revilest thou God's high priest? *Ib.* 4

17 I am a Pharisee, the son of a Pharisee. *Ib.* 6

18 A conscience void of offence toward God, and toward men. *Ib.* xxiv. 16

19 I appeal unto Cæsar. *Ib.* xxv. 11

20 Hast thou appealed unto Cæsar? unto Cæsar shalt thou go. *Ib.* 12

21 I think myself happy, king Agrippa. *Ib.* xxvi. 2

22 After the most straitest sect of our religion I lived a Pharisee. *Ib.* 5

23 Paul, thou art beside thyself; much learning doth make thee mad. *Ib.* 24

24 Words of truth and soberness. *Ib.* 25

25 For this thing was not done in a corner. *Ib.* 26

26 Almost thou persuadest me to be a Christian. *Ib.* 28

27 I would to God, that not only thou, but also all that hear me this day, were both almost, and altogether such as I am, except these bonds. *Ib.* 29

28 They used helps, undergirding the ship. *Ib.* xxvii. 17

29 They cast four anchors out of the stern, and wished for the day. *Ib.* 29

30 Without ceasing I make mention of you always in my prayers. *The Epistle of Paul to the Romans* i. 9

31 The just shall live by faith. *Ib.* 17

32 Worshipped and served the creature more than the Creator. *Ib.* 25

33 Patient continuance in well doing. *Ib.* ii. 7

34 For there is no respect of persons with God. *Ib.* 11

35 These . . . are a law unto themselves. *Ib.* 14

36 Let God be true, but every man a liar. *Ib.* iii. 4

37 Let us do evil, that good may come. *Romans* iii. 8

38 For all have sinned, and come short of the glory of God. *Ib.* 23

39 For where no law is, there is no transgression.
Ib. iv. 15

40 Who against hope believed in hope. *Ib.* 18

41 Hope maketh not ashamed. *Ib.* v. 5

42 Where sin abounded, grace did much more abound.
Ib. 20

43 Shall we continue in sin, that grace may abound?
Ib. vi. 1

44 We also should walk in newness of life. *Ib.* 4

45 Christ being raised from the dead dieth no more; death hath no more dominion over him.
For in that he died, he died unto sin once: but in that he liveth, he liveth unto God. *Ib.* 9

46 The wages of sin is death. *Ib.* 23

47 Is the law sin? God forbid. Nay, I had not known sin, but by the law. *Ib.* vii. 7

48 Now then it is no more I that do it, but sin that dwelleth in me. *Ib.* 17

49 For the good that I would I do not: but the evil which I would not, that I do. *Ib.* 19

50 I find then a law, that, when I would do good, evil is present with me. *Ib.* 21

51 O wretched man that I am! who shall deliver me from the body of this death? *Ib.* 24

52 They that are after the flesh do mind the things of the flesh; but they that are after the Spirit the things of the Spirit.
For to be carnally minded is death. *Ib.* viii. 5

53 For ye have not received the spirit of bondage again to fear; but ye have received the Spirit of adoption, whereby we cry, Abba, Father. *Ib.* 15

54 We are the children of God:
And if children, then heirs; heirs of God, and joint-heirs with Christ. *Ib.* 16

55 For we know that the whole creation groaneth and travaileth in pain together until now. *Ib.* 22

56 All things work together for good to them that love God. *Ib.* 28

57 If God be for us, who can be against us? *Ib.* 31

58 For I am persuaded, that neither death, nor life, nor angels, nor principalities, nor powers, nor things present, nor things to come,
Nor height, nor depth, nor any other creature, shall be able to separate us from the love of God, which is in Christ Jesus our Lord. *Ib.* 38

59 I could wish that myself were accursed from Christ for my brethren, my kinsmen according to the flesh. *Ib.* ix. 3

60 Hath not the potter power over the clay, of the same lump to make one vessel unto honour, and another unto dishonour? *Ib.* 21

61 A zeal of God, but not according to knowledge.
Ib. x. 2

62 I beseech you therefore, brethren, by the mercies of God, that ye present your bodies a living sacrifice, holy, acceptable unto God. *Ib.* xii. 1

1 Let love be without dissimulation.
The Epistle of Paul to the Romans xii. 9

2 Be kindly affectioned one to another with brotherly love; in honour preferring one another;
Not slothful in business; fervent in spirit; serving the Lord. *Ib.* 10

3 Given to hospitality. *Ib.* 13

4 Rejoice with them that do rejoice, and weep with them that weep. *Ib.* 15

5 Mind not high things, but condescend to men of low estate. Be not wise in your own conceits. *Ib.* 16

6 Vengeance is mine; I will repay, saith the Lord. *Ib.* 19

7 Be not overcome of evil, but overcome evil with good. *Ib.* 21

8 Let every soul be subject unto the higher powers. *Ib.* xiii. 1

9 The powers that be are ordained of God. *Ib.*

10 For rulers are not a terror to good works, but to the evil. *Ib.* 3

11 Render therefore to all their dues: tribute to whom tribute is due; custom to whom custom; fear to whom fear; honour to whom honour.
Owe no man anything, but to love one another: for he that loveth another hath fulfilled the law. *Ib.* 7

12 Love is the fulfilling of the law. *Ib.* 10

13 Now it is high time to awake out of sleep: for now is our salvation nearer than when we believed.
The night is far spent, the day is at hand: let us therefore cast off the works of darkness, and let us put on the armour of light. *Ib.* 11

14 Make not provision for the flesh, to fulfil the lusts thereof. *Ib.* 14

15 Doubtful disputations. *Ib.* xiv. 1

16 Let every man be fully persuaded in his own mind. *Ib.* 5

17 We then that are strong ought to bear the infirmities of the weak, and not to please ourselves. *Ib.* xv. 1

18 Salute one another with an holy kiss. *Ib.* xvi. 16

19 The foolishness of preaching.
The First Epistle of Paul to the Corinthians i. 21

20 God hath chosen the foolish things of the world to confound the wise; and God hath chosen the weak things of the world to confound the things which are mighty. *Ib.* 27

21 I determined not to know any thing among you, save Jesus Christ, and him crucified. *Ib.* ii. 2

22 I have planted, Apollos watered; but God gave the increase. *Ib.* iii. 6

23 Every man's work shall be made manifest. *Ib.* 13

24 Stewards of the mysteries of God. *Ib.* iv. 1

25 A spectacle unto the world, and to angels. *Ib.* 9

26 Absent in body, but present in spirit. *Ib.* v. 3

27 Know ye not that a little leaven leaveneth the whole lump? *Ib.* 6

28 Christ our passover is sacrificed for us:
Therefore let us keep the feast, not with the old leaven, neither with the leaven of malice and wickedness; but with the unleavened bread of sincerity and truth. *Ib.* 7

29 Your body is the temple of the Holy Ghost.
I *Corinthians* vi. 19

30 It is better to marry than to burn. *Ib.* vii. 9

31 The unbelieving husband is sanctified by the wife. *Ib.* 14

32 The fashion of this world passeth away. *Ib.* 31

33 Knowledge puffeth up, but charity edifieth. *Ib.* viii. 1

34 Who goeth a warfare any time at his own charges? who planteth a vineyard, and eateth not of the fruit thereof? *Ib.* ix. 7

35 I am made all things to all men. *Ib.* 22

36 Know ye not that they which run in a race run all, but one receiveth the prize? *Ib.* 24

37 Now they do it to obtain a corruptible crown; but we an incorruptible.
I therefore so run, not as uncertainly; so fight I, not as one that beateth the air:
But I keep under my body, and bring it into subjection: lest that by any means, when I have preached to others, I myself should be a castaway. *Ib.* 25

38 Let him that thinketh he standeth take heed lest he fall.
There hath no temptation taken you but such as is common to man: but God is faithful, who will not suffer you to be tempted above that ye are able; but will with the temptation also make a way to escape, that ye may be able to bear it. *Ib.* x. 12

39 All things are lawful for me, but all things are not expedient. *Ib.* 23

40 For the earth is the Lord's, and the fulness thereof. *Ib.* 26

41 Whether therefore ye eat, or drink, or whatsoever ye do, do all to the glory of God. *Ib.* 31

42 If a woman have long hair, it is a glory to her. *Ib.* xi. 15

43 Now there are diversities of gifts, but the same Spirit. *Ib.* xii. 4

44 Though I speak with the tongues of men and of angels, and have not charity, I am become as sounding brass, or a tinkling cymbal. *Ib.* xiii. 1

45 Though I have all faith, so that I could remove mountains, and have not charity, I am nothing.
And though I bestow all my goods to feed the poor, and though I give my body to be burned, and have not charity, it profiteth me nothing.
Charity suffereth long, and is kind; charity envieth not; charity vaunteth not itself, is not puffed up,
Doth not behave itself unseemly, seeketh not her own, is not easily provoked, thinketh no evil;
Rejoiceth not in iniquity, but rejoiceth in the truth;
Beareth all things, believeth all things, hopeth all things, endureth all things.
Charity never faileth: but whether there be prophecies, they shall fail; whether there be tongues, they shall cease; whether there be knowledge, it shall vanish away.
For we know in part, and we prophesy in part. *Ib.* 2

46 When I was a child, I spake as a child, I understood as a child, I thought as a child: but when I became a man, I put away childish things.

For now we see through a glass, darkly; but then face to face: now I know in part; but then shall I know even as also I am known.

And now abideth faith, hope, charity, these three; but the greatest of these is charity.

The First Epistle of Paul to the Corinthians xiii. 11

1 If the trumpet give an uncertain sound, who shall prepare himself to the battle? *Ib.* xiv. 8

2 Let your women keep silence in the churches: for it is not permitted unto them to speak. *Ib.* 34

3 If they will learn any thing, let them ask their husbands at home: for it is a shame for women to speak in the church. *Ib.* 35

4 Let all things be done decently and in order. *Ib.* 40

5 Last of all he was seen of me also, as of one born out of due time.

For I am the least of the apostles, that am not meet to be called an apostle, because I persecuted the church of God.

But by the grace of God I am what I am. *Ib.* xv. 8

6 I laboured more abundantly than they all: yet not I, but the grace of God which was with me. *Ib.* 10

7 We are of all men most miserable. *Ib.* 19

8 But now is Christ risen from the dead, and become the firstfruits of them that slept.

For since by man came death, by man came also the resurrection of the dead.

For as in Adam all die, even so in Christ shall all be made alive. *Ib.* 20

9 The last enemy that shall be destroyed is death. *Ib.* 26

10 If after the manner of men I have fought with beasts at Ephesus. *Ib.* 32

11 Let us eat and drink; for to morrow we die. *Ib.*

12 Evil communications corrupt good manners. *Ib.* 33

13 One star differeth from another star in glory. *Ib.* 41

14 It is sown in corruption; it is raised in incorruption. *Ib.* 42

15 The first man is of the earth, earthy. *Ib.* 47

16 Behold, I shew you a mystery; We shall not all sleep, but we shall all be changed,

In a moment, in the twinkling of an eye, at the last trump. *Ib.* 51

17 For this corruptible must put on incorruption, and this mortal must put on immortality. *Ib.* 53

18 O death, where is thy sting? O grave, where is thy victory? *Ib.* 55

19 Quit you like men, be strong. *Ib.* xvi. 13

20 Let him be Anathema Maran-atha. *Ib.* 22

21 Fleshy tables of the heart.

The Second Epistle of Paul to the Corinthians iii. 3

22 Not of the letter, but of the spirit: for the letter killeth, but the spirit giveth life. *Ib.* 6

23 We have this treasure in earthen vessels. *Ib.* iv. 7

24 An house not made with hands, eternal in the heavens. *Ib.* v. 1

25 We walk by faith, not by sight. *Ib.* 7

26 The love of Christ constraineth us. *Ib.* 14

27 Now is the accepted time. *Ib.* vi. 2

28 By honour and dishonour, by evil report and good report. II *Corinthians* vi. 8

29 As having nothing, and yet possessing all things. *Ib.* 10

30 Without were fightings, within were fears. *Ib.* vii. 5

31 God loveth a cheerful giver. *Ib.* ix. 7

32 For ye suffer fools gladly, seeing ye yourselves are wise. *Ib.* xi. 19

33 Are they Hebrews? so am I. Are they Israelites? so am I. Are they the seed of Abraham? so am I.

Are they ministers of Christ? (I speak as a fool) I am more. *Ib.* 22

34 Five times received I forty stripes save one. *Ib.* 24

35 In perils in the city, in perils in the wilderness, in perils in the sea, in perils among false brethren. *Ib.* 26

36 Whether in the body, I cannot tell; or whether out of the body, I cannot tell: God knoweth. *Ib.* xii. 2

37 There was given to me a thorn in the flesh, the messenger of Satan to buffet me. *Ib.* 7

38 My strength is made perfect in weakness. *Ib.* 9

39 In the mouth of two or three witnesses shall every word be established. *Ib.* xiii. 1

40 The right hands of fellowship.

The Epistle of Paul to the Galatians ii. 9

41 O foolish Galatians, who hath bewitched you? *Ib.* iii. 1

42 Weak and beggarly elements. *Ib.* iv. 9

43 Which things are an allegory. *Ib.* 24

44 Ye are fallen from grace. *Ib.* v. 4

45 For the flesh lusteth against the Spirit, and the Spirit against the flesh ... so that ye cannot do the things that ye would. *Ib.* 17

46 But the fruit of the Spirit is love, joy, peace, long-suffering, gentleness, goodness, faith,

Meekness, temperance. *Ib.* 22

47 Be not deceived; God is not mocked: for whatsoever a man soweth, that shall he also reap. *Ib.* vi. 7

48 Let us not be weary in well doing: for in due season we shall reap, if we faint not. *Ib.* 9

49 Ye see how large a letter I have written unto you with mine own hand. *Ib.* 11

50 You hath he quickened, who were dead in trespasses and sins. *The Epistle of Paul to the Ephesians* ii. 1

51 Preached peace to you which were afar off, and to them that were nigh. *Ib.* 17

52 The unsearchable riches of Christ. *Ib.* iii. 8

53 To be strengthened with might by his Spirit in the inner man. *Ib.* 16

54 The love of Christ, which passeth knowledge. *Ib.* 19

55 Him that is able to do exceeding abundantly above all that we ask or think. *Ib.* 20

56 Worthy of the vocation wherewith ye are called. *Ib.* iv. 1

57 Carried about with every wind of doctrine. *Ib.* 14

58 We are members one of another. *Ib.* 25

1 Be ye angry, and sin not: let not the sun go down upon your wrath.
The Epistle of Paul to the Ephesians iv. 26

2 Nor foolish talking, nor jesting, which are not convenient. *Ib.* v. 4

3 Let no man deceive you with vain words: for because of these things cometh the wrath of God upon the children of disobedience. *Ib.* 6

4 Redeeming the time, because the days are evil. *Ib.* 16

5 Psalms and hymns and spiritual songs. *Ib.* 19

6 Wives, submit yourselves unto your own husbands, as unto the Lord. *Ib.* 22

7 The first commandment with promise. *Ib.* vi. 2

8 Ye fathers, provoke not your children to wrath. *Ib.* 4

9 Not with eyeservice, as menpleasers. *Ib.* 6

10 Put on the whole armour of God. *Ib.* 11

11 For we wrestle not against flesh and blood, but against principalities, against powers, against the rulers of the darkness of this world, against spiritual wickedness in high places.
Wherefore take unto you the whole armour of God, that ye may be able to withstand in the evil day, and having done all, to stand. *Ib.* 12

12 Your feet shod with the preparation of the gospel of peace. *Ib.* 15

13 The shield of faith, wherewith ye shall be able to quench all the fiery darts of the wicked. *Ib.* 16

14 I thank my God upon every remembrance of you.
The Epistle of Paul to the Philippians i. 3.

15 For to me to live is Christ, and to die is gain. *Ib.* 21

16 Having a desire to depart, and to be with Christ; which is far better. *Ib.* 23

17 But made himself of no reputation, and took upon him the form of a servant, and was made in the likeness of men. *Ib.* ii. 7

18 Given him a name which is above every name:
That at the name of Jesus every knee should bow. *Ib.* 9

19 Work out your own salvation with fear and trembling. *Ib.* 12

20 An Hebrew of the Hebrews; as touching the law, a Pharisee. *Ib.* iii. 5

21 But what things were gain to me, those I counted loss for Christ. *Ib.* 7

22 If by any means I might attain unto the resurrection of the dead. *Ib.* 11

23 Forgetting those things which are behind, and reaching forth unto those things which are before,
I press toward the mark. *Ib.* 13

24 Whose God is their belly, and whose glory is in their shame. *Ib.* 19

25 Rejoice in the Lord alway: and again I say, Rejoice. *Ib.* iv. 4

26 The peace of God, which passeth all understanding. *Ib.* 7

27 Whatsoever things are true, whatsoever things are honest, whatsoever things are just, whatsoever things are pure, whatsoever things are lovely, whatsoever things are of good report; if there be any

virtue, and if there be any praise, think on these things. *Philippians* iv. 8

28 I can do all things through Christ which strengtheneth me. *Ib.* 13

29 Touch not; taste not; handle not.
The Epistle of Paul to the Colossians ii. 21

30 Set your affection on things above, not on things on the earth. *Ib.* iii. 2

31 Where there is neither Greek nor Jew, circumcision nor uncircumcision, Barbarian, Scythian, bond nor free: but Christ is all, and in all. *Ib.* 11

32 Husbands, love your wives, and be not bitter against them. *Ib.* 19

33 Let your speech be alway with grace, seasoned with salt. *Ib.* iv. 6

34 Luke, the beloved physician. *Ib.* 14

35 Labour of love.
The First Epistle of Paul to the Thessalonians i. 3

36 Study to be quiet, and to do your own business. *Ib.* iv. 11

37 Pray without ceasing. *Ib.* v. 17

38 Prove all things; hold fast that which is good. *Ib.* 21

39 If any would not work, neither should he eat.
The Second Epistle of Paul to the Thessalonians iii. 10

40 Be not weary in well doing. *Ib.* 13

41 Fables and endless genealogies.
The First Epistle of Paul to Timothy i. 4

42 I did it ignorantly in unbelief. *Ib.* 13

43 Sinners; of whom I am chief. *Ib.* 15

44 If a man desire the office of a bishop, he desireth a good work. *Ib.* iii. 1

45 Not greedy of filthy lucre. *Ib.* 3

46 For every creature of God is good, and nothing to be refused, if it be received with thanksgiving. *Ib.* iv. 4

47 Old wives' fables. *Ib.* 7

48 Worse than an infidel. *Ib.* v. 8

49 Tattlers also and busybodies, speaking things which they ought not. *Ib.* 13

50 Drink no longer water, but use a little wine for thy stomach's sake and thine often infirmities. *Ib.* 23

51 For we brought nothing into this world, and it is certain we can carry nothing out. *Ib.* vi. 7

52 The love of money is the root of all evil. *Ib.* 10

53 Fight the good fight of faith, lay hold on eternal life. *Ib.* 12

54 Rich in good works. *Ib.* 18

55 Science falsely so called. *Ib.* 20

56 For God hath not given us the spirit of fear; but of power, and of love, and of a sound mind.
The Second Epistle of Paul to Timothy i. 7

57 Hold fast the form of sound words. *Ib.* 13

58 From a child thou hast known the holy scriptures. *Ib.* iii. 15

59 Be instant in season, out of season. *Ib.* iv. 2

60 I have fought a good fight, I have finished my course, I have kept the faith. *Ib.* 7

1 For Demas hath forsaken me, having loved this present world.
The Second Epistle of Paul to Timothy iv. 10

2 Only Luke is with me. *Ib.* 11

3 Alexander the coppersmith did me much evil: the Lord reward him according to his works. *Ib.* 14

4 Unto the pure all things are pure.
The Epistle of Paul to Titus i. 15

5 Being such an one as Paul the aged, and now also a prisoner of Jesus Christ.
The Epistle of Paul to Philemon 9

6 At sundry times and in divers manners.
The Epistle of Paul to the Hebrews i. 1

7 The brightness of his glory, and the express image of his person. *Ib.* 3

8 For the word of God is quick, and powerful, and sharper than any twoedged sword, piercing even to the dividing asunder of soul and spirit.
Ib. iv. 12

9 They crucify to themselves the Son of God afresh, and put him to an open shame. *Ib.* vi. 6

10 Without shedding of blood is no remission.
Ib. ix. 22

11 Not forsaking the assembling of ourselves together, as the manner of some is. *Ib.* x. 25

12 It is a fearful thing to fall into the hands of the living God. *Ib.* 31

13 Faith is the substance of things hoped for, the evidence of things not seen. *Ib.* xi. 1

14 For he looked for a city which hath foundations.
Ib. 10

15 These all died in faith. *Ib.* 13

16 Esteeming the reproach of Christ greater riches than the treasures in Egypt. *Ib.* 26

17 Of whom the world was not worthy. *Ib.* 38

18 Wherefore seeing we also are compassed about with so great a cloud of witnesses, let us lay aside every weight, and the sin which doth so easily beset us, and let us run with patience the race that is set before us,
Looking unto Jesus the author and finisher of our faith. *Ib.* xii. 1

19 Whom the Lord loveth he chasteneth. *Ib.* 6

20 He found no place of repentance, though he sought it carefully with tears. *Ib.* 17

21 The spirits of just men made perfect. *Ib.* 23

22 Let brotherly love continue.
Be not forgetful to entertain strangers: for thereby some have entertained angels unawares. *Ib.* xiii. 1

23 Jesus Christ the same yesterday, and to day, and for ever. *Ib.* 8

24 For here have we no continuing city, but we seek one to come. *Ib.* 14

25 To do good and to communicate forget not. *Ib.* 16

26 Let patience have her perfect work.
The General Epistle of James i. 4

27 If any of you lack wisdom, let him ask of God, that giveth to all men liberally, and upbraideth not. *Ib.* 5

28 Blessed is the man that endureth temptation: for when he is tried, he shall receive the crown of life.
James i. 12

29 Every good gift and every perfect gift is from above, and cometh down from the Father of lights, with whom is no variableness, neither shadow of turning.
Ib. 17

30 Be swift to hear, slow to speak, slow to wrath:
For the wrath of man worketh not the righteousness of God. *Ib.* 19

31 Superfluity of naughtiness. *Ib.* 21

32 Be ye doers of the word, and not hearers only.
Ib. 22

33 If any be a hearer of the word, and not a doer, he is like unto a man beholding his natural face in a glass:
For he beholdeth himself, and goeth his way, and straightway forgetteth what manner of man he was.
Ib. 23

34 If any man among you seem to be religious, and bridleth not his tongue, but deceiveth his own heart, this man's religion is vain.
Pure religion and undefiled before God and the Father is this, To visit the fatherless and widows in their affliction, and to keep himself unspotted from the world. *Ib.* 26

35 Faith without works is dead. *Ib.* ii. 20

36 How great a matter a little fire kindleth! *Ib.* iii. 5

37 The tongue can no man tame; it is an unruly evil.
Ib. 8

38 Doth a fountain send forth at the same place sweet water and bitter? *Ib.* 11

39 This wisdom descendeth not from above, but is earthly, sensual, devilish. *Ib.* 15

40 Resist the devil, and he will flee from you. *Ib.* iv. 7

41 For what is your life? It is even a vapour, that appeareth for a little time, and then vanisheth away. *Ib.* 14

42 Ye have heard of the patience of Job. *Ib.* v. 11

43 Let your yea be yea; and your nay, nay. *Ib.* 12

44 The effectual fervent prayer of a righteous man availeth much. *Ib.* 16

45 Whom having not seen, ye love.
The First Epistle General of Peter i. 8

46 All flesh is as grass, and all the glory of man as the flower of grass. The grass withereth, and the flower thereof falleth away. *Ib.* 24

47 As newborn babes, desire the sincere milk of the word.
Ib. ii. 2

48 But ye are a chosen generation, a royal priesthood, an holy nation, a peculiar people. *Ib.* 9

49 Abstain from fleshly lusts, which war against the soul.
Ib. 11

50 Honour all men. Love the brotherhood. Fear God. Honour the king. *Ib.* 17

51 For what glory is it, if, when ye be buffeted for your faults, ye shall take it patiently? but if, when ye do well, and suffer for it, ye take it patiently, this is acceptable with God. *Ib.* 20

52 The Shepherd and Bishop of your souls. *Ib.* 25

1 **Ornament** of a meek and quiet spirit.
The First Epistle General of Peter iii. 4

2 Giving honour unto the wife, as unto the weaker vessel. *Ib.* 7

3 Not rendering evil for evil, or railing for railing: but contrariwise blessing. *Ib.* 9

4 The end of all things is at hand. *Ib.* iv. 7

5 Charity shall cover the multitude of sins. *Ib.* 8

6 Be sober, be vigilant; because your adversary the devil, as a roaring lion, walketh about, seeking whom he may devour. *Ib.* v. 8

7 And the day star arise in your hearts.
The Second Epistle General of Peter i. 19

8 Not afraid to speak evil of dignities. *Ib.* ii. 10

9 The dog is turned to his own vomit again. *Ib.* 22

10 If we say that we have no sin, we deceive ourselves, and the truth is not in us.
The First Epistle General of John i. 8

11 But whoso hath this world's good, and seeth his brother have need, and shutteth up his bowels of compassion from him, how dwelleth the love of God in him? *Ib.* iii. 17

12 He that loveth not knoweth not God; for God is love.
Ib. iv. 8

13 No man hath seen God at any time. *Ib.* 12

14 There is no fear in love; but perfect love casteth out fear. *Ib.* 18

15 If a man say, I love God, and hateth his brother, he is a liar: for he that loveth not his brother whom he hath seen, how can he love God whom he hath not seen? *Ib.* 20

16 The elder unto the elect lady.
The Second Epistle of John 1

17 Yet Michael the archangel, when contending with the devil he disputed about the body of Moses, durst not bring against him a railing accusation.
The General Epistle of Jude 9

18 Spots in your feasts of charity. *Ib.* 12

19 Clouds they are without water, carried about of winds. *Ib.*

20 Raging waves of the sea, foaming out their own shame; wandering stars, to whom is reserved the blackness of darkness for ever. *Ib.* 13

21 John to the seven churches which are in Asia: Grace be unto you, and peace, from him which is, and which was, and which is to come.
The Revelation of St. John the Divine i. 4

22 Behold, he cometh with clouds; and every eye shall see him, and they also which pierced him: and all kindreds of the earth shall wail because of him. Even so, Amen.
I am Alpha and Omega, the beginning and the ending, saith the Lord. *Ib.* 7

23 I John, who also am your brother, and companion in tribulation, and in the kingdom and patience of Jesus Christ, was in the isle that is called Patmos, for the word of God, and for the testimony of Jesus Christ.
I was in the Spirit on the Lord's day, and heard behind me a great voice, as of a trumpet. *Ib.* 9

24 What thou seest, write in a book, and send it unto the seven churches which are in Asia. *Revelation* i. 11

25 Being turned, I saw seven golden candlesticks. *Ib.* 12

26 Clothed with a garment down to the foot, and girt about the paps with a golden girdle. *Ib.* 13

27 His head and his hairs were white like wool, as white as snow; and his eyes were as a flame of fire;
And his feet like unto fine brass, as if they burned in a furnace; and his voice as the sound of many waters.
And he had in his right hand seven stars: and out of his mouth went a sharp twoedged sword: and his countenance was as the sun shineth in his strength.
And when I saw him, I fell at his feet as dead. *Ib.* 14

28 I am he that liveth, and was dead; and, behold, I am alive for evermore, Amen; and have the keys of hell and of death. *Ib.* 18

29 I have somewhat against thee, because thou hast left thy first love. *Ib.* ii. 4

30 Be thou faithful unto death, and I will give thee a crown of life. *Ib.* 10

31 I . . . will give him a white stone, and in the stone a new name written, which no man knoweth saving he that receiveth it. *Ib.* 17

32 I will not blot out his name out of the book of life.
Ib. iii. 5

33 I will write upon him my new name. *Ib.* 12

34 I know thy works, that thou art neither cold nor hot: I would thou wert cold or hot.
So then because thou art lukewarm, and neither cold nor hot, I will spue thee out of my mouth. *Ib.* 15

35 Behold, I stand at the door, and knock. *Ib.* 20

36 And he that sat was to look upon like a jasper and a sardine stone: and there was a rainbow round about the throne, in sight like unto an emerald. *Ib.* iv. 3

37 And before the throne there was a sea of glass like unto crystal: and in the midst of the throne, and round about the throne, were four beasts full of eyes before and behind. *Ib.* 6

38 They were full of eyes within: and they rest not day and night, saying, Holy, holy, holy, Lord God Almighty, which was, and is, and is to come. *Ib.* 8

39 Thou hast created all things, and for thy pleasure they are and were created. *Ib.* 11

40 Who is worthy to open the book, and to loose the seals thereof? *Ib.* v. 2

41 A Lamb as it had been slain, having seven horns and seven eyes. *Ib.* 6

42 Golden vials full of odours, which are the prayers of saints. *Ib.* 8

43 He went forth conquering, and to conquer. *Ib.* vi. 2

44 A measure of wheat for a penny, and three measures of barley for a penny; and see thou hurt not the oil and the wine. *Ib.* 6

45 And I looked, and behold a pale horse: and his name that sat on him was Death. *Ib.* 8

46 How long, O Lord, holy and true, dost thou not judge and avenge our blood on them that dwell on the earth? *Ib.* 10

1 And the stars of heaven fell unto the earth, even as a fig tree casteth her untimely figs, when she is shaken of a mighty wind.

The Revelation of St. John the Divine vi. 13

2 Said to the mountains and rocks, Fall on us, and hide us from the face of him that sitteth on the throne, and from the wrath of the Lamb. *Ib.* 16

3 A great multitude, which no man could number, of all nations, and kindreds, and people, and tongues.

Ib. vii. 9

4 And all the angels stood round about the throne, and about the elders and the four beasts, and fell before the throne on their faces, and worshipped God.

Ib. 11

5 And one of the elders answered, saying unto me, What are these which are arrayed in white robes? and whence came they? *Ib.* 13

6 These are they which came out of great tribulation, and have washed their robes, and made them white in the blood of the Lamb. *Ib.* 14

7 They shall hunger no more, neither thirst any more; neither shall the sun light on them, nor any heat.

Ib. 16

8 God shall wipe away all tears from their eyes. *Ib.* 17

9 There was silence in heaven about the space of half an hour. *Ib.* viii. 1

10 And the name of the star is called Wormwood. *Ib.* 11

11 Those men which have not the seal of God in their foreheads. *Ib.* ix. 4

12 And in those days shall men seek death, and shall not find it; and shall desire to die, and death shall flee from them. *Ib.* 6

13 And there were stings in their tails. *Ib.* 10

14 It was in my mouth sweet as honey: and as soon as I had eaten it, my belly was bitter. *Ib.* x. 10

15 The kingdoms of this world are become the kingdoms of our Lord, and of his Christ. *Ib.* xi. 15

16 And there appeared a great wonder in heaven; a woman clothed with the sun, and the moon under her feet, and upon her head a crown of twelve stars.

Ib. xii. 1

17 And there was war in heaven: Michael and his angels fought against the dragon; and the dragon fought and his angels. *Ib.* 7

18 The devil is come down unto you, having great wrath, because he knoweth that he hath but a short time.

Ib. 12

19 A time, and times, and half a time. *Ib.* 14

20 Who is like unto the beast? who is able to make war with him? *Ib.* xiii. 4

21 And that no man might buy or sell, save he that had the mark, or the name of the beast, or the number of his name. *Ib.* 17

22 The number of the beast: for it is the number of a man; and his number is Six hundred threescore and six. *Ib.* 18

23 They sung as it were a new song . . . and no man could learn that song but the hundred and forty and four thousand, which were redeemed from the earth.

Ib. xiv. 3

24 And in their mouth was found no guile: for they are without fault before the throne of God. *Ib.* 5

25 Babylon is fallen, is fallen, that great city.

Revelation xiv. 8

26 And the smoke of their torment ascendeth up for ever and ever: and they have no rest day nor night, who worship the beast and his image. *Ib.* 11

27 Blessed are the dead which die in the Lord from henceforth: Yea, saith the Spirit, that they may rest from their labours; and their works do follow them. *Ib.* 13

28 And I saw as it were a sea of glass mingled with fire.

Ib. xv. 2

29 Behold, I come as a thief. *Ib.* xvi. 15

30 And he gathered them together into a place called in the Hebrew tongue Armageddon. *Ib.* 16

31 I will shew unto thee the judgment of the great whore that sitteth upon many waters. *Ib.* xvii. 1

32 MYSTERY, BABYLON THE GREAT, THE MOTHER OF HARLOTS AND ABOMINATIONS OF THE EARTH.

And I saw the woman drunken with the blood of the saints. *Ib.* 5

33 And a mighty angel took up a stone like a great millstone, and cast it into the sea, saying, Thus with violence shall that great city Babylon be thrown down, and shall be found no more at all.

Ib. xviii. 21

34 Blessed are they which are called unto the marriage supper of the Lamb. *Ib.* xix. 9

35 And I fell at his feet to worship him. And he said unto me, See thou do it not: I am thy fellow-servant. *Ib.* 10

36 And I saw heaven opened, and behold a white horse; and he that sat upon him was called Faithful and True. *Ib.* 11

37 And he hath on his vesture and on his thigh a name written, KING OF KINGS, AND LORD OF LORDS. *Ib.* 16

38 The key of the bottomless pit. *Ib.* xx. 1

39 And he laid hold on the dragon, that old serpent, which is the Devil, and Satan, and bound him a thousand years. *Ib.* 2

40 On such the second death hath no power. *Ib.* 6

41 And I saw a great white throne. *Ib.* 11

42 And I saw the dead, small and great, stand before God; and the books were opened. *Ib.* 12

43 And the sea gave up the dead which were in it. *Ib.* 13

44 And I saw a new heaven and a new earth: for the first heaven and the first earth were passed away; and there was no more sea.

And I John saw the holy city, new Jerusalem, coming down from God out of heaven, prepared as a bride adorned for her husband. *Ib.* xxi. 1

45 And God shall wipe away all tears from their eyes; and there shall be no more death, neither sorrow, nor crying, neither shall there be any more pain: and the former things are passed away.

And he that sat upon the throne said, Behold, I make all things new. And he said unto me, Write: for these words are true and faithful. *Ib.* 4

46 I will give unto him that is athirst of the fountain of the water of life freely. *Ib.* 6

47 The city was pure gold, like unto clear glass. *Ib.* 18

1 The first foundation was jasper; the second, sapphire; the third, a chalcedony; the fourth, an emerald;

The fifth, sardonyx; the sixth, sardius; the seventh, chrysolyte; the eighth, beryl; the ninth, a topaz; the tenth, a chrysoprasus; the eleventh, a jacinth; the twelfth, an amethyst.

The Revelation of St. John the Divine xxi. 19

2 The twelve gates were twelve pearls. *Ib.* 21

3 The street of the city was pure gold. *Ib.*

4 And I saw no temple therein. *Ib.* 22

5 And the city had no need of the sun, neither of the moon, to shine in it: for the glory of God did lighten it, and the Lamb is the light thereof. *Ib.* 23

6 And he shewed me a pure river of water of life, clear as crystal, proceeding out of the throne of God and of the Lamb. *Ib.* xxii. 1

7 And the leaves of the tree were for the healing of the nations. *Ib.* 2

8 He that is unjust, let him be unjust still: and he which is filthy, let him be filthy still: and he that is righteous, let him be righteous still: and he that is holy, let him be holy still.

And, behold, I come quickly. *Ib.* 11

9 Whosoever loveth and maketh a lie. *Ib.* 15

10 I am the root and the offspring of David, and the bright and morning star.

And the Spirit and the bride say, Come. And let him that heareth say, Come. And let him that is athirst come. And whosoever will, let him take the water of life freely. *Ib.* 16

11 If any man shall add unto these things, God shall add unto him the plagues that are written in this book. *Ib.* 18

12 God shall take away his part out of the book of life, and out of the holy city, and from the things which are written in this book. *Ib.* 19

13 Amen. Even so, come, Lord Jesus. *Ib.* 20

ISAAC BICKERSTAFFE
1735?–1812?

14 Perhaps it was right to dissemble your love,
But—why did you kick me downstairs?
An Expostulation

15 There was a jolly miller once,
Lived on the river Dee;
He worked and sang from morn till night;
No lark more blithe than he.
Love in a Village, I. v

16 And this the burthen of his song,
For ever us'd to be,
I care for nobody, not I,
If no one cares for me. *Ib.*

17 We all love a pretty girl—under the rose. *Ib.* II. ii

18 In every port he finds a wife.
Thomas and Sally (1761), ii

EDWARD HENRY BICKERSTETH
1825–1906

19 Peace, perfect peace, in this dark world of sin?
The Blood of Jesus whispers peace within.
Songs in the House of Pilgrimage (1875)

ROGER BIGOD,
EARL OF NORFOLK
1245–1306

20 (Edward I: 'By God, earl, you shall either go or hang!')
'O King, I will neither go nor hang!'
Hemingburgh's Chronicle, ii. 121

JOSH BILLINGS
see
HENRY WHEELER SHAW

LAURENCE BINYON
1869–1943

21 Now is the time for the burning of the leaves.
The Burning of the Leaves

22 With proud thanksgiving, a mother for her children,
England mourns for her dead across the sea.
Poems For the Fallen

23 They shall grow not old, as we that are left grow old:
Age shall not weary them, nor the years condemn.
At the going down of the sun and in the morning
We will remember them. *Ib.*

24 That many-memoried name. *Tristram's End*

FREDERICK EDWIN SMITH,
EARL OF BIRKENHEAD
1872–1930

25 The world continues to offer glittering prizes to those who have stout hearts and sharp swords.
Rectorial Address, Glasgow University, 7 Nov. 1923

AUGUSTINE BIRRELL
1850–1933

26 That great dust-heap called 'history'.
Obiter Dicta. Carlyle

27 In the name of the Bodleian. *Ib. Dr. Johnson*

28 What then did happen at the Reformation?
Title of Essay

OTTO VON BISMARCK
1815–1898

29 Die Politik ist keine exakte Wissenschaft.
Politics are not an exact science.
Speech, Prussian Chamber, 18 Dec. 1863

30 Nach Canossa gehen wir nicht.
We will not go to Canossa.
Speech, Reichstag, 14 May 1872

31 Die gesunden Knochen eines einzigen pommerschen Musketiers.
The healthy bones of a single Pomeranian grenadier.
Ib. 5 Dec. 1876

32 Ehrlicher Makler.
An honest broker. *Ib. 19 Feb. 1878*

33 Blut und Eisen.
Blood and iron.
Speech, Prussian House of Deputies, 28 Jan. 1886
(Legt eine möglichst starke militärische Kraft . . . in die Hand des Königs von Preussen, dann wird er die Politik machen können, die Ihr wünscht; mit

Reden und Schützenfesten und Liedern macht sie sich nicht, sie macht sich nur durch Blut und Eisen.

Place in the hands of the King of Prussia the strongest possible military power, then he will be able to carry out the policy you wish; this policy cannot succeed through speeches, and shooting-matches, and songs; it can only be carried out through blood and iron.)

1 I may avail myself of the opportunity of denying once more the truth of the story that Prince Bismarck had ever likened Lord Salisbury to a lath of wood painted to look like iron.

Sidney Whitman, *Personal Reminiscences of Prince Bismarck* (1902), p. 252.

VALENTINE BLACKER
1778–1823

2 'Put your trust in God, my boys, and keep your powder dry.' *Oliver's Advice*

SIR WILLIAM BLACKSTONE
1723–1780

3 Man was formed for society.
Commentaries on the Laws of England, introd. § 2

4 Mankind will not be reasoned out of the feelings of humanity. *Ib.* bk. i. 5

5 The king never dies. *Ib.* 7

6 The royal navy of England hath ever been its greatest defence and ornament; it is its ancient and natural strength; the floating bulwark of the island. *Ib.* 13

7 Time whereof the memory of man runneth not to the contrary. *Ib.* 18

8 That the king can do no wrong, is a necessary and fundamental principle of the English constitution. *Ib.* iii. 17

9 It is better that ten guilty persons escape than one innocent suffer. *Ib.* iv. 27

HELEN SELINA BLACKWOOD, LADY DUFFERIN
1807–1867

10 I'm sitting on the stile, Mary,
Where we sat, side by side.
Lament of the Irish Emigrant

11 The corn was springing fresh and green,
And the lark sang loud and high,
And the red was on your lip, Mary,
The love-light in your eye. *Ib.*

12 They say there's bread and work for all,
And the sun shines always there:
But I'll not forget old Ireland,
Were it fifty times as fair. *Ib.*

ROBERT BLAIR
1699–1746

13 The good he scorn'd
Stalk'd off reluctant, like an ill-us'd ghost,
Not to return; or if it did, its visits
Like those of angels, short, and far between.
The Grave, l. 586

CHARLES DUPEE BLAKE
1846–1903

14 Rock-a-bye-baby on the tree top,
When the wind blows the cradle will rock,
When the bough bends the cradle will fall,
Down comes the baby, cradle and all.
Attr., but see Corrigenda, *p. 587*

WILLIAM BLAKE
1757–1827

15 The errors of a wise man make your rule,
Rather than the perfections of a fool.
On Art and Artists, viii

16 When Sir Joshua Reynolds died
All Nature was degraded:
The King dropped a tear into the Queen's ear,
And all his pictures faded. *Ib.* xxi

17 I understood Christ was a carpenter
And not a brewer's servant, my good Sir. *Ib.* xxvi

18 To see a World in a Grain of Sand,
And a Heaven in a Wild Flower,
Hold Infinity in the palm of your hand,
And Eternity in an hour. *Auguries of Innocence*

19 A Robin Redbreast in a Cage
Puts all Heaven in a Rage. *Ib.*

20 A dog starv'd at his master's gate
Predicts the ruin of the State,
A horse misus'd upon the road
Calls to Heaven for human blood.
Each outcry of the hunted hare
A fibre from the brain does tear,
A skylark wounded in the wing,
A cherubim does cease to sing.

21 The bat that flits at close of eve
Has left the brain that won't believe. *Ib.*

22 He who shall hurt the little wren
Shall never be belov'd by men.
He who the ox to wrath has mov'd
Shall never be by woman lov'd. *Ib.*

23 The caterpillar on the leaf
Repeats to thee thy mother's grief.
Kill not the moth nor butterfly,
For the Last Judgement draweth nigh. *Ib.*

24 A truth that's told with bad intent
Beats all the lies you can invent.
It is right it should be so;
Man was made for Joy and Woe;
And when this we rightly know,
Thro' the World we safely go,
Joy and woe are woven fine,
A clothing for the soul divine. *Ib.*

25 Every tear from every eye
Becomes a babe in Eternity. *Ib.*

26 The bleat, the bark, bellow, and roar
Are waves that beat on Heaven's shore. *Ib.*

27 The strongest poison ever known
Came from Caesar's laurel crown. *Ib.*

28 He who doubts from what he sees
Will ne'er believe, do what you please.
If the Sun and Moon should doubt,
They'd immediately go out.
To be in a passion you good may do,
But no good if a passion is in you.

The whore and gambler, by the state
Licensed, build that nation's fate.
The harlot's cry from street to street
Shall weave old England's winding sheet.
Auguries of Innocence

1 God appears, and God is Light,
To those poor souls who dwell in Night;
But does a Human Form display
To those who dwell in realms of Day. *Ib.*

2 Does the Eagle know what is in the pit
Or wilt thou go ask the Mole?
Can Wisdom be put in a silver rod,
Or Love in a golden bowl?
Book of Thel, Thel's motto.

3 Everything that lives,
Lives not alone, nor for itself. *Ib.* II

4 My brother John, the evil one.
To Thomas Butts. 'With Happiness stretch'd across the Hills', l. 15

5 For double the vision my eyes do see,
And a double vision is always with me.
With my inward eye 'tis an Old Man grey,
With my outward, a Thistle across my way.
Ib. l. 27

6 'What,' it will be questioned, 'when the sun rises, do you not see a round disc of fire somewhat like a guinea?' 'O no, no, I see an innumerable company of the heavenly host crying, "Holy, Holy, Holy is the Lord God Almighty!"'
Descriptive Catalogue, 1810. *The Vision of Judgment*

7 He has observ'd the golden rule,
Till he's become the golden fool.
Miscellaneous Epigrams, ii

8 Wondrous the gods, more wondrous are the men,
More wondrous, wondrous still, the cock and hen,
More wondrous still the table, stool and chair;
But oh! more wondrous still the charming fair.
Ib. xiii. *Imitation of Pope*

9 To Chloe's breast young Cupid slyly stole,
But he crept in at Myra's pocket-hole. *Ib.* xv

10 The Vision of Christ that thou dost see
Is my vision's greatest enemy.
Thine has a great hook nose like thine,
Mine has a snub nose like to mine.
The Everlasting Gospel. a

11 Both read the Bible day and night,
But thou read'st black where I read white. *Ib.*

12 This life's five windows of the soul
Distorts the Heavens from pole to pole,
And leads you to believe a lie
When you see with, not thro', the eye. *Ib.* γ

13 Jesus was sitting in Moses' chair.
They brought the trembling woman there.
Moses commands she be ston'd to death.
What was the sound of Jesus' breath?
He laid His hand on Moses' law;
The ancient Heavens, in silent awe,
Writ with curses from pole to pole,
All away began to roll. *Ib.* ξ

14 I am sure this Jesus will not do,
Either for Englishman or Jew. *Ib. Epilogue*

15 [Of Hayley's birth]
Of H—'s birth this was the happy lot:
His mother on his father him begot.
On Friends and Foes, iv

16 [On Hayley]
To forgive enemies H— does pretend,
Who never in his life forgave a friend,
And when he could not act upon my wife
Hired a villain to bereave my life. *Ib.* v

17 To H[ayley]
Thy friendship oft has made my heart to ache:
Do be my enemy—for friendship's sake. *Ib.* vi

18 On H[ayle]y's Friendship.
When H—y finds out what you cannot do,
That is the very thing he'll set you to. *Ib.* vii

19 [On Cromek]
A petty sneaking knave I knew—
O! Mr. Cr—, how do ye do? *Ib.* xxi

20 [On William Haines]
The Sussex men are noted fools,
And weak is their brain-pan;
I wonder if H— the painter
Is not a Sussex man? *Ib.* xxiii

21 Mutual Forgiveness of each vice,
Such are the Gates of Paradise.
The Gates of Paradise, prologue

22 Truly, my Satan, thou art but a dunce,
And dost not know the garment from the man;
Every harlot was a virgin once,
Nor canst thou ever change Kate into Nan.

Tho' thou art worshipp'd by the names divine
Of Jesus and Jehovah, thou art still
The Son of Morn in weary Night's decline,
The lost traveller's dream under the hill.
Ib. epilogue

23 Great things are done when men and mountains meet;
This is not done by jostling in the street.
Gnomic Verses, i

24 If you have form'd a circle to go into,
Go into it yourself, and see how you would do.
Ib. ii. *To God*

25 Abstinence sows sand all over
The ruddy limbs and flaming hair,
But Desire gratified
Plants fruits of life and beauty there. *Ib.* x

26 The sword sung on the barren heath,
The sickle in the fruitful field:
The sword he sung a song of death,
But could not make the sickle yield. *Ib.* xiv

27 He who bends to himself a Joy
Doth the winged life destroy;
But he who kisses the Joy as it flies
Lives in Eternity's sunrise. *Ib.* xvii. 1

28 What is it men in women do require?
The lineaments of gratified desire.
What is it women do in men require?
The lineaments of gratified desire. *Ib.* xvii. 4

29 Since all the riches of this world
May be gifts from the Devil and earthly kings,
I should suspect that I worshipp'd the Devil
If I thank'd my God for worldly things. *Ib.* xix

1 The Angel that presided o'er my birth
 Said 'Little creature, form'd of joy and mirth,
 Go, love without the help of anything on earth.'
 Gnomic Verses, xxi

2 I must Create a System, or be enslav'd by another
 Man's;
 I will not Reason and Compare: my business is to
 Create. *Jerusalem*, f. 10, l. 20

3 Near mournful
 Ever-weeping Paddington. *Ib.* f. 12, l. 27

4 The fields from Islington to Marybone,
 To Primrose Hill and Saint John's Wood,
 Were builded over with pillars of gold;
 And there Jerusalem's pillars stood. *Ib.* f. 27

5 Pancras and Kentish Town repose
 Among her golden pillars high,
 Among her golden arches which
 Shine upon the starry sky. *Ib.*

6 For a tear is an intellectual thing,
 And a sigh is the sword of an Angel King,
 And the bitter groan of the martyr's woe
 Is an arrow from the Almighty's bow. *Ib.* f. 52

7 He who would do good to another must do it in
 Minute Particulars.
 General Good is the plea of the scoundrel, hypocrite,
 and flatterer;
 For Art and Science cannot exist but in minutely
 organized Particulars. *Ib.* f. 55, l. 54

8 I give you the end of a golden string;
 Only wind it into a ball,
 It will lead you in at Heaven's gate,
 Built in Jerusalem's wall. *Ib.* f. 77

9 O ye Religious, discountenance every one among you
 who shall pretend to despise Art and Science! *Ib.*

10 Let every Christian, as much as in him lies, engage
 himself openly and publicly, before all the World,
 in some mental pursuit for the Building up of
 Jerusalem. *Ib.*

11 England! awake! awake! awake!
 Jerusalem thy sister calls!
 Why wilt thou sleep the sleep of death,
 And close her from thy ancient walls? *Ib.*

12 And now the time returns again:
 Our souls exult, and London's towers
 Receive the Lamb of God to dwell
 In England's green and pleasant bowers. *Ib.*

13 I care not whether a man is Good or Evil; all that I
 care
 Is whether he is a Wise man or a Fool. Go! put off
 Holiness,
 And put on Intellect. *Ib.* f. 91

14 Father, O father! what do we here
 In this land of unbelief and fear?
 The Land of Dreams is better far,
 Above the light of the morning star.
 The Land of Dreams

15 Little Mary Bell had a Fairy in a nut,
 Long John Brown had the Devil in his gut.
 Long John Brown and Little Mary Bell

16 And did those feet in ancient time
 Walk upon England's mountains green?
 And was the holy Lamb of God
 On England's pleasant pastures seen?

And did the Countenance Divine
 Shine forth upon our clouded hills?
 And was Jerusalem builded here
 Among these dark Satanic mills?

Bring me my bow of burning gold!
 Bring me my arrows of desire!
 Bring me my spear! O clouds, unfold!
 Bring me my chariot of fire!

I will not cease from Mental Fight,
 Nor shall my Sword sleep in my hand,
 Till we have built Jerusalem,
 In England's green & pleasant Land.
 Milton, preface

17 Mock on, mock on, Voltaire, Rousseau;
 Mock on, mock on, 'tis all in vain!
 You throw the sand against the wind,
 And the wind blows it back again.
 Mock on, mock on, Voltaire

18 Whether on Ida's shady brow,
 Or in the chambers of the East,
 The chambers of the sun, that now
 From ancient melody have ceas'd;

Whether in Heaven ye wander fair,
 Or the green corners of the earth,
 Or the blue regions of the air
 Where the melodious winds have birth;

Whether on crystal rocks ye rove,
 Beneath the bosom of the sea
 Wand'ring in many a coral grove,
 Fair Nine, forsaking Poetry!

How have you left the ancient love
 That bards of old enjoy'd in you!
 The languid strings do scarcely move!
 The sound is forc'd, the notes are few!
 To the Muses

19 My Spectre around me night and day
 Like a wild beast guards my way;
 My Emanation far within
 Weeps incessantly for my sin.
 My Spectre around Me Night and Day, i

20 And throughout all Eternity
 I forgive you, you forgive me.
 As our dear Redeemer said:
 'This the Wine, and this the Bread.' *Ib.* xiv

21 Never seek to tell thy love,
 Love that never told can be;
 For the gentle wind does move
 Silently, invisibly. *Never Seek to Tell Thy Love*

22 Soon as she was gone from me,
 A traveller came by,
 Silently, invisibly:
 He took her with a sigh. *Ib.*

23 Hear the voice of the Bard!
 Who present, past, and future sees.
 Songs of Experience, introduction

24 Tiger! Tiger! burning bright
 In the forests of the night,
 What immortal hand or eye
 Could frame thy fearful symmetry?

In what distant deeps or skies
 Burnt the fire of thine eyes?
 On what wings dare he aspire?
 What the hand dare seize the fire?

And what shoulder, and what art,
Could twist the sinews of thy heart?
And when thy heart began to beat,
What dread hand? and what dread feet?

What the hammer? What the chain?
In what furnace was thy brain?
What the anvil? what dread grasp
Dare its deadly terrors clasp?

When the stars threw down their spears,
And water'd heaven with their tears,
Did he smile his work to see?
Did he who made the Lamb make thee?

Tiger! Tiger! burning bright
In the forests of the night,
What immortal hand or eye,
Dare frame thy fearful symmetry?
Songs of Experience. The Tiger

1 Children of the future age,
Reading this indignant page,
Know that in a former time,
Love, sweet love, was thought a crime.
Ib. A Little Girl Lost

2 Love seeketh not itself to please,
Nor for itself hath any care,
But for another gives its ease,
And builds a Heaven in Hell's despair.
Ib. The Clod and the Pebble

3 Love seeketh only Self to please,
To bind another to its delight,
Joys in another's loss of ease,
And builds a Hell in Heaven's despite. *Ib.*

4 Then the Parson might preach, and drink, and sing,
And we'd be as happy as birds in the spring;
And modest Dame Lurch, who is always at church,
Would not have bandy children, nor fasting, nor
birch. *Ib. The Little Vagabond*

5 I was angry with my friend
I told my wrath, my wrath did end.
I was angry with my foe:
I told it not, my wrath did grow.
Ib. A Poison Tree

6 Youth of delight, come hither,
And see the opening morn,
Image of truth new-born.
Ib. Voice of the Ancient Bard

7 Ah, Sun-flower! weary of time,
Who countest the steps of the Sun;
Seeking after that sweet golden clime,
Where the traveller's journey is done;

Where the Youth pined away with desire,
And the pale Virgin shrouded in snow,
Arise from their graves and aspire
Where my Sun-flower wishes to go.
Ib. Ah, Sun-Flower!

8 My mother groan'd, my father wept,
Into the dangerous world I leapt;
Helpless, naked, piping loud,
Like a fiend hid in a cloud. *Ib. Infant Sorrow*

9 Piping down the valleys wild,
Piping songs of pleasant glee,
On a cloud I saw a child,
And he laughing said to me:

'Pipe a song about a Lamb!'
So I piped with merry cheer.
'Piper, pipe that song again;'
So I piped: he wept to hear.

'Drop thy pipe, thy happy pipe;
Sing thy songs of happy cheer:'
So I sang the same again,
While he wept with joy to hear.

'Piper, sit thee down and write
In a book, that all may read.'
So he vanish'd from my sight,
And I pluck'd a hollow reed.

And I made a rural pen,
And I stain'd the water clear,
And I wrote my happy songs
Every child may joy to hear.
Songs of Innocence introduction

10 Little Lamb, who made thee?
Dost thou know who made thee?
Gave thee life, and bid thee feed,
By the stream and o'er the mead;
Gave thee clothing of delight,
Softest clothing, woolly, bright;
Gave thee such a tender voice,
Making all the vales rejoice?
Little Lamb, who made thee?
Dost thou know who made thee?

Little Lamb, I'll tell thee,
Little Lamb, I'll tell thee:
He is callèd by thy name,
For He calls Himself a Lamb,
He is meek, and He is mild;
He became a little child.
I a child, and thou a lamb,
We are callèd by His name.
Little Lamb, God bless thee!
Little Lamb, God bless thee! *Ib. The Lamb*

11 How sweet is the Shepherd's sweet lot!
Ib. The Shepherd

12 'I have no name:
I am but two days old.'
What shall I call thee?
'I happy am,
Joy is my name.'
Sweet joy befall thee! *Ib. Infant Joy*

13 My mother bore me in the southern wild,
And I am black, but O! my soul is white;
White as an angel is the English child,
But I am black, as if bereav'd of light.
Ib. The Little Black Boy

14 When the voices of children are heard on the green,
And laughing is heard on the hill. *Ib. Nurse's Song*

15 'Twas on a Holy Thursday, their innocent faces clean,
The children walking two and two, in red and blue
and green. *Ib. Holy Thursday*

16 Then cherish pity, lest you drive an angel from your
door. *Ib.*

17 When my mother died I was very young,
And my father sold me while yet my tongue
Could scarcely cry, ''weep! 'weep! 'weep! 'weep!'
So your chimneys I sweep, and in soot I sleep.
Ib. The Chimney Sweeper

18 To Mercy, Pity, Peace, and Love
All pray in their distress. *Ib. The Divine Image*

[76]

1 For Mercy has a human heart,
  Pity a human face,
  And Love, the human form divine,
  And Peace, the human dress.
          Songs of Innocence. The Divine Image

2 And there the lion's ruddy eyes
  Shall flow with tears of gold,
  And pitying the tender cries,
  And walking round the fold,
  Saying, 'Wrath, by His meekness,
  And, by His health, sickness,
  Is driven away
  From our immortal day.'   *Ib. Night*

3 Can I see another's woe,
  And not be in sorrow too?
  Can I see another's grief,
  And not seek for kind relief?
          Ib. On Another's Sorrow

4 Cruelty has a human heart,
  And Jealousy a human face;
  Terror the human form divine,
  And Secrecy the human dress.
          Appendix to Songs of Innocence and of Experience. A Divine Image

5 Good English hospitality, O then it did not fail!
          Songs from an Island in the Moon, xi

6 Energy is Eternal Delight.
          Marriage of Heaven and Hell: The Voice of the Devil

7 The reason Milton wrote in fetters when he wrote of
  Angels and God, and at liberty when of Devils and
  Hell, is because he was a true Poet, and of the
  Devil's party without knowing it.   *Ib. note*

8 The road of excess leads to the palace of wisdom.
          Ib. Proverbs of Hell

9 Prudence is a rich, ugly, old maid courted by Incapacity.   *Ib.*

10 He who desires but acts not, breeds pestilence.   *Ib.*

11 A fool sees not the same tree that a wise man sees.   *Ib.*

12 Eternity is in love with the productions of time.   *Ib.*

13 Bring out number, weight, and measure in a year of
  dearth.   *Ib.*

14 If the fool would persist in his folly he would become
  wise.   *Ib.*

15 Prisons are built with stones of Law, brothels with
  bricks of Religion.   *Ib.*

16 The pride of the peacock is the glory of God.
  The lust of the goat is the bounty of God.
  The wrath of the lion is the wisdom of God.
  The nakedness of woman is the work of God.   *Ib.*

17 The tigers of wrath are wiser than the horses of instruction.   *Ib.*

18 Damn braces. Bless relaxes.   *Ib.*

19 Sooner murder an infant in its cradle than nurse
  unacted desires.   *Ib.*

20 Truth can never be told so as to be understood, and
  not be believ'd.   *Ib.*

21 Then I asked: 'Does a firm persuasion that a thing is
  so, make it so?'
  He replied: 'All Poets believe that it does, and in ages
  of imagination this firm persuasion removed mountains; but many are not capable of a firm persuasion
  of anything.'   *Ib. A Memorable Fancy*

SUSANNA BLAMIRE
1747–1794

22 And ye shall walk in silk attire,
  And siller ha'e to spare.   *The Siller Crown*

PHILIPP BLISS
1838–1876

23 Hold the fort, for I am coming.
          The Charm. Ho, My Comrades, See the Signal!

ROBERT BLOOMFIELD
1766–1823

24 Strange to the world, he wore a bashful look,
  The Fields his study, Nature was his book.
          Farmer's Boy. Spring, l. 31

HENRY BLOSSOM
1866–1919

25 I want what I want when I want it.
          Title of song in Mlle. Modiste

GEBHARD LEBERECHT BLÜCHER
1742–1819

26 Was für plündern!
  What a place to plunder!
          On his visit to London in 1814. Attributed

EDMUND BLUNDEN
1896–

27 All things they have in common being so poor,
  And their one fear, Death's shadow at the door.
  Each sundown makes them mournful, each sunrise
  Brings back the brightness in their failing eyes.
          Almswomen

28 These were men of pith and thew,
  Whom the city never called;
  Scarce could read or hold a quill,
  Built the barn, the forge, the mill.   *Forefathers*

29 I am for the woods against the world,
  But are the woods for me?   *The Kiss*

30 How shines your tower, the only one
  Of that especial site and stone!
  And even the dream's confusion can
  Sustain to-morrow's road.   *The Survival*

WILFRID SCAWEN BLUNT
1840–1922

31 God! to hear the shrill
  Sweet treble of her fifes upon the breeze,
  And at the summons of the rock gun's roar
  To see her red coats marching from the hill!
          Gibraltar

32 I would not, if I could, be called a poet.
  I have no natural love of the 'chaste muse'.
  If aught be worth the doing I would do it;
  And others, if they will, may tell the news.
          Love Sonnets of Proteus, xcv

33 I like the hunting of the hare
  Better than that of the fox.   *The Old Squire*

34 I like to be as my fathers were,
  In the days ere I was born.   *Ib.*

1 To-day, all day, I rode upon the Down,
With hounds and horsemen, a brave company.
St. Valentine's Day

2 Your face my quarry was. For it I rode,
My horse a thing of wings, myself a god.   *Ib.*

JOHN ERNEST BODE
1816–1874

3 I see the sights that dazzle.
The tempting sounds I hear.
*Hymns from the Gospel for the Day. O Jesus,
I Have Promised*

BOETHIUS
?480–524

4 Nam in omni adversitate fortunae infelicissimum
genus est infortunii, fuisse felicem.

For truly in adverse fortune the worst sting of
misery is to *have been* happy.
Consolation of Philosophy, bk. ii, prose 4 (H. R.
James's translation). (*See 168:22*)

NICOLAS BOILEAU
1636–1711

5 Enfin Malherbe vint, et, le premier en France,
Fit sentir dans les vers une juste cadence.

At last comes Malherbe, and, the first to do so in
France, makes verse run smoothly.
L'Art Poétique, i. 131–2

6 Qu'en un lieu, qu'en un jour, un seul fait accompli
Tienne jusqu'à la fin le théâtre rempli.

One action, in one place, one day perpend
And you will hold your audience till the end.
Ib. iii. 45–6

7 Si j'écris quatre mots, j'en effacerai trois.

Of every four words I write, I strike out three.
Satires, ii

HENRY ST. JOHN, VISCOUNT BOLINGBROKE
1678–1751

8 The Idea of a Patriot King.   *Title of Book*

9 What a world is this, and how does fortune banter us!
Letter, 3 Aug. 1714

10 Pests of society; because their endeavours are
directed to loosen the bands of it, and to take at least
one curb out of the mouth of that wild beast man.
Ib. 12 Sept. 1724

11 Truth lies within a little and certain compass, but
error is immense.   *Reflections upon Exile*

12 They make truth serve as a stalking-horse to error.
On the Study of History, letter 1

13 I have read somewhere or other—in Dionysius of
Halicarnassus, I think—that History is Philosophy
teaching by examples.   *Ib.* letter 2

14 Nations, like men, have their infancy.   *Ib.* letter 4

15 They [Thucydides and Xenophon] maintained the
dignity of history.   *Ib.* letter 5

HORATIUS BONAR
1808–1889

16 A few more years shall roll,
A few more seasons come,
And we shall be with those that rest,
Asleep within the tomb.
Songs for the Wilderness. A Few More Years

CARRIE JACOBS BOND
1862–

17 And we find at the end of a perfect day
The soul of a friend we've made.
A Perfect Day, st. 2

BARTON BOOTH
1681–1733

18 True as the needle to the pole,
Or as the dial to the sun.   *Song*

'GENERAL' WILLIAM BOOTH
1829–1912

19 This Submerged Tenth—is it, then, beyond the reach
of the nine-tenths in the midst of whom they live.
In Darkest England (1890), I. ii. 23

GEORGE BORROW
1803–1881

20 The author of 'Amelia', the most singular genius
which their island ever produced, whose works it
has long been the fashion to abuse in public and to
read in secret.   *The Bible in Spain*, ch. 1

21 My favourite, I might say, my only study, is man.
Ib. ch. 5

22 The genuine spirit of localism.   *Ib.* ch. 31

23 There are no countries in the world less known by
the British than these selfsame British Islands.
Lavengro, preface

24 There's night and day, brother, both sweet things;
sun, moon, and stars, brother, all sweet things;
there's likewise a wind on the heath. Life is very
sweet, brother; who would wish to die? *Ib.* ch. 25

25 There's the wind on the heath, brother; if I could only
feel that, I would gladly live for ever.   *Ib.*

26 Let no one sneer at the bruisers of England. What
were the gladiators of Rome, or the bull-fighters of
Spain, in its palmiest days, compared to England's
bruisers?   *Ib.* ch. 26

27 A losing trade, I assure you, sir: literature is a drug.
Ib. ch. 30

28 Good ale, the true and proper drink of Englishmen.
He is not deserving of the name of Englishman who
speaketh against ale, that is good ale.   *Ib.* ch. 48

29 Youth will be served, every dog has his day, and mine
has been a fine one.   *Ib.* ch. 92

30 Fear God, and take your own part.
The Romany Rye, ch. 16

31 Tip them Long Melford.   *Ib.*

MARÉCHAL BOSQUET
1810–1861

1 C'est magnifique, mais ce n'est pas la guerre.

It is magnificent, but it is not war.
Remark on the Charge of the Light Brigade, 1854

JOHN COLLINS BOSSIDY
1860–1928

2 And this is good old Boston,
   The home of the bean and the cod,
Where the Lowells talk to the Cabots,
   And the Cabots talk only to God.
On the Aristocracy of Harvard

GORDON BOTTOMLEY
1874–1948

3 When you destroy a blade of grass
You poison England at her roots:
Remember no man's foot can pass
Where evermore no green life shoots.
To Ironfounders and Others

BOULAY DE LA MEURTHE
1761–1840

4 C'est pire qu'un crime, c'est une faute.

It is worse than a crime, it is a blunder.
On hearing of the execution of the Duc d'Enghien,
1804

FRANCIS WILLIAM BOURDILLON
1852–1921

5 The night has a thousand eyes,
   And the day but one;
Yet the light of the bright world dies,
   With the dying sun.

The mind has a thousand eyes,
   And the heart but one;
Yet the light of a whole life dies,
   When love is done.   *Light*

W. ST. HILL BOURNE
1846–1929

6 The sower went forth sowing,
   The seed in secret slept.
Church Bells. The Sower Went Forth Sowing

CHARLES, BARON BOWEN
1835–1894

7 The rain it raineth on the just
   And also on the unjust fella:
But chiefly on the just, because
   The unjust steals the just's umbrella.
Walter Sichel, *Sands of Time*

8 *On a metaphysician:* A blind man in a dark room
—looking for a black hat—which isn't there.
Attr. See Notes and Queries, clxxxii. 153

EDWARD ERNEST BOWEN
1836–1901

9 Forty years on, when afar and asunder
Parted are those who are singing to-day.
Forty Years On. Harrow School Song

10 Follow up! Follow up! Follow up! Follow up!
   Follow up!
Till the field ring again and again,
With the tramp of the twenty-two men,
Follow up!   *Ib.*

WILLIAM LISLE BOWLES
1762–1850

11 The cause of Freedom is the cause of God!
Edmund Burke, l. 78

JOHN BRADFORD
1510?–1555

12 But for the grace of God there goes John Bradford.
Exclamation on seeing some criminals taken to
execution. Dict. of Nat. Biog.

F. H. BRADLEY
1846–1924

13 A ballet dance of bloodless categories.   *Logic*

JOHN BRADSHAW
1602–1659

14 Rebellion to tyrants is obedience to God.
Suppositious epitaph. Randall's *Life of Jeffer-*
son, vol. iii, appendix No. IV, p. 585

JOHN BRAHAM
1774?–1856

15 England, home and beauty.
The Americans (1811). Song, *The Death of*
Nelson

HARRY BRAISTED
nineteenth century

16 If you want to win her hand,
   Let the maiden understand
That she's not the only pebble on the beach.
You're Not the Only Pebble on the Beach

REV. JAMES BRAMSTON
1694?–1744

17 What's not destroy'd by Time's devouring hand?
Where's Troy, and where's the Maypole in the
   Strand?   *Art of Politics,* l. 71

RICHARD BRATHWAITE
1588?–1673

18 To Banbury came I, O profane one!
Where I saw a Puritane-one
Hanging of his cat on Monday,
For killing of a mouse on Sunday.
Barnabee's Journal, pt. i

JANE BRERETON

1685–1740

1 The picture plac'd the busts between,
  Adds to the thought much strength,
Wisdom, and wit are little seen,
  But folly's at full length.
    *Poems. On Mr. Nash's Picture at full Length
    between the Busts of Sir Isaac Newton and
    Mr. Pope. (Attr. also to Lord Chesterfield)*

NICHOLAS BRETON

1545?–1626?

2 We rise with the lark and go to bed with the lamb.
    The Court and Country, par. 8

3 I wish my deadly foe, no worse
Than want of friends, and empty purse.
    A Farewell to Town

4 Who can live in heart so glad
As the merry country lad. *The Happy Countryman*

5 A Mad World, My Masters. *Title of Dialogue*, 1635

6 He is as deaf as a door. *Miseries of Mavillia*, v.

7 In the merry month of May,
In a morn by break of day,
Forth I walked by the wood side,
Whenas May was in his pride:
There I spied all alone,
Phillida and Coridon.
Much ado there was, God wot,
He would love, and she would not.

She said never man was true,
He said, none was false to you.
He said, he had lov'd her long,
She said, Love should have no wrong.
Coridon would kiss her then,
She said, Maids must kiss no men,
Till they did for good and all. *Phillida and Coridon*

8 Come little babe, come silly soul,
Thy father's shame, thy mother's grief,
Born as I doubt to all our dole,
And to thy self unhappy chief:
  Sing lullaby and lap it warm,
  Poor soul that thinks no creature harm.
    A Sweet Lullaby

ROBERT BRIDGES

1844–1930

9 All women born are so perverse
No man need boast their love possessing.
    All Women Born Are So Perverse

10 Wanton with long delay the gay spring leaping
  cometh;
The blackthorn starreth now his bough on the eve of
  May. *April 1885*

11 Awake, my heart, to be loved, awake, awake!
    Awake, My Heart, To Be Loved

12 Awake, the land is scattered with light, and see,
Uncanopied sleep is flying from field and tree:
And blossoming boughs of April in laughter shake.
    Ib.

13 Clear and gentle stream!
Known and loved so long. *Clear and Gentle Stream*

14 The cliff-top has a carpet
Of lilac, gold and green:
The blue sky bounds the ocean,
The white clouds scud between. *The Cliff-Top*

15 Above my head the heaven,
The sea beneath my feet. *Ib.*

16 Were I a cloud I'd gather
My skirts up in the air,
And fly I well know whither,
And rest I well know where. *Ib. The Ocean*

17 Wherefore to-night so full of care,
My soul, revolving hopeless strife,
Pointing at hindrance, and the bare
Painful escapes of fitful life? *Dejection*

18 O soul, be patient: thou shalt find
A little matter mend all this;
Some strain of music to thy mind,
Some praise for skill not spent amiss. *Ib.*

19 O bold majestic downs, smooth, fair and lonely;
O still solitude, only matched in the skies.
Perilous in steep places,
Soft in the level races. *The Downs*

20 Gay Robin is seen no more:
He is gone with the snow.
    Gay Robin Is Seen No More

21 The whole world now is but the minister
Of thee to me. *Growth of Love*, 3

22   That old feud
'Twixt things and me is quash'd in our new truce.
    Ib.

23 The very names of things belov'd are dear,
And sounds will gather beauty from their sense,
As many a face thro' love's long residence
Groweth to fair instead of plain and sere. *Ib.* 4

24 Thus may I think the adopting Muses chose
Their sons by name, knowing none would be heard
Or writ so oft in all the world as those,—
Dan Chaucer, mighty Shakespeare, then for third
The classic Milton, and to us arose
Shelley with liquid music in the word. *Ib.*

25 And hither tempt the pilgrim steps of spring. *Ib.* 6

26   Beauty being the best of all we know
Sums up the unsearchable and secret aims
Of nature. *Ib.* 8

27 Winter was not unkind because uncouth;
His prison'd time made me a closer guest,
And gave thy graciousness a warmer zest,
Biting all else with keen and angry tooth. *Ib.* 10

28 There's many a would-be poet at this hour,
Rhymes of a love that he hath never woo'd,
And o'er his lamp-lit desk in solitude
Deems that he sitteth in the Muses' bower. *Ib.* 11

29 Lo, Shakespeare, since thy time nature is loth
To yield to art her fair supremacy;
In conquering one thou hast so enrichèd both.
What shall I say? for God—whose wise decree
Confirmeth all He did by all He doth—
Doubled His whole creation making thee. *Ib.* 21

30 I would be a bird, and straight on wings I arise,
And carry purpose up to the ends of the air. *Ib.* 22

31 The dark and serious angel, who so long
Vex'd his immortal strength in charge of me. *Ib.* 61

1 What make ye and what strive for? keep ye thought
Of us, or in new excellence divine
Is old forgot? or do ye count for nought
What the Greek did and what the Florentine?
Growth of Love, 64

2 Ah heavenly joy! But who hath ever heard,
Who hath seen joy, or who shall ever find
Joy's language? There is neither speech nor word;
Nought but itself to teach it to mankind. *Ib.* 65

3 Eternal Father, who didst all create,
In whom we live, and to whose bosom move,
To all men be Thy name known, which is Love,
Till its loud praises sound at heaven's high gate.
Ib. 69

4 Christ with His lamp of truth
Sitteth upon the hill
Of everlasting youth,
And calls His saints around. *Hymn of Nature*, v

5 Gird on thy sword, O man, thy strength endue,
In fair desire thine earth-born joy renew.
Live thou thy life beneath the making sun
Till Beauty, Truth, and Love in thee are one.
Ib. vii

6 And every eve I say,
Noting my step in bliss,
That I have known no day
In all my life like this. *The Idle Life I Lead*

7 I have loved flowers that fade,
Within whose magic tents
Rich hues have marriage made
With sweet unmemoried scents.
I Have Loved Flowers That Fade

8 I heard a linnet courting
His lady in the spring:
His mates were idly sporting,
Nor stayed to hear him sing
His song of love.—
I fear my speech distorting
His tender love. *I Heard a Linnet Courting*

9 I love all beauteous things,
I seek and adore them;
God hath no better praise,
And man in his hasty days
Is honoured for them.

I too will something make
And joy in the making;
Altho' to-morrow it seem
Like the empty words of a dream
Remembered on waking.
I Love All Beauteous Things

10 I made another song,
In likeness of my love:
And sang it all day long,
Around, beneath, above:
I told my secret out,
That none might be in doubt. *I Made Another Song*

11 I never shall love the snow again
Since Maurice died.
I Never Shall Love the Snow Again

12 I will not let thee go.
Ends all our month-long love in this?
Can it be summed up so,
Quit in a single kiss?
I will not let thee go. *I Will Not Let Thee Go*

13 I will not let thee go.
Had not the great sun seen, I might;
Or were he reckoned slow
To bring the false to light,
Then might I let thee go. *I Will Not Let Thee Go*

14 Thou sayest farewell, and lo!
I have thee by the hands,
And will not let thee go. *Ib.*

15 When men were all asleep the snow came flying,
In large white flakes falling on the city brown,
Stealthily and perpetually settling and loosely lying.
London Snow

16 'O look at the trees!' they cried, 'O look at the trees!'
Ib.

17 My delight and thy delight
Walking, like two angels white,
In the gardens of the night.
My Delight and Thy Delight

18 Beautiful must be the mountains whence ye come,
And bright in the fruitful valleys the streams, where-
from
Ye learn your song:
Where are those starry woods? O might I wander
there,
Among the flowers, which in that heavenly air
Bloom the year long! *Nightingales*

19 Nay, barren are those mountains and spent the
streams:
Our song is the voice of desire, that haunts our
dreams.
A throe of the heart. *Ib.*

20 As night is withdrawn
From these sweet-springing meads and bursting
boughs of May,
Dream, while the innumerable choir of day
Welcome the dawn. *Ib.*

21 Rejoice ye dead, where'er your spirits dwell,
Rejoice that yet on earth your fame is bright,
And that your names, remembered day and night,
Live on the lips of those who love you well.
Ode to Music

22 Perfect little body, without fault or stain on thee,
With promise of strength and manhood full and fair!
On a Dead Child

23 He
Must gather his faith together, and his strength make
stronger. *Ib.*

24 O youth whose hope is high,
Who dost to Truth aspire,
Whether thou live or die,
O look not back nor tire.
O Youth Whose Hope is High

25 If thou canst Death defy,
If thy Faith is entire,
Press onward, for thine eye
Shall see thy heart's desire. *Ib.*

26 Whither, O splendid ship, thy white sails crowding,
Leaning across the bosom of the urgent West,
That fearest nor sea rising, nor sky clouding,
Whither away, fair rover, and what thy quest?
A Passer-By

1 Since to be loved endures,
    To love is wise:
Earth hath no good but yours,
    Brave, joyful eyes:
Earth hath no sin but thine,
    Dull eye of scorn:
O'er thee the sun doth pine
    And angels mourn.   *Since to be Loved Endures*

2 So sweet love seemed that April morn,
When first we kissed beside the thorn,
So strangely sweet, it was not strange
We thought that love could never change.

But I can tell—let truth be told—
That love will change in growing old;
Though day by day is nought to see,
So delicate his motions be.   *So Sweet Love Seemed*

3 I wonder, bathed in joy complete,
How love so young could be so sweet.   *Ib.*

4   Back on budding boughs
Come birds, to court and pair,
    Whose rival amorous vows
Amaze the scented air.   *Spring*, ode i. 1

5 And country life I praise,
And lead, because I find
The philosophic mind
Can take no middle ways.   *Ib.* 7

6 With ecstasies so sweet
As none can even guess,
Who walk not with the feet
Of joy in idleness.   *Ib.* 10

7 Spring goeth all in white,
Crowned with milk-white may:
In fleecy flocks of light
O'er heaven the white clouds stray:

White butterflies in the air;
White daisies prank the ground:
The cherry and hoary pear
Scatter their snow around.   *Spring Goeth All in White*

8 Now will the Orientals make hither in return
Outlandish pilgrimage: their wiseacres have seen
The electric light i' the West, and come to worship.
        The Testament of Beauty, l. 592

9 There is a hill beside the silver Thames,
Shady with birch and beech and odorous pine:
And brilliant underfoot with thousand gems
Steeply the thickets to his floods decline.
        There is a Hill

10 Fight, to be found fighting: nor far away
Deem, nor strange thy doom.
Like this sorrow 'twill come,
And the day will be to-day.   *Weep Not To-Day*

11 When Death to either shall come,—
    I pray it be first to me,—
Be happy as ever at home,
    If so, as I wish, it be.
Possess thy heart, my own;
    And sing to the child on thy knee,
Or read to thyself alone
    The songs that I made for thee.
     When Death to Either Shall Come

12 When first we met we did not guess
That Love would prove so hard a master.
   When First We Met We Did Not Guess

13 When June is come, then all the day
I'll sit with my love in the scented hay:
And watch the sunshot palaces high,
That the white clouds build in the breezy sky.
        When June is Come

14   That
Sheep-worry of Europe. [Napoleon]
        Wintry Delights, l. 121

JOHN BRIGHT
1811–1889

15 My opinion is that the Northern States will manage
somehow to muddle through.
    During the American Civil War. Quoted in Justin
    McCarthy: *Reminiscences* (1899)

16 The knowledge of the ancient languages is mainly a
luxury.   *Letter in* Pall Mall Gaz., 30 Nov. 1886

17 The angel of death has been abroad throughout the
land; you may almost hear the beating of his wings.
    Speech, House of Commons, 23 Feb. 1855

18 I am for 'Peace, retrenchment, and reform', the
watchword of the great Liberal party 30 years ago.
       Ib. Birmingham, 28 Apr. 1859

19 England is the mother of Parliaments.
        Ib. 18 Jan. 1865

20 The right hon. Gentleman . . . has retired into what
may be called his political Cave of Adullam—and he
has called about him every one that was in distress
and every one that was discontented.
      Ib. House of Commons, 13 Mar. 1866

21 This party of two is like the Scotch terrier that was
so covered with hair that you could not tell which
was the head and which was the tail.   *Ib.*

22 Force is not a remedy.   *Ib. Birmingham, 16 Nov. 1880*

ALEXANDER BROME
1620–1666

23 Something there is moves me to love, and I
Do know I love, but know not how, nor why.
        Love's without Reason, v

24 I have been in love, and in debt, and in drink,
This many and many a year.   *The Mad Lover*, l. 1

RICHARD BROME
d. 1652?

25 You rose o' the wrong side to-day.
        The Court-Beggar, Act II

26 I am a gentleman, though spoiled i' the breeding.
The Buzzards are all gentlemen. We came in with
the Conqueror.   *English Moor*, III. ii

J. BROMFIELD
fl. 1840

27   'Tis a very good world we live in,
    To spend, and to lend, and to give in;
But to beg, or to borrow, or ask for our own,
  'Tis the very worst world that ever was known.
    The Gatherer, The Mirror, 12 Sept. 1840

ISAAC HILL BROMLEY
1833–1898

1 Conductor, when you receive a fare,
Punch in the presence of the passenjare!—
Punch, brothers! Punch with care!
Punch in the presence of the passenjare!
Punch, Brother, Punch. N. G. Osborn's *Isaac H. Bromley*

2 John A. Logan is the Head Centre, the Hub, the King Pin, the Main Spring, Mogul, and Mugwump of the final plot.
New York Tribune, 16 Feb. 1877

ANNE BRONTË
1820–1849

3 Oh, I am very weary,
Though tears no longer flow;
My eyes are tired of weeping,
My heart is sick of woe.
Appeal

4 Because the road is rough and long,
Shall we despise the skylark's song?
Views of Life

CHARLOTTE BRONTË
1816–1855

5 Reader, I married him.
Jane Eyre, ch. 38

6 Alfred and I intended to be married in this way almost from the first; we never meant to be spliced in the humdrum way of other people.
Villette, ch. 42

EMILY BRONTË
1818–1848

7 No coward soul is mine,
No trembler in the world's storm-troubled sphere:
I see Heaven's glories shine,
And faith shines equal, arming me from fear.
Last Lines

8 O God within my breast,
Almighty! ever-present Deity!
Life—that in me has rest,
As I—undying Life—have power in Thee!
Ib.

9 Vain are the thousand creeds
That move men's hearts: unutterably vain;
Worthless as withered weeds,
Or idlest froth amid the boundless main.
Ib.

10 So surely anchor'd on
The steadfast rock of immortality.
Ib.

11 Though earth and man were gone,
And suns and universes ceased to be,
And Thou wert left alone,
Every existence would exist in Thee.
Ib.

12 There is not room for Death,
Nor atom that his might could render void:
Thou—THOU art Being and Breath,
And what THOU art may never be destroy'd.
Ib.

13 Oh! dreadful is the check—intense the agony—
When the ear begins to hear, and the eye begins to see;
When the pulse begins to throb, the brain to think again;
The soul to feel the flesh, and the flesh to feel the chain.
The Prisoner

14 Cold in the earth—and fifteen wild Decembers,
From those brown hills, have melted into spring.
Remembrance

15 I lingered round them, under that benign sky: watched the moths fluttering among the heath and hare-bells; listened to the soft wind breathing through the grass; and wondered how any one could ever imagine unquiet slumbers for the sleepers in that quiet earth.
Wuthering Heights. Last Words

HENRY BROOKE
1703?–1783

16 For righteous monarchs,
Justly to judge, with their own eyes should see;
To rule o'er freemen, should themselves be free.
Earl of Essex, 1

RUPERT BROOKE
1887–1915

17 The hawthorn hedge puts forth its buds,
And my heart puts forth its pain.
All Suddenly the Spring Comes Soft

18 And I shall find some girl perhaps,
And a better one than you,
With eyes as wise, but kindlier,
And lips as soft, but true.
And I daresay she will do.
The Chilterns

19 Blow out, you bugles, over the rich Dead!
There's none of these so lonely and poor of old,
But, dying, has made us rarer gifts than gold.
These laid the world away; poured out the red
Sweet wine of youth; gave up the years to be
Of work and joy, and that unhoped serene,
That men call age; and those who would have been,
Their sons, they gave, their immortality.
The Dead

20 Honour has come back, as a king, to earth,
And paid his subjects with a royal wage;
And Nobleness walks in our ways again;
And we have come into our heritage.
Ib.

21 The cool kindliness of sheets, that soon
Smooth away trouble; and the rough male kiss of blankets.
The Great Lover

22 The benison of hot water.
Ib.

23 Fish say, they have their stream and pond;
But is there anything beyond?
Heaven

24 One may not doubt that, somehow, good
Shall come of water and of mud;
And, sure, the reverent eye must see
A purpose in liquidity.
Ib.

25 But somewhere, beyond space and time,
Is wetter water, slimier slime!
Ib.

26 Immense, of fishy form and mind,
Squamous, omnipotent, and kind;
And under that Almighty Fin,
The littlest fish may enter in.
Ib.

27 Oh! never fly conceals a hook,
Fish say, in the Eternal Brook,
But more than mundane weeds are there,
And mud, celestially fair.
Ib.

1 Unfading moths, immortal flies,
And the worm that never dies.
And in that Heaven of all their wish,
There shall be no more land, say fish. *Heaven*

2 Breathless, we flung us on the windy hill,
Laughed in the sun, and kissed the lovely grass.
The Hill

3 'We are Earth's best, that learnt her lesson here.
Life is our cry. We have kept the faith!' we said;
'We shall go down with unreluctant tread
Rose-crowned into the darkness!' *Ib.*

4 —And then you suddenly cried, and turned away.
Ib.

5 With snuffle and sniff and handkerchief,
And dim and decorous mirth,
With ham and sherry, they'll meet to bury
The lordliest lass of earth.
Lines Written in the Belief that the Ancient Roman Festival of the Dead was called Ambarvalia

6 Spend in pure converse our eternal day;
Think each in each, immediately wise;
Learn all we lacked before; hear, know, and say
What this tumultuous body now denies;
And feel, who have laid our groping hands away;
And see, no longer blinded by our eyes.
Not With Vain Tears

7 Oh! Death will find me, long before I tire
Of watching you; and swing me suddenly
Into the shade and loneliness and mire
Of the last land! *Oh! Death Will Find Me*

8 Oh! there the chestnuts, summer through,
Beside the river make for you
A tunnel of green gloom, and sleep
Deeply above. *The Old Vicarage, Grantchester*

9 Here tulips bloom as they are told;
Unkempt about those hedges blows
An English unofficial rose. *Ib.*

10 And there the unregulated sun
Slopes down to rest when day is done,
And wakes a vague unpunctual star,
A slippered Hesper. *Ib.*

11 Curates, long dust, will come and go
On lissom, clerical, printless toe;
And oft between the boughs is seen
The sly shade of a Rural Dean. *Ib.*

12 God! I will pack, and take a train,
And get me to England once again!
For England's the one land, I know,
Where men with splendid hearts may go;
And Cambridgeshire, of all England,
The shire for men who understand;
And of *that* district I prefer
The lovely hamlet Grantchester. *Ib.*

13 For Cambridge people rarely smile,
Being urban, squat, and packed with guile. *Ib.*

14 They love the Good; they worship Truth;
They laugh uproariously in youth;
(And when they get to feeling old,
They up and shoot themselves, I'm told.) *Ib.*

15 Stands the Church clock at ten to three?
And is there honey still for tea? *Ib.*

16 Now, God be thanked Who has matched us with His hour,
And caught our youth, and wakened us from sleeping.
Peace

17 Leave the sick hearts that honour could not move,
And half-men, and their dirty songs and dreary,
And all the little emptiness of love. *Ib.*

18 Naught broken save this body, lost but breath;
Nothing to shake the laughing heart's long peace there
But only agony, and that has ending;
And the worst friend and enemy is but Death. *Ib.*

19   Safe shall be my going,
Secretly armed against all death's endeavour;
Safe though all safety's lost; safe where men fall;
And if these poor limbs die, safest of all. *Safety*

20 Some white tremendous daybreak. *Second Best*

21 If I should die, think only this of me:
That there's some corner of a foreign field
That is for ever England. There shall be
In that rich earth a richer dust concealed;
A dust whom England bore, shaped, made aware,
Gave, once, her flowers to love, her ways to roam,
A body of England's, breathing English air,
Washed by the rivers, blest by suns of home.
And think, this heart, all evil shed away,
A pulse in the eternal mind, no less
Gives somewhere back the thoughts by England given.
Her sights and sounds; dreams happy as her day;
And laughter, learnt of friends; and gentleness,
In hearts at peace, under an English heaven.
The Soldier

22 But there's wisdom in women, of more than they have known,
And thoughts go blowing through them, are wiser than their own. *There's Wisdom in Women*

23 And there's an end, I think, of kissing,
When our mouths are one with Mouth.
Tiare Tahiti

PHILLIPS BROOKS
1835–1893

24 O little town of Bethlehem,
How still we see thee lie;
Above thy deep and dreamless sleep
The silent stars go by.
The Church Porch. O Little Town of Bethlehem

25 Yet in the dark streets shineth
The everlasting light;
The hopes and fears of all the years
Are met in thee to-night. *Ib.*

THOMAS BROOKS
1608–1680

26 For (magna est veritas et prævalebit) great is truth, and shall prevail.
The Crown and Glory of Christianity (1662), p. 407

ROBERT BARNABAS BROUGH
1828–1860

27 My Lord Tomnoddy is thirty-four;
The Earl can last but a few years more.

My Lord in the Peers will take his place:
Her Majesty's councils his words will grace.
Office he'll hold and patronage sway;
Fortunes and lives he will vote away;
And what are his qualifications?—ONE!
He's the Earl of Fitzdotterel's eldest son.
My Lord Tomnoddy

HENRY, BARON BROUGHAM
1778–1868

1 In my mind, he was guilty of no error,—he was chargeable with no exaggeration,—he was betrayed by his fancy into no metaphor, who once said, that all we see about us, Kings, Lords, and Commons, the whole machinery of the State, all the apparatus of the system, and its varied workings, end in simply bringing twelve good men into a box.
Speech on the Present State of the Law, 7 Feb. 1828, p. 5

2 Look out, gentlemen, the schoolmaster is abroad!
Attr. to Speech, London Mechanics' Institute, 1825

3 Education makes a people easy to lead, but difficult to drive; easy to govern, but impossible to enslave.
Attr.

JOHN BROWN
1715–1766

4 Truth's sacred Fort th' exploded laugh shall win;
And Coxcombs vanquish Berkley by a grin.
Essay on Satire. On the Death of Pope, l. 223

5 Altogether upon the high horse.
Letter to Garrick, 27 Oct. 1765. Correspondence of Garrick (1831), vol. i, p. 205

JOHN BROWN
1800–1859

6 I, John Brown, am now quite certain that the crimes of this guilty land will never be purged away but with blood.
Last Statement, 2 Dec. 1859. R. J. Hinton, John Brown and His Men

JOHN BROWN
1810–1882

7 'Dish or no dish', rejoined the Caledonian [to an Englishman,] 'there's a deal of fine confused feedin' about it, [a singed sheep's-head,] let me tell you.'
Horae Subsecivae ('With brains, Sir')

THOMAS BROWN
1663–1704

8 In the reign of King Charles the Second, a certain worthy Divine at Whitehall, thus address'd himself to the auditory at the conclusion of his sermon: 'In short, if you don't live up to the precepts of the Gospel, but abandon your selves to your irregular appetites, you must expect to receive your reward in a certain place, which 'tis not good manners to mention here.'
Laconics

9 A little before you made a leap into the dark.
Letters from the Dead

10 I do not love you, Dr. Fell,
But why I cannot tell;
But this I know full well,
I do not love you, Dr. Fell.
(trans. of *Martial, Epigrams*, i. 32.) *Works* (1719), vol. iv, p. 113

THOMAS EDWARD BROWN
1830–1897

11 O blackbird, what a boy you are!
How you do go it. *The Blackbird*

12 A garden is a lovesome thing, God wot!
My Garden

13 Not God! in gardens! when the eve is cool?
Nay, but I have a sign;
'Tis very sure God walks in mine. *Ib.*

CHARLES FARRAR BROWNE
see
ARTEMUS WARD

SIR THOMAS BROWNE
1605–1682

14 He who discommendeth others obliquely commendeth himself. *Christian Morals, pt. i, § xxxiv*

15 That unextinguishable laugh in heaven.
The Garden of Cyrus, ch. 2

16 Life itself is but the shadow of death, and souls departed but the shadows of the living. All things fall under this name. The sun itself is but the dark *simulacrum*, and light but the shadow of God.
Ib. ch. 4

17 Flat and flexible truths are beat out by every hammer; but Vulcan and his whole forge sweat to work out Achilles his armour. *Ib. ch. 5*

18 But the quincunx of heaven runs low, and 'tis time to close the five ports of knowledge. *Ib.*

19 All things began in order, so shall they end, and so shall they begin again; according to the ordainer of order and mystical mathematics of the city of heaven. *Ib.*

20 Nor will the sweetest delight of gardens afford much comfort in sleep; wherein the dullness of that sense shakes hands with delectable odours; and though in the bed of Cleopatra, can hardly with any delight raise up the ghost of a rose. *Ib.*

21 Though Somnus in Homer be sent to rouse up Agamemnon, I find no such effects in these drowsy approaches of sleep. To keep our eyes open longer were but to act our Antipodes. The huntsmen are up in America, and they are already past their first sleep in Persia. But who can be drowsy at that hour which freed us from everlasting sleep? or have slumbering thoughts at that time, when sleep itself must end, and, as some conjecture, all shall awake again? *Ib.*

22 Dreams out of the ivory gate, and visions before midnight. *On Dreams (Works* [1835], vol. iv, p. 359)

23 Half our days we pass in the shadow of the earth; and the brother of death exacteth a third part of our lives. *Ib.*

1 I dare, without usurpation, assume the honourable style of a Christian. *Religio Medici*, pt. i, § 1

2 At my devotion I love to use the civility of my knee, my hat, and hand. *Ib.* § 3

3 I could never divide my self from any man upon the difference of an opinion, or be angry with his judgment for not agreeing with me in that, from which perhaps within a few days I should dissent my self. *Ib.* § 6

4 Many . . . have too rashly charged the troops of error, and remain as trophies unto the enemies of truth. *Ib.*

5 A man may be in as just possession of truth as of a city, and yet be forced to surrender. *Ib.*

6 Methinks there be not impossibilities enough in Religion for an active faith. *Ib.* § 9

7 As for those wingy mysteries in divinity, and airy subtleties in religion, which have unhinged the brains of better heads, they never stretched the *pia mater* of mine. *Ib.*

8 I love to lose myself in a mystery; to pursue my reason to an *O altitudo!* *Ib.* § 10

9 Who can speak of eternity without a solecism, or think thereof without an ecstasy? Time we may comprehend, 'tis but five days elder than ourselves. *Ib.* § 11

10 I have often admired the mystical way of Pythagoras, and the secret magic of numbers. *Ib.* § 12

11 We carry within us the wonders we seek without us: There is all Africa and her prodigies in us. *Ib.* § 15

12 All things are artificial, for nature is the art of God. *Ib.* § 16

13 'Twill be hard to find one that deserves to carry the buckler unto Samson. *Ib.* § 21

14 Obstinacy in a bad cause, is but constancy in a good. *Ib.* § 25

15 Persecution is a bad and indirect way to plant religion. *Ib.*

16 There are many (questionless) canonized on earth, that shall never be Saints in Heaven. *Ib.* § 26

17 Not pickt from the leaves of any author, but bred amongst the weeds and tares of mine own brain. *Ib.* § 35

18 This reasonable moderator and equal piece of justice, Death. *Ib.* § 37

19 I am not so much afraid of death, as ashamed thereof; 'tis the very disgrace and ignominy of our natures. *Ib.* § 39

20 Certainly there is no happiness within this circle of flesh, nor is it in the optics of these eyes to behold felicity; the first day of our Jubilee is death. *Ib.* § 43

21 I have tried if I could reach that great resolution . . . to be honest without a thought of Heaven or Hell. *Ib.* § 46

22 To believe only possibilities, is not faith, but mere Philosophy. *Ib.*

23 There is no road or ready way to virtue. *Ib.* § 53

24 My desires only are, and I shall be happy therein, to be but the last man, and bring up the rear in heaven. *Religio Medici*, pt. i, § 57

25 I am of a constitution so general, that it consorts and sympathiseth with all things. I have no antipathy, or rather idiosyncrasy, in diet, humour, air, any thing. *Ib.* pt. ii, § 1

26 If there be any among those common objects of hatred I do contemn and laugh at, it is that great enemy of reason, virtue, and religion, the multitude; that numerous piece of monstrosity, which, taken asunder, seem men, and the reasonable creatures of God, but, confused together, make but one great beast, and a monstrosity more prodigious than Hydra. *Ib.*

27 I feel not in myself those common antipathies that I can discover in others; those national repugnances do not touch me, nor do I behold with prejudice the French, Italian, Spaniard, or Dutch; but where I find their actions in balance with my countrymen's, I honour, love and embrace them in the same degree. *Ib.*

28 All places, all airs make unto me one country; I am in England, everywhere, and under any meridian. *Ib.*

29 It is the common wonder of all men, how among so many millions of faces, there should be none alike. *Ib.* § 2

30 No man can justly censure or condemn another, because indeed no man truly knows another. *Ib.* § 4

31 Charity begins at home, is the voice of the world. *Ib.*

32 Sure there is music even in the beauty, and the silent note which Cupid strikes, far sweeter than the sound of an instrument. For there is a music wherever there is a harmony, order or proportion; and thus far we may maintain the music of the spheres; for those well ordered motions, and regular paces, though they give no sound unto the ear, yet to the understanding they strike a note most full of harmony. *Ib.* § 9

33 For even that vulgar and tavern music, which makes one man merry, another mad, strikes in me a deep fit of devotion, and a profound contemplation of the first Composer, there is something in it of divinity more than the ear discovers. *Ib.*

34 I could be content that we might procreate like trees, without conjunction, or that there were any way to perpetuate the World without this trivial and vulgar way of coition: it is the foolishest act a wise man commits in all his life; nor is there any thing that will more deject his cool'd imagination, when he shall consider what an odd and unworthy piece of folly he hath committed. *Ib.*

35 We all labour against our own cure, for death is the cure of all diseases. *Ib.*

36 For the world, I count it not an inn, but an hospital, and a place, not to live, but to die in. *Ib.* § 12

37 There is surely a piece of divinity in us, something that was before the elements, and owes no homage unto the sun. *Ib.*

38 [Sleep is] in fine, so like death, I dare not trust it without my prayers. *Ib.* § 13

1 Sleep is a death, O make me try,
By sleeping what it is to die.
And as gently lay my head
On my grave, as now my bed. *Religio Medici*, pt. ii, § 31

2 Conclude in a moist relentment. *Urn Burial*, ch. 1

3 With rich flames, and hired tears, they solemnized
their obsequies. *Ib.* ch. 3

4 Hercules is not only known by his foot. *Ib.*

5 Men have lost their reason in nothing so much as their
religion, wherein stones and clouts make martyrs.
Ib. ch. 4

6 They carried them out of the world with their feet
forward. *Ib.*

7 Were the happiness of the next world as closely
apprehended as the felicities of this, it were a
martyrdom to live. *Ib.*

8 These dead bones have . . . quietly rested under the
drums and tramplings of three conquests. *Ib.* ch. 5

9 Time, which antiquates antiquities, and hath an art
to make dust of all things, hath yet spared these
minor monuments. *Ib.*

10 The long habit of living indisposeth us for dying. *Ib.*

11 Misery makes Alcmena's nights. *Ib.*

12 What song the Syrens sang, or what name Achilles
assumed when he hid himself among women,
though puzzling questions, are not beyond all
conjecture. *Ib.*

13 Circles and right lines limit and close all bodies, and
the mortal right-lined circle, must conclude and
shut up all. *Ib.*

14 Old families last not three oaks. *Ib.*

15 To be nameless in worthy deeds exceeds an infamous
history. *Ib.*

16 But the iniquity of oblivion blindly scattereth her
poppy, and deals with the memory of men without
distinction to merit of perpetuity. *Ib.*

17 Herostratus lives that burnt the Temple of Diana—
he is almost lost that built it. *Ib.*

18 The night of time far surpasseth the day, and who
knows when was the equinox? *Ib.*

19 Mummy is become merchandise, Mizraim cures
wounds, and Pharaoh is sold for balsams. *Ib.*

20 Man is a noble animal, splendid in ashes, and pom-
pous in the grave. *Ib.*

21 Ready to be any thing, in the ecstasy of being ever,
and as content with six foot as the *moles* of Adrianus.
Ib.

WILLIAM BROWNE
1591–1643

22 And all the former causes of her moan
Did therewith bury in oblivion.
Britannia's Pastorals, bk. i, Song 2

23 Well languag'd Daniel. *Ib.* bk. ii, Song 2

24 Underneath this sable hearse
Lies the subject of all verse,
Sidney's sister, Pembroke's mother;
Death! ere thou hast slain another,
Fair and learn'd, and good as she,
Time shall throw a dart at thee.
Epitaph. On the Countess of Pembroke

25 May! Be thou never grac'd with birds that sing,
Nor Flora's pride!
In thee all flowers and roses spring,
Mine only died. *In Obitum M.S. x°. Maij*

SIR WILLIAM BROWNE
1692–1774

26 The King to Oxford sent a troop of horse,
For Tories own no argument but force:
With equal skill to Cambridge books he sent,
For Whigs admit no force but argument.
Reply to Trapp's epigram 'The King, observing
with judicious eyes' (*see* 548:20)
Nichols' Literary Anecdotes, vol. ii, p. 330

ELIZABETH BARRETT BROWNING
1806–1861

27 Here's God down on us! what are you about?
How all those workers start amid their work,
Look round, look up, and feel, a moment's space,
That carpet-dusting, though a pretty trade,
Is not the imperative labour after all.
Aurora Leigh, bk. i

28 Near all the birds
Will sing at dawn,—and yet we do not take
The chaffering swallow for the holy lark. *Ib.*

29 God answers sharp and sudden on some prayers,
And thrusts the thing we have prayed for in our face,
A gauntlet with a gift in't. *Ib.* bk. ii

30 The music soars within the little lark,
And the lark soars. *Ib.* bk. iii

31 I think it frets the saints in heaven to see
How many desolate creatures on the earth
Have learnt the simple dues of fellowship
And social comfort, in a hospital. *Ib.*

32 Now may the good God pardon all good men!
Ib. bk. iv

33 Since when was genius found respectable? *Ib.* bk. vi

34 The devil's most devilish when respectable.
Ib. bk. vii

35 Earth's crammed with heaven,
And every common bush afire with God;
But only he who sees, takes off his shoes,
The rest sit round it and pluck blackberries,
And daub their natural faces unaware
More and more from the first similitude. *Ib.*

36 'Jasper first,' I said,
'And second sapphire; third chalcedony;
The rest in order,—last an amethyst.' *Ib.* bk. ix

37 Speak low to me, my Saviour, low and sweet
From out the hallelujahs, sweet and low,
Lest I should fear and fall, and miss Thee so
Who art not missed by any that entreat. *Comfort*

38 O poets, from a maniac's tongue was poured the
deathless singing!
O Christians, at your cross of hope, a hopeless hand
was clinging!
O men, this man in brotherhood your weary paths
beguiling,
Groaned inly while he taught you peace, and died
while ye were smiling. *Cowper's Grave*

39 And kings crept out again to feel the sun.
Crowned and Buried

1 Do ye hear the children weeping, O my brothers,
Ere the sorrow comes with years?
The Cry of the Children

2 But the young, young children, O my brothers,
They are weeping bitterly!
They are weeping in the playtime of the others,
In the country of the free. *Ib.*

3 And lips say, 'God be pitiful,'
Who ne'er said, 'God be praised.'
Cry of the Human

4 And that dismal cry rose slowly
And sank slowly through the air,
Full of spirit's melancholy
And eternity's despair!
And they heard the words it said—
Pan is dead! great Pan is dead!
Pan, Pan is dead! *The Dead Pan*

5 Oh, the little birds sang east, and the little birds sang
west, *Toll slowly*.
And I smiled to think God's greatness flowed around
our incompleteness,—
Round our restlessness, His rest.
Rime of the Duchess May, last stanza

6 Thou large-brained woman and large-hearted man.
To George Sand. A Desire

7 Or from Browning some 'Pomegranate', which, if
cut deep down the middle,
Shows a heart within blood-tinctured, of a veined
humanity. *Lady Geraldine's Courtship*, xli

8 By thunders of white silence, overthrown.
Hiram Power's Greek Slave

9 'Yes,' I answered you last night;
'No,' this morning, sir, I say.
Colours seen by candle-light
Will not look the same by day. *The Lady's Yes*

10 In the pleasant orchard closes,
'God bless all our gains,' say we;
But 'May God bless all our losses,'
Better suits with our degree. *The Lost Bower*

11 What was he doing, the great god Pan,
Down in the reeds by the river?
Spreading ruin and scattering ban,
Splashing and paddling with hoofs of a goat,
And breaking the golden lilies afloat
With the dragon-fly on the river.
A Musical Instrument

12 Yet half a beast is the great god Pan,
To laugh as he sits by the river,
Making a poet out of a man:
The true gods sigh for the cost and pain,—
For the reed which grows nevermore again
As a reed with the reeds in the river. *Ib.*

13 And her smile, it seems half holy,
As if drawn from thoughts more far
Than our common jestings are.

And if any poet knew her,
He would sing of her with falls
Used in lovely madrigals. *A Portrait*

14 God keeps a niche
In Heaven, to hold our idols: and albeit
He brake them to our faces, and denied
That our close kisses should impair their white,—

I know we shall behold them raised, complete,
The dust swept from their beauty,—glorified,
New Memnons singing in the great God-light.
Sonnets. Futurity

15 I tell you, hopeless grief is passionless.
Sonnets. Grief

16 Straightway I was 'ware,
So weeping, how a mystic shape did move
Behind me, and drew me backward by the hair
And a voice said in mastery while I strove, . . .
'Guess now who holds thee?'—'Death', I said, but
there
The silver answer rang, . . . 'Not Death, but Love.'
Sonnets from the Portuguese, 1

17 The face of all the world is changed, I think,
Since first I heard the footsteps of thy soul
Move still, oh, still, beside me, as they stole
Betwixt me and the dreadful outer brink
Of obvious death, where I, who thought to sink,
Was caught up into love, and taught the whole
Of a new rhythm. *Ib.* 7

18 If thou must love me, let it be for naught
Except for love's sake only. *Ib.* 14

19 When our two souls stand up erect and strong
Face to face, silent, drawing nigh and nigher. *Ib.* 22

20 Let us stay
Rather on earth, Beloved—where the unfit
Contrarious moods of men recoil away
And isolate pure spirits, and permit
A place to stand and love in for a day,
With darkness and the death-hour rounding it. *Ib.*

21 God's gifts put man's best dreams to shame. *Ib.* 26

22 First time he kissed me, he but only kissed
The fingers of this hand wherewith I write;
And, ever since, it grew more clean and white. *Ib.* 38

23 And think it soon when others cry, 'Too late'. *Ib.* 40

24 How do I love thee? Let me count the ways.
I love thee to the depth and breadth and height
My soul can reach, when feeling out of sight
For the ends of Being and ideal Grace.
I love thee to the level of every day's
Most quiet need, by sun and candle light.
I love thee freely, as men strive for Right;
I love thee purely, as they turn from Praise.
I love thee with the passion put to use
In my old griefs, and with my childhood's faith.
I love thee with a love I seemed to lose
With my lost saints—I love thee with the breath,
Smiles, tears, of all my life!—and, if God choose,
I shall but love thee better after death. *Ib.* 43

25 Of all the thoughts of God that are
Borne inward unto souls afar,
Along the Psalmist's music deep,
Now tell me if that any is,
For gift or grace, surpassing this—
'He giveth His beloved, sleep.' *The Sleep*

26 O earth, so full of dreary noises!
O men, with wailing in your voices!
O delvèd gold, the wailers heap!
O strife, O curse, that o'er it fall!
God strikes a silence through you all,
And giveth His belovèd, sleep. *Ib.*

1 Let One, most loving of you all,
  Say, 'Not a tear must o'er her fall;
  He giveth His belovèd, sleep.' *The Sleep*

2 There Shakespeare, on whose forehead climb
  The crowns o' the world. Oh, eyes sublime,
  With tears and laughters for all time!
  A Vision of Poets, verse 100

3 Life treads on life, and heart on heart:
  We press too close in church and mart
  To keep a dream or grave apart. *Ib.* (conclusion)

4 Knowledge by suffering entereth;
  And Life is perfected by Death. *Ib.*

5 And the rolling anapaestic
  Curled like vapour over shrines!
  Wine of Cyprus, x

6 Our Euripides, the human,
  With his droppings of warm tears,
  And his touches of things common
  Till they rose to touch the spheres! *Ib.* xii

ROBERT BROWNING
1812–1889

7 Burrow awhile and build, broad on the roots of things.
  Abt Vogler, ii

8 On the earth the broken arcs; in the heaven, a perfect
  round. *Ib.* ix

9 All we have willed or hoped or dreamed of good shall
  exist. *Ib.* x

10 The high that proved too high, the heroic for earth too
  hard,
  The passion that left the ground to lose itself in the
  sky,
  Are music sent up to God by the lover and the bard;
  Enough that he heard it once: we shall hear it by and
  by. *Ib.*

11 But God has a few of us whom he whispers in the
  ear;
  The rest may reason and welcome; 'tis we musicians
  know. *Ib.* xi

12 The C Major of this life. *Ib.* xii

13 How he lies in his rights of a man!
  Death has done all death can. *After*

14 So free we seem, so fettered fast we are!
  Andrea del Sarto

15 Ah, but a man's reach should exceed his grasp,
  Or what's a heaven for? *Ib.*

16 Four great walls in the New Jerusalem,
  Meted on each side by the angel's reed,
  For Leonard, Rafael, Agnolo and me
  To cover. *Ib.*

17 Again the Cousin's whistle! Go, my Love. *Ib.*

18 It all comes to the same thing at the end.
  Any Wife to Any Husband

19 Why need the other women know so much? *Ib.*

20 A minute's success pays the failure of years.
  Apollo and the Fates, prologue

21 The Doric little Morgue! *Apparent Failure*

22 It's wiser being good than bad;
  It's safer being meek than fierce:
  It's fitter being sane than mad.
  My own hope is, a sun will pierce

The thickest cloud earth ever stretched;
  That, after Last, returns the First,
  Though a wide compass round be fetched;
  That what began best can't end worst,
  Nor what God blessed once, prove accurst.
  Apparent Failure

23 But, thanks to wine-lees and democracy,
  We've still our stage where truth calls spade a spade!
  Aristophanes' Apology, l. 392

24 He lies now in the little valley, laughed
  And moaned about by those mysterious streams.
  Ib. l. 5679

25 There up spoke a brisk little somebody,
  Critic and whippersnapper, in a rage
  To set things right.
  Balaustion's Adventure, pt. i, l. 308

26 A man can have but one life and one death,
  One heaven, one hell. *In a Balcony*, l. 13

27 I count life just a stuff
  To try the soul's strength on. *Ib.* l. 651

28 Truth that peeps
  Over the glass's edge when dinner's done,
  And body gets its sop and holds its noise
  And leaves soul free a little.
  Bishop Blougram's Apology

29 A piano-forte is a fine resource,
  All Balzac's novels occupy one shelf,
  The new edition fifty volumes long. *Ib.*

30 The funny type
  They get up well at Leipsic. *Ib.*

31 Just when we're safest, there's a sunset-touch,
  A fancy from a flower-bell, some one's death,
  A chorus-ending from Euripides,
  And that's enough for fifty hopes and fears,—
  The grand Perhaps. *Ib.*

32 All we have gained then by our unbelief
  Is a life of doubt diversified by faith,
  For one of faith diversified by doubt:
  We called the chess-board white—we call it black. *Ib.*

33 Demireps
  That love and save their souls in new French books.
  Ib.

34 You, for example, clever to a fault,
  The rough and ready man that write apace,
  Read somewhat seldomer, think perhaps even less.
  Ib.

35 Be a Napoleon and yet disbelieve!
  Why, the man's mad, friend, take his light away. *Ib.*

36 And that's what all the blessed Evil's for. *Ib.*

37 Set you square with Genesis again. *Ib.*

38 No, when the fight begins within himself,
  A man's worth something. *Ib.*

39 Gigadibs the literary man. *Ib.*

40 He said true things, but called them by wrong names.
  Ib.

41 By this time he has tested his first plough,
  And studied his last chapter of St. John. *Ib.*

42 Saint Praxed's ever was the church for peace.
  The Bishop Orders His Tomb

43 Mistresses with great smooth marbly limbs. *Ib.*

44 See God made and eaten all day long. *Ib.*

45 Good, strong, thick, stupefying incense-smoke. *Ib.*

1 Aha, ELUCESCEBAT quoth our friend?
No Tully, said I, Ulpian at the best.
The Bishop Orders His Tomb

2 There's a woman like a dew-drop, she's so purer than
the purest. *A Blot in the 'Scutcheon*, I. iii

3 Morning, evening, noon and night,
'Praise God!' sang Theocrite.
The Boy and the Angel

4 How well I know what I mean to do
When the long dark autumn-evenings come.
By the Fireside, i

5 Not verse now, only prose! *Ib.* ii

6 O woman-country, wooed not wed. *Ib.* vi

7   That great brow
And the spirit-small hand propping it. *Ib.* xxiii

8 We two stood there with never a third. *Ib.* xxxviii

9 Oh, the little more, and how much it is!
And the little less, and what worlds away!
Ib. xxxix

10 If you join two lives, there is oft a scar.
They are one and one, with a shadowy third;
One near one is too far. *Ib.* xlvi

11 One born to love you, sweet! *Ib.* li

12 Letting the rank tongue blossom into speech.
Caliban upon Setebos, l. 23

13 Setebos, Setebos, and Setebos!
'Thinketh, He dwelleth i' the cold o' the moon.
'Thinketh He made it, with the sun to match,
But not the stars; the stars came otherwise. *Ib.* l. 24

14 'Let twenty pass, and stone the twenty-first.
Loving not, hating not, just choosing so. *Ib.* l. 103

15 A bitter heart that bides its time and bites. *Ib.* l. 167

16 Kentish Sir Byng stood for his King,
Bidding the crop-headed Parliament swing:
And, pressing a troop unable to stoop
And see the rogues flourish and honest folk droop,
Marched them along, fifty-score strong,
Great-hearted gentlemen, singing this song.

God for King Charles! Pym and such carles
To the Devil that prompts 'em their treasonous parles!
Cavalier Tunes, i. *Marching Along*

17 King Charles, and who'll do him right now?
King Charles, and who's ripe for fight now?
Give a rouse: here's, in Hell's despite now,
King Charles! *Ib.* 2. *Give a Rouse*

18 To whom used my boy George quaff else,
By the old fool's side that begot him?
For whom did he cheer and laugh else,
While Noll's damned troopers shot him? *Ib.*

19 Boot, saddle, to horse, and away!
Ib. 3. *Boot and Saddle*

20 'Tis the Last Judgment's fire must cure this place,
Calcine its clods and set my prisoners free.
Childe Roland, xi

21 One stiff blind horse, his every bone a-stare. *Ib.* xiii

22 I never saw a brute I hated so;
He must be wicked to deserve such pain. *Ib.* xiv

23 Dauntless the slug-horn to my lips I set,
And blew. *Childe Roland to the Dark Tower came.*
Ib. xxxiv

24 Out of the little chapel I burst
Into the fresh night-air again. *Christmas Eve,* i

25 The preaching man's immense stupidity. *Ib.* iii

26 In the natural fog of the good man's mind. *Ib.* iv

27 He was there.
He himself with his human air. *Ib.* viii

28 Our best is bad, nor bears Thy test;
Still, it should be our very best. *Ib.*

29 Some thrilling view of the surplice-question. *Ib.* xiv

30 The exhausted air-bell of the Critic. *Ib.* xvi

31 While I watched my foolish heart expand
In the lazy glow of benevolence,
O'er the various modes of man's belief. *Ib.* xx

32 The raree-show of Peter's successor. *Ib.* xxii

33 For the preacher's merit or demerit,
It were to be wished the flaws were fewer
In the earthen vessel, holding treasure,
Which lies as safe in a golden ewer;
But the main thing is, does it hold good measure?
Heaven soon sets right all other matters! *Ib.*

34   The sprinkled isles,
Lily on lily, that o'erlace the sea.
And laugh their pride when the light wave lisps
'Greece'. *Cleon*, l. 1

35 I have written three books on the soul,
Proving absurd all written hitherto,
And putting us to ignorance again. *Ib.* l. 57

36 What is he buzzing in my ears?
'Now that I come to die,
Do I view the world as a vale of tears?'
Ah, reverend sir, not I! *Confessions*

37 To mine, it serves for the old June weather
Blue above lane and wall;
And that farthest bottle labelled 'Ether'
Is the house o'ertopping all. *Ib.*

38 How sad and bad and mad it was—
But then, how it was sweet! *Ib.*

39 There are flashes struck from midnights,
There are fire-flames noondays kindle,
Whereby piled-up honours perish,
Whereby swollen ambitions dwindle,
While just this or that poor impulse,
Which for once had play unstifled,
Seems the sole work of a life-time
That away the rest have trifled. *Cristina*, 4

40 Stung by the splendour of a sudden thought.
A Death in the Desert, l. 59

41 Such ever was love's way: to rise, it stoops. *Ib.* l. 134

42 For life, with all it yields of joy and woe,
And hope and fear,—believe the aged friend—
Is just a chance o' the prize of learning love.
Ib. l. 245

43 I say, the acknowledgement of God in Christ
Accepted by thy reason, solves for thee
All questions in the earth and out of it. *Ib.* l. 474

44 For I say, this is death and the sole death,
When a man's loss comes to him from his gain,
Darkness from light, from knowledge ignorance,
And lack of love from love made manifest. *Ib.* l. 482

1 Progress, man's distinctive mark alone,
Not God's, and not the beasts': God is, they are,
Man partly is and wholly hopes to be.
A Death in the Desert, l. 586

2 But 'twas Cerinthus that is lost. *Ib.* last line

3 Your ghost will walk, you lover of trees,
(If our loves remain)
In an English lane. *De Gustibus*

4 The bean-flowers' boon. *Ib.*

5 A castle, precipice-encurled,
In a gash of the wind-grieved Apennine. *Ib.*

6 Italy, my Italy!
Queen Mary's saying serves for me—
(When fortune's malice
Lost her—Calais)—
Open my heart and you will see
Graved inside of it, 'Italy'. *Ib.*

7 Reads verse and thinks she understands.
Dis aliter visum, iv

8 Schumann's our music-maker now. *Ib.* viii

9 Ingres's the modern man who paints. *Ib.*

10 Heine for songs; for kisses, how? *Ib.*

11 Sure of the Fortieth spare Arm-chair
When gout and glory seat me there. *Ib.* xii

12 With loves and doves, at all events
With money in the Three per Cents. *Ib.* xiii

13 Here comes my husband from his whist. *Ib.* xxx

14 That one Face, far from vanish, rather grows,
Or decomposes but to recompose,
Become my universe that feels and knows.
Dramatis Personae, epilogue, third speaker, xii

15 How very hard it is to be
A Christian! *Easter Day*, i

16 'Tis well averred,
A scientific faith's absurd. *Ib.* vi

17 A fierce vindictive scribble of red. *Ib.* xv

18 'Condemned to earth for ever, shut
From heaven!'
    But Easter-Day breaks! But
Christ rises! Mercy every way
Is infinite—and who can say? *Ib.* xxxiii

19 Karshish, the picker-up of learning's crumbs.
An Epistle

20 Beautiful Evelyn Hope is dead! *Evelyn Hope*

21 Your mouth of your own geranium's red. *Ib.*

22 You will wake, and remember, and understand. *Ib.*

23 What if this friend happen to be—God?
Fears and Scruples, xii

24 Truth never hurts the teller.
Fifine at the Fair, xxxii

25 'What, and is it really you again?' quoth I:
'I again, what else did you expect?' quoth she.
Ib. epilogue, i

26 I chanced upon a new book yesterday:
I opened it, and where my finger lay
'Twixt page and uncut page those words I read,
Some six or seven at most, and learned thereby
That you, FitzGerald, whom by ear and eye
She never knew, 'thanked God my wife was dead.'

Ay, dead! and were yourself alive, good Fitz,
How to return your thanks would pass my wits.
Kicking you seems the common lot of curs—
While more appropriate greeting lends you grace:
Surely to spit there glorifies your face—
Spitting from lips once sanctified by Hers.
Rejoinder to a remark (see 207:33) by Edward
FitzGerald on the death of E. B. Browning.
Athenaeum, No. 3220 (*13 July 1889*), p. 64

27 When the liquor's out why clink the cannikin?
The Flight of the Duchess, xvi

28 You're my friend—
What a thing friendship is, world without end!
Ib. xvii

29 I must learn Spanish, one of these days,
Only for that slow sweet name's sake.
The Flower's Name

30 Is there no method to tell her in Spanish
June's twice June since she breathed it with me? *Ib.*

31 If you get simple beauty and nought else,
You get about the best thing God invents.
Fra Lippo Lippi, l. 217

32 You should not take a fellow eight years old
And make him swear to never kiss the girls. *Ib.* l. 224

33   This world's no blot for us,
Nor blank; it means intensely, and means good:
To find its meaning is my meat and drink. *Ib.* l. 313

34 [*Christianity*]
'Tis the faith that launched point-blank her dart
At the head of a lie—taught Original Sin,
The corruption of Man's Heart. *Gold Hair*

35 The moth's kiss, first!
Kiss me as if you made believe
You were not sure, this eve,
How my face, your flower, had pursed
Its petals up. . . .
The bee's kiss, now!
Kiss me as if you entered gay
My heart at some noonday. *In a Gondola*

36 Let us begin and carry up this corpse,
Singing together. *A Grammarian's Funeral*, l. 1

37 He's for the morning. *Ib.* l. 24

38 This is our master, famous, calm, and dead,
Borne on our shoulders. *Ib.* l. 27

39 Yea, this in him was the peculiar grace . . .
That before living he'd learn how to live. *Ib.* l. 75

40 He said, 'What's time? leave Now for dogs and apes!
Man has Forever.' *Ib.* l. 83

41 That low man seeks a little thing to do,
Sees it and does it:
This high man, with a great thing to pursue,
Dies ere he knows it.
That low man goes on adding one to one,
His hundred's soon hit:
This high man, aiming at a million,
Misses an unit.
That, has the world here—should he need the next,
Let the world mind him!
This, throws himself on God, and unperplext
Seeking shall find Him. *Ib.* l. 113

42 He settled *Hoti's* business—let it be!—
Properly based *Oun*—
Gave us the doctrine of the enclitic *De*,
Dead from the waist down. *Ib.* l. 129

1 Lofty designs must close in like effects.
A Grammarian's Funeral, l. 145

2 O, world, as God has made it! all is beauty.
The Guardian Angel

3 This is Ancona, yonder is the sea.   *Ib.*

4 Infinite mercy, but, I wis,
As infinite a justice too.
The Heretic's Tragedy, i

5 (And wanteth there grace of lute or clavicithern, ye
shall say to confirm him who singeth—)
We bring John now to be burned alive.   *Ib.* ii

6 Forth John's soul flared into the dark.   *Ib.* x

7 God help all poor souls lost in the dark!   *Ib.*

8 I liken his Grace to an acorned hog.
Holy-Cross Day, iv

9 The Lord will have mercy on Jacob yet,
And again in his border see Israel set.   *Ib.* xiii

10 Thou! if thou wast He, who at mid-watch came,
By the starlight, naming a dubious name!   *Ib.* xvi

11 We gave the Cross, when we owed the Throne.   *Ib.*

12 We withstood Christ then? Be mindful how
At least we withstand Barabbas now!   *Ib.* xviii

13   We march, thy band,
South, East, and on to the Pleasant Land.   *Ib.* xx

14 Oh, to be in England
Now that April's there,
And whoever wakes in England
Sees, some morning, unaware,
That the lowest boughs and the brushwood sheaf
Round the elm-tree bole are in tiny leaf,
While the chaffinch sings on the orchard bough
In England—now!   *Home-thoughts, from Abroad*

15 That's the wise thrush; he sings each song twice over,
Lest you should think he never could recapture
The first fine careless rapture!   *Ib.*

16 All will be gay when noontide wakes anew
The buttercups, the little children's dower
—Far brighter than this gaudy melon-flower!   *Ib.*

17 Nobly, nobly Cape St. Vincent to the North-west
died away;
Sunset ran, one glorious blood-red, reeking into
Cadiz Bay.
Home-thoughts, from the Sea

18 'Here and here did England help me: how can I help
England?'—say,
Whoso turns as I, this evening, turn to God to praise
and pray,
While Jove's planet rises yonder, silent over Africa.
Ib

19   'With this same key
Shakespeare unlocked his heart' once more!
Did Shakespeare? If so, the less Shakespeare he!
House, x

20 How it strikes a Contemporary.   *Title*

21 He took such cognizance of men and things.
How it Strikes a Contemporary, l. 30

22 I sprang to the stirrup, and Joris, and he;
I galloped, Dirck galloped, we galloped all three.
How they brought the Good News from Ghent to Aix

23 You know, we French stormed Ratisbon.
Incident of the French Camp

24 'You're wounded!' 'Nay,' the soldier's pride
Touched to the quick, he said:
'I'm killed, Sire!' And his chief beside
Smiling the boy fell dead.   *Incident of the French Camp*

25 Ignorance is not innocence but sin.
The Inn Album, v

26 Just my vengeance complete,
The man sprang to his feet,
Stood erect, caught at God's skirts, and prayed!
—So, *I* was afraid!   *Instans Tyrannus*

27 The swallow has set her six young on the rail,
And looks seaward.   *James Lee*, III. i

28 Oh, good gigantic smile o' the brown old earth.
Ib. VII. i

29 I should be dead of joy, James Lee.
Ib. IX. viii

30 There's heaven above, and night by night
I look right through its gorgeous roof.
Johannes Agricola in Meditation

31 I said—Then, dearest, since 'tis so,
Since now at length my fate I know,
Since nothing all my love avails,
Since all, my life seemed meant for, fails,
Since this was written and needs must be—
My whole heart rises up to bless
Your name in pride and thankfulness!
Take back the hope you gave,—I claim
Only a memory of the same.
The Last Ride Together, i

32 Who knows but the world may end to-night?   *Ib.* ii

33 Hush! if you saw some western cloud
All billowy-bosomed, over-bowed
By many benedictions—sun's
And moon's and evening-star's at once.   *Ib.* iii

34   My soul
Smoothed itself out, a long-cramped scroll
Freshening and fluttering in the wind.   *Ib.* iv

35 Might she have loved me? just as well
She might have hated, who can tell!   *Ib.*

36 The petty done, the undone vast.   *Ib.* v

37 What hand and brain went ever paired?   *Ib.* vi

38 They scratch his name on the Abbey-stones.
My riding is better, by their leave.   *Ib.*

39 Sing, riding's a joy! For me, I ride.   *Ib.* vii

40 Ride, ride together, for ever ride?   *Ib.* x

41 Escape me?
Never—
Beloved!   *Life in a Love*

42 To dry one's eyes and laugh at a fall,
And, baffled, get up and begin again.   *Ib.*

43 No sooner the old hope goes to ground
Than a new one, straight to the self-same mark,
I shape me—
Ever
Removed!   *Ib.*

44 So I gave her eyes my own eyes to take,
My hand sought hers as in earnest need,
And round she turned for my noble sake,
And gave me herself indeed.   *A Light Woman*

45 'Tis an awkward thing to play with souls,
And matter enough to save one's own.   *Ib.*

46 And, Robert Browning, you writer of plays,
Here's a subject made to your hand!   *Ib.*

1 A face to lose youth for, to occupy age
  With the dream of, meet death with.   *A Likeness*

2 Just for a handful of silver he left us,
  Just for a riband to stick in his coat.
                                  The Lost Leader

3 We that had loved him so, followed him, honoured
    him,
  Lived in his mild and magnificent eye,
  Learned his great language, caught his clear accents,
  Made him our pattern to live and to die!   *Ib.*

4 Shakespeare was of us, Milton was for us,
  Burns, Shelley, were with us—they watch from their
    graves!   *Ib.*

5 We shall march prospering,—not thro' his presence;
  Songs may inspirit us,—not from his lyre;
  Deeds will be done,—while he boasts his quiescence,
  Still bidding crouch whom the rest bade aspire. *Ib.*

6 One more devils'-triumph and sorrow for angels,
  One wrong more to man, one more insult to God!
                                                Ib.

7 Never glad confident morning again!   *Ib.*

8 All's over, then; does truth sound bitter
  As one at first believes?   *The Lost Mistress*

9 I will hold your hand but as long as all may,
  Or so very little longer!   *Ib.*

10 Where the quiet-coloured end of evening smiles.
                              Love among the Ruins

11   Earth's returns
  For whole centuries of folly, noise and sin!   *Ib.*

12 Love is best.   *Ib.*

13 How the March sun feels like May! *A Lovers' Quarrel*

14 Oppression makes the wise man mad.   *Luria*, iv

15 But a bird's weight can break the infant tree
  Which after holds an aery in its arms.   *Ib.*

16   The only fault's with time;
  All men become good creatures: but so slow! *Ib.* v

17 Argument's hot to the close.
                  Master Hugues of Saxe-Gotha, xiii

18 One dissertates, he is candid;
  Two must discept,—has distinguished.   *Ib.* xiv

19   A poor devil has ended his cares
  At the foot of your rotten-runged rat-riddled stairs?
  Do I carry the moon in my pocket?   *Ib.* xxix

20 As I gain the cove with pushing prow,
  And quench its speed i' the slushy sand.
                              Meeting at Night

21 A mile of warm sea-scented beach.   *Ib.*

22 A tap at the pane, the quick sharp scratch
  And blue spurt of a lighted match,
  And a voice less loud, thro' its joys and fears,
  Than the two hearts beating each to each!   *Ib.*

23 Ah, did you once see Shelley plain,
    And did he stop and speak to you
  And did you speak to him again?
    How strange it seems, and new!   *Memorabilia*

24 A moulted feather, an eagle-feather!
  Well, I forget the rest.   *Ib.*

25 Have you found your life distasteful?
    My life did, and does, smack sweet.
  Was your youth of pleasure wasteful?
    Mine I saved and hold complete.

Do your joys with age diminish?
  When mine fail me, I'll complain.
Must in death your daylight finish?
  My sun sets to rise again.   *At the 'Mermaid'*

26 I find earth not grey but rosy,
  Heaven not grim but fair of hue.
    Do I stoop? I pluck a posy.
  Do I stand and stare? All's blue.   *Ib.*

27 'Next Poet'—(Manners, Ben!)   *Ib.*

28 If such as came for wool, sir, went home shorn,
  Where is the wrong I did them?
                  Mr. Sludge, 'The Medium', l. 630

29   Solomon of saloons
  And philosophic diner-out.   *Ib.* l. 773

30 This trade of mine—I don't know, can't be sure
  But there was something in it, tricks and all!
  Really, I want to light up my own mind.   *Ib.* l. 809

31 Boston's a hole, the herring-pond is wide,
  V-notes are something, liberty still more.
  Beside, is he the only fool in the world?
                                      Ib. last lines

32 This is a spray the bird clung to.   *Misconceptions*

33 This is a heart the Queen leant on.   *Ib.*

34 That's my last Duchess painted on the wall.
                              My Last Duchess, I. i

35 What matter to me if their star is a world?
  Mine has opened its soul to me; therefore I love it.
                                              My Star

36 Give me of Nelson only a touch.
                          Nationality in Drinks

37 All I can say is—I saw it!   *Natural Magic*

38 Never the time and the place
    And the loved one all together!
                      Never the Time and the Place

39   A lion who dies of an ass's kick,
  The wronged great soul of an ancient Master
                      Old Pictures in Florence, vi

40 What's come to perfection perishes.
  Things learned on earth, we shall practise in heaven.
  Works done least rapidly, Art most cherishes.
                                              Ib. xvii

41 There remaineth a rest for the people of God:
  And I have had troubles enough, for one.   *Ib.* xxii

42 All June I bound the rose in sheaves.
                                  One Way of Love

43 Lose who may—I still can say,
  Those who win heaven, blest are they!   *Ib.*

44 There they are, my fifty men and women.
                                One Word More, i

45 Rafael made a century of sonnets,
  Made and wrote them in a certain volume
  Dinted with the silver-pointed pencil
  Else he only used to draw Madonnas.   *Ib.* ii

46 Suddenly, as rare things will, it vanished.   *Ib.* iv

47 Dante once prepared to paint an angel:
  Whom to please? You whisper 'Beatrice'.   *Ib.* v

48 Dante, who loved well because he hated,
  Hated wickedness that hinders loving.   *Ib.*

49 Does he paint? he fain would write a poem—
  Does he write? he fain would paint a picture.
                                          Ib. viii

1 Heaven's gift takes earth's abatement.
One Word More, ix

2 Even he, the minute makes immortal,
Proves, perchance, but mortal in the minute. *Ib.*

3 Never dares the man put off the prophet. *Ib.* x

4 Other heights in other lives, God willing:
All the gifts from all the heights, your own, Love!
Ib. xii

5 He who blows thro' bronze, may breathe thro' silver.
Ib. xiii

6 I am mine and yours—the rest be all men's. *Ib.* xiv

7 Where my heart lies, let my brain lie also. *Ib.*

8 Lo, the moon's self!
Here in London, yonder late in Florence,
Still we find her face, the thrice-transfigured.
Curving on a sky imbrued with colour,
Drifted over Fiesole by twilight,
Came she, our new crescent of a hair's-breadth.
Full she flared it, lamping Samminiato,
Rounder 'twixt the cypresses and rounder,
Perfect till the nightingales applauded. *Ib.* xv

9 Blank to Zoroaster on his terrace,
Blind to Galileo on his turret,
Dumb to Homer, dumb to Keats—him, even!
Ib. xvi

10 God be thanked, the meanest of his creatures
Boasts two soul-sides, one to face the world with,
One to show a woman when he loves her! *Ib.* xvii

11 Silent silver lights and darks undreamed of,
Where I hush and bless myself with silence. *Ib.* xviii

12 Oh, their Rafael of the dear Madonnas,
Oh, their Dante of the dread Inferno,
Wrote one song—and in my brain I sing it,
Drew one angel—borne, see, on my bosom! *Ib.* xix

13 I see my way as birds their trackless way,
I shall arrive! what time, what circuit first,
I ask not: but unless God send his hail
Or blinding fireballs, sleet or stifling snow,
In some time, his good time, I shall arrive:
He guides me and the bird. In His good time!
Paracelsus, pt. I

14 Truth is within ourselves. *Ib.*

15 PARACELSUS:
    I am he that aspired to *know*: and thou?
APRILE:
    I would *love* infinitely, and be loved! *Ib.* pt. II

16   God is the perfect poet,
Who in his person acts his own creations. *Ib.*

17 Measure your mind's height by the shade it casts!
Ib. pt. III

18 Heap cassia, sandal-buds and stripes
Of labdanum, and aloe-balls. *Ib.* pt. IV

19 As when a queen, long dead, was young. *Ib.*

20 Over the sea our galleys went. *Ib.*

21 All at once they leave you, and you know them!
Ib. pt. V

22 I give the fight up: let there be an end,
A privacy, an obscure nook for me.
I want to be forgotten even by God. *Ib.*

23   Progress is
The law of life, man is not man as yet. *Ib.*

24 Thus the Mayne glideth
Where my Love abideth.
Sleep's no softer. *Paracelsus,* pt. V

25 Like plants in mines which never saw the sun,
But dream of him, and guess where he may be,
And do their best to climb and get to him. *Ib.*

26   If I stoop
Into a dark tremendous sea of cloud,
It is but for a time; I press God's lamp
Close to my breast; its splendour, soon or late,
Will pierce the gloom: I shall emerge one day. *Ib.*

27 Round the Cape of a sudden came the sea,
And the sun looked over the mountain's rim;
And straight was a path of gold for him,
And the need of a world of men for me.
Parting at Morning

28 It was roses, roses, all the way. *The Patriot*

29 The air broke into a mist with bells. *Ib.*

30 Sun-treader, life and light be thine for ever!
(Shelley) Pauline, l. 148

31 Ah, thought which saddens while it soothes!
Pictor Ignotus

32 Hamelin Town's in Brunswick,
    By famous Hanover city;
The river Weser, deep and wide,
    Washes its walls on the southern side.
The Pied Piper of Hamelin, st. i

33   Shrieking and squeaking
In fifty different sharps and flats. *Ib.* ii

34 A plate of turtle green and glutinous. *Ib.* iv

35 Anything like the sound of a rat
Makes my heart go pit-a-pat! *Ib.*

36 In did come the strangest figure! *Ib.* v

37 So munch on, crunch on, take your nuncheon,
Breakfast, supper, dinner, luncheon. *Ib.* vii

38 So, Willy, let me and you be wipers
Of scores out with all men, especially pipers! *Ib.* xv

39 Day! Faster and more fast,
O'er night's brim, day boils at last.
Pippa Passes, introduction

40 The year's at the spring,
And day's at the morn;
Morning's at seven;
The hill-side's dew-pearled;
The lark's on the wing;
The snail's on the thorn:
    God's in his heaven—
All's right with the world! *Ib.* pt. I

41 God must be glad one loves His world so much!
Ib. pt. III

42 Some unsuspected isle in the far seas!
Some unsuspected isle in far-off seas! *Ib.*

43 In the morning of the world,
When earth was nigher heaven than now. *Ib.*

44 No need that sort of king should ever die! *Ib*

45 You'll look at least on love's remains,
    A grave's one violet:
Your look?—that pays a thousand pains.
    What's death? You'll love me yet! *Ib.*

46 All service ranks the same with God—
With God, whose puppets, best and worst,
Are we; there is no last nor first. *Ib.* pt. IV

1 Stand still, true poet that you are!
I know you; let me try and draw you.
Some night you'll fail us: when afar
You rise, remember one man saw you,
Knew you, and named a star!   *Popularity*

2   With ardours manifold,
The bee goes singing to her groom,
Drunken and overbold.   *Ib.*

3   Who fished the murex up?
What porridge had John Keats?   *Ib.*

4 The rain set early in to-night.   *Porphyria's Lover*

5   All her hair
In one long yellow string I wound
Three times her little throat around,
And strangled her. No pain felt she;
I am quite sure she felt no pain.   *Ib.*

6 And all night long we have not stirred,
And yet God has not said a word!   *Ib.*

7 But flame? The bush is bare.   *Prologue (Asolando)*

8 Fear death?—to feel the fog in my throat,
  ` The mist in my face.   *Prospice*

9 Where he stands, the Arch Fear in a visible form.
                                                             Ib.

10 I was ever a fighter, so—one fight more,
The best and the last!
I would hate that death bandaged my eyes, and for-
    bore,
And bade me creep past.   *Ib.*

11 No! let me taste the whole of it, fare like my peers
The heroes of old,
Bear the brunt, in a minute pay glad life's arrears
Of pain, darkness and cold.   *Ib.*

12 O thou soul of my soul! I shall clasp thee again,
          And with God be the rest!   *Ib.*

13   Grow old along with me!
The best is yet to be,
The last of life, for which the first was made:
Our times are in His hand
Who saith, 'A whole I planned,
Youth shows but half; trust God: see all, nor be
    afraid!'   *Rabbi ben Ezra, i*

14 Irks care the crop-full bird? Frets doubt the maw-
    crammed beast?   *Ib. iv*

15   Then, welcome each rebuff
That turns earth's smoothness rough,
Each sting that bids nor sit nor stand but go!
Be our joys three-parts pain!
Strive, and hold cheap the strain;
Learn, nor account the pang; dare, never grudge the
    throe!   *Ib. vi*

16   For thence,—a paradox
Which comforts while it mocks,—
Shall life succeed in that it seems to fail:
What I aspired to be,
And was not, comforts me.
A brute I might have been, but would not sink i' the
    scale.   *Ib. vii*

17   Let us not always say
'Spite of this flesh to-day
I strove, made head, gained ground upon the whole!'
As the bird wings and sings,
Let us cry 'All good things
Are ours, nor soul helps flesh more, now, than flesh
    helps soul.'   *Ib. xii*

18 Once more on my adventure brave and new.
                                          Rabbi ben Ezra, xiv

19   When evening shuts,
          A certain moment cuts
The deed off, calls the glory from the grey.   *Ib. xvi*

20   Now, who shall arbitrate?
     Ten men love what I hate,
Shun what I follow, slight what I receive:
     Ten, who in ears and eyes
     Match me: we all surmise,
They, this thing, and I, that: whom shall my soul
     believe?   *Ib. xxii*

21 Fancies that broke through language and escaped.
                                                             Ib. xxv

22   All that is, at all,
     Lasts ever, past recall;
Earth changes, but thy soul and God stand sure.
                                                             Ib. xxvii

23 Time's wheel runs back or stops: potter and clay
     endure.   *Ib.*

24 He fixed thee mid this dance
Of plastic circumstance.   *Ib. xxviii*

25 Look not thou down but up!
To uses of a cup.   *Ib. xxx*

26 My times be in Thy hand!
Perfect the cup as planned!
Let age approve of youth, and death complete the
     same!   *Ib. xxxii*

27 Do you see this square old yellow Book, I toss
I' the air, and catch again.
                              The Ring and the Book, bk. i, l. 33

28 The Life, Death, Miracles of Saint Somebody,
Saint Somebody Else, his Miracles, Death and Life.
                                                             Ib. l. 80

29 Well, British Public, ye who like me not,
(God love you!).   *Ib. l. 410*

30 'Go get you manned by Manning and new-manned
By Newman and, mayhap, wise-manned to boot
By Wiseman.'   *Ib. l. 444*

31   A dusk mis-featured messenger,
No other than the angel of this life,
Whose care is lest men see too much at once.
                                                             Ib. l. 593

32 Let this old woe step on the stage again!   *Ib. l. 824*

33   Youth means love,
Vows can't change nature, priests are only men.
                                                             Ib. l. 1056

34 O lyric Love, half angel and half bird
And all a wonder and a wild desire.   *Ib. l. 1391*

35 Boldest of hearts that ever braved the sun,
Took sanctuary within the holier blue,
And sang a kindred soul out to his face,—
Yet human at the red-ripe of the heart.   *Ib. l. 1393*

36 This is the same voice: can thy soul know change?
                                                             Ib. l. 1401

37 Never may I commence my song, my due
To God who best taught song by gift of thee,
Except with bent head and beseeching hand.
                                                             Ib. l. 1403

38 Their utmost up and on.   *Ib. l. 1413*

39 The story always old and always new.
                                          Ib. bk. ii, l. 214

1 But facts are facts and flinch not.
   The Ring and the Book, bk. ii, l. 1049

2   Go practise if you please
With men and women: leave a child alone
For Christ's particular love's sake!—so I say.
   Ib. bk. iii. l. 88

3 In the great right of an excessive wrong. *Ib.* l. 1055

4 Everyone soon or late comes round by Rome.
   Ib. bk. v, l. 296

5 'Twas a thief said the last kind word to Christ:
Christ took the kindness and forgave the theft.
   Ib. bk. vi, l. 869

6 O great, just, good God! Miserable me! *Ib.* l. 2105

7 The uncomfortableness of it all. *Ib.* bk. vii, l. 400

8 True life is only love, love only bliss. *Ib.* l. 960

9 O lover of my life, O soldier-saint. *Ib.* l. 1786

10   Through such souls alone
God stooping shows sufficient of His light
For us i' the dark to rise by. And I rise. *Ib.* l. 1843

11 Faultless to a fault. *Ib.* bk. ix, l. 1177

12   Of what I call God,
And fools call Nature. *Ib.* bk. x, l. 1073

13 Why comes temptation but for man to meet
And master and make crouch beneath his foot,
And so be pedestalled in triumph? *Ib.* l. 1185

14 White shall not neutralize the black, nor good
Compensate bad in man, absolve him so:
Life's business being just the terrible choice.
   Ib. l. 1236

15   There's a new tribunal now,
Higher than God's—the educated man's! *Ib.* l. 1976

16 That sad obscure sequestered state
Where God unmakes but to remake the soul
He else made first in vain; which must not be.
   Ib. l. 2130

17 Abate,—Cardinal,—Christ,—Maria,—God, . . .
Pompilia, will you let them murder me?
   Ib. bk. xi, l. 2424

18   It is the glory and good of Art,
That Art remains the one way possible
Of speaking truths, to mouths like mine at least.
   Ib. bk. xii, l. 842

19 Thy rare gold ring of verse (the poet praised)
Linking our England to his Italy. *Ib.* l. 873

20 Good, to forgive;
    Best, to forget!
Living, we fret;
Dying, we live. *La Saisiaz*, dedication

21 How good is man's life, the mere living! how fit to
   employ
All the heart and the soul and the senses, for ever in
   joy! *Saul*, ix

22 All's love, yet all's law. *Ib.* xvii

23 'Tis not what man does which exalts him, but what
   man would do! *Ib.* xviii

24   It is by no breath,
Turn of eye, wave of hand, that salvation joins issue
   with death!
As thy Love is discovered almighty, almighty be
   proved
Thy power, that exists with and for it, of being
   beloved! *Ib.*

25   O Saul, it shall be
A Face like my face that receives thee; a Man like to
   me,
Thou shalt love and be loved by, for ever: a Hand like
   this hand
Shall throw open the gates of new life to thee! See
   the Christ stand! *Saul*, xviii

26 Because a man has shop to mind
In time and place, since flesh must live,
   Needs spirit lack all life behind,
All stray thoughts, fancies fugitive,
All loves except what trade can give?
   Shop, xx

27 I want to know a butcher paints,
A baker rhymes for his pursuit,
Candlestick-maker much acquaints
His soul with song, or, haply mute,
Blows out his brains upon the flute. *Ib.* xxi

28 Nay but you, who do not love her,
Is she not pure gold, my mistress? *Song*

29 Who will, may hear Sordello's story told.
   Sordello, bk. i

30 Sidney's self, the starry paladin. *Ib.*

31   whence the grieved and obscure waters slope
Into a darkness quieted by hope;
Plucker of amaranths grown beneath God's eye
In gracious twilights where his chosen lie. *Ib.*

32 Still more labyrinthine buds the rose. *Ib.*

33   A touch divine—
And the scaled eyeball owns the mystic rod;
Visibly through his garden walketh God. *Ib.*

34   Any nose
May ravage with impunity a rose. *Ib.* bk. vi

35 Who would has heard Sordello's story told. *Ib.*

36 You are not going to marry your old friend's love,
   after all? *A Soul's Tragedy*, Act II

37 I have known *Four*-and-twenty leaders of revolts.
   Ib. last words

38 Gr-r-r- there go, my heart's abhorrence!
Water your damned flower-pots, do!
   Soliloquy of the Spanish Cloister

39 I the Trinity illustrate,
   Drinking watered orange-pulp—
In three sips the Arian frustrate;
   While he drains his at one gulp. *Ib.*

40 There's a great text in Galatians,
   Once you trip on it, entails
Twenty-nine distinct damnations,
   One sure, if another fails. *Ib.*

41 My scrofulous French novel
On grey paper with blunt type! *Ib.*

42 'St, there's Vespers! Plena gratiâ
Ave, Virgo! Gr-r-r—you swine! *Ib.*

43 The glory dropped from their youth and love,
And both perceived they had dreamed a dream.
   The Statue and the Bust

44 The world and its ways have a certain worth. *Ib.*

45 The soldier-saints, who row on row,
Burn upward each to his point of bliss. *Ib.*

46 The sin I impute to each frustrate ghost
Is—the unlit lamp and the ungirt loin,
Though the end in sight was a vice, I say. *Ib.*

1 All the breath and the bloom of the year in the bag of one bee. *Summum Bonum (Asolando)*

2 At the midnight in the silence of the sleep-time,
When you set your fancies free. *Ib.* epilogue

3 Greet the unseen with a cheer. *Ib.*

4 One who never turned his back but marched breast forward,
Never doubted clouds would break,
Never dreamed, though right were worsted, wrong would triumph,
Held we fall to rise, are baffled to fight better,
Sleep to wake. *Ib.*

5 I've a Friend, over the sea;
I like him, but he loves me.
It all grew out of the books I write;
Time's Revenges

6 There may be heaven; there must be hell;
Meantime, there is our earth here—well! *Ib.*

7 Hark, the dominant's persistence till it must be answered to! *A Toccata of Galuppi's*, viii

8 What of soul was left, I wonder, when the kissing had to stop? *Ib.* xiv

9 Dear dead women, with such hair, too—what's become of all the gold
Used to hang and brush their bosoms? I feel chilly and grown old. *Ib.* xv

10 As I ride, as I ride.
Through the Metidja to Abd-el-kadr

11 Grand rough old Martin Luther
Bloomed fables—flowers on furze,
The better the uncouther:
Do roses stick like burrs? *The Twins*

12 Only I discern—
Infinite passion, and the pain
Of finite hearts that yearn. *Two in the Campagna*

13 Sky—what a scowl of cloud
Till, near and far,
Ray on ray split the shroud
Splendid, a star! *The Two Poets of Croisic*

14 Bang-whang-whang goes the drum, tootle-te-tootle the fife. *Up at a Villa—Down in the City*

15 Wanting is—what?
Summer redundant,
Blueness abundant,
—Where is the blot? *Wanting—is what?*

16 What's become of Waring
Since he gave us all the slip? *Waring*, I. i

17 Monstr'-inform'-ingens-horrend-ous
Demoniaco-seraphic
Penman's latest piece of graphic. *Ib.* iv

18 Some lost lady of old years. *Ib.*

19 In Vishnu-land what Avatar? *Ib.* vi

20 'When I last saw Waring . . .'
(How all turned to him who spoke!
You saw Waring? Truth or joke?
In land-travel or sea-faring?) *Ib.* II. i

21 Oh, never star
Was lost here but it rose afar! *Ib.* iii

22 But little do or can the best of us:
That little is achieved through Liberty.
In Andrew Reid's *Why I am a Liberal*

23 Let's contend no more, **Love**,
Strive nor weep:
All be as before, Love,
—Only sleep! *A Woman's Last Word*

24 What so wild as words are? *Ib.*

25 Where the apple reddens,
Never pry:
Lest we lose our Edens,
Eve and I. *Ib.*

26 That shall be to-morrow
Not to-night:
I must bury sorrow
Out of sight. *Ib.*

27 I knew you once: but in Paradise,
If we meet, I will pass nor turn my face.
The Worst of It, xix

28 We have not sighed deep, laughed free,
Starved, feasted, despaired,—been happy.
Youth and Art

29 And nobody calls you a dunce,
And people suppose me clever:
This could but have happened once,
And we missed it, lost it for ever. *Ib.*

MICHAEL BRUCE
1746–1767

30 Sweet bird! thy bower is ever green,
Thy sky is ever clear:
Thou hast no sorrow in thy song,
No winter in thy year!
To the Cuckoo. (Also attr. to John Logan)

GEORGE BRYAN BRUMMELL
1778–1840

31 Who's your fat friend? [Of the Prince of Wales.]
Gronow, *Reminiscences* (1862), p. 63

JEAN DE LA BRUYÈRE
1645–1696

32 Tout est dit et l'on vient trop tard depuis plus de sept mille ans qu'il y a des hommes et qui pensent.

Everything has been said, and we are more than seven thousand years of human thought too late. *Les Caractères (Ouvrages de l'Esprit)*

33 Le peuple n'a guère d'esprit et les grands n'ont point d'âme . . . faut-il opter, je ne balance pas, je veux être peuple.

The people have little intelligence, the great no heart . . . if I had to choose I should have no hesitation in choosing the people. *Ib. (Des Grands)*

34 Entre le bon sens et le bon goût il y a la différence de la cause et son effet.

Between good sense and good taste there is the same difference as between cause and effect.
Ib. (Des Jugements)

ALFRED BRYAN
nineteenth century

35 Who paid the rent for Mrs. Rip Van Winkle
When Rip Van Winkle went away?
Who Paid the Rent for Mrs. Rip Van Winkle?

WILLIAM JENNINGS BRYAN
1860–1925

1 The humblest citizen of all the land, when clad in the armor of a righteous cause, is stronger than all the hosts of error.
Speech at the National Democratic Convention, Chicago, 1896

2 You shall not press down upon the brow of labor this crown of thorns, you shall not crucify mankind upon a cross of gold. *Ib.*

WILLIAM CULLEN BRYANT
1794–1878

3 So live, that when thy summons comes to join
The innumerable caravan, which moves
To that mysterious realm, where each shall take
His chamber in the silent halls of death,
Thou go not, like the quarry-slave at night,
Scourged to his dungeon, but, sustained and soothed
By an unfaltering trust, approach thy grave
Like one who wraps the drapery of his couch
About him, and lies down to pleasant dreams.
Thanatopsis, l. 73

4 They seemed
Like old companions in adversity.
A Winter Piece, l. 26

ROBERT WILLIAMS BUCHANAN
1841–1901

5 The Fleshly School of Poetry.
Title of article in The Contemporary Review, *Oct. 1871. (Applied to Swinburne, William Morris, D. G. Rossetti, and others.)*

6 She just wore
Enough for modesty—no more.
White Rose and Red, 1. v, l. 60

7 The sweet post-prandial cigar. *De Berny*

GEORGE VILLIERS, SECOND DUKE OF BUCKINGHAM
1628–1687

8 The world is made up for the most part of fools and knaves. *To Mr. Clifford, on his Humane Reason*

9 What the devil does the plot signify, except to bring in fine things? *The Rehearsal, III. i*

10 Ay, now the plot thickens very much upon us.
Ib. ii

JOHN SHEFFIELD, FIRST DUKE OF BUCKINGHAM AND NORMANBY
1648–1721

11 Read Homer once, and you can read no more,
For all books else appear so mean, so poor,
Verse will seem prose; but still persist to read,
And Homer will be all the books you need.
An Essay on Poetry

12 A faultless monster which the world ne'er saw. *Ib.*

HENRY J. BUCKOLL
1803–1871

13 Lord, behold us with Thy blessing
Once again assembled here.
Psalms and Hymns for the Use of Rugby School Chapel. Lord, Behold us with Thy Blessing

14 Lord, dismiss us with Thy blessing,
Thanks for mercies past receive.
Ib. Lord, Dismiss us with Thy Blessing

JOHN BALDWIN BUCKSTONE
1802–1879

15 On such an occasion as this,
All time and nonsense scorning,
Nothing shall come amiss,
And we won't go home till morning.
Billy Taylor, 1. ii

EUSTACE BUDGELL
1686–1737

16 What Cato did, and Addison approved
Cannot be wrong.
Lines found on his desk after his suicide, 4 May 1737

GEORGES-LOUIS LECLERC DE BUFFON
1707–1788

17 Le style est l'homme même.
Style is the man himself. *Discours sur le Style*

18 Le génie n'est qu'une grande aptitude à la patience.
Genius is only a great aptitude for patience.
Attr. to Buffon by Hérault de Séchelles in Voyage à Montbard

ARTHUR BULLER
1874–1944

19 There was a young lady named Bright,
Whose speed was far faster than light;
She set out one day
In a relative way,
And returned home the previous night.
Limerick in Punch, *19 Dec. 1923*

EDWARD GEORGE BULWER-LYTTON
see
BARON LYTTON

EDWARD ROBERT BULWER, EARL OF LYTTON
see
OWEN MEREDITH

ALFRED BUNN
1796?–1860

20 Alice, where art thou? *Title of Song*

21 I dreamt that I dwelt in marble halls,
With vassals and serfs at my side.
Bohemian Girl, Act II

22 When other lips, and other hearts,
Their tales of love shall tell. *Ib. Act III*

1 The light of other days is faded,
And all their glory past.
The Maid of Artois, Act II

JOHN BUNYAN
1628–1688

2 Mr. Badman died . . . as they call it, like a Chrisom-child, quietly and without fear.
Life and Death of Mr. Badman

3 As I walk'd through the wilderness of this world.
Pilgrim's Progress, pt. i

4 The name of the one was Obstinate and the name of the other Pliable. *Ib.*

5 The name of the slough was Despond. *Ib.*

6 The gentleman's name was Mr. Worldly-Wise-Man. *Ib.*

7 Set down my name, Sir. *Ib.*

8 Come in, come in;
Eternal glory thou shalt win. *Ib.*

9 And behold there was a very stately palace before him, the name of which was Beautiful. *Ib.*

10 The valley of Humiliation. *Ib.*

11 A foul Fiend coming over the field to meet him; his name is Apollyon. *Ib.*

12 Then Apollyon straddled quite over the whole breadth of the way. *Ib.*

13 Set your faces like a flint. *Ib.*

14 It beareth the name of Vanity-Fair, because the town where 'tis kept, is lighter than vanity. *Ib.*

15 So soon as the man overtook me, he was but a word and a blow. *Ib.*

16 Hanging is too good for him, said Mr. Cruelty. *Ib.*

17 Yet my great-grandfather was but a water-man, looking one way, and rowing another: and I got most of my estate by the same occupation.
[*Mr. By-Ends.*] *Ib.*

18 They came at a delicate plain, called Ease, where they went with much content; but that plain was but narrow, so they went quickly over it. *Ib.*

19 A castle, called Doubting-Castle, the owner whereof was Giant Despair. *Ib.*

20 Now Giant Despair had a wife, and her name was Diffidence. *Ib.*

21 A grievous crab-tree cudgel. *Ib.*

22 They came to the Delectable Mountains. *Ib.*

23 Sleep is sweet to the labouring man. *Ib.*

24 A great horror and darkness fell upon Christian. *Ib.*

25 Then I saw that there was a way to hell, even from the gates of heaven. *Ib.*

26 So I awoke, and behold it was a dream. *Ib.*

27 A man that could look no way but downwards, with a muckrake in his hand. *Ib.* pt. ii

28 One leak will sink a ship, and one sin will destroy a sinner. *Ib.*

29 A young Woman her name was Dull. *Ib.*

30 One Great-heart. *Ib.*

31 He that is down needs fear no fall,
He that is low no pride.
He that is humble ever shall
Have God to be his guide.
I am content with what I have,
Little be it, or much:
And, Lord, contentment still I crave,
Because Thou savest such.
Fulness to such, a burden is,
That go on pilgrimage;
Here little, and hereafter bliss,
Is best from age to age.
Pilgrim's Progress, pt. ii. *Shepherd Boy's Song in the Valley of Humiliation*

32 A man there was, tho' some did count him mad,
The more he cast away, the more he had. *Ib.*

33 An ornament to her profession. *Ib.*

34 Whose name is Valiant-for-Truth. *Ib.*

35 Who would true valour see,
Let him come hither;
One here will constant be,
Come wind, come weather.
There's no discouragement
Shall make him once relent
His first avow'd intent
To be a pilgrim.

[*Altered version in 'English Hymnal'*:
He who would valiant be
'Gainst all disaster,
Let him in constancy
Follow the Master. &c.] *Ib.*

36 Who so beset him round
With dismal stories,
Do but themselves confound—
His strength the more is. *Ib.*

37 Then fancies flee away!
I'll fear not what men say,
I'll labour night and day
To be a pilgrim. *Ib.*

38 Mr. Standfast. *Ib.*

39 My sword, I give to him that shall succeed me in my pilgrimage, and my courage and skill to him that can get it. [*Mr. Valiant-for-Truth.*] *Ib.*

40 I have formerly lived by hearsay, and faith, but now I go where I shall live by sight, and shall be with Him in whose company I delight myself. [*Mr. Standfast.*] *Ib.*

41 So he passed over, and all the trumpets sounded for him on the other side. *Ib.*

SAMUEL DICKINSON BURCHARD
1812–1891

42 We are Republicans and don't propose to leave our party and identify ourselves with the party whose antecedents are rum, Romanism, and rebellion.
Speech, New York City, 29 Oct. 1884

GELETT BURGESS
1866–1951

43 Are you a bromide?
Title of Essay in Smart Set, *1906*

1 I never saw a Purple Cow,
　I never hope to see one;
　But I can tell you, anyhow,
　　I'd rather see than be one!
　　　Burgess Nonsense Book. The Purple Cow

2 Ah, yes! I wrote the 'Purple Cow'—
　I'm sorry, now, I wrote it!
　But I can tell you anyhow,
　　I'll kill you if you quote it!　　*Ib.*

REV. JOHN WILLIAM BURGON
1813–1888

3 A rose-red city—'half as old as Time'! *Petra, l. 132*

JOHN BURGOYNE
1722–1792

4 You have only, when before your glass, to keep pronouncing to yourself nimini-pimini—the lips cannot fail of taking their plie.　　*The Heiress,* III. ii

EDMUND BURKE
1729–1797

5 Would twenty shillings have ruined Mr. Hampden's
fortune? No! but the payment of half twenty
shillings, on the principle it was demanded, would
have made him a slave.
　　Speech on American Taxation, 1774

6 It is the nature of all greatness not to be exact. *Ib.*

7 Falsehood has a perennial spring.　　*Ib.*

8 It did so happen that persons had a single office
divided between them, who had never spoken to
each other in their lives; until they found themselves, they knew not how, pigging together, heads
and points, in the same truckle-bed.　　*Ib.*

9 For even then, sir, even before this splendid orb was
entirely set, and while the western horizon was in a
blaze with his descending glory, on the opposite
quarter of the heavens arose another luminary,
and, for his hour, became lord of the ascendant. *Ib.*

10 Great men are the guide-posts and landmarks in the
state.　　*Ib.*

11 Passion for fame; a passion which is the instinct of all
great souls.　　*Ib.*

12 To tax and to please, no more than to love and to be
wise, is not given to men.　　*Ib.*

13 The only liberty I mean, is a liberty connected with
order; that not only exists along with order and
virtue, but which cannot exist at all without them.
　　Speech at his arrival at Bristol, 13 Oct. 1774

14 Parliament is not a *congress* of ambassadors from
different and hostile interests; which interests each
must maintain, as an agent and advocate, against
other agents and advocates; but parliament is a
deliberative assembly of *one* nation, with *one*
interest, that of the whole; where, not local purposes, not local prejudices ought to guide, but the
general good, resulting from the general reason of
the whole. You choose a member indeed; but
when you have chosen him, he is not member of
Bristol, but he is a member of *parliament.*
　　Speech to the Electors of Bristol, 3 Nov. 1774

15 Applaud us when we run; console us when we fall;
cheer us when we recover: but let us pass on—for
God's sake, let us pass on!
　　Speech at Bristol previous to the Election, 1780

16 Bad laws are the worst sort of tyranny.　　*Ib.*

17 The worthy gentleman [Mr. Coombe], who has been
snatched from us at the moment of the election,
and in the middle of the contest, whilst his desires
were as warm, and his hopes as eager as ours, has
feelingly told us, what shadows we are, and what
shadows we pursue.
　　Speech at Bristol on Declining the Poll, 1780

18 The cold neutrality of an impartial judge.
　　Preface to the Address of M. Brissot, 1794

19 I have in general no very exalted opinion of the virtue
of paper government.
　　*Speech on Conciliation with America, 22 Mar.
1775*

20 The noble lord in the blue riband. [Lord North, the
Prime Minister.]
　　*Ib. (the 'blue riband' being the badge of the Order
of the Garter)*

21 The concessions of the weak are the concessions of
fear.　　*Ib.*

22 Young man, there is America—which at this day
serves for little more than to amuse you with stories
of savage men, and uncouth manners; yet shall,
before you taste of death, show itself equal to the
whole of that commerce which now attracts the
envy of the world.　　*Ib.*

23 When we speak of the commerce with our colonies,
fiction lags after truth; invention is unfruitful,
and imagination cold and barren.　　*Ib.*

24 A people who are still, as it were, but in the gristle
and not yet hardened into the bone of manhood. *Ib.*

25 Through a wise and salutary neglect [of the colonies],
a generous nature has been suffered to take her
own way to perfection; when I reflect upon these
effects, when I see how profitable they have been to
us, I feel all the pride of power sink and all pre-
sumption in the wisdom of human contrivances
melt and die away within me. My rigour relents.
I pardon something to the spirit of liberty.　　*Ib.*

26 The use of force alone is but *temporary*. It may subdue for a moment; but it does not remove the
necessity of subduing again: and a nation is not
governed, which is perpetually to be conquered.
　　Ib.

27 Nothing less will content me, than *whole America.*
　　Ib.

28 Abstract liberty, like other mere abstractions, is not
to be found.　　*Ib.*

29 All protestantism, even the most cold and passive, is
a sort of dissent. But the religion most prevalent in
our northern colonies is a refinement on the principle of resistance: it is the dissidence of dissent,
and the protestantism of the Protestant religion.
　　Ib.

30 In no country perhaps in the world is the law so
general a study. . . . This study renders men acute,
inquisitive, dexterous, prompt in attack, ready in
defence, full of resources. . . . They augur misgovernment at a distance, and snuff the approach
of tyranny in every tainted breeze.　　*Ib.*

1 The mysterious virtue of wax and parchment.
   Speech on Conciliation with America, 22 Mar. 1775.

2 I do not know the method of drawing up an indictment against an whole people. *Ib.*

3 It is not, what a lawyer tells me I *may* do; but what humanity, reason, and justice, tell me I ought to do. *Ib.*

4 Govern two millions of men, impatient of servitude, on the principles of freedom. *Ib.*

5 I am not determining a point of law; I am restoring tranquillity. *Ib.*

6 The march of the human mind is slow. *Ib.*

7 Freedom and not servitude is the cure of anarchy; as religion, and not atheism, is the true remedy for superstition. *Ib.*

8 Instead of a standing revenue, you will have therefore a perpetual quarrel. *Ib.*

9 Parties must ever exist in a free country. *Ib.*

10 My hold of the colonies is in the close affection which grows from common names, from kindred blood, from similar privileges, and equal protection. These are ties which, though light as air, are as strong as links of iron. *Ib.*

11 Slavery they can have anywhere. It is a weed that grows in every soil. *Ib.*

12 Deny them this participation of freedom, and you break that sole bond, which originally made, and must still preserve the unity of the empire. *Ib.*

13 It is the love of the people; it is their attachment to their government, from the sense of the deep stake they have in such a glorious institution, which gives you your army and your navy, and infuses into both that liberal obedience, without which your army would be a base rabble, and your navy nothing but rotten timber. *Ib.*

14 Magnanimity in politics is not seldom the truest wisdom; and a great empire and little minds go ill together. *Ib.*

15 By adverting to the dignity of this high calling, our ancestors have turned a savage wilderness into a glorious empire: and have made the most extensive, and the only honourable conquests, not by destroying, but by promoting the wealth, the number, the happiness of the human race. *Ib.*

16 The people never give up their liberties but under some delusion.
   Speech at County Meeting of Buckinghamshire, 1784

17 Corrupt influence, which is itself the perennial spring of all prodigality, and of all disorder; which loads us, more than millions of debt; which takes away vigour from our arms, wisdom from our councils, and every shadow of authority and credit from the most venerable parts of our constitution.
   Speech on the Economical Reform, 1780

18 Individuals pass like shadows; but the commonwealth is fixed and stable. *Ib.*

19 The people are the masters. *Ib.*

20 A rapacious and licentious soldiery.
   Speech on Fox's East India Bill, 1783

21 He has put to hazard his ease, his security, his interest, his power, even his darling popularity, for the benefit of a people whom he has never seen. *Ib.*

22 What the greatest inquest of the nation has begun, its highest Tribunal [the British House of Commons] will accomplish.
   Impeachment of Warren Hastings, 15 Feb. 1788

23 Religious persecution may shield itself under the guise of a mistaken and over-zealous piety.
   Ib. 17 Feb. 1788

24 An event has happened, upon which it is difficult to speak, and impossible to be silent.
   Ib. 5 May 1789

25 Resolved to die in the last dyke of prevarication.
   Ib. 7 May 1789

26 There is but one law for all, namely, that law which governs all law, the law of our Creator, the law of humanity, justice, equity—the law of nature, and of nations. *Ib. 28 May 1794*

27 I impeach him in the name of the people of India, whose rights he has trodden under foot, and whose country he has turned into a desert. Lastly, in the name of human nature itself, in the name of both sexes, in the name of every age, in the name of every rank, I impeach the common enemy and oppressor of all!
   Impeachment of Warren Hastings, as recorded by Macaulay in his essay on Warren Hastings

28 His virtues were his arts.
   Inscription on the statue of the Marquis of Rockingham in Wentworth Park

29 The greater the power, the more dangerous the abuse.
   Speech on the Middlesex Election, 1771

30 It is not a predilection to mean, sordid, home-bred cares, that will avert the consequences of a false estimation of our interest, or prevent the shameful dilapidation, into which a great empire must fall, by mean reparations upon mighty ruins.
   Speech on the Nabob of Arcot's Debts

31 Old religious factions are volcanoes burnt out.
   Speech on the Petition of the Unitarians, 1792

32 Dangers by being despised grow great. *Ib.*

33 To complain of the age we live in, to murmur at the present possessors of power, to lament the past, to conceive extravagant hopes of the future, are the common dispositions of the greatest part of mankind.
   Thoughts on the Cause of the Present Discontents

34 The power of the crown, almost dead and rotten as Prerogative, has grown up anew, with much more strength, and far less odium, under the name of Influence. *Ib.*

35 The wisdom of our ancestors. *Ib.*

36 When bad men combine, the good must associate; else they will fall, one by one, an unpitied sacrifice in a contemptible struggle. *Ib.*

37 Of this stamp is the cant of *Not men, but measures*; a sort of charm by which many people get loose from every honourable engagement. *Ib.*

38 There is, however, a limit at which forbearance ceases to be a virtue.
   Observations on a Publication, 'The present state of the nation'

1 Well stored with pious frauds, and, like most discourses of the sort, much better calculated for the private advantage of the preacher than the edification of the hearers.
Observations on a Publication, 'The present state of the nation'

2 It is a general popular error to imagine the loudest complainers for the public to be the most anxious for its welfare. *Ib.*

3 I flatter myself that I love a manly, moral, regulated liberty as well as any gentleman.
Reflections on the Revolution in France

4 Whenever our neighbour's house is on fire, it cannot be amiss for the engines to play a little on our own. *Ib.*

5 Politics and the pulpit are terms that have little agreement. No sound ought to be heard in the church but the healing voice of Christian charity. . . . Surely the church is a place where one day's truce ought to be allowed to the dissensions and animosities of mankind. *Ib.*

6 A state without the means of some change is without the means of its conservation. *Ib.*

7 Make the Revolution a parent of settlement, and not a nursery of future revolutions. *Ib.*

8 The confused jargon of their Babylonian pulpits. *Ib.*

9 People will not look forward to posterity, who never look backward to their ancestors. *Ib.*

10 Government is a contrivance of human wisdom to provide for human *wants*. Men have a right that these wants should be provided for by this wisdom. *Ib.*

11 It is now sixteen or seventeen years since I saw the Queen of France, then the Dauphiness, at Versailles; and surely never lighted on this orb, which she hardly seemed to touch, a more delightful vision. I saw her just above the horizon, decorating and cheering the elevated sphere she just began to move in,—glittering like the morning star, full of life, and splendour, and joy. . . . Little did I dream that I should have lived to see disasters fallen upon her in a nation of gallant men, in a nation of men of honour, and of cavaliers. I thought ten thousand swords must have leaped from their scabbards to avenge even a look that threatened her with insult. But the age of chivalry is gone. That of sophisters, economists, and calculators, has succeeded; and the glory of Europe is extinguished for ever. *Ib.*

12 The unbought grace of life, the cheap defence of nations, the nurse of manly sentiment and heroic enterprise is gone! *Ib.*

13 It is gone, that sensibility of principle, that chastity of honour, which felt a stain like a wound. *Ib.*

14 Vice itself lost half its evil, by losing all its grossness. *Ib.*

15 The offspring of cold hearts and muddy understandings. *Ib.*

16 In the groves of *their* academy, at the end of every vista, you see nothing but the gallows. *Ib.*

17 Kings will be tyrants from policy, when subjects are rebels from principle. *Ib.*

18 Learning will be cast into the mire, and trodden down under the hoofs of a swinish multitude. *Ib.*

19 France has always more or less influenced manners in England: and when your fountain is choked up and polluted, the stream will not run long, or will not run clear with us, or perhaps with any nation.
Reflections on the Revolution in France

20 Because half a dozen grasshoppers under a fern make the field ring with their importunate chink, whilst thousands of great cattle, reposed beneath the shadow of the British oak, chew the cud and are silent, pray do not imagine that those who make the noise are the only inhabitants of the field; that, of course, they are many in number; or that, after all, they are other than the little, shrivelled, meagre, hopping, though loud and troublesome *insects* of the hour. *Ib.*

21 Who now reads Bolingbroke? Who ever read him through? Ask the booksellers of London what is become of all these lights of the world. *Ib.*

22 Man is by his constitution a religious animal. *Ib.*

23 A perfect democracy is therefore the most shameless thing in the world. *Ib.*

24 The men of England, the men, I mean, of light and leading in England. *Ib.*

25 Nobility is a graceful ornament to the civil order. It is the Corinthian capital of polished society. *Ib.*

26 Superstition is the religion of feeble minds. *Ib.*

27 He that wrestles with us strengthens our nerves, and sharpens our skill. Our antagonist is our helper. *Ib.*

28 Our patience will achieve more than our force. *Ib.*

29 Good order is the foundation of all good things. *Ib.*

30 The delicate and refined play of the imagination.
On the Sublime and Beautiful, introduction

31 I am convinced that we have a degree of delight, and that no small one, in the real misfortunes and pains of others. *Ib*. pt. i, § xiv

32 No passion so effectually robs the mind of all its powers of acting and reasoning as fear.
Ib. pt. ii, § ii

33 Custom reconciles us to everything.
Ib. pt. iv, § xviii

34 Laws, like houses, lean on one another.
Tracts on the Popery Laws, ch. 3, pt. i

35 In all forms of Government the people is the true legislator. *Ib.*

36 And having looked to government for bread, on the very first scarcity they will turn and bite the hand that fed them. *Thoughts and Details on Scarcity*

37 The writers against religion, whilst they oppose every system, are wisely careful never to set up any of their own.
A Vindication of Natural Society, preface

38 The fabric of superstition has in our age and nation received much ruder shocks than it had ever felt before; and through the chinks and breaches of our prison we see such glimmerings of light, and feel such refreshing airs of liberty, as daily raise our ardour for more.
A Vindication of Natural Society

39 A good parson once said, that where mystery begins, religion ends. Cannot I say, as truly at least, of human laws, that where mystery begins, justice ends? *Ib.*

1 The lucrative business of mystery.
A Vindication of Natural Society

2 The only infallible criterion of wisdom to vulgar judgments—success.
Letter to a Member of the National Assembly

3 Those who have been once intoxicated with power, and have derived any kind of emolument from it, even though but for one year, can never willingly abandon it. *Ib.*

4 Cromwell was a man in whom ambition had not wholly suppressed, but only suspended the sentiments of religion. *Ib.*

5 Tyrants seldom want pretexts. *Ib.*

6 You can never plan the future by the past. *Ib.*

7 To innovate is not to reform.
A Letter to a Noble Lord, 1796

8 These gentle historians, on the contrary, dip their pens in nothing but the milk of human kindness. *Ib.*

9 The king, and his faithful subjects, the lords and commons of this realm,—the triple cord, which no man can break. *Ib.*

10 The coquetry of public opinion, which has her caprices, and must have her way.
Letter to Thos. Burgh, New Year's Day, 1780

11 The arrogance of age must submit to be taught by youth. *Letter to Fanny Burney, 29 July 1782*

12 People crushed by law have no hopes but from power. If laws are their enemies, they will be enemies to laws; and those, who have much to hope and nothing to lose, will always be dangerous, more or less. *Letter to the Hon. C. J. Fox, 8 Oct. 1777*

13 The grand Instructor, Time.
Letter to Sir H. Langrishe, 26 May 1795

14 All men that are ruined are ruined on the side of their natural propensities.
Letters on a Regicide Peace, letter 1

15 Example is the school of mankind, and they will learn at no other. *Ib.*

16 Never, no, never, did Nature say one thing and Wisdom say another. *Ib. No. 3*

17 Well is it known that ambition can creep as well as soar. *Ib.*

18 He [the Duke of Richmond] was a host of debaters in himself.
Letter to the Marquis of Rockingham, 10 Jan. 1773

19 I know many have been taught to think that moderation, in a case like this, is a sort of treason.
Letter to the Sheriffs of Bristol

20 Between craft and credulity, the voice of reason is stifled. *Ib.*

21 If any ask me what a free government is, I answer, that for any practical purpose, it is what the people think so. *Ib.*

22 Liberty, too, must be limited in order to be possessed. *Ib.*

23 Nothing in progression can rest on its original plan. We may as well think of rocking a grown man in the cradle of an infant. *Ib.*

24 Among a people generally corrupt, liberty cannot long exist. *Ib.*

25 Nothing is so fatal to religion as indifference, which is, at least, half infidelity.
Letter to Wm. Smith, 29 Jan. 1795

26 The silent touches of time. *Ib.*

27 Somebody has said, that a king may make a nobleman, but he cannot make a gentleman. *Ib.*

28 Not merely a chip of the old 'block', but the old block itself. *On Pitt's First Speech, 1781*

29 Mr. Burke observed that Johnson had been very great that night; Mr. Langton . . . could have wished to hear more from another person; (plainly intimating that he meant Mr. Burke). 'O, no (said Mr. Burke), it is enough for me to have rung the bell to him.' *Boswell's Life of Johnson, vol. iv, p. 26*

30 'No, no,' said he, 'it is not a good imitation of Johnson; it has all his pomp, without his force; it has all the nodosities of the oak without its strength; it has all the contortions of the Sibyl without the inspiration.'
Remark to Boswell who had spoken of Croft's Life of Dr. Young *as a good imitation of Johnson's style.* Boswell's *Life of Johnson, vol. iv, p. 59*

WILLIAM CECIL, LORD BURLEIGH
1520–1598

31 What! all this for a song?
To Queen Elizabeth (when ordered to give a pension of £100 to Spenser). Birch, Life of Spenser, p. xiii

SIR FRANCIS COWLEY BURNAND
1836–1917

32 It's no matter what you do
If your heart be only true,
And his heart *was* true to Poll. *True to Poll*

BISHOP GILBERT BURNET
1643–1715

33 There was a sure way never to see it lost, and that was to die in the last ditch.
History of his own Times (1715), i. 457 (1766)

34 He [Halifax] had said he had known many kicked down stairs, but he never knew any kicked up stairs before. *Original Memoirs, c. 1697*

FANNY BURNEY [MME D'ARBLAY]
1752–1840

35 In the bosom of her respectable family resided Camilla. *Camilla, bk. i, ch. 1*

36 Travelling is the ruin of all happiness! There's no looking at a building here after seeing Italy. [*Mr. Meadows.*] *Cecilia, ed. 1904, bk. iv, ch. 2*

37 'True, very true, ma'am,' said he [Mr. Meadows], yawning, 'one really lives no where; one does but vegetate, and wish it all at an end.'
Ib. bk. vii, ch. 5

38 Indeed, the freedom with which Dr. Johnson condemns whatever he disapproves is astonishing.
Diary, 23 Aug. 1778

1 **All** the delusive seduction of martial music.
Diary, Ce 4 florial, 1802

2 'Do you come to the play without knowing what it is?' [*Mr. Lovell*]. 'O yes, Sir, yes, very frequently: I have no time to read play-bills; one merely comes to meet one's friends, and show that one's alive.'
Evelina, letter 20

JOHN BURNS
1858–1943

3 Every drop of the Thames is liquid 'istory.
Attrib. by Sir Frederick Whyte, K.C.S.I.

ROBERT BURNS
1759–1796

4 O thou! whatever title suit thee,
Auld Hornie, Satan, Nick, or Clootie.
Address to the Deil

5 But fare you weel, auld Nickie-ben!
O wad ye tak a thought an' men'!
Ye aiblins might—I dinna ken—
      Still hae a stake:
I'm wae to think upo' yon den,
      Ev'n for your sake!   *Ib.*

6 Ye're aiblins nae temptation.
Address To the Unco Guid

7 Then gently scan your brother man,
Still gentler sister woman;
Tho' they may gang a kennin wrang,
To step aside is human.   *Ib.*

8 Then at the balance let's be mute,
      We never can adjust it;
What's done we partly may compute,
      But know not what's resisted.   *Ib.*

9 Ae fond kiss, and then we sever.   *Ae Fond Kiss*

10 But to see her was to love her,
Love but her, and love for ever.   *Ib.*

11 Had we never lov'd sae kindly,
Had we never lov'd sae blindly,
Never met—or never parted,
We had ne'er been broken-hearted.   *Ib.*

12 Should auld acquaintance be forgot,
      And never brought to mind?   *Auld Lang Syne*

13 We twa hae run about the braes,
      And pu'd the gowans fine.   *Ib.*

14 We'll tak' a right gude-willie waught
For auld lang syne.   *Ib.*

15 We'll tak a cup o' kindness yet,
For auld lang syne.   *Ib.*

16 And there's a hand, my trusty fiere,
      And gie's a hand o' thine.   *Ib.*

17 But tell me whisky's name in Greek,
      I'll tell the reason.
The Author's Earnest Cry and Prayer, xxx

18 Freedom and Whisky gang thegither!   *Ib. xxxi*

19 Sleep I can get nane
      For thinking on my dearie.   *Ay Waukin O*

20 The poor inhabitant below
Was quick to learn and wise to know
And keenly felt the friendly glow

And softer flame;
But thoughtless follies laid him low,
      And stain'd his name!   *A Bard's Epitaph*

21 Know prudent cautious self-control
      Is wisdom's root.   *Ib.*

22 Come, Firm Resolve, take thou the van,
Thou stalk o' carl-hemp in man!
And let us mind, faint heart ne'er wan
A lady fair;
Wha does the utmost that he can,
Will whyles do mair.   *To Dr. Blacklock*

23 To make a happy fire-side clime
      To weans and wife,
That's the true pathos and sublime
      Of human life.   *Ib.*

24 But aye the tear comes in my ee,
To think on him that's far awa.
The Bonnie Lad that's far awa

25 O saw ye bonnie Lesley
      As she gaed o'er the border?
She's gane, like Alexander,
      To spread her conquests farther.
To see her is to love her,
      And love but her for ever,
For Nature made her what she is,
      And ne'er made anither!   *Bonnie Lesley*

26 The Deil he could na scaith thee,
      Or aught that wad belang thee;
He'd look into thy bonnie face,
      And say, 'I canna wrang thee'.   *Ib.*

27 Bonnie wee thing, cannie wee thing,
      Lovely wee thing, wert thou mine,
I wad wear thee in my bosom,
      Lest my jewel it should tine.
The Bonnie Wee Thing

28 Your poor narrow foot-path of a street,
Where twa wheel-barrows tremble when they meet.
The Brigs of Ayr

29 Hark! the mavis' evening sang
Sounding Clouden's woods amang;
Then a-faulding let us gang,
      My bonnie dearie.   *Ca' the Yowes*

30 She draiglet a' her petticoatie,
      Coming through the rye
      Coming through the Rye (taken from an old song,
      The Bob-tailed Lass).

31 Gin a body meet a body
      Coming through the rye;
Gin a body kiss a body,
      Need a body cry?   *Ib.*

32 Contented wi' little and cantie wi' mair.
Contented wi' Little

33 Th' expectant wee-things, toddlin', stacher through
      To meet their Dad, wi' flichterin' noise an' glee.
His wee bit ingle, blinkin bonnilie,
      His clean hearth-stane, his thrifty wifie's smile,
The lisping infant prattling on his knee,
      Does a' his weary kiaugh and care beguile,
An' makes him quite forget his labour an' his toil.
The Cotter's Saturday Night, iii

34 The mother, wi' her needle an' her sheers,
Gars auld claes look amaist as weel's the new.   *Ib. v*

35 They never sought in vain that sought the Lord
      aright!   *Ib. vi*

1 A wretch, a villain, lost to love and truth.
The Cotter's Saturday Night, x

2 The halesome parritch, chief of Scotia's food. *Ib.* xi

3 The sire turns o'er, wi' patriarchal grace,
The big ha'-Bible, ance his father's pride. *Ib.* xii

4 He wales a portion with judicious care,
And 'Let us worship God!' he says with solemn air.
Ib.

5 From scenes like these old Scotia's grandeur springs,
That makes her loved at home, revered abroad:
Princes and lords are but the breath of kings,
'An honest man's the noblest work of God.' *Ib.* xix

6 Ev'n ministers, they hae been kenn'd,
In holy rapture,
A rousing whid at times to vend,
And nail't wi' Scripture.
Death and Dr. Hornbook, i

7 I wasna fou, but just had plenty. *Ib.* iii

8 The auld kirk-hammer strak the bell
Some wee short hour ayont the twal. *Ib.* xxxi

9 On ev'ry hand it will allow'd be,
He's just—nae better than he should be.
A Dedication to Gavin Hamilton, l. 25

10 The De'il's Awa' Wi' the Exciseman. *Title of Song*

11 But Facts are chiels that winna ding,
An' downa be disputed. *A Dream*

12 Yet aft a ragged cowt's been known
To mak a noble aiver. *Ib.*

13 Duncan Gray cam here to woo,
Ha, ha, the wooing o't,
On blithe Yule-night when we were fou,
Ha, ha, the wooing o't.
Maggie coost her head fu' high,
Look'd asklent and unco skeigh,
Gart poor Duncan stand abeigh;
Ha, ha, the wooing o't. *Duncan Gray*

14 Meg was deaf as Ailsa Craig,
Ha, ha, the wooing o't,
Duncan sighed baith out and in,
Grat his een baith bleer't and blin',
Spak o' lowpin o'er a linn;
Ha, ha, the wooing o't. *Ib.*

15 How it comes let doctors tell,
Ha, ha, the wooing o't,
Meg grew sick as he grew haill,
Ha, ha, the wooing o't. *Ib.*

16 A Gentleman who held the patent for his honours
immediately from Almighty God.
Elegy on Capt. Matthew Henderson: from the title

17 Perhaps it may turn out a sang,
Perhaps turn out a sermon.
Epistle to a Young Friend, 1786

18 But still keep something to yoursel
Ye scarcely tell to ony. *Ib.*

19 I wa[i]ve the quantum o' the sin,
The hazard of concealing;
But och; it hardens a' within,
And petrifies the feeling! *Ib.*

20 An atheist-laugh's a poor exchange
For Deity offended. *Ib.*

21 And may ye better reck the rede
Than ever did th' adviser! *Ib.*

22 The heart aye's the part aye
That makes us right or wrang. *Epistle to Davie*

23 What's a' your jargon o' your schools,
Your Latin names for horns and stools;
If honest Nature made you fools,
What sairs your grammars?
First Epistle to John Lapraik

24 Gie me ae spark o' Nature's fire,
That's a' the learning I desire. *Ib.*

25 For thus the royal mandate ran,
When first the human race began,
'The social, friendly, honest man,
Whate'er he be,
'Tis he fulfils great Nature's plan,
And none but he!'
Second Epistle to Lapraik

26 My barmie noddle's working prime.
Epistle to James Smith

27 Some rhyme a neebor's name to lash;
Some rhyme (vain thought!) for needfu' cash;
Some rhyme to court the country clash,
An' raise a din;
For me, an aim I never fash;
I rhyme for fun. *Ib.*

28 Farewell dear, deluding Woman,
The joy of joys! *Ib.*

29 Flow gently, sweet Afton, among thy green braes,
Flow gently, I'll sing thee a song in thy praise.
My Mary's asleep by thy murmuring stream,
Flow gently, sweet Afton, disturb not her dream.
Flow gently, sweet Afton

30 The rank is but the guinea's stamp;
The man's the gowd for a' that!
For a' that and a' that

31 A man's a man for a' that. *Ib.*

32 A prince can mak a belted knight,
A marquis, duke, and a' that;
But an honest man's aboon his might,
Guid faith he mauna fa' that! *Ib.*

33 It's coming yet, for a' that,
That man to man the warld o'er
Shall brothers be for a' that. *Ib.*

34 My heart is sair, I daur na tell,
My heart is sair for Somebody.
For the Sake of Somebody

35 There's Death in the cup—so beware! *On a Goblet*

36 Go fetch to me a pint o' wine,
An' fill it in a silver tassie. *Go Fetch to Me a Pint*

37 Green grow the rashes O,
Green grow the rashes O;
The sweetest hours that e'er I spend,
Are spent amang the lasses O!

There's nought but care on ev'ry han',
In ev'ry hour that passes O;
What signifies the life o' man,
An 'twere na for the lasses O.
Green Grow the Rashes

38 But gie me a canny hour at e'en,
My arms about my dearie O;
An' warly cares, an' warly men,
May a' gae tapsalteerie O! *Ib.*

1 The wisest man the warl' saw,
  He dearly lov'd the lasses O.
    Green Grow the Rashes

2 Auld nature swears, the lovely dears
  Her noblest work she classes O;
  Her prentice han' she tried on man,
  An' then she made the lasses O. *Ib.*

3 That I for poor auld Scotland's sake,
  Some usefu' plan or beuk could make,
  Or sing a sang at least.
    To the Guidwife of Wauchope-House

4 Fair fa' your honest sonsie face,
  Great chieftain o' the puddin'-race!
  Aboon them a' ye tak your place,
      Painch, tripe, or thairm:
  Weel are ye wordy o' a grace
      As lang's my arm. *To a Haggis*

5 His spindle shank a guid whip-lash,
  His nieve a nit. *Ib.*

6 It's guid to be merry and wise,
  It's guid to be honest and true,
  It's guid to support Caledonia's cause,
  And bide by the buff and the blue.
    Here's a Health to Them that's Awa'

7 O, gie me the lass that has acres o' charms,
  O, gie me the lass wi' the weel-stockit farms.
    Hey for a Lass wi' a Tocher

8 Then hey, for a lass wi' a tocher—
  The nice yellow guineas for me! *Ib.*

9 The golden hours on angel wings
  Flew o'er me and my dearie;
  For dear to me as light and life
  Was my sweet Highland Mary. *Highland Mary*

10 But oh! fell death's untimely frost,
  That nipt my flower sae early! *Ib.*

11 Here some are thinkin' on their sins,
  An' some upo' their claes. *The Holy Fair*, x

12 Leeze me on drink! it gi'es us mair
  Than either school or college. *Ib.* xix

13 There's some are fou o' love divine,
  There's some are fou o' brandy. *Ib.* xxvii

14 I hae a wife o' my ain. *I Hae a Wife o' My Ain*

15 Naebody cares for me,
  I care for naebody. *Ib.*

16 It was a' for our rightfu' King
  We left fair Scotland's strand.
    It was a' for our Rightfu' King

17 Now a' is done that men can do,
  And a' is done in vain. *Ib.*

18 He turn'd him right and round about
  Upon the Irish shore;
  And gae his bridle-reins a shake,
  With adieu for evermore, My dear,
  Adieu for evermore. *Ib.*

19 John Anderson my jo, John,
  When we were first acquent,
  Your locks were like the raven,
  Your bonny brow was brent.
    John Anderson My Jo

20 John Anderson my jo, John,
  We clamb the hill thegither;
  And mony a canty day, John,
  We've had wi' ane anither:

Now we maun totter down, John,
  And hand in hand we'll go,
  And sleep thegither at the foot,
  John Anderson, my jo. *John Anderson My Jo*

21 There were three kings into the east,
  Three kings both great and high;
  And they hae sworn a solemn oath
  John Barleycorn should die. *John Barleycorn*

22 Partly wi' love o'ercome sae sair,
  And partly she was drunk.
    The Jolly Beggars, l. 221

23 Their tricks an' craft hae put me daft,
  They've ta'en me in, an' a' that,
  But clear your decks, an' '*here's the Sex!*'
  I like the jads for a' that. *Ib. l. 266*

24 A fig for those by law protected!
  Liberty's a glorious feast!
  Courts for cowards were erected,
  Churches built to please the priest. *Ib. l. 292*

25 Life is all a variorum,
  We regard not how it goes;
  Let them cant about decorum
  Who have characters to lose. *Ib. l. 308*

26 As cauld a wind as ever blew,
  A caulder kirk, and in't but few;
  A caulder preacher never spak;—
  Ye'se a' be het ere I come back.
    The Kirk of Lamington

27 I've seen sae mony changefu' years,
  On earth I am a stranger grown;
  I wander in the ways of men,
  Alike unknowing and unknown.
    Lament for James, Earl of Glencairn

28 The mother may forget the child
  That smiles sae sweetly on her knee;
  But I'll remember thee, Glencairn,
  And a' that thou hast done for me. *Ib.*

29 O had she been a country maid,
  And I the happy country swain.
    The Lass of Ballochmyle

30 When o'er the hill the eastern star
  Tells bughtin-time is near, my jo;
  I'll meet thee on the lea-rig,
  My ain kind dearie O. *The Lea-Rig*

31 True it is, she had one failing,
  Had a woman ever less?
    Lines written under the Picture of Miss Burns

32 Ha! whare ye gaun, ye crowlin' ferlie!
  Your impudence protects you sairly:
  I canna say but ye strunt rarely,
      Owre gauze and lace;
  Tho' faith! I fear ye dine but sparely
      On sic a place. *To a Louse*

33 O wad some Pow'r the giftie gie us
  To see oursels as others see us!
  It wad frae mony a blunder free us,
      And foolish notion. *Ib.*

34 Their sighin', cantin', grace-proud faces,
  Their three-mile prayers, and half-mile graces.
    To the Rev. John M'Math

35 May coward shame distain his name,
  The wretch that dares not die!
    Macpherson's Farewell

1   Nature's law,
That man was made to mourn.
Man was made to Mourn

2 Man's inhumanity to man
Makes countless thousands mourn!   *Ib.*

3 O Death, the poor man's dearest friend,
The kindest and the best!   *Ib.*

4 Thou lingering star, with lessening ray,
That lov'st to greet the early morn,
Again thou usherest in the day
My Mary from my soul was torn.
To Mary in Heaven

5 Time but the impression deeper makes,
As streams their channels deeper wear.   *Ib.*

6 I sigh'd, and said amang them a',
'Ye are na Mary Morison.'   *Mary Morison*

7 Wee modest crimson-tippèd flow'r.
To a Mountain Daisy

8 Ev'n thou who mourn'st the Daisy's fate,
That fate is thine—no distant date;
Stern Ruin's ploughshare drives elate
  Full on thy bloom,
Till crush'd beneath the furrow's weight
  Shall be thy doom!   *Ib.*

9 Wee, sleekit, cow'rin', tim'rous beastie,
O what a panic's in thy breastie!
Thou need na start awa sae hasty,
      Wi' bickering brattle!
I wad be laith to rin an' chase thee,
    Wi' murd'ring pattle!   *To a Mouse*

10 I'm truly sorry Man's dominion
Has broken Nature's social union,
An' justifies th' ill opinion
  Which makes thee startle
At me, thy poor, earth-born companion
  An' fellow-mortal!   *Ib.*

11 The best laid schemes o' mice an' men
  Gang aft a-gley.   *Ib.*

12 My heart's in the Highlands, my heart is not here;
My heart's in the Highlands a-chasing the deer;
Chasing the wild deer, and following the roe,
My heart's in the Highlands, wherever I go.
My Heart's in the Highlands. But see 420:24 in
Corrigenda, p. 587

13 Farewell to the Highlands, farewell to the North,
The birth-place of valour, the country of worth. *Ib.*

14 O, my Luve's like a red red rose
  That's newly sprung in June:
O my Luve's like the melodie
  That's sweetly play'd in tune.
My Love is like a Red Red Rose

15 The minister kiss'd the fiddler's wife,
An' could na preach for thinkin' o't.
My Love she's but a Lassie yet

16 She is a winsome wee thing,
She is a handsome wee thing,
She is a lo'esome wee thing,
  This sweet wee wife o' mine.
My Wife's a Winsome Wee Thing

17 Of a' the airts the wind can blaw,
I dearly like the west.   *Of a' the Airts*

18 If there's another world, he lives in bliss;
If there is none, he made the best of this.
On a Friend. Epitaph on Wm. Muir

19 He ne'er was gi'en to great misguidin',
Yet coin his pouches wad na bide in.
On a Scotch Bard

20 Hear, Land o' Cakes, and brither Scots.
On Captain Grose's Peregrinations

21 If there's a hole in a' your coats,
  I rede you tent it:
A chield's amang you taking notes,
    And, faith, he'll prent it.   *Ib.*

22 He has a fouth o' auld nick-nackets.   *Ib.*

23 An idiot race to honour lost,
Who know them best, despise them most.
On Seeing Sterling Palace in Ruins

24 O, wert thou in the cauld blast,
  On yonder lea, on yonder lea,
My plaidie to the angry airt,
  I'd shelter thee, I'd shelter thee.
O, Wert Thou in the Cauld Blast

25 Thy bield should be my bosom,
  To share it a', to share it a'.   *Ib.*

26 Or were I in the wildest waste,
  Sae black and bare, sae black and bare,
The desert were a paradise,
  If thou wert there, if thou wert there.   *Ib.*

27 The teeth o' Time may gnaw Tantallan,
  But thou's for ever!   *To Pastoral Poetry*

28 The mair they talk I'm kent the better.
E'en Let Them Clash

29 O Luve will venture in, where it daur na weel be
  seen.   *The Posie*

30 And I will pu' the pink, the emblem o' my dear,
For she's the pink o' womankind, and blooms without a peer.   *Ib.*

31 It's aye the cheapest lawyer's fee,
  To taste the barrel.   *Scotch Drink*

32 Scots, wha hae wi' Wallace bled,
Scots, wham Bruce has aften led,
Welcome to your gory bed,
  Or to victorie!
Now's the day, and now's the hour;
See the front o' battle lour!
See approach proud Edward's power—
    Chains and slaverie!   *Scots, Wha Hae*

33 Liberty's in every blow!
  Let us do or die!   *Ib.*

34 Some hae meat, and canna eat,
  And some wad eat that want it;
But we hae meat and we can eat,
  And sae the Lord be thankit.
The Selkirk Grace. As attributed to Burns

35 The Muse, nae poet ever fand her,
Till by himself he learned to wander
Adown some trotting burn's meander,
    An' no think lang;
To William Simpson

36 Good Lord, what is man! for as simple he looks,
Do but try to develop his hooks and his crooks,
With his depths and his shallows, his good and his
  evil,
All in all, he's a problem must puzzle the devil.
Sketch: inscribed to C. J. Fox

1 Tho' poor in gear, we're rich in love.
The Soldier's Return

2 Whare sits our sulky sullen dame,
Gathering her brows like gathering storm,
Nursing her wrath to keep it warm.
Tam o' Shanter, l. 10

3 Auld Ayr, wham ne'er a town surpasses
For honest men and bonnie lasses. *Ib. l. 15*

4 Ah, gentle dames! It gars me greet
To think how mony counsels sweet,
How mony lengthen'd sage advices,
The husband frae the wife despises! *Ib. l. 33*

5 His ancient, trusty, drouthy crony;
Tam lo'ed him like a vera brither;
They had been fou for weeks thegither. *Ib. l. 43*

6 Kings may be blest, but Tam was glorious,
O'er a' the ills o' life victorious! *Ib. l. 57*

7 But pleasures are like poppies spread—
You seize the flow'r, its bloom is shed;
Or like the snow falls in the river—
A moment white—then melts for ever. *Ib. l. 59*

8 Nae man can tether time or tide. *Ib. l. 67*

9 That hour, o' night's black arch the key-stane.
Ib. l. 69

10 Inspiring bold John Barleycorn!
What dangers thou canst make us scorn!
Wi' tippenny, we fear nae evil;
Wi' usquebae, we'll face the devil! *Ib. l. 105*

11 The mirth and fun grew fast and furious. *Ib. l. 143*

12 But Tam kent what was what fu' brawlie. *Ib. l. 163*

13 Ev'n Satan glowr'd, and fidg'd fu' fain,
An' hotched an' blew wi' might an' main:
Till first ae caper, syne anither,
Tam tint his reason a' thegither,
And roars out, 'Weel done, Cutty-sark!' *Ib. l. 185*

14 Ah, Tam! ah, Tam! thou'll get thy fairin'!
In hell they'll roast thee like a herrin'! *Ib. l. 201*

15 He'll hae misfortunes great and sma',
But aye a heart aboon them a'; *There was a Lad*

16 A man may drink and no be drunk;
A man may fight and no be slain;
A man may kiss a bonnie lass,
And aye be welcome back again.
There was a Lass, they ca'd her Meg

17 We labour soon, we labour late,
To feed the titled knave, man,
And a' the comfort we're to get,
Is that ayont the grave, man.
The Tree of Liberty, attributed to Burns

18 His lockèd, lettered, braw brass collar,
Shew'd him the gentleman and scholar.
The Twa Dogs, l. 13

19 The fient a pride na pride had he. *Ib. l. 16*

20 And there began a lang digression
About the lords of the creation. *Ib. l. 45*

21 But human bodies are sic fools,
For a' their colleges and schools,
That when nae real ills perplex them,
They mak enow themsels to vex them. *Ib. l. 195*

22 But hear their absent thoughts o' ither,
They're a' run deils an' jads thegither.
The Twa Dogs, l. 221

23 Rejoiced they were na men but dogs. *Ib. l. 236*

24 Up in the morning's no' for me,
Up in the morning early. *Up in the Morning*

25 Misled by fancy's meteor ray,
By passion driven;
But yet the light that led astray
Was light from Heaven. *The Vision, Duan II, xviii*

26 What can a young lassie, what shall a young lassie,
What can a young lassie do wi' an auld man?
What can a Young Lassie

27 And then his auld brass 'ill buy me a new pan. *Ib.*

28 O whistle, and I'll come to you, my lad:
O whistle, and I'll come to you, my lad:
Tho' father and mither and a' should gae mad,
O whistle, and I'll come to you, my lad.
Whistle, and I'll come to you, my Lad

29 Now we're married—speir nae mair—
Whistle owre the lave o't. *Whistle owre the lave o't*

30 We are na fou, we're nae that fou,
But just a drappie in our ee.
Willie Brewed a Peck o' Maut

31 It is the moon, I ken her horn,
That's blinkin' in the lift sae hie;
She shines sae bright to wyle us hame,
But, by my sooth! she'll wait a wee. *Ib.*

32 Sic a wife as Willie had,
I wad na gie a button for her! *Willie's Wife*

33 Her nose and chin they threaten ither. *Ib.*

34 Her face wad fyle the Logan-water. *Ib.*

35 The heart benevolent and kind
The most resembles God. *A Winter Night*

36 Ye banks and braes o' bonny Doon,
How can ye bloom sae fresh and fair?
How can ye chant, ye little birds,
And I sae weary fu' o' care?
Ye Banks and Braes o' Bonny Doon

37 Thou minds me o' departed joys,
Departed never to return. *Ib.*

38 And ilka bird sang of its love,
And fondly sae did I o' mine. *Ib.*

39 And my fause lover stole my rose,
But ah! he left the thorn wi' me. *Ib.*

40 Don't let the awkward squad fire over me.
*A. Cunningham's Works of Burns; with his Life,
1834, vol. i, p. 344*

JEREMIAH BURROUGHS

1599–1646

41 We use to say, it's a woman's reason to say, I will do
such a thing, because I will do it.
On Hosea, vol. iv, p. 80

BENJAMIN HAPGOOD BURT

nineteenth century

42 When you're all dressed up and no place to go.
Title of Song

HENRY BURTON
fl. 1886

1 Have you had a kindness shown?
   Pass it on!
   'Twas not given for thee alone,
   Pass it on!
   Let it travel down the years,
   Let it wipe another's tears,
   Till in Heaven the deed appears—
   Pass it on!   *Pass It On*

ROBERT BURTON
1577–1640

2 All my joys to this are folly,
   Naught so sweet as Melancholy.
   Anatomy of Melancholy. Author's Abstract of Melancholy

3 They lard their lean books with the fat of others' works.   *Ib. Democritus to the Reader*

4 We can say nothing but what hath been said. . . . Our poets steal from Homer. . . . Divines use Austin's words *verbatim* still, and our story-dressers do as much, he that comes last is commonly best.   *Ib.*

5 I had no time to lick it into form, as she [a bear] doth her young ones.   *Ib.*

6 Like watermen, that row one way and look another.   *Ib.*

7 Him that makes shoes go barefoot himself.   *Ib.*

8 All poets are mad.   *Ib.*

9 A loose, plain, rude writer.   *Ib.*

10 Cookery is become an art, a noble science: cooks are gentlemen.   *Ib. pt. i, § 2, memb. 2, subsect. 2*

11 Die to save charges.   *Ib. memb. 3, subsect. 12*

12 I may not here omit those two main plagues, and common dotages of human kind, wine and women, which have infatuated and besotted myriads of people. They go commonly together.   *Ib. subsect. 13*

13 Hinc quam sit calamus sævior ense patet.
   From this it is clear how much the pen is worse than the sword.   *Ib. memb. 4, subsect. 4*

14 One was never married, and that's his hell; another is, and that's his plague.   *Ib. subsect. 7*

15 [Fabricius] finds certain spots and clouds in the sun.   *Ib. pt. ii, § 2, memb. 3*

16 Seneca thinks he takes delight in seeing thee. The gods are well pleased when they see great men contending with adversity.   *Ib. § 3, memb. 1, subsect. 1*

17 Every thing, saith Epictetus, hath two handles, the one to be held by, the other not.   *Ib. memb. 3*

18 Who cannot give good counsel? 'tis cheap, it costs them nothing.   *Ib.*

19 What is a ship but a prison?   *Ib. memb. 4*

20 All places are distant from Heaven alike.   *Ib.*

21 The Commonwealth of Venice in their armoury have this inscription, 'Happy is that city which in time of peace thinks of war.'   *Ib. memb. 6*

22 Tobacco, divine, rare, superexcellent tobacco, which goes far beyond all their panaceas, potable gold, and philosopher's stones, a sovereign remedy to all diseases. . . . But, as it is commonly abused by most men, which take it as tinkers do ale, 'tis a plague, a mischief, a violent purger of goods, lands, health, hellish, devilish, and damned tobacco, the ruin and overthrow of body and soul.   *Anatomy of Melancholy*, pt. ii, § 4, memb. 2, subsect. 1

23 Let me not live, saith Aretine's Antonia, if I had not rather hear thy discourse than see a play!   *Ib. pt. iii, § 1, memb. 1, subsect. 1*

24 And this is that Homer's golden chain, which reacheth down from Heaven to earth, by which every creature is annexed, and depends on his Creator.   *Ib. subsect. 2*

25 To enlarge or illustrate this—is to set a candle in the sun.   *Ib. § 2, memb. 1, subsect. 2*

26 Cornelia kept her in talk till her children came from school, and these, said she, are my jewels.   *Ib. memb. 2, subsect. 3*

27 To these crocodile's tears, they will add sobs, fiery sighs, and sorrowful countenance.   *Ib. subsect. 4*

28 Diogenes struck the father when the son swore. *Ib.*

29 England is a paradise for women, and hell for horses: Italy a paradise for horses, hell for women, as the diverb goes.   *Ib. § 3, memb. 1, subsect. 2*

30 The miller sees not all the water that goes by his mill.   *Ib. memb. 4, subsect. 1*

31 The fear of some divine and supreme powers, keeps men in obedience. *Ib. § 4, memb. 1, subsect. 2*

32 One religion is as true as another.
       Ib. memb. 2, subsect. 1

33 Be not solitary, be not idle.   *Ib. Last words*

COMTE DE BUSSY-RABUTIN
1681–1693

34 L'absence est à l'amour ce qu'est au feu le vent; il éteint le petit, il allume le grand.

   Absence is to love what wind is to fire; it extinguishes the small, it enkindles the great.
   Histoire amoureuse des Gaules, Maximes d'Amours

BISHOP JOSEPH BUTLER
1692–1752

35 It has come, I know not how, to be taken for granted, by many persons, that Christianity is not so much as a subject of inquiry; but that it is, now at length, discovered to be fictitious.
   The Analogy of Religion (1756), *Advertisement*

36 But to *us*, probability is the very guide of life.
       Ib. Introduction

37 Things and actions are what they are, and the consequences of them will be what they will be: why then should we desire to be deceived?
       Fifteen Sermons. No. 7, § 16

38 Sir, the pretending to extraordinary revelations and gifts of the Holy Ghost is a horrid thing, a very horrid thing. [To John Wesley.]
       Wesley, Works, xiii. 449

NICHOLAS MURRAY BUTLER
1862–

1 ... a society like ours [U.S.A.] of which it is truly said to be often but three generations 'from shirt-sleeves to shirt-sleeves'. *True and False Democracy*

SAMUEL BUTLER
1612–1680

2 When civil fury first grew high,
And men fell out they knew not why.
Hudibras, pt. i, c. 1, l. 1

3 And pulpit, drum ecclesiastic,
Was beat with fist, instead of a stick. *Ib.* l. 11

4 Beside, 'tis known he could speak Greek,
As naturally as pigs squeak:
That Latin was no more difficile,
Than to a black-bird 'tis to whistle. *Ib.* l. 51

5 He was in logic a great critic,
Profoundly skill'd in analytic.
He could distinguish, and divide
A hair 'twixt south and south-west side.
On either which he would dispute,
Confute, change hands, and still confute. *Ib.* l. 65

6 He'd run in debt by disputation,
And pay with ratiocination. *Ib.* l. 77

7 For rhetoric he could not ope
His mouth, but out there flew a trope. *Ib.* l. 81

8 For all a rhetorician's rules
Teach nothing but to name his tools. *Ib.* l. 89

9 A Babylonish dialect
Which learned pedants much affect. *Ib.* l. 93

10 For he, by geometric scale,
Could take the size of pots of ale; ...
And wisely tell what hour o' th' day
The clock doth strike, by algebra. *Ib.* l. 121

11 Beside, he was a shrewd philosopher,
And had read ev'ry text and gloss over. *Ib.* l. 127

12 What ever sceptic could inquire for;
For every why he had a wherefore. *Ib.* l. 131

13 He knew what's what, and that's as high
As metaphysic wit can fly. *Ib.* l. 149

14 Such as take lodgings in a head
That's to be let unfurnished. *Ib.* l. 160

15 He could raise scruples dark and nice,
And after solve 'em in a trice:
As if Divinity had catch'd
The itch, of purpose to be scratch'd. *Ib.* l. 163

16 'T was Presbyterian true blue. *Ib.* l. 189

17 Such as do build their faith upon
The holy text of pike and gun. *Ib.* l. 193

18 And prove their doctrine orthodox
By apostolic blows and knocks. *Ib.* l. 197

19 And still be doing, never done:
As if Religion were intended
For nothing else but to be mended. *Ib.* l. 202

20 Compound for sins, they are inclin'd to
By damning those they have no mind to. *Ib.* l. 213

21 The trenchant blade, Toledo trusty,
For want of fighting was grown rusty,
And eat into it self, for lack
Of some body to hew and hack. *Ib.* l. 357

22 For rhyme the rudder is of verses,
With which like ships they steer their courses.
Hudibras, pt. i, c. 1, l. 457

23 For what is Worth in anything,
But so much Money as 'twill bring. *Ib.* l. 465

24 He ne'er consider'd it, as loth
To look a gift-horse in the mouth. *Ib.* l. 483

25 Quoth Hudibras, I smell a rat;
Ralpho, thou dost prevaricate. *Ib.* l. 815

26 Great actions are not always true sons
Of great and mighty resolutions. *Ib.* l. 885

27 There was an ancient sage philosopher,
That had read Alexander Ross over. *Ib.* c. 2, l. 1

28 Through perils both of wind and limb,
Through thick and thin she follow'd him. *Ib.* l. 369

29 Ay me! what perils do environ
The man that meddles with cold iron! *Ib.* c. 3, l. 1

30   I'll make the fur
Fly 'bout the ears of the old cur. *Ib.* l. 277

31 These reasons made his mouth to water. *Ib.* l. 379

32 Then while the honour thou hast got
Is spick and span-new, piping hot. *Ib.* l. 398

33 Cheer'd up himself with ends of verse,
And sayings of philosophers. *Ib.* l. 1011

34 Cleric before, and Lay behind;
A lawless linsy-woolsy brother,
Half of one order, half another. *Ib.* l. 1226

35 Learning, that cobweb of the brain,
Profane, erroneous, and vain. *Ib.* l. 1339

36 For nothing goes for sense, or light,
That will not with old rules jump right;
As if rules were not in the schools
Derived from truth, but truth from rules. *Ib.* l. 1353

37 Quoth Hudibras, Friend Ralph, thou hast
Outrun the constable at last. *Ib.* l. 1367

38 Not by your individual whiskers,
But by your dialect and discourse.
Ib. pt. ii, c. 1, l. 155

39 Some have been beaten till they know
What wood a cudgel's of by th' blow;
Some kick'd, until they can feel whether
A shoe be Spanish or neats-leather. *Ib.* l. 221

40 Such great achievements cannot fail,
To cast salt on a woman's tail. *Ib.* l. 277

41 She that with poetry is won
Is but a desk to write upon. *Ib.* l. 591

42 Love is a boy, by poets styl'd,
Then spare the rod, and spoil the child. *Ib.* l. 844

43 The sun had long since in the lap
Of Thetis, taken out his nap,
And like a lobster boil'd, the morn
From black to red began to turn. *Ib.* c. 2, l. 29

44 And after many circumstances,
Which vulgar authors in romances
Do use to spend their time and wits on,
To make impertinent description. *Ib.* l. 41

45 Have always been at daggers-drawing,
And one another clapper-clawing. *Ib.* l. 79

46 Oaths are but words, and words but wind. *Ib.* l. 107

1 For saints may do the same things by
The Spirit, in sincerity,
Which other men are tempted to.
Hudibras, pt. ii, c. 2. l. 235

2   As the ancients
Say wisely, Have a care o' th' main chance,
And look before you ere you leap;
For, as you sow, you are like to reap.   *Ib. l. 501*

3 Doubtless the pleasure is as great
Of being cheated, as to cheat.
As lookers-on feel most delight,
That least perceive a juggler's sleight,
And still the less they understand,
The more th' admire his sleight of hand.
Ib. c. 3, l. 1

4 He made an instrument to know
If the moon shine at full or no   *Ib. l. 261*

5 And fire a mine in China, here,
With sympathetic gunpowder.   *Ib. l. 295*

6 To swallow gudgeons ere th'are catch'd,
And count their chickens ere th'are hatch'd.
Ib. l. 923

7 T'enforce a desperate amour.   *Ib. pt. iii, c. 1, l. 2*

8 Still amorous, and fond, and billing,
Like Philip and Mary on a shilling.   *Ib. l. 687*

9 For in what stupid age or nation
Was marriage ever out of fashion?   *Ib. l. 817*

10 Discords make the sweetest airs.   *Ib. l. 919*

11 What makes all doctrines plain and clear?
About two hundred pounds a year.
And that which was prov'd true before,
Prove false again? Two hundred more.   *Ib. l. 1277*

12 With crosses, relics, crucifixes,
Beads, pictures, rosaries, and pixes,
The tools of working out salvation
By mere mechanic operation.   *Ib. l. 1495*

13 The saints engage in fierce contests
About their carnal interests.   *Ib. c. 2, introd.*

14 Both parties join'd to do their best
To damn the public interest.   *Ib. l. 147*

15 Neither have the hearts to stay,
Nor wit enough to run away.   *Ib. l. 569*

16 For if it be but half denied,
'Tis half as good as justified.   *Ib. l. 803*

17 For, those that fly, may fight again,
Which he can never do that's slain.   *Ib. c. 3, l. 243*

18 He that complies against his will,
Is of his own opinion still.   *Ib. l. 547*

19 For Justice, though she's painted blind,
Is to the weaker side inclin'd.   *Ib. l. 709*

20 For money has a power above
The stars and fate, to manage love.   *Ib. l. 1279*

21 And counted *breaking Priscian's head* a thing
More capital than to behead a king.
*Genuine Remains: Satire on the Imperfection of
Human Learning, pt. 2, l. 149*

22 The best of all our actions tend
To the preposterousest end.
*Ib. Satire upon the Weakness and Misery of
Man, l. 41*

23 The greatest saints and sinners have been made
The proselytes of one another's trade.
Miscellaneous Thoughts

24 All love at first, like generous wine,
Ferments and frets until 'tis fine;
But when 'tis settled on the lee,
And from th' impurer matter free,
Becomes the richer still the older,
And proves the pleasanter the colder.   *Ib.*

25 The souls of women are so small,
That some believe they've none at all.   *Ib.*

26 The law can take a purse in open court,
While it condemns a less delinquent for't.   *Ib.*

27 For trouts are tickled best in muddy water.
On a Hypocritical Nonconformist, iv

SAMUEL BUTLER
1835–1902

28 It has been said that although God cannot alter the
past, historians can; it is perhaps because they can
be useful to Him in this respect that He tolerates
their existence.   *Erewhon, ch. 14*

29 A wound in the solicitor is a very serious thing.
The Humour of Homer. Ramblings in Cheapside

30 I keep my books at the British Museum and at
Mudie's.   *Ib.*

31 The most perfect humour and irony is generally quite
unconscious.   *Life and Habit, ch. 2*

32 Life is one long process of getting tired.
Note Books. Life, vii

33 Life is the art of drawing sufficient conclusions from
insufficient premises.   *Ib. ix*

34 All progress is based upon a universal innate desire
on the part of every organism to live beyond its
income.   *Ib. xvi*

35 When the righteous man turneth away from his
righteousness that he hath committed and doeth
that which is neither quite lawful nor quite right,
he will generally be found to have gained in
amiability what he has lost in holiness.
Ib. Elementary Morality. Counsels of Imperfection

36 It costs a lot of money to die comfortably.
Ib. A Luxurious Death

37 The healthy stomach is nothing if not conservative.
Few radicals have good digestions.
Ib. Mind and Matter. Indigestion

38 The history of art is the history of revivals.
Ib. Handel and Music. Anachronism

39 Though wisdom cannot be gotten for gold, still less
can it be gotten without it. Gold, or the value of
what is equivalent to gold, lies at the root of wisdom,
and enters so largely into the very essence of the
Holy Ghost that 'no gold, no Holy Ghost' may pass
as an axiom. *Ib. Cash and Credit. Modern Simony*

40 Genius . . . has been defined as a supreme capacity
for taking trouble. . . . It might be more fitly
described as a supreme capacity for getting its
possessors into trouble of all kinds and keeping
them therein so long as the genius remains.
Ib. Genius, i

1 The phrase 'unconscious humour' is the one contribution I have made to the current literature of the day.
Note Books. The Position of a Homo Unius Libri. Myself and 'Unconscious Humour'

2 We were saying what a delightful dispensation of providence it was that prosperous people will write their memoirs. We hoped Tennyson was writing his. (1890.)
P.S. We think his son has done nearly as well. (1898.)
Ib. The Enfant Terrible of Literature

3 An apology for the Devil: It must be remembered that we have only heard one side of the case. God has written all the books.
Ib. Higgledy-Piggledy. An Apology for the Devil

4 God is Love, I dare say. But what a mischievous devil Love is. *Ib. God is Love*

5 To live is like love, all reason is against it, and all healthy instinct for it. *Ib. Life and Love*

6 The public buys its opinions as it buys its meat, or takes in its milk, on the principle that it is cheaper to do this than to keep a cow. So it is, but the milk is more likely to be watered.
Ib. Material for a Projected Sequel to Alps and Sanctuaries. Public Opinion

7 I do not mind lying, but I hate inaccuracy.
Ib. Truth and Convenience. Falsehood, iv

8 The world will, in the end, follow only those who have despised as well as served it.
Ib. Life of the World to Come. The World

9 An honest God's the noblest work of man.
Further Extracts from the Note-Books (1934), p. 26. See also Festing Jones, *Memoir* (1919), vol. i, p. 212. (*See also* 267:16)

10 'Man wants but little here below' but likes that little good—and not too long in coming. *Ib. p. 61*

11 Dulce et decorum est desipere in loco.
Ib. p. 92. (Horace, *Odes*, III. ii. 14, and IV. xii. 28.)

12 Jesus! with all thy faults I love thee still. *Ib. p. 117*

13 Taking numbers into account, I should think more mental suffering had been undergone in the streets leading from St. George's, Hanover Square, than in the condemned cells of Newgate.
The Way of All Flesh, ch. 13

14 The advantage of doing one's praising for oneself is that one can lay it on so thick and exactly in the right places. *Ib. ch. 34*

15 There's many a good tune played on an old fiddle.
Ib. ch. 61

16 'Tis better to have loved and lost, than never to have lost at all. *Ib. ch. 77*

17 O God! Oh Montreal! *Psalm of Montreal*

18 Preferrest thou the gospel of Montreal to the gospel of Hellas,
The gospel of thy connexion with Mr. Spurgeon's haberdasher to the gospel of the Discobolus?
Yet none the less blasphemed he beauty saying, 'The Discobolus hath no gospel,
But my brother-in-law is haberdasher to Mr. Spurgeon.' *Ib.*

19 Yet meet we shall, and part, and meet again,
Where dead men meet on lips of living men.
Poems. Life after Death

20 I would not be—not quite—so pure as you.
Ib. A Prayer

WILLIAM BUTLER
1535–1618

21 Doubtless God could have made a better berry [strawberry], but doubtless God never did.
Walton, *Compleat Angler*, pt. i, ch. 5

JOHN BYROM
1692–1763

22 Some say, that Signor Bononcini,
Compar'd to Handel's a mere ninny;
Others aver, to him, that Handel
Is scarcely fit to hold a candle.
Strange! that such high dispute shou'd be
'Twixt Tweedledum and Tweedledee.
Epigram on the Feuds between Handel and Bononcini

23 I shall prove it—as clear as a whistle.
Epistle to Lloyd, 1. xii

24 Christians awake, salute the happy morn,
Whereon the Saviour of the world was born.
Hymn for Christmas Day

25 God bless the King, I mean the Faith's Defender;
God bless—no harm in blessing—the Pretender;
But who Pretender is, or who is King,
God bless us all—that's quite another thing.
To an Officer in the Army

GEORGE GORDON BYRON, LORD BYRON
1788–1824

26 The 'good old times'—all times when old are good—
Are gone. *The Age of Bronze, i*

27 For what were all these country patriots born?
To hunt, and vote, and raise the price of corn?
Ib. xiv

28 Year after year they voted cent. per cent.,
Blood, sweat, and tear-wrung millions—why? for rent! *Ib.*

29 Woe is me, Alhama! *Siege and Conquest of Alhama, i*

30 And thou art dead, as young and fair
As aught of mortal birth. *And Thou Art Dead*

31 And wilt thou weep when I am low?
And Wilt Thou Weep?

32 Like the lost Pleiad seen no more below.
Beppo, xiv

33 Just like a coffin clapt in a canoe. [A gondola.] *Ib. xix*

34 In short, he was a perfect cavaliero,
And to his very valet seem'd a hero. *Ib. xxxiii*

35 His heart was one of those which most enamour us,
Wax to receive, and marble to retain. *Ib. xxxiv*

36 Besides, they always smell of bread and butter.
Ib. xxxix

37 I am ashes where once I was fire.
To the Countess of Blessington

1 Know ye the land where the cypress and myrtle
　Are emblems of deeds that are done in their clime?
Where the rage of the vulture, the love of the turtle,
　Now melt into sorrow, now madden to crime!
　　　　　　　　　　Bride of Abydos, c. I. i

2 Where the virgins are soft as the roses they twine,
And all, save the spirit of man, is divine? *Ib.*

3 The blind old man of Scio's rocky isle. *Ib.* c. II. ii

4 Mark! where his carnage and his conquests cease!
He makes a solitude, and calls it—peace! *Ib.* xx

5 Hark! to the hurried question of Despair:
　'Where is my child?'—an echo answers—
　　　　'Where?' *Ib.* xxvii

6 Adieu, adieu! my native shore
　Fades o'er the waters blue.
　　　　　　　　Childe Harold, c. I. xiii

7 My native land—Good Night! *Ib.*

8 In Biscay's sleepless bay. *Ib.* xiv

9 Here all were noble, save Nobility. *Ib.* lxxxv

10 War, war is still the cry, 'War even to the knife!'
　　　　　　　　　　Ib. lxxxvi

11 A schoolboy's tale, the wonder of an hour! *Ib.* c. II. ii

12 The dome of Thought, the palace of the Soul. *Ib.* vi

13 Well didst thou speak, Athena's wisest son!
'All that we know is, nothing can be known.' *Ib.* vii

14 Ah! happy years! once more who would not be a boy?
　　　　　　　　　　Ib. xxiii

15 None are so desolate but something dear,
　Dearer than self, possesses or possess'd
A thought, and claims the homage of a tear. *Ib.* xxiv

16 　The joys and sorrows sailors find,
Coop'd in their winged sea-girt citadel. *Ib.* xxviii

17 Fair Greece! sad relic of departed worth!
Immortal, though no more; though fallen, great!
　　　　　　　　　　Ib. lxxiii

18 Hereditary bondsmen! know ye not
Who would be free themselves must strike the blow?
　　　　　　　　　　Ib. lxxvi

19 Where'er we tread 'tis haunted, holy ground.
　　　　　　　　　　Ib. lxxxviii

20 What is the worst of woes that wait on age?
　What stamps the wrinkle deeper on the brow?
To view each loved one blotted from life's page,
　And be alone on earth, as I am now. *Ib.* xcviii

21 Ada! sole daughter of my house and heart. *Ib.* c. III. i

22 Once more upon the waters! yet once more!
And the waves bound beneath me as a steed
That knows his rider. *Ib.* ii

23 　　　　Years steal
Fire from the mind as vigour from the limb;
And life's enchanted cup but sparkles near the brim.
　　　　　　　　　　Ib. viii

24 Stop!—for thy tread is on an Empire's dust!
An earthquake's spoil is sepulchred below! *Ib.* xvii

25 There was a sound of revelry by night,
　And Belgium's capital had gather'd then
Her beauty and her chivalry, and bright
　The lamps shone o'er fair women and brave men;
A thousand hearts beat happily; and when

Music arose with its voluptuous swell,
Soft eyes look'd love to eyes which spake **again,**
　And all went merry as a marriage bell;
But hush! hark! a deep sound strikes like a rising knell!
　　　　　　　　Childe Harold, c. III. xxi

26 Did ye not hear it?—No; 'twas but the wind,
　Or the car rattling o'er the stony street;
On with the dance! let joy be unconfined;
　No sleep till morn, when Youth and Pleasure meet
To chase the glowing Hours with flying feet.
　　　　　　　　　　Ib. xxii

27 Arm! Arm! it is—it is—the cannon's opening roar!
　　　　　　　　　　Ib.

28 Within a window'd niche of that high hall
Sate Brunswick's fated chieftain. *Ib.* xxiii

29 He rush'd into the field, and, foremost fighting, fell.
　　　　　　　　　　Ib.

30 And there was mounting in hot haste. *Ib.* xxv

31 　Swiftly forming in the ranks of war;
And the deep thunder peal on peal afar. *Ib.*

32 Or whispering, with white lips—'The foe! they come!
　they come!' *Ib.*

33 Grieving, if aught inanimate e'er grieves,
　Over the unreturning brave,—alas! *Ib.* xxvii

34 Burning with high hope, shall moulder cold and low.
　　　　　　　　　　Ib.

35 Battle's magnificently stern array! *Ib.* xxviii

36 Rider and horse,—friend, foe,—in one red burial
　blent! *Ib.*

37 Bright names will hallow song. *Ib.* xxix

38 The tree will wither long before it fall. *Ib.* xxxii

39 Like to the apples on the Dead Sea's shore,
All ashes to the taste. *Ib.* xxxiv

40 There sunk the greatest, nor the worst of men,
Whose spirit, antithetically mixt,
One moment of the mightiest, and again
On little objects with like firmness fixt. [Napoleon.]
　　　　　　　　　　Ib. xxxvi

41 That untaught innate philosophy. *Ib.* xxxix

42 Quiet to quick bosoms is a hell. *Ib.* xlii

43 The castled crag of Drachenfels
Frowns o'er the wide and winding Rhine. *Ib.* lv

44 But these are deeds which should not pass away,
And names that must not wither. *Ib.* lxvii

45 Lake Leman woos me with its crystal face. *Ib.* lxviii

46 To fly from, need not be to hate, mankind. *Ib.* lxix

47 I live not in myself, but I become
Portion of that around me; and to me
High mountains are a feeling, but the hum
Of human cities torture. *Ib.* lxxii

48 The self-torturing sophist, wild Rousseau. *Ib.* lxxvii

49 Sapping a solemn creed with solemn sneer. [Gibbon.]
　　　　　　　　　　Ib. cvii

50 I have not loved the world, nor the world me;
　I have not flatter'd its rank breath, nor bow'd
To its idolatries a patient knee. *Ib.* cxiii

51 　　　　I stood
Among them, but not of them; in a shroud
Of thoughts which were not their thoughts. *Ib.*

1 I stood in Venice, on the Bridge of Sighs;
A palace and a prison on each hand.
Childe Harold, c. IV. i

2 Where Venice sate in state, throned on her hundred isles! *Ib.*

3 The spouseless Adriatic mourns her lord. *Ib.* xi

4 Oh for an hour of blind old Dandolo. *Ib.* xii

5   It may be a sound—
A tone of music—summer's eve—or spring—
A flower—the wind—the Ocean—which shall wound,
Striking the electric chain wherewith we are darkly
bound. *Ib.* xxiii

6 The moon is up, and yet it is not night;
Sunset divides the sky with her; a sea
Of glory streams along the Alpine height
Of blue Friuli's mountains; Heaven is free
From clouds, but of all colours seems to be,—
Melted to one vast Iris of the West,—
Where the day joins the past Eternity. *Ib.* xxvii

7 The Ariosto of the North. [Scott.] *Ib.* xl

8 Italia! oh Italia! thou who hast
The fatal gift of beauty. *Ib.* xlii

9 Let these describe the undescribable. *Ib.* liii

10 Love watching Madness with unalterable mien.
Ib. lxxii

11 Then farewell, Horace; whom I hated so,
Not for thy faults, but mine. *Ib.* lxxvii

12 Oh Rome! my country! city of the soul! *Ib.* lxxviii

13 The Niobe of nations! there she stands,
Childless and crownless, in her voiceless woe.
Ib. lxxix

14 Yet, Freedom! yet thy banner, torn, but flying,
Streams like the thunder-storm *against* the wind.
Ib. xcviii

15 Alas! our young affections run to waste,
Or water but the desert. *Ib.* cxx

16 Of its own beauty is the mind diseased. *Ib.* cxxii

17 Time, the avenger! *Ib.* cxxx

18 The arena swims around him—he is gone,
Ere ceased the inhuman shout which hail'd the wretch
who won. *Ib.* cxl

19 He heard it, but he heeded not—his eyes
Were with his heart, and that was far away;
He reck'd not of the life he lost nor prize,
But where his rude hut by the Danube lay,
There were his young barbarians all at play,
There was their Dacian mother—he, their sire,
Butcher'd to make a Roman holiday. *Ib.* cxli

20 A ruin—yet what ruin! from its mass
Walls, palaces, half-cities, have been rear'd.
Ib. cxliii

21 While stands the Coliseum, Rome shall stand;
When falls the Coliseum, Rome shall fall;
And when Rome falls—the World. *Ib.* cxlv

22   Spared and blest by time;
Looking tranquillity. *Ib.* cxlvi

23 The Lord of the unerring bow,
The God of life, and poesy, and light. *Ib.* clxi

24   So young, so fair,
Good without effort, great without a foe. *Ib.* clxxii

25 Oh! that the desert were my dwelling-place,
With one fair spirit for my minister,
That I might all forget the human race,
And, hating no one, love but only her!
Childe Harold, c. IV. clxxvii

26 There is a pleasure in the pathless woods,
There is a rapture on the lonely shore,
There is society, where none intrudes,
By the deep sea, and music in its roar:
I love not man the less, but Nature more,
From these our interviews, in which I steal
From all I may be, or have been before,
To mingle with the Universe, and feel
What I can ne'er express, yet cannot all conceal.
Ib. clxxviii

27 Roll on, thou deep and dark blue Ocean—roll!
Ten thousand fleets sweep over thee in vain;
Man marks the earth with ruin—his control
Stops with the shore. *Ib.* clxxix

28 He sinks into thy depths with bubbling groan,
Without a grave, unknell'd, uncoffin'd, and unknown.
Ib.

29 Time writes no wrinkle on thine azure brow:
Such as creation's dawn beheld, thou rollest now.
Ib. clxxxii

30 Thou glorious mirror, where the Almighty's form
Glasses itself in tempests. *Ib.* clxxxiii

31 Dark-heaving—boundless, endless, and sublime,
The image of eternity. *Ib.*

32 And I have loved thee, Ocean! and my joy
Of youthful sports was on thy breast to be
Borne, like thy bubbles, onward: from a boy
I wanton'd with thy breakers, . . .
And trusted to thy billows far and near,
And laid my hand upon thy mane—as I do here.
Ib. clxxxiv

33 Eternal spirit of the chainless mind!
Brightest in dungeons, Liberty! thou art.
Sonnet on Chillon

34 Chillon! thy prison is a holy place,
    And thy sad floor an altar—for 'twas trod,
Until his very steps have left a trace
    Worn, as if thy cold pavement were a sod,
By Bonnivard! May none those marks efface!
    For they appeal from tyranny to God. *Ib.*

35 My hair is grey, but not with years,
      Nor grew it white
      In a single night,
As men's have grown from sudden fears.
The Prisoner of Chillon, i

36 Regain'd my freedom with a sigh. *Ib.* xiv

37 The comet of a season. *Churchill's Grave*

38 The glory and the nothing of a name. *Ib.*

39 We were a gallant company,
Riding o'er land, and sailing o'er sea.
Oh! but we went merrily! *Siege of Corinth*, prologue

40 Thus was Corinth lost and won! *Ib.* xxxiii

41 The fatal facility of the octo-syllabic verse.
The Corsair, preface

42 O'er the glad waters of the dark blue sea,
Our thoughts as boundless, and our souls as free.
Ib. c. I. i

43 She walks the waters like a thing of life. *Ib.* iii

1 Such hath it been—shall be—beneath the sun
The many still must labour for the one.
The Corsair, c. I. viii

2 There was a laughing devil in his sneer. *Ib.* ix

3 Much hath been done, but more remains to do—
Their galleys blaze—why not their city too?
Ib. c. II. iv

4 The weak alone repent. *Ib.* x

5 Oh! too convincing—dangerously dear—
In woman's eye the unanswerable tear! *Ib.* xv

6 She for him had given
Her all on earth, and more than all in heaven!
Ib. c. III. xvii

7 He left a Corsair's name to other times,
Link'd with one virtue, and a thousand crimes.
Ib. xxiv

8 Slow sinks, more lovely ere his race be run,
Along Morea's hills the setting sun;
Not, as in northern climes, obscurely bright,
But one unclouded blaze of living light.
Curse of Minerva, I. 1, and *The Corsair*, III. i

9 I had a dream, which was not all a dream. *Darkness*

10 I tell thee, be not rash; a golden bridge
Is for a flying enemy.
The Deformed Transformed, pt. II, sc. ii

11 Through life's road, so dim and dirty,
I have dragg'd to three-and-thirty.
What have these years left to me?
Nothing—except thirty-three.
Diary, 21 Jan. 1821. In Moore's *Life of Byron*,
vol. ii, p. 414 (1st ed.).

12 I wish he would explain his explanation.
Don Juan, c. I, dedication ii

13 The intellectual eunuch Castlereagh. *Ib.* xi

14 My way is to begin with the beginning. *Ib.* vii

15 In virtues nothing earthly could surpass her,
Save thine 'incomparable oil', Macassar! *Ib.* xvii

16 But—Oh! ye lords of ladies intellectual,
Inform us truly, have they not hen-peck'd you all?
Ib. xxii

17 She
Was married, charming, chaste, and twenty-three.
Ib. lix

18 Her stature tall—I hate a dumpy woman. *Ib.* lxi

19 What men call gallantry, and gods adultery,
Is much more common where the climate's sultry.
Ib. lxiii

20 Christians have burnt each other, quite persuaded
That all the Apostles would have done as they did.
Ib. lxxxiii

21 A little still she strove, and much repented,
And whispering 'I will ne'er consent'—consented.
Ib. cxvii

22 'Tis sweet to hear the watch-dog's honest bark
Bay deep-mouth'd welcome as we draw near home;
'Tis sweet to know there is an eye will mark
Our coming, and look brighter when we come.
Ib. cxxiii

23 Sweet is revenge—especially to women. *Ib.* cxxiv

24 Pleasure's a sin, and sometimes sin's a pleasure.
Ib. cxxxiii

25 Man's love is of man's life a thing apart,
'Tis woman's whole existence.
Don Juan, c. I. cxciv

26 My grandmother's review—the British. *Ib.* ccix

27 So for a good old-gentlemanly vice,
I think I must take up with avarice. *Ib.* ccxvi

28 There's nought, no doubt, so much the spirit calms
As rum and true religion. *Ib.* c. II. xxxiv

29 'Twas twilight, and the sunless day went down
Over the waste of waters. *Ib.* xlix

30 A solitary shriek, the bubbling cry
Of some strong swimmer in his agony. *Ib.* liii

31 If this be true, indeed,
Some Christians have a comfortable creed. *Ib.* lxxxvi

32 He could, perhaps, have pass'd the Hellespont,
As once (a feat on which ourselves we prided)
Leander, Mr. Ekenhead, and I did. *Ib.* cv

33 Let us have wine and women, mirth and laughter,
Sermons and soda-water the day after. *Ib.* clxxviii

34 Man, being reasonable, must get drunk;
The best of life is but intoxication. *Ib.* clxxix

35 Alas! they were so young, so beautiful,
So lonely, loving, helpless. *Ib.* cxcii

36 A group that's quite antique,
Half naked, loving, natural, and Greek. *Ib.* cxciv

37 Alas! the love of women! it is known
To be a lovely and a fearful thing! *Ib.* cxcix

38 In her first passion woman loves her lover,
In all the others all she loves is love. *Ib.* c. III. iii

39 Romances paint at full length people's wooings,
But only give a bust of marriages;
For no one cares for matrimonial cooings,
There's nothing wrong in a connubial kiss:
Think you, if Laura had been Petrarch's wife,
He would have written sonnets all his life? *Ib.* viii

40 Dreading that climax of all human ills,
The inflammation of his weekly bills. *Ib.* xxxv

41 He was the mildest manner'd man
That ever scuttled ship or cut a throat,
With such true breeding of a gentleman,
You never could divine his real thought. *Ib.* xli

42 But Shakspeare also says, 'tis very silly
'To gild refined gold, or paint the lily.' *Ib.* lxxvi

43 The isles of Greece, the isles of Greece!
Where burning Sappho loved and sung,
Where grew the arts of war and peace,
Where Delos rose, and Phœbus sprung!
Eternal summer gilds them yet,
But all, except their sun, is set. *Ib.* lxxxvi. 1

44 The mountains look on Marathon—
And Marathon looks on the sea;
And musing there an hour alone,
I dream'd that Greece might still be free. *Ib.* 3

45 A king sate on the rocky brow
Which looks o'er sea-born Salamis;
And ships, by thousands, lay below,
And men in nations;—all were his!
He counted them at break of day—
And when the sun set where were they? *Ib.* 4

46 Earth! render back from out thy breast
A remnant of our Spartan dead!
Of the three hundred grant but three,
To make a new Thermopylæ! *Ib.* 7

1 Fill high the cup with Samian wine!
Don Juan, c. III. lxxxvi. 9

2 You have the Pyrrhic dance as yet;
　Where is the Pyrrhic phalanx gone!
Of two such lessons, why forget
　The nobler and the manlier one?
You have the letters Cadmus gave—
Think ye he meant them for a slave?　*Ib.* 10

3 Place me on Sunium's marbled steep,
　Where nothing, save the waves and I,
May hear our mutual murmurs sweep;
　There, swan-like, let me sing and die:
A land of slaves shall ne'er be mine—
Dash down yon cup of Samian wine!　*Ib.* 16

4 Milton's the prince of poets—so we say;
　A little heavy, but no less divine.　*Ib.* xci

5 A drowsy frowzy poem, call'd the 'Excursion',
Writ in a manner which is my aversion.　*Ib.* xciv

6 We learn from Horace, 'Homer sometimes sleeps';
We feel without him, Wordsworth sometimes wakes.
　　　　Ib. xcviii

7 Ave Maria! 'tis the hour of prayer!
Ave Maria! 'tis the hour of love!　*Ib.* ciii

8 Imagination droops her pinion.　*Ib.* c. IV. iii

9 And if I laugh at any mortal thing,
　'Tis that I may not weep.　*Ib.* iv

10 'Whom the gods love die young' was said of yore.
　　　　Ib. xii

11 'Arcades ambo', *id est*—blackguards both.　*Ib.* xciii

12 I've stood upon Achilles' tomb,
　And heard Troy doubted; time will doubt of Rome.
　　　　Ib. ci

13 Oh! 'darkly, deeply, beautifully blue',
　As some one somewhere sings about the sky. *Ib.* cx

14 When amatory poets sing their loves
　In liquid lines mellifluously bland,
And pair their rhymes as Venus yokes her doves.
　　　　Ib. c. v. i

15 I have a passion for the name of 'Mary',
　For once it was a magic sound to me:
And still it half calls up the realms of fairy,
　Where I beheld what never was to be.　*Ib.* iv

16 A lady in the case.　*Ib.* xix

17 And put himself upon his good behaviour.　*Ib.* xlvii

18 That all-softening, overpowering knell,
　The tocsin of the soul—the dinner-bell.　*Ib.* xlix

19 Not to admire is all the art I know.　*Ib.* ci
　　　(See 257:1, 386:33)

20 Why don't they knead two virtuous souls for life
Into that moral centaur, man and wife?　*Ib.* clviii

21 There is a tide in the affairs of women,
　Which, taken at the flood, leads—God knows
　where.　*Ib.* c. VI. ii

22 A lady of a 'certain age', which means
Certainly aged.　*Ib.* lxix

23 A 'strange coincidence', to use a phrase
By which such things are settled now-a-days.
　　　　Ib. lxxviii

24 'Let there be light!' said God, 'and there was light!'
'Let there be blood!' says man, and there's a sea!
　　　　Ib. c. VII. xli

25 'Carnage, (so Wordsworth tells you), is God's
　daughter.'　*Don Juan*, c. VIII. ix

26 Oh, Wellington! (or 'Villainton')—for Fame
Sounds the heroic syllables both ways.　*Ib.* c. IX. i

27 Call'd 'Saviour of the Nations'—not yet saved,
And 'Europe's Liberator'—still enslaved. [Welling-
ton.]　*Ib.* v

28 Never had mortal man such opportunity,
Except Napoleon, or abused it more.　*Ib.* ix

29 That water-land of Dutchmen and of ditches.
　　　　Ib. c. X. lxiii

30 When Bishop Berkeley said 'there was no matter',
　And proved it—'twas no matter what he said.
　　　　Ib. c. XI. i

31 But Tom's no more—and so no more of Tom.
　　　　Ib. xx

32 And, after all, what is a lie? 'Tis but
　The truth in masquerade.　*Ib.* xxxvii

33 　I—albeit I'm sure I did not know it,
　Nor sought of foolscap subjects to be king.—
　Was reckon'd, a considerable time,
　The grand Napoleon of the realms of rhyme. *Ib.* lv

34 But Juan was my Moscow, and Faliero
　My Leipsic, and my Mont Saint Jean seems Cain.
　　　　Ib. lvi

35 John Keats, who was kill'd off by one critique,
　Just as he really promised something great,
　If not intelligible, without Greek
　Contrived to talk about the Gods of late,
　Much as they might have been supposed to speak.
　Poor fellow! His was an untoward fate;
　'Tis strange the mind, that very fiery particle,
　Should let itself be snuff'd out by an article. *Ib.* lx

36 Nought's permanent among the human race,
　Except the Whigs *not* getting into place.　*Ib.* lxxxii

37 Love rules the camp, the court, the grove—for love
Is heaven, and heaven is love.　*Ib.* c. XII. xiii

38 And hold up to the sun my little taper.　*Ib.* xxi

39 For talk six times with the same single lady,
　And you may get the wedding dresses ready. *Ib.* lix

40 　　Merely innocent flirtation,
Not quite adultery, but adulteration.　*Ib.* lxiii

41 A Prince . . .
With fascination in his very bow.　*Ib.* lxxxiv

42 A finish'd gentleman from top to toe.　*Ib.*

43 Beauteous, even where beauties most abound.
　　　　Ib. c. XIII. ii

44 Now hatred is by far the longest pleasure;
Men love in haste, but they detest at leisure.　*Ib.* vi

45 Cervantes smiled Spain's chivalry away.　*Ib.* xi

46 I hate to hunt down a tired metaphor.　*Ib.* xxxvi

47 The English winter—ending in July,
　To recommence in August.　*Ib.* xlii

48 Society is now one polish'd horde,
　Form'd of two mighty tribes, the *Bores* and *Bored*.
　　　　Ib. xcv

49 I for one venerate a petticoat.　*Ib.* c. XIV. xxvi

50 Of all the horrid, hideous notes of woe,
　Sadder than owl-songs or the midnight blast,
Is that portentous phrase, 'I told you so.'　*Ib.* l

1 'Tis strange—but true; for truth is always strange;
Stranger than fiction.   *Don Juan*, c. xiv. ci

2 A lovely being, scarcely form'd or moulded,
A rose with all its sweetest leaves yet folded.
          Ib. c. xv. xliii

3 The antique Persians taught three useful things,
To draw the bow, to ride, and speak the truth.
          Ib. c. xvi. i

4 Not so her gracious, graceful, graceless Grace.
          Ib. xlix

5 The loudest wit I e'er was deafen'd with.   *Ib.* lxxxi

6 And both were young, and one was beautiful.
          The Dream, ii

7 A change came o'er the spirit of my dream.   *Ib.* v

8 Still must I hear?—shall hoarse Fitzgerald bawl
His creaking couplets in a tavern hall.
          English Bards and Scotch Reviewers, l. 1

9   I'll publish, right or wrong:
Fools are my theme, let satire be my song.   *Ib.* l. 5

10 'Tis pleasant, sure, to see one's name in print;
A book's a book, although there's nothing in 't.
          Ib. l. 51

11 A man must serve his time to every trade
Save censure—critics all are ready made.   *Ib.* l. 63

12 With just enough of learning to misquote.   *Ib.* l. 66

13   As soon
Seek roses in December—ice in June;
Hope constancy in wind, or corn in chaff;
Believe a woman or an epitaph,
Or any other thing that's false, before
You trust in critics, who themselves are sore. *Ib.* l. 75

14 Better to err with Pope, than shine with Pye. *Ib.* l. 102

15 Sense and wit with poesy allied.   *Ib.* l. 105

16 Who both by precept and example, shows
That prose is verse, and verse is merely prose.
          Ib. l. 241

17 Be warm, but pure: be amorous, but be chaste.
          Ib. l. 306

18 Perverts the Prophets, and purloins the Psalms.
          Ib. l. 326

19 Oh, Amos Cottle!—Phoebus! what a name
To fill the speaking trump of future fame!
          Ib. l. 399

20 The petrifactions of a plodding brain.   *Ib.* l. 416

21 To sanction Vice, and hunt Decorum down.
          Ib. l. 621

22 To live like Clodius, and like Falkland fall.
          Ib. l. 686

23 Lords too are bards, such things at times befall,
And 'tis some praise in peers to write at all.
          Ib. l. 719

24 Forsook the labours of a servile state.
Stemm'd the rude storm, and triumph'd over fate.
          Ib. l. 779

25 [*Kirke White*:]
'Twas thine own genius gave the final blow,
And help'd to plant the wound that laid thee low:
So the struck eagle, stretch'd upon the plain,
No more through rolling clouds to soar again,
View'd his own feather on the fatal dart,
And wing'd the shaft that quiver'd in his heart;

Keen were his pangs, but keener far to feel
He nursed the pinion which impell'd the steel;
While the same plumage that had warm'd his nest
Drank the last life-drop of his bleeding breast.
          English Bards and Scotch Reviewers, l. 839

26 Yet Truth sometimes will lend her noblest fires,
And decorate the verse herself inspires:
This fact in Virtue's name let Crabbe attest;
Though nature's sternest painter, yet the best.
          Ib. l. 855

27 The mighty master of unmeaning rhyme. [Darwin.]
          Ib. l. 894

28 Let simple Wordsworth chime his childish verse,
And brother Coleridge lull the babe at nurse.
          Ib. l. 917

29 Glory, like the phoenix 'midst her fires,
Exhales her odours, blazes, and expires.   *Ib.*

30 I too can hunt a poetaster down.   *Ib.*

31 The world is a bundle of hay,
          Mankind are the asses who pull;
Each tugs it a different way,
          And the greatest of all is John Bull.   *Epigram.*

32 My sister! my sweet sister! if a name
Dearer and purer were, it should be thine.
          Epistle to Augusta

33 And know, whatever thou hast been,
'Tis something better not to be.   *Euthanasia*

34 Fare thee well! and if for ever,
Still for ever, fare thee well.   *Fare Thee Well!*

35 I only know we loved in vain—
I only feel—Farewell!—Farewell!
          Farewell! if ever Fondest Prayer

36 Nor be, what man should ever be,
The friend of Beauty in distress?   *To Florence*

37 Clime of the unforgotten brave!
          The Giaour, l. 103

38 For Freedom's battle once begun,
Bequeath'd by bleeding Sire to Son,
Though baffled oft is ever won.   *Ib.* l. 123

39 Dark tree, still sad when others' grief is fled,
The only constant mourner o'er the dead! [A cypress.]
          Ib. l. 286

40 And lovelier things have mercy shown
To every failing but their own,
And every woe a tear can claim
Except an erring sister's shame.   *Ib.* l. 418

41 The harp the monarch minstrel swept.   *Title*

42 Or lend fresh interest to a twice-told tale.
          Hints from Horace, l. 184

43 Friendship is Love without his wings!
          Hours of Idleness. L'Amitié

44 I have tasted the sweets and the bitters of love.
          Ib. To Rev. J. T. Becher

45 Though women are angels, yet wedlock's the devil.
          Ib. To Eliza

46 Then receive him as best such an advent becomes,
With a legion of cooks, and an army of slaves!
          The Irish Avatar

47 More happy, if less wise.   *The Island*, c. ii. xi

1 Jack was embarrassed—never hero more,
And as he knew not what to say, he swore.
The Island, c. IV. v

2 Who killed John Keats?
'I,' says the Quarterly,
So savage and Tartarly;
''Twas one of my feats.'   *John Keats*

3 Weep, daughter of a royal line.
Lines to a Lady Weeping

4 Left by his sire, too young such loss to know,
Lord of himself—that heritage of woe.
Lara, c. I. ii

5 His madness was not of the head, but heart.
Ib. xviii

6 Maid of Athens, ere we part,
Give, oh give me back my heart!
Or, since that has left my breast,
Keep it now, and take the rest!   *Maid of Athens*

7 Mont Blanc is the monarch of mountains;
They crown'd him long ago
On a throne of rocks, in a robe of clouds,
With a diadem of snow.   *Manfred, I. i*

8 When the moon is on the wave,
And the glow-worm in the grass,
And the meteor on the grave,
And the wisp on the morass;
When the falling stars are shooting,
And the answer'd owls are hooting,
And the silent leaves are still
In the shadow of the hill.   *Ib.*

9 By that most seeming-virtuous eye.   *Ib.*

10 The heart ran o'er
With silent worship of the great of old—
The dead but sceptred sovereigns, who still rule
Our spirits from their urns.   *Ib. III. iv*

11 Old man! 'tis not so difficult to die.   *Ib.*

12 You have deeply ventured;
But all must do so who would greatly win.
Marino Faliero, I. ii

13 'Bring forth the horse!'—the horse was brought;
In truth, he was a noble steed.   *Mazeppa, ix. I*

14 My boat is on the shore,
And my bark is on the sea;
But, before I go, Tom Moore,
Here's a double health to thee!   *To Thomas Moore*

15 Here's a sigh to those who love me,
And a smile to those who hate;
And, whatever sky 's above me,
Here's a heart for every fate.   *Ib.*

16 My Murray.   *To Mr. Murray*

17 There be none of Beauty's daughters
With a magic like thee.
*Stanzas for Music. 'There be none of Beauty's
daughters'*

18 There's not a joy the world can give like that it takes
away.   *Ib. 'There's not a joy the world can give'*

19 'Tis done—but yesterday a King!
And arm'd with Kings to strive—
And now thou art a nameless thing:
So abject—yet alive!   *Ode to Napoleon Bonaparte*

20 The Arbiter of others' fate
A Suppliant for his own!   *Ib.*

21 The Cincinnatus of the West. [Washington.]
Ode to Napoleon Bonaparte

22 But the poor dog, in life the firmest friend,
The first to welcome, foremost to defend.
Inscription on a Newfoundland Dog

23 Oh! snatched away in beauty's bloom,
On thee shall press no ponderous tomb;
But on thy turf shall roses rear
Their leaves, the earliest of the year.
Oh! Snatched Away in Beauty's Bloom

24 It is not in the storm nor in the strife
We feel benumb'd, and wish to be no more,
But in the after-silence on the shore,
When all is lost, except a little life.
On Hearing Lady Byron was Ill

25 The moral Clytemnestra of thy lord.   *Ib.*

26 My days are in the yellow leaf;
The flowers and fruits of love are gone;
The worm, the canker, and the grief
Are mine alone!
On This Day I Complete my Thirty-Sixth Year

27 Seek out—less often sought than found—
A soldier's grave, for thee the best;
Then look around, and choose thy ground,
And take thy rest.   *Ib.*

28 It is the hour when from the boughs
The nightingale's high note is heard;
It is the hour when lovers' vows
Seem sweet in every whisper'd word.   *Parisina*

29 Yet in my lineaments they trace
Some features of my father's face.   *Ib.*

30 Thy Godlike crime was to be kind,
To render with thy precepts less
The sum of human wretchedness.   *Prometheus*

31 Man in portions can foresee
His own funereal destiny.   *Ib.*

32 Oh, talk not to me of a name great in story;
The days of our youth are the days of our glory;
And the myrtle and ivy of sweet two-and-twenty
Are worth all your laurels, though ever so plenty.
*Stanzas Written on the Road between Florence
and Pisa.*

33 Oh Fame!—if I e'er took delight in thy praises,
'Twas less for the sake of thy high-sounding phrases,
Than to see the bright eyes of the dear one discover,
She thought that I was not unworthy to love her.   *Ib.*

34 I knew it was love, and I felt it was glory.   *Ib.*

35 By all that's good and glorious take this counsel.
Sardanapalus, I. ii

36 I am the very slave of circumstance
And impulse—borne away with every breath!
Ib. IV. i

37 The Assyrian came down like the wolf on the fold,
And his cohorts were gleaming in purple and gold;
And the sheen of their spears was like stars on the sea,
When the blue wave rolls nightly on deep Galilee.
Destruction of Sennacherib

38 For the Angel of Death spread his wings on the
blast.   *Ib.*

39 And the might of the Gentile, unsmote by the sword,
Hath melted like snow in the glance of the Lord! *Ib.*

1 She walks in beauty, like the night
  Of cloudless climes and starry skies;
And all that's best of dark and bright
  Meet in her aspect and her eyes:
Thus mellow'd to that tender light
  Which heaven to gaudy day denies.
                Hebrew Melodies. She Walks in Beauty

2 And on that cheek, and o'er that brow,
  So soft, so calm, yet eloquent,
The smiles that win, the tints that glow
  But tell of days in goodness spent,
A mind at peace with all below,
  A heart whose love is innocent!   *Ib.*

3 Born in the garret, in the kitchen bred,
Promoted thence to deck her mistress' head.
                                    A Sketch

4 So, we'll go no more a roving
  So late into the night,
Though the heart be still as loving,
  And the moon be still as bright.
              So, We'll Go No More a Roving

5 For the sword outwears its sheath,
  And the soul wears out the breast.
And the heart must pause to breathe,
  And love itself have rest.   *Ib.*

6 Though the night was made for loving,
  And the day returns too soon,
Yet we'll go no more a-roving
  By the light of the moon.   *Ib.*

7 Could Love for ever
  Run like a river.   *Stanzas*

8 Part in friendship—and bid good-night. *Ib.*

9 Though the day of my destiny's over,
  And the star of my fate hath declined.
              Stanzas to Augusta

10 In the desert a fountain is springing,
   In the wide waste there still is a tree,
And a bird in the solitude singing,
   Which speaks to my spirit of *thee*.   *Ib.*

11 And Freedom hallows with her tread
   The silent cities of the dead.
           On the Star of 'The Legion of Honour'

12 And when we think we lead, we are most led.
                The Two Foscari, II. i

13 The Mede is at his gate!
   The Persian on his throne!   *Vision of Belshazzar*

14 Saint Peter sat by the celestial gate:
   His keys were rusty, and the lock was dull.
                Vision of Judgement, i

15 The angels all were singing out of tune,
   And hoarse with having little else to do,
Excepting to wind up the sun and moon,
   Or curb a runaway young star or two.   *Ib.* ii

16 Each day too slew its thousands six or seven
   Till at the crowning carnage, Waterloo,
They threw their pens down in divine disgust—
   The page was so besmear'd with blood and dust.
                                    Ib. v

17 A better farmer ne'er brushed dew from lawn,
   A worse king never left a realm undone.   *Ib.* viii

18 It seem'd the mockery of hell to fold
   The rottenness of eighty years in gold.   *Ib.* x

19 In whom his qualities are reigning still,
Except that household virtue, most uncommon,
Of constancy to a bad, ugly woman.
                Vision of Judgement, xii

20   'Midst them an old man
With an old soul, and both extremely blind. *Ib.* xxiii

21 As he drew near, he gazed upon the gate
Ne'er to be entered more by him or Sin,
With such a glance of supernatural hate
As made Saint Peter wish himself within;
He patter'd with his keys at a great rate,
And sweated through his apostolic skin:
Of course his perspiration was but ichor,
Or some such other spiritual liquor.
                                    Ib. xxv

22 Yet still between his Darkness and his Brightness
There pass'd a mutual glance of great politeness.
                                    Ib. xxxv

23 The Archangel bow'd, not like a modern beau.
                                    Ib. xxxvi

24   Satan met his ancient friend
With more hauteur, as might an old Castilian
Poor noble meet a mushroom rich civilian   *Ib.*

25 When Michael saw this host, he first grew pale,
As angels can; next, like Italian twilight,
He turn'd all colours—as a peacock's tail,
Or sunset streaming through a Gothic skylight
In some old abbey, or a trout not stale,
Or distant lightning on the horizon *by* night
Or a fresh rainbow, or a grand review
Of thirty regiments in red, green, and blue.
                                    Ib. lxi

26 And when the tumult dwindled to a calm,
I left him practising the hundredth psalm.   *Ib.* cvi

27 Seductive Waltz!   *The Waltz*

28 Voluptuous Waltz!   *Ib.*

29 When we two parted
     In silence and tears,
   Half broken-hearted
     To sever for years,
Pale grew thy cheek and cold,
   Colder thy kiss.   *When We Two Parted*

30 If I should meet thee
   After long years,
How should I greet thee?—
   With silence and tears.   *Ib.*

31 The fault was Nature's fault not thine,
   Which made thee fickle as thou art.
                To a Youthful Friend

32 No *Manual*, no letters, no tooth-powder, no *extract*
   from Moore's *Italy* concerning Marino Falieri, no
   nothing—as a man hallooed out at one of Burdett's
   elections, after a long ululatus of No Bastille! No
   Governor Aris! No '—God knows what';—but his
   ne plus ultra was, 'no nothing!'
                Letter to Murray, 4 June 1817

33 I am sure my bones would not rest in an English
   grave, or my clay mix with the earth of that country.
   I believe the thought would drive me mad on my
   deathbed, could I suppose that any of my friends
   would be base enough to convey my carcass back
   to your soil.   *Ib. 7 June 1819*

34 The Princess of Parallelograms.
   (*Speaking of Annabella Milbanke to Lady Melbourne*)

1 As he [Lord Byron] himself briefly described it in his Memoranda, 'I awoke one morning and found myself famous.'—Moore's *Life of Byron, 1830*, vol. i, p. 347 (referring to the instantaneous success of *Childe Harold*)

HENRY JAMES BYRON
1834-1884

2 Life's too short for chess.　　　*Our Boys*, Act I

3 He's up to these grand games, but one of these days I'll loore him on to skittles—and astonish him.
　　　　　　　　　　　　　　Ib. Act II

JAMES BRANCH CABELL
1879-

4 I am willing to taste any drink once.　*Jurgen*, ch. 1

5 A man possesses nothing certainly save a brief loan of his own body: and yet the body of man is capable of much curious pleasure.　*Ib.* ch. 20

6 The optimist proclaims that we live in the best of all possible worlds; and the pessimist fears this is true.　　　*The Silver Stallion*, bk. iv, ch. 26

AUGUSTUS CAESAR
63 B.C.–A.D. 14

7 Quintili Vare, legiones redde.
　　Quintilius Varus, give me back my legions.
　　　　　　Suetonius, *Divus Augustus*, 23

8 Urbem . . . excoluit adeo, ut iure sit gloriatus marmoream se relinquere, quam latericiam accepisset.
　　He so improved the city that he justly boasted that he found it brick and left it marble.　*Ib.* 28

9 Ad Graecas Kalendas soluturos.
　　They will pay at the Greek Kalends.　*Ib.* 87

JULIUS CAESAR
102?-44 B.C.

10 Gallia est omnis divisa in partes tres.
　　Gaul as a whole is divided into three parts.
　　　　　　　　　De Bello Gallico, I. i

11 Fere libenter homines id quod volunt credunt.
　　Men willingly believe what they wish. *Ib.* iii. 18

12 Et tu, Brute?
　　You also, Brutus?
　　Of unknown origin. Quoted by Shakespeare, '*Julius Caesar*', III. i, *perhaps from the (lost) Latin play* '*Caesar Interfectus*', *probably from* '*The True Tragedie of Richard Duke of York.*' '*Some have written that as M. Brutus came running upon him, he said "καὶ σύ, τέκνον", "and you, my son."*' (Holland's *Suetonius*, p. 33)

13 Veni, vidi, vici.
　　I came, I saw, I conquered.
　　Suetonius, *Divus Julius*, xxxvii. 2.
　　(*Inscription displayed in Caesar's Pontic triumph, or, according to Plutarch, l. 2, written in a letter by Caesar, announcing the victory of Zela which concluded the Pontic campaign*)

14 Iacta alea est.
　　The die is cast.　　　　　　*Ib.* xxxii
　　　　　　At the crossing of the Rubicon

15 Caesar's wife must be above suspicion.
　　Traditional, based on Plutarch, *Life of Julius Caesar*, x. 6

16 Thou hast Caesar and his fortune with thee.
　　Plutarch, *Life of Julius Caesar*, xxxviii. 3. Trans. by North.

PEDRO CALDERÓN DE LA BARCA
1600-1681

17 No se pierde
　　El hacer bien, aun en sueños.
　　Don't relinquish right-doing, even in dreams.
　　　　　　　　La Vida es Sueño, sc. iv

CALIGULA
A.D. 12-41

18 Utinam populus Romanus unam cervicem haberet!
　　Would that the Roman people had but one neck!
　　　　　　Suetonius, *Life of Caligula*, 30

CALLIMACHUS
fl. 250 B.C.

19 μέγα βιβλίον μέγα κακόν.
　　Great book, great evil.
　　Proverb derived from Callimachus, *Fragments*, 359

CHARLES STUART CALVERLEY
1831-1884

20 The auld wife sat at her ivied door,
　　(*Butter and eggs and a pound of cheese*)
　　A thing she had frequently done before;
　　And her spectacles lay on her apron'd knees.
　　　　　　　　　　　　　　Ballad

21 The farmer's daughter hath soft brown hair;
　　(*Butter and eggs and a pound of cheese*)
　　And I met with a ballad, I can't say where,
　　Which wholly consisted of lines like these.　*Ib.*

22 And this song is consider'd a perfect gem,
　　And as to the meaning, it's what you please.　*Ib.*

23 O Beer! O Hodgson, Guinness, Allsopp, Bass!
　　Names that should be on every infant's tongue! *Beer*

24 When 'Dulce est desipere in loco'
　　Was written, real Falernian winged the pen.　*Ib.*

25 I cannot sing the old songs now!
　　It is not that I deem them low;
　　'Tis that I can't remember how
　　　　They go.　　　　　　　　*Changed*

26 Sikes, housebreaker, of Houndsditch,
　　　Habitually swore;
　　But so surpassingly profane
　　　He never was before.　　　*Charades*, vi

27 Aspect anything but bland.　　　　　*Ib.*

28 You see this pebble-stone? It's a thing I bought
　　Of a bit of a chit of a boy i' the mid o' the day—
　　I like to dock the smaller parts-o'-speech,
　　As we curtail the already curtail'd cur
　　(You catch the paronomasia, play 'po' words?).
　　　　　　　　　The Cock and the Bull

29 The basis or substratum—what you will—
　　Of the impending eighty thousand lines.　*Ib.*

1 Donn'd galligaskins, antigropeloes.
The Cock and the Bull

2 Ombrifuge (Lord love you!), case o' rain. *Ib.*

3 A bare-legg'd beggarly son of a gun. *Ib.*

4 Fiddlepin's end! Get out, you blazing ass!
Gabble o' the goose. Don't bugaboo-baby *me!* *Ib.*

5 Pretty i' the Mantuan! *Ib.*

6 It takes up about eighty thousand lines,
A thing imagination boggles at:
And might, odds-bobs, sir! in judicious hands,
Extend from here to Mesopotamy. *Ib.*

7 Life is with such all beer and skittles;
They are not difficult to please
About their victuals. *Contentment*

8 'Twas ever thus from childhood's hour!
My fondest hopes would not decay:
I never loved a tree or flower
Which was the first to fade away! *Disaster*

9 For king-like rolls the Rhine,
And the scenery 's divine,
And the victuals and the wine
Rather good. *Dover to Munich*

10 Forever! 'Tis a single word!
Our rude forefathers deemed it two:
Can you imagine so absurd
A view? *Forever*

11 Wherefore bless ye, O beloved ones:—
Now unto mine inn must I,
Your 'poor moralist', betake me,
In my 'solitary fly'. *'Hic Vir, Hic Est'*

12 For I've read in many a novel that, unless they've
souls that grovel,
Folks *prefer* in fact a hovel to your dreary marble
halls. *In the Gloaming*

13 Grinder, who serenely grindest
At my door the Hundredth Psalm.
Lines on Hearing the Organ

14 Meaning, however, is no great matter.
Lovers, and a Reflection

15 Thro' the rare red heather we danced together,
(O love my Willie!) and smelt for flowers:
I must mention again it was gorgeous weather,
Rhymes are so scarce in this world of ours. *Ib.*

16 Study first propriety. *Of Propriety*

17 How Eugene Aram, though a thief, a liar, and a
murderer,
Yet, being intellectual, was amongst the noblest of
mankind. *Of Reading*

18 Thou, who when fears attack,
Bidst them avaunt, and Black
Care, at the horseman's back
Perching, unseatest;
Sweet, when the morn is grey;
Sweet, when they've cleared away
Lunch; and at close of day
Possibly sweetest. *Ode to Tobacco*

19 I have a liking old
For thee, though manifold
Stories, I know, are told
Not to thy credit. *Ib.*

20 How they who use fusees
All grow by slow degrees
Brainless as chimpanzees,
Meagre as lizards;
Go mad, and beat their wives;
Plunge (after shocking lives)
Razors and carving knives
Into their gizzards. *Ode to Tobacco*

21 Jones—(who, I'm glad to say,
Asked leave of Mrs. J.)—
Daily absorbs a clay
After his labours. *Ib.*

22 Cats may have had their goose
Cooked by tobacco-juice;
Still why deny its use
Thoughtfully taken?
We're not as tabbies are:
Smith, take a fresh cigar!
Jones, the tobacco-jar!
Here 's to thee, Bacon! *Ib.*

RICHARD OWEN CAMBRIDGE
1717-1802

23 What is the worth of anything,
But for the happiness 'twill bring? *Learning, l. 23*

PIERRE-JACQUES, BARON DE CAMBRONNE
1770-1842

24 La Garde meurt, mais ne se rend pas.
The Guards die but do not surrender.
*Attr. to Cambronne when called upon to sur-
render by Col. Halkett. Cambronne denied the
saying at a banquet at Nantes, 1835*

WILLIAM CAMDEN
1551-1623

25 My friend, judge not me,
Thou seest I judge not thee.
Betwixt the stirrup and the ground
Mercy I asked, mercy I found.
*Remains. Epitaph for a Man Killed by Falling
from His Horse*

HERBERT CAMPBELL

26 Now we sha'n't be long. *Title of Song*

JANE MONTGOMERY CAMPBELL
1817-1878

27 We plough the fields, and scatter
The good seed on the land,
But it is fed and watered
By God's Almighty Hand;
He sends the snow in winter,
The warmth to swell the grain,
The breezes and the sunshine,
And soft refreshing rain.
All good gifts around us
Are sent from Heaven above,
Then thank the Lord, O thank the Lord,
For all His love.
We Plough the Fields. Tr. from the German.
C. S. Bere's Garland of Songs

1 He paints the wayside flower,
He lights the evening star.
We Plough the Fields. Tr. from the German.
C. S. Bere's *Garland of Songs*

THOMAS CAMPBELL
1777–1844

2 'Tis Lethe's gloom, but not its quiet,—
The pain without the peace of death! *Absence*

3 Of Nelson and the North
Sing the glorious day's renown,
When to battle fierce came forth
All the might of Denmark's crown,
And her arms along the deep proudly shone,—
By each gun the lighted brand
In a bold determined hand;
And the Prince of all the land
Led them on. *Battle of the Baltic*

4 There was silence deep as death,
And the boldest held his breath
For a time. *Ib.*

5 Again! again! again!
And the havoc did not slack,
Till a feeble cheer the Dane
To our cheering sent us back. *Ib.*

6 Out spoke the victor then
As he hailed them o'er the wave,
'Ye are brothers! ye are men!
And we conquer but to save;
So peace instead of death let us bring:
But yield, proud foe, thy fleet
With the crews at England's feet,
And make submission meet
To our King.' *Ib.*

7 Let us think of them that sleep,
Full many a fathom deep,
By thy wild and stormy steep,
Elsinore! *Ib.*

8 O leave this barren spot to me!
Spare, woodman, spare the beechen tree.
The Beech-Tree's Petition

9 The lordly, lovely Rhine. *The Child and the Hind*

10 There came to the beach a poor Exile of Erin.
Exile of Erin

11 He sang the bold anthem of 'Erin go bragh!' *Ib.*

12 Gay lilied fields of France.
Gertrude of Wyoming, pt. ii. 15

13 When Transatlantic Liberty arose. *Ib.* pt. iii. 6

14 To-morrow let us do or die! *Ib.* 37

15 To live in hearts we leave behind
Is not to die *Hallowed Ground*

16 On the green banks of Shannon, when Sheelah was
nigh,
No blithe Irish lad was so happy as I;
No harp like my own could so cheerily play,
And wherever I went was my poor dog Tray.
The Harper

17 On Linden, when the sun was low,
All bloodless lay the untrodden snow,
And dark as winter was the flow
Of Iser, rolling rapidly. *Hohenlinden*

18 Then shook the hills with thunder riven,
Then rushed the steed to battle driven,
And louder than the bolts of heaven
Far flashed the red artillery. *Hohenlinden*

19 The combat deepens. On, ye brave,
Who rush to glory, or the grave!
Wave, Munich! all thy banners wave,
And charge with all thy chivalry! *Ib.*

20 Few, few shall part where many meet!
The snow shall be their winding-sheet,
And every turf beneath their feet
Shall be a soldier's sepulchre. *Ib.*

21 Better be courted and jilted
Than never be courted at all. *The Jilted Nymph*

22 'Tis the sunset of life gives me mystical lore,
And coming events cast their shadows before.
Lochiel's Warning

23 A chieftain to the Highlands bound
Cries, 'Boatman, do not tarry!
And I'll give thee a silver pound
To row us o'er the ferry.' *Lord Ullin's Daughter*

24 'O, I'm the chief of Ulva's isle,
And this Lord Ullin's daughter.' *Ib.*

25 Then who will cheer my bonny bride
When they have slain her lover? *Ib.*

26 I'll meet the raging of the skies,
But not an angry father. *Ib.*

27 One lovely hand she stretched for aid,
And one was round her lover. *Ib.*

28 'Come back! come back!' he cried in grief
Across the stormy water:
'And I'll forgive your Highland chief,
My daughter! oh my daughter!' *Ib.*

29 The waters wild went o'er his child,
And he was left lamenting. *Ib.*

30 With Freedom's lion-banner
Britannia rules the waves. *Ode to the Germans*

31 'Tis distance lends enchantment to the view,
And robes the mountain in its azure hue.
Pleasures of Hope, pt. i, l. 7

32 The proud, the cold untroubled heart of stone,
That never mused on sorrow but its own. *Ib.* l. 185

33 Hope, for a season, bade the world farewell,
And Freedom shrieked—as Kosciusko fell!
Ib. l. 381

34 Who hath not owned, with rapture-smitten frame,
The power of grace, the magic of a name?
Ib. pt. ii, l. 5

35 And muse on Nature with a poet's eye. *Ib.* l. 98

36 What millions died—that Caesar might be great!
Ib. l. 174

37 Who hail thee, Man! the pilgrim of a day,
Spouse of the worm, and brother of the clay.
Ib. l. 305

38 Truth, ever lovely,—since the world began
The foe of tyrants, and the friend of man. *Ib.* l. 347

39 But, sad as angels for the good man's sin,
Weep to record, and blush to give it in! *Ib.* l. 357

40 Cease, every joy, to glimmer on my mind,
But leave, oh! leave the light of Hope behind!

What though my wingèd hours of bliss have been,
Like angel-visits, few and far between?
Pleasures of Hope, pt. ii, l. 375

1 Well can ye mouth fair Freedom's classic line.
And talk of Constitutions o'er your wine.
On Poland, l. 65

2 One moment may with bliss repay
Unnumbered hours of pain;
Such was the throb and mutual sob
Of the knight embracing Jane. *The Ritter Bann*

3 And the sentinel stars set their watch in the sky.
The Soldier's Dream

4 Drink ye to her that each loves best,
And, if you nurse a flame
That 's told but to her mutual breast,
We will not ask her name.
Song. Drink Ye To Her

5 Can you keep the bee from ranging,
Or the ringdove's neck from changing?
No! nor fettered Love from dying
In the knot there 's no untying.
Song. How Delicious is the Winning

6 Again to the battle, Achaians!
Our hearts bid the tyrants defiance;
Our land, the first garden of Liberty's tree—
It has been, and shall yet be, the land of the free!
Song of the Greeks

7 Her women fair; her men robust for toil;
Her vigorous souls, high-cultured as her soil:
Her towns, where civic independence flings
The gauntlet down to senates, courts, and kings.
Theodric, l. 160

8 It was not strange; for in the human breast
Two master-passions cannot co-exist. *Ib.* l. 488

9 'Twas the hour when rites unholy
Called each Paynim voice to prayer.
The Turkish Lady

10 Ye Mariners of England
That guard our native seas,
Whose flag has braved, a thousand years,
The battle and the breeze—
Your glorious standard launch again
To match another foe!
And sweep through the deep,
While the stormy winds do blow,—
While the battle rages loud and long,
And the stormy winds do blow.
Ye Mariners of England

11 Britannia needs no bulwarks,
No towers along the steep;
Her march is o'er the mountain waves,
Her home is on the deep. *Ib.*

12 The meteor flag of England
Shall yet terrific burn,
Till danger's troubled night depart
And the star of peace return. *Ib.*

13 An original something, fair maid, you would win me
To write—but how shall I begin?
For I fear I have nothing original in me—
Excepting Original Sin.
*To a Young Lady, Who Asked Me to Write
Something Original for Her Album*

14 Now Barabbas was a publisher.
Often attributed to Byron

SIR HENRY CAMPBELL-BANNERMAN
1836–1908

15 When was a war not a war? When it was carried on
by methods of barbarism.
*Speech at Dinner of National Reform Union,
14 June 1901*

THOMAS CAMPION
d. 1620

16 Rose-cheeked Laura, come;
Sing thou smoothly with thy beauty's
Silent music, either other
Sweetly gracing.
Observations in the Art of English Poesie. Laura

17 Lovely forms do flow
From conceit divinely framed;
Heaven is music, and thy beauty's
Birth is heavenly. *Ib.*

18 Only beauty purely loving
Knows no discord,
But still moves delight,
Like clear springs renewed by flowing,
Ever perfect, ever in them-
selves eternal. *Ib.*

19 My sweetest Lesbia let us live and love,
And though the sager sort our deeds reprove,
Let us not weigh them: Heav'n's great lamps do dive
Into their west, and straight again revive,
But soon as once set is our little light,
Then must we sleep one ever-during night.
A Book of Airs, i

20 Follow thy fair sun, unhappy shadow,
Though thou be black as night,
And she made all of light,
Yet follow thy fair sun, unhappy shadow. *Ib. iv*

21 When to her lute Corinna sings,
Her voice revives the leaden strings,
And both in highest notes appear,
As any challeng'd echo clear.
But when she doth of mourning speak,
Ev'n with her sighs the strings do break. *Ib. vi*

22 Follow your Saint, follow with accents sweet;
Haste you, sad notes, fall at her flying feet. *Ib. x*

23 The man of life upright,
Whose guiltless heart is free
From all dishonest deeds
Or thought of vanity *Ib. xviii*

24 He only can behold
With unaffrighted eyes
The horrors of the deep
And terrors of the skies. *Ib.*

25 Good thoughts his only friends,
His wealth a well-spent age,
The earth his sober inn
And quiet pilgrimage. *Ib.*

26 Hark, all you ladies that do sleep;
The fairy Queen Proserpina
Bids you awake and pity them that weep. *Ib. xix*

27 When thou must home to shades of under ground,
And there arriv'd, a new admired guest,
The beauteous spirits do ingirt thee round,
White Iope, blithe Helen, and the rest,
To hear the stories of thy finisht love
From that smooth tongue whose music hell can move.
Ib. xx

1 Never weather-beaten sail more willing bent to shore,
Never tired pilgrim's limbs affected slumber more.
Two Books of Airs. Divine and Moral Songs, xi.

2 Kind are her answers,
But her performance keeps no day;
Breaks time, as dancers
From their own Music when they stray.
Third Book of Airs, vii

3 Lost is our freedom,
When we submit to women so:
Why do we need them,
When in their best they work our woe? *Ib.*

4 There is a garden in her face,
Where roses and white lilies grow;
A heav'nly paradise is that place,
Wherein all pleasant fruits do flow.
There cherries grow, which none may buy
Till 'Cherry ripe' themselves do cry.
Fourth Book of Airs, vii

5 Those cherries fairly do enclose
Of orient pearl a double row;
Which when her lovely laughter shows,
They look like rosebuds fill'd with snow.
Yet them nor peer nor prince can buy,
Till 'Cherry ripe' themselves do cry. *Ib.*

GEORGE CANNING
1770–1827

6 In matters of commerce the fault of the Dutch
Is offering too little and asking too much.
The French are with equal advantage content,
So we clap on Dutch bottoms just twenty per cent.
*Dispatch, in Cipher, To Sir Charles Bagot,
English Ambassador at The Hague, 31 Jan. 1826*

7 Needy Knife-grinder! whither are you going?
Rough is the road, your wheel is out of order—
Bleak blows the blast;—your hat has got a hole in't.
So have your breeches.
The Friend of Humanity and the Knife-Grinder

8 Story! God bless you! I have none to tell, Sir. *Ib.*

9 I give thee sixpence! I will see thee damn'd first—
Wretch! whom no sense of wrongs can rouse to ven-
geance;
Sordid, unfeeling, reprobate, degraded,
Spiritless outcast! *Ib.*

10 So down thy hill, romantic Ashbourne, glides
The Derby dilly, carrying *Three* Insides.
The Loves of the Triangles, l. 178

11 A steady patriot of the world alone,
The friend of every country but his own. [The Jacobin.]
New Morality, l. 113

12 And finds, with keen discriminating sight,
Black's not so black;—nor white so very white.
Ib. l. 199

13 Give me the avowed, erect and manly foe;
Firm I can meet, perhaps return the blow;
But of all plagues, good Heaven, thy wrath can send,
Save me, oh, save me, from the candid friend.
Ib. l. 207

14 Pitt is to Addington
As London is to Paddington.
The Oracle, c. 1803–4

15 Man, only—rash, refined, presumptuous man,
Starts from his rank, and mars creation's plan.
Progress of Man, l. 55

16 A sudden thought strikes me, let us swear an eternal
friendship. *The Rovers*, I. i

17 Whene'er with haggard eyes I view
This Dungeon, that I'm rotting in,
I think of those Companions true
Who studied with me at the U-
-NIVERSITY of GOTTINGEN,-
-NIVERSITY of GOTTINGEN. *Song*

18 Sun, moon, and thou vain world, adieu. *Ib.*

19 (*Pitt*:)
When our perils are past, shall our gratitude sleep?
No,—here's to the pilot that weathered the storm.
*Song for the inauguration of the Pitt Club,
25 May 1802.*

20 Away with the cant of 'Measures not men'!—the idle
supposition that it is the harness and not the horses
that draw the chariot along. If the comparison must
be made, if the distinction must be taken, men are
everything, measures comparatively nothing.
Speech, House of Commons, 1801

21 I called the New World into existence, to redress the
balance of the Old. *Speech, 12 Dec. 1826*

CANUTE
994?–1035

22 Merrily sang the monks in Ely
When Cnut, King, rowed thereby;
Row, my knights, near the land,
And hear we these monks' song.
Attr. *Song of the Monks of Ely*, *Historia Eliensis*
(1066). Green, *Conquest of England*, ix

FRANCESCO CARACCIOLI
1752–1799

23 Il y a en Angleterre soizante sectes religieuses dif-
férentes, et une seule sauce.

In England there are sixty different religions,
and only one sauce. *Attrib.*

RICHARD CAREW
1555–1620

24 Take the miracle of our age, Sir Philip Sidney.
An Epistle on the Excellency of the English Tongue

THOMAS CAREW
1595?–1639?

25 He that loves a rosy cheek,
Or a coral lip admires,
Or, from star-like eyes, doth seek
Fuel to maintain his fires;
As old Time makes these decay,
So his flames must waste away.
Disdain Returned

26 Here lies a King that rul'd, as he thought fit
The universal monarchy of wit;
Here lies two Flamens, and both those the best:
Apollo's first, at last the true God's priest.
Elegy on the Death of Donne

1 Know, Celia (since thou art so proud,)
'Twas I that gave thee thy renown.
Thou had'st in the forgotten crowd
Of common beauties liv'd unknown,
Had not my verse extoll'd thy name,
And with it imped the wings of fame.
Ingrateful Beauty Threatened

2 Wise poets that wrapt Truth in tales,
Knew he themselves through all her veils. *Ib.*

3 An untimely grave.
Inscription on Tomb of the Duke of Buckingham

4 Good to the poor, to kindred dear,
To servants kind, to friendship clear,
To nothing but herself severe.
Inscription on Tomb of Lady Mary Wentworth

5 So though a virgin, yet a bride
To every Grace, she justified
A chaste polygamy, and died. *Ib.*

6 The purest soul that e'er was sent
Into a clayey tenement.
On the Lady Mary Villiers

7 Give me more love or more disdain;
The torrid or the frozen zone:
Bring equal ease unto my pain;
The temperate affords me none.
Mediocrity in Love Rejected

8 When thou, poor excommunicate
From all the joys of love, shalt see
The full reward and glorious fate
Which my strong faith shall purchase me,
Then curse thine own inconstancy.
To My Inconstant Mistress

9 Ask me no more where Jove bestows,
When June is past, the fading rose;
For in your beauty's orient deep
These flowers, as in their causes, sleep. *A Song*

10 Ask me no more whither doth haste
The nightingale when May is past;
For in your sweet dividing throat
She winters and keeps warm her note. *Ib.*

11 Ask me no more if east or west
The Phoenix builds her spicy nest;
For unto you at last she flies,
And in your fragrant bosom dies. *Ib.*

HENRY CAREY
1693?–1743

12 Aldiborontiphoscophornio!
Where left you Chrononhotonthologos?
Chrononhotonthologos, I. i

13 His cogitative faculties immers'd
In cogibundity of cogitation. *Ib.*

14 To thee, and gentle Rigdum-Funnidos,
Our gratulations flow in streams unbounded. *Ib. iii*

15 God save our gracious king!
Long live our noble king!
God save the king! *God Save the King. (But
see 6:13, 250:14, and Corrigenda, p. 587)*

16 Confound their politics,
Frustrate their knavish tricks. *Ib.*

17 Of all the girls that are so smart
There's none like pretty Sally,
She is the darling of my heart,
And she lives in our alley. *Sally in our Alley*

18 When she is by I leave my work,
(I love her so sincerely)
My master comes like any Turk,
And bangs me most severely. *Sally in our Alley*

19 Of all the days that's in the week
I dearly love but one day—
And that's the day that comes betwixt
A Saturday and Monday. *Ib.*

WILLIAM CARLETON
1794–1869

20 Things at home are crossways, and Betsey and I
are out. *Farm Ballads. Betsey and I Are Out*

21 We arg'ed the thing at breakfast, we arg'ed the thing
at tea,
And the more we arg'ed the question, the more we
didn't agree. *Ib.*

THOMAS CARLYLE
1795–1881

22 A well-written Life is almost as rare as a well-
spent one.
Critical and Miscellaneous Essays, vol. i. Richter

23 'Providence has given to the French the empire of
the land, to the English that of the sea, to the
Germans that of—the air!'
(Quoting a remark of J. P. F. Richter.) Ib.

24 The three great elements of modern civilization,
Gunpowder, Printing, and the Protestant Religion.
Ib. State of German Literature

25 The 'golden-calf of Self-love.' *Ib. Burns*

26 So here has been dawning
Another blue day. *Ib. To-day*

27 Out of Eternity
This new Day is born;
Into Eternity
At night, will return. *Ib.*

28 It is the Age of Machinery, in every outward and
inward sense of that word.
Ib. vol. ii. Signs of the Times

29 The Bible-Society . . . is found, on inquiry, to be . . .
a machine for converting the Heathen. *Ib.*

30 Thought, he [Dr. Cabanis] is inclined to hold, is
still secreted by the brain; but then Poetry and
Religion (and it is really worth knowing) are 'a
product of the smaller intestines'! *Ib.*

31 What is all knowledge too but recorded experience,
and a product of history; of which, therefore,
reasoning and belief, no less than action and
passion, are essential materials? *Ib. On History*

32 History is the essence of innumerable biographies. *Ib.*

33 The foul sluggard's comfort: 'It will last my time.'
Ib. vol. iii. Count Cagliostro. Flight Last

34 This Mirabeau's work, then, is done. He sleeps with
the primeval giants. He has gone over to the
majority: *Abiit ad plures. Ib. Mirabeau*

35 There is no life of a man, faithfully recorded, but is
a heroic poem of its sort, rhymed or unrhymed.
Ib. vol. iv. Sir Walter Scott

1 Under all speech that is good for anything there lies a silence that is better. Silence is deep as Eternity; speech is shallow as Time.
Critical and Miscellaneous Essays, vol. iv. *Sir Walter Scott*

2 To the very last, he [Napoleon] had a kind of idea; that, namely, of *La carrière ouverte aux talents*, The tools to him that can handle them. *Ib.*

3 It can be said of him [Scott], When he departed, he took a man's life along with him. No sounder piece of British manhood was put together in that eighteenth century of Time. *Ib.*

4 A witty statesman said, you might prove anything by figures. *Ib. Chartism*, ch. 2

5 Surely of all 'rights of man', this right of the ignorant man to be guided by the wiser, to be, gently or forcibly, held in the true course by him, is the indisputablest. *Ib.* ch. 6

6 In epochs when cash payment has become the sole nexus of man to man. *Ib.*

7 Thou wretched fraction, wilt thou be the ninth part even of a tailor? *Ib. Francia*

8 This idle habit of 'accounting for the moral sense', as they phrase it. . . . The moral sense, thank God, is a thing you never will 'account for'. . . . By no greatest happiness principle, greatest nobleness principle, or any principle whatever, will you make that in the least clearer than it already is.
Ib. vol. v. *Shooting Niagara: and After?*

9 'Genius' (which means transcendent capacity of taking trouble, first of all).
Frederick the Great, bk. iv, ch. 3

10 If they could forget, for a moment, the correggiosity of Correggio, and the learned babble of the sale-room and varnishing auctioneer.
Ib. ch. 6. (*See 513:15*)

11 Happy the people whose annals are blank in history-books! *Ib.* bk. xvi, ch. 1

12 France was long a despotism tempered by epigrams.
History of the French Revolution, pt. 1, bk. i, ch. 1

13 Indeed it is well said, 'in every object there is inexhaustible meaning; the eye sees in it what the eye brings means of seeing'. *Ib.* ch. 2

14 Is not every meanest day 'the conflux of two eternities!' *Ib.* bk. iv, ch. 4

15 A whiff of grapeshot. *Ib.* bk. v, ch. 3

16 History a distillation of rumour. *Ib.* bk. vii, ch. 5

17 The gospel according to Jean Jacques.
Ib. pt. ii, bk. i, ch. 6

18 The difference between Orthodoxy or My-doxy and Heterodoxy or Thy-doxy. *Ib.* bk. iv, ch. 2

19 The seagreen Incorruptible. [Robespierre.] *Ib.* ch. 4

20 Aristocracy of the Moneybag. *Ib.* bk. vii, ch. 7

21 It is well said, in every sense, that a man's religion is the chief fact with regard to him.
Heroes and Hero-Worship, i. *The Hero as Divinity*.

22 Worship is transcendent wonder. *Ib.*

23 No sadder proof can be given by a man of his own littleness than disbelief in great men. *Ib.*

24 No great man lives in vain. The history of the world is but the biography of great men. *Ib.*

25 The greatest of faults, I should say, is to be conscious of none.
Heroes and Hero-Worship, ii. *The Hero as Prophet*

26 The Hero can be Poet, Prophet, King, Priest or what you will, according to the kind of world he finds himself born into. *Ib.* iii. *The Hero as Poet*

27 In books lies the *soul* of the whole Past Time; the articulate audible voice of the Past, when the body and material substance of it has altogether vanished like a dream. *Ib.* v. *The Hero as Man of Letters*

28 The true University of these days is a collection of books. *Ib.*

29 Burke said there were Three Estates in Parliament; but, in the Reporters' Gallery yonder, there sat a *Fourth Estate* more important far than they all. *Ib.*

30 Adversity is sometimes hard upon a man; but for one man who can stand prosperity, there are a hundred that will stand adversity. *Ib.*

31 I hope we English will long maintain our *grand talent pour le silence*. *Ib.* vi. *The Hero as King*

32 Maid-servants, I hear people complaining, are getting instructed in the 'ologies'.
Inaugural Address at Edinburgh, 1866

33 Speech is human, silence is divine, yet also brutish and dead: therefore we must learn both arts.
Journal

34 Respectable Professors of the Dismal Science. [Political Economy.]
Latter-Day Pamphlets, No. 1. *The Present Time*

35 Little other than a redtape Talking-machine, and unhappy Bag of Parliamentary Eloquence. *Ib.*

36 A healthy hatred of scoundrels.
Ib. No. 2. *Model Prisons*

37 Idlers, game-preservers and mere human clothes-horses. [Exodus from Houndsditch.]
Ib. No. 3. *Downing Street*

38 Nature admits no lie. *Ib.* No. 5. *Stump Orator*

39 A Parliament speaking through reporters to Buncombe and the twenty-seven millions mostly fools.
Ib. No. 6. *Parliaments*

40 'May the Devil fly away with the fine arts!' exclaimed . . . in my hearing, one of our most distinguished public men. *Ib.* No. 8

41 Mother of dead dogs.
Letter to John Carlyle, 11 Sept. 1840 (Froude's *Carlyle, 1884*, vol. i, p. 196)

42 The unspeakable Turk should be immediately struck out of the question.
Letter to G. Howard, 24 Nov. 1876

43 Transcendental moonshine.
Life of John Sterling, pt. i, ch. 15

44 The progress of human society consists . . . in . . . the better and better apportioning of wages to work.
Past and Present, bk. i, ch. 3

45 Brothers, I am sorry I have got no Morrison's Pill for curing the maladies of Society. *Ib.* ch. 4

46 Thou and I, my friend, can, in the most flunkey world, make, each of us, *one* non-flunkey, one hero, if we like: that will be two heroes to begin with.
Ib. ch. 6

1 Cash-payment is not the sole nexus of man with man. *Past and Present*, bk. iii, ch. 9

2 Blessed is he who has found his work; let him ask no other blessedness. *Ib.* ch. 11

3 Captains of industry. *Ib.* bk. iv, title of ch. 4

4 The sunny plains and deep indigo transparent skies of Italy are all indifferent to the great sick heart of a Sir Walter Scott: on the back of the Apennines, in wild spring weather, the sight of bleak Scotch firs, and snow-spotted heath and desolation, brings tears into his eyes. *Ib.* ch. 5

5 Upwards of five-hundred-thousand two-legged animals without feathers lie round us, in horizontal positions; their heads all in nightcaps, and full of the foolishest dreams. *Sartor Resartus*, bk. i, ch. 3

6 He who first shortened the labour of copyists by device of *Movable Types* was disbanding hired armies, and cashiering most Kings and Senates, and creating a whole new democratic world: he had invented the art of printing. *Ib.* ch. 5

7 Man is a tool-using animal. . . . Without tools he is nothing, with tools he is all. *Ib.*

8 Whoso has sixpence is sovereign (to the length of sixpence) over all men; commands cooks to feed him, philosophers to teach him, kings to mount guard over him,—to the length of sixpence. *Ib.*

9 Lives the man that can figure a naked Duke of Windlestraw addressing a naked House of Lords? *Ib.* ch. 9

10 Language is called the garment of thought: however, it should rather be, language is the flesh-garment, the body, of thought. *Ib.* ch. 11

11 What printed thing soever I could meet with I read. *Ib.* bk. ii, ch. 3

12 The end of man is an action, and not a thought, though it were the noblest. *Ib.* ch. 6

13 The everlasting No. *Ib.* ch. 7, title

14 The folly of that impossible precept, 'Know thyself'; till it be translated into this partially possible one, 'Know what thou canst work at'. *Ib.*

15 My spiritual new-birth, or Baphometic Fire-baptism. *Ib.*

16 Great men are the inspired [speaking and acting] texts of that divine Book of Revelations, whereof a chapter is completed from epoch to epoch, and by some named History. *Ib.* ch. 8

17 The everlasting Yea. *Ib.* ch. 9, title

18 Man's unhappiness, as I construe, comes of his greatness; it is because there is an Infinite in him, which with all his cunning he cannot quite bury under the Finite. *Ib.*

19 Close thy Byron; open thy Goethe. *Ib.*

20 'Do the duty which lies nearest thee', which thou knowest to be a duty! Thy second duty will already have become clearer. *Ib.*

21 Be no longer a chaos, but a world, or even worldkin. Produce! Produce! Were it but the pitifullest infinitesimal fraction of a product, produce it in God's name! 'Tis the utmost thou hast in thee: out with it, then. *Ib.*

22 As the Swiss Inscription says: *Sprechen ist silbern, Schweigen ist golden* (Speech is silvern, Silence is golden); or as I might rather express it: Speech is of Time, Silence is of Eternity. *Sartor Resartus*, bk. iii, ch. 3

23 Two men I honour, and no third. *Ib.* ch. 4

24 I don't pretend to understand the Universe—it's a great deal bigger than I am. . . . People ought to be modester. *Remark to Wm. Allingham.* D. A. Wilson's and D. Wilson MacArthur's *Carlyle in Old Age*

25 If Jesus Christ were to come to-day, people would not even crucify him. They would ask him to dinner, and hear what he had to say, and make fun of it. *Remark.* D. A. Wilson's *Carlyle at his Zenith*

26 It were better to perish than to continue schoolmastering. *Remark.* D. A. Wilson's *Carlyle Till Marriage*

27 Macaulay is well for a while, but one wouldn't *live* under Niagara. *Remark.* R. M. Milnes's *Notebook, 1838*

28 A good book is the purest essence of a human soul. *Speech in support of the London Library, 1840.* F. Harrison's *Carlyle and the London Library*

29 '"Thou's gey" [pretty, pronounced *gyei*] "ill to deal wi"—Mother's allocution to me once, in some unreasonable moment of mine', is Carlyle's note on this phrase (which, indeed, is an old-fashioned country formula), cited by his wife in a letter to his mother in Dec. 1835. . . . The readers of Mr. Froude's *Life of Carlyle* will remember that he harps upon this phrase, using it as a sort of refrain, but always with the significant change of the word 'deal' to 'live'—'gey ill to *live* wi'. C. Eliot Norton, *Letters of Thomas Carlyle* (1888), I. 44

30 Who never ate his bread in sorrow,
Who never spent the darksome hours
Weeping and watching for the morrow
He knows ye not, ye heavenly Powers.
Translation of Goethe's Wilhelm Meister's Apprenticeship, bk. ii, ch. 13

31 Carlyle and Milnes were talking . . . of the Administration just formed by Sir Robert Peel, and Milnes was evincing some disappointment . . . that he had not been offered a post in it. 'No, no,' said Carlyle, 'Peel knows what he is about; there is only one post fit for you, and that is the office of perpetual president of the Heaven and Hell Amalgamation Society.' T. E. Wemyss Reid, *The Life of Lord Houghton* (1890), p. 187

32 MARGARET FULLER:
I accept the universe.
CARLYLE:
Gad! she'd better! *Attrib.*

JULIA CARNEY
1823–1908

33 Little drops of water, little grains of sand,
Make the mighty ocean, and the pleasant land.
So the little minutes, humble though they be,
Make the mighty ages of eternity.
Little Things. (Attr. also to E. C. Brewer, D. C. Colesworthy, and F. S. Osgood)

1 Little deeds of kindness, little words of love,
Help to make earth happy, like the heaven above.
(Changed by later compilers to 'make this earth an
Eden'.)   *Little Things*

JOSEPH EDWARDS CARPENTER
1813–?

2 What are the wild waves saying
Sister, the whole day long,
That ever amid our playing,
I hear but their low lone song?
What are the Wild Waves Saying?

3 Yes! but there's something greater,
That speaks to the heart alone;
The voice of the great Creator,
Dwells in that mighty tone!   *Ib.*

LEWIS CARROLL
[CHARLES LUTWIDGE DODGSON]
1832–1898

4 What I tell you three times is true.
Hunting of the Snark, Fit 1. The Landing

5 He had forty-two boxes, all carefully packed,
With his name painted clearly on each:
But, since he omitted to mention the fact,
They were all left behind on the beach.   *Ib.*

6 He would answer to 'Hi!' or to any loud cry,
Such as 'Fry me!' or 'Fritter-my-wig!'   *Ib.*

7 His intimate friends called him 'Candle-ends',
And his enemies, 'Toasted-cheese'.   *Ib.*

8 Then the bowsprit got mixed with the rudder sometimes.   *Ib.*

9 But the principal failing occurred in the sailing,
And the Bellman, perplexed and distressed,
Said he *had* hoped, at least, when the wind blew due
East,
That the ship would *not* travel due West!
Ib. Fit 2. The Bellman's Speech

10 But oh, beamish nephew, beware of the day,
If your Snark be a Boojum! For then
You will softly and suddenly vanish away,
And never be met with again!
Ib. Fit. 3. The Baker's Tale

11 They sought it with thimbles, they sought it with care;
They pursued it with forks and hope;
They threatened its life with a railway-share;
They charmed it with smiles and soap.
Ib. Fit 5. The Beaver's Lesson

12 Recollecting with tears how, in earlier years,
It had taken no pains with its sums.   *Ib.*

13 And in charity-meetings it stands at the door,
And collects—though it does not subscribe.   *Ib.*

14 For the Snark *was* a Boojum, you see.
Ib. Fit 8. The Vanishing

15 He thought he saw an Elephant,
That practised on a fife:
He looked again, and found it was
A letter from his wife.
'At length I realize,' he said,
'The bitterness of life!'   *Sylvie and Bruno, ch. 5*

16 He thought he saw a Buffalo
Upon the chimney-piece:
He looked again, and found it was
His sister's husband's niece.
'Unless you leave this house,' he said,
'I'll send for the Police!'   *Sylvie and Bruno, ch. 6*

17 He thought he saw a Rattlesnake
That questioned him in Greek,
He looked again and found it was
The Middle of Next Week.
'The one thing I regret,' he said,
'Is that it cannot speak!'   *Ib.*

18 He thought he saw a Banker's Clerk
Descending from the bus:
He looked again, and found it was
A Hippopotamus:
'If this should stay to dine,' he said,
'There won't be much for us.'   *Ib. ch. 7*

19 He thought he saw an Albatross
That fluttered round the lamp:
He looked again, and found it was
A penny-postage-stamp.
'You'd best be getting home,' he said,
'The nights are very damp.'   *Ib. ch. 12*

20 'What is the use of a book', thought Alice, 'without
pictures or conversations?'
Alice in Wonderland, ch. 1

21 Do cats eat bats? . . . Do bats eat cats?   *Ib.*

22 'Curiouser and curiouser!' cried Alice.   *Ib. ch. 2*

23 How doth the little crocodile
Improve his shining tail,
And pour the waters of the Nile
On every golden scale!   *Ib.*

24 How cheerfully he seems to grin,
How neatly spreads his claws,
And welcomes little fishes in
With gently smiling jaws!   *Ib.*

25 'I'll be judge, I'll be jury,' said cunning old Fury;
'I'll try the whole cause, and condemn you to death.'
Ib. ch. 3

26 The Duchess! The Duchess!
O my dear paws! Oh my fur and whiskers! *Ib. ch. 4*

27 'I can't explain *myself*, I'm afraid, sir,' said Alice,
'because I'm not myself, you see.' 'I don't see,'
said the Caterpillar.   *Ib. ch. 5*

28 'You are old, Father William,' the young man said,
'And your hair has become very white;
And yet you incessantly stand on your head—
Do you think, at your age, it is right?'

'In my youth,' Father William replied to his son.
'I feared it might injure the brain;
But now that I'm perfectly sure I have none,
Why, I do it again and again.'   *Ib.*

29 'I have answered three questions, and that is enough,'
Said his father; 'don't give yourself airs!
Do you think I can listen all day to such stuff?
Be off, or I'll kick you downstairs!'   *Ib.*

30 'I shall sit here,' he said, 'on and off, for days and
days.'   *Ib. ch. 6*

31 'If everybody minded their own business,' said the
Duchess in a hoarse growl, 'the world would go
round a deal faster than it does.'   *Ib.*

1 Speak roughly to your little boy,
And beat him when he sneezes;
He only does it to annoy,
Because he knows it teases.
Alice in Wonderland, ch. 6

2 For he can thoroughly enjoy
The pepper when he pleases! *Ib.*

3 'Did you say pig, or fig?' said the Cat. *Ib.*

4 This time it vanished quite slowly, beginning with the end of the tail, and ending with the grin, which remained some time after the rest of it had gone. [The Cheshire Cat.] *Ib.*

5 'Have some wine,' the March Hare said in an encouraging tone. Alice looked all round the table, but there was nothing on it but tea. 'I don't see any wine,' she remarked. 'There isn't any,' said the March Hare. *Ib.* ch. 7

6 'Then you should say what you mean,' the March Hare went on. 'I do,' Alice hastily replied; 'at least —at least I mean what I say—that's the same thing, you know.'
'Not the same thing a bit!' said the Hatter. 'Why, you might just as well say that "I see what I eat" is the same thing as "I eat what I see!"' *Ib.*

7 'It was the *best* butter,' the March Hare meekly replied. *Ib.*

8 Twinkle, twinkle, little bat!
How I wonder what you're at!
Up above the world you fly!
Like a teatray in the sky. *Ib.*

9 'Take some more tea,' the March Hare said to Alice, very earnestly.
'I've had nothing yet,' Alice replied in an offended tone, 'so I can't take more.'
'You mean you can't take *less*,' said the Hatter: 'it's very easy to take *more* than nothing.' *Ib.*

10 Let's all move one place on. *Ib.*

11 'But they were *in* the well,' Alice said to the Dormouse. . . . 'Of course they were,' said the Dormouse,—'well in.' *Ib.*

12 'They drew all manner of things—everything that begins with an M——' 'Why with an M?' said Alice. 'Why not?' said the March Hare. *Ib.*

13 The Queen was in a furious passion, and went stamping about, and shouting, 'Off with his head!' or 'Off with her head!' about once in a minute.
Ib. ch. 8

14 'A cat may look at a king,' said Alice. *Ib.*

15 And the moral of that is—'Oh, 'tis love, 'tis love, that makes the world go round!' *Ib.* ch. 9

16 Everything's got a moral, if you can only find it. *Ib.*

17 Take care of the sense, and the sounds will take care of themselves. *Ib.*

18 'That's nothing to what I could say if I chose,' the Duchess replied. *Ib.*

19 'Just about as much right,' said the Duchess, 'as pigs have to fly.' *Ib.*

20 I only took the regular course . . . the different branches of Arithmetic—Ambition, Distraction, Uglification, and Derision. *Ib.*

21 'That's the reason they're called lessons,' the Gryphon remarked: 'because they lessen from day to day.' *Ib.*

22 'Will you walk a little faster?' said a whiting to a snail, 'There's a porpoise close behind us, and he's treading on my tail.' *Alice in Wonderland*, ch. 10

23 Will you, won't you, will you, won't you, will you join the dance? *Ib.*

24 The further off from England the nearer is to France—
Then turn not pale, beloved snail, but come and join the dance. *Ib.*

25 'Tis the voice of the lobster; I heard him declare, 'You have baked me too brown, I must sugar my hair.' *Ib.*

26 Soup of the evening, beautiful Soup! *Ib.*

27 The Queen of Hearts, she made some tarts,
All on a summer day:
The Knave of Hearts, he stole those tarts,
And took them quite away! *Ib.* ch. 11

28 'Write that down,' the King said to the jury, and the jury eagerly wrote down all three dates on their slates, and then added them up, and reduced the answer to shillings and pence. *Ib.*

29 Here one of the guinea-pigs cheered, and was immediately suppressed by the officers of the court. *Ib.*

30 'Where shall I begin, please your Majesty?' he asked. 'Begin at the beginning,' the King said, gravely, 'and go on till you come to the end: then stop.' *Ib.*

31 '*Un*important, of course, I meant,' the King hastily said, and went on to himself in an undertone, 'important— unimportant— unimportant— important—' as if he were trying which word sounded best. *Ib.* ch. 12

32 'That's not a regular rule: you invented it just now.' 'It's the oldest rule in the book,' said the King. 'Then it ought to be Number One,' said Alice. *Ib.*

33 They told me you had been to her,
And mentioned me to him:
She gave me a good character,
But said I could not swim. *Ib.*

34 The jury all wrote down on their slates, '*She* doesn't believe there's an atom of meaning in it.' *Ib.*

35 No! No! Sentence first—verdict afterwards. *Ib.*

36 'Do I look like it?' said the Knave. (Which he certainly did *not*, being made entirely of cardboard.) *Ib.*

37 'The horror of that moment,' the King went on, 'I shall never, *never* forget!' 'You will, though,' the Queen said, 'if you don't make a memorandum of it.' *Through the Looking-Glass*, ch. 1

38 'My precious Lily! My imperial kitten!'—
'Imperial fiddlestick!' *Ib.*

39 'Twas brillig, and the slithy toves
Did gyre and gimble in the wabe;
All mimsy were the borogoves,
And the mome raths outgrabe.

'Beware the Jabberwock, my son!
The jaws that bite, the claws that catch!
Beware the Jubjub bird, and shun
The frumious Bandersnatch!'

He took his vorpal sword in hand:
Long time the manxome foe he sought—
So rested he by the Tumtum tree,
And stood awhile in thought.

And as in uffish thought he stood,
The Jabberwock, with eyes of flame,
Came whiffling through the tulgey wood,
And burbled as it came!

One, two! One, two! And through and through
The vorpal blade went snicker-snack!
He left it dead, and with its head
He went galumphing back.

'And hast thou slain the Jabberwock?
Come to my arms, my beamish boy!
O frabjous day! Callooh! Callay!'
He chortled in his joy.
Through the Looking-Glass, ch. 1

1 Curtsey while you're thinking what to say. It saves
time. *Ib.* ch. 2

2 Speak in French when you can't think of the English
for a thing. *Ib.*

3 'Now! Now!' cried the Queen. 'Faster! Faster!' *Ib.*

4 Now, *here*, you see, it takes all the running *you* can
do, to keep in the same place. If you want to get
somewhere else, you must run at least twice as
fast as that! *Ib.*

5 'Sap and sawdust,' said the Gnat. *Ib.* ch. 3

6 Tweedledum and Tweedledee
Agreed to have a battle;
For Tweedledum said Tweedledee
Had spoiled his nice new rattle.

Just then flew down a monstrous crow,
As black as a tar-barrel;
Which frightened both the heroes so,
They quite forgot their quarrel. *Ib.* ch. 4

7 If you think we're wax-works, you ought to pay, you
know. Wax-works weren't made to be looked at for
nothing. Nohow! *Ib.*

8 'Contrariwise,' continued Tweedledee, 'if it was so,
it might be; and if it were so, it would be: but as
it isn't, it ain't. That's logic.' *Ib.*

9 The sun was shining on the sea,
Shining with all his might:
He did his very best to make
The billows smooth and bright—
And this was odd, because it was
The middle of the night.
Ib. The Walrus and the Carpenter

10 'It's very rude of him,' she said
'To come and spoil the fun!' *Ib.*

11 You could not see a cloud, because
No cloud was in the sky:
No birds were flying overhead—
There were no birds to fly. *Ib.*

12 The Walrus and the Carpenter
Were walking close at hand;
They wept like anything to see
Such quantities of sand:
'If this were only cleared away,'
They said, 'it would be grand!'

'If seven maids with seven mops
Swept it for half a year,
Do you suppose,' the Walrus said,
'That they could get it clear?'
'I doubt it,' said the Carpenter,
And shed a bitter tear.
Through the Looking-Glass, ch. 4. *The Walrus
and the Carpenter*

13 But four young Oysters hurried up,
All eager for the treat:
Their coats were brushed, their faces washed,
Their shoes were clean and neat—
And this was odd, because, you know,
They hadn't any feet. *Ib.*

14 And thick and fast they came at last,
And more, and more, and more. *Ib.*

15 The Walrus and the Carpenter
Walked on a mile or so,
And then they rested on a rock
Conveniently low:
And all the little Oysters stood
And waited in a row.

'The time has come,' the Walrus said,
'To talk of many things:
Of shoes—and ships—and sealing wax—
Of cabbages—and kings—
And why the sea is boiling hot—
And whether pigs have wings.' *Ib.*

16 'For some of us are out of breath,
And all of us are fat!' *Ib.*

17 'A loaf of bread,' the Walrus said,
'Is what we chiefly need:
Pepper and vinegar besides
Are very good indeed—
Now if you're ready, Oysters dear,
We can begin to feed.' *Ib.*

18 'The night is fine,' the Walrus said.
'Do you admire the view?' *Ib.*

19 The Carpenter said nothing but
'The butter's spread too thick!' *Ib.*

20 'I weep for you,' the Walrus said:
'I deeply sympathize.'
With sobs and tears he sorted out
Those of the largest size,
Holding his pocket-handkerchief
Before his streaming eyes. *Ib.*

21 But answer came there none—
And this was scarcely odd because
They'd eaten every one. *Ib.*

22 'Fit to snore his head off!' as Tweedledum remarked. *Ib.*

23 'Let's fight till six, and then have dinner,' said
Tweedledum. *Ib.*

24 'You know,' he said very gravely, 'it's one of the most
serious things that can possibly happen to one in a
battle—to get one's head cut off.' *Ib.*

25 'I'm very brave generally,' he went on in a low voice:
'only to-day I happen to have a headache.' *Ib.*

26 Twopence a week, and jam every other day.
Ib. ch. 5

27 The rule is, jam to-morrow and jam yesterday—but
never jam to-day. *Ib.*

28 'It's a poor sort of memory that only works backwards,' the Queen remarked. *Ib.*

1 Consider anything, only don't cry!
Through the Looking-Glass, ch. 5

2 'I can't believe *that*!' said Alice. 'Can't you?' the Queen said in a pitying tone. 'Try again: draw a long breath, and shut your eyes.' Alice laughed. 'There's no use trying,' she said: 'one *can't* believe impossible things.' 'I daresay you haven't had much practice,' said the Queen. 'When I was your age, I always did it for half-an-hour a day. Why, sometimes I've believed as many as six impossible things before breakfast.' *Ib.*

3 'It's very provoking,' Humpty Dumpty said after a long silence,—'to be called an egg—*very!*' *Ib. ch.* 6

4 With a name like yours, you might be any shape, almost. *Ib.*

5 They gave it me,—for an un-birthday present. *Ib.*

6 'There's glory for you!' 'I don't know what you mean by "glory",' Alice said. 'I meant, "there's a nice knock-down argument for you!"' 'But "glory" doesn't mean "a nice knock-down argument",' Alice objected. 'When *I* use a word,' Humpty Dumpty said in a rather scornful tone, 'it means just what I choose it to mean,—neither more nor less.' *Ib.*

7 'The question is,' said Humpty Dumpty, 'which is to be master—that's all.' *Ib.*

8 I can explain all the poems that ever were invented—and a good many that haven't been invented just yet. *Ib.*

9 '*I* can repeat poetry as well as other folk if it comes to that—' 'Oh, it needn't come to that!' Alice hastily said. *Ib.*

10 The little fishes of the sea,
They sent an answer back to me.

The little fishes' answer was
'We cannot do it, Sir, because——' *Ib.*

11 I took a kettle large and new,
Fit for the deed I had to do. *Ib.*

12 I said it very loud and clear;
I went and shouted in his ear.

But he was very stiff and proud;
He said 'You needn't shout so loud!'

And he was very proud and stiff;
He said 'I'd go and wake them, if——' *Ib.*

13 You see it's like a portmanteau—there are two meanings packed up into one word. *Ib.*

14 He's an Anglo-Saxon Messenger—and those are Anglo-Saxon attitudes. *Ib. ch.* 7

15 The other Messenger's called Hatta. I must have *two* you know—to come and go. One to come, and one to go. *Ib.*

16 'There's nothing like eating hay when you're faint.' ... 'I didn't say there was nothing *better*,' the King replied, 'I said there was nothing *like* it.' *Ib.*

17 'I'm sure nobody walks much faster than I do!' 'He can't do that,' said the King, 'or else he'd have been here first.' *Ib.*

18 It's as large as life, and twice as natural! *Ib.*

19 If you'll believe in me, I'll believe in you. *Ib.*

20 The [White] Knight said ... 'It's my own invention.' *Ib.*

21 But you've no idea what a difference it makes, mixing it with other things—such as gunpowder and sealing-wax. *Through the Looking-Glass, ch.* 7

22 I'll tell thee everything I can:
There's little to relate.
I saw an aged, aged man,
A-sitting on a gate.

'Who are you, aged man?' I said.
'And how is it you live?'
And his answer trickled through my head
Like water through a sieve.

He said, 'I look for butterflies
That sleep among the wheat:
I make them into mutton-pies,
And sell them in the street.' *Ib.*

23 I cried, 'Come, tell me how you live!'
And thumped him on the head. *Ib.*

24 He said, 'I hunt for haddocks' eyes
Among the heather bright,
And work them into waistcoat-buttons
In the silent night.

And these I do not sell for gold
Or coin of silvery shine,
But for a copper halfpenny,
And that will purchase nine.

I sometimes dig for buttered rolls,
Or set limed twigs for crabs;
I sometimes search the grassy knolls
For wheels of hansom-cabs.' *Ib.*

25 Or madly squeeze a right-hand foot
Into a left-hand shoe. *Ib.*

26 'Speak when you're spoken to!' the Red Queen sharply interrupted her. *Ib. ch.* 9

27 No admittance till the week after next! *Ib.*

28 It isn't etiquette to cut any one you've been introduced to. Remove the joint. *Ib.*

29 Un-dish-cover the fish, or dishcover the riddle. *Ib.*

WILLIAM HERBERT CARRUTH
1859–1924

30 Some call it evolution,
And others call it God.
Each In His Own Tongue, and Other Poems, 1908

PHOEBE CARY
1824–1871

31 And though hard be the task,
'Keep a stiff upper lip'. *Keep a Stiff Upper Lip*

32 Nearer my Father's house,
Where the many mansions be,
Nearer the great white throne,
Nearer the crystal sea. *Nearer Home*

HARRY CASTLING

33 What-Ho! She bumps! *Title of Song*

34 Let's all go down the Strand. *Title of Song*

REV. EDWARD CASWALL
1814-1878

1 Come, Thou Holy Spirit, come;
And from Thy celestial home
Shed a ray of light Divine;
Come, Thou Father of the poor,
Come, Thou source of all our store,
Come, within our bosoms shine.
*Hymns and Poems. Come, Thou Holy Spirit, Come
(trans. from Latin)*

2 In our labour rest most sweet,
Grateful coolness in the heat,
Solace in the midst of woe.   *Ib.*

(*As adapted in 'Hymns Ancient and Modern'*):

3 Days and moments quickly flying,
Blend the living with the dead;
Soon will you and I be lying
Each within our narrow bed.
Ib. Days and Moments Quickly Flying

4 Earth has many a noble city;
Bethlehem, thou dost all excel.
Ib. Earth Has Many a Noble City

5 Hark! a thrilling voice is sounding;
'Christ is nigh,' it seems to say.
Ib. Hark! A Thrilling Voice is Sounding

6 Jesu, the very thought of Thee
With sweetness fills the breast.
Ib. Jesu, The Very Thought of Thee (trans. from Latin)

7 My God, I love Thee; not because
I hope for heaven thereby.
Ib. My God, I Love Thee (trans. from Latin)

CATO THE ELDER
234-149 B.C.

8 Delenda est Carthago.

Carthage must be destroyed.

Plutarch, Life of Cato

CATULLUS
87-54? B.C.

9 Cui dono lepidum novum libellum
Arido modo pumice expolitum?

Here's my small book out, nice and new,
Fresh-bound—whom shall I give it to?
Carmina, i, trans. by Sir W. Marris

10   Namque tu solebas
Meas esse aliquid putare nugas.

To you [Cornelius], who of yore
Upon my trifles set some store.   *Ib.*

11 Plus uno maneat perenne saeclo.

May it outlive an hundred year.   *Ib.*

12 Lugete, O Veneres Cupidinesque,
Et quantum est hominum venustiorum.
Passer mortuus est meae puellae,
Passer, deliciae meae puellae.

Come, all ye Loves and Cupids, haste
To mourn, and all ye men of taste;
My lady's sparrow, O, he's sped,
The bird my lady loved is dead!   *Ib. iii*

13 Qui nunc it per iter tenebricosum
Illuc, unde negant redire quenquam.

And now he treads the gloomy track
Whence no one, so they say, comes back.
Carmina, iii

14 Sed haec prius fuere.

All this is over now.   *Ib. iv*

15 Vivamus, mea Lesbia, atque amemus,
Rumoresque senum severiorum
Omnes unius aestimemus assis.
Soles occidere et redire possunt:
Nobis cum semel occidit brevis lux
Nox est perpetua una dormienda.

Lesbia mine, let's live and love!
Give no doit for tattle of
Crabbed old censorious men;
Suns may set and rise again,
But when our short day takes flight
Sleep we must one endless night.   *Ib. v*

16 Da mi basia mille.

Kiss me times a thousand o'er.   *Ib.*

17 Miser Catulle, desinas ineptire.

Forgo your dream, poor fool of love.   *Ib. viii*

18 At tu, Catulle, destinatus obdura.

But bide, Catullus, firm and set.   *Ib.*

19 Nec meum respectet, ut ante, amorem,
Qui illius culpa cecidit velut prati
Ultimi flos, praetereunte postquam
Tactus aratro est.

But ne'er look back again to find my love,
My love, which for her fault has wilted now,
Like meadow flower, upon the marge thereof,
Touched by a passing plough.   *Ib. xi*

20 Totum ut te faciant, Fabulle, nasum.

To make you nose and only nose.   *Ib. xiii*

21 O quid solutis est beatius curis?
Cum mens onus reponit, ac peregrino
Labore fessi venimus larem ad nostrum,
Desideratoque acquiescimus lecto.
Hoc est quod unum est pro laboribus tantis.
Salve O venusta Sirmio atque hero gaude;
Gaudete vosque O Lydiae lacus undae;
Ridete quidquid est domi cachinnorum.

What joy is like it? to be quit of care
And drop my load, and after weary miles
Come home, and sink upon the bed that so
I used to dream of: this one thing is worth
All that long service. Hail, sweet Sirmio!
Welcome thy lord with laughter, and give back
Your laughter, waters of the Lydian lake:
Laugh, home of mine, with all your maddest mirth.
Ib. xxxi

22   Quidquid est, ubicumque est,
Quodcumque agit, renidet: hunc habet morbum,
Neque elegantem, ut arbitror, neque urbanum.

Whate'er the case, where'er he be,
Or does, he smiles; with him it is a vice,
And not, I think, a pretty one, nor nice. *Ib. xxxix*

23 Nam risu inepto res ineptior nulla est.

Untimely grinning is the silliest sin.   *Ib.*

24 Iam ver egelidos refert tepores.

Now Spring restores the balmy days.   *Ib. xlvi*

1 Gratias tibi maximas Catullus
Agit pessimus omnium poeta,
Tanto pessimus omnium poeta,
Quanto tu optimus omnium's patronum.

 Catullus gives you warmest thanks,
 And he the worst of poets ranks;
 As much the worst of bards confessed,
 As you of advocates the best. *Carmina*, xlix

2 Ille mi par esse deo videtur,
Ille, si fas est, superare divos,
Qui sedens adversus identidem te
 Spectat et audit
Dulce ridentem, misero quod omnis
Eripit sensus mihi.

 Like to a god he seems to me,
 Above the gods, if so may be,
 Who sitting often close to thee
  May see and hear
 Thy lovely laugh: ah, luckless man! *Ib*. li

3 Quid est, Catulle? quid moraris emori?
 How now? why not be quick and die? *Ib*. lii

4 Salaputium disertum!
 He can talk, that little cuss! *Ib*. liii

5 Caeli, Lesbia nostra, Lesbia illa,
Illa Lesbia, quam Catullus unam
Plus quam se atque suos amavit omnes,
Nunc in quadruviis et angiportis
Glubit magnanimis Remi nepotes.

 My Lesbia,—Lesbia, whom once
 Catullus loved of girls alone
 Above himself and all his own—
 Now into lanes and corners runs
 To traffic with proud Remus' sons. *Ib*. lviii

6 Torquatus volo parvulus
Matris e gremio suae
Porrigens teneras manus,
Dulce rideat ad patrem
Semihiante labello.

 Sit suo similis patri
Manlio et facile inscieis
Noscitetur ab omnibus,
Et pudicitiam suo
Matris indicet ore.

 I'd a wee Torquatus see
 Stretch soft finger-tips
 From his mother's lap, and smile
 Sweetly at his sire the while
  With half-parted lips;

 To his father Manlius so
 Very alike, in sooth
 Even strangers him shall know,
 And his face alone shall show
  Forth his mother's truth. *Ib*. lxi. 209

7 Vesper adest, iuvenes, consurgite: Vesper Olympo
Exspectata diu vix tandem lumina tollit.

 Up, lads! 'tis Eve at last: to longing eyes
 Upon Olympus Hesper lifts his ray. *Ib*. lxii. 1

8 Quid datur a divis felici optatius hora?
 What gift hath heaven to match thy happy hour?
          Ib. 30

9 Ut flos in saeptis secretus nascitur hortis,
Ignotus pecori, nullo contusus aratro,
Quem muicent aurae, firmat sol, educat imber;
Multi millu pueri, multae optavere puellae.

 As grows a flower within a garden close,
 Known to no cattle, by no ploughshare smit,
 Suns give it strength, rain growth, and air repose,
 And many lads and lasses long for it.
         Carmina, lxii. 39

10 Omnia fanda nefanda malo permixta furore,
Iustificam nobis mentem avertere deorum.

 Then right and wrong confused and all at odds
 Turned from us the just judgment of the gods.
         Ib. lxiv. 406

11 Sed mulier cupido quod dicit amanti,
In vento et rapida scribere oportet aqua.

  But a woman's sayings to her lover,
 Should be in wind and running water writ. *Ib*. lxx

12 Desine de quoquam quicquam bene velle mereri,
Aut aliquem fieri posse putare pium.

 Cease to expect to win men's gratitude,
 To think that human beings can be grateful.
         Ib. lxxiij

13 Siqua recordanti benefacta priora voluptas
Est homini.

 If it be good to mind each kindly act. *Ib*. lxxvi

14 Difficile est longum subito deponere amorem.
 'Tis hard to drop at once old-standing love. *Ib*.

15 Si vitam puriter egi.
 If my life be fair.   *Ib*.

16 O di, reddite mi hoc pro pietate mea.
 Gods, grant me this thing for my piety. *Ib*.

17 Chommoda dicebat, si quando commoda vellet
Dicere.

 'Hallowances' said Arrius (meaning 'allowances').
         Ib. lxxxiv

18 Odi et amo: quare id faciam, fortasse requiris.
Nescio, sed fieri sentio et excrucior.

 I hate, I love—the cause thereof
 Belike you ask of me:
 I do not know, but feel 'tis so,
 And I'm in agony.   *Ib*. lxxxv

19 Si quicquam mutis gratum acceptumve sepulcris
Accidere a nostro, Calve, dolore potest.

 If the dumb grave, my Calvus, can receive
 Aught that is dear or grateful from our grief.
         Ib. xcvi

20 Multas per gentes et multa per aequora vectus
Advenio has miseras, frater, ad inferias,
Ut te postremo donarem munere mortis
Et mutam nequiquam alloquerer cinerem.
Quandoquidem fortuna mihi tete abstulit ipsum,
Heu miser indigne frater adempte mihi,
Nunc tamen interea haec prisco quae more parentum
Tradita sunt tristi munere ad inferias,
Accipe fraterno multum manantia fletu,
Atque in perpetuum, frater, ave atque vale.

 By many lands and over many a wave
 I come, my brother, to your piteous grave,
 To bring you the last offering in death
 And o'er dumb dust expend an idle breath;

For fate has torn your living self from me,
And snatched you, brother, O, how cruelly!
Yet take these gifts, brought as our fathers bade
For sorrow's tribute to the passing shade;
A brother's tears have wet them o'er and o'er;
And so, my brother, hail, and farewell evermore!
Carmina, ci

1 At non effugies meos iambos.

You shan't evade
These rhymes I've made.
Fragments, trans. Sir W. Marris

EDITH CAVELL
1865–1915

2 I realize that patriotism is not enough. I must have no hatred or bitterness towards anyone.
Last Words, 12 Oct. 1915. The Times, 23 Oct. 1915

CAMILLO BENSO CAVOUR
1810–1861

3 Noi siamo pronti a proclamare nell' Italia questo gran principio: Libera Chiesa in libero Stato.

We are ready to proclaim throughout Italy the great principle of a free church in a free state.
Speech, 27 Mar. 1861. William de la Rive, *Remin. of Life and Character of Count Cavour* (1862), ch. 13, p. 276

ROBERT CECIL
see
SALISBURY

THOMAS OF CELANO
c. 1250

4 Dies irae, dies illa
Solvet saeclum in favilla,
Teste David cum Sibylla.

Day of wrath and doom impending,
David's word with Sibyl's blending
Heaven and earth in ashes ending!
Analecta Hymnica, liv, p. 269. (Trans. by Dr. W. J. Irons in *The English Hymnal*)

SUSANNAH CENTLIVRE
1667?–1723

5 The real Simon Pure. *Bold Stroke for a Wife*, v. i.
6 And lash the vice and follies of the age.
The Man's Bewitched, prologue
7 He is as melancholy as an unbrac'd drum.
Wonder, II. i

MIGUEL DE CERVANTES
1547–1616

8 El Caballero de la Triste Figura.

The Knight of the Sorrowful Countenance.
Don Quixote, pt. i, ch. 19. *Trans. by* Smollett
9 La mejor salsa del mundo es el hambre.

The best sauce in the world is hunger.
Ib. pt. ii, ch. 5

10 El pan comido y la compañía deshecha.

Where there's no more bread, boon companions melt away. *Don Quixote*, pt. ii, ch. 7
11 Muchos pocos hacen un mucho.

Many a pickle makes a mickle. *Ib.*
12 [*Sancho asks whether, to get to heaven, we ought not all to become monks.*]

No todos podemos ser frailes y muchos son los caminos por donde lleva Dios a los suyos al cielo. Religión *es* la caballería.

We cannot all be friars, and many are the ways by which God leads His children home. Religion *is* knight-errantry. *Ib.* ch. 8
13 [*Sancho, on his master*]

Es un entreverado loco, lleno de lúcidos intervalos.

He's a muddled fool, full of lucid intervals.
Ib. ch. 18
14 Dos linages sólos hay en el mundo, como decía una abuela mia, que son el tener y el no tener.

There are but two families in the world, as my grandmother used to say, the Haves and the Have-nots. *Ib.* ch. 20
15 Digo, paciencia y barajar.

Patience, and shuffle the cards. *Ib.* ch. 23
16 Del dicho al hecho hay gran trecho.

It's a far cry from speech to deed. *Ib.* ch. 34
17 La diligencia es madre de la buena ventura y la pereza, su contrario, jamás llegó al término que pide un buen deseo.

Diligence is the mother of good fortune, and idleness, its opposite, never brought a man to the goal of any of his best wishes. *Ib.*
18 Bien haya el que inventó el sueño, capa que cubre todos los humanos pensamientos, manjar que quita la hambre, agua que ahuyenta la sed, fuego que calienta el frío, frío que templa el ardor, y, finalmente, moneda general con que todas las cosas se compran, balanza y peso que iguala al pastor con el rey y al simple con el discreto.

Blessings on him who invented sleep, the mantle that covers all human thoughts, the food that appeases hunger, the drink that quenches thirst, the fire that warms cold, the cold that moderates heat, and, lastly, the general coin that purchases all things, the balance and weight that equals the shepherd with the king, and the simple with the wise. *Ib.* ch. 68. Trans. by Jervas
19 Los buenos pintores imitan la naturaleza, pero los malos la vomitan.

Good painters imitate nature, bad ones vomit it.
El Licenciado Vidriera
20 Puesto ya el pie en el estribo.

With one foot already in the stirrup.
Preface to 'Persiles y Sigismunda' (4 days before his death.)

JOHN CHALKHILL
fl. 1600

21 Oh, the sweet contentment
The countryman doth find. *Coridon's Song*

PATRICK REGINALD CHALMERS
1872–

1 'I find,' said 'e, 'things very much as 'ow I've always
  found,
  For mostly they goes up and down or else goes round
  and round.'
  *Green Days and Blue Days: Roundabouts and
  Swings*

2 What's lost upon the roundabouts we pulls up on the
  swings! *Ib.*

JOSEPH CHAMBERLAIN
1836–1914

3 But the cup is nearly full. The career of high-handed
  wrong is coming to an end. *Speech, 20 Oct. 1884*

4 Provided that the City of London remains as it is at
  present, the clearing-house of the world.
  Ib. Guildhall, London, 19 Jan. 1904

5 Learn to think Imperially. *Ib.*

6 The day of small nations has long passed away. The
  day of Empires has come.
  Ib. Birmingham, 12 May 1904

7 We are not downhearted. The only trouble is, we
  cannot understand what is happening to our neighbours. *Ib. Smethwick, 18 Jan. 1906*

NEVILLE CHAMBERLAIN
1869–1940

8 In war, whichever side may call itself the victor, there
  are no winners, but all are losers.
  Speech at Kettering, 3 July 1938

9 I believe it is peace for our time . . . peace with
  honour.
  *Radio Speech after Munich Agreement. 1 Oct.
  1938*

10 Hitler has missed the bus.
  Speech. House of Commons. 4 April 1940

CHARLES HADDON CHAMBERS
1860–1921

11 The long arm of coincidence.
  Captain Swift, Act II

JOHN CHANDLER
1806–1876

12 Conquering kings their titles take
  From the foes they captive make:
  Jesu, by a nobler deed,
  From the thousands He hath freed.
  As in Hymns Ancient and Modern. *Conquering
  Kings Their Titles Take*, trans. from Latin

ARTHUR CHAPMAN
1873–

13 Out where the handclasp's a little stronger,
  Out where the smile dwells a little longer,
  That's where the West begins.
  Out where the West Begins

GEORGE CHAPMAN
1559?–1634?

14 I know an Englishman,
  Being flatter'd, is a lamb; threaten'd, a lion;
  Alphonsus, Emperor of Germany, I. ii

15 Berenice's ever-burning hair.
  Blind Beggar of Alexandria

16 Speed his plough. *Bussy D'Ambois*, I. i

17 Who to himself is law, no law doth need,
  Offends no law, and is a king indeed. *Ib.* II. i

18 Terror of darkness! O, thou king of flames! *Ib.* v. i

19 Give me a spirit that on this life's rough sea
  Loves t'have his sails fill'd with a lusty wind,
  Even till his sail-yards tremble, his masts crack,
  And his rapt ship run on her side so low
  That she drinks water, and her keel ploughs air;
  There is no danger to a man, that knows
  What life and death is; there's not any law,
  Exceeds his knowledge; neither is it lawful
  That he should stoop to any other law.
  He goes before them, and commands them all,
  That to himself is a law rational.
  Byron's Conspiracy, III. i

20 O incredulity! the wit of fools,
  That slovenly will spit on all things fair,
  The coward's castle, and the sluggard's cradle.
  De Guiana, l. 82

21 We have watered our horses in Helicon.
  May-Day, III. iii

22 For one heat, all know, doth drive out another,
  One passion doth expel another still.
  Monsieur D'Olive, v. i

23 They're only truly great who are truly good.
  Revenge for Honour, v. ii

24 A poem, whose subject is not truth, but things like
  truth. *Revenge of Bussy D'Ambois*, dedication

25 Danger, the spur of all great minds. *Ib.* v. i

26 And let a scholar all Earth's volumes carry,
  He will be but a walking dictionary.
  Tears of Peace, l. 266

CHARLES I OF GREAT BRITAIN
1600–1649

27 Never make a defence of apology before you be
  accused. *Letter to Lord Wentworth, 3 Sept. 1636*

28 As to the King, the Laws of the Land will clearly
  instruct you for that. . . . For the People; and truly
  I desire their Liberty and Freedom, as much as
  any Body: but I must tell you, that their Liberty
  and Freedom consists in having the Government
  of those Laws, by which their Life and their Goods
  may be most their own; 'tis not for having share in
  Government [Sirs] that is nothing pertaining to
  'em. A Subject and a Sovereign are clean different
  things. . . . If I would have given way to an arbitrary
  way, for to have all Laws chang'd according to the
  Power of the Sword, I needed not to have come
  here; and therefore I tell you (and I pray God it be
  not laid to your Charge) that I am the Martyr of
  the People.
  Speech on the scaffold, 30 Jan. 1649. Rushworth's
  Historical Collections (1703–8), vol. vi

1 I die a Christian, according to the Profession of the Church of England, as I found it left me by my Father.
Speech on the scaffold, 30 Jan. 1649. Rushworth's *Historical Collections (1703–8), vol. vi*

CHARLES II OF GREAT BRITAIN
1630–1685

2 It is upon the navy under the Providence of God that the safety, honour, and welfare of this realm do chiefly attend.   *Articles of War.* Preamble

3 Better than a play.
(*On the Debates in the House of Lords on Lord Ross's Divorce Bill, 1670.*) A. Bryant, *King Charles II*

4 This is very true: for my words are my own, and my actions are my ministers'.
Reply to Lord Rochester's Epitaph on him [q.v.]

5 He [Charles II] said once to myself, he was no atheist, but he could not think God would make a man miserable only for taking a little pleasure out of the way.
Burnet, *History of My Own Time*, vol. 1, bk. ii, ch. 1

6 He [Lauderdale] told me, the king spoke to him to let that [Presbytery] go, for it was not a religion for gentlemen.   *Ib.* ch. 2

7 King Charles gave him [Godolphin] a short character when he was page, which he maintained to his life's end, of being never *in* the way, nor *out* of the way.
Ib. vol. II, bk. iii, ch. II, n. (*The Earl of Dartmouth*)

8 Let not poor Nelly starve.   *Ib.* ch. 17

9 Brother, I am too old to go again to my travels.
Hume's *History of Great Britain*, vol. ii, 1757, ch. 7

10 I am sure no man in England will take away my life to make you King. [To his brother James.]
W. King's *Political & Lit. Anecdotes*

11 He had been, he said, an unconscionable time dying; but he hoped that they would excuse it.
Macaulay's *Hist. England*, 1849, vol. i, ch. 4, p. 437

12 His nonsense suits their nonsense.
On a certain preacher

CHARLES V
1500–1558

13 Je parle espagnol à Dieu, italien aux femmes, français aux hommes et allemand à mon cheval.
To God I speak Spanish, to women Italian, to men French, and to my horse—German.   *Attrib.*

SALMON PORTLAND CHASE
1808–1873

14 No more slave States: no slave Territories.
Platform of the Free Soil National Convention, 1848

15 The Constitution, in all its provisions, looks to an indestructible Union composed of indestructible States. *Decision in Texas v. White*, 7 Wallace, 725

16 The way to resumption is to resume.
Letter to Horace Greeley, 17 May 1866

EARL OF CHATHAM
see
WILLIAM PITT

THOMAS CHATTERTON
1752–1770

17 O! synge untoe mie roundelaie,
  O! droppe the brynie teare wythe mee,
  Daunce ne moe atte hallie daie,
  Lycke a reynynge ryver bee;
    Mie love ys dedde,
    Gon to hys death-bedde,
    Al under the wyllowe-tree.   *Mynstrelles Songe*

FRANÇOIS-RENÉ DE CHATEAUBRIAND
1768–1848

18 L'écrivain original n'est pas celui qui n'imite personne, mais celui que personne ne peut imiter.
The original writer is not he who refrains from imitating others, but he who can be imitated by none.   *Génie du Christianisme*

GEOFFREY CHAUCER
1340?–1400

19 Singest with vois memorial in the shade.
Anelida and Arcite, proem

20 Flee fro the prees, and dwelle with sothfastnesse. . .
  Forth, pilgrim, forth! Forth, beste, out of thy stal!
  Know thy contree, look up, thank God of al!
  Hold the hye wey, and lat thy gost thee lede;
  And trouthe shal delivere, hit is no drede.
Balade de Bon Conseyl

21 Whanne that Aprille with his shoures sote
  The droghte of Marche hath perced to the rote.
Canterbury Tales. Prologue, l. 1

22 And smale fowles maken melodye,
  That slepen al the night with open yë,
  (So priketh hem nature in hir corages):
  Than longen folk to goon on pilgrimages.   *Ib.* l. 9

23   He loved chivalrye,
  Trouthe and honour, freedom and curteisye. *Ib.* l. 45

24 He was a verray parfit gentil knight.   *Ib.* l. 72

25 He was as fresh as is the month of May.   *Ib.* l. 92

26 He coude songes make and wel endyte.   *Ib.* l. 95

27 Curteys he was, lowly, and servisable,
  And carf biforn his fader at the table.   *Ib.* l. 99

28 Hir gretteste ooth was but by sëynt Loy.   *Ib.* l. 120

29 Ful wel she song the service divyne,
  Entuned in hir nose ful semely;
  And Frensh she spak ful faire and fetisly,
  After the scole of Stratford atte Bowe,
  For Frensh of Paris was to hir unknowe.   *Ib.* l. 122

30 She wolde wepe, if that she sawe a mous
  Caught in a trappe, if it were deed or bledde.
  Of smale houndes had she, that she fedde
  With rosted flesh, or milk and wastel-breed.
  But sore weep she if oon of hem were deed.
Ib. l. 144

31 He yaf nat of that text a pulled hen,
  That seith, that hunters been nat holy men.
Ib. l. 177

1 A Frere ther was, a wantown and a merye.
Canterbury Tales. Prologue, l. 208

2 He knew the tavernes wel in every toun. *Ib.* l. 240

3 He was the best beggere in his hous. *Ib.* l. 252

4 Somwhat he lipsed, for his wantownesse,
To make his English swete up-on his tonge.
Ib. l. 264

5 A Clerk ther was of Oxenford also. *Ib.* l. 285

6 For him was lever have at his beddes heed
Twenty bokes, clad in blak or reed,
Of Aristotle and his philosophye,
Than robes riche, or fithele, or gay sautrye.
But al be that he was a philosophre,
Yet hadde he but litel gold in cofre. *Ib.* l. 293

7 And gladly wolde he lerne, and gladly teche.
Ib. l. 308

8 No-wher so bisy a man as he ther nas,
And yet he semed bisier than he was. *Ib.* l. 321

9 For he was Epicurus owne sone. *Ib.* l. 336

10 It snewed in his hous of mete and drinke. *Ib.* l. 345

11 A Shipman was ther, woning fer by weste:
For aught I woot, he was of Dertemouthe. *Ib.* l. 388

12 And, certeinly, he was a good felawe. *Ib.* l. 395

13 Of nyce conscience took he no keep.
If that he faught, and hadde the hyer hond,
By water he sente hem hoom to every lond.
Ib. l. 398

14 His studie was but litel on the bible. *Ib.* l. 438

15 She was a worthy womman al hir lyve,
Housbondes at chirche-dore she hadde fyve,
Withouten other companye in youthe;
But therof nedeth nat to speke as nouthe.
And thryes hadde she been at Jerusalem;
She hadde passed many a straunge streem;
At Rome she hadde been, and at Boloigne,
In Galice at seint Jame, and at Cologne. *Ib.* l. 459

16 A good man was ther of religioun,
And was a povre Persoun of a toun. *Ib.* l. 477

17 This noble ensample to his sheep he yaf,
That first he wroghte, and afterward he taughte.
Ib. l. 496

18 But Cristes lore, and his apostles twelve,
He taughte, but first he folwed it him-selve.
Ib. l. 527

19 That hadde a fyr-reed cherubinnes face. *Ib.* l. 624

20 Wel loved he garleek, oynons, and eek lekes,
And for to drinken strong wyn, reed as blood.
Ib. l. 634

21 His walet lay biforn him in his lappe,
Bret-ful of pardoun come from Rome al hoot.
Ib. l. 686

22 He hadde a croys of latoun, ful of stones,
And in a glas he hadde pigges bones.
But with thise relikes, whan that he fond
A povre person dwelling up-on lond,
Up-on a day he gat him more moneye
Than that the person gat in monthes tweye.
And thus, with feyned flaterye and japes,
He made the person and the peple his apes.
Ib. l. 699

23 Who-so shal telle a tale after a man,
He moot reherce, as ny as ever he can,
Everich a word, if it be in his charge,
Al speke he never so rudeliche and large;
Or elles he moot telle his tale untrewe,
Or feyne thing, or finde wordes newe.
Canterbury Tales. Prologue, l. 731

24 Thus with hir fader, for a certeyn space,
Dwelleth this flour of wyfly pacience,
That neither by hir wordes ne hir face
Biforn the folk, ne eek in hir absence,
Ne shewed she that hir was doon offence.
Ib. The Clerkes Tale, l. 862

25 O stormy peple! unsad and ever untrewe. *Ib.* l. 939

26 Trouthe is the hyeste thing that man may kepe.
Ib. The Frankeleyns Tale, l. 751

27 The carl spak oo thing, but he thoghte another.
Ib. The Freres Tale, l. 270

28 And therfore, at the kinges court, my brother,
Ech man for him-self, ther is non other.
Ib. Knightes Tale, l. 323

29 And whan a beest is deed, he hath no peyne;
But man after his deeth moot wepe and pleyne.
Ib. l. 461

30 The bisy larke, messager of day. *Ib.* l. 633

31 For pitee renneth sone in gentile herte. *Ib.* l. 903

32 The smyler with the knyf under the cloke.
Ib. l. 1141

33 Up roos the sonne, and up roos Emelye. *Ib.* l. 1415

34 What is this world? what asketh men to have?
Now with his love, now in his colde grave
Allone, with-outen any companye. *Ib.* l. 1919

35 She is mirour of alle curteisye.
Ib. Tale of the Man of Lawe, l. 68

36 Lat take a cat, and fostre him wel with milk,
And tendre flesh, and make his couche of silk,
And lat him seen a mous go by the wal;
Anon he weyveth milk, and flesh, and al,
And every deyntee that is in that hous,
Swich appetyt hath he to ete a mous.
Ib. The Maunciples Tale, l. 71

37 What is bettre than wisdom? Womman. And what is
bettre than a good womman? No-thing.
Ib. The Tale of Melibeus, § 15

38 Ful wys is he that can him-selven knowe.
Ib. The Monkes Tale, l. 149

39 Redeth the grete poete of Itaille,
That highte Dant, for he can al devyse
Fro point to point, nat o word wol he faille.
Ib. l. 470

40 The month in which the world bigan,
That highte March, whan god first maked man.
Ib. The Nonne Preestes Tale, l. 367

41 Daun Russel the fox sterte up at ones. *Ib.* l. 514

42 And on a Friday fil al this meschaunce. *Ib.* l. 521

43 And lightly as it comth, so wol we spende.
Ib. Pardoners Tale, l. 453

44 He can nat stinte of singing by the weye.
Ib. The Prioresses Tale, l. 105

45 Yet in our asshen olde is fyr y-reke.
Ib. The Reves Prologue, l. 28

1 The gretteste clerkes been noght the wysest men.
 Canterbury Tales. The Reves Tale, l. 134

2 So was hir joly whistle wel y-wet.   *Ib.* l. 235

3 He wolde sowen som difficultee,
Or springen cokkel in our clene corn.
 Ib. The Shipmannes Prologue, l. 20

4 A doghter hadde this worthy king also,
That yongest was, and highte Canacee.
 Ib. The Squieres Tale, l. 24

5 'Thou lokest as thou woldest finde an hare,
For ever up-on the ground I see thee stare.'
 Ib. Prologue to Sir Thopas, l. 6

6 The bacoun was nat fet for hem, I trowe,
That som men han in Essex at Dunmowe.
 Ib. The Prologue of the Wyves' Tale of Bathe, l. 217

7 And for to see, and eek for to be seye. *Ib.* l. 552

8 But yet I hadde alwey a coltes tooth.
Gat-tothed I was, and that bicam me weel.
           Ib. l. 602

9 This is a long preamble of a tale. *Ib.* l. 831

10 As thikke as motes in the sonne-beem.
 Ib. Tale of the Wyf of Bathe, l. 12

11 'My lige lady, generally,' quod he,
'Wommen desyren to have sovereynte
As well over hir housbond as hir love.' *Ib.* l. 181

12 He is gentil that doth gentil dedis *Ib.* l. 314

13 Ful craftier to pley she was
Than Athalus, that made the game
First of the ches: so was his name.
 The Book of the Duchesse, l. 662

14 O litel book, thou art so unconning,
How darst thou put thy-self in prees for drede?
 The Flower and the Leaf, l. 591

15   Venus clerk, Ovyde,
That hath y-sowen wonder wyde
The grete god of Loves name.
 The Hous of Fame, iii, l. 397

16 And as for me, thogh that I can but lyte,
On bokes for to rede I me delyte,
And to hem yeve I feyth and ful credence,
And in myn herte have hem in reverence
So hertely, that ther is game noon,
That fro my bokes maketh me to goon,
But hit be seldom, on the holyday;
Save, certeynly, whan that the month of May
Is comen, and that I here the foules singe,
And that the floures ginnen for to springe,
Farwel my book and my devocion.
 Legend of Good Women. Prologue, l. 29

17   Of alle the floures in the mede,
Than love I most these floures whyte and rede,
Swiche as men callen daysies in our toun. *Ib.* l. 41

18 Til that myn herte dye.   *Ib.* l. 57

19 That wel by reson men hit calle may
The 'dayesye' or elles the 'ye of day,'
The emperice and flour of floures alle.
I pray to god that faire mot she falle,
And alle that loven floures, for hir sake! *Ib.* l. 183

20 Fo lo, the gentil kind of the lioun!
For whan a flye offendeth him or byteth,
He with his tayl awey the flye smyteth

Al esily; for, of his genterye,
Him deyneth nat to wreke him on a flye,
As doth a curre or elles another beste.
 Legend of Good Women. Prologue, l. 377

21 And she was fair as is the rose in May.
 Ib. Legend of Cleopatra, l. 34

22 The lyf so short, the craft so long to lerne,
Thassay so hard, so sharp the conquering.
 The Parlement of Foules, l. 1

23 For out of olde feldes, as men seith,
Cometh al this newe corn fro yeer to yere;
And out of olde bokes, in good feith,
Cometh al this newe science that men lere. *Ib.* l. 22

24 Thou shalt make castels than in Spayne,
And dreme of joye, al but in vayne.
 Romaunt of the Rose, B. l. 2573

25 But the Troyane gestes, as they felle,
In Omer, or in Dares, or in Dyte,
Who-so that can, may rede hem as they wryte.
 Troilus and Criseyde, i, l. 145

26 For it is seyd, 'man maketh ofte a yerde
With which the maker is him-self y-beten.' *Ib.* l. 740

27 Unknowe, unkist, and lost that is unsought.
          Ib. l. 809

28 O wind, O wind, the weder ginneth clere. *Ib.* ii, l. 2

29 Til crowes feet be growe under your yë. *Ib.* l. 403

30 And we shal speke of thee som-what, I trowe,
Whan thou art goon, to do thyne eres glowe!
          Ib. l. 1021

31 It is nought good a sleping hound to wake.
         Ib. iii, l. 764

32 For I have seyn, of a ful misty morwe,
Folwen ful ofte a mery someres day. *Ib.* l. 1060

33 Right as an aspes leef she gan to quake. *Ib.* l. 1200

34 And as the newe abaysshed nightingale,
That stinteth first whan she biginneth singe.
          Ib. l. 1233

35 For of fortunes sharp adversitee
The worst kinde of infortune is this,
A man to have ben in prosperitee,
And it remembren, when it passed is. *Ib.* l. 1625

36 Oon ere it herde, at the other out it wente.
         Ib. iv, l. 434

37 But manly set the world on sixe and sevene;
And, if thou deye a martir, go to hevene. *Ib.* l. 622

38 For tyme y-lost may not recovered be. *Ib.* l. 1283

39 Ye, fare-wel al the snow of ferne yere! *Ib.* v, l. 1176

40 Eek greet effect men wryte in place lyte. [i.e. little space]
Th'entente is al, and nought the lettres space.
          Ib. l. 1629

41 Go, litel book, go litel myn tragedie. *Ib.* l. 1786

42 O yonge fresshe folkes, he or she. *Ib.* l. 1835

43 O moral Gower, this book I directe
To thee.   *Ib.* l. 1856

NIVELLE DE LA CHAUSSÉE
1692–1754

44 Quand tout le monde a tort, tout le monde a raison.
 When every one is wrong, every one is right.
        La Gouvernante, I. iii

ANDREW CHERRY

1762–1812

1 Loud roar'd the dreadful thunder,
The rain a deluge show'r'd. *The Bay of Biscay*

2 Till next day,
There she lay,
In the Bay of Biscay, O! *Ib.*

PHILIP DORMER STANHOPE, EARL OF CHESTERFIELD

1694–1773

3 The dews of the evening most carefully shun,
Those tears of the sky for the loss of the sun.
Advice to a Lady in Autumn

4 Unlike my subject will I frame my song,
It shall be witty and it sha'n't be long.
Epigram on 'Long' Sir Thomas Robinson. *D.N.B.*

5 The picture plac'd the busts between,
Adds to the thought much strength;
Wisdom and Wit are little seen,
But Folly's at full length.
*Wit and Wisdom of Lord Chesterfield. Epigrams.
On the Picture of Richard Nash . . . between the
Busts of . . . Newton and . . . Pope . . . at Bath.
(Attr. also to Mrs. Jane Brereton)*

6 In scandal, as in robbery, the receiver is always
thought as bad as the thief.
Advice to his Son. Rules for Conversation, Scandal

7 In my mind, there is nothing so illiberal and so ill-
bred, as audible laughter. *Ib. Graces, Laughter*

8 In my opinion, parsons are very like other men, and
neither the better nor the worse for wearing a
black gown. *Letter to his Son, 5 Apr. 1746*

9 The knowledge of the world is only to be acquired
in the world, and not in a closet. *Ib. 4 Oct. 1746*

10 An injury is much sooner forgotten than an insult.
Ib. 9 Oct. 1746

11 Courts and camps are the only places to learn the
world in. *Ib. 2 Oct. 1747*

12 There is a Spanish proverb, which says very justly,
Tell me whom you live with, and I will tell you who
you are. *Ib. 9 Oct. 1747*

13 Take the tone of the company that you are in. *Ib.*

14 Do as you would be done by is the surest method
that I know of pleasing. *Ib. 16 Oct. 1747*

15 I recommend you to take care of the minutes: for
hours will take care of themselves. *Ib. 6 Nov. 1747*

16 Advice is seldom welcome; and those who want it
the most always like it the least. *Ib. 29 Jan. 1748*

17 Speak of the moderns without contempt, and of the
ancients without idolatry. *Ib. 22 Feb. 1748*

18 Wear your learning, like your watch, in a private
pocket: and do not merely pull it out and strike it;
merely to show that you have one. *Ib.*

19 Sacrifice to the Graces. *Ib. 9 Mar. 1748*

20 I am neither of a melancholy nor a cynical disposition,
and am as willing and as apt to be pleased as anybody; but I am sure that, since I have had the full
use of my reason, nobody has ever heard me laugh.
Ib.

21 If Shakespeare's genius had been cultivated, those
beauties, which we so justly admire in him, would
have been undisgraced by those extravagancies, and
that nonsense, with which they are so frequently
accompanied. *Letter to his Son, 1 Apr. 1748*

22 Women, then, are only children of a larger growth:
they have an entertaining tattle, and sometimes
wit; but for solid, reasoning good-sense, I never
knew in my life one that had it, or who reasoned
or acted consequentially for four and twenty hours
together. *Ib. 5 Sept. 1748*

23 A man of sense only trifles with them [women], plays
with them, humours and flatters them, as he does
with a sprightly and forward child; but he neither
consults them about, nor trusts them with, serious
matters. *Ib.*

24 It must be owned, that the Graces do not seem to be
natives of Great Britain; and I doubt, the best of us
here have more of rough than polished diamond.
Ib. 18 Nov. 1748

25 Idleness is only the refuge of weak minds.
Ib. 20 July 1749

26 Women are much more like each other than men:
they have, in truth, but two passions, vanity and
love; these are their universal characteristics.
Ib. 19 Dec. 1749

27 Knowledge may give weight, but accomplishments
give lustre, and many more people see than weigh.
Ib. 8 May 1750

28 Is it possible to love such a man? No. The utmost
I can do for him is to consider him as a respectable
Hottentot. [Lord Lyttelton.] *Ib. 28 Feb. 1751*

29 It is commonly said, and more particularly by Lord
Shaftesbury, that ridicule is the best test of truth.
Ib. 6 Feb. 1752

30 Every woman is infallibly to be gained by every sort
of flattery, and every man by one sort or other.
Ib. 16 Mar. 1752

31 A chapter of accidents. *Ib. 16 Feb. 1753*

32 In matters of religion and matrimony I never give
any advice; because I will not have anybody's
torments in this world or the next laid to my
charge. *Letter to A. C. Stanhope, 12 Oct. 1765*

33 Religion is by no means a proper subject of conversation in a mixed company.
Undated Letter to his Godson, No. 112

34 I assisted at the birth of that most significant word,
flirtation, which dropped from the most beautiful
mouth in the world. *The World, No. 101*

35 Tyrawley and I have been dead these two years; but
we don't choose to have it known.
Boswell's Johnson, 3 Apr. 1773

36 He once exclaimed to Anstis, Garter King at Arms,
'You foolish man, you do not even know your own
foolish business.'
*Jesse's Memoirs of the Court of England from
1688 to Geo. II, vol. ii*

37 Give Dayrolles a chair.
Last Words. W. H. Craig, Life of Chesterfield

CHESTERTON

GILBERT KEITH CHESTERTON
1874-1936

1 Are they clinging to their crosses,
　　F. E. Smith?
　　　　Antichrist, or the Reunion of Christendom

2 Talk about the pews and steeples
　And the cash that goes therewith!
But the souls of Christian peoples . . .
　　Chuck it, Smith! 　　　　*Ib.*

3 Heaven shall forgive you Bridge at dawn,
　The clothes you wear—or do not wear—
　　　　Ballade d'une Grande Dame

4 But for the virtuous things you do,
　The righteous work, the public care,
It shall not be forgiven you. 　　*Ib.*

5 They spoke of progress spiring round,
　Of Light and Mrs. Humphry Ward—
It is not true to say I frowned,
Or ran about the room and roared;
I might have simply sat and snored—
I rose politely in the club
And said, 'I feel a little bored;
Will some one take me to a pub?'
　　　　A Ballade of an Anti-Puritan

6 I'll read 'Jack Redskin on the Quest'
　And feed my brain with better things.
　　　　A Ballade of a Book Reviewer

7 Prince, Prince-Elective on the modern plan,
Fulfilling such a lot of people's Wills,
You take the Chiltern Hundreds while you can—
A storm is coming on the Chiltern Hills.
　　　　A Ballade of the First Rain

8 The gallows in my garden, people say,
Is new and neat and adequately tall.
　　　　A Ballade of Suicide

9 The strangest whim has seized me. . . . After all
　I think I will not hang myself to-day. 　*Ib.*

10 Prince, I can hear the trumpet of Germinal,
The tumbrils toiling up the terrible way;
Even to-day your royal head may fall—
I think I will not hang myself to-day. 　*Ib.*

11 Before the gods that made the gods
　Had seen their sunrise pass,
The White Horse of the White Horse Vale
　Was cut out of the grass.
　　　　Ballad of the White Horse, bk. i

12 There was not English armour left,
　Nor any English thing,
When Alfred came to Athelney
　To be an English king. 　　*Ib.*

13 I tell you naught for your comfort,
　Yea, naught for your desire,
Save that the sky grows darker yet
　And the sea rises higher. 　　*Ib.*

14 Last of a race in ruin—
　He spoke the speech of the Gaels. 　*Ib. bk. ii*

15 For the great Gaels of Ireland
　Are the men that God made mad,
For all their wars are merry,
　And all their songs are sad. 　　*Ib.*

16 The thing on the blind side of the heart,
　On the wrong side of the door,
The green plant groweth, menacing
　Almighty lovers in the spring;
There is always a forgotten thing,
　And love is not secure.
　　　　Ballad of the White Horse, bk. iii

17 We have more lust again to lose
　Than you to win again. 　　*Ib.*

18 And when the last arrow
　　Was fitted and was flown,
When the broken shield was hung on the breast,
And the hopeless lance was laid in rest,
　And the hopeless horn blown,
The King looked up. 　　*Ib. bk. vii*

19 Nelson turned his blindest eye
　On Naples and on liberty.
　　　　Blessed are the Peacemakers

20 The Christ-child stood at Mary's knee,
　His hair was like a crown,
And all the flowers looked up at Him,
　And all the stars looked down. 　*A Christmas Carol*

21 When fishes flew and forests walked
　And figs grew upon thorn,
Some moment when the moon was blood
　Then surely I was born.

With monstrous head and sickening cry
　And ears like errant wings,
The devil's walking parody
　On all four-footed things. 　　*The Donkey*

22 Fools! For I also had my hour;
　One far fierce hour and sweet:
There was a shout about my ears,
　And palms before my feet. 　　*Ib.*

23 There is one creed: 'neath no world-terror's wing
　Apples forget to grow on apple-trees. 　*Ecclesiastes*

24 The men that worked for England
　They have their graves at home:

And they that rule in England,
　In stately conclave met,
Alas, alas for England
　They have no graves as yet.
　　　　Elegy in a Country Churchyard

25 But since he stood for England
　And knew what England means,
Unless you give him bacon
　You must not give him beans. 　*The Englishman*

26 Lady, the stars are falling pale and small,
Lady, we will not live if life be all,
Forgetting those good stars in heaven hung;
When all the world was young.
For more than gold was in a ring, and love was not a
　little thing
Between the trees in Ivywood, when all the world was
　young. 　　*The Flying Inn, ch. 24*

27 Mr. Mandragon, the Millionaire.
　　　　The Good Rich Man

28 When Man is the Turk, and the Atheist,
　Essene, Erastian Whig,
And the Thug and the Druse and the Catholic
　And the crew of the Captain's gig.
　　　　The Higher Unity

1 But our rest is as far as the fire-drake swings
  And our peace is put in impossible things
  Where clashed and thundered unthinkable wings
  Round an incredible star. *The House of Christmas*

2 Or must Fate act the same grey farce again,
  And wait, till one, amid Time's wrecks and scars,
  Speaks to a ruin here, 'What poet-race
  Shot such Cyclopean arches at the stars?'
  King's Cross Station

3 White founts falling in the courts of the sun,
  And the Soldan of Byzantium is smiling as they run.
  Lepanto

4 The cold queen of England is looking in the glass;
  The shadow of the Valois is yawning at the Mass.
  Ib.

5 Strong gongs groaning as the drums beat far. *Ib.*

6 Don John of Austria is going to the war. *Ib.*

7 It is he that saith not 'Kismet'; it is he that knows
  not fate;
  It is Richard, it is Raymond, it is Godfrey in the gate!
  Ib.

8 Cervantes on his galley sets the sword back in the
  sheath,
  (Don John of Austria rides homeward with a wreath.)
  Ib.

9 And he smiles, but not as Sultans smile, and settles
  back the blade. . . .
  (But Don John of Austria rides home from the
  Crusade.)
  Ib.

10 For I come from Castlepatrick, and me heart is on me
  sleeve,
  But a lady stole it from me on St. Gallowglass's Eve.
  Me Heart

11 The folk that live in Liverpool, their heart is in their
  boots;
  They go to hell like lambs, they do, because the
  hooter hoots.
  Ib.

12 And they think we're burning witches when we're
  only burning weeds.
  Ib.

13 You saw the moon from Sussex Downs,
  A Sussex moon, untravelled still,
  I saw a moon that was the town's,
  The largest lamp on Campden Hill.
  The Napoleon of Notting Hill, dedication

14 This did not end by Nelson's urn
  Where an immortal England sits—
  Nor where your tall young men in turn
  Drank death like wine at Austerlitz.
  Ib.

15 Yes, Heaven is everywhere at home,
  The big blue cap that always fits.
  Ib.

16 The legend of an epic hour
  A child I dreamed, and dream it still,
  Under the great grey water-tower
  That strikes the stars on Campden Hill.
  Ib.

17 John Grubby, who was short and stout
  And troubled with religious doubt,
  Refused about the age of three
  To sit upon the curate's knee. *The New Freethinker*

18 From all the easy speeches
  That comfort cruel men. *O God of Earth and Altar*

19 'What of vile dust?' the preacher said.
  Methought the whole world woke.
  The Praise of Dust

20 Walter, be wise, avoid the wild and new!
  The Constitution is the game for you.
  The Revolutionary, or Lines to a Statesman (Rt.
  Hon. Walter Long)

21 Before the Roman came to Rye or out to Severn
  strode,
  The rolling English drunkard made the rolling
  English road. *The Rolling English Road*

22 That night we went to Birmingham by way of Beachy
  Head. *Ib.*

23 My friends, we will not go again or ape an ancient rage,
  Or stretch the folly of our youth to be the shame of
  age. *Ib.*

24 For there is good news yet to hear and fine things to
  be seen.
  Before we go to Paradise by way of Kensal Green. *Ib.*

25 And a few men talked of freedom, while England
  talked of ale. *The Secret People*

26 But the squire seemed struck in the saddle; he was
  foolish, as if in pain.
  He leaned on a staggering lawyer, he clutched a
  cringing Jew,
  He was stricken; it may be, after all, he was stricken
  at Waterloo. *Ib.*

27 We only know the last sad squires ride slowly towards
  the sea,
  And a new people takes the land: and still it is not
  we. *Ib.*

28 Smile at us, pay us, pass us; but do not quite forget.
  For we are the people of England, that never have
  spoken yet. *Ib.*

29 Lord Lilac thought it rather rotten
  That Shakespeare should be quite forgotten,
  And therefore got on a Committee
  With several chaps out of the City.
  The Shakespeare Memorial

30 The souls most fed with Shakespeare's flame
  Still sat unconquered in a ring,
  Remembering him like anything. *Ib.*

31 But not with that grand constancy
  Of Clement Shorter, Herbert Tree,
  Lord Rosebery and Comyns Carr
  And all the other names there are;
  Who stuck like limpets to the spot,
  Lest they forgot, lest they forgot.

  Lord Lilac was of slighter stuff;
  Lord Lilac had had quite enough. *Ib.*

32 God made the wicked Grocer
  For a mystery and a sign,
  That men might shun the awful shop
  And go to inns to dine. *Song Against Grocers*

33 The evil-hearted Grocer
  Would call his mother 'Ma'am,'
  And bow at her and bob at her,
  Her aged soul to damn. *Ib.*

34 He crams with cans of poisoned meat
  The subjects of the King,
  And when they die by thousands
  Why, he laughs like anything. *Ib.*

35 He keeps a lady in a cage
  Most cruelly all day,
  And makes her count and calls her 'Miss'
  Until she fades away. *Ib.*

1 The righteous minds of innkeepers
Induce them now and then
To crack a bottle with a friend
Or treat unmoneyed men,

But who hath seen the Grocer
Treat housemaids to his teas
Or crack a bottle of fish-sauce
Or stand a man a cheese? *Song Against Grocers*

2 And I dream of the days when work was scrappy,
And rare in our pockets the mark of the mint,
And we were angry and poor and happy,
And proud of seeing our names in print.
A Song of Defeat

3 And sword in hand upon Afric's passes
Her last republic cried to God. *Ib.*

4 And the faith of the poor is faint and partial,
And the pride of the rich is all for sale,
And the chosen heralds of England's Marshal
Are the sandwich-men of the *Daily Mail*. *Ib.*

5 They haven't got no noses,
The fallen sons of Eve. *The Song of Quoodle*

6 And goodness only knowses
The Noselessness of Man. *Ib.*

7 But I, I cannot read it
(Although I run and run)
Of them that do not have the faith,
And will not have the fun.
The Song of the Strange Ascetic

8 Where his aunts, who are not married,
Demand to be divorced. *Ib.*

9 Tea, although an Oriental,
Is a gentleman at least;
Cocoa is a cad and coward,
Cocoa is a vulgar beast.
The Song of Right and Wrong

10 When old unbroken Pickwick walked
Among the broken men.
When I Came Back to Fleet Street

11 Still he that scorns and struggles
Sees, frightful and afar,
All that they leave of rebels
Rot high on Temple Bar. *Ib.*

12 And Noah he often said to his wife when he sat down
to dine,
'I don't care where the water goes if it doesn't get
into the wine.' *Wine and Water*

13 Step softly, under snow or rain,
To find the place where men can pray;
The way is all so very plain
That we may lose the way. *The Wise Men*

14 Call upon the wheels, master, call upon the wheels;
We are taking rest, master, finding how it feels.
Song of the Wheels

15. And that is the meaning of Empire Day.
Songs of Education. Geography

16 All slang is metaphor, and all metaphor is poetry.
The Defendant. A Defence of Slang

17 The human race, to which so many of my readers
belong... *The Napoleon of Notting Hill*, ch. 1

18 There is nothing the matter with Americans except
their ideals. The real American is all right; it is
the ideal American who is all wrong.
New York Times, 1 Feb. 1931. Reprinted in
Sidelights

19 Hardy went down to botanize in the swamp, while
Meredith climbed towards the sun. Meredith
became, at his best, a sort of daintily dressed Walt
Whitman: Hardy became a sort of village atheist
brooding and blaspheming over the village idiot.
The Victorian Age in Literature, ch. 2

20 He [Tennyson] could not think up to the height of
his own towering style. *Ib.* ch. 3

ALBERT CHEVALIER
1861–1923

21 'Wot's the good of Hanyfink? Why—Nuffink!'
Cockney Complaint

22 We've been together now for forty years,
An' it don't seem a day too much;
There ain't a lady livin' in the land
As I'd 'swop' for my dear old Dutch! *My Old Dutch*

23 Knocked 'em in the Old Kent Road. *Title of Song*

WILLIAM CHILLINGWORTH
1602–1644

24 The Bible and the Bible only is the religion of Protestants. *The Religion of Protestants*

RUFUS CHOATE
1799–1859

25 Its constitution the glittering and sounding generalities of natural right which make up the Declaration
of Independence.
*Letter to the Maine Whig State Central Com-
mittee, 9 Aug. 1856 (see 201:21)*

HENRY FOTHERGILL CHORLEY
1808–1872

26 God the All-terrible! King, Who ordainest
Great winds Thy clarions, the lightnings Thy sword.
Hullah's Part Music. God The All-Terrible!

DAVID CHRISTY
1802–?

27 Cotton is King. *Title of Book*, 1855

CHARLES CHURCHILL
1731–1764

28 Greatly his foes he dreads, but more his friends;
He hurts me most who lavishly commends.
The Apology, l. 19

29 Though by whim, envy, or resentment led,
They damn those authors whom they never read.
The Candidate, l. 57

30 The only difference, after all their rout,
Is, that the one is in, the other out.
The Conference, l. 165

31 If all, if all alas! were well at home. *Ib. l. 226*

32 Be England what she will,
With all her faults, she is my country still.
The Farewell, l. 27

33 It can't be Nature, for it is not sense. *Ib. l. 200*

1 England—a happy land we know,
Where follies naturally grow. *The Ghost*, bk. i, l. 111

2 Fame
Is nothing but an empty name. *Ib.* l. 229

3 And adepts in the speaking trade
Keep a cough by them ready made. *Ib.* bk. ii, l. 545

4 Who wit with jealous eye surveys,
And sickens at another's praise. *Ib.* l. 663

5 Just to the windward of the law. *Ib.* bk. iii, l. 56

6 [*Johnson:*] He for subscribers baits his hook,
And takes your cash; but where's the book?
No matter where; wise fear, you know,
Forbids the robbing of a foe;
But what, to serve our private ends,
Forbids the cheating of our friends? *Ib.* l. 801

7 A joke's a very serious thing. *Ib.* bk. iv, l. 1386

8 Railing at life, and yet afraid of death.
Gotham, i, l. 215

9 The danger chiefly lies in acting well;
No crime's so great as daring to excel.
Epistle to William Hogarth, l. 51

10 Candour, who, with the charity of Paul,
Still thinks the best, whene'er she thinks at all,
With the sweet milk of human kindness bless'd,
The furious ardour of my zeal repress'd. *Ib.* l. 55

11 By different methods different men excel;
But where is he who can do all things well?
Ib. l. 573

12 Keep up appearances; there lies the test;
The world will give thee credit for the rest.
Outward be fair, however foul within;
Sin if thou wilt, but then in secret sin. *Night*, l. 311

13 As one with watching and with study faint,
Reel in a drunkard, and reel out a saint. *Ib.* l. 323

14 Who often, but without success, have pray'd
For apt Alliteration's artful aid.
The Prophecy of Famine, l. 85

15 A heart to pity, and a hand to bless. *Ib.* l. 178

16 He sicken'd at all triumphs but his own.
The Rosciad, l. 64

17 Ne'er blush'd unless, in spreading Vice's snares,
She blunder'd on some virtue unawares. *Ib.* l. 137

18 Genius is of no country. *Ib.* l. 207

19 He mouths a sentence, as curs mouth a bone.
Ib. l. 322

20 Fashion!—a word which knaves and fools may use,
Their knavery and folly to excuse. *Ib.* l. 455

21 So much they talk'd, so very little said. *Ib.* l. 550

22 Learn'd without sense, and venerably dull. *Ib.* l. 572

23 Not without art, but yet to nature true. *Ib.* l. 699

24 But, spite of all the criticizing elves,
Those who would make us feel, must feel themselves.
Ib. l. 961

25 The two extremes appear like man and wife,
Coupled together for the sake of strife. *Ib.* l. 1005

26 Where he falls short, 'tis Nature's fault alone;
Where he succeeds, the merit's all his own.
Ib. l. 1025

27 The best things carried to excess are wrong.
Ib. l. 1039

28 With the persuasive language of a tear.
The Times, l. 308

LORD RANDOLPH SPENCER CHURCHILL
1849–1894

29 Ulster will fight; Ulster will be right.
Letter, 7 May 1886

30 The old gang. [Members of the Conservative
Government.]
Speech, House of Commons, 7 Mar. 1878

31 He [Gladstone] told them that he would give them
and all other subjects of the Queen much legislation, great prosperity, and universal peace, and he
has given them nothing but chips. Chips to the
faithful allies in Afghanistan, chips to the trusting
native races of South Africa, chips to the Egyptian
fellah, chips to the British farmer, chips to the
manufacturer and the artisan, chips to the agri-
cultural labourer, chips to the House of Commons
itself. *Ib. 24 Jan. 1884*

32 An old man in a hurry. [Gladstone.]
*Ib. To the Electors of South Paddington, June
1886*

33 All great men make mistakes. Napoleon forgot
Blücher, I forgot Goschen.
*Leaves from the Notebooks of Lady Dorothy
Nevill, p. 21*

34 The duty of an Opposition is to oppose.
1830. Quoted by Lord Randolph Churchill. W. S.
Churchill, *Lord Randolph Churchill*, vol. i, ch 5

35 (*Decimal points:*) I never could make out what those
damned dots meant. *Ib.* (1906), vol. ii, p. 184

WINSTON LEONARD SPENCER CHURCHILL
1874–

36 It cannot in the opinion of His Majesty's Government
be classified as slavery in the extreme acceptance
of the word without some risk of terminological
inexactitude.
Speech, House of Commons, 22 Feb. 1906

37 The maxim of the British people is 'Business as
usual'. *Speech at Guildhall, 9 Nov. 1914*

38 I would say to the House, as I said to those who have
joined this Government, 'I have nothing to offer
but blood, toil, tears and sweat'.
Speech, House of Commons, 13 May 1940

39 Victory at all costs, victory in spite of all terror, victory however long and hard the road may be; for
without victory there is no survival. *Ib.*

40 We shall not flag or fail. We shall fight in France, we
shall fight on the seas and oceans, we shall fight with
growing confidence and growing strength in the
air, we shall defend our island, whatever the cost
may be, we shall fight on the beaches, we shall fight
on the landing grounds, we shall fight in the fields
and in the streets, we shall fight in the hills; we
shall never surrender. *Ib. 4 June 1940*

41 Let us therefore brace ourselves to our duties, and so
bear ourselves that, if the British Empire and its
Commonwealth last for a thousand years, men will
still say: 'This was their finest hour'.
Ib. 18 June 1940

1 Never in the field of human conflict was so much owed by so many to so few.
Speech, House of Commons, 20 Aug. 1940

2 The British Empire and the United States will have to be somewhat mixed up together in some of their affairs for the mutual and general advantage. For my own part, looking out upon the future, I do not view the process with any misgivings. I could not stop it if I wished; no one can stop it. Like the Mississippi, it just keeps rolling along. Let it roll. Let it roll on full flood, inexorable, irresistible, benignant, to broader lands and better days. *Ib.*

3 We are waiting for the long-promised invasion. So are the fishes.
Radio Broadcast to the French people, 21 Oct. 1940

4 I do not resent criticism, even when, for the sake of emphasis, it parts for the time with reality.
Speech, House of Commons, 22 Jan. 1941

5 Give us the tools, and we will finish the job.
Radio Broadcast. (Addressing President Roosevelt.) 9 Feb. 1941

6 This whipped jackal [Mussolini], who, to save his own skin, has made of Italy a vassal state of Hitler's Empire, is frisking up by the side of the German tiger with yelps not only of appetite—that could be understood—but even of triumph.
Speech, House of Commons, Apr. 1941

7 Do not let us speak of darker days; let us rather speak of sterner days. These are not dark days: these are great days—the greatest days our country has ever lived; and we must all thank God that we have been allowed, each of us according to our stations, to play a part in making these days memorable in the history of our race.
Address to the boys of Harrow School, 29 Oct. 1941

8 What kind of people do they [the Japanese] think we are? *Speech to U.S. Congress, 24 Dec. 1941*

9 When I warned them [the French Government] that Britain would fight on alone whatever they did, their Generals told their Prime Minister and his divided Cabinet: 'In three weeks England will have her neck wrung like a chicken.'
Some chicken! Some neck!
Speech to the Canadian Parliament, 30 Dec. 1941

10 This is not the end. It is not even the beginning of the end. But it is, perhaps, the end of the beginning.
Speech at the Mansion House, 10 Nov. 1942. (Of the Battle of Egypt)

11 I have not become the King's First Minister in order to preside over the liquidation of the British Empire. *Ib.*

12 The soft under-belly of the Axis.
Report on the War Situation, House of Commons, 11 Nov. 1942

13 Not a seat but a springboard.
Radio Broadcast, 29 Nov. 1942. (On North Africa)

14 There is no finer investment for any community than putting milk into babies. *Ib. 21 Mar. 1943*

15 An iron curtain has descended across the Continent.
Address at Westminster College, Fulton, U.S.A., 5 Mar. 1946

16 By being so long in the lowest form [at Harrow] I gained an immense advantage over the cleverer boys . . . I got into my bones the essential structure of the normal British sentence—which is a noble thing. Naturally I am biased in favour of boys learning English; and then I would let the clever ones learn Latin as an honour, and Greek as a treat.
My Early Life (1930), Roving Commission

17 On the night of the tenth of May [1940], at the outset of this mighty battle, I acquired the chief power in the State, which henceforth I wielded in ever-growing measure for five years and three months of world war, at the end of which time, all our enemies having surrendered unconditionally or being about to do so, I was immediately dismissed by the British electorate from all further conduct of their affairs.
The Second World War, vol. i, The Gathering Storm (1948), p. 526

18 No one can guarantee success in war, but only deserve it. *Ib. vol. ii, Their Finest Hour (1949), p. 484.*

19 Dictators ride to and fro upon tigers which they dare not dismount. And the tigers are getting hungry.
While England Slept (1936)

20 I have watched this famous island descending incontinently, fecklessly, the stairway which leads to a dark gulf. It is a fine broad stairway at the beginning, but after a bit the carpet ends. A little farther on there are only flagstones, and a little farther on still these break beneath your feet. *Ib.*

COLLEY CIBBER
1671–1757

21 O say! What is that thing called Light,
Which I can ne'er enjoy. *The Blind Boy*

22 Whilst thus I sing, I am a King,
Altho' a poor blind boy. *Ib.*

23 Oh! how many torments lie in the small circle of a wedding-ring! *The Double Gallant, I. ii*

24 Dumb's a sly dog. *Love Makes a Man, IV. i*

25 One had as good be out of the world, as out of the fashion. *Love's Last Shift, Act II*

26 Off with his head—so much for Buckingham.
Richard III, altered, IV. iii

27 A weak invention of the enemy. *Ib. v. iii*

28 Conscience avaunt, *Richard's* himself again:
Hark! the shrill trumpet sounds, to horse, away,
My soul's in arms, and eager for the fray. *Ib.*

29 Perish the thought! *Ib. v*

30 Losers must have leave to speak.
The Rival Fools, Act I

31 Stolen sweets are best. *Ib.*

32 This business will never hold water.
She Would and She Would Not, Act IV

33 Persuasion tips his tongue whene'er he talks,
And he has chambers in the King's Bench Walks.
Parody of Pope's lines on William Murray, Lord Mansfield, in Satires and Epistles of Horace Imitated, bk. i, Ep. vi (see 386:11)

MARCUS TULLIUS CICERO
106–43 B.C.

1 In Romuli faece.

Among the dregs of Romulus. *Ad Atticum*, II. i. 8

2 Spartam nactus es: hanc (ex)orna.

Sparta is your inheritance: make the best of her.
Ib. IV. vi. 2

3 Nihil tam absurde dici potest, quod non dicatur ab aliquo philosophorum.

There is nothing so absurd but some philosopher has said it. *De Divinatione*, ii. 58

4 Vulgo enim dicitur: Iucundi acti labores.

For it is commonly said: accomplished labours are pleasant. *De Finibus*, ii. 105

5 Salus populi suprema est lex.

The good of the people is the chief law.
De Legibus, III. iii. 8

6 'Ipse dixit.' 'Ipse' autem erat Pythagoras.

'He himself said it', and this 'he himself', it seems, was Pythagoras. *De Natura Deorum*, I. v.10

7 Summum bonum.

The highest good. *De Officiis*, I. ii. 5

8 Cedant arma togae, concedant laurea laudi.

Let wars yield to peace, laurels to paeans.
Ib. I. xxii. 82

9 Numquam se minus otiosum esse quam cum otiosus, nec minus solum quam cum solus esset.

Never less idle than when wholly idle, nor less alone than when wholly alone. *Ib.* III. i. 1

10 Mens cuiusque is est quisque.

The mind of each man is the man himself.
De Republica, vi. 26

11 Quousque tandem abutere, Catilina, patientia nostra?

How long will you abuse our patience, Catiline?
In Catilinam, I. i. 1

12 O tempora, O mores!

O what times, O what habits! *Ib.*

13 Abiit, excessit, evasit, erupit.

He departed, he withdrew, he strode off, he broke forth. *Ib.* II. i. 1

14 Civis Romanus sum.

I am a Roman citizen. *In Verrem*, V. lvii. 147

15 Omnes artes quae ad humanitatem pertinent habent quoddam commune vinclum et quasi cognatione quadam inter se continentur.

All arts which have anything to do with man have a common bond and as it were contain within themselves a certain affinity. *Pro Archia*, I. ii

16 Haec studia adulescentiam acuunt, senectutem oblectant, secundas res ornant, adversis perfugium ac solacium praebent, delectant domi, non impediunt foris, pernoctant nobiscum, peregrinantur, rusticantur.

These studies are an impetus to youth, and a delight to age; they are an adornment to good fortune, refuge and relief in trouble; they enrich private and do not hamper public life; they are with us by night, they are with us on long journeys, they are with us in the depths of the country.
Ib. VII. xvi

17 Oderint, dum metuant.

Let them hate so long as they fear.
Philippic, I. 14 (*quoted from the tragedian Accius*)

18 Quod di omen avertant.

May the gods avert this omen. *Ib.* III. xiv. 35

19 Silent enim leges inter arma.

Laws are inoperative in war. *Pro Milone*, IV. xi

20 Cui bono.

To whose profit. *Ib.* XII. xxxii

21 Ne quid res publica detrimenti caperet.

That no harm come to the state.
Ib. XXVI. lxx, *quoting the senatorial 'ultimate decree',
beginning 'caveant consules' (let the consuls see to it).*

22 Id quod est praestantissimum maximeque optabile omnibus sanis et bonis et beatis, cum dignitate otium.

The thing which is the most outstanding and the most desirable to all healthy and good and well-off persons, is a peaceful life with honour.
Pro Sestio, xlv. 98

23 Errare, mehercule, malo cum Platone ... quam cum istis vera sentire.

I would rather be wrong with Plato than right with such men as these [the Pythagoreans].
Tusculanae disputationes, I. xvii. 39

24 O fortunatam natam me consule Romam!

O happy Rome, born when I was consul!
Quoted in Juvenal, x. 122

EDWARD HYDE, EARL OF CLARENDON
1609–1674

25 Without question, when he [Hampden] first drew the sword, he threw away the scabbard.
History of the Rebellion, ed. W. Dunn Macray (1888), III. vii. 84

26 He [Hampden] had a head to contrive, a tongue to persuade, and a hand to execute any mischief. *Ib.*

27 He [Falkland] ... would, with a shrill and sad accent, ingeminate the word *Peace, Peace.* *Ib.* 233

28 So enamoured on peace that he would have been glad the King should have bought it at any price.
Ib.

29 He [Cromwell] will be looked upon by posterity as a brave bad man. *Ib.* xv. last line

JAMES STANIER CLARKE
1765?–1834

30 Perhaps when you again appear in print you may choose to dedicate your volumes to Prince Leopold: any historical romance, illustrative of the history of the august House of Cobourg, would just now be very interesting.
Letter to Jane Austen, 27 March 1816. *Jane Austen's Letters*, ed. R. W. Chapman (1932), p. 451

JOHN CLARKE
fl. 1639

31 He that would thrive
Must rise at five;
He that hath thriven
May lie till seven.
Paraemiologia Anglo-Latina (1639)

1 Home is home, though it be never so homely.
Parœmiologia Anglo-Latina (1639)

HENRY CLAY
1777–1852

2 I had rather be right than be President.
To Senator Preston of South Carolina, 1839

3 The gentleman [Josiah Quincy] can not have forgotten his own sentiments, uttered even on the floor of this House, 'peaceably if we can, forcibly if we must'.
Speech, 8 Jan. 1813

SAMUEL LANGHORNE CLEMENS
see
MARK TWAIN

JOHN CLEVELAND
1613–1658

4 Had Cain been Scot, God would have changed his doom,
Nor forced him wander, but confined him home.
The Rebel Scot

STEPHEN GROVER CLEVELAND
1837–1908

5 I have considered the pension list of the republic a roll of honour.
Veto of Dependent Pension Bill, 5 July 1888

ROBERT CLIVE, LORD CLIVE
1725–1774

6 By God, Mr. Chairman, at this moment I stand astonished at my own moderation!
Reply during Parliamentary cross-examination, 1773

7 I feel that I am reserved for some end or other.
Words when his pistol failed to go off twice, in his attempt to commit suicide. G. R. Gleig, Life, ch. 1

ARTHUR HUGH CLOUGH
1819–1861

8 Rome, believe me, my friend, is like its own Monte Testaceo,
Merely a marvellous mass of broken and castaway wine-pots. *Amours de Voyage, c. I. ii*

9 The horrible pleasure of pleasing inferior people.
Ib. xi

10 Juxtaposition, in short; and what is juxtaposition?
Ib.

11 Allah is great, no doubt, and Juxtaposition his prophet. *Ib. III. vi*

12 Mild monastic faces in quiet collegiate cloisters.
Ib. ix

13 Tibur is beautiful, too, and the orchard slopes, and the Anio
Falling, falling yet, to the ancient lyrical cadence.
Ib. xi

14 Whither depart the souls of the brave that die in the battle,
Die in the lost, lost fight, for the cause that perishes with them? *Amours de Voyage, v. vi.*

15 Say, 'I am flitting about many years from brain unto brain of
Feeble and restless youths born to inglorious days:
But,' so finish the word, 'I was writ in a Roman chamber,
When from Janiculan heights thundered the cannon of France.' *Ib. end*

16 The grave man, nicknamed Adam.
The Bothie of Tober-na-Vuolich, i

17 Over a ledge of granite
Into a granite bason the amber torrent descended.
Ib.

18 Good, too, Logic, of course; in itself, but not in fine weather. *Ib. ii*

19 Petticoats up to the knees, or even, it might be, above them. *Ib.*

20 Hope an Antinoüs mere, Hyperion of calves the Piper. *Ib.*

21 Sesquipedalian blackguard. *Ib.*

22 *Thicksides* and *hairy* Aldrich. *Ib.*

23 Gay in the mazy
Moving, imbibing the rosy, and pointing a gun at the horny! *Ib. iii*

24 Grace is given of God, but knowledge is bought in the market. *Ib. iv*

25 Bright October was come, the misty-bright October.
Ib. vi

26 Dangerous Corryvreckan. *Ib. ix*

27 This Rachel-and-Leah is marriage. *Ib.*

28 They are married, and gone to New Zealand. *Ib.*

29 Delicious. Ah!
What else is like the gondola? *Dipsychus, pt. I. iv*

30 How pleasant it is to have money, heigh-ho!
How pleasant it is to have money. *Ib.*

31 'There is no God,' the wicked saith,
'And truly it's a blessing,
For what he might have done with us
It's better only guessing.' *Ib. v*

32 But country folks who live beneath
The shadow of the steeple;
The parson and the parson's wife,
And mostly married people;

Youths green and happy in first love,
So thankful for illusion;
And men caught out in what the world
Calls guilt, in first confusion;

And almost every one when age,
Disease, or sorrows strike him,
Inclines to think there is a God,
Or something very like Him. *Ib.*

33 Home, Rose, and home, Provence and La Palie.
Les Vaches

34 Thou shalt have one God only; who
Would be at the expense of two?
The Latest Decalogue

35 Thou shalt not kill; but need'st not strive
Officiously to keep alive. *Ib.*

1 Do not adultery commit;
Advantage rarely comes of it.   *The Latest Decalogue*

2 Thou shalt not steal; an empty feat,
When it's so lucrative to cheat.   *Ib.*

3 Thou shalt not covet; but tradition
Approves all forms of competition.   *Ib.*

4 Lo, here is God, and there is God!
Believe it not, O Man.   *When Israel came out of Egypt*

5 What voice did on my spirit fall,
Peschiera, when thy bridge I crost?
''Tis better to have fought and lost,
Than never to have fought at all.'   *Peschiera*

6 As ships, becalmed at eve, that lay
With canvas drooping, side by side,
Two towers of sail at dawn of day
Are scarce long leagues apart descried.
                    Qua Cursum Ventus

7 O bounding breeze, O rushing seas!
At last, at last, unite them there!   *Ib.*

8 Say not the struggle naught availeth,
The labour and the wounds are vain,
The enemy faints not, nor faileth,
And as things have been, things remain.

If hopes were dupes, fears may be liars;
It may be, in yon smoke concealed,
Your comrades chase e'en now the fliers,
And, but for you, possess the field.

For while the tired waves, vainly breaking,
Seem here no painful inch to gain,
Far back through creeks and inlets making
Comes silent, flooding in, the main.

And not by eastern windows only,
When daylight comes, comes in the light,
In front the sun climbs slow, how slowly,
But westward, look, the land is bright.
                    Say Not the Struggle Naught Availeth

9 To finger idly some old Gordian knot,
Unskilled to sunder, and too weak to cleave,
And with much toil attain to half-believe.
                    Songs in Absence, Come back, Come back

10 Green fields of England! whereso'er
Across this watery waste we fare,
Your image at our hearts we bear,
Green fields of England, everywhere.
                    Ib. Green Fields of England!

11 Some future day when what is now is not,
When all old faults and follies are forgot.
                    Ib. Some Future Day

12 That out of sight is out of mind
Is true of most we leave behind.
                    Ib. That Out of Sight

13 Where lies the land to which the ship would go?
Far, far ahead, is all her seamen know.
And where the land she travels from? Away,
Far, far behind, is all that they can say.
                    Ib. Where Lies the Land

14 It fortifies my soul to know
That, though I perish, Truth is so:
That, howsoe'er I stray and range,
Whate'er I do, Thou dost not change.
I steadier step when I recall
That, if I slip, Thou dost not fall.
                    With Whom Is No Variableness

SIR WILLIAM LAIRD CLOWES
1856–1905

15 The Glorious First of June.
Page-heading in The Royal Navy: a History
(1899), vol. iv, p. 225. Taken from explanatory
pamphlet accompanying Cleveley's prints of the
action: *Two prints . . . representing the Glorious
and Memorable Action of the First of June 1794*

WILLIAM COBBETT
1762–1835

16 The slavery of the tea and coffee and other slop-
kettle.   *Advice to Young Men, letter i, 31*

17 Nouns of number, or multitude, such as *Mob,*
Parliament, Rabble, House of Commons, Regiment, Court of King's Bench, Den of Thieves,
and the like.
*English Grammar, letter xvii, Syntax as Relating
to Pronouns*

18 All is vulgar, all clumsy, all dull, all torpid inanity.
            Ib. letter xxiv, Six Lessons, Lesson 4

19 From a very early age, I had imbibed the opinion,
that it was every man's duty to do all that lay in
his power to leave his country as good as he had
found it.   *Political Register, 22 Dec. 1832*

20 But what is to be the fate of the great wen [London]
of all? The monster, called . . . 'the metropolis of
the empire'?   *Rural Rides, 1821*

RICHARD COBDEN
1804–1865

21 I believe it has been said that one copy of *The Times*
contains more useful information than the whole
of the historical works of Thucydides.
            Speech, Manchester, 27 Dec. 1850

CHARLES COBORN
1852–1945

22 Two lovely black eyes,
Oh! what a surprise!
Only for telling a man he was wrong,
Two lovely black eyes!   *Two Lovely Black Eyes*

ALISON COCKBURN
1713–1794

23 I've seen the smiling of Fortune beguiling,
I've felt all its favours and found its decay.
                    The Flowers of the Forest

24 I've seen the forest adorn'd the foremost,
With flowers of the fairest, most pleasant and gay:
Sae bonny was their blooming, their scent the air
perfuming;
But now they are wither'd and weeded away.   *Ib.*

25 For the flowers of the forest are withered away.   *Ib.*

SIR ASTON COKAYNE
1608–1684

26 Sydney, whom we yet admire
Lighting our little torches at his fire.
                    Funeral Elegy on Mr. Michael Drayton

DESMOND F. T. COKE
1879–1931

1 His blade struck the water a full second before any other . . . until . . . as the boats began to near the winning-post, his own was dipping into the water *twice* as often as any other.
> *Sandford of Merton* (1903), ch. xii. *Often quoted as* 'All rowed fast but none so fast as stroke', *and attrib. to* Ouida.

SIR EDWARD COKE
1552–1634

2 Magna Charta is such a fellow, that he will have no sovereign.
> *On the Lords' Amendment to the Petition of Right, 17 May 1628.* Rushworth's *Hist. Coll.,* 1659, i

3 How long soever it hath continued, if it be against reason, it is of no force in law.
> *Institutes: Commentary upon Littleton. First Institute,* § 80

4 Reason is the life of the law, nay the common law itself is nothing else but reason. . . . The law, which is perfection of reason. *Ib.* § 138

5 The gladsome light of Jurisprudence. *Ib. epilogus*

6 Syllables govern the world. *Ib.*

7 For a man's house is his castle, *et domus sua cuique est tutissimum refugium. Ib. Third Institute,* cap. 73

8 Six hours in sleep, in law's grave study six,
Four spend in prayer, the rest on Nature fix.
> *Pandects,* lib. ii, tit. iv, *De in Jus vocando*

9 The house of every one is to him as his castle and fortress. *Semayne's Case,* 5 Rep. 91b

10 They [corporations] cannot commit treason, nor be outlawed, nor excommunicate, for they have no souls. *Sutton's Hospital Case,* 10 Rep. 32b

HARTLEY COLERIDGE
1796–1849

11 But what is Freedom? Rightly understood,
A universal licence to be good. *Liberty*

12 She is not fair to outward view
As many maidens be;
Her loveliness I never knew
Until she smiled on me.
Oh! then I saw her eye was bright,
A well of love, a spring of light. *Song. She is not Fair*

13 Her very frowns are fairer far,
Than smiles of other maidens are. *Ib.*

14 Old times unqueen thee, and old loves endear thee.
> *To a Lofty Beauty, from her Poor Kinsman*

SIR JOHN COLERIDGE, BARON COLERIDGE
1820–1894

15 I speak not of this college or of that, but of the University as a whole; and, gentlemen, what a *whole* Oxford is!
> G. W. E. Russell's *Collections and Recollections,* ch. 29

MARY ELIZABETH COLERIDGE
1861–1907

16 Mother of God! no lady thou:
Common woman of common earth! *Our Lady*

17 We were young, we were merry, we were very, very wise,
And the door stood open at our feast,
When there passed us a woman with the West in her eyes,
And a man with his back to the East. *Unwelcome*

SAMUEL TAYLOR COLERIDGE
1772–1834

18 It is an ancient Mariner,
And he stoppeth one of three.
'By thy long grey beard and glittering eye,
Now wherefore stopp'st thou me?'
> *The Ancient Mariner,* pt. i

19 The guests are met, the feast is set:
May'st hear the merry din. *Ib.*

20 He holds him with his skinny hand,
'There was a ship,' quoth he.
'Hold off! unhand me, grey-beard loon!'
Eftsoons his hand dropt he.

He holds him with his glittering eye—
The Wedding-Guest stood still,
And listens like a three years' child:
The Mariner hath his will.

The Wedding-Guest sat on a stone:
He cannot choose but hear;
And thus spake on that ancient man,
The bright-eyed Mariner. *Ib.*

21 The ship was cheered, the harbour cleared,
Merrily did we drop
Below the kirk, below the hill,
Below the lighthouse top.

The Sun came up upon the left.
Out of the sea came he!
And he shone bright, and on the right
Went down into the sea. *Ib.*

22 The Wedding-Guest here beat his breast,
For he heard the loud bassoon. *Ib.*

23 The bride hath paced into the hall,
Red as a rose is she. *Ib.*

24 As who pursued with yell and blow
Still treads the shadow of his foe,
And forward bends his head. *Ib.*

25 And ice, mast-high, came floating by,
As green as emerald. *Ib.*

26 The ice was here, the ice was there,
The ice was all around:
It cracked and growled, and roared and howled,
Like noises in a swound! *Ib.*

27 It ate the food it ne'er had eat,
And round and round it flew.

The ice did split with a thunder-fit;
The helmsman steered us through! *Ib.*

28 And a good south wind sprung up behind;
The Albatross did follow,
And every day, for food or play,
Came to the mariner's hollo! *Ib.*

1 'God save thee, ancient Mariner!
From the fiends that plague thee thus!—
Why look'st thou so?'—With my cross-bow
I shot the Albatross.   *The Ancient Mariner*, pt. i

2 Nor dim nor red, like God's own head,
The glorious Sun uprist.   *Ib.* pt. ii

3 We were the first that ever burst
Into that silent sea.   *Ib.*

4 All in a hot and copper sky,
The bloody Sun, at noon,
Right up above the mast did stand,
No bigger than the Moon.   *Ib.*

5 As idle as a painted ship
Upon a painted ocean.   *Ib.*

6 Water, water, every where,
And all the boards did shrink;
Water, water, every where.
Nor any drop to drink.

The very deep did rot: O Christ!
That ever this should be!
Yea, slimy things did crawl with legs
Upon the slimy sea.

About, about, in reel and rout
The death-fires danced at night;
The water, like a witch's oils,
Burnt green, and blue and white.   *Ib.*

7 Nine fathom deep he had followed us
From the land of mist and snow.   *Ib.*

8 There passed a weary time. Each throat
Was parched, and glazed each eye.
A weary time! a weary time!
How glazed each weary eye.   *Ib.* pt. iii

9 I bit my arm, I sucked the blood,
And cried, A sail! a sail!   *Ib.*

10 Gramercy! they for joy did grin,
And all at once their breath drew in,
As they were drinking all.   *Ib.*

11 When that strange shape drove suddenly
Betwixt us and the Sun.   *Ib.*

12 And straight the Sun was flecked with bars,
(Heaven's Mother send us grace!)
As if through a dungeon-grate he peered
With broad and burning face.   *Ib.*

13 *Her* lips were red, *her* looks were free,
Her locks were yellow as gold:
Her skin was white as leprosy,
The Night-mare LIFE-IN-DEATH was she,
Who thicks man's blood with cold.

The naked hulk alongside came,
And the twain were casting dice;
'The game is done! I've won! I've won!'
Quoth she, and whistles thrice.   *Ib.*

14 The Sun's rim dips; the stars rush out:
At one stride comes the dark;
With far-heard whisper, o'er the sea,
Off shot the spectre-bark.   *Ib.*

15 We listened and looked sideways up!   *Ib.*

16 The hornèd Moon, with one bright star
Within the nether tip.   *Ib.*

17 Each turned his face with a ghastly pang,
And cursed me with his eye.   *Ib.*

18 And every soul, it passed me by,
Like the whizz of my cross-bow!
          The Ancient Mariner, pt. iii

19 'I fear thee, ancient Mariner!
I fear thy skinny hand!
And thou art long, and lank, and brown,
As is the ribbed sea-sand.'   *Ib.* pt. iv

20 Alone, alone, all, all alone,
Alone on a wide wide sea!
And never a saint took pity on
My soul in agony.   *Ib.*

21 And a thousand thousand slimy things
Lived on; and so did I.   *Ib.*

22 An orphan's curse would drag to hell
A spirit from on high;
But oh! more horrible than that
Is the curse in a dead man's eye.   *Ib.*

23 The moving Moon went up the sky,
And no where did abide:
Softly she was going up,
And a star or two beside.   *Ib.*

24 And everywhere the blue sky belongs to them, and
is their appointed rest and their native country
and their own natural homes, which they enter un-
announced, as lords that are certainly expected,
and yet there is a silent joy at their arrival [the
stars].   *Ib.* (gloss)

25 But where the ship's huge shadow lay,
The charmed water burned alway
A still and awful red.   *Ib.*

26 A spring of love gushed from my heart,
And I blessed them unaware.   *Ib.*

27 Oh Sleep! it is a gentle thing,
Beloved from pole to pole,
To Mary Queen the praise be given!
She sent the gentle sleep from Heaven,
That slid into my soul.   *Ib.* pt. v

28 The silly buckets on the deck,
That had so long remained,
I dreamt that they were filled with dew;
And when I awoke, it rained.   *Ib.*

29 Sure I had drunken in my dreams,
And still my body drank.   *Ib.*

30 Beneath the lightning and the Moon
The dead men gave a groan.   *Ib.*

31 It had been strange, even in a dream,
To have seen those dead men rise.   *Ib.*

32 We were a ghastly crew.   *Ib.*

33 The body of my brother's son
Stood by me, knee to knee:
The body and I pulled at one rope,
But he said nought to me.   *Ib.*

34 How they seemed to fill the sea and air
With their sweet jargoning!   *Ib.*

35 It ceased; yet still the sails made on
A pleasant noise till noon,
A noise like of a hidden brook
In the leafy month of June,
That to the sleeping woods all night
Singeth a quiet tune.   *Ib.*

36 With a short uneasy motion.   *Ib.*

37 Quoth he, 'The man hath penance done,
And penance more will do.'   *Ib.*

1 The air is cut away before,
And closes from behind. *The Ancient Mariner*, pt. vi

2 Like one, that on a lonesome road
Doth walk in fear and dread,
And having once turned round walks on,
And turns no more his head;
Because he knows, a frightful fiend
Doth close behind him tread. *Ib.*

3 It raised my hair, it fanned my cheek
Like a meadow-gale of spring. *Ib.*

4 Oh! dream of joy! is this indeed
The lighthouse top I see?
Is this the hill? is this the kirk?
Is this mine own countree? *Ib.*

5 O let me be awake, my God!
Or let me sleep alway. *Ib.*

6 A man all light, a seraph-man,
On every corse there stood.

This seraph-band, each waved his hand:
It was a heavenly sight!
They stood as signals to the land,
Each one a lovely light. *Ib.*

7 No voice; but oh! the silence sank
Like music on my heart. *Ib.*

8 This Hermit good lives in that wood
Which slopes down to the sea.
How loudly his sweet voice he rears!
He loves to talk with marineres
That come from a far countree.

He kneels at morn, and noon, and eve—
He hath a cushion plump:
It is the moss that wholly hides
The rotted old oak-stump. *Ib.* pt. vii

9 Brown skeletons of leaves that lag
My forest-brook along;
When the ivy-tod is heavy with snow,
And the owlet whoops to the wolf below,
That eats the she-wolf's young. *Ib.*

10 Under the water it rumbled on,
Still louder and more dread:
It reached the ship, it split the bay;
The ship went down like lead. *Ib.*

11 I moved my lips—the Pilot shrieked
And fell down in a fit;
The holy Hermit raised his eyes,
And prayed where he did sit.

I took the oars: the Pilot's boy,
Who now doth crazy go,
Laughed loud and long, and all the while
His eyes went to and fro.
'Ha! ha!' quoth he, 'full plain I see,
The Devil knows how to row'. *Ib.*

12 I pass, like night, from land to land;
I have strange power of speech;
That moment that his face I see,
I know the man that must hear me:
To him my tale I teach. *Ib.*

13 And hark the little vesper-bell,
Which biddeth me to prayer! *Ib.*

14 O Wedding-Guest! this soul hath been
Alone on a wide wide sea:
So lonely 'twas, that God himself
Scarce seemed there to be. *Ib.*

15 O sweeter than the marriage-feast,
'Tis sweeter far to me,
To walk together to the kirk
With a goodly company.
To walk together to the kirk,
And all together pray,
While each to his great Father bends,
Old men, and babes, and loving friends
And youths and maidens gay!
The Ancient Mariner, pt. vii

16 He prayeth well, who loveth well
Both man and bird and beast.

He prayeth best, who loveth best
All things both great and small;
For the dear God who loveth us,
He made and loveth all. *Ib.*

17 He went like one that hath been stunned,
And is of sense forlorn:
A sadder and a wiser man,
He rose the morrow morn. *Ib.*

18 That he sings, and he sings; and for ever sings he—
'I love my Love, and my Love loves me!'
Answer to a Child's Question

19 And the Spring comes slowly up this way,
Christabel, pt. i

20 I guess, 'twas frightful there to see
A lady so richly clad as she—
Beautiful exceedingly! *Ib.*

21 Carved with figures strange and sweet,
All made out of the carver's brain. *Ib.*

22 A sight to dream of, not to tell! *Ib.*

23 But this she knows, in joys and woes,
That saints will aid if men will call:
For the blue sky bends over all! *Ib.*

24 Each matin bell, the Baron saith,
Knells us back to a world of death. *Ib.* pt. ii

25 Alas! they had been friends in youth;
But whispering tongues can poison truth. *Ib.*

26 And constancy lives in realms above;
And life is thorny; and youth is vain;
And to be wroth with one we love
Doth work like madness in the brain. *Ib.*

27 They stood aloof, the scars remaining,
Like cliffs which had been rent asunder;
A dreary sea now flows between. *Ib.*

28 In Köhln, a town of monks and bones,
And pavements fang'd with murderous stones
And rags, and hags, and hideous wenches;
I counted two and seventy stenches,
All well defined, and several stinks!
Ye Nymphs that reign o'er sewers and sinks,
The river Rhine, it is well known,
Doth wash your city of Cologne;
But tell me, Nymphs, what power divine
Shall henceforth wash the river Rhine? *Cologne*

29 My eyes make pictures, when they are shut.
A Day-Dream

30 Well! If the Bard was weatherwise, who made
The grand old ballad of Sir Patrick Spence.
Dejection: an Ode

31 A grief without a pang, void, dark and drear,
A stifled, drowsy, unimpassioned grief,
Which finds no natural outlet, no relief,
In word, or sigh, or tear. *Ib.*

1 And those thin clouds above, in flakes and bars,
 That give away their motion to the stars.
 Dejection: an Ode

2 I see them all so excellently fair,
 I see, not feel, how beautiful they are!

3 I may not hope from outward forms to win
 The passion and the life, whose fountains are within.
 Ib.

4 O Lady! we receive but what we give,
 And in our life alone does Nature live. *Ib.*

5 A light, a glory, a fair luminous cloud
 Enveloping the Earth. *Ib.*

6 Joy is the sweet voice, joy the luminous cloud—
 We in ourselves rejoice!
 And thence flows all that charms or ear or sight,
 All melodies the echoes of that voice,
 All colours a suffusion from that light. *Ib.*

7 From his brimstone bed at break of day
 A walking the Devil is gone,
 To visit his snug little farm the earth,
 And see how his stock goes on.
 The Devil's Thoughts. (See 507: 19–22)

8 And backward and forward he switched his long tail
 As a gentleman switches his cane. *Ib.*

9 His jacket was red and his breeches were blue,
 And there was a hole where the tail came through.
 Ib.

10 He saw a Lawyer killing a viper
 On a dunghill hard by his own stable;
 And the Devil smiled, for it put him in mind
 Of Cain and his brother, Abel. *Ib.*

11 He saw a cottage with a double coach-house,
 A cottage of gentility;
 And the Devil did grin, for his darling sin
 Is pride that apes humility. *Ib.*

12 As he went through Cold-Bath Fields he saw
 A solitary cell;
 And the Devil was pleased, for it gave him a hint
 For improving his prisons in Hell. *Ib.*

13 With Donne, whose muse on dromedary trots,
 Wreathe iron pokers into true-love knots.
 On Donne's Poetry

14 What is an Epigram? a dwarfish whole,
 Its body brevity, and wit its soul. *Epigram*

15 Swans sing before they die—'twere no bad thing
 Did certain persons die before they sing.
 Epigram on a Volunteer Singer

16 Stop, Christian passer-by!—Stop, child of God.
 Epitaph for Himself

17 That he who many a year with toil of breath
 Found death in life, may here find life in death. *Ib.*

18 Ere sin could blight or sorrow fade,
 Death came with friendly care:
 The opening bud to Heaven convey'd,
 And bade it blossom *there. Epitaph on an Infant*

19 Forth from his dark and lonely hiding-place
 (Portentous sight!) the owlet Atheism,
 Sailing on obscene wings athwart the noon,
 Drops his blue-fringèd lids, and holds them close,
 And hooting at the glorious sun in Heaven,
 Cries out, 'Where is it?' *Fears in Solitude*

20 Letters four do form his name. [Pitt.]
 Fire, Famine and Slaughter

21 With what deep worship I have still adored
 The spirit of divinest Liberty. *France*

22 So for the mother's sake the child was dear,
 And dearer was the mother for the child.
 *Sonnet to a Friend Who Asked How I Felt When
 the Nurse First Presented My Infant to Me*

23 The frost performs its secret ministry,
 Unhelped by any wind. *Frost at Midnight*

24 Only that film, which fluttered on the grate,
 Still flutters there, the sole unquiet thing. *Ib.*

25 Therefore all seasons shall be sweet to thee,
 Whether the summer clothe the general earth
 With greenness, or the redbreast sit and sing
 Betwixt the tufts of snow on the bare branch
 Of mossy apple-tree, while the nigh thatch
 Smokes in the sun-thaw; whether the eave-drops
 fall
 Heard only in the trances of the blast,
 Or if the secret ministry of frost
 Shall hang them up in silent icicles,
 Quietly shining to the quiet moon. *Ib.*

26 It sounds like stories from the land of spirits
 If any man obtain that which he merits
 Or any merit that which he obtains.
 The Good, Great Man

27 'Tis sweet to him who all the week
 Through city-crowds must push his way,
 To stroll alone through fields and woods,
 And hallow thus the Sabbath-day. *Home-Sick*

28 Hast thou a charm to stay the morning-star
 In his steep course?
 Hymn before Sun-rise, in the Vale of Chamouni

29 And visited all night by troops of stars. *Ib.*

30 Earth, with her thousand voices, praises God. *Ib.*

31 The Knight's bones are dust,
 And his good sword rust;—
 His soul is with the saints, I trust.
 The Knight's Tomb

32 In Xanadu did Kubla Khan
 A stately pleasure-dome decree:
 Where Alph, the sacred river, ran
 Through caverns measureless to man
 Down to a sunless sea.
 So twice five miles of fertile ground
 With walls and towers were girdled round:
 And there were gardens bright with sinuous rills,
 Where blossomed many an incense-bearing tree;
 And here were forests ancient as the hills,
 Enfolding sunny spots of greenery.
 But oh! that deep romantic chasm which slanted
 Down the green hill athwart a cedarn cover!
 A savage place! as holy and enchanted
 As e'er beneath a waning moon was haunted
 By woman wailing for her demon-lover!
 And from this chasm, with ceaseless turmoil seething,
 As if this earth in fast thick pants were breathing,
 A mighty fountain momently was forced.
 Kubla Khan

33 And 'mid these dancing rocks at once and ever
 It flung up momently the sacred river.
 Five miles meandering with a mazy motion
 Through wood and dale the sacred river ran,
 Then reached the caverns measureless to man,
 And sank in tumult to a lifeless ocean:

And 'mid this tumult Kubla heard from far
Ancestral voices prophesying war!

The shadow of the dome of pleasure
Floated midway on the waves;
Where was heard the mingled measure
From the fountain and the caves.
It was a miracle of rare device,
A sunny pleasure-dome with caves of ice!

A damsel with a dulcimer
In a vision once I saw:
It was an Abyssinian maid,
And on her dulcimer she played,
Singing of Mount Abora.
Could I revive within me
Her symphony and song,
To such a deep delight 'twould win me,
That with music loud and long,
I would build that dome in air,
That sunny dome! those caves of ice!
And all who heard should see them there,
And all should cry, Beware! Beware!
His flashing eyes, his floating hair!
Weave a circle round him thrice,
And close your eyes with holy dread,
For he on honey-dew hath fed,
And drunk the milk of Paradise.   *Kubla Khan*

1 This Lime-Tree Bower my Prison.   *Title*

2   A charm
For thee, my gentle-hearted Charles, to whom
No sound is dissonant which tells of Life.   *Ib.* l. 74

3 All thoughts, all passions, all delights,
   Whatever stirs this mortal frame,
   All are but ministers of Love,
   And feed his sacred flame.   *Love*

4 Trochee trips from long to short.   *Metrical Feet*

5 Iambics march from short to long;—
   With a leap and a bound the swift Anapaests throng.
                                              Ib.

6 Choose thou whatever suits the line;
   Call me Sappho, call me Chloris,
   Call me Lalage or Doris,
   Only, only call me thine.   *Names*

7 'Most musical, most melancholy' bird!
   A melancholy bird? Oh! idle thought!
   In Nature there is nothing melancholy.
                                       The Nightingale

8 In the hexameter rises the fountain's silvery column;
   In the pentameter aye falling in melody back.
                                    Ovidian Elegiac Metre

9 The fair humanities of old religion.   *Piccolomini*, II. iv

10 But still the heart doth need a language, still
   Doth the old instinct bring back the old names. *Ib.*

11 Something childish, but very natural.   *Title*

12 O! I do love thee, meek *Simplicity*!
   Sonnets Attempted in the Manner of Contemporary Writers. 2. To Simplicity

13 And this reft house is that the which he built,
   Lamented Jack!
   Ib. 3. *On a Ruined House in a Romantic Country*

14 A mother is a mother still,
   The holiest thing alive.   *The Three Graves*, pt. III. x

15 We ne'er can be
   Made happy by compulsion.
                              The Three Graves, pt. IV. xii

16 Never, believe me,
   Appear the Immortals,
      Never alone.
                      Visit of the Gods (Imit. from Schiller)

17 All Nature seems at work. Slugs leave their lair—
   The bees are stirring—birds are on the wing—
   And Winter slumbering in the open air,
   Wears on his smiling face a dream of Spring!
   And I the while, the sole unbusy thing,
   Nor honey make, nor pair, nor build, nor sing.
                                       Work Without Hope

18 Work without hope draws nectar in a sieve,
   And hope without an object cannot live.   *Ib.*

19 Poor little Foal of an oppressed race!
   I love the languid patience of thy face.
                                         To a Young Ass

20 Verse, a breeze mid blossoms straying,
   Where Hope clung feeding, like a bee—
   Both were mine! Life went a-maying
      With Nature, Hope, and Poesy,
         When I was young!   *Youth and Age*

21 Like some poor nigh-related guest,
   That may not rudely be dismist;
   Yet hath outstay'd his welcome while,
   And tells the jest without the smile.   *Ib.*

22 He who begins by loving Christianity better than
   Truth will proceed by loving his own sect or church
   better than Christianity, and end by loving himself
   better than all.
      Aids to Reflection: Moral and Religious Aphorisms, xxv

23 The most happy marriage I can picture or imagine to
   myself would be the union of a deaf man to a blind
   woman.   T. Allsop's *Recollections* (1836)

24 If men could learn from history, what lessons it might
   teach us! But passion and party blind our eyes,
   and the light which experience gives is a lantern on
   the stern, which shines only on the waves behind
   us!   *Ib.* (*18 Dec. 1831*)

25 Until you understand a writer's ignorance, presume
   yourself ignorant of his understanding.
                              Biographia Literaria, ch. 12

26 That willing suspension of disbelief for the moment,
   which constitutes poetic faith.   *Ib.* ch. 14

27 Our *myriad-minded* Shakespeare. Note Ἀνὴρ μυριόνους,
   a phrase which I have borrowed from a Greek
   monk, who applies it to a Patriarch of Constantinople.   *Ib.* ch. 15

28 No man was ever yet a great poet, without being at the
   same time a profound philosopher.   *Ib.*

29 The dwarf sees farther than the giant, when he has the
   giant's shoulder to mount on.
                              The Friend, § i, Essay 8

30 Reviewers are usually people who would have been
   poets, historians, biographers, &c., if they could;
   they have tried their talents at one or at the other,
   and have failed; therefore they turn critics.
                   Lectures on Shakespeare and Milton, i

31 Summer has set in with its usual severity.
   Remark quoted in Lamb's Letter to V. Novello, 9 May 1826

1 The last speech, [Iago's soliloquy] the motive-hunting of motiveless malignity—how awful!
Notes on the Tragedies of Shakespeare, Othello

2 From whatever place I write you will expect that part of my 'Travels' will consist of excursions in my own mind.
Satyrane's Letters, ii. [The Friend, 7 Dec. 1809 No. 16. Biographia Literaria]

3 Schiller has the material sublime.
Table Talk, 29 Dec. 1822

4 You abuse snuff! Perhaps it is the final cause of the human nose.
Ib. 4 Jan. 1823

5 To see him [Kean] act, is like reading Shakespeare by flashes of lightning.
Ib. 27 Apr. 1823

6 I wish our clever young poets would remember my homely definitions of prose and poetry; that is, prose = words in their best order;—poetry = the *best* words in the best order.
Ib. 12 July 1827

7 The man's desire is for the woman; but the woman's desire is rarely other than for the desire of the man.
Ib. 23 July 1827

8 My mind is in a state of philosophical doubt as to animal magnetism.
Ib. 30 Apr. 1830

9 Poetry is certainly something more than good sense, but it must be good sense at all events; just as a palace is more than a house, but it must be a house, at least.
Ib. 9 May 1830

10 Swift was *anima Rabelaisii habitans in sicco*—the soul of Rabelais dwelling in a dry place.
Ib. 15 June 1830

11 The misfortune is, that he [Tennyson] has begun to write verses without very well understanding what metre is.
Ib. 24 Apr. 1833

12 When I was a boy, I was fondest of Æschylus; in youth and middle-age I preferred Euripides; now in my declining years I prefer Sophocles. I can now at length see that Sophocles is the most perfect. Yet he never rises to the sublime simplicity of Æschylus—a simplicity of design, I mean—nor diffuses himself in the passionate outpourings of Euripides.
Ib. 1 July 1833

13 That passage is what I call the sublime dashed to pieces by cutting too close with the fiery four-in-hand round the corner of nonsense.
Ib. 20 Jan. 1834

14 I believe Shakespeare was not a whit more intelligible in his own day than he is now to an educated man, except for a few local allusions of no consequence. He is of no age—nor of any religion, or party or profession. The body and substance of his works came out of the unfathomable depths of his own oceanic mind: his observation and reading, which was considerable, supplied him with the drapery of his figures.
Ib. 15 Mar. 1834

15 This dark frieze-coated, hoarse, teeth-chattering Month.
Watchman, No. 6. Apr. 1796

16 Poor Lamb, if he wants any *knowledge*, he may apply to me.
Ascribed by Lamb in a Letter to Southey, 28 July 1798

JESSE COLLINGS
1831–1920

17 Three acres and a cow.
Phrase used in his land-reform propaganda of 1885. (See 339:2)

JOHN CHURTON COLLINS
1848–1908

18 To ask advice is in nine cases out of ten to tout for flattery.
Maxims and Reflections, No. 59

MORTIMER COLLINS
1827–1876

19 A man is as old as he's feeling,
A woman as old as she looks.
The Unknown Quantity

WILLIAM COLLINS
1721–1759

20 Fair Fidele's grassy tomb.
Dirge in Cymbeline

21 And rifle all the breathing Spring.
Ib.

22 Each lonely scene shall thee restore,
For thee the tear be duly shed;
Belov'd till life can charm no more,
And mourn'd, till Pity's self be dead.
Ib.

23 If aught of oaten stop, or pastoral song,
May hope, O pensive Eve, to soothe thine ear.
Ode to Evening

24 While now the bright-haired sun
Sits in yon western tent, whose cloudy skirts,
With brede ethereal wove,
O'erhang his wavy bed:
Now air is hush'd, save where the weak-ey'd bat,
With short shrill shriek flits by on leathern wing,
Or where the beetle winds
His small but sullen horn,
As oft he rises 'midst the twilight path,
Against the pilgrim borne in heedless hum.
Ib.

25 Hamlets brown, and dim-discover'd spires.
Ib.

26 Bathe thy breathing tresses, meekest Eve!
Ib.

27 Round the moist marge of each cold Hebrid isle.
Ode on the Popular Superstitions of the Highlands

28 Tho' taste, tho' genius bless,
To some divine excess,
Faints the cold work till thou inspire the whole.
Ode to Simplicity

29 How sleep the brave, who sink to rest,
By all their country's wishes blest!
Ode Written in the Year 1746

30 By fairy hands their knell is rung,
By forms unseen their dirge is sung;
There Honour comes, a pilgrim grey,
To bless the turf that wraps their clay,
And Freedom shall awhile repair,
To dwell a weeping hermit there!
Ib.

31 When Music, heav'nly maid, was young.
The Passions, an Ode for Music

1 With eyes up-rais'd, as one inspir'd,
Pale Melancholy sate retir'd,
And from her wild sequester'd seat,
In notes by distance made more sweet,
Pour'd thro' the mellow horn her pensive soul.
The Passions, an Ode for Music

2 In hollow murmurs died away. *Ib.*

3 O Music, sphere-descended maid. *Ib.*

4 Too nicely Jonson knew the critic's part,
Nature in him was almost lost in Art.
Verses to Sir Thomas Hanmer

GEORGE COLMAN
1732–1794

5 Love and a cottage! Eh, Fanny! Ah, give me indifference and a coach and six!
The Clandestine Marriage, I. ii

GEORGE COLMAN
1762–1836

6 Mum's the word. *Battle of Hexham*, II. i

7 Praise the bridge that carried you over.
Heir-at-Law, I. i

8 Lord help you! Tell 'em Queen Anne's dead. *Ib.*

9 Oh, London is a fine town,
A very famous city,
Where all the streets are paved with gold,
And all the maidens pretty. *Ib.* ii

10 Not to be sneezed at. *Ib.* II. i

11 Oh, Miss Bailey! Unfortunate Miss Bailey!
Love Laughs at Locksmiths, Act II, *Song*

12 Says he, 'I am a handsome man, but I'm a gay
deceiver.' *Ib.*

13 Johnson's style was grand and Gibbon's elegant; the
stateliness of the former was sometimes pedantic,
and the polish of the latter was occasionally finical.
Johnson marched to kettle-drums and trumpets;
Gibbon moved to flutes and hautboys: Johnson
hewed passages through the Alps, while Gibbon
levelled walks through parks and gardens.
Random Records (1830), i. 121

14 My father was an eminent button maker—but I had
a soul above buttons—I panted for a liberal profession. *Sylvester Daggerwood*, I. x

15 His heart runs away with his head.
Who Wants a Guinea?, I. i

16 Impaling worms to torture fish.
Lady of the Wreck, c. II. l. 18

17 Mynheer Vandunck, though he never was drunk,
Sipped brandy and water gayly.
Mynheer Vandunck

18 Like two single gentlemen roll'd into one.
*My Nightgown and Slippers. Lodgings for Single
Gentlemen*

19 When taken, To be well shaken.
Ib. Newcastle Apothecary

CHARLES CALEB COLTON
1780?–1832

20 When you have nothing to say, say nothing.
Lacon, vol. i, No. 183

21 Examinations are formidable even to the best prepared, for the greatest fool may ask more than the
wisest man can answer. *Ib.* No. 322

22 If you would be known, and not know, vegetate in
a village; if you would know, and not be known,
live in a city. *Lacon*, vol. i, No. 334

23 Man is an embodied paradox, a bundle of contra-
dictions. *Ib.* No. 408

24 The debt which cancels all others. *Ib.* vol. ii, No. 66

PRINCE DE CONDÉ
1621–1686

25 Silence! Voilà l'ennemi!
Hush! Here comes the enemy!
As Bourdaloue mounted the pulpit at St. Sulpice

WILLIAM CONGREVE
1670–1729

26 Is there in the world a climate more uncertain than
our own? And, which is a natural consequence,
is there any where a people more unsteady, more
apt to discontent, more *saturnine, dark,* and *melan-
cholic* than our selves? Are we not of all people
the most unfit to be alone, and most unsafe to be
trusted with our selves? . . .'
*Amendments of Mr. Collier's False and Im-
perfect Citations*

27 Careless she is with artful care,
Affecting to seem unaffected. *Amoret*

28 She likes her self, yet others hates
For that which in herself she prizes;
And while she laughs at them, forgets
She is the thing that she despises. *Ib.*

29 It is the business of a comic poet to paint the vices
and follies of human kind.
The Double Dealer, Epistle Dedicatory

30 Retired to their tea and scandal, according to their
ancient custom. *Ib.* I. i

31 There is nothing more unbecoming a man of quality
than to laugh; Jesu, 'tis such a vulgar expression
of the passion! *Ib.* iv

32 Tho' marriage makes man and wife one flesh, it leaves
'em still two fools. *Ib.* II. iii

33 She lays it on with a trowel. *Ib.* III. x

34 When people walk hand in hand there's neither over-
taking nor meeting. *Ib.* IV. ii

35 See how love and murder will out. *Ib.* vi

36 No mask like open truth to cover lies,
As to go naked is the best disguise. *Ib.* v. iv

37 I cannot help it, if I am naturally more delighted
with any thing that is amiable, than with any thing
that is wonderful. *Preface to Dryden*

38 What he [Dryden] has done in any one species, or
distinct kind, would have been sufficient to have
acquired him a great name. If he had written
nothing but his Prefaces, or nothing but his Songs,
or his Prologues, each of them would have intituled
him to the preference and distinction of excelling
in his kind. *Ib.*

39 O Sleep! thou flatterer of happy minds.
Elegy to Sleep

40 The good receiv'd, the giver is forgot.
Epistle to Lord Halifax, l. 40

1 Music alone with sudden charms can bind
The wand'ring sense, and calm the troubled mind.
Hymn to Harmony

2 Ah! Madam, . . . you know every thing in the world
but your perfections, and you only know not
those, because 'tis the top of perfection not to
know them. *Incognita*

3 I am always of the opinion with the learned, if they
speak first. *Ib.*

4 For 'tis some virtue, virtue to commend.
To Sir Godfrey Kneller

5 But soon as e'er the beauteous idiot spoke,
Forth from her coral lips such folly broke,
Like balm the trickling nonsense heal'd my wound,
And what her eyes enthral'd, her tongue unbound.
Lesbia

6 I confess freely to you, I could never look long upon
a monkey, without very mortifying reflections.
*Letter to Dennis, concerning Humour in Comedy,
1695*

7 If I can give that Cerberus a sop, I shall be at rest
for one day. *Love for Love*, I. iv

8 I warrant you, if he danced till doomsday, he thought
I was to pay the piper. *Ib.* II. v

9 Ferdinand Mendez Pinto was but a type of thee, thou
liar of the first magnitude. *Ib.*

10 Has he not a rogue's face? . . . a hanging-look
to me . . . has a damn'd Tyburn-face, without the
benefit o' the Clergy. . . . *Ib.* vii

11 I came upstairs into the world; for I was born in a
cellar. *Ib.*

12 What, wouldst thou have me turn pelican, and feed
thee out of my own vitals? *Ib.*

13 Oh fie, Miss, you must not kiss and tell. *Ib.* x

14 He that first cries out stop thief, is often he that has
stoln the treasure. *Ib.* III. xiv

15 Women are like tricks by slight of hand,
Which, to admire, we should not understand.
Ib. IV. xxi

16 A branch of one of your antediluvian families,
fellows that the flood could not wash away.
Ib. v. ii

17 To find a young fellow that is neither a wit in his
own eye, nor a fool in the eye of the world, is a
very hard task. *Ib.*

18 Music has charms to sooth a savage breast.
The Mourning Bride, I. i

19 How reverend is the face of this tall pile,
Whose ancient pillars rear their marble heads,
To bear aloft its arch'd and pond'rous roof,
By its own weight made stedfast and immoveable,
Looking tranquillity. It strikes an awe
And terror on my aching sight. *Ib.* II. iii

20 Heav'n has no rage, like love to hatred turn'd,
Nor Hell a fury, like a woman scorn'd. *Ib.* III. viii

21 Is he then dead?
What, dead at last, quite, quite for ever dead!
Ib. v. xi

22 In my conscience I believe the baggage loves me,
for she never speaks well of me her self, nor
suffers any body else to rail at me.
The Old Bachelor, I. i

23 One of love's April-fools. *Ib.*

24 The Devil watches all opportunities. *Ib.* vi

25 Man was by Nature Woman's cully made:
We never are, but by ourselves, betrayed. *Ib.* III. i

26 Bilbo's the word, and slaughter will ensue.
Ib. vii

27 Ask all the tyrants of thy sex, if their fools are not
known by this party-coloured livery—I am
melancholy when thou art absent; look like an ass
when thou art present; wake for thee, when I
should sleep, and even dream of thee, when I am
awake; sigh much, drink little, eat less, court
solitude, am grown very entertaining to my self,
and (as I am informed) very troublesome to everybody else. If this be not love, it is madness, and
then it is pardonable—Nay yet a more certain sign
than all this; I give thee my money. *Ib.* x

28 Eternity was in that moment. *Ib.* IV. vii

29 You were about to tell me something, child—but
you left off before you began. *Ib.* viii

30 Now am I slap-dash down in the mouth. *Ib.* ix.

31 Well, Sir Joseph, you have such a winning way with
you. *Ib.* v. vii

32 SHARPER.
Thus grief still treads upon the heels of pleasure:
Marry'd in haste, we may repent at leisure.
SETTER.
Some by experience find those words mis-plac'd:
At leisure marry'd, they repent in haste.
Ib. viii *and* ix

33 I could find it in my heart to marry thee, purely to
be rid of thee. *Ib.* x

34 Courtship to marriage, as a very witty prologue to
a very dull Play. *Ib.*

35 O Sleep, why dost thou leave me?
Why thy visionary joys remove?
O Sleep, again deceive me,
To my arms restore my wand'ring Love.
Semele, II. ii

36 Whom she refuses, she treats still
With so much sweet behaviour,
That her refusal, through her skill,
Looks almost like a favour. *Song: Doris*

37 False though she be to me and love,
I'll ne'er pursue revenge;
For still the charmer I approve,
Tho' I deplore her change.
Song: False Though She Be

38 Wou'd I were free from this restraint,
Or else had hopes to win her;
Wou'd she cou'd make of me a saint,
Or I of her a sinner.
Song: Pious Selinda Goes to Prayers

39 Alack he's gone the way of all flesh.
'Squire Bickerstaff Detected. (Attr. to Congreve)

40 Say what you will, 'tis better to be left than never to
have been loved. *The Way of the World*, II. i

1 Here she comes i' faith full sail, with her fan spread and streamers out, and a shoal of fools for tenders.
The Way of the World, II. iv

2 O ay, letters—I had letters—I am persecuted with letters—I hate letters—no body knows how to write letters; and yet one has 'em, one does not know why—They serve one to pin up one's hair. . . .
Ib.

3 WITWOUD.
Pray, Madam, do you pin up your hair with all your letters: I find I must keep copies.
MILLAMANT.
Only with those in verse, Mr. Witwoud. I never pin up my hair with prose.
Ib.

4 MILLAMANT.
I believe I gave you some pain.
MIRABEL.
Does that please you?
MILLAMANT.
Infinitely; I love to give pain.
MIRABEL.
You wou'd affect a cruelty which is not in your nature; your true vanity is in the power of pleasing.
MILLAMANT.
O I ask your pardon for that—one's cruelty is one's power, and when one parts with one's cruelty, one parts with one's power; and when one has parted with that, I fancy one's old and ugly.
Ib.

5 Beauty is the lover's gift.
Ib.

6 Lord, what is a lover, that it can give? Why one makes lovers as fast as one pleases, and they live as long as one pleases, and they die as soon as one pleases: and then if one pleases one makes more.
Ib.

7 Fools never wear out—they are such *drap-de-berry* things.
Ib. III. x

8 Love's but a frailty of the mind
When 'tis not with ambition join'd.
Ib. xii

9 O, nothing is more alluring than a levee from a couch in some confusion.
Ib. IV. i

10 I nauseate walking; 'tis a country diversion, I loathe the country.
Ib. iv

11 O, I hate a lover that can dare to think he draws a moment's air, independent on the bounty of his mistress. There is not so impudent a thing in Nature, as the saucy look of an assured man, confident of success.
Ib. v

12 My dear liberty, shall I leave thee? My faithful solitude, my darling contemplation, must I bid you then adieu? Ay-h adieu—My morning thoughts, agreeable wakings, indolent slumbers, all ye *douceurs*, ye *sommeils du matin*, adieu—I can't do't, 'tis more than impossible.
Ib.

13 Don't let us be familiar or fond, nor kiss before folks, like my Lady Fadler and Sir Francis: Nor go to Hyde-Park together the first Sunday in a new chariot, to provoke eyes and whispers, and then never be seen there together again; as if we were proud of one another the first week, and asham'd of one another ever after. . . . Let us be very strange and well-bred: Let us be as strange as if we had been married a great while, and as well-bred as if we were not married at all.
Ib.

14 These articles subscrib'd, if I continue to endure you a little longer, I may by degrees dwindle into a wife.
The Way of the World, iv. v

15 O horrid provisos!
Ib.

16 Wilfull will do't.
Ib. x

17 I hope you do not think me prone to any iteration of nuptials.
Ib. xii

T. W. CONNOR
nineteenth century

18 She was one of the early birds,
And I was one of the worms.
She Was A Dear Little Dickie-bird

HENRY CONSTABLE
1562–1613

19 Diaphenia, like the daffadowndilly,
White as the sun, fair as the lily,
Heigh ho, how I do love thee!
I do love thee as my lambs
Are beloved of their dams;
How blest were I if thou wouldst prove me!
[Damelus' Song to his] Diaphenia

CONSTANTINE
288?–337

20 In hoc signo vinces.
In this sign shalt thou conquer.
Words of Constantine's vision. Eusebius, *Life of Constantine*, i. 28

ELIZA COOK
1818–1889

21 I love it, I love it; and who shall dare
To chide me for loving that old arm-chair?
The Old Arm-chair

22 Better build schoolrooms for 'the boy',
Than cells and gibbets for 'the man'.
A Song for the Ragged Schools

CALVIN COOLIDGE
1872–1933

23 I do not choose to run for President in 1928.
Announcement in 1927

24 He said he was against it.
On being asked what had been said by a clergyman who preached on sin

25 The business of America is business.
Speech before Society of American Newspaper Editors, 17 Jan. 1925

26 They hired the money, didn't they?
With reference to the war debts incurred by England and others (1925)

SIR A. DUFF COOPER
1890–

27 Not lust of conquest but love of order is at the basis of Empire.
United Empire (1948)

GEORGE COOPER
1840–1927

1 O Genevieve, sweet Genevieve,
    The days may come, the days may go,
    But still the hands of mem'ry weave
    The blissful dreams of long ago.   *Sweet Genevieve*

JAMES FENIMORE COOPER
1789–1851

2 The Last of the Mohicans.   *Title of Novel*

BISHOP RICHARD CORBET
1582–1635

3 Farewell rewards and fairies.   *The Fairy's Farewell*

4   Who of late for cleanliness,
Finds sixpence in her shoe?   *Ib.*

5 Let others write for glory or reward,
Truth is well paid when she is sung and heard.
    Elegy on Lord Howard, Baron of Effingham

PIERRE CORNEILLE
1606–1684

6 À vaincre sans péril, on triomphe sans gloire,
    When there is no peril in the fight, there is no glory
    in the triumph.   *Le Cid*, ii. 2

7 Faites votre devoir et laissez faire aux dieux.
    Do your duty, and leave the issue to the Gods.
    Horace, ii. 8

FRANCES CROFTS CORNFORD
1886–

8 A young Apollo, golden-haired,
Stands dreaming on the verge of strife,
Magnificently unprepared
For the long littleness of life.   *Rupert Brooke*

9 O fat white woman whom nobody loves,
Why do you walk through the fields in gloves,

Missing so much and so much?
    To a Fat Lady Seen from a Train

FRANCIS MACDONALD CORNFORD
1874–1943

10 Every public action which is not customary, either is
wrong or, if it is right, is a dangerous precedent.
It follows that nothing should ever be done for the
first time.   *Microcosmographia Academica*, vii

MME CORNUEL
1605–1694

11 Il n'y a point de héros pour son valet de chambre.
    No man is a hero to his valet.
    Lettres de Mlle Aïssé, xii, 13 août 1728

BARRY CORNWALL
[BRYAN WALLER PROCTER]
1787–1874

12 The sea! the sea! the open sea!
The blue, the fresh, the ever free!   *The Sea*

CORONATION SERVICE

13 We present you with this Book, the most valuable
thing that this world affords. Here is wisdom; this
is the royal Law; these are the lively Oracles of
God.   *The Presenting of the Holy Bible*

ANTONIO CORREGGIO
1494–1534

14 Anch' io sono pittore!
    I, too, am a painter.
    *On seeing Raphael's 'St. Cecilia' at Bologna, c.
    1525*

WILLIAM JOHNSON CORY
1823–1892

15 They told me, Heraclitus, they told me you were
    dead,
They brought me bitter news to hear and bitter tears
    to shed.   *Heraclitus*

16   How often you and I
Had tired the sun with talking and sent him down
    the sky.   *Ib.*

17 A handful of grey ashes, long long ago at rest.   *Ib.*

18 You promise heavens free from strife.
    Mimnermus in Church

19 This warm kind world is all I know.   *Ib.*

20 But oh, the very reason why
    I clasp them, is because they die.   *Ib.*

NATHANIEL COTTON
1705–1788

21 Yet still we hug the dear deceit.   *Visions, iv, Content*

ÉMILE COUÉ
1857–1926

22 Tous les jours, à tous points de vue, je vais de mieux
en mieux.

    Every day, in every way, I am getting better and
    better.   *Formula in his clinic at Nancy*

VICTOR COUSIN
1792–1867

23 L'art pour l'art.
    Art for art's sake.   *Lecture at the Sorbonne*

THOMAS COVENTRY, BARON COVENTRY
1578–1640

24 The wooden walls are the best walls of this kingdom.
    *Speech to the Judges, 17 June 1635, given in
    Rushworth's* Hist. Coll. (1680), vol. ii, p. 297

NOEL COWARD
1899–

25 Mad dogs and Englishmen go out in the mid-day sun;
The Japanese don't care to, the Chinese wouldn't
    dare to;
Hindus and Argentines sleep firmly from twelve to
    one,
But Englishmen detest a siesta.
    Mad Dogs and Englishmen

ABRAHAM COWLEY
1618-1667

1 Love in her sunny eyes does basking play;
Love walks the pleasant mazes of her hair;
Love does on both her lips for ever stray;
And sows and reaps a thousand kisses there.
In all her outward parts Love's always seen;
   But, oh, he never went within. *The Change*

2 Nothing is there to come, and nothing past,
But an eternal Now does always last.
   Davideis, bk. i, l. 361

3 Poet and Saint! to thee alone are given
The two most sacred names of earth and Heaven.
   On the Death of Mr. Crashaw

4   Thou
Wert living the same poet which thou'rt now,
Whilst Angels sing to thee their airs divine,
And joy in an applause so great as thine.
Equal society with them to hold,
Thou need'st not make new songs, but say the old.
   Ib.

5 His faith perhaps, in some nice tenents might
Be wrong; his life, I'm sure, was in the right. *Ib.*

6 Hail, Bard triumphant! and some care bestow
On us, the Poets Militant below! *Ib.*

7 The thirsty earth soaks up the rain,
And drinks, and gapes for drink again.
The plants suck in the earth, and are
With constant drinking fresh and fair. *Drinking*

8 Fill all the glasses there, for why
Should every creature drink but I,
Why, man of morals, tell me why? *Ib.*

9 God the first garden made, and the first city Cain.
   The Garden

10 Ye fields of Cambridge, our dear Cambridge, say,
Have ye not seen us walking every day?
Was there a tree about which did not know
   The love betwixt us two? *On William Harvey*

11 The world's a scene of changes, and to be
Constant, in Nature were inconstancy. *Inconstancy*

12 Well then; I now do plainly see
This busy world and I shall ne'er agree;
The very honey of all earthly joy
Does of all meats the soonest cloy,
   And they (methinks) deserve my pity,
Who for it can endure the stings,
The crowd, and buz, and murmurings
   Of this great hive, the city.
   The Mistress, or Love Verses

13 Ah, yet, e'er I descend to th' grave
May I a small house, and large garden have!
And a few friends, and many books, both true,
   Both wise, and both delightful too!
   And since Love ne'er will from me flee,
A Mistress moderately fair,
And good as guardian angels are,
   Only belov'd, and loving me! *Ib.*

14 What shall I do to be for ever known,
And make the age to come my own? *The Motto*

15 This only grant me, that my means may lie
Too low for envy, for contempt too high.
   Of Myself

16 Acquaintance I would have, but when't depends
Not on the number, but the choice of friends.
   Of Myself

17 I would not fear nor wish my fate,
   But boldly say each night,
To-morrow let my sun his beams display,
Or in clouds hide them; I have lived to-day. *Ib.*

18 Nothing so soon the drooping spirits can raise
As praises from the men, whom all men praise.
   Ode upon a Copy of Verses of My Lord Broghill's

19 Who lets slip Fortune, her shall never find.
Occasion once pass'd by, is bald behind.
   Pyramus and Thisbe, xv

20 Lukewarmness I account a sin
As great in love as in religion. *The Request*

21 Life is an incurable disease. *To Dr. Scarborough*, vi

22 Let but thy wicked men from out thee go,
And all the fools that crowd thee so,
Even thou, who dost thy millions boast,
A village less than Islington wilt grow,
A solitude almost. *Of Solitude*, xii

23 The Dangers of an Honest Man in much Company.
   *Discourses by Way of Essays, in Verse and
Prose*, 8, title

24 Hence, ye profane; I hate ye all;
Both the great vulgar, and the small.
   Trans. of Horace, bk. iii, ode 1

HANNAH COWLEY
1743-1809

25 Five minutes! Zounds! I have been five minutes too
late all my life-time! *The Belle's Stratagem*, I. i

26 Vanity, like murder, will out. *Ib.* iv

27 But what is woman?—only one of Nature's agreeable
blunders. *Who's the Dupe?*, II

WILLIAM COWPER
1731-1800

28 Let my obedience then excuse
My disobedience now. *Beau's Reply*

29 When the British warrior queen,
   Bleeding from the Roman rods,
Sought with an indignant mien,
   Counsel of her country's gods,

Sage beneath a spreading oak
Sat the Druid, hoary chief. *Boadicea*

30 Rome shall perish—write that word
In the blood that she has spilt. *Ib.*

31 Hark! the Gaul is at her gates! *Ib.*

32 Regions Caesar never knew
   Thy posterity shall sway,
Where his eagles never flew,
   None invincible as they. *Ib.*

33 Ruffians, pitiless as proud,
Heav'n awards the vengeance due;
Empire is on us bestow'd,
Shame and ruin wait for you. *Ib.*

1 Obscurest night involv'd the sky,
　Th' Atlantic billows roar'd,
When such a destin'd wretch as I,
　Wash'd headlong from on board,
Of friends, of hope, of all bereft,
His floating home for ever left. *The Castaway*

2 But misery still delights to trace
Its semblance in another's case. *Ib.*

3 　We perish'd, each alone:
But I beneath a rougher sea,
And whelm'd in deeper gulphs than he. *Ib.*

4 Truth is the golden girdle of the globe. *Charity*, l. 86

5 Grief is itself a med'cine. *Ib.* l. 159

6 He found it inconvenient to be poor. *Ib.* l. 189

7 India's spicy shores. *Ib.* l. 442

8 Pelting each other for the public good. *Ib.* l. 623

9 Spare the poet for his subject's sake. *Ib.* l. 636

10 But strive to be a man before your mother.
Motto to Connoisseur, No. 111

11 Not more distinct from harmony divine,
The constant creaking of a country sign.
Conversation, l. 9

12 Though syllogisms hang not on my tongue,
I am not surely always in the wrong!
'Tis hard if all is false that I advance—
A fool must now and then be right, by chance.
Ib. l. 93

13 But still remember, if you mean to please,
To press your point with modesty and ease.
Ib. l. 103

14 A noisy man is always in the right. *Ib.* l. 114

15 A moral, sensible, and well-bred man
Will not affront me, and no other can. *Ib.* l. 193

16 A tale should be judicious, clear, succinct;
The language plain, and incidents well link'd;
Tell not as new what ev'ry body knows;
And, new or old, still hasten to a close. *Ib.* l. 235

17 The pipe, with solemn interposing puff,
Makes half a sentence at a time enough;
The dozing sages drop the drowsy strain,
Then pause, and puff—and speak, and pause again.
Ib. l. 245

18 Pernicious weed! whose scent the fair annoys,
Unfriendly to society's chief joys,
Thy worst effect is banishing for hours
The sex whose presence civilizes ours. *Ib.* l. 251

19 A fine puss-gentleman that's all perfume. *Ib.* l. 284

20 His wit invites you by his looks to come,
But when you knock it never is at home. *Ib.* l. 303

21 Our wasted oil unprofitably burns,
Like hidden lamps in old sepulchral urns. *Ib.* l. 357

22 Whose only fit companion is his horse. *Ib.* l. 412

23 A poet does not work by square or line. *Ib.* l. 789

24 　　　What appears
In England's case to move the muse to tears?
Expostulation, l. 1

25 Th' embroid'ry of poetic dreams. *Ib.* l. 234

26 War lays a burden on the reeling state,
And peace does nothing to relieve the weight.
Ib. l. 306

27 The busy trifler. *Expostulation*, l. 32

28 A pick-lock to a place. *Ib.* l. 379

29 　　　Thousands . . .
Kiss the book's outside who ne'er look within.
Ib. l. 389

30 Religion, if in heav'nly truths attir'd,
Needs only to be seen to be admired. *Ib.* l. 492

31 The man that hails you Tom or Jack,
And proves by thumps upon your back
　　How he esteems your merit,
Is such a friend, that one had need
Be very much his friend indeed
　　To pardon or to bear it. *Friendship*

32 John Gilpin was a citizen
　Of credit and renown,
A train-band captain eke was he
　Of famous London town.

John Gilpin's spouse said to her dear—
　Though wedded we have been
These twice ten tedious years, yet we
　No holiday have seen. *John Gilpin*

33 To-morrow is our wedding-day,
　And we will then repair
Unto the Bell at Edmonton
　All in a chaise and pair.

My sister and my sister's child,
　Myself and children three,
Will fill the chaise; so you must ride
　On horseback after we. *Ib.*

34 He soon replied—I do admire
　Of womankind but one,
And you are she, my dearest dear,
　Therefore it shall be done.

I am a linen-draper bold,
　As all the world doth know,
And my good friend the calender
　Will lend his horse to go. *Ib.*

35 　O'erjoy'd was he to find
That, though on pleasure she was bent,
　She had a frugal mind. *Ib.*

36 　　　And all agog
To dash through thick and thin! *Ib.*

37 John Gilpin at his horse's side
　Seiz'd fast the flowing mane,
And up he got, in haste to ride,
　But soon came down again. *Ib.*

38 So down he came; for loss of time,
　Although it griev'd him sore,
Yet loss of pence, full well he knew,
　Would trouble him much more. *Ib.*

39 Good lack! quoth he—yet bring it me,
　My leathern belt likewise,
In which I bear my trusty sword
　When I do exercise. *Ib.*

40 So, fair and softly, John he cried,
　But John he cried in vain. *Ib.*

41 So stooping down, as needs he must
　Who cannot sit upright,
He grasp'd the mane with both his hands,
　And eke with all his might. *Ib.*

1 His horse, who never in that sort
  Had handled been before,
What thing upon his back had got
  Did wonder more and more.

  Away went Gilpin, neck or nought,
  Away went hat and wig!   *John Gilpin*

2 The dogs did bark, the children scream'd.
  Up flew the windows all;
And ev'ry soul cried out—Well done!
  As loud as he could bawl.

  Away went Gilpin—who but he?
  His fame soon spread around—
He carries weight! he rides a race!
  'Tis for a thousand pound!   *Ib.*

3 The dinner waits, and we are tired:
  Said Gilpin—So am I   *Ib.*

4   Which brings me to
The middle of my song.   *Ib.*

5 My hat and wig will soon be here—
  They are upon the road.   *Ib.*

6 The calender, right glad to find
  His friend in merry pin.   *Ib.*

7 My head is twice as big as yours,
  They therefore needs must fit.   *Ib.*

8 Said John—It is my wedding-day,
  And all the world would stare,
If wife should dine at Edmonton
  And I should dine at Ware.   *Ib.*

9 'Twas for your pleasure you came here,
  You shall go back for mine.   *Ib.*

10 Nor stopp'd till where he had got up
  He did again get down.   *Ib.*

11 Now let us sing—Long live the king,
  And Gilpin long live he;
And, when he next doth ride abroad,
  May I be there to see!   *Ib.*

12 An honest man, close-button'd to the chin,
Broad-cloth without, and a warm heart within.
    Epistle to Jos. Hill, l. 62

13 No dancing bear was so genteel,
  Or half so dégagé.   *Of Himself*

14 Painful passage o'er a restless flood.   *Hope*, l. 3

15 Men deal with life as children with their play,
Who first misuse, then cast their toys away.
    Ib. l. 127

16 Some eastward, and some westward, and all wrong.
    Ib. l. 281

17 Could he with reason murmur at his case,
Himself sole author of his own disgrace? *Ib.* l. 316

18 And diff'ring judgements serve but to declare
That truth lies somewhere, if we knew but where.
    Ib. l. 423

19 Seek to delight, that they may mend mankind,
And, while they captivate, inform the mind.
    Ib. l. 758

20 Absence from whom we love is worse than death,
And frustrate hope severer than despair.
    'Hope, Like the Short-Liv'd Ray'

21 The twentieth year is well-nigh past,
Since first our sky was overcast;
Ah would that this might be the last!
    My Mary!   *To Mary*

22 Thy needles, once a shining store,
For my sake restless heretofore,
Now rust disus'd, and shine no more,
    My Mary!   *Ib.*

23 Partakers of thy sad decline,
Thy hands their little force resign;
Yet, gently prest, press gently mine,
    My Mary!   *Ib.*

24 Greece, sound thy Homer's, Rome thy Virgil's name,
But England's Milton equals both in fame.
    To John Milton

25 Oh that those lips had language! Life has pass'd
With me but roughly since I heard thee last.
Those lips are thine—thy own sweet smiles I see,
The same that oft in childhood solac'd me.
    On the Receipt of My Mother's Picture, l. 1

26 Blest be the art that can immortalize.   *Ib.* l. 8

27 Wretch even then, life's journey just begun.
    Ib. l. 24

28 Perhaps thou gav'st me, though unseen, a kiss;
Perhaps a tear, if souls can weep in bliss. *Ib.* l. 25

29 Disappointed still, was still deceiv'd.   *Ib.* l. 39

30 Where once we dwelt our name is heard no more,
Children not thine have trod my nursery floor;
And where the gard'ner Robin, day by day,
Drew me to school along the public way,
Delighted with my bauble coach, and wrapt
In scarlet mantle warm, and velvet capt,
'Tis now become a history little known. *Ib.* l. 46

31 Thy morning bounties ere I left my home,
The biscuit, or confectionary plum.   *Ib.* l. 60

32 The fragrant waters on my cheek bestow'd. *Ib.* l. 62

33 Not scorn'd in heaven, though little notic'd here.
    Ib. l. 73

34   I should ill requite thee to constrain
Thy unbound spirit into bonds again.   *Ib.* l. 86

35 Me howling winds drive devious, tempest toss'd,
Sails ript, seams op'ning wide, and compass lost.
    Ib. l. 102

36 Some people are more nice than wise.
    Mutual Forbearance, l. 20

37 Oh, fond attempt to give a deathless lot
To names ignoble, born to be forgot!
    On Observing Some Names of Little Note
    Recorded in the Biographia Britannica

38 There goes the parson, oh! illustrious spark,
And there, scarce less illustrious, goes the clerk! *Ib.*

39 Thought again—but knew not what to think.
    The Needless Alarm, l. 54

40 Beware of desp'rate steps. The darkest day
(Live till to-morrow) will have pass'd away.
    Ib. l. 132

41 Hence jarring sectaries may learn
Their real int'rest to discern;
That brother should not war with brother,
And worry and devour each other.
    The Nightingale and Glow-Worm

1 Oh! for a closer walk with God,
  A calm and heav'nly frame;
A light to shine upon the road
  That leads me to the Lamb!   *Olney Hymns*, 1

2 What peaceful hours I once enjoy'd!
  How sweet their mem'ry still!
But they have left an aching void,
  The world can never fill.   *Ib.*

3 The dearest idol I have known,
  Whate'er that idol be;
Help me to tear it from thy Throne,
  And worship only thee.   *Ib.*

4 Nor sword nor spear the stripling took,
But chose a pebble from the brook.   *Ib.* 4

5 O make this heart rejoice, or ache;
  Decide this doubt for me;
And if it be not broken, break,
  And heal it, if it be.   *Ib.* 9

6 So unaccustom'd to the yoke,
So backward to comply.   *Ib.* 12

7 There is a fountain fill'd with blood.   *Ib.* 15

8 When this poor lisping stammering tongue
  Lies silent in the grave.   *Ib.*

9 Hark, my soul! it is the Lord;
  'Tis thy Saviour, hear his word;
Jesus speaks, and speaks to thee;
  'Say, poor sinner, lov'st thou me?'   *Ib.* 18

10 I deliver'd thee when bound,
And, when bleeding, heal'd thy wound;
Sought thee wand'ring, set thee right,
Turn'd thy darkness into light.   *Ib.*

11 'Can a woman's tender care
  Cease, towards the child she bare?
Yes, she may forgetful be,
  Yet will I remember thee.'   *Ib.*

12 Mine is an unchanging love,
  Higher than the heights above;
Deeper than the depths beneath,
  Free and faithful, strong as death.   *Ib.*

13 Lord, it is my chief complaint,
  That my love is weak and faint;
Yet I love thee and adore,
  Oh for grace to love thee more!   *Ib.*

14 What various hindrances we meet
  In coming to a mercy-seat!   *Ib.* 29

15 And Satan trembles, when he sees
  The weakest saint upon his knees.   *Ib.*

16 While Moses stood with arms spread wide,
  Success was found on Israel's side;
But when thro' weariness they fail'd,
  That moment Amalek prevail'd.   *Ib.*

17 I seem forsaken and alone,
  I hear the lion roar;
And ev'ry door is shut but one,
  And that is mercy's door.   *Ib.* 33

18 God moves in a mysterious way
  His wonders to perform;
He plants his footsteps in the sea,
  And rides upon the storm.

Deep in unfathomable mines
  Of never failing skill
He treasures up his bright designs,
  And works his sovereign will.

Ye fearful saints fresh courage take,
  The clouds ye so much dread
Are big with mercy, and shall break
  In blessings on your head.

Judge not the Lord by feeble sense,
  But trust him for his grace;
Behind a frowning providence
  He hides a smiling face.   *Olney Hymns*, 35

19 The bud may have a bitter taste,
  But sweet will be the flow'r.   *Ib.*

20 Blind unbelief is sure to err,
  And scan his work in vain;
God is his own interpreter,
  And he will make it plain.   *Ib.*

21 Sometimes a light surprises
  The Christian while he sings;
It is the Lord who rises
  With healing in his wings;
When comforts are declining,
  He grants the soul again
A season of clear shining
  To cheer it after rain.   *Ib.* 44

22 I shall not ask Jean Jacques Rousseau,
  If birds confabulate or no. *Pairing Time Anticipated*

23 The poplars are fell'd, farewell to the shade
And the whispering sound of the cool colonnade.
             The Poplar-Field

24 Unmiss'd but by his dogs and by his groom.
            Progress of Error, l. 95

25 Oh, laugh or mourn with me the rueful jest,
A cassock'd huntsman and a fiddling priest!
             Ib. l. 110

26 Himself a wand'rer from the narrow way,
His silly sheep, what wonder if they stray? *Ib.* l. 118

27 Remorse, the fatal egg by pleasure laid.   *Ib.* l. 239

28 Woman, lovely woman, does the same.   *Ib.* l. 274

29 Caesar's image is effac'd at last.   *Ib.* l. 280

30 As creeping ivy clings to wood or stone,
And hides the ruin that it feeds upon.   *Ib.* l. 285

31 How much a dunce that has been sent to roam
Excels a dunce that has been kept at home. *Ib.* l. 415

32 Talks of darkness at noon-day.   *Ib.* l. 451

33 Thou god of our idolatry, the press.   *Ib.* l. 461

34 The nobler tenants of the flood.   *Ib.* l. 482

35 Laugh at all you trembled at before.   *Ib.* l. 592

36 Pleasure is labour too, and tires as much.
              Hope, l. 20

37 He blam'd and protested, but join'd in the plan;
He shar'd in the plunder, but pitied the man.
          Pity for Poor Africans

38 Then, shifting his side, (as a lawyer knows how).
        Report of an Adjudged Case

39 But vers'd in arts that, while they seem to stay
A falling empire, hasten its decay. *Retirement*, l. 383

40 The disencumber'd Atlas of the state.   *Ib.* l. 394

41 Prison'd in a parlour snug and small,
Like bottled wasps upon a southern wall. *Ib.* l. 493

42 Play the fool, but at a cheaper rate.   *Ib.* l. 562

1 He likes the country, but in truth must own,
  Most likes it, when he studies it in town.
  Retirement, l. 573

2   Philologists who chase
  A panting syllable through time and space,
  Start it at home, and hunt it in the dark,
  To Gaul, to Greece, and into Noah's ark. *Ib.* l. 619

3 Absence of occupation is not rest,
  A mind quite vacant is a mind distress'd. *Ib.* l. 623

4 [Voltaire:]
  Built God a church, and laugh'd his word to scorn.
  Ib. l. 688

5 Beggars invention and makes fancy lame. *Ib.* l. 709

6 I praise the Frenchman, his remark was shrewd—
  How sweet, how passing sweet, is solitude!
  But grant me still a friend in my retreat,
  Whom I may whisper—solitude is sweet. *Ib.* l. 739

7 Fast by the banks of the slow winding Ouse.
  Ib. l. 804

8 The tear that is wip'd with a little address,
  May be follow'd perhaps by a smile. *The Rose*

9 Toll for the brave—
    The brave! that are no more:
  All sunk beneath the wave,
    Fast by their native shore.
  Loss of the Royal George

10 A land-breeze shook the shrouds,
    And she was overset;
  Down went the Royal George,
    With all her crew complete. *Ib.*

11 Toll for the brave—
    Brave Kempenfelt is gone,
  His last sea-fight is fought,
    His work of glory done.
  It was not in the battle,
    No tempest gave the shock,
  She sprang no fatal leak,
    She ran upon no rock;
  His sword was in the sheath,
    His fingers held the pen,
  When Kempenfelt went down
    With twice four hundred men. *Ib.*

12 Weigh the vessel up,
    Once dreaded by our foes. *Ib.*

13 He and his eight hundred
  Must plough the wave no more. *Ib.*

14 Oh, happy shades—to me unblest!
  Friendly to peace, but not to me! *The Shrubbery*

15 Chief monster that hast plagued the nations yet.
  Table Talk, l. 38

16 The lie that flatters I abhor the most. *Ib.* l. 88

17 Th' unwashed artificer. *Ib.* l. 152

18 As if the world and they were hand and glove.
  Ib. l. 173

19 Admirals, extoll'd for standing still,
  Or doing nothing with a deal of skill. *Ib.* l. 192

20 The leathern ears of stock-jobbers and Jews.
  Ib. l. 197

21 The Frenchman, easy, debonair, and brisk,
  Give him his lass, his fiddle, and his frisk,
  Is always happy, reign whoever may,
  And laughs the sense of mis'ry far away. *Ib.* l. 236

22 Freedom has a thousand charms to show,
  That slaves, howe'er contented, never know.
  Table Talk, l. 260

23 Stamps God's own name upon a lie just made,
  To turn a penny in the way of trade. *Ib.* l. 420

24 Suspend your mad career. *Ib.* l. 435

25 Feels himself spent, and fumbles for his brains.
  Ib. l. 537

26 Ages elaps'd ere Homer's lamp appear'd,
  And ages ere the Mantuan swan was heard:
  To carry nature lengths unknown before,
  To give a Milton birth, ask'd ages more. *Ib.* l. 556

27 By low ambition and the thirst of praise. *Ib.* l. 591

28 [Pope:]
  But he (his musical finesse was such,
  So nice his ear, so delicate his touch)
  Made poetry a mere mechanic art;
  And ev'ry warbler has his tune by heart. *Ib.* l. 654

29 Pity religion has so seldom found
  A skilful guide into poetic ground! *Ib.* l. 716

30 Hail Sternhold, then; and Hopkins, hail! *Ib.* l. 759

31 I sing the Sofa. *The Task*, bk. i, *The Sofa*, l. 1

32 The Fair commands the song. *Ib.* l. 7

33 So sit two kings of Brentford on one throne.
  Ib. l. 78

34 Thus first necessity invented stools,
  Convenience next suggested elbow-chairs,
  And luxury the accomplish'd Sofa last. *Ib.* l. 86

35 The nurse sleeps sweetly, hir'd to watch the sick,
  Whom, snoring, she disturbs. *Ib.* l. 89

36 Nor rural sights alone, but rural sounds,
  Exhilarate the spirit, and restore
  The tone of languid Nature. *Ib.* l. 181

37 Toils much to earn a monumental pile,
  That may record the mischiefs he has done.
  Ib. l. 276

38 God made the country, and man made the town.
  Ib. l. 749

39 There is a public mischief in your mirth. *Ib.* l. 769

40 Oh for a lodge in some vast wilderness,
  Some boundless contiguity of shade,
  Where rumour of oppression and deceit,
  Of unsuccessful or successful war,
  Might never reach me more.
  Ib. bk. ii, *The Timepiece*, l. 1

41   Mountains interpos'd
  Make enemies of nations, who had else,
  Like kindred drops, been mingled into one. *Ib.* l. 17

42 Slaves cannot breathe in England, if their lungs
  Receive our air, that moment they are free;
  They touch our country, and their shackles fall.
  Ib. l. 40

43 England, with all thy faults, I love thee still—
  My country! *Ib.* l. 206

44 I would not yet exchange thy sullen skies,
  And fields without a flow'r, for warmer France
  With all her vines. *Ib.* l. 212

45 Presume to lay their hand upon the ark
  Of her magnificent and awful cause. *Ib.* l. 231

1　　　　Praise enough
To fill th' ambition of a private man,
That Chatham's language was his mother tongue,
And Wolfe's great name compatriot with his own.
　　　The Task, bk. ii, *The Timepiece*, l. 235

2 Chatham heart-sick of his country's shame.
　　　　　　　　　　　　　Ib. l. 244

3 There is a pleasure in poetic pains
Which only poets know.　　　　*Ib.* l. 285

4 Variety's the very spice of life,
That gives it all its flavour.　　*Ib.* l. 606

5　　　　　　His head,
Not yet by time completely silver'd o'er,
Bespoke him past the bounds of freakish youth,
But strong for service still, and unimpair'd. *Ib.* l. 702

6 Domestic happiness, thou only bliss
Of Paradise that has surviv'd the fall!
　　　　Ib. bk. iii, *The Garden*, l. 41

7 Guilty splendour.　　　　　　*Ib.* l. 70

8 I was a stricken deer, that left the herd
Long since.　　　　　　　　　*Ib.* l. 108

9　　　　　　Charge
His mind with meanings that he never had.
　　　　　　　　　　　　　Ib. l. 148

10 Great contest follows, and much learned dust
Involves the combatants.　　　*Ib.* l. 161

11 From reveries so airy, from the toil
Of dropping buckets into empty wells,
And growing old in drawing nothing up! *Ib.* l. 188

12 Exercise all functions of a man.　*Ib.* l. 198

13　　　　Newton, childlike sage!
Sagacious reader of the works of God.　*Ib.* l. 252

14 Riches have wings.　　　　　*Ib.* l. 263

15 The only amaranthine flower on earth
Is virtue.　　　　　　　　　*Ib.* l. 268

16　　　　Detested sport,
That owes its pleasures to another's pain. *Ib.* l. 326

17 Studious of laborious ease.　　*Ib.* l. 361

18 Who loves a garden loves a greenhouse too.
　　　　　　　　　　　　　Ib. l. 566

19 To combat may be glorious, and success
Perhaps may crown us; but to fly is safe. *Ib.* l. 686

20 He comes, the herald of a noisy world,
With spatter'd boots, strapp'd waist, and frozen locks;
News from all nations lumb'ring at his back.
　　　　Ib. bk. iv, *The Winter Evening*, l. 5

21 Now stir the fire, and close the shutters fast,
Let fall the curtains, wheel the sofa round,
And, while the bubbling and loud-hissing urn
Throws up a steamy column, and the cups,
That cheer but not inebriate, wait on each,
So let us welcome peaceful ev'ning in. *Ib.* l. 34

22 Katterfelto, with his hair on end
At his own wonders, wond'ring for his bread.
　　　　　　　　　　　　　Ib. l. 85

23 'Tis pleasant through the loopholes of retreat
To peep at such a world; to see the stir
Of the great Babel, and not feel the crowd. *Ib.* l. 88

24 O Winter, ruler of th' inverted year. *Ib.* l. 120

25 I love thee, all unlovely as thou seem'st
And dreaded as thou art.
　　　The Task, bk. iv, *The Winter Evening*, l. 128

26 I crown thee king of intimate delights,
Fire-side enjoyments, home-born happiness.
　　　　　　　　　　　　　Ib. l. 139

27　　　A Roman meal;
. . . .
　　　a radish and an egg.　　*Ib.* ll. 168–73

28 The slope of faces, from the floor to th' roof,
(As if one master-spring controll'd them all),
Relax'd into a universal grin.　*Ib.* l. 202

29 With spots quadrangular of di'mond form,
Ensanguin'd hearts, clubs typical of strife,
And spades, the emblem of untimely graves.
　　　　　　　　　　　　　Ib. l. 217

30 In indolent vacuity of thought.　*Ib.* l. 297

31 It seems the part of wisdom.　*Ib.* l. 336

32 All learned, and all drunk!　*Ib.* l. 478

33 Gloriously drunk, obey th' important call! *Ib.* l. 510

34 Sidney, warbler of poetic prose.　*Ib.* l. 516

35 I never fram'd a wish, or form'd a plan,
That flatter'd me with hopes of earthly bliss,
But there I laid the scene.　　*Ib.* l. 695

36 Entangled in the cobwebs of the schools. *Ib.* l. 726

37　　　　　　The fragrant weed,
The Frenchman's darling. [Mignonette.] *Ib.* l. 764

38 Prepost'rous sight! the legs without the man.
　　　Ib. bk. v, *The Winter Morning Walk*, l. 20

39 Half lurcher and half cur.　　*Ib.* l. 46

40 Silently as a dream the fabric rose;—
No sound of hammer or of saw was there. *Ib.* l. 144

41 Great princes have great playthings. *Ib.* l. 175

42 But war's a game, which, were their subjects wise,
Kings would not play at.　　　*Ib.* l. 187

43 And the first smith was the first murd'rer's son.
　　　　　　　　　　　　　Ib. l. 219

44 The beggarly last doit.　　　*Ib.* l. 316

45　　　　All constraint,
Except what wisdom lays on evil men,
Is evil.　　　　　　　　　　*Ib.* l. 448

46 He is the freeman whom the truth makes free.
　　　　　　　　　　　　　Ib. l. 733

47 Give what thou canst, without thee we are poor;
And with thee rich, take what thou wilt away.
　　　　　　　　　　　　　Ib. l. 905

48 There is in souls a sympathy with sounds;
And, as the mind is pitch'd the ear is pleas'd
With melting airs, or martial, brisk, or grave:
Some chord in unison with what we hear,
Is touch'd within us, and the heart replies.
　　　Ib. bk. vi, *The Winter Walk at Noon*, l. 1

49　　　　Knowledge dwells
In heads replete with thoughts of other men;
Wisdom in minds attentive to their own. *Ib.* l. 89

50 Knowledge is proud that he has learn'd so much;
Wisdom is humble that he knows no more. *Ib.* l. 96

51 Books are not seldom talismans and spells. *Ib.* l. 98

52 Nature is but a name for an effect,
Whose cause is God.　　　　*Ib.* l. 223

1 A cheap but wholesome salad from the brook.
The Task, bk. vi, *The Winter Walk at Noon*, l. 304

2 Anger insignificantly fierce. *Ib.* l. 320

3 I would not enter on my list of friends
(Tho' grac'd with polish'd manners and fine sense,
Yet wanting sensibility) the man
Who needlessly sets foot upon a worm. *Ib.* l. 560

4 The crested worm. *Ib.* l. 780

5   Stillest streams
Oft water fairest meadows, and the bird
That flutters least is longest on the wing. *Ib.* l. 929

6 Public schools 'tis public folly feeds.
Tirocinium, l. 250

7 We love the play-place of our early days. *Ib.* l. 297

8 The little ones, unbutton'd, glowing hot,
Playing our games, and on the very spot;
As happy as we once, to kneel and draw
The chalky ring, and knuckle down at taw;
To pitch the ball into the grounded hat,
Or drive it devious with a dex'trous pat. *Ib.* l. 304

9 The parson knows enough who knows a duke.
Ib. l. 403

10   As a priest,
A piece of mere church furniture at best. *Ib.* l. 425

11 His fav'rite stand between his father's knees.
Ib. l. 570

12   Tenants of life's middle state,
Securely plac'd between the small and great.
Ib. l. 807

13 If it chance, as sometimes chance it will,
That, though school-bred, the boy be virtuous still.
Ib. l. 839

14 Humility may clothe an English dean. *Truth*, l. 118

15 He has no hope who never had a fear. *Ib.* l. 298

16 Just knows, and knows no more, her Bible true—
A truth the brilliant Frenchman never knew. [Voltaire.] *Ib.* l. 327

17 Envy, ye great, the dull unletter'd small. *Ib.* l. 375

18 One who wears a coronet, and prays. *Ib.* l. 378

19 His mind his kingdom, and his will his law.
Ib. l. 406

20 Mary! I want a lyre with other strings.
Sonnet to Mrs. Unwin

21 Verse, that immortalizes whom it sings! *Ib.*

22 I am monarch of all I survey,
  My right there is none to dispute;
From the centre all round to the sea
  I am lord of the fowl and the brute.
Oh, solitude! where are the charms
  That sages have seen in thy face?
Better dwell in the midst of alarms,
  Than reign in this horrible place.
Verses Supposed to be Written by Alexander Selkirk

23 Never hear the sweet music of speech. *Ib.*

24 Society, friendship, and love,
  Divinely bestow'd upon man. *Ib.*

25 But the sound of the church-going bell
  These valleys and rocks never heard,
Ne'er sigh'd at the sound of a knell,
  Or smil'd when a sabbath appear'd. *Ib.*

26 [On Johnson's inadequate treatment of *Paradise Lost*]
Oh! I could thresh his old jacket till I made his
pension jingle in his pockets.
Letters, To the Rev. W. Unwin, 31 Oct. 1779

27 Our severest winter, commonly called the spring.
Ib. 8 June 1783

28 He kissed likewise the maid in the kitchen, and
seemed upon the whole a most loving, kissing,
kind-hearted gentleman.
Ib. To the Rev. J. Newton, 29 Mar. 1784

GEORGE CRABBE
1754–1832

29 What is a church?—Our honest sexton tells,
'Tis a tall building, with a tower and bells.
The Borough, letter ii, *The Church*, l. 11

30 Virtues neglected then, adored become,
And graces slighted, blossom on the tomb. *Ib.* l. 133

31 Intrigues half-gather'd, conversation-scraps,
Kitchen-cabals, and nursery-mishaps.
Ib. letter iii, *The Vicar*, l. 71

32 Habit with him was all the test of truth,
'It must be right: I've done it from my youth.'
Ib. l. 138

33 Lo! the poor toper whose untutor'd sense,
Sees bliss in ale, and can with wine dispense;
Whose head proud fancy never taught to steer,
Beyond the muddy ecstasies of beer.
Inebriety, l. 120 (*Imitation of Pope*)

34 This, books can do—nor this alone: they give
New views to life, and teach us how to live;
They soothe the grieved, the stubborn they chastise;
Fools they admonish, and confirm the wise.
Their aid they yield to all: they never shun
The man of sorrow, nor the wretch undone;
Unlike the hard, the selfish, and the proud,
They fly not sullen from the suppliant crowd;
Nor tell to various people various things,
But show to subjects, what they show to kings.
The Library, l. 41

35 Here come the grieved, a change of thought to find,
The curious here, to feed a craving mind;
Here the devout their peaceful temple choose;
And here the poet meets his favouring muse.
With awe around these silent walks I tread:
These are the lasting mansions of the dead.
Ib. l. 101

36 And mighty folios first, a lordly band,
Then quartos, their well-order'd ranks maintain,
And light octavos fill a spacious plain;
See yonder, ranged in more frequented rows,
A humbler band of duodecimos. *Ib.* l. 128

37 Hence, in these times, untouch'd the pages lie,
And slumber out their immortality. *Ib.* l. 157

38 Fashion, though Folly's child, and guide of fools,
Rules e'en the wisest, and in learning rules. *Ib.* l. 167

39 Against her foes Religion well defends
Her sacred truths, but often fears her friends.
Ib. l. 249

40 Coldly profane, and impiously gay. *Ib.* l. 265

41 The murmuring poor, who will not fast in peace.
The Newspaper, l. 158

1 A master-passion is the love of news.
The Newspaper, l. 279

2 Hold their glimmering tapers to the sun.
The Parish Register, introd. to pt. I, l. 92

3 Our farmers round, well pleased with constant gain,
Like other farmers, flourish and complain.
Ib. pt. i, *Baptisms*, l. 273

4 I preach for ever; but I preach in vain!
Ib. pt. ii, *Marriages*, l. 130

5 When from the cradle to the grave I look,
Mine I conceive a melancholy book.
Ib. pt. iii, *Burials*, l. 21

6 Grave Jonas Kindred, Sybil Kindred's sire,
Was six feet high, and look'd six inches higher.
Tales, vi, *The Frank Courtship*, l. 1

7 When the coarse cloth she saw, with many a stain,
Soil'd by rude hinds who cut and came again.
Ib. vii, *The Widow's Tale*, l. 25

8 Who often reads, will sometimes wish to write.
Ib. xi, *Edward Shore*, l. 109

9 The wife was pretty, trifling, childish, weak;
She could not think, but would not cease to speak.
Ib. xiv, *Struggles of Conscience*, l. 343

10 But 'twas a maxim he had often tried,
That right was right, and there he would abide.
Ib. xv, *The Squire and the Priest*, l. 365

11 That all was wrong because not all was right.
Ib. xix, *The Convert*, l. 313

12 He tried the luxury of doing good.
Tales of the Hall, iii, *Boys at School*, l. 139

13 Secrets with girls, like loaded guns with boys,
Are never valued till they make a noise.
Ib. xi, *The Maid's Story*, l. 84

14 'The game', he said, 'is never lost till won.'
Ib. xv, *Gretna Green*, l. 334

15 The face the index of a feeling mind.
Ib. xvi, *Lady Barbara*, l. 124

16 Love warps the mind a little from the right.
Ib. xxi, *Smugglers and Poachers*, l. 216

17 Lo! where the heath, with withering brake grown o'er,
Lends the light turf that warms the neighbouring
poor;
From thence a length of burning sand appears,
Where the thin harvest waves its wither'd ears;
Rank weeds, that every art and care defy,
Reign o'er the land, and rob the blighted rye:
There thistles stretch their prickly arms afar,
And to the ragged infant threaten war;
There poppies, nodding, mock the hope of toil;
There the blue bugloss paints the sterile soil;
Hardy and high, above the slender sheaf,
The slimy mallow waves her silky leaf,
O'er the young shoot the charlock throws a shade,
And clasping tares cling round the sickly blade.
The Village, bk. i, l. 63

18 I sought the simple life that Nature yields. *Ib.* l. 110

19 And the cold charities of man to man. *Ib.* l. 245

20 A potent quack, long versed in human ills,
Who first insults the victim whom he kills;
Whose murd'rous hand a drowsy Bench protect,
And whose most tender mercy is neglect. *Ib.* l. 282

21 The ring so worn, as you behold,
So thin, so pale, is yet of gold:
The passion such it was to prove;
Worn with life's cares, love yet was love.
His Mother's Wedding Ring

MRS. DINAH MARIA CRAIK
1826–1887

22 Douglas, Douglas, tender and true.
Songs of Our Youth, 'Douglas, Douglas, Tender and True'

STEPHEN CRANE
1871–1900

23 The Red Badge of Courage. *Title*

ARCHBISHOP THOMAS CRANMER
1489–1556

24 This hand hath offended.
Strype's *Memorials of Cranmer*, 1694, vol. iii

RICHARD CRASHAW
1612?–1649

25 Nympha pudica Deum vidit, et erubuit.
The conscious water saw its God, and blushed.
Epigrammata Sacra. Aquae in Vinum Versae
(His own translation.)

26 All those fair and flagrant things.
The Flaming Heart upon the Book of Saint Teresa, l. 34

27 Love's passives are his activ'st part.
The wounded is the wounding heart. *Ib.* l. 73

28 O thou undaunted daughter of desires! *Ib.* l. 93

29 By all the eagle in thee, all the dove. *Ib.* l. 95

30 By thy large draughts of intellectual day. *Ib.* l. 97

31 By the full kingdom of that final kiss
That seized thy parting soul, and seal'd thee His;
By all the Heavens thou hast in Him—
Fair sister of the Seraphim!—
By all of Him we have in thee;
Leave nothing of myself in me.
Let me so read thy life, that I
Unto all life of mine may die! *Ib.* l. 101

32 I would be married, but I'd have no wife,
I would be married to a single life. *On Marriage*

33 I sing the Name which none can say
But touch'd with an interior ray.
To the Name Above Every Name, l.

34 Narrow, and low, and infinitely less. *Ib.* l. 22

35 Come; and come strong,
To the conspiracy of our spacious song. *Ib.* l. 70

36 Gloomy night embrac'd the place
Where the noble Infant lay.
The Babe look't up and shew'd his face;
In spite of darkness, it was day.
It was Thy day, sweet! and did rise
Not from the East, but from thine eyes.
Hymn of the Nativity, l. 17

1 Poor World (said I) what wilt thou do
To entertain this starry stranger?
Is this the best thou canst bestow?
A cold, and not too cleanly, manger?
Contend, ye powers of heav'n and earth
To fit a bed for this huge birth.
Hymn of the Nativity, l. 37

2 Proud world, said I; cease your contest
And let the mighty Babe alone.
The phoenix builds the phoenix' nest.
Love's architecture is his own. *Ib.* l. 44

3 I saw the curl'd drops, soft and slow,
Come hovering o'er the place's head;
Off'ring their whitest sheets of snow
To furnish the fair Infant's bed.
Forbear, said I; be not too bold.
Your fleece is white but 'tis too cold. *Ib.* l. 50

4 I saw the obsequious Seraphims
Their rosy fleece of fire bestow.
For well they now can spare their wings
Since Heaven itself lies here below.
Well done, said I: but are you sure
Your down so warm, will pass for pure? *Ib.* l. 58

5 We saw thee in thy balmy nest,
Young dawn of our eternal day!
We saw thine eyes break from their East
And chase the trembling shades away.
We saw thee; and we blest the sight
We saw thee by thine own sweet light. *Ib.* l. 71

6 Welcome, all wonders in one sight!
Eternity shut in a span. *Ib.* l. 79

7 Love's great artillery. *Prayer*, l. 15

8 Lo here a little volume, but large book.
On a Prayer-Book Sent to Mrs. M. R.

9 Happy soul, she shall discover
What joy, what bliss,
How many heavens at once it is,
To have a God become her lover. *Ib.*

10 Two walking baths; two weeping motions;
Portable, and compendious oceans.
Saint Mary Magdalene, or The Weeper, xix

11 Love, thou art absolute sole Lord
Of life and death.
*Hymn to the Name & Honour of the Admirable
Saint Teresa*, l. 1

12 Farewell house, and farewell home!
She's for the Moors, and martyrdom. *Ib.* l. 63

13 Two went to pray? O rather say
One went to brag, th'other to pray:
. . . . .
One nearer to God's Altar trod,
The other to the Altar's God.
*Steps to the Temple, Two Went up into the
Temple to Pray*

14 All is Caesar's; and what odds
So long as Caesar's self is God's? *Ib. Mark* 12

15 And when life's sweet fable ends,
Soul and body part like friends;
No quarrels, murmurs, no delay;
A kiss, a sigh, and so away. *Temperance*

16 Why, 'tis a point of faith. Whate'er it be,
I'm sure it is no point of charity.
On a Treatise of Charity

17 Whoe'er she be,
That not impossible she
That shall command my heart and me;
Where'er she lie,
Lock'd up from mortal eye,
In shady leaves of destiny.
Wishes to His Supposed Mistress

18 Meet you her my wishes,
Bespeak her to my blisses,
And be ye call'd my absent kisses.
I wish her beauty,
That owes not all his duty
To gaudy tire, or glist'ring shoe-tie. *Ib.*

19 Life, that dares send
A challenge to his end,
And when it comes say 'Welcome Friend'. *Ib.*

20 Sydnaean showers
Of sweet discourse, whose powers
Can crown old Winter's head with flowers. *Ib.*

21 'Tis she, and here
Lo I unclothe and clear,
My wishes' cloudy character. *Ib.*

22 Let her full Glory,
My fancies, fly before ye,
Be ye my fictions; but her story. *Ib.*

MRS. EDMUND CRASTER
d. 1874

23 The Centipede was happy quite,
Until the Toad in fun
Said 'Pray which leg goes after which?'
And worked her mind to such a pitch,
She lay distracted in the ditch
Considering how to run. *Attrib.*

JULIA CRAWFORD
fl. 1835

24 Kathleen Mavourneen! the grey dawn is breaking,
The horn of the hunter is heard on the hill;
The lark from her light wing the bright dew is
shaking;
Kathleen Mavourneen! what, slumbering still?
Oh! hast thou forgotten how soon we must sever?
Oh! hast thou forgotten this day we must part?
It may be for years, and it may be for ever,
Oh! why art thou silent, thou voice of my heart?
Kathleen Mavourneen. Metropolitan Magazine,
London, 1835

BISHOP MANDELL CREIGHTON
1843–1901

25 No people do so much harm as those who go about
doing good. *Life* (1904), vol. ii, p. 503

JOHN WILSON CROKER
1780–1857

26 We now are, as we always have been, decidedly and
conscientiously attached to what is called the Tory,
and which might with more propriety be called the
Conservative, party.
Article, Quarterly Review, Jan. 1830, p. 276

1 A game which a sharper once played with a dupe, entitled, 'Heads I win, tails you lose.'
Croker Papers, iii. 59

OLIVER CROMWELL
1599–1658

2 A few honest men are better than numbers.
Letter to Sir W. Spring, Sept. 1643

3 Such men as had the fear of God before them and as made some conscience of what they did . . . the plain russet-coated captain that knows what he fights for and loves what he knows.
Letter of Sept. 1643. In Carlyle, Letters and Speeches of Oliver Cromwell

4 I beseech you, in the bowels of Christ, think it possible you may be mistaken.
Letter to the General Assembly of the Church of Scotland, 3 Aug. 1650

5 The dimensions of this mercy are above my thoughts. It is, for aught I know, a crowning mercy.
Letter for the Honourable William Lenthall, 4 Sept. 1651

6 Not what they want but what is good for them.
Attr. remark

7 Mr. Lely, I desire you would use all your skill to paint my picture truly like me, and not flatter me at all; but remark all these roughnesses, pimples, warts, and everything as you see me, otherwise I will never pay a farthing for it.
Remark, Walpole's Anecdotes of Painting, ch. 12

8 Take away these baubles.
Remark, Sydney Papers (1825), p. 141

9 It is not fit that you should sit here any longer! . . . you shall now give place to better men.
Speech to the Rump Parliament, 22 Jan. 1654

10 It's a maxim not to be despised, 'Though peace be made, yet it's interest that keeps peace.'
Speech to Parliament, 4 Sept. 1654

11 Necessity hath no law. Feigned necessities, imaginary necessities, . . . are the greatest cozenage that men can put upon the Providence of God, and make pretences to break known rules by.
Ib. 12 Sept. 1654

12 Your poor army, those poor contemptible men, came up hither.
Ib. 21 Apr. 1657

13 You have accounted yourselves happy on being environed with a great ditch from all the world beside.
Ib. 25 Jan. 1658

14 My design is to make what haste I can to be gone.
Last Words. Morley, Life, v, ch. 10

THOMAS W. H. CROSLAND
1868–1924

15 The Unspeakable Scot.
Title of satirical essay

RICHARD ASSHETON, VISCOUNT CROSS
1823–1914

16 [When the House of Lords laughed at his speech in favour of Spiritual Peers]
I hear a smile.
G. W. E. Russell's Collections and Recollections, ch. 29

JOHN CROWNE
1640?–1703?

17 River Thames, attended by two nymphs, representing Peace and Plenty.
Calisto, prologue, stage directions

JOHANN CRÜGER
1598–1662

18 Nun danket alle Gott.
Now thank we all our God.
Hymn

BISHOP RICHARD CUMBERLAND
1631–1718

19 It is better to wear out than to rust out.
G. Horne, The Duty of Contending for the Faith

ALLAN CUNNINGHAM
1784–1842

20 A wet sheet and a flowing sea,
A wind that follows fast
And fills the white and rustling sail
And bends the gallant mast.
A Wet Sheet and a Flowing Sea

21 While the hollow oak our palace is,
Our heritage the sea.
Ib.

22 It's hame and it's hame, hame fain wad I be,
O, hame, hame, hame to my ain countree!
It's hame and It's hame. Hogg includes this poem among his Jacobite Relics, i. 135. In his notes, i. 294, he says he took it from Cromek's Galloway and Nithsdale Relics, and supposes that it owed much to Allan Cunningham

23 The lark shall sing me hame in my ain countree. *Ib.*

24 But the sun through the mirk blinks blithe in my e'e,
'I'll shine on ye yet in your ain countree.' *Ib.*

WILL CUPPY
1884–

25 The Dodo never had a chance. He seems to have been invented for the sole purpose of becoming extinct and that was all he was good for.
How to Become Extinct

JOHN PHILPOT CURRAN
1750–1817

26 The condition upon which God hath given liberty to man is eternal vigilance; which condition if he break, servitude is at once the consequence of his crime, and the punishment of his guilt.
Speech on the Right of Election of Lord Mayor of Dublin, 10 July 1790

GEORGE NATHANIEL CURZON, MARQUESS OF KEDLESTON
1859–1925

27 I do not exclude the intelligent anticipation of facts even before they occur.
Speech, House of Commons, 29 Mar. 1898

HENRY CUST
1861–1917

1 Let Hell afford
The pavement of her Heaven. *Non Nobis, Domine*

HARRY DACRE
fl. 1892

2 Daisy, Daisy, give me your answer, do!
I'm half crazy, all for the love of you!
It won't be a stylish marriage,
I can't afford a carriage,
But you'll look sweet upon the seat
Of a bicycle made for two! *Daisy Bell*

CHARLES ANDERSON DANA
1819–1897

3 When a dog bites a man that is not news, but when
a man bites a dog that is news.
What is News? The New York Sun, 1882

SAMUEL DANIEL
1562–1619

4   Princes in this case
Do hate the traitor, though they love the treason.
Tragedy of Cleopatra, iv. i

5 Unless above himself he can
Erect himself, how poor a thing is man!
To the Lady Margaret, Countess of Cumberland,
xii

6 Custom that is before all law, Nature that is above
all art. *A Defence of Rhyme*

7 Love is a sickness full of woes,
All remedies refusing:
A plant that with most cutting grows,
Most barren with best using.
Why so?
More we enjoy it, more it dies,
If not enjoy'd, it sighing cries,
Hey ho.
Hymen's Triumph, i. v

8 This is the thing that I was born to do.
Musophilus, l. 577

9 And who, in time, knows whither we may vent
The treasure of our tongue, to what strange shores
This gain of our best glory shall be sent,
T'enrich unknowing nations with our stores?
What worlds in th'yet unformed Occident
May come refin'd with th'accents that are ours?
Ib. l. 957

10 But years hath done this wrong,
To make me write too much, and live too long.
Philotas, [Ded.] To the Prince, l. 108

11 Pity is sworn servant unto love:
And this be sure, wherever it begin
To make the way, it lets your master in.
The Queen's Arcadia, ii. i

12 Care-charmer Sleep, son of the sable Night,
Brother to Death, in silent darkness born:
Relieve my languish, and restore the light,
With dark forgetting of my care return,
And let the day be time enough to mourn

The shipwreck of my ill adventured youth:
Let waking eyes suffice to wail their scorn,
Without the torment of the night's untruth.
Sonnets to Delia, liv

13 Come worthy Greek, Ulysses come
Possess these shores with me:
The winds and seas are troublesome,
And here we may be free.
Here may we sit, and view their toil
That travail on the deep,
And joy the day in mirth the while,
And spend the night in sleep.
Ulysses and the Siren

JOHN JEREMIAH DANIELL
1819–1898

14 Sing, boys, in joyful chorus
Your hymn of praise to-day,
And sing, ye gentle maidens,
Your sweet responsive lay.
*Hymns Ancient & Modern, Come, Sing with
Holy Gladness.*

DANTE ALIGHIERI
1265–1321

15 Nel mezzo del cammin di nostra vita.
In the middle of the road of our life.
Divine Comedy. Inferno, i. 1

16 Or se' tu quel Virgilio?
Art thou then that Virgil? *Ib. 79*

17 Lasciate ogni speranza voi ch'entrate!
All hope abandon, ye who enter here. *Ib. iii. 9*

18 Non ragioniam di lor, ma guarda, e passa.
Let us not speak of them, but look, and pass on.
Ib. 51

19 Il gran rifiuto.
The great refusal. *Ib. 60*

20 Onorate l'altissimo poeta.
Honour to the greatest poet. *Ib. iv. 80*

21 Il Maestro di color che sanno.
The Master of them that know. [Aristotle.]
Ib. 131

22   Nessun maggior dolore,
Che ricordarsi del tempo felice
Nella miseria.
There is no greater sorrow than to recall a time of
happiness in misery. *Ib. v. 121. (See 78:4)*

23 Galeotto fu il libro e chi lo scrisse:
Quel giorno più non vi leggemmo avante.
Galeotto was the book and writer too: that day
therein we read no more. *Ib. 137*

24 E quindi uscimmo a riveder le stelle.
Thence we came forth to rebehold the stars.
Ib. xxxiv. 139

25 Puro e disposto a salire alle stelle.
Pure and made apt for mounting to the stars.
Ib. Purgatorio, xxxiii. 145

26 E'n la sua volontade è nostra pace.
In His will is our peace. *Ib. Paradiso, iii. 85*

Tu proverai sì come sa di sale
Lo pane altrui, e com' è duro calle
Lo scendere e il salir per l'altrui scale.

You shall find out how salt is the taste of another's
bread, and how hard a path the going down and
going up another's stairs.
Divine Comedy. Paradiso, xvii. 58

2 L'amor che muove il sole e l'altre stelle.

The love that moves the sun and the other stars.
Ib. xxxiii. 145

GEORGES JACQUES DANTON
1759–1794

3 De l'audace, et encore de l'audace, et toujours de
l'audace!

Boldness, and again boldness, and always boldness!
*Speech to the Legislative Committee of General
Defence, 2 Sept. 1792. Le Moniteur, 4 Sept.
1792*

CHARLES ROBERT DARWIN
1809–1882

4 A hairy quadruped, furnished with a tail and pointed
ears, probably arboreal in its habits.
Descent of Man, ch. 21

5 We must, however, acknowledge, as it seems to me,
that man with all his noble qualities, . . . still bears
in his bodily frame the indelible stamp of his lowly
origin.
Ib. last words

6 I have called this principle, by which each slight
variation, if useful, is preserved, by the term of
Natural Selection.
The Origin of Species, ch. 3

7 We will now discuss in a little more detail the struggle
for existence.
Ib.

8 The expression often used by Mr. Herbert Spencer
of the Survival of the Fittest is more accurate, and
is sometimes equally convenient.
Ib.

CHARLES DAVENANT
1656–1714

9 Custom, that unwritten law,
By which the people keep even kings in awe.
Circe, II. iii

SIR WILLIAM DAVENANT
1606–1668

10 Had laws not been, we never had been blam'd;
For not to know we sinn'd is innocence.
Dryden Miscellany, vi. l. 226

11 I shall sleep like a top.
The Rivals, Act III

12 For I must go where lazy Peace
Will hide her drowsy head;
And, for the sport of kings, increase
The number of the dead.
The Soldier Going to the Field

13 The lark now leaves his wat'ry nest,
And climbing, shakes his dewy wings;
He takes this window for the east;
And to implore your light, he sings,
Awake, awake, the morn will never rise,
Till she can dress her beauty at your eyes.
Song

JOHN DAVIDSON
1857–1909

14 When the pods went pop on the broom, green broom.
A Runnable Stag

15 A runnable stag, a kingly crop.
Ib.

SIR JOHN DAVIES
1569–1626

16 Skill comes so slow, and life so fast doth fly,
We learn so little and forget so much.
Nosce Teipsum, introduction, xix

17 Wit to persuade, and beauty to delight. *Orchestra*, v

18 Why should your fellowship a trouble be,
Since man's chief pleasure is society?
Ib. xxxii

19 Judge not the play before the play be done.
Respice Finem

SCROPE BERDMORE DAVIES
c. 1783–1852

20 Babylon in all its desolation is a sight not so awful
as that of the human mind in ruins.
Letter to Thomas Raikes, May 1835. See
Journal of T. Raikes, 1831 to 1847, 1856, vol. ii

WILLIAM HENRY DAVIES
1870–1940

21 A rainbow and a cuckoo's song
May never come together again;
May never come
This side the tomb.
A Great Time

22 The simple bird that thinks two notes a song.
April's Charms

23 The little hunchback of the snow.
In the Snow

24 What is this life if, full of care,
We have no time to stand and stare?
Leisure

25 Sweet Stay-at-Home, sweet Well-content.
Sweet Stay-at-Home

JEFFERSON DAVIS
1808–1889

26 All we ask is to be let alone.
*Attr. Remark in Inaugural Address as President
of the Confederate States of America, 18 Feb.
1861*

THOMAS OSBORNE DAVIS
1814–1845

27 Come in the evening, or come in the morning,
Come when you're looked for, or come without
warning.
The Welcome

STEPHEN DECATUR
1779–1820

28 Our country! In her intercourse with foreign nations,
may she always be in the right; but our country,
right or wrong.
A. S. Mackenzie, Life of Decatur, ch. xiv

MARQUISE DU DEFFAND

1697–1780

1 La distance n'y fait rien; il n'y a que le premier pas qui coûte.

The distance is nothing; it is only the first step that is difficult.

Remark on the legend that St. Denis, carrying his head in his hands, walked two leagues. Letter to d'Alembert, 7 July 1763

DANIEL DEFOE

1661?–1731

2 The best of men cannot suspend their fate:
The good die early, and the bad die late.
Character of the late Dr. S. Annesley

3 We lov'd the doctrine for the teacher's sake. *Ib.*

4 Nature has left this tincture in the blood,
That all men would be tyrants if they could.
The Kentish Petition, addenda, l. 11

5 I was born in the year 1632, in the city of York, of a good family, though not of that county, my father being a foreigner of Bremen, who settled first at Hull.
The Life and Adventures of Robinson Crusoe, pt. i

6 Robin, Robin, Robin Crusoe, poor Robin Crusoe!
Where are you, Robin Crusoe? Where are you?
Where have you been? [*The parrot.*] *Ib.*

7 It happened one day, about noon, going towards my boat, I was exceedingly surprised with the print of a man's naked foot on the shore, which was very plain to be seen in the sand. I stood like one thunderstruck, or as if I had seen an apparition. *Ib.*

8 I takes my man Friday with me. *Ib.*

9 In trouble to be troubl'd
Is to have your trouble doubl'd.
Robinson Crusoe, The Farther Adventures

10 Necessity makes an honest man a knave.
Serious Reflections of Robinson Crusoe, ch. 2

11 Wherever God erects a house of prayer,
The Devil always builds a chapel there;
And 'twill be found, upon examination,
The latter has the largest congregation.
The True-Born Englishman, pt. i, l. 1

12 From this amphibious ill-born mob began
That vain, ill-natur'd thing, an Englishman.
Ib. l. 132

13 Your Roman-Saxon-Danish-Norman English.
Ib. l. 139

14 Great families of yesterday we show,
And lords whose parents were the Lord knows who.
Ib. l. 374

15 In their religion they are so uneven,
That each man goes his own By-way to heaven.
Ib. l. 104

16 And of all plagues with which mankind are curst,
Ecclesiastic tyranny's the worst. *Ib. pt. ii, l. 299*

17 When kings the sword of justice first lay down,
They are no kings, though still they possess the crown.
Titles are shadows, crowns are empty things,
The good of subjects is the end of kings. *Ib. l. 313*

THOMAS DEKKER

1570?–1641?

18 The best of men
That e'er wore earth about him, was a sufferer,
A soft, meek, patient, humble, tranquil spirit,
The first true gentleman that ever breath'd.
The Honest Whore, pt. i. I. ii

19 That great fishpond. [The sea.] *Ib.*

20 This principle is old, but true as fate,
Kings may love treason, but the traitor hate.
Ib. pt. iv. IV

21 Art thou poor, yet hast thou golden slumbers?
Oh sweet content!
Art thou rich, yet is thy mind perplexed?
Oh, punishment!
Dost thou laugh to see how fools are vexed
To add to golden numbers, golden numbers?
O, sweet content, O, sweet, O, sweet content!
Work apace, apace, apace, apace;
Honest labour bears a lovely face;
Then hey nonny, nonny; hey nonny, nonny.
Patient Grissil, Act 1

22 Canst drink the waters of the crisped spring?
O sweet content!
Swim'st thou in wealth, yet sink'st in thine own tears?
O punishment! *Ib.*

23 Golden slumbers kiss your eyes,
Smiles awake you when you rise:
Sleep, pretty wantons, do not cry,
And I will sing a lullaby:
Rock them, rock them, lullaby.

Care is heavy, therefore sleep you;
You are care, and care must keep you. *Ib. IV. ii*

24 Cold's the wind, and wet's the rain,
Saint Hugh be our good speed:
Ill is the weather that bringeth no gain,
Nor helps good hearts in need.

Trowle the bowl, the jolly nut-brown bowl,
And here kind mate to thee:
Let's sing a dirge for Saint Hugh's soul,
And down it merrily.
Shoemaker's Holiday, Second Three-man's Song

WALTER DE LA MARE

1873–

25 Ann, Ann!
Come! quick as you can!
There's a fish that *talks*
In the frying-pan.
Out of the fat,
As clear as glass,
He put up his mouth
And moaned 'Alas!'
Oh, most mournful,
'Alas, alack!'
Then turned to his sizzling,
And sank him back. *Alas, Alack*

26 Oh, no man knows
Through what wild centuries
Roves back the rose. *All That's Past*

1 Very old are we men;
Our dreams are tales
Told in dim Eden
By Eve's nightingales;
We wake and whisper awhile,
But, the day gone by,
Silence and sleep like fields
Of amaranth lie.   *All That's Past*

2 Far are the shades of Arabia,
Where the Princes ride at noon.   *Arabia*

3 He is crazed with the spell of far Arabia,
They have stolen his wits away.   *Ib.*

4 What can a tired heart say,
Which the wise of the world have made dumb?
Save to the lonely dreams of a child,
    'Return again, come!'   *Dreams*

5 Bright towers of silence. [Clouds.]   *England*

6 Here lies a most beautiful lady,
    Light of step and heart was she;
I think she was the most beautiful lady
    That ever was in the West Country.
But beauty vanishes; beauty passes;
    However rare—rare it be;
And when I crumble, who will remember
    This lady of the West Country?   *Epitaph*

7 When I lie where shades of darkness
Shall no more assail mine eyes.   *Fare Well*, i

8 Memory fades, must the remembered
Perishing be?   *Ib.*

9 Look thy last on all things lovely,
Every hour—let no night
Seal thy sense in deathly slumber
Till to delight
Thou hast paid thy utmost blessing;
Since that all things thou wouldst praise
Beauty took from those who loved them
In other days.   *Ib.* iii

10 In Hans' old Mill his three black cats
Watch the bins for the thieving rats.
Whisker and claw, they crouch in the night,
Their five eyes smouldering green and bright:

Jekkel, and Jessup, and one-eyed Jill.   *Five Eyes*

11 Three jolly gentlemen,
In coats of red,
Rode their horses
Up to bed.   *The Huntsmen*

12 Do diddle di do,
Poor Jim Jay
Got stuck fast
In Yesterday.   *Jim Jay*

13 'Is there anybody there?' said the traveller,
Knocking on the moonlit door.   *The Listeners*

14 'Tell them I came, and no one answered,
That I kept my word,' he said.   *Ib.*

15 Never the least stir made the listeners.   *Ib.*

16 Ay, they heard his foot upon the stirrup,
And the sound of iron on stone,
And how the silence surged softly backward,
When the plunging hoofs were gone.   *Ib.*

17 It's a very odd thing—
As odd as can be—
That whatever Miss T. eats
Turns into Miss T.
Porridge and apples,
Mince, muffins and mutton,
Jam, junket, jumbles—
Not a rap, not a button
It matters; the moment
They're out of her plate,
Though shared by Miss Butcher
And sour Mr. Bate,
Tiny and cheerful,
And neat as can be,
Whatever Miss T. eats
Turns into Miss T.   *Miss T.*

18 'Won't you look out of your window, Mrs. Gill?'
Quoth the Fairy, nidding, nodding in the garden.
                    The Mocking Fairy

19 Never more, Sailor,
Shalt thou be
Tossed on the wind-ridden
Restless sea.   *Never More, Sailor*

20 No robin ever
On the deep
Hopped with his song
To haunt thy sleep.   *Ib.*

21 Thistle and darnel and dock grew there,
    And a bush, in the corner, of may,
On the orchard wall I used to sprawl,
    In the blazing heat of the day;
Half asleep and half awake,
    While the birds went twittering by,
And nobody there my line to share
    But Nicholas Nye.

Nicholas Nye was lean and grey,
    Lame of a leg and old,
More than a score of donkey's years
    He had seen since he was foaled;
He munched the thistles, purple and spiked,
    Would sometimes stoop and sigh,
And turn his head, as if he said,
    'Poor Nicholas Nye!'

But dusk would come in the apple boughs,
    The green of the glow-worm shine,
The birds in nest would crouch to rest,
    And home I'd trudge to mine;
And there, in the moonlight, dark with dew,
    Asking not wherefore nor why,
Would brood like a ghost, and as still as a post,
    Old Nicholas Nye.   *Nicholas Nye*

22 Three jolly Farmers
Once bet a pound
Each dance the others would
Off the ground.   *Off the Ground*

23 Old Sallie Worm from her hole doth peep;
'Come!' said Old Shellover,
'Ay!' said Creep.   *Old Shellover*

24 Lone and alone she lies,
    Poor Miss 7,
Five steep flights from the earth,
    And one from heaven;
Dark hair and dark brown eyes,—
Not to be sad she tries,
Still—still it's lonely lies
Poor Miss 7.   *Poor 'Miss 7'*

1 And still would remain
  My wit to try—
My worn reeds broken,
  The dark tarn dry,
All words forgotten—
  Thou, Lord, and I.   *The Scribe*

2 Slowly, silently, now the moon
Walks the night in her silver shoon.   *Silver*

3 Some one came knocking
  At my wee, small door;
Some one came knocking,
  I'm sure—sure—sure.   *Some One*

4 Ages and ages have fallen on me—
On the wood and the pool and the elder tree.
    Song of Enchantment

5 And quiet did quiet remain.   *The Song of Finis*

6 Of all the trees in England,
  Oak, Elder, Elm and Thorn,
The Yew alone burns lamps of peace
  For them that lie forlorn.   *Trees*

7 Of all the trees in England,
  Her sweet three corners in,
Only the Ash, the bonnie Ash
  Burns fierce while it is green.   *Ib.*

8 And not a single one can see
My tiny watching eye.   *The Window*

SIR JOHN DENHAM
1615–1669

9 Where, with like haste, though several ways they run;
Some to undo, and some to be undone.
    Cooper's Hill, l. 31

10 Oh, could I flow like thee, and make thy stream
My great example, as it is my theme!
Though deep, yet clear; though gentle, yet not dull;
Strong without rage, without o'erflowing full.
    Ib. l. 189

11 Youth, what man's age is like to be doth show;
We may our ends by our beginnings know.
    Of Prudence, l. 225

THOMAS, LORD DENMAN
1779–1854

12 Trial by jury itself, instead of being a security to
persons who are accused, will be a delusion, a
mockery, and a snare.
    *Judgement in O'Connell v. the Queen, 4 Sept.
1844*

CLARENCE JAMES DENNIS
1876–1938

13 Me name is Mud.
    The Sentimental Bloke: A Spring Song, st. 2
(1916)

JOHN DENNIS
1657–1734

14 A man who could make so vile a pun would not
scruple to pick a pocket.
    The Gentleman's Magazine (1781), p. 324 (Edit.
note)

15 Damn them! They will not let my play run, but they
steal my thunder!
    W. S. Walsh, *Handy-book of Literary Curiosities*

THOMAS DE QUINCEY
1785–1859

16 Set up as a theatrical scarecrow for superstitious
terrors.
    Confessions of an English Opium Eater. Preface,
(1856)

17 The burden of the incommunicable.   *Ib.* pt. i

18 So, then, Oxford Street, stony-hearted stepmother,
thou that listenest to the sighs of orphans, and
drinkest the tears of children, at length I was dismissed from thee.   *Ib.*

19 Thou hast the keys of Paradise, oh just, subtle, and
mighty opium! *Ib.* pt. ii, *The Pleasures of Opium*

20 An Iliad of woes.   *Ib.* pt. iii, *The Pains of Opium*

21 Everlasting farewells! and again, and yet again
reverberated—everlasting farewells!   *Ib.*

22 Murder Considered as One of the Fine Arts.
    Title of Essay

23 If once a man indulges himself in murder, very soon
he comes to think little of robbing; and from robbing he comes next to drinking and sabbath-break-
ing, and from that to incivility and procrastination.
    Ib. Supplementary Papers

24 There is first the literature of *knowledge*, and secondly,
the literature of *power*. *Essays on the Poets; Pope*

25 Books, we are told, propose to *instruct* or to *amuse*.
Indeed! . . . The true antithesis to knowledge, in
this case, is not *pleasure*, but *power*. All that is
literature seeks to communicate power; all that is
not literature, to communicate knowledge.
    Letters to a Young Man, letter iii. *De Quincey
adds that he is indebted for this distinction to
'many years' conversation with Mr. Wordsworth'*

RENÉ DESCARTES
1596–1650

26 Cogito, ergo sum.
    I think, therefore I am. *Le Discours de la Méthode*

27 Le bon sens est la chose du monde la mieux partagée,
car chacun pense en être bien pourvu.
    Common sense is the most widely shared com-
modity in the world, for every man is convinced
that he is well supplied with it.   *Ib.*

CAMILLE DESMOULINS
1760–1794

28 My age is that of the *bon Sansculotte Jésus*; an age
fatal to Revolutionists.
    Answer at his trial. Carlyle, *French Revolution*,
bk. vi, ch. 2

PHILIPPE NÉRICAULT dit DESTOUCHES
1680–1754

29 Les absents ont toujours tort.
    The absent are always in the wrong.
    L'Obstacle imprévu, i. vi

EDWARD DE VERE, EARL OF OXFORD

1550–1604

1 If women could be fair and yet not fond.
Women's Changeableness

ROBERT DEVEREUX, EARL OF ESSEX

see

ESSEX

GEORGE DEWEY

1837–1917

2 You may fire when you are ready, Gridley.
Dewey's *Autobiography*

CHARLES DIBDIN

1745–1814

3 Did you ever hear of Captain Wattle?
He was all for love and a little for the bottle.
Captain Wattle and Miss Roe

4 For a soldier I listed, to grow great in fame,
And be shot at for sixpence a-day. *Charity*

5 In every mess I finds a friend,
In every port a wife. *Jack in his Element*

6 What argufies sniv'ling and piping your eye?
Poor Jack

7 For they say there's a Providence sits up aloft,
To keep watch for the life of poor Jack! *Ib.*

8 But the standing toast that pleased the most
Was—The wind that blows, the ship that goes,
And the lass that loves a sailor! *The Round Robin*

9 Spanking Jack was so comely, so pleasant, so jolly,
Though winds blew great guns, still he'd whistle
and sing;
Jack lov'd his friend, and was true to his Molly,
And if honour gives greatness, was great as a king.
The Sailor's Consolation

10 Here, a sheer hulk, lies poor Tom Bowling,
The darling of our crew. *Tom Bowling*

11 Faithful, below, he did his duty;
But now he's gone aloft. *Ib.*

12 And did you not hear of a jolly young waterman,
Who at Blackfriars Bridge used for to ply;
And he feather'd his oars with such skill and dexterity,
Winning each heart, and delighting each eye.
The Waterman

13 As he row'd along, thinking of nothing at all. *Ib.*

14 Then farewell, my trim-built wherry!
Oars, and coat, and badge, farewell. *Ib.*

THOMAS JOHN DIBDIN

1771–1841

15 Oh! what a snug little Island,
A right little, tight little Island!
The Snug Little Island

16 Then a very great war-man call'd Billy the Norman
Cried 'D—n it, I never lik'd *my* land.' *Ib.*

CHARLES DICKENS

1812–1870

17 Rather a tough customer in argeyment, Joe, if anybody
was to try and tackle him. [*Parkes.*]
Barnaby Rudge, ch. 1

18 Something will come of this. I hope it mayn't be
human gore. [*Simon Tappertit.*] *Ib.* ch. 4

19 Polly put the kettle on, we'll all have tea. [*Grip.*]
Ib. ch. 17

20 'There are strings,' said Mr. Tappertit, ' . . . in the
human heart that had better not be wibrated.'
Ib. ch. 22

21 Oh gracious, why wasn't I born old and ugly?
[*Miss Miggs.*] *Ib.* ch. 70

22 Jarndyce and Jarndyce still drags its dreary length
before the Court, perennially hopeless.
Bleak House, ch. 1

23 This is a London particular. . . . A fog, miss.
Ib. ch. 3

24 Educating the natives of Borrioboola-Gha, on the
left bank of the Niger. [*Mrs. Jellyby.*] *Ib.* ch. 4

25 The wind's in the east. . . . I am always conscious of
an uncomfortable sensation now and then when
the wind is blowing in the east. [*Mr. Jarndyce.*]
Ib. ch. 6

26 I only ask to be free. The butterflies are free. Mankind
will surely not deny to Harold Skimpole what it
concedes to the butterflies! *Ib.*

27 'Not to put too fine a point upon it'—a favourite
apology for plain-speaking with Mr. Snagsby.
Ib. ch. 11

28 He wos wery good to me, he wos ! [*Jo.*] *Ib.*

29 He [Mr. Turveydrop] is celebrated, almost everywhere, for his Deportment. [*Caddy.*] *Ib.* ch. 14

30 'It was a maxim of Captain Swosser's', said Mrs.
Badger, 'speaking in his figurative naval manner,
that when you make pitch hot, you cannot make it
too hot; and that if you only have to swab a plank,
you should swab it as if Davy Jones were after
you.' *Ib.* ch. 17

31 The Professor made the same remark, Miss Summer-
son, in his last illness; when (his mind wandering)
he insisted on keeping his little hammer under the
pillow, and chipping at the countenances of the
attendants. The ruling passion! [*Mrs. Badger.*] *Ib.*

32 What is peace? Is it war? No. Is it strife? No.
[*Mr. Chadband.*] *Ib.* ch. 19

33 The Chadband style of oratory is widely received
and much admired. *Ib.*

34 You are a human boy, my young friend. A human
boy. O glorious to be a human boy! . . .
O running stream of sparkling joy
To be a soaring human boy! [*Mr. Chadband.*] *Ib.*

35 Jobling, there *are* chords in the human mind. [*Guppy.*]
Ib. ch. 20

36 'It is,' says Chadband, 'the ray of rays, the sun of
suns, the moon of moons, the star of stars. It is the
light of Terewth.' *Ib.* ch. 25

37 Lo, the city is barren, I have seen but an eel. *Ib.*

1 It's my old girl that advises. She has the head. But I never own to it before her. Discipline must be maintained. [*Mr. Bagnet.*]   *Bleak House*, ch. 27

2 It is a melancholy truth that even great men have their poor relations.   *Ib.* ch. 28

3 Never have a mission, my dear child. [*Mr. Jellyby.*]   *Ib.* ch. 30

4 England has been in a dreadful state for some weeks. Lord Coodle would go out, and Sir Thomas Doodle wouldn't come in, and there being nobody in Great Britain (to speak of) except Coodle and Doodle, there has been no Government.   *Ib.* ch. 40

5 She's Colour-Sergeant of the Nonpareil battalion. [*Mr. Bagnet.*]   *Ib.* ch. 52

6 A smattering of everything, and a knowledge of nothing. [*Minerva House.*]   *Sketches by Boz. Tales*, ch. 3. *Sentiment*

7 Grief never mended no broken bones, and as good people's wery scarce, what I says is, make the most on 'em.   *Ib. Scenes*, ch. 22, *Gin-Shops*

8 O let us love our occupations,
Bless the squire and his relations,
Live upon our daily rations,
And always know our proper stations.
     The Chimes, 2nd Quarter

9 In came a fiddler—and tuned like fifty stomach-aches. In came Mrs. Fezziwig, one vast substantial smile.   *A Christmas Carol*, stave 2

10 'God bless us every one!' said Tiny Tim, the last of all.   *Ib.* stave 3

11 It *was* a turkey! He could never have stood upon his legs, that bird. He would have snapped 'em off short in a minute, like sticks of sealing-wax.   *Ib.* stave 5

12 'Somebody's sharp.' 'Who is?' asked the gentleman, laughing. I looked up quickly; being curious to know. 'Only Brooks of Sheffield,' said Mr. Murdstone. I was relieved to find that it was only Brooks of Sheffield; for, at first, I really thought it was I.   *David Copperfield*, ch. 2

13 'I am a lone lorn creetur',' were Mrs. Gummidge's words, . . . 'and everythink goes contrairy with me.'   *Ib.* ch. 3

14 'I feel it more than other people,' said Mrs. Gummidge.   *Ib.*

15 I'd better go into the house, and die and be a riddance! [*Mrs. Gummidge.*]   *Ib.*

16 She's been thinking of the old 'un! [*Mr. Peggotty, of Mrs. Gummidge.*]   *Ib.*

17 Barkis is willin'.   *Ib.* ch. 5

18 'There was a gentleman here yesterday,' he said— 'a stout gentleman, by the name of Topsawyer . . . he came in here, . . . ordered a glass of this ale— *would* order it—I told him not—drank it, and fell dead. It was too old for him. It oughtn't to be drawn; that's the fact.' [*The Waiter.*]   *Ib.*

19 I live on broken wittles—and I sleep on the coals. [*The Waiter.*]   *Ib.*

20 'When a man says he's willin',' said Mr. Barkis, . . . 'it's as much as to say, that a man's waitin' for a answer.'   *Ib.* ch. 8

21 Experientia does it—as papa used to say. [*Mrs. Micawber.*]   *David Copperfield*, ch. 11

22 I have known him [Micawber] come home to supper with a flood of tears, and a declaration that nothing was now left but a jail; and go to bed making a calculation of the expense of putting bow-windows to the house, 'in case anything turned up,' which was his favourite expression.   *Ib.*

23 I never will desert Mr. Micawber. [*Mrs. Micawber.*]   *Ib.* ch. 12

24 Annual income twenty pounds, annual expenditure nineteen nineteen six, result happiness. Annual income twenty pounds, annual expenditure twenty pounds ought and six, result misery. [*Mr. Micawber.*]   *Ib.*

25 Mr. Dick had been for upwards of ten years endeavouring to keep King Charles the First out of the Memorial; but he had been constantly getting into it, and was there now.   *Ib.* ch. 14

26 I am well aware that I am the 'umblest person going. . . . My mother is likewise a very 'umble person. We live in a numble abode. [*Uriah Heep.*]   *Ib.* ch. 16

27 The mistake was made of putting some of the trouble out of King Charles's head into my head.   *Ib.* ch. 17

28 We are so very 'umble. [*Uriah Heep.*]   *Ib.*

29 'Orses and dorgs is some men's fancy. They're wittles and drink to me—lodging, wife, and children—reading, writing and 'rithmetic—snuff, tobacker, and sleep.   *Ib.* ch. 19

30 I only ask for information. [*Miss Rosa Dartle.*]   *Ib.* ch. 20

31 'It was as true', said Mr. Barkis, '. . . as taxes is. And nothing's truer than them.'   *Ib.* ch. 21

32 What a world of gammon and spinnage it is, though, ain't it! [*Miss Mowcher.*]   *Ib.* ch. 22

33 The whole social system . . . is a system of Prince's nails. [*Miss Mowcher.*]   *Ib.*

34 'Oh, surely! surely!' said Mr. Spenlow. . . . 'I should be happy, myself, to propose two months, . . . but I have a partner. Mr. Jorkins.'   *Ib.* ch. 23

35 Other things are all very well in their way, but give me Blood! [*Mr. Waterbrook.*]   *Ib.* ch. 25

36 I assure you she's the dearest girl. [*Traddles.*]   *Ib.* ch. 27

37 Accidents will occur in the best-regulated families; and in families not regulated by that pervading influence which sanctifies while it enhances the —a—I would say, in short, by the influence of Woman, in the lofty character of Wife, they may be expected with confidence, and must be borne with philosophy. [*Mr. Micawber.*]   *Ib.* ch. 28

38 He told me, only the other day, that it was provided for. That was Mr. Micawber's expression, 'Provided for.' [*Traddles.*]   *Ib.*

39 'People can't die, along the coast,' said Mr. Peggotty, 'except when the tide's pretty nigh out. They can't be born, unless it's pretty nigh in—not properly born, till flood. He's a going out with the tide.'   *Ib.* ch. 30

1 Mrs. Crupp had indignantly assured him that there wasn't room to swing a cat there; but, as Mr. Dick justly observed to me, sitting down on the foot of the bed, nursing his leg, 'You know, Trotwood, I don't want to swing a cat. I never do swing a cat. Therefore, what does that signify to *me!*'
David Copperfield, ch. 35

2 It's only my child-wife. [*Dora.*] *Ib.* ch. 44

3 Circumstances beyond my individual control. [*Mr. Micawber.*] *Ib.* ch. 49

4 I'm Gormed—and I can't say no fairer than that! [*Mr. Peggotty.*] *Ib.* ch. 63

5 He's tough, ma'am, tough, is J. B. Tough, and devilish sly! [*Major Bagstock.*] *Dombey and Son*, ch. 7

6 There was no light nonsense about Miss Blimber. . . . She was dry and sandy with working in the graves of deceased languages. None of your live languages for Miss Blimber. They must be dead—stone dead—and then Miss Blimber dug them up like a Ghoul. *Ib.* ch. 11

7 As to Mr. Feeder, B.A., Doctor Blimber's assistant, he was a kind of human barrel-organ, with a little list of tunes at which he was continually working, over and over again, without any variation. *Ib.*

8 If I could have known Cicero, and been his friend, and talked with him in his retirement at Tusculum (beautiful Tusculum!), I could have died contented. [*Mrs. Blimber.*] *Ib.*

9 'Wal'r, my boy,' replied the Captain, 'in the Proverbs of Solomon you will find the following words, "May we never want a friend in need, nor a bottle to give him!" When found, make a note of.' [*Captain Cuttle.*] *Ib.* ch. 15

10 Train up a fig-tree in the way it should go, and when you are old sit under the shade of it. [*Captain Cuttle.*] *Ib.* ch. 19

11 Cows are my passion. [*Mrs. Skewton.*] *Ib.* ch. 21

12 Mr. Toots devoted himself to the cultivation of those gentle arts which refine and humanize existence, his chief instructor in which was an interesting character called the Game Chicken, who was always to be heard of at the bar of the Black Badger, wore a shaggy white great-coat in the warmest weather, and knocked Mr. Toots about the head three times a week. *Ib.* ch. 22

13 It's of no consequence. [*Mr. Toots.*] *Ib.*

14 The bearings of this observation lays in the application on it. [*Bunsby.*] *Ib.* ch. 23

15 Say, like those wicked Turks, there is no What's-his-name but Thingummy, and What-you-may-call-it is his prophet! [*Mrs. Skewton.*] *Ib.* ch. 27

16 I positively adore Miss Dombey;—I—I am perfectly sore with loving her. [*Mr. Toots.*] *Ib.* ch. 30

17 If you could see my legs when I take my boots off, you'd form some idea of what unrequited affection is. [*Mr. Toots.*] *Ib.* ch. 48

18 Stranger, pause and ask thyself the question, Canst thou do likewise? If not, with a blush retire.
Edwin Drood, ch. 4

19 'Dear me,' said Mr. Grewgious, peeping in, 'it's like looking down the throat of Old Time.' *Ib.* ch. 9

20 'Umps', said Mr. Grewgious. *Ib.* ch. 11

21 Your sister is given to government. [*Joe Gargery.*]
Great Expectations, ch. 7

22 I had cherished a profound conviction that her bringing me up by hand, gave her no right to bring me up by jerks. *Ib.* ch. 8

23 On the Rampage, Pip, and off the Rampage, Pip; such is Life! [*Joe Gargery.*] *Ib.* ch. 15

24 Get hold of portable property. [*Wemmick.*]
Ib. ch. 24

25 You don't object to an aged parent, I hope? [*Wemmick.*] *Ib.* ch. 25

26 'Have you seen anything of London, yet?' [*Herbert.*] 'Why, yes: Sir—but we didn't find that it come up to its likeness in the red bills—it is there drawd too architectooralooral.' [*Joe Gargery.*] *Ib.* ch. 27

27 'Halloa! Here's a church! . . . Let's go in! . . . Here's Miss Skiffins! Let's have a wedding.' [*Wemmick.*]
Ib. ch. 55

28 Now, what I want is, Facts. . . . Facts alone are wanted in life. [*Mr. Gradgrind.*]
Hard Times, bk. i, ch. 1

29 Whatever was required to be done, the Circumlocution Office was beforehand with all the public departments in the art of perceiving—HOW NOT TO DO IT. *Little Dorrit*, bk. i, ch. 10

30 Look here. Upon my soul you mustn't come into the place saying you want to know, you know. [*Barnacle Junior.*] *Ib.*

31 One remark . . . I wish to make, one explanation I wish to offer, when your Mama came and made a scene of it with my Papa and when I was called down into the little breakfast-room where they were looking at one another with your Mama's parasol between them seated on two chairs like mad bulls what was I to do? [*Flora Finching.*]
Ib. ch. 13

32 The Great Fire of London was not the fire in which your Uncle George's workshops was burned down. [*Mr. F.'s Aunt.*] *Ib.*

33 I hate a fool! [*Mr. F.'s Aunt.*] *Ib.*

34 Take a little time—count five-and-twenty, Tattycoram. [*Mr. Meagles.*] *Ib.* ch. 16

35 There's milestones on the Dover Road! [*Mr. F.'s Aunt.*] *Ib.* ch. 23

36 You can't make a head and brains out of a brass knob with nothing in it. You couldn't when your Uncle George was living; much less when he's dead. [*Mr. F.'s Aunt.*] *Ib.*

37 He [Mr. Finching] proposed seven times once in a hackney-coach once in a boat once in a pew once on a donkey at Tunbridge Wells and the rest on his knees. [*Flora Finching.*] *Ib.* ch. 24

38 I revere the memory of Mr. F. as an estimable man and most indulgent husband, only necessary to mention Asparagus and it appeared or to hint at any little delicate thing to drink and it came like magic in a pint bottle it was not ecstasy but it was comfort. [*Flora Finching.*] *Ib.*

39 E please. Double good! [*Mrs. Plornish.*] *Ib.* ch. 25

1 Father is rather vulgar, my dear. The word Papa, besides, gives a pretty form to the lips. Papa, potatoes, poultry, prunes and prism, are all very good words for the lips; especially prunes and prism. [*Mrs. General.*]   *Little Dorrit*, bk. ii, ch. 5

2 Dante—known to that gentleman [Mr. Sparkler] as an eccentric man in the nature of an Old File, who used to put leaves round his head, and sit upon a stool for some unaccountable purpose, outside the cathedral at Florence.   *Ib. ch.* 6

3 Once a gentleman, and always a gentleman. [*Rigaud.*]   *Ib. ch.* 28

4 The Lord No Zoo. [*Toby Chuzzlewit.*]   *Martin Chuzzlewit*, ch. 1

5 'The name of those fabulous animals (pagan, I regret to say) who used to sing in the water, has quite escaped me.' Mr. George Chuzzlewit suggested 'Swans.' 'No,' said Mr. Pecksniff. 'Not swans. Very like swans, too. Thank you.' The nephew . . . propounded 'Oysters.' 'No,' said Mr. Pecksniff, . . . 'nor oysters. But by no means unlike oysters; a very excellent idea; thank you, my dear sir, very much. Wait. Sirens! Dear me! sirens, of course.'   *Ib. ch.* 4

6 Any man may be in good spirits and good temper when he's well dressed. There an't much credit in that. [*Mark Tapley.*]   *Ib. ch.* 5

7 Some credit in being jolly. [*Mark Tapley.*]   *Ib.*

8 A highly geological home-made cake.   *Ib.*

9 'Let us be merry.' Here he took a captain's biscuit. [*Mr. Pecksniff.*]   *Ib.*

10 With affection beaming in one eye, and calculation shining out of the other. [*Mrs. Todgers.*]   *Ib. ch.* 8

11 Oh, Todgers' could do it when it chose! Mind that.   *Ib. ch.* 9

12 Charity and Mercy. Not unholy names, I hope? [*Mr. Pecksniff.*]   *Ib.*

13 'Do not repine, my friends,' said Mr. Pecksniff, tenderly. 'Do not weep for me. It is chronic.'   *Ib.*

14 Let us be moral. Let us contemplate existence. [*Mr. Pecksniff.*]   *Ib.*

15 Here's the rule for bargains: 'Do other men, for they would do you.' That's the true business precept. [*Jonas Chuzzlewit.*]   *Ib. ch.* 11

16 'Mrs. Harris,' I says, 'leave the bottle on the chimley-piece, and don't ask me to take none, but let me put my lips to it when I am so disposed.' [*Mrs. Gamp.*]   *Ib. ch.* 19

17 Some people . . . may be Rooshans, and others may be Prooshans; they are born so, and will please themselves. Them which is of other naturs thinks different. [*Mrs. Gamp.*]   *Ib.*

18 Therefore I *do* require it, which I makes confession, to be brought reg'lar and draw'd mild. [*Mrs. Gamp.*]   *Ib. ch.* 25

19 'She's the sort of woman now,' said Mould, . . . 'one would almost feel disposed to bury for nothing: and do it neatly, too!'   *Ib.*

20 He'd make a lovely corpse. [*Mrs. Gamp.*]   *Ib.*

21 All the wickedness of the world is print to him. [*Mrs. Gamp.*]   *Ib. ch.* 26

22 'Sairey,' says Mrs. Harris, 'sech is life. Vich likeways is the hend of all things!' [*Mrs. Gamp.*]   *Martin Chuzzlewit*, ch. 29

23 Our backs is easy ris. We must be cracked-up, or they rises, and we snarls. . . . You'd better crack up, you had! [*Chollop.*]   *Ib. ch.* 33

24 Our fellow-countryman is a model of a man, quite fresh from Natur's mould! . . . Rough he may be. So air our Barrs. Wild he may be. So air our Buffalers. [*Pogram.*]   *Ib. ch.* 34

25 'To be presented to a Pogram,' said Miss Codger, 'by a Hominy, indeed, a thrilling moment is it in its impressiveness on what we call our feelings.'   *Ib.*

26 'Mind and matter,' said the lady in the wig, 'glide swift into the vortex of immensity. Howls the sublime, and softly sleeps the calm Ideal, in the whispering chambers of Imagination.'   *Ib.*

27 'The Ankworks package,' . . . 'I wish it was in Jonadge's belly, I do,' cried Mrs. Gamp; appearing to confound the prophet with the whale in this miraculous aspiration.   *Ib. ch.* 40

28 Oh Sairey, Sairey, little do we know wot lays afore us! [*Mrs. Gamp.*]   *Ib.*

29 I know'd she wouldn't have a cowcumber! [*Betsey Prig.*]   *Ib. ch.* 49

30 'Who deniges of it?' Mrs. Gamp enquired.   *Ib.*

31 Ever since afore her First, which Mr. Harris who was dreadful timid went and stopped his ears in a empty dog-kennel, and never took his hands away or come out once till he was showed the baby, wen bein' took with fits, the doctor collared him and laid him on his back upon the airy stones, and she was told to ease her mind, his owls was organs. [*Mrs. Gamp.*]   *Ib.*

32 No, Betsey! Drink fair, wotever you do! [*Mrs. Gamp.*]   *Ib.*

33 'Bother Mrs. Harris!' said Betsey Prig. . . . 'I don't believe there's no sich a person!'   *Ib.*

34 The words she spoke of Mrs. Harris, lambs could not forgive . . . nor worms forget. [*Mrs. Gamp.*] *Ib.*

35 Which fiddle-strings is weakness to expredge my nerves this night! [*Mrs. Gamp.*]   *Ib. ch.* 51

36 Farewell! Be the proud bride of a ducal coronet, and forget me! . . . Unalterably, never yours, Augustus. [*Augustus Moddle.*]   *Ib. ch.* 54

37 United Metropolitan Improved Hot Muffin and Crumpet Baking and Punctual Delivery Company.   *Nicholas Nickleby*, ch. 2

38 EDUCATION.—At Mr. Wackford Squeers's Academy, Dotheboys Hall, at the delightful village of Dotheboys, near Greta Bridge in Yorkshire, Youth are boarded, clothed, booked, furnished with pocket-money, provided with all necessaries, instructed in all languages living and dead, mathematics, orthography, geometry, astronomy, trigonometry, the use of the globes, algebra, single stick (if required), writing, arithmetic, fortification, and every other branch of classical literature. Terms, twenty guineas per annum. No extras, no vacations, and diet unparalleled.   *Ib. ch.* 3

1 He had but one eye, and the popular prejudice runs in favour of two. [*Mr. Squeers.*]
Nicholas Nickleby, ch. 4

2 Serve it right for being so dear. [*Mr. Squeers.*]
Ib. ch. 5

3 Subdue your appetites, my dears, and you've conquered human natur. [*Mr. Squeers.*] *Ib.*

4 Here's richness! [*Mr. Squeers.*] *Ib.*

5 C-l-e-a-n, clean, verb active, to make bright, to scour. W-i-n, win, d-e-r, der, winder, a casement. When the boy knows this out of the book, he goes and does it. [*Mr. Squeers.*] *Ib.* ch. 8

6 As she frequently remarked when she made any such mistake, it would be all the same a hundred years hence. [*Mrs. Squeers.*] *Ib.* ch. 9

7 There are only two styles of portrait painting; the serious and the smirk. [*Miss La Creevy.*]
Ib. ch. 10

8 Oh! they're too beautiful to live, much too beautiful! [*Mrs. Kenwigs.*] *Ib.* ch. 14

9 Sir, My pa requests me to write to you, the doctors considering it doubtful whether he will ever recuvver the use of his legs which prevents his holding a pen. [*Fanny Squeers.*] *Ib.* ch. 15

10 One mask of brooses both blue and green. [*Fanny Squeers.*] *Ib.*

11 I am screaming out loud all the time I write and so is my brother which takes off my attention rather and I hope will excuse mistakes. [*Fanny Squeers.*]
Ib.

12 I pity his ignorance and despise him. [*Fanny Squeers.*]
Ib.

13 This is all very well, Mr. Nickleby, and very proper, so far as it goes—so far as it goes, but it doesn't go far enough. [*Mr. Gregsbury.*] *Ib.* ch. 16

14 We've got a private master comes to teach us at home, but we ain't proud, because ma says it's sinful. [*Mrs. Kenwigs.*] *Ib.*

15 'What's the water in French, sir?' '*L'eau*,' replied Nicholas. 'Ah!' said Mr. Lillywick, shaking his head mournfully. 'I thought as much. Lo, eh? I don't think anything of that language—nothing at all.' *Ib.*

16 'It's very easy to talk,' said Mrs. Mantalini.
'Not so easy when one is eating a demnition egg,' replied Mr. Mantalini; 'for the yolk runs down the waistcoat, and yolk of egg does not match any waistcoat but a yellow waistcoat, demmit.'
Ib. ch. 17

17 Language was not powerful enough to describe the infant phenomenon. *Ib.* ch. 23

18 'I hope you have preserved the unities, sir?' said Mr. Curdle. . . .
'The unities, sir, . . . are a completeness—a kind of a universal dovetailedness with regard to place and time.' *Ib.* ch. 24

19 She's the only sylph I ever saw, who could stand upon one leg, and play the tambourine on her other knee, like a sylph. [*Mr. Crummles.*] *Ib.* ch. 25

20 The two countesses had no outlines at all, and the dowager's was a demd outline. [*Mr. Mantalini.*]
Ib. ch. 34

21 I am a demd villain! I will fill my pockets with change for a sovereign in half-pence and drown myself in the Thames . . . I will become a demd, damp, moist, unpleasant body! [*Mr. Mantalini.*]
Nicholas Nickleby, ch. 34

22 In the absence of the planet Venus, who has gone on business to the Horse Guards. [*The Gentleman in the Small-clothes.*] *Ib.* ch. 41

23 Bring in the bottled lightning, a clean tumbler, and a corkscrew. [*The Gentleman in the Small-clothes.*]
Ib. ch. 49

24 All is gas and gaiters. [*The Gentleman in the Small-clothes.*] *Ib.*

25 My life is one demd horrid grind! [*Mr. Mantalini.*]
Ib. ch. 64

26 He has gone to the demnition bow-wows. [*Mr. Mantalini.*] *Ib.*

27 Is the old min agreeable? [*Dick Swiveller.*]
The Old Curiosity Shop, ch. 2

28 What is the odds so long as the fire of soul is kindled at the taper of conwiviality, and the wing of friendship never moults a feather! [*Dick Swiveller.*] *Ib.*

29 Fan the sinking flame of hilarity with the wing of friendship; and pass the rosy wine. [*Dick Swiveller.*] *Ib.* ch. 7

30 Codlin's the friend, not Short. [*Codlin.*] *Ib.* ch. 19

31 If I know'd a donkey wot wouldn't go
To see Mrs. Jarley's waxwork show,
Do you think I'd acknowledge him,
   Oh no no!   *Ib.* ch. 27

32 I believe, Sir, that you desire to look at these apartments. They are very charming apartments, Sir. They command an uninterrupted view of—of over the way, and they are within one minute's walk of—of the corner of the street. [*Dick Swiveller.*]
Ib. ch. 34

33 I never nursed a dear Gazelle, to glad me with its soft black eye, but when it came to know me well, and love me, it was sure to marry a market-gardener. [*Dick Swiveller.*] *Ib.* ch. 56

34 'Did you ever taste beer?' 'I had a sip of it once,' said the small servant. 'Here's a state of things!' cried Mr. Swiveller. . . . 'She *never* tasted it—it can't be tasted in a sip!' *Ib.* ch. 57

35 It was a maxim with Foxey—our revered father, gentlemen—'Always suspect everybody.' [*Sampson Brass.*] *Ib.* ch. 66

36 Oliver Twist has asked for more! [*Bumble.*]
Oliver Twist, ch. 2

37 Known by the *sobriquet* of 'The artful Dodger.'
Ib. ch. 8

38 'Hard,' replied the Dodger. 'As nails,' added Charley Bates. *Ib.* ch. 9

39 There is a passion for hunting something deeply implanted in the human breast. *Ib.* ch. 10

40 I'll eat my head. [*Mr. Grimwig.*] *Ib.* ch. 14

41 I only know two sorts of boys. Mealy boys, and beef-faced boys. [*Mr. Grimwig.*] *Ib.*

42 Oh, Mrs. Corney, what a prospect this opens! What a opportunity for a jining of hearts and housekeepings! [*Bumble.*] *Ib.* ch. 27

1 'If the law supposes that,' said Mr. Bumble . . . 'the law is a ass—a idiot.' *Oliver Twist,* ch. 51

2 A literary man—*with* a wooden leg. [*Mr. Boffin on Silas Wegg.*] *Our Mutual Friend,* bk. i, ch. 5

3 Professionally he declines and falls, and as a friend he drops into poetry. [*Mr. Boffin on Silas Wegg.*] *Ib.*

4 Why then we should drop into poetry. [*Boffin.*] *Ib.*

5 Decline-and-Fall-Off-The-Rooshan-Empire. [*Mr. Boffin.*] *Ib.*

6 'Mrs. Boffin, Wegg,' said Boffin, 'is a highflyer at Fashion.' *Ib.*

7 Meaty jelly, too, especially when a little salt, which is the case when there's ham, is mellering to the organ. [*Silas Wegg.*] *Ib.*

8 'It is Rooshan; ain't it, Wegg?'
'No, sir. Roman. Roman.'
'What's the difference, Wegg?'
'The difference, sir?—There you place me in a difficulty, Mr. Boffin. Suffice it to observe, that the difference is best postponed to some other occasion when Mrs. Boffin does not honour us with her company.' *Ib.*

9 I didn't think this morning there was half so many Scarers in Print. [*Boffin.*] *Ib.*

10 Mr. Podsnap settled that whatever he put behind him he put out of existence. . . . Mr. Podsnap had even acquired a peculiar flourish of his right arm in often clearing the world of its most difficult problems, by sweeping them behind him. *Ib.* ch. 11

11 The question [with Mr. Podsnap] about everything was, would it bring a blush into the cheek of the young person? *Ib.*

12 The gay, the gay and festive scene,
The halls, the halls of dazzling light. [*Mrs. Boffin.*] *Ib.* ch. 15

13 Oh! *I* know their tricks and their manners. [*Fanny Cleaver.*] *Ib.* bk. ii, ch. 1

14 I think . . . that it is the best club in London. [*Mr. Twemlow, on the House of Commons.*] *Ib.* ch. 3

15 I don't care whether I am a Minx, or a Sphinx. [*Lavvy.*] *Ib.* ch. 8

16 A slap-up gal in a bang-up chariot. *Ib.*

17 Queer Street is full of lodgers just at present. [*Fledgeby.*] *Ib.* bk. iii, ch. 1

18 O Mrs. Higden, Mrs. Higden, you was a woman and a mother, and a mangler in a million million. [*Sloppy.*] *Ib.* ch. 9

19 He'd be sharper than a serpent's tooth, if he wasn't as dull as ditch water. [*Fanny Cleaver.*] *Ib.* ch. 10

20 T'other governor. [*Mr. Riderhood.*] *Ib.* bk. iv, ch. 1

21 The dodgerest of the dodgers. [*Mr. Fledgeby.*] *Ib.* ch. 8

22 The Golden Dustman. *Ib.* ch. 11

23 He had used the word in its Pickwickian sense. . . . He had merely considered him a humbug in a Pickwickian point of view. [*Mr. Blotton.*] *Pickwick Papers,* ch. 1

24 Heads, heads . . .! . . . five children—mother—tall lady, eating sandwiches—forgot the arch—crash—knock—children look round—mother's head off—sandwich in her hand—no mouth to put it in—head of a family off—shocking, shocking! [*Jingle.*] *Pickwick Papers,* ch. 2

25 'I am ruminating,' said Mr. Pickwick, 'on the strange mutability of human affairs.'
'Ah! I see—in at the palace door one day, out at the window the next. Philosopher, sir?'
'An observer of human nature, sir,' said Mr. Pickwick. *Ib.*

26 Half-a-crown in the bill, if you look at the waiter.—Charge you more if you dine at a friend's than they would if you dined in the coffee-room. [*Jingle.*] *Ib.*

27 Not presume to dictate, but broiled fowl and mushrooms—capital thing! [*Jingle.*] *Ib.*

28 Kent, sir—everybody knows Kent—apples, cherries, hops, and women. [*Jingle.*] *Ib.*

29 'It wasn't the wine,' murmured Mr. Snodgrass, in a broken voice. 'It was the salmon.' *Ib.* ch. 8

30 I wants to make your flesh creep. [*The Fat Boy.*] *Ib.*

31 'It's always best on these occasions to do what the mob do.' 'But suppose there are two mobs?' suggested Mr. Snodgrass. 'Shout with the largest,' replied Mr. Pickwick. *Ib.* ch. 13

32 'Can I unmoved see thee dying
On a log,
Expiring frog!' [*Mrs. Leo Hunter.*] *Ib.* ch. 15

33 'Sir,' said Mr. Tupman, 'you're a fellow.' 'Sir,' said Mr. Pickwick, 'you're another!' *Ib.*

34 Tongue; well that's a wery good thing when it an't a woman's. [*Mr. Weller.*] *Ib.* ch. 19

35 Mr. Weller's knowledge of London was extensive and peculiar. *Ib.* ch. 20

36 Be wery careful o' vidders all your life. [*Mr. Weller.*] *Ib.*

37 The wictim o' connubiality, as Blue Beard's domestic chaplain said, with a tear of pity, ven he buried him. [*Mr. Weller.*] *Ib.*

38 'It's a wery remarkable circumstance, sir,' said Sam, 'that poverty and oysters always seem to go together.' *Ib.* ch. 22

39 It's over, and can't be helped, and that's one consolation, as they always says in Turkey, ven they cuts the wrong man's head off. [*Sam Weller.*] *Ib.* ch. 23

40 Dumb as a drum vith a hole in it, sir. [*Sam Weller.*] *Ib.* ch. 25

41 Wery glad to see you, indeed, and hope our acquaintance may be a long 'un, as the gen'l'm'n said to the fi' pun' note. [*Sam Weller.*] *Ib.*

42 Wen you're a married man, Samivel, you'll understand a good many things as you don't understand now; but vether it's worth while goin' through so much to learn so little, as the charity-boy said ven he got to the end of the alphabet, is a matter o' taste. [*Mr. Weller.*] *Ib.* ch. 27

43 Our noble society for providing the infant negroes in the West Indies with flannel waistcoats and moral pocket handkerchiefs. *Ib.* ch. 27

1 'Eccentricities of genius, Sam,' said Mr. Pickwick.
Pickwick Papers, ch. 30

2 Keep yourself *to* yourself. [*Mr. Raddle.*]   *Ib.* ch. 32

3 Pursuit of knowledge under difficulties, Sammy?
[*Mr. Weller.*]   *Ib.* ch. 33

4 A double glass o' the inwariable. [*Mr. Weller.*] *Ib.*

5 Poetry's unnat'ral; no man ever talked poetry 'cept
a beadle on boxin' day, or Warren's blackin' or
Rowland's oil, or some o' them low fellows. [*Mr.
Weller.*]   *Ib.*

6 Wot's the good o' callin' a young 'ooman a Wenus or
a angel, Sammy? [*Mr. Weller.*]   *Ib.*

7 'That's rather a sudden pull up, ain't it, Sammy?'
inquired Mr. Weller.
'Not a bit on it,' said Sam; 'she'll vish there wos more,
and that's the great art o' letter writin'.'   *Ib.*

8 If your governor don't prove a alleybi, he'll be what
the Italians call reg'larly flummoxed. [*Mr. Weller.*]
Ib.

9 She's a swellin' wisibly before my wery eyes. [*Mr.
Weller.*]   *Ib.*

10 It's my opinion, sir, that this meeting is drunk, sir!
[*Mr. Stiggins.*]   *Ib.*

11 A Being, erect upon two legs, and bearing all the outward semblance of a man, and not of a monster.
[*Buzfuz.*]   *Ib.* ch. 34

12 Chops and Tomata sauce. Yours, Pickwick.   *Ib.*

13 'Do you spell it with a "V" or a "W"?' inquired the
judge.
'That depends upon the taste and fancy of the speller,
my Lord,' replied Sam.   *Ib.*

14 Put it down a we, my Lord, put it down a we. [*Mr.
Weller.*]   *Ib.*

15 'Little to do, and plenty to get, I suppose?' said
Sergeant Buzfuz, with jocularity.
'Oh, quite enough to get, sir, as the soldier said ven
they ordered him three hundred and fifty lashes,'
replied Sam.
'You must not tell us what the soldier, or any other
man, said, sir,' interposed the judge; 'it's not
evidence.'   *Ib.*

16 'Yes, I have a pair of eyes,' replied Sam, 'and that's
just it. If they wos a pair o' patent double million
magnifyin' gas microscopes of hextra power, p'raps
I might be able to see through a flight o' stairs and
a deal door; but bein' only eyes, you see my wision's
limited.'   *Ib.*

17 Oh Sammy, Sammy, vy worn't there a alleybi! [*Mr.
Weller.*]   *Ib.*

18 Miss Bolo rose from the table considerably agitated,
and went straight home, in a flood of tears and a
Sedan chair.   *Ib.* ch. 35

19 A friendly swarry, consisting of a boiled leg of mutton
with the usual trimmings.   *Ib.* ch. 37

20 'You disliked the killibeate taste, perhaps?'
'I don't know much about that 'ere,' said Sam. 'I
thought they'd a wery strong flavour o' warm flat-
irons.'
'That *is* the killibeate, Mr. Weller,' observed Mr.
John Smauker, contemptuously.   *Ib.*

21 'That 'ere young lady,' replied Sam. 'She knows wot's
wot, she does.'   *Pickwick Papers*, ch. 37

22 *We* know, Mr. Weller—we, who are men of the world
—that a good uniform must work its way with the
women, sooner or later.   *Ib.*

23 You're a amiably-disposed young man, sir, I don't
think. [*Sam Weller.*]   *Ib.* ch. 38

24 'And a bird-cage, sir,' says Sam. 'Veels vithin veels,
a prison in a prison.'   *Ib.* ch. 40

25 'It would make anyone go to sleep, that bedstead
would, whether they wanted to or not.' [*Mr.
Roker.*]
'I should think,' said Sam, . . . 'poppies was nothing
to it.'   *Ib.* ch. 41

26 *They* don't mind it; it's a regular holiday to them—
all porter and skittles. [*Sam Weller.*]   *Ib.*

27 The have-his-carcase, next to the perpetual motion, is
vun of the blessedest things as wos ever made.
[*Sam Weller.*]   *Ib.* ch. 43

28 Anythin' for a quiet life, as the man said wen he took
the sitivation at the lighthouse. [*Sam Weller.*] *Ib.*

29 Wich puts me in mind o' the man as killed hisself on
principle, wich o' course you've heerd on, sir.
[*Sam Weller.*]   *Ib.* ch. 44

30 Which is your partickler wanity? Vich wanity do you
like the flavour on best, sir? [*Sam Weller.*]
Ib. ch. 45

31 You've got the key of the street, my friend. [*Lowten.*]
Ib. ch. 47

32 'Never . . . see . . . a dead postboy, did you?' inquired
Sam . . . 'No,' rejoined Bob, 'I never did.' 'No!'
rejoined Sam triumphantly. 'Nor never vill; and
there's another thing that no man never see, and
that's a dead donkey.'   *Ib.* ch. 51

33 'Vell, gov'ner, ve must all come to it, one day or
another.'
'So we must, Sammy,' said Mr. Weller the elder.
'There's a Providence in it all,' said Sam.
'O' course there is,' replied his father with a nod of
grave approval. 'Wot 'ud become of the undertakers vithout it, Sammy?'   *Ib.* ch. 52

34 ''Cos a coachman's a privileged indiwidual,' replied
Mr. Weller, looking fixedly at his son. ''Cos a
coachman may do vithout suspicion wot other men
may not; 'cos a coachman may be on the wery
amicablest terms with eighty mile o' females, and
yet nobody think that he ever means to marry any
vun among them.'   *Ib.*

35 I pass my whole life, miss, in turning an immense
pecuniary Mangle. [*Mr. Lorry.*]
A Tale of Two Cities, bk. 1, ch. 4

36 If you must go flopping yourself down, flop in favour
of your husband and child, and not in opposition
to 'em. [*Jerry Cruncher.*]   *Ib.* bk. ii, ch. 1

37 'I tell thee,' said madame—'that although it is a long
time on the road, it is on the road and coming. I
tell thee it never retreats, and never stops.' [*Mme
Defarge.*]

38 'It is possible—that it may not come, during our
lives. . . . We shall not see the triumph.' [*Defarge.*]
'We shall have helped it,' returned madame.
Ib. ch. 16

1 There might be medical doctors . . . a cocking their medical eyes. [*Jerry Cruncher.*]
A Tale of Two Cities, bk. iii, ch. 9

2 It is a far, far better thing that I do, than I have ever done; it is a far, far better rest that I go to, than I have ever known. [*Sidney Carton.*] *Ib.* ch. 15

EMILY DICKINSON
1830–1886

3 Parting is all we know of heaven,
And all we need of hell. *Poems. Parting*

JOHN DICKINSON
1732–1808

4 Our cause is just. Our union is perfect.
Declaration on Taking Up Arms in 1775

5 Then join in hand brave Americans all,
By uniting we stand, by dividing we fall.
The Liberty Song. Memoirs of the Historical Soc. of Pennsylvania, vol. xiv

DENIS DIDEROT
1713–1784

6 L'esprit de l'escalier.

Staircase wit.
An untranslatable phrase, the meaning of which is that one only thinks on one's way downstairs of the smart retort one might have made in the drawing-room. Paradoxe sur le Comédien

WENTWORTH DILLON, EARL OF ROSCOMMON
1633?–1685

7 But words once spoke can never be recall'd.
Art of Poetry, l. 438

8 Choose an author as you choose a friend.
Essay on Translated Verse, l. 96

9 Immodest words admit of no defence,
For want of decency is want of sense. *Ib.* l. 113

10 The multitude is always in the wrong. *Ib.* l. 183

DIOGENES
fl. c. 380 B.C.

11 "μικρόν", εἶπεν, "ἀπὸ τοῦ ἡλίου μετάστηθι."

Alexander . . . asked him if he lacked anything. 'Yea,' said he, 'that I do: that you stand out of my sun a little.'
Plutarch, *Life of Alexander*, 14 (*North's translation*)

DIONYSIUS OF HALICARNASSUS
c. 40–8 B.C.

12 History is philosophy teaching by examples.
Antiquities of Rome

BENJAMIN DISRAELI, EARL OF BEACONSFIELD
1804–1881

13 Though I sit down now, the time will come when you will hear me.
Maiden Speech, 7 Dec. 1837. Meynell, *Disraeli*, i. 43

14 The Continent will not suffer England to be the workshop of the world.
Speech, House of Commons, 15 Mar. 1838

15 The noble Lord [Lord Stanley] is the Rupert of Parliamentary discussion. *Ib. 24 Apr. 1844*

16 The right hon. Gentleman [Sir Robert Peel] caught the Whigs bathing, and walked away with their clothes. *Ib. 28 Feb. 1845*

17 Protection is not a principle, but an expedient.
Ib. 17 Mar. 1845

18 A Conservative Government is an organized hypocrisy. *Ib.*

19 He traces the steam-engine always back to the tea-kettle. *Ib. 11 Apr. 1845*

20 A precedent embalms a principle. *Ib. 22 Feb. 1848*

21 Justice is truth in action. *Ib. 11 Feb. 1851*

22 I read this morning an awful, though monotonous, manifesto in the great organ of public opinion, which always makes me tremble: Olympian bolts; and yet I could not help fancying amid their rumbling terrors I heard the plaintive treble of the Treasury Bench. *Ib. 13 Feb. 1851*

23 England does not love coalitions. *Ib. 16 Dec. 1852*

24 Finality is not the language of politics.
Ib. 28 Feb. 1859

25 This shows how much easier it is to be critical than to be correct. *Ib. 24 Jan. 1860*

26 The Church of England is not a mere depositary of doctrine. *Ib. 27 Feb. 1861*

27 To put an end to these bloated armaments.
Ib. 8 May 1862

28 He seems to think that posterity is a pack-horse, always ready to be loaded. *Ib. 3 June 1862*

29 Colonies do not cease to be colonies because they are independent. *Ib. 5 Feb. 1863*

30 You are not going, I hope, to leave the destinies of the British Empire to prigs and pedants. *Ib.*

31 Never take anything for granted.
Ib. at Salthill, 5 Oct. 1864

32 I hold that the characteristic of the present age is craving credulity.
Ib. at Meeting of Society for Increasing Endowments of Small Livings in the Diocese of Oxford, 25 Nov. 1864

33 Man, my Lord [Bishop Wilberforce], is a being born to believe. *Ib.*

34 Party is organized opinion. *Ib.*

35 Is man an ape or an angel? Now I am on the side of the angels. *Ib.*

36 Assassination has never changed the history of the world. *Ib. House of Commons, 1 May 1865*

37 Change is inevitable. In a progressive country change is constant. *Ib. Edinburgh, 29 Oct. 1867*

38 I had to prepare the mind of the country, and . . . to educate our party. *Ib.*

39 We have legalized confiscation, consecrated sacrilege, and condoned high treason.
Ib. House of Commons, 27 Feb. 1871

1 I believe that without party Parliamentary government is impossible. *Speech, Manchester, 3 Apr. 1872*

2 As I sat opposite the Treasury Bench the ministers reminded me of one of those marine landscapes not very unusual on the coasts of South America. You behold a range of exhausted volcanoes. *Ib.*

3 Increased means and increased leisure are the two civilizers of man. *Ib.*

4 A University should be a place of light, of liberty, and of learning. *Ib. House of Commons, 11 Mar. 1873*

5 An author who speaks about his own books is almost as bad as a mother who talks about her own children. *Ib. at Banquet given by Glasgow to Lord Rector, 19 Nov. 1873*

6 King Louis Philippe once said to me that he attributed the great success of the British nation in political life to their talking politics after dinner. *Ib.*

7 Upon the education of the people of this country the fate of this country depends. *Ib. House of Commons, 15 June 1874*

8 He is a great master of gibes and flouts and jeers. *Referring to his colleague, the Marquis of Salisbury. Ib. 5 Aug. 1874*

9 Cosmopolitan critics, men who are the friends of every country save their own. *Ib. Guildhall, 9 Nov. 1877*

10 Lord Salisbury and myself have brought you back peace—but a peace I hope with honour. *Ib. House of Commons, 16 July 1878*

11 A series of congratulatory regrets. [Lord Harrington's Resolution on the Berlin Treaty.] *Ib. at Banquet in Riding School, Knightsbridge, 27 July 1878*

12 A sophistical rhetorician, inebriated with the exuberance of his own verbosity. [Gladstone.] *Ib.*

13 The hare-brained chatter of irresponsible frivolity. *Ib. Guildhall, London, 9 Nov. 1878*

14 One of the greatest of Romans, when asked what were his politics, replied, *Imperium et Libertas*. That would not make a bad programme for a British Ministry. *Ib. Mansion House, London, 10 Nov. 1879*

15 The key of India is in London. *Ib. House of Lords, 5 Mar. 1881*

16 Damn your principles! Stick to your party. *Attr. Remark to Bulwer Lytton* (Latham, *Famous Sayings*)

17 Protection is not only dead, but damned. (*c. 1850*) Monypenny and Buckle, *Life of Disraeli*, iii. 241

18 Pray remember, Mr. Dean, no dogma, no Dean. *Ib. iv. 368*

19 There is no reason to doubt the story which represents him as using more than once, in conversation with Her Majesty on literary subjects, the words: 'We authors, Ma'am.' *Ib. v. 49*

20 'I am dead: dead, but in the Elysian fields,' was Benjamin's reply to an acquaintance among the peers, who, when welcoming him to the Lords, expressed a fear lest he should miss the excitement of the Commons. *Ib. 522*

21 When I want to read a novel I write one. Monypenny and Buckle, *Life of Disraeli*, vi. 636

22 Everyone likes flattery; and when you come to Royalty you should lay it on with a trowel. *Remark to Matthew Arnold.* G. W. E. Russell, *Collections and Recollections*, ch. 23.

23 She is an excellent creature, but she never can remember which came first, the Greeks or the Romans. [Of his wife.] *Ib. ch. 1*

24 Your Majesty is the head of the literary profession. *Remark to Queen Victoria. Ib. ch. 23*

25 Never complain and never explain. *J. Morley, Life of Gladstone, i. 122*

26 Between ourselves, I could floor them all. This *entre nous*: I was never more confident of anything than that I could carry everything before me in that House. The time will come. *Letters, 7 Feb. 1833*

27 In the 'Town' yesterday, I am told 'some one asked Disraeli, in offering himself for Marylebone, on what he intended *to stand*. "On my head," was the reply.' *Ib. 8 Apr. 1833*

28 There can be no economy where there is no efficiency. *Ib. To Constituents, 3 Oct. 1868*

29 Tadpole and Taper were great friends. Neither of them ever despaired of the Commonwealth. *Coningsby, bk. i, ch. 1*

30 No Government can be long secure without a formidable Opposition. *Ib. bk. ii, ch. 1*

31 . . . the Arch-Mediocrity who presided, rather than ruled, over this Cabinet of Mediocrities. *Ib.*

32 Conservatism discards Prescription, shrinks from Principle, disavows Progress; having rejected all respect for antiquity, it offers no redress for the present, and makes no preparation for the future. *Ib. ch. 5*

33 'A sound Conservative government,' said Taper, musingly. 'I understand: Tory men and Whig measures.' *Ib. ch. 6*

34 Adventures are to the adventurous. *Ib. bk. iii, ch. 1*

35 The still hissing bacon and the eggs that looked like tufts of primroses. *Ib.*

36 Almost everything that is great has been done by youth. *Ib.*

37 Youth is a blunder; Manhood a struggle; Old Age a regret. *Ib.*

38 It seems to me a barren thing this Conservatism—an unhappy cross-breed, the mule of politics that engenders nothing. *Ib. ch. 5*

39 I have been ever of opinion that revolutions are not to be evaded. *Ib. bk. iv, ch. 11*

40 The depositary of power is always unpopular. *Ib.*

41 Where can we find faith in a nation of sectaries? *Ib. ch. 13*

42 Man is only truly great when he acts from the passions. *Ib.*

43 I grew intoxicated with my own eloquence. *Contarini Fleming, pt. i, ch. 7*

44 Read no history: nothing but biography, for that is life without theory. *Ib. ch. 23*

1 The practice of politics in the East may be defined by one word—dissimulation.
Contarini Fleming, pt. v, ch. 10

2 He flits across the stage a transient and embarrassed phantom. *Endymion*, bk. i, ch. 3

3 His Christianity was muscular. *Ib.* ch. 14

4 The Athanasian Creed is the most splendid ecclesiastical lyric ever poured forth by the genius of man.
Ib. ch. 54

5 'As for that,' said Waldershare, 'sensible men are all of the same religion.' 'And pray, what is that?' inquired the prince. 'Sensible men never tell.'
Ib. ch. 81

6 The sweet simplicity of the three per cents.
Ib. ch. 91

7 I believe they went out, like all good things, with the Stuarts. *Ib.* ch. 99

8 What we anticipate seldom occurs; what we least expect generally happens. *Ib.* bk. ii, ch. 4

9 Time is the great physician. *Ib.* bk. vi, ch. 9

10 They [the Furies] mean well; their feelings are strong, but their hearts are in the right place.
The Infernal Marriage, pt. i, 1

11 The blue ribbon of the turf. [The Derby.]
Life of Lord George Bentinck, ch. 26

12 Every day when he looked into the glass, and gave the last touch to his consummate toilette, he offered his grateful thanks to Providence that his family was not unworthy of him. *Lothair*, ch. 1

13 'I could have brought you some primroses, but I do not like to mix violets with anything.'
'They say primroses make a capital salad,' said Lord St. Jerome. *Ib.* ch. 13

14 A Protestant, if he wants aid or advice on any matter, can only go to his solicitor. *Ib.* ch. 27

15 London; a nation, not a city. *Ib.*

16 The gondola of London. [A hansom.] *Ib.*

17 When a man fell into his anecdotage it was a sign for him to retire from the world. *Ib.* ch. 28

18 He was not an intellectual Crœsus, but his pockets were full of sixpences. *Ib.*

19 What I admire in the order to which you belong is that they do live in the air; that they excel in athletic sports; that they can only speak one language; and that they never read. This is not a complete education, but it is the highest education since the Greek. *Ib.* ch. 29

20 Every woman should marry—and no man.
Ib. ch. 30

21 You know who the critics are? The men who have failed in literature and art. *Ib.* ch. 35

22 'My idea of an agreeable person,' said Hugo Bohun, 'is a person who agrees with me.' *Ib.* ch. 41

23 St. Aldegonde had a taste for marriages and public executions. *Ib.* ch. 88

24 'I rather like bad wine,' said Mr. Mountchesney; 'one gets so bored with good wine.'
Sybil, bk. i, ch. 1

25 The Egremonts had never said anything that was remembered, or done anything that could be recalled. *Ib.* ch. 3

26 To do nothing and get something, formed a boy's ideal of a manly career. *Sybil*, bk. i, ch. 5

27 Little things affect little minds. *Ib.* bk. iii, ch. 2

28 Mr. Kremlin himself was distinguished for ignorance, for he had only one idea,—and that was wrong.
Ib. bk. iv, ch. 5

29 I was told that the Privileged and the People formed Two Nations. *Ib.* ch. 8

30 A public man of light and leading in the country.
Ib. bk. v, ch. 1

31 The Youth of a Nation are the trustees of Posterity.
Ib. bk. vi, ch. 13

32 Guanoed her mind by reading French novels.
Tancred, bk. ii, ch. 9

33 That fatal drollery called a representative government.
Ib. ch. 13

34 A majority is always the best repartee. *Ib.* ch. 14

35 All is race; there is no other truth. *Ib.*

36 The East is a career. *Ib.*

37 London is a modern Babylon. *Ib.* bk. v, ch. 5

38 The microcosm of a public school.
Vivian Grey, bk. i, ch. 2

39 I hate definitions. *Ib.* bk. ii, ch. 6

40 Information upon points of practical politics.
Ib. ch. 15

41 Experience is the child of Thought, and Thought is the child of Action. We cannot learn men from books. *Ib.* bk. v, ch. 1

42 There is moderation even in excess.
Ib. bk. vi, ch. 1

43 I repeat . . . that all power is a trust—that we are accountable for its exercise—that, from the people, and for the people, all springs, and all must exist.
Ib. ch. 7

44 All Paradise opens! Let me die eating ortolans to the sound of soft music!
The Young Duke, bk. i, ch. 10

45 A *dark* horse, which had never been thought of, and which the careless St. James had never even observed in the list, rushed past the grand stand in sweeping triumph.
Ib. bk. ii, ch. 5

46 'The age of chivalry is past,' said May Dacre. 'Bores have succeeded to dragons.' *Ib.*

47 A man may speak very well in the House of Commons, and fail very completely in the House of Lords. There are two distinct styles requisite: I intend, in the course of my career, if I have time, to give a specimen of both. *Ib.* bk. v, ch. 6

ISAAC D'ISRAELI
1766–1848

48 He wreathed the rod of criticism with roses. [Bayle.]
Curiosities of Literature, 1834, vol. i, p. 20

49 There is an art of reading, as well as an art of thinking, and an art of writing. *Literary Character*, ch. 11

SYDNEY THOMPSON DOBELL
1824–1874

1 The murmur of the mourning ghost
That keeps the shadowy kine,
'Oh, Keith of Ravelston,
The sorrows of thy line!'   *A Nuptial Eve*

HENRIETTA OCTAVIA DE LISLE DOBREE
1831–1894

2 Safely, safely gather'd in,
Far from sorrow, far from sin.
Children's Hymn Book, 1881. *Safely, Safely
Gather'd In.*

HENRY AUSTIN DOBSON
1840–1921

3 And I wove the thing to a random rhyme,
For the Rose is Beauty, the Gardener, Time.
A Fancy from Fontenelle

4 It may be that he could not count
The sires and sons to Jesse's fount,—
He liked the 'Sermon on the Mount,'—
And more, he read it.
A Gentleman of the Old School

5 All passes. Art alone
Enduring stays to us;
The Bust outlasts the throne,—
The Coin, Tiberius.
Ars Victrix. (See Théophile Gautier, 214:3)

6 And where are the galleons of Spain?
Ballad to Queen Elizabeth

7 O, Love's but a dance,
Where Time plays the fiddle!
See the couples advance,—
O, Love's but a dance!
A whisper, a glance,—
'Shall we twirl down the middle?'
O, Love's but a dance,
Where Time plays the fiddle!   *Cupid's Alley*

8 Ah, would but one might lay his lance in rest,
And charge in earnest . . . were it but a mill!
Don Quixote

9 Fame is a food that dead men eat,—
I have no stomach for such meat.
Fame is a Food that Dead Men Eat

10 He held his pen in trust
To Art, not serving shame or lust.   *In After Days*

11 The ladies of St. James's!
They're painted to the eyes,
Their white it stays for ever,
Their red it never dies:
But Phyllida, my Phyllida!
Her colour comes and goes;
It trembles to a lily,—
It wavers to a rose.   *The Ladies of St. James's*

12 The ladies of St. James's!
They have their fits and freaks;
They smile on you—for seconds;
They frown on you—for weeks.   *Ib.*

13 But Phyllida, my Phyllida!
She takes her buckled shoon,
When we go out a-courting
Beneath the harvest moon.   *Ib.*

14 For I respectfully decline
To dignify the Serpentine,
And make *hors-d'œuvres* for fishes.
To 'Lydia Languish'

15 Time goes, you say? Ah no!
Alas, Time stays, *we* go.   *The Paradox of Time*

16 I intended an Ode,
And it turned to a Sonnet.
It began *à la mode,*
I intended an Ode;
But Rose crossed the road
In her latest new bonnet;
I intended an Ode;
And it turned to a Sonnet.   *Rose-Leaves*

17 Rose kissed me to-day.
Will she kiss me to-morrow?
Let it be as it may,
Rose kissed me to-day,
But the pleasure gives way
To a savour of sorrow;—
Rose kissed me to-day,—
Will she kiss me to-morrow?   *Ib.*

18 This was the Pompadour's Fan!
*On a Fan that belonged to the Marquise de
Pompadour*

PHILIP DODDRIDGE
1702–1751

19 Hark, the glad sound! The Saviour comes,
The Saviour promised long.
Hymns (1755). Hark, The Glad Sound

20 O God of Bethel, by whose hand
Thy people still are fed,
Who through this weary pilgrimage
Hast all our fathers led:

Our vows, our prayers, we now present
Before thy throne of grace,
God of our fathers, be the God
Of their succeeding race.   *Ib. O God of Bethel*

21 Ye servants of the Lord,
Each in his office wait,
Observant of His heav'nly Word,
And watchful at His Gate.
Ib. Ye Servants of the Lor

MARY ABIGAIL DODGE
see
GAIL HAMILTON

CHARLES LUTWIDGE DODGSON
see
LEWIS CARROLL

GEORGE BUBB DODINGTON, BARON MELCOMBE
1691–1762

22 Love thy country, wish it well,
Not with too intense a care,
'Tis enough, that when it fell,
Thou its ruin didst not share.   *Spence's Anecdotes*

CHARLES FLETCHER DOLE
1845–?

1 Democracy is on trial in the world, on a more colossal scale than ever before. *The Spirit of Democracy*

ALFRED DOMETT
1811–1887

2 It was the calm and silent night!—
  Seven hundred years and fifty-three
Had Rome been growing up to might,
  And now was Queen of land and sea!
No sound was heard of clashing wars;
  Peace brooded o'er the hushed domain;
Apollo, Pallas, Jove and Mars,
  Held undisturbed their ancient reign,
    In the solemn midnight
      Centuries ago! *Christmas Hymn*

ÆLIUS DONATUS
fl. 4th cent. A.D.

3 Huic quid simile sententiae et Comicus ait: 'nihil est dictum, quod non est dictum prius.' (Terent. in *Prolog. Eunuchi.*) Unde preceptor meus Donatus, cum istum versiculum exponeret: Pereant, inquit, qui ante nos nostra dixerunt.

  The same idea is said by the comic poet: 'Nothing is said which has not been said before.' Whence my teacher Donatus, when he was speaking of that verse, said, 'Confound those who have said our remarks before us.'
  St. Jerome, *Commentary on Ecclesiastes*, cap. i. Migne's *Patrologiae Lat. Cursus*, xxiii. 390

JOHN DONNE
1571?–1631

4 Twice or thrice had I loved thee,
Before I knew thy face or name.
So in a voice, so in a shapeless flame,
Angels affect us oft, and worshipped be.
  Air and Angels

5   Just such disparity
  As is 'twixt air and Angels' purity,
'Twixt women's love, and men's will ever be. *Ib.*

6 All other things, to their destruction draw,
Only our love hath no decay;
This, no to-morrow hath, nor yesterday,
Running it never runs from us away,
But truly keeps his first, last, everlasting day.
  The Anniversary

7 Let us love nobly, and live, and add again
Years and years unto years, till we attain
To write threescore: this is the second of our reign.
  Ib.

8 Come live with me, and be my love,
And we will some new pleasures prove
Of golden sands, and crystal brooks,
With silken lines, and silver hooks. *The Bait*

9 A naked thinking heart, that makes no show,
Is to a woman, but a kind of ghost. *The Blossom*

10 The day breaks not, it is my heart.
  Break of Day (Attr. also to John Dowland)

11 For God's sake hold your tongue, and let me love.
  The Canonization

12 Dear love, for nothing less than thee
Would I have broke this happy dream,
  It was a theme
For reason, much too strong for fantasy,
Therefore thou wak'd'st me wisely; yet
My dream thou brok'st not, but continued'st it.
  The Dream

13 Love built on beauty, soon as beauty, dies.
  Elegies, No. 2. *The Anagram*

14 The grim eight-foot-high iron-bound serving-man,
That oft names God in oaths, and only then.
  Ib. No. 4. *The Perfume*

15 She, and comparisons are odious.
  Ib. No. 8. *The Comparison*

16 No Spring, nor Summer beauty hath such grace,
As I have seen in one Autumnal face.
  Ib. No. 9. *The Autumnal*

17 So, if I dream I have you, I have you,
For, all our joys are but fantastical.
  Ib. No. 10. *The Dream*

18 By our first strange and fatal interview.
  Ib. No. 16. *On His Mistress*

19   All will spy in thy face
  A blushing womanly discovering grace. *Ib.*

20 Whoever loves, if he do not propose
The right true end of love, he's one that goes
To sea for nothing but to make him sick.
  Ib. No. 18. *Love's Progress*

21   The straight Hellespont between
  The Sestos and Abydos of her breasts. *Ib.*

22 Those set our hairs, but these our flesh upright.
  Ib. No. 19. *On Going to Bed*

23 O my America! my new-found-land. *Ib.*

24 Where harmless fish monastic silence keep.
  Epicedes and Obsequies. Elegy on Mrs. Boulstred,
  l. 14

25 O strong and long-liv'd death, how cam'st thou in?
  Ib. l. 21

26 Hail, Bishop Valentine, whose day this is,
  All the air is thy Diocese.
  Epithalamions. 1, *On the Lady Elizabeth and Count Palatine being Married on St. Valentine's Day.*

27 The household bird, with the red stomacher. *Ib.*

28 So, so, break off this last lamenting kiss,
Which sucks two souls, and vapours both away,
Turn thou ghost that way, and let me turn this,
And let our selves benight our happiest day.
  The Expiration

29 Where, like a pillow on a bed,
A pregnant bank swelled up, to rest
The violet's reclining head,
Sat we two, one another's best. *The Extasy*

30 So to'entergraft our hands, as yet
Was all the means to make us one,
And pictures in our eyes to get
Was all our propagation. *Ib.*

31 And whilst our souls negotiate there,
We like sepulchral statues lay;
All day, the same our postures were,
And we said nothing, all the day. *Ib.*

1 But O alas, so long, so far
Our bodies why do we forbear?
They're ours, though they're not we, we are
The intelligencies, they the sphere.   *The Extasy*

2 So must pure lovers' souls descend
T' affections, and to faculties,
Which sense may reach and apprehend,
Else a great Prince in prison lies.   *Ib.*

3 She, she is dead; she's dead; when thou know'st this,
Thou know'st how dry a cinder this world is.
           The First Anniversary, l. 427

4 Who ever comes to shroud me, do not harm
Nor question much
That subtle wreath of hair, which crowns my arm;
The mystery, the sign you must not touch,
   For 'tis my outward soul,
Viceroy to that, which then to heaven being gone,
   Will leave this to control,
And keep these limbs, her Province, from dissolution.
                     The Funeral

5 What ere she meant by it, bury it with me,
   For since I am
Love's martyr, it might breed idolatry,
If into other's hands these relics came;
   As 'twas humility
To afford to it all that a soul can do,
   So, 'tis some bravery,
That since you would save none of me, I bury some
   of you.   *Ib.*

6 I wonder by my troth, what thou, and I
Did, till we lov'd? were we not wean'd till then?
But suck'd on country pleasures, childishly?
                     The Good-Morrow

7 And now good morrow to our waking souls,
Which watch not one another out of fear.   *Ib.*

8 Without sharp North, without declining West.   *Ib.*

9 That All, which always is All everywhere.
                  Holy Sonnets. Annunciation

10 Immensity cloistered in thy dear womb.   *Ib.*

11 As due by many titles I resign
My self to thee, O God, first I was made
By thee, and for thee, and when I decayed
Thy blood bought that, the which before was thine.
                     Ib. ii

12 I am a little world made cunningly
Of elements, and an angelic sprite.   *Ib.* v

13 At the round earth's imagined corners, blow
Your trumpets, Angels, and arise, arise.   *Ib.* vii

14 All whom war, dearth, age, agues, tyrannies,
Despair, law, chance, hath slain.   *Ib.*

15 Death be not proud, though some have called thee
Mighty and dreadful, for, thou art not so,
For, those, whom thou think'st, thou dost overthrow,
Die not, poor death.   *Ib.* x

16 One short sleep past, we wake eternally,
And death shall be no more; death, thou shalt die.
                     Ib.

17 What if this present were the world's last night?
                     Ib. xiii

18 Batter my heart, three person'd God; for, you
As yet but knock, breathe, shine, and seek to mend.
                     Ib. xiv

19 Take me to you, imprison me, for I
Except you enthrall me, never shall be free,
Nor ever chaste, except you ravish me.
                  Holy Sonnets, xiv

20 Show me, dear Christ, thy spouse, so bright and
   clear.   *Ib.* xviii

21   As thou
Art jealous, Lord, so I am jealous now,
Thou lov'st not, till from loving more, thou free
My soul: whoever gives, takes liberty:
   O, if thou car'st not whom I love
   Alas, thou lov'st not me.
      *Hymn to Christ, at the author's last going into
      Germany*

22 Seal then this bill of my Divorce to all.   *Ib.*

23 To see God only, I go out of sight:
   And to scape stormy days, I choose
   An everlasting night.   *Ib.*

24 Wilt thou forgive that sin, where I begun,
Which is my sin, though it were done before?
Wilt thou forgive those sins through which I run
And do them still, though still I do deplore?
When thou hast done, thou hast not done,
   For I have more.

Wilt thou forgive that sin, by which I'have won
Others to sin, and made my sin their door?
Wilt thou forgive that sin which I did shun
A year or two, but wallowed in a score?
When thou hast done, thou hast not done,
   For I have more.

I have a sin of fear that when I have spun
My last thread, I shall perish on the shore;
Swear by thy self that at my death, thy Sun
Shall shine as it shines now, and heretofore;
And having done that, thou hast done,
   I have no more.   *Hymn to God the Father*

25 Since I am coming to that holy room,
Where, with thy quire of Saints for evermore,
I shall be made thy Music; as I come
I tune the instrument here at the door,
And what I must do then, think here before.
                  Hymn to God in My Sickness

26 Will no other vice content you?   *The Indifferent*

27 Rob me, but bind me not, and let me go.   *Ib.*

28 And by Love's sweetest part, Variety, she swore. *Ib.*

29 And said, alas, some two or three
Poor heretics in love there be,
Which think to stablish dangerous constancy.   *Ib.*

30 Stand still, and I will read to thee
A lecture, Love, in love's philosophy.
                  A Lecture upon the Shadow

31 When I died last, and, Dear, I die
As often as from thee I go,
Though it be but an hour ago,
And lovers' hours be full eternity.   *The Legacy*

32 Love is a growing or full constant light;
And his first minute, after noon, is night.   *Ib.*

33 If yet I have not all thy love,
Dear, I shall never have it all.   *Lovers' Infiniteness*

34 I long to talk with some old lover's ghost,
Who died before the god of love was born.
                     Love's Deity

1 Rebel and Atheist too, why murmur I,
As though I felt the worst that love could do?
Love's Deity

2 'Tis the year's midnight, and it is the day's.
Nocturnal upon St. Lucy's Day

3 The world's whole sap is sunk:
The general balm th' hydroptic earth hath drunk. *Ib.*

4 I sing the progress of a deathless soul.
Progress of the Soul, i

5 Great Destiny the Commissary of God. *Ib.* iv

6 To my six lustres almost now outwore. *Ib.* v

7 This soul to whom Luther, and Mahomet were
Prisons of flesh. *Ib.* vii

8 When my grave is broke up again
Some second guest to entertain,
(For graves have learnt that woman-head
To be to more than one a bed). *The Relic*

9 A bracelet of bright hair about the bone. *Ib.*

10 On a huge hill,
Cragged, and steep, Truth stands, and he that will
Reach her, about must, and about must go.
Satyre iii. l. 79

11 As till God's great *Venite* change the song.
The Second Anniversary, l. 44

12 Think then, my soul, that death is but a groom,
Which brings a taper to the outward room. *Ib.* l. 85

13 Her pure and eloquent blood
Spoke in her cheeks, and so distinctly wrought,
That one might almost say, her body thought.
Ib. l. 244

14 Whose twilights were more clear, than our mid-day.
Ib. l. 463

15 Sweetest love, I do not go,
For weariness of thee,
Nor in hope the world can show
A fitter Love for me;
But since that I
Must die at last, 'tis best,
To use my self in jest
Thus by feigned deaths to die. *Song*

16 Go, and catch a falling star,
Get with child a mandrake root,
Tell me, where all past years are,
Or who cleft the Devil's foot.
Song, Go and Catch a Falling Star

17 And swear
No where
Lives a woman true and fair. *Ib.*

18 Though she were true, when you met her,
And last, till you write your letter,
Yet she
Will be
False, ere I come, to two, or three. *Ib.*

19 Busy old fool, unruly Sun,
Why dost thou thus,
Through windows, and through curtains call on us?
Must to thy motions lovers' seasons run?
The Sun Rising

20 Love, all alike, no season knows, nor clime,
Nor hours, days, months, which are the rags of time.

21 I am two fools, I know,
For loving, and for saying so
In whining Poetry. *The Triple Fool*

22 Who are a little wise, the best fools be. *Ib.*

23 I have done one braver thing
Than all the Worthies did,
And yet a braver thence doth spring,
Which is, to keep that hid. *The Undertaking*

24 So let us melt, and make no noise,
No tear-floods, nor sigh-tempests move,
'Twere profanation of our joys
To tell the laity our love.
A Valediction Forbidding Mourning

25 Dull sublunary lovers' love
(Whose soul is sense) cannot admit
Absence, because it doth remove
Those things which elemented it.

But we, by a love so much refined,
That ourselves know not what it is,
Inter-assured of the mind,
Care less, eyes, lips, and hands to miss.

Our two souls therefore, which are one,
Though I must go, endure not yet
A breach, but an expansion,
Like gold to airy thinness beat.

If they be two, they are two so
As stiff twin compasses are two,
Thy soul the fixt foot, makes no show
To move, but doth, if the other do.

And though it in the centre sit,
Yet when the other far doth roam,
It leans, and hearkens after it,
And grows erect, as that comes home.

Such wilt thou be to me, who must
Like th' other foot, obliquely run;
Thy firmness makes my circle just,
And makes me end, where I begun. *Ib.*

26 But I do nothing upon my self, and yet I am mine
own *Executioner*. *Devotions*

27 No man is an *Island*, entire of it self. *Ib.*

28 Any man's *death* diminishes *me*, because I am involved
in *Mankind*; And therefore never send to know for
whom the *bell* tolls; It tolls for *thee*. *Ib.*

29 John Donne, Anne Donne, Un-done.
Letter to his Wife

30 Poor intricated soul! Riddling, perplexed, labyrin-
thical soul! *Sermons*, i, p. 486, No. xlviii

31 A Day that hath no *pridie*, nor *postridie*, yesterday
doth not usher it in, nor tomorrow shall not drive
it out. Methusalem, with all his hundreds of
years, was but a mushroom of a night's growth,
to this Day, and all the four Monarchies, with all
their thousands of years, and all the powerful
Kings and Queens of this world, were but as a
bed of flowers, some gathered at six, some at
seven, some at eight, all in one morning, in respect
of this Day. *Ib.* p. 747, No. lxxiii. *Eternity*

32 I throw myself down in my chamber, and I call in,
and invite God, and his Angels thither, and when
they are there, I neglect God and his Angels, for
the noise of a fly, for the rattling of a coach, for the
whining of a door.
Ib. p. 800, No. lxxx. *At the Funeral of Sir*
William Cokayne

JULIA CAROLINE RIPLEY DORR
1825–1913

1 O true, brave heart! God bless thee, wheresoe'er
In God's great universe thou art to-day!
*Friar Anselm and other Poems. How Can I
Cease to Pray for Thee?*

CHARLES SACKVILLE, EARL OF DORSET
1638–1706

2 To all you ladies now at land,
We men, at sea, indite.
To All You Ladies Now at Land

SARAH DOUDNEY
1843–1926

3 But the waiting time, my brothers,
Is the hardest time of all.
Psalms of Life, The Hardest Time of All

BISHOP GAVIN DOUGLAS
1474?–1522

4 Dame naturis menstralis, on that other part,
Thar blysfull bay entonyng every art,
To beyt thir amorus of thar nychtis baill,
The merl, the mavys, and the nychtyngale,
With mery notis myrthfully furth brest,
Enforcying thame quha mycht do clynk it best.
Eneados, bk. xii, prol. l. 231

5 And all small fowlys singis on the spray:
Welcum the lord of lycht and lamp of day. *Ib.* l. 251

WILLIAM DOUGLAS
1672–1748

6 And for bonnie Annie Laurie
I'd lay me doun and dee.   *Annie Laurie*

LORENZO DOW
1777–1834

7 Observing the doctrine of Particular Election . . . and
those who preached it up to make the Bible clash
and contradict itself, by preaching somewhat like
this:
You can and you can't—You shall and you shan't—
You will and you won't—And you will be damned
if you do—
And you will be damned if you don't.
Reflections on the Love of God, vi (1836), 30

ERNEST DOWSON
1867–1900

8 And I was desolate and sick of an old passion.
Non Sum Qualis Eram

9 I have been faithful to thee, Cynara! in my fashion.
Ib.

10 I have forgot much, Cynara! gone with the wind,
Flung roses, roses, riotously, with the throng,
Dancing, to put thy pale, lost lilies out of mind. *Ib.*

11 They are not long, the weeping and the laughter,
Love and desire and hate;
I think they have no portion in us after
We pass the gate.   *Vitae Summa Brevis*

SIR ARTHUR CONAN DOYLE
1859–1930

12 What of the bow?
The bow was made in England:
Of true wood, of yew-wood,
The wood of English bows.   *Song of the Bow*

13 'It seems . . . to be one of those simple cases which
are so extremely difficult.' 'That sounds a little
paradoxical.' 'But it is profoundly true. Singularity is almost invariably a clue. The more
featureless and commonplace a crime is, the more
difficult is it to bring it home.'
*The Adventures of Sherlock Holmes. The Bos-
combe Valley Mystery*

14 A little monograph on the ashes of one hundred and
forty different varieties of pipe, cigar, and cigarette
tobacco.   *Ib.*

15 The husband was a teetotaller, there was no other
woman, and the conduct complained of was that
he had drifted into the habit of winding up every
meal by taking out his false teeth and hurling
them at his wife.   *Ib. A Case of Identity*

16 It has long been an axiom of mine that the little
things are infinitely the most important.   *Ib.*

17 It is my belief, Watson, founded upon my experience, that the lowest and vilest alleys of London
do not present a more dreadful record of sin than
does the smiling and beautiful countryside.
Ib. Copper Beeches

18 A man should keep his little brain attic stocked with
all the furniture that he is likely to use, and the rest
he can put away in the lumber-room of his library,
where he can get it if he wants it.
Ib. Five Orange Pips

19 It is quite a three-pipe problem.
Ib. The Red-Headed League

20 I have nothing to do to-day. My practice is never
very absorbing.   *Ib.*

21 To Sherlock Holmes she [Irene Adler] is always *the*
woman.   *Ib. Scandal in Bohemia*

22 It is a capital mistake to theorize before one has data.
Ib.

23 You know my methods, Watson.
*The Memoirs of Sherlock Holmes. The Crooked
Man*

24 'Excellent!' I [Dr. Watson] cried. 'Elementary,' said
he [Holmes].   *Ib.*

25 'It is my duty to warn you that it will be used
against you,' cried the Inspector, with the magnificent fair play of the British criminal law.
Ib. Dancing Men

26 He [Professor Moriarty] is the Napoleon of crime.
Ib. The Final Problem

27 'The practice is quiet,' said I [Dr. Watson], 'and I
have an accommodating neighbour.'   *Ib.*

28 You know my methods in such cases, Watson.
Ib. The Musgrave Ritual

29 My practice could get along very well for a day or
two.   *Ib. The Naval Treaty*

1 You mentioned your name as if I should recognize it, but beyond the obvious facts that you are a bachelor, a solicitor, a Freemason, and an asthmatic, I know nothing whatever about you.
The Memoirs of Sherlock Holmes. The Norwood Builder

2 'Arrest you!' said Holmes. 'This is really most grati—most interesting!' *Ib.*

3 These are much deeper waters than I had thought.
Ib. Reigate Squires

4 A long shot, Watson; a very long shot!
Ib. Silver Blaze

5 'Is there any point to which you would wish to draw my attention?'
'To the curious incident of the dog in the night-time.'
'The dog did nothing in the night-time.'
'That was the curious incident,' remarked Sherlock Holmes. *Ib.*

6 We have not yet met our Waterloo, Watson, but this is our Marengo.
The Return of Sherlock Holmes. Abbey Grange

7 You will ruin no more lives as you ruined mine. You will wring no more hearts as you wrung mine. I will free the world of a poisonous thing. Take that, you hound, and that!—and that!—and that!—and that! *Ib. Charles Augustus Milverton*

8 Now, Watson, the fair sex is your department.
Ib. The Second Stain

9 There is a spirituality about the face, however . . . which the typewriter does not generate. The lady is a musician. *Ib. The Solitary Cyclist*

10 All other men are specialists, but his specialism is omniscience.
Hist Last Bow. Bruce-Partington Plans

11 I thought I knew my Watson. *Ib. The Devil's Foot*

12 'I [Sherlock Holmes] followed you—' 'I saw no one.' 'That is what you may expect to see when I follow you.' *Ib.*

13 Good old Watson! You are the one fixed point in a changing age. *Ib. His Last Bow*

14 But here, unless I am mistaken, is our client.
Ib. Wisteria Lodge

15 There is but one step from the grotesque to the horrible. *Ib.*

16 The giant rat of Sumatra, a story for which the world is not yet prepared.
The Case Book. Sussex Vampire

17 They were the footprints of a gigantic hound!
The Hound of the Baskervilles, ch. 2

18 Detection is, or ought to be, an exact science, and should be treated in the same cold and unemotional manner. You have attempted to tinge it with romanticism, which produces much the same effect as if you worked a love-story or an elopement into the fifth proposition of Euclid.
The Sign of Four

19 An experience of women which extends over many nations and three separate continents. *Ib.*

20 How often have I said to you that when you have eliminated the impossible, whatever remains, *however improbable*, must be the truth? *Ib.*

21 You know my methods. Apply them.
The Sign of Four

22 The Baker Street irregulars. *Ib.*

23 London, that great cesspool into which all the loungers of the Empire are irresistibly drained.
A Study in Scarlet

24 'Wonderful!' I [Dr. Watson] ejaculated. 'Commonplace,' said Holmes. *Ib.*

25 'I should have more faith,' he said; 'I ought to know by this time that when a fact appears opposed to a long train of deductions it invariably proves to be capable of bearing some other interpretation.' *Ib.*

26 'I am inclined to think—' said I [Dr. Watson]. 'I should do so,' Sherlock Holmes remarked, impatiently. *The Valley of Fear*

27 The vocabulary of 'Bradshaw' is nervous and terse, but limited. *Ib.*

28 Mediocrity knows nothing higher than itself, but talent instantly recognizes genius. *Ib.*

SIR FRANCIS HASTINGS CHARLES DOYLE
1810–1888

29 Last night, among his fellow roughs, He jested, quaff'd, and swore.
The Private of the Buffs

30 *To-day*, beneath the foeman's frown, He stands in Elgin's place, Ambassador from Britain's crown And type of all her race. *Ib.*

31 Poor, reckless, rude, low-born, untaught, Bewilder'd, and alone, A heart with English instinct fraught He yet can call his own. *Ib.*

32 Vain, mightiest fleets of iron framed; Vain, those all-shattering guns; Unless proud England keep, untamed, The strong heart of her sons. *Ib.*

33 A man of mean estate, Who died, as firm as Sparta's king, Because his soul was great. *Ib.*

34 His creed no parson ever knew, For this was still his 'simple plan,' To have with clergymen to do As little as a Christian can.
The Unobtrusive Christian

SIR FRANCIS DRAKE
1540?–1596

35 There is plenty of time to win this game, and to thrash the Spaniards too. *Attr. in the Dict. of Nat. Biog.*

'The tradition goes, that Drake would needs see the game up; but was soon prevail'd on to go and play out the rubber with the Spaniards.' W. Oldys' *Life of Ralegh* in Ralegh's *Hist. of the World*, 1736.

36 I remember Drake, in the vaunting style of a soldier, would call the Enterprise [of Cadiz, 1587] the singeing of the King of Spain's Beard.
Bacon, *Considerations touching a War with Spain* (*Harleian Misc.* 1745, vol. v, p. 85, col. 1)

1 I must have the gentleman to haul and draw with the
mariner, and the mariner with the gentleman. . . .
I would know him, that would refuse to set his hand
to a rope, but I know there is not any such here.
Corbett, Drake and the Tudor Navy, i. 249

MICHAEL DRAYTON
1563–1631

2 Ill news hath wings, and with the wind doth go,
Comfort's a cripple and comes ever slow.
The Barrons' Wars, bk. II, xxviii

3 He was a man (then boldly dare to say)
In whose rich soul the virtues well did suit,
In whom so mix'd the elements all lay,
That none to one could sovereignty impute,
As all did govern yet all did obey;
He of a temper was so absolute,
As that it seem'd when Nature him began,
She meant to shew all, that might be in man.
Ib. bk. III, xl

4 The mind is free, whate'er afflict the man,
A King's a King, do Fortune what she can.
Ib. bk. v, xxxvi

5 Thus when we fondly flatter our desires,
Our best conceits do prove the greatest liars.
Ib. bk. VI, xciv

6 Fair stood the wind for France
When we our sails advance,
Nor now to prove our chance
Longer will tarry.
To the Cambro-Britons. Agincourt

7 They now to fight are gone,
Armour on armour shone,
Drum now to drum did groan,
To hear, was wonder;
That with the cries they make,
The very earth did shake,
Trumpet to trumpet spake,
Thunder to thunder. *Ib.*

8 Suffolk his axe did ply,
Beaumont and Willoughby
Bare them right doughtily,
Ferrers and Fanhope.

Upon Saint Crispin's Day
Fought was this noble fray,
Which fame did not delay
To England to carry.
O when shall English men
With such acts fill a pen?
Or England breed again
Such a King Harry? *Ib.*

9 Care draws on care, woe comforts woe again,
Sorrow breeds sorrow, one grief brings forth twain.
*England's Heroical Epistles. Henry Howard, Earl
of Surrey, to the Lady Geraldine, l. 87*

10 When Time shall turn those amber locks to grey,
My verse again shall gild and make them gay.
Ib. l. 123

11 Had in him those brave translunary things,
That the first poets had. [Marlowe.]
To Henry Reynolds, of Poets and Poesy, l. 106

12 For that fine madness still he did retain
Which rightly should possess a poet's brain.
Ib. l. 109

13 Next these, learn'd Jonson, in this list I bring,
Who had drunk deep of the Pierian spring.
To Henry Reynolds, of Poets and Poesy, l. 129

14 I pray thee leave, love me no more,
Call home the heart you gave me,
I but in vain the saint adore,
That can, but will not, save me.
To His Coy Love

15 These poor half-kisses kill me quite. *Ib.*

16 He made him turn and stop, and bound,
To gallop, and to trot the round,
He scarce could stand on any ground,
He was so full of mettle.
Nymphidia, The Court of Fairy, lxv

17 That shire which we the heart of England well may
call. *Poly-olbion, song xiii, l. 2*

18 Crave the tuneful nightingale to help you with her lay,
The ousel and the throstlecock, chief music of our
May. *Shepherd's Garland, eclogue iii, 17–18*

19 How many paltry, foolish, painted things,
That now in coaches trouble ev'ry street,
Shall be forgotten, whom no poet sings,
Ere they be well wrapped in their winding sheet?
Where I to thee Eternity shall give,
When nothing else remaineth of these days,
And Queens hereafter shall be glad to live
Upon the alms of thy superfluous praise.
Sonnets. Idea, vi

20 Since there's no help, come let us kiss and part,
Nay, I have done: you get no more of me,
And I am glad, yea glad with all my heart,
That thus so cleanly, I myself can free,
Shake hands for ever, cancel all our vows,
And when we meet at any time again,
Be it not seen in either of our brows,
That we one jot of former love retain;
Now at the last gasp of Love's latest breath,
When his pulse failing, Passion speechless lies,
When Faith is kneeling by his bed of death,
And Innocence is closing up his eyes,
Now if thou wouldst, when all have given him over,
From death to life, thou might'st him yet recover.
Ib. lxi

WILLIAM DRENNAN
1754–1820

21 The men of the Emerald Isle. *Erin*

JOHN DRINKWATER
1882–1937

22 He comes on chosen evenings,
My blackbird bountiful. *Blackbird*

23 Moon-washed apples of wonder. *Moonlit Apples*

THOMAS DRUMMOND
1797–1840

24 Property has its duties as well as its rights.
Letter to the Earl of Donoughmore, 22 May 1838

WILLIAM DRUMMOND
1585–1649

25 This fair volume which we World do name.
The World. Flowers of Sion

1 Or if by chance our minds do muse on ought,
It is some picture on the margin wrought.
The World. Flowers of Sion

2 The last and greatest herald of Heaven's King.
Poems. For the Baptist

3 Only the echoes which he made relent,
Ring from their marble caves, repent, repent.   *Ib.*

4 Phœbus, arise,
And paint the sable skies,
With azure, white, and red.   *Ib. Song* (ii)

5 I long to kiss the image of my death.
Ib. sonnet ix, *Sleep, Silence Child*

6   A morn
Of bright carnations did o'erspread her face. *Ib.* xlvi

JOHN DRYDEN
1631–1700

7 In pious times, ere priestcraft did begin,
Before polygamy was made a sin.
Absalom and Achitophel, pt. i, l. 1

8   And, wide as his command,
Scatter'd his Maker's image through the land.
Ib. l. 9

9 Whate'er he did was done with so much ease,
In him alone, 'twas natural to please.   *Ib.* l. 27

10 The Jews, a headstrong, moody, murmuring race
As ever tried the extent and stretch of grace,
God's pampered people, whom, debauched with ease,
No king could govern nor no God could please.
Ib. l. 45

11 Plots, true or false, are necessary things,
To raise up commonwealths and ruin kings.
Ib. l. 83

12 For priests of all religions are the same:
Of whatsoe'er descent their Godhead be,
Stock, stone, or other homely pedigree,
In his defence his servants are as bold,
As if he had been born of beaten gold.   *Ib.* l. 99

13 Of these the false Achitophel was first,
A name to all succeeding ages curst.
For close designs and crooked counsels fit,
Sagacious, bold, and turbulent of wit,
Restless, unfixed in principles and place,
In power unpleas'd, impatient of disgrace;
A fiery soul, which working out its way,
Fretted the pigmy body to decay:
And o'er informed the tenement of clay.
A daring pilot in extremity;
Pleased with the danger, when the waves went high
He sought the storms; but for a calm unfit,
Would steer too nigh the sands to boast his wit.
Great wits are sure to madness near alli'd,
And thin partitions do their bounds divide.
Ib. l. 150

14 Bankrupt of life, yet prodigal of ease.   *Ib.* l. 168

15 And all to leave what with his toil he won
To that unfeather'd two-legg'd thing, a son.
Ib. l. 169

16 Resolv'd to ruin or to rule the state.   *Ib.* l. 174

17 And Heav'n had wanted one immortal song.
Ib. l. 197

18 The people's prayer, the glad diviner's theme,
The young men's vision and the old men's dream!
Absalom and Achitophel, pt. i, l. 238

19 All empire is no more than power in trust.
Ib. l. 411

20 Better one suffer, than a nation grieve.   *Ib.* l. 416

21 But far more numerous was the herd of such
Who think too little and who talk too much.
Ib. l. 533

22 A man so various that he seem'd to be
Not one, but all mankind's epitome.
Stiff in opinions, always in the wrong;
Was everything by starts, and nothing long:
But, in the course of one revolving moon,
Was chemist, fiddler, statesman, and buffoon.
Ib. l. 545

23 So over violent, or over civil,
That every man, with him, was God or Devil.
Ib. l. 557

24 In squandering wealth was his peculiar art:
Nothing went unrewarded, but desert.
Beggar'd by fools, whom still he found too late:
He had his jest, and they had his estate.   *Ib.* l. 559

25 During his office treason was no crime,
The sons of Belial had a glorious time.   *Ib.* l. 597

26 His tribe were God Almighty's gentlemen.
Ib. l. 645

27 Youth, beauty, graceful action seldom fail:
But common interest always will prevail:
And pity never ceases to be shown
To him, who makes the people's wrongs his own.
Ib. l. 723

28 For who can be secure of private right,
If sovereign sway may be dissolv'd by might?
Nor is the people's judgement always true:
The most may err as grossly as the few.   *Ib.* l. 779

29 Never was patriot yet, but was a fool.   *Ib.* l. 968

30 Beware the fury of a patient man.   *Ib.* l. 1005

31 Henceforth a series of new time began,
The mighty years in long procession ran:
Once more the God-like David was restored,
And willing nations knew their lawful lord.
Ib. l. 1028

32 Doeg, though without knowing how or why,
Made still a blund'ring kind of melody;
Spurr'd boldly on, and dash'd through thick and thin,
Through sense and nonsense, never out nor in;
Free from all meaning, whether good or bad,
And in one word, heroically mad.   *Ib.* pt. ii, l. 412

33 Rhyme is the rock on which thou art to wreck.
Ib. l. 486

34   The god-like hero sate
On his imperial throne;
His valiant peers were plac'd around;
Their brows with roses and with myrtles bound.
(So should desert in arms be crowned:)
The lovely Thais by his side,
Sate like a blooming Eastern bride
In flow'r of youth and beauty's pride.
Happy, happy, happy pair!
None but the brave,
None but the brave,
None but the brave deserves the fair.
Alexander's Feast, l. 4

1 Assumes the god,
Affects to nod,
And seems to shake the spheres.
Alexander's Feast, l. 44

2 Bacchus ever fair, and ever young. *Ib.* l. 48

3 Sound the trumpets; beat the drums;
Flush'd with a purple grace
He shows his honest face:
Now give the hautboys breath; he comes, he comes.
Ib. l. 50

4 Drinking is the soldier's pleasure. *Ib.* l. 57

5 Rich the treasure;
Sweet the pleasure;
Sweet is pleasure after pain. *Ib.* l. 58

6 And thrice he routed all his foes, and thrice he slew
the slain. *Ib.* l. 68

7 Fallen from his high estate,
And welt'ring in his blood:
Deserted at his utmost need
By those his former bounty fed;
On the bare earth expos'd he lies,
With not a friend to close his eyes. *Ib.* l. 78

8 Revolving in his alter'd soul
The various turns of chance below. *Ib.* l. 85

9 Softly sweet, in Lydian measures,
Soon he sooth'd his soul to pleasures.
War, he sung, is toil and trouble;
Honour but an empty bubble.
Never ending, still beginning,
Fighting still, and still destroying,
If the world be worth thy winning,
Think, oh think, it worth enjoying.
Lovely Thais sits beside thee,
Take the good the gods provide thee. *Ib.* l. 97

10 Sigh'd and look'd, and sigh'd again. *Ib.* l. 120

11 And, like another Helen, fir'd another Troy.
Ib. l. 154

12 Could swell the soul to rage, or kindle soft desire.
Ib. l. 160

13 Let old Timotheus yield the prize,
Or both divide the crown:
He rais'd a mortal to the skies;
She drew an angel down. *Ib.* l. 177

14 All For Love, or the World Well Lost.
Title of Play

15 My love's a noble madness. *All For Love*, II. i

16 Fool that I was, upon my eagle's wings
I bore this wren, till I was tired with soaring,
And now he mounts above me. *Ib.*

17 Give, you gods,
Give to your boy, your Caesar,
The rattle of a globe to play withal,
This gewgaw world, and put him cheaply off:
I'll not be pleased with less than Cleopatra. *Ib.*

18 The wretched have no friends. *Ib.* III. i

19 Nature has cast me in so soft a mould,
That but to hear a story, feigned for pleasure,
Of some sad lover's death, moistens my eyes,
And robs me of my manhood. *Ib.* IV. i

20 Men are but children of a larger growth;
Our appetites as apt to change as theirs,
And full as craving too, and full as vain. *Ib.*

21 Your Cleopatra; Dolabella's Cleopatra; every man's
Cleopatra. *All For Love*, IV. i

22 Welcome, thou kind deceiver!
Thou best of thieves; who, with an easy key,
Dost open life, and, unperceived by us,
Even steal us from ourselves. *Ib.* V. i

23 A knock-down argument; 'tis but a word and a blow.
Amphitryon, I. i

24 I am devilishly afraid, that's certain; but . . . I'll sing,
that I may seem valiant. *Ib.* II. i

25 Whistling to keep myself from being afraid. *Ib.* III. i

26 I never saw any good that came of telling truth. *Ib.*

27 I am the true Amphitryon. *Ib.* V. i

28 As one that neither seeks, nor shuns his foe.
Annus Mirabilis, xli

29 By viewing nature, nature's handmaid art,
Makes mighty things from small beginnings grow:
Thus fishes first to shipping did impart,
Their tail the rudder, and their head the prow.
Ib. clv

30 And on the lunar world securely pry. *Ib.* clxiv

31 An horrid stillness first invades the ear,
And in that silence we the tempest fear.
Astræa Redux, l. 7

32 He made all countries where he came his own.
Ib. l. 76

33 Death, in itself, is nothing; but we fear,
To be we know not what, we know not where.
Aureng-Zebe, IV. i

34 When I consider life, 'tis all a cheat;
Yet, fool'd with hope, men favour the deceit;
Trust on, and think to-morrow will repay:
To-morrow's falser than the former day;
Lies worse, and, while it says, we shall be blest
With some new joys, cuts off what we possest.
Strange cozenage! None would live past years again,
Yet all hope pleasure in what yet remain;
And, from the dregs of life, think to receive,
What the first sprightly running could not give. *Ib.*

35 From harmony, from heavenly harmony
This universal frame began:
From harmony to harmony
Through all the compass of the notes it ran,
The diapason closing full in Man. *St. Cecilia's Day*, i

36 What passion cannot Music raise and quell? *Ib.* ii

37 The trumpet's loud clangour
Excites us to arms. *Ib.* iii

38 The soft complaining flute. *Ib.* iv

39 The trumpet shall be heard on high,
The dead shall live, the living die,
And Music shall untune the sky. *Ib.* Grand Chorus

40 And made almost a sin of abstinence.
Character of a Good Parson, l. 11

41 I am as free as nature first made man,
Ere the base laws of servitude began,
When wild in woods the noble savage ran.
The Conquest of Granada, pt. i, I. i

42 Forgiveness to the injured does belong;
But they ne'er pardon, who have done the wrong.
Ib. pt. ii, I. ii

1 Thou strong seducer, opportunity!
The Conquest of Granada, pt. i, IV. iii

2 For he was great, ere fortune made him so.
Death of Oliver Cromwell, vi

3 Old as I am, for ladies' love unfit,
The power of beauty I remember yet.
Cymon and Iphigenia, l. 1

4 When beauty fires the blood, how love exalts the mind. *Ib.* l. 41

5 He trudg'd along unknowing what he sought,
And whistled as he went, for want of thought.
Ib. l. 84

6 She hugg'd th' offender, and forgave th' offence,
Sex to the last. *Ib.* l. 367

7 Ill fortune seldom comes alone. *Ib.* l. 392

8 Of seeming arms to make a short essay,
Then hasten to be drunk, the business of the day.
Ib. l. 407

9 Theirs was the giant race before the flood.
Epistles. To Mr. Congreve, l. 5

10 Our builders were with want of genius curst;
The second temple was not like the first;
Till you, the best Vitruvius, come at length,
Our beauties equal, but excel our strength.
Ib. l. 13

11 For Tom the Second reigns like Tom the First.
Ib. l. 48

12 Heav'n, that but once was prodigal before,
To Shakespeare gave as much; she could not give him more. *Ib.* l. 62

13 How blessed is he, who leads a country life,
Unvex'd with anxious cares, and void of strife!
Who studying peace, and shunning civil rage,
Enjoy'd his youth, and now enjoys his age:
All who deserve his love, he makes his own;
And, to be lov'd himself, needs only to be known.
Ib. To John Driden of Chesterton, l. 1

14 Lord of yourself, uncumber'd with a wife. *Ib.* l. 18

15 Better to hunt in fields, for health unbought,
Than fee the doctor for a nauseous draught.
The wise, for cure, on exercise depend;
God never made his work, for man to mend.
Ib. l. 92

16 Ev'n victors are by victories undone. *Ib.* l. 164

17 His colours laid so thick on every place,
As only showed the paint, but hid the face.
Ib. To Sir R. Howard, l. 75

18 Here lies my wife: here let her lie!
Now she's at rest, and so am I.
Epitaph Intended for Dryden's Wife

19 He had brought me to my last legs; I was fighting as low as ever was Squire Widdrington.
An Evening's Love, II. i

20 She fear'd no danger, for she knew no sin.
The Hind and the Panther, pt. i, l. 4

21 And doom'd to death, though fated not to die.
Ib. l. 8

22 For truth has such a face and such a mien
As to be lov'd needs only to be seen. *Ib.* l. 33

23 My thoughtless youth was winged with vain desires,
My manhood, long misled by wandering fires,

Followed false lights; and when their glimpse was gone
My pride struck out new sparkles of her own.
Such was I, such by nature still I am;
Be Thine the glory, and be mine the shame!
Good life be now my task: my doubts are done;
(What more could fright my faith than Three in One?) *The Hind and the Panther*, pt. i, l. 72

24 Reason to rule, but mercy to forgive:
The first is law, the last prerogative. *Ib.* l. 261

25 For all have not the gift of martyrdom. *Ib.* pt. ii, l. 59

26 Either be wholly slaves or wholly free. *Ib.* l. 285

27 Much malice mingled with a little wit. *Ib.* pt. iii, l. 1

28 Think you your new French proselytes are come
To starve abroad, because they starv'd at home?
Your benefices twinkl'd from afar,
They found the new Messiah by the star. *Ib.* l. 173

29 For present joys are more to flesh and blood
Than a dull prospect of a distant good. *Ib.* l. 364

30 By education most have been misled;
So they believe, because they so were bred.
The priest continues what the nurse began,
And thus the child imposes on the man. *Ib.* l. 389

31 The wind was fair, but blew a mack'rel gale.
Ib. l. 456

32 T' abhor the makers, and their laws approve,
Is to hate traitors and the treason love. *Ib.* l. 706

33 For those whom God to ruin has design'd,
He fits for fate, and first destroys their mind.
Ib. l. 1093

34 And love's the noblest frailty of the mind.
The Indian Emperor, II. ii

35 Repentance is the virtue of weak minds. *Ib.* III. i

36 For all the happiness mankind can gain
Is not in pleasure, but in rest from pain. *Ib.* IV. i

37 Thou youngest virgin-daughter of the skies,
Made in the last promotion of the blest.
To the Memory of Mrs. Killigrew, l. 1

38 Since heav'n's eternal year is thine. *Ib.* l. 15

39 While yet a young probationer,
And candidate of heav'n. *Ib.* l. 21

40 When rattling bones together fly
From the four corners of the sky. *Ib.* l. 184

41 That fairy kind of writing which depends only upon the force of imagination.
King Arthur, Dedication

42 All heiresses are beautiful. *Ib.* I. i

43 War is the trade of kings. *Ib.* II. ii

44 Fairest Isle, all isles excelling,
Seat of pleasures, and of loves;
Venus here will choose her dwelling,
And forsake her Cyprian groves.
Ib. v. *Song of Venus*

45 Ovid, the soft philosopher of love.
Love Triumphant, II. i

46 Thou tyrant, tyrant Jealousy,
Thou tyrant of the mind!
Song of Jealousy. Love Triumphant

1 All human things are subject to decay,
And, when fate summons, monarchs must obey.
Mac Flecknoe, l. 1

2 The rest to some faint meaning make pretence,
But Shadwell never deviates into sense.
Some beams of wit on other souls may fall,
Strike through and make a lucid interval;
But Shadwell's genuine night admits no ray,
His rising fogs prevail upon the day.   *Ib.* l. 19

3 And torture one poor word ten thousand ways.
Ib. l. 208

4 I am resolved to grow fat and look young till forty,
and then slip out of the world with the first wrinkle
and the reputation of five-and-twenty.
The Maiden Queen, III. i

5 I am to be married within these three days; married
past redemption.   *Marriage à la Mode*, I. i

6 For secrets are edged tools,
And must be kept from children and from fools.
Sir Martin Mar-All, II. ii

7 We loathe our manna, and we long for quails.
The Medal, l. 131

8 But treason is not own'd when 'tis descried;
Successful crimes alone are justified.   *Ib.* l. 207

9 Three poets, in three distant ages born,
Greece, Italy and England did adorn.
The first in loftiness of thought surpass'd;
The next in majesty, in both the last:
The force of nature could no farther go;
To make a third she join'd the former two.
Lines Under Portrait of Milton

10 Whatever is, is in its causes just.   *Oedipus*, III. i

11   Wit will shine
Through the harsh cadence of a rugged line.
To the Memory of Mr. Oldham

12 But love's a malady without a cure.
Palamon and Arcite, bk. ii, l. 110

13 Fool, not to know that love endures no tie,
And Jove but laughs at lovers' perjury.   *Ib.* l. 148

14 And Antony, who lost the world for love.   *Ib.* l. 607

15 Unsham'd, though foil'd he does the best he can.
Ib. bk. iii, l. 741

16 Repentance is but want of power to sin.   *Ib.* l. 813

17 Since ev'ry man who lives is born to die,
And none can boast sincere felicity,
With equal mind, what happens, let us bear,
Nor joy nor grieve too much for things beyond our
care.
Like pilgrims to th' appointed place we tend;
The world's an inn, and death the journey's end.
Ib. l. 883

18 A virgin-widow and a *Mourning Bride*.   *Ib.* l. 927

19 Happy who in his verse can gently steer,
From grave to light; from pleasant to severe.
The Art of Poetry, c. i, l. 75

20 Errors, like straws, upon the surface flow;
He who would search for pearls must dive below.
Prologues and Epilogues: Prologue, All For Love

21   Bold knaves thrive without one grain of sense,
But good men starve for want of impudence.
Ib. Epilogue, Constantine the Great

22 For, Heaven be thank'd we live in such an age,
When no man dies for love, but on the stage.
Prologues and Epilogues: Epilogue, Mithridates

23 But 'tis the talent of our English nation,
Still to be plotting some new reformation.
Ib. Prologue, Sophonisba, l. 9

24 So poetry, which is in Oxford made
An art, in London only is a trade.
Prologue to the University of Oxford

25 Oxford to him a dearer name shall be,
Than his own mother University.
Thebes did his green unknowing youth engage,
He chooses Athens in his riper age.   *Ib.*

26 And this unpolished rugged verse I chose
As fittest for discourse and nearest prose.
Religio Laici, ad fin.

27 I strongly wish for what I faintly hope:
Like the day-dreams of melancholy men,
I think and think on things impossible,
Yet love to wander in that golden maze.
Rival Ladies, III. i

28 Learn to write well, or not to write at all.
Essay on Satire, l. 281

29 This is the porcelain of humankind.
Don Sebastian, I. i

30 Brutus and Cato might discharge their souls,
And give them furloughs for another world;
But we, like sentries, are obliged to stand
In starless nights, and wait the 'pointed hour.
Ib. II. i

31 A very merry, dancing, drinking,
Laughing, quaffing, and unthinking time.
Secular Masque, l. 39

32 Joy rul'd the day, and Love the night.   *Ib.* l. 81

33   There is a pleasure sure,
In being mad, which none but madmen know!
The Spanish Friar I. i (see also 203:27)

34 Lord of humankind.   *Ib.* II. ii

35 And, dying, bless the hand that gave the blow.   *Ib.*

36 They say everything in the world is good for something.   *Ib.* III. ii

37 Or break the eternal Sabbath of his rest.   *Ib.* V. ii

38 The clouds dispell'd, the sky resum'd her light,
And Nature stood recover'd of her fright.
But fear, the last of ills, remain'd behind,
And horror heavy sat on ev'ry mind.
Theodore and Honoria, l. 336

39 And that one hunting which the Devil design'd,
For one fair female, lost him half the kind.
Ib. l. 427

40 Mute and magnificent, without a tear.
Threnodia Augustalis, ii

41 Men met each other with erected look,
The steps were higher that they took;
Friends to congratulate their friends made haste;
And long inveterate foes saluted as they passed.
Ib. iv

42 Freedom which in no other land will thrive,
Freedom an English subject's sole prerogative. *Ib.* x

43 And he, who servilely creeps after sense,
Is safe, but ne'er will reach an excellence.
Tyrannic Love, Prologue

1 All delays are dangerous in war. *Tyrannic Love*, I. i

2 Pains of love be sweeter far
Than all other pleasures are. *Ib.* IV. i

3 We must beat the iron while it is hot, but we may polish it at leisure. *Dedication of the Aeneis*

4 I trade both with the living and the dead, for the enrichment of our native language. *Ib.*

5 A thing well said will be wit in all languages. *Essay of Dramatic Poesy*

6 He was the man who of all modern, and perhaps ancient poets, had the largest and most comprehensive soul. . . . He was naturally learn'd; he needed not the spectacles of books to read Nature; he looked inwards, and found her there. . . . He is many times flat, insipid; his comic wit degenerating into clenches, his serious swelling into bombast. But he is always great, when some occasion is presented to him. [Shakespeare.] *Ib.*

7 The consideration of this made Mr. Hales of Eaton say, that there was no subject of which any poet ever writ, but he would produce it much better done in Shakespeare. *Ib.*

8 He invades authors like a monarch; and what would be theft in other poets, is only victory in him. [Ben Jonson.] *Ib.*

9 If by the people you understand the multitude, the *hoi polloi*, 'tis no matter what they think; they are sometimes in the right, sometimes in the wrong: their judgement is a mere lottery. *Ib.*

10 He [Shakespeare] is the very Janus of poets; he wears almost everywhere two faces; and you have scarce begun to admire the one, ere you despise the other.
Essay on the Dramatic Poetry of the Last Age

11 One of the greatest, most noble, and most sublime poems which either this age or nation has produced. [Paradise Lost.] *Essays, Apology for Heroic Poetry*

12 What judgment I had increases rather than diminishes; and thoughts, such as they are, come crowding in so fast upon me, that my only difficulty is to choose or reject; to run them into verse or to give them the other harmony of prose.
Preface to Fables

13 'Tis sufficient to say [of Chaucer], according to the proverb, that here is God's plenty. *Ib.*

14 It becomes not me to draw my pen in defence of a bad cause, when I have so often drawn it for a good one. *Ib.*

15 He [Chaucer] is a perpetual fountain of good sense. *Ib.*

16 One of our late great poets is sunk in his reputation, because he could never forgive any conceit which came in his way; but swept like a drag-net, great and small. There was plenty enough, but the dishes were ill-sorted; whole pyramids of sweetmeats, for boys and women; but little of solid meat for men. *Ib.*

17 How easy it is to call rogue and villain, and that wittily! But how hard to make a man appear a fool, a blockhead, or a knave, without using any of those opprobrious terms! To spare the grossness of the names, and to do the thing yet more severely, is to draw a full face, and to make the nose and cheeks stand out, and yet not to employ any depth of shadowing. *Of Satire*

18 Sure the poet . . . spewed up a good lump of clotted nonsense at once. *On Settle*

19 A man may be capable, as Jack Ketch's wife said of his servant, of a plain piece of work, a bare hanging; but to make a malefactor die sweetly was only belonging to her husband. *Ib.*

20 Happy the man, and happy he alone,
He, who can call to-day his own:
He who, secure within, can say,
To-morrow do thy worst, for I have lived to-day.
Trans. of Horace, bk. iii, ode xxix

21 Not Heav'n itself upon the past has pow'r;
But what has been, has been, and I have had my hour. *Ib.*

22 I can enjoy her while she's kind;
But when she dances in the wind,
And shakes the wings, and will not stay,
I puff the prostitute away. [Fortune.] *Ib.*

23 Look round the habitable world! how few
Know their own good; or knowing it, pursue.
Trans. of Juvenal, x

24 To see and to be seen, in heaps they run;
Some to undo, and some to be undone.
Trans. of Ovid, Art of Love, I. 109

25 Thus, while the mute creation downward bend
Their sight, and to their earthly mother tend,
Man looks aloft; and with erected eyes
Beholds his own hereditary skies.
Trans. of Ovid, Metamorphoses, I. 107

26 Who, for false quantities, was whipt at school.
Trans. of Persius, Satires, I. 135

27 Swear, fool, or starve; for the dilemma's even;
A tradesman thou! and hope to go to heaven?
Ib. v. 204

28 She knows her man, and when you rant and swear,
Can draw you to her *with a single hair*. *Ib.* 246

29 Arms, and the man I sing, who, forced by fate,
And haughty Juno's unrelenting hate. . . .
Trans. of Virgil, Æneid, I. i

30 Cousin Swift, you will never be a poet.
Johnson's Lives of the Poets: Swift

GEORGE DUFFIELD
1818–1888

31 Stand up!—stand up for Jesus!
The Psalmist. Stand Up, Stand Up for Jesus

ALEXANDRE DUMAS
1803–1870

32 Cherchons la femme.
Let us look for the woman.
Les Mohicans de Paris, vol. ii, ch. 2
(Cherchez la femme. Attributed to Joseph Fouché.)

33 Tous pour un, un pour tous.
All for one, one for all.
Les Trois Mousquetiers, passim

MARÉCHAL DUMOURIEZ
1739–1823

1 Les courtisans qui l'entourent n'ont rien oublié et n'ont rien appris.

The courtiers who surround him have forgotten nothing and learnt nothing.
Of Louis XVIII, at the time of the Declaration of Verona, Sept. 1795. Examen. See also Talleyrand

WILLIAM DUNBAR
1465?–1530?

2 Timor mortis conturbat me.
Lament for the Makaris

3 London, thou art of townes *A per se.* London, l. 1

4 Thou lusty Troynovaunt. *Ib.* l. 9

5 London, thou art the flower of cities all!
Gemme of all joy, jasper of jocunditie. *Ib.* l. 16

6 Fair be their wives, right lovesom, white and small. *Ib.* l. 46

7 Thy famous Maire, by pryncely governaunce,
With sword of justice thee ruleth prudently.
No Lord of Parys, Venyce, or Floraunce
In dignitye or honour goeth to hym nigh. *Ib.* l. 49

8 All love is lost but upon God alone.
The Merle and the Nightingale, ii

FINLEY PETER DUNNE
1867–1936

9 'Th' American nation in th' Sixth Ward is a fine people,' he says. 'They love th' eagle,' he says, 'on th' back iv a dollar.'
Mr. Dooley in Peace and War. Oratory on Politics

JAMES DUPORT
1606–1679

10 Quem Juppiter vult perdere dementat prius.
Whom God would destroy He first sends mad.

THOMAS D'URFEY
1653–1723

11 Neighbours o'er the Herring Pond.
Pills to Purge Melancholy, 1719, vol. ii, p. 333. *Fable of the Lady, the Lurcher, and the Marrow-Puddings,* xiv

SIR EDWARD DYER
c. 1540–1607

12 My mind to me a kingdom is,
Such present joys therein I find,
That it excels all other bliss
That earth affords or grows by kind.
Though much I want which most would have,
Yet still my mind forbids to crave.
My Mind to Me a Kingdom Is

13 Some have too much, yet still do crave;
I little have, and seek no more.
They are but poor, though much they have,
And I am rich with little store.
They poor, I rich; they beg, I give;
They lack, I leave; they pine, I live. *Ib.*

JOHN DYER
1700?–1758

14 A little rule, a little sway,
A sunbeam in a winter's day,
Is all the proud and mighty have
Between the cradle and the grave.
Grongar Hill, l. 89

15 There is a kindly mood of melancholy,
That wings the soul and points her to the skies.
The Ruins of Rome, l. 347

JOHN DYER
fl. 1714

16 And he that will this health deny,
Down among the dead men let him lie.
Toast: Here's a Health to the King

MARIA EDGEWORTH
1767–1849

17 Well! some people talk of morality, and some of religion, but give me a little snug property.
The Absentee, ch. 2

18 And all the young ladies . . . said . . . that to be sure a love match was the only thing for happiness, where the parties could any way afford it.
Castle Rackrent (Continuation of Memoirs)

19 I've a great fancy to see my own funeral afore I die.
Ib.

20 Come when you're called;
And do as you're bid;
Shut the door after you;
And you'll never be chid. *The Contrast,* ch. 1

21 Business was his aversion; pleasure was his business.
Ib. ch. 2

THOMAS ALVA EDISON
1847–1931

22 Genius is one per cent. inspiration and ninety-nine per cent. perspiration.
Newspaper Interview. Life (1932), ch. 24

JAMES EDMESTON
1791–1867

23 Lead us, Heavenly Father, lead us
O'er the world's tempestuous sea;
Guard us, guide us, keep us, feed us,
For we have no help but Thee.
Sacred Lyrics, Set 2. Lead Us, Heavenly Father

EDWARD III OF ENGLAND
1312–1377

24 Let the boy win his spurs.
Of the Black Prince at Crécy, 1345

Also say to them, that they suffre hym this day to wynne his spurres, for if god be pleased, I woll this iourney be his, and the honoure therof.
Lord Berners, Froissart's Chron., 1812, I. cxxx. 158.

EDWARD VII OF GREAT BRITAIN
1841–1910

25 We are all Socialists now-a-days.
Speech at Mansion House, 5 Nov. 1895

EDWARD VIII OF GREAT BRITAIN

1894-

1 I have found it impossible to carry the heavy burden of responsibility and to discharge my duties as King as I would wish to do without the help and support of the woman I love. *Broadcast, 11 Dec. 1936*

RICHARD EDWARDES

1523?-1566

2 In going to my naked bed, as one that would have slept,
I heard a wife sing to her child, that long before had wept.
She sighed sore, and sang full sweet, to bring the babe to rest,
That would not cease, but cried still in sucking at her breast.
She was full weary of her watch and grieved with her child,
She rocked it, and rated it, till that on her it smiled.
Then did she say, 'Now have I found this proverb true to prove:
The falling out of faithful friends, renewing is of love.' *Amantium Irae, ed. 1580*

JONATHAN EDWARDS

1629-1712

3 The bodies of those that made such a noise and tumult when alive, when dead, lie as quietly among the graves of their neighbours as any others.
Procrastination

OLIVER EDWARDS

1711-1791

4 I have tried too in my time to be a philosopher; but, I don't know how, cheerfulness was always breaking in. *Boswell's Johnson, 17 Apr. 1778*

5 For my part, now, I consider supper as a turnpike through which one must pass, in order to get to bed. [Boswell's *Note*: I am not absolutely sure but this was my own suggestion, though it is truly in the character of Edwards.] *Ib.*

'GEORGE ELIOT'
[MARY ANN CROSS]

1819-1880

6 A prophetess? Yea, I say unto you, and more than a prophetess—a uncommon pretty young woman.
Adam Bede, ch. 1

7 It's but little good you'll do a-watering the last year's crop. *Ib. ch. 18*

8 It was a pity he couldna be hatched o'er again, an' hatched different. *Ib.*

9 Our deeds determine us, as much as we determine our deeds. *Ib. ch. 29*

10 Mrs. Poyser 'has her say out'. *Ib. title of ch. 32*

11 It's them as take advantage that get advantage i' this world. *Ib. ch. 32*

12 A maggot must be born i' the rotten cheese to like it. *Ib.*

13 He was like a cock who thought the sun had risen to hear him crow. *Adam Bede, ch. 33*

14 We hand folks over to God's mercy, and show none ourselves. *Ib. ch. 42*

15 I'm not one o' those as can see the cat i' the dairy, an' wonder what she's come after. *Ib. ch. 52*

16 I'm not denyin' the women are foolish: God Almighty made 'em to match the men. *Ib. ch. 53*

17 A difference of taste in jokes is a great strain on the affections. *Daniel Deronda, bk. ii, ch. 15*

18 Men's men: gentle or simple, they're much of a muchness. *Ib. bk. iv, ch. 31*

19 Friendships begin with liking or gratitude—roots that can be pulled up. *Ib. ch. 32*

20 Prophecy is the most gratuitous form of error.
Middlemarch, ch. 10

21 Our deeds still travel with us from afar,
And what we have been makes us what we are.
Ib. heading to ch. 70

22 The law's made to take care o' raskills.
The Mill on the Floss, bk. iii, ch. 4

23 This is a puzzling world, and Old Harry's got a finger in it. *Ib. ch. 9*

24 The small old-fashioned book, for which you need only pay sixpence at a bookstall, works miracles to this day, turning bitter waters into sweetness. . . . It was written down by a hand that waited for the heart's prompting: it is the chronicle of a solitary hidden anguish, struggle, trust and triumph. [*The Imitation of Christ.*] *Ib. bk. iv, ch. 3*

25 I've never any pity for conceited people, because I think they carry their comfort about with them.
Ib. bk. v, ch. 4

26 The happiest women, like the happiest nations, have no history. *Ib. bk. vi, ch. 3*

27 If you please to take the privilege o' sitting down.
Ib. ch. 4

28 I should like to know what is the proper function of women, if it is not to make reasons for husbands to stay at home, and still stronger reasons for bachelors to go out. *Ib. ch. 6*

29 'Character', says Novalis, in one of his questionable aphorisms—'character is destiny'. *Ib.*

30 In every parting there is an image of death.
Scenes of Clerical Life, Amos Barton, ch. 10

31 Animals are such agreeable friends—they ask no questions, they pass no criticisms.
Mr. Gilfil's Love-Story, ch. 7

32 Nothing is so good as it seems beforehand.
Silas Marner, ch. 18

33 Debasing the moral currency.
Title of essay in 'Theophrastus Such' (1879)

34 Oh may I join the choir invisible
Of those immortal dead who live again
In minds made better by their presence.
Poems: Oh May I Join the Choir Invisible

35 So shall I join the choir invisible
Whose music is the gladness of the world. *Ib.*

Wise books

36 For half the truths they hold are honoured tombs.
Ib. The Spanish Gypsy, bk. ii

1   'Tis God gives skill,
But not without men's hands: He could not make
Antonio Stradivari's violins
Without Antonio.   *Poems: Stradivarius*, l. 140

THOMAS STEARNS ELIOT
1888-

2 Because I do not hope to turn again
Because I do not hope
Because I do not hope to turn.   *Ash Wednesday*

3   Turning
Wearily, as one would turn to nod good-bye to
   Rochefoucauld,
If the street were time and he at the end of the street.
      The Boston Evening Transcript

4 Time present and time past
Are both perhaps present in time future,
And time future contained in time past.
      Burnt Norton

5   Human kind
Cannot bear very much reality.   *Ib.*

6 At the still point of the turning world.   *Ib.*

7 In my beginning is my end.   *East Coker*

8 That was a way of putting it—not very satisfactory:
A periphrastic study in a worn-out poetical fashion,
Leaving one still with the intolerable wrestle
With words and meanings.   *Ib.*

9   Each venture
Is a new beginning, a raid on the inarticulate
With shabby equipment always deteriorating
In the general mess of imprecision of feeling.   *Ib.*

10 We are the hollow men
We are the stuffed men
Leaning together.   *The Hollow Men*

11 Between the idea
And the reality
Between the motion
And the act
Falls the Shadow.   *Ib.*

12 This is the way the world ends
Not with a bang but a whimper.   *Ib.*

13 A cold coming we had of it,
Just the worst time of the year
For a journey, and such a long journey:
The ways deep and the weather sharp,
The very dead of winter.   *Journey of the Magi*

14   Last season's fruit is eaten
And the fullfed beast shall kick the empty pail.
For last year's words belong to last year's language
And next year's words await another voice.
      Little Gidding

15 When the evening is spread out against the sky
Like a patient etherized upon a table.
      Love Song of J. Alfred Prufrock

16 In the room the women come and go
Talking of Michelangelo.   *Ib.*

17 The yellow fog that rubs its back upon the window-
   panes.   *Ib.*

18 I have measured out my life with coffee spoons.   *Ib.*

19 I should have been a pair of ragged claws
Scuttling across the floors of silent seas.   *Ib.*

20 And I have seen the eternal Footman hold my coat
   and snicker,
And in short, I was afraid.
      Love Song of J. Alfred Prufrock

21 I grow old . . . I grow old . . .
I shall wear the bottoms of my trousers rolled.   *Ib.*

22 I have heard the mermaids singing, each to each;
I do not think that they will sing to me.   *Ib.*

23 I am aware of the damp souls of housemaids
Sprouting despondently at area gates.
      Morning at the Window

24 The sapient sutlers of the Lord.
      Mr. Eliot's Sunday Morning Service

25 The last temptation is the greatest treason:
To do the right deed for the wrong reason.
      Murder in the Cathedral, pt. 1

26 The nightingales are singing near
The Convent of the Sacred Heart
And sang within the bloody wood
When Agamemnon cried aloud.
      Sweeney Among the Nightingales

27 April is the cruellest month, breeding
Lilacs out of the dead land, mixing
Memory and desire, stirring
Dull roots with spring rain.
      The Waste Land, i. *The Burial of the Dead*

28 And I will show you something different from either
Your shadow at morning striding behind you,
Or your shadow at evening rising to meet you
I will show you fear in a handful of dust.   *Ib.*

29 'Jug Jug' to dirty ears.   *Ib.* ii. *A Game of Chess*

30 Musing upon the king my brother's wreck
And on the king my father's death before him.
      Ib. iii. *The Fire Sermon*

31 O the moon shines bright on Mrs. Porter
And on her daughter
They wash their feet in soda water.   *Ib.*

32 When lovely woman stoops to folly and
Paces about her room again, alone,
She smoothes her hair with automatic hand,
And puts a record on the gramophone.   *Ib.*

33 Webster was much possessed by death.
      Whispers of Immortality

34 Donne, I suppose, was such another
Who found no substitute for sense,
To seize and clutch and penetrate;
Expert beyond experience.   *Ib.*

QUEEN ELIZABETH I
1533-1603

35 'Twas God the word that spake it,
He took the Bread and brake it;
And what the word did make it;
That I believe, and take it.
   *Answer on being asked her opinion of Christ's
presence in the Sacrament.* S. Clarke's *Marrow
of Ecclesiastical History*, pt. ii, *Life of Queen
Elizabeth*, ed. 1675

36 The queen of Scots is this day leichter of a fair son,
   and I am but a barren stock.
   J. B. Black, *The Reign of Elizabeth (Oxford History of England)*, ch. 3, p. 75

1 Good-morning, gentlemen both. [To a delegation of eighteen tailors.]
    Chamberlin, *Sayings of Queen Elizabeth*, p. 28

2 To your text, Mr. Dean! to your text!   *Ib.* p. 137

3 I am your anointed Queen. I will never be by violence constrained to do anything. I thank God I am endued with such qualities that if I were turned out of the Realm in my petticoat I were able to live in any place in Christome.   *Ib.* p. 142

4 I will make you shorter by the head.
    Recueil des Dépôts, trans. by Cooper, vol. ii, p. 169, *cit.* Chamberlin, p. 224

5 The daughter of debate, that eke discord doth sow. [Mary Queen of Scots.]
    Chamberlin, *Sayings of Queen Elizabeth*, p. 301

6 Madam I may not call you; mistress I am ashamed to call you; and so I know not what to call you; but howsoever, I thank you. [To the wife of the Archbishop of Canterbury. The Queen did not approve of married clergy.]
    Harington, *Brief View of the State of the Church*, 1607

7 God may forgive you, but I never can. [To the Countess of Nottingham.]
    The Queen . . . crying to her that God might pardon her, but she never could.
    Hume, *History of England under the House of Tudor*, vol. ii, ch. 7

8 If thy heart fails thee, climb not at all.
    Lines written on a window after Sir Walter Ralegh's line 'Fain would I climb, yet fear I to fall.' Fuller, *Worthies of England*, vol. i, p. 419

9 Semper eadem.   *Motto*

10 As for me, I see no such great cause why I should either be fond to live or fear to die. I have had good experience of this world, and I know what it is to be a subject and what to be a sovereign. Good neighbours I have had, and I have met with bad: and in trust I have found treason.
    Speech to Parliament, 1586. Camden's *Annals*, p. 98

11 I know I have the body of a weak and feeble woman, but I have the heart and stomach of a king, and of a king of England too; and think foul scorn that Parma or Spain, or any prince of Europe, should dare to invade the borders of my realm.
    Speech to the Troops at Tilbury on the Approach of the Armada, 1588

12 Though God hath raised me high, yet this I count the glory of my crown: that I have reigned with your loves.
    The Golden Speech, 1601. D'Ewes's *Journal*, p. 659

13 Must! Is *must* a word to be addressed to princes? Little man, little man! thy father, if he had been alive, durst not have used that word.
    To Robert Cecil. On her death-bed. J. R. Green, *A Short History of the English People*, ch. vii

JOHN ELLERTON
1826–1893

14 Now the labourer's task is o'er;
Now the battle-day is past;

Now upon tne farther shore
Lands the voyager at last.
    Hymns for the Society for Promoting Christian Knowledge. Now the Labourer's Task

15 Father, in Thy gracious keeping
Leave we now Thy servant sleeping.   *Ib.*

16 We stand to bless Thee ere our worship cease;
Then, lowly kneeling, wait Thy word of peace.
    Hymns Ancient and Modern. Saviour, Again to Thy Dear Name We Raise

17 The day Thou gavest, Lord, is ended,
The darkness falls at Thy behest.
    A Liturgy for Missionary Meetings. The Day Thou Gavest

JANE ELLIOT
1727–1805

18 I've heard them lilting, at the ewe milking.
Lasses a' lilting, before dawn of day;
But now they are moaning, on ilka green loaning;
The flowers of the forest are a' wede away.
    The Flowers of the Forest

CHARLOTTE ELLIOTT
1789–1871

19 'Christian! seek not yet repose,'
Hear thy guardian angel say;
Thou art in the midst of foes—
    'Watch and pray.'
    Morning and Evening Hymns. Christian! Seek Not Yet Repose

20 Just as I am, without one plea
But that Thy blood was shed for me,
And that Thou bidd'st me come to Thee,
O Lamb of God, I come!
    Invalid's Hymn Book. Just As I Am

EBENEZER ELLIOTT
1781–1849

21 What is a communist? One who hath yearnings
For equal division of unequal earnings.
    Poetical Works. Epigram

22 When wilt thou save the people?
Oh, God of Mercy! when?
The people, Lord, the people!
Not thrones and crowns, but men!
    Ib. The People's Anthem

GEORGE ELLIS
see
SIR GREGORY GANDER

HENRY HAVELOCK ELLIS
1859–1939

23 Every artist writes his own autobiography.
    The New Spirit. Tolstoi II

ELSTOW

24 Elstow ['One Elstow, a friar of the order of Observant Friars'] smiling said . . . 'With thanks to God we know the way to heaven, to be as ready by water as by land, and therefore we care not which way we go.'
    When threatened with drowning by Henry VIII.
    Stow, *Annales*, 1615, p. 543.

RALPH WALDO EMERSON
1803–1882

1 There is no great and no small
  To the Soul that maketh all:
And where it cometh, all things are;
  And it cometh everywhere.　*The Absorbing Soul*

2 I am the owner of the sphere,
  Of the seven stars and the solar year,
Of Caesar's hand, and Plato's brain,
  Of Lord Christ's heart, and Shakespeare's strain. *Ib.*

3 If the red slayer think he slays,
  Or if the slain think he is slain,
They know not well the subtle ways
  I keep, and pass, and turn again.　*Brahma*

4 Far or forgot to me is near.　*Ib.*

5 I am the doubter and the doubt,
  And I the hymn the Brahmin sings.　*Ib.*

6 But thou, meek lover of the good!
  Find me, and turn thy back on heaven.　*Ib.*

7 By the rude bridge that arched the flood,
  Their flag to April's breeze unfurled,
Here once the embattled farmers stood,
  And fired the shot heard round the world.
    *Hymn Sung at the Completion of the Concord
    Monument*

8 Knows he who tills this lonely field,
  To reap its scanty corn,
What mystic fruit his acres yield
  At midnight and at morn?　*Dirge. Concord, 1838*

9 Nor knowest thou what argument
  Thy life to thy neighbour's creed has lent.
All are needed by each one;
  Nothing is fair or good alone.　*Each and All*

10 O fair and stately maid, whose eyes
  Were kindled in the upper skies
At the same torch that lighted mine.　*To Eva*

11 Hast thou named all the birds without a gun?
    Forbearance

12 Give all to love:
  Obey thy heart;
Friends, kindred, days,
Estate, good fame,
Plans, credit, and the Muse,—
Nothing refuse.　*Give All to Love*

13 Cling with life to the maid;
But when the surprise,
First vague shadow of surmise
Flits across her bosom young
Of a joy apart from thee,
Free be she, fancy-free.　*Ib.*

14 Heartily know,
When half-gods go,
The gods arrive.　*Ib.*

15 Good-bye, proud world! I'm going home:
Thou art not my friend, and I'm not thine. *Good-bye*

16 For what are they all in their high conceit,
When man in the bush with God may meet?　*Ib.*

17 A subtle chain of countless rings
The next unto the farthest brings,
And, striving to be man, the worm
Mounts through all the spires of form.　*May Day*

18 The mountain and the squirrel
  Had a quarrel;
And the former called the latter 'Little Prig'.
Bun replied,
'You are doubtless very big;
But all sorts of things and weather
Must be taken in together,
To make up a year
And a sphere.'
    Fable, The Mountain and the Squirrel

19 Things are in the saddle,
  And ride mankind.
    Ode, Inscribed to W. H. Channing

20 Olympian bards who sung
  Divine ideas below,
Which always find us young,
  And always keep us so.　*The Poet*

21 I like a church; I like a cowl;
I love a prophet of the soul;
And on my heart monastic aisles
Fall like sweet strains, or pensive smiles;
Yet not for all his faith can see,
Would I that cowlèd churchman be.　*The Problem*

22 Not from a vain or shallow thought
His awful Jove young Phidias brought.　*Ib.*

23 The hand that rounded Peter's dome,
And groined the aisles of Christian Rome,
Wrought in a sad sincerity;
Himself from God he could not free;
He builded better than he knew;—
The conscious stone to beauty grew.　*Ib.*

24 Taylor, the Shakespeare of divines.　*Ib.*

25 Some of your hurts you have cured,
  And the sharpest you still have survived,
But what torments of grief you endured
  From evils which never arrived!
    Quatrains. Borrowing (from the French)

26 Rhodora! if the sages ask thee why
This charm is wasted on the earth and sky,
Tell them, dear, that if eyes were made for seeing,
Then Beauty is its own excuse for being.　*The Rhodora*

27 Though love repine, and reason chafe,
  There came a voice without reply,—
''Tis man's perdition to be safe,
  When for the truth he ought to die.'　*Sacrifice*

28 The frolic architecture of the snow. *The Snowstorm*

29 Wilt thou seal up the avenues of ill?
Pay every debt, as if God wrote the bill.　*Solution*

30 It is time to be old,
To take in sail.　*Terminus*

31 House and tenant go to ground,
Lost in God, in Godhead found.　*Threnody*

32 So nigh is grandeur to our dust,
  So near is God to man,
When Duty whispers low, *Thou must*,
  The youth replies, *I can*.　*Voluntaries*, iii

33 There is no way to success in our art but to take off
your coat, grind paint, and work like a digger on
the railroad, all day and every day.
    Conduct of Life. Power

34 Art is a jealous mistress.　*Ib. Wealth*

EMERSON

1 The louder he talked of his honour, the faster we counted our spoons. *Conduct of Life. Worship*

2 London is the epitome of our times, and the Rome of to-day. *English Traits*, xviii. *Result*

3 So . . . I feel in regard to this aged England . . . pressed upon by transitions of trade and . . . competing populations,—I see her not dispirited, not weak, but well remembering that she has seen dark days before;—indeed, with a kind of instinct that she sees a little better in a cloudy day, and that, in storm of battle and calamity, she has a secret vigour and a pulse like a cannon.
Ib. ch. 19 (*Speech at Manchester, 1847*)

4 Nothing astonishes men so much as common-sense and plain dealing. *Essays*, xii. *Art*

5 Though we travel the world over to find the beautiful we must carry it with us or we find it not. *Ib.*

6 Those who listened to Lord Chatham felt that there was something finer in the man, than anything which he said. *Ib.* xv. *Character*

7 Beware when the great God lets loose a thinker on this planet. *Ib.* x. *Circles*

8 People wish to be settled: only as far as they are unsettled is there any hope for them. *Ib.*

9 Nothing great was ever achieved without enthusiasm. *Ib.*

10 Men are better than this theology.
Ib. iii. *Compensation*

11 I knew a witty physician who found the creed in the biliary duct, and used to affirm that if there was disease in the liver, the man became a Calvinist, and if that organ was sound, he became a Unitarian.
Ib. xiv. *Experience*

12 To fill the hour—that is happiness. *Ib.*

13 The wise through excess of wisdom is made a fool. *Ib.*

14 The years teach much which the days never know. *Ib.*

15 Yet these uneasy pleasures and fine pains are for curiosity, and not for life. *Ib.* vi. *Friendship*

16 A friend may well be reckoned the masterpiece of Nature. *Ib.*

17 Tart, cathartic virtue. *Ib.* viii. *Heroism*

18 O friend, never strike sail to a fear! Come into port greatly, or sail with God the seas. *Ib.*

19 It was a high counsel that I once heard given to a young person, 'Always do what you are afraid to do.' *Ib.*

20 Every reform was once a private opinion, and when it shall be a private opinion again it will solve the problem of the age. *Ib.* i. *History*

21 There is properly no history; only biography. *Ib.*

22 God offers to every mind its choice between truth and repose. *Ib.* xi. *Intellect*

23 He in whom the love of truth predominates . . . submits to the inconvenience of suspense and imperfect opinion; but he is a candidate for truth . . . and respects the highest law of his being. *Ib.*

24 All mankind love a lover. *Ib.* v. *Love*

25 Men are conservatives when they are least vigorous, or when they are most luxurious. They are conservatives after dinner.
Essays, New England Reformers

26 The reward of a thing well done, is to have done it. *Ib.*

27 We are wiser than we know. *Ib.* ix. *The Over-Soul*

28 Converse with a mind that is grandly simple, and literature looks like word-catching. *Ib.*

29 Words and deeds are quite indifferent modes of the divine energy. Words are also actions, and actions are a kind of words. *Ib.* xiii. *The Poet*

30 It is not metres, but a metre-making argument, that makes a poem. *Ib.*

31 We are symbols, and inhabit symbols. *Ib.*

32 Language is fossil poetry. *Ib.*

33 The poet knows that he speaks adequately, then, only when he speaks somewhat wildly, or, 'with the flower of the mind.' *Ib.*

34 Good men must not obey the laws too well.
Ib. xix. *Politics*

35 In skating over thin ice, our safety is in our speed.
Ib. vii. *Prudence*

36 To believe your own thought, to believe that what is true for you in your private heart is true for all men,—that is genius. *Ib.* ii. *Self-Reliance*

37 To-morrow a stranger will say with masterly good sense precisely what we have thought and felt all the time, and we shall be forced to take with shame our own opinion from another. *Ib.*

38 Society everywhere is in conspiracy against the manhood of every one of its members. *Ib.*

39 Whoso would be a man must be a nonconformist. *Ib.*

40 A foolish consistency is the hobgoblin of little minds, adored by little statesmen and philosophers and divines. With consistency a great soul has simply nothing to do. . . . Speak what you think to-day in words as hard as cannon-balls, and to-morrow speak what to-morrow thinks in hard words again, though it contradict every thing you said to-day. *Ib.*

41 Is it so bad, then, to be misunderstood? Pythagoras was misunderstood, and Socrates, and Jesus, and Luther, and Copernicus, and Galileo, and Newton, and every pure and wise spirit that ever took flesh. To be great is to be misunderstood. *Ib.*

42 Shoves Jesus and Judas equally aside. *Ib.*

43 I like the silent church before the service begins, better than any preaching. *Ib.*

44 As men's prayers are a disease of the will so are their creeds a disease of the intellect. *Ib.*

45 Every Stoic was a Stoic; but in Christendom where is the Christian? *Ib.*

46 There are not in the world at any one time more than a dozen persons who read and understand Plato:— never enough to pay for an edition of his works; yet to every generation these come duly down, for the sake of those few persons, as if God brought them written in his hand. *Ib.* iv. *Spiritual Laws*

47 If you would not be known to do anything, never do it. *Ib.*

1 We are always getting ready to live, but never living.
Journals, 13 Apr. 1834

2 I hate quotations. *Ib. May 1849*

3 Man does not live by bread alone, but by faith, by admiration, by sympathy.
Lectures and Biographical Sketches. The Sovereignty of Ethics

4 Great men are they who see that spiritual is stronger than any material force, that thoughts rule the world.
Letters and Social Aims. Progress of Culture, Phi Beta Kappa Address, 18 July 1876

5 By necessity, by proclivity,—and by delight, we all quote. *Ib. Quotation and Originality*

6 Next to the originator of a good sentence is the first quoter of it. *Ib.*

7 I have heard with admiring submission the experience of the lady who declared that the sense of being well-dressed gives a feeling of inward tranquillity which religion is powerless to bestow. [Miss C. F. Forbes, 1817–1911.] *Ib. Social Aims*

8 When Nature has work to be done, she creates a genius to do it. *Method of Nature*

9 Every hero becomes a bore at last.
Representative Men. Uses of Great Men

10 Talent alone cannot make a writer. There must be a man behind the book. *Ib. Goethe*

11 Is not marriage an open question, when it is alleged, from the beginning of the world, that such as are in the institution wish to get out; and such as are out wish to get in. *Ib. Montaigne*

12 Belief consists in accepting the affirmations of the soul; Unbelief, in denying them. *Ib.*

13 Never read any book that is not a year old.
Society and Solitude. Books

14 Hitch your wagon to a star. *Ib. Civilization*

15 We boil at different degrees. *Ib. Eloquence*

16 One of our statesmen said, 'The curse of this country is eloquent men.' *Ib.*

17 America is a country of young men. *Ib. Old Age*

18 'Tis the good reader that makes the good book.
Ib. Success

19 Invention breeds invention. *Ib. Works and Days*

20 'Well,' said Red Jacket [to someone complaining that he had not enough time], 'I suppose you have all there is.' *Ib.*

21 Glittering generalities! They are blazing ubiquities.
Attr. remark on Rufus Choate (see 142 : 25 sneering at the ideas of the Declaration of Independence as 'glittering generalities'

22 If a man write a better book, preach a better sermon, or make a better mouse-trap than his neighbour, tho' he build his house in the woods, the world will make a beaten path to his door.
Mrs. Sarah S. B. Yule (1856–1916) credits the quotation to Emerson in her Borrowings *(1889), stating in* The Docket, *Feb. 1912, that she copied this in her handbook from a lecture delivered by Emerson. The 'mouse-trap' quotation was the occasion of a long controversy, owing to Elbert Hubbard's claim to its authorship.*

23 He who has a thousand friends has not a friend to spare,
And he who has one enemy will meet him everywhere.
Translations. From Omar Chiam

THOMAS DUNN ENGLISH
1819–1902

24 Oh! don't you remember sweet Alice, Ben Bolt,
Sweet Alice, whose hair was so brown,
Who wept with delight when you gave her a smile,
And trembled with fear at your frown? *Ben Bolt*

ENNIUS
239–169 B.C.

25 Moribus antiquis res stat Romana virisque.
The Roman state stands by ancient customs, and its manhood. *Annals*

26 Unus homo nobis cunctando restituit rem.
One man by delaying saved the state for us.
Cicero, De Senectute, iv. 10

HENRY ERSKINE
1746–1817

27 In the garb of old Gaul, wi' the fire of old Rome.
In the Garb of Old Gaul

THOMAS ERSKINE, BARON ERSKINE
1750–1823

28 The uncontrouled licentiousness of a brutal and insolent soldiery.
Report (1796) of Erskine's defence of William Stone

ROBERT DEVEREUX, EARL OF ESSEX
1566–1601

29 Reasons are not like garments, the worse for wearing.
To Lord Willoughby, 4 Jan. 1598–9. See Notes and Queries, Ser. X, vol. ii, p. 23

HENRI ESTIENNE
1531–1598

30 Si jeunesse savoit; si vieillesse pouvoit.
If youth knew; if age could.
Les Prémices, Épigramme cxci

SIR GEORGE ETHEREGE
1635 ?–1691

31 I must confess I am a fop in my heart; ill customs influence my very senses, and I have been so used to affectation that without the help of the air of the court what is natural cannot touch me.
Letter to Mr. Poley, 2/12 Jan. 1687/8

32 Few of our plays can boast of more wit than I have heard him speak at a supper. [Sir Charles Sedley.]
Letter to Mr. Will. Richards, undated

33 I walk within the purlieus of the Law.
Love in a Tub, I. iii

34 What a pretty lisp he has! *The Man of Mode, I. i*

1 Do not vow—Our love is frail as is our life, and full as little in our power; and are you sure you shall out-live this day? *The Man of Mode*, II. i

2 When love grows diseas'd, the best thing we can do is to put it to a violent death; I cannot endure the torture of a lingring and consumptive passion.
Ib. ii

3 Writing, Madam, 's a mechanic part of wit! A gentleman should never go beyond a song or a billet.
Ib. IV. i

4 None ever had so strange an art
His passion to convey
Into a listening virgin's heart,
And steal her soul away.

Fly, fly betimes, for fear you give
Occasion for your fate.
In vain, said she, in vain I strive,
Alas! 'tis now too late! *Ib.* v. i

5 What e'er you say, I know all beyond High-Park's a desart to you. *Ib.* ii

EUCLID
fl. c. 300 B.C.

6 Quod erat demonstrandum (trans. from the Greek).
Which was to be proved.

7 A line is length without breadth.

8 There is no 'royal road' to geometry.
(*Said to Ptolemy I.* Proclus, *Comment on Euclid*, Prol. G. 20.)

EURIPIDES
480–406 B.C.

9 ἡ γλῶσσ' ὀμώμοχ', ἡ δὲ φρὴν ἀνώμοτος.

'Twas but my tongue, 'twas not my soul that swore.
Hippolytus, 612. Trans. by Gilbert Murray

ABEL EVANS
1679–1737

10 When Tadlow walks the streets, the paviours cry,
'God bless you, Sir!' and lay their rammers by.
Epigram. On Dr. Tadlow

11 Under this stone, Reader, survey
Dead Sir John Vanbrugh's house of clay.
Lie heavy on him, Earth! for he
Laid many heavy loads on thee!
Epitaph on Sir John Vanbrugh, Architect of Blenheim Palace

JOHN EVELYN
1620–1706

12 This knight was indeed a valiant gentleman; but not a little given to romance, when he spake of himself. *Diary, 6 Sept. 1651*

13 Mulberry Garden, now the only place of refreshment about the town for persons of the best quality to be exceedingly cheated at. *Ib. 10 May 1654*

14 That miracle of a youth, Mr. Christopher Wren.
Ib. 11 July 1654

15 I saw Hamlet Prince of Denmark played, but now the old plays began to disgust this refined age.
Diary, 26 Nov. 1661

DAVID EVERETT
1769–1813

16 You'd scarce expect one of my age
To speak in public on the stage;
And if I chance to fall below
Demosthenes or Cicero,
Don't view me with a critic's eye,
But pass my imperfections by.
Large streams from little fountains flow,
Tall oaks from little acorns grow.
Lines Written for a School Declamation

VISCOUNT EVERSLEY
[CHARLES SHAW-LEFEVRE]
1794–1888

17 What is that fat gentleman in such a passion about?
Remark as a child on hearing Mr. Fox speak in Parliament. G. W. E. Russell, *Collections and Recollections*, ch. 11

WILLIAM NORMAN EWER
1885–

18 I gave my life for freedom—This I know:
For those who bade me fight had told me so.
Five Souls, 1917

19 How odd
Of God
To choose
The Jews. *How Odd*

FREDERICK WILLIAM FABER
1814–1863

20 Have mercy on us worms of earth.
Jesus and Mary. Have Mercy on Us, God Most High

21 My God, how wonderful Thou art!
Thy majesty how bright,
How beautiful Thy mercy-seat
In depths of burning light!
Ib. My God, How Wonderful Thou Art!

22 Thine endless wisdom, boundless power,
And awful purity! *Ib.*

23 Hark! Hark! my soul, angelic songs are swelling
O'er earth's green fields and ocean's wave-beat shore!
How sweet the truth those blessed strains are telling
Of that new life when sin shall be no more!
Oratory Hymns. The Pilgrims of the Night

24 The music of the Gospel leads us home. *Ib.*

25 Rest comes at length; though life be long and dreary,
The day must dawn, and darksome night be passed.
Ib.

26 O Paradise! O Paradise!
Who doth not crave for rest? *Ib. Paradise*

27 Faith of our fathers! holy faith!
We will be true to thee till death.
Ib. A Pledge of Faithfulness

ROBERT FABYAN

d. 1513

1 Finally he paid the debt of nature.
Chronicles, pt. ii, xli

LUCIUS CARY, VISCOUNT FALKLAND

1610?-1643

2 When it is not necessary to change, it is necessary not to change.
A Speech concerning Episcopacy [delivered 1641].
A Discourse of Infallibility, 1660

AUGUST HEINRICH HOFFMANN VON FALLERSLEBEN

1798-1874

3 Deutschland, Deutschland über alles.
Germany, Germany over all.   *Title of Song*

GEORGE FARQUHAR

1678-1707

4 Sir, you shall taste my *Anno Domini*.
The Beaux' Stratagem, i. i

5 I have fed purely upon ale; I have eat my ale, drank my ale, and I always sleep upon ale.   *Ib.*

6 My Lady Bountiful.   *Ib.*

7 Says little, thinks less, and does—nothing at all, faith.
Ib.

8 'Tis still my maxim, that there is no scandal like rags, nor any crime so shameful as poverty.   *Ib.*

9 There's some diversion in a talking blockhead; and since a woman must wear chains, I would have the pleasure of hearing 'em rattle a little.   *Ib.* ii. ii

10 No woman can be a beauty without a fortune.   *Ib.*

11 I believe they talked of me, for they laughed consumedly.   *Ib.* iii. i

12 'Twas for the good of my country that I should be abroad.—Anything for the good of one's country—I'm a Roman for that.   *Ib.* ii

13 Captain is a good travelling name, and so I take it. *Ib.*

14 AIMWELL:
Then you understand Latin, Mr. Bonniface?

BONNIFACE:
Not I, Sir, as the saying is, but he talks it so very fast that I'm sure it must be good.   *Ib.*

15 There are secrets in all families.   *Ib.* iii

16 How a little love and good company improves a woman!   *Ib.* iv. i

17 It is a maxim that man and wife should never have it in their power to hang one another.   *Ib.* ii

18 Spare all I have, and take my life.   *Ib.* v. ii

19 I hate all that don't love me, and slight all that do.
The Constant Couple, i. ii

20 Grant me some wild expressions, Heavens, or I shall burst— . . . Words, words or I shall burst. *Ib.* v. iii

21 Charming women can true converts make,
We love the precepts for the teacher's sake.   *Ib.*

22 Crimes, like virtues, are their own rewards.
The Inconstant, iv. ii

23 'Tis an old saying, Like master, like man; why not as well, Like mistress, like maid?
Love and a Bottle, i. i

24 Money is the sinews of love, as of war.   *Ib.* ii. i

25 Poetry's a mere drug, Sir.   *Ib.* iii. ii

26 He answered the description the page gave to a T, Sir.   *Ib.* iv. iii

27 And there's a pleasure in being mad,
Which none but madmen know.
The Recruiting Officer, i. iii (see also 193:33)

28 Hanging and marriage, you know, go by Destiny.
Ib. iii. ii

29 I cou'd be mighty foolish, and fancy my self mighty witty; Reason still keeps its throne, but it nods a little, that's all.   *Ib.*

30 A lady, if undrest at Church, looks silly,
One cannot be devout in dishabilly.
The Stage Coach, prologue

31 I'm privileg'd to be very impertinent, being an Oxonian.   *Sir Harry Wildair*, ii. i

32 The King of Spain is dead.   *Ib.* ii

REV. FREDERICK WILLIAM FARRAR

1831-1903

33 Russell . . . acted invariably from the highest principles.   *Eric, or Little by Little*, pt. i, ch. 3

34 Russell, let me always call you Edwin, and call me Eric.   *Ib.* ch. 4

35 'What a surly devil that is,' said Eric, . . .
'A surly—? Oh, Eric, that's the first time I ever heard you swear.'   *Ib.* ch. 8

36 'By heavens, this is *too* bad!' he exclaimed, stamping his foot with anger. 'What have I ever done to you young blackguards, that you should treat me thus?'
Ib. pt. ii, ch. 1

37 They all drank his health with the usual honours:—
'. . . For he's a jolly good fe-el-low, which nobody can deny.'   *Julian Home*, ch. 21

EMPEROR FERDINAND I

1503-1564

38 Fiat justitia, et pereat mundus.
Let justice be done, though the world perish.
Saying

JOHN FERRIAR

1761-1815

39 Now cheaply bought for thrice their weight in gold
Illustrations of Sterne. Bibliomania, l. 65

WILLIAM PITT FESSENDEN

1806-1869

40 Repudiate the repudiators.
Presidential Campaign Slogan, 1868

EUGENE FIELD
1850–1895

1 But I, when I undress me
　Each night, upon my knees
Will ask the Lord to bless me
　With apple pie and cheese.　*Apple Pie and Cheese*

2 When I demanded of my friend what viands he
　preferred,
He quoth: 'A large cold bottle, and a small hot bird!'
　The Bottle and the Bird

3 A little peach in an orchard grew,—
A little peach of emerald hue;
Warmed by the sun and wet by the dew,
　It grew.　*The Little Peach*

4 Listen to my tale of woe.　*Ib.*

5 Wynken, Blynken, and Nod one night
　Sailed off in a wooden shoe—
Sailed on a river of crystal light,
　Into a sea of dew.　*Wynken, Blynken, and Nod*

HENRY FIELDING
1707–1754

6 '*Tace*, madam,' answered Murphy, 'is Latin for a
　candle.'　*Amelia*, bk. i, ch. 10

7 It hath been often said, that it is not death, but dying,
　which is terrible.　*Ib.* bk. iii, ch. 4

8 When widows exclaim loudly against second mar-
　riages, I would always lay a wager, that the man, if
　not the wedding-day, is absolutely fixed on.
　Ib. bk. vi, ch. 8

9 One fool at least in every married couple.
　Ib. bk. ix, ch. 4

10 There is not in the universe a more ridiculous, nor
　a more contemptible animal, than a proud clergy-
　man.　*Ib.* ch. 10

11 One of my illustrious predecessors.
　Covent-Garden Journal, No. 3, 11 Jan. 1752

12 I am as sober as a Judge.
　Don Quixote in England, iii. xiv

13 Oh! The roast beef of England,
And old England's roast beef.
　The Grub Street Opera, iii. iii

14 He in a few minutes ravished this fair creature, or at
　least would have ravished her, if she had not, by
　a timely compliance, prevented him.
　Jonathan Wild, bk. iii, ch. 7

15 But pray, Mr. Wild, why bitch?　*Ib.* ch. 8

16 To whom nothing is given, of him can nothing be
　required.　*Joseph Andrews*, bk. ii, ch. 8

17 I describe not men, but manners; not an individual,
　but a species.　*Ib.* bk. iii, ch. 1

18 They are the affectation of affectation.　*Ib.* ch. 3

19 Public schools are the nurseries of all vice and im-
　morality.　*Ib.* ch. 5

20 Some folks rail against other folks, because other
　folks have what some folks would be glad of.
　Ib. bk. iv, ch. 6

21 Love and scandal are the best sweeteners of tea.
　Love in Several Masques, iv. xi

22 Yes, I had two strings to my bow; both golden ones,
　agad! and both cracked.
　Love in Several Masques, v. xiii

23 Map me no maps, sir, my head is a map, a map of the
　whole world.　*Rape upon Rape*, i. v

24 Every physician almost hath his favourite disease.
　Tom Jones, bk. ii, ch. 9

25 Thwackum was for doing justice, and leaving mercy
　to heaven.　*Ib.* bk. iii, ch. 10

26 A late facetious writer, who told the public that when-
　ever he was dull they might be assured there was
　a design in it.　*Ib.* bk. v, ch. 1

27 O! more than Gothic ignorance.　*Ib.* bk. vii, ch. 3

28 'I did not mean to abuse the cloth; I only said your
　conclusion was a *non sequitur*.'—
'You are another,' cries the sergeant, 'an you come to
　that, no more a *sequitur* than yourself.'
　Ib. bk. ix, ch. 6

29 An amiable weakness.　*Ib.* bk. x, ch. 8

30 His designs were strictly honourable, as the phrase
　is; that is, to rob a lady of her fortune by way of
　marriage.　*Ib.* bk. xi, ch. 4

31 Composed that monstrous animal a husband and wife.
　Ib. bk. xv, ch. 9

32 Nay, you may call me coward if you will; but if that
　little man there upon the stage is not frightened,
　I never saw any man frightened in my life.
　Ib. bk. xvi, ch. 5

33 'He the best player!' cries Partridge, with a contemp-
　tuous sneer. 'Why, I could act as well as he myself.
　I am sure, if I had seen a ghost, I should have
　looked in the very same manner, and done just as
　he did. . . . The king for my money! He speaks
　all his words distinctly, half as loud again as the
　other. Anybody may see he is an actor.'　*Ib.*

34 All Nature wears one universal grin.
　Tom Thumb the Great, i. i

35 To sun my self in Huncamunca's eyes.　*Ib.* iii

36 When I'm not thank'd at all, I'm thank'd enough,
I've done my duty, and I've done no more.　*Ib.*

37 The dusky night rides down the sky,
　And ushers in the morn;
The hounds all join in glorious cry,
　The huntsman winds his horn:
And a-hunting we will go.
　A-Hunting We Will Go

L'ABBÉ EDGEWORTH DE FIRMONT
1745–1807

38 Fils de Saint Louis, montez au ciel.
Son of Saint Louis, ascend to heaven.
　*Attr. words to Louis XVI as he mounted the
　steps of the guillotine at his execution, 1793.
　No documentary proof at all.*

JOHN ARBUTHNOT FISHER, LORD FISHER
1841–1920

39 You will always be fools! We shall never be gentle-
　men!
　*The Times, 26 June 1919. Quoted by him as
　'the apposite words spoken by a German naval*

officer to his English confrère . . . On the whole I think I prefer to be the fool—even as a matter of business.'

1 Sack the lot! *The Times*, 2 Sept. 1919

ALBERT H. FITZ

2 You are my honey, honey-suckle,
I am the bee. *The Honey-Suckle and the Bee*

CHARLES FITZGEFFREY
1575?–1638

3 And bold and hard adventures t' undertake,
Leaving his country for his country's sake.
Life and Death of Sir Francis Drake (1596), ccxiii

EDWARD FITZGERALD
1809–1883

4 Awake! for Morning in the Bowl of Night
Has flung the Stone that puts the Stars to Flight:
And Lo! the Hunter of the East has caught
The Sultan's Turret in a Noose of Light.
Omar Khayyám, ed. 1, i

5 Wake! For the Sun, who scatter'd into flight
The Stars before him from the Field of Night,
Drives Night along with them from Heav'n, and strikes
The Sultan's Turret with a Shaft of Light. *Ib.* ed. 4, i

6 Dreaming when Dawn's Left Hand was in the Sky
I heard a Voice within the Tavern cry,
'Awake, my Little ones, and fill the Cup
Before Life's Liquor in its Cup be dry.' *Ib.* ed. 1, ii

7 Before the phantom of False Morning died,
Methought a Voice within the Tavern cried,
'When all the Temple is prepared within,
Why nods the drowsy Worshipper outside?'
Ib. ed. 4, ii

8 Now the New Year reviving old Desires,
The thoughtful Soul to Solitude retires,
Where the White Hand of Moses on the Bough
Puts out, and Jesus from the Ground suspires.
Ib. eds. 1 and 4, iv

9 Iram indeed is gone with all its Rose,
And Jamshyd's Sev'n-ring'd Cup where no one knows;
But still the Vine her ancient Ruby yields,
And still a Garden by the Water blows. *Ib.* ed. 1, v

10 Iram indeed is gone with all his Rose. *Ib.* ed. 4, v

11 But still a Ruby kindles in the Vine,
And many a Garden by the Water blows. *Ib.*

12 In divine
High piping Pehlevi, with 'Wine! Wine! Wine!
Red Wine!'—the Nightingale cries to the Rose
That yellow Cheek of hers to incarnadine.
Ib. ed. 1, vi

13 That sallow cheek of hers to incarnadine.
Ib. ed. 4, vi

14 Come, fill the Cup, and in the Fire of Spring
The Winter Garment of Repentance fling:
The Bird of Time has but a little way
To fly—and Lo! the Bird is on the Wing.
Ib. ed. 1, vii

15 Come, fill the Cup, and in the fire of Spring
Your Winter-garment of Repentance fling:
The Bird of Time has but a little way
To flutter—and the Bird is on the wing.
Omar Khayyám, ed. 4, vii

16 The Wine of Life keeps oozing drop by drop,
The Leaves of Life keep falling one by one.
Ib. ed. 4, viii. Not in ed. 1

17 And look—a thousand Blossoms with the Day
Woke—and a thousand scatter'd into Clay.
Ib. ed. 1, viii

18 Each Morn a thousand Roses brings, you say;
Yes, but where leaves the Rose of Yesterday?
And this first Summer month that brings the Rose,
Shall take Jamshyd and Kaikobad away.
Ib. ed. 4, ix

19 But come with old Khayyám, and leave the Lot
Of Kaikobad and Kaikhosru forgot:
Let Rustum lay about him as he will,
Or Hatim Tai cry Supper—heed them not.
Ib. ed. 1, ix

20 Well, let it take them! What have we to do
With Kaikobad the Great, or Kaikhosru?
Let Zal and Rustum bluster as they will,
Or Hatim call to Supper—heed not you. *Ib.* ed. 4, x

21 And pity Sultan Mahmud on his Throne.
Ib. ed. 1, x

22 And Peace to Mahmud on his golden Throne.
Ib. ed. 4, xi

23 Here with a Loaf of Bread beneath the bough,
A Flask of Wine, a Book of Verse—and Thou
Beside me singing in the Wilderness—
And Wilderness is Paradise enow. *Ib.* ed. 1, xi

24 A Book of Verses underneath the Bough,
A Jug of Wine, a Loaf of Bread—and Thou
Beside me singing in the Wilderness—
Oh, Wilderness were Paradise enow! *Ib.* ed. 4, xii

25 Ah, take the Cash in hand and waive the Rest;
Oh, the brave Music of a *distant* Drum!
Ib. ed. 1, xii

26 Ah, take the Cash, and let the Credit go,
Nor heed the rumble of a distant Drum!
Ib. ed. 4, xiii

27 The Worldly Hope men set their Hearts upon
Turns Ashes—or it prospers; and anon,
Like Snow upon the Desert's dusty Face
Lighting a little Hour or two—is gone.
Ib. ed. 1, xiv; ed. 4, xvi

28 And those who husbanded the Golden Grain,
And those who flung it to the Winds like Rain,
Alike to no such aureate Earth are turn'd
As, buried once, Men want dug up again.
Ib. eds. 1 and 4, xv

29 Think, in this batter'd Caravanserai
Whose Doorways are alternate Night and Day,
How Sultan after Sultan with his Pomp
Abode his Hour or two, and went his way.
Ib. ed. 1, xv

30 Think, in this batter'd Caravanserai
Whose Portals are alternate Night and Day,
How Sultan after Sultan with his Pomp
Abode his destin'd Hour, and went his way.
Ib. ed. 4, xvii

1 They say the Lion and the Lizard keep
The Courts where Jamshýd gloried and drank deep:
And Bahram, that great Hunter—the Wild Ass
Stamps o'er his Head, and he lies fast asleep.
Omar Khayyám, ed. 1, xvii

2 Stamps o'er his Head, but cannot break his Sleep.
Ib. ed. 4, xviii

3 I sometimes think that never blows so red
The Rose as where some buried Caesar bled;
That every Hyacinth the Garden wears
Dropt in her Lap from some once lovely Head.
Ib. ed. 1, xviii; ed. 4, xix

4 And this reviving Herb whose tender Green
Fledges the River-Lip on which we lean—
Ah! lean upon it lightly! for who knows
From what once lovely Lip it springs unseen!
Ib. ed. 4, xx

5 Ah, my Belovéd, fill the Cup that clears
To-DAY of past Regrets and Future Fears:
To-morrow!—Why, To-morrow I may be
Myself with Yesterday's Sev'n thousand Years.
Ib. ed. 1, xx; ed. 4, xxi

6 Lo! some we loved, the loveliest and best
That Time and Fate of all their Vintage prest,
Have drunk their Cup a Round or two before,
And one by one crept silently to Rest. *Ib.* ed. 1, xxi

7 For some we loved, the loveliest and the best
That from his Vintage rolling Time hath prest.
Ib. ed. 4, xxii

8 Ah, make the most of what we yet may spend,
Before we too into the Dust descend;
Dust into Dust, and under Dust, to lie,
Sans Wine, sans Song, sans Singer, and—sans End!
Ib. ed. 1, xxiii; ed. 4, xxiv

9 Oh, come with old Khayyám, and leave the Wise
To talk; one thing is certain, that Life flies;
One thing is certain, and the Rest is Lies;
The Flower that once hath blown for ever dies.
Ib. ed. 1, xxvi

10 Myself when young did eagerly frequent
Doctor and Saint, and heard great argument
About it and about: but evermore
Came out by the same Door as in I went. *Ib.* xxvii

11 Came out by the same Door wherein I went.
Ib. ed. 4, xxvii

12 With them the Seed of Wisdom did I sow,
And with mine own hand wrought to make it grow;
And this was all the Harvest that I reap'd—
'I came like Water, and like Wind I go.'
Ib. eds. 1 and 4, xxviii

13 Into this Universe, and *Why* not knowing
Nor *Whence*, like Water willy-nilly flowing;
And out of it, as Wind along the Waste,
I know not *Whither*, willy-nilly blowing. *Ib.* xxix

14 What, without asking, hither hurried *whence*?
And, without asking, *whither* hurried hence!
Another and another Cup to drown
The Memory of this Impertinence! *Ib.* ed. 1, xxx

15 Oh, many a Cup of this forbidden Wine
Must drown the memory of that insolence!
Ib. ed. 4, xxx

16 There was a Door to which I found no Key:
There was a Veil past which I could not see:
Some little Talk awhile of ME and THEE
There seem'd—and then no more of THEE and ME.
Omar Khayyám, ed. 1, xxxii

17 There was the Door to which I found no Key;
There was the Veil through which I might not see:
Some little talk awhile of ME and THEE
There was—and then no more of THEE and ME.
Ib. ed. 4, xxxii

18 For in the Market-place, one Dusk of Day,
I watch'd the Potter thumping his wet clay:
And with its all obliterated Tongue
It murmur'd—'Gently, Brother, gently, pray!'
Ib. ed. 1, xxxvi. Not in ed. 4

19 Ah, fill the Cup:—what boots it to repeat
How Time is slipping underneath our Feet:
Unborn To-MORROW, and dead YESTERDAY,
Why fret about them if To-DAY be sweet!
Ib. ed. 1, xxxvii. Not in ed. 4

20 One Moment in Annihilation's Waste,
One Moment, of the Well of Life to taste—
The Stars are setting and the Caravan
Starts for the Dawn of Nothing—Oh, make haste!
Ib. ed. 1, xxxviii

21 A Moment's Halt—a momentary taste
Of BEING from the Well amid the Waste—
And lo!—the phantom Caravan has reach'd
The Nothing it set out from—Oh, make haste!
Ib. ed. 4, xlviii

22 Waste not your Hour, nor in the vain pursuit
Of This and That endeavour and dispute;
Better be jocund with the fruitful Grape
Than sadden after none, or bitter, Fruit. *Ib.* liv

23 You know, my Friends, with what a brave Carouse
I made a Second Marriage in my house;
Divorced old barren Reason from my Bed,
And took the Daughter of the Vine to Spouse. *Ib.* lv

24 Was never deep in anything but—Wine.
Ib. ed. 1, xli; ed. 4, lvi

25 The Grape that can with Logic absolute
The Two-and-Seventy jarring Sects confute.
Ib. ed. 1, xliii; ed. 4, lix

26 Oh threats of Hell and Hopes of Paradise!
One thing at least is certain—*This* Life flies;
One thing is certain and the rest is Lies;
The Flower that once has blown for ever dies.
Ib. ed. 4, lxiii

27 Strange, is it not? that of the myriads who
Before us pass'd the door of Darkness through,
Not one returns to tell us of the Road,
Which to discover we must travel too. *Ib.* lxiv

28 'Tis all a Chequer-board of Nights and Days
Where Destiny with Men for Pieces plays:
Hither and thither moves, and mates, and slays,
And one by one back in the Closet lays.
Ib. ed. 1, xlix

29 But helpless Pieces of the Game He plays
Upon this Chequer-board of Nights and Days;
Hither and thither moves, and checks, and slays,
And one by one back in the Closet lays.
Ib. ed. 4, lxix

1 The Ball no question makes of Ayes and Noes,
  But Here or There as strikes the Player goes;
    And He that toss'd you down into the Field,
  He knows about it all—HE knows—HE knows!
                    Omar Khayyám, ed. 4, lxx

2 The Moving Finger writes; and, having writ,
  Moves on: nor all thy Piety nor Wit
    Shall lure it back to cancel half a Line,
  Nor all thy Tears wash out a Word of it. *Ib. ed. 1, li*
  [Ed. 4, lxxi, reads 'your' instead of 'thy'.]

3 And that inverted Bowl we call The Sky,
  Whereunder crawling coop't we live and die,
    Lift not thy hands to *It* for help—for It
  Rolls impotently on as Thou or I.   *Ib.* lii

4 And that inverted Bowl they call the Sky.
                          Ib. ed. 4, lxxii

5 As impotently moves as you or I.   *Ib.*

6 With Earth's first Clay They did the Last Man knead,
  And there of the Last Harvest sow'd the Seed:
    And the first Morning of Creation wrote
  What the last Dawn of Reckoning shall read.
                    Ib. ed. 1, liii; ed. 4, lxxiii

7 Drink! for you know not whence you came, nor
      why:
  Drink! for you know not why you go, nor where.
                Ib. ed. 4, lxxiv. Not in ed. 1

8 One glimpse of it within the Tavern caught
  Better than in the Temple lost outright. *Ib. ed.1, lvi*

9 One Flash of it within the Tavern caught.
                          Ib. ed. 4, lxxvii

10 O Thou, who didst with Pitfall and with Gin
   Beset the Road I was to wander in,
     Thou wilt not with Predestination round
   Enmesh me, and impute my Fall to Sin?
                          Ib. ed. 1, lvii

11 Thou wilt not with Predestined Evil round
   Enmesh, and then impute my Fall to Sin!
                          Ib. ed. 4, lxxx

12 Oh, Thou, who Man of baser Earth didst make,
   And who with Eden didst devise the Snake;
     For all the Sin wherewith the Face of Man
   Is blacken'd, Man's Forgiveness give—and take!
                          Ib. ed. 1, lviii

13 And even with Paradise devise the Snake.
                          Ib. ed. 4, lxxxi

14 Then said a Second—'Ne'er a peevish Boy
   Would break the Bowl from which he drank in joy;
     And He that with his hand the Vessel made
   Will surely not in after Wrath destroy.'   *Ib.* lxxxv

15 After a momentary silence spake
   Some Vessel of a more ungainly Make;
     'They sneer at me for leaning all awry;
   What! did the Hand then of the Potter shake?'
                          Ib. lxxxvi

16 'Who *is* the Potter, pray, and who the Pot?'
                    Ib. ed. 1, lx; ed. 4, lxxxvii

17 Then said another—'Surely not in vain
   My Substance from the common Earth was ta'en,
     That He who subtly wrought me into Shape
   Should stamp me back to common Earth again.'
                          Ib. ed. 1, lxi

18 Another said—'Why, ne'er a peevish Boy,
   Would break the Vessel from which he drank in Joy;
     Shall He that *made* the Vessel in pure Love
   And Fancy, in an after Rage destroy!'
                    Omar Khayyám, ed. 1, lxii

19 Said one—'Folks of a surly Tapster tell,
   And daub his Visage with the Smoke of Hell;
     They talk of some strict Testing of us—Pish!
   He's a Good Fellow, and 'twill all be well.'
                    Ib. lxiv; ed. 4, lxxxviii

20 Indeed the Idols I have loved so long
   Have done my credit in this World much wrong:
     Have drown'd my Glory in a Shallow Cup
   And sold my Reputation for a Song.   *Ib. ed. 4, xciii*

21 Indeed, indeed, Repentance oft before
   I swore—but was I sober when I swore?
     And then and then came Spring, and Rose-in-hand
   My thread-bare Penitence apieces tore.   *Ib.* xciv

22 And much as Wine has play'd the Infidel,
   And robb'd me of my Robe of Honour—Well,
     I often wonder what the Vintners buy
   One half so precious as the Goods they sell.
                          Ib. ed. 1, lxxi

23 One half so precious as the stuff they sell.
                          Ib. ed. 4, xcv

24 Alas, that Spring should vanish with the Rose!
   That Youth's sweet-scented Manuscript should close!
     The Nightingale that in the Branches sang,
   Ah, whence, and whither flown again, who knows!
                          Ib. ed. 1, lxxii

25 Yet Ah, that Spring should vanish with the Rose!
                          Ib. ed. 4, xcvi

26 Ah Love! could thou and I with Fate conspire
   To grasp this sorry Scheme of Things entire,
     Would not we shatter it to bits—and then
   Re-mould it nearer to the Heart's Desire!
                          Ib. ed. 1, lxxiii

27 Ah Love! could you and I with Him conspire.
                          Ib. ed. 4, xcix

28 Ah, Moon of my Delight who know'st no wane,
   The Moon of Heav'n is rising once again:
     How oft hereafter rising shall she look
   Through this same Garden after me—in vain!
                          Ib. ed. 1, lxxiv

29 Yon rising Moon that looks for us again.
   How oft hereafter will she wax and wane;
     How oft hereafter rising look for us
   Through this same Garden—and for *one* in vain!
                          Ib. ed. 4, c

30 And when Thyself with shining Foot shall pass
   Among the Guests Star-scattered on the Grass,
     And in thy joyous Errand reach the Spot
   Where I made one—turn down an empty Glass!
                          Ib. ed. 1, lxxv

31 And when like her, O Saki, you shall pass.
                          Ib. ed. 4, ci

32 And in your joyous errand reach the spot.   *Ib.*

33 Mrs. Browning's death is rather a relief to me, I must
     say: no more Aurora Leighs, thank God!
       *Letter, 15 July 1861 (see 91:26 for Browning's
       rejoinder)*

34 Taste is the feminine of genius.
                    Ib. To J. R. Lowell, Oct. 1877

1 A Mr Wilkinson, a clergyman.
  Hallam Tennyson's Tennyson, *ii. 276. An imitation of Wordsworth's worst style*

JAMES ELROY FLECKER
1884–1915

2 Voiced like a great bell swinging in a dome.
  The Bridge of Fire, iv

3 For pines are gossip pines the wide world through.
  Brumana

4 Half to forget the wandering and the pain,
  Half to remember days that have gone by,
  And dream and dream that I am home again! *Ib.*

5 Noon strikes on England, noon on Oxford town,
  Beauty she was statue cold—there's blood upon her gown:
  Noon of my dreams, O noon!
  Proud and godly kings had built her, long ago,
  With her towers and tombs and statues all arow,
  With her fair and floral air and the love that lingers there,
  And the streets where the great men go.
  The Dying Patriot

6 Evening on the olden, the golden sea of Wales,
  When the first star shivers and the last wave pales:
  O evening dreams! *Ib.*

7 West of these out to seas colder than the Hebrides I must go
  Where the fleet of stars is anchored and the young star-captains glow. *Ib.*

8 The dragon-green, the luminous, the dark, the serpent-haunted sea.
  The Gates of Damascus. West Gate

9 We who with songs beguile your pilgrimage
  And swear that Beauty lives though lilies die,
  We Poets of the proud old lineage
  Who sing to find your hearts, we know not why,—
  What shall we tell you? Tales, marvellous tales
  Of ships and stars and isles where good men rest.
  The Golden Journey to Samarkand, Prologue

10 When the great markets by the sea shut fast
  All that calm Sunday that goes on and on:
  When even lovers find their peace at last,
  And Earth is but a star, that once had shone. *Ib.*

11 How splendid in the morning glows the lily; with what grace he throws
  His supplication to the rose. *Hassan*, I. i

12 And some to Meccah turn to pray, and I toward thy bed, Yasmin. *Ib.* ii

13   For one night or the other night
  Will come the Gardener in white, and gathered flowers are dead, Yasmin. *Ib.*

14 For lust of knowing what should not be known,
  We take the Golden Road to Samarkand. *Ib.* v. ii

15 And with great lies about his wooden horse
  Set the crew laughing, and forgot his course.
  The Old Ships

16 It was so old a ship—who knows, who knows?
  And yet so beautiful, I watched in vain
  To see the mast burst open with a rose,
  And the whole deck put on its leaves again. *Ib.*

17 And old Mæonides the blind
  Said it three thousand years ago.
  To a Poet a Thousand Years Hence

18 And walk with you, and talk with you, like any other boy. *Rioupéroux*

19 A ship, an isle, a sickle moon—
  With few but with how splendid stars
  The mirrors of the sea are strewn
  Between their silver bars.
  A Ship, an Isle, and a Sickle Moon

RICHARD FLECKNOE
d. 1678?

20 Still-born Silence! thou that art
  Floodgate of the deeper heart. *Poems*, 1653

MARJORIE FLEMING
1803–1811

21 A direful death indeed they had
  That would put any parent mad
  But she was more than usual calm
  She did not give a singel dam. *Journal, p. 29*

22 The most devilish thing is 8 times 8 and 7 times 7
  it is what nature itselfe cant endure. *Ib. p. 47*

23 To-day I pronounced a word which should never come
  out of a lady's lips it was that I called John a
  Impudent Bitch. *Ib. p. 51*

24 I am going to turn over a new life and am going to be
  a very good girl and be obedient to Isa Keith, here
  there is plenty of gooseberries which makes my
  teeth watter. *Ib. p. 76*

25 I hope I will be religious again but as for regaining
  my character I despare. *Ib. p. 80*

26 An annibabtist is a thing I am not a member of.
  Ib. p. 99

27 Sentiment is what I am not acquainted with. *Ib.*

28 My dear Isa,
   I now sit down on my botom to answer all your
  kind and beloved letters which you was so good as to
  write to me. *Letters. I, To Isabella*

29 O lovely O most charming pug
  Thy graceful air and heavenly mug. . . .
  His noses cast is of the roman
  He is a very pretty weoman
  I could not get a rhyme for roman
  And was obliged to call it weoman. *Poems*

PAUL FLEMING
1609–1640

30 Des großen Vaters Helm ist viel zu weit dem Sohne.
   The mighty father's helm is far too big for his son.
  Sonnet (Die jetzigen Deutschen)

ANDREW FLETCHER OF SALTOUN
1655–1716

31 I knew a very wise man so much of Sir Chr—'s sentiment, that he believed if a man were permitted to
  make all the ballads, he need not care who should
  make the laws of a nation.
   Letter to the Marquis of Montrose, and Others.
  Political Works

PHINEAS FLETCHER
1582–1650

1 Poorly (poor man) he liv'd; poorly (poor man) he
di'd.　　　　　*The Purple Island*, I. xix

2 His little son into his bosom creeps,
The lively picture of his father's face.　*Ib.* XII. vi

3 Drop, drop, slow tears,
And bathe those beauteous feet,
Which brought from Heav'n
The news and Prince of Peace.　　*An Hymn*

4 In your deep floods
Drown all my faults and fears;
Not let His eye
See sin, but through my tears.　　*Ib.*

5 Love is like linen often chang'd, the sweeter.
Sicelides, III. v

6 The coward's weapon, poison.　　*Ib.* v. iii

7 Love's tongue is in the eyes.
Piscatory Eclogues, eclog. v, xiii

JOHN FLORIO
1553?–1625

8 England is the paradise of women, the purgatory of
men, and the hell of horses.　　*Second Frutes*

MARÉCHAL FOCH
1851–1929

9 Mon centre cède, ma droite recule, situation excel-
lente. J'attaque!

My centre is giving way, my right is in retreat;
situation excellent. I shall attack.
Sir G. Aston, *Biography of Foch* (1929), ch. 13,
p. 122

JEAN DE LA FONTAINE
1621–1695

10 Aide-toi, le ciel t'aidera.
Help yourself, and heaven will help you.
Fables, vi. 18. *Le Chartier Embourbé*

11 Je plie et ne romps pas.
I bend and I break not.
Ib. i. 22. *Le Chêne et le Roseau*

12 C'est double plaisir de tromper le trompeur.
It is doubly pleasing to trick the trickster.
Ib. ii. 15. *Le Coq et le Renard*

13 Il connaît l'univers et ne se connaît pas.
He knows the world and does not know himself.
Ib. viii. 26. *Démocrite et les Abdéritains*

14 La raison du plus fort est toujours la meilleure.
The reason of the strongest is always the best.
Ib. i. 10. *Le Loup et l'Agneau*

15 La mort ne surprend point le sage,
Il est toujours prêt à partir.
Death never takes the wise man by surprise; he is
always ready to go.
Ib. viii. 1. *La Mort et le Mourant*

BERNARD LE BOVIER DE FONTENELLE
1657–1757

16 Si j'avais les mains pleines de vérités, je me garderais
de les ouvrir.
If my hands were filled with truths, I should be
careful not to open them.

SAMUEL FOOTE
1720–1777

17 Born in a cellar, . . . and living in a garret.
The Author, II

18 So she went into the garden to cut a cabbage-leaf, to
make an apple-pie; and at the same time a great
she-bear, coming up the street, pops its head into
the shop. 'What! no soap?' So he died, and she
very imprudently married the barber; and there
were present the Picninnies, and the Joblillies, and
the Garyalies, and the grand Panjandrum himself,
with the little round button at top, and they all fell
to playing the game of catch as catch can, till the
gun powder ran out at the heels of their boots.
In Maria Edgeworth, *Harry and Lucy Concluded*

19 For as the old saying is,
When house and land are gone and spent
Then learning is most excellent.　*Taste*, I. i

20 He is not only dull in himself, but the cause of dullness in others. *Remark.* Boswell's *Life of Johnson*,
ed. Powell, IV, p. 178. Parody of Shakespeare,
Henry IV, Part II, I. ii. 7

HENRY FORD
1863–1947

21 History is bunk.
In the witness box during his libel suit v. *the
Chicago Tribune, July 1919*

JOHN FORD
1586–1639?

22 Hairs as gay as are Apollo's locks.
The Broken Heart, I. ii

23 Tempt not the stars, young man, thou canst not play
With the severity of fate.　　*Ib.* iii

24 I am . . . a mushroom
On whom the dew of heaven drops now and then.
Ib.

25 The joys of marriage are the heaven on earth,
Life's paradise, great princess, the soul's quiet,
Sinews of concord, earthly immortality,
Eternity of pleasures; no restoratives
Like to a constant woman.　　*Ib.* II. ii

26 I have not thoughts
Enough to think.　　*Ib.* IV. ii

27 He hath shook hands with time.　　*Ib.* v. ii

28 We can drink till all look blue.
The Lady's Trial, IV. ii

29 Tell us, pray, what devil
This melancholy is, which can transform
Men into monsters.　　*Ib.* III. i

1 Parthenophil is lost, and I would see him;
For he is like to something I remember,
A great while since, a long, long time ago.
The Lover's Melancholy

2 'Tis Pity She's a Whore. *Title of Play*

3   Why, I hold fate
Clasp'd in my fist, and could command the course
Of time's eternal motion, hadst thou been
One thought more steady than an ebbing sea.
'Tis Pity She's a Whore, v. iv

LENA GUILBERT FORD
d. 1916?

4 Keep the home fires burning, while your hearts are
    yearning,
Though your lads are far away they dream of home;
There's a silver lining through the dark cloud shining;
Turn the dark cloud inside out, till the boys come
    home. *Keep the Home Fires Burning*

THOMAS FORD
c. 1580–1648

5 There is a lady sweet and kind,
Was never face so pleased my mind;
I did but see her passing by,
And yet I love her till I die.
There is a Lady. (*Music of Sundry Kinds*,
1607, IX. i.) *But see* Corrigenda, *p. 587*

HOWELL FORGY
1908–

6 Praise the Lord, and pass the ammunition.
*Attr. when a Naval Lt., at Pearl Harbour,
7 Dec. 1941*

E. M. FORSTER
1879–

7 Beethoven's Fifth Symphony is the most sublime
noise that has ever penetrated into the ear of man.
Howards End (1910), ch. 5

VENANTIUS FORTUNATUS
530–609

8 Vexilla regis prodeunt
Fulget crucis mysterium.

The royal banners forward go
The cross shines forth in mystic glow.
Durham Rituale. Trans. by J. M. Neale

SAM WALTER FOSS
1858–1911

9 I say the very things that make the greatest stir,
An' the most interestin' things, are things that didn't
occur.
Back Country Poems. Things That Didn't Occur

10 W'en you see a man in woe,
Walk right up and say 'hullo';
Say 'hullo' and 'how d'ye do.
How's the world a-usin' you?' *Hullo*

CHARLES FOSTER
1828–1904

11 Isn't this a billion dollar country?
*At the 51st Congress; retorting to a Democratic
gibe about a 'million dollar Congress'*

SIR GEORGE EULAS FOSTER
1847–1931

12 In these somewhat troublesome days when the great
Mother Empire stands splendidly isolated in
Europe.
*Speech, Canadian House of Commons, 16 Jan.
1896*

STEPHEN COLLINS FOSTER
1826–1864

13 I come down dah wid my hat caved in,
    Doodah! doodah!
I go back home wid a pocket full of tin,
    Oh! doodah day!
Gwine to run all night!
Gwine to run all day!
I'll bet my money on de bob-tail nag,
Somebody bet on de bay. *Camptown Races*

14 De blind hoss stick'n in a big mud hole,
    Doodah! doodah!
Can't touch de bottom wid a ten-foot pole,
    Oh! doodah day! *Ib.*

15 Weep no more, my lady,
Oh! weep no more to-day!
We will sing one song for the old Kentucky Home,
For the old Kentucky Home far away.
My Old Kentucky Home

16 'Way down upon de Swanee Ribber,
    Far, far away,
Dere's where my heart is turning ebber:
    Dere's where de old folks stay.
All up and down de whole creation
    Sadly I roam,
Still longing for de old plantation,
    And for de old folks at home.
Old Folks at Home (*Swanee Ribber*)

17 I'm coming, I'm coming,
For my head is bending low,
I hear their gentle voices calling
'Poor old Joe.' *Poor Old Joe*

18 He had no wool on de top of his head,
In de place where de wool ought to grow. *Uncle Ned*

19 Dere's no more hard work for poor old Ned,
He's gone whar de good niggers go. *Ib.*

CHARLES JAMES FOX
1749–1806

20 How much the greatest event it is that ever happened
in the world! and how much the best!
*On the Fall of the Bastille. Letter to Fitzpatrick,
30 July 1789. Russell's Life and Times of C. J.
Fox, vol. ii, p. 361*

21 He was uniformly of an opinion which, though not a
popular one, he was ready to aver, that the right of
governing was not property, but a trust.
*On Pitt's scheme of Parliamentary Reform.
J. L. Hammond, C. J. Fox (1903), p. 75*

1 No man could be so wise as Thurlow looked.
  Campbell's *Lives of the Lord Chancellors*, 1846,
  vol. v, p. 661.

2 I die happy.
  Last Words. Russell, *op. cit.*, vol. iii, ch. 69

HENRY FOX
see
FIRST BARON HOLLAND

HENRY RICHARD VASSALL FOX
see
THIRD BARON HOLLAND

ANATOLE FRANCE
1844–1924

3 Le bon critique est celui qui raconte les aventures de
  son âme au milieu des chefs-d'œuvre.

  The good critic is he who relates the adventures of
  his soul among masterpieces.
  La Vie littéraire, preface

FRANCOIS Ier
1508–1565

4 Tout est perdu fors l'honneur.

  All is lost save honour.
  *Traditional words in a letter to his mother after
  his defeat at Pavia, 1525. The actual words
  were:* 'De toutes choses ne m'est demeuré que
  l'honneur et la vie qui est saulve.' *Collection des
  Documents Inédits sur l'Histoire de France*, vol. i,
  1847, p. 129

BENJAMIN FRANKLIN
1706–1790

5 Remember, that time is money.
  Advice to Young Tradesman, 1748. Writings,
  vol. ii

6 No nation was ever ruined by trade.
  Essays. Thoughts on Commercial Subjects

7 Be in general virtuous, and you will be happy.
  Ib. On Early Marriages

8 There never was a good war, or a bad peace.
  Letter to Quincy, 11 Sept. 1783

9 But in this world nothing can be said to be certain,
  except death and taxes.
  *Letter to Jean Baptiste Le Roy, 13 Nov. 1789.
  Writings*, vol. x

10 A little neglect may breed mischief, . . . for want of a
  nail, the shoe was lost; for want of a shoe the
  horse was lost; and for want of a horse the rider
  was lost.
  Maxims . . . Prefixed to Poor Richard's Almanac,
  (1758)

11 Some are weather-wise, some are otherwise.
  Poor Richard's Almanac, Feb. 1735

12 Necessity never made a good bargain. *Ib. Apr. 1735*

13 Three may keep a secret, if two of them are dead.
  Ib. July 1735

14 At twenty years of age, the will reigns; at thirty, the
  wit; and at forty, the judgement.
  Poor Richard's Almanac, June 1741

15 Dost thou love life? Then do not squander time, for
  that's the stuff life is made of. *Ib. June 1746*

16 Many have been ruined by buying good pennyworths.
  Ib. Sept. 1747

17 He that lives upon hope will die fasting.
  Ib. 1758, preface

18 We must indeed all hang together, or, most assuredly,
  we shall all hang separately.
  *Remark to John Hancock, at Signing of the
  Declaration of Independence, 4 July 1776*

19 Poor man, said I, you pay too much for your whistle.
  The Whistle, 10 Nov. 1779

20 Man is a tool-making animal.
  Boswell's Life of Johnson, 7 Apr. 1778.

21   The body of
       Benjamin Franklin, printer,
     (Like the cover of an old book,
         Its contents worn out,
   And stript of its lettering and gilding)
       Lies here, food for worms!
     Yet the work itself shall not be lost,
   For it will, as he believed, appear once more
             In a new
       And more beautiful edition,
         Corrected and amended
       By its Author! *Epitaph for himself*

FREDERICK THE GREAT
1712–1786

22 My people and I have come to an agreement which
  satisfies us both. They are to say what they please,
  and I am to do what I please.   *Ascribed.*

23 Ihr Racker, wollt ihr ewig leben?

  Rascals, would you live for ever?
  *When the Guards hesitated, at Kolin, 18 June
  1757*

EDWARD AUGUSTUS FREEMAN
1823–1892

24 A saying which fell from myself in one of the debates
  in Congregation on the Modern Language Statute
  has been quoted in several places . . . 'chatter about
  Shelley' . . . I mentioned that I had lately read a
  review of a book about Shelley in which the critic
  . . . praised or blamed the author . . . for his 'treatment of the Harriet problem'.
  Contemporary Review, Oct. 1887: 'Literature
  and Language'
  *The two phrases are often telescoped as 'chatter about
  Harriet'.*

JOHN HOOKHAM FRERE
1769–1846

25 The feather'd race with pinions skim the air—
  Not so the mackerel, and still less the bear!
  Progress of Man, l. 34. *Poetry of the Anti-
  Jacobin, 1799*

26 Ah! who has seen the mailed lobster rise,
  Clap her broad wings, and soaring claim the skies?
  Ib. l. 44

CHARLES FROHMAN
1860–1915

1 Why fear death? It is the most beautiful adventure in life.
His last words before going down in the Lusitania, *7 May 1915.* I. F. Marcosson and D. Frohman, *Charles Frohman, ch. 19*

ROBERT FROST
1875–

2 Something there is that doesn't love a wall.
North of Boston. Mending Wall

3 My apple trees will never get across
And eat the cones under his pines, I tell him.
He only says, 'Good fences make good neighbours.'
Ib.

JAMES ANTHONY FROUDE
1818–1894

4 Wild animals never kill for sport. Man is the only one to whom the torture and death of his fellow-creatures is amusing in itself.
Oceana, ch. 5

5 Men are made by nature unequal. It is vain, therefore, to treat them as if they were equal.
Short Studies on Great Subjects. 3rd Ser. Party Politics

6 Experience teaches slowly, and at the cost of mistakes.
Ib.

7 Fear is the parent of cruelty.
Ib.

THOMAS FULLER
1608–1661

8 Thus this brook hath conveyed his [Wickliff's] ashes into Avon; Avon into Severn; Severn into the narrow seas; they, into the main ocean. And thus the ashes of Wickliff are the emblem of his doctrine, which now, is dispersed all the world over.
The Church History (1655), bk. iv, sec. ii, par. 53, p. 171

9 It is a silly game where nobody wins.
Gnomologia, No. 2880

10 A proverb is much matter decocted into few words.
The History of the Worthies of England, ch. 2

11 Know most of the rooms of thy native country before thou goest over the threshold thereof.
The Holy and Profane State (1642), bk. ii, ch. 4, p. 159. *Of Travelling*

12 A little skill in antiquity inclines a man to Popery; but depth in that study brings him about again to our religion.
Ib. ch. 6, p. 69. The True Church Antiquary

13 Light (God's eldest daughter).
Ib. ch. 7, p. 167. Of Building

14 But our captain counts the Image of God nevertheless his image, cut in ebony as if done in ivory.
Ib. ch. 20. The Good Sea-Captain

15 Learning hath gained most by those books by which the printers have lost.
Ib. bk. iii, ch. 18, p. 200. Of Books

16 He was one of a lean body and visage, as if his eager soul, biting for anger at the clog of his body, desired to fret a passage through it.
The Holy and Profane State, bk. v, ch. 19, p. 441. Life of the Duke of Alva

17 Worldly wealth he cared not for, desiring only to make both ends meet. [Of Edmund Grindall.]
Worthies of England. Worthies of Cumberland

18 Many were the wit-combats betwixt him [Shakespeare] and Ben Jonson, which two I behold like a Spanish great gallion, and an English man of war: Master Jonson (like the former) was built far higher in learning; solid, but slow, in his performances. Shakespeare, with the English man of war, lesser in bulk, but lighter in sailing, could turn with all the tides, tack about, and take advantage of all winds, by the quickness of his wit and invention.
Ib. Worthies of Warwickshire

HENRY FUSELI
[JOHANN HEINRICH FUESSLI]
1741–1825

19 Blake is damned good to steal from!
Gilchrist's Life of Blake (1863), ch. vii

ROSE FYLEMAN
1877–

20 There are fairies at the bottom of our garden.
Fairies

THOMAS GAINSBOROUGH
1727–1788

21 We are all going to heaven, and Vandyke is of the company.
Attr. Last Words. Boulton, *Thomas Gainsborough, ch. 9*

REV. THOMAS GAISFORD
1779–1855

22 Nor can I do better, in conclusion, than impress upon you the study of Greek literature, which not only elevates above the vulgar herd, but leads not infrequently to positions of considerable emolument.
Christmas Day Sermon in the Cathedral, Oxford. Rev. W. Tuckwell, *Reminiscences of Oxford* (2nd ed., 1907), p. 124.

GAIUS
fl. c. 110–*c.* 180

23 Damnosa hereditas.
Ruinous inheritance.
Inst. ii. 163

GALILEO GALILEI
1564–1642

24 E pur si muove.
But it does move.
Attr. to Galileo after his recantation in 1632. The earliest appearance of the phrase is 1761 (see E. R. Hull, *Galileo), and it is generally conceded to be apocryphal.*

RICHARD GALL
1776–1801

1 Baloo, baloo, my wee wee thing.   *Poems and Songs*

JOHN GALSWORTHY
1867–1933

2 If on a Spring night I went by
And God were standing there,
What is the prayer that I would cry
To Him? This is the prayer:
O God of Courage grave,
O Master of this night of Spring!
Make firm in me a heart too brave
To ask Thee anything.   *The Prayer*

3 He [Jolyon] was afflicted by the thought that where
Beauty was, nothing ever ran quite straight, which,
no doubt, was why so many people looked on it as
immoral.   *In Chancery*, ch. 13

4 Nobody tells me anything. [*James Forsyte.*]
The Man of Property, pt. 1, ch. i

SIR GREGORY GANDER
[GEORGE ELLIS]
1745–1815

5 Snowy, Flowy, Blowy,
Showery, Flowery, Bowery,
Hoppy, Croppy, Droppy,
Breezy, Sneezy, Freezy.   *The Twelve Months*

AUGUSTUS P. GARDNER
1865–1918

6 Wake up, America.   *Speech, 16 Oct. 1916*

JAMES ABRAM GARFIELD
1831–1881

7 Fellow-citizens: God reigns, and the Government at
Washington lives!
Speech on Assassination of Lincoln, 1865

DAVID GARRICK
1717–1779

8 Prologues precede the piece—in mournful verse;
As undertakers—walk before the hearse.
Apprentice, prologue

9 Are these the choice dishes the Doctor has sent us?
Is this the great poet whose works so content us?
This Goldsmith's fine feast, who has written fine
books?
Heaven sends us good meat, but the Devil sends
cooks.
On Doctor Goldsmith's Characteristical Cookery

10 Come, cheer up, my lads! 'tis to glory we steer,
To add something more to this wonderful year;
To honour we call you, not press you like slaves,
For who are so free as the sons of the waves?
  Heart of oak are our ships,
  Heart of oak are our men:
    We always are ready;
    Steady, boys, steady;
We'll fight and we'll conquer again and again.
Heart of Oak

11 We ne'er see our foes but we wish 'em to stay,
They never see us but they wish us away;
If they run, why, we follow, and run 'em ashore,
For if they won't fight us, we cannot do more.
Heart of Oak

12 Here lies Nolly Goldsmith, for shortness call'd Noll,
Who wrote like an angel, but talk'd like poor Poll.
Impromptu Epitaph

13 I've that within—for which there are no plaisters.
Prologue to Goldsmith's She Stoops to Conquer

14 A fellow-feeling makes one wond'rous kind.
*An Occasional Prologue on Quitting the Theatre,
10 June 1776*

15 Kitty, a fair, but frozen maid,
  Kindled a flame I still deplore;
The hood-wink'd boy I call'd in aid,
Much of his near approach afraid.
  So fatal to my suit before.
A Riddle. Lady's Magazine, June 1762

16 That blessed word Mesopotamia.
*Garrick tells of the power of George White-
field's voice, that 'he could make men either
laugh or cry by pronouncing the word Mesopotamia'. Related by Francis Jacox. A story
goes (Harvey's Companion to English Literature)
that an old woman told her pastor that she
found great support in that comfortable word
Mesopotamia.*
Notes and Queries, *Ser.* XI, i. 458

WILLIAM LLOYD GARRISON
1805–1879

17 I am in earnest—I will not equivocate—I will not
excuse—I will not retreat a single inch—and I will
be heard!
*Salutatory Address of The Liberator, 1 Jan.
1831*

18 Our country is the world—our countrymen are all
mankind. *Prospectus of The Liberator, 15 Dec. 1837*

19 The compact which exists between the North and the
South is 'a covenant with death and an agreement
with hell'.
*Resolution adopted by the Massachusetts Anti-
Slavery Society, 27 Jan. 1843*

SIR SAMUEL GARTH
1661–1719

20 Hard was their lodging, homely was their food;
For all their luxury was doing good.
Claremont, l. 148

21 A barren superfluity of words.
The Dispensary, c. 2, l. 95

ELIZABETH CLEGHORN GASKELL
1810–1865

22 Get her a flannel waistcoat and flannel drawers,
ma'am, if you wish to keep her alive. But my
advice is, kill the poor creature at once. [*Capt.
Brown on Miss Betsey Barker's cow.*]
Cranford, ch. 1

23 We were none of us musical, though Miss Jenkyns
beat time, out of time, by way of appearing to be so.
Ib.

1 Bombazine would have shown a deeper sense of her loss. [*Miss Jenkyns.*]   *Cranford*, ch. 7

JOSÉ ORTEGA Y GASSET
1883–

2 Orden no es una presión que desde fuera se ejerce sobre la sociedad, sino un equilibrio que se suscita en su interior.

Order is not a pressure which is imposed on society from without, but an equilibrium which is set up from within.
Mirabeau o el Político

THÉOPHILE GAUTIER
1811–1872

3 Tout passe.—L'art robuste
Seul a l'éternité,
Le buste
Survit à la cité.
See Henry Austin Dobson, *183:5. L'Art*

4 Je suis un homme pour qui le monde extérieur existe.

I am a man for whom the outside world exists.
Journal des Goncourt, 1 May 1857

GAVARNI
1801–1866

5 Les enfants terribles.

The embarrassing young. *Title of a series of prints*

JOHN GAY
1685–1732

6 I rage, I melt, I burn,
The feeble God has stabb'd me to the heart.
Acis and Galatea, ii

7 Bring me an hundred reeds of decent growth,
To make a pipe for my capacious mouth.   *Ib.*

8 O ruddier than the cherry,
O sweeter than the berry.   *Ib.*

9 Wou'd you gain the tender creature?
Softly, gently, kindly treat her,
Suff'ring is the lover's part.
Beauty by constraint, possessing
You enjoy but half the blessing,
Lifeless charms, without the heart.   *Ib.*

10 Love sounds the alarm, and Fear is a flying.   *Ib.*

11 How, like a moth, the simple maid
Still plays about the flame!
The Beggar's Opera, Act I, sc. iv, air iv

12 Our Polly is a sad slut! nor heeds what we have taught her.
I wonder any man alive will ever rear a daughter!
Ib. viii, air vii

13 Do you think your mother and I should have liv'd comfortably so long together, if ever we had been married?   *Ib.*

14 Can Love be controll'd by advice?   *Ib.* air viii

15 O Polly, you might have toy'd and kist,
By keeping men off, you keep them on.   *Ib.* air ix

16 Well, Polly; as far as one woman can forgive another, I forgive thee.
The Beggar's Opera, Act I, sc. viii, air ix

17 POLLY.
Then all my sorrows are at an end.
MRS. PEACHUM.
A mighty likely speech, in troth, for a wench who is just married!   *Ib.*

18 Money, wife, is the true fuller's earth for reputations, there is not a spot or a stain but what it can take out.
Ib. ix

19 A fox may steal your hens, sir
. . . .
If lawyer's hand is fee'd, sir
He steals your whole estate.   *Ib.* air xi

20 The comfortable estate of widowhood, is the only hope that keeps up a wife's spirits.   *Ib.* x

21 Oh, ponder well! be not severe;
So save a wretched wife:
For on the rope that hangs my dear
Depends poor Polly's life.   *Ib.* air xii

22 Away, hussy. Hang your husband and be dutiful. *Ib.*

23 Even butchers weep!   *Ib.* xii

24 Pretty Polly, say,
When I was away,
Did your fancy never stray
To some newer lover?   *Ib.* xiii, air xiv

25 I sipt each flower,
I chang'd ev'ry hour,
But here ev'ry flower is united.   *Ib.* air xv

26 If with me you'd fondly stray.
Over the hills and far away.   *Ib.* air xvi

27 O what pain it is to part!   *Ib.* air xvii

28 We retrench the superfluities of mankind.   *Ib.* II. i

29 Fill ev'ry glass, for wine inspires us,
And fires us
With courage, love and joy.
Women and wine should life employ.
Is there ought else on earth desirous?   *Ib.* air xix

30 If the heart of a man is deprest with cares,
The mist is dispell'd when a woman appears.
Ib. iii, air xxi

31 I must have women. There is nothing unbends the mind like them.   *Ib.*

32 Youth's the season made for joys,
Love is then our duty.   *Ib.* iv, air xxii

33 To cheat a man is nothing; but the woman must have fine parts indeed who cheats a woman!   *Ib.*

34 Man may escape from rope and gun;
Nay, some have outliv'd the doctor's pill:
Who takes a woman must be undone,
That basilisk is sure to kill.
The fly that sips treacle is lost in the sweets,
So he that tastes woman, woman, woman,
He that tastes woman, ruin meets. *Ib.* viii, air xxvi

35 MACHEATH.
Have you no bowels, no tenderness, my dear Lucy, to see a husband in these circumstances?

LUCY.
A husband!

MACHEATH.
In ev'ry respect but the form.   *Ib.* ix

1 I am ready, my dear Lucy, to give you satisfaction— if you think there is any in marriage?
The Beggar's Opera, Act II, sc. ix

2 In one respect indeed, our employment may be reckoned dishonest, because, like great Statesmen, we encourage those who betray their friends. *Ib.* x

3 I think you must ev'n do as other widows—buy yourself weeds, and be cheerful. *Ib.* xi

4 How happy could I be with either,
Were t'other dear charmer away!
But while ye thus tease me together,
To neither a word will I say. *Ib.* xiii, air xxxv

5 One wife is too much for one husband to hear,
But two at a time there's no mortal can bear.
This way, and that way, and which way I will,
What would comfort the one, t'other wife would take ill. *Ib.* III. xi, air liii

6 The charge is prepar'd; the lawyers are met;
The Judges all rang'd (a terrible show!). *Ib.* air lvii

7 That that Jemmy Twitcher should peach me, I own surprised me! *Ib.* xiv

8 She who has never lov'd, has never liv'd.
The Captives, II. i

9 If e'er your heart has felt the tender passion
You will forgive this just, this pious fraud. *Ib.* IV. x

10 She who trifles with all
Is less likely to fall
Than she who but trifles with one.
The Coquet Mother and the Coquet Daughter

11 Then nature rul'd, and love, devoid of art,
Spoke the consenting language of the heart.
Dione, prologue

12 Behold the victim of Parthenia's pride!
He saw, he sigh'd, he lov'd, was scorn'd and died.
Ib. I. i

13 He best can pity who has felt the woe. *Ib.* II. ii

14 Woman's mind
Oft' shifts her passions, like th'inconstant wind;
Sudden she rages, like the troubled main,
Now sinks the storm, and all is calm again. *Ib.* v

15 A woman's friendship ever ends in love. *Ib.* IV. vi

16 Behold the bright original appear.
Epistle to a Lady, l. 85

17 Praising all alike, is praising none. *Ib.* l. 114

18 One always zealous for his country's good. *Ib.* l. 118

19 Variety's the source of joy below.
Epistle to Bernard Lintott, l. 41

20 Life is a jest; and all things show it.
I thought so once; but now I know it.
My Own Epitaph

21 Whence is thy learning? Hath thy toil
O'er books consum'd the midnight oil?
Fables. Series I, introduction, l. 15

22 Where yet was ever found a mother,
Who'd give her booby for another?
Ib. The Mother, the Nurse, and the Fairy, iii, l. 33

23 Envy's a sharper spur than pay,
No author ever spar'd a brother,
Wits are gamecocks to one another.
Ib. The Elephant and the Bookseller, l. 74

24 An open foe may prove a curse,
But a pretended friend is worse.
Fables, xvii. *The Shepherd's Dog and the Wolf*, l. 33

25 Where there is life, there's hope, he cried,
Then why such haste? so groan'd and died.
Ib. xxvii. *The Sick Man and the Angel*, l. 49

26 Those who in quarrels interpose,
Must often wipe a bloody nose.
Ib. xxxiv. *The Mastiff*, l. 1

27 How many saucy airs we meet
From Temple-bar to Aldgate-street.
Ib. xxxv. *The Barley-Mow and Dunghill*, l. 1

28 Fools may our scorn, not envy raise,
For envy is a kind of praise.
Ib. xliv. *The Hound and the Huntsman*, l. 29

29 Friendship, like love, is but a name.
Ib. l. *The Hare and Many Friends*, l. 1

30 And when a lady's in the case,
You know, all other things give place. *Ib.* l. 41

31 Give me, kind heaven, a private station,
A mind serene for contemplation.
Ib. Series II, ii. *The Vulture, the Sparrow, and Other Birds*, l. 69

32 Studious of elegance and ease.
Ib. viii. *The Man, the Cat, the Dog, and the Fly*, l. 127

33 Whoever heard a man of fortune in England talk of the necessaries of life? . . . Whether we can afford it or no, we must have superfluities. *Polly*, I. i

34 How little are our customs known on this side of the herring-pond! *Ib.*

35 No, sir, tho' I was born and bred in England, I can dare to be poor, which is the only thing now-a-days men are asham'd of. *Ib.* xi

36 An inconstant woman, tho' she has no chance to be very happy, can never be very unhappy. *Ib.* xiv

37 Sleep, O Sleep,
With thy rod of incantation
Charm my imagination.

What's to sleep?
'Tis a visionary blessing;
A dream that's past expressing;
Our utmost wish possessing
So may I always keep. *Ib.* II. i

38 And one slight hair the mighty bulk commands.
Rural Sports, c. 1, l. 244

39 All in the Downs the fleet was moor'd,
The streamers waving in the wind,
When black-ey'd Susan came aboard.
Sweet William's Farewell to Black-Eyed Susan

40 We only part to meet again.
Change, as ye list, ye winds; my heart shall be
The faithful compass that still points to thee. *Ib.*

41 They'll tell thee, sailors, when away,
In ev'ry port a mistress find. *Ib.*

42 If to far India's coast we sail,
Thy eyes are seen in di'monds bright,
Thy breath is Africk's spicy gale,
Thy skin is ivory, so white.
Thus ev'ry beauteous object that I view,
Wakes in my soul some charm of lovely Sue. *Ib.*

1 Adieu, she cries! and wav'd her lily hand.
Sweet William's Farewell to Black-Eyed Susan

2 A miss for pleasure, and a wife for breed.
The Toilette

3 Now Cynthia nam'd, fair regent of the Night.
Trivia, bk. iii, l. 4

4 Dispute the reign of some luxurious mire. *Ib.* l. 48

5 'Twas when the seas were roaring
With hollow blasts of wind;
A damsel lay deploring,
All on a rock reclin'd.
The What D'ye Call It, II. viii

SIR ERIC GEDDES
1875–1937

6 We will get everything out of her [Germany] that you
can squeeze out of a lemon and a bit more. . . . I will
squeeze her until you can hear the pips squeak.
Speech at the Drill Hall, Cambridge, 9 Dec. 1918

DAVID LLOYD GEORGE, EARL OF DWYFOR
1863–1945

7 The stern hand of fate has scourged us to an elevation where we can see the great everlasting things
that matter for a nation; the great peaks of honour
we had forgotten—duty and patriotism clad in glittering white; the great pinnacle of sacrifice pointing
like a rugged finger to Heaven.
Speech, Queen's Hall, London, 19 Sept. 1914

8 What is our task? To make Britain a fit country for
heroes to live in.
Speech, Wolverhampton, 24 Nov. 1918

HENRY GEORGE
1839–1897

9 So long as all the increased wealth which modern
progress brings goes but to build up great fortunes,
to increase luxury and make sharper the contrast
between the House of Have and the House of Want,
progress is not real and cannot be permanent.
Progress and Poverty. Introductory, The Problem

GEORGE I OF GREAT BRITAIN
1660–1727

10 I hate all Boets and Bainters.
Campbell, *Lives of the Chief Justices*, ch. 30,
Lord Mansfield

GEORGE II OF GREAT BRITAIN
1683–1760

11 Non, j'aurai des maîtresses.
No, I shall have mistresses.
*Reply to Queen Caroline when, as she lay dying,
she urged him to marry again. Her reply to this
was* 'Ah! mon Dieu! cela n'empêche pas'. Hervey,
Memoirs of George the Second (1848), vol. ii

12 Oh! he is mad, is he? Then I wish he would *bite*
some other of my generals.
*Reply to one who complained that General Wolfe
was a madman. F. Thackeray, History of William
Pitt*, vol. i, ch. 15, note

GEORGE III OF GREAT BRITAIN
1738–1820

13 Born and educated in this country I glory in the name
of Briton. *Speech from the Throne, 1760*

14 'Was there ever,' cried he, 'such stuff as great part of
Shakespeare? Only one must not say so! But what
think you?—what?—Is there not sad stuff?
what?—what?
To Fanny Burney (in her Diary, 19 Dec. 1785)

GEORGE V OF GREAT BRITAIN
1865–1936

15 Wake up, England.
*Title of a reprint in 1911 of a speech made by the
King when Prince of Wales in the Guildhall on
5 Dec. 1901 on his return from a tour of the
Empire*

I venture to allude to the impression which seemed
generally to prevail among their brethren across
the seas, that the old country must wake up if she
intends to maintain her old position of pre-
eminence in her colonial trade against foreign
competitors. *Speech.*

16 How is the Empire?
Last Words. The Times, 21 Jan. 1936

EDWARD GIBBON
1737–1794

17 The successors of Charles the Fifth may disdain their
brethren of England; but the romance of *Tom
Jones*, that exquisite picture of human manners,
will outlive the palace of the Escurial and the
imperial eagle of the house of Austria.
Autobiography (World's Classics ed.), p. 4

18 My early and invincible love of reading, which I
would not exchange for the treasures of India.
Ib. p. 27

19 To the University of Oxford I acknowledge no
obligation; and she will as cheerfully renounce me
for a son, as I am willing to disclaim her for a
mother. I spent fourteen months at Magdalen
College: they proved the fourteen months the most
idle and unprofitable of my whole life. *Ib.* p. 36

20 The monks of Magdalen. *Ib.* p. 40

21 Decent easy men, who supinely enjoyed the gifts of
the founder. *Ib.*

22 Their dull and deep potations excused the brisk in-
temperance of youth. *Ib.*

23 Dr. — well remembered that he had a salary to receive, and only forgot that he had a duty to perform.
Ib. p. 44

24 It was here that I suspended my religious inquiries
(*aged 17*). *Ib.* p. 63

25 I saw and loved. *Ib.* p. 83

26 I sighed as a lover, I obeyed as a son. *Ib.*

27 [Of London.]
Crowds without company, and dissipation without
pleasure. *Ib.* p. 90

28 The captain of the Hampshire grenadiers . . . has not
been useless to the historian of the Roman empire.
Ib. p. 106

1 It was at Rome, on the 15th of October, 1764, as I sat musing amidst the ruins of the Capitol, while the barefoot friars were singing vespers in the Temple of Jupiter, that the idea of writing the decline and fall of the city first started to my mind.
Autobiography, p. 160

2 The first of earthly blessings, independence.
Ib. p. 176

3 I will not dissemble the first emotions of joy on the recovery of my freedom, and, perhaps, the establishment of my fame. But my pride was soon humbled, and a sober melancholy was spread over my mind, by the idea that I had taken an ever-lasting leave of an old and agreeable companion, and that whatsoever might be the future date of my History, the life of the historian must be short and precarious.
Ib. p. 205

4 My English text is chaste, and all licentious passages are left in the decent obscurity of a learned language.
Ib. p. 212

5 The various modes of worship, which prevailed in the Roman world, were all considered by the people as equally true; by the philosopher, as equally false; and by the magistrate, as equally useful.
Decline and Fall of the Roman Empire, ch. 2

6 The principles of a free constitution are irrecoverably lost, when the legislative power is nominated by the executive.
Ib. ch. 3

7 Titus Antoninus Pius. . . . His reign is marked by the rare advantage of furnishing very few materials for history; which is, indeed, little more than the register of the crimes, follies, and misfortunes of mankind.
Ib.

8 If a man were called to fix the period in the history of the world during which the condition of the human race was most happy and prosperous, he would, without hesitation, name that which elapsed from the death of Domitian to the accession of Commodus.
Ib.

9 All taxes must, at last, fall upon agriculture. *Ib.* ch. 8

10 Corruption, the most infallible symptom of constitutional liberty.
Ib. ch. 21

11 In every deed of mischief he [Comenus] had a heart to resolve, a head to contrive, and a hand to execute.
Ib. ch. 48

12 A victorious line of march had been prolonged above a thousand miles from the rock of Gibraltar to the banks of the Loire; the repetition of an equal space would have carried the Saracens to the confines of Poland and the Highlands of Scotland: the Rhine is not more impassable than the Nile or Euphrates, and the Arabian fleet might have sailed without a naval combat into the mouth of the Thames. Perhaps the interpretation of the Koran would now be taught in the schools of Oxford, and her pulpits might demonstrate to a circumcised people the sanctity and truth of the revelation of Mahomet.
Ib. ch. 52

13 Vicissitudes of fortune, which spares neither man nor the proudest of his works, which buries empires and cities in a common grave.
Ib. ch. 71

14 All that is human must retrograde if it does not advance.
Ib.

STELLA GIBBONS

1902–

15 Something nasty in the woodshed.
Cold Comfort Farm, passim

HUMPHREY GIFFORD

1550–1600

16 Ye curious carpet knights, that spend the time in sport and play,
Abroad, and see new sights, your country's cause calls you away. *For Soldiers. Posie of Gilloflowers*

REV. RICHARD GIFFORD

1725–1807

17 Verse softens toil, however rude the sound;
She feels no biting pang the while she sings;
Nor, as she turns the giddy wheel around,
Revolves the sad vicissitude of things.
Contemplation

WILLIAM GIFFORD

1756–1826

18 In all the sad variety of woe. *The Baviad*, l. 164

19 The insatiate itch of scribbling.
Trans. of Juvenal, vii. 79

20 Virtue alone is true nobility. *Ib.* viii. 32

FRED GILBERT

1850–1903

21 At Trinity Church I met my doom. *Title of Song*

22 Woa, mare! Woa, mare!
You've earned your little bit o' corn! *Down the Road*

23 As I walk along the Bois Bou-long,
With an independent air,
You can hear the girls declare,
'He must be a millionaire';
You can hear them sigh and wish to die,
You can see them wink the other eye
At the man who broke the Bank at Monte Carlo.
The Man Who Broke the Bank at Monte Carlo

SIR HUMPHREY GILBERT

1539?–1583

24 We are as near to heaven by sea as by land!
Hakluyt's Voyages, iii (1600), p. 159

SIR WILLIAM SCHWENCK GILBERT

1836–1911

25 Among them was a Bishop, who
Had lately been appointed to
The balmy isle of Rum-ti-Foo,
And Peter was his name.
The 'Bab' Ballads, The Bishop of Rum-ti-Foo

26 It is my duty, and I will. *Ib. Captain Reece*

27 It was their duty, and they did. *Ib.*

28 A very good girl was Emily Jane,
Jimmy was good and true,
John was a very good man in the main
(And I am a good man too.)
Ib. Emily, John, James, and I

[217]

1 Down went the owners—greedy men whom hope of gain allured:
Oh, dry the starting tear, for they were heavily insured. *The 'Bab' Ballads, Etiquette*

2 He had often eaten oysters, but had never had enough. *Ib.*

3 There were captains by the hundred, there were baronets by dozens. *Ib. Ferdinando and Elvira*

4 Only find out who it is that writes those lovely cracker mottoes! *Ib.*

5 The padre said, 'Whatever have you been and gone and done?' *Ib. Gentle Alice Brown*

6 The other night, from cares exempt,
I slept—and what d'you think I dreamt?
I dreamt that somehow I had come
To dwell in Topsy-Turveydom!—
Where vice is virtue—virtue, vice:
Where nice is nasty—nasty, nice:
Where right is wrong and wrong is right—
Where white is black and black is white.
Ib. My Dream

7 From a highly impossible tree
In a highly impossible scene.
Ib. Only a Dancing Girl

8 The mildest curate going. *Ib. The Rival Curates*

9 Strike the concertina's melancholy string!
Blow the spirit-stirring harp like anything!
Let the piano's martial blast
Rouse the Echoes of the Past,
For of Agib, Prince of Tartary, I sing!
Ib. Story of Prince Agib

10 Which is pretty, but I don't know what it means. *Ib.*

11 Then they began to sing
That extremely lovely thing,
'*Scherzando! ma non troppo ppp.*' *Ib.*

12 Roll on, thou ball, roll on!
Through pathless realms of Space
Roll on!
What though I'm in a sorry case?
What though I cannot meet my bills?
What though I suffer toothache's ills?
What though I swallow countless pills?
Never *you* mind!
Roll on! *Ib. To the Terrestrial Globe*

13 It's true I've got no shirts to wear;
It's true my butcher's bill is due;
It's true my prospects all look blue—
But don't let that unsettle you!
Never *you* mind!
Roll on! (*It rolls on.*) *Ib.*

14 Oh, I am a cook and a captain bold,
And the mate of the *Nancy* brig,
And a bo'sun tight, and a midshipmite,
And the crew of the captain's gig.
Ib. The Yarn of the 'Nancy Bell'

15 In all the woes that curse our race
There is a lady in the case. *Fallen Fairies, II*

16 He led his regiment from behind—
He found it less exciting. *The Gondoliers, I*

17 That celebrated,
Cultivated,
Underrated
Nobleman,
The Duke of Plaza Toro! *The Gondoliers, I*

18 Of that there is no manner of doubt—
No probable, possible shadow of doubt—
No possible doubt whatever. *Ib.*

19 His terrible taste for tippling. *Ib.*

20 A taste for drink, combined with gout,
Had doubled him up for ever. *Ib.*

21 Oh, 'tis a glorious thing, I ween,
To be a regular Royal Queen!
No half-and-half affair, I mean,
But a right-down regular Royal Queen! *Ib.*

22 All shall equal be.
The Earl, the Marquis, and the Dook,
The Groom, the Butler, and the Cook,
The Aristocrat who banks with Coutts,
The Aristocrat who cleans the boots. *Ib.*

23 But the privilege and pleasure
That we treasure beyond measure
Is to run on little errands for the Ministers of State.
Ib. II

24 With the gratifying feeling that our duty has been done! *Ib.*

25 Take a pair of sparkling eyes. *Ib.*

26 Take my counsel, happy man;
Act upon it, if you can! *Ib.*

27 He wished all men as rich as he
(And he was rich as rich could be),
So to the top of every tree
Promoted everybody. *Ib.*

28 Dukes were three a penny. *Ib.*

29 When every blessed thing you hold
Is made of silver, or of gold,
You long for simple pewter.
When you have nothing else to wear
But cloth of gold and satins rare,
For cloth of gold you cease to care—
Up goes the price of shoddy. *Ib.*

30 When every one is somebodee,
Then no one's anybody. *Ib.*

31 I see no objection to stoutness, in moderation.
Iolanthe, I

32 For I'm to be married to-day—to-day—
Yes, I'm to be married to-day! *Ib.*

33 Thou the singer; I the song! *Ib.*

34 Bow, bow, ye lower middle classes!
Bow, bow, ye tradesmen, bow, ye masses. *Ib.*

35 The Law is the true embodiment
Of everything that's excellent.
It has no kind of fault or flaw,
And I, my Lords, embody the Law. *Ib.*

36 Pretty young wards in Chancery. *Ib.*

37 A pleasant occupation for
A rather susceptible Chancellor! *Ib.*

38 For I'm not so old, and not so plain,
And I'm quite prepared to marry again. *Ib.*

1 Spurn not the nobly born With love affected,
Nor treat with virtuous scorn The well-connected.
Iolanthe, 1

2 Hearts just as pure and fair
May beat in Belgrave Square
As in the lowly air
Of Seven Dials. *Ib.*

3 When I went to the Bar as a very young man,
(Said I to myself, said I). *Ib.*

4 My son in tears—and on his wedding day! *Ib.*

5 He exercises of his brains,
That is, assuming that he's got any. *Ib.* II

6 I am an intellectual chap,
And think of things that would astonish you.
I often think it's comical
How Nature always does contrive
That every boy and every gal,
That's born into the world alive,
Is either a little Liberal,
Or else a little Conservative! *Ib.*

7 The House of Peers, throughout the war,
Did nothing in particular,
And did it very well:
Yet Britain set the world ablaze
In good King George's glorious days! *Ib.*

8 Oh, Captain Shaw!
Type of true love kept under!
Could thy Brigade
With cold cascade
Quench my great love, I wonder! *Ib.*

9 When you're lying awake with a dismal headache,
and repose is taboo'd by anxiety,
I conceive you may use any language you choose
to indulge in, without impropriety. *Ib.*

10 For you dream you are crossing the Channel, and
tossing about in a steamer from Harwich—
Which is something like a large bathing machine
and a very small second class carriage. *Ib.*

11 And you're giving a treat (penny ice and cold meat)
to a party of friends and relations—
They're a ravenous horde—and they all came on
board at Sloane Square and South Kensington
Stations.
And bound on that journey you find your attorney
(who started that morning from Devon);
He's a bit undersized, and you don't feel surprised
when he tells you he's only eleven. *Ib.*

12 In your shirt and your socks (the black silk with gold
clocks), crossing Salisbury Plain on a bicycle. *Ib.*

13 From the greengrocer tree you get grapes and green
pea, cauliflower, pineapple, and cranberries,
While the pastrycook plant cherry brandy will grant,
apple puffs, and three-corners, and Banburys. *Ib.*

14 Faint heart never won fair lady!
Nothing venture, nothing win—
Blood is thick, but water's thin—
In for a penny, in for a pound—
It's Love that makes the world go round! *Ib.*

15 A wandering minstrel I—
A thing of shreds and patches,
Of ballads, songs and snatches,
And dreamy lullaby! *The Mikado*, 1

16 Are you in sentimental mood?
I'll sigh with you. *Ib.*

17 But the happiest hour a sailor sees
Is when he's down
At an inland town,
With his Nancy on his knees, yo ho!
And his arm around her waist! *The Mikado*, 1

18 And I am right,
And you are right,
And all is right as right can be! *Ib.*

19 I can trace my ancestry back to a protoplasmal primordial atomic globule. Consequently, my family
pride is something in-conceivable. I can't help it.
I was born sneering. *Ib.*

20 It revolts me, but I do it! *Ib.*

21 I accept refreshment at any hands, however lowly.
Ib.

22 And the brass will crash,
And the trumpets bray,
And they'll cut a dash
On their wedding day. *Ib.*

23 I am happy to think that there will be no difficulty
in finding plenty of people whose loss will be a
distinct gain to society at large. *Ib.*

24 As some day it may happen that a victim must be
found,
I've got a little list—I've got a little list
Of society offenders who might well be under ground
And who never would be missed—who never
would be missed! *Ib.*

25 The idiot who praises, with enthusiastic tone,
All centuries but this, and every country but his own.
Ib.

26 They wouldn't be sufficiently degraded in their own
estimation unless they were insulted by a very
considerable bribe. *Ib.*

27 Three little maids from school are we,
Pert as a schoolgirl well can be,
Filled to the brim with girlish glee. *Ib.*

28 Life is a joke that's just begun. *Ib.*

29 Three little maids who, all unwary,
Come from a ladies' seminary. *Ib.*

30 Modified rapture! *Ib.*

31 Awaiting the sensation of a short, sharp shock,
From a cheap and chippy chopper on a big black
block. *Ib.*

32 For he's going to marry Yum-Yum—
Yum-Yum. *Ib.*

33 There's not a trace
Upon her face
Of diffidence or shyness. *Ib.* II

34 Ah, pray make no mistake,
We are not shy;
We're very wide awake,
The moon and I! *Ib.*

35 Brightly dawns our wedding day;
Joyous hour, we give thee greeting! *Ib.*

36 Sing a merry madrigal. *Ib.*

37 Here's a how-de-doo! *Ib.*

38 Matrimonial devotion
Doesn't seem to suit her notion. *Ib.*

1 Ha! ha! Family Pride, how do you like *that*, my buck?
   The Mikado, II

2 My object all sublime
   I shall achieve in time—
   To let the punishment fit the crime—
   The punishment fit the crime.   *Ib.*

3 A source of innocent merriment!
   Of innocent merriment.   *Ib.*

4 Sent to hear sermons
   From mystical Germans
   Who preach from ten till four.   *Ib.*

5 The music-hall singer attends a series
   Of masses and fugues and 'ops'
   By Bach, interwoven
   With Spohr and Beethoven,
   At classical Monday Pops.   *Ib.*

6 The billiard sharp whom any one catches,
   His doom's extremely hard—
   He's made to dwell—
   In a dungeon cell
   On a spot that's always barred.
   And there he plays extravagant matches
   In fitless finger-stalls
   On a cloth untrue
   With a twisted cue
   And elliptical billiard balls.   *Ib.*

7 The criminal cried, as he dropped him down,
   In a state of wild alarm—
   With a frightful, frantic, fearful frown,
   I bared my big right arm.   *Ib.*

8 I drew my snickersnee!   *Ib.*

9 Her terrible tale
   You can't assail,
   With truth it quite agrees;
   Her taste exact
   For faultless fact
   Amounts to a disease.   *Ib.*

10 Though trunkless, yet
    It couldn't forget
    The deference due to me!   *Ib.*

11 I have a left shoulder-blade that is a miracle of love-
    liness. People come miles to see it. My right elbow
    has a fascination that few can resist.   *Ib.*

12 Something lingering, with boiling oil in it, I fancy. *Ib.*

13 Merely corroborative detail, intended to give artistic
    verisimilitude to an otherwise bald and uncon-
    vincing narrative.   *Ib.*

14 She has a left elbow which people come miles to see!
    Ib.

15 The flowers that bloom in the spring,
            Tra la,
    Have nothing to do with the case.   *Ib.*

16 I've got to take under my wing,
            Tra la,
    A most unattractive old thing,
            Tra la,
    With a caricature of a face.
    And that's what I mean when I say, or I sing,
    'Oh bother the flowers that bloom in the spring.' *Ib.*

17 On a tree by a river a little tom-tit
    Sang 'Willow, titwillow, titwillow!'
    And I said to him, 'Dicky-bird, why do you sit
    Singing 'Willow, titwillow, titwillow?'   *Ib.*

18 'Is it weakness of intellect, birdie?' I cried,
    'Or a rather tough worm in your little inside?'
    With a shake of his poor little head he replied,
    'Oh, willow, titwillow, titwillow!'
    The Mikado, II

19 He sobbed and he sighed, and a gurgle he gave,
    Then he plunged himself into the billowy wave,
    And an echo arose from the suicide's grave—
    'Oh willow, titwillow, titwillow!'   *Ib.*

20 There's a fascination frantic
    In a ruin that's romantic;
    Do you think you are sufficiently decayed?   *Ib.*

21 When your Majesty says, 'Let a thing be done,' it's
    as good as done—practically, it *is* done—because
    your Majesty's will is law.   *Ib.*

22 Twenty love-sick maidens we,
    Love-sick all against our will.   *Patience*, I

23 When I first put this uniform on.   *Ib.*

24 Am I alone,
    And unobserved? I am!   *Ib.*

25 If you're anxious for to shine in the high aesthetic line
    as a man of culture rare.   *Ib.*

26 You must lie upon the daisies and discourse in novel
    phrases of your complicated state of mind,
    The meaning doesn't matter if it's only idle chatter of
    a transcendental kind.
        And everyone will say,
        As you walk your mystic way,
    'If this young man expresses himself in terms too
    deep for *me*,
    Why, what a very singularly deep young man this
    deep young man must be!'   *Ib.*

27 For Art stopped short in the cultivated court of the
    Empress Josephine.   *Ib.*

28 Then a sentimental passion of a vegetable fashion
    must excite your languid spleen,
    An attachment à la Plato for a bashful young potato,
    or a not too French French bean!
    Though the Philistines may jostle, you will rank as an
    apostle in the high aesthetic band,
    If you walk down Piccadilly with a poppy or a lily in
    your medieval hand.
        And everyone will say,
        As you walk your flowery way,
    'If he's content with a vegetable love which would
    certainly not suit *me*,
    Why, what a most particularly pure young man this
    pure young man must be!'   *Ib.*

29 Prithee, pretty maiden—prithee, tell me true.   *Ib.*

30 Nobody I care for comes a-courting me.   *Ib.*

31 Prithee, pretty maiden, will you marry me?
    (Hey, but I'm hopeful, willow, willow, waly!)
    I may say, at once, I'm a man of propertee—
        Hey willow waly O!
    Money, I despise it;
    Many people prize it,
    Hey willow waly O!   *Ib.*

32 The pain that is all but a pleasure will change
    For the pleasure that's all but pain.   *Ib.*

33 There will be too much of me
    In the coming by and by!   *Ib.* II

1 While this magnetic,
　Peripatetic
Lover, he lived to learn,
　By no endeavour
　Can magnet ever
Attract a Silver Churn! *Patience*, II

2 Sing 'Hey to you—good day to you'—
Sing 'Bah to you—ha! ha! to you'—
Sing 'Booh to you—pooh, pooh to you'. *Ib.*

3 He will have to be contented
With our heartfelt sympathy! *Ib.*

4 'High diddle diddle'
Will rank as an idyll,
If I pronounce it chaste! *Ib.*

5 Who's fond of his dinner
And doesn't get thinner
On bottled beer and chops. *Ib.*

6 Francesca di Rimini, miminy, piminy,
Je-ne-sais-quoi young man! *Ib.*

7 A greenery-yallery, Grosvenor Gallery,
Foot-in-the-grave young man! *Ib.*

8 A Sewell & Cross young man,
A Howell & James young man,
A pushing young particle—'What's the next article?'
Waterloo House young man! *Ib.*

9 I'm called Little Buttercup—dear Little Buttercup,
Though I could never tell why. *H.M.S. Pinafore*, I

10 I am the Captain of the *Pinafore*;
And a right good captain too! *Ib.*

11 And I'm never, never sick at sea!
　What, never?
　No, never!
　What, *never*?
　Hardly ever!
He's hardly ever sick at sea!
Then give three cheers, and one cheer more,
For the hardy Captain of the *Pinafore*! *Ib.*

12 You're exceedingly polite,
And I think it only right
To return the compliment. *Ib.*

13 I never use a big, big D. *Ib.*

14 And so do his sisters, and his cousins and his aunts!
　His sisters and his cousins,
　Whom he reckons up by dozens,
　And his aunts! *Ib.*

15 When I was a lad I served a term
As office boy to an Attorney's firm.
I cleaned the windows and I swept the floor,
And I polished up the handle of the big front door.
I polished up that handle so carefullee
That now I am the Ruler of the Queen's Navee! *Ib.*

16 And I copied all the letters in a big round hand. *Ib.*

17 I always voted at my party's call,
And I never thought of thinking for myself at all. *Ib.*

18 Stick close to your desks and never go to sea,
And you all may be Rulers of the Queen's Navee! *Ib.*

19 His energetic fist should be ready to resist
A dictatorial word. *Ib.*

20 His bosom should heave and his heart should glow,
And his fist be ever ready for a knock-down blow. *Ib.*

21 Things are seldom what they seem,
Skim milk masquerades as cream. *H.M.S. Pinafore*, II

22 The merry maiden and the tar. *Ib.*

23 It was the cat! *Ib.*

24 He is an Englishman!
For he himself has said it,
And it's greatly to his credit,
That he is an Englishman! *Ib.*

25 For he might have been a Roosian,
A French, or Turk, or Proosian,
　Or perhaps Ital-ian!
But in spite of all temptations
To belong to other nations,
He remains an Englishman! *Ib.*

26 The other, upper crust,
A regular patrician. *Ib.*

27 It is, it is a glorious thing
To be a Pirate King. *Pirates of Penzance*, I

28 The question is, had he not been
A thing of beauty,
Would she be swayed by quite as keen
A sense of duty? *Ib.*

29 Poor wandering one!
Though thou hast surely strayed,
Take heart of grace,
Thy steps retrace,
Poor wandering one! *Ib.*

30 Take heart, fair days will shine;
Take any heart, take mine! *Ib.*

31 I am the very model of a modern Major-General. *Ib.*

32 I'm very good at integral and differential calculus;
I know the scientific names of beings animalculous. *Ib.*

33 When the foeman bares his steel,
　Tarantara, tarantara!
We uncomfortable feel,
　Tarantara. *Ib.* II

34 When constabulary duty's to be done,
The policeman's lot is not a happy one. *Ib.*

35 When the enterprising burglar's not a-burgling. *Ib.*

36 When the coster's finished jumping on his mother—
He loves to lie a-basking in the sun. *Ib.*

37 No Englishman unmoved that statement hears,
Because, with all our faults, we love our House of
Peers. *Ib.*

38 Politics we bar,
They are not our bent:
On the whole we are
Not intelligent. *Princess Ida*, I

39 Yet everybody says I'm such a disagreeable man!
And I can't think why! *Ib.*

40 To everybody's prejudice I know a thing or two;
I can tell a woman's age in half a minute—and I do! *Ib.*

41 Man is Nature's sole mistake! *Ib.* II

42 My natural instinct teaches me
　(And instinct is important, O!)
You're everything you ought to be,
　And nothing that you oughtn't, O! *Ib.*

1 Oh, don't the days seem lank and long
   When all goes right and nothing goes wrong,
   And isn't your life extremely flat
   With nothing whatever to grumble at!
                   Princess Ida, III

2 All baronets are bad.   *Ruddigore*, I

3 I'll wager in their joy they kissed each other's cheek
   (Which is what them furriners do).   *Ib.*

4 You must stir it and stump it,
    And blow your own trumpet,
   Or trust me, you haven't a chance.   *Ib.*

5 He combines the manners of a Marquis with the
   morals of a Methodist.   *Ib.*

6 When he's excited he uses language that would make
   your hair curl.   *Ib.*

7 For duty, duty must be done;
   The rule applies to everyone.   *Ib.*

8 For you are such a smart little craft—
   Such a neat little, sweet little craft,
   Such a bright little, tight little,
   Slight little, light little,
   Trim little, prim little craft!   *Ib.* II

9 If a man can't forge his own will, whose will can he
   forge?   *Ib.*

10 Desperate deeds of derring do.   *Ib.*

11 Some word that teems with hidden meaning—like
   Basingstoke.   *Ib.*

12 This particularly rapid, unintelligible patter
   Isn't generally heard, and if it is it doesn't matter. *Ib.*

13 Time was when Love and I were well acquainted.
                   The Sorcerer, I

14 Forsaking even military men.   *Ib.*

15 I was a pale young curate then.   *Ib.*

16   Oh! My name is John Wellington Wells,
   I'm a dealer in magic and spells.   *Ib.*

17 If anyone anything lacks,
   He'll find it all ready in stacks,
    If he'll only look in
    On the resident Djinn,
   Number seventy, Simmery Axe!   *Ib.*

18 Now for the tea of our host,
    Now for the rollicking bun,
   Now for the muffin and toast,
    Now for the gay Sally Lunn!   *Ib.*

19 So I fell in love with a rich attorney's
   Elderly ugly daughter.   *Trial by Jury*

20 She may very well pass for forty-three
   In the dusk with a light behind her!   *Ib.*

21 And many a burglar I've restored
   To his friends and his relations.   *Ib.*

22 For now I am a Judge,
   And a good Judge too.   *Ib.*

23 And a good job too!   *Ib.*

24 Oh never, never, never, since I joined the human race,
   Saw I so exquisitely fair a face.   *Ib.*

25 Is life a boon?
   If so, it must befall
   That Death, whene'er he call,
   Must call too soon.   *The Yeomen of the Guard*, I

26 I have a song to sing O!
   Sing me your song, O!   *The Yeomen of the Guard*, I

27 It's a song of a merryman, moping mum,
   Whose soul was sad, and whose glance was glum
   Who sipped no sup, and who craved no crumb,
   As he sighed for the love of a ladye.   *Ib.*

28 His pains were o'er, and he sighed no more,
   For he lived in the love of a ladye!   *Ib.*

29 The prisoner comes to meet his doom.   *Ib.*

30 'Tis ever thus with simple folk—an accepted wit has
   but to say 'Pass the mustard', and they roar their
   ribs out!   *Ib.* II

THOMAS GILLESPIE
1777–1844

31 An attitude, not only of defence, but defiance.
   The Mountain Storm. (Wilson's *Tales of the
   Borders*, No. 145.)
   'Defence not defiance' *became the motto of
   the Volunteer Movement in 1859.*

JAMES GILLRAY
1757–1815

32 Political Ravishment, or, The Old Lady of Thread-
   needle Street in Danger.   *Title of Caricature*, 1797

CHARLOTTE PERKINS STETSON GILMAN
1860–?

33 I do not want to be a fly!
   I want to be a worm!
      In This Our World. A Conservative

WILLIAM EWART GLADSTONE
1809–1898

34 You cannot fight against the future. Time is on our
   side.   *Speech on the Reform Bill, 1866*

35 [The Turks] one and all, bag and baggage, shall, I
   hope, clear out from the province they have deso-
   lated and profaned.
      Speech, House of Commons, 7 May 1877

36 Out of the range of practical politics.
      Ib. at Dalkeith, 26 Nov. 1879

37 The resources of civilization are not yet exhausted.
      Ib. Leeds, Speech at Banquet, 7 Oct. 1881

38 [The Irish Land League]. It is perfectly true that
   these gentlemen wish to march through rapine to
   disintegration and dismemberment of the Empire,
   and, I am sorry to say, even to the placing of
   different parts of the Empire in direct hostility
   one with the other.   *Ib. Knowsley, 27 Oct. 1881*

39 I would tell them of my own intention to keep my own
   counsel . . . and I will venture to recommend them,
   as an old Parliamentary hand, to do the same.
      Ib. House of Commons, 21 Jan. 1886

40 All the world over, I will back the masses against the
   classes.   *Ib. Liverpool, 28 June 1886*

41 We are part of the community of Europe, and we must
   do our duty as such. *Ib. Carnarvon, 10 Apr. 1888*

1 This is the negation of God erected into a system of Government.
First Letter to the Earl of Aberdeen on the State persecutions of the Neapolitan Government, § 8, 1851, p. 9, n.

2 The impregnable rock of Holy Scripture.
Title of Book, 1890

3 Throw his mind into the common stock.
Phrase. G. W. E. Russell, *Collections and Recollections*, ch. 33

HANNAH GLASSE
fl. 1747

4 Take your hare when it is cased. . . .
Art of Cookery
Usually misquoted as 'First catch your hare'.

WILLIAM HENRY, DUKE OF GLOUCESTER
1743–1805

5 Another damned, thick, square book! Always scribble, scribble, scribble! Eh! Mr. Gibbon?
Best's *Literary Memorials*. (Boswell's *Johnson*, vol. ii, p. 2, n.)

JOHN A. GLOVER-KIND

6 I Do Like To Be Beside the Seaside.
Title of song (1909)

ALFRED DENIS GODLEY
1856–1925

7 What asks the Bard? He prays for nought
But what the truly virtuous crave:
That is, the things he plainly ought
To have . . .

His taste in residence is plain:
No palaces his heart rejoice:
A cottage in a lane (Park Lane
For choice)—
Lyra Frivola, 'After Horace'

8 What is this that roareth thus?
Can it be a Motor Bus?
Yes, the smell and hideous hum
Indicat Motorem Bum.

How shall wretches live like us
Cincti Bis Motoribus?
Domine, defende nos
Contra hos Motores Bos!
The Motor Bus. Letter to C.R.L.F., *10 Jan. 1914*

HANNAH GODWIN

9 Good sense without vanity, a penetrating judgement without a disposition to satire, good nature and humility, with about as much religion as my William likes, struck me with a wish that she was my William's wife.
Letter of 29 June 1784 to her brother William, recommending Miss Gay. C. Kegan Paul, *William Godwin*, vol. i

WILLIAM GODWIN
1756–1836

10 The log was burning brightly,
'Twas a night that should banish all sin,
For the bells were ringing the Old Year out,
And the New Year in. *The Miner's Dream of Home*

HERMANN GOERING
1893–1946

11 Guns will make us powerful; butter will only make us fat. *Radio Broadcast, summer of 1936*

12 When I hear anyone talk of Culture, I reach for my revolver.

JOHANN WOLFGANG VON GOETHE
1749–1832

13 Lord Byron ist nur groß, wenn er dichtet; sobald er reflektiert ist er ein Kind.
Lord Byron is only great as a poet; as soon as he reflects, he is a child.
Conversations with Eckermann, 18 Jan. 1825

14 Im übrigen ist es zuletzt die größte Kunst, sich zu beschränken und zu isolieren.
For the rest of it, the last and greatest art is to limit and isolate oneself. *Ib. 20 Apr. 1825*

15 Es irrt der Mensch, so lang er strebt.
Man errs, 'till his strife is over.
Faust, pt. i. *Prolog im Himmel*

16 Zwei Seelen wohnen, ach! in meiner Brust.
Two souls dwell, alas! in my breast.
Ib. Vor dem Thor

17 Ich bin der Geist der stets verneint.
I am the spirit that always denies.
Ib. Studierzimmer

18 Entbehren sollst Du! sollst entbehren!
Das ist der ewige Gesang.
Deny yourself! You must deny yourself!
That is the song that never ends. *Ib.*

19 Grau, teurer Freund, ist alle Theorie
Und grün des Lebens goldner Baum.
All theory, dear friend, is grey, but the golden tree of actual life springs ever green. *Ib.*

20 Meine Ruh' ist hin,
Mein Herz ist schwer.
My peace is gone,
My heart is heavy. *Ib. Gretchen am Spinnrad*

21 Die Tat ist alles, nicht der Ruhm.
The deed is everything, its repute nothing.
Ib. pt. ii. Großer Vorhof

22 Das Ewig-Weibliche zieht uns hinan.
That which is eternal in Woman lifts us above.
Ib. last line

23 Du musst herrschen und gewinnen,
Oder dienen und verlieren,
Leiden oder triumphiren
Amboss oder Hammer sein.
You must either conquer and rule or lose and serve, suffer or triumph, and be the anvil or the hammer.
Der Gross-Cophta, Act ii

1 Ein unnütz Leben ist ein früher Tod.
  A useless life is an early death.　　*Iphigenie*, i. 2

2 Ich singe, wie der Vogel singt,
  Der in den Zweigen wohnet.

  I sing but as the bird there sings,
  High in the treetops nesting.　　*Der Sänger*

3 Der Aberglaube is die Poesie des Lebens.

  Superstition is the poetry of life.
  　　　　　　Sprüche in Prosa (1819), iii

4 Es bildet ein Talent sich in der Stille,
  Sich ein Charakter in dem Strom der Welt.

  Genius develops in quiet places,
  Character out in the full current of human life.
  　　　　　　Tasso, i. 2

5 Über allen Gipfeln
  Ist Ruh'.

  Over all the mountain tops is peace.
  　　　　　　Wanderers Nachtlied

6 Kennst du das Land, wo die Zitronen blühn?
  Im dunkeln Laub die Gold-Orangen glühn,
  Ein sanfter Wind vom blauen Himmel weht,
  Die Myrte still und hoch der Lorbeer steht—
  Kennst du es wohl?

  　　　　　　Dahin! Dahin!
  Möcht ich mit dir, o mein Geliebter, ziehn!

  Know you the land where the lemon-trees bloom?
  In the dark foliage the gold oranges glow; a soft
  wind hovers from the sky, the myrtle is still and
  the laurel stands tall—do you know it well?
  There, there, I would go, O my beloved, with
  thee!　　*Wilhelm Meisters Lehrjahre*, III. i

7 Mehr Licht!

  More light!
  　　Attr. dying words. (Actually: 'Macht doch den
  zweiten Fensterladen auch auf, damit mehr
  Licht hereinkomme': 'Open the second shutter,
  so that more light can come in.')

8 Ohne Hast, aber ohne Rast.

  Without haste, but without rest.　　*Motto*

OLIVER GOLDSMITH
1728-1774

9 For he who fights and runs away
  May live to fight another day;
  But he who is in battle slain
  Can never rise and fight again.
  　　Art of Poetry on a New Plan. Written by New-
  bery, revised by Goldsmith

10 To the last moment of his breath
  On hope the wretch relies;
  And e'en the pang preceding death
  Bids expectation rise.

  Hope, like the gleaming taper's light,
  Adorns and cheers our way;
  And still, as darker grows the night,
  Emits a brighter ray.　　*The Captivity*, II

11 A night-cap decked his brows instead of bay;
  A cap by night—a stocking all the day!
  　　Description of an Author's Bedchamber. In
  Citizen of the World, letter 30. *The Author's
  Club* (1760)

12 Sweet Auburn! loveliest village of the plain.
  　　　　　　The Deserted Village, l. 1

13 The bashful virgin's side-long looks of love,
  The matron's glance that would those looks reprove.
  　　　　　　Ib. l. 29

14 Ill fares the land, to hast'ning ills a prey,
  Where wealth accumulates, and men decay;
  Princes and lords may flourish, or may fade;
  A breath can make them, as a breath has made;
  But a bold peasantry, their country's pride,
  When once destroy'd, can never be supplied.
  A time there was, ere England's griefs began,
  When every rood of ground maintain'd its man;
  For him light labour spread her wholesome store,
  Just gave what life requir'd, but gave no more;
  His best companions, innocence and health;
  And his best riches, ignorance of wealth.　　*Ib.* l. 51

15 How happy he who crowns in shades like these,
  A youth of labour with an age of ease.　　*Ib.* l. 99

16 Bends to the grave with unperceiv'd decay,
  While resignation gently slopes the way;
  And, all his prospects bright'ning to the last,
  His heaven commences ere the world be pass'd.
  　　　　　　Ib. l. 109

17 The watchdog's voice that bay'd the whisp'ring wind,
  And the loud laugh that spoke the vacant mind.
  　　　　　　Ib. l. 121

18 A man he was to all the country dear,
  And passing rich with forty pounds a year;
  Remote from towns he ran his godly race,
  Nor e'er had chang'd nor wished to change his place;
  Unpractis'd he to fawn, or seek for power,
  By doctrines fashion'd to the varying hour;
  Far other aims his heart had learned to prize,
  More skill'd to raise the wretched than to rise.
  　　　　　　Ib. l. 141

19 He chid their wand'rings, but reliev'd their pain.
  　　　　　　Ib. l. 150

20 The broken soldier, kindly bade to stay,
  Sat by his fire, and talk'd the night away;
  Wept o'er his wounds, or tales of sorrow done,
  Shoulder'd his crutch, and show'd how fields were
  won.　　　　　　*Ib.* l. 155

21 Careless their merits, or their faults to scan,
  His pity gave ere charity began.
  Thus to relieve the wretched was his pride,
  And e'en his failings lean'd to Virtue's side.
  But in his duty prompt at every call,
  He watch'd and wept, he pray'd and felt, for all.
  And, as a bird each fond endearment tries
  To tempt its new-fledg'd offspring to the skies,
  He tried each art, reprov'd each dull delay,
  Allur'd to brighter worlds, and led the way.
  　　　　　　Ib. l. 161

22 At church, with meek and unaffected grace,
  His looks adorn'd the venerable place;
  Truth from his lips prevail'd with double sway,
  And fools, who came to scoff, remain'd to pray.
  　　　　　　Ib. l. 177

23 Even children follow'd with endearing wile,
  And pluck'd his gown, to share the good man's smile.
  　　　　　　Ib. l. 183

1 A man severe he was, and stern to view;
I knew him well, and every truant knew;
Well had the boding tremblers learn'd to trace
The day's disasters in his morning face;
Full well they laugh'd with counterfeited glee,
At all his jokes, for many a joke had he;
Full well the busy whisper, circling round,
Convey'd the dismal tidings when he frown'd;
Yet he was kind; or if severe in aught,
The love he bore to learning was in fault.
The Deserted Village, l. 197

2 In arguing too, the parson own'd his skill,
For e'en though vanquish'd, he could argue still;
While words of learned length, and thund'ring sound
Amazed the gazing rustics rang'd around,
And still they gaz'd, and still the wonder grew,
That one small head could carry all he knew.
Ib. l. 211

3 The white-wash'd wall, the nicely sanded floor,
The varnish'd clock that click'd behind the door;
The chest contriv'd a double debt to pay,
A bed at night, a chest of drawers by day. *Ib.* l. 227

4 The twelve good rules, the royal game of goose.
Ib. l. 232

5 And, e'en while fashion's brightest arts decoy,
The heart distrusting asks, if this be joy. *Ib.* l. 263

6   How wide the limits stand
Between a splendid and a happy land. *Ib.* l. 267

7 Her modest looks the cottage might adorn,
Sweet as the primrose peeps beneath the thorn.
Ib. l. 329

8 In all the silent manliness of grief. *Ib.* l. 384

9 Thou source of all my bliss, and all my woe,
That found'st me poor at first, and keep'st me so.
Ib. l. 413

10 The fat was so white, and the lean was so ruddy.
The Haunch of Venison, l. 4

11 Turn, gentle Hermit of the dale,
   And guide my lonely way,
To where yon taper cheers the vale
   With hospitable ray.
Edwin and Angelina, or The Hermit

12 No flocks that range the valleys free
   To slaughter I condemn.
Taught by the Power that pities me,
   I learn to pity them. *Ib.*

13 Man wants but little here below,
   Nor wants that little long. *Ib.*

14 The sigh that rends thy constant heart,
   Shall break thy Edwin's too. *Ib.*

15 The king himself has follow'd her,—
   When she has walk'd before.
Elegy on Mrs. Mary Blaize

16 The doctor found, when she was dead,—
   Her last disorder mortal. *Ib.*

17 Good people all, of every sort,
   Give ear unto my song;
And if you find it wond'rous short,
   It cannot hold you long.
Elegy on the Death of a Mad Dog

18 That still a godly race he ran,
   Whene'er he went to pray *Ib.*

19 The naked every day he clad,
   When he put on his clothes.
Elegy on the Death of a Mad Dog

20 And in that town a dog was found,
   As many dogs there be,
Both mongrel, puppy, whelp, and hound,
   And curs of low degree. *Ib.*

21 The dog, to gain some private ends,
   Went mad and bit the man. *Ib.*

22 And swore the dog had lost his wits,
   To bite so good a man. *Ib.*

23 The man recover'd of the bite,
   The dog it was that died. *Ib.*

24 Brutes never meet in bloody fray,
   Nor cut each other's throats, for pay.
Logicians Refuted, l. 39

25 Our Garrick's a salad; for in him we see
Oil, vinegar, sugar, and saltness agree.
Retaliation, l. 11

26 Who mix'd reason with pleasure, and wisdom with mirth:
If he had any faults, he has left us in doubt. [Dr. Barnard, Dean of Derry.] *Ib.* l. 24

27 Here lies our good Edmund, whose genius was such,
We scarcely can praise it, or blame it too much;
Who, born for the Universe, narrow'd his mind,
And to party gave up what was meant for mankind.
Though fraught with all learning, yet straining his throat
To persuade Tommy Townshend to lend him a vote;
Who, too deep for his hearers, still went on refining,
And thought of convincing, while they thought of dining;
Though equal to all things, for all things unfit,
Too nice for a statesman, too proud for a wit.
[Edmund Burke.] *Ib.* l. 29

28 Too fond of the *right* to pursue the *expedient*.
[Edmund Burke.] *Ib.* l. 40

29 His conduct still right, with his argument wrong.
[William Burke.] *Ib.* l. 46

30 Here lies David Garrick, describe me, who can,
An abridgement of all that was pleasant in man.
Ib. l. 93

31 As a wit, if not first, in the very first line. [Garrick.]
Ib. l. 96

32 On the stage he was natural, simple, affecting;
'Twas only that when he was off he was acting.
[Garrick.] *Ib.* l. 101

33 He cast off his friends as a huntsman his pack,
For he knew when he pleas'd he could whistle them back.
Of praise a mere glutton, he swallow'd what came,
And the puff of a dunce he mistook it for fame.
[Garrick.] *Ib.* l. 107

34 Here Reynolds is laid, and to tell you my mind,
He has not left a better or wiser behind:
His pencil was striking, resistless, and grand;
His manners were gentle, complying, and bland;
Still born to improve us in every part,
His pencil our faces, his manners our heart. *Ib.* l. 137

35 When they talk'd of their Raphaels, Correggios, and stuff,
He shifted his trumpet, and only took snuff. [Reynolds.] *Ib.* l. 145

1 Thou best-humour'd man with the worst-humour'd muse. [Whiteford.] *Retaliation*, l. 174

2 Let schoolmasters puzzle their brain,
  With grammar, and nonsense, and learning,
Good liquor, I stoutly maintain,
  Gives genius a better discerning.
    She Stoops to Conquer, i. i, song

3 Remote, unfriended, melancholy, slow,
Or by the lazy Scheldt, or wandering Po.
    The Traveller, l. 1

4 Where'er I roam, whatever realms to see,
My heart untravell'd fondly turns to thee;
Still to my brother turns with ceaseless pain,
And drags at each remove a lengthening chain.
    Ib. l. 7

5 And learn the luxury of doing good. *Ib.* l. 22

6 These little things are great to little man. *Ib.* l. 42

7 Such is the patriot's boast, where'er we roam,
His first, best country ever is, at home. *Ib.* l. 73

8 Where wealth and freedom reign, contentment fails,
And honour sinks where commerce long prevails.
    Ib. l. 91

9 Man seems the only growth that dwindles here.
    Ib. l. 126

10 But winter ling'ring chills the lap of May. *Ib.* l. 172

11 At night returning, every labour sped,
He sits him down the monarch of a shed;
Smiles by his cheerful fire, and round surveys
His children's looks, that brighten at the blaze;
While his lov'd partner, boastful of her hoard,
Displays her cleanly platter on the board. *Ib.* l. 191

12 They please, are pleas'd; they give to get esteem,
Till, seeming bless'd, they grow to what they seem.
    Ib. l. 265

13 To men of other minds my fancy flies,
Embosom'd in the deep where Holland lies.
Methinks her patient sons before me stand,
Where the broad ocean leans against the land.
    Ib. l. 282

14 Pride in their port, defiance in their eye,
I see the lords of human kind pass by. *Ib.* l. 327

15 The land of scholars, and the nurse of arms.
    Ib. l. 356

16 Laws grind the poor, and rich men rule the law.
    Ib. l. 386

17 In every government, though terrors reign,
Though tyrant kings, or tyrant laws restrain,
How small, of all that human hearts endure,
That part which laws or kings can cause or cure!
    Ib. l. 427

18 When lovely woman stoops to folly
  And finds too late that men betray,
What charm can soothe her melancholy,
  What art can wash her guilt away?
The only art her guilt to cover,
  To hide her shame from every eye,
To give repentance to her lover.
  And wring his bosom—is to die.
    Song. From the *Vicar of Wakefield*, ch. 29

19 As writers become more numerous, it is natural for readers to become more indolent.
    The Bee, No. 175. *Upon Unfortunate Merit*

20 The volume of nature is the book of knowledge.
    Citizen of the World, letter 4

21 'The Republic of Letters' is a very common expression among the Europeans. *Ib.* letter 20

22 He writes indexes to perfection. *Ib.* letter 29

23 To a philosopher no circumstance, however trifling, is too minute. *Ib.* letter 30

24 'Did I say so?' replied he coolly; 'to be sure, if I said so, it was so.' *Ib.* letter 54

25 Had Caesar or Cromwell exchanged countries, the one might have been a sergeant, and the other an exciseman. *Essays*, i. *Introductory Paper*

26 The true use of speech is not so much to express our wants as to conceal them.
    Ib. v. *The Use of Language*

27 Bacon, that great and hardy genius.
    Ib. xviii. *Travel in Asia*

28 Here's to the memory of Shakespeare, Falstaff, and all the merry men of East-cheap.
    Ib. xix. *At The Boar's Head Tavern*

29 I hate the French because they are all slaves, and wear wooden shoes.
    Ib. xxiv. *Distresses of a Common Soldier*

30 This same philosophy is a good horse in the stable, but an arrant jade on a journey.
    The Good-Natured Man, 1

31 We must touch his weaknesses with a delicate hand. There are some faults so nearly allied to excellence, that we can scarce weed out the fault without eradicating the virtue. *Ib.*

32 All his faults are such that one loves him still the better for them. *Ib.*

33 I'm now no more than a mere lodger in my own house. *Ib.*

34 Friendship is a disinterested commerce between equals; love, an abject intercourse between tyrants and slaves. *Ib.*

35 Don't let us make imaginary evils, when you know we have so many real ones to encounter. *Ib.*

36 LEONTINE:
An only son, sir, might expect more indulgence.
CROAKER:
An only father, Sir, might expect more obedience.
    Ib.

37 I am told he makes a very handsome corpse, and becomes his coffin prodigiously. *Ib.*

38 Silence is become his mother tongue. *Ib.* 11

39 All men have their faults; too much modesty is his.
    Ib.

40 You, that are going to be married, think things can never be done too fast; but we, that are old, and know what we are about, must elope methodically, madam. *Ib.*

41 She stoops to conquer. *Title of play*

42 In my time, the follies of the town crept slowly among us, but now they travel faster than a stage-coach. *She Stoops to Conquer*, 1

43 I love every thing that's old; old friends, old times, old manners, old books, old wines. *Ib.*

1 As for disappointing them I should not so much mind; but I can't abide to disappoint myself.
She Stoops to Conquer, 1

2 Is it one of my well-looking days, child? Am I in face to-day? *Ib.*

3 The very pink of perfection. *Ib.*

4 In a concatenation accordingly. *Ib.*

5 I'll be with you in the squeezing of a lemon. *Ib.*

6 It's a damned long, dark, boggy, dirty, dangerous way. *Ib.*

7 Your worship must not tell the story of Ould Grouse in the gun-room. I can't help laughing at that . . . We have laughed at that these twenty years. *Ib.* II

8 This is Liberty-Hall, gentlemen. *Ib.*

9 The first blow is half the battle. *Ib.*

10 We are the boys
That fears no noise
Where the thundering cannons roar. *Ib.*

11 Was there ever such a cross-grained brute? *Ib.* III

12 Women and music should never be dated. *Ib.*

13 As for murmurs, mother, we grumble a little now and then, to be sure. But there's no love lost between us. *Ib.* IV

14 A book may be amusing with numerous errors, or it may be very dull without a single absurdity.
The Vicar of Wakefield, advertisement

15 I was ever of opinion, that the honest man who married and brought up a large family, did more service than he who continued single and only talked of population. *Ib.* ch. 1

16 I chose my wife, as she did her wedding gown, not for a fine glossy surface, but such qualities as would wear well. *Ib.*

17 All our adventures were by the fire-side, and all our migrations from the blue bed to the brown. *Ib.*

18 A mutilated courtesy. *Ib.*

19 The virtue which requires to be ever guarded is scarcely worth the sentinel. *Ib.* ch. 5

20 I find you want me to furnish you with argument and intellects too. No, Sir, there I protest you are too hard for me. *Ib.* ch. 7

21 'Very well,' cried I, 'that's a good girl, I find you are perfectly qualified for making converts, and so go help your mother to make the gooseberry-pie.' *Ib.*

22 By the living jingo, she was all of a muck of sweat. *Ib.* ch. 9

23 With other fashionable topics, such as pictures, taste, Shakespeare, and the musical glasses. *Ib.*

24 Mr. Burchell . . . at the conclusion of every sentence would cry out 'Fudge!'—an expression which displeased us all. *Ib.* ch. 11

25 Conscience is a coward, and those faults it has not strength enough to prevent it seldom has justice enough to accuse. *Ib.* ch. 13

26 It seemed to me pretty plain, that they had more of love than matrimony in them. *Ib.* ch. 16

27 There is no arguing with Johnson; for when his pistol misses fire, he knocks you down with the butt end of it.
Remark. Boswell's *Life of Johnson, 26 Oct. 1769*

28 As I take my shoes from the shoemaker, and my coat from the tailor, so I take my religion from the priest.
Boswell's *Life of Johnson, 9 Apr. 1773*

29 [To Johnson who was laughing when he said that the little fishes in a proposed fable should talk like little fishes.]
Why, Dr. Johnson, this is not so easy as you seem to think; for if you were to make little fishes talk, they would talk like whales.
Ib. 27 Apr. 1773

30 [To Boswell, for talking of Johnson as entitled to the honour of unquestionable superiority.]
Sir, you are for making a monarchy of what should be a republic. *Ib. 7 May 1773*

31 [To Boswell, of Johnson.]
Is he like Burke, who winds into a subject like a serpent? *Ib. 10 May 1773*

32 He [Johnson] has nothing of the bear but his skin.
Ib. ii. 66 (Birkbeck Hill edn.)

SAMUEL GOLDWYN
1882–

33 In two words: im-possible.
Quoted in Alva Johnson: *The Great Goldwyn*

ADAM LINDSAY GORDON
1833–1870

34 Question not, but live and labour
Till yon goal be won,
Helping every feeble neighbour,
Seeking help from none;
Life is mostly froth and bubble,
Two things stand like stone,
Kindness in another's trouble,
Courage in your own.
Ye Wearie Wayfarer, Fytte 8

SIR THOMAS EDWARD GORDON
1832–1914

35 The roof of the world. *Title of a book, 1876*

EVA GORE-BOOTH
1872–1926

36 The little waves of Breffny go stumbling through my soul. *Poems. The Little Waves of Breffny*

GEORGE JOACHIM, FIRST VISCOUNT GOSCHEN
1831–1907

37 I have the courage of my opinions, but I have not the temerity to give a political blank cheque to Lord Salisbury. *Speech, House of Commons, 19 Feb. 1884*

38 If so we shall make our wills and do our duty.
Speech, 14 Apr. 1886

39 We have stood alone in that which is called isolation—our splendid isolation, as one of our colonial friends was good enough to call it. [See G. E. Foster.]
Speech at Lewes, 26 Feb. 1896

SIR EDMUND GOSSE
1849–1928

1 Papa, don't tell me that she's a Paedobaptist?
Father and Son, ch. 10

REV. EDWARD MEYRICK GOULBURN
1818–1897

2 Let the scintillations of your wit be like the corus-
cations of summer lightning, lambent but in-
nocuous.
Sermon at Rugby. Rev. W. Tuckwell, *Reminiscences of Oxford* (2nd ed., 1907), p. 272

JOHN GOWER
1325?–1408

3 It hath and schal ben evermor
That love is maister wher he wile.
Confessio Amantis, prologue, l. 34

RICHARD GRAFTON
?–1572?

4 Thirty days hath November,
April, June, and September,
February hath twenty-eight alone,
And all the rest have thirty-one.
Abridgement of the Chronicles of England (1570),
introductory matter, sig. 1 ¶ j. b

CHARLES GRAHAM

5 Two little girls in blue, lad,
Two little girls in blue,
They were sisters, we were brothers,
And learned to love the two.
Two Little Girls In Blue

HARRY GRAHAM
1874–1936

6 Auntie, did you feel no pain
Falling from that apple-tree?
Would you do it, please, again?
Cos my friend here didn't see.
*Ruthless Rhymes for Heartless Homes. Apprecia-
tion*

7 O'er the rugged mountain's brow
Clara threw the twins she nursed,
And remarked, 'I wonder now
Which will reach the bottom first?'
Ib. Calculating Clara

8 Aunt Jane observed, the second time
She tumbled off a bus,
The step is short from the Sublime
To the Ridiculous.
Ib. Equanimity

9 'There's been an accident!' they said,
'Your servant's cut in half; he's dead!'
'Indeed!' said Mr. Jones, 'and please
Send me the half that's got my keys.' *Ib. Mr. Jones*

10 Philip, foozling with his cleek,
Drove his ball through Helen's cheek;
Sad they bore her corpse away,
Seven up and six to play.
Ib. Philip

11 Billy, in one of his nice new sashes,
Fell in the fire and was burnt to ashes;
Now, although the room grows chilly,
I haven't the heart to poke poor Billy.
Ruthless Rhymes. Tender-Heartedness

ROBERT CUNNINGHAME-GRAHAM
1735–1797

12 If doughty deeds my lady please,
Right soon I'll mount my steed.
*If Doughty Deeds My Lady Please, or O Tell
Me How To Woo Thee*

13 For you alone I ride the ring. *Ib.*

JAMES GRAHAME
1765–1811

14 Hail, Sabbath! thee I hail, the poor man's day.
The Sabbath, l. 29

KENNETH GRAHAME
1859–1932

15 'Aunt Maria flung herself on him [the curate]. "O
Mr. Hodgitts!" I heard her cry, "you are brave! for
my sake do not be rash!" He was not rash.'
The Golden Age, 'The Burglars'

16 Believe me, my young friend, there is *nothing*—
absolutely nothing—half so much worth doing as
simply messing about in boats.
The Wind in the Willows, ch. 1

17 The clever men at Oxford
Know all that there is to be knowed.
But they none of them know one half as much
As intelligent Mr. Toad. *Ib. ch. x*

JAMES GRAINGER
1721?–1766

18 What is fame? an empty bubble;
Gold? a transient, shining trouble. *Solitude*, l. 96

19 Now, Muse, let's sing of rats.
The Sugar Cane. MS. quoted in Boswell's *Life
of Johnson, 21 March 1776*. The passage was
not printed

SIR ROBERT GRANT
1779–1838

20 The Ancient of Days,
Pavilioned in splendour,
And girded with praise.
Bickersteth's *Church Psalmody. O Worship the
King*

21 His chariots of wrath The deep thunder clouds form,
And dark is his path On the wings of the storm. *Ib.*

22 Frail children of dust,
And feeble as frail. *Ib.*

ULYSSES SIMPSON GRANT
1822–1885

23 I know no method to secure the repeal of bad or
obnoxious laws so effective as their stringent
execution. *Inaugural Address, 4 Mar. 1869*

1 I purpose to fight it out on this line, if it takes all
summer.
*Dispatch to Washington, From Head-Quarters
in the Field, 11 May 1864*

2 Let no guilty man escape, if it can be avoided. . . .
No personal considerations should stand in the way
of performing a public duty.
*Indorsement of a Letter relating to the Whiskey
Ring, 29 July 1875*

3 Let us have peace.
*Letter of Acceptance of Nomination, 29 May
1868*

4 No terms except unconditional and immediate surrender can be accepted. I propose to move immediately upon your works.
*To Simon Bolivar Buckner, whom he was besieging
in Fort Donelson, 16 Feb. 1862*

GEORGE GRANVILLE, BARON LANSDOWNE
1667-1735

5 I'll be this abject thing no more;
Love, give me back my heart again.
Adieu l'Amour

6 Who to a woman trusts his peace of mind,
Trusts a frail bark, with a tempestuous wind.
The British Enchanters, II. i

7 Of all the plagues with which the world is curst,
Of every ill, a woman is the worst. *Ib.*

8 Marriage the happiest bond of love might be,
If hands were only joined when hearts agree. *Ib. v. i*

9 O Love! thou bane of the most generous souls!
Thou doubtful pleasure, and thou certain pain.
Heroic Love, II. i

10 'Tis the talk, and not the intrigue, that's the crime.
The She Gallants, III. i

11 Cowards in scarlet pass for men of war. *Ib. v*

12 Whimsey, not reason, is the female guide.
The Vision, l. 81

ALFRED PERCEVAL GRAVES
1846-1931

13 Of priests we can offer a charmin' variety,
Far renowned for larnin' and piety. *Father O'Flynn*

14 Powerfulest preacher and tinderest teacher
And kindliest creature in ould Donegal. *Ib.*

15 Checkin' the crazy ones, coaxin' onaisy ones,
Liftin' the lazy ones on wid the stick. *Ib.*

JOHN WOODCOCK GRAVES
1795-1886

16 D'ye ken John Peel with his coat so gray?
D'ye ken John Peel at the break of the day?
D'ye ken John Peel when he's far far away
With his hounds and his horn in the morning?
'Twas the sound of his horn called me from my bed,
And the cry of his hounds has me oft-times led;
For Peel's view-hollo would waken the dead,
Or a fox from his lair in the morning. *John Peel*

ROBERT GRAVES
1895-

17 Goodbye to all that. *Title of book*

THOMAS GRAY
1716-1771

18 The social smile, the sympathetic tear.
Alliance of Education and Government, l. 37

19 When love could teach a monarch to be wise,
And gospel-light first dawn'd from Bullen's eyes.
Ib. l. 108

20 Ruin seize thee, ruthless King!
Confusion on thy banners wait,
Tho' fann'd by Conquest's crimson wing
They mock the air with idle state. *The Bard, I. i*

21 To high-born Hoel's harp, or soft Llewellyn's lay.
Ib. ii

22 Weave the warp, and weave the woof,
The winding-sheet of Edward's race.
Give ample room, and verge enough
The characters of hell to trace. *Ib. II. i*

23 Fair laughs the morn, and soft the zephyr blows,
While proudly riding o'er the azure realm
In gallant trim the gilded vessel goes,
Youth on the prow, and Pleasure at the helm;
Regardless of the sweeping whirlwind's sway,
That, hush'd in grim repose, expects his evening
prey. *Ib. ii*

24 Ye towers of Julius, London's lasting shame,
With many a foul and midnight murther fed. *Ib. iii*

25 Visions of glory, spare my aching sight,
Ye unborn ages, crowd not on my soul! *Ib. III. i*

26 And Truth severe, by fairy Fiction drest. *Ib. ii*

27 Now my weary lips I close;
Leave me, leave me to repose! *Descent of Odin, l. 71*

28 The curfew tolls the knell of parting day,
The lowing herd wind slowly o'er the lea,
The ploughman homeward plods his weary way,
And leaves the world to darkness and to me.

Now fades the glimmering landscape on the sight,
And all the air a solemn stillness holds,
Save where the beetle wheels his droning flight,
And drowsy tinklings lull the distant folds.
Elegy Written in a Country Churchyard, i–ii

29 Save that from yonder ivy-mantled tow'r,
The moping owl does to the moon complain.
Ib. iii

30 Each in his narrow cell for ever laid,
The rude forefathers of the hamlet sleep. *Ib. iv*

31 The breezy call of incense-breathing Morn,
The swallow twitt'ring from the straw-built shed,
The cock's shrill clarion, or the echoing horn,
No more shall rouse them from their lowly bed.

For them no more the blazing hearth shall burn,
Or busy housewife ply her evening care:
No children run to lisp their sire's return,
Or climb his knees the envied kiss to share.
Ib. v–vi

1 Let not ambition mock their useful toil,
   Their homely joys, and destiny obscure;
Nor grandeur hear with a disdainful smile,
   The short and simple annals of the poor.

The boast of heraldry, the pomp of pow'r,
   And all that beauty, all that wealth e'er gave,
Awaits alike th' inevitable hour,
   The paths of glory lead but to the grave.
     Elegy Written in a Country Churchyard, viii–ix

2 Where thro' the long-drawn aisle and fretted vault
The pealing anthem swells the note of praise.
                       Ib. x

3 Can storied urn or animated bust
   Back to its mansion call the fleeting breath?
Can honour's voice provoke the silent dust,
   Or flatt'ry soothe the dull cold ear of death?
                       Ib. xi

4 Hands, that the rod of empire might have sway'd,
   Or wak'd to ecstasy the living lyre.   *Ib.* xii

5 But knowledge to their eyes her ample page
   Rich with the spoils of time did ne'er unroll;
Chill penury repress'd their noble rage,
   And froze the genial current of the soul.

Full many a gem of purest ray serene,
   The dark unfathom'd caves of ocean bear:
Full many a flower is born to blush unseen,
   And waste its sweetness on the desert air.

Some village-Hampden, that with dauntless breast
   The little tyrant of his fields withstood;
Some mute inglorious Milton here may rest,
   Some Cromwell guiltless of his country's blood.

Th' applause of list'ning senates to command,
   The threats of pain and ruin to despise,
To scatter plenty o'er a smiling land,
   And read their hist'ry in a nation's eyes.
                    Ib. xiii–xvi

6 Forbad to wade through slaughter to a throne,
   And shut the gates of mercy on mankind. *Ib.* xvii

7 Far from the madding crowd's ignoble strife,
   Their sober wishes never learn'd to stray;
Along the cool sequester'd vale of life
   They kept the noiseless tenor of their way.

Yet ev'n these bones from insult to protect
   Some frail memorial still erected nigh,
With uncouth rhymes and shapeless sculpture deck'd,
   Implores the passing tribute of a sigh. *Ib.* xix–xx

8 And many a holy text around she strews,
   That teach the rustic moralist to die.   *Ib.* xxi

9 For who to dumb Forgetfulness a prey,
   This pleasing anxious being e'er resign'd,
Left the warm precincts of the cheerful day,
   Nor cast one longing ling'ring look behind?

On some fond breast the parting soul relies,
   Some pious drops the closing eye requires;
Ev'n from the tomb the voice of Nature cries,
   Ev'n in our ashes live their wonted fires.
                   Ib. xxii–xxiii

10 Mindful of th' unhonour'd dead.   *Ib.* xxiv

11 Brushing with hasty steps the dews away
   To meet the sun upon the upland lawn. *Ib.* xxv

12 His listless length at noontide would he stretch,
   And pore upon the brook that babbles by. *Ib.* xxvi

13 Here rests his head upon the lap of Earth
   A youth to fortune and to fame unknown.
Fair Science frown'd not on his humble birth,
   And Melancholy mark'd him for her own.

Large was his bounty, and his soul sincere,
   Heav'n did a recompense as largely send:
He gave to Mis'ry all he had, a tear,
   He gain'd from Heav'n ('twas all he wish'd) a
     friend.

No farther seek his merits to disclose,
   Or draw his frailties from their dread abode,
(There they alike in trembling hope repose),
   The bosom of his Father and his God.
     Elegy written in a Country Churchyard, xxx–xxxii

14 Iron-sleet of arrowy shower
   Hurtles in the darken'd air.   *The Fatal Sisters*

15 Daughter of Jove, relentless power,
   Thou tamer of the human breast,
Whose iron scourge and tort'ring hour
   The bad affright, afflict the best.
                Hymn to Adversity, l. 1

16 What sorrow was, thou bad'st her know,
   And from her own, she learn'd to melt at others' woe.
                    Ib. l. 15

17 And leave us leisure to be good.   *Ib.* l. 20

18 Rich windows that exclude the light,
   And passages, that lead to nothing. *A Long Story*, ii

19 Full oft within the spacious walls,
   When he had fifty winters o'er him,
My grave Lord-Keeper led the brawls;
   The Seal, and Maces, danc'd before him. *Ib.* iii

20 What female heart can gold despise?
   What cat's averse to fish?
          Ode on the Death of a Favourite Cat

21 A fav'rite has no friend!   *Ib.*

22 Not all that tempts your wand'ring eyes
   And heedless hearts, is lawful prize;
Nor all, that glisters, gold.   *Ib.*

23 Ye distant spires, ye antique towers,
   That crown the wat'ry glade.
    Ode on a Distant Prospect of Eton College, l. 1

24 Urge the flying ball.   *Ib.* l. 30

25 Still as they run they look behind,
   They hear a voice in every wind,
   And snatch a fearful joy.   *Ib.* l. 38

26 Alas, regardless of their doom,
   The little victims play!
No sense have they of ills to come,
   Nor care beyond to-day.   *Ib.* l. 51

27 Ah, tell them, they are men.   *Ib.* l. 60

28 Grim-visag'd comfortless Despair.   *Ib.* l. 69

29 Slow-consuming Age.   *Ib.* l. 90

30 To each his suff'rings: all are men,
   Condemn'd alike to groan;
The tender for another's pain,
   Th' unfeeling for his own.

Yet ah! why should they know their fate?
Since sorrow never comes too late,
   And happiness too swiftly flies.
Thought would destroy their paradise.
   No more; where ignorance is bliss,
   'Tis folly to be wise.   *Ib.* l. 91

1 Hence, avaunt ('tis holy ground)
Comus, and his midnight-crew.
Ode for Music, or Installation Ode, l. 1

2 Servitude that hugs her chain. *Ib.* l. 6

3 There sit the sainted sage, the bard divine,
The few, whom genius gave to shine
Thro' every unborn age, and undiscover'd clime.
Ib. l. 15

4 Their tears, their little triumphs o'er,
Their human passions now no more. *Ib.* l. 48

5 The meanest flowret of the vale,
The simplest note that swells the gale,
The common sun, the air, and skies,
To him are opening paradise.
Ode. On the Pleasure Arising from Vicissitude,
l. 49

6 The Attic warbler pours her throat,
Responsive to the cuckoo's note.
Ode on the Spring, l. 5

7 How vain the ardour of the crowd,
How low, how little are the proud,
How indigent the great! *Ib.* l. 18

8 Contemplation's sober eye. *Ib.* l. 31

9 The bloom of young desire and purple light of love.
The Progress of Poesy, i. 3

10 Nature's darling. [Shakespeare.] *Ib.* iii. 1

11   The dauntless child
Stretched forth his little arms, and smiled.
[Shakespeare.] *Ib.*

12 Or ope the sacred source of sympathetic tears. *Ib.*

13 Nor second he, that rode sublime
Upon the seraph-wings of ecstasy,
The secrets of th' abyss to spy.
He pass'd the flaming bounds of place and time:
The living throne, the sapphire-blaze,
Where angels tremble, while they gaze,
He saw; but blasted with excess of light,
Closed his eyes in endless night. [Milton.] *Ib.* iii. 2

14 Two coursers of ethereal race,
With necks in thunder clothed, and long-resounding
pace. *Ib.*

15 Bright-eyed Fancy, hovering o'er,
Scatters from her pictured urn
Thoughts, that breathe, and words, that burn. *Ib.* 3

16 Beyond the limits of a vulgar fate,
Beneath the good how far—but far above the great.
Ib.

17 Too poor for a bribe, and too proud to importune,
He had not the method of making a fortune.
Sketch of his own Character

18 To warm their little loves the birds complain.
Sonnet on the Death of Richard West

19 And weep the more because I weep in vain. *Ib.*

20 Now as the paradisaical pleasures of the Mahometans
consist in playing upon the flute and lying with
Houris, be mine to read eternal new romances of
Marivaux and Crebillon.
Letters. 103, *To West* [8] *Apr.,* [*1742*]

21 The language of the age is never the language of
poetry, except among the French, whose verse,
where the thought or image does not support it,
differs in nothing from prose. *Ib.*

22 It has been usual to catch a mouse or two (for form's
sake) in public once a year. [On refusing the
Laureateship.] *Letter. 259, To Mason, 19 Dec. 1757*

23 Any fool may write a most valuable book by chance,
if he will only tell us what he heard and saw
with veracity. *Ib. 475, To Walpole, 25 Feb. 1768*

24 I shall be but a shrimp of an author.
Ib. (Seventeen years after the publication of *An
Elegy Written in a Country Churchyard*)

MATTHEW GREEN
1696–1737

25 I live by pulling off the hat.
On Barclay's Apology, 1. 84

26 They politics like ours profess,
The greater prey upon the less. *The Grotto*, 1. 69

27 Fling but a stone, the giant dies.
Laugh and be well. *The Spleen*, 1. 92

28 Or to some coffee-house I stray,
For news, the manna of a day,
And from the hipp'd discourses gather
That politics go by the weather. *Ib.* 1. 168

29 Experience joined with common sense,
To mortals is a providence. *Ib.* 1. 312

30 Who their ill-tasted, home-brewed prayer
To the State's mellow forms prefer. *Ib.* 1. 336

31 By happy alchemy of mind
They turn to pleasure all they find. *Ib.* 1. 610

ROBERT GREENE
1560?–1592

32 A noble mind disdains to hide his head,
And let his foes triumph in his overthrow.
Alphonso, King of Aragon, 1

33 Cupid abroad was lated in the night,
His wings were wet with ranging in the rain.
Sonnet: Cupid Abroad was Lated

34 Friar Bacon and Friar Bungay. *Title of play*

35 Hangs in the uncertain balance of proud time.
Friar Bacon and Friar Bungay, III. i

36 Sweet Adon, darest not glance thine eye
N'oserez vous, mon bel ami?
Upon thy Venus that must die?
Je vous en prie, pity me:
*N'oserez vous, mon bel, mon bel,
N'oserez vous, mon bel ami? Infida's Song*

37 Ah! were she pitiful as she is fair,
Or but as mild as she is seeming so.
Dorastus in Praise of Fawnia. Pandosto, ed. 1694

38 O glorious sun, imagine me the west!
Shine in my arms, and set thou in my breast! *Ib.*

39 Love in my bosom like a bee
Doth suck his sweet;
Now with his wings he plays with me,
Now with his feet.
Within mine eyes he makes his nest,
His bed amid my tender breast;
My kisses are his daily feast,
And yet he robs me of my rest.
Ah, wanton, will ye? *Rosalind's Madrigal*

1 Like to Diana in her summer weed,
Girt with a crimson robe of brightest dye,
   Goes fair Samela.
Whiter than be the flocks that straggling feed,
When washed by Arethusa's fount they lie,
   Is fair Samela.   *Samela*

2 Weep not, my wanton, smile upon my knee;
When thou art old there's grief enough for thee.
   Mother's wag, pretty boy,
   Father's sorrow, father's joy.
   When thy father first did see
   Such a boy by him and me,
   He was glad, I was woe:
   Fortune changed made him so,
   When he left his pretty boy,
   Last his sorrow, first his joy.   *Sephestia's Song*

3 The wanton smiled, father wept;
   Mother cried, baby lept;
   More he crowed, more we cried;
   Nature could not sorrow hide.
   He must go, he must kiss
   Child and mother, baby bliss;
   For he left his pretty boy,
   Father's sorrow, father's joy.   *Ib.*

4 The swain did woo, she was nice,
Following fashion nayed him twice.
        The Shepherd's Ode

5 Ah! what is love! It is a pretty thing,
As sweet unto a shepherd as a king,
   And sweeter too;
For kings have cares that wait upon a crown,
And cares can make the sweetest love to frown.
   Ah then, ah then,
If country loves such sweet desires do gain,
What lady would not love a shepherd swain?
       The Shepherd's Wife's Song

6 For there is an upstart crow, beautified with our
feathers, that with his tiger's heart wrapped in a
player's hide, supposes he is as well able to bum-
bast out a blank verse as the best of you; and
being an absolute *Iohannes fac totum*, is in his
own conceit the only Shake-scene in a country.
*The Groatsworth of Wit Bought with a Million
of Repentance*

GREGORY I
540–604

7 Quasi quidam quippe est fluvius, ut ita dixerim,
planus et altus, in quo et agnus ambulet et elephas
natet.
   This is as it were a river, if I may so use the expression, in which a lamb may walk and an elephant
   may swim.
     Moralia in Job. Epistola Miseria, ch. 4

8 Responsum est, quod Angli vocarentur. At ille:
'Bene,' inquit; 'nam et angelicam habent faciem, et
tales angelorum in caelis decet esse coheredes.'
   They answered that they were called Angles. 'It
   is well,' he said, 'for they have the faces of
   angels, and such should be the co-heirs of the
   angels in heaven.'
   Traditionally quoted: 'Non Angli sed Angeli.'
     Bede, *Historia Ecclesiastica*, II. i

GREGORY VII
1020–1085

9 Dilexi iustitiam et odi iniquitatem, propterea morior
in exilio.
   I have loved justice and hated iniquity: therefore
   I die in exile.   Bowden, *Life*, iii, ch. 20

STEPHEN GRELLET
1773–1855

10 I expect to pass through this world but once; any
good thing therefore that I can do, or any kindness
that I can show to any fellow-creature, let me do it
now; let me not defer or neglect it, for I shall not
pass this way again.
   Attr. 'Treasure Trove', *collected by John o'
   London, 1925.* Many other claimants to authorship

FULKE GREVILLE, FIRST BARON BROOKE
1554–1628

11 More than most fair, full of that heavenly fire,
   Kindled above to show the Maker's glory;
Beauty's first-born, in whom all powers conspire
   To write the Graces' life, and Muses' story:
If in my heart all saints else be defaced,
Honour the shrine, where you alone are placed.
       Cælica, sonnet iii

12 Fire and people do in this agree,
They both good servants, both ill masters be.
      Inquisition upon Fame, lxvii

13 Do what you can: mine shall subsist by me:
I am the measure of Felicity.
    Mustapha. Chorus Tertius, Eternity

14 Oh wearisome condition of humanity!
Born under one law, to another bound.
        Mustapha, v. iv

15 Silence augmenteth grief, writing increaseth rage,
Stal'd are my thoughts, which loved and lost, the
   wonder of our age,
Yet quick'ned now with fire, though dead with frost
   ere now,
Enraged I write, I know not what: dead, quick, I
   know not how.
    Elegy on the Death of Sir Philip Sidney

16 Fulke Greville, Servant to Queen Elizabeth, Coun-
cillor to King James, and Friend to Sir Philip
Sidney.
   *Epitaph Written for Himself, on his Monument in
   Warwick*

EDWARD, VISCOUNT GREY OF FALLODON
1862–1933

17 The British Army should be a projectile to be fired
by the British Navy. *Lord Fisher, Memories*, ch. 1

18 The lamps are going out all over Europe; we shall
not see them lit again in our lifetime.
   3 Aug. 1914. Twenty-Five Years, vol. ii, ch. 18

GERALD GRIFFIN
1803–1840

19 I knew a gentle maid,
Flower of the hazel glade,—
   Eileen Aroon.   *Eileen Aroon*

1 Dear were her charms to me,
Dearer her laughter free,
Dearest her constancy,—
Eileen Aroon!   *Eileen Aroon*

NICHOLAS GRIMALD
1519–1562

2 Of all the heavenly gifts that mortal men commend,
What trusty treasure in the world can countervail a
friend?   *Of Friendship*

3 In working well, if travail you sustain,
Into the wind shall lightly pass the pain;
But of the deed the glory shall remain,
And cause your name with worthy wights to reign.
In working wrong, if pleasure you attain,
The pleasure soon shall fade, and void as vain;
But of the deed throughout the life the shame
Endures, defacing you with foul defame.
Musonius the Philosopher's Saying

GEORGE GROSSMITH
1847–1912
and
WALTER WEEDON GROSSMITH
1854–1919

4 What's the good of a home if you are never in it?
The Diary of a Nobody, ch. 1

5 I . . . recognized her as a woman who used to work
years ago for my old aunt at Clapham. It only
shows how small the world is.   *Ib.* ch. 2

6 He [Gowing] suggested we should play 'Cutlets', a
game we never heard of. He sat on a chair, and
asked Carrie to sit on his lap, an invitation which
dear Carrie rightly declined.   *Ib.* ch. 7

7 One, two, three; go! Have you an estate in Greenland?   *Ib.* ch. 10

8 That's right.   *Ib.* ch. 11

9 Without an original there can be no imitation.   *Ib.*

10 I left the room with silent dignity, but caught my
foot in the mat.   *Ib.* ch. 12

11 I am a poor man, but I would gladly give ten shillings
to find out who sent me the insulting Christmas
card I received this morning.   *Ib.* ch. 13

12 What's the matter with Gladstone? He's all right.
Ib. ch. 17

PHILIP GUEDALLA
1889–1944

13 The little ships, the unforgotten Homeric catalogue
of *Mary Jane* and *Peggy IV*, of *Folkestone Belle*,
Boy Billy, and *Ethel Maud*, of *Lady Haig* and
Skylark . . . the little ships of England brought the
Army home.
Mr. Churchill. [Evacuation of Dunkirk.]

14 The work of Henry James has always seemed
divisible by a simple dynastic arrangement into
three reigns: James I, James II, and the Old Pretender.
Collected Essays, vol. iv. *Men of Letters: Mr.
Henry James*

YVETTE GUILBERT

15 Linger longer Lucy,
Linger longer Lou.   *Song*

TEXAS GUINAN
1884–1933

16 Fifty million Frenchmen can't be wrong.
Attr. New York World-Telegram, 21 Mar. 1931

DOROTHY FRANCES GURNEY
1858–1932

17 The kiss of the sun for pardon,
The song of the birds for mirth,
One is nearer God's Heart in a garden
Than anywhere else on earth.   *God's Garden*

18 O perfect Love, all human thought transcending,
Lowly we kneel in prayer before Thy throne.
Hymn. O Perfect Love

HADRIAN
A.D. 76–138

19 Animula vagula blandula,
Hospes comesque corporis,
Quae nunc abibis in loca
Pallidula rigida nudula,
Nec ut soles dabis iocos!

Little soul, wandering, pleasant, guest and companion of the body, into what places wilt thou
now go, pale, stiff, naked, nor wilt thou play any
longer as thou art wont.
.   Duff, *Minor Latin Poems* (Loeb, 1934), 445

DOUGLAS HAIG, EARL HAIG
1861–1928

20 Every position must be held to the last man: there
must be no retirement. With our backs to the wall,
and believing in the justice of our cause, each one
of us must fight on to the end.
*Order to the British Troops, 12 Apr. 1918. The
Times, 13 Apr.*

RICHARD BURDON HALDANE, VISCOUNT
HALDANE
1856–1928

21 I had gone to Germany too often, and had read her
literature too much, not to give ground to narrow-
minded people to say that Germany was my
'spiritual home'.   *An Autobiography*, p. 285

SIR MATTHEW HALE
1609–1676

22 Christianity is part of the Common Law of England.
Historia Placitorum Coronae (1736). Also in
Blackstone's *Commentaries on the Laws of
England*, iv, 1765

SARAH JOSEPHA HALE
1788–1879

23 Mary had a little lamb,
Its fleece was white as snow,
And everywhere that Mary went
The lamb was sure to go.

'What makes the lamb love Mary so?'
  The eager children cry.
'Oh, Mary loves the lamb, you know,'
  The teacher did reply.
        Poems for Our Children. Mary's Little Lamb

THOMAS CHANDLER HALIBURTON
1796–1865

1 I want you to see Peel, Stanley, Graham, Shiel, Russell, Macaulay, Old Joe, and so on. These men are all upper crust here.
        Sam Slick in England, ch. 24

GEORGE SAVILE, MARQUIS OF HALIFAX
1633–1695

2 Love is a passion that hath friends in the garrison.
        Advice to a Daughter: Behaviour and Conversation

3 This innocent word 'Trimmer' signifies no more than this, that if men are together in a boat, and one part of the company would weigh it down on one side, another would make it lean as much to the contrary.
        Character of a Trimmer, preface

4 He would rather die, than see a piece of English grass trampled down by a foreign Trespasser.
        Character of a Trimmer

5 Men are not hanged for stealing horses, but that horses may not be stolen.
        Political Thoughts and Reflections: Of Punishment

6 To the question, What shall we do to be saved in this World? there is no other answer but this, Look to your Moat. *A Rough Draft of a New Model at Sea*

CHARLES SPRAGUE HALL
fl. 1860

7 John Brown's body lies a mould'ring in the grave, His soul is marching on!
        John Brown's Body. Nicholas Smith's *Stories of Great National Songs*

BISHOP JOSEPH HALL
1574–1656

8 Ah me! how seldom see we sons succeed
  Their fathers' praise, in prowess and great deed.
        Satires, bk. iv, no. 3

9 I first adventure, follow me who list
  And be the second English satirist.
        Virgidemiae, Prologue

10 Perfection is the child of Time.
        Works (1625), p. 670

11 All his dealings are square, and above the board.
        Virtues and Vices (1608), bk. i, p. 15

OWEN HALL [JAMES DAVIS]
d. 1907

12 Tell me, pretty maiden, are there any more at home like you?
        Florodora. Act ii

FITZ-GREENE HALLECK
1790–1867

13 Forever, float that standard sheet!
  Where breathes the foe but falls before us,
  With Freedom's soil beneath our feet,
  And Freedom's banner streaming o'er us?
        The American Flag
        Attr. also to Joseph Rodman Drake, 1795–1820.

14 They love their land because it is their own,
  And scorn to give aught other reason why;
  Would shake hands with a king upon his throne,
  And think it kindness to his Majesty. *Connecticut*

15 Green be the turf above thee,
  Friend of my better days!
  None knew thee but to love thee,
  Nor named thee but to praise.
        On the Death of J. R. Drake

16 Come to the bridal-chamber, Death!
  Come to the mother's, when she feels,
  For the first time, her first-born's breath.
        Marco Bozzaris

FRIEDRICH HALM [FRANZ VON MÜNCH-BELLINGHAUSEN]
1806–1871

17 Mein Herz ich will dich fragen:
  Was ist denn Liebe? Sag'!—
  'Zwei Seelen und ein Gedanke,
  Zwei Herzen und ein Schlag!'

  What love is, if thou wouldst be taught,
  Thy heart must teach alone,—
  Two souls with but a single thought,
  Two hearts that beat as one.
        Der Sohn der Wildniss, Act ii *ad fin.*
        Trans. by Maria Lovell in *Ingomar the Barbarian*

WILLIAM FREDERICK HALSEY
1882–

18 Our ships have been salvaged and are retiring at high speed toward the Japanese fleet.
        Radio Message, Oct. 1944 after Japanese claims that most of the American Third Fleet had been sunk or were retiring

PHILIP GILBERT HAMERTON
1834–1894

19 The art of reading is to skip judiciously.
        Intellectual Life, pt. iv, letter iv

ALEXANDER HAMILTON
1757–1804

20 A national debt, if it is not excessive, will be to us a national blessing.
        Letter to Robert Morris, 30 Apr. 1781

GAIL HAMILTON
1838–1896

21 The total depravity of inanimate things. *Epigram*

[234]

WILLIAM HAMILTON
1704–1754

1 Busk ye, busk ye, my bonny bonny bride,
Busk ye, busk ye, my winsome marrow.
Poetical Works. The Braes of Yarrow

WILLIAM GERARD HAMILTON
1729–1796

2 Johnson is dead.—Let us go to the next best:—There is nobody; no man can be said to put you in mind of Johnson.
Boswell's Life of Johnson (1934), vol. iv, p. 420

SIR WILLIAM HAMILTON
1788–1856

3 Truth, like a torch, the more it's shook it shines.
Discussions on Philosophy, title-page

4 On earth there is nothing great but man; in man there is nothing great but mind.
Lectures on Metaphysics

OSCAR HAMMERSTEIN
1895–

5 The last time I saw Paris, her heart was warm and gay,
I heard the laughter of her heart in every street café.
Song. The Last Time I Saw Paris

PERCY HAMMOND
1873–1936

6 The human knee is a joint and not an entertainment.
Mark Sullivan, *Our Times*, vol. iii, ch. 10

RICHARD ROLLE DE HAMPOLE
1290?–1349

7 When Adam dalfe and Eve spane
So spire if thou may spede,
Whare was than the pride of man,
That nowe merres his mede?
Religious Pieces in Prose and Verse, vii. *Early English Text Society, Original Series*, No. 26. *An altered form was used by John Ball (d. 1381) as the text of his revolutionary sermon on the outbreak of the Peasants' Revolt, 1381:*
When Adam delved and Eve span,
Who was then the gentleman?

JOHN HANCOCK
1737–1793

8 There, I guess King George will be able to read that.
Remark on signing the Declaration of Independence, 4 July 1776

MINNY MAUD HANFF
fl. 1900

9 Since then they called him Sunny Jim.
Sunny Jim. Advertisement for Force, a breakfast food

KATHERINE HANKEY
1834–1911

10 Tell me the old, old story,
Of unseen things above.
The Story Wanted. Tell Me the Old, Old Story

PHILIP YORKE, EARL OF HARDWICKE
1690–1764

11 His doubts are better than most people's certainties.
[Referring to the book *Dirleton's Doubts*.]
Boswell's Johnson (1934), iii, p. 205

E. J. HARDY
12 How To Be Happy Though Married.
Title of book (1910)

THOMAS HARDY
1840–1928

13 'He was a man who used to notice such things.'
Afterwards

14 Some nocturnal blackness, mothy and warm,
When the hedgehog travels furtively over the lawn.
Ib.

15 As the hope-hour stroked its sum.
A Broken Appointment

16 Twin halves of one august event.
Convergence of the Twain

17 An aged thrush, frail, gaunt, and small,
In blast-beruffled plume.   *The Darkling Thrush*

18 So little cause for carolings
Of such ecstatic sound
Was written on terrestrial things
Afar or nigh around,
That I could think there trembled through
His happy good-night air
Some blessed Hope, whereof he knew
And I was unaware.   *Ib.*

19 And foreign constellations west
Each night above his mound.   *Drummer Hodge*

20 What of the Immanent Will and its designs?—
It works unconsciously as heretofore,
Eternal artistries in Circumstance.
The Dynasts, pt. i. *Fore-Scene*

21   Like a knitter drowsed,
Whose fingers play in skilled unmindfulness,
The Will has woven with an absent heed
Since life first was; and ever so will weave.   *Ib.*

22 The nether sky opens, and Europe is disclosed as a prone and emaciated figure, the Alps shaping like a backbone, and the branching mountain-chains like ribs, the peninsular plateau of Spain forming a head. Broad and lengthy lowlands stretch from the north of France across Russia like a grey-green garment hemmed by the Ural mountains and the glistening Arctic Ocean.
The point of view then sinks downwards through space, and draws near to the surface of the perturbed countries, where the peoples, distressed by events which they did not cause, are seen writhing, crawling, heaving, and vibrating in their various cities and nationalities.
Ib. Stage Direction

1 A local cult called Christianity. *The Dynasts*, I. vi

2 My argument is that War makes rattling good history; but Peace is poor reading. *Ib.* II. v

3 But O, the intolerable antilogy
Of making figments feel! *Ib.* IV. vi

4 Each captain, petty officer, and man
Is only at his post when under fire. *Ib.* v. i

5 The all-urging Will, raptly magnipotent. *Ib.* VI. viii

6 But—a stirring thrills the air
Like to sounds of joyance there
    That the rages
    Of the ages
Shall be cancelled, and deliverance offered from the darts that were,
Consciousness the Will informing, till It fashion all
    things fair! *Ib.* pt. iii, last lines

7 The selfsame bloody mode. *Embarcation*

8 William Dewy, Tranter Reuben, Farmer Ledlow late at plough,
Robert's kin, and John's, and Ned's,
And the Squire, and Lady Susan, lie in Mellstock
    churchyard now! *Friends Beyond*

9 Mothy curfew-tide. *Ib.*

10 A lone cave's stillicide. *Ib.*

11 If ye break my best blue china, children, I shan't care
or ho. *Ib.*

12 And shakes this fragile frame at eve
With throbbings of noontide. *I Look Into My Glass*

13 If way to the Better there be, it exacts a full look at the
worst. *In Tenebris*

14 Only a man harrowing clods
    In a slow silent walk
With an old horse that stumbles and nods
    Half asleep as they stalk.

Only thin smoke without flame
    From the heaps of couch grass;
Yet this will go onward the same
    Though Dynasties pass.

Yonder a maid and her wight
    Come whispering by:
War's annals will cloud into night
    Ere their story die.
In Time of 'The Breaking of Nations'

15 That long drip of human tears.
On an Invitation to the United States

16 Let me enjoy the earth no less
Because the all-enacting Might
That fashioned forth its loveliness
Had other aims than my delight.
Let Me Enjoy the Earth

17 Here's not a modest maiden elf
    But dreads the final Trumpet,
Lest half of her should rise herself,
    And half some sturdy strumpet!
The Levelled Churchyard

18 What of the faith and fire within us
    Men who march away
    Ere the barn-cocks say
Night is growing gray? *Men Who March Away*

19 Your face, and the God-curst sun, and a tree,
And a pond edged with grayish leaves.
Neutral Tones

20 And both of us, scorning parochial ways,
Had lived like the wives in the patriarchs' days.
Over the Coffin

21 Christmas Eve, and twelve of the clock.
    'Now they are all on their knees,'
An elder said as we sat in a flock
    By the embers in hearthside ease. *The Oxen*

22 So fair a fancy few would weave
    In these years! *Ib.*

23 I should go with him in the gloom,
    Hoping it might be so. *Ib.*

24 Read that moderate man Voltaire.
The Respectable Burgher

25 I have lived with Shades so long.
Retrospect: I Have Lived with Shades

26 Love is lame at fifty years. *The Revisitation*

27 A little ball of feather and bone. *Shelley's Skylark*

28 Patiently adjust, amend, and heal. *The Sleep-Worker*

29 And the spirits of those who were homing
    Passed on, rushingly,
Like the Pentecost Wind. *Souls of the Slain*

30 This is the weather the cuckoo likes,
    And so do I. *Weathers*

31 And maids come forth sprig-muslin drest. *Ib.*

32 This is the weather the shepherd shuns,
    And so do I. *Ib.*

33 Rooks in families homeward go. *Ib.*

34 When I set out for Lyonnesse,
    A hundred miles away.
When I Set Out for Lyonnesse

35 When I came back from Lyonnesse
    With magic in my eyes. *Ib.*

36 Goodbye is not worth while. *Without Ceremony*

37 Life offers—to deny! *Yellham-Wood's Story*

38 The kingly brilliance of Sirius pierced the eye with a steely glitter, the star called Capella was yellow, Aldebaran and Betelgueux shone with a fiery red. To persons standing alone on a hill during a clear midnight such as this, the roll of the world eastward is almost a palpable movement.
Far From the Madding Crowd, ch. 2

39 A nice unparticular man. *Ib.* ch. 8

40 We ought to feel deep cheerfulness that a happy Providence kept it from being any worse. *Ib.*

41 Ah! stirring times we live in—stirring times.
Ib. ch. 15

42 Five decades hardly modified the cut of a gaiter, the embroidery of a smock-frock, by the breadth of a hair. Ten generations failed to alter the turn of a single phrase. In these Wessex nooks the busy outsider's ancient times are only old; his old times are still new; his present is futurity.
Ib. ch. 22

1 'And the people of Bath', continued Cain, 'never need to light their fires except as a luxury, for the water springs up out of the earth ready boiled for use.' ''Tis true as the light', testified Matthew Moon. 'I've heard other navigators say the same thing.'
Far From the Madding Crowd, ch. 33

2 Ethelberta breathed a sort of exclamation, not right out, but stealthily, like a parson's damn.
The Hand of Ethelberta

3 Done because we are too menny.
Jude the Obscure, pt. vi, ch. 2

4 Life's Little Ironies.
Title

5 'Well, poor soul; she's helpless to hinder that or anything now,' answered Mother Cuxsom. 'And all her shining keys will be took from her, and her cupboards opened, and things a' didn't wish seen, anybody will see; and her little wishes and ways will all be as nothing.'
The Mayor of Casterbridge, ch. 18

6 Dialect words—those terrible marks of the beast to the truly genteel.
Ib. ch. 20

7 Michael Henchard's Will.
That Elizabeth-Jane Farfrae be not told of my death, or made to grieve on account of me.
& that I be not buried in consecrated ground.
& that no sexton be asked to toll the bell.
& that nobody is wished to see my dead body.
& that no murners walk behind me at my funeral.
& that no flours be planted on my grave.
& that no man remember me.
To this I put my name.
Ib. ch. 45

8 The heaven being spread with this pallid screen and the earth with the darkest vegetation, their meeting-line at the horizon was clearly marked. In such contrast the heath wore the appearance of an instalment of night which had taken up its place before its astronomical hour was come: darkness had to a great extent arrived hereon, while day stood distinct in the sky.
The Return of the Native, ch. 1

9 In fact, precisely at this transitional point of its nightly roll into darkness the great and particular glory of the Egdon waste began, and nobody could be said to understand the heath who had not been there at such a time.
Ib.

10 The great inviolate place had an ancient permanence which the sea cannot claim. Who can say of a particular sea that it is old? Distilled by the sun, kneaded by the moon, it is renewed in a year, in a day, or in an hour. The sea changed, the fields changed, the rivers, the villages, and the people changed, yet Egdon remained.
Ib.

11 A little one-eyed, blinking sort o' place.
Tess of the D'Urbervilles, ch. 1

12 Always washing, and never getting finished. *Ib.* ch. 4

13 The New Testament was less a Christiad than a Pauliad to his intelligence.
Ib. ch. 25

14 The President of the Immortals (in Æschylean phrase) had ended his sport with Tess. *Ib.* ch. 59

15 The courses of the *Victory* were absorbed into the main, then her topsails went, and then her top-gallants. She was now no more than a dead fly's wing on a sheet of spider's web; and even this fragment diminished. Anne could hardly bear to see the end, and yet she resolved not to flinch. The admiral's flag sank behind the watery line, and in a minute the very truck of the last main-mast stole away. The *Victory* was gone.
The Trumpet Major, ch. 34

16 Good, but not religious-good.
Under the Greenwood Tree, ch. 2

17 Silent? Ah, he is silent! He can keep silence well. That man's silence is wonderful to listen to.
Ib. ch. 14

18 You was a good man, and did good things.
The Woodlanders, ch. 48

JULIUS CHARLES HARE
1795–1855
and
AUGUSTUS WILLIAM HARE
1792–1834

19 Man without religion is the creature of circumstances.
Guesses at Truth, Series 1

20 Truth, when witty, is the wittiest of all things. *Ib.*

21 The ancients dreaded death: the Christian can only fear dying. *Ib.*

22 Half the failures in life arise from pulling in one's horse as he is leaping. *Ib.*

23 Purity is the feminine, Truth the masculine, of Honour. *Ib.*

24 Every Irishman, the saying goes, has a potato in his head. *Ib.*

25 Everybody has his own theatre, in which he is manager, actor, prompter, playwright, sceneshifter, boxkeeper, doorkeeper, all in one, and audience into the bargain. *Ib.* Series 2

MAURICE EVAN HARE
1889–

26 There once was a man who said, 'Damn!
It is borne in upon me I am
An engine that moves
In predestinate grooves,
I'm not even a bus I'm a tram.'
Written, as above, at St. John's College, Oxford, in 1905

FRANCIS HARGRAVE
1741?–1821

27 A soil whose air is deemed too pure for slaves to breathe in. [England.]
Argument on Sommersett Habeas Corpus Case, 14 May 1772. James Sommersett was a negro slave from Jamaica, who accompanied his master to England and claimed his freedom. See Cobbett's State Trials, vol. xx

WILLIAM HARGREAVES

28 I'm Burlington Bertie:
I rise at ten-thirty.
Burlington Bertie. First sung by Ella Shields in October 1914 at the Argyle Theatre, Birkenhead.

1 I walk down the Strand
With my gloves on my hand
And I walk down again
With them off. *Burlington Bertie*

SIR JOHN HARINGTON
1561–1612

2   When I make a feast,
I would my guests should praise it, not the cooks.
Epigrams, bk. i, No. 5. *Against Writers that Carp at Other Men's Books*

3 Treason doth never prosper: what's the reason?
For if it prosper, none dare call it treason.
Ib. bk. iv, No. 5. *Of Treason*

ROBERT GOODLOE HARPER
1765–1825

4 Millions for defence but not a cent for tribute.
Toast at the dinner given by Congress at Philadelphia, 18 June 1798. Claypoole's *American Daily Advertiser, 20 June 1798.* A. J. Beveridge's *Life of John Marshall*, vol. ii.

CHARLES K. HARRIS
1865–1930

5 After the ball is over. *After the Ball*

6 Somewhere the sun is shining. *Somewhere*

CLIFFORD HARRIS

7 You called me Baby Doll a year ago. *A Broken Doll*

8 You left behind a broken doll. *Ib.*

JOEL CHANDLER HARRIS
1848–1908

9 'Law, Brer Tarrypin!' sez Brer Fox, sezee, 'you ain't see no trouble yit. Ef you wanter see sho' nuff trouble, you des oughter go 'longer me; I'm de man w'at kin show you trouble,' sezee.
Nights with Uncle Remus, ch. 17

10 W'en folks git ole en strucken wid de palsy, dey mus' speck ter be laff'd at. *Ib.* ch. 23

11 Hit look lak sparrer-grass, hit feel like sparrer-grass, hit tas'e lak sparrer-grass, en I bless ef 'taint sparrer-grass. *Ib.* ch. 27

12 All by my own-alone self. *Ib.* ch. 36

13 No 'pollygy aint gwine ter make h'ar come back whar de b'iling water hit. *Ib.* ch. 45

14 We er sorter po'ly, Sis Tempy, I'm 'blige ter you. You know w'at de jay-bird say ter der squinch-owl! 'I'm sickly but sassy.' *Ib.* ch. 50

15 A contrapshun what he call a Tar-Baby. *Uncle Remus. Legends of the Old Plantation,* ch. 2. *Tar-Baby Story*

16 How duz yo' sym'tums seem ter segashuate? *Ib.*

17 Tar-baby ain't sayin' nuthin', en Brer Fox, he lay low. *Ib.*

18 Bred en bawn in a brier-patch! *Ib.* ch. 4

19 Lounjun 'roun' en suffer'n'. *Ib.* ch. 12

20 Ole man Know-All died las' year.
Uncle Remus, ch. 34. *Plantation Proverbs*

21 Licker talks mighty loud w'en it git loose fum de jug. *Ib.*

22 Hongry rooster don't cackle w'en he fine a wum. *Ib.*

23 Youk'n hide de fier, but w'at you gwine do wid de smoke? *Ib.*

24 Oh, whar shill we go w'en de great day comes,
Wid de blowin' er de trumpits en de bangin' er de drums?
How many po' sinners'll be kotched out late
En find no latch ter de golden gate?
Uncle Remus. His Songs, i

FRANCIS BRETT HART
or
BRET HARTE
1839–1902

25 He read aloud the book wherein the Master
Had writ of Little Nell.
Dickens in Camp

26 And on that grave where English oak and holly
And laurel wreaths entwine
Deem it not all a too presumptuous folly,—
This spray of Western pine! *Ib.*

27 You see this yer Dow
Hed the worst kind of luck;
He slipped up somehow
On each thing thet he struck.
Why, ef he'd a straddled that fence-rail, the derned thing 'ed get up and buck. *Dow's Flat*

28 Thar ain't no sense
In gittin' riled! *Jim*

29 Over the trackless past, somewhere,
Lie the lost days of our tropic youth,
Only regained by faith and prayer,
Only recalled by prayer and plaint:
Each lost day has its patron saint! *The Lost Galleon*

30 For there be women fair as she,
Whose verbs and nouns do more agree.
Mrs. Judge Jenkins

31 If, of all words of tongue and pen,
The saddest are, 'It might have been,'
More sad are these we daily see:
'It is, but hadn't ought to be!' *Ib.*

32 Which I wish to remark,
And my language is plain,
That for ways that are dark
And for tricks that are vain,
The heathen Chinee is peculiar,
Which the same I would rise to explain.
Plain Language from Truthful James

33 But his smile it was pensive and childlike. *Ib.*

34 But he smiled as he sat by the table,
With the smile that was childlike and bland. *Ib.*

35 And the same with intent to deceive. *Ib.*

36 We are ruined by Chinese cheap labour. *Ib.*

37 And we found on his nails, which were taper,
What is frequent in tapers—that's wax. *Ib.*

38 He wore, I think, a chasuble, the day when first we met. *The Ritualist*

1 I reside at Table Mountain, and my name is Truthful James. *The Society upon the Stanislaus*

2 And he smiled a kind of sickly smile, and curled up on the floor,
And the subsequent proceedings interested him no more. *Ib.*

3 With unpronounceable awful names.
The Tale of a Pony

MINNIE LOUISE HASKINS
1875–

4 And I said to the man who stood at the gate of the year: 'Give me a light that I may tread safely into the unknown'. And he replied: 'Go out into the darkness and put your hand into the hand of God. That shall be to you better than light and safer than a known way.'
God Knows. Quoted by King George VI in a Christmas Broadcast. 25 Dec. 1939

STEPHEN HAWES
fl. 1502–1521

5 When the lytle byrdes swetely dyd syng
Laudes to their maker early in the mornyng.
Passetyme of Pleasure, cap. 33, xxxiii

6 For though the day be never so longe,
At last the belles ringeth to evensonge. *Ib.* cap. 42

ROBERT STEPHEN HAWKER
1803–1875

7 And have they fixed the where and when?
And shall Trelawny die?
Here's twenty thousand Cornish men
Will know the reason why!
Song of the Western Men. The last three lines have existed since the imprisonment by James II, 1688, of the seven Bishops, including Trelawny, Bishop of Bristol

SIR ANTHONY HOPE HAWKINS
see
ANTHONY HOPE

NATHANIEL HAWTHORNE
1804–1864

8 Dr. Johnson's morality was as English an article as a beefsteak. *Our Old Home. Lichfield and Uttoxeter*

LORD CHARLES HAY
?–1760

9 Gentlemen of the French Guard, fire first! (Messieurs les gardes françaises, tirez.)
Battle of Fontenoy, 1745. E. Fournier, L'Esprit dans l'Histoire (1883), ch. 52, p. 349

WILLIAM HAZLITT
1778–1830

10 His sayings are generally like women's letters; all the pith is in the postscript. [Charles Lamb.]
Conversations of Northcote. Boswell Redivivus

11 The only specimen of Burke is, *all that he wrote*.
English Literature, ch. ix. *Character of Mr Burke*

12 He writes as fast as they can read, and he does not write himself down. *Ib.* ch. xiv. *Sir Walter Scott*

13 His worst is better than any other person's best. *Ib.*

14 His works (taken together) are almost like a new edition of human nature. This is indeed to be an author! *Ib.*

15 The round-faced man in black entered, and dissipated all doubts on the subject, by beginning to talk. He did not cease while he stayed; nor has he since, that I know of. [Coleridge.]
Ib. ch. xvii. *My First Acquaintance with Poets*

16 'For those two hours,' he [Coleridge] afterwards was pleased to say, 'he was conversing with W. H.'s forehead!' *Ib.*

17 He [Coleridge] lamented that Wordsworth was not prone enough to belief in the traditional superstitions of the place, and that there was a something corporeal, a *matter-of-fact-ness*, a clinging to the palpable, or often to the petty, in his poetry, in consequence. *Ib.*

18 At Godwin's . . . they [Lamb, Holcroft, and Coleridge] were disputing fiercely which was the best— Man as he was, or man as he is to be. 'Give me,' says Lamb, 'man as he is *not* to be.' This saying was the beginning of a friendship between us, which I believe still continues. *Ib.*

19 You will hear more good things on the outside of a stagecoach from London to Oxford than if you were to pass a twelvemonth with the undergraduates, or heads of colleges, of that famous university. *The Ignorance of the Learned*

20 The temple of fame stands upon the grave: the flame that burns upon its altars is kindled from the ashes of great men.
Lectures on the English Poets. Lecture viii, On the Living Poets

21 He [Coleridge] talked on for ever; and you wished him to talk on for ever. *Ib.*

22 The dupe of friendship, and the fool of love; have I not reason to hate and to despise myself? Indeed I do; and chiefly for not having hated and despised the world enough.
The Plain Speaker. On the Pleasure of Hating

23 The love of liberty is the love of others; the love of power is the love of ourselves.
Political Essays. 'The Times' Newspaper

24 Those who make their dress a principal part of themselves, will, in general, become of no more value than their dress. *Ib. On the Clerical Character*

25 There is nothing good to be had in the country, or, if there is, they will not let you have it.
Ib. 1817. Observations on Mr. Wordsworth's Excursion

26 The art of pleasing consists in being pleased.
Round Table, vol. i. On Manner

27 The greatest offence against virtue is to speak ill of it.
Sketches and Essays. On Cant and Hypocrisy

28 The most fluent talkers or most plausible reasoners are not always the justest thinkers.
Ib. On Prejudice

1 We never do anything well till we cease to think about the manner of doing it.
Sketches and Essays. On Prejudice

2 There is an unseemly exposure of the mind, as well as of the body.   *Ib. On Disagreeable People*

3 A nickname is the heaviest stone that the devil can throw at a man.   *Ib. Nicknames*

4 Rules and models destroy genius and art.
Ib. On Taste

5 But of all footmen the lowest class is *literary footmen*.
Ib. Footmen

6 His [Leigh Hunt's] light, agreeable, polished style . . . hits off the faded graces of 'an Adonis of fifty'.
The Spirit of the Age: Mr. Leigh Hunt

7 Cavanagh's blows were not undecided and ineffectual —lumbering like Mr. Wordsworth's epic poetry, nor wavering like Mr. Coleridge's lyric prose, nor short of the mark like Mr. Brougham's speeches, nor wide of it like Mr. Canning's wit, nor foul like the *Quarterly*, nor *let* balls like the *Edinburgh Review*. Cobbett and Junius together would have made a Cavanagh.
Table Talk, vii. *The Indian Jugglers*

8 When I am in the country I wish to vegetate like the country.   *Ib. xix. On Going a Journey*

9 Give me the clear blue sky over my head, and the green turf beneath my feet, a winding road before me, and a three hours' march to dinner—and then to thinking! It is hard if I cannot start some game on these lone heaths.   *Ib.*

10 The English (it must be owned) are rather a foul-mouthed nation.   *Ib. xxii. On Criticism*

11 We can scarcely hate any one that we know.   *Ib.*

12 Venerate art as art.   *Ib. xxx*

13 So have I loitered my life away, reading books, looking at pictures, going to plays, hearing, thinking, writing on what pleased me best. I have wanted only one thing to make me happy, but wanting that have wanted everything.
Winterslow. My First Acquaintance with Poets

14 Well, I've had a happy life.
Last words. W. C. Hazlitt's *Memoirs of William Hazlitt*, 1867

BISHOP REGINALD HEBER
1783–1826

15 Brightest and best of the sons of the morning! Dawn on our darkness and lend us Thine aid!
Hymns, &c. Brightest and Best

16 By cool Siloam's shady rill
How sweet the lily grows!   *Ib. By Cool Siloam's*

17 From Greenland's icy mountains,
From India's coral strand,
Where Afric's sunny fountains
Roll down their golden sand.
Ib. From Greenland's Icy Mountains

18 What though the spicy breezes
Blow soft o'er Ceylon's isle;
Though every prospect pleases,
And only man is vile:

In vain with lavish kindness
The gifts of God are strown;
The heathen in his blindness
Bows down to wood and stone.
This is the most familiar version. Bishop Heber originally wrote 'The savage in his blindness'. *He altered this, and also altered* 'Ceylon's' *to* 'Java's'.
Hymns. From Greenland's Icy Mountains

19 Holy, Holy, Holy! Lord God Almighty!
Early in the morning our song shall rise to Thee:
Holy, Holy, Holy! Merciful and Mighty!
God in Three Persons, Blessed Trinity!

Holy, Holy, Holy! all the Saints adore Thee,
Casting down their golden crowns around the glassy sea.   *Ib. Holy, Holy, Holy!*

20 The Son of God goes forth to war,
A Kingly crown to gain;
His blood-red banner streams afar:—
Who follows in His train?
Ib. The Son of God Goes Forth

21 A noble army, men and boys,
The matron and the maid,
Around the Saviour's throne rejoice
In robes of light array'd.   *Ib.*

22 They climb'd the steep ascent of Heav'n
Through peril, toil and pain;
O God, to us may grace be given
To follow in their train.   *Ib.*

GEORG WILHELM HEGEL
1770–1831

23 What experience and history teach is this—that people and governments never have learned anything from history, or acted on principles deduced from it.
Philosophy of History. Introduction. Used by Shaw in his *Revolutionist's Handbook* and in the preface to *Heartbreak House*

HEINRICH HEINE
1797–1856

24 Ich grolle nicht, und wenn das Herz auch bricht.
I do not murmur, even if my heart break.
Buch der Lieder. Title of song

25 Ich weiss nicht, was soll es bedeuten,
Dass ich so traurig bin;
Ein Märchen aus alten Zeiten,
Das kommt mir nicht aus dem Sinn.

I know not why I am so sad; I cannot get out of my head a fairy-tale of olden times.   *Die Lorelei*

26 Auf Flügeln des Gesanges.
On the wings of song.   *Title of song*

27 Dieu me pardonnera. C'est son métier.
God will pardon me. It is His trade.
On his Deathbed

SIR ARTHUR HELPS
1813–1875

28 Somebody, I suppose, was excusing something on the score of temper, to which the bishop replied, 'Temper is nine-tenths of Christianity.'
Friends in Council, bk. i, ch. 8

1 Reading is sometimes an ingenious device for avoiding thought. *Friends in Council*, bk. ii, ch. 1

2 What a blessing this smoking is! perhaps the greatest that we owe to the discovery of America.
Ib. series II, 1859, vol. i, ch. 1, *Worry*

3 There is one statesman of the present day, of whom I always say that he would have escaped making the blunders that he has made if he had only ridden more in omnibuses.
Ib. vol. ii, ch. 9, *On Government*

FELICIA DOROTHEA HEMANS
1793–1835

4 Not there, not there, my child!   *The Better Land*

5 The boy stood on the burning deck
Whence all but he had fled;
The flame that lit the battle's wreck
Shone round him o'er the dead.   *Casabianca*

6 There came a burst of thunder sound—
The boy—oh! where was he?   *Ib.*

7 Oh! call my brother back to me!
I cannot play alone;
The summer comes with flower and bee—
Where is my brother gone?
The Child's First Grief

8 They grew in beauty, side by side,
They fill'd one home with glee;—
Their graves are sever'd, far and wide,
By mount, and stream, and sea.
The Graves of a Household

9 One sleeps where Southern vines are drest
Above the noble slain;
He wrapt his colours round his breast
On a blood-red field of Spain.   *Ib.*

10 She faded 'midst Italian flowers—
The last of that bright band.   *Ib.*

11 He Never Smiled Again!   *Title*

12 The stately homes of England,
How beautiful they stand!
Amidst their tall ancestral trees,
O'er all the pleasant land.   *The Homes of England*

13 The cottage homes of England!
By thousands on her plains.   *Ib.*

14 Leaves have their time to fall,
And flowers to wither at the north wind's breath,
And stars to set—but all,
Thou hast *all* seasons for thine own, O Death!
The Hour of Death

15 In the busy haunts of men.
Tale of the Secret Tribunal, pt. i, l. 203

JOHN HEMING
d. 1630
and
HENRY CONDELL
d. 1627

16 His mind and hand went together. What he thought he uttered with that earnestness that we have scarce received from him a blot in his papers.
Preface to the First Folio Shakespeare, 1623

ERNEST HEMINGWAY
1898–

17 The world is a fine place and worth fighting for.
For Whom the Bell Tolls, 1940

WILLIAM ERNEST HENLEY
1849–1903

18 Out of the night that covers me,
Black as the Pit from pole to pole,
I thank whatever gods may be
For my unconquerable soul.

In the fell clutch of circumstance,
I have not winced nor cried aloud:
Under the bludgeonings of chance
My head is bloody, but unbowed.
Echoes, iv. *Invictus. In Mem. R. T. H. B*

19 It matters not how strait the gate,
How charged with punishments the scroll,
I am the master of my fate:
I am the captain of my soul.   *Ib.*

20 The friendly and comforting breast
Of the old nurse, Death.   *Ib.* xxix. *To R. L. S.*

21 A late lark twitters from the quiet skies.
Ib. xxxv. *Margaritæ Sororis*

22 Night with her train of stars
And her great gift of sleep.   *Ib*

23 So be my passing!
My task accomplished and the long day done,
My wages taken, and in my heart
Some late lark singing,
Let me be gathered to the quiet west,
The sundown splendid and serene,
Death.   *Ib.*

24 Or ever the Knightly years were gone
With the old world to the grave,
I was a King in Babylon
And you were a Christian Slave.
Ib. xxxvii. *To W. A.*

25 What have I done for you,
England, my England?
What is there I would not do,
England, my own?
For England's Sake, iii. *Pro Rege Nostro*

26 Ever the faith endures,
England, my England:—
'Take and break us: we are yours,
England, my own!
Life is good, and joy runs high
Between English earth and sky;
Death is death; but we shall die
To the Song on your bugles blown, England.'   *Ib.*

27   Far in the stillness a cat
Languishes loudly.   *In Hospital*, vii. *Vigil*

28 Much is she worth, and even more is made of her.
Ib. viii. *Staff Nurse: Old Style*

29 Valiant in velvet, light in ragged luck,
Most vain, most generous, sternly critical,
Buffoon and poet, lover and sensualist:
A deal of Ariel, just a streak of Puck,
Much Antony, of Hamlet most of all,
And something of the Shorter-Catechist. [Stevenson.]
Ib. xxv. *Apparition*

30 Gulls in an aery morrice.   *Rhymes and Rhythms*, xi

HENRI IV

1553–1610

1 Je veux qu'il n'y ait si pauvre paysan en mon royaume qu'il n'ait tous les dimanches sa poule au pot.

I want there to be no peasant in my kingdom so poor that he is unable to have a chicken in his pot every Sunday.

Hardouin de Péréfixe, *Hist. de Henry le Grand*, 1681

2 Pends-toi, brave Crillon; nous avons combattu à Arques et tu n'y étais pas.

Hang yourself, brave Crillon; we fought at Arques and you were not there.

Traditional form given by Voltaire to a letter of Henri to Crillon. Lettres missives de Henri IV, Collection des documents inédits de l'histoire de France, vol. iv, 1847, p. 848

3 Paris vaut bien une messe.

Paris is well worth a mass.

Attr. either to Henry IV or to his minister Sully, in conversation with Henry. Caquets de l'Accouchée, 1622

4 The wisest fool in Christendom.

Of James I of England. Remark attr. to Henry IV and Sully. The French is not known

MATTHEW HENRY

1662–1714

5 Many a dangerous temptation comes to us in gay, fine colours, that are but skin-deep.

Commentaries, Genesis III. i

6 The better day, the worse deed. *Ib. vi*

7 To their own second and sober thoughts.

Ib. Job VI. xxix

8 He rolls it under his tongue as a sweet morsel.

Ib. Ps. XXXVI. ii

9 They that die by famine die by inches.

Ib. Ps. LIX. xv

10 Men of polite learning and a liberal education.

Ib. Acts X. i

11 All this and heaven too. *Life of Philip Henry, p. 70*

O. HENRY [WILLIAM SYDNEY PORTER]

1862–1910

12 Life is made up of sobs, sniffles, and smiles, with sniffles predominating. *Gifts of the Magi*

13 'Little old New York's good enough for us'—that's what they sing. *A Tempered Wind*

14 The Four Million. *Title*

15 Turn up the lights, I don't want to go home in the dark.

Last words, quoting popular song. C. A. Smith's O. Henry, ch. 9

PATRICK HENRY

1736–1799

16 Caesar had his Brutus—Charles the First, his Cromwell—and George the Third—('Treason,' cried the Speaker) ... *may profit by their example.* If this be treason, make the most of it.

Speech in the Virginia Convention, 1765. W. Wirt's Patrick Henry (1818), p. 65

17 I am not a Virginian, but an American.

Speech in the Virginia Convention, Sept. 1774

18 I know not what course others may take; but as for me, give me liberty, or give me death!

Ib. 23 Mar. 1775. W. Wirt's Patrick Henry (1818), p. 123.

PHILIP HENRY

1631–1696

19 They are not amissi, but praemissi.
[Not lost, but gone before.]

Matthew Henry, Life of Philip Henry, ch. 5, ed. 1825, p. 111

HENRY II OF ENGLAND

1133–1189

20 Who will free me from this turbulent priest? [Becket.]

History books

21 What a parcel of fools and dastards have I nourished in my house, that not one of them will avenge me of this one upstart clerk!

K. Norgate, in Dict. of Nat. Biog.

HENRY VIII OF ENGLAND

1491–1547

22 [Anne of Cleves.] The King found her so different from her picture ... that ... he swore they had brought him a Flanders mare.

Smollett, Hist. of England (ed. 3, 1759), vi. 68

23 This man hath the right sow by the ear.

Of Cranmer

HERACLEITUS

fl. 513 B.C.

24 πάντα ῥεῖ, οὐδὲν μένει.

All is flux, nothing is stationary.

Alluded to by Aristotle in De Caelo, 3. 1. 18 (ed. Weise) and elsewhere

SIR ALAN PATRICK HERBERT

1890–

25 Don't let's go to the dogs to-night,
For mother will be there. *Don't Let's Go to the Dogs*

26 Don't tell my mother I'm living in sin,
Don't let the old folks know:
Don't tell my twin that I breakfast on gin,
He'd never survive the blow.
Don't Tell My Mother

27 I'm not a jealous woman, but I *can't* see what he sees in her,
I can't see *what* he sees in her, I can't see what he *sees* in her!
I Can't Think What He Sees in Her

28 It may be life, but ain't it slow? *It May Be Life*

29 I wouldn't be too ladylike in love if I were you.
I Wouldn't Be Too Ladylike

30 Let's stop somebody from doing something!
Let's Stop Somebody

1 Let's find out what everyone is doing,
And then stop everyone from doing it.
Let's Stop Somebody

2 As my poor father used to say
In 1863,
Once people start on all this Art
Good-bye, moralitee!
And what my father used to say
Is good enough for me. *Lines for a Worthy Person*

3 This high official, all allow,
Is grossly overpaid.
There wasn't any Board; and now
There isn't any trade.
On the President of the Board of Trade

4 Saturday night!
Saturday night!
I want to make Hammersmith hum. *Saturday Night*

5 Harriet, Hi!
Light of my eye!
Come to the pictures and have a good cry,
For it's jolly old Saturday,
Mad-as-a-hatter-day,
Nothing-much-matter-day-night! *Ib.*

6 Well, fancy giving money to the Government!
Might as well have put it down the drain.
Fancy giving money to the Government!
Nobody will see the stuff again.
Well, they've no idea what money's for—
Ten to one they'll start another war.
I've heard a lot of silly things, but, Lor'!
Fancy giving money to the Government!
Too Much!

7 Holy Deadlock.
Title of a novel satirizing the Divorce Law

8 He didn't ought to come to bed in boots.
Riverside Nights

9 The Common Law of England has been laboriously
built about a mythical figure—the figure of 'The
Reasonable Man'. *Uncommon Law* (1935), p. 1

10 People must not do things for fun. We are not here
for fun. There is no reference to fun in any Act of
Parliament. *Ib.* p. 28

11 If elderly bishops were seen leaving the Athenaeum
with jugs of stout in their hands the casual observer would form an impression of the character
of that institution which would be largely unjust.
Ib. p. 33

12 *Counsel*: But is the jury to understand, Mr. Haddock,
that in your opinion the highbrow is necessarily of
the feminine gender?
Witness: Of course. It is one of the special diseases
of women. *Ib.* p. 50

13 The critical period in matrimony is breakfast-time.
Ib. p. 98

14 The Englishman never enjoys himself except for a
noble purpose. *Ib.* p. 198

15 For any ceremonial purposes the otherwise excellent
liquid, water, is unsuitable in colour and other
respects. *Ib.* p. 272

16 An Act of God was defined as *something which no
reasonable man could have expected. Ib.* p. 316

17 A dull speaker, like a plain woman, is credited with
all the virtues, for we charitably suppose that a surface so unattractive must be compensated by
interior blessings. *Ib.* p. 412

EDWARD HERBERT, BARON HERBERT OF CHERBURY
1583–1648

18 Now that the April of your youth adorns
The garden of your face.
Poems. Ditty: Now That the April

GEORGE HERBERT
1593–1633

19 The book of books, the storehouse and magazine of
life and comfort, the holy Scriptures.
A Priest to the Temple. ch. 4

20 I read, and sigh, and wish I were a tree—
For sure then I should grow
To fruit or shade; at least some bird would trust
Her household to me, and I should be just.
The Temple. Affliction

21 Ah, my dear God, though I am clean forgot,
Let me not love Thee, if I love Thee not. *Ib.*

22 How well her name an 'Army' doth present.
In whom the 'Lord of Hosts' did pitch His tent!
Ib. Anagram, Mary

23 Like summer-friends,
Flies of estates and sunshine. *Ib. The Answer*

24 Let all the world in ev'ry corner sing
My God and King.
The heav'ns are not too high,
His praise may thither fly;
The earth is not too low,
His praises there may grow.
Let all the world in ev'ry corner sing
My God and King.
The Church with psalms must shout,
No door can keep them out:
But above all, the heart
Must bear the longest part. *Ib. Antiphon*

25 Hearken unto a Verser, who may chance
Rhyme thee to good, and make a bait of pleasure:
A verse may find him who a sermon flies,
And turn delight into a sacrifice.
Ib. The Church Porch, i

26 Drink not the third glass—which thou canst not tame
When once it is within thee. *Ib.* v

27 Dare to be true: nothing can need a lie;
A fault, which needs it most, grows two thereby.
Ib. xiii

28 Chase brave employment with a naked sword
Throughout the world. *Ib.* xv

29 O England, full of sin, but most of sloth;
Spit out thy phlegm, and fill thy breast with glory.
Ib. xvi

30 Think the king sees thee still; for his King does.
Ib. xxi

31 Never was scraper brave man. Get to live;
Then live, and use it. *Ib.* xxvi

32 Wit's an unruly engine, wildly striking
Sometimes a friend, sometimes the engineer. *Ib.* xli

33 Towards great persons use respective boldness.
Ib. xliii

34 But love is lost, the way of friendship's gone,
Though David had his Jonathan, Christ his John.
Ib. xlvi

1 **Be calm** in arguing; for fierceness makes
  Error a fault and truth discourtesy.
  The Temple. The Church Porch, lii

2 Calmness is great advantage; he that lets
  Another chafe, may warm him at his fire.   *Ib.* liii

3   Who aimeth at the sky
  Shoots higher much than he that means a tree.
                                    Ib. lvi

4 Man is God's image; but a poor man is
  Christ's stamp to boot.   *Ib.* lxiv

5 Kneeling ne'er spoil'd silk stocking; quit thy state;
  All equal are within the Church's gate.   *Ib.* lxviii

6   O, be drest;
  Stay not for th' other pin! Why, thou hast lost
  A joy for it worth worlds.   *Ib.* lxix

7 Judge not the preacher, for he is thy Judge;
  If thou mislike him, thou conceiv'st him not:
  God calleth preaching folly: do not grudge
  To pick out treasures from an earthen pot:
  The worst speaks something good; if all want sense,
  God takes a text, and preacheth patience.   *Ib.* lxxii

8 Look not on pleasures as they come, but go.
                                    Ib. lxxvii

9 I struck the board, and cried, 'No more;
            I will abroad.'
  What, shall I ever sigh and pine?
  My lines and life are free; free as the road,
  Loose as the wind, as large as store.
            Shall I be still in suit?
  Have I no harvest but a thorn
  To let me blood, and not restore
  What I have lost with cordial fruit?
            Sure there was wine
  Before my sighs did dry it; there was corn
  Before my tears did drown it;
  Is the year only lost to me?
  Have I no bays to crown it?   *Ib. The Collar*

10   Away! take heed;
            I will abroad.
  Call in thy death's-head there, tie up thy fears;
            He that forbears
  To suit and serve his need
            Deserves his load.
  But as I rav'd and grew more fierce and wild
            At every word,
  Methought I heard one calling, 'Child';
            And I replied, 'My Lord.'   *Ib.*

11 SAVIOUR:
  That as I did freely part
  With my glory and desert,
  Left all joys to feel all smart—
  MAN:
  Ah, no more: Thou break'st my heart. *Ib. Dialogue*

12 Throw away Thy rod,
  Throw away Thy wrath;
            O my God,
  Take the gentle path.   *Ib. Discipline*

13 Love is swift of foot;
  Love's a man of war,
            And can shoot,
  And can hit from far.   *Ib.*

14 I got me flowers to strew Thy way,
  I got me boughs off many a tree;
  But Thou wast up by break of day,
  And brought'st Thy sweets along with Thee.
                                    Ib. Easter Song

15 Teach me, my God and King,
  In all things Thee to see,
  And what I do in any thing
  To do it as for Thee.

  A man that looks on glass,
  On it may stay his eye;
  Or if he pleaseth, through it pass,
  And then the heaven espy.
                          The Temple. The Elixir

16 A servant with this clause
  Makes drudgery divine;
  Who sweeps a room as for Thy laws
  Makes that and th' action fine.   *Ib.*

17 Oh that I were an orange-tree,
            That busy plant!
  Then I should ever laden be,
            And never want
  Some fruit for Him that dressed me. *Ib. Employment*

18 And now in age I bud again,
  After so many deaths I live and write;
  I once more smell the dew and rain,
  And relish versing: O, my only Light,
            It cannot be
            That I am he
  On whom Thy tempests fell all night.
                                    Ib. The Flower

19 Death is still working like a mole,
  And digs my grave at each remove.   *Ib. Grace*

20 I made a posy while the day ran by;
  Here will I smell my remnant out, and tie
     My life within this band;
  But Time did beckon to the flow'rs, and they
  By noon most cunningly did steal away,
     And wither'd in my hand.   *Ib. Life*

21 Love bade me welcome; yet my soul drew back,
            Guilty of dust and sin.
  But quick-ey'd Love, observing me grow slack
            From my first entrance in,
  Drew nearer to me, sweetly questioning
            If I lack'd any thing.   *Ib. Love*

22 'You must sit down,' says Love, 'and taste My meat.'
            So I did sit and eat.   *Ib.*

23   For us the winds do blow,
  The earth resteth, heav'n moveth, fountains flow;
     Nothing we see but means our good,
     As our delight or as our treasure;
  The whole is either our cupboard of food
     Or cabinet of pleasure.   *Ib. Man*

24 Oh mighty love! Man is one world, and hath
     Another to attend him.   *Ib.*

25 King of glory, King of peace,
            I will love Thee;
  And, that love may never cease,
            I will move Thee.   *Ib. Praise*

26 Sev'n whole days, not one in seven,
            I will praise Thee;
  In my heart, though not in heaven,
            I can raise Thee.   *Ib.*

27 He would adore my gifts instead of Me,
  And rest in Nature, not the God of Nature:
            So both should losers be. *Ib. The Pulley*

[244]

1 Yet let him keep the rest,
But keep them with repining restlessness;
Let him be rich and weary, that at least,
If goodness lead him not, yet weariness
May toss him to My breast.
The Temple, The Pulley

2 My God, my verse is not a crown,
No point of honour, or gay suit,
No hawk, no banquet, or renown,
Nor a good sword, nor yet a lute. *Ib. The Quiddity*

3 But Thou shalt answer, Lord, for me. *Ib. The Quip*

4 But who does hawk at eagles with a dove?
Ib. The Sacrifice, xxiii

5 Lord, with what care Thou hast begirt us round!
Parents first season us; then schoolmasters
Deliver us to laws; they send us, bound
To rules of reason, holy messengers,

Pulpits and Sundays, sorrow dogging sin,
Afflictions sorted, anguish of all sizes,
Fine nets and stratagems to catch us in,
Bibles laid open, millions of surprises. *Ib. Sin*

6 Yet all these fences and their whole array
One cunning bosom sin blows quite away. *Ib.*

7 Grasp not at much, for fear thou losest all.
Ib. The Size

8 The Sundays of man's life,
Threaded together on Time's string,
Make bracelets to adorn the wife
Of the eternal glorious King:
On Sunday heaven's gate stands ope;
Blessings are plentiful and rife,
More plentiful than hope. *Ib. Sunday*

9 Enrich my heart, mouth, hands in me,
With faith, with hope, with charity,
That I may run, rise, rest with Thee.
Ib. Trinity Sunday

10 The God of love my Shepherd is,
And He that doth me feed,
While He is mine, and I am His,
What can I want or need? *Ib. 23rd Psalm*

11 Lord, make me coy and tender to offend:
In friendship, first I think if that agree
Which I intend
Unto my friend's intent and end;
I would not use a friend as I use Thee.
Ib. Unkindness

12 My friend may spit upon my curious floor;
Would he have gold? I lend it instantly;
But let the poor,
And Thou within them, starve at door:
I cannot use a friend as I use Thee. *Ib.*

13 Sweet day, so cool, so calm, so bright,
The bridal of the earth and sky,
The dew shall weep thy fall to-night;
For thou must die.

Sweet rose, whose hue angry and brave
Bids the rash gazer wipe his eye,
Thy root is ever in its grave,
And thou must die.

Sweet spring, full of sweet days and roses,
A box where sweets compacted lie. *Ib. Virtue*

14 Only a sweet and virtuous soul,
Like season'd timber, never gives;
But though the whole world turn to coal,
Then chiefly lives. *Ib.*

HERODOTUS
484–424? B.C.

15 οὐ φροντὶς Ἱπποκλείδῃ.

Hippocleides doesn't care. *Histories,* vi. 129. 4

ROBERT HERRICK
1591–1674

16 With thousand such enchanting dreams, that meet
To make sleep not so sound, as sweet.
*Hesperides. A Country Life: to his Brother,
M. Tho. Herrick*

17 I sing of brooks, of blossoms, birds, and bowers:
Of April, May, of June, and July-flowers.
I sing of May-poles, Hock-carts, wassails, wakes,
Of bride-grooms, brides, and of their bridal-cakes.
Ib. Argument of his Book

18 A little saint best fits a little shrine,
A little prop best fits a little vine,
As my small cruse best fits my little wine.
*Ib. A Ternary of Littles, upon a Pipkin of Jelly
sent to a Lady*

19 A little stream best fits a little boat;
A little lead best fits a little float;
As my small pipe best fits my little note.

A little meat best fits a little belly,
As sweetly, Lady, give me leave to tell ye,
This little pipkin fits this little jelly. *Ib.*

20 Fair pledges of a fruitful tree,
Why do ye fall so fast?
Your date is not so past;
But you may stay yet here a while,
To blush and gently smile;
And go at last. *Ib. Blossoms*

21 Cherry ripe, ripe, ripe, I cry,
Full and fair ones; come and buy:
If so be, you ask me where
They do grow? I answer, there,
Where my Julia's lips do smile;
There's the land, or cherry-isle. *Ib. Cherry Ripe*

22 What needs complaints
When she a place
Has with the race
Of Saints?
In endless mirth,
She thinks not on
What's said or done
In earth.
Ib. Comfort to a Youth that had Lost his Love

23 Nor do's she mind,
Or think on't now
That ever thou
Wast kind. *Ib.*

24 Get up, get up for shame, the blooming morn
Upon her wings presents the god unshorn.
Ib. Corinna's Going a-Maying

25 Get up, sweet Slug-a-bed, and see
The dew bespangling herb and tree. *Ib.*

26 'Tis sin,
Nay, profanation to keep in. *Ib.*

27 Come, let us go, while we are in our prime;
And take the harmless folly of the time. *Ib.*

1 So when or you or I are made
A fable, song, or fleeting shade;
All love, all liking, all delight
Lies drown'd with us in endless night.
Then while time serves, and we are but decaying;
Come, my Corinna, come, let's go a-Maying.
Hesperides. Corinna's Going a-Maying

2 Fair daffodils, we weep to see
You haste away so soon:
As yet the early-rising sun
Has not attain'd his noon.
Stay, stay,
Until the hasting day
Has run
But to the even-song;
And, having pray'd together, we
Will go with you along. *Ib. Daffodils*

3 We have short time to stay, as you,
We have as short a Spring;
As quick a growth to meet decay,
As you or any thing. *Ib.*

4 A sweet disorder in the dress
Kindles in clothes a wantonness:
A lawn about the shoulders thrown
Into a fine distraction:
An erring lace, which here and there
Enthrals the crimson stomacher:
A cuff neglectful, and thereby
Ribbands to flow confusedly:
A winning wave (deserving note)
In the tempestuous petticoat:
A careless shoe-string, in whose tie
I see a wild civility:
Do more bewitch me, than when Art
Is too precise in every part. *Ib. Delight in Disorder*

5 Here a solemn Fast we keep,
While all beauty lies asleep
Husht be all things; (no noise here)
But the toning of a tear:
Or a sigh of such as bring
Cowslips for her covering. *Ib. Epitaph upon a Virgin*

6 Only a little more
I have to write,
Then I'll give o'er,
And bid the world Good-night.
Ib. His Poetry his Pillar

7 O time that cut'st down all
And scarce leav'st here
Memorial
Of any men that were. *Ib.*

8 Roses at first were white,
Till thy co'd not agree,
Whether my Sappho's breast,
Or they more white sho'd be.
Ib. How Roses Came Red.

9 'Twixt kings and tyrants there's this difference known;
Kings seek their subjects' good: tyrants their own.
Ib. Kings and Tyrants

10 You say, to me-wards your affection's strong;
Pray love me little, so you love me long.
Ib. Love me Little, Love me Long

11 Love is a circle that doth restless move
In the same sweet eternity of love.
Ib. Love What It Is

12 Night makes no difference 'twixt the Priest and Clerk;
Joan as my Lady is as good i' th' dark.
Hesperides. No Difference i' th' Dark

13 I do love I know not what;
Sometimes this, and sometimes that.
Ib. No Luck in Love

14 Made us nobly wild, not mad.
Ib. Ode for Ben Jonson

15 Out-did the meat, out-did the frolic wine. *Ib.*

16 Fain would I kiss my Julia's dainty leg,
Which is as white and hairless as an egg.
Ib. On Julia's Legs

17 Men are suspicious; prone to discontent:
Subjects still loathe the present Government.
Ib. Present Government Grievous

18 The readiness of doing, doth express
No other, but the doer's willingness. *Ib. Readiness*

19 Attempt the end, and never stand to doubt;
Nothing's so hard, but search will find it out.
Ib. Seek and Find

20 And once more yet (ere I am laid out dead)
Knock at a star with my exalted head.
Ib. The Bad Season Makes the Poet Sad

21 It is the end that crowns us, not the fight.
Ib. The End

22 Good morrow to the day so fair;
Good morning, Sir, to you:
Good morrow to mine own torn hair
Bedabbled with the dew. *Ib. The Mad Maid's Song*

23 Her eyes the glow-worm lend thee,
The shooting-stars attend thee;
And the elves also,
Whose little eyes glow,
Like the sparks of fire, befriend thee.

No Will-o'-th'-Wisp mislight thee;
Nor snake, or slow-worm bite thee:
But on, on thy way
Not making a stay,
Since ghost there's none to affright thee.
Ib. The Night-Piece, to Julia

24 Praise they that will times past, I joy to see
My self now live: this age best pleaseth me.
Ib. The Present Time Best Pleaseth

25 Some ask'd how pearls did grow, and where?
Then spoke I to my girl,
To part her lips, and shew'd them there
The quarelets of pearl.
Ib. The Rock of Rubies, and the Quarry of Pearls

26 Now is the time, when all the lights wax dim;
And thou (Anthea) must withdraw from him
Who was thy servant.
Ib. To Anthea: Now is the Time

27 For my Embalming (Sweetest) there will be
No Spices wanting, when I'm laid by thee. *Ib.*

28 Give me a kiss, and to that kiss a score;
Then to that twenty, add a hundred more:
A thousand to that hundred: so kiss on,
To make that thousand up a million.
Treble that million, and when that is done,
Let's kiss afresh, as when we first begun.
Ib. To Anthea: Ah, My Anthea!

1 Bid me to live, and I will live
  Thy Protestant to be:
Or bid me love, and I will give
  A loving heart to thee.

A heart as soft, a heart as kind,
  A heart as sound and free,
As in the whole world thou canst find,
  That heart I'll give to thee.
    Hesperides. To Anthea, Who May Command Him
    Anything

2 Bid me to weep, and I will weep,
  While I have eyes to see.   *Ib.*

3 Bid me despair, and I'll despair,
  Under that cypress tree:
Or bid me die, and I will dare
  E'en Death, to die for thee.   *Ib.*

4 Thou art my life, my love, my heart,
  The very eyes of me:
And hast command of every part,
  To live and die for thee.   *Ib.*

5 No marigolds yet closed are;
  No shadows great appear.
    Ib. To Daisies, not to Shut so Soon

6 Sweet, be not proud of those two eyes,
  Which star-like sparkle in their skies.
         Ib. To Dianeme

7 That ruby which you wear
Sunk from the tip of your soft ear
Will last to be a precious stone
When all your world of beauty's gone.   *Ib.*

8 I dare not ask a kiss;
  I dare not beg a smile;
Lest having that, or this,
  I might grow proud the while.

No, no, the utmost share
  Of my desire, shall be
Only to kiss that air,
  That lately kissed thee.   *Ib. To Electra*

9 He loves his bonds, who when the first are broke,
  Submits his neck unto a second yoke. *Ib. To Love*

10 Gather ye rosebuds while ye may,
  Old Time is still a-flying:
And this same flower that smiles to-day,
  To-morrow will be dying.

The glorious lamp of Heaven, the sun,
  The higher he's a getting;
The sooner will his race be run,
  And nearer he's to setting.

That age is best, which is the first,
  When youth and blood are warmer;
But being spent, the worse, and worst
  Times, still succeed the former.

Then be not coy, but use your time;
  And while ye may, go marry:
For having lost but once your prime,
  You may for ever tarry.
    Ib. To Virgins, to Make Much of Time

11 Welcome maids of honour,
    You do bring
    In the Spring;
And wait upon her.   *Ib. To Violets*

12 Her pretty feet
  Like snails did creep
  A little out, and then,
As if they started at bo-peep,
  Did soon draw in agen.   *Hesperides. Upon her Feet*

13 Whenas in silks my Julia goes,
Then, then (methinks) how sweetly flows
That liquefaction of her clothes.

Next, when I cast mine eyes and see
That brave vibration each way free;
O how that glittering taketh me!
    Ib. Upon Julia's Clothes

14 So smooth, so sweet, so silv'ry is thy voice,
As, could they hear, the damn'd would make no noise,
But listen to thee (walking in thy chamber)
Melting melodious words, to lutes of amber.
    Ib. Upon Julia's Voice

15 Here a little child I stand,
Heaving up my either hand;
Cold as paddocks though they be,
Here I lift them up to Thee,
For a benison to fall
On our meat, and on us all. Amen.
    Noble Numbers. Another Grace for a Child

16 Lord, Thou hast given me a cell
    Wherein to dwell,
A little house, whose humble roof
    Is weather-proof;
Under the spars of which I lie
    Both soft, and dry.
    Ib. A Thanksgiving to God for his House

17 A little buttery, and therein
    A little bin,
Which keeps my little loaf of bread
    Unchipt, unflead:
Some brittle sticks of thorn or briar
    Make me a fire,
Close by whose living coal I sit,
    And glow like it.   *Ib.*

18 When the artless doctor sees
No one hope, but of his fees,
And his skill runs on the lees;
    Sweet Spirit, comfort me!

When his potion and his pill,
Has, or none, or little skill,
Meet for nothing, but to kill;
    Sweet Spirit, comfort me!
    Ib. His Litany to the Holy Spirit

19 In prayer the lips ne'er act the winning part,
Without the sweet concurrence of the heart.
    Ib. The Heart

20 But, for Man's fault, then was the thorn,
Without the fragrant rose-bud, born;
But ne'er the rose without the thorn. *Ib. The Rose*

21 To work a wonder, God would have her shown,
At once, a bud, and yet a rose full-blown.
    Ib. The Virgin Mary

22 If any thing delight me for to print
My book, 'tis this; that Thou, my God, art in't.
    Ib. To God

JAMES HERVEY
1714-1758

1 E'en crosses from his sov'reign hand
Are blessings in disguise.
Works. Reflections on a Flower-Garden

HESIOD
c. 735 B.C.

2 πλέον ἥμισυ παντός.

The half is greater than the whole.
Works and Days, 40

JOHN HEYWOOD
1497?-1580?

3 All a green willow, willow;
All a green willow is my garland. *The Green Willow*

THOMAS HEYWOOD
d. 1650?

4 Seven cities warr'd for Homer, being dead,
Who, living, had no roof to shroud his head.
Hierarchie of the Blessed Angels

5 Pack, clouds, away, and welcome day,
With night we banish sorrow;
Sweet air blow soft, mount larks aloft
To give my Love good-morrow!
Pack, Clouds, Away, st. 1

6 A Woman Killed with Kindness. *Title of play*

EMILY HENRIETTA HICKEY
1845-1924

7 Beloved, it is morn!
A redder berry on the thorn,
A deeper yellow on the corn,
For this good day new-born:
Pray, Sweet, for me
That I may be
Faithful to God and thee.
Beloved, It Is Morn

WILLIAM EDWARD HICKSON
1803-1870

8 'Tis a lesson you should heed,
Try, try again.
If at first you don't succeed,
Try, try again. *Try and Try Again*

'DR. BREWSTER HIGLEY'
nineteenth century

9 Oh give me a home where the buffalo roam,
Where the deer and the antelope play,
Where seldom is heard a discouraging word
And the skies are not cloudy all day.
Home on the Range. (1873)

AARON HILL
1685-1750

10 Tender-handed stroke a nettle,
And it stings you for your pains;
Grasp it like a man of mettle,
And it soft as silk remains.
Verses Written on Window

ROWLAND HILL
1744-1833

11 He did not see any reason why the devil should have
all the good tunes.
E. W. Broome, *Rev. Rowland Hill*, vii

ARTHUR CLEMENT HILTON
1851-1877

12 The papers they had finished lay
In piles of blue and white,
They answered everything they could,
And wrote with all their might,
But though they wrote it all by rote,
They did not write it right.
The Vulture and the Husbandman. After Lewis
Carroll

HIPPOCRATES
c. 460-357 B.C.

13 ὁ βίος βραχύς, ἡ δὲ τέχνη μακρή.

The life so short, the craft so long to learn.
Aphorisms, I. i. Trans. by Chaucer

ADOLF HITLER
1889-1945

14 My patience is now at an end. *Speech, 26 Sept. 1938*

15 It is the last territorial claim which I have to make in
Europe. *Ib.*

PRINCE HOARE
1755-1834

16 The saucy Arethusa. *Song: The Arethusa*

THOMAS HOBBES
1588-1679

17 Geometry (which is the only science that it hath
pleased God hitherto to bestow on mankind).
Leviathan, pt. i, ch. 4

18 The condition of man . . . is a condition of war of
everyone against everyone. *Ib.*

19 Words are wise men's counters, they do but reckon
with them, but they are the money of fools. *Ib.*

20 They that approve a private opinion, call it opinion;
but they that mislike it, heresy: and yet heresy
signifies no more than private opinion. *Ib.* ch. 11

21 No arts; no letters; no society; and which is worst of
all, continual fear and danger of violent death; and
the life of man, solitary, poor, nasty, brutish, and
short. *Ib.* ch. 13

22 Force, and fraud, are in war the two cardinal virtues.
Ib.

23 The Papacy is not other than the Ghost of the
deceased Roman Empire, sitting crowned upon the
grave thereof. *Ib.* pt. iv, ch. 47

24 Laughter is nothing else but sudden glory arising
from some sudden conception of some eminency
in ourselves, by comparison with the infirmity of
others, or with our own formerly.
On Human Nature, ix. (1650)

1 He was wont to say that if he had read as much as other men, he should have known no more than other men.   Aubrey, *Life of Hobbes*

2 I am about to take my last voyage, a great leap in the dark.
Last Words. Watkins, *Anecdotes of Men of Learning*

JOHN CAM HOBHOUSE, BARON BROUGHTON
1786–1869

3 When I invented the phrase 'His Majesty's Opposition' [Canning] paid me a compliment on the fortunate hit.   *Recollections of a Long Life*, ii, ch. 12

EDWARD WALLIS HOCH
1849–1925

4 There is so much good in the worst of us,
And so much bad in the best of us,
That it hardly becomes any of us
To talk about the rest of us.
Good and Bad. Attr. to many other authors

RALPH HODGSON
1871–

5 'Twould ring the bells of Heaven
The wildest peal for years,
If Parson lost his senses
And people came to theirs,
And he and they together
Knelt down with angry prayers
For tamed and shabby tigers
And dancing dogs and bears,
And wretched, blind, pit ponies,
And little hunted hares.   *Poems. The Bells of Heaven*

6 See an old unhappy bull,
Sick in soul and body both.   *Ib. The Bull*

7 Eve, with her basket, was
Deep in the bells and grass,
Wading in bells and grass
Up to her knees,
Plucking a dish of sweet
Berries and plums to eat,
Down in the bells and grass
Under the trees.   *Ib. Eve*

8 Picture that orchard sprite,
Eve, with her body white,
Supple and smooth to her
Slim finger tips.   *Ib.*

9 But oh, the den of wild things in
The darkness of her eyes!   *Ib. The Gipsy Girl*

10 I did not pray him to lay bare
The mystery to me;
Enough the rose was heaven to smell,
And His own face to see.   *Ib. The Mystery*

11 Reason has moons, but moons not hers,
Lie mirror'd on her sea,
Confounding her astronomers,
But, O! delighting me.   *Ib. Reason Has Moons*

12 God loves an idle rainbow,
No less than labouring seas.   *Ib.*

13 I climbed a hill as light fell short,
And rooks came home in scramble sort,
And filled the trees and flapped and fought
And sang themselves to sleep.
    Poems. The Song of Honour

14 Hear flocks of shiny pleiades
Among the plums and apple trees
Sing in the summer day.   *Ib.*

15 When stately ships are twirled and spun
Like whipping tops and help there's none
And mighty ships ten thousand ton
Go down like lumps of lead.   *Ib.*

16 I stood upon that silent hill
And stared into the sky until
My eyes were blind with stars and still
I stared into the sky.   *Ib.*

17 Time, you old gypsy man,
  Will you not stay,
Put up your caravan
  Just for one day? *Ib. Time, You Old Gypsy Man*

HEINRICH HOFFMAN
1809–1874

18 Augustus was a chubby lad;
Fat ruddy cheeks Augustus had:
And everybody saw with joy
The plump and hearty, healthy boy.
He ate and drank as he was told,
And never let his soup get cold.
But one day, one cold winter's day,
He screamed out, 'Take the soup away!
O take the nasty soup away!
I won't have any soup to-day.'
    Struwwelpeter. Augustus

19 Here is cruel Frederick, see!
A horrid wicked boy was he.   *Ib. Cruel Frederick*

20 The trough was full, and faithful Tray
  Came out to drink one sultry day;
He wagged his tail, and wet his lip.   *Ib.*

21 At this, good Tray grew very red,
And growled, and bit him till he bled.   *Ib.*

22 But good dog Tray is happy now;
He has no time to say 'Bow-wow!'
He seats himself in Frederick's chair
And laughs to see the good things there:
The soup he swallows, sup by sup—
And eats the pies and puddings up.   *Ib.*

23 Let me see if Philip can
Be a little gentleman;
Let me see, if he is able
To sit still for once at table.   *Ib. Fidgety Philip*

24 But fidgety Phil,
He won't sit still;
He wriggles
And giggles,
And then, I declare,
Swings backwards and forwards,
And tilts up his chair.   *Ib.*

25 It almost makes me cry to tell
What foolish Harriet befell.
    Ib. Harriet and the Matches

1 Now tall Agrippa lived close by—
So tall, he almost touch'd the sky;
He had a mighty inkstand, too,
In which a great goose-feather grew.
Struwwelpeter. The Inky Boys

2 Look at little Johnny there,
Little Johnny Head-In-Air! *Ib. Johnny Head-In-Air*

3 Silly little Johnny, look,
You have lost your writing-book! *Ib.*

4 The door flew open, in he ran,
The great, long, red-legged scissor-man.
Ib. The Little Suck-a-Thumb

5 'Ah!' said Mamma, 'I knew he'd come
To naughty little Suck-a-Thumb.' *Ib.*

6 He finds it hard, without a pair
Of spectacles, to shoot the hare.
The hare sits snug in leaves and grass,
And laughs to see the green man pass.
Ib. The Man Who Went Out Shooting

7 And now she's trying all she can,
To shoot the sleepy, green-coat man. *Ib.*

8 Help! Fire! Help! The Hare! The Hare! *Ib.*

9 The hare's own child, the little hare. *Ib.*

10 Anything to me is sweeter
Than to see Shock-headed Peter.
Ib. Shock-Headed Peter

JAMES HOGG
1770–1835

11 And hey, then, up go we.
Jacobite Relics of Scotland, i. 15. *Title*

12 Wha the deil hae we goten for a King
But a wee wee German lairdie?
And when we gade to bring him hame,
He was delving in his kail-yardie.
Ib. 83. The Wee, Wee German Lairdie

13 Listen a while, and I'll tell you a tale,
Of a new device of a Protestant Flail.
Ib. 324. The Protestant Flail

14 God bless our Lord the King!
God save our lord the king!
God save the king!
Make him victorious,
Happy, and glorious,
Long to reign over us:
God save the king! *Ib. ii. 50. God Save The King.*
(*But see* 6:13, 125:15, *and Corrigenda, p. 587*)

15 We'll o'er the water, we'll o'er the sea,
We'll o'er the water to Charlie;
Come weel, come wo, we'll gather and go,
And live or die wi' Charlie.
Ib. 76. O'er the Water to Charlie

16 There grows a bonny brier bush in our kail yard.
Ib. 78. An You Be He

17 'Twas on a Monday morning,
Right early in the year,
That Charlie came to our town,
The young Chevalier.
And Charlie he's my darling,
My darling, my darling.
And Charlie he's my darling,
The young Chevalier.
Ib. 93. The Young Chevalier. (*See also* 360:15)

18 Cock up your beaver, and cock it fu' sprush;
We'll over the Border and gi'e them a brush;
There's somebody there we'll teach better behaviour.
Hey, Johnnie lad, cock up your beaver!
Jacobite Relics, ii. 127. *Cock Up Your Beaver*

19 Will you no come back again?
Better lo'ed you'll never be,
And will you no come back again?
Ib. 195. Will You No Come Back Again?

20 My love she's but a lassie yet. *Title of song*

21 Bonny Kilmeny gaed up the glen.
The Queen's Wake, ii. *Kilmeny. Thirteenth Bard's Song*, l. 1

22 Late, late in the gloamin' Kilmeny came hame!
Ib. l. 24

23 For Kilmeny had been she knew not where,
And Kilmeny had seen what she could not declare.
Ib. l. 38

HENRY FOX, FIRST BARON HOLLAND
1705–1774

24 If Mr. Selwyn calls again, shew him up; if I am alive
I shall be delighted to see him; and if I am dead he
would like to see me.
Last Words. J. H. Jesse, *George Selwyn and his Contemporaries*, 1844, vol. iii, p. 50

HENRY RICHARD VASSALL FOX, THIRD BARON HOLLAND
1733–1840

25 Nephew of Fox, and friend of Grey,—
Enough my meed of fame
If those who deign'd to observe me say
I injur'd neither name.
Memoir of Rev. Sydney Smith (1855), i. 334

SIR RICHARD HOLLAND
c. 1450

26 O Dowglas, O Dowglas,
tendir and trewe! *Buke of the Howlat*, xxxi

JOHN HAYNES HOLMES
1879–

27 The universe is not hostile, nor yet is it friendly. It is
simply indifferent.
Sensible Man's View of Religion

OLIVER WENDELL HOLMES
1809–1894

28 Lean, hungry, savage anti-everythings.
Poems. A Modest Request

29 Sweet is the scene where genial friendship plays
The pleasing game of interchanging praise.
Ib. An After-Dinner Poem

30 Uncursed by doubt, our earliest creed we take;
We love the precepts for the teacher's sake.
Ib. A Rhymed Lesson (Urania)

31 And, when you stick on conversation's burrs,
Don't strew your pathway with those dreadful urs.
Ib.

1 Man wants but little drink below,
But wants that little strong.
Poems: A Song of other Days. Parody on Goldsmith

2 Day hath put on his jacket, and around
His burning bosom buttoned it with stars.
Ib. Evening

3 We greet the monarch-peasant.
Ib. For the Burns Centennial Celebration

4 Wisdom has taught us to be calm and meek,
To take one blow, and turn the other cheek;
It is not written what a man shall do
If the rude caitiff smite the other too!
Ib. Non-Resistance

5 Ay, tear her tattered ensign down!
Long has it waved on high,
And many an eye has danced to see
That banner in the sky;
Beneath it rung the battle shout,
And burst the cannon's roar;—
The meteor of the ocean air
Shall sweep the clouds no more. *Ib. Old Ironsides*

6 Have you heard of the wonderful one-hoss shay,
That was built in such a logical way
It ran a hundred years to a day?
Ib. The Deacon's Masterpiece

7 A general flavor of mild decay. *Ib.*

8 When the last reader reads no more.
Ib. The Last Reader

9 Feels the same comfort while his acrid words
Turn the sweet milk of kindness into curds.
Ib. The Moral Bully

10 And silence, like a poultice, comes
To heal the blows of sound. *Ib. The Music Grinders*

11 Call him not old, whose visionary brain
Holds o'er the past its undivided reign.
For him in vain the envious seasons roll
Who bears eternal summer in his soul.
Ib. The Old Player

12 To be seventy years young is sometimes far more
cheerful and hopeful than to be forty years old.
On the Seventieth Birthday of Julia Ward Howe

13 Man has his will,—but woman has her way.
The Autocrat of the Breakfast-Table, ch. 1

14 I think I said, I can make it plain to Benjamin
Franklin here that there are at least six person-
alities distinctly to be recognized as taking part in
that dialogue between John and Thomas.

Three Johns. { 1. The real John; known only to
his Maker.
2. John's ideal John; never the
real one, and often very unlike
him.
3. Thomas' ideal John; never the
real John, nor John's John,
but often very unlike either.

Three Thomases. { 1. The real Thomas.
2. Thomas' ideal Thomas.
3. John's ideal Thomas.
Ib. ch. 3

15 Build thee more stately mansions, O my soul,
As the swift seasons roll!
Leave thy low-vaulted past!
Let each new temple, nobler than the last,
Shut thee from heaven with a dome more vast,
Till thou at length art free,
Leaving thine outgrown shell by life's unresting sea!
*The Autocrat of the Breakfast Table, ch. 4. The
Chambered Nautilus*

16 Boston State-House is the hub of the solar system.
You couldn't pry that out of a Boston man if you
had the tire of all creation straightened out for a
crowbar. *Ib. ch. 6*

17 The axis of the earth sticks out visibly through the
centre of each and every town or city. *Ib.*

18 The world's great men have not commonly been great
scholars, nor its great scholars great men. *Ib.*

19 His humid front the cive, anheling, wipes.
And dreams of erring on ventiferous ripes.
Ib. ch. 11. Aestivation

20 Depart,—be off,—excede,—evade,—erump! *Ib.*

21 Fate tried to conceal him by naming him Smith.
[Samuel Francis Smith.] *The Boys*

22 It is the province of knowledge to speak and it is the
privilege of wisdom to listen.
The Poet at the Breakfast Table, ch. 10

23 It is the folly of the world, constantly, which confounds
its wisdom.
The Professor at the Breakfast Table, ch. 1

24 A moment's insight is sometimes worth a life's experience. *Ib. ch. 10*

JOHN HOME

1722–1808

25 In the first days
Of my distracting grief, I found myself—
As women wish to be, who love their lords.
Douglas, I. 1

26 My name is Norval; on the Grampian hills
My father feeds his flocks; a frugal swain,
Whose constant cares were to increase his store.
Ib. II. 1

27 He seldom errs
Who thinks the worst he can of womankind.
Ib. III. iii

28 Like Douglas conquer, or like Douglas die. *Ib. v*

29 Bold and erect the Caledonian stood,
Old was his mutton and his claret good;
Let him drink port, the English statesman cried—
He drank the poison and his spirit died.
Lockhart, Life of Scott, IV, ch. v

HOMER

c. 900 B.C.

30 μῆνιν ἄειδε, θεά, Πηληϊάδεω Ἀχιλῆος
οὐλομένην, ἣ μυρί' Ἀχαιοῖς ἄλγε' ἔθηκε.

The wrath of Peleus' son, the direful spring
Of all the Grecian woes, O Goddess, sing!
Iliad, i. 1. Trans. by Pope

31 τὸν δ' ἀπαμειβόμενος.

To him in answer spake. . . *Ib. 84*

32 οἵη περ φύλλων γενεή, τοίη δὲ καὶ ἀνδρῶν.

As the generation of leaves, so is that of men.
Ib. vi. 146

1 αἰὲν ἀριστεύειν καὶ ὑπείροχον ἔμμεναι ἄλλων.

Always to be best, and distinguished above the
rest. *Iliad*, vi. 208.

2 δακρυόεν γελάσασα.

Smiling through her tears. *Ib.* 484

3 εἷς οἰωνὸς ἄριστος, ἀμύνεσθαι περὶ πάτρης.

One omen is best, to fight in defence of one's
country. *Ib.* xii. 243

4 ἄνδρα μοι ἔννεπε, Μοῦσα, πολύτροπον.

Tell me, Muse, of the man of many wiles. [Odys-
seus.] *Odyssey*, i. 1

5 πολλῶν δ' ἀνθρώπων ἴδεν ἄστεα καὶ νόον ἔγνω.

He saw the cities of many men, and knew their
mind. *Ib.* 3

6 ὡς ἀπόλοιτο καὶ ἄλλος ὅτις τοιαῦτά γε ῥέζοι.

So perish all who do the like again. *Ib.* 47

7 βουλοίμην κ' ἐπάρουρος ἐὼν θητευέμεν ἄλλῳ
ἀνδρὶ παρ' ἀκλήρῳ, ᾧ μὴ βίοτος πολὺς εἴη,
ἢ πᾶσιν νεκύεσσι καταφθιμένοισιν ἀνάσσειν.

Rather would I, in the sun's warmth divine,
Serve a poor churl who drags his days in grief,
Than the whole lordship of the dead were mine.
Ib. xi. 489

WILLIAM HONE
1780–1842

8 A good lather is half the shave.
Every-Day Book, vol. i, 1269

9 John Jones may be described as 'one of the *has* beens.'
Ib. vol. ii, 820

THOMAS HOOD
1799–1845

10 When Eve upon the first of Men
The apple press'd with specious cant,
Oh! what a thousand pities then
That Adam was not Adamant! *A Reflection*

11 It was not in the winter
Our loving lot was cast!
It was the time of roses,
We plucked them as we passed!
Ballad: It Was Not in the Winter

12 One more Unfortunate,
Weary of breath,
Rashly importunate,
Gone to her death!

Take her up tenderly,
Lift her with care;
Fashion'd so slenderly,
Young, and so fair!

Look at her garments
Clinging like cerements. *The Bridge of Sighs*

13 Loving, not loathing. *Ib.*

14 All that remains of her
Now is pure womanly. *Ib.*

15 Past all dishonour,
Death has left on her
Only the beautiful. *Ib.*

16 Still, for all slips of hers,
One of Eve's family. *The Bridge of Sighs*

17 Was there a dearer one
Still, and a nearer one
Yet, than all other? *Ib.*

18 Alas! for the rarity
Of Christian charity
Under the sun!
Oh! it was pitiful!
Near a whole city full,
Home had she none! *Ib.*

19 Even God's providence
Seeming estranged. *Ib.*

20 Mad from life's history,
Glad to death's mystery,
Swift to be hurl'd—
Anywhere, anywhere,
Out of the world! *Ib.*

21 Picture it—think of it,
Dissolute man!
Lave in it, drink of it,
Then, if you can! *Ib.*

22 Owning her weakness,
Her evil behaviour,
And leaving, with meekness,
Her sins to her Saviour! *Ib.*

23 Our very hopes belied our fears,
Our fears our hopes belied—
We thought her dying when she slept,
And sleeping when she died! *The Death Bed*

24 Much study had made him very lean,
And pale, and leaden-ey'd.
The Dream of Eugene Aram

25 But Guilt was my grim Chamberlain
That lighted me to bed. *Ib.*

26 Two stern-faced men set out from Lynn,
Through the cold and heavy mist;
And Eugene Aram walked between,
With gyves upon his wrist. *Ib.*

27 Where folks that ride a bit of blood,
May break a bit of bone. *The Epping Hunt*, l. 99

28 O saw ye not fair Inez? *Fair Inez*

29 Ben Battle was a soldier bold,
And used to war's alarms:
But a cannon-ball took off his legs,
So he laid down his arms! *Faithless Nelly Gray*

30 For here I leave my second leg,
And the Forty-second Foot! *Ib.*

31 The love that loves a scarlet coat
Should be more uniform. *Ib.*

32 His death, which happen'd in his berth,
At forty-odd befell:
They went and told the sexton, and
The sexton toll'd the bell. *Faithless Sally Brown*

33 I remember, I remember,
The house where I was born,
The little window where the sun
Came peeping in at morn;
He never came a wink too soon,
Nor brought too long a day,
But now, I often wish the night
Had borne my breath away! *I Remember*

1 I remember, I remember,
The roses, red and white,
The vi'lets, and the lily-cups,
Those flowers made of light!
The lilacs where the robin built,
And where my brother set
The laburnum on his birthday,—
The tree is living yet!   *I Remember*

2 I remember, I remember,
The fir trees dark and high;
I used to think their slender tops
Were close against the sky:
It was a childish ignorance,
But now 'tis little joy
To know I'm farther off from heav'n
Than when I was a boy.   *Ib.*

3 He never spoils the child and spares the rod,
But spoils the rod and never spares the child.
    The Irish Schoolmaster, xii

4 But evil is wrought by want of thought,
As well as want of heart!   *The Lady's Dream*

5 For that old enemy the gout
Had taken him in toe!   *Lieutenant Luff*

6 Alas! my everlasting peace
Is broken into pieces.   *Mary's Ghost*

7 And then, in the fulness of joy and hope,
Seem'd washing his hands with invisible soap,
In imperceptible water.
    Miss Kilmansegg. Her Christening

8 There's Bardus, a six-foot column of fop,
A lighthouse without any light atop.
    Ib. Her First Step

9 For one of the pleasures of having a rout,
Is the pleasure of having it over.   *Ib. Her Dream*

10 Home-made dishes that drive one from home.
    Ib. Her Misery

11 No sun—no moon!
No morn—no noon
No dawn—no dusk—no proper time of day.   *No!*

12 No warmth, no cheerfulness, no healthful ease,
No comfortable feel in any member—
No shade, no shine, no butterflies, no bees,
No fruits, no flowers, no leaves, no birds,—
November!   *Ib.*

13 I saw old Autumn in the misty morn
Stand shadowless like Silence, listening
To silence.   *Ode: Autumn*

14 Not one of those self-constituted saints,
Quacks—not physicians—in the cure of souls.
    Ode to Rae Wilson, l. 13

15 Dear bells! how sweet the sound of village bells
When on the undulating air they swim!
Now loud as welcomes! faint, now, as farewells!
    Ib. l. 159

16 The shrill sweet lark.
    The Plea of the Midsummer Fairies, xxx

17   The bird forlorn,
That singeth with her breast against a thorn.   *Ib.*

18 We will not woo foul weather all too soon,
Or nurse November on the lap of June.   *Ib.* xcii

19 She stood breast high amid the corn,
Clasp'd by the golden light of morn,
Like the sweetheart of the sun,
Who many a glowing kiss had won.   *Ruth*

20 Thus she stood amid the stooks,
Praising God with sweetest looks.   *Ib.*

21 Sure, I said, heav'n did not mean,
Where I reap thou shouldst but glean,
Lay thy sheaf adown and come,
Share my harvest and my home.   *Ib.*

22 With fingers weary and worn,
With eyelids heavy and red,
A woman sat, in unwomanly rags,
Plying her needle and thread—
Stitch! stitch! stitch!
In poverty, hunger, and dirt.   *The Song of the Shirt*

23 O! men with sisters dear,
   O! men with mothers and wives!
It is not linen you're wearing out,
   But human creatures' lives!   *Ib.*

24 Sewing at once, with a double thread,
A shroud as well as a shirt.   *Ib.*

25 Oh! God! that bread should be so dear,
And flesh and blood so cheap!   *Ib.*

26 No blessed leisure for love or hope,
But only time for grief!   *Ib.*

27 My tears must stop, for every drop
Hinders needle and thread!   *Ib.*

28 There is a silence where hath been no sound,
There is a silence where no sound may be,
In the cold grave—under the deep deep sea,
Or in wide desert where no life is found.
    Sonnet. Silence

29 A wife who preaches in her gown,
And lectures in her night-dress!
    The Surplice Question

30 Our hands have met, but not our hearts;
Our hands will never meet again.   *To a False Friend*

31 There are three things which the public will always
clamour for, sooner or later: namely, Novelty,
novelty, novelty.
    Announcement of Comic Annual for 1836

32 The sedate, sober, silent, serious, sad-coloured sect.
[Quakers.]   *The Doves and the Crows*

33 'Extremes meet', as the whiting said with its tail in
its mouth.   *Ib.*

34 Holland . . . lies so low they're only saved by being
dammed.   *Up the Rhine. To Rebecca Page*

RICHARD HOOKER
1554?–1600

35 He that goeth about to persuade a multitude, that
they are not so well governed as they ought to be,
shall never want attentive and favourable hearers.
    Ecclesiastical Polity, bk. i, § 1

36 Of Law there can be no less acknowledged, than that
her seat is the bosom of God, her voice the harmony of the world: all things in heaven and earth
do her homage, the very least as feeling her care,
and the greatest as not exempted from her power.
    Ib. § xvi

1 Change is not made without inconvenience, even from worse to better.

Quoted by Johnson, as from Hooker, in the Preface to the 'English Dictionary'

ELLEN STURGIS HOOPER
1816–1841

2 I slept, and dreamed that life was Beauty;
I woke, and found that life was Duty.   *Life a Duty*

HERBERT CLARK HOOVER
1874–

3 The American system of rugged individualism.
Campaign speech, New York, 22 Oct. 1928

4 Our country has deliberately undertaken a great social and economic experiment, noble in motive and far-reaching in purpose. [The Eighteenth Amendment, enacting Prohibition.]
Letter to Senator W. H. Borah, 28 Feb. 1928

ANTHONY HOPE [SIR ANTHONY HOPE HAWKINS]
1863–1933

5 Economy is going without something you do want in case you should, some day, want something you probably won't want. *The Dolly Dialogues*, No. 12

6 'You oughtn't to yield to temptation.'
'Well, somebody must, or the thing becomes absurd.'
Ib. No. 14

7 'Boys will be boys——'
'And even that ... wouldn't matter if we could only prevent girls from being girls.'   *Ib.* No. 16

8 '*Bourgeois*,' I observed, 'is an epithet which the riff-raff apply to what is respectable, and the aristocracy to what is decent.'   *Ib.* No. 17

9 He is very fond of making things which he doesn't want, and then giving them to people who have no use for them.   *Ib.*

10 I wish you would read a little poetry sometimes. Your ignorance cramps my conversation.
Ib. No. 22

11 I may not understand, but I am willing to admire.
Ib.

12 Good families are generally worse than any others.
Prisoner of Zenda, ch. 1

13 His foe was folly and his weapon wit.
Inscription on the tablet to W. S. Gilbert, Victoria Embankment, London (1915)

LAURENCE HOPE [ADELA FLORENCE NICOLSON]
1865–1904

14 Pale hands I loved beside the Shalimar,
Where are you now? Who lies beneath your spell?
Indian Love Lyrics. Pale Hands I Loved

15 Pale hands, pink-tipped, like lotus-buds that float
On those cool waters where we used to dwell,
I would have rather felt you round my throat
Crushing out life than waving me farewell.   *Ib.*

16 Less than the dust beneath thy chariot wheel,
Less than the weed that grows beside thy door,
Less than the rust that never stained thy sword,
Less than the need thou hast in life of me,
  Even less am I.
Indian Love Lyrics. Less than the Dust

GERARD MANLEY HOPKINS
1844–1889

17 Wild air, world-mothering air,
Nestling me everywhere.
The Blessed Virgin Compared to the Air We Breathe

18 Some candle clear burns somewhere I came by.
I muse at how its being puts blissful back
With yellowy moisture mild night's blear-all black,
Or to-fro tender trambeams truckle at the eye.
The Candle Indoors

19 Not, I'll not, carrion comfort, Despair, not feast on thee;
Not untwist—slack they may be—these last strands of man
In me or, most weary, cry *I can no more.* I can;
Can something, hope, wish day come, not choose not to be.   *Carrion Comfort*

20   That night, that year
Of now done darkness I wretch lay wrestling with (my God!) my God.   *Ib.*

21 Towery city and branchy between towers.
Duns Scotus' Oxford

22 Cuckoo-echoing, bell-swarmèd, lark-charmèd, rook-racked, river-rounded.   *Ib.*

23 Didst fettle for the great grey drayhorse his bright and battering sandal!   *Felix Randal*

24 The world is charged with the grandeur of God.
God's Grandeur

25   Because the Holy Ghost over the bent
World broods with warm breast and with ah! bright wings.   *Ib.*

26 Elected Silence, sing to me
And beat upon my whorlèd ear,
Pipe me to pastures still and be
The music that I care to hear.
The Habit of Perfection

27 Palate, the hutch of tasty lust,
Desire not to be rinsed with wine:
The can must be so sweet, the crust
So fresh that come in fasts divine!   *Ib.*

28 And you unhouse and house the Lord.   *Ib.*

29   I have desired to go
    Where springs not fail,
To fields where flies no sharp and sided hail
    And a few lilies blow.

    And I have asked to be
    Where no storms come,
Where the green swell is in the havens dumb,
    And out of the swing of the sea.
Heaven-Haven

30 What would the world be, once bereft
Of wet and of wildness? Let them be left,
O let them be left, wildness and wet;
Long live the weeds and the wilderness yet.
Inversnaid

1   All
Life death does end and each day dies with sleep.
No Worst, There Is None

2 Glory be to God for dappled things.   *Pied Beauty*

3 All things counter, original, spare, strange;
Whatever is fickle, freckled (who knows how?)
With swift, slow; sweet, sour; adazzle, dim;
He fathers-forth whose beauty is past change:
          Praise him.   *Ib.*

4 The glassy peartree leaves and blooms, they brush
The descending blue; that blue is all in a rush.
                           Spring

5 Look at the stars! look, look up at the skies!
O look at all the fire-folk sitting in the air!
The bright boroughs, the circle-citadels there!
              The Starlight Night

6 Ah well! it is all a purchase, all is a prize.
Buy then! bid then!—What?—Prayer, patience, alms,
vows.
Look, look: a May-mess, like on orchard boughs!
Look! March-bloom, like on mealed-with-yellow
sallows!
These are indeed the barn; withindoors house
The shocks.   This piece-bright paling shuts the
spouse
Christ home, Christ and his mother and all his
hallows.   *Ib.*

7 I am all at once what Christ is, since he was what I
am, and
This Jack, joke, poor potsherd, patch, matchwood,
immortal diamond,
Is immortal diamond.
      That Nature is a Heraclitean Fire

8 Thou art indeed just, Lord, if I contend
With thee; but, sir, so what I plead is just.
Why do sinners' ways prosper? and why must
Disappointment all I endeavour end?
         Thou Art Indeed Just, Lord

9 Birds build—but not I build; no, but strain,
Time's eunuch, and not breed one work that wakes.
Mine, O thou lord of life, send my roots rain. *Ib.*

10 To What Serves Mortal Beauty?   *Title*

11 I caught this morning morning's minion, kingdom of
daylight's dauphin, dapple-dawn-drawn Falcon.
               The Windhover

12 The achieve of, the mastery of the thing!   *Ib.*

JOSEPH HOPKINSON
1770–1842

13 Hail, Columbia! happy land!
Hail, ye heroes! heaven-born band! *Hail, Columbia!*

HORACE
65–8 B.C.

14   Ut turpiter atrum
Desinat in piscem mulier formosa superne.
   Make what at the top was a beautiful woman have
      ugly ending in a black fish's tail.
      Ars Poetica, 4. Trans. by Wickham

15 'Pictoribus atque poetis
Quidlibet audendi semper fuit aequa potestas.'
Scimus, et hanc veniam petimusque damusque
vicissim.

'Poets and painters,' you say, 'have always had
an equal licence in daring invention.' We know
it: this liberty we claim for ourselves and give
again to others.   *Ars Poetica*, 9

16 Inceptis gravibus plerumque et magna professis
Purpureus, late qui splendeat, unus et alter
Adsuitur pannus.
   Often on a work of grave purpose and high promises
     is tacked a purple patch or two to give an effect
     of colour.   *Ib.* 14

17   Amphora coepit
Institui: currente rota cur urceus exit?
   It was a wine-jar that was to be moulded: as the
     wheel runs round why does it come out a pitcher?
                    Ib. 21

18   Brevis esse laboro,
Obscurus fio.
   It is when I am struggling to be brief that I be-
     come unintelligible.   *Ib.* 25

19 Dixeris egregie notum si callida verbum
Reddiderit iunctura novum.
   You may gain the finest effects in language by the
     skilful setting which makes a well-known word
     new.   *Ib.* 47

20 Multa renascentur quae iam cecidere, cadentque
Quae nunc sunt in honore vocabula, si volet usus,
Quem penes arbitrium est et ius et norma loquendi.
   Many a term which has fallen from use shall have
     a second birth, and those shall fall that are now
     in high honour, if so Usage shall will it, in whose
     hands is the arbitrament, the right and rule of
     speech.   *Ib.* 70

21 Grammatici certant et adhuc sub iudice lis est.
   Scholars dispute, and the case is still before the
     courts.   *Ib.* 78

22 Proicit ampullas et sesquipedalia verba.
   Throws aside his paint-pots and his words a foot
     and a half long.   *Ib.* 97

23   Si vis me flere, dolendum est
Primum ipsi tibi.
   If you wish to draw tears from me, you must first
     feel pain yourself.   *Ib.* 102

24   Servetur ad imum
Qualis ab incepto processerit, et sibi constet.
Difficile est proprie communia dicere.
   See that it [a fresh character in a play] is kept to
     the end such as it starts at the beginning and
     is self-consistent. It is a hard task to treat what is
     common in a way of your own. *Ib.* 126

25 Parturient montes, nascetur ridiculus mus.
   Mountains will be in labour, the birth will be a
     single laughable little mouse.   *Ib.* 139

26 Dic mihi, Musa, virum, captae post tempora Troiae
Qui mores hominum multorum vidit et urbis.
   Of him, my Muse, who, when Troy's ramparts fell,
     Saw many cities and men's manners, tell. *Ib.* 141

27 Non fumum ex fulgore, sed ex fumo dare lucem
Cogitat.
   His thought is not to give flame first and then
     smoke, but from smoke to let light break out.
                    Ib. 143

1 Semper ad eventum festinat et in medias res
Non secus ac notas auditorem rapit.

He ever hastens to the issue, and hurries his hearers
into the midst of the story as if they knew it before.   *Ars Poetica*, 148. Trans. by Wickham

2 Difficilis, querulus, laudator temporis acti
Se puero, castigator, censorque minorum.
Multa ferunt anni venientes commoda secum,
Multa recedentes adimunt.

Testy, a grumbler, inclined to praise the way the
world went when he was a boy, to play the critic
and censor of the new generation. The tide of
years as it rises brings many conveniences, as it
ebbs carries many away.   *Ib.* 173

3 Ne pueros coram populo Medea trucidet.

You will not let Medea slay her boys before the
audience.   *Ib.* 185

4 Quodcumque ostendis mihi sic, incredulus odi.

Anything that you thus thrust upon my sight, I
discredit and revolt at.   *Ib.* 188

5 Nec deus intersit, nisi dignus vindice nodus
Inciderit.

Neither should a god intervene, unless a knot be-
falls worthy of his interference.   *Ib.* 191

6   Vos exemplaria Graeca
Nocturna versate manu, versate diurna.

For yourselves, do you thumb well by night and
day Greek models.   *Ib.* 268

7   Fungar vice cotis, acutum
Reddere quae ferrum valet exsors ipsa secandi.

So I will play the part of a whetstone which can
make steel sharp, though it has no power itself of
cutting.   *Ib.* 304

8 Grais ingenium, Grais dedit ore rotundo
Musa loqui.

It was the Greeks who had at the Muse's hand
the native gift, the Greeks who had the utterance
of finished grace.   *Ib.* 323

9 Omne tulit punctum qui miscuit utile dulci,
Lectorem delectando pariterque monendo.

He has gained every vote who has mingled profit
with pleasure by delighting the reader at once
and instructing him.   *Ib.* 343

10 Indignor quandoque bonus dormitat Homerus.

But if Homer, usually good, nods for a moment,
I think it shame.   *Ib.* 359

11 Ut pictura poesis.
As with the painter's work, so with the poet's.
Ib. 361

12   Mediocribus esse poetis
Non homines, non di, non concessere columnae.

To poets to be second-rate is a privilege which
neither men, nor gods, nor bookstalls ever allowed.   *Ib.* 372

13 Tu nihil invita dices faciesve Minerva.

You will say nothing, do nothing, unless Minerva
pleases.   *Ib.* 385

14 Nonumque prematur in annum.

Let it be kept quiet till the ninth year.   *Ib.* 388

15 Solve senescentem mature sanus equum, ne
Peccet ad extremum ridendus et ilia ducat.

Be wise in time, and turn your horse out to grass
when he shows signs of age, lest he end in a ludicrous breakdown with straining flanks.
Epistles, I. i. 8. Trans. by Wickham

16 Nullius addictus iurare in verba magistri,
Quo me cumque rapit tempestas, deferor hospes.

I am not bound over to swear allegiance to any
master: where the wind carries me, I put into
port and make myself at home.   *Ib.* 14

17 Virtus est vitium fugere, et sapientia prima
Stultitia caruisse.

To flee vice is the beginning of virtue, and the beginning of wisdom is to have got rid of folly.
Ib. 41

18   Hic murus aeneus esto,
Nil conscire sibi, nulla pallescere culpa.

Be this your wall of brass, to have no guilty secrets,
no wrong-doing that makes you turn pale. *Ib.* 60

19 Si possis recte, si non, quocumque modo rem.

Money by right means if you can, if not, by any
means, money.   *Ib.* 66

20 Olim quod vulpes aegroto cauta leoni
Respondit referam: 'quia me vestigia terrent,
Omnia te adversum spectantia, nulla retrorsum.'

The wary fox in the fable answered the sick lion:
'Because I am frightened at seeing that all the
footprints point towards your den and none the
other way.'   *Ib.* 73

21 Qui quid sit pulchrum, quid turpe, quid utile, quid
non,
Planius ac melius Chrysippo et Crantore dicit.

Who shows us what is fair, what is foul, what is
profitable, what not, more plainly and better than
a Chrysippus or a Crantor.   *Ib.* ii. 3

22 Quidquid delirant reges plectuntur Achivi.

For every folly of their princes the Greeks feel the
scourge.   *Ib.* 14

23 Rursus quid virtus et quid sapientia possit
Utile proposuit nobis exemplar Ulixen.

Again, of the power of virtue and of wisdom he has
given us a profitable example in Ulysses. *Ib.* 17

24 Nos numerus sumus et fruges consumere nati.

We are the ciphers, fit for nothing but to eat our
share of earth's fruits.   *Ib.* 27

25 Dimidium facti qui coepit habet: sapere aude.

He who has begun his task has half done it. Have
the courage to be wise.   *Ib.* 40

26 Ira furor brevis est.
Anger is a short madness.   *Ib.* 62

27 Omnem crede diem tibi diluxisse supremum.
Grata superveniet quae non sperabitur hora.
Me pinguem et nitidum bene curata cute vises
Cum ridere voles Epicuri de grege porcum.

Hold for yourself the belief that each day that
dawns is your last: the hour to which you do not
look forward will be a pleasant surprise. If you
ask of myself, you will find me, whenever you
want something to laugh at, in good case, fat and
sleek, a true hog of Epicurus' herd.   *Ib.* iv. 13

1 Nil admirari prope res est una, Numici,
Solaque quae possit facere et servare beatum.

Nought to admire is perhaps the one and only
thing, Numicius, that can make a man happy and
keep him so. *Epistles*, I. vi. 1

2 Naturam expellas furca, tamen usque recurret.

If you drive nature out with a pitchfork, she will
soon find a way back. *Ib.* x. 24

3 Tamen illic vivere vellem,
Oblitusque meorum obliviscendus et illis.

Yet I could find it in my heart to live there, forgetting my friends and forgotten by them.
Ib. xi. 8

4 Caelum non animum mutant qui trans mare currunt,
Strenua nos exercet inertia: navibus atque
Quadrigis petimus bene vivere. Quod petis hic est,
Est Ulubris, animus si te non deficit aequus.

They change their sky, not their soul, who run
across the sea. We work hard at doing nothing:
we seek happiness in yachts and four-horse
coaches. What you seek is here—is at Ulubrae—
if an even soul does not fail you. *Ib.* 27

5 Concordia discors.

Harmony in discord. *Ib.* xii. 19

6 Principibus placuisse viris non ultima laus est.
Non cuivis homini contingit adire Corinthum.

To have found favour with leaders of mankind is
not the meanest of glories. It is not every one
that can get to Corinth. *Ib.* xvii. 35

7 Et semel emissum volat irrevocabile verbum.

A word once let out of the cage cannot be whistled
back again. *Ib.* xviii. 71

8 Nam tua res agitur, paries cum proximus ardet.

It is your own interest that is at stake when your
next neighbour's wall is ablaze. *Ib.* 80

9 Tu, dum tua navis in alto est,
Hoc age, ne mutata retrorsum te ferat aura.
Oderunt hilarem tristes tristemque iocosi.

For yourself, my friend, while your bark is on the
sea, give all heed lest the breeze shift and turn
your course back again. The gloomy hate the
cheerful, the mirthful the gloomy. *Ib.* 87

10 Fallentis semita vitae.

The untrodden paths of life. *Ib.* 103

11 Sit mihi quod nunc est, etiam minus, et mihi vivam
Quod superest aevi, si quid superesse volunt di;
Sit bona librorum et provisae frugis in annum
Copia, neu fluitem dubiae spe pendulus horae.
Sed satis est orare Iovem qui ponit et aufert,
Det vitam, det opes: aequum mi animum ipse parabo.

Give me what I have, or even less; and therewith
let me live to myself for what remains of life,
if the gods will that anything remain. Let me
have a generous supply of books and of food
stored a year ahead; nor let me hang and tremble
on the hope of the uncertain hour. Nay, it is
enough to ask Jove, who gives them and takes
them away, that he grant life and subsistence; a
balanced mind I will find for myself. *Ib.* 107

12 Prisco si credis, Maecenas docte, Cratino,
Nulla placere diu nec vivere carmina possunt
Quae scribuntur aquae potoribus.

You know, Maecenas, as well as I, that, if you
trust old Cratinus, no poems can please long,
nor live, which are written by water-drinkers.
Epistles, I. xix. 1

13 O imitatores, servum pecus.

O imitators, you slavish herd. *Ib.* 19

14 Graecia capta ferum victorem cepit et artes
Intulit agresti Latio.

When Greece had been enslaved she made a slave
of her rough conqueror, and introduced the arts
into Latium, still rude. *Ib.* II. i. 156

15 Si foret in terris, rideret Democritus.

If he were on earth, Democritus would laugh at
the sight. *Ib.* 194

16 Atque inter silvas Academi quaerere verum.

And seek for truth in the garden of Academus.
Ib. ii. 45

17 Singula de nobis anni praedantur euntes.

Years as they pass plunder us of one thing after
another. *Ib.* 55

18 Multa fero, ut placem genus irritabile vatum.

I have to submit to much in order to pacify the
sensitive race of poets. *Ib.* 102

19 At qui legitimum cupiet fecisse poema,
Cum tabulis animum censoris sumet honesti.

But the man who shall desire to leave behind him
a poem true to the laws of art, when he takes
his tables to write will take also the spirit of an
honest censor. *Ib.* 109

20 Obscurata diu populo bonus eruet atque
Proferet in lucem speciosa vocabula rerum,
Quae priscis memorata Catonibus atque Cethegis
Nunc situs informis premit et deserta vetustas.

Phrases of beauty that have been lost to popular
view he will kindly disinter and bring into the
light, phrases which, though they were on the
lips of a Cato and a Cethegus of old time, now
lie uncouth because out of fashion and disused
because old. *Ib.* 115

21 Quid te exempta iuvat spinis de pluribus una?
Vivere si recte nescis, decede peritis.
Lusisti satis, edisti satis atque bibisti:
Tempus abire tibi est.

How does it relieve you to pluck one thorn out of
many? If you do not know how to live aright,
make way for those who do. You have played
enough, have eaten and drunk enough. It is time
for you to leave the scene. *Ib.* 212

22 Beatus ille, qui procul negotiis,
Ut prisca gens mortalium,
Paterna rura bubus exercet suis,
Solutus omni faenore.

Happy the man who far from schemes of business,
like the early generations of mankind, ploughs
and ploughs again his ancestral land with oxen
of his own breeding, with no yoke of usury on
his neck! *Epodes*, ii. 1. Trans. by Wickham

23 Maecenas atavis edite regibus,
O et praesidium et dulce decus meum.

Maecenas, in lineage the child of kings, but oh! to
me, my protector, pride, and joy.
Odes, I. i. 1. Trans. by Wickham

1 Indocilis pauperiem pati.

To be content without wealth he finds too hard
a lesson. *Odes*, I. i. 18

2 Quodsi me lyricis vatibus inseres,
Sublimi feriam sidera vertice.

But if you give me a place among the bards of the
lyre, I shall lift my head till it strikes the stars.
Ib. 35

3 Audiet pugnas vitio parentum
Rara iuventus.

How they fought shall be told to a young generation scant in number for their parents' crimes.
Ib. ii. 23

4 Animae dimidium meae.

The half of my own life. *Ib.* iii. 8

5 Illi robur et aes triplex
Circa pectus erat, qui fragilem truci
Commisit pelago ratem
Primus.

His heart was mailed in oak and triple brass who
was the first to commit a frail bark to the rough
seas. *Ib.* 9

6 Audax omnia perpeti
Gens humana ruit per vetitum nefas.

In its boldness to bear and to dare all things, the
race of man rushes headlong into sin, despite of
law. *Ib.* 25

7 Nil mortalibus ardui est.

No height is too arduous for mortal men. *Ib.* 37

8 Pallida Mors aequo pulsat pede pauperum tabernas
Regumque turris.

Pale Death with impartial foot knocks at the doors
of poor men's hovels and of kings' palaces.
Ib. iv. 13

9 Vitae summa brevis spem nos vetat incohare longam.

Life's short span forbids us to enter on far-reaching
hopes. *Ib.* 15

10 Quis multa gracilis te puer in rosa
Perfusus liquidis urget odoribus
Grato, Pyrrha, sub antro?
Cui flavam religas comam,
Simplex munditiis?

What delicate stripling is it, Pyrrha, that now,
steeped in liquid perfumes, is wooing thee on
the heaped rose-leaves in some pleasant grot?
For whose eyes dost thou braid those flaxen
locks, so trim, so simple? *Ib.* v. 1

11 Nil desperandum Teucro duce et auspice Teucro.

No lot is desperate under Teucer's conduct and
Teucer's star. *Ib.* vii. 27

12 Cras ingens iterabimus aequor.

To-morrow we set out once more upon the boundless sea. *Ib.* 32

13 Permitte divis cetera.

All else leave to the gods. *Ib.* ix. 9

14 Quid sit futurum cras fuge quaerere et
Quem Fors dierum cumque dabit lucro
Appone.

What shall be to-morrow, think not of asking.
Each day that Fortune gives you, be it what it
may, set down for gain. *Ib.* 13

15 Donec virenti canities abest
Morosa.

So long as youth is green and testy old age is far
off. *Odes*, I. ix. 17

16 Tu ne quaesieris, scire nefas.

Pray, ask not,—such knowledge is not for us.
Ib. xi. 1

17 Dum loquimur, fugerit invida
Aetas: carpe diem, quam minimum credula postero.

Even while we speak, Time, the churl, will have
been running. Snatch the sleeve of to-day and
trust as little as you may to to-morrow. *Ib.* 7

18 Velut inter ignis
Luna minores.

As shines the moon among the lesser fires.
Ib. xii. 47

19 Felices ter et amplius
Quos irrupta tenet copula nec malis
Divulsus querimoniis
Suprema citius solvet amor die.

Thrice happy they, and more than thrice, whom
an unbroken bond holds fast, and whom love,
never torn asunder by foolish quarrellings, will
not loose till life's last day! *Ib.* xiii. 17

20 O matre pulchra filia pulchrior.

O fairer daughter of a fair mother. *Ib.* xvi. 1

21 Mater saeva Cupidinum.

The imperious mother of Loves. *Ib.* xix. 1

22 Integer vitae scelerisque purus.

He that is unstained in life and pure from guilt.
Ib. xxii. 1

23 Dulce ridentem Lalagen amabo,
Dulce loquentem.

Still shall I love Lalage and her sweet laughter,
Lalage and her sweet prattle. *Ib.* 23

24 Quis desiderio sit pudor aut modus
Tam cari capitis?

What shame or measure should there be in grief
for one so dear? *Ib.* xxiv. 1

25 Multis ille bonis flebilis occidit.

Many a good man may weep for his death. *Ib.* 9

26 Durum: sed levius fit patientia
Quidquid corrigere est nefas.

'Tis hard. But what may not be altered is made
lighter by patience. *Ib.* 19

27 Parcus deorum cultor et infrequens.

A grudging and infrequent worshipper of the gods.
Ib. xxxiv. 1

28 Nunc est bibendum, nunc pede libero
Pulsanda tellus.

Now we must drink, now beat the earth with free
step. *Ib.* xxxvii. 1

29 Persicos odi, puer, apparatus.

Persian luxury, boy, I hate. *Ib.* xxxviii. 1

30 Mitte sectari, rosa quo locorum
Sera moretur.

Cease your efforts to find where the last rose lingers.
Ib. 3

1   Incedis per ignis
Suppositos cineri doloso.

> You tread over fires hidden under a treacherous
> crust of ashes.   *Odes*, II. i. 7

2 Crescit indulgens sibi dirus hydrops.

> The dread dropsy grows by indulging itself.
>   *Ib.* ii. 13

3 Aequam memento rebus in arduis
Servare mentem.

> Remember when life's path is steep to keep your
> mind even.   *Ib.* iii. 1

4 Omnes eodem cogimur.

> We all are driven one road.   *Ib.* 25

5 Ille terrarum mihi praeter omnis
Angulus ridet.

> That nook of earth's surface has a smile for me be-
> fore all other places.   *Ib.* vi. 13

6 Auream quisquis mediocritatem
Diligit.

> Whoso loves well the golden mean.   *Ib.* x. 5

7 Sperat infestis, metuit secundis
Alteram sortem bene praeparatum
Pectus.

> The heart that is well forearmed hopes when times
> are adverse, and when they are favourable fears,
> a change of fortune.   *Ib.* 13

8   Neque semper arcum
Tendit Apollo.

> Nor keeps Apollo his bow for ever strung.   *Ib.* 19

9 Eheu fugaces, Postume, Postume,
Labuntur anni.

> Ah me, Postumus, Postumus, the fleeting years
> are slipping by.   *Ib.* xiv. 1

10   Domus et placens
Uxor.

> House and wife of our choice.   *Ib.* 21

11   Nihil est ab omni
Parte beatum.

> No lot is happy on all sides.   *Ib.* xvi. 27

12   Credite posteri.

> Believe it, after-years!   *Ib.* xix. 2

13 Compesce clamorem ac sepulcri
Mitte supervacuos honores.

> Check all cries, and let be the meaningless honours
> of the tomb.   *Ib.* xx. 23

14 Odi profanum vulgus et arceo;
Favete linguis; carmina non prius
Audita Musarum sacerdos
Virginibus puerisque canto.

> I hate the uninitiate crowd and bid them avaunt.
> Listen all in silence! Strains unheard before I,
> the Muses' hierophant, now chant to maidens
> and to boys.   *Ib.* III. i. 1

15 Omne capax movet urna nomen.

> Every name alike is shaken in her roomy urn. *Ib.* 16

16 Post equitem sedet atra Cura.

> Black Care mounts on the horseman's pillion.
>   *Ib.* 40

17 Cur valle permutem Sabina
Divitias operosiores?

> Why should I exchange my Sabine valley for
> wealth which adds to trouble?   *Odes*, III. i. 47

18 Dulce et decorum est pro patria mori.

> To die for fatherland is a sweet thing and be-
> coming.   *Ib.* ii. 13

19 Virtus repulsae nescia sordidae
Intaminatis fulget honoribus,
Nec sumit aut ponit securis
Arbitrio popularis aurae.

> Virtue, which cannot know the disgrace of rejection,
> shines bright with honours that have no stain on
> them, nor takes nor resigns the rods at the shift-
> ing breath of the people's pleasure.   *Ib.* 17

20 Raro antecedentem scelestum
Deseruit pede Poena claudo.

> Rarely has Punishment, though halt of foot, left
> the track of the criminal in the way before her.
>   *Ib.* 31

21 Iustum et tenacem propositi virum
Non civium ardor prava iubentium,
Non vultus instantis tyranni
Mente quatit solida.

> The just man and firm of purpose not the heat of
> fellow citizens clamouring for what is wrong,
> nor presence of threatening tyrant can shake in
> his rocklike soul.   *Ib.* iii. 1

22 Si fractus illabatur orbis,
Impavidum ferient ruinae.

> If the round sky should crack and fall upon him,
> the wreck will strike him fearless still.   *Ib.* 7

23 Aurum irrepertum et sic melius situm.

> The gold unfound, and so the better placed. *Ib.* 49

24 Non hoc iocosae conveniet lyrae:
Quo, Musa, tendis?

> This will not suit a mirthful lyre. Whither away,
> my Muse?   *Ib.* 69

25 Auditis an me ludit amabilis
Insania?

> Do you hear it? Or is it a delightful madness that
> makes sport of me?   *Ib.* iv. 5

26 Non sine dis animosus infans.

> A brave babe, surely, and some god's special care.
>   *Ib.* 20

27 Fratresque tendentes opaco
Pelion imposuisse Olympo.

> The brothers who strove to leave Pelion set on the
> top of leafy Olympus.   *Ib.* 51

28 Vis consili expers mole ruit sua.

> Force without mind falls by its own weight.
>   *Ib.* 65

29 O magna Carthago, probrosis
Altior Italiae ruinis!

> O mighty Carthage, lifted higher for the shameful
> downfall of Italy!   *Ib.* v. 39

30 Delicta maiorum immeritus lues.

> For the sins of your sires albeit you had no hand
> in them, you must suffer.   *Ib.* vi. 1

1 Aetas parentum peior avis tulit
Nos nequiores, mox daturos
Progeniem vitiosiorem.

Our sires' age was worse than our grandsires'.
We their sons are more worthless than they: so
in our turn we shall give the world a progeny
yet more corrupt. *Odes*, III. vi. 46

2 Docte sermones utriusque linguae.

Learned . . . in the lore of either tongue.
Ib. viii. 5

3 Donec gratus eram tibi.

So long as I found favour in your sight. *Ib.* ix. 1

4 Tecum vivere amem, tecum obeam libens.

With you I should love to live, with you be ready
to die. *Ib.* 24

5 Splendide mendax et in omne virgo
Nobilis aevum.

With glorious falsehood . . ., a maid famous to
all time. *Ib.* xi. 35

6 Miserarum est neque amori dare ludum neque dulci
Mala vino lavere.

Poor maidens! who may neither let love have his
way, nor wash away their troubles in sweet wine.
Ib. xii. 1

7 O fons Bandusiae splendidior vitro.

O spring of Bandusia, more brilliant than glass.
Ib. xiii. 1

8 Non ego hoc ferrem calidus iuventa
Consule Planco.

I should not have borne it in my youth's hot blood
when Plancus was consul. *Ib.* xiv. 27

9 Magnas inter opes inops.

A pauper in the midst of wealth. *Ib.* xvi. 28

10 O nata mecum consule Manlio
. . . pia testa.

O born with me when Manlius was consul, . . .
my gentle wine-jar. *Ib.* xxi. 1

11 Quid leges sine moribus
Vanae proficiunt?

What profit laws, which without lives are empty?
Ib. xxiv. 35

12 Vixi puellis nuper idoneus
Et militavi non sine gloria;
Nunc arma defunctumque bello
Barbiton hic paries habebit.

Though that life is past, I was but now still meet
for ladies' love, and fought my battles not without
glory. Now my armour and the lute, whose campaigns are over, will hang here on yonder wall.
Ib. xxvi. 1

13 Fumum et opes strepitumque Romae.

The smoke, and the grandeur and the noise . . .
of Rome. *Ib.* xxix. 12

14 Ille potens sui
Laetusque deget, cui licet in diem
Dixisse 'vixi: cras vel atra
Nube polum Pater occupato
Vel sole puro'.

He will through life be master of himself and a
happy man who from day to day can have said,
'I have lived: to-morrow the Sire may fill the
sky with black clouds or with cloudless sunshine.'
Odes, III. xxix. 41

15 Exegi monumentum aere perennius.

My work is done, the memorial more enduring than
brass. *Ib.* xxx. 1

16 Non omnis moriar.

I shall not all die. *Ib.* 6

17 Non sum qualis eram bonae
Sub regno Cinarae. Desine, dulcium
Mater saeva Cupidinum.

I am other than I was when poor Cinara was queen.
Try no more, 'imperious mother of sweet loves'.
Ib. IV. i. 3. (*Cf. 258:21*)

18 Numerisque fertur
Lege solutis.

As he [Pindar] pours along in lawless rhythms.
Ib. ii. 11

19 Quod spiro et placeo, si placeo, tuum est.

Breath of song and power to please, if please I
may, are alike of thee. *Ib.* iii. 24

20 Fortes creantur fortibus et bonis.

Gallant sons spring from the gallant and good.
Ib. iv. 29

21 Duris ut ilex tonsa bipennibus
Nigrae feraci frondis in Algido,
Per damna, per caedis, ab ipso
Ducit opes animumque ferro.

Like the holm-oak shorn by ruthless axes on Al-
gidus where black leaves grow thick, through
loss, through havoc, from the very edge of the
steel draws new strength and heart. *Ib.* 57

22 Merses profundo: pulchrior evenit.

Plunge it in the depth—it comes forth the fairer.
Ib. 65

23 Occidit, occidit
Spes omnis et fortuna nostri
Nominis Hasdrubale interempto.

Fallen, fallen is all our hope and the fortune of
our name in the death of Hasdrubal. *Ib.* 70

24 Diffugere nives, redeunt iam gramina campis
Arboribusque comae.

The snows have scattered and fled; already the
grass comes again in the fields and the leaves on
the trees. *Ib.* vii. 1

25 Immortalia ne speres, monet annus et almum
Quae rapit hora diem.

That you hope for nothing to last for ever, is the
lesson of the revolving year and of the flight of
time which snatches from us the sunny days.
Ib. 7

26 Damna tamen celeres reparant caelestia lunae:
Nos ubi decidimus
Quo pater Aeneas, quo Tullus dives et Ancus,
Pulvis et umbra sumus.

Yet change and loss in the heavens the swift moons
make up again. For us, when we have descended
where is father Aeneas, where are rich old Tullus
and Ancus, we are but some dust and a shadow.
Ib. 13

1 Dignum laude virum Musa vetat mori.

The hero who is worthy of her praise the Muse
will not let die. *Odes*, IV. viii. 28

2 Vixere fortes ante Agamemnona
Multi; sed omnes illacrimabiles
Urgentur ignotique longa
Nocte, carent quia vate sacro.

Gallant heroes lived before Agamemnon, not a
few; but on all alike, unwept and unknown,
eternal night lies heavy because they lack a
sacred poet. *Ib.* ix. 25

3 Quotiens bonus atque fidus
Iudex honestum praetulit utili.

So often as, on a judgement-seat, generous and leal,
he has set honour before expediency. *Ib.* 40

4 Non possidentem multa vocaveris
Recte beatum: rectius occupat
Nomen beati, qui deorum
Muneribus sapienter uti
Duramque callet pauperiem pati
Peiusque leto flagitium timet.

It is not the possessor of many things whom you
will rightly call happy. The name of the happy
man is claimed more justly by him who has
learnt the art wisely to use what the gods give,
and who can endure the hardships of poverty,
who dreads disgrace as something worse than
death. *Ib.* 45

5 Misce stultitiam consiliis brevem:
Dulce est desipere in loco.

Mix with your sage counsels some brief folly. In
due place to forget one's wisdom is sweet.
Ib. xii. 27

6 Qui fit, Maecenas, ut nemo, quam sibi sortem
Seu ratio dederit seu fors obiecerit, illa
Contentus vivat, laudet diversa sequentes?

How comes it, Maecenas, that, whether it be self-
chosen or flung to him by chance, every one is
discontented with his own lot and keeps his
praises for those who tread some other path?
Satires, I. i. 1. Trans. by Wickham

7 Quamquam ridentem dicere verum
Quid vetat? Ut pueris olim dant crustula blandi
Doctores, elementa velint ut discere prima.

And yet, why may one not be telling truth while
one laughs, as teachers sometimes give little boys
cakes to coax them into learning their letters?
Ib. 24

8 Mutato nomine de te
Fabula narratur.

Change but the name, and it is of yourself that tale
is told. *Ib.* 69

9 Est modus in rebus, sunt certi denique fines,
Quos ultra citraque nequit consistere rectum.

There is measure in everything. There are fixed
limits beyond which and short of which right
cannot find resting-place. *Ib.* 106

10 Hoc genus omne.

All their kith and kin. *Ib.* ii. 2

11 At ingenium ingens
Inculto latet hoc sub corpore.

But under that uncouth outside are hidden vast
gifts of mind. *Satires*, I. iii. 33

12 Stans pede in uno.

Without effort. *Ib.* iv. 10

13 Faenum habet in cornu.

He carries hay on his horns. *Ib.* 34

14 Etiam disiecti membra poetae.

Even in his dismembered state, the limbs of a poet.
Ib. 62

15 Hic niger est, hunc tu, Romane, caveto.

That man is black at heart: mark and avoid him,
if you are a Roman indeed. *Ib.* 85

16 Ad unguem
Factus homo.

The pink of accomplishment. *Ib.* v. 32

17 Credat Iudaeus Apella,
Non ego.

Apella the Jew must believe it, not I. *Ib.* 100

18 Naso suspendis adunco
Ignotos.

Hang on the crook of your nose those of unknown
origin. *Ib.* vi. 5

19 Sic me servavit Apollo.

So Apollo bore me from the fray. *Ib.* ix. 78

20 Satis est equitem mihi plaudere, ut audax
Contemptis aliis explosa Arbuscula dixit.

It is enough for me if the knights applaud—I care
not a fig for the rest of the house.
[The actress Arbuscula, as she was being hissed
from the stage.] *Ib.* x. 76

21 Solventur risu tabulae, tu missus abibis.

In a tempest of laughter the Tables will go to
pieces. You will leave the court without a stain
on your character. *Ib.* II. i. 86

22 Nec meus hic sermo est, sed quae praecepit Ofellus
Rusticus, abnormis sapiens crassaque Minerva.

This is no talk of my own, but the teaching of Ofellus, the countryman, a philosopher, though not
from the schools, but of home-spun wit.
Ib. ii. 2

23 Par nobile fratrum.

A noble pair of brothers. *Ib.* iii. 243

24 Hoc erat in votis: modus agri non ita magnus,
Hortus ubi et tecto vicinus iugis aquae fons
Et paulum silvae super his foret.

This used to be among my prayers—a portion of
land not so very large, but which should contain
a garden, and near the homestead a spring of
ever-flowing water, and a bit of forest to complete it. *Ib.* vi. 1

25 O rus, quando ego te aspiciam? quandoque licebit
Nunc veterum libris, nunc somno et inertibus horis,
Ducere sollicitae iucunda oblivia vitae?

O country home, when shall I look on you again!
when shall I be allowed, between my library of
classics and sleep and hours of idleness, to drink
the sweet draughts that make us forget the troubles of life? *Ib.* 60

26 O noctes cenaeque deum!

O nights and suppers of gods! *Ib.* 65

1 Responsare cupidinibus, contemnere honores
Fortis, et in se ipso totus, teres, atque rotundus.

> Who has courage to say no again and again to de-
> sires, to despise the objects of ambition, who is a
> whole in himself, smoothed and rounded.
> *Satires*, II. vii. 85

RICHARD HENRY ['HENGIST'] HORNE
1803–1884

2 'Tis always morning somewhere in the world.
Orion, bk. iii, c. ii

3 Ye rigid Ploughmen! Bear in mind
Your labour is for future hours.
Advance! Spare not! Nor look behind!
Plough deep and straight with all your powers!
The Plough

BISHOP SAMUEL HORSLEY
1733–1806

4 The people have nothing to do with the laws but to
obey them. *Speech in the House of Lords*

JOHN HOSKINS
1566–1638

5 Absence, hear thou my protestation
Against thy strength,
Distance and length:
Do what thou canst for alteration,
For hearts of truest mettle
Absence doth join, and time doth settle.
Absence: A Poetical Rhapsody. Attr.

6 By absence this good means I gain,
That I can catch her,
Where none can watch her,
In some close corner of my brain:
There I embrace and kiss her,
And so I both enjoy and miss her. *Ib.*

RICHARD MONCKTON MILNES,
BARON HOUGHTON
1809–1885

7 'Lady Moon, Lady Moon, where are you roving?'
'Over the sea.'
'Lady Moon, Lady Moon, whom are you loving?'
'All that love me.' *A Child's Song: Lady Moon*

8 A fair little girl sat under a tree,
Sewing as long as her eyes could see;
Then smoothed her work, and folded it right,
And said, 'Dear work! Good Night! Good Night!'
Good Night and Good Morning

9 I wander'd by the brookside,
I wander'd by the mill,—
I could not hear the brook flow,
The noisy wheel was still;
There was no burr of grasshopper,
No chirp of any bird,
But the beating of my own heart
Was all the sound I heard. *Song: The Brookside*

ALFRED EDWARD HOUSMAN
1859–1936

10 Loveliest of trees, the cherry now
Is hung with bloom along the bough,
And stands about the woodland ride
Wearing white for Eastertide.

Now, of my threescore years and ten,
Twenty will not come again,
And take from seventy springs a score,
It only leaves me fifty more.

And since to look at things in bloom
Fifty springs are little room,
About the woodlands I will go
To see the cherry hung with snow.
A Shropshire Lad, ii

11 There sleeps in Shrewsbury jail to-night,
Or wakes, as may betide,
A better lad, if things went right,
Than most that sleep outside. *Ib.* ix

12 And naked to the hangman's noose
The morning clocks will ring
A neck God made for other use
Than strangling in a string. *Ib.*

13 In farm and field through all the shire
The eye beholds the heart's desire;
Ah, let not only mine be vain
For lovers should be loved again. *Ib.* x

14 Lovers lying two and two
Ask not whom they sleep beside,
And the bridegroom all night through
Never turns him to the bride. *Ib.* xii

15 When I was one-and-twenty
I heard a wise man say,
'Give crowns and pounds and guineas
But not your heart away.' *Ib.* xiii

16 But I was one-and-twenty,
No use to talk to me. *Ib.*

17 When I was one-and-twenty
I heard him say again,
'The heart out of the bosom
Was never given in vain;
'Tis paid with sighs a plenty
And sold for endless rue.'
And I am two-and-twenty,
And oh, 'tis true, 'tis true. *Ib.*

18 His folly has not fellow
Beneath the blue of day
That gives to man or woman
His heart and soul away. *Ib.* xiv

19 Oh, when I was in love with you,
Then I was clean and brave,
And miles around the wonder grew
How well did I behave.

And now the fancy passes by,
And nothing will remain,
And miles around they'll say that I
Am quite myself again. *Ib.* xviii

20 The garland briefer than a girl's. *Ib.* xix

21 In summertime on Bredon
The bells they sound so clear;
Round both the shires they ring them
In steeples far and near,
A happy noise to hear.

Here of a Sunday morning
　My love and I would lie,
And see the coloured counties,
　And hear the larks so high
　About us in the sky.　　　*A Shropshire Lad*, xxi

1 And I would turn and answer
　　Among the springing thyme,
　'Oh, peal upon our wedding,
　　And we will hear the chime,
　　And come to church in time.'　　*Ib.*

2 They tolled the one bell only,
　　Groom there was none to see,
　The mourners followed after,
　　And so to church went she,
　　And would not wait for me.

　The bells they sound on Bredon,
　　And still the steeples hum.
　'Come all to church, good people,'—
　　Oh, noisy bells, be dumb;
　　I hear you, I will come.　　　*Ib.*

3 The lads that will die in their glory and never be old.
　　　　　　　　　　　　　　Ib. xxiii

4 Is my team ploughing,
　　That I was used to drive?　　*Ib.* xxvii

5 Ay, the horses trample,
　　The harness jingles now;
　No change though you lie under
　　The land you used to plough.　　*Ib.*

6 The goal stands up, the keeper
　　Stands up to keep the goal.　　*Ib.*

7 Yes, lad, I lie easy,
　　I lie as lads would choose;
　I cheer a dead man's sweetheart,
　　Never ask me whose.　　　*Ib.*

8 The tree of man was never quiet:
　　Then 'twas the Roman; now 'tis I.　　*Ib.* xxxi

9 To-day the Roman and his trouble
　　Are ashes under Uricon.　　*Ib.*

10 'Oh, go where you are wanted, for you are not wanted
　　here.'
　And that was all the farewell when I parted from my
　　dear.　　　　　　　　　　　　*Ib.* xxxiv

11 And the enemies of England they shall see me and
　　be sick.　　　　　　　　　　　*Ib.*

12 White in the moon the long road lies,
　　The moon stands blank above;
　White in the moon the long road lies
　　That leads me from my love.　　*Ib.* xxxvi

13 Oh tarnish late on Wenlock Edge,
　　Gold that I never see;
　Lie long, high snowdrifts in the hedge
　　That will not shower on me.　　*Ib.* xxxix

14 Into my heart an air that kills
　　From yon far country blows.
　What are those blue remembered hills,
　　What spires, what farms are those?

　That is the land of lost content,
　　I see it shining plain,
　The happy highways where I went
　　And cannot come again.　　　*Ib.* xl

15 But play the man, stand up and end you,
　　When your sickness is your soul.　　*Ib.* xlv

16 Be still, be still, my soul; it is but for a season;
　　Let us endure an hour and see injustice done.
　　　　　　　　　　　A Shropshire Lad, xlviii

17 Oh why did I awake? When shall I sleep again? *Ib.*

18 Think no more, lad; laugh, be jolly:
　　Why should men make haste to die?
　Empty heads and tongues a-talking
　Make the rough road easy walking,
　And the feather pate of folly
　　Bears the falling sky.

　Oh, 'tis jesting, dancing, drinking
　　Spins the heavy world around.
　If young hearts were not so clever,
　Oh, they would be young for ever:
　Think no more; 'tis only thinking
　　Lays lads underground.　　　*Ib.* xlix

19 Far in a western brookland
　　That bred me long ago
　The poplars stand and tremble
　　By pools I used to know.　　*Ib.* lii

20 There, by the starlit fences,
　　The wanderer halts and hears
　My soul that lingers sighing
　　About the glimmering weirs.　　*Ib*

21 Many a rose-lipt maiden
　　And many a lightfoot lad.　　*Ib.* liv

22 I shall have lived a little while
　　Before I die for ever.　　*Ib.* lvii

23 In all the endless road you tread
　　There's nothing but the night.　　*Ib.* lx

24 Say, for what were hop-yards meant,
　　Or why was Burton built on Trent?　　*Ib.* lxii

25 Malt does more than Milton can,
　　To justify God's ways to man.　　*Ib.*

26 Mithridates, he died old.　　　*Ib.*

27 We'll to the woods no more,
　　The laurels all are cut. *Last Poems*, introductory.

28 And lads are in love with the grave.　　*Ib.* iv

29 Peace is come and wars are over,
　　Welcome you and welcome all.　　*Ib.* viii

30 May will be fine next year as like as not:
　　Oh ay, but then we shall be twenty-four.　*Ib.* ix

31 We for a certainty are not the first
　　Have sat in taverns while the tempest hurled
　Their hopeful plans to emptiness, and cursed
　　Whatever brute and blackguard made the world.
　　　　　　　　　　　　　　　Ib.

32 The troubles of our proud and angry dust
　　Are from eternity, and shall not fail.
　Bear them we can, and if we can we must.
　　Shoulder the sky, my lad, and drink your ale. *Ib.*

33 Pass me the can, lad; there's an end of May. *Ib.*

34 But men at whiles are sober
　And think by fits and starts.
　And if they think, they fasten
　　Their hands upon their hearts.　　*Ib.* x

35 I, a stranger and afraid
　　In a world I never made.　　*Ib.* xii

36 Made of earth and sea
　　His overcoat for ever,
　　And wears the turning globe.　　*Ib.* xx

1 The fairies break their dances
    And leave the printed lawn,
    And up from India glances
    The silver sail of dawn.

    The candles burn their sockets,
    The blinds let through the day,
    The young man feels his pockets
    And wonders what's to pay.   *Last Poems*, xxi

2 See, in mid heaven the sun is mounted; hark,
    The belfries tingle to the noonday chime.
    'Tis silent, and the subterranean dark
    Has crossed the nadir, and begins to climb.
                                Ib. xxxvi

3 To air the ditty,
    And to earth I.   *Ib.* xli

4 These, in the day when heaven was falling,
    The hour when earth's foundations fled,
    Followed their mercenary calling
    And took their wages and are dead.

    Their shoulders held the sky suspended;
    They stood, and earth's foundations stay;
    What God abandoned, these defended,
    And saved the sum of things for pay.
    Ib. xxxvii. *Epitaph on an Army of Mercenaries*

5 By Sestos town, in Hero's tower
    On Hero's heart Leander lies;
    The signal torch has burned his hour,
    And splutters as it dies.   *More Poems*, xv

6 Experience has taught me, when I am shaving of a
    morning, to keep watch over my thoughts, because,
    if a line of poetry strays into my memory, my skin
    bristles so that the razor ceases to act.
                    The Name and Nature of Poetry

RICHARD HOVEY
1864–1900

7 I do not know beneath what sky
    Nor on what seas shall be thy fate;
    I only know it shall be high,
    I only know it shall be great.   *Unmanifest Destiny*

BISHOP WILLIAM WALSHAM HOW
1823–1897

8 For all the Saints who from their labours rest,
    Who Thee by faith before the world confess'd,
    Thy name, O Jesu, be for ever blest,
                                Alleluia!
    Earl Nelson's *Hymns For Saints' Days: For All
    the Saints*

9 And when the strife is fierce, the warfare long,
    Steals on the ear the distant triumph-song,
    And hearts are brave again, and arms are strong.
                                Alleluia!   *Ib.*

10 From earth's wide bounds, from ocean's farthest
    coast,
    Through gates of pearl streams in the countless host,
    Singing to Father, Son, and Holy Ghost,
                                Alleluia!   *Ib.*

11 O Lord, stretch forth thy mighty hand
    And guard and bless our fatherland.
    Church Hymns, 1871. *To Thee, Our God, We Fly*

12 O Jesu, thou art standing
    Outside the fast-closed door.
                    Psalms and Hymns, 1867

13 Shame on us, Christian brethren,
    His Name and sign who bear.   *Ib.*

SAMUEL HOWARD
1710–1782

14 Gentle Shepherd, tell me where.   *Song*

JULIA WARD HOWE
1819–1910

15 Mine eyes have seen the glory of the coming of the
    Lord:
    He is trampling out the vintage where the grapes of
    wrath are stored.
                Battle Hymn of the American Republic

16 His truth is marching on.   *Ib.*

17 Oh, be swift, my soul, to answer Him, be jubilant,
    my feet!   *Ib.*

18 In the beauty of the lilies Christ was born, across the
    sea,
    With a glory in His bosom that transfigures you and
    me:
    As He died to make men holy, let us die to make men
    free.   *Ib.*

JAMES HOWELL
1594?–1666

19 Some hold translations not unlike to be
    The wrong side of a Turkey tapestry.
                    Familiar Letters, bk. i, let. 6

20 One hair of a woman can draw more than a hundred
    pair of oxen.   *Ib.* bk. ii, let. 4

21 This life at best is but an inn,
    And we the passengers.   *Ib.* let. 73

MARY HOWITT
1799–1888

22 Buttercups and daisies,
    Oh, the pretty flowers;
    Coming ere the Springtime,
    To tell of sunny hours.   *Buttercups and Daisies*

23 'Will you walk into my parlour?' said a spider to a fly:
    ''Tis the prettiest little parlour that ever you did spy.'
                        The Spider and the Fly

EDMOND HOYLE
1672–1769

24 When in doubt, win the trick.
    *Hoyle's Games. Whist. Twenty-four Short Rules
    for Learners*

ELBERT HUBBARD
1859–1915

25 Life is just one damned thing after another.
                    A Thousand and One Epigrams, p. 137

THOMAS HUGHES
1822–1896

1 He never wants anything but what's right and fair; only when you come to settle what's right and fair, it's everything that he wants and nothing that you want. And that's his idea of a compromise. Give me the Brown compromise when I'm on his side.
Tom Brown's Schooldays, pt. ii, ch. 2

2 It's more than a game. It's an institution. [Cricket.]
Ib. ch. 7

VICTOR HUGO
1802–1885

3 Souffrons, mais souffrons sur les cimes.
If we must suffer, let us suffer nobly.
Contemplations: Les Malheureux

DAVID HUME
1711–1776

4 Avarice, the spur of industry.
Essays. Of Civil Liberty

5 Beauty in things exists in the mind which contemplates them.
Ib. Of Tragedy

6 A miracle may be accurately defined, a transgression of a law of nature by a particular volition of the Deity, or by the interposition of some invisible agent.
On Miracles, pt. 1, note

7 No testimony is sufficient to establish a miracle, unless the testimony be of such a kind, that its falsehood would be more miraculous than the fact which it endeavours to establish: and even in that case there is a mutual destruction of arguments, and the superior only gives us an assurance suitable to that degree of force which remains after deducting the inferior.
Ib. pt. 1

8 There is not to be found, in all history, any miracle attested by a sufficient number of men, of such unquestioned good sense, education, and learning, as to secure us against all delusion in themselves; of such undoubted integrity, as to place them beyond all suspicion of any design to deceive others; of such credit and reputation in the eyes of mankind, as to have a great deal to lose in case of their being detected in any falsehood; and at the same time attesting facts, performed in such a public manner, and in so celebrated a part of the world, as to render the detection unavoidable.
Ib. pt. 2

9 The usual propensity of mankind towards the marvellous.
Ib.

10 The Christian religion not only was at first attended with miracles, but even at this day cannot be believed by any reasonable person without one. Mere reason is insufficient to convince us of its veracity: and whoever is moved by faith to assent to it, is conscious of a continued miracle in his own person, which subverts all the principles of his understanding, and gives him a determination to believe what is most contrary to custom and experience.
Ib.

11 Custom, then, is the great guide of human life.
Inquiry Concerning Human Understanding, sec. 5, pt. 1

12 Never literary attempt was more unfortunate than my Treatise of Human Nature. It fell *dead-born from the press*.
My Own Life, ch. 1

13 Opposing one species of superstition to another, set them a quarrelling; while we ourselves, during their fury and contention, happily make our escape into the calm, though obscure, regions of philosophy.
The Natural History of Religion

MARGARET WOLFE HUNGERFORD
1855?–1897

14 Beauty is in the eye of the beholder.
Quoted in *Molly Bawn* (1878). (*See* 557:18)

G. W. HUNT
fl. 1878

15 We don't want to fight, but, by jingo if we do,
We've got the ships, we've got the men, we've got the money too.
We've fought the Bear before, and while Britons shall be true,
The Russians shall not have Constantinople.
We Don't Want to Fight. Music Hall Song, 1878

JAMES HENRY LEIGH HUNT
1784–1859

16 Abou Ben Adhem (may his tribe increase!)
Awoke one night from a deep dream of peace,
And saw, within the moonlight in his room,
Making it rich, and like a lily in bloom,
An angel writing in a book of gold:—
Exceeding peace had made Ben Adhem bold,
And to the presence in the room he said,
'What writest thou?'—The vision raised its head,
And with a look made of all sweet accord,
Answered, 'The names of those who love the Lord.'
Abou Ben Adhem and the Angel

17   'I pray thee then,
Write me as one that loves his fellow-men.' *Ib.*

18 And lo! Ben Adhem's name led all the rest. *Ib.*

19 A Venus grown fat! *Blue-stocking Revels*

20 'By God!' said Francis, 'rightly done!' and he rose from where he sat:
'No love,' quoth he, 'but vanity, sets love a task like that.'
The Glove and the Lions

21 Green little vaulter in the sunny grass.
To the Grasshopper and the Cricket

22 It flows through old hushed Egypt and its sands,
Like some great mighty thought threading a dream,
And times and things, as in that vision, seem
Keeping along it their eternal stands. *The Nile*

23 The laughing queen that caught the world's great hands. *Ib.*

24 If you become a nun, dear,
A friar I will be.
In any cell you run, dear,
Pray look behind for me. *The Nun*

25 Jenny kissed me when we met,
Jumping from the chair she sat in;
Time, you thief, who love to get
Sweets into your list, put that in:

Say I'm weary, say I'm sad,
Say that health and wealth have missed me,
Say I'm growing old, but add,
Jenny kissed me.   *Rondeau*

1 Stolen sweets are always sweeter,
Stolen kisses much completer,
Stolen looks are nice in chapels,
Stolen, stolen, be your apples.
                 Song of Fairies Robbing an Orchard

2 Where the light woods go seaward from the town.
                        The Story of Rimini, i, l. 18

3 But most he loved a happy human face.
                                    Ib. iii, l. 110

4 The two divinest things this world has got,
A lovely woman in a rural spot!   *Ib.* l. 257

5 Places of nestling green, for poets made.   *Ib.* l. 430

6 This Adonis in loveliness was a corpulent man of
fifty. [The Prince Regent.]
                        The Examiner, 22 Mar. 1812

7 A pleasure so exquisite as almost to amount to pain.
            Letter to Alexander Ireland, 2 June 1848

ANNE HUNTER
1742–1821

8 My mother bids me bind my hair
  With bands of rosy hue,
Tie up my sleeves with ribbons rare,
  And lace my bodice blue.

'For why,' she cries, 'sit still and weep,
  While others dance and play?'
Alas! I scarce can go or creep
  While Lubin is away.
                    My Mother Bids Me Bind My Hair

JOHN HUSS
1373–1415

9 O sancta simplicitas!
  O holy simplicity!
  *At the stake, seeing an old peasant bringing a fag-
  got to throw on the pile.* Zincgreff-Weidner,
  Apophthegmata, pub. in Amsterdam 1653,
  pt. iii, p. 383. Geo. Büchmann, *Geflügelte
  Worte* (1898), p. 509

FRANCIS HUTCHESON
1694–1746

10 Wisdom denotes the pursuing of the best ends by the
best means.
    *Inquiry into the Original of our Ideas of Beauty
    and Virtue*, 1725. Treatise I, sec. v, § 18

11 That action is best, which procures the greatest happiness for the greatest numbers.
    Ib. Treatise II. *Concerning Moral Good and
    Evil*, sec. 3, § 8. (*See 42:21*)

ALDOUS LEONARD HUXLEY
1894–

12   But when the wearied Band
Swoons to a waltz, I take her hand,
And there we sit in peaceful calm,
Quietly sweating palm to palm.   *Frascati's*

13 Seated upon the convex mound
Of one vast kidney, Jonah prays
And sings his canticles and hymns,
Making the hollow vault resound
God's goodness and mysterious ways,
Till the great fish spouts music as he swims.   *Jonah*

14 Bewildered furrows deepen the Thunderer's scowl;
This world so vast, so variously foul—
Who can have made its ugliness? In what
Revolting fancy were the Forms begot
Of all these monsters? What strange deity—
So barbarously not a Greek was he?   *Leda*

15 Your maiden modesty would float face down,
And men would weep upon your hinder parts.   *Ib.*

16 Beauty for some provides escape,
Who gain a happiness in eyeing
The gorgeous buttocks of the ape
Or Autumn sunsets exquisitely dying.
                        The Ninth Philosopher's Song

17 Then brim the bowl with atrabilious liquor!
We'll pledge our Empire vast across the flood:
For Blood, as all men know, than water's thicker,
But water's wider, thank the Lord, than Blood.   *Ib.*

THOMAS HENRY HUXLEY
1825–1895

18 Science is nothing but trained and organized common sense, differing from the latter only as a
veteran may differ from a raw recruit: and its
methods differ from those of common sense only
as far as the guardsman's cut and thrust differ from
the manner in which a savage wields his club.
        Collected Essays, iv. *The Method of Zadig*

19 The great tragedy of Science—the slaying of a
beautiful hypothesis by an ugly fact.
            Ib. viii. *Biogenesis and Abiogenesis*

20 The chess-board is the world; the pieces are the
phenomena of the universe; the rules of the game
are what we call the laws of Nature. The player on
the other side is hidden from us. We know that
his play is always fair, just, and patient. But also
we know, to our cost, that he never overlooks a
mistake, or makes the smallest allowance for ignorance.   *Lay Sermons, &c.*, iii. *A Liberal Education*

21 If some great Power would agree to make me always
think what is true and do what is right, on condition
of being turned into a sort of clock and wound
up every morning before I got out of bed, I should
instantly close with the offer.
        *On Descartes' Discourse on Method. Method &
        Results*, iv

22 Logical consequences are the scarecrows of fools and
the beacons of wise men.
        Science and Culture, ix. *On the Hypothesis that
        Animals are Automata*

23 Irrationally held truths may be more harmful than
reasoned errors.
        Ib. xii. *The Coming of Age of the Origin of Species*

24 It is the customary fate of new truths to begin as
heresies and to end as superstitions.   *Ib.*

25 I took thought, and invented what I conceived to be
the appropriate title of 'agnostic'.
            Science and Christian Tradition, ch. 7

EDWARD HYDE

see

EARL OF CLARENDON

HENRIK IBSEN

1828–1906

1 The minority is always right.
An Enemy of the People, Act IV

2 One should never put on one's best trousers to go out to battle for freedom and truth. *Ib.* Act V

3 Vine-leaves in his hair. *Hedda Gabler*, Act II

4 People don't do such things. *Ib.* Act IV

5 The younger generation will come knocking at my door. *The Master-Builder*, Act I

WILLIAM RALPH INGE

1860–

6 Democracy is only an experiment in government, and it has the obvious disadvantage of merely counting votes instead of weighing them.
Possible Recovery?

7 Literature flourishes best when it is half a trade and half an art. *The Victorian Age* (1922), p. 49

8 A man may build himself a throne of bayonets, but he cannot sit on it.
Marchant, *Wit and Wisdom of Dean Inge*, No. 108

9 The nations which have put mankind and posterity most in their debt have been small states—Israel, Athens, Florence, Elizabethan England.
Ib. No. 181

JEAN INGELOW

1820–1897

10 But two are walking apart for ever,
And wave their hands for a mute farewell.
Divided

11 When sparrows build, and the leaves break forth,
My old sorrow wakes and cries. *Supper at the Mill*

12 Play uppe 'The Brides of Enderby'.
The High Tide on the Coast of Lincolnshire, 1571

13 Come uppe, Whitefoot, come uppe Lightfoot,
Come uppe Jetty, rise and follow,
Jetty, to the milking shed. *Ib.*

14 A sweeter woman ne'er drew breath
Than my sonne's wife, Elizabeth. *Ib.*

15 And didst Thou love the race that loved not Thee?
Hymn

ROBERT GREEN INGERSOLL

1833–1899

16 An honest God is the noblest work of man.
Gods, pt. 1, p. 2. (*See also 112:9*)

17 In nature there are neither rewards nor punishments—there are consequences.
Lectures & Essays, 3rd Series. *Some Reasons Why*, viii

JOHN KELLS INGRAM

1823–1907

18 Who fears to speak of Ninety-Eight?
The Nation, April 1843

WASHINGTON IRVING

1783–1859

19 A tart temper never mellows with age, and a sharp tongue is the only edged tool that grows keener with constant use. *Rip Van Winkle*

20 They who drink beer will think beer.
The Sketch Book. Stratford

21 A woman's whole life is a history of the affections.
Ib. The Broken Heart

22 Free-livers on a small scale; who are prodigal within the compass of a guinea. *The Stout Gentleman*

23 I am always at a loss to know how much to believe of my own stories.
Tales of a Traveller, To the Reader

24 There is a certain relief in change, even though it be from bad to worse; as I have found in travelling in a stage-coach, that it is often a comfort to shift one's position and be bruised in a new place. *Ib.*

25 The almighty dollar, that great object of universal devotion throughout our land, seems to have no genuine devotees in these peculiar villages.
Wolfert's Roost. The Creole Village

ANDREW JACKSON

1767–1845

26 You are uneasy; you never sailed with *me* before, I see.
J. Parton's *Life of Jackson*, vol. iii, ch. 35

27 Our Federal Union: it must be preserved.
Toast given on the Jefferson Birthday Celebration, 13 Apr. 1830. Benton, *Thirty Years' View*, vol. I

RICHARD JAGO

1715–1781

28 With leaden foot time creeps along
While Delia is away. *Absence: With Leaden Foot*

JAMES I OF ENGLAND AND VI OF SCOTLAND

1566–1625

29 A branch of the sin of drunkenness, which is the root of all sins. *A Counterblast to Tobacco* (1604)

30 A custom loathsome to the eye, hateful to the nose, harmful to the brain, dangerous to the lungs, and in the black, stinking fume thereof, nearest resembling the horrible Stygian smoke of the pit that is bottomless. *Ib.*

31 Herein is not only a great vanity, but a great contempt of God's good gifts, that the sweetness of man's breath, being a good gift of God, should be wilfully corrupted by this stinking smoke. *Ib.*

32 Dr. Donne's verses are like the peace of God; they pass all understanding.
Saying recorded by Archdeacon Plume (1630–1704)

HENRY JAMES
1843–1916

1 It takes a great deal of history to produce a little literature. *Life of Nathaniel Hawthorne*

2 [Thoreau] was worse than provincial—he was parochial. *Ib. ch. 4*

3 Dramatise, dramatise!
Prefaces. Altar of the Dead, and elsewhere

4 The note I wanted; that of the strange and sinister embroidered on the very type of the normal and easy. *Ib.*

5 The terrible *fluidity* of self-revelation.
Ib. The Ambassadors

6 The deep well of unconscious cerebration.
Ib. The American

7 The historian, essentially, wants more documents than he can really use; the dramatist only wants more liberties than he can really take.
Ib. The Aspern Papers, &c.

8 I have always fondly remembered a remark that I heard fall years ago from the lips of Ivan Turgenieff in regard to his own experience of the usual origin of the fictive picture. It began for him almost always with the vision of some person or persons, who hovered before him, soliciting him, as the active or passive figure, interesting him and appealing to him just as they were and by what they were. He saw them in that fashion, as *disponibles*, saw them subject to the chances, the complications of existence, and saw them vividly, but then had to find for them the right relations, those that would bring them out. *Ib. The Portrait of a Lady*

9 The fatal futility of Fact.
Ib. The Spoils of Poynton, &c.

10 The Real Right Thing. *Story-title*

11 The only obligation to which in advance we may hold a novel, without incurring the accusation of being arbitrary, is that it be interesting.
The Art of Fiction. Partial Portraits

12 Experience is never limited, and it is never complete; it is an immense sensibility, a kind of huge spider-web of the finest silken threads suspended in the chamber of consciousness, and catching every air-borne particle in its tissue. *Ib.*

13 What is character but the determination of incident? what is incident but the illustration of character?
Ib.

14 We must grant the artist his subject, his idea, his *donné*: our criticism is applied only to what he makes of it. *Ib.*

15 Vereker's secret, my dear man—the general intention of his books: the string the pearls were strung on, the buried treasure, the figure in the carpet.
The Figure in the Carpet, ch. 11

16 Cats and monkeys, monkeys and cats—all human life is there. *The Madonna of the Future*

17 Tennyson was not Tennysonian. *The Middle Years*

18 Print it as it stands—beautifully.
Terminations. The Death of the Lion, x

THOMAS JEFFERSON
1743–1826

19 We hold these truths to be sacred and undeniable; that all men are created equal and independent, that from that equal creation they derive rights inherent and inalienable, among which are the preservation of life, and liberty, and the pursuit of happiness.
Original draft for the *Declaration of Independence.* (*See 11:11*)

20 In the full tide of successful experiment.
First Inaugural Address, 4 March 1801

21 Peace, commerce, and honest friendship with all nations—entangling alliances with none. *Ib.*

22 A little rebellion now and then is a good thing.
Letter to James Madison, 30 Jan. 1787

23 The tree of liberty must be refreshed from time to time with the blood of patriots and tyrants. It is its natural manure.
Ib. To W. S. Smith, 13 Nov. 1787

24 Whenever a man has cast a longing eye on them [offices], a rottenness begins in his conduct.
Ib. To Tench Coxe, 1799

25 To seek out the best through the whole Union we must resort to other information, which, from the best of men, acting disinterestedly and with the purest motives, is sometimes incorrect.
Letter to Elias Shipman and others of New Haven, 12 July 1801

26 If a due participation of office is a matter of right, how are vacancies to be obtained? Those by death are few; by resignation, none.
Usually quoted, 'Few die and none resign'. *Ib.*

27 Indeed I tremble for my country when I reflect that God is just.
Notes on Virginia, Query xviii. Manners

28 When a man assumes a public trust, he should consider himself as public property.
Remark to Baron von Humboldt, 1807. Rayner's Life of Jefferson, p. 356

29 No duty the Executive had to perform was so trying as to put the right man in the right place.
J. B. MacMaster, *History of the People of the U.S.*; vol. ii, ch. 13, p. 586

CHARLES JEFFERYS
1807–1865

30 I have heard the mavis singing
His love-song to the morn;
I have seen the dew-drop clinging
To the rose just newly born. *Mary of Argyle*

FRANCIS, LORD JEFFREY
1773–1850

31 This will never do.
On Wordsworth's '*Excursion*'. *Edinburgh Review, Nov. 1814, p. 1*

JEROME KLAPKA JEROME
1859–1927

32 It is impossible to enjoy idling thoroughly unless one has plenty of work to do.
Idle Thoughts of an Idle Fellow. On Being Idle

1 Love is like the measles; we all have to go through it.
Idle Thoughts of an Idle Fellow. On Being in Love

2 George goes to sleep at a bank from ten to four each day, except Saturdays, when they wake him up and put him outside at two.
Three Men in a Boat, ch. 2

3 But there, everything has its drawbacks, as the man said when his mother-in-law died, and they came down on him for the funeral expenses. *Ib.* ch. 3

4 My tooth-brush is a thing that haunts me when I'm travelling, and makes my life a misery. *Ib.* ch. 4

5 I like work: it fascinates me. I can sit and look at it for hours. I love to keep it by me: the idea of getting rid of it nearly breaks my heart. *Ib.* ch. 15

6 The Passing of the Third Floor Back. *Title of play*

DOUGLAS WILLIAM JERROLD
1803–1857

7 Honest bread is very well—it's the butter that makes the temptation. *The Catspaw*, Act III

8 Religion's in the heart, not in the knees.
The Devil's Ducat, I. ii

9 Mrs. Caudle's Curtain Lectures. *Title of Book*

10 He is one of those wise philanthropists who, in a time of famine, would vote for nothing but a supply of toothpicks.
Wit and Opinions of Douglas Jerrold (1859), p. 2.
A Philanthropist

11 Love's like the measles—all the worse when it comes late in life. *Ib.* p. 6

12 The best thing I know between France and England is—the sea. *Ib.* p. 13. *The Anglo-French Alliance*

13 That fellow would vulgarize the day of judgment.
Ib. A Comic Author

14 The ugliest of trades have their moments of pleasure. Now, if I were a grave-digger, or even a hangman, there are some people I could work for with a great deal of enjoyment. *Ib.* p. 14. *Ugly Trades*

15 Earth is here [Australia] so kind, that just tickle her with a hoe and she laughs with a harvest.
Ib. A Land of Plenty

16 Some people are so fond of ill-luck that they run half-way to meet it.
Ib. Meeting Troubles Half-way

17 He was so good he would pour rose-water over a toad. *Ib.* p. 17. *A Charitable Man*

18 Talk to him of Jacob's ladder, and he would ask the number of the steps.
Ib. p. 29. *A Matter-of-fact Man*

19 We love peace, as we abhor pusillanimity; but not peace at any price. There is a peace more destructive of the manhood of living man than war is destructive of his material body. Chains are worse than bayonets. *Ib.* p. 155. *Peace*

20 If an earthquake were to engulf England to-morrow, the English would manage to meet and dine somewhere among the rubbish, just to celebrate the event.
Remark. Blanchard Jerrold's *Life of D. Jerrold*, ch. 14

21 The only athletic sport I ever mastered was back-gammon.
W. Jerrold, *Douglas Jerrold* (1914), vol. i, ch. 1, p. 22

BISHOP JOHN JEWEL
1522–1571

22 In old time we had treen chalices and golden priests, but now we have treen priests and golden chalices.
Certain Sermons Preached Before the Queen's Majesty, 1609, p. 176

JOHN OF SALISBURY
see
SALISBURY

ANDREW JOHNSON
1808–1875

23 We are swinging round the circle.
Speech on the Presidential Reconstruction, August 1866

LIONEL PIGOT JOHNSON
1867–1902

24 There Shelley dream'd his white Platonic dreams.
Oxford

25 In her ears the chime
Of full, sad bells brings back her old springtide. *Ib.*

26 I know you: solitary griefs,
Desolate passions, aching hours.
The Precept of Silence

27 The saddest of all Kings
Crown'd, and again discrown'd.
By the Statue of King Charles I at Charing Cross

28 Stars in their stations set;
And every wandering star. *Ib.*

29 The fair and fatal King. *Ib.*

30 Speak after sentence? Yea:
And to the end of time. *Ib.*

31 King, tried in fires of woe!
Men hunger for thy grace:
And through the night I go,
Loving thy mournful face. *Ib.*

PHILANDER CHASE JOHNSON
1866–

32 Cheer up, the worst is yet to come.
Shooting Stars. See *Everybody's Magazine*, May 1920

SAMUEL JOHNSON
1709–1784

33 The rod produces an effect which terminates in itself. A child is afraid of being whipped, and gets his task, and there's an end on't; whereas, by exciting emulation and comparisons of superiority, you lay the foundation of lasting mischief; you make brothers and sisters hate each other.
Boswell's *Life of Johnson* (L. F. Powell's *revision of G. B. Hill's edition*), vol. i, p. 46

1 **In** my early years I read very hard. It is a sad reflection, but a true one, that I knew almost as much at eighteen as I do now.
Boswell's *Life of Johnson*, vol. i, p. 56. *20 July 1763*

2 *Johnson*: I had no notion that I was wrong or irreverent to my tutor.
Boswell: That, Sir, was great fortitude of mind.
Johnson: No, Sir; stark insensibility.
Ib. p. 60. 5 Nov. 1728

3 Sir, we are a nest of singing birds. *Ib. p. 75. 1730*

4 If you call a dog *Hervey*, I shall love him.
Ib. p. 106. 1737

5 My old friend, Mrs. Carter, could make a pudding as well as translate Epictetus. *Ib. p. 123 n. 1738*

6 Sleep, undisturb'd, within this peaceful shrine,
Till angels wake thee with a note like thine!
Ib. p. 149. 1741

7 Great George's acts let tuneful Cibber sing;
For Nature form'd the Poet for the King. *Ib.*

8 Tom Birch is as brisk as a bee in conversation; but no sooner does he take a pen in his hand, than it becomes a torpedo to him, and benumbs all his faculties. *Ib. p. 159. 1743*

9 [When asked how he felt upon the ill success of *Irene*]
Like the Monument. *Ib. p. 199. Feb. 1749*

10 I'll come no more behind your scenes, David; for the silk stockings and white bosoms of your actresses excite my amorous propensities. *Ib. p. 201. 1750*

11 A man may write at any time, if he will set himself doggedly to it. *Ib. p. 203. Mar. 1750*

12 [Of F. Lewis]
Sir, he lived in London, and hung loose upon society.
Ib. p. 226. 1750

13 [To Beauclerk]
Thy body is all vice, and thy mind all virtue.
Ib. p. 250. 1752

14 [On being knocked up at 3 a.m. by Beauclerk and Langton]
What, is it you, you dogs! I'll have a frisk with you.
Ib.

15 Wretched un-idea'd girls. *Ib. p. 251. 1753*

16 I had done all I could; and no man is well pleased to have his all neglected, be it ever so little.
Ib. p. 261. Letter to Lord Chesterfield, 7 Feb. 1755

17 The shepherd in Virgil grew at last acquainted with Love, and found him a native of the rocks. *Ib.*

18 Is not a Patron, my Lord, one who looks with unconcern on a man struggling for life in the water, and, when he has reached ground, encumbers him with help? The notice which you have been pleased to take of my labours, had it been early, had been kind; but it has been delayed till I am indifferent, and cannot enjoy it; till I am solitary, and cannot impart it; till I am known, and do not want it. *Ib.*

19 A fly, Sir, may sting a stately horse and make him wince; but one is but an insect, and the other is a horse still. *Ib. p. 263, n. 3*

20 [Of Lord Chesterfield]
This man I thought had been a Lord among wits; but, I find, he is only a wit among Lords.
Ib. p. 266. 1754

21 [Of Lord Chesterfield's *Letters*]
They teach the morals of a whore, and the manners of a dancing master. Boswell's *Life*, vol. i, p. 266. *1754*

22 [Of Bolingbroke and his editor, Mallet]
Sir, he was a scoundrel, and a coward: a scoundrel, for charging a blunderbuss against religion and morality; a coward, because he had not resolution to fire it off himself, but left half a crown to a beggarly Scotchman, to draw the trigger after his death! *Ib. p. 268. 6 Mar. 1754*

23 Mr. Millar, bookseller, undertook the publication of Johnson's Dictionary. When the messenger who carried the last sheet to Millar returned, Johnson asked him, 'Well, what did he say?' 'Sir,' answered the messenger, 'he said, thank God I have done with him.'
'I am glad', replied Johnson, with a smile, 'that he thanks God for any thing.' *Ib. p. 287. Apr. 1755*

24 I respect Millar, Sir; he has raised the price of literature. *Ib. p. 288. 1755*

25 There are two things which I am confident I can do very well: one is an introduction to any literary work, stating what it is to contain, and how it should be executed in the most perfect manner; the other is a conclusion, shewing from various causes why the execution has not been equal to what the author promised to himself and to the public. *Ib. p. 292. 1755*

26 [When asked by a lady why he defined 'pastern' as the 'knee' of a horse, in his Dictionary]
Ignorance, madam, pure ignorance. *Ib. p. 293. 1755*

27 Lexicographer: a writer of dictionaries, a harmless drudge. *Ib. p. 296. 1755*

28 I have protracted my work till most of those whom I wished to please have sunk into the grave; and success and miscarriage are empty sounds.
Ib. p. 297. 1755

29 A man, Sir, should keep his friendship in constant repair. *Ib. p. 300. 1755*

30 The booksellers are generous liberal-minded men.
Ib. p. 304. 1756

31 The worst of Warburton is, that he has a rage for saying something, when there's nothing to be said.
Ib. p. 329. 1758

32 No man will be a sailor who has contrivance enough to get himself into a jail; for being in a ship is being in a jail, with the chance of being drowned. . . . A man in a jail has more room, better food, and commonly better company. *Ib. p. 348. 16 Mar. 1759*

33 'Are you a botanist, Dr. Johnson?'
'No, Sir, I am not a botanist; and (alluding, no doubt, to his near sightedness) should I wish to become a botanist, I must first turn myself into a reptile.'
Ib. p. 377. 20 July 1762

34 *Boswell*: I do indeed come from Scotland, but I cannot help it. . . .
Johnson: That, Sir, I find, is what a very great many of your countrymen cannot help.
Ib. p. 392. 16 May 1763

35 When a butcher tells you that *his heart bleeds for his country* he has, in fact, no uneasy feeling.
Ib. p. 394. 16 May 1763

1 [On Dr. Blair's asking whether any man of a modern age could have written *Ossian*]
Yes, Sir, many men, many women, and many children.   Boswell's *Life*, vol. i, p. 396. *24 May 1763*

2 Sir, it was like leading one to talk of a book when the author is concealed behind the door.   *Ib.*

3 He insisted on people praying with him; and I'd as lief pray with Kit Smart as any one else.
Ib. p. 397. *24 May 1763*

4 [Of Kit Smart]
He did not love clean linen; and I have no passion for it.   *Ib.*

5 [Of literary criticism]
You may scold a carpenter who has made you a bad table, though you cannot make a table.   It is not your trade to make tables.   *Ib.* p. 409. *25 June 1763*

6 [Of Dr. John Campbell]
I am afraid he has not been in the inside of a church for many years; but he never passes a church without pulling off his hat.   This shews that he has good principles.   *Ib.* p. 418. *1 July 1763*

7 [Of Dr. John Campbell]
He is the richest author that ever grazed the common of literature.   *Ib.* n.

8 Norway, too, has noble wild prospects; and Lapland is remarkable for prodigious noble wild prospects. But, Sir, let me tell you, the noblest prospect which a Scotchman ever sees, is the high road that leads him to England!   *Ib.* p. 425. *6 July 1763*

9 A man ought to read just as inclination leads him; for what he reads as a task will do him little good.
Ib. p. 428. *14 July 1763*

10 But if he does really think that there is no distinction between virtue and vice, why, Sir, when he leaves our houses let us count our spoons.
Ib. p. 432. *14 July 1763*

11 Truth, Sir, is a cow, which will yield such people [sceptics] no more milk, and so they are gone to milk the bull.   *Ib.* p. 444. *21 July 1763*

12 Your levellers wish to level *down* as far as themselves; but they cannot bear levelling *up* to themselves.
Ib. p. 448. *21 July 1763*

13 Sir, it is no matter what you teach them [children] first, any more than what leg you shall put into your breeches first.   *Ib.* p. 452. *26 July 1763*

14 Why, Sir, Sherry [Thomas Sheridan] is dull, naturally dull; but it must have taken him a great deal of pains to become what we now see him.   Such an excess of stupidity, Sir, is not in Nature.
Ib. p. 453. *28 July 1763*

15 [Of Thomas Sheridan's influence on the English language]
Sir, it is burning a farthing candle at Dover, to shew light at Calais.   *Ib.* p. 454. *28 July 1763*

16 Sir, a woman's preaching is like a dog's walking on his hinder legs.   It is not done well; but you are surprised to find it done at all.
Ib. p. 463. *31 July 1763*

17 I look upon it, that he who does not mind his belly will hardly mind anything else.
Ib. p. 467. *5 Aug. 1763*

18 This was a good dinner enough, to be sure; but it was not a dinner to *ask* a man to.
Boswell's *Life*, vol. i, p. 470. *5 Aug. 1763*

19 Sir, we could not have had a better dinner had there been a *Synod of Cooks*.   *Ib.*

20 [Boswell happened to say it would be terrible if Johnson should not find a speedy opportunity of returning to London, from Harwich]
Don't, Sir, accustom yourself to use big words for little matters.   It would *not* be *terrible*, though I *were* to be detained some time here.
Ib. p. 471. *6 Aug. 1763*

21 [Talking of Bishop Berkeley's theory of the non-existence of matter, Boswell observed that though they were satisfied it was not true, they were unable to refute it.   Johnson struck his foot against a large stone, till he rebounded from it, saying]
I refute it *thus*.   *Ib.*

22 [Of Sir John Hawkins]
A very unclubable man.   *Ib.* p. 480 n. *1764*

23 Our tastes greatly alter.   The lad does not care for the child's rattle, and the old man does not care for the young man's whore.
Ib. vol. ii, p. 14. *Spring, 1766*

24 It was not for me to bandy civilities with my Sovereign.   *Ib.* p. 35. *Feb. 1767*

25 Sir, I love Robertson, and I won't talk of his book.
Ib. p. 53. *1768*

26 *Johnson*: Well, we had a good talk.
Boswell: Yes, Sir; you tossed and gored several persons.   *Ib.* p. 66. *1769*

27 Let me smile with the wise, and feed with the rich.
Ib. p. 79. *6 Oct. 1769*

28 Sir, We *know* our will is free, and *there's* an end on't.
Ib. p. 82. *16 Oct. 1769*

29 Inspissated gloom.   *Ib.*

30 I do not know, Sir, that the fellow is an infidel; but if he be an infidel, he is an infidel as a dog is an infidel; that is to say, he has never thought upon the subject.   *Ib.* p. 95. *19 Oct. 1769*

31 Shakespeare never had six lines together without a fault.   Perhaps you may find seven, but this does not refute my general assertion.
Ib. p. 96. *19 Oct. 1769*

32 I would not *coddle* the child.
Ib. p. 101. *26 Oct. 1769*

33 Let fanciful men do as they will, depend upon it, it is difficult to disturb the system of life.
Ib. p. 102. *26 Oct. 1769*

34 *Boswell*: So, Sir, you laugh at schemes of political improvement?
Johnson: Why, Sir, most schemes of political improvement are very laughable things.   *Ib.*

35 It matters not how a man dies, but how he lives.
Ib. p. 106. *26 Oct. 1769*

36 Burton's *Anatomy of Melancholy*, he said, was the only book that ever took him out of bed two hours sooner than he wished to rise.   *Ib.* p. 121. *1770*

1 [On Jonas Hanway, who followed his *Travels to Persia* with *An Eight Day's Journey from London to Portsmouth*]
Jonas acquired some reputation by travelling abroad, but lost it all by travelling at home.
Boswell's Life of Johnson, vol. ii, p. 122. *1770*

2 Want of tenderness is want of parts, and is no less a proof of stupidity than depravity. *Ib.*

3 That fellow seems to me to possess but one idea, and that is a wrong one. *Ib.* p. 126. *1770*

4 A gentleman who had been very unhappy in marriage, married immediately after his wife died: Johnson said, it was the triumph of hope over experience.
Ib. p. 128. *1770*

5 Every man has a lurking wish to appear considerable in his native place.
Ib. p. 141. *Letter to Sir Joshua Reynolds, 17 July 1771*

6 It is so far from being natural for a man and woman to live in a state of marriage that we find all the motives which they have for remaining in that connection, and the restraints which civilized society imposes to prevent separation, are hardly sufficient to keep them together. *Ib.* p. 165. *31 Mar. 1772*

7 Nobody can write the life of a man, but those who have eat and drunk and lived in social intercourse with him. *Ib.* p. 166. *31 Mar. 1772*

8 I would not give half a guinea to live under one form of government rather than another. It is of no moment to the happiness of an individual.
Ib. p. 170. *31 Mar. 1772*

9 [To Sir Adam Fergusson]
Sir, I perceive you are a vile Whig. *Ib.*

10 There is a remedy in human nature against tyranny, that will keep us safe under every form of government. *Ib.*

11 A man who is good enough to go to heaven, is good enough to be a clergyman. *Ib.* p. 171. *5 Apr. 1772*

12 Sir, there is more knowledge of the heart in one letter of Richardson's, than in all *Tom Jones*.
Ib. p. 174. *6 Apr. 1772*

13 Why, Sir, if you were to read Richardson for the story, your impatience would be so much fretted that you would hang yourself.
Ib. p. 175. *6 Apr. 1772*

14 [On Lord Mansfield, who was educated in England]
Much may be made of a Scotchman, if he be *caught* young. *Ib.* p. 194. *Spring 1772*

15 [On Goldsmith's apology in the *London Chronicle* for beating Evans the bookseller]
It is a foolish thing well done.
Ib. p. 210. *3 Apr. 1773*

16 *Elphinston*: What, have you not read it through? . . .
Johnson: No, Sir, do *you* read books *through*?
Ib. p. 226. *19 Apr. 1773*

17 [Quoting a college tutor]
Read over your compositions, and where ever you meet with a passage which you think is particularly fine, strike it out. *Ib.* p. 237. *30 Apr. 1773*

18 He [Goldsmith] is now writing a Natural History and will make it as entertaining as a Persian Tale. *Ib.*

19 [Of Lady Diana Beauclerk]
The woman's a whore, and there's an end on't.
Boswell's Life, vol. ii, p. 247. *7 May 1773*

20 I hope I shall never be deterred from detecting what I think a cheat, by the menaces of a ruffian.
Ib. p. 298. *Letter to James Macpherson, 20 Jan. 1775*

21 [To Dr. Barnard, Bishop of Killaloe]
The Irish are a fair people;—they never speak well of one another. *Ib.* p. 307. *1775*

22 [To William Strahan]
There are few ways in which a man can be more innocently employed than in getting money.
Ib. p. 323. *27 Mar. 1775*

23 He [Thomas Gray] was dull in a new way, and that made many people think him *great*.
Ib. p. 327. *28 Mar. 1775*

24 I never think I have hit hard, unless it rebounds.
Ib. p. 335. *2 Apr. 1775*

25 I think the full tide of human existence is at Charing-Cross. *Ib.* p. 337. *2 Apr. 1775*

26 Most vices may be committed very genteelly: a man may debauch his friend's wife genteelly: he may cheat at cards genteelly. *Ib.* p. 340. *6 Apr. 1775*

27 George the First knew nothing, and desired to know nothing; did nothing, and desired to do nothing; and the only good thing that is told of him is, that he wished to restore the crown to its hereditary successor. *Ib.* p. 342. *6 Apr. 1775*

28 A man will turn over half a library to make one book.
Ib. p. 344. *6 Apr. 1775*

29 Patriotism is the last refuge of a scoundrel.
Ib. p. 348. *7 Apr. 1775*

30 That is the happiest conversation where there is no competition, no vanity, but a calm quiet interchange of sentiments. *Ib.* p. 359. *14 Apr. 1775*

31 [On the Scotch]
Their learning is like bread in a besieged town: every man gets a little, but no man gets a full meal.
Ib. p. 363. *18 Apr. 1775*

32 Knowledge is of two kinds. We know a subject ourselves, or we know where we can find information upon it. *Ib.* p. 365. *18 Apr. 1775*

33 Politics are now nothing more than a means of rising in the world. *Ib.* p. 369. *1775*

34 Players, Sir! I look upon them as no better than creatures set upon tables and joint stools to make faces and produce laughter, like dancing dogs.
Ib. p. 404. *1775*

35 In lapidary inscriptions a man is not upon oath.
Ib. p. 407. *1775*

36 There is now less flogging in our great schools than formerly, but then less is learned there; so that what the boys get at one end they lose at the other. *Ib.*

37 When men come to like a sea-life, they are not fit to live on land. *Ib.* p. 438. *18 Mar. 1776*

38 Sir, it is a great thing to dine with the Canons of Christ-Church. *Ib.* p. 445. *20 Mar. 1776*

39 There is nothing which has yet been contrived by man, by which so much happiness is produced as by a good tavern or inn. *Ib.* p. 452. *21 Mar. 1776*

1 Marriages would in general be as happy, and often more so, if they were all made by the Lord Chancellor.   Boswell's *Life*, vol. ii, p. 461. *22 Mar. 1776*

2 Questioning is not the mode of conversation among gentlemen.   *Ib.* p. 472. *Mar. 1776*

3 Fine clothes are good only as they supply the want of other means of procuring respect.
Ib. p. 475. *27 Mar. 1776*

4 [Johnson had observed that a man is never happy for the present, but when he is drunk, and Boswell said: 'Will you not add,—or when driving rapidly in a post-chaise?']
No, Sir, you are driving rapidly *from* something, or *to* something.   *Ib.* vol. iii, p. 5. *29 Mar. 1776*

5 If a madman were to come into this room with a stick in his hand, no doubt we should pity the state of his mind; but our primary consideration would be to take care of ourselves. We should knock him down first, and pity him afterwards.
Ib. p. 11. *3 Apr. 1776*

6 Consider, Sir, how should you like, though conscious of your innocence, to be tried before a jury for a capital crime, once a week.   *Ib.*

7 We would all be idle if we could.
Ib. p. 13. *3 Apr. 1776*

8 No man but a blockhead ever wrote, except for money.   *Ib.* p. 19. *5 Apr. 1776*

9 It is better that some should be unhappy than that none should be happy, which would be the case in a general state of equality. *Ib.* p. 26. *7 Apr. 1776*

10 His [Lord Shelburne's] parts, Sir, are pretty well for a Lord; but would not be distinguished in a man who had nothing else but his parts.
Ib. p. 35. *11 Apr. 1776*

11 A man who has not been in Italy, is always conscious of an inferiority.   *Ib.* p. 36. *11 Apr. 1776*

12 'Does not Gray's poetry tower above the common mark?'
'Yes, Sir, but we must attend to the difference between what men in general cannot do if they would, and what every man may do if he would. Sixteen-string Jack towered above the common mark.'
Ib. p. 38. *12 Apr. 1776*

13 'Sir, what is poetry?'
'Why, Sir, it is much easier to say what it is not. We all *know* what light is; but it is not easy to *tell* what it is.'   *Ib.*

14 [To Mrs. Thrale, who had interrupted him and Boswell by a lively extravagant sally on the expense of clothing children]
Nay, Madam, when you are declaiming, declaim; and when you are calculating, calculate.
Ib. p. 49. *26 Apr. 1776*

15 Every man of any education would rather be called a rascal, than accused of deficiency in *the graces*.
Ib. p. 54. *May 1776*

16 Sir, you have but two topics, yourself and me. I am sick of both.   *Ib.* p. 57. *May 1776*

17 Dine with Jack Wilkes, Sir! I'd as soon dine with Jack Ketch.   *Ib.* p. 66. *15 May 1776*

18 Sir, it is not so much to be lamented that Old England is lost, as that the Scotch have found it.
Ib. p. 78. *15 May 1776*

19 Olivarii Goldsmith, Poetae, Physici, Historici, Qui nullum fere scribendi genus non tetigit, Nullum quod tetigit non ornavit.
To Oliver Goldsmith, A Poet, Naturalist, and Historian, who left scarcely any style of writing untouched, and touched nothing that he did not adorn.
Boswell's *Life*, vol. iii, p. 82. *22 June 1776.*
Epitaph on Goldsmith

20 That distrust which intrudes so often on your mind is a mode of melancholy, which, if it be the business of a wise man to be happy, it is foolish to indulge; and if it be a duty to preserve our faculties entire for their proper use, it is criminal.
Ib. p. 135. *Letter to Boswell, 11 Sept. 1777*

21 If I had no duties, and no reference to futurity, I would spend my life in driving briskly in a post-chaise with a pretty woman.
Ib. p. 162. *19 Sept. 1777*

22 Depend upon it, Sir, when a man knows he is to be hanged in a fortnight, it concentrates his mind wonderfully.   *Ib.* p. 167. *19 Sept. 1777*

23 No, Sir, when a man is tired of London, he is tired of life; for there is in London all that life can afford.
Ib. p. 178. *20 Sept. 1777*

24 He was so generally civil, that nobody thanked him for it.   *Ib.* p. 183. *21 Sept. 1777*

25 He who praises everybody praises nobody.
Ib. p. 225 n.

26 Round numbers are always false.
Ib. p. 226, n. 4. *30 Mar. 1778.* Wks. *1787*

27 Accustom your children (said he) constantly to this; if a thing happened at one window and they, when relating it, say that it happened at another, do not let it pass, but instantly check them; you do not know where deviation from truth will end.
Ib. p. 228. *31 Mar. 1778*

28 [Of the appearance of the spirit of a person after death]
All argument is against it; but all belief is for it.
Ib. p. 230. *31 Mar. 1778*

29 John Wesley's conversation is good, but he is never at leisure. He is always obliged to go at a certain hour. This is very disagreeable to a man who loves to fold his legs and have out his talk, as I do.   *Ib.*

30 Though we cannot out-vote them we will out-argue them.   *Ib.* p. 234. *3 Apr. 1778*

31 [To a clergyman who asked: 'Were not Dodd's sermons addressed to the passions?']
They were nothing, Sir, be they addressed to what they may.   *Ib.* p. 248. *7 Apr. 1778*

32 Seeing Scotland, Madam, is only seeing a worse England.   *Ib.*

33 Goldsmith, however, was a man, who, whatever he wrote, did it better than any other man could do.
Ib. p. 253. *9 Apr. 1778*

34 Every man thinks meanly of himself for not having been a soldier, or not having been at sea.
Ib. p. 265. *10 Apr. 1778*

35 A mere antiquarian is a rugged being.
Ib. p. 278. *Letter to Boswell, 23 Apr. 1778*

1 Johnson had said that he could repeat a complete chapter of 'The Natural History of Iceland', from the Danish of Horrebow, the whole of which was exactly thus:—'CHAP. LXXII. *Concerning snakes.* 'There are no snakes to be met with throughout the whole island.'
Boswell's *Life of Johnson*, vol. iii, p. 279. *13 Apr. 1778*

2 A country governed by a despot is an inverted cone.
Ib. p. 283. *14 Apr. 1778*

3 I am willing to love all mankind, *except an American.*
Ib. p. 290. *15 Apr. 1778*

4 As the Spanish proverb says, 'He, who would bring home the wealth of the Indies, must carry the wealth of the Indies with him.' So it is in travelling; a man must carry knowledge with him, if he would bring home knowledge.
Ib. p. 302. *17 Apr. 1778*

5 All censure of a man's self is oblique praise. It is in order to shew how much he can spare.
Ib. p. 323. *25 Apr. 1778*

6 [On Boswell's expressing surprise at finding a Staffordshire Whig]
Sir, there are rascals in all countries.
Ib. p. 326. *28 Apr. 1778*

7 I have always said, the first Whig was the Devil. *Ib.*

8 It is thus that mutual cowardice keeps us in peace. Were one half of mankind brave and one half cowards, the brave would be always beating the cowards. Were all brave, they would lead a very uneasy life; all would be continually fighting; but being all cowards, we go on very well. *Ib.*

9 The King of Siam sent ambassadors to Louis XIV, but Louis XIV sent none to the King of Siam.
Ib. p. 336. *29 Apr. 1778*

10 Were it not for imagination, Sir, a man would be as happy in the arms of a chambermaid as of a Duchess. *Ib.* p. 341. *9 May 1778*

11 Dr. Mead lived more in the broad sunshine of life than almost any man. *Ib.* p. 355. *16 May 1778*

12 Claret is the liquor for boys; port for men; but he who aspires to be a hero must drink brandy.
Ib. p. 381. *7 Apr. 1779*

13 A man who exposes himself when he is intoxicated, has not the art of getting drunk.
Ib. p. 389. *24 Apr. 1779*

14 Remember that all tricks are either knavish or childish.
Ib. p. 396. *Letter to Boswell, 9 Sept. 1779*

15 *Boswell*: Is not the Giant's-Causeway worth seeing? *Johnson*: Worth seeing? yes; but not worth going to see. *Ib.* p. 410. *12 Oct. 1779*

16 If you are idle, be not solitary; if you are solitary, be not idle.
Ib. p. 415. *Letter to Boswell, 27 Oct. 1779*

17 Sir, among the anfractuosities of the human mind, I know not if it may not be one, that there is a superstitious reluctance to sit for a picture.
Ib. vol. iv, p. 4. *1780*

18 [Of Kitty Clive]
Clive, sir, is a good thing to sit by; she always understands what you say. *Ib.* p. 7. *1780*

19 [On being asked why Pope had written:
Let modest Foster, if he will, excel
Ten metropolitans in preaching well]
Sir, he hoped it would vex somebody.
Boswell's *Life*, vol. iv, p. 9. *1780*

20 A Frenchman must be always talking, whether he knows anything of the matter or not; an Englishman is content to say nothing, when he has nothing to say. *Ib.* p. 15. *1780*

21 Greek, Sir, is like lace; every man gets as much of it as he can. *Ib.* p. 23. *1780*

22 Are we alive after all this satire! *Ib.* p. 29. *1780*

23 [Of Goldsmith]
No man was more foolish when he had not a pen in his hand, or more wise when he had. *Ib.*

24 Depend upon it that if a man talks of his misfortunes there is something in them that is not disagreeable to him; for where there is nothing but pure misery there never is any recourse to the mention of it.
Ib. p. 31. *1780*

25 [Mr. Fowke once observed to Dr. Johnson that, in his opinion, the Doctor's literary strength lay in writing biography, in which he infinitely exceeded all his contemporaries]
'Sir', said Johnson, 'I believe that is true. The dogs don't know how to write trifles with dignity.'
Ib. p. 34. n. 5

26 Mrs. Montagu has dropt me. Now, Sir, there are people whom one should like very well to drop, but would not wish to be dropped by.
Ib. p. 73. *Mar. 1781*

27 This merriment of parsons is mighty offensive.
Ib. p. 76. *Mar. 1781*

28 [Of Lord North]
He fills a chair. *Ib.* p. 81. *1 Apr. 1781*

29 [At the sale of Thrale's brewery]
We are not here to sell a parcel of boilers and vats, but the potentiality of growing rich, beyond the dreams of avarice. *Ib.* p. 87. *6 Apr. 1781*

30 'The woman had a bottom of good sense.'
The word '*bottom*' thus introduced, was so ludicrous, . . . that most of us could not forbear tittering . . .
'Where's the merriment? . . . I say the *woman* was *fundamentally* sensible.' *Ib.* p. 99. *20 Apr. 1781*

31 Classical quotation is the *parole* of literary men all over the world. *Ib.* p. 102. *8 May 1781*

32 [To Miss Monckton, afterwards Lady Corke, who said that Sterne's writings affected her]
Why, that is, because, dearest, you're a dunce.
Ib. p. 109. *May 1781*

33 Sir, I have two very cogent reasons for not printing any list of subscribers;—one, that I have lost all the names,—the other, that I have spent all the money. *Ib.* p. 111. *May 1781*

34 My friend [Johnson] was of opinion, that when a man of rank appeared in that character [as an author], he deserved to have his merit handsomely allowed.
Ib. p. 114. *May 1781*

35 A wise Tory and a wise Whig, I believe, will agree. Their principles are the same, though their modes of thinking are different.
Ib. p. 117. *Written statement given to Boswell, May 1781*

1 Officious, innocent, sincere,
Of every friendless name the friend.

Yet still he fills affection's eye,
Obscurely wise, and coarsely kind.
  Boswell's Life, vol. iv, p. 127. *20 Jan. 1782.*
  On the death of Mr. Levett

2 In Misery's darkest caverns known,
His ready help was ever nigh.   *Ib.*

3 His virtues walk'd their narrow round,
Nor made a pause, nor left a void;
And sure th' Eternal Master found
His single talent well employ'd.   *Ib.*

4 Then, with no throbs of fiery pain,
No cold gradations of decay,
Death broke at once the vital chain,
And freed his soul the nearest way.   *Ib.*

5 Resolve not to be poor: whatever you have, spend less.
Poverty is a great enemy to human happiness; it certainly destroys liberty, and it makes some virtues impracticable and others extremely difficult.
    Ib. p. 157. 7 Dec. 1782

6 I never have sought the world; the world was not to seek me.   *Ib. p. 172. 23 Mar. 1783*

7 Thurlow is a fine fellow; he fairly puts his mind to yours.   *Ib. p. 179. 1783*

8 [Of Ossian]
Sir, a man might write such stuff for ever, if he would *abandon* his mind to it. *Ib. p. 183. 1783*

9 [When Dr. Adam Smith was expatiating on the beauty of Glasgow, Johnson had cut him short by saying, 'Pray, Sir, have you ever seen Brentford?']
Boswell: My dear Sir, surely that was *shocking*?
Johnson: Why, then, Sir, *you* have never seen Brentford.   *Ib. p. 186. 1783*

10 [To Maurice Morgann who asked him whether he reckoned Derrick or Smart the better poet]
Sir, there is no settling the point of precedency between a louse and a flea. *Ib. p. 192. 1783*

11 When I observed he was a fine cat, saying, 'why yes, Sir, but I have had cats whom I liked better than this'; and then as if perceiving Hodge to be out of countenance, adding, 'but he is a very fine cat, a very fine cat indeed.'   *Ib. p. 197. 1783*

12 [Johnson had said 'public affairs vex no man', and Boswell had suggested that the growing power of the Whigs vexed Johnson]
Sir, I have never slept an hour less, nor eat an ounce less meat. I would have knocked the factious dogs on the head, to be sure; but I was not *vexed*.
    Ib. p. 220. 15 May 1783

13 Clear your *mind* of cant. *Ib. p. 221. 15 May 1783*

14 Sir, he is a cursed Whig, a *bottomless* Whig, as they all are now.   *Ib. p. 223. 26 May 1783*

15 As I know more of mankind I expect less of them, and am ready now to call a man *a good man*, upon easier terms than I was formerly.
    Ib. p. 239. Sept. 1783

16 Boswell is a very clubable man. *Ib. p. 254 n. 1783*

17 [Of George Psalmanazar, whom he reverenced for his piety]
I should as soon think of contradicting a Bishop.
    Ib. p. 274. 15 May 1784

18 [To Bennet Langton who brought him texts on Christian charity when he was ill]
What is your drift, Sir?
  Boswell's Life, vol. iv, p. 281. *30 May 1784*

19 [On the roast mutton he had for dinner at an inn]
It is as bad as bad can be: it is ill-fed, ill-killed, ill-kept, and ill-drest. *Ib. p. 284. 3 June 1784*

20 *Johnson*: As I cannot be sure that I have fulfilled the conditions on which salvation is granted, I am afraid I may be one of those who shall be damned (looking dismally).
Dr Adams: What do you mean by damned?
Johnson (passionately and loudly): Sent to Hell, Sir, and punished everlastingly. *Ib. p. 299. 1784*

21 [To Miss Hannah More, who had expressed a wonder that the poet who had written *Paradise Lost* should write such poor Sonnets]
Milton, Madam, was a genius that could cut a Colossus from a rock; but could not carve heads upon cherry-stones. *Ib. p. 305. 13 June 1784*

22 Don't cant in defence of savages.
    Ib. p. 308. 15 June 1784

23 [On hearing the line in Brooke's *Earl of Essex*
'Who rules o'er freemen should himself be free']
It might as well be 'Who drives fat oxen should himself be fat.'   *Ib. p. 313. June 1784*

24 Sir, I have found you an argument; but I am not obliged to find you an understanding.   *Ib.*

25 [On Sir Joshua Reynolds's observing that the real character of a man was found out by his amusements]
Yes, Sir; no man is a hypocrite in his pleasures.
    Ib. p. 316. June 1784

26 Blown about by every wind of criticism.
    Ib. p. 319. June 1784

27 Talking of the Comedy of 'The Rehearsal', he [Johnson] said, 'It has not wit enough to keep it sweet.' This was easy;—he therefore caught himself, and pronounced a more rounded sentence; 'It has not vitality enough to preserve it from putrefaction.'   *Ib. p. 320. June 1784*

28 Who can run the race with Death?
  Ib. p. 360. Letter to Dr. Burney, 2 Aug. 1784

29 Sir, I look upon every day to be lost, in which I do not make a new acquaintance. *Ib. p. 374. Nov. 1784*

30 I will be conquered; I will not capitulate. *Ib.*

31 Are you sick or are you sullen?
  Ib. p. 380. Letter to Boswell, 3 Nov. 1784

32 A lawyer has no business with the justice or injustice of the cause which he undertakes, unless his client asks his opinion, and then he is bound to give it honestly. The justice or injustice of the cause is to be decided by the judge.
  Boswell, Tour to the Hebrides, 15 Aug. 1773, p. 175

33 Let him go abroad to a distant country; let him go to some place where he is *not* known. Don't let him go to the devil where he is known!
    Ib. 18 Aug., p. 194

34 I wonder, however, that so many people have written who might have let it alone. *Ib. 19 Aug.,* p. 197

1 [To Boswell who would excuse Sir Alexander Gordon's boring of them by saying it was all kindness]
True, Sir; but sensation is sensation.
Boswell, Tour to the Hebrides, 23 Aug., p. 219

2 I have, all my life long, been lying till noon; yet I tell all young men, and tell them with great sincerity, that nobody who does not rise early will ever do any good. *Ib. 14 Sept.,* p. 299

3 I inherited a vile melancholy from my father, which has made me mad all my life, at least not sober.
Ib. 16 Sept., p. 302

4 I am always sorry when any language is lost, because languages are the pedigree of nations.
Ib. 18 Sept., p. 310

5 [Johnson, railing against Scotland, said that the wine the Scots had before the Union would not make them drunk. Boswell assured Johnson there was much drunkenness]
No, Sir; there were people who died of dropsies, which they contracted in trying to get drunk.
Ib. 23 Sept., p. 326

6 I do not like much to see a Whig in any dress; but I hate to see a Whig in a parson's gown.
Ib. 24 Sept., p. 331

7 It was said to old Bentley upon the attacks against him, 'Why, they'll write you down.' 'No, Sir,' he replied, 'depend upon it, no man was ever written down but by himself.' *Ib. 1 Oct.,* p. 344

8 The known style of a dedication is flattery: it professes to flatter. *Ib. 4 Oct.,* p. 352

9 A cucumber should be well sliced, and dressed with pepper and vinegar, and then thrown out, as good for nothing. *Ib. 5 Oct.,* p. 354

10 [Calling for a gill of whisky]
Come, let me know what it is that makes a Scotchman happy! *Ib. 23 Oct.,* p. 393

11 Sir, are you so grossly ignorant of human nature, as not to know that a man may be very sincere in good principles, without having good practice?
Ib. 25 Oct., p. 403

12 I am sorry I have not learned to play at cards. It is very useful in life: it generates kindness and consolidates society. *Ib. 21 Nov.,* p. 433

13 This world where much is to be done and little to be known.
Johnsonian Miscellanies ed. G. B. Hill (1897), vol. i. *Prayers and Meditations. Against inquisitive and perplexing Thoughts,* p. 118

14 Wheresoe'er I turn my view,
All is strange, yet nothing new;
Endless labour all along,
Endless labour to be wrong;
Phrase that time hath flung away,
Uncouth words in disarray,
Trick'd in antique ruff and bonnet,
Ode, and elegy, and sonnet.
Ib. Anecdotes of Johnson by Mrs. Piozzi, p. 190

15 Hermit hoar, in solemn cell,
Wearing out life's evening gray;
Strike thy bosom, sage! and tell
What is bliss, and which the way?

Thus I spoke, and speaking sigh'd,
Scarce repress'd the starting tear,
When the hoary Sage reply'd,
'Come, my lad, and drink some beer.'
Johnsonian Miscellanies, vol. i, p. 193

16 If the man who turnips cries,
Cry not when his father dies,
'Tis a proof that he had rather
Have a turnip than his father
Ib. Burlesque of Lopez de Vega's lines, 'Se acquien los leones vence,' &c.

17 He [Charles James Fox] talked to me at club one day concerning Catiline's conspiracy—so I withdrew my attention, and thought about Tom Thumb.
Ib. p. 202

18 Dear Bathurst (said he to me one day) was a man to my very heart's content: he hated a fool, and he hated a rogue, and he hated a whig; he was a very good hater. *Ib.* p. 204

19 [Of a Jamaica gentleman, then lately dead]
He will not, whither he is now gone, find much difference, I believe, either in the climate or the company. *Ib.* p. 211

20 One day at Streatham . . . a young gentleman called to him suddenly, and I suppose he thought disrespectfully, in these words: 'Mr. Johnson, would you advise me to marry?' 'I would advise no man to marry, Sir,' returns for answer in a very angry tone Dr Johnson, 'who is not likely to propagate understanding.' *Ib.* p. 213

21 [To a Quaker:]
Oh, let us not be found, when our Master calls us, ripping the lace off our waistcoats, but the spirit of contention from our souls and tongues!
Ib. p. 222

22 *Goldsmith*: Here's such a stir about a fellow that has written one book [Beattie's *Essay on Truth*], and I have written many.
Johnson: Ah, Doctor, there go two-and-forty sixpences you know to one guinea. *Ib.* p. 269

23 It is very strange, and very melancholy, that the paucity of human pleasures should persuade us ever to call hunting one of them. *Ib.* p. 288

24 You could not stand five minutes with that man [Edmund Burke] beneath a shed while it rained, but you must be convinced you had been standing with the greatest man you had ever yet seen.
Ib. p. 290

25 Johnson observed that he 'did not care to speak ill of any man behind his back, but he believed the gentleman was an *attorney*'. *Ib.* p. 327, n.

26 Was there ever yet anything written by mere man that was wished longer by its readers, excepting *Don Quixote, Robinson Crusoe,* and the *Pilgrim's Progress*? *Ib.* p. 332

27 [On his Parliamentary reports]
I took care that the *Whig Dogs* should not have the best of it.
Ib. An Essay on Johnson, by Arthur Murphy, p. 379

28 Books that you may carry to the fire, and hold readily in your hand, are the most useful after all.
Ib. vol. ii. *Apophthegms from Hawkins's edition of Johnson's works,* p. 2

1 A man is in general better pleased when he has a good dinner upon his table, than when his wife talks Greek. *Johnsonian Miscellanies*, vol. ii, p. 11

2 I would rather see the portrait of a dog that I know, than all the allegorical paintings they can shew me in the world. *Ib.* p. 15

3 There is a time of life, Sir, when a man requires the repairs of a table. *Ib. Anecdotes by Joseph Cradock*, p. 64

4 I have heard him assert, that a tavern chair was the throne of human felicity. *Ib. Extracts from Hawkins's Life of Johnson*, p. 91.

5 I dogmatise and am contradicted, and in this conflict of opinions and sentiments I find delight. *Ib.* p. 92

6 Abstinence is as easy to me, as temperance would be difficult. *Ib. Anecdotes by Hannah More*, p. 197

7 Of music Dr. Johnson used to say that it was the only sensual pleasure without vice. *Ib. Anecdotes by William Seward*, p. 301

8 [Of the performance of a celebrated violinist] Difficult do you call it, Sir? I wish it were impossible. *Ib. p.* 308

9 What is written without effort is in general read without pleasure. *Ib.* p. 309

10 As with my hat upon my head
   I walk'd along the Strand,
   I there did meet another man
   With his hat in his hand.
   Ib. Anecdotes by George Steevens, p. 315

11 Where you see a Whig you see a rascal. *Ib. Anecdotes by the Rev. W. Cole*, p. 393

12 Love is the wisdom of the fool and the folly of the wise. *Ib. William Cooke's Life of Samuel Foote*, p. 393

13 Fly fishing may be a very pleasant amusement; but angling or float fishing I can only compare to a stick and a string, with a worm at one end and a fool at the other. *Attributed to Johnson by Hawker in* Instructions to Young Sportsmen, 1859, p. 197. *Not found in his works. See* Notes and Queries, *11 Dec. 1915*

14 Madam, before you flatter a man so grossly to his face, you should consider whether or not your flattery is worth his having. *Remark to Hannah More*. Mme D'Arblay's *Diary and Letters* (1891), vol. i, ch. ii, p. 55

15 I know not, madam, that you have a right, upon moral principles, to make your readers suffer so much. *To Mrs. Sheridan, after publication of her novel* Memoirs of Miss Sydney Biddulph (1763)

16 Sir, your wife, under pretence of keeping a bawdy-house, is a receiver of stolen goods. *To a Thames waterman, reported by Bennet Langton to James Boswell, 1780*

17 Nobody speaks in earnest, Sir; there is no serious conversation. *Attrib.*

18 A book should teach us to enjoy life, or to endure it. *Attrib.*

19 No two men can be half an hour together, but one shall acquire an evident superiority over the other. *See* Corrigenda, *p. 587*

20 In all pointed sentences, some degree of accuracy must be sacrificed to conciseness. *On the Bravery of the English Common Soldier. Works* (1787), vol. x, p. 286

21 I am not yet so lost in lexicography, as to forget that words are the daughters of earth, and that things are the sons of heaven. *Dictionary of the English Language.* Preface

22 Every quotation contributes something to the stability or enlargement of the language. *Ib.*

23 But these were the dreams of a poet doomed at last to wake a lexicographer. *Ib.*

24 If the changes that we fear be thus irresistible, what remains but to acquiesce with silence, as in the other insurmountable distresses of humanity? It remains that we retard what we cannot repel, that we palliate what we cannot cure. *Ib.*

25 The chief glory of every people arises from its authors. *Ib.*

26 To make dictionaries is dull work. *Ib. Dull. 8*

27 *Excise.* A hateful tax levied upon commodities. *Ib.*

28 *Net.* Anything reticulated or decussated at equal distances, with interstices between the intersections. *Ib.*

29 *Oats.* A grain, which in England is generally given to horses, but in Scotland supports the people. *Ib.*

30 *Patron.* Commonly a wretch who supports with insolence, and is paid with flattery. *Ib.*

31 *Pension.* An allowance made to anyone without an equivalent. In England it is generally understood to mean pay given to a state hireling for treason to his country. *Ib.*

32 *Whig.* The name of a faction. *Ib.*

33 Every man is, or hopes to be, an idler. *The Idler*, No. 1

34 When two Englishmen meet, their first talk is of the weather. *Ib.* No. 11

35 Promise, large promise, is the soul of an advertisement. *Ib.* No. 41

36 He is no wise man who will quit a certainty for an uncertainty. *Ib.* No. 57

37 A Scotchman must be a very sturdy moralist who does not love Scotland better than truth. *Journey to the Western Islands. Col.*

38 At seventy-seven it is time to be in earnest. *Ib.*

39 Whatever withdraws us from the power of our senses; whatever makes the past, the distant, or the future, predominate over the present, advances us in the dignity of thinking beings. *Ib. Inch Kenneth*

40 Grief is a species of idleness. *Letters of Johnson (ed. G. B. Hill, 1892)*, vol. i, p. 212. No. 302, *to Mrs. Thrale, 17 Mar. 1773*

41 There is no wisdom in useless and hopeless sorrow. *Ib.* vol. ii, p. 215. No. 722, *to Mrs. Thrale, 12 Apr. 1781*

42 I am very ready to repay for that kindness which soothed twenty years of a life radically wretched. *Ib.* p. 407. No. 972, *to Mrs. Thrale, 8 July 1784*

1 A hardened and shameless tea-drinker, who has for twenty years diluted his meals with only the infusion of this fascinating plant; whose kettle has scarcely time to cool; who with tea amuses the evening, with tea solaces the midnight, and with tea welcomes the morning.
Review in the 'Literary Magazine', vol. ii. No. xiii. 1757

2 The true genius is a mind of large general powers, accidentally determined to some particular direction.
Lives of the English Poets, 1905, ed. G. B. Hill, vol. i, Cowley, § 3, p. 2

3 Language is the dress of thought.   *Ib. § 181, p. 58*

4 An acrimonious and surly republican.
Ib. Milton, § 168, p. 156

5 The great source of pleasure is variety.
Ib. Butler, § 35, p. 212

6 The father of English criticism. [Dryden]
Ib. Dryden, § 193, p. 410

7 But what are the hopes of man! I am disappointed by that stroke of death, which has eclipsed the gaiety of nations and impoverished the public stock of harmless pleasure. [Garrick's death.]
Ib. vol. ii, Edmund Smith, § 76, p. 21

8 About things on which the public thinks long it commonly attains to think right.
Ib. Addison, § 136, p. 132

9 Whoever wishes to attain an English style, familiar but not coarse, and elegant but not ostentatious, must give his days and nights to the volumes of Addison.   *Ib. § 168, p. 150*

10 By the common sense of readers uncorrupted with literary prejudices . . . must be finally decided all claim to poetical honours.   *Ib. Gray, § 51, p. 441*

11 He washed himself with oriental scrupulosity.
Ib. vol. iii, Swift, § 122, p. 55

12 There are minds so impatient of inferiority that their gratitude is a species of revenge, and they return benefits, not because recompense is a pleasure, but because obligation is a pain.
The Rambler, 15 Jan. 1751

13 I have laboured to refine our language to grammatical purity, and to clear it from colloquial barbarisms, licentious idioms, and irregular combinations.
Ib. 14 Mar. 1752

14 Ye who listen with credulity to the whispers of fancy, and pursue with eagerness the phantoms of hope; who expect that age will perform the promises of youth, and that the deficiencies of the present day will be supplied by the morrow; attend to the history of Rasselas, Prince of Abyssinia.
Rasselas, ch. 1

15 The business of a poet, said Imlac, is to examine, not the individual, but the species; . . . he does not number the streaks of the tulip, or describe the different shades in the verdure of the forest.   *Ib. ch. 10*

16 Human life is everywhere a state in which much is to be endured, and little to be enjoyed.   *Ib. ch. 11*

17 Marriage has many pains, but celibacy has no pleasures.   *Ib. ch. 26*

18 Example is always more efficacious than precept.
Ib. ch. 29

19 Integrity without knowledge is weak and useless, and knowledge without integrity is dangerous and dreadful.   *Rasselas, ch. 41*

20 The endearing elegance of female friendship.
Ib. ch. 45

21 The power of punishment is to silence, not to confute.
Sermons, No. xxiii

22 Notes are often necessary, but they are necessary evils.
Shakespeare (1765), preface.

23 A quibble is to Shakespeare what luminous vapours are to the traveller: he follows it at all adventures; it is sure to lead him out of his way and sure to engulf him in the mire.   *Ib.*

24 It must be at last confessed that, as we owe everything to him [Shakespeare], he owes something to us; that, if much of our praise is paid by perception and judgement, much is likewise given by custom and veneration. We fix our eyes upon his graces and turn them from his deformities, and endure in him what we should in another loathe or despise.   *Ib.*

25 I have always suspected that the reading is right which requires many words to prove it wrong, and the emendation wrong that cannot without so much labour appear to be right.   *Ib.*

26 How is it that we hear the loudest yelps for liberty among the drivers of negroes?
Taxation No Tyranny

27 Unmov'd tho' witlings sneer and rivals rail;
Studious to please, yet not asham'd to fail.
Irene, prologue

28 Learn that the present hour alone is man's.
Ib. III. ii. 33

29 How small, of all that human hearts endure,
That part which laws or kings can cause or cure!
Still to ourselves in every place consigned,
Our own felicity we make or find:
With secret course, which no loud storms annoy,
Glides the smooth current of domestic joy.
Lines added to Goldsmith's 'Traveller'

30 Here falling houses thunder on your head,
And here a female atheist talks you dead.
London, l. 17

31 And, bid him go to Hell, to Hell he goes.   *Ib. l. 116*

32 Of all the griefs that harrass the distress'd,
Sure the most bitter is a scornful jest;
Fate never wounds more deep the gen'rous heart,
Than when a blockhead's insult points the dart.
Ib. l. 166

33 This mournful truth is ev'rywhere confess'd,
Slow rises worth by poverty depress'd.   *Ib. l. 176*

34 When learning's triumph o'er her barb'rous foes
First rear'd the Stage, immortal Shakespeare rose;
Each change of many-colour'd life he drew,
Exhausted worlds, and then imagin'd new:
Existence saw him spurn her bounded reign,
And panting Time toil'd after him in vain.
Prologue at the Opening of the Theatre in Drury Lane, 1747

35 Cold approbation gave the ling'ring bays,
For those who durst not censure, scarce could praise.
Ib.

36 The wild vicissitudes of taste.   *Ib.*

1 The stage but echoes back the public voice.
The drama's laws the drama's patrons give,
For we that live to please, must please to live.
Prologue at the Opening of Drury Lane

2 Let observation with extensive view,
Survey mankind, from China to Peru;
Remark each anxious toil, each eager strife,
And watch the busy scenes of crowded life.
Vanity of Human Wishes, l. 1

3 Our supple tribes repress their patriot throats,
And ask no questions but the price of votes. *Ib.* l. 95

4 Deign on the passing world to turn thine eyes,
And pause awhile from letters to be wise;
There mark what ills the scholar's life assail,
Toil, envy, want, the patron, and the jail.
See nations slowly wise, and meanly just,
To buried merit raise the tardy bust. *Ib.* l. 157

5 A frame of adamant, a soul of fire,
No dangers fright him and no labours tire. *Ib.* l. 193

6 His fall was destined to a barren strand,
A petty fortress, and a dubious hand;
He left the name, at which the world grew pale,
To point a moral, or adorn a tale. *Ib.* l. 219

7 'Enlarge my life with multitude of days!'
In health, in sickness, thus the suppliant prays:
Hides from himself its state, and shuns to know,
That life protracted is protracted woe.
Time hovers o'er, impatient to destroy,
And shuts up all the passages of joy. *Ib.* l. 225

8 An age that melts with unperceiv'd decay,
And glides in modest innocence away. *Ib.* l. 293

9 Superfluous lags the vet'ran on the stage. *Ib.* l. 308

10 In life's last scene what prodigies surprise,
Fears of the brave, and follies of the wise!
From Marlb'rough's eyes the streams of dotage flow,
And Swift expires a driv'ler and a show. *Ib.* l. 315

11 What ills from beauty spring. *Ib.* l. 321

12 Still raise for good the supplicating voice,
But leave to Heaven the measure and the choice,
Ib. l. 351

13 Secure, whate'er he gives, he gives the best. *Ib.* l. 356

14 Faith, that, panting for a happier seat,
Counts death kind Nature's signal of retreat. *Ib.* l. 363

15 With these celestial Wisdom calms the mind,
And makes the happiness she does not find. *Ib.* l. 367

JOHN BENN JOHNSTONE
1803–1891

16 I want you to assist me in forcing her on board the
lugger; once there, I'll frighten her into marriage.

(*Since quoted as:* Once aboard the lugger and the maid
is mine.) *The Gipsy Farmer*

AL JOLSON
1886–1950

17 You ain't heard nothin' yet, folks.
*Remark in the first talking film, 'The Jazz Singer',
July* 1927

JOHN PAUL JONES
1747–1792

18 I have not yet begun to fight.
*Remark on being hailed to know whether he had
struck his flag, as his ship was sinking, 23 Sept.
1779. De Koven's Life and Letters of J. P.
Jones, vol.* i

SIR WILLIAM JONES
1746–1794

19 On parent knees, a naked new-born child,
Weeping thou sat'st, when all around thee smil'd;
So live, that, sinking in thy last long sleep,
Calm thou may'st smile, while all around thee weep.
Persian Asiatick Miscellany (1786), *vol.* ii, p.
374, *A Moral Tetrastich*

20 My opinion is, that power should always be distrusted,
in whatever hands it is placed.
Lord Teignmouth's Life of Sir W. Jones (1835),
vol. i. *Letter to Lord Althorpe, 5 Oct. 1782*

21 Seven hours to law, to soothing slumber seven,
Ten to the world allot, and *all* to Heaven.
Ib. vol. ii. *Lines in Substitution for Sir E. Coke's
lines:* Six hours in sleep, [&c.]. (*See* 148:8)

BEN JONSON
1573–1637

22 Fortune, that favours fools. *The Alchemist*, prologue

23 I will eat exceedingly, and prophesy.
Bartholomew Fair, I. vi

24 Neither do thou lust after that tawney weed tobacco.
Ib. II. vi

25 When I mock poorness, then heaven make me poor.
The Case is Altered, III. i

26 PEOPLE:
The Voice of Cato is the voice of Rome.
CATO:
The voice of Rome is the consent of heaven!
Catiline his Conspiracy, III. i

27 Where it concerns himself,
Who's angry at a slander makes it true. *Ib.*

28 Slow, slow, fresh fount, keep time with my salt tears:
Yet, slower, yet; O faintly, gentle springs:
List to the heavy part the music bears,
Woe weeps out her division, when she sings.
Cynthia's Revels, I. i

29 So they be ill men,
If they spake worse, 'twere better: for of such
To be dispraised, is the most perfect praise. *Ib.* III. ii

30 True happiness
Consists not in the multitude of friends,
But in the worth and choice. *Ib.*

31 Queen and huntress, chaste and fair,
Now the sun is laid to sleep,
Seated in thy silver chair,
State in wonted manner keep:
Hesperus entreats thy light,
Goddess, excellently bright. *Ib.* V. iii

32 If he were
To be made honest by an act of parliament,
I should not alter in my faith of him.
The Devil is An Ass, IV. i

1 I remember the players have often mentioned it as an honour to Shakespeare that in his writing (whatsoever he penned) he never blotted out a line. My answer hath been 'Would he had blotted a thousand'. Which they thought a malevolent speech. I had not told posterity this, but for their ignorance, who chose that circumstance to commend their friend by wherein he most faulted; and to justify mine own candour: for I loved the man, and do honour his memory, on this side idolatry, as much as any. He was (indeed) honest, and of an open and free nature; had an excellent phantasy, brave notions, and gentle expressions; wherein he flowed with that facility, that sometimes it was necessary he should be stopped: *sufflaminandus erat*, as Augustus said of Haterius. His wit was in his own power, would the rule of it had been so too. . . . But he redeemed his vices with his virtues. There was ever more in him to be praised than to be pardoned.

Discoveries. De Shakespeare Nostrati. Augustus in Haterium

2 His hearers could not cough, or look aside from him, without loss. . . . The fear of every man that heard him was, lest he should make an end. [Bacon.]
Ib. lxxviii. *Dominus Verulamius*

3 In his adversity I ever prayed, that God would give him strength; for greatness he could not want.
Ib. lxxx. *De Augmentis Scientiarum,—Lord St. Alban*

4 Yet the best pilots have needs of mariners, besides sails, anchor, and other tackle.
Ib. Illiteratus Princeps

5 Talking and eloquence are not the same: to speak, and to speak well, are two things.
Ib. Praecept. Element

6 Alas, all the castles I have, are built with air, thou know'st. *Eastward Ho*, II. ii. 226

7 Still to be neat, still to be drest,
As you were going to a feast;
Still to be powder'd, still perfum'd,
Lady, it is to be presumed,
Though art's hid causes are not found,
All is not sweet, all is not sound.

Give me a look, give me a face,
That makes simplicity a grace;
Robes loosely flowing, hair as free:
Such sweet neglect more taketh me,
Than all the adulteries of art;
They strike mine eyes, but not my heart.
Epicoene, I. i

8 HAUGHTY:
Is this the silent woman?
CENTAURE:
Nay, she has found her tongue since she was married.
Ib. III. vi

9 But that which most doth take my Muse and me,
Is a pure cup of rich Canary wine,
Which is the Mermaid's now, but shall be mine:
Of which, had Horace or Anacreon tasted,
Their lives, as do their lines, till now had lasted.
Epigrams, ci. *Inviting a Friend to Supper*

10 Weep with me, all you that read
This little story:
And know for whom a tear you shed
Death's self is sorry.
'Twas a child that so did thrive
In grace and feature,
As Heaven and Nature seem'd to strive
Which own'd the creature.
Years he number'd scarce thirteen
When Fates turn'd cruel,
Yet three fill'd Zodiacs had he been
The stage's jewel;
And did act, what now we moan,
Old men so duly,
As sooth the Parcae thought him one,
He play'd so truly.
So, by error, to his fate
They all consented;
But viewing him since, alas, too late!
They have repented:
And have sought (to give new birth)
In baths to steep him;
But being so much too good for earth,
Heaven vows to keep him.
Epigrams, cxx. *An Epitaph on Salomon Pavy, a Child of Queen Elizabeth's Chapel*

11 Underneath this stone doth lie
As much beauty as could die;
Which in life did harbour give
To more virtue than doth live.
If at all she had a fault,
Leave it buried in this vault.
One name was Elizabeth,
The other let it sleep with death:
Fitter, where it died, to tell,
Than that it lived at all! Farewell!
Ib. cxxiv. *Epitaph on Elizabeth L. H.*

12 Helter skelter hang sorrow, care'll kill a cat, up-tails all, and a louse for the hangman.
Every Man in His Humour, I. iii

13 As sure as death. *Ib.* II. i

14 Ods me, I marvel what pleasure or felicity they have in taking their roguish tobacco. It is good for nothing but to choke a man, and fill him full of smoke and embers. *Ib.* III. v

15 I do honour the very flea of his dog. *Ib.* IV. ii

16 I have it here in black and white. *Ib.*

17 It must be done like lightning. *Ib.* v

18 There shall be no love lost.
Every Man out of His Humour, II. i

19 Blind Fortune still
Bestows her gifts on such as cannot use them. *Ib.* ii

20 Follow a shadow, it still flies you,
Seem to fly it, it will pursue:
So court a mistress, she denies you;
Let her alone, she will court you.
Say, are not women truly, then,
Styl'd but the shadows of us men?
The Forest, vii. *Song: That Women are but Men's Shadows*

21 Drink to me only with thine eyes,
And I will pledge with mine;
Or leave a kiss but in the cup,
And I'll not look for wine.

The thirst that from the soul doth rise
  Doth ask a drink divine;
But might I of Jove's nectar sup,
  I would not change for thine.

I sent thee late a rosy wreath,
  Not so much honouring thee,
As giving it a hope that there
  It could not wither'd be.
But thou thereon didst only breathe,
  And sent'st it back to me;
Since when it grows and smells, I swear,
  Not of itself, but thee.   *The Forest*, ix. *To Celia*

1 How near to good is what is fair!
  Which we no sooner see,
But with the lines and outward air,
  Our senses taken be.
    Love Freed from Ignorance and Folly

2 Thou art not to learn the humours and tricks of that
  old bald cheater, Time.   *The Poetaster*, I. i

3 Ramp up my genius, be not retrograde;
  But boldly nominate a spade a spade.   *Ib.* v. i

4 Detraction is but baseness' varlet;
  And apes are apes, though clothed in scarlet.   *Ib.*

5 This is Mab, the Mistress-Fairy
  That doth nightly rob the dairy.   *The Satyr*

6 She that pinches country wenches
  If they rub not clean their benches.   *Ib.*

7 But if so they chance to feast her,
  In a shoe she drops a tester.   *Ib.*

8   Tell proud Jove,
Between his power and thine there is no odds:
'Twas only fear first in the world made gods.
    Sejanus, II. ii

9 This figure that thou here seest put,
It was for gentle Shakespeare cut,
Wherein the graver had a strife
With Nature, to out-do the life:
O could he but have drawn his wit
As well in brass, as he has hit
His face; the print would then surpass
All that was ever writ in brass:
But since he cannot, reader, look
Not on his picture, but his book.
  On the Portrait of Shakespeare, To the Reader

10 While I confess thy writings to be such,
As neither man, nor muse, can praise too much.
  To the Memory of My Beloved, the Author, Mr.
  William Shakespeare

11   Soul of the Age!
The applause! delight! the wonder of our stage!
My Shakespeare, rise; I will not lodge thee by
Chaucer, or Spenser, or bid Beaumont lie
A little further, to make thee a room:
Thou art a monument, without a tomb,
And art alive still, while thy book doth live,
And we have wits to read, and praise to give.   *Ib.*

12 Marlowe's mighty line.   *Ib.*

13 And though thou hadst small Latin, and less Greek.
                            Ib.

14 Call forth thundering Aeschylus.   *Ib.*

15   To hear thy buskin tread,
And shake a stage: or, when thy socks were on,
Leave thee alone, for the comparison
Of all, that insolent Greece, or haughty Rome
Sent forth, or since did from their ashes come.   *Ib.*

16 He was not of an age, but for all time!   *Ib.*

17 For a good poet's made, as well as born.   *Ib.*

18 Sweet Swan of Avon! what a sight it were
To see thee in our waters yet appear,
And make those flights upon the banks of Thames,
That so did take Eliza, and our James!   *Ib.*

19 THOMAS:
They write here, one Cornelius-Son
Hath made the Hollanders an invisible eel
To swim the haven at Dunkirk, and sink all
The shipping there. . . .
CYMBAL:
It is an automa, runs under water,
With a snug nose, and has a nimble tail
Made like an auger, with which tail she wriggles
Betwixt the costs of a ship, and sinks it straight.
    The Staple of News, III. i

20 Well, they talk we shall have no more Parliaments,
  God bless us!   *Ib.*

21   Hark you, John Clay, if you have
Done any such thing, tell troth and shame the devil.
    Tale of a Tub, II. i

22 Mother, the still sow eats up all the draff.   *Ib.* III. v

23 I sing the birth was born to-night,
  The author both of life and light.
    Underwoods. Poems of Devotion, iii. *Hymn on the*
    Nativity

24 Have you seen but a bright lily grow,
  Before rude hands have touch'd it?
Have you mark'd but the fall o' the snow
  Before the soil hath smutch'd it?

O so white! O so soft! O so sweet is she!
  Ib. Celebration of Charis, iv. *Her Triumph*

25 She is Venus when she smiles;
But she's Juno when she walks,
And Minerva when she talks.   *Ib.* v

26 Greek was free from rhyme's infection,
Happy Greek, by this protection,
  Was not spoiled:
Whilst the Latin, queen of tongues,
Is not yet free from rhyme's wrongs,
  But rests foiled.
    Ib. xlviii. *A Fit of Rhyme against Rhyme*

27 Vulgar languages that want
Words, and sweetness, and be scant
  Of true measure,
Tyrant rhyme hath so abused,
That they long since have refused
  Other cesure.
He that first invented thee,
May his joints tormented be,
  Cramp'd for ever;
Still may syllabes jar with time,
Still may reason war with rhyme,
  Resting never!   *Ib.*

28 England's high Chancellor: the destin'd heir,
In his soft cradle, to his father's chair.
  Ib. lxx. *On Lord Bacon's [Sixtieth] Birthday*

1 It is not growing like a tree
　In bulk, doth make men better be;
　Or standing long an oak, three hundred **year**,
　To fall a log at last, dry, bald, and sere:
　　A lily of a day,
　　Is fairer far in May,
　Although it fall and die that night;
　It was the plant and flower of light.
　In small proportions we just beauties see;
　And in short measures, life may perfect be.
　　Underwoods, lxxxviii. *A Pindaric Ode on the
　　Death of Sir H. Morison*

2 What gentle ghost, besprent with April dew,
　Hails me so solemnly to yonder yew?
　　Ib. ci. *Elegy on the Lady Jane Pawlet*

3 The voice so sweet, the words so fair,
　As some soft chime had stroked the air;
　And though the sound were parted thence,
　Still left an echo in the sense. *Ib*. *Eupheme*, iv

4 Calumnies are answered best with silence.
　　Volpone, II. ii

5 Come, my Celia, let us prove,
　While we can, the sports of love. *Ib*. III. v

6 Suns, that set, may rise again;
　But if once we lose this light,
　'Tis with us perpetual night. *Ib*.

7 You have a gift, sir, (thank your education,)
　Will never let you want, while there are men,
　And malice, to breed causes. [To a lawyer.] *Ib*. v. i

8 　　　　　　Mischiefs feed
　Like beasts, till they be fat, and then they bleed.
　　Ib. viii

9 O rare Ben Jonson.
　　*Epitaph written on his tombstone in Westminster
　　Abbey, by Jack Young. See* Aubrey's *Brief
　　Lives, Ben Jonson*

DOROTHEA JORDAN
1762–1816

10 'Oh where, and Oh! where is your Highland laddie
　gone?'
　'He's gone to fight the French, for King George
　upon the throne,
　And it's Oh! in my heart, how I wish him safe at
　home!' *The Blue Bells of Scotland*

JOSEPH JOUBERT
1754–1824

11 S'il est un homme tourmenté par la maudite ambition
　de mettre tout un livre dans une page, toute une
　page dans une phrase, et cette phrase dans un mot,
　c'est moi.

　If there be any man cursed with the itch to com-
　press a whole book into a page, a whole page into
　a phrase, and that phrase into a word, it is I.
　　Pensées

BENJAMIN JOWETT
1817–1893

12 The lie in the Soul is a true lie.
　　From the Introduction to his translation of Plato's
　　Republic, bk. ii

13 One man is as good as another until he has written a
　book.
　　Campbell and Abbott, *Life and Letters of B.
　　Jowett*, i. 248

JAMES JOYCE
1882–1941

14 A portrait of the artist as a young man. *Title of Book*

JULIAN
c. 331–363

15 Vicisti, Galilæe.
　Thou hast conquered, O Galilean.
　　Dying words. Latin translation of Theodoret,
　　Hist. Eccles. iii. 20

JUNIUS
fl. 1770

16 The liberty of the press is the *Palladium* of all the
　civil, political, and religious rights of an English-
　man. *Letters*, dedication

17 The right of election is the very essence of the consti-
　tution. *Ib*. Letter 11, *24 Apr. 1769*

18 Is this the wisdom of a great minister? or is it the
　ominous vibration of a pendulum?
　　Ib. Letter 12, *30 May 1769*

19 There is a holy mistaken zeal in politics as well as in
　religion. By persuading others, we convince our-
　selves. *Ib*. Letter 35, *19 Dec. 1769*

20 Whether it be the heart to conceive, the understand-
　ing to direct, or the hand to execute.
　　Ib. Letter 37, *19 Mar. 1770*

21 The injustice done to an individual is sometimes of
　service to the public. *Ib*. Letter 41, *14 Nov. 1770*

EMPEROR JUSTINIAN
527–565

22 Justitia est constans et perpetua voluntas jus suum
　cuique tribuens.
　Justice is the constant and perpetual wish to render
　to every one his due. *Institutiones*, I. i. 1

JUVENAL
A.D. 60–c. 130

23 Probitas laudatur et alget.
　Honesty is commended, and starves.
　　Satires, i. 74. Trans. by Lewis Evans

24 Si natura negat, facit indignatio versum.
　If nature denies the power, indignation would give
　birth to verses. *Ib*. 79

25 Quidquid agunt homines, votum timor ira voluptas
　Gaudia discursus nostri farrago libelli est.
　All that men are engaged in, their wishes, fears,
　anger, pleasures, joys, and varied pursuits, form
　the hotch-potch of my book. *Ib*. 85

26 Quis tulerat Gracchos de seditione querentis?
　Who shall endure the Gracchi complaining about
　sedition? *Ib*. ii. 24

1 Dat veniam corvis, vexat censura columbas.

Censure acquits the raven, but falls foul of the
dove. *Satires*, ii. 63

2 Nemo repente fuit turpissimus.

No one ever reached the climax of vice at one step.
Ib. 83

3 Grammaticus rhetor geometres pictor aliptes
Augur schoenobates medicus magus, omnia novit
Graeculus esuriens; in caelum miseris, ibit.
(*Alternative reading of last line*: in coelum
iusseris, ibit.)

Grammarian, rhetorician, geometer, painter, trainer,
soothsayer, rope-dancer, physician, wizard—he
knows everything. Bid the hungry Greekling go
to heaven! He'll go. *Ib*. iii. 76

4 Nil habet infelix paupertas durius in se
Quam quod ridiculos homines facit.

Poverty, bitter though it be, has no sharper pang
than this, that it makes men ridiculous. *Ib*. 152

5 Haud facile emergunt quorum virtutibus opstat
Res angusta domi.

Difficult indeed is it for those to emerge from obscurity whose noble qualities are cramped by
narrow means at home. *Ib*. 164

6 Omnia Romae
Cum pretio.

Everything at Rome is coupled with high price.
Ib. 183

7 Credo Pudicitiam Saturno rege moratam
In terris visamque diu.

I believe that while Saturn still was king, Chastity
lingered upon earth, and was long seen there.
Ib. vi. 1

8 Rara avis in terris nigroque simillima cycno.

A rare bird on the earth and very like a black
swan. *Ib*. 165

9 Hoc volo, sic iubeo, sit pro ratione voluntas.

I will it, I insist on it! Let my will stand instead
of reason. *Ib*. 223

10 Nunc patimur longae pacis mala, saevior armis
Luxuria incubuit victumque ulciscitur orbem.

Now we are suffering all the evils of long-continued
peace. Luxury, more ruthless than war, broods
over Rome, and exacts vengeance for a conquered world. *Ib*. 292

11 'Pone seram, prohibe.' Sed quis custodiet ipsos
Custodes? Cauta est et ab illis incipit uxor.

'Put on a lock! keep her in confinement!' But who
is to guard the guards themselves? Your wife
is as cunning as you, and begins with them.
Ib. 347

12 Tenet insanabile multos
Scribendi cacoethes et aegro in corde senescit.

An inveterate itch of writing, now incurable, clings
to many, and grows old in their distempered
body. *Ib*. vii. 51

13 Occidit miseros crambe repetita magistros.

It is the reproduction of the cabbage that wears
out the master's life. [i.e. cabbage twice cooked.]
Ib. 154

14 Summum crede nefas animam praeferre pudori
Et propter vitam vivendi perdere causas.

Deem it to be the summit of impiety to prefer existence to honour, and for the sake of life to
sacrifice life's only end. *Satires*, viii. 83

15 Omnibus in terris, quae sunt a Gadibus usque
Auroram et Gangen, pauci dinoscere possunt
Vera bona atque illis multum diversa, remota
Erroris nebula.

In all the regions which extend from Gades even
to the farthest east and Ganges, there are but few
that can discriminate between real blessings and
those that are widely different, all the mist of
error being removed. *Ib*. x. 1

16 Nocitura toga, nocitura petuntur
Militia.

Our prayers are put up for what will injure us
in peace, and injure us in war. *Ib*. 8

17 Cantabit vacuus coram latrone viator.

The traveller with empty pockets will sing even in
the robber's face. *Ib*. 22

18 Verbosa et grandis epistula venit
A Capreis.

A wordy and lengthy epistle came from Capreae.
Ib. 71

19 Duas tantum res anxius optat,
Panem et circenses.

Limits its [i.e. the Roman people's] anxious longings to two things only—bread, and the games
of the circus. *Ib*. 80

20 Expende Hannibalem: quot libras in duce summo
invenies?

Put Hannibal in the scales: and how many pounds
of flesh will you find in that famous general?
Ib. 147

21 I demens et saevas curre per Alpes,
Ut pueris placeas et declamatio fias.

Go then, madman, and hurry over the rugged
Alps, that you may be the delight of boys, and
furnish subjects for declamations. *Ib*. 166

22 Mors sola fatetur
Quantula sint hominum corpuscula.

Death alone discloses how very small are the puny
bodies of men. *Ib*. 172

23 Da spatium vitae, multos da, Iuppiter, annos.

Grant length of life, great Jove, and many years.
Ib. 188

24 Orandum est ut sit mens sana in corpore sano.
Fortem posce animum mortis terrore carentem,
Qui spatium vitae extremum inter munera ponat
Naturae.

Your prayer must be that you may have a sound
mind in a sound body. Pray for a bold spirit,
free from all dread of death; that reckons the
closing scene of life among Nature's kindly
boons. *Ib*. 356

25 Nullum numen habes si sit prudentia, nos te,
Nos facimus, Fortuna, deam caeloque locamus.

If we have wise foresight, thou, Fortune, hast
no divinity. It is we that make thee a deity, and
place thy throne in heaven! *Ib*. 365

1   Prima est haec ultio quod se
Iudice nemo nocens absolvitur.

    This is the punishment that first lights upon him,
that by the verdict of his own breast no guilty
man is acquitted.   *Satires*, xiii. 2

2   Quippe minuti
Semper et infirmi est animi exiguique voluptas
Ultio. Continuo sic collige, quod vindicta
Nemo magis gaudet quam femina.

    Since revenge is ever the pleasure of a paltry spirit,
a weak and abject mind! Draw this conclusion
at once from the fact, that no one delights in revenge more than a woman.   *Ib.* 189

3 Maxima debetur puero reverentia, siquid
Turpe paras, nec tu pueri contempseris annos.

    The greatest reverence is due to a child! If you
are contemplating a disgraceful act, despise not
your child's tender years.   *Ib.* xiv. 47

IMMANUEL KANT
1724–1804

4 Zwei Dinge erfüllen das Gemüth mit immer neuer
und zunehmender Bewunderung und Ehrfurcht,
je öfter und anhaltender sich das Nachdenken
damit beschäftigt: der bestirnte Himmel über mir,
und das moralische Gesetz in mir.

    Two things fill the mind with ever-increasing won-
der and awe, the more often and the more intensely the mind of thought is drawn to them:
the starry heavens above me and the moral law
within me.
          Critique of Practical Reason, conclusion

5 There is ... but one categorical imperative: 'Act only
on that maxim whereby thou canst at the same
time will that it should become a universal law.'
      Trans. by A. D. Lindsay, from *Fundamental
Principles of ... Morals*, p. 421

6 I ought, therefore I can.   *Attrib.*

ALPHONSE KARR
1808–1890

7 Plus ça change, plus c'est la même chose.

    The more things change, the more they are the
same.   *Les Guêpes, Jan. 1849*, vi

8 Si l'on veut abolir la peine de mort en ce cas, que
MM. les assassins commencent.

    If we are to abolish the death penalty, I should like
to see the first step taken by our friends the
murderers.   *Ib.*

DENIS KEARNEY
1847–1907

9 Horny-handed sons of toil.
          Speech. San Francisco, c. 1878

JOHN KEATS
1795–1821

10 Season of mists and mellow fruitfulness,
Close bosom-friend of the maturing sun;
Conspiring with him how to load and bless
With fruit the vines that round the thatch-eaves run.
          To Autumn

11   To set budding more
And still more later flowers for the bees,
Until they think warm days will never cease,
For Summer has o'erbrimmed their clammy cells.
          To Autumn

12 Who hath not seen thee oft amid thy store?
Sometimes whoever seeks abroad may find
Thee sitting careless on a granary floor,
Thy hair soft-lifted by the winnowing wind;
Or on a half-reap'd furrow sound asleep,
Drows'd with the fume of poppies, while thy hook
Spares the next swath and all its twined flowers. *Ib.*

13 Where are the songs of Spring? Ay, where are they?
          Ib.

14 Then in a wailful choir the small gnats mourn
Among the river sallows, borne aloft
Or sinking as the light wind lives or dies. *Ib.*

15 The red-breast whistles from a garden-croft;
And gathering swallows twitter in the skies. *Ib.*

16 Bards of Passion and of Mirth,
Ye have left your souls on earth!
Have ye souls in heaven too?
    *Written on the blank page before Beaumont
and Fletcher's* Fair Maid of the Inn. *Bards of
Passion and of Mirth*

17 Where the nightingale doth sing
Not a senseless, tranced thing,
But divine melodious truth.   *Ib.*

18 The imagination of a boy is healthy, and the mature
imagination of a man is healthy; but there is a space
of life between, in which the soul is in a ferment,
the character undecided, the way of life uncertain,
the ambition thick-sighted: thence proceeds maw-
kishness.   *Endymion*, preface

19 A thing of beauty is a joy for ever:
Its loveliness increases; it will never
Pass into nothingness; but still will keep
A bower quiet for us, and a sleep
Full of sweet dreams, and health, and quiet breathing.
          Ib. bk. i, l. 1

20   The inhuman dearth
Of noble natures.   *Ib.* l. 8

21   The grandeur of the dooms
We have imagined for the mighty dead. *Ib.* l. 20

22 They must be always with us, or we die. *Ib.* l. 33

23   The unimaginable lodge
For solitary thinkings; such as dodge
Conception to the very bourne of heaven,
Then leave the naked brain.   *Ib.* l. 293

24 O magic sleep! O comfortable bird,
That broodest o'er the troubled sea of the mind
Till it is hush'd and smooth!   *Ib.* l. 453

25 Wherein lies happiness? In that which becks
Our ready minds to fellowship divine,
A fellowship with essence.   *Ib.* l. 777

26   The crown of these
Is made of love and friendship, and sits high
Upon the forehead of humanity.   *Ib.* l. 800

1   Who, of men, can tell
That flowers would bloom, or that green fruit would
 swell
To melting pulp, that fish would have bright mail,
The earth its dower of river, wood, and vale,
The meadows runnels, runnels pebble-stones,
The seed its harvest, or the lute its tones,
Tones ravishment, or ravishment its sweet
If human souls did never kiss and greet?
       Endymion, bk. i, l. 835

2   Never, I aver,
Since Ariadne was a vintager. *Ib.* bk. ii, l. 442

3 O Sorrow,
  Why dost borrow
Heart's lightness from the merriment of May?
       Ib. bk. iv, l. 164

4 To Sorrow,
  I bade good-morrow,
And thought to leave her far away behind;
  But cheerly, cheerly,
  She loves me dearly;
She is so constant to me, and so kind. *Ib.* l. 173

5 Come hither, lady fair, and joined be
  To our wild minstrelsy!   *Ib.* l. 236

6 Great Brahma from his mystic heaven groans,
And all his priesthood moans. *Ib.* l. 265

7   Their smiles,
Wan as primroses gather'd at midnight
By chilly finger'd spring.   *Ib.* l. 969

8 Sweet are the pleasures that to verse belong,
And doubly sweet a brotherhood in song.
      Epistle to G. F. Mathew

9   Oh, never will the prize,
High reason, and the love [?lore] of good and ill,
Be my award! *Epistle to J. H. Reynolds*, l. 74

10 Lost in a sort of Purgatory blind. *Ib.* l. 80

11   It is a flaw
In happiness, to see beyond our bourn,—
It forces us in summer skies to mourn,
It spoils the singing of the nightingale. *Ib.* l. 82

12 St. Agnes' Eve—Ah, bitter chill it was!
The owl, for all his feathers, was a-cold;
The hare limp'd trembling through the frozen grass,
And silent was the flock in woolly fold.
     The Eve of Saint Agnes, i

13 The sculptur'd dead on each side seem to freeze,
Emprison'd in black, purgatorial rails. *Ib.* ii

14 The silver, snarling trumpets 'gan to chide. *Ib.* iv

15 Upon the honey'd middle of the night. *Ib.* vi

16 The music, yearning like a God in pain. *Ib.* vii

17 A poor, weak, palsy-stricken, churchyard thing.
         Ib. xviii

18 Out went the taper as she hurried in;
Its little smoke, in pallid moonshine, died. *Ib.* xxiii

19 A casement high and triple-arch'd there was,
All garlanded with carven imag'ries
Of fruits, and flowers, and bunches of knot-grass,
And diamonded with panes of quaint device,
Innumerable of stains and splendid dyes,
As are the tiger-moth's deep-damask'd wings;
And in the midst, 'mong thousand heraldries,
And twilight saints, and dim emblazonings,
A shielded scutcheon blush'd with blood of queens
 and kings.   *Ib.* xxiv

20 Full on this casement shone the wintry moon,
And threw warm gules on Madeline's fair breast.
     The Eve of Saint Agnes, xxv

21 By degrees
Her rich attire creeps rustling to her knees.
         Ib. xxvi

22 Her soft and chilly nest.   *Ib.* xxvii

23 As though a rose should shut, and be a bud again.
          Ib.

24 And still she slept an azure-lidded sleep,
In blanched linen, smooth, and lavender'd. *Ib.* xxx

25 And lucent syrops, tinct with cinnamon;
Manna and dates, in argosy transferr'd
From Fez; and spiced dainties, every one,
From silken Samarcand to cedar'd Lebanon. *Ib.*

26 He play'd an ancient ditty, long since mute,
In Provence call'd, 'La belle dame sans mercy'.
         Ib. xxxiii

27 And the long carpets rose along the gusty floor.
          Ib. xl

28 And they are gone: aye, ages long ago
These lovers fled away into the storm. *Ib.* xlii

29 The Beadsman, after thousand aves told,
For aye unsought-for slept among his ashes cold. *Ib.*

30 Upon a Sabbath-day it fell;
Twice holy was the Sabbath-bell,
That call'd the folk to evening prayer.
     The Eve of Saint Mark, l. 1

31 Dry your eyes—O dry your eyes,
For I was taught in Paradise
To ease my breast of melodies.
     Fairy Song: Shed No Tear

32 Fanatics have their dreams, wherewith they weave
A paradise for a sect. *The Fall of Hyperion*, l. 1

33 'None can usurp this height', return'd that shade,
'But those to whom the miseries of the world
Are misery, and will not let them rest.' *Ib.* l. 147

34   They are no dreamers weak,
They seek no wonder but the human face;
No music but a happy-noted voice. *Ib.* l. 162

35 The poet and the dreamer are distinct,
Diverse, sheer opposite, antipodes.
The one pours out a balm upon the world,
The other vexes it.   *Ib.* l. 199

36 His flaming robes stream'd out beyond his heels,
And gave a roar, as if of earthly fire,
That scared away the meek ethereal hours,
And made their dove-wings tremble. On he flared.
       Ib. c. ii, l. 58

37 Ever let the fancy roam,
Pleasure never is at home.   *Fancy*, l. 1

38 O sweet Fancy! let her loose;
Summer's joys are spoilt by use. *Ib.* l. 9

39 Where's the cheek that doth not fade,
Too much gaz'd at? Where's the maid
Whose lip mature is ever new? *Ib.* l. 69

40   Where's the face
One would meet in every place? *Ib.* l. 73

1 Where—where slept thine ire,
When like a blank idiot I put on thy wreath,
  Thy laurel, thy glory,
  The light of thy story,
Or was I a worm—too low crawling, for death?
  O Delphic Apollo!   *Hymn to Apollo*

2 Far from the fiery noon, and eve's one star.
           Hyperion, bk. i, l. 3

3   No stir of air was there,
Not so much life as on a summer's day
Robs not one light seed from the feather'd grass,
But where the dead leaf fell, there did it rest. *Ib.* l. 7

4   The Naiad 'mid her reeds
Press'd her cold finger closer to her lips.   *Ib.* l. 13

5 How beautiful, if sorrow had not made
Sorrow more beautiful than Beauty's self.   *Ib.* l. 35

6 That large utterance of the early Gods.   *Ib.* l. 51

7 O aching time! O moments big as years!   *Ib.* l. 64

8 As when, upon a trancèd summer-night,
Those green-rob'd senators of mighty woods,
Tall oaks, branch-charmèd by the earnest stars,
Dream, and so dream all night without a stir.
              Ib. l. 72

9 And all those acts which Deity supreme
Doth ease its heart of love in.   *Ib.* l. 111

10 Unseen before by Gods or wondering men.
              Ib. l. 183

11 Instead of sweets, his ample palate took
Savour of poisonous brass and metal sick. *Ib.* l. 188

12 He entered, but he enter'd full of wrath. *Ib.* l. 213

13 For as in theatres of crowded men
Hubbub increases more they call out, 'Hush!'
              Ib. l. 253

14 And still they were the same bright, patient stars.
              Ib. l. 353

15 Who cost her mother Tellus keener pangs,
Though feminine, than any of her sons.
           Ib. bk. ii, l. 54

16 Now comes the pain of truth, to whom 'tis pain;
O folly! for to bear all naked truths,
And to envisage circumstance, all calm,
That is the top of sovereignty.   *Ib.* l. 202

17 A solitary sorrow best befits
Thy lips, and antheming a lonely grief.
           Ib. bk. iii, l. 5

18   Point me out the way
To any one particular beauteous star,
And I will flit into it with my lyre,
And make its silvery splendour pant with bliss.
              Ib. l. 99

19 Knowledge enormous makes a God of me. *Ib.* l. 113

20 But, for the general award of love,
The little sweet doth kill much bitterness.
           Isabella, xiii

21 Why were they proud? again we ask aloud,
Why in the name of Glory were they proud? *Ib.* xvi

22 So the two brothers and their murder'd man
Rode past fair Florence.   *Ib.* xxvii

23 And she forgot the stars, the moon, the sun,
  And she forgot the blue above the trees,
And she forgot the dells where waters run,
  And she forgot the chilly autumn breeze;
She had no knowledge when the day was done,
  And the new moon she saw not: but in peace
Hung over her sweet Basil evermore.   *Isabella*, liii

24   'For cruel 'tis,' said she,
'To steal my Basil-pot away from me.'   *Ib.* lxii

25 I stood tip-toe upon a little hill.   *Title*

26   And then there crept
A little noiseless noise among the leaves,
Born of the very sigh that silence heaves.
    I Stood Tip-toe upon a Little Hill

27 Here are sweet peas, on tiptoe for a flight. *Ib.*

28 Oh what can ail thee, Knight at arms
  Alone and palely loitering;
The sedge is wither'd from the lake,
  And no birds sing.   *La Belle Dame Sans Merc*

29 I see a lily on thy brow,
  With anguish moist and fever dew;
And on thy cheek a fading rose
  Fast withereth too.   *Ib.*

30 I met a lady in the meads
  Full beautiful, a faery's child;
Her hair was long, her foot was light,
  And her eyes were wild.   *Ib.*

31 I set her on my pacing steed,
  And nothing else saw all day long;
For sideways would she lean, and sing
  A faery's song.   *Ib.*

32 She look'd at me as she did love,
  And made sweet moan.   *Ib.*

33 And sure in language strange she said,
  'I love thee true!'   *Ib.*

34 And there I shut her wild, wild eyes
  With kisses four.   *Ib.* (Ld. Houghton's version)

35   La belle Dame sans Merci
Hath thee in thrall!   *Ib.*

36 I saw their starv'd lips in the gloam
  With horrid warning gapèd wide,
And I awoke, and found me here
  On the cold hill side.   *Ib.*

37 She was a gordian shape of dazzling hue,
Vermilion-spotted, golden, green, and blue;
Striped like a zebra, freckled like a pard,
Eyed like a peacock, and all crimson barr'd.
           Lamia, pt. i, l. 47

38 Real are the dreams of Gods, and smoothly pass
Their pleasures in a long immortal dream. *Ib.* l. 127

39 Love in a hut, with water and a crust,
Is—Love, forgive us!—cinders, ashes, dust;
Love in a palace is perhaps at last
More grievous torment than a hermit's fast.
           Ib. pt. ii, l. 1

40 That purple-lined palace of sweet sin. *Ib.* l. 31

41 In pale contented sort of discontent. *Ib.* l. 135

42   Do not all charms fly
At the mere touch of cold philosophy?
There was an awful rainbow once in heaven:
We know her woof, her texture; she is given
In the dull catalogue of common things.
Philosophy will clip an Angel's wings. *Ib.* l. 229

1 Souls of poets dead and gone,
What Elysium have ye known,
Happy field or mossy cavern,
Choicer than the Mermaid Tavern?
Have ye tippled drink more fine
Than mine host's Canary wine?
Lines on the Mermaid Tavern

2 Pledging with contented smack
The Mermaid in the Zodiac. *Ib.*

3 This living hand, now warm and capable
Of earnest grasping, would, if it were cold
And in the icy silence of the tomb,
So haunt thy days and chill thy dreaming nights
That thou wouldst wish thine own heart dry of blood
So in my veins red life might stream again,
And thus be conscience-calm'd—see here it is—
I hold it towards you.
*Lines Supposed to have been Addressed to Fanny
Brawne*

4 Old Meg was brave as Margaret Queen
And tall as Amazon:
An old red blanket cloak she wore;
A chip hat had she on. *Meg Merrilies*

5 Let none profane my Holy See of love,
Or with a rude hand break
The sacramental cake. *Ode to Fanny*

6 Thou still unravish'd bride of quietness,
Thou foster-child of silence and slow time.
Ode on a Grecian Urn

7 What men or gods are these? What maidens loth?
What mad pursuit? What struggle to escape?
What pipes and timbrels? What wild ecstasy? *Ib.*

8 Heard melodies are sweet, but those unheard
Are sweeter; therefore, ye soft pipes, play on;
Not to the sensual ear, but, more endear'd,
Pipe to the spirit ditties of no tone. *Ib.*

9 For ever wilt thou love, and she be fair! *Ib.*

10 For ever piping songs for ever new. *Ib.*

11 All breathing human passion far above. *Ib.*

12 Who are these coming to the sacrifice?
To what green altar, O mysterious priest,
Lead'st thou that heifer lowing at the skies,
And all her silken flanks with garlands drest?
What little town by river or sea shore,
Or mountain-built with peaceful citadel,
Is emptied of this folk, this pious morn? *Ib.*

13 O Attic shape! Fair attitude! *Ib.*

14 Thou, silent form, dost tease us out of thought
As doth eternity: Cold Pastoral! *Ib.*

15 'Beauty is truth, truth beauty,'—that is all
Ye know on earth, and all ye need to know. *Ib.*

16 For I would not be dieted with praise,
A pet-lamb in a sentimental farce! *Ode on Indolence*

17 By bards who died content on pleasant sward,
Leaving great verse unto a little clan. *Ode to Maia*

18 Rich in the simple worship of a day. *Ib.*

19 No, no, go not to Lethe, neither twist
Wolf's-bane, tight-rooted, for its poisonous wine.
Ode on Melancholy

20 Nor let the beetle, nor the death-moth be
Your mournful Psyche. *Ib.*

21 She dwells with Beauty—Beauty that must die;
And Joy, whose hand is ever at his lips
Bidding adieu; and aching Pleasure nigh,
Turning to Poison while the bee-mouth sips:
Ay, in the very temple of delight
Veil'd Melancholy has her sovran shrine.
Though seen of none save him whose strenuous
tongue
Can burst Joy's grape against his palate fine;
His soul shall taste the sadness of her might,
And be among her cloudy trophies hung.
Ode on Melancholy

22 My heart aches, and a drowsy numbness pains
My sense. *Ode to a Nightingale*

23 'Tis not through envy of thy happy lot,
But being too happy in thine happiness,—
That thou, light-winged Dryad of the trees,
In some melodious plot
Of beechen green, and shadows numberless,
Singest of summer in full-throated ease. *Ib.*

24 O, for a draught of vintage! that hath been
Cool'd a long age in the deep-delved earth,
Tasting of Flora and the country green,
Dance, and Provençal song, and sunburnt mirth!
O for a beaker full of the warm South,
Full of the true, the blushful Hippocrene,
With beaded bubbles winking at the brim,
And purple-stained mouth;
That I might drink, and leave the world unseen,
And with thee fade away into the forest dim. *Ib.*

25 Fade far away, dissolve, and quite forget
What thou among the leaves hast never known,
The weariness, the fever, and the fret,
Here, where men sit and hear each other groan. *Ib.*

26 Where youth grows pale, and spectre-thin, and dies.
Ib.

27 Where but to think is to be full of sorrow
And leaden-eyed despairs,
Where Beauty cannot keep her lustrous eyes,
Or new Love pine at them beyond to-morrow. *Ib.*

28 Away! away! for I will fly to thee,
Not charioted by Bacchus and his pards,
But on the viewless wings of Poesy,
Though the dull brain perplexes and retards. *Ib.*

29 But here there is no light,
Save what from heaven is with the breezes blown
Through verdurous glooms and winding mossy ways.
Ib.

30 I cannot see what flowers are at my feet,
Nor what soft incense hangs upon the boughs. *Ib.*

31 Fast fading violets cover'd up in leaves;
And mid-May's eldest child,
The coming musk-rose, full of dewy wine,
The murmurous haunt of flies on summer eves. *Ib.*

32 Darkling I listen; and, for many a time
I have been half in love with easeful Death,
Call'd him soft names in many a mused rhyme,
To take into the air my quiet breath;
Now more than ever seems it rich to die,
To cease upon the midnight with no pain,
While thou art pouring forth thy soul abroad
In such an ecstasy!
Still wouldst thou sing, and I have ears in vain—
To thy high requiem become a sod.

1 Thou wast not born for death, immortal Bird!
No hungry generations tread thee down;
The voice I hear this passing night was heard
In ancient days by emperor and clown:
Perhaps the self-same song that found a path
Through the sad heart of Ruth, when sick for home,
She stood in tears amid the alien corn;
    The same that oft-times hath
Charm'd magic casements, opening on the foam
Of perilous seas, in faery lands forlorn.
                        Ode to a Nightingale

2 Forlorn! the very word is like a bell
To toll me back from thee to my sole self!
Adieu! the fancy cannot cheat so well
As she is fam'd to do, deceiving elf.
Adieu! adieu! thy plaintive anthem fades
Past the near meadows, over the still stream,
Up the hill-side; and now 'tis buried deep
    In the next valley-glades:
Was it a vision, or a waking dream?
Fled is that music:—Do I wake or sleep?   *Ib.*

3 'Mid hush'd, cool-rooted flowers, fragrant-eyed,
Blue, silver-white, and budded Tyrian.
                            Ode to Psyche

4 O latest-born and loveliest vision far
Of all Olympus' faded hierarchy!   *Ib.*

5   To make delicious moan
Upon the midnight hours.   *Ib.*

6 Thy voice, thy lute, thy pipe, thy incense sweet
From swinged censer teeming;
Thy shrine, thy grove, thy oracle, thy heat
Of pale-mouth'd prophet dreaming.   *Ib.*

7 Yes, I will be thy priest, and build a fane
In some untrodden region of my mind,
Where branched thoughts, new grown with pleasant
pain,
Instead of pines shall murmur in the wind.   *Ib.*

8 With buds, and bells, and stars without a name,
With all the gardener Fancy e'er could feign,
Who breeding flowers, will never breed the same. *Ib.*

9 A bright torch, and a casement ope at night,
To let the warm Love in.   *Ib.*

10 Stop and consider! life is but a day;
A fragile dew-drop on its perilous way
From a tree's summit; a poor Indian's sleep
While his boat hastens to the monstrous steep
Of Montmorenci.   *Sleep and Poetry*, l. 85

11 O for ten years, that I may overwhelm
Myself in poesy; so I may do the deed
That my own soul has to itself decreed.   *Ib.* l. 96

12 They sway'd about, upon a rocking horse,
And thought it Pegasus.   *Ib.* l. 186

13   The blue
Bared its eternal bosom, and the dew
Of summer nights collected still to make
The morning precious.   *Ib.* l. 189

14   A drainless shower
Of light is poesy; 'tis the supreme of power;
'Tis might half slumb'ring on its own right arm.
                                      Ib. l. 235

15   The great end
Of poesy, that it should be a friend
To soothe the cares, and lift the thoughts of man.
                                      Ib. l. 245

16 They shall be accounted poet kings
Who simply tell the most heart-easing things.
                        Sleep and Poetry, l. 267

17 Bright star, would I were steadfast as thou art—
Not in lone splendour hung aloft the night
And watching, with eternal lids apart,
Like nature's patient, sleepless Eremite,
The moving waters at their priestlike task
Of pure ablution round earth's human shores.
                            Sonnet. Bright Star

18 Still, still to hear her tender-taken breath,
And so live ever—or else swoon to death.   *Ib.*

19 Much have I travell'd in the realms of gold,
And many goodly states and kingdoms seen;
Round many western islands have I been
Which bards in fealty to Apollo hold.
Oft of one wide expanse had I been told
That deep-brow'd Homer ruled as his demesne;
Yet did I never breathe its pure serene
Till I heard Chapman speak out loud and bold:
Then felt I like some watcher of the skies
When a new planet swims into his ken;
Or like stout Cortez when with eagle eyes
He star'd at the Pacific—and all his men
Look'd at each other with a wild surmise—
Silent, upon a peak in Darien.
        Ib. On First Looking into Chapman's Homer

20 O Chatterton! how very sad thy fate!
                            Ib. To Chatterton

21   Mortality
Weighs heavily on me like unwilling sleep.
                    Ib. On Seeing the Elgin Marbles

22 The poetry of earth is never dead:
When all the birds are faint with the hot sun,
And hide in cooling trees, a voice will run
From hedge to hedge about the new-mown mead.
                Ib. On the Grasshopper and Cricket

23 Happy is England! I could be content
To see no other verdure than its own;
To feel no other breezes than are blown
Through its tall woods with high romances blent.
                        Ib. Happy is England!

24 Happy is England, sweet her artless daughters;
Enough their simple loveliness for me.   *Ib.*

25   Other spirits there are standing apart
Upon the forehead of the age to come.
        Ib. To Haydon, ii.   *Great Spirits Now On Earth*

26 There is a budding morrow in midnight.
                                Ib. To Homer

27 Four seasons fill the measure of the year.
                                Ib. Human Seasons

28 Glory and loveliness have pass'd away.
                                Ib. To Leigh Hunt

29 Son of the old moon-mountains African!
Chief of the Pyramid and Crocodile! *Ib. To the Nile*

30 It keeps eternal whisperings around
Desolate shores, and with its mighty swell
Gluts twice ten thousand Caverns.   *Ib. On the Sea*

31 O soft embalmer of the still midnight. *Ib. To Sleep*

32 Turn the key deftly in the oiled wards,
And seal the hushed casket of my soul.   *Ib.*

33 The sweet converse of an innocent mind.
                                Ib. To Solitude

1 The day is gone, and all its sweets are gone!
Sweet voice, sweet lips, soft hand, and softer breast.
Sonnet. The Day Is Gone

2 To one who has been long in city pent;
'Tis very sweet to look into the fair
And open face of heaven.
Ib. To One Who Has Been Long

3 A debonair
And gentle tale of love and languishment. *Ib.*

4 When I have fears that I may cease to be
Before my pen has glean'd my teeming brain.
Ib. When I Have Fears

5 When I behold upon the night's starr'd face,
Huge cloudy symbols of a high romance. *Ib.*

6 Then on the shore
Of the wide world I stand alone, and think
Till love and fame to nothingness do sink. *Ib.*

7 In a drear-nighted December,
Too happy, happy tree,
Thy branches ne'er remember
Their green felicity.
Stanzas. In a Drear-nighted December

8 But were there ever any
Writh'd not at passing joy?
To know the change and feel it,
When there is none to heal it,
Nor numbed sense to steel it,
Was never said in rhyme. *Ib.*

9 O fret not after knowledge—I have none,
And yet my song comes native with the warmth.
O fret not after knowledge—I have none,
And yet the Evening listens. *What the Thrush Said*

10 Woman! when I behold thee flippant, vain,
Inconstant, childish, proud, and full of fancies.
Woman! When I Behold Thee

11 Like a whale's back in the sea of prose.
Letters (ed. M. B. Forman, 1935), 14. *To Leigh
Hunt, 10 May 1817*

12 What a thing to be in the mouth of fame. *Ib.*

13 I remember your saying that you had notions of a
good Genius presiding over you. I have of late
had the same thought—for things which [I] do
half at random are afterwards confirmed by my
judgment in a dozen features of propriety. Is it
too daring to fancy Shakespeare this Presider?
Ib. 15. To B. R. Haydon, 10–11 May 1817

14 I am quite disgusted with literary men.
Ib. 25. To Benjamin Bailey, 8 Oct. 1817

15 A long poem is a test of invention which I take to
be the Polar star of poetry, as fancy is the sails,
and imagination the rudder. *Ib.*

16 A man should have the fine point of his soul taken
off to become fit for this world.
Ib. 30. To J. H. Reynolds, 22 Nov. 1817

17 I am certain of nothing but the holiness of the heart's
affections and the truth of imagination—what the
imagination seizes as beauty must be truth—
whether it existed before or not.
Ib. 31. To Benjamin Bailey, 22 Nov. 1817

18 I have never yet been able to perceive how anything
can be known for truth by consecutive reasoning—
and yet it must be. *Ib.*

19 O for a life of sensations rather than of thoughts! *Ib.*

20 The excellency of every art is its intensity, capable
of making all disagreeables evaporate, from their
being in close relationship with beauty and truth.
Letters, 32. To G. and T. Keats, 21 Dec. 1817

21 Negative Capability, that is, when a man is capable
of being in uncertainties, mysteries, doubts, without any irritable reaching after fact and reason—
Coleridge, for instance, would let go by a fine
isolated verisimilitude caught from the Penetralium
of mystery, from being incapable of remaining content with half-knowledge. *Ib.*

22 There is nothing stable in the world; uproar's your
only music.
Ib. 37. To G. and T. Keats, 13 Jan. 1818

23 So I do believe . . . that works of genius are the first
things in this world. *Ib.*

24 For the sake of a few fine imaginative or domestic
passages, are we to be bullied into a certain
philosophy engendered in the whims of an egotist.
Ib. 44. To J. H. Reynolds, 3 Feb. 1818

25 We hate poetry that has a palpable design upon us—
and if we do not agree, seems to put its hand in its
breeches pocket. Poetry should be great and unobtrusive, a thing which enters into one's soul, and
does not startle or amaze it with itself, but with its
subject. *Ib.*

26 When man has arrived at a certain ripeness in intellect any one grand and spiritual passage serves
him as a starting-post towards all 'the two-and-
thirty palaces'.
Ib. 48. To J. H. Reynolds, 19 Feb. 1818

27 Poetry should surprise by a fine excess, and not by
singularity; it should strike the reader as a wording
of his own highest thoughts, and appear almost a
remembrance. Its touches of beauty should never
be half-way, thereby making the reader breathless,
instead of content. The rise, the progress, the
setting of imagery should, like the sun, come
natural to him.
Ib. 51. To John Taylor, 27 Feb. 1818

28 If poetry comes not as naturally as leaves to a tree it
had better not come at all. *Ib.*

29 I have good reason to be content, for thank God I
can read and perhaps understand Shakespeare to
his depths. *Ib.*

30 Scenery is fine—but human nature is finer.
Ib. 53. To Benjamin Bailey, 13 Mar. 1818

31 As if the roots of the earth were rotten, cold, and
drenched. *Ib. 60. To J. H. Reynolds, 9 Apr. 1818*

32 A country which is continually under hatches.
Ib. 61. To J. H. Reynolds, 10 Apr. 1818

33 I have been hovering for some time between the
exquisite sense of the luxurious and a love for
philosophy—were I calculated for the former I
should be glad—but as I am not I shall turn all
my soul to the latter.
Ib. 62. To John Taylor, 24 Apr. 1818

34 Axioms in philosophy are not axioms until they are
proved upon our pulses: we read fine things but
never feel them to the full until we have gone the
same steps as the author.
Ib. 64. To J. H. Reynolds, 3 May 1818

1 I am in that temper that if I were under water I would scarcely kick to come to the top.
Letters, 66. To Benjamin Bailey, 21 May 1818

2 Were it in my choice I would reject a petrarchal coronation—on account of my dying day, and because women have cancers.
Ib. 69. To Benjamin Bailey, 10 June 1818

3 I do think better of womankind than to suppose they care whether Mister John Keats five feet high likes them or not.
Ib. 79. To Benjamin Bailey, 18 July 1818

4 His identity presses upon me.
Ib. 86. To C. W. Dilke, 21 Sept. 1818

5 I never was in love—yet the voice and the shape of a woman has haunted me these two days.
Ib. 87. To J. H. Reynolds, 22 Sept. 1818

6 There is an awful warmth about my heart like a load of immortality.
Ib.

7 In Endymion, I leaped headlong into the sea, and thereby have become better acquainted with the soundings, the quicksands, and the rocks, than if I had stayed upon the green shore, and piped a silly pipe, and took tea and comfortable advice.
Ib. 90. To James Hessey, 9 Oct. 1818

8 I would sooner fail than not be among the greatest.
Ib.

9 As to the poetical character itself (I mean that sort of which, if I am anything, I am a member; that sort distinguished from the Wordsworthian or egotistical sublime; which is a thing *per se* and stands alone) it is not itself—it has no self. . . . It has as much delight in conceiving an Iago as an Imogen.
Ib. 93. To Richard Woodhouse, 27 Oct. 1818

10 A poet is the most unpoetical of anything in existence, because he has no identity; he is continually [informing] and filling some other body.
Ib.

11 I think I shall be among the English Poets after my death.
Ib. 94. To George and Georgiana Keats, 14 Oct. 1818

12 The roaring of the wind is my wife and the stars through the window pane are my children. The mighty abstract idea I have of beauty in all things stifles the more divided and minute domestic happiness. . . . The opinion I have of the generality of women—who appear to me as children to whom I would rather give a sugar plum than my time, forms a barrier against matrimony which I rejoice in.
Ib.

13 I never can feel certain of any truth but from a clear perception of its beauty.
Ib. 98. To George and Georgiana Keats, 16 Dec. 1818–4 Jan. 1819

14 I have come to this resolution—never to write for the sake of writing or making a poem, but from running over with any little knowledge or experience which many years of reflection may perhaps give me; otherwise I shall be dumb.
Ib. 115. To B. R. Haydon, 8 Mar. 1819

15 It is true that in the height of enthusiasm I have been cheated into some fine passages; but that is not the thing.
Ib.

16 I should like the window to open onto the Lake of Geneva—and there I'd sit and read all day like the picture of somebody reading.
Letters, 116. To Fanny Keats, 13 Mar. 1819

17 A man's life of any worth is a continual allegory.
Ib. 123. To George and Georgiana Keats, 14 Feb.–3 May 1819

18 Shakespeare led a life of allegory: his works are the comments on it.
Ib.

19 Nothing ever becomes real till it is experienced—even a proverb is no proverb to you till your life has illustrated it.
Ib.

20 Call the world if you please 'The vale of Soul-making'.
Ib.

21 I have met with women whom I really think would like to be married to a poem, and to be given away by a novel.
Ib. 136. To Fanny Brawne, 8 July 1819

22 I have two luxuries to brood over in my walks, your loveliness and the hour of my death. O that I could have possession of them both in the same minute.
Ib. 139. To Fanny Brawne, 25 July 1819

23 I am convinced more and more day by day that fine writing is next to fine doing, the top thing in the world. *Ib. 145. To J. H. Reynolds, 24 Aug. 1819*

24 Give me books, fruit, french wine and fine weather and a little music out of doors, played by somebody I do not know.
Ib. 146. To Fanny Keats, 29 Aug. 1819

25 All clean and comfortable I sit down to write.
Ib. 156. To George and Georgiana Keats, 17 Sept. 1819

26 I have but lately been on my guard against Milton. Life to him would be death to me. Miltonic verse cannot be written but it [*for* in] the vein of art—I wish to devote myself to another sensation. *Ib.*

27 The only means of strengthening one's intellect is to make up one's mind about nothing—to let the mind be a thoroughfare for all thoughts. Not a select party. *Ib.*

28 You have ravished me away by a power I cannot resist; and yet I could resist till I saw you; and even since I have seen you I have endeavoured often 'to reason against the reason of my Love'.
Ib. 160. To Fanny Brawne, 13 Oct. 1819

29 'If I should die', said I to myself, 'I have left no immortal work behind me—nothing to make my friends proud of my memory—but I have loved the principle of beauty in all things, and if I had had time I would have made myself remembered.'
Ib. 186. To Fanny Brawne, Feb. 1820?

30 I long to believe in immortality. . . . If I am destined to be happy with you here—how short is the longest life. I wish to believe in immortality—I wish to live with you for ever.
Ib. 223. To Fanny Brawne, July 1820

31 I wish you could invent some means to make me at all happy without you. Every hour I am more and more concentrated in you; every thing else tastes like chaff in my mouth.
Ib. 224. To Fanny Brawne, Aug. 1820

1 You, I am sure, will forgive me for sincerely remarking that you might curb your magnanimity, and be more of an artist, and load every rift of your subject with ore. *Letters, 227. To Shelley, Aug. 1820*

2 He already seemed to feel the flowers growing over him.
Words reported by Severn. W. Sharp, *Life and Letters of Severn,* ch. 4

3 Here lies one whose name was writ in water.
Epitaph. Lord Houghton, *Life of Keats,* ii. 91

JOHN KEBLE
1792–1866

4 New every morning is the love
Our wakening and uprising prove.
The Christian Year. Morning

5 If on our daily course our mind
Be set to hallow all we find,
New treasures still, of countless price,
God will provide for sacrifice. *Ib.*

6 We need not bid, for cloister'd cell,
Our neighbour and our work farewell.
Nor strive to wind ourselves too high
For sinful man beneath the sky. *Ib.*

7 The trivial round, the common task,
Would furnish all we ought to ask;
Room to deny ourselves; a road
To bring us, daily, nearer God. *Ib.*

8 And help us, this and every day,
To live more nearly as we pray. *Ib.*

9 Sun of my soul! Thou Saviour dear,
It is not night if Thou be near. *Ib. Evening*

10 Abide with me from morn till eve,
For without Thee I cannot live:
Abide with me when night is nigh,
For without Thee I dare not die. *Ib.*

11 Like infant slumbers, pure and light. *Ib.*

12 There is a book, who runs may read,
Which heavenly truth imparts,
And all the lore its scholars need,
Pure eyes and Christian hearts. *Ib. Septuagesima*

13 Bless'd are the pure in heart,
For they shall see our God. *Ib. The Purification*

14 Still to the lowly soul
He doth Himself impart,
And for His cradle and His throne
Chooseth the pure in heart. *Ib.*

15 The voice that breathed o'er Eden.
Poems. Holy Matrimony

16 The English *Virgil.* [Spenser.]
Lectures on Poetry, lect. v, 1912, vol. i, p. 82

FRANK BILLINGS KELLOGG
1856–1937

17 The high contracting parties solemnly declare in the names of their respective peoples that they condemn recourse to war for the solution of international controversies, and renounce it as an instrument of national policy in their relations with one another. The high contracting parties agree that the settlement or solution of all disputes or conflicts of whatever nature or of whatever origin they may be, which may rise among them, shall never be sought except by pacific means.
Peace Pact, signed at Paris 27 Aug. 1928

THOMAS KELLY
1769–1854

18 The Head that once was crowned with thorns
Is crowned with glory now.
Hymns on Various Passages of Scripture (1820).
The Head that Once Was Crowned

THOMAS À KEMPIS
1380–1471

19 Opto magis sentire compunctionem quam scire eius definitionem.
I had rather feel compunction, than understand the definition thereof.
Imitatio Christi, ch. 1, § iii. Trans. by Anthony Hoskins.

20 Nam homo proponit, sed Deus disponit.
Man proposes but God disposes. *Ib.* § xix

21 Sic transit gloria mundi.
O, how quickly doth the glory of the world pass away! *Ib.* ch. 3, § vi

22 Passione interdum movemur et zelum putamus.
We are sometimes moved with passion, and we think it to be zeal. Quoted in *ib.* ch. 5, § i

23 Multo tutius est stare in subiectione quam in praelatura.
It is much safer to obey, than to govern.
Ib. ch. 9, § i

24 Si libenter crucem portas portabit te.
If thou bear the Cross cheerfully, it will bear thee.
Ib. ch. 12, § v

25 Nunquam sis ex toto otiosus, sed aut legens, aut scribens, aut orans, aut meditans, aut aliquid utilitatis pro communi laborans.
Never be entirely idle: but either be reading, or writing, or praying, or meditating, or endeavouring something for the public good.
Ib. ch. 19, § iv

26 Utinam per unam diem essemus bene conversati in hoc mundo.
O that we had spent but one day in this world thoroughly well! *Ib.* ch. 23, § ii

JOHN KEMPTHORNE
1775–1838

27 Praise the Lord! ye heavens adore Him,
Praise Him, Angels in the height;
Sun and moon, rejoice before Him,
Praise Him, all ye stars and light.
Hymns of Praise. For Foundling Apprentices (1796). *Praise the Lord! Ye Heavens Adore Him*

BISHOP THOMAS KEN
1637–1711

1 Awake my soul, and with the sun
Thy daily stage of duty run;
Shake off dull sloth, and joyful rise
To pay thy morning sacrifice.
Morning Hymn (1709). *Awake My Soul*

2 Teach me to live, that I may dread
The grave as little as my bed.
Evening Hymn. Glory to Thee My God This Night

3 Praise God, from whom all blessings flow,
Praise Him, all creatures here below,
Praise Him above, ye heavenly host,
Praise Father, Son, and Holy Ghost.
Morning and Evening Hymn

LLOYD KENYON, FIRST BARON KENYON
1732–1802

4 The Christian religion is part of the law of the land.
[England.]   *Decision in William's Case. 1797*

LADY CAROLINE KEPPEL
1735–?

5 What's this dull town to me?
Robin's not near.
He whom I wished to see,
Wished for to hear;
Where's all the joy and mirth
Made life a heaven on earth?
O! they're all fled with thee,
Robin Adair.   *Robin Adair*

JOSEPH KESSELRING
1902–

6 Arsenic and Old Lace.   *Title of Play.* (1941)

WILLIAM KETHE
d. 1608?

7 All people that on earth do dwell,
Sing to the Lord with cheerful voice;
Him serve with fear, His praise forth tell,
Come ye before Him, and rejoice.

The Lord, ye know, is God indeed;
Without our aid He did us make.
Daye's Psalter (1560). *All People That on Earth*

8 For it is seemly so to do.   *Ib.*

9 For why? The Lord our God is good.   *Ib.*

RALPH KETTELL
1563–1643

10 Here is Hey for Garsington! and Hey for Cuddesdon!
and Hey Hockley! but here's nobody cries, Hey
for God Almighty!
Sermon at Garsington Revel. Aubrey's Brief Lives,
vol. ii

FRANCIS SCOTT KEY
1779–1843

11 'Tis the star-spangled banner; O long may it wave
O'er the land of the free, and the home of the brave!
The Star-Spangled Banner

JOYCE KILMER
1888–1918

12 I think that I shall never see
A poem lovely as a tree.
Poems, Essays, and Letters, 1917, i. *Trees*

13 Poems are made by fools like me,
But only God can make a tree.   *Ib.*

BENJAMIN FRANKLIN KING
1857–1894

14 Nothing to do but work,
Nothing to eat but food,
Nothing to wear but clothes
To keep one from going nude.   *The Pessimist*

15 Nothing to breathe but air,
Quick as a flash 'tis gone;
Nowhere to fall but off,
Nowhere to stand but on!   *Ib.*

HARRY KING

16 Young men taken in and done for.   *Title of Song*

BISHOP HENRY KING
1592–1669

17 Nature's true-born child, who sums his years
(Like me) with no arithmetic but tears.
The Anniverse. Elegy

18 Accept, thou shrine of my dead Saint,
Instead of dirges this complaint;
And for sweet flowers to crown thy hearse,
Receive a strew of weeping verse
From thy griev'd friend, whom thou might'st see
Quite melted into tears for thee.   *The Exequy*

19 Sleep on, my Love, in thy cold bed,
Never to be disquieted!
My last good night! Thou wilt not wake
Till I thy fate shall overtake:
Till age, or grief, or sickness must
Marry my body to that dust
It so much loves; and fill the room
My heart keeps empty in thy tomb.
Stay for me there; I will not fail
To meet thee in that hollow vale.
And think not much of my delay;
I am already on the way,
And follow thee with all the speed
Desire can make, or sorrows breed.   *Ib.*

20 'Tis true, with shame and grief I yield,
Thou like the van first took'st the field,
And gotten hast the victory
In thus adventuring to die
Before me, whose more years might crave
A just precedence in the grave.
But hark! My pulse like a soft drum
Beats my approach, tells thee I come;
And slow howe'er my marches be,
I shall at last sit down by thee.   *Ib.*

21 We that did nothing study but the way
To love each other, with which thoughts the day
Rose with delight to us, and with them set,
Must learn the hateful art, how to forget.
The Surrender

STODDARD KING

1889–1933

1 There's a long, long trail a-winding
Into the land of my dreams,
Where the nightingales are singing
And a white moon beams:
There's a long, long night of waiting
Until my dreams all come true;
Till the day when I'll be going down
That long long trail with you. *The Long, Long Trail*

ALEXANDER WILLIAM KINGLAKE

1809–1891

2 Soon the men of the column began to see that though
the scarlet line was slender, it was very rigid and
exact. *Invasion of the Crimea*, vol. ii, p. 455

CHARLES KINGSLEY

1819–1875

3 Airly Beacon, Airly Beacon;
Oh the pleasant sight to see
Shires and towns from Airly Beacon,
While my love climb'd up to me! *Airly Beacon*

4 Airly Beacon, Airly Beacon;
Oh the weary haunt for me,
All alone on Airly Beacon,
With his baby on my knee! *Ib.*

5 And no one but the baby cried for poor Lorraine,
Lorrèe. *Ballad: 'Lorraine, Lorraine, Lorrèe'*

6 My fairest child, I have no song to give you;
No lark could pipe in skies so dull and grey.
A Farewell. To C. E. G.

7 Be good, sweet maid, and let who can be clever;
Do lovely things, not dream them, all day long;
And so make Life, and Death, and that For Ever,
One grand sweet song. *Ib.*

8 It was Earl Haldan's daughter,
She looked across the sea.
It Was Earl Haldan's Daughter

9 The locks of six princesses
Must be my marriage fee,
'So hey bonny boat, and ho bonny boat!
Who comes a-wooing me?' *Ib.*

10 Leave to Robert Browning
Beggars, fleas, and vines;
Leave to squeamish Ruskin
Popish Apennines,
Dirty stones of Venice
And his gas-lamps seven;
We've the stones of Snowdon
And the lamps of heaven. *Letter to Thomas Hughes*

11 What we can we will be,
Honest Englishmen.
Do the work that's nearest,
Though it's dull at whiles,
Helping, when we meet them,
Lame dogs over stiles. *Ib.*

12 Welcome, wild North-easter!
Shame it is to see
Odes to every zephyr;
Ne'er a verse to thee. *Ode to the North-East Wind*

13 Jovial wind of winter
Turn us out to play! *Ode to the North-East Wind*

14 Chime, ye dappled darlings,
Down the roaring blast;
You shall see a fox die
Ere an hour be past. *Ib.*

15 'Tis the hard grey weather
Breeds hard English men. *Ib.*

16 Come; and strong within us
Stir the Vikings' blood;
Bracing brain and sinew;
Blow, thou wind of God! *Ib.*

17 I once had a sweet little doll, dears,
The prettiest doll in the world;
Her cheeks were so red and so white, dears,
And her hair was so charmingly curled.
Songs from The Water Babies. My Little Doll

18 Yet, for old sakes' sake she is still, dears,
The prettiest doll in the world. *Ib.*

19 When all the world is young, lad,
And all the trees are green;
And every goose a swan, lad,
And every lass a queen;
Then hey for boot and horse, lad,
And round the world away:
Young blood must have its course, lad,
And every dog his day.

When all the world is old, lad,
And all the trees are brown;
And all the sport is stale, lad,
And all the wheels run down;
Creep home, and take your place there,
The spent and maimed among:
God grant you find one face there,
You loved when all was young. *Ib. Young and Old*

20 The merry brown hares came leaping
Over the crest of the hill,
Where the clover and corn lay sleeping
Under the moonlight still. *The Bad Squire*

21 Oh! that we two were Maying
Down the stream of the soft Spring breeze;
Like children with violets playing,
In the shade of the whispering trees.
The Saint's Tragedy, II. ix.

22 'O Mary, go and call the cattle home,
And call the cattle home,
And call the cattle home,
Across the sands of Dee:'
The western wind was wild and dank with foam,
And all alone went she. *The Sands of Dee*

23 The western tide crept up along the sand,
And o'er and o'er the sand,
And round and round the sand,
As far as eye could see.
The rolling mist came down and hid the land:
And never home came she. *Ib.*

24 The cruel crawling foam. *Ib.*

25 Three fishers went sailing away to the west,
Away to the west as the sun went down;
Each thought on the woman who loved him the best,
And the children stood watching them out of the
town. *The Three Fishers*

26 And the night-rack came rolling up ragged and
brown. *Ib.*

1 For men must work, and women must weep,
And there's little to earn, and many to keep,
Though the harbour bar be moaning.
The Three Fishers

2 For men must work, and women must weep,
And the sooner it's over, the sooner to sleep;
And good-bye to the bar and its moaning. *Ib.*

3 To be discontented with the divine discontent, and to be ashamed with the noble shame, is the very germ and first upgrowth of all virtue.
Health and Education (1874), p. 20

4 Truth, for its own sake, had never been a virtue with the Roman clergy.
Review of Froude's History of England, *in* Macmillan's Magazine *for Jan. 1864*

5 He did not know that a keeper is only a poacher turned outside in, and a poacher a keeper turned inside out. *The Water Babies, ch. 1*

6 As thorough an Englishman as ever coveted his neighbour's goods. *Ib. ch. 4*

7 And still the lobster held on. *Ib. ch. 5*

8 Mrs. Bedonebyasyoudid is coming. *Ib.*

9 The loveliest fairy in the world; and her name is Mrs. Doasyouwouldbedoneby. *Ib.*

10 All the butterflies and cockyolybirds would fly past me. *Ib. ch. 8*

11 Till the coming of the Cocqcigrues. *Ib.*

12 Don Desperado
Walked on the Prado,
And there he met his enemy. *Westward Ho, ch. 12*

13 More ways of killing a cat than choking her with cream. *Ib. ch. 20*

14 Eustace is a man no longer; he is become a thing, a tool, a Jesuit. *Ib. ch. 23*

15 What, then, does Dr. Newman mean?
Title of a pamphlet, 1864

16 Some say that the age of chivalry is past, that the spirit of romance is dead. The age of chivalry is never past, so long as there is a wrong left unredressed on earth. *Life* (1879), vol. ii, ch. 28

RUDYARD KIPLING
1865–1936

17 When you've shouted 'Rule Britannia', when you've sung 'God save the Queen',
When you've finished killing Kruger with your mouth. *The Absent-Minded Beggar*

18 He's an absent-minded beggar, and his weaknesses are great—
But we and Paul must take him as we find him—
He's out on active service, wiping something off a slate—
And he's left a lot of little things behind him! *Ib.*

19 Duke's son—cook's son—son of a hundred Kings—
(Fifty thousand horse and foot going to Table Bay!) *Ib.*

20 Pass the hat for your credit's sake, and pay—pay—pay! *Ib.*

21 If you'd go to Mother Carey
(Walk her down to Mother Carey!),
Oh, we're bound to Mother Carey where she feeds her chicks at sea! *Anchor Song*

22 England's on the anvil—hear the hammers ring—
Clanging from the Severn to the Tyne!
Never was a blacksmith like our Norman King—
England's being hammered, hammered, hammered into line! *The Anvil*

23 Back to the Army again. *Title*

24 A-layin' on to the Sergeant I don't know a gun from a bat. *Back to the Army Again*

25 I 'eard the feet on the gravel—the feet o' the men what drill—
An' I sez to my flutterin' 'eart-strings, I sez to 'em, 'Peace, be still!' *Ib.*

26 Rolling down the Ratcliffe Road drunk and raising Cain. *The Ballad of the 'Bolivar'*

27 Oh, East is East, and West is West, and never the twain shall meet,
Till Earth and Sky stand presently at God's great Judgment Seat;
But there is neither East nor West, Border, nor Breed, nor Birth,
When two strong men stand face to face, though they come from the ends of the earth!
The Ballad of East and West

28 With the mouth of a bell and the heart of Hell and the head of the gallows-tree. *Ib.*

29 And the talk slid north, and the talk slid south,
With the sliding puffs from the hookah-mouth.
Four things greater than all things are,—
Women and Horses and Power and War.
Ballad of the King's Jest

30 It was not part of their blood,
It came to them very late
With long arrears to make good,
When the English began to hate. *The Beginnings*

31 There's peace in a Larañaga, there's calm in a Henry Clay. *The Betrothed*

32 And a woman is only a woman, but a good cigar is a Smoke. *Ib.*

33 Gentlemen unafraid.
Beyond the Path of the Outmost Sun. (Barrack-Room Ballads: Dedication)

34 'Oh, where are you going to, all you Big Steamers,
With England's own coal, up and down the salt seas?'
'We are going to fetch you your bread and your butter,
Your beef, pork, and mutton, eggs, apples, and cheese.' *Big Steamers*

35 'Oh, the Channel's as bright as a ball-room already,
And pilots are thicker than pilchards at Looe.' *Ib.*

36 'For the bread that you eat and the biscuits you nibble,
The sweets that you suck and the joints that you carve,
They are brought to you daily by all us Big Steamers—
And if any one hinders our coming you'll starve!' *Ib.*

37 We're foot—slog—slog—slog—sloggin' over Africa—
Foot—foot—foot—foot—sloggin' over Africa—
(Boots—boots—boots—boots—movin' up an' down again!)
There's no discharge in the war! *Boots*

1 Try—try—try—try—to think o' something different—
Oh—my—God—keep—me from goin' lunatic!
(Boots—boots—boots—boots—movin' up an' down again!) *Boots*

2 O ye who tread the Narrow Way
By Tophet-flare to Judgement Day.
Buddha at Kamakura

3 I've a head like a concertina, I've a tongue like a button-stick,
I've a mouth like an old potato, and I'm more than a little sick,
But I've had my fun o' the Corp'ral's Guard; I've made the cinders fly,
And I'm here in the Clink for a thundering drink and blacking the Corporal's eye. *Cells*

4 'Drunk and resisting the Guard!'
Mad drunk and resisting the Guard—
'Strewth, but I socked it them hard!
So it's pack-drill for me and a fortnight's C.B.
For 'drunk and resisting the Guard'. *Ib.*

5 Take of English earth as much
As either hand may rightly clutch.
In the taking of it breathe
Prayer for all who lie beneath. . . .
Lay thy earth upon thy heart,
And thy sickness shall depart! *A Charm*

6 Land of our birth, we pledge to thee
Our love and toil in the years to be;
When we are grown and take our place,
As men and women with our race.

Father in Heaven who lovest all,
Oh, help Thy children when they call;
That they may build from age to age
An undefilèd heritage.

Teach us to bear the yoke in youth,
With steadfastness and careful truth;
That, in our time, Thy Grace may give
The truth whereby the nations live.
The Children's Song

7 That we, with Thee, may walk uncowed
By fear or favour of the crowd. *Ib.*

8 That, under Thee, we may possess
Man's strength to comfort man's distress.

Teach us delight in simple things,
And mirth that has no bitter springs;
Forgiveness free of evil done,
And love to all men 'neath the sun!

Land of our birth, our faith, our pride,
For whose dear sake our fathers died;
O Motherland, we pledge to thee
Head, heart, and hand through the years to be! *Ib.*

9 High noon behind the tamarisks—the sun is hot above us—
As at Home the Christmas Day is breaking wan.
They will drink our healths at dinner—those who tell us how they love us,
And forget us till another year be gone!
Christmas in India

10 So Time, that is o'er-kind,
To all that be,
Ordains us e'en as blind,
As bold as she:

That in our very death,
And burial sure,
Shadow to shadow, well persuaded, saith,
'See how our works endure!'
Cities and Thrones and Powers (Puck of Pook's Hill)

11 We must go back with Policeman Day—
Back from the City of Sleep! *The City of Sleep*

12 The coastwise lights of England watch the ships of England go! *The Coastwise Lights*

13 They know the worthy General as 'that most immoral man'. *A Code of Morals*

14 Gold is for the mistress—silver for the maid—
Copper for the craftsman cunning at his trade.
'Good!' said the Baron, sitting in his hall,
'But Iron—Cold Iron—is master of them all.'
Cold Iron

15 We have learned to whittle the Eden Tree to the shape of a surplice-peg,
We have learned to bottle our parents twain in the yolk of an addled egg,
We know that the tail must wag the dog, for the horse is drawn by the cart;
But the Devil whoops, as he whooped of old: 'It's clever, but is it Art?'
The Conundrum of the Workshops

16 Our father Adam sat under the Tree and scratched with a stick in the mould;
And the first rude sketch that the world had seen was joy to his mighty heart.
Till the Devil whispered behind the leaves, 'It's pretty, but is it Art?' *Ib.*

17 By the favour of God we might know as much—
as our father Adam knew! *Ib.*

18 And that is called paying the Dane-geld;
But we've proved it again and again,
That if once you have paid him the Dane-geld
You never get rid of the Dane. *Dane-Geld*

19 'What are the bugles blowin' for?' said Files-on-Parade.
'To turn you out, to turn you out,' the Colour-Sergeant said. *Danny Deever*

20 'For they're hangin' Danny Deever, you can hear the Dead March play,
The Regiment's in 'ollow square—they're hangin' 'im to-day;
They've taken of 'is buttons off an' cut 'is stripes away,
An' they're hangin' Danny Deever in the mornin'.'
Ib.

21 The 'eathen in 'is blindness bows down to wood an' stone;
'E don't obey no orders unless they is 'is own;
'E keeps 'is side-arms awful: 'e leaves 'em all about,
An' then comes up the Regiment an' pokes the 'eathen out. *The 'Eathen*

22 All along o' dirtiness, all along o' mess,
All along o' doin' things rather-more-or-less,
All along of abby-nay*, kul†, an' hazar-ho‡,
Mind you keep your rifle an' yourself jus' so! *Ib.*

  * not now † to-morrow ‡ wait a bit.

23 The 'eathen in 'is blindness must end where 'e began,
But the backbone of the Army is the Non-commissioned man! *Ib.*

1 The first dry rattle of new-drawn steel
Changes the world to-day! *Edgehill Fight*

2 Who are neither children nor Gods, but men in a
world of men! *England's Answer to the Cities*

3 Winds of the World, give answer! They are whim-
pering to and fro—
And what should they know of England who only
England know? *The English Flag*

4 I barred my gates with iron, I shuttered my doors
with flame,
Because to force my ramparts your nutshell navies
came. *Ib.*

5 Never was isle so little, never was sea so lone,
But over the scud and the palm-trees an English Flag
was flown. *Ib.*

6 I could not look on Death, which being known,
Men led me to him, blindfold and alone.
Epitaphs of the War. The Coward

7 All that pentecostal crew. *Et Dona Ferentes*

8 But it never really mattered till the English grew
polite. *Ib.*

9 Something lost behind the Ranges. *The Explorer*

10 Your 'Never-never country'. *Ib.*

11 Anybody might have found it, but—His Whisper
came to me! *Ib.*

12 For the Red Gods call us out and we must go!
The Feet of the Young Men

13 When the Hymalayan peasant meets the he-bear in
his pride,
He shouts to scare the monster, who will often turn
aside.
But the she-bear thus accosted rends the peasant
tooth and nail
For the female of the species is more deadly than the
male. *The Female of the Species*

14 Man propounds negotiations, Man accepts the com-
promise.
Very rarely will he squarely push the logic of a fact
To its ultimate conclusion in unmitigated act. *Ib.*

15 Buy my English posies!
Kent and Surrey may—
Violets of the Undercliff
Wet with Channel spray;
Cowslips from a Devon combe—
Midland furze afire—
Buy my English posies
And I'll sell your heart's desire! *The Flowers*

16 Take the flower and turn the hour, and kiss your love
again! *Ib.*

17 So it's knock out your pipes an' follow me!
An' it's finish up your swipes an' follow me!
Oh, 'ark to the big drum callin',
Follow me—follow me 'ome! *Follow Me 'Ome*

18 For it's 'Three rounds blank' an' follow me,
An' it's 'Thirteen rank' an' follow me;
Oh, passin' the love o' women,
Follow me—follow me 'ome! *Ib.*

19 For all we have and are,
For all our children's fate,
Stand up and take the war.
The Hun is at the gate! *For All We Have and Are*

20 There is but one task for all—
One life for each to give.
What stands if Freedom fall?
Who dies if England live? *For All We Have and Are*

21 Ford, ford, ford o' Kabul river,
Ford o' Kabul river in the dark!
There's the river up an' brimmin', an' there's 'arf a
squadron swimmin'
'Cross the ford o' Kabul river in the dark.
Ford o' Kabul River

22 For to admire an' for to see,
For to be'old this world so wide
It never done no good to me,
But I can't drop it if I tried! *For to Admire*

23 So 'ere's to you, Fuzzy-Wuzzy, at your 'ome in the
Soudan;
You're a pore benighted 'eathen but a first-class
fightin' man;
An' 'ere's to you, Fuzzy-Wuzzy, with your 'ayrick
'ead of 'air—
You big black boundin' beggar—for you broke a
British square! *Fuzzy-Wuzzy*

24 'E's all 'ot sand an' ginger when alive,
An' 'e's generally shammin' when 'e's dead. *Ib.*

25 'E's the only thing that doesn't give a damn
For a Regiment o' British Infantree! *Ib.*

26 To the legion of the lost ones, to the cohort of the
damned. *Gentlemen Rankers*

27 Gentlemen-rankers out on the spree,
Damned from here to Eternity. *Ib.*

28 We have done with Hope and Honour, we are lost to
Love and Truth,
We are dropping down the ladder rung by rung;
And the measure of our torment is the measure of our
youth.
God help us, for we knew the worst too young! *Ib.*

29 The wild hawk to the wind-swept sky,
The deer to the wholesome wold,
And the heart of a man to the heart of a maid,
As it was in the days of old. *The Gipsy Trail*

30 Our England is a garden that is full of stately views,
Of borders, beds and shrubberies and lawns and
avenues,
With statues on the terraces and peacocks strutting
by;
But the Glory of the Garden lies in more than meets
the eye. *The Glory of the Garden*

31 The Glory of the Garden it abideth not in words. *Ib.*

32 Our England is a garden, and such gardens are not
made
By singing:—'Oh, how beautiful!' and sitting in the
shade,
While better men than we go out and start their
working lives
At grubbing weeds from gravel paths with broken
dinner-knives. *Ib.*

33 Then seek your job with thankfulness and work till
further orders,
If it's only netting strawberries or killing slugs on
borders;
And when your back stops aching and your hands
begin to harden,
You will find yourself a partner in the Glory of the
Garden.

Oh, Adam was a gardener, and God who made him sees
That half a proper gardener's work is done upon his knees,
So when your work is finished, you can wash your hands and pray
For the Glory of the Garden, that it may not pass away!
And the Glory of the Garden it shall never pass away!
The Glory of the Garden

1 You may talk o' gin an' beer
When you're quartered safe out 'ere,
An' you're sent to penny-fights an' Aldershot it;
But when it comes to slaughter
You will do your work on water,
An' you'll lick the bloomin' boots of 'im that's got it.
Gunga Din

2 The uniform 'e wore
Was nothin' much before,
An' rather less than 'arf o' that be'ind. *Ib.*

3 An' for all 'is dirty 'ide
'E was white, clear white, inside
When 'e went to tend the wounded under fire! *Ib.*

4 So I'll meet 'im later on
At the place where 'e is gone—
Where it's always double drills and no canteen. *Ib.*

5 'E'll be squattin' on the coals
Givin' drink to poor damned souls,
An' I'll get a swig in Hell from Gunga Din. *Ib.*

6 Though I've belted you an' flayed you,
By the livin' Gawd that made you,
You're a better man than I am, Gunga Din! *Ib.*

7 But O, 'tis won'erful good for the Prophet!
Hal o' the Draft. (Puck of Pook's Hill)

8 Ere yet we loose the legions—
Ere yet we draw the blade,
Jehovah of the Thunders,
Lord God of Battles, aid! *Hymn Before Action*

9 There are nine and sixty ways of constructing tribal lays,
And—every—single—one—of—them—is—right!
In the Neolithic Age

10 If you can keep your head when all about you
Are losing theirs and blaming it on you,
If you can trust yourself when all men doubt you,
But make allowance for their doubting too;
If you can wait and not be tired by waiting,
Or being lied about, don't deal in lies,
Or being hated, don't give way to hating,
And yet don't look too good, nor talk too wise:

If you can dream—and not make dreams your master;
If you can think—and not make thoughts your aim;
If you can meet with Triumph and Disaster
And treat those two impostors just the same. *If—*

11 If you can make one heap of all your winnings
And risk it on one turn of pitch-and-toss,
And lose, and start again at your beginnings
And never breathe a word about your loss. *Ib.*

12 If you can talk with crowds and keep your virtue,
Or walk with Kings—nor lose the common touch,
If neither foes nor loving friends can hurt you,
If all men count with you, but none too much;

If you can fill the unforgiving minute
With sixty seconds' worth of distance run,
Yours is the Earth and everything that's in it,
And—which is more—you'll be a Man, my son!
If—

13 I have eaten your bread and salt,
I have drunk your water and wine.
I Have Eaten Your Bread. (Departmental Ditties: Prelude)

14 Dear hearts across the seas. *Ib.*

15 No doubt but ye are the People. *The Islanders*

16 Then ye returned to your trinkets; then ye contented your souls
With the flannelled fools at the wicket or the muddied oafs at the goals. *Ib.*

17 Given to strong delusion, wholly believing a lie. *Ib.*

18 He wrote that monarchs were divine,
And left a son who—proved they weren't! *James I*

19 Jane went to Paradise:
That was only fair,
Good Sir Walter met her first,
And led her up the stair.
Henry and Tobias,
And Miguel of Spain,
Stood with Shakespeare at the top
To welcome Jane. *Jane's Marriage*

20 Jane lies in Winchester, blessèd be her shade!
Praise the Lord for making her, and her for all she made.
And, while the stones of Winchester—or Milsom Street—remain,
Glory, Love, and Honour unto England's Jane! *Ib.*

21 Cold, commanded lust. *Justice*

22 Let them relearn the Law. *Ib.*

23 I've never sailed the Amazon,
I've never reached Brazil.
Just-So Stories. Beginning of the Armadilloes

24 Yes, weekly from Southampton,
Great steamers, white and gold,
Go rolling down to Rio
(Roll down—roll down to Rio!).
And I'd like to roll to Rio
Some day before I'm old! *Ib.*

25 I've never seen a Jaguar,
Nor yet an Armadill-
o dilloing in his armour,
And I s'pose I never will. *Ib.*

26 The Camel's hump is an ugly lump
Which well you may see at the Zoo;
But uglier yet is the Hump we get
From having too little to do.
Ib. How the Camel Got His Hump

27 We get the Hump—
Cameelious Hump—
The Hump that is black and blue! *Ib.*

28 The cure for this ill is not to sit still,
Or frowst with a book by the fire;
But to take a large hoe and a shovel also,
And dig till you gently perspire. *Ib.*

29 Old Man Kangaroo first, Yellow-Dog Dingo behind.
Ib. Sing-Song of Old Man Kangaroo

1 'Confound Romance!' . . . And all unseen
Romance brought up the nine-fifteen.　*The King*

2 For Allah created the English mad—the maddest of
all mankind!　*Kitchener's School*

3 I've taken my fun where I've found it,
An' now I must pay for my fun,
For the more you 'ave known o' the others
The less will you settle to one;
An' the end of it's sittin' an' thinkin',
An' dreamin' Hell-fires to see.
So be warned by my lot (which I know you will not),
An' learn about women from me!　*The Ladies*

4 An' I learned about women from 'er!　*Ib.*

5 But the things you will learn from the Yellow an'
Brown,
They'll 'elp you a lot with the White!　*Ib.*

6 For the Colonel's Lady an' Judy O'Grady
Are sisters under their skins!　*Ib.*

7 Have it jest *as* you've a mind to, but, if I was you, I'd
dreen.　*The Land*

8 'Hev it just as you've a mind to, *but*'—and here he
takes command.
For whoever pays the taxes old Mus' Hobden owns
the land.　*Ib.*

9 Thus said the Lord in the vault above the Cherubim,
Calling to the Angels and the Souls in their degree.
The Last Chantey

10 Then said the soul of the Angel of the Off-shore
Wind.　*Ib.*

11 And Ye take mine honour from me if Ye take away
the sea!　*Ib.*

12 Then cried the soul of the stout Apostle Paul to God.
Ib.

13 When they learned Thy Grace and Glory under
Malta by the sea!　*Ib.*

14 Loud sang the souls of the jolly, jolly mariners,
Plucking at their harps, and they plucked unhandily:
'Our thumbs are rough and tarred,
And the tune is something hard—
May we lift a Deepsea Chantey such as seamen use
at sea?'　*Ib.*

15 Heave or sink it, leave or drink it, we were masters
of the sea!　*Ib.*

16 Then stooped the Lord, and He called the good sea
up to Him,
And 'stablishèd its borders unto all eternity,
That such as have no pleasure
For to praise the Lord by measure,
They may enter into galleons and serve Him on the
Sea.　*Ib.*

17 And the ships shall go abroad
To the Glory of the Lord
Who heard the silly sailor-folk and gave them back
their sea!　*Ib.*

18 I ha' harpit ye up to the Throne o' God,
I ha' harpit your midmost soul in three.
I ha' harpit ye down to the Hinges o' Hell,
And—ye—would—make—a Knight o' me!
The Last Rhyme of True Thomas

19 Now this is the Law of the Jungle—as old and as true
as the sky.　*The Law of the Jungle*

20 This is the sorrowful story
Told as the twilight fails
And the monkeys walk together
Holding their neighbours' tails.
The Legends of Evil

21 Thin Noah spoke him fairly, thin talked to him
sevairely,
An' thin he cursed him squarely to the glory av the
Lord:—
'Divil take the ass that bred you, an' the greater ass
that fed you!
Divil go wid you, ye spalpeen!' an' the Donkey wint
aboard.　*Ib.*

22 Till Noah said:—'There's wan av us that hasn't paid
his fare!'　*Ib.*

23 We have had an Imperial lesson; it may make us an
Empire yet!　*The Lesson*

24 And that's how it all began, my dears,
And that's how it all began!
The Light that Failed, chapter heading

25 The Liner she's a lady, an' she never looks nor
'eeds—
The Man-o'-War's 'er 'usband, an' 'e gives 'er all
she needs;
But, oh, the little cargo-boats, that sail the wet sea
roun',
They're just the same as you an' me a-plyin' up an'
down!　*The Liner She's a Lady*

26 There's a whisper down the field where the year has
shot her yield,
And the ricks stand grey to the sun,
Singing:—'Over then, come over, for the bee has quit
the clover,
And your English summer's done.'　*The Long Trail*

27 You have heard the beat of the off-shore wind,
And the thresh of the deep-sea rain;
You have heard the song—how long? how long?
Pull out on the trail again!
Ha' done with the Tents of Shem, dear lass,
We've seen the seasons through,
And it's time to turn on the old trail, our own trail,
the out trail,
Pull out, pull out, on the Long Trail—the trail that
is always new!　*Ib.*

28 It's North you may run to the rime-ringed sun,
Or South to the blind Horn's hate;
Or East all the way into Mississippi Bay,
Or West to the Golden Gate.　*Ib.*

29 The Queen was in her chamber, and she was middling
old,
Her petticoat was satin, and her stomacher was gold.
Backwards and forwards and sideways did she pass,
Making up her mind to face the cruel looking-glass.
The cruel looking-glass that will never show a lass
As comely or as kindly or as young as what she was!
The Looking Glass

30 The Queen was in her chamber, her sins were on her
head.
She looked the spirits up and down and statelily she
said:—
'Backwards and forwards and sideways though I've
been,
Yet I am Harry's daughter and I am England's
Queen!'　*Ib.*

1 There's a Legion that never was 'listed.
The Lost Legion

2 To go and find out and be damned
(Dear boys!),
To go and get shot and be damned. *Ib.*

3 Lord, Thou hast made this world below the shadow
of a dream,
An', taught by time, I tak' it so—exceptin' always
Steam.
From coupler-flange to spindle-guide I see Thy
Hand, O God—
Predestination in the stride o' yon connectin'-rod.
McAndrew's Hymn

4 Alone wi' God an' these
My engines. *Ib.*

5 Yon's strain, hard strain, o' head an' hand, for though
Thy Power brings
All skill to naught, Ye'll understand a man must
think o' things. *Ib.*

6 Ye thought? Ye are not paid to think. *Ib.*

7 Mister McAndrew, don't you think steam spoils
romance at sea? *Ib.*

8 Romance! Those first-class passengers they like it
very well,
Printed an' bound in little books; but why don't
poets tell? *Ib.*

9 While, out o' touch o' vanity, the sweatin' thrust-
block says:
'Not unto us the praise, or man—not unto us the
praise!' *Ib.*

10 By the old Moulmein Pagoda, lookin' eastward to the
sea,
There's a Burma girl a-settin', and I know she thinks
o' me;
For the wind is in the palm-trees, an' the temple-
bells they say:
'Come you back, you British soldier; come you back
to Mandalay!'
Come you back to Mandalay,
Where the old Flotilla lay:
Can't you 'ear their paddles chunkin' from Rangoon
to Mandalay?
On the road to Mandalay,
Where the flyin'-fishes play,
An' the dawn comes up like thunder outer China
'crost the Bay! *Mandalay*

11 An' I seed her first a-smokin' of a whackin' white
cheroot,
An' a-wastin' Christian kisses on an 'eathen idol's
foot. *Ib.*

12 When the mist was on the rice-fields an' the sun was
droppin' slow,
She'd git 'er little banjo an' she'd sing 'Kulla-lo-lo!'
Ib.

13 But that's all shove be'ind me—long ago an' fur away,
An' there ain' no 'buses runnin' from the Bank to
Mandalay;
An' I'm learnin' 'ere in London wot the ten-year
soldier tells:
'If you've 'eard the East a-callin', you won't never
'eed naught else.' *Ib.*

14 I am sick o' wastin' leather on these gritty pavin'-
stones,
An' the blasted English drizzle wakes the fever in my
bones;
Tho' I walks with fifty 'ousemaids outer Chelsea to
the Strand,
An' they talks a lot o' lovin', but wot do they under-
stand?
Beefy face an' grubby 'and—
Law! Wot do they understand?
I've a neater, sweeter maiden in a cleaner, greener
land! *Mandalay*

15 Ship me somewheres east of Suez, where the best is
like the worst,
Where there aren't no Ten Commandments, an' a
man can raise a thirst:
For the temple-bells are callin', an' it's there that I
would be—
By the old Moulmein Pagoda, looking lazy at the sea.
Ib.

16 Ten thousand men on the pay-roll, and forty
freighters at sea! *The 'Mary Gloster'*

17 Harrer an' Trinity College! I ought to ha' sent you
to sea. *Ib.*

18 For you muddled with books and pictures, an' china
an' etchin's an' fans,
And your rooms at college was beastly—more like a
whore's than a man's. *Ib.*

19 I've seen your carriages blocking the half o' the
Cromwell Road,
But never the doctor's brougham to help the missus
unload. *Ib.*

20 For a man he must go with a woman, which women
don't understand—
Or the sort that say they can see it, they aren't the
marrying brand. *Ib.*

21 I'm sick of the hired women. I'll kiss my girl on her
lips! *Ib.*

22 Nice while it lasted, an' now it is over—
Tear out your 'eart an' good-bye to your lover!
What's the use o' grievin', when the mother that bore
you
(Mary, pity women!) knew it all before you?
Mary, Pity Women

23 There runs a road by Merrow Down—
A grassy track to-day it is—
An hour out of Guildford town,
Above the river Wey it is. *Merrow Down*

24 But as the faithful years return
And hearts unwounded sing again,
Comes Taffy dancing through the fern
To lead the Surrey spring again. *Ib.*

25 Mines reported in the fairway,
Warn all traffic and detain.
'Sent up *Unity, Claribel, Assyrian, Stormcock,* and
Golden Gain. *Mine Sweepers*

26 Good rest to all
That keep the Jungle Law.
Morning Song in the Jungle

27 If I were hanged on the highest hill,
Mother o' mine, O mother o' mine!
I know whose love would follow me still,
Mother o' mine, O mother o' mine!
Mother O' Mine

1 If I were damned of body and soul,
I know whose prayers would make me whole,
Mother o' mine, O mother o' mine! *Mother O'Mine*

2 'Have you news of my boy Jack?'
Not this tide.
'When d'you think that he'll come back?'
Not with this wind blowing, and this tide.
My Boy Jack

3 My new-cut ashlar takes the light
Where crimson-blank the windows flare.
My New-cut Ashlar

4 The depth and dream of my desire,
The bitter paths wherein I stray—
Thou knowest Who hast made the Fire,
Thou knowest Who hast made the Clay. *Ib.*

5 One stone the more swings into place
In that dread Temple of Thy worth.
It is enough that, through Thy Grace,
I saw nought common on Thy Earth. *Ib.*

6 Now it is not good for the Christian's health to hustle
the Aryan brown,
For the Christian riles, and the Aryan smiles, and it
weareth the Christian down;
And the end of the fight is a tombstone white with
the name of the late deceased,
And the epitaph drear: 'A Fool lies here who tried to
hustle the East.' *Naulahka*, heading of ch. 5

7 The Saxon is not like us Normans. His manners are
not so polite.
But he never means anything serious till he talks
about justice and right,
When he stands like an ox in the furrow with his
sullen set eyes on your own,
And grumbles, 'This isn't fair dealing,' my son, leave
the Saxon alone. *Norman and Saxon*

8 The 'orse 'e knows above a bit, the bullock's but a
fool,
The elephant's a gentleman, the battery-mule's a
mule;
But the commissariat cam-u-el, when all is said an'
done,
'E's a devil an' a ostrich an' a orphan-child in one.
Oonts

9 Excellent herbs had our fathers of old—
Excellent herbs to ease their pain.
Our Fathers of Old

10 Anything green that grew out of the mould
Was an excellent herb to our fathers of old. *Ib.*

11 A Nation spoke to a Nation,
A Throne sent word to a Throne:
'Daughter am I in my mother's house,
But mistress in my own.
The gates are mine to open,
As the gates are mine to close,
And I abide by my Mother's House.'
Said our Lady of the Snows. *Our Lady of the Snows*

12 In the Name of the Empress, the Overland Mail!
The Overland Mail

13 The toad beneath the harrow knows
Exactly where each tooth-point goes;
The butterfly upon the road
Preaches contentment to that toad. *Pagett M.P.*

14 Pagett, M.P., was a liar, and a fluent liar therewith.
Ib.

15 After me cometh a Builder. Tell him, I too have
known. *The Palace*

16 Can't! Don't! Sha'n't! Won't!
Pass it along the line!
Somebody's pack has slid from his back,
'Wish it were only mine!
Somebody's load has tipped off in the road—
Cheer for a halt and a row!
Urrh! Yarrh! Grr! Arrh!
Somebody's catching it now!
Parade-Song of the Camp-Animals. Commissariat Camels

17 But a man in khaki kit who could handle men a bit,
With his bedding labelled Sergeant Whatsisname.
Pharaoh and the Sergeant

18 He drank strong waters and his speech was coarse;
He purchased raiment and forbore to pay;
He stuck a trusting junior with a horse,
And won gymkhanas in a doubtful way,
Then, 'twixt a vice and folly, turned aside
To do good deeds—and straight to cloak them, lied.
Plain Tales from the Hills. Chapter heading to
A Bank Fraud

19 The Three in One, the One in Three? Not so!
To my own Gods I go.
It may be they shall give me greater ease
Than your cold Christ and tangled Trinities.
Ib. Chapter heading to *Lispeth*

20 Bade farewell to Minnie Boffkin in one last, long
lingering fit. *The Post that Fitted*

21 Year by year, in pious patience, vengeful Mrs. Boffkin sits
Waiting for the Sleary babies to develop Sleary's fits.
Ib.

22 There is sorrow enough in the natural way
From men and women to fill our day;
But when we are certain of sorrow in store,
Why do we always arrange for more?
Brothers and Sisters, I bid you beware
Of giving your heart to a dog to tear.
The Power of the Dog

23 Valour and Innocence
Have latterly gone hence
To certain death by certain shame attended.
The Queen's Men

24 God of our fathers, known of old,
Lord of our far-flung battle-line,
Beneath whose awful Hand we hold
Dominion over palm and pine—
Lord God of Hosts, be with us yet,
Lest we forget—lest we forget!

The tumult and the shouting dies;
The Captains and the Kings depart:
Still stands Thine ancient sacrifice,
An humble and a contrite heart.
Lord God of Hosts, be with us yet,
Lest we forget—lest we forget! *Recessional*

25 Lo, all our pomp of yesterday
Is one with Nineveh and Tyre! *Ib.*

26 If, drunk with sight of power, we loose
Wild tongues that have not Thee in awe,
Such boastings as the Gentiles use,
Or lesser breeds without the Law. *Ib.*

1 For heathen heart that puts her trust
  In reeking tube and iron shard,
  All valiant dust that builds on dust,
  And, guarding, calls not Thee to guard,
  For frantic boast and foolish word—
  Thy mercy on Thy People, Lord!   *Recessional*

2 If England was what England seems,
  An' not the England of our dreams,
  But only putty, brass, an' paint,
  'Ow quick we'd drop 'er! But she ain't!
                                          The Return

3 There's never a law of God or man runs north of the
  Fifty-Three.   *The Rhyme of the Three Sealers*

4 English they be and Japanee that hang on the Brown
  Bear's flank,
  And some be Scot, but the worst of the lot, and the
  boldest thieves, be Yank!   *Ib.*

5 And I've lost Britain, and I've lost Gaul,
  And I've lost Rome and, worst of all,
  I've lost Lalage!   *Rimini*

6 I walk my beat before London Town,
  Five hours up and seven down,
  Up I go till I end my run
  At Tide-end-town, which is Teddington.
                                          The River's Tale

7 Brother, thy tail hangs down behind!
                          Road Song of the Bandar-Log

8 Smokin' my pipe on the mountings, sniffin' the
  mornin' cool,
  I walks in my old brown gaiters along o' my old brown
  mule
  With seventy gunners be'ind me, an' never a beggar
  forgets
  It's only the pick of the Army that handles the dear
  little pets—
  For you all love the Screw-guns—the Screw-guns
  they all love you!
  So when we call round with a few guns, o' course
  you'll know what to do—
  Just send in your Chief an' surrender—it's worse if
  you fights or you runs:
  You can go where you please, you can skid up the
  trees, but you don't get away from the guns!
                                          Screw-guns

9 Who hath desired the Sea?—the sight of salt water
  unbounded.   *The Sea and the Hills*

10 So and no otherwise—so and no otherwise—hillmen
  desire their Hills!   *Ib.*

11 Cheer for the Sergeant's weddin'—
  Give 'em one cheer more!
  Grey gun-'orses in the lando,
  An' a rogue is married to a whore.
                                          The Sergeant's Weddin'

12 Shillin' a day,
  Bloomin' good pay—
  Lucky to touch it, a shillin' a day!   *Shillin' a Day*

13 Give 'im a letter—
  Can't do no better,
  Late Troop-Sergeant-Major an'—runs with a letter!
  Think what 'e's been,
  Think what 'e's seen.
  Think of 'is pension an'—
  GAWD SAVE THE QUEEN!   *Ib.*

14 So it was 'Rounds! What Rounds?' at two of a frosty
  night.
  'E's 'oldin' on by the Sergeant's sash, but, sentry,
  shut your eye.   *The Shut-Eye Sentry*

15 But you ought to 'ave 'eard 'em markin' time
  To 'ide the things 'e said!   *Ib.*

16 There was two-an'-thirty Sergeants,
  There was Corp'rals forty-one,
  There was just nine 'undred rank an' file
  To swear to a touch o' sun.   *Ib.*

17 We'll 'elp 'im for 'is mother, an' 'e'll 'elp us by-an'-
  by!   *Ib.*

18 Them that asks no questions isn't told a lie.
  Watch the wall, my darling, while the Gentlemen go
  by!
  Five and twenty ponies
  Trotting through the dark—
  Brandy for the Parson,
  'Baccy for the Clerk;
  Laces for a lady, letters for a spy,
  Watch the wall, my darling, while the Gentlemen go
  by!   *A Smuggler's Song*

19 Sez 'e, 'I'm a Jolly—'Er Majesty's Jolly—soldier an'
  sailor too!'   *Soldier an' Sailor too!*

20 'E's a kind of a giddy harumfrodite—soldier an'
  sailor too!   *Ib.*

21 I'm the Prophet of the Utterly Absurd,
  Of the Patently Impossible and Vain.
                                          The Song of the Banjo

22 I am all that ever went with evening dress!   *Ib.*

23 There's never a wave of all her waves
  But marks our English dead. *The Song of the Dead*, ii

24 If blood be the price of admiralty,
  Lord God, we ha' paid in full!   *Ib.*

25 For the Lord our God Most High
  He hath made the deep as dry,
  He hath smote for us a pathway to the ends of all the
  earth!   *A Song of the English*

26 Keep ye the Law—be swift in all obedience—
  Clear the land of evil, drive the road and bridge the
  ford.
  Make ye sure to each his own
  That he reap where he hath sown;
  By the peace among our peoples let men know we
  serve the Lord!   *Ib.*

27 Ere Mor the Peacock flutters, ere the Monkey People
  cry,
  Ere Chil the Kite swoops down a furlong sheer,
  Through the Jungle very softly flits a shadow and a
  sigh—
  He is Fear, O Little Hunter, he is Fear!
                                          The Song of the Little Hunter

28 But thy throat is shut and dried, and thy heart against
  thy side
  Hammers: 'Fear, O Little Hunter—this is Fear!'   *Ib.*

29 Mithras, God of the Morning, our trumpets waken
  the Wall!
  'Rome is above the Nations, but Thou art over all!'
                                          A Song to Mithras

1 The Sons of Mary seldom bother, for they have inherited that good part;
But the Sons of Martha favour their Mother of the
careful soul and the troubled heart.
And because she lost her temper once, and because
she was rude to the Lord her Guest,
Her Sons must wait upon Mary's Sons, world without
end, reprieve, or rest. *The Sons of Martha*

2 They do not preach that their God will rouse them a
little before the nuts work loose.
They do not teach that His Pity allows them to leave
their job when they damn-well choose. *Ib.*

3 They sit at the Feet—they hear the Word—they see
how truly the Promise runs.
They have cast their burden upon the Lord, and—
the Lord He lays it on Martha's Sons! *Ib.*

4 'Let us now praise famous men'—
Men of little showing—
For their work continueth,
And their work continueth,
Broad and deep continueth,
Greater than their knowing!
Stalky & Co. A School Song

5 An' it all goes into the laundry,
But it never comes out in the wash,
'Ow we're sugared about by the old men
('Eavy-sterned amateur old men!)
That 'amper an' 'inder an' scold men
For fear o' Stellenbosch! *Stellenbosch*

6 You may carve it on his tombstone, you may cut it
on his card,
That a young man married is a young man marred.
The Story of the Gadsbys

7 No tender-hearted garden crowns,
No bosomed woods adorn
Our blunt, bow-headed whale-backed Downs,
But gnarled and writhen thorn. *Sussex*

8 Half-wild and wholly tame,
The wise turf cloaks the white cliff-edge
As when the Romans came. *Ib.*

9 The barrow and the camp abide,
The sunlight and the sward. *Ib.*

10 And here the sea-fogs lap and cling
And here, each warning each,
The sheep-bells and the ship-bells ring
Along the hidden beach. *Ib.*

11 Little, lost, Down churches praise
The Lord who made the hills. *Ib.*

12 Huge oaks and old, the which we hold
No more than Sussex weed. *Ib.*

13 God gives all men all earth to love,
But, since man's heart is small,
Ordains for each one spot shall prove
Belovèd over all.
Each to his choice, and I rejoice
The lot has fallen to me
In a fair ground—in a fair ground—
Yea, Sussex by the sea! *Ib.*

14 Till I 'eard a beggar squealin' out for quarter as 'e
ran,
An' I thought I knew the voice an'—it was me!
That Day

15 Once on a time there was a Man.
Things and the Man

16 And, Thomas, here's my best respects to you!
*To Thomas Atkins. Prelude to Barrack-Room
Ballads*

17 One man in a thousand, Solomon says,
Will stick more close than a brother.
The Thousandth Man

18 But the Thousandth Man will stand by your side
To the gallows-foot—and after! *Ib.*

19 With maids of matchless beauty and parentage un-
guessed,
And a Church of England parson for the Islands of
the Blest. *The Three-Decker*

20 Till he heard as the roar of a rain-fed ford the roar of
the Milky Way. *Tomlinson*

21 Stand up, stand up now, Tomlinson, and answer
loud and high
The good that ye did for the sake of men or ever ye
came to die. *Ib.*

22 But now ye wait at Heaven's Gate and not in Berkeley Square. *Ib.*

23 Though we called your friend from his bed this night,
he could not speak to you,
For the race is run by one and one and never by two
and two. *Ib.*

24 'Ye have read, ye have heard, ye have thought,' he
said, 'and the tale is yet to run:
By the worth of the body that once ye had, give
answer—what ha' ye done?' *Ib.*

25 Oh, this I have felt, and this I have guessed, and
this I have heard men say,
And this they wrote that another man wrote of a carl
in Norroway. *Ib.*

26 And—the faith that ye share with Berkeley Square
uphold you, Tomlinson! *Ib.*

27 The Wind that blows between the Worlds, it nipped
him to the bone,
And he yearned to the flare of Hell-gate there as the
light of his own hearth-stone. *Ib.*

28 For the sin ye do by two and two ye must pay for one
by one! *Ib.*

29 Once I ha' laughed at the power of Love and twice at
the grip of the Grave,
And thrice I ha' patted my God on the head that men
might call me brave. *Ib.*

30 Have ye sinned one sin for the pride o' the eye or the
sinful lust of the flesh? *Ib.*

31 Then Tomlinson he gripped the bars and yammered,
'Let me in—
For I mind that I borrowed my neighbour's wife to
sin the deadly sin.'
The Devil he grinned behind the bars, and banked
the fires high:
'Did ye read of that sin in a book?' said he; and
Tomlinson said 'Ay!' *Ib.*

32 The Devil he blew upon his nails, and the little devils
ran. *Ib.*

33 'Ye have scarce the soul of a louse,' he said, 'but the
roots of sin are there.' *Ib.*

34 And—the God that you took from a printed book be
with you, Tomlinson! *Ib.*

1 Oh, it's Tommy this, an' Tommy that, an' 'Tommy, go away';
But it's 'Thank you, Mister Atkins,' when the band begins to play. *Tommy*

2 It's Tommy this, an' Tommy that, an' 'Chuck him out, the brute!'
But it's 'Saviour of 'is country' when the guns begin to shoot. *Ib.*

3 Then it's Tommy this, an' Tommy that, an' 'Tommy, 'ow's yer soul?'
But it's 'Thin red line of 'eroes' when the drums begin to roll. *Ib.*

4 We aren't no thin red 'eroes, nor we aren't no black-guards too.
But single men in barricks, most remarkable like you;
An' if sometimes our conduck isn't all your fancy paints,
Why, single men in barricks don't grow into plaster saints. *Ib.*

5 Of all the trees that grow so fair,
Old England to adorn,
Greater are none beneath the Sun,
Than Oak, and Ash, and Thorn. *A Tree Song*

6 England shall bide till Judgement Tide,
By Oak, and Ash, and Thorn! *Ib.*

7 I tell this tale, which is strictly true,
Just by way of convincing you
How very little, since things were made,
Things have altered in the building trade. *A Truthful Song*

8 Your glazing is new and your plumbing's strange,
But otherwise I perceive no change;
And in less than a month, if you do as I bid,
I'd learn you to build me a Pyramid! *Ib.*

9 The old man kindly answered them:
'It might be Japheth, it might be Shem,
Or it might be Ham (though his skin was dark),
Whereas it is Noah, commanding the Ark.'

Your wheel is new and your pumps are strange,
But otherwise I perceive no change;
And in less than a week, if she did not ground,
I'd sail this hooker the wide world round! *Ib.*

10 Much I owe to the Lands that grew—
More to the Lives that fed—
But most to Allah Who gave me two
Separate sides to my head. *The Two-Sided Man*

11 The dark eleventh hour
Draws on and sees us sold. *Ulster*

12 A fool there was and he made his prayer
(Even as you and I!)
To a rag and a bone and a hank of hair
(We called her the woman who did not care)
But the fool he called her his lady fair—
(Even as you and I!) *The Vampire*

13 But a fool must follow his natural bent
(Even as you and I!) *Ib.*

14 Oh, was there ever sailor free to choose,
That didn't settle somewhere near the sea? *The Virginity*

15 They that have wrought the end unthought
Be neither saint nor sage,
But only men who did the work
For which they drew the wage. *The Wage-Slaves*

16 They shut the road through the woods
Seventy years ago. *The Way Through the Woods*

17 Steadily cantering through
The misty solitudes,
As though they perfectly knew
The old lost road through the woods—
But there is no road through the woods! *Ib.*

18 Father, Mother, and Me,
Sister and Auntie say
All the people like us are We,
And every one else is They. *We and They*

19 When Earth's last picture is painted and the tubes are twisted and dried,
When the oldest colours have faded, and the youngest critic has died,
We shall rest, and, faith, we shall need it—lie down for an æon or two,
Till the Master of All Good Workmen shall put us to work anew. *When Earth's Last Picture*

20 And those that were good shall be happy: they shall sit in a golden chair;
They shall splash at a ten-league canvas with brushes of comets' hair. *Ib.*

21 And only The Master shall praise us, and only The Master shall blame;
And no one shall work for money, and no one shall work for fame,
But each for the joy of the working, and each, in his separate star,
Shall draw the Thing as he sees It for the God of Things as They are! *Ib.*

22 When 'Omer smote 'is bloomin' lyre,
'E'd 'eard men sing by land an' sea;
An' what 'e thought 'e might require,
'E went an' took—the same as me!
When 'Omer Smote. (Barrack-Room Ballads: Introduction)

23 They knew 'e stole; 'e knew they knowed.
They didn't tell, nor make a fuss,
But winked at 'Omer down the road,
An' 'e winked back—the same as us! *Ib.*

24 Take up the White Man's burden—
Send forth the best ye breed—
Go, bind your sons to exile
To serve your captives' need;
To wait in heavy harness
On fluttered folk and wild—
Your new-caught, sullen peoples,
Half-devil and half-child. *The White Man's Burden*

25 By all ye cry or whisper,
By all ye leave or do,
The silent, sullen peoples
Shall weigh your Gods and you. *Ib.*

26 Take up the White Man's burden—
And reap his old reward:
The blame of those ye better,
The hate of those ye guard. *Ib.*

27 'Ave you 'eard o' the Widow at Windsor
With a hairy gold crown on 'er 'ead?
She 'as ships on the foam—she 'as millions at 'ome,
An' she pays us poor beggars in red. *The Widow at Windsor*

1 Take 'old o' the Wings o' the Mornin',
An' flop round the earth till you're dead;
But you won't get away from the tune that they play
To the bloomin' old rag over 'ead.
The Widow at Windsor

2 Down to Gehenna or up to the Throne,
He travels the fastest who travels alone.
The Winners

3 When the 'arf-made recruity goes out to the East
'E acts like a babe an' 'e drinks like a beast,
An' 'e wonders because 'e is frequent deceased
Ere 'e's fit for to serve as a soldier.
The Young British Soldier

4 When you're wounded and left on Afghanistan's
plains,
An' the women come out to cut up what remains,
Jest roll to your rifle an' blow out your brains
An' go to your Gawd like a soldier. *Ib.*

5 How can I crown thee further, O Queen of the
Sovereign South? *The Young Queen*

6 'Ha! Ha!' said the duck, laughing.
The Day's Work. The Brushwood Boy

7 What shall I do when I see you in the light? *Ib.*

8 Good hunting! *The Jungle Book. Kaa's Hunting*

9 We be of one blood, thou and I. *Ib.*

10 'Nice,' said the small 'stute Fish. 'Nice but nubbly.'
Just-So Stories. How the Whale Got His Throat

11 You must *not* forget the Suspenders, Best Beloved.
Ib.

12 A man of infinite-resource-and-sagacity. *Ib.*

13 Most 'scruciating idle.
Ib. How the Camel Got His Hump

14 'Humph yourself!'
And the Camel humphed himself. *Ib.*

15 There lived a Parsee from whose hat the rays of the
sun were reflected in more-than-oriental-splen-
dour. *Ib. How the Rhinoceros Got His Skin*

16 An Elephant's Child—who was full of 'satiable
curtiosity. *Ib. The Elephant's Child*

17 The great grey-green, greasy Limpopo River, all set
about with fever-trees. *Ib.*

18 Led go! You are hurtig be! *Ib.*

19 This is too butch for be! *Ib.*

20 He was a Tidy Pachyderm. *Ib.*

21 The Cat. He walked by himself, and all places were
alike to him.
Ib. The Cat That Walked By Himself

22 He went back through the Wet Wild Woods, waving
his wild tail, and walking by his wild lone. But he
never told anybody. *Ib.*

23 Tho' tay is not my diversion.
Life's Handicap. The Courting of Dinah Shadd

24 Glory's no compensation for a belly-ache. *Ib.*

25 What's the good of argifying? *Ib. On Greenhow Hill*

26 I hold by the Ould Church, for she's the mother of
them all—ay, an' the father, too. I like her bekaze
she's most remarkable regimental in her fittings. *Ib.*

27 Asia is not going to be civilized after the methods of
the West. There is too much Asia and she is too
old. *Ib. The Man Who Was*

28 Let it be clearly understood that the Russian is a delightful person till he tucks in his shirt.
Life's Handicap. The Man Who Was

29 Man that is born of woman is small potatoes and few
in the hill. *Ib. The Head of the District*

30 Some were married, which was bad, and some did
other things which were worse.
Ib. The Mark of the Beast

31 You haf too much Ego in your Cosmos.
Ib. Bertran and Bimi

32 He did not rave, as do many bridegrooms, over the
strangeness and delight of seeing his own true love
sitting down to breakfast with him every morning
'as though it were the most natural thing in the
world'. 'He had been there before', as the Americans say. *Ib. Georgie Porgie*

33 The Light that Failed. *Title of Novel*

34 Every one is more or less mad on one point.
*Plain Tales from the Hills. On the Strength of
a Likeness*

35 Open and obvious devotion from any sort of man is
always pleasant to any sort of woman. *Ib.*

36 He gave way to the queer, savage feeling that sometimes takes by the throat a husband twenty years'
married, when he sees, across the table, the same
face of his wedded wife, and knows that, as he has
sat facing it, so must he continue to sit until the
day of its death or his own.
Ib. The Bronckhurst Divorce Case

37 Twas like a battle field wid all the glory missin.
Ib. The Daughter of the Regiment

38 Take my word for it, the silliest woman can manage
a clever man; but it needs a very clever woman to
manage a fool. *Ib. Three and—an Extra*

39 But that is another story. *Ib.*

40 Lalun is a member of the most ancient profession in
the world. *Soldiers Three. On the City Wall*

41 Being kissed by a man who didn't wax his moustache
was—like eating an egg without salt.
Ib. The Gadsbys. Poor Dear Mamma

42 Steady the Buffs. *Ib.*

43 Been trotting out the Gorgonzola! *Ib.*

44 Almost inevitable Consequences. *Ib. Fatima*

45 I gloat! Hear me gloat! *Stalky and Co., ch. i*

46 Your Uncle Stalky. *Ib.*

47 We ain't goin' to have any beastly Erickin'.
Ib. The Moral Reformers

48 'This man,' said M'Turk, with conviction, 'is *the
Gadarene Swine*.' *Ib. The Flag of Their Country*

49 It's boy; only boy. *Ib. An Unsavoury Interlude*

50 'Tisn't beauty, so to speak, nor good talk necessarily. It's just IT. Some women'll stay in a man's
memory if they once walked down a street.
Traffics and Discoveries. Mrs. Bathurst

51 The Waddy is an infectious disease herself.
Wee Willie Winkie. A Second-Rate Woman

52 Once upon a time there was a Man and his Wife and
a Tertium Quid. *Ib. At the Pit's Mouth*

53 Gawd knows, an' 'E won't split on a pal.
Ib. Drums of the Fore and Aft

HORATIO HERBERT KITCHENER, EARL KITCHENER
1850–1916

1 You are ordered abroad as a soldier of the King to help our French comrades against the invasion of a common enemy. You have to perform a task which will need your courage, your energy, your patience. Remember that the honour of the British Army depends on your individual conduct. It will be your duty not only to set an example of discipline and perfect steadiness under fire but also to maintain the most friendly relations with those whom you are helping in this struggle. In this new experience you may find temptations both in wine and women. You must entirely resist both temptations, and, while treating all women with perfect courtesy, you should avoid any intimacy. Do your duty bravely. Fear God. Honour the King.

A message to the soldiers of the British Expeditionary Force, 1914, to be kept by each soldier in his Active Service Pay-Book. Sir G. Arthur's *Life of Kitchener*, vol. iii, p. 27.

FRIEDRICH VON KLINGER
1752–1831

2 Sturm und Drang.

Storm and stress. *Title of Play* (1775)

CHARLES KNIGHT

3 Here we are! here we are!! here we are again!!! There's Pat and Mac and Tommy and Jack and Joe. When there's trouble brewing, When there's something doing, Are we downhearted? No! let 'em all come!

Here We Are! Here We Are Again!!

MARY KNOWLES
1733–1807

4 He [Dr. Johnson] gets at the substance of a book directly; he tears out the heart of it.

Boswell's *Johnson* (ed. 1934), vol. iii, p. 284. *15 Apr. 1778*

JOHN KNOX
1505–1572

5 Un homme avec Dieu est toujours dans la majorité.

A man with God is always in the majority. *Inscription on the Reformation Monument, Geneva, Switzerland*

6 The First Blast of the Trumpet Against the Monstrous Regiment of Women. *Title of Pamphlet,* 1558

RONALD ARBUTHNOT KNOX
1888–

7 When suave politeness, tempering bigot zeal, Corrected *I believe* to *One does feel.*

Absolute and Abitofhell

8 O God, for as much as without Thee We are not enabled to doubt Thee, Help us all by Thy grace To convince the whole race It knows nothing whatever about Thee.

Attr. Langford Reed, *The Limerick Book*

9 There was a young man of Devizes, Whose ears were of different sizes; The one that was small Was no use at all, But the other won several prizes.

Attr. Langford Reed, *The Limerick Book*

10 There was once a man who said 'God Must think it exceedingly odd If he finds that this tree Continues to be When there's no one about in the Quad.'

Ib. For the answer see 5:27

PAUL KRUGER
1825–1904

11 A bill of indemnity . . . for raid by Dr. Jameson and the British South Africa Company's troops. The amount falls under two heads—first material damage, total of claim, £577,938 3s. 3d.; second, moral or intellectual damage, total of claim, £1,000,000.

Communicated to House of Commons by Joseph Chamberlain, 18 Feb. 1897

THOMAS KYD
1557?–1595?

12 In time the savage bull sustains the yoke, In time all haggard hawks will stoop to lure, In time small wedges cleave the hardest oak, In time the flint is pierced with softest shower.

The Spanish Tragedy, I. vi. 3

13 What outcries pluck me from my naked bed?

Ib. II. v. I

14 Oh eyes, no eyes, but fountains fraught with tears; Oh life, no life, but lively form of death; Oh world, no world, but mass of public wrongs.

Ib. III. ii. I

15 Thus must we toil in other men's extremes, That know not how to remedy our own. *Ib.* vi. I

16 I am never better than when I am mad. Then methinks I am a brave fellow; then I do wonders. But reason abuseth me, and there's the torment, there's the hell. *Ib.* vii a. 169 (1602 edn.)

17 My son—and what's a son? A thing begot Within a pair of minutes, thereabout, A lump bred up in darkness. *Ib.* xi. Additions, l. 5

18   Duly twice a morning Would I be sprinkling it with fountain water. At last it grew, and grew, and bore, and bore, Till at the length It grew a gallows and did bear our son, It bore thy fruit and mine: O wicked, wicked plant.

Ib. xii. Additions, l. 66

19 For what's a play without a woman in it?

Ib. IV. i. 96

HENRY LABOUCHERE
1831–1912

20 He [Labouchere] did not object, he once said, to Gladstone's always having the ace of trumps up his sleeve, but only to his pretence that God had put it there.

Dict. of Nat. Biog., 1912–1921. Cf. Thorold's *Life of Labouchere,* p. 375

ARTHUR J. LAMB
1870–1928

1 She's a bird in a gilded cage. *Song (1900)*

LADY CAROLINE LAMB
1785–1828

2 Mad, bad, and dangerous to know.
Of Byron, in her Journal

CHARLES LAMB
1775–1834

3 I have no ear. *Essays of Elia. A Chapter on Ears*

4 I even think that sentimentally I am disposed to harmony. But organically I am incapable of a tune. *Ib.*

5 'Presents', I often say, 'endear Absents.'
Ib. A Dissertation upon Roast Pig

6 It argues an insensibility. *Ib.*

7 We are not of Alice, nor of thee, nor are we children at all. The children of Alice call Bartrum father. We are nothing; less than nothing, and dreams. We are only what might have been, and must wait upon the tedious shores of Lethe millions of ages before we have existence, and a name.
Ib. Dream Children

8 Why have we none [i.e. no grace] for books, those spiritual repasts—a grace before Milton—a grace before Shakspeare—a devotional exercise proper to be said before reading the Faerie Queene?
Ib. Grace Before Meat

9 Coleridge holds that a man cannot have a pure mind who refuses apple-dumplings. I am not certain but he is right. *Ib.*

10 I am, in plainer words, a bundle of prejudices—made up of likings and dislikings.
Ib. Imperfect Sympathies

11 I have been trying all my life to like Scotchmen, and am obliged to desist from the experiment in despair. *Ib.*

12 'A clear fire, a clean hearth, and the rigour of the game.' This was the celebrated wish of old Sarah Battle (now with God), who, next to her devotions, loved a good game at whist.
Ib. Mrs. Battle's Opinions on Whist

13 All people have their blind side—their superstitions; and I have heard her declare, under the rose, that Hearts was her favourite suit. *Ib.*

14 She unbent her mind afterwards—over a book. *Ib.*

15 Methinks it is better that I should have pined away seven of my goldenest years, when I was thrall to the fair hair, and fairer eyes, of Alice W - - n, than that so passionate a love-adventure should be lost.
Ib. New Year's Eve

16 In everything that relates to science, I am a whole Encyclopaedia behind the rest of the world.
Ib. The Old and the New Schoolmaster

17 He is awkward, and out of place, in the society of his equals. . . . He cannot meet you on the square.
Ib.

18 A votary of the desk—a notched and cropt scrivener—one that sucks his substance, as certain sick people are said to do, through a quill.
Essays of Elia. Oxford in the Vacation

19 The human species, according to the best theory I can form of it, is composed of two distinct races, *the men who borrow*, and *the men who lend*.
Ib. The Two Races of Men

20 What a liberal confounding of those pedantic distinctions of *meum* and *tuum*! *Ib.*

21 I mean your *borrowers of books*—those mutilators of collections, spoilers of the symmetry of shelves, and creators of odd volumes. *Ib.*

22 To lose a volume to C[oleridge] carries some sense and meaning in it. You are sure that he will make one hearty meal on your viands, if he can give no account of the platter after it. *Ib.*

23 That princely woman, the thrice noble Margaret Newcastle. *Ib.*

24 I counsel thee, shut not thy heart, nor thy library, against S. T. C[oleridge]. *Ib.*

25 I love to lose myself in other men's minds. When I am not walking, I am reading; I cannot sit and think. Books think for me.
Last Essays of Elia. Detached Thoughts on Books and Reading

26 I can read any thing which I call a book. There are things in that shape which I cannot allow for such. In this catalogue of books which are no books—biblia a-biblia—I reckon Court Calendars, Directories . . . the works of Hume, Gibbon, Robertson, Beattie, Soame Jenyns, and, generally, all those volumes which 'no gentleman's library should be without'. *Ib.*

27 Things in books' clothing. *Ib.*

28 Milton almost requires a solemn service of music to be played before you enter upon him. *Ib.*

29 A poor relation—is the most irrelevant thing in nature. *Ib. Poor Relations*

30 An Oxford scholar, meeting a porter who was carrying a hare through the streets, accosts him with this extraordinary question: 'Prithee, friend, is that thy own hare, or a wig?'
Ib. Popular Fallacies. That the Worst Puns are the Best

31 Cultivate simplicity, Coleridge.
Letter to Coleridge, 8 Nov. 1796

32 I could forgive a man for not enjoying Milton; but I would not call that man my friend who should be offended with 'the divine chit-chat of Cowper'.
Quoting Coleridge's own phrase in Letter to Coleridge, 5 Dec. 1796

33 The scene for the most part laid in a Brothel. O tempora, O mores! but as friend Coleridge said when he was talking bawdy to Miss — 'to the pure all things are pure'. *Letter to Southey, July 1798*

34 An old woman clothed in grey,
Whose daughter was charming and young,
And she was deluded away
By Roger's false flattering tongue.
Quoted in letter to Southey, 29 Oct. 1798

1 I came home . . . hungry as a hunter.
Letter to Coleridge, probably 16 or 17 Apr. 1800

2 Oh, her lamps of a night! her rich goldsmiths, print-shops, toy-shops, mercers, hardware-men, pastry-cooks, St. Paul's Churchyard, the Strand, Exeter Change, Charing Cross, with a man upon a black horse! These are thy gods, O London!
Letter to Thomas Manning, 28 Nov. 1800

3 Separate from the pleasure of your company, I don't much care if I never see another mountain in my life. *Letter to William Wordsworth, 30 Jan. 1801*

4 The man must have a rare recipe for melancholy, who can be dull in Fleet Street.
The Londoner, in letter to Thomas Manning, 15 Feb. 1802

5 Nursed amid her noise, her crowds, her beloved smoke—what have I been doing all my life, if I have not lent out my heart with usury to such scenes? *Ib.*

6 It was Lamb who, when Dr. Parr asked him how he managed to emit so much smoke, replied that he had toiled after it as other men after virtue. And Macready relates that he remarked in his presence that he wished to draw his last breath through a pipe and exhale it in a pun.
Letter to W. and D. Wordsworth, 28 Sept. 1805, note by E. V. Lucas

7 A little thin, flowery border round, neat, not gaudy.
Letter to Wordsworth, June 1806

8 To do this it will be necessary to leave off Tobacco. But I had some thoughts of doing that before, for I sometimes think it does not agree with me.
Letter to W. Wordsworth, 26 June 1806

9 I have made a little scale, supposing myself to receive the following various accessions of dignity from the king, who is the fountain of honour—As at first, 1, Mr. C. Lamb; . . . 10th, Emperor Lamb; 11th, Pope Innocent, higher than which is nothing but the Lamb of God.
Letter to Thomas Manning, 2 Jan. 1810

10 Nothing puzzles me more than time and space; and yet nothing troubles me less, as I never think about them. *Ib.*

11 I was at Hazlitt's marriage, and had like to have been turned out several times during the ceremony. Anything awful makes me laugh. I misbehaved once at a funeral. *Letter to Southey, 9 Aug. 1815*

12 This very night I am going to leave off tobacco! Surely there must be some other world in which this unconquerable purpose shall be realized. The soul hath not her generous aspirings implanted in her in vain. *Letter to Thomas Manning, 26 Dec. 1815*

13 His face when he repeats his verses hath its ancient glory, an Archangel a little damaged. [Coleridge.]
Letter to W. Wordsworth, 26 Apr. 1816

14 The rogue gives you Love Powders, and then a strong horse drench to bring 'em off your stomach that they mayn't hurt you. [Coleridge.]
Letter to Wordsworth, 23 Sept. 1816

15 Fanny Kelly's divine plain face.
Letter to Mrs. Wordsworth, 18 Feb. 1818

16 How I like to be liked, and what I do to be liked!
Letter to D. Wordsworth, 8 Jan. 1821

17 Who first invented Work—and tied the free
And holy-day rejoicing spirit down
To the ever-haunting importunity
Of business, in the green fields, and the town—
To plough—loom—anvil—spade—and, oh, most sad,
To this dry drudgery of the desk's dead wood?
Letter to Barton, Sept. 1822

18 Those fellows hate us. [Booksellers and authors.]
Letter to Barton, 9 Jan. 1823

19 Old as I am waxing, in his eyes I was still the child he [Randall Norris] first knew me. To the last he called me Charley. I have none to call me Charley now. *Letter to Robinson, 20 Jan. 1827*

20 We should be modest for a modest man—as he is for himself. *Letter to Mrs. Montagu, Summer 1827*

21 You are knee deep in clover.
Letter to C. C. Clarke, Dec. 1828

22 When my sonnet was rejected, I exclaimed, 'Damn the age; I will write for Antiquity!'
Letter to B. W. Procter, 22 Jan. 1829

23 Books of the true sort, not those things in boards that moderns mistake for books—what they club for at book clubs. *Letter to J. Gillman, 30 Nov. 1829*

24 The golden works of the dear, fine, silly old angel. [Thomas Fuller.] *Letter to J. Gillman, 1830*

25 Some cry up Haydn, some Mozart,
Just as the whim bites. For my part,
I do not care a farthing candle
For either of them, or for Handel.
Letter to Mrs. William Hazlitt, 24 May 1830

26 Did G[eorge] D[yer] send his penny tract to me to convert me to Unitarianism? Dear blundering soul! why I am as old a one-Goddite as himself.
Letter to Moxon, 24 Oct. 1831

27 Half as sober as a judge.
Letter to Mr. and Mrs. Moxon, Aug. 1833

28 The greatest pleasure I know, is to do a good action by stealth, and to have it found out by accident.
Table Talk by the late Elia. The Athenæum, 4 Jan. 1834

29 What a lass that were to go a-gipseying through the world with.
The Jovial Crew. The Examiner, July 1819

30 The uncommunicating muteness of fishes.
A Quakers' Meeting

31 For thy sake, Tobacco, I
Would do any thing but die.
A Farewell to Tobacco, l. 122

32 Gone before
To that unknown and silent shore. *Hester*

33 By myself walking,
To myself talking. *Hypochondriacus*

34 Riddle of destiny, who can show
What thy short visit meant, or know
What thy errand here below?
On an Infant Dying as soon as Born

35 Slow journeying on
To the green plains of pleasant Hertfordshire.
Sonnet: The Lord of Light Shakes Off

1 I have had playmates, I have had companions,
In my days of childhood, in my joyful school-days,—
All, all are gone, the old familiar faces.
The Old Familiar Faces

2 Free from self-seeking, envy, low design,
I have not found a whiter soul than thine.
To Martin Charles Burney

3 I like you, and your book, ingenious Hone!
To the Editor of the Every-Day Book

4 Truths, which transcend the searching School-men's
vein,
And half had stagger'd that stout Stagirite.
Written at Cambridge

5 If ever I marry a wife,
I'll marry a landlord's daughter,
For then I may sit in the bar,
And drink cold brandy and water.
Written in a copy of Coelebs in Search of a Wife

6 Martin, if dirt were trumps, what hands you would
hold!
Leigh Hunt's *Lord Byron and his Contemporaries*
(1828), p. 299

7 I do not [know the lady]; but damn her at a venture.
E. V. Lucas, *Charles Lamb* (1905), vol. i, p. 320,
note

MARY LAMB
1764–1847

8 He [Henry Crabb Robinson] says he never saw a man
so happy in *three wives* as Mr. Wordsworth is.
Letter to Sarah Hutchinson, Nov. 1816

9 A child's a plaything for an hour.
Parental Recollections

10 Thou straggler into loving arms,
Young climber up of knees,
When I forget thy thousand ways,
Then life and all shall cease. *Ib.*

JOHN GEORGE LAMBTON,
FIRST EARL OF DURHAM
1792–1840

11 ... one of his sublimities ... too good to be lost ... he
said he considered £40,000 a year a moderate income—such a one as a man *might jog on with.*
The Creevey Papers (13 Sept. 1821), ii. 32

LETITIA ELIZABETH LANDON
1802–1838

12 Few, save the poor, feel for the poor. *The Poor*

WALTER SAVAGE LANDOR
1775–1864

13 Around the child bend all the three
Sweet Graces; Faith, Hope, Charity.
Around the man bend other faces;
Pride, Envy, Malice, are his Graces.
Around the Child

14 Ah, what avails the sceptred race!
Ah, what the form divine!
What every virtue, every grace!
Rose Aylmer, all were thine.

Rose Aylmer, whom these wakeful eyes
May weep, but never see,
A night of memories and of sighs
I consecrate to thee. *Rose Aylmer*

15 There is delight in singing, tho' none hear
Beside the singer. *To Robert Browning*

16 Shakespeare is not our poet, but the world's,
Therefore on him no speech! *Ib.*

17 Browning! Since Chaucer was alive and hale,
No man hath walked along our roads with step
So active, so inquiring eye, or tongue
So varied in discourse. But warmer climes
Give brighter plumage, stronger wing: the breeze
Of Alpine heights thou playest with, borne on
Beyond Sorrento and Amalfi, where
The Siren waits thee, singing song for song. *Ib.*

18 Such stains there are—as when a Grace
Sprinkles another's laughing face
With nectar, and runs on. *On Catullus*

19 Child of a day, thou knowest not
The tears that overflow thy urn. *Child of a Day*

20 The witty and the tender Hood.
Confessions of Jealousy

21 Hail, ye indomitable heroes, hail!
Despite of all your generals ye prevail.
The Crimean Heroes

22 Stand close around, ye Stygian set,
With Dirce in one boat convey'd!
Or Charon, seeing, may forget
That he is old and she a shade. *Dirce*

23 Death stands above me, whispering low
I know not what into my ear;
Of his strange language all I know
Is, there is not a word of fear. *Epigrams, c. Death*

24 Wearers of rings and chains!
Pray do not take the pains
To set me right.
In vain my faults ye quote;
I write as others wrote
On Sunium's height. *Ib. ci*

25 I strove with none; for none was worth my strife;
Nature I loved, and, next to Nature, Art;
I warmed both hands before the fire of life;
It sinks, and I am ready to depart. *Finis*

26 I have sinuous shells, of pearly hue.
Gebir, bk. 1, l. 170

27 Apply
Its polished lips to your attentive ear. *Ib. l. 174*

28 And it remembers its august abodes,
And murmurs as the ocean murmurs there. *Ib.*

29 Is this the mighty ocean? is this all?
Ib. bk. v, l. 130

30 From you, Ianthe, little troubles pass
Like little ripples down a sunny river.
Ianthe's Troubles

31 In his own image the Creator made,
His own pure sunbeam quickened thee, O man!
Thou breathing dial! since thy day began
The present hour was ever mark'd with shade!
In His own Image the Creator Made

1 I loved him not; and yet now he is gone
   I feel I am alone.
I check'd him while he spoke; yet, could he speak,
   Alas! I would not check.   *The Maid's Lament*

2 Mother, I cannot mind my wheel.   *Title*

3 No longer could I doubt him true—
   All other men may use deceit;
He always said my eyes were blue,
   And often swore my lips were sweet.
      Mother, I Cannot Mind My Wheel

4 Proud word you never spoke, but you will speak
   Four not exempt from pride some future day.
Resting on one white hand a warm wet cheek
   Over my open volume you will say,
'This man loved *me!*' then rise and trip away.
      Proud Word You Never Spoke

5 We are what suns and winds and waters make us;
The mountains are our sponsors, and the rills
Fashion and win their nursling with their smiles.
      Regeneration

6 Well I remember how you smiled
   To see me write your name upon
The soft sea-sand—'O! what a child!
   You think you're writing upon stone!'

I have since written what no tide
   Shall ever wash away, what men
Unborn shall read o'er ocean wide
   And find Ianthe's name again.
      Well I Remember How You Smiled

7 I know not whether I am proud,
But this I know, I hate the crowd.   *With an Album*

8 Chatting on deck was Dryden too,
The Bacon of our rhyming crew.
   To Wordsworth: Those Who Have Laid the Harp
   Aside

9 Tho' never tender nor sublime,
He struggles with and conquers Time. [Dryden.]
      Ib.

10 Thee gentle Spenser fondly led;
But me he mostly sent to bed.   *Ib.*

11 George the First was always reckoned
   Vile, but viler George the Second;
And what mortal ever heard
   Any good of George the Third?
When from earth the Fourth descended
   God be praised, the Georges ended!
   Epigram in *The Atlas*, 28 Apr. 1855. See *Notes*
   and Queries, 3 May 1902, pp. 318, 354

12 Laodameia died; Helen died; Leda, the beloved of
   Jupiter, went before.
   Imaginary Conversations, Æsop and Rhodope, ii

13 There are no fields of amaranth on this side of the
   grave: there are no voices, O Rhodopè! that are not
   soon mute, however tuneful: there is no name, with
   whatever emphasis of passionate love repeated, of
   which the echo is not faint at last.   *Ib.*

14 He who first praises a book becomingly is next in
   merit to the author.   *Ib. Alfieri and Salomon*, ii

15 Prose on certain occasions can bear a great deal of
   poetry: on the other hand, poetry sinks and swoons
   under a moderate weight of prose.
      Ib. Archdeacon Hare and Walter Landor

16 I hate false words, and seek with care, difficulty, and
   moroseness, those that fit the thing.
   Imaginary Conversations. Bishop Burnet and
   Humphrey Hardcastle

17 Goodness does not more certainly make men happy
   than happiness makes them good.
      Ib. Lord Brooke and Sir Philip Sidney

18 LEONORA:
But tell him, tell Torquato . . . go again; entreat,
persuade, command him, to forget me.
PANIGAROLA:
Alas! even the command, even the command from
   you and from above, might not avail perhaps.
   You smile, Madonna!
LEONORA:
I die happy.   *Ib. Leonora di Este and Panigarola*

19 States, like men, have their growth, their manhood,
   their decrepitude, their decay.   *Ib.*

20 When it was a matter of wonder how Keats, who was
   ignorant of Greek, could have written his 'Hyperion', Shelley, whom envy never touched, gave
   as a reason, 'Because he *was* a Greek'.
      Ib. Southey and Landor, ii

21 Clear writers, like fountains, do not seem so deep as
   they are; the turbid look the most profound.
      Ib. Southey and Porson

22 Fleas know not whether they are upon the body of a
   giant or upon one of ordinary stature.   *Ib.*

ANDREW LANG
1844–1912

23 St. Andrews by the Northern Sea,
   That is a haunted town to me!   *Almae Matres*

24 The surge and thunder of the Odyssey.
   As One that for a Weary Space has Lain

25 There's a joy without canker or cark,
   There's a pleasure eternally new,
'Tis to gloat on the glaze and the mark
   Of china that's ancient and blue.
      Ballade of Blue China

26 Here's a pot with a cot in a park,
   In a park where the peach-blossoms blew,
Where the lovers eloped in the dark,
   Lived, died, and were changed into two
   Bright birds that eternally flew
Through the boughs of the may, as they sang.
   'Tis a tale was undoubtedly true
   In the reign of the Emperor Hwang.   *Ib.*

27 If the wild bowler thinks he bowls,
   Or if the batsman thinks he's bowled,
They know not, poor misguided souls,
   They too shall perish unconsoled.
I am the batsman and the bat,
   I am the bowler and the ball,
The umpire, the pavilion cat,
   The roller, pitch, and stumps, and all.
      Brahma (in imitation of Emerson)

28 But he shaved with a shell when he chose,—
   'Twas the manner of Primitive Man.
      Double Ballade of Primitive Man

FREDERICK LANGBRIDGE
1849–1923

1 Two men look out through the same bars:
One sees the mud, and one the stars.
A Cluster of Quiet Thoughts, 1896 (*Religious Tract Society Publication*)

JOHN LANGHORNE
1735–1779

2 Cold on Canadian hills, or Minden's plain,
Perhaps that parent mourn'd her soldier slain;
. . . . . .
The child of misery, baptiz'd in tears!
The Country Justice, pt. i. *Apology for Vagrants*

WILLIAM LANGLAND
1330?–1400?

3 In a somer seson whan soft was the sonne.
The Vision of William concerning Piers the Plowman (ed. Skeat), B Text, Prologue, l. 1.

4 A glotoun of wordes. *Ib*. l. 139

5 Bakers and brewers, bouchers and cokes—
For thees men doth most harme to the mene puple.
Ib. C Text, Passus 4, l. 80

6 Grammere, that grounde is of alle.
Ib. Passus 18, l. 107

7 'After sharpest shoures,' quath Pees [Peace] 'most sheene is the sonne;
Ys no weder warmer than after watery cloudes.'
Ib. Passus 21, l. 456

8 Dowel, Dobet, and Dobest.
Ib. MS. *Laud 581*, Passus 8, heading

ARCHBISHOP STEPHEN LANGTON
d. 1228

9 Veni Sancte, Spiritus,
Et emitte coelitus
Lucis tuae radium.

Come, thou holy Paraclete,
And from thy celestial seat
Send thy light and brilliancy.
Trans. by J. M. Neale

SIDNEY LANIER
1842–1881

10 Into the woods my Master went,
Clean forspent, forspent.
Into the woods my Master came,
Forspent with love and shame.
Poems. A Ballad of Trees and the Master

BISHOP HUGH LATIMER
1485?–1555

11 Be of good comfort Master Ridley, and play the man. We shall this day light such a candle by God's grace in England, as (I trust) shall never be put out.
Foxe, *Actes and Monuments* (1570), p. 1937

SIR HARRY LAUDER
1870–1950

12 I love a lassie. *Title of Song*

13 Just a wee doch-an' dorris
Before we gang awa' . . .
If y' can say
It's a braw brecht moonlecht necht,
Yer a' recht, that's a'. *Song*

14 Keep right on to the end of the road. *Title of Song*

15 O! it's nice to get up in the mornin'
But it's nicer to lie in bed. *Song*

16 Roamin' in the Gloamin'. *Title of Song*

WILLIAM L. LAURENCE
1888–

17 At first it was a giant column that soon took the shape of a supramundane mushroom.
Report in The New York Times, *26 Sept. 1945, on the first atomic explosion test held in New Mexico, U.S.A.*

ANDREW BONAR LAW
1858–1923

18 If, therefore, war should ever come between these two countries [Great Britain and Germany], which Heaven forbid! it will not, I think, be due to irresistible natural laws, it will be due to the want of human wisdom.
Speech, House of Commons, 27 Nov. 1911

19 I said [in 1911] that if ever war arose between Great Britain and Germany it would not be due to inevitable causes, for I did not believe in inevitable war. I said it would be due to human folly.
Speech, House of Commons, 6 Aug. 1914

DAVID HERBERT LAWRENCE
1885–1930

20 The terror, the agony, the nostalgia of the heathen past was a constant torture to her mediumistic soul. *The Lost Girl*, ch. 15

21 She is dear to me in the middle of my being. But the gold and flowing serpent is coiling up again, to sleep at the root of my tree.
The Man Who Died, pt. ii

22 Be a good animal, true to your animal instincts.
The White Peacock, pt. ii, ch. 2

23 Along the avenue of cypresses,
All in their scarlet cloaks and surplices
Of linen, go the chanting choristers,
The priests in gold and black, the villagers.
Giorno dei Morti

24 The silence of the many villagers,
The candle-flame beside the surplices. *Ib*.

SIR AUSTEN HENRY LAYARD
1817–1894

25 I have always believed that successes would be the inevitable result if the two services, the army and navy, had fair play, and if we sent the right man to fill the right place.
Speech in Parliament, 15 Jan. 1855

STEPHEN BUTLER LEACOCK
1869–1944

1 Lord Ronald . . . flung himself upon his horse and rode madly off in all directions.
Nonsense Novels. Gertrude the Governess

EDWARD LEAR
1812–1888

2 There was an Old Man with a beard,
Who said, 'It is just as I feared!—
Two Owls and a Hen,
Four Larks and a Wren,
Have all built their nests in my beard!'
Book of Nonsense

3 There was an Old Man in a tree,
Who was horribly bored by a bee;
When they said, 'Does it buzz?'
He replied, 'Yes, it does!
It's a regular brute of a bee!' *Ib.*

4 There was an Old Man in a boat,
Who said, 'I'm afloat, I'm afloat!'
When they said, 'No, you ain't!'
He was ready to faint,
That unhappy Old Man in a boat. *Ib.*

5 There was an Old Person of Basing,
Whose presence of mind was amazing;
He purchased a steed,
Which he rode at full speed,
And escaped from the people of Basing. *Ib.*

6 There was an old Lady of Chertsey,
Who made a remarkable curtsey:
She whirled round and round,
Till she sunk underground,
Which distressed all the people of Chertsey. *Ib.*

7 There was an old man who said, 'Hush!
I perceive a young bird in this bush!'
When they said, 'Is it small?'
He replied, 'Not at all!
It is four times as big as the bush!' *Ib.*

8 Nasticreechia Krorluppia. *Nonsense Botany*

9 'How pleasant to know Mr. Lear!'
Who has written such volumes of stuff!
Some think him ill-tempered and queer,
But a few think him pleasant enough.
Nonsense Songs, preface

10 He drinks a good deal of Marsala
But never gets tipsy at all. *Ib.*

11 His body is perfectly spherical,
He weareth a runcible hat. *Ib.*

12 On the coast of Coromandel
Where the early pumpkins blow,
In the middle of the woods
Lived the Yonghy-Bonghy-Bò.
Two old chairs, and half a candle,—
One old jug without a handle,—
These were all his worldly goods.
Ib. The Courtship of the Yonghy-Bonghy-Bò

13 'Lady Jingly! Lady Jingly!
Sitting where the pumpkins blow,
Will you come and be my wife?'
Said the Yonghy-Bonghy-Bò. *Ib.*

14 One never more can go to court,
Because his legs have grown too short;
The other cannot sing a song
Because his legs have grown too long!
Nonsense Songs. The Daddy Long-Legs and the Fly

15 When awful darkness and silence reign
Over the great Gromboolian plain,
Through the long, long wintry nights.
When the angry breakers roar
As they beat on the rocky shore;—
When Storm-clouds brood on the towering heights
Of the Hills of the Chankly Bore.
Ib. The Dong with the Luminous Nose

16 Slowly it wanders,—pauses,—creeps,—
Anon it sparkles,—flashes and leaps;
And ever as onward it gleaming goes
A light on the Bong-tree stem it throws:
And those who watch at that midnight hour
From Hall or Terrace or lofty Tower,
Cry as the wild light passes along,—
'The Dong!—the Dong!
The wandering Dong through the forest goes!
The Dong!—the Dong!
The Dong with the Luminous Nose!' *Ib.*

17 A Nose as strange as a Nose could be!
Of vast proportions and painted red,
And tied with cords to the back of his head.
—In a hollow rounded space it ended
With a luminous Lamp within suspended,
All fenced about
With a bandage stout
To prevent the wind from blowing it out. *Ib.*

18 And who so happy,—O who,
As the Duck and the Kangaroo?
Ib. The Duck and the Kangaroo

19 O My agèd Uncle Arly!
Sitting on a heap of Barley
Thro' the silent hours of night,—
Close beside a leafy thicket:—
On his nose there was a Cricket,—
In his hat a Railway-Ticket;—
(But his shoes were far too tight.)
Ib. Incidents in the Life of my Aged Uncle Arly

20 Every evening found him gazing,—
Singing,—'Orb! you're quite amazing!
How I wonder what you are!' *Ib.*

21 Far and few, far and few,
Are the lands where the Jumblies live;
Their heads are green, and their hands are blue,
And they went to sea in a Sieve. *Ib. The Jumblies*

22 In spite of all their friends could say,
On a winter's morn, on a stormy day,
In a Sieve they went to sea! *Ib.*

23 Suppose we should fall down flumpetty
Just like pieces of stone!
Ib. Mr. and Mrs. Discobbolos

24 The Owl and the Pussy-Cat went to sea
In a beautiful pea-green boat.
They took some honey, and plenty of money,
Wrapped up in a five-pound note.
The Owl looked up to the Stars above
And sang to a small guitar,
'O lovely Pussy! O Pussy, my love,
What a beautiful Pussy you are.'
Ib. The Owl and the Pussy-Cat

1 Pussy said to the Owl, 'You elegant fowl!
How charmingly sweet you sing!
O let us be married! too long we have tarried:
But what shall we do for a ring?'
They sailed away for a year and a day,
To the land where the Bong-tree grows,
And there in a wood a Piggy-wig stood
With a ring at the end of his nose.
Nonsense Songs. The Owl and the Pussy-Cat

2 'Dear Pig, are you willing to sell for one shilling
Your ring?' Said the Piggy, 'I will'.   *Ib.*

3 They dined on mince, and slices of quince,
Which they ate with a runcible spoon;
And hand in hand, on the edge of the sand,
They danced by the light of the moon.   *Ib.*

4 We think so then, and we thought so still!
Ib. The Pelican Chorus

5 The Pobble who has no toes
Had once as many as we;
When they said, 'Some day you may lose them all';—
He replied,—'Fish fiddle de-dee!'
Ib. The Pobble Who Has No Toes

6 His Aunt Jobiska made him drink
Lavender water tinged with pink,
For she said, 'The world in general knows
There's nothing so good for a Pobble's toes!'   *Ib.*

7 For his Aunt Jobiska said, 'No harm
Can come to his toes if his nose is warm,
And it's perfectly known that a Pobble's toes
Are safe, provided he minds his nose.'   *Ib.*

8   When boats or ships came near him
He tinkledy-binkledy-winkled a bell.   *Ib.*

9 He has gone to fish, for his Aunt Jobiska's
Runcible Cat with crimson whiskers!   *Ib.*

10   It's a fact the whole world knows,
That Pobbles are happier without their toes.   *Ib.*

11 'But the longer I live on this Crumpetty Tree
The plainer than ever it seems to me
That very few people come this way
And that life on the whole is far from gay!'
Said the Quangle-Wangle Quee.
Ib. The Quangle-Wangle's Hat

12 Two old Bachelors were living in one house;
One caught a Muffin, the other caught a Mouse.
Ib. The Two Old Bachelors

13 Who, or why, or which, or what,
Is the Akond of Swat?
Ib. 1888 edn. The Akond of Swat

14 There was an old person of Slough,
Who danced at the end of a bough;
But they said, 'If you sneeze,
You might damage the trees,
You imprudent old person of Slough.'
One Hundred Nonsense Pictures and Rhymes

15 There was an old man in a Marsh,
Whose manners were futile and harsh.   *Ib.*

16 There was an old man at a Junction,
Whose feelings were wrung with compunction.   *Ib.*

17 There was an old person of Pett,
Who was partly consumed by regret.   *Ib.*

18 There was an old person of Ware,
Who rode on the back of a bear:
When they asked,—'Does it trot?'—
He said 'Certainly not!
He's a Moppsikon Floppsikon bear.'
One Hundred Nonsense Pictures and Rhymes

19 There was an old person of Dean,
Who dined on one pea and one bean;
For he said, 'More than that,
Would make me too fat,'
That cautious old person of Dean.   *Ib.*

20 There was an old person of Ealing,
Who was wholly devoid of good feeling;
He drove a small gig,
With three Owls and a Pig,
Which distressed all the people of Ealing.   *Ib.*

21 There was an old man of Thermopylae,
Who never did anything properly;
But they said, 'If you choose
To boil eggs in your shoes,
You shall never remain in Thermopylae.'   *Ib.*

22 There was an old man on the Border,
Who lived in the utmost disorder.   *Ib.*

MARY ELIZABETH LEASE
1853–1933

23 Kansas had better stop raising corn and begin raising
hell.   *Attr.*

WILLIAM EDWARD HARTPOLE LECKY
1838–1903

24 The stately ship is seen no more,
The fragile skiff attains the shore;
And while the great and wise decay,
And all their trophies pass away,
Some sudden thought, some careless rhyme,
Still floats above the wrecks of Time.
On an Old Song

HENRY LEE
1756–1818

25 First in war, first in peace, first in the hearts of his
fellow citizens.
*Resolution in the House of Representatives on the
death of Washington, 26 Dec. 1799*

NATHANIEL LEE
1653?–1692

26 When the sun sets, shadows, that showed at noon
But small, appear most long and terrible.
Œdipus, IV. i

27 Man, false man, smiling, destructive man.
Theodosius, III. ii

28 He speaks the kindest words, and looks such things,
Vows with so much passion, swears with so much
grace.
That 'tis a kind of Heaven to be deluded by him.
The Rival Queens, Act I

29 'Tis beauty calls and glory leads the way.   *Ib.*

30 Then he will talk, Good Gods,
How he will talk.   *Ib. Act III*

1 When Greeks joined Greeks, then was the tug of war!
The Rival Queens, IV. ii

2 Philip fought men, but Alexander women. *Ib.*

RICHARD LE GALLIENNE
1866–1947

3 The cry of the Little Peoples goes up to God in vain.
The Cry of the Little Peoples

4 Give back the little nation leave to live.
Christmas in War-Time

5 Loud mockers in the roaring street
Say Christ is crucified again:
Twice pierced His gospel-bearing feet,
Twice broken His great heart in vain,
The Second Crucifixion

6 The Quest of the Golden Girl. *Title of Novel*

HENRY SAMBROOKE LEIGH
1837–1883

7 In form and feature, face and limb,
I grew so like my brother
That folks got taking me for him
And each for one another.
Carols of Cockayne, The Twins

8 For one of us was born a twin
And not a soul knew which. *Ib.*

9 The rapturous, wild, and ineffable pleasure
Of drinking at somebody else's expense.
Ib. Stanzas to an Intoxicated Fly

10 I know where little girls are sent
For telling taradiddles. *Ib. Only Seven*

CHARLES GODFREY LELAND
1824–1903

11 Hans Breitmann gife a barty—
Vhere ish dat barty now? *Hans Breitmann's Party*

12 All goned afay mit de lager-beer—
Afay in de ewigkeit! *Ib.*

13 Und efery dime she gife a shoomp
She make der vinders sound. *Ib.*

14 They saw a Dream of Loveliness descending from
the train. *Brand New Ballads. The Masher*

WILLIAM LENTHALL
1591–1662

15 I have neither eye to see, nor tongue to speak here,
but as the House is pleased to direct me.
Rushworth's *Historical Collections*, iv. 238

LUIS DE LEÓN
c. 1528–1591

16 Dicebamus hesterna die.
We were saying yesterday.
*On resuming a lecture at Salamanca University
after five years' imprisonment.* A. F. G. Bell, *Luis
de León*, ch. 8

GOTTHOLD EPHRAIM LESSING
1729–1781

17 Ein einziger dankbarer Gedanke gen Himmel ist das
vollkommenste Gebet.
One single grateful thought raised to heaven is a
perfect prayer. *Minna von Barnhelm*, ii. 7

18 Wenn Gott in seiner Rechten alle Wahrheit und in
seiner Linken den einzigen, immer regen Trieb
nach Wahrheit, obgleich mit dem Zusatz, mich
immer und ewig zu irren, verschlossen hielte und
sprach zu mir: Wähle! ich fiele ihm mit Demut
in seine Linke und sagte: Vater, gieb! Die reine
Wahrheit ist ja doch nur für Dich allein.
If God were to hold out enclosed in His right hand
all Truth, and in His left hand just the active
search for Truth, though with the condition that
I should ever err therein, and should say to me:
Choose! I should humbly take His left hand and
say: Father! Give me this one; absolute Truth
belongs to Thee alone. *Wolfenbüttler Fragmente*

SIR ROGER L'ESTRANGE
1616–1704

19 It is with our passions as it is with fire and water, they
are good servants, but bad masters.
Æsop's Fables, no. 38, *Reflection*

20 Though this may be play to you, 'tis death to us.
Ib. no. 398

GEORGE LEVESON-GOWER, EARL GRANVILLE
1815–1891

21 Spheres of action.
Letter to Count Münster, 29 April 1885 (Sir
Edward Hertslet, *Map of Africa by Treaty*
(1894), vol. ii, p. 596)

GEORGE HENRY LEWES
1817–1878

22 Many a genius has been slow of growth. Oaks that
flourish for a thousand years do not spring up into
beauty like a reed. *Spanish Drama*, ch. 2

23 Murder, like talent, seems occasionally to run in
families. *The Physiology of Common Life*, ch. 12

24 We must never assume that which is incapable of
proof. *Ib.* ch. 13

SIR GEORGE CORNEWALL LEWIS
1806–1863

25 Life would be tolerable were it not for its amuse-
ments.
*According to Lord Grey of Fallodon, in his
Twenty-Five Years*

CHARLES-JOSEPH, PRINCE DE LIGNE
1735–1814

26 Le congrès ne marche pas, il danse.
The Congress makes no progress; but it dances.
*Comment on the Congress of Vienna to Comte
Auguste de La Garde-Chambonas.* La Garde-
Chambonas, *Souvenirs du Congrès de Vienne,
1814–1815*, c. 1.

GEORGE LILLO
1693–1739

1 There's sure no passion in the human soul,
But finds its food in music.   *Fatal Curiosity*, I. ii

ABRAHAM LINCOLN
1809–1865

2 I think the necessity of being *ready* increases.—Look
to it.
> *Speeches and Letters* (1907). *The whole of a letter
> to Governor Andrew Curtin of Pennsylvania,
> 8 Apr. 1861*

3 I intend no modification of my oft-expressed personal
wish that all men everywhere could be free.
> *Ib. Letter to H. Greeley, 22 Aug. 1862*

4 I claim not to have controlled events, but confess
plainly that events have controlled me.
> *Ib. Letter to A. G. Hodges, 4 Apr. 1864*

5 The ballot is stronger than the bullet.
> *Ib. Speech, 19 May 1856*

6 'A house divided against itself cannot stand.' I believe this government cannot endure permanently,
half slave and half free. *Ib. Speech, 17 June 1858*

7 What is conservatism? Is it not adherence to the old
and tried, against the new and untried?
> *Ib. Speech, 27 Feb. 1860*

8 Let us have faith that right makes might; and in that
faith let us to the end, dare to do our duty as we
understand it.   *Ib.*

9 I take the official oath to-day with no mental reserva-
tions, and with no purpose to construe the Constitution or laws by any hypercritical rules.
> *Ib. First Inaugural Address, 4 Mar. 1861*

10 The mystic chords of memory, stretching from every
battlefield and patriot grave to every living heart
and hearthstone all over this broad land, will yet
swell the chorus of the Union when again touched,
as surely they will be, by the better angels of our
nature.   *Ib.*

11 In giving freedom to the slave, we assure freedom to
the free,—honourable alike in what we give and
what we preserve.
> *Ib. Annual Message to Congress, 1 Dec. 1862*

12 Fourscore and seven years ago our fathers brought
forth upon this continent a new nation, conceived
in liberty, and dedicated to the proposition that
all men are created equal. Now we are engaged
in a great civil war, testing whether that nation,
or any nation so conceived and so dedicated, can
long endure. We are met on a great battlefield of
that war. We have come to dedicate a portion of
that field as a final resting-place of those who
here gave their lives that that nation might live.
It is altogether fitting and proper that we should
do this. But in a larger sense we cannot dedicate,
we cannot consecrate, we cannot hallow this
ground. The brave men, living and dead, who
struggled here, have consecrated it far above our
power to add or detract. The world will little note,
nor long remember, what we say here, but it can
never forget what they did here. It is for us, the
living, rather to be dedicated here to the unfinished
work they have thus far so nobly advanced. It is

rather for us to be here dedicated to the great task
remaining before us, that from these honoured
dead we take increased devotion to that cause for
which they here gave the last full measure of
devotion; that we here highly resolve that the
dead shall not have died in vain, that this nation,
under God, shall have a new birth of freedom;
and that government of the people, by the people,
and for the people, shall not perish from the earth.
> *Speeches and Letters* (1907). *Address at Dedication
> of National Cemetery at Gettysburg, 19 Nov. 1863*

13 With malice toward none; with charity for all; with
firmness in the right, as God gives us to see the
right. *Ib. Second Inaugural Address, 4 Mar. 1865*

14 You can fool all the people some of the time, and some
of the people all the time, but you can not fool all
the people all of the time.
> *Attr. words in a speech at Clinton, 8 Sept. 1858.
> N. W. Stephenson, Autobiography of A. Lincoln
> (1927). Attr. also to Phineas Barnum, 1810–91*

15 It is not best to swap horses while crossing the river.
> *Reply to National Union League, 9 June 1864.
> J. E. Nicolay and J. Hay, Abraham Lincoln,
> bk. ix*

16 As President, I have no eyes but constitutional eyes;
I cannot see you.
> *Attr. reply to the South Carolina Commissioners*

17 People who like this sort of thing will find this the
sort of thing they like.
> *Judgement on a book. G. W. E. Russell, Collec-
> tions and Recollections, ch. 30*

GEORGE LINLEY
1798–1865

18 Ever of thee I'm fondly dreaming,
Thy gentle voice my spirit can cheer.
> *Poems. Ever of Thee*

19 Among our ancient mountains,
And from our lovely vales,
Oh, let the prayer re-echo:
'God bless the Prince of Wales!'
> *Ib. God Bless the Prince of Wales*

20 Thou art gone from my gaze like a beautiful dream,
And I seek thee in vain by the meadow and stream.
> *Ib. Thou Art Gone*

21 Tho' lost to sight, to mem'ry dear
Thou ever wilt remain.
> *Song. Attr. to Linley. Notes and Queries, Ser.
> 5, vol. x, p. 417*

SIR THOMAS LITTLETON
1422–1481

22 [From] time whereof the memory of man runneth not
to the contrary.   *Tenures (?1481), § 170*

LIVY
59 B.C.–A.D. 17

23 Vae victis.
> Woe to the vanquished.   *History*, v. xlviii. 9

MARIE LLOYD
1870–1922

1 A little of what you fancy does you good.
Title of Song

2 I'm one of the ruins that Cromwell knocked about a bit. *Ib.*

3 Oh, mister porter, what shall I do?
Ib. (words actually by Thomas Le Brunn)

ROBERT LLOYD
1733–1764

4 Slow and steady wins the race.
Poems. The Hare and the Tortoise

JOHN LOCKE
1632–1704

5 New opinions are always suspected, and usually opposed, without any other reason but because they are not already common.
Essay on the Human Understanding, dedicatory epistle

6 Nature never makes excellent things for mean or no uses. *Ib.* bk. ii, ch. 1, sec. 15

7 No man's knowledge here can go beyond his experience. *Ib.* sec. 19

8 It is one thing to show a man that he is in an error, and another to put him in possession of truth.
Ib. bk. iv, ch. 7, sec. 11

9 All men are liable to error; and most men are, in many points, by passion or interest, under temptation to it. *Ib.* ch. 20, sec. 17

FREDERICK LOCKER-LAMPSON
1821–1895

10 The world's as ugly, ay, as sin,
And almost as delightful. *The Jester's Plea*

11 And many are afraid of God—
And more of Mrs. Grundy. *Ib.*

12 Some men are good for righting wrongs,—
And some for writing verses. *Ib.*

13 If you lift a guinea-pig up by the tail
His eyes drop out! *A Garden Lyric*

JOHN GIBSON LOCKHART
1794–1854

14 Here lies that peerless peer Lord Peter,
Who broke the laws of God and man and metre.
Epitaph for Patrick ('Peter'), Lord Robertson.
Scott's *Journal*, vol. i, p. 259, n. 2

FRANCIS LOCKIER
1667–1740

15 In all my travels I never met with any one Scotchman but what was a man of sense. I believe everybody of that country that has any, leaves it as fast as they can. *Spence's Anecdotes* (1858), p. 55

THOMAS LODGE
1558?–1625

16 Devils are not so black as they are painted.
A Margarite of America

17 Love, in my bosom, like a bee,
Doth suck his sweet. *Love, In My Bosom*

18 Heigh ho, would she were mine!
Rosalind's Description

JOHN LOGAN
1748–1788

19 Behold congenial Autumn comes,
The sabbath of the year!
Ode on a Visit to the Country in Autumn

20 For never on thy banks shall I
Behold my love, the flower of Yarrow.
The Braes of Yarrow

21 Sweet bird! thy bow'r is ever green,
Thy sky is ever clear;
Thou hast no sorrow in thy song,
No winter in thy year!
To the Cuckoo. Attr. (See *Notes and Queries*, April 1902, p. 309; 14 June, 1902, p. 469.) *Attr. also to Michael Bruce*

FRIEDRICH VON LOGAU
1605–1655

22 Gottesmühlen mahlen langsam, mahlen aber trefflich klein;
Ob aus Langmut Er sich säumet, bringt mit Schärf' Er alles ein.

Though the mills of God grind slowly, yet they grind exceeding small;
Though with patience He stands waiting, with exactness grinds He all.
Sinngedichte, III. ii. 24 (trans. H. W. Longfellow)

JACK LONDON
[JOHN GRIFFITH LONDON]
1876–1916

23 The Call of the Wild. *Title*

HENRY WADSWORTH LONGFELLOW
1807–1882

24 I shot an arrow into the air,
It fell to earth, I knew not where.
The Arrow and the Song

25 And the song, from beginning to end,
I found again in the heart of a friend. *Ib.*

26 I know a maiden fair to see,
Take care!
She can both false and friendly be,
Beware! Beware!
Trust her not,
She is fooling thee! *Beware!* (From the German)

27 I stood on the bridge at midnight,
As the clocks were striking the hour. *The Bridge*

28 In the elder days of Art,
Builders wrought with greatest care
Each minute and unseen part;
For the Gods see everywhere. *The Builders*

29 Build me straight, O worthy Master!
Staunch and strong, a goodly vessel,
That shall laugh at all disaster,
And with wave and whirlwind wrestle!
The Building of the Ship

1 Thou, too, sail on, O Ship of State!
Sail on, O Union, strong and great!
Humanity with all its fears,
With all the hopes of future years,
Is hanging breathless on thy fate!
The Building of the Ship

2 Ye are better than all the ballads
That ever were sung or said;
For ye are living poems,
And all the rest are dead. *Children*

3 Between the dark and the daylight,
When the night is beginning to lower,
Comes a pause in the day's occupations,
That is known as the Children's Hour.
The Children's Hour

4 Singing the Hundredth Psalm, the grand old Puritan
anthem. *The Courtship of Miles Standish*, iii

5 Archly the maiden smiled, and, with eyes overrunning
with laughter,
Said, in a tremulous voice, 'Why don't you speak for
yourself, John?' *Ib.*

6 God had sifted three kingdoms to find the wheat for
this planting. *Ib.* iv

7 The day is done, and the darkness
Falls from the wings of Night,
As a feather is wafted downward
From an eagle in his flight. *The Day is Done*

8 A feeling of sadness and longing,
That is not akin to pain,
And resembles sorrow only
As the mist resembles the rain. *Ib.*

9 The bards sublime,
Whose distant footsteps echo
Through the corridors of Time. *Ib.*

10 The cares that infest the day
Shall fold their tents, like the Arabs,
And as silently steal away. *Ib.*

11 If you would hit the mark, you must aim a little above
it;
Every arrow that flies feels the attraction of earth.
Elegiac Verse

12 This is the forest primeval.
Evangeline, introduction, l. 1

13 When she had passed, it seemed like the ceasing of
exquisite music. *Ib.* pt. i. i, l. 62

14 Talk not of wasted affection, affection never was
wasted;
If it enrich not the heart of another, its waters, returning
Back to their springs, like the rain, shall fill them full
of refreshment. *Ib.* pt. ii. i, l. 55

15 Sorrow and silence are strong, and patient endurance
is godlike. *Ib.* l. 60

16 And, as she looked around, she saw how Death, the
consoler,
Laying his hand upon many a heart, had healed it for
ever. *Ib.* v, l. 88

17 The shades of night were falling fast,
As through an Alpine village passed
A youth, who bore, 'mid snow and ice,
A banner with the strange device,
Excelsior! *Excelsior*

18 In happy homes he saw the light
Of household fires gleam warm and bright. *Ib.*

19 'Try not the Pass!' the old man said;
'Dark lowers the tempest overhead.' *Excelsior*

20 'O stay,' the maiden said, 'and rest
Thy weary head upon this breast!' *Ib.*

21 'Beware the pine-tree's withered branch!
Beware the awful avalanche!' *Ib.*

22 A traveller, by the faithful hound,
Half-buried in the snow was found. *Ib.*

23 Spake full well, in language quaint and olden,
One who dwelleth by the castled Rhine,
When he called the flowers, so blue and golden,
Stars, that in earth's firmament do shine. *Flowers*

24 That is best which lieth nearest;
Shape from that thy work of art. *Gaspar Becerra*

25 Giotto's tower,
The lily of Florence blossoming in stone.
Giotto's Tower

26 I like that ancient Saxon phrase, which calls
The burial-ground God's-Acre! *God's-Acre*

27 Ah, the souls of those that die
Are but sunbeams lifted higher.
The Golden Legend, pt. iv. *The Cloisters*

28 I heard the trailing garments of the Night
Sweep through her marble halls! *Hymn to the Night*

29 Hold the fleet angel fast until he bless thee. *Kavanagh*

30 Saint Augustine! well hast thou said,
That of our vices we can frame
A ladder, if we will but tread
Beneath our feet each deed of shame!
The Ladder of Saint Augustine

31 The heights by great men reached and kept
Were not attained by sudden flight,
But they, while their companions slept,
Were toiling upward in the night. *Ib.*

32 Live I, so live I,
To my Lord heartily,
To my Prince faithfully
To my Neighbour honestly,
Die I, so die I.
*Law of Life. From the Sinngedichte of Fried-
rich von Logau*

33 Know how sublime a thing it is
To suffer and be strong. *The Light of Stars*

34 Standing, with reluctant feet,
Where the brook and river meet,
Womanhood and childhood fleet! *Maidenhood*

35 You would attain to the divine perfection,
And yet not turn your back upon the world.
Michael Angelo, pt. i. v

36 Would seem angelic in the sight of God,
Yet not too saint-like in the eyes of men;
In short, would lead a holy Christian life
In such a way that even your nearest friend
Would not detect therein one circumstance
To show a change from what it was before. *Ib.*

37 The men that women marry,
And why they marry them, will always be
A marvel and a mystery to the world. *Ib.* vi

38 A boy's will is the wind's will,
And the thoughts of youth are long, long thoughts.
My Lost Youth

[316]

1 A solid man of Boston.
A comfortable man, with dividends,
And the first salmon, and the first green peas.
New England Tragedies, John Endicott, IV. i

2 *Emigravit* is the inscription on the tombstone where
he lies;
Dead he is not, but departed,—for the artist never
dies.   *Nuremberg*, xiii

3 Listen, my children, and you shall hear
Of the midnight ride of Paul Revere,
On the eighteenth of April in Seventy-five.
Paul Revere's Ride

4 Not in the clamour of the crowded street,
Not in the shouts and plaudits of the throng,
But in ourselves, are triumph and defeat. *The Poets*

5 Tell me not, in mournful numbers,
Life is but an empty dream!
For the soul is dead that slumbers,
And things are not what they seem.

Life is real! Life is earnest!
And the grave is not its goal;
Dust thou art, to dust returnest,
Was not spoken of the soul.   *A Psalm of Life*

6 Art is long, and Time is fleeting,
And our hearts, though stout and brave,
Still, like muffled drums, are beating
Funeral marches to the grave.   *Ib.*

7 Trust no Future, howe'er pleasant!
Let the dead Past bury its dead!
Act,—act in the living Present!
Heart within, and God o'erhead!   *Ib.*

8 Lives of great men all remind us
We can make our lives sublime,
And, departing, leave behind us
Footprints on the sands of time.

Footprints, that perhaps another,
Sailing o'er life's solemn main,
A forlorn and shipwrecked brother,
Seeing, shall take heart again.

Let us, then, be up and doing,
With a heart for any fate;
Still achieving, still pursuing,
Learn to labour and to wait.   *Ib.*

9 There is a Reaper, whose name is Death,
And, with his sickle keen,
He reaps the bearded grain at a breath,
And the flowers that grow between.
The Reaper and the Flowers

10 Oh, not in cruelty, not in wrath,
The Reaper came that day;
'Twas an angel visited the green earth,
And took the flowers away.   *Ib.*

11 There is no flock, however watched and tended,
But one dead lamb is there!
There is no fireside, howsoe'er defended,
But has one vacant chair!   *Resignation*

12 There is no Death! What seems so is transition;
This life of mortal breath
Is but a suburb of the life elysian,
Whose portal we call Death.   *Ib.*

13 Though the mills of God grind slowly, yet they grind
exceeding small;
Though with patience he stands waiting, with exactness grinds he all.
*Retribution. From the Sinngedichte of Friedrich
von Logau*

14 A Lady with a Lamp shall stand
In the great history of the land,
A noble type of good,
Heroic womanhood.   *Santa Filomena*

15 'Wouldst thou'—so the helmsman answered,—
'Learn the secret of the sea?
Only those who brave its dangers
Comprehend its mystery!'   *The Secret of the Sea*

16 Beside the ungather'd rice he lay,
His sickle in his hand.   *The Slave's Dream*

17 He did not feel the driver's whip,
Nor the burning heat of day;
For Death had illumined the Land of Sleep,
And his lifeless body lay
A worn-out fetter, that the soul
Had broken and thrown away!   *Ib.*

18 Stay, stay at home, my heart, and rest;
Home-keeping hearts are happiest.
Song: Stay, Stay at Home

19 Should you ask me, whence these stories?
Whence these legends and traditions?
The Song of Hiawatha, introduction

20 I should answer, I should tell you,
'From the forests and the prairies,
From the great lakes of the Northland,
From the land of the Ojibways,
From the land of the Dacotahs,
From the mountains, moors, and fenlands,
Where the heron, the Shuh-shuh-gah,
Feeds among the reeds and rushes.'   *Ib.*

21 Gitche Manito, the mighty.   *Ib.* i. *The Peace-Pipe*

22 By the shore of Gitche Gumee,
By the shining Big-Sea-Water,
Stood the wigwam of Nokomis,
Daughter of the Moon, Nokomis.
Dark behind it rose the forest,
Rose the black and gloomy pine-trees,
Rose the firs with cones upon them;
Bright before it beat the water,
Beat the clear and sunny water,
Beat the shining Big-Sea-Water.
Ib. iii. *Hiawatha's Childhood*

23 Ewa-yea! my little owlet!
Who is this, that lights the wigwam?
With his great eyes lights the wigwam?   *Ib.*

24 Called them 'Hiawatha's Chickens'.   *Ib.*

25 And his heart was hot within him,
Like a living coal his heart was.
Ib. iv. *Hiawatha and Mudjekeewis*

26 From the waterfall he named her,
Minnehaha, Laughing Water.   *Ib.*

27 As unto the bow the cord is,
So unto the man is woman;
Though she bends him, she obeys him,
Though she draws him, yet she follows;
Useless each without the other!
Ib. x. *Hiawatha's Wooing*

1 Onaway! Awake, beloved!
The Song of Hiawatha. xi. *Hiawatha's Wedding-feast*

2 He is dead, the sweet musician!
He the sweetest of all singers!
He has gone from us for ever,
He has moved a little nearer
To the Master of all music,
To the Master of all singing!
O my brother, Chibiabos!
Ib. xv. *Hiawatha's Lamentation*

3 The secret anniversaries of the heart.
Sonnets. Holidays

4 Stars of the summer night!
Far in yon azure deeps,
Hide, hide your golden light!
She sleeps!
My lady sleeps!
Sleeps! *The Spanish Student,* I. iii

5 Dreams of the summer night!
Tell her, her lover keeps
Watch! while in slumbers light
She sleeps! *Ib.*

6 Thinking the deed, and not the creed,
Would help us in our utmost need.
Tales of a Wayside Inn, pt. 1, Prelude, l. 221

7 At all feasts where ale was strongest
Sat the merry monarch longest,
First to come and last to go.
Ib. The Musician's Tale. The Saga of King Olaf, ii

8 He seemed the incarnate 'Well, I told you so!'
Ib. The Poet's Tale. The Birds of Killingworth

9 Our ingress into the world
Was naked and bare;
Our progress through the world
Is trouble and care;
Our egress from the world
Will be nobody knows where;
But if we do well here
We shall do well there;
And I could tell you no more,
Should I preach a whole year!
Ib. pt. II. *The Student's Tale. The Cobbler of Hagenau*

10 Ships that pass in the night, and speak each other in passing;
Only a signal shown and a distant voice in the darkness;
So on the ocean of life we pass and speak one another,
Only a look and a voice; then darkness again and a silence.
Ib. pt. III. *The Theologian's Tale. Elizabeth,* iv

11 Under the spreading chestnut tree
The village smithy stands;
The smith, a mighty man is he,
With large and sinewy hands;
And the muscles of his brawny arms
Are strong as iron bands.
The Village Blacksmith

12 He earns whate'er he can,
And looks the whole world in the face,
For he owes not any man. *Ib.*

13 Toiling,—rejoicing,—sorrowing,
Onward through life he goes;

Each morning sees some task begin,
Each evening sees it close;
Something attempted, something done,
Has earned a night's repose.
The Village Blacksmith

14 It was the schooner Hesperus,
That sailed the wintry sea;
And the skipper had taken his little daughter,
To bear him company.
The Wreck of the Hesperus

15 But the father answered never a word,
A frozen corpse was he. *Ib.*

16 And fast through the midnight dark and drear,
Through the whistling sleet and snow,
Like a sheeted ghost, the vessel swept
Towards the reef of Norman's Woe. *Ib.*

17 There was a little girl
Who had a little curl
Right in the middle of her forehead,
When she was good
She was very, very good,
But when she was bad she was horrid.
B. R. T. Machetta, *Home Life of Longfellow*

18 In this world a man must be either anvil or hammer.
Hyperion, ch. iv

ANITA LOOS
1893–

19 Gentlemen Prefer Blondes. *Title of Novel*

LOUIS XIV
1638–1715

20 Il n'y a plus de Pyrénées.
The Pyrenees have ceased to exist.
At the accession of his grandson to the throne of Spain, 1700. Attr. by Voltaire *in Siècle de Louis XIV, ch. 28*

21 L'État c'est moi.
I am the State.
Attr. remark before the Parlement de Paris, 13 April 1655. Dulaure, Histoire de Paris

22 Toutes les fois que je donne une place vacante, je fais cent mécontents et un ingrat.
Every time I make an appointment, I make one ungrateful person and a hundred with a grievance.
Voltaire: *Siècle de Louis XIV,* ch. 26

LOUIS XVIII
1755–1824

23 L'exactitude est la politesse des rois.
Punctuality is the politeness of kings. *Attr.*

RICHARD LOVELACE
1618–1658

24 Am not I shot
With the self-same artillery?
Amyntor from Beyond the Sea to Alexis

25 Lucasta that bright northern star. *Ib.*

26 And when she ceas'd, we sighing saw
The floor lay pav'd with broken hearts.
Gratiana Dancing and Singing

1 So did she move; so did she sing
 Like the harmonious spheres that bring
 Unto their rounds their music's aid;
 Which she performed such a way,
 As all th' inamour'd world will say
 The Graces danced, and Apollo play'd.

Gratiana Dancing and Singing

2 Forbear, thou great good husband, little ant.

The Ant

3 Cease, large example of wise thrift a while. *Ib.*

4 When Love with unconfined wings
 Hovers within my gates;
 And my divine Althea brings
 To whisper at the grates:
 When I lie tangled in her hair,
 And fettered to her eye;
 The Gods, that wanton in the air,
 Know no such liberty. *To Althea, From Prison*

5 When flowing cups run swiftly round
 With no allaying Thames. *Ib.*

6 When thirsty grief in wine we steep,
 When healths and draughts go free,
 Fishes, that tipple in the deep,
 Know no such liberty. *Ib.*

7 When (like committed linnets) I
 With shriller throat shall sing
 The sweetness, mercy, majesty,
 And glories of my King;
 When I shall voice aloud, how good
 He is, how great should be;
 Enlarged winds that curl the flood,
 Know no such liberty.

 Stone walls do not a prison make
 Nor iron bars a cage;
 Minds innocent and quiet take
 That for an hermitage;
 If I have freedom in my love,
 And in my soul am free;
 Angels alone, that soar above,
 Enjoy such liberty. *Ib.*

8 If to be absent were to be
 Away from thee;
 Or that when I am gone,
 You or I were alone;
 Then my Lucasta might I crave
 Pity from blust'ring wind, or swallowing wave.

To Lucasta, Going Beyond the Seas

9 And greet as angels greet. *Ib.*

10 Tell me not (Sweet) I am unkind,
 That from the nunnery
 Of thy chaste breast, and quiet mind,
 To war and arms I fly.

 True; a new mistress now I chase,
 The first foe in the field;
 And with a stronger faith embrace
 A sword, a horse, a shield.

 Yet this inconstancy is such,
 As you too shall adore;
 I could not love thee (Dear) so much,
 Lov'd I not honour more.

To Lucasta, Going to the Wars

[319]

SAMUEL LOVER
1797–1868

11 When once the itch of literature comes over a man,
 nothing can cure it but the scratching of a pen.
Handy Andy, ch. 36

12 'Now women are mostly troublesome cattle to deal
 with mostly', said Goggins. *Ib.*

JAMES RUSSELL LOWELL
1819–1891

13 An' you've gut to git up airly
 Ef you want to take in God.
The Biglow Papers, First Series, No. 1

14 God'll send the bill to you. *Ib.*

15 You've a darned long row to hoe. *Ib.*

16 This goin' ware glory waits ye haint one agreeable
 feetur. *Ib. No. 2*

17 But John P.
 Robinson he
 Sez they didn't know everythin' down in Judee.
Ib. No. 3

18 A marciful Providence fashioned us holler,
 O' purpose thet we might our principles swaller.
Ib. No. 4

19 I du believe in Freedom's cause,
 Ez fur away ez Payris is;
 I love to see her stick her claws
 In them infarnal Phayrisees;
 It's wal enough agin a king
 To dror resolves an' triggers,—
 But libbaty's a kind o' thing
 Thet don't agree with niggers.
Ib. No. 6. The Pious Editor's Creed

20 An' in convartin' public trusts
 To very privit uses. *Ib.*

21 I *don't* believe in princerple,
 But O, I *du* in interest. *Ib.*

22 It ain't by princerples nor men
 My preudunt course is steadied,—
 I scent wich pays the best, an' then
 Go into it baldheaded. *Ib.*

23 God makes sech nights, all white an' still
 Fur'z you can look or listen,
 Moonshine an' snow on field an' hill,
 All silence an' all glisten.
Ib. Introduction to the Second Series. The Courtin'.

24 'Twas kin' o' kingdom-come to look
 On sech a blessed cretur. *Ib.*

25 She thought no v'ice hed sech a swing
 Ez hisn in the choir;
 My! when he made Ole Hunderd ring,
 She *knowed* the Lord was nigher. *Ib.*

26 His heart kep' goin' pity-pat,
 But hern went pity Zekle. *Ib.*

27 I tell ye wut, my jedgement is you're pooty sure to
 fail,
 Ez long 'z the head keeps turnin' back for counsel to
 the tail. *Ib. Second Series*, No. 3, l. 223

28 We've a war, an' a debt, an' a flag; an' ef this
 Ain't to be inderpendunt, why, wut on irth is?
Ib. No. 4

1 But somehow, when the dogs hed gut asleep,
Their love o' mutton beat their love o' sheep.
The Biglow Papers. Second Series, Ib. No. 11,
l. 291

2 In life's small things be resolute and great
To keep thy muscle trained: know'st thou when Fate
Thy measure takes, or when she'll say to thee,
'I find thee worthy; do this deed for me'? *Epigram*

3 They believed—faith, I'm puzzled—I think I may
call
Their belief a believing in nothing at all,
Or something of that sort; I know they all went
For a general union of total dissent.
A Fable for Critics, l. 733

4 There comes Poe with his raven like Barnaby Rudge,
Three-fifths of him genius, and two-fifths sheer fudge.
Ib. l. 1215

5 No man is born into the world, whose work
Is not born with him; there is always work,
And tools to work withal, for those who will:
And blessèd are the horny hands of toil!
A Glance Behind the Curtain, l. 201

6 These pearls of thought in Persian gulfs were bred,
Each softly lucent as a rounded moon;
The diver Omar plucked them from their bed,
Fitzgerald strung them on an English thread.
In a Copy of Omar Khayyám

7 The birch, most shy and ladylike of trees.
An Indian-Summer Reverie

8 Before Man made us citizens, great Nature made us
men.   *On the Capture of Fugitive Slaves*

9 Once to every man and nation comes the moment to
decide,
In the strife of Truth with Falsehood, for the good or
evil side.   *The Present Crisis*

10 Truth forever on the scaffold, Wrong forever on the
throne.   *Ib.*

11   Behind the dim unknown,
Standeth God within the shadow, keeping watch
above his own.   *Ib.*

12 Then to side with Truth is noble when we share her
wretched crust,
Ere her cause bring fame and profit, and 'tis prosper-
ous to be just;
Then it is the brave man chooses, while the coward
stands aside,
Doubting in his abject spirit, till his Lord is crucified.
Ib.

13 New occasions teach new duties: Time makes ancient
good uncouth;
They must upward still, and onward, who would
keep abreast of Truth.   *Ib.*

14 They are slaves who fear to speak
For the fallen and the weak.   *Stanzas on Freedom*

15 They are slaves who dare not be
In the right with two or three.   *Ib.*

16 May is a pious fraud of the almanac.
Under the Willows, l. 21

17 And what is so rare as a day in June?
Then, if ever, come perfect days;
Then Heaven tries earth if it be in tune,
And over it softly her warm ear lays.
Vision of Sir Launfal, pt. 1, prelude

18 Who gives himself with his alms feeds three,—
Himself, his hungering neighbour, and Me.
Vision of Sir Launfal, pt. 11. viii

19 A wise scepticism is the first attribute of a good critic.
Among My Books. Shakespeare Once More

20 Let us be of good cheer, however, remembering that
the misfortunes hardest to bear are those which
never come.
Democracy and Addresses. Democracy

21 There is no good in arguing with the inevitable. The
only argument available with an east wind is to put
on your overcoat.   *Ib.*

LUCAN

A.D. 39–65

22 Victrix causa deis placuit, sed victa Catoni.
The conquering cause was pleasing to the Gods,
but the conquered one to Cato.
Works, 1. 128. Trans. by Ridley

23 Stat magni nominis umbra.
There stands the shadow of a glorious name.
Ib. 135

24 Nil actum credens, dum quid superesset agendum.
Thinking nothing done while anything remained to
be done.   *Ib.* ii. 657

25   Clarum et venerabile nomen
Gentibus.
A name illustrious and revered by nations.
Ib. ix. 203

26 Estne Dei sedes nisi terra, et pontus, et aer,
Et coelum, et virtus? Superos quid quaerimus ultra?
Jupiter est quodcumque vides, quocumque moveris.
The abode of God, too, is, wherever is earth and
sea and air, and sky, and virtue. Why further
do we seek the Gods of heaven? Whatever
thou dost behold and whatever thou dost touch,
that is Jupiter.   *Ib.* 578

LUCRETIUS

99–55 B.C.

27 Ergo vivida vis animi pervicit, et extra
Processit longe flammantia moenia mundi
Atque omne immensum peragravit, mente animoque.
And so it was that the lively force of his mind won
its way, and he passed on far beyond the fiery
walls of the world, and in mind and spirit
traversed the boundless whole.
De Rerum Natura, i. 72. Trans. by Bailey

28 Tantum religio potuit suadere malorum.
Such evil deeds could religion prompt.   *Ib.* 101

29   Nil posse creari
De nilo.
Nothing can be created out of nothing.   *Ib.* 155

30 Suave, mari magno turbantibus aequora ventis,
E terra magnum alterius spectare laborem,
Non quia vexari quemquamst iucunda voluptas,
Sed quibus ipse malis careas quia cernere suave est.
Suave etiam belli certamina magna tueri
Per campos instructa tua sine parte pericli.
Sed nil dulcius est, bene quam munita tenere
Edita doctrina sapientum templa serena,

Despicere unde queas alios passimque videre
Errare atque viam palantis quaerere vitae,
Certare ingenio, contendere nobilitate,
Noctes atque dies niti praestante labore
Ad summas emergere opes rerumque potiri.

Sweet it is, when on the great sea the winds are
buffeting the waters, to gaze from the land on
another's great struggles; not because it is pleasure or joy that any one should be distressed,
but because it is sweet to perceive from what misfortune you yourself are free. Sweet is it too, to
behold great contests of war in full array over
the plains, when you have no part in the danger.
But nothing is more gladdening than to dwell
in the calm high places, firmly embattled on the
heights by the teaching of the wise, whence you
can look down on others, and see them wandering hither and thither, going astray as they seek
the way of life, in strife matching their wits or
rival claims of birth, struggling night and day
by surpassing effort to rise up to the height of
power and gain possession of the world.
De Rerum Natura, ii. 1

1   Sic rerum summa novatur
Semper, et inter se mortales mutua vivunt.
Augescunt aliae gentes, aliae minuuntur,
Inque brevi spatio mutantur saecla animantum
Et quasi cursores vitai lampada tradunt.

Thus the sum of things is ever being replenished,
and mortals live one and all by give and take.
Some races wax and others wane, and in a short
space the tribes of living things are changed, and
like runners hand on the torch of life.   *Ib.* 75

2   Medio de fonte leporum
Surgit amari aliquid quod in ipsis floribus angat.

From the heart of this fountain of delights wells
up some bitter taste to choke them even amid
the flowers.   *Ib.* iv. 1133

MARTIN LUTHER
1483–1546

3 Esto peccator et pecca fortiter, sed fortius fide et gaude
in Christo.

Be a sinner and sin strongly, but more strongly
have faith and rejoice in Christ.
Letter to Melanchthon. Epistolæ M. Lutheri
(Ienae (1556), i. 345)

4 Ich kann nicht anders.

I can do no other.
*Speech at the Diet of Worms, 18 Apr. 1521. On
his monument at Worms*

5 Wer nicht liebt Wein, Weib und Gesang,
Der bleibt ein Narr sein Leben lang.

Who loves not woman, wine, and song
Remains a fool his whole life long.
*Attr. to Luther. Written in the Luther room in the
Wartburg, but no proof exists of its authorship*

6 Ein feste Burg ist unser Gott,
Ein gute Wehr und Waffen.

A safe stronghold our God is still,
A trusty shield and weapon.
Klug'sche Gesangbuch (1529), *Ein Feste Burg.*
Trans. by Carlyle

7 Wenn ich gewisst hätte, dass so viel Teufel auf mich
gezielet hätten, als Ziegel auf den Dächern waren
zu Worms, wäre ich dennoch eingeritten.

If I had heard that as many devils would set on me
in Worms as there are tiles on the roofs, I should
none the less have ridden there.
Luthers Sämmtliche Schriften (1745), xvi. 14

JOHN LYDGATE
1370?–1451?

8 Woord is but wynd; leff woord and tak the dede.
Secrees of old Philisoffres, l. 1224

9 Sithe off oure language he [Chaucer] was the lode-
sterre.   *The Fall of Princes*, prol. l. 252

10 Sithe he off Inglissh in makyng was the beste,
Preie onto God to yiue his soule good reste. *Ib.* l. 356

11 Comparisouns doon offte gret greuaunce.
Ib. bk. iii, l. 2188

12 Love is mor than gold or gret richesse.
The Siege of Thebes, pt. III, l. 2716

JOHN LYLY
1554?–1606

13 CAMPASPE:
Were women never so fair, men would be false.
APELLES:
Were women never so false, men would be fond.
Campaspe, III. iii

14 Cupid and my Campaspe play'd
At cards for kisses, Cupid paid;
He stakes his quiver, bow, and arrows,
His mother's doves, and team of sparrows;
Loses them too; then, down he throws
The coral of his lip, the rose
Growing on 's cheek (but none knows how);
With these, the crystal of his brow,
And then the dimple on his chin:
All these did my Campaspe win.
At last he set her both his eyes;
She won, and Cupid blind did rise.
O Love! has she done this to thee?
What shall, alas! become of me?   *Ib.* III. v

15 What bird so sings, yet so does wail?
O 'tis the ravish'd nightingale.
Jug, jug, jug, jug, tereu, she cries,
And still her woes at midnight rise.   *Ib.* v. i

16 How at heaven's gates she claps her wings,
The morn not waking till she sings.   *Ib.*

17 Be valiant, but not too venturous. Let thy attire be
comely, but not costly.
Euphues, Anatomy of Wit (Arber), p. 39

18 Night hath a thousand eyes.
Maides Metamorphose, III. i

19 If all the earth were paper white
And all the sea were ink
'Twere not enough for me to write
As my poor heart doth think.
Poems, Early Autobiographical. Lyly's *Works*,
ed. Bond (1902), vol. iii, p. 452

HENRY FRANCIS LYTE

1793-1847

1 Abide with me; fast falls the eventide;
The darkness deepens; Lord, with me abide;
When other helpers fail, and comforts flee,
Help of the helpless, O, abide with me.

Swift to its close ebbs out life's little day;
Earth's joys grow dim, its glories pass away;
Change and decay in all around I see;
O Thou, who changest not, abide with me.
Remains. Abide with Me

2 I fear no foe with Thee at hand to bless;
Ills have no weight, and tears no bitterness;
Where is death's sting? Where, grave, thy victory?
I triumph still, if Thou abide with me.

Hold Thou Thy Cross before my closing eyes;
Shine through the gloom, and point me to the skies;
Heaven's morning breaks, and earth's vain shadows flee;
In life, in death, O Lord, abide with me. *Ib.*

GEORGE LYTTELTON, BARON LYTTELTON

1709-1773

3 What is your sex's earliest, latest care,
Your heart's supreme ambition?—To be fair.
Advice to a Lady, l. 17

4 Seek to be good, but aim not to be great;
A woman's noblest station is retreat. *Ib.* l. 51

5 Where none admire, 'tis useless to excel;
Where none are beaux, 'tis vain to be a belle.
Soliloquy of a Beauty in the Country

6 Tell me, my heart, if this be love?
Song. When Delia

EDWARD GEORGE BULWER-LYTTON, BARON LYTTON

1803-1873

7 Ah, never can fall from the days that have been
A gleam on the years that shall be! *A Lament*

8 When stars are in the quiet skies,
Then most I pine for thee;
Bend on me, then, thy tender eyes,
As stars look on the sea!
Ernest Maltravers, bk. iii, ch. i

9 Here Stanley meets,—how Stanley scorns, the glance!
The brilliant chief, irregularly great,
Frank, haughty, rash,—the Rupert of Debate.
The New Timon, pt. I. vi

10 Out-babying Wordsworth and out-glittering Keats.
[Tennyson.] *Ib.*

11 Beneath the rule of men entirely great
The pen is mightier than the sword. *Richelieu*, II. ii

12 In the lexicon of youth, which Fate reserves
For a bright manhood, there is no such word
As—*fail*! *Ib.*

13 Poverty has strange bedfellows.
The Caxtons, pt. iv, ch. 4

14 There is no man so friendless but what he can find
a friend sincere enough to tell him disagreeable
truths.
What Will He Do With It?, bk. iii, ch. 15
(heading)

EDWARD ROBERT BULWER, EARL OF LYTTON

see

OWEN MEREDITH

WARD McALLISTER

1827-1895

15 There are only about four hundred people in New
York society.
Interview with Charles H. Crandall in the New
York Tribune, *1888*

DOUGLAS MacARTHUR

1880-

16 I shall return.
Message on leaving Corregidor for Australia.
11 Mar. 1942

THOMAS BABINGTON MACAULAY, BARON MACAULAY

1800-1859

17 Attend, all ye who list to hear our noble England's
praise;
I tell of the thrice famous deeds she wrought in
ancient days. *The Armada*

18 Night sank upon the dusky beach, and on the purple
sea,
Such night in England ne'er had been, nor e'er again
shall be. *Ib.*

19 The rugged miners poured to war from Mendip's
sunless caves. *Ib.*

20 The sentinel on Whitehall gate looked forth into the
night. *Ib.*

21 At once on all her stately gates arose the answering
fires;
At once the wild alarum clashed from all her reeling
spires. *Ib.*

22 And broader still became the blaze, and louder still
the din,
As fast from every village round the horse came spurring in;
And eastward straight from wild Blackheath the warlike errand went,
And roused in many an ancient hall the gallant squires
of Kent. *Ib.*

23 Till Belvoir's lordly terraces the sign to Lincoln sent,
And Lincoln sped the message on o'er the wide vale
of Trent;
Till Skiddaw saw the fire that burned on Gaunt's em-
battled pile,
And the red glare on Skiddaw roused the burghers of
Carlisle. *Ib.*

24 Obadiah Bind - their - kings - in - chains - and - their -
nobles-with-links-of-iron. *The Battle of Naseby*

25 Oh, wherefore come ye forth in triumph from the
north,
With your hands, and your feet, and your raiment
all red?
And wherefore doth your rout send forth a joyous
shout?
And whence be the grapes of the wine-press which
ye tread? *Ib.*

1 And the Man of Blood was there, with his long
  essenced hair,
And Astley, and Sir Marmaduke, and Rupert of the
  Rhine.   *The Battle of Naseby*

2 For God! for the Cause! for the Church! for the
  laws!
For Charles King of England, and Rupert of the
  Rhine!   *Ib.*

3 The furious German comes, with his clarions and
  his drums.   *Ib.*

4 He looked upon his people, and a tear was in his eye;
He looked upon the traitors, and his glance was stern
  and high.   *Ivry*

5 'Press where ye see my white plume shine, amidst the
  ranks of war,
And be your oriflamme to-day the helmet of Navarre.'
                                                  Ib.

6 Their ranks are breaking like thin clouds before a
  Biscay gale.   *Ib.*

7 To my true king I offer'd free from stain
Courage and faith; vain faith, and courage vain.
                                    A Jacobite's Epitaph

8 And pined by Arno for my lovelier Tees.   *Ib.*

9 By those white cliffs I never more must see,
By that dear language which I spake like thee,
Forget all feuds, and shed one English tear
O'er English dust. A broken heart lies here.   *Ib.*

10 Lars Porsena of Clusium
   By the nine gods he swore
That the great house of Tarquin
   Should suffer wrong no more.
By the Nine Gods he swore it,
   And named a trysting day,
And bade his messengers ride forth,
   East and west and south and north,
   To summon his array.
              Lays of Ancient Rome. Horatius, i

11 From lordly Volaterræ,
   Where scowls the far-famed hold
Piled by the hands of giants
   For godlike kings of old.   *Ib. iv*

12 The harvests of Arretium,
   This year, old men shall reap.
This year, young boys in Umbro
   Shall plunge the struggling sheep;
And in the vats of Luna,
   This year, the must shall foam
Round the white feet of laughing girls
   Whose sires have marched to Rome.   *Ib. viii*

13 A proud man was Lars Porsena
   Upon the trysting day.   *Ib. xi*

14 And with a mighty following
   To join the muster came
The Tusculan Mamilius,
   Prince of the Latian name.   *Ib. xii*

15 And plainly and more plainly
   Now might the burghers know,
By port and vest, by horse and crest,
   Each warlike Lucumo.   *Ib. xxiii*

16 But the Consul's brow was sad,
   And the Consul's speech was low,
And darkly looked he at the wall,
   And darkly at the foe.   *Ib. xxvi*

17 Then out spake brave Horatius,
   The Captain of the Gate:
'To every man upon this earth
   Death cometh soon or late.
And how can man die better
   Than facing fearful odds,
For the ashes of his fathers,
   And the temples of his Gods?'   *Horatius, xxvii*

18 To save them from false Sextus
   That wrought the deed of shame.   *Ib. xxviii*

19 'Now who will stand on either hand,
   And keep the bridge with me?'   *Ib. xxix*

20 And straight against that great array
   Forth went the dauntless Three.   *Ib. xxxi*

21 Then none was for a party;
   Then all were for the state;
Then the great man helped the poor,
   And the poor man loved the great:
Then lands were fairly portioned;
   Then spoils were fairly sold:
The Romans were like brothers
   In the brave days of old.   *Ib. xxxi*

22 Was none who would be foremost
   To lead such dire attack;
But those behind cried 'Forward!'
   And those before cried 'Back!'   *Ib. l*

23 Thrice looked he at the city;
   Thrice looked he at the dead;
And thrice came on in fury,
   And thrice turned back in dread.   *Ib. lii*

24 'Come back, come back, Horatius!'
   Loud cried the Fathers all.
'Back, Lartius! back, Herminius!
   Back, ere the ruin fall!'   *Ib. liii*

25 But when they turned their faces,
   And on the farther shore
Saw brave Horatius stand alone,
   They would have crossed once more.   *Ib. liv*

26 Round turned he, as not deigning
   Those craven ranks to see;
Nought spake he to Lars Porsena,
   To Sextus nought spake he;
But he saw on Palatinus
   The white porch of his home!
And he spake to the noble river
   That rolls by the towers of Rome.   *Ib. lviii*

27 'Oh, Tiber! father Tiber!
   To whom the Romans pray,
A Roman's life, a Roman's arms,
   Take thou in charge this day!'   *Ib. lix*

28 And even the ranks of Tuscany
   Could scarce forbear to cheer.   *Ib. lx*

29 Never, I ween, did swimmer,
   In such an evil case,
Struggle through such a raging flood
   Safe to the landing place.   *Ib. lxii*

30 'Heaven help him!' quoth Lars Porsena,
   'And bring him safe to shore;
For such a gallant feat of arms
   Was never seen before.'   *Ib. lxiii*

31 When the oldest cask is opened,
   And the largest lamp is lit.   *Ib. lxix*

1 With weeping and with laughter
   Still is the story told,
How well Horatius kept the bridge
   In the brave days of old.
         Lays of Ancient Rome. Horatius, lxx

2 In lordly Lacedaemon,
   The city of two kings.
         Ib. The Battle of Lake Regillus, ii

3 Those trees in whose dim shadow
   The ghastly priest doth reign,
The priest who slew the slayer,
   And shall himself be slain.   *Ib. x*

4 Herminius glared on Sextus.   *Ib. xv*

5 Ah! woe is me for the good house
   That loves the people well!   *Ib. xvii*

6 For aye Valerius loathed the wrong,
   And aye upheld the right.   *Ib. xviii*

7 Away, away went Auster
   Like an arrow from the bow:
Black Auster was the fleetest steed
   From Aufidus to Po.   *Ib. xxv*

8 One of us two, Herminius,
   Shall never more go home.
I will lay on for Tusculum
   And lay thou on for Rome!   *Ib. xxvii*

9 Herminius smote Mamilius
   Through breast-plate and through breast;
And fast flowed out the purple blood
   Over the purple vest.
Mamilius smote Herminius
   Through headpiece and through head;
And side by side those chiefs of pride
   Together fell down dead.   *Ib. xxviii*

10 The pass was steep and rugged,
   The wolves they howled and whined;
But he ran like a whirlwind up the pass,
   And he left the wolves behind.   *Ib. xxix*

11 'The furies of thy brother
   With me and mine abide,
If one of your accursed house
   Upon black Auster ride!'   *Ib. xxx*

12 So spake he; and was buckling
   Tighter black Auster's band,
When he was aware of a princely **pair**
   That rode at his right hand.
So like they were, no mortal
   Might one from other know:
White as snow their armour was:
   Their steeds were white as snow.   *Ib. xxxii*

13 And all who saw them trembled,
   And pale grew every cheek.   *Ib. xxxiii*

14 Let no man stop to plunder,
   But slay, and slay, and slay;
The Gods who live for ever
   Are on our side to-day.   *Ib. xxxv*

15 And fliers and pursuers
   Were mingled in a mass;
And far away the battle
   Went roaring through the pass.   *Ib. xxxvi*

16 These be the great Twin Brethren
   To whom the Dorians pray.   *Ib. xl*

17   Thou, through all change,
Fix thy firm gaze on virtue and on me.
         Lines Written in August

18 From all the angelic ranks goes forth a groan,
   'How long, O Lord, how long?'
The still small voice makes answer 'Wait and see,
   O sons of glory, what the end shall be'.
         Marriage of Tirzah and Ahirad

19 Ye diners-out from whom we guard our spoons.
   Political Georgics. See his letter to Hannah Macaulay, 29 June 1831

20 Knowledge advances by steps, and not by leaps.
         Essays and Biographies. History

21 The business of everybody is the business of nobody.
   Historical Essays Contributed to the 'Edinburgh Review'. Hallam's Constitutional History (Sept. 1828)

22 The gallery in which the reporters sit has become a fourth estate of the realm.   *Ib.*

23 He knew that the essence of war is violence, and that moderation in war is imbecility. [John Hampden.]
   Ib. Lord Nugent's Memorials of Hampden (Dec. 1831)

24 The reluctant obedience of distant provinces generally costs more than it [the territory] is worth.
   Ib. Lord Mahon's War of the Succession (Jan. 1833)

25 The highest intellects, like the tops of mountains, are the first to catch and to reflect the dawn.
   Ib. Sir J. Mackintosh's History of the Revolution (July 1835)

26 The history of England is emphatically the history of progress.   *Ib.*

27 The rising hope of those stern and unbending Tories.
   Ib. Gladstone on Church and State (April 1839)

28 Every schoolboy knows who imprisoned Montezuma, and who strangled Atahualpa.
         Ib. Lord Clive (Jan. 1840)

29 They [the Nabobs] raised the price of everything in their neighbourhood, from fresh eggs to rotten boroughs.   *Ib.*

30 A savage old Nabob, with an immense fortune, a tawny complexion, a bad liver, and a worse heart. [Clive.]   *Ib.*

31 When some traveller from New Zealand shall, in the midst of a vast solitude, take his stand on a broken arch of London Bridge to sketch the ruins of St. Paul's.   *Ib. Von Ranke* (Oct. 1840)

32 The Chief Justice was rich, quiet, and infamous.
         Ib. Warren Hastings (Oct. 1841)

33 The great Proconsul.   *Ib.*

34 In order that he might rob a neighbour whom he had promised to defend, black men fought on the coast of Coromandel, and red men scalped each other by the Great Lakes of North America.
         Ib. Frederic the Great (Apr. 1842)

35 We hardly know any instance of the strength and weakness of human nature so striking, and so grotesque, as the character of this haughty, vigilant, resolute, sagacious blue-stocking, half Mithridates and half Trissotin, bearing up against a world in arms, with an ounce of poison in one pocket and a quire of bad verses in the other. [Frederick.]   *Ib.*

36 *Lues Boswelliana*, or disease of admiration.
         Ib. Earl of Chatham (Jan. 1834)

1 The dust and silence of the upper shelf.
Literary Essays Contributed to the 'Edinburgh Review'. Milton (Aug. 1825)

2 As civilization advances, poetry almost necessarily declines. *Ib.*

3 Perhaps no person can be a poet, or can even enjoy poetry, without a certain unsoundness of mind. *Ib.*

4 Nobles by the right of an earlier creation, and priests by the imposition of a mightier hand. *Ib.*

5 That propensity which, for want of a better name, we will venture to christen Boswellism. *Ib.*

6 Out of his surname they have coined an epithet for a knave, and out of his Christian name a synonym for the Devil. *Ib. Machiavelli* (Mar. 1827)

7 Nothing is so useless as a general maxim. *Ib.*

8 We have heard it said that five per cent. is the natural interest of money.
Ib. Southey's Colloquies (Jan. 1830)

9 His writing bears the same relation to poetry which a Turkey carpet bears to a picture. There are colours in the Turkey carpet out of which a picture might be made. There are words in Mr. Montgomery's writing which, when disposed in certain orders and combinations, have made, and will make again, good poetry. But, as they now stand, they seem to be put together on principle in such a manner as to give no image of anything 'in the heavens above, or in the earth beneath, or in the waters under the earth.'
Ib. Mr. Robert Montgomery's Poems (Apr. 1830)

10 The use of a mirror, we submit, is not to be painted upon. *Ib.*

11 But Mr. Robert Montgomery's readers must take such grammar as they can get, and be thankful. *Ib.*

12 We take this to be, on the whole, the worst similitude in the world. In the first place, no stream meanders, or can possibly meander, level with its fount. In the next place, if streams did meander level with their founts, no two motions can be less like each other than that of meandering level and that of mounting upwards. *Ib.*

13 His theory is therefore this, that God made the thunder, but that the lightning made itself. *Ib.*

14 He had a head which statuaries loved to copy, and a foot the deformity of which the beggars in the street mimicked.
Ib. Moore's Life of Lord Byron (June 1830)

15 We know no spectacle so ridiculous as the British public in one of its periodical fits of morality. *Ib.*

16 We prefer a gipsy by Reynolds to his Majesty's head on a sign-post. *Ib.*

17 The world, we believe, is pretty well agreed in thinking that the shorter a prize poem is, the better. *Ib.*

18 From the poetry of Lord Byron they drew a system of ethics, compounded of misanthropy and voluptuousness, a system in which the two great commandments were, to hate your neighbour, and to love your neighbour's wife. *Ib.*

19 Very few and very weary are those who are in at the death of the Blatant Beast.
Ib. Southey's Edition of Pilgrim's Progress (Dec. 1830)

20 What schoolboy of fourteen is ignorant of this remarkable circumstance?
Ib. Sir William Temple (Oct. 1838)

21 There is a vile phrase of which bad historians are exceedingly fond, 'the dignity of history'. *Ib.*

22 The conformation of his mind was such that whatever was little seemed to him great, and whatever was great seemed to him little.
Ib. Horace Walpole (Oct. 1833)

23 With the dead there is no rivalry. In the dead there is no change. Plato is never sullen. Cervantes is never petulant. Demosthenes never comes unseasonably. Dante never stays too long. No difference of political opinion can alienate Cicero. No heresy can excite the horror of Bossuet.
Ib. Lord Bacon (July 1837)

24 An acre in Middlesex is better than a principality in Utopia. *Ib.*

25 The checkered spectacle of so much glory and so much shame. *Ib.*

26 The Life of Johnson is assuredly a great, a very great work. Homer is not more decidedly the first of heroic poets, Shakespeare is not more decidedly the first of dramatists, Demosthenes is not more decidedly the first of orators, than Boswell is the first of biographers.
Ib. Boswell's Life of Johnson (Sept. 1831)

27 They knew luxury; they knew beggary; but they never knew comfort. *Ib.*

28 In the foreground is that strange figure which is as familiar to us as the figures of those among whom we have been brought up, the gigantic body, the huge massy face, seamed with the scars of disease, the brown coat, the black worsted stockings, the grey wig with the scorched foretop, the dirty hands, the nails bitten and pared to the quick. *Ib.*

29 Like Sir Condy Rackrent in the tale, she survived her own wake, and overheard the judgment of posterity. *Ib. Madame D'Arblay* (Jan. 1843)

30 A sort of broken Johnsonese. *Ib.*

31 He was a rake among scholars, and a scholar among rakes. [Richard Steele.]
Ib. Aikin's Life of Addison (July 1843)

32 The old philosopher is still among us in the brown coat with the metal buttons and the shirt which ought to be at wash, blinking, puffing, rolling his head, drumming with his fingers, tearing his meat like a tiger, and swallowing his tea in oceans.
Life of Johnson (ad fin.)

33 I shall cheerfully bear the reproach of having descended below the dignity of history.
History of England, vol. i, ch. 1

34 Thus our democracy was, from an early period, the most aristocratic, and our aristocracy the most democratic in the world. *Ib.*

35 Persecution produced its natural effect on them. It found them a sect; it made them a faction. *Ib.*

36 It was a crime in a child to read by the bedside of a sick parent one of those beautiful collects which had soothed the griefs of forty generations of Christians. *Ib. ch. 2*

1 The Puritan hated bear-baiting, not because it gave pain to the bear, but because it gave pleasure to the spectators. *History of England*, vol. i, ch. 2

2 There were gentlemen and there were seamen in the navy of Charles the Second. But the seamen were not gentlemen; and the gentlemen were not seamen. *Ib.* ch. 3

3 The English Bible, a book which, if everything else in our language should perish, would alone suffice to show the whole extent of its beauty and power. *Edinburgh Review*, Jan. 1828. *On John Dryden*

4 His imagination resembled the wings of an ostrich. It enabled him to run, though not to soar. *Ib.*

5 It is not easy to make a simile go on all fours. *Ib.* Dec. 1830. *On John Bunyan*

6 The object of oratory alone is not truth, but persuasion. *Works* (1898), vol. xi. *Essay on Athenian Orators*

7 History, abounding with kings thirty feet high, and reigns thirty thousand years long—and geography made up of seas of treacle and seas of butter. *Minute, as Member of Supreme Council of India, 2 Feb. 1835*

8 Dark and terrible beyond any season within my remembrance of political affairs was the day of their flight. Far darker and far more terrible will be the day of their return. [The Tory Government, defeated in Nov. 1830.] *Speech, 20 Sept. 1831*

9 A broken head in Cold Bath Fields produces a greater sensation among us than three pitched battles in India. *Ib. 10 July 1833*

10 Thank you, madam, the agony is abated. [Reply, aged four.] Trevelyan's *Life and Letters of Macaulay*, ch. 1

11 I shall not be satisfied unless I produce something which shall for a few days supersede the last fashionable novel on the tables of young ladies. *Ib.* ch. 13

ANTHONY CLEMENT McAULIFFE
1898–

12 Nuts! *Reply to German demand for surrender of 101st Airborne Division men trapped at Bastogne, Belgium, 23 Dec. 1944*

JOSEPH McCARTHY
contemporary

13 You made me love you, I didn't want to do it. *You Made Me Love You*

GEORGE McCLELLAN
1826–1885

14 All quiet along the Potomac. *Attr. in the American Civil War*

JOHN McCRAE
d. 1918

15 We shall not sleep, though poppies grow In Flanders fields. *In Flanders Fields*. (*Punch*, vol. cxlix, 8 Dec. 1915)

CHARLES BAIRD MACDONALD
1885–

16 When ye come to play golf ye maun hae a heid! *Scotland's Gift—Golf*, 1928

(A caddy at St. Andrews named Lang Willie was teaching one of the professors of the university the noble game. The professor was not a promising pupil.—Willie fairly got out of patience and said to him: 'Ye see, Professor, as long as ye are learning thae lads at the College Latin and Greek it is easy work, but when ye come to play golf ye maun hae a heid!')

GEORGE MACDONALD
1824–1905

17 Where did you come from, baby dear? Out of the everywhere into here. *At the Back of the North Wind*, xxxiii, *Song*

18 Where did you get your eyes so blue? Out of the sky as I came through. *Ib.*

19 Here lie I, Martin Elginbrodde: Hae mercy o' my soul, Lord God; As I wad do, were I Lord God, And ye were Martin Elginbrodde. *David Elginbrod*, bk. i, ch. 13

20 Alas, how easily things go wrong! A sigh too much, or a kiss too long, And there follows a mist and a weeping rain, And life is never the same again. *Phantastes: Down the Lane*

21 They all were looking for a king To slay their foes, and lift them high; Thou cam'st, a little baby thing, That made a woman cry. *That Holy Thing*

CHARLES MACKAY
1814–1889

22 Cheer! Boys, cheer! *Title of Song*

23 There's a good time coming, boys, A good time coming. *The Good Time Coming*

24 Old Tubal Cain was a man of might In the days when earth was young. *Tubal Cain*

HENRY MACKENZIE
1745–1831

25 The Man of Feeling. *Title of Novel*

SIR JAMES MACKINTOSH
1765–1832

26 Men are never so good or so bad as their opinions. *Ethical Philosophy*, § 6. *Bentham*

27 The frivolous work of polished idleness. *Ib. Remarks on Thomas Brown*

28 The Commons, faithful to their system, remained in a wise and masterly inactivity. *Vindiciæ Gallicæ*, § 1

MURDOCH McLENNAN

fl. 1715

1 There's some say that we wan, some say that they
    wan,
  Some say that nane wan at a', man;
  But one thing I'm sure, that at Sheriffmuir
  A battle there was which I saw, man:
  And we ran, and they ran, and they ran, and we ran,
  And we ran; and they ran awa', man!
    Sheriffmuir. Roxburghe Ballads (1889), vol. vi.
    In Hogg's *Jacobite Relics*, 1821, vol. ii, the last
    line is: 'But Florence ran fastest of a', man.'
    (Florence was the Marquis of Huntley's horse)

IRENE RUTHERFORD McLEOD

1891–

2 I'm a lean dog, a keen dog, a wild dog, and alone.
    Lone Dog, st. 1

NORMAN MACLEOD

1812–1872

3 Courage, brother! do not stumble,
  Though thy path is dark as night;
  There's a star to guide the humble:
  'Trust in God, and do the Right.'
    Edinburgh Christian Magazine, Jan. 1857

MAURICE DE MACMAHON

1808–1893

4 J'y suis, j'y reste.
  Here I am, and here I stay.
    Attr. remark at the taking of the Malakoff, 8 Sept.
    1855

LEONARD McNALLY

1752–1820

5 This lass so neat, with smiles so sweet,
  Has won my right good-will,
  I'd crowns resign to call thee mine,
  Sweet lass of Richmond Hill.
    The Lass of Richmond Hill. E. Duncan, *Minstrelsy*
    of England (1905), i. 254. Attr. also to W. Upton
    in *Oxford Song Book*, and to W. Hudson in
    Baring-Gould, *English Minstrelsie* (1895), iii. 54

SAMUEL MADDEN

1686–1765

6 Words are men's daughters, but God's sons are things.
    Boulter's Monument, l. 377

MAURICE DE MAETERLINCK

1862–

7 Il n'y a pas de morts.
  There are no dead.   *L'Oiseau bleu*, IV. ii

ARCHBISHOP WILLIAM CONNOR MAGEE

1821–1891

8 I'd rather that England should be free than that
  England should be compulsorily sober.
    Sermon at Peterborough, 1868

MAGNA CARTA

1215

9 Nisi per legale iudicium parium suorum vel per legem
  terrae.
  Except by the legal judgement of his peers or the law
    of the land.   *Clause 39*

SIR JOHN PENTLAND MAHAFFY

1839–1919

10 [On distinguishing the Irish bull from similar freaks
  of language.] The Irish bull is always pregnant.

ALFRED THAYER MAHAN

1840–1914

11 Those far distant, storm-beaten ships, upon which
  the Grand Army never looked, stood between it
  and the dominion of the world.
    The Influence of Sea Power upon the French
    Revolution and Empire, 1793–1812 (1892), ii.
    118

FRANCIS SYLVESTER MAHONY

see

FATHER PROUT

SIR HENRY JAMES SUMNER MAINE

1822–1888

12 Except the blind forces of Nature, nothing moves in
  this world which is not Greek in its origin.
    Rede Lecture, 1875. Village Communities

JOSEPH DE MAISTRE

1753–1821

13 Toute nation a le gouvernement qu'elle mérite.
  Every country has the government it deserves.
    Lettres et Opuscules Inédits, i, p. 215, 15 août
    1811

DAVID MALLET

1705?–1765

14 O grant me, Heaven, a middle state,
  Neither too humble nor too great;
  More than enough, for nature's ends,
  With something left to treat my friends.
    Imitation of Horace, bk. ii, sat. vi

SIR THOMAS MALORY

fl. 1470

15 It is notoriously known through the universal world
  that there be nine worthy and the best that ever
  were. That is to wit three paynims, three Jews,
  and three Christian men. As for the paynims they
  were . . . the first Hector of Troy, . . . the second
  Alexander the Great; and the third Julius Caesar.
  . . . As for the three Jews . . . the first was Duke
  Joshua . . .; the second David, King of Jerusalem;
  and the third Judas Maccabaeus. . . . And sith the
  said Incarnation . . . was first the noble Arthur. . . .
  The second was Charlemagne or Charles the
  Great . . .; and the third and last was Godfrey of
  Bouillon.
    Le Morte D'Arthur, Caxton's Original Preface

1 I, according to my copy, have done set it in imprint, to the intent that noble men may see and learn the noble acts of chivalry, the gentle and virtuous deeds that some knights used in those days.
Le Morte D'Arthur. Caxton's Original Preface

2 Wherein they shall find many joyous and pleasant histories, and noble and renowned acts of humanity, gentleness, and chivalries. For herein may be seen noble chivalry, courtesy, humanity, friendliness, hardiness, love, friendship, cowardice, murder, hate, virtue, and sin. Do after the good and leave the evil, and it shall bring you to good fame and renown. *Ib.*

3 Whoso pulleth out this sword of this stone and anvil is rightwise King born of all England.
Ib. bk. i, ch. 4

4 This beast went to the well and drank, and the noise was in the beast's belly like unto the questing of thirty couple hounds, but all the while the beast drank there was no noise in the beast's belly.
Ib. ch. 19

5 Me repenteth, said Merlin; because of the death of that lady thou shalt strike a stroke most dolorous that ever man struck, except the stroke of our Lord, for thou shalt hurt the truest knight and the man of most worship that now liveth, and through that stroke three kingdoms shall be in great poverty, misery and wretchedness twelve years, and the knight shall not be whole of that wound for many years. *Ib. bk. ii, ch. 8*

6 What, nephew, said the king, is the wind in that door? *Ib. bk. vii, ch. 34*

7 Ah, my little son, thou hast murdered thy mother! And therefore I suppose thou that art a murderer so young, thou art full likely to be a manly man in thine age . . . when he is christened let call him Tristram, that is as much to say as a sorrowful birth. *Ib. bk. viii, ch. 1*

8 The questing beast. *Ib. bk. ix, ch. 12*

9 God defend me, said Dinadan, for the joy of love is too short, and the sorrow thereof, and what cometh thereof, dureth over long. *Ib. bk. x, ch. 56*

10 It is his day, said Dinadan. *Ib. ch. 70*

11 Nay, by my knighthood, said Palomides, I never espied that ever she loved me more than all the world, nor never had I pleasure with her, but the last day she gave me the greatest rebuke that ever I had, the which shall never go from my heart.
Ib. ch. 82.

12 Now I thank God, said Sir Launcelot, for His great mercy of that I have seen, for it sufficeth me. For, as I suppose, no man in this world hath lived better than I have done, to achieve that I have done.
Ib. bk. xvii, ch. 16

13 Fair lord, salute me to my lord, Sir Launcelot, my father, and as soon as ye see him, bid him remember of this unstable world. *Ib. ch. 22*

14 Thus endeth the story of the Sangreal, that was briefly drawn out of French into English, the which is a story chronicled for one of the truest and the holiest that is in this world. *Ib. ch. 23, end*

15 And thus it passed on from Candlemass until after Easter, that the month of May was come, when every lusty heart beginneth to blossom, and to bring forth fruit; for like as herbs and trees bring forth fruit and flourish in May, in likewise every lusty heart that is in any manner a lover, springeth and flourisheth in lusty deeds.
Le Morte D'Arthur, bk. xviii, ch. 25

16 Therefore all ye that be lovers call unto your remembrance the month of May, like as did Queen Guenevere, for whom I make here a little mention, that while she lived she was a true lover, and therefore she had a good end. *Ib.*

17 Through this man and me hath all this war been wrought, and the death of the most noblest knights of the world; for through our love that we have loved together is my most noble lord slain. *Ib. bk. xxi, ch. 9*

18 Therefore, Sir Launcelot, I require thee and beseech thee heartily, for all the love that ever was betwixt us, that thou never see me more in the visage. *Ib.*

19 Wherefore, madam, I pray you kiss me and never no more. Nay, said the queen, that shall I never do, but abstain you from such works: and they departed. But there was never so hard an hearted man but he would have wept to see the dolour that they made. *Ib. ch. 10*

20 And Sir Launcelot awoke, and went and took his horse, and rode all that day and all night in a forest, weeping. *Ib.*

21 Then Sir Launcelot saw her visage, but he wept not greatly, but sighed. *Ib. ch. 11*

22 Then Sir Launcelot never after ate but little meat, ne drank, till he was dead. *Ib. ch. 12*

23 I saw the angels heave up Sir Launcelot unto heaven, and the gates of heaven opened against him. *Ib.*

24 Said Sir Ector . . . Sir Launcelot . . . thou wert never matched of earthly knight's hand; and thou wert the courteoust knight that ever bare shield; and thou wert the truest friend to thy lover that ever bestrad horse; and thou wert the truest lover of a sinful man that ever loved woman; and thou wert the kindest man that ever struck with sword; and thou wert the goodliest person that ever came among press of knights; and thou wert the meekest man and the gentlest that ever ate in hall among ladies; and thou wert the sternest knight to thy mortal foe that ever put spear in the rest.
Ib. ch. 13

THOMAS ROBERT MALTHUS
1766–1834

25 Population, when unchecked, increases in a geometrical ratio. Subsistence only increases in an arithmetical ratio. *The Principle of Population*, 1

W. R. MANDALE
nineteenth century

26 Up and down the City Road,
In and out the Eagle,
That's the way the money goes—
Pop goes the weasel! *Pop Goes the Weasel*

JAMES CLARENCE MANGAN
1803–1849

1 There's wine from the royal Pope
    Upon the ocean green;
And Spanish ale shall give you hope,
    My Dark Rosaleen!   *Dark Rosaleen*

2 Your holy delicate white hands
    Shall girdle me with steel.   *Ib.*

3 The fair hills of Eiré, O.   *Title of Poem*

4 Roll forth, my song, like the rushing river.
    The Nameless One

5 He, too, had tears for all souls in trouble
    Here, and in hell.   *Ib.*

MANILIUS
A.D. 1st cent.

6 Eripuit caelo fulmen, mox sceptra tyrannis.

    He snatched the thunderbolt from heaven, soon
    the sceptres from tyrants.
    i. 104. (*Inscribed on Benjamin Franklin's Statue*)

MRS. MARY DE LA RIVIERE MANLEY
1663–1724

7 No time like the present.   *The Lost Lover*, IV. i

HORACE MANN
1796–1859

8 The object of punishment is, prevention from evil; it
never can be made impulsive to good.
    Lectures and Reports on Education, 1867, lecture
    vii

9 Lost, yesterday, somewhere between Sunrise and
Sunset, two golden hours, each set with sixty
diamond minutes. No reward is offered, for they
are gone forever.   *Lost, Two Golden Hours*

LORD JOHN MANNERS, DUKE OF RUTLAND
1818–1906

10 Let wealth and commerce, laws and learning die,
But leave us still our old nobility!
    England's Trust, pt. III, l. 227

WILLIAM MURRAY, EARL OF MANSFIELD
1705–1793

11 Consider what you think justice requires, and decide
accordingly. But never give your reasons; for your
judgement will probably be right, but your reasons
will certainly be wrong.
    Advice. Campbell's *Lives of the Chief Justices*,
    1874, vol. iv, p. 26

RICHARD MANT
1776–1848

12 Bright the vision that delighted
Once the sight of Judah's seer.
    Ancient Hymns. Bright the Vision

JOHANNES MANTUANUS

13 Semel insanivimus omnes.

    We have all been mad once.   *Eclogue*, i. 217

WALTER MAP or MAPES
fl. 1200

14 If die I must, let me die drinking in an inn.
    De nugis curialium

MARCUS AURELIUS ANTONINUS
A.D. 121–180

15 The poet says, Dear city of Cecrops; and wilt not
thou say, Dear City of Zeus?   *Trans. by* G. Long

WILLIAM LEARNED MARCY
1786–1857

16 To the victor belong the spoils of the enemy.
    Parton's *Life of Jackson* (1860), vol. iii, p. 378

JUAN DE MARIANA
1535–1624

17 La última camisa de que se despojan los sabios es la
soberbia.

    The last shirt your wise man will abandon is pride.

MARIE-ANTOINETTE
1755–1793

18 Qu'ils mangent de la brioche.

    Let them eat cake.
    On being told that her people had no bread.
    Attributed to Marie-Antoinette, but much older.
    Rousseau refers in his Confessions, *1740, to*
    a similar remark, as a well-known saying

EDWIN MARKHAM
1852–1940

19 Bowed by the weight of centuries he leans
Upon his hoe and gazes on the ground,
The emptiness of ages in his face,
And on his back the burden of the world.
    The Man with the Hoe

CHRISTOPHER MARLOWE
1564–1593

20 My men, like satyrs grazing on the lawns,
Shall with their goat feet dance an antic hay.
    Edward II, I. i. 59

21 Live and die in Aristotle's works.   *Faustus*, l. 33

22 Sweet Analytics, 'tis thou hast ravished me. *Ib.* l. 34

23 I'll have them fly to India for gold,
Ransack the ocean for orient pearl.   *Ib.* l. 110

24 I'll have them wall all Germany with brass,
And make swift Rhine circle fair Wertenberg.
I'll have them fill the public schools with silk,
Wherewith the students shall be bravely clad.
    Ib. l. 116

25 For when we hear one rack the name of God,
Abjure the Scriptures, and his Saviour Christ,
We fly, in hope to get his glorious soul.   *Ib.* l. 282

1 MEPHISTOPHELES:
    O by aspiring pride and insolence,
    For which God threw him from the face of heaven.
    FAUSTUS:
    And what are you that live with Lucifer?
    MEPHISTOPHELES:
    Unhappy spirits that fell with Lucifer,
    Conspired against our God with Lucifer,
    And are for ever damned with Lucifer. *Faustus*, l. 303

2 Why this is hell, nor am I out of it:
    Thinkst thou that I who saw the face of God,
    And tasted the eternal joys of heaven,
    Am not tormented with ten thousand hells
    In being deprived of everlasting bliss! *Ib.* l. 312

3   When all the world dissolves,
    And every creature shall be purified,
    All places shall be hell that are not heaven. *Ib.* l. 556

4 Have not I made blind Homer sing to me?
                          Ib. l. 637

5 Was this the face that launch'd a thousand ships,
    And burnt the topless towers of Ilium?
    Sweet Helen, make me immortal with a kiss!
    Her lips suck forth my soul: see, where it flies!
    Come Helen, come give me my soul again.
    Here will I dwell, for heaven be in these lips,
    And all is dross that is not Helena. *Ib.* l. 1328

6 O thou art fairer than the evening air,
    Clad in the beauty of a thousand stars,
    Brighter art thou than flaming Jupiter,
    When he appeared to hapless Semele,
    More lovely than the monarch of the sky
    In wanton Arethusa's azured arms,
    And none but thou shalt be my paramour. *Ib.* l. 1341

7 Now hast thou but one bare hour to live,
    And then thou must be damned perpetually;
    Stand still you ever-moving spheres of heaven,
    That time may cease, and midnight never come.
    Fair nature's eye, rise, rise again and make
    Perpetual day, or let this hour be but
    A year, a month, a week, a natural day,
    That Faustus may repent and save his soul.
    O lente, lente currite noctis equi:
    The stars move still, time runs, the clock will strike,
    The devil will come, and Faustus must be damn'd.
    O I'll leap up to my God: who pulls me down?
    See see where Christ's blood streams in the firmament.
    One drop would save my soul, half a drop, ah my
    Christ. *Ib.* l. 1420

8 Mountains and hills, come, come and fall on me,
    And hide me from the heavy wrath of God.
                           Ib. l. 1438

9 You stars that reigned at my nativity,
    Whose influence hath allotted death and hell,
    Now draw up Faustus like a foggy mist,
    Into the entrails of yon labouring cloud,
    That when you vomit forth into the air,
    My limbs may issue from your smoky mouths,
    So that my soul may but ascend to heaven.
                          Ib. l. 1443

10 Ah, Pythagoras' metempsychosis. *Ib.* l. 1461

11 O soul, be changed into little water drops,
    And fall into the ocean, ne'er be found:
    My God, my God, look not so fierce on me.
                          Ib. l. 1472

12 Cut is the branch that might have grown full straight,
    And burnèd is Apollo's laurel bough,
    That sometime grew within this learned man.
                         Faustus, l. 1478

13 It lies not in our power to love, or hate,
    For will in us is over-rul'd by fate.
    When two are stripped, long ere the course begin,
    We wish that one should lose, the other win;
    And one especially do we affect
    Of two gold ingots, like in each respect.
    The reason no man knows; let it suffice,
    What we behold is censured by our eyes.
    Where both deliberate, the love is slight;
    Who ever loved that loved not at first sight?
    Hero and Leander. First Sestiad, l. 167

14 I count religion but a childish toy,
    And hold there is no sin but ignorance.
                   The Jew of Malta, l. 14

15 And as their wealth increases, so enclose
    Infinite riches in a little room. *Ib.* l. 71

16 As for myself, I walk abroad o' nights
    And kill sick people groaning under walls:
    Sometimes I go about and poison wells. *Ib.* l. 939

17 Come live with me, and be my love,
    And we will all the pleasures prove,
    That valleys, groves, hills and fields,
    Woods or steepy mountain yields.
    The Passionate Shepherd to his Love

18 By shallow rivers, to whose falls
    Melodious birds sing madrigals. *Ib.*

19 And I will make thee beds of roses
    And a thousand fragrant posies. *Ib.*

20 Jigging veins of rhyming mother wits.
    Conquests of Tamburlaine, prologue

21 Zenocrate, lovelier than the Love of Jove,
    Brighter than is the silver Rhodope,
    Fairer than whitest snow on Scythian hills.
                   Ib. pt. 1, l. 283

22 Our swords shall play the orators for us. *Ib.* l. 328

23 With Nature's pride, and richest furniture,
    His looks do menace heaven and dare the Gods.
                         Ib. l. 351

24 His deep affections make him passionate. *Ib.* l. 359

25 These are the men that all the world admires.
                          Ib. l. 418

26 Accurst be he that first invented war. *Ib.* l. 664

27 Is it not passing brave to be a King,
    And ride in triumph through Persepolis? *Ib.* l. 758

28 Nature that fram'd us of four elements,
    Warring within our breasts for regiment,
    Doth teach us all to have aspiring minds:
    Our souls, whose faculties can comprehend
    The wondrous Architecture of the world:
    And measure every wand'ring planet's course,
    Still climbing after knowledge infinite,
    And always moving as the restless Spheres,
    Will us to wear ourselves and never rest,
    Until we reach the ripest fruit of all,
    That perfect bliss and sole felicity,
    The sweet fruition of an earthly crown. *Ib.* l. 869

29 Virtue is the fount whence honour springs. *Ib.* l. 1769

1 Ah fair Zenocrate, divine Zenocrate,
Fair is too foul an epithet for thee.
Conquests of Tamburlaine, pt. 1, l. 1916

2 What is beauty saith my sufferings then?
If all the pens that ever poets held,
Had fed the feeling of their masters' thoughts,
And every sweetness that inspir'd their hearts,
Their minds, and muses on admired themes:
If all the heavenly quintessence they still
From their immortal flowers of Poesy,
Wherein as in a mirror we perceive
The highest reaches of a human wit.
If these had made one poem's period
And all combin'd in beauty's worthiness,
Yet should there hover in their restless heads,
One thought, one grace, one wonder at the least,
Which into words no virtue can digest.
But how unseemly is it for my sex,
My discipline of arms and chivalry,
My nature and the terror of my name,
To harbour thoughts effeminate and faint!
Save only that in Beauty's just applause,
With whose instinct the soul of man is touched;
And every warrior that is rapt with love
Of fame, of valour, and of victory,
Must needs have beauty beat on his conceits:
I thus conceiving and subduing both,
That which hath stoopt the tempest of the Gods,
Even from the fiery-spangled veil of heaven,
To feel the lovely warmth of shepherds' flames
And march in cottages of strowed weeds,
Shall give the world to note, for all my birth,
That Virtue solely is the sum of glory,
And fashions men with true nobility.   *Ib.* l. 1941

3 Now walk the angels on the walls of heaven,
As sentinels to warn th' immortal souls,
To entertain divine Zenocrate.   *Ib.* pt. 11, l. 2983

4 Yet let me kiss my Lord before I die,
And let me die with kissing of my Lord. *Ib.* l. 3037

5 Helen, whose beauty summoned Greece to arms,
And drew a thousand ships to Tenedos. *Ib.* l. 3055

6 More childish valourous than manly wise. *Ib.* l. 3690

7 Holla, ye pampered Jades of Asia:
What, can ye draw but twenty miles a day?
Ib. l. 3980

8 Tamburlaine, the Scourge of God, must die.
Ib. l. 4641

9 I'm arm'd with more than complete steel—
The justice of my quarrel.
Lust's Dominion, iv. iii. (*Play probably not by
Marlowe. See* 7:7)

SHACKERLEY MARMION
1603–1639

10 Familiarity begets boldness.   *The Antiquary*, Act 1

11 Great joys, like griefs, are silent.
Holland's Leaguer, v. 1

DONALD ROBERT PERRY MARQUIS
1878–1937

12 toujours gai, archy, toujours gai.
archy's life of mehitabel, i. *the life of mehitabel the
cat*

13   the great open spaces
where cats are cats.
archy's life of mehitabel, xiv. *mehitabel has an
adventure*

FREDERICK MARRYAT
1792–1848

14 There's no getting blood out of a turnip.
Japhet in Search of a Father, ch. 4

15 If you please, ma'am, it was a very little one. [The
nurse excusing her illegitimate baby.]
Midshipman Easy, ch. 3

16 All zeal . . . all zeal, Mr. Easy.   *Ib.* ch. 9

17 As savage as a bear with a sore head.
The King's Own, ch. 26

18 I never knows the children. It's just six of one and
half-a-dozen of the other.   *The Pirate*, ch. 4

19 I think it much better that . . . every man paddle his
own canoe.   *Settlers in Canada*, ch. 8

20 I haven't the gift of the gab, my sons—because I'm
bred to the sea.   *The Old Navy*, st. 1

JOHN MARSTON
1575?–1634

21 Who winks and shuts his apprehension up.
Antonio's Revenge, prologue

MARTIAL
b. A.D. 43

22 Non est, crede mihi, sapientis dicere 'Vivam':
Sera nimis vita est crastina: vive hodie.

It sorts not, believe me, with wisdom to say 'I
shall live'. Too late is to-morrow's life; live thou
to-day.   *Epigrammata*, i. xv. Trans. by Ker

23 Sunt bona, sunt quaedam mediocria, sunt mala plura
Quae legis hic: aliter non fit, Avite, liber.

There are good things, there are some indifferent,
there are more things bad that you read here.
Not otherwise, Avitus, is a book produced.
Ib. xvi

24 Non amo te, Sabidi, nec possum dicere quare:
Hoc tantum possum dicere, non amo te.

I do not love you, Sabidius, and I can't say why.
This only I can say, I do not love you. *Ib.* xxxii

25 Laudant illa sed ista legunt.

Those they praise, but they read the others.
Ib. iv. xlix

26   Bonosque
Soles effugere atque abire sentit,
Qui nobis pereunt et imputantur.

And he feels the good days are flitting and passing
away, our days that perish and are scored to our
account.   *Ib.* v. xx

27 Non est vivere, sed valere vita est.

Life is not living, but living in health.   *Ib.* vi. lxx

28 Rus in urbe.

The country in town.   *Ib.* xii. lvii

ANDREW MARVELL
1621–1678

1 Where the remote Bermudas ride
In th' ocean's bosom unespied.   *Bermudas*

2   Orange bright,
Like golden lamps in a green night.   *Ib.*

3 And makes the hollow seas, that roar,
Proclaim the ambergris on shore.
He cast (of which we rather boast)
The Gospel's pearls upon our coast.   *Ib.*

4 Echo beyond the Mexique Bay.   *Ib.*

5 My love is of a birth as rare
As 'tis for object strange and high:
It was begotten by despair
Upon impossibility.

Magnanimous Despair alone
Could show me so divine a thing,
Where feeble Hope could ne'er have flown
But vainly flapt its tinsel wing.   *Definition of Love*

6 As lines so loves oblique may well
Themselves in every angle greet
But ours so truly parallel,
Though infinite can never meet.

Therefore the love which us doth bind,
But Fate so enviously debars,
Is the conjunction of the mind,
And opposition of the stars.   *Ib.*

7 Earth cannot shew so brave a sight
As when a single soul does fence
The batteries of alluring sense,
And Heaven views it with delight.
          *Dialogue between the Resolved Soul and Created
          Pleasure*

8 All this fair, and soft, and sweet,
Which scatteringly doth shine,
Shall within one Beauty meet,
And she be only thine.   *Ib.*

9 And want new worlds to buy.   *Ib.*

10 Not full sails hasting loaden home,
Nor the chaste lady's pregnant womb,
Nor Cynthia teeming shows so fair,
As two eyes swoln with weeping are.   *Eyes and Tears*

11 Thus let your streams o'erflow your springs,
Till eyes and tears be the same things:
And each the other's difference bears;
These weeping eyes, those seeing tears.   *Ib.*

12 Choosing each stone, and poising every weight,
Trying the measures of the breadth and height;
Here pulling down, and there erecting new,
Founding a firm state by proportions true.
          *The First Anniversary of the Government under
          Oliver Cromwell*, l. 245

13 How vainly men themselves amaze
To win the palm, the oak, or bays;
And their uncessant labours see
Crown'd from some single herb or tree,
Whose short and narrow vergèd shade
Does prudently their toils upbraid;
While all flowers and all trees do close
To weave the garlands of repose.   *The Garden*

14 Fair quiet, have I found thee here,
And Innocence thy Sister dear!   *Ib.*

15 Society is all but rude,
To this delicious solitude.   *The Garden*

16 The Gods, that mortal beauty chase,
Still in a tree did end their race.
Apollo hunted Daphne so,
Only that she might laurel grow.
And Pan did after Syrinx speed,
Not as a nymph, but for a reed.   *Ib.*

17 What wond'rous life is this I lead!
Ripe apples drop about my head;
The luscious clusters of the vine
Upon my mouth do crush their wine;
The nectarine and curious peach,
Into my hands themselves do reach;
Stumbling on melons, as I pass,
Insnar'd with flow'rs, I fall on grass.   *Ib.*

18 Meanwhile the mind, from pleasure less,
Withdraws into its happiness.   *Ib.*

19 Annihilating all that's made
To a green thought in a green shade.   *Ib.*

20 Here at the fountain's sliding foot,
Or at some fruit-tree's mossy root,
Casting the body's vest aside,
My soul into the boughs does glide:
There like a bird it sits, and sings,
Then whets, and combs its silver wings;
And, till prepar'd for longer flight,
Waves in its plumes the various light.   *Ib.*

21 Such was that happy garden-state,
While man there walk'd without a mate.   *Ib.*

22 But 'twas beyond a mortal's share
To wander solitary there:
Two Paradises 'twere in one
To live in Paradise alone.   *Ib.*

23 Of a tall stature and of sable hue,
Much like the son of Kish that lofty Jew,
Twelve years complete he suffer'd in exile
And kept his father's asses all the while.
          An Historical Poem

24 [*Charles I*]
He nothing common did or mean
Upon that memorable scene:
     But with his keener eye
     The axe's edge did try.
          *Horatian Ode upon Cromwell's Return from Ire-
          land*, l. 57

25 But bowed his comely head,
Down as upon a bed.   *Ib.*

26 And now the Irish are ashamed
To see themselves in one year tamed:
     So much one man can do
     That does both act and know.   *Ib.* l. 75

27 Ye living lamps, by whose dear light
     The nightingale does sit so late,
And studying all the summer night,
     Her matchless songs does meditate.
          The Mower to the Glow-worms

28 The wanton troopers riding by
Have shot my fawn and it will die.
          Nymph Complaining for the Death of her Fawn

29 Thy love was far more better than
The love of false and cruel men.   *Ib.*

1 It is a wond'rous thing, how fleet
  'Twas on those little silver feet.
  With what a pretty skipping grace,
  It oft would challenge me the race:
  And when 't had left me far away,
  'Twould stay, and run again, and stay.
  For it was nimbler much than hinds;
  And trod, as on the four winds.
  Nymph Complaining for the Death of her Fawn

2 I have a garden of my own,
  But so with roses overgrown,
  And lilies, that you would it guess
  To be a little wilderness. *Ib.*

3 Had it liv'd long, it would have been
  Lilies without, roses within. *Ib.*

4 The Picture of little T.C. in a Prospect of Flowers.
  Title of Poem

5 Who can foretell for what high cause
  This darling of the Gods was born?
  The Picture of Little T.C.

6 For though the whole world cannot shew such
  another,
  Yet we'd better by far have him than his brother.
  Statue in Stocks-Market

7 He is Translation's thief that addeth more,
  As much as he that taketh from the store
  Of the first author. *To Dr. Witty*

8 Had we but world enough, and time,
  This coyness, Lady, were no crime.
  We would sit down, and think which way
  To walk, and pass our long love's day.
  Thou by the Indian Ganges' side
  Shouldst rubies find: I by the tide
  Of Humber would complain. I would
  Love you ten years before the Flood:
  And you should if you please refuse
  Till the conversion of the Jews.
  My vegetable love should grow
  Vaster than empires, and more slow.
  To His Coy Mistress

9 But at my back I always hear
  Time's wingèd chariot hurrying near.
  And yonder all before us lie
  Deserts of vast eternity.
  Thy beauty shall no more be found;
  Nor, in thy marble vault, shall sound
  My echoing song: then worms shall try
  That long preserved virginity:
  And your quaint honour turn to dust;
  And into ashes all my lust.
  The grave's a fine and private place,
  But none I think do there embrace. *Ib.*

10 Thrice happy he who, not mistook,
   Hath read in Nature's mystic book.
   Upon Appleton House. To My Lord Fairfax,
   lxxiii

KARL MARX
1818–1883

11 Die Proletarier haben nichts in ihr zu verlieren als
   ihre Ketten. Sie haben eine Welt zu gewinnen.
   Proletarier aller Länder, vereinigt euch!

   The workers have nothing to lose in this [revo-
   lution] but their chains. They have a world to gain.
   Workers of the world, unite!
   The Communist Manifesto (1848), last words

12 Jeder nach seinen Fähigkeiten, jedem nach seinen
   Bedürfnissen.

   From each according to his abilities, to each accord-
   ing to his needs.
   Criticism of the Gotha programme, 1875.
   (See 29:14)

13 Die Religion . . . ist das Opium des Volkes.
   Religion . . . is the opium of the people.
   Kritik der Hegelschen Rechtsphilosophie, Intro-
   duction

14 The dictatorship of the proletariat.
   '*Used more than once*', according to Mr. and Mrs.
   Sidney Webb

MARY TUDOR
1516–1558

15 When I am dead and opened, you shall find 'Calais'
   lying in my heart.   Holinshed, *Chron.* iii. 1160

THEOPHILE JULIUS HENRY MARZIALS
1850–1920

16 Ahoy! and Oho, and it's who's for the ferry?
   (The briar's in bud and the sun going down:)
   And I'll row ye so quick and I'll row ye so steady,
   And 'tis but a penny to Twickenham Town.
   Twickenham Ferry

JOHN MASEFIELD
1874–

17 Over the grasses of the ancient way
   Rutted this morning by the passing guns.
   August 1914

18 Coming in solemn beauty like slow old tunes of Spain.
   Beauty

19 But the loveliest things of beauty God ever has
   showed to me,
   Are her voice, and her hair, and eyes, and the dear red
   curve of her lips. *Ib.*

20 Quinquireme of Nineveh from distant Ophir
   Rowing home to haven in sunny Palestine,
   With a cargo of ivory,
   And apes and peacocks,
   Sandalwood, cedarwood, and sweet white wine.
   Cargoes

21 Dirty British coaster with a salt-caked smoke stack,
   Butting through the Channel in the mad March days,
   With a cargo of Tyne coal,
   Road-rail, pig-lead,
   Firewood, iron-ware, and cheap tin trays. *Ib.*

22 Oh some are fond of Spanish wine, and some are fond
   of French,
   And some'll swallow tay and stuff fit only for a wench.
   Captain Stratton's Fancy

23 And fifteen arms went round her waist.
   (And then men ask, Are Barmaids chaste?)
   The Everlasting Mercy

24 To get the whole world out of bed
   And washed, and dressed, and warmed, and fed,
   To work, and back to bed again,
   Believe me, Saul, costs worlds of pain. *Ib.*

1 And he who gives a child a treat
Makes joy-bells ring in Heaven's street,
And he who gives a child a home
Builds palaces in Kingdom come,
And she who gives a baby birth
Brings Saviour Christ again to Earth.
The Everlasting Mercy

2 O Christ, the plough, O Christ, the laughter
Of holy white birds flying after.   *Ib.*

3 The corn that makes the holy bread
By which the soul of man is fed,
The holy bread, the food unpriced,
Thy everlasting mercy, Christ.   *Ib.*

4 Death opens unknown doors. It is most grand to die.
Pompey the Great. i. *The Chief Centurions.* 'Man
is a sacred city'

5 He passed the spring where the rushes spread,
And there in the stones was his earth ahead.
One last short burst upon failing feet—
There life lay waiting, so sweet, so sweet,
Rest in a darkness, balm for aches.

.   .   .   .   .   .

The earth was stopped. It was barred with stakes.
Reynard the Fox

6 Then the moon came quiet and flooded full
Light and beauty on clouds like wool,
On a feasted fox at rest from hunting,
In the beech-wood grey where the brocks were
grunting.
The beech-wood grey rose dim in the night
With moonlight fallen in pools of light,
The long dead leaves on the ground were rimed;
A clock struck twelve and the church-bells chimed.
Ib.

7   The house is falling,
The beaten men come into their own.
The Rider at the Gate

8 One road leads to London,
One road runs to Wales,
My road leads me seawards
To the white dipping sails.   *Roadways*

9 My road calls me, lures me
West, east, south, and north;
Most roads lead men homewards,
My road leads me forth.   *Ib.*

10 I must down to the seas again, to the lonely sea and
the sky,
And all I ask is a tall ship and a star to steer her by,
And the wheel's kick and the wind's song and the
white sail's shaking,
And a grey mist on the sea's face and a grey dawn
breaking.   *Sea Fever*

11 I must down to the seas again, for the call of the
running tide
Is a wild call and a clear call that may not be denied.
Ib.

12 I must down to the seas again, to the vagrant gypsy
life,
To the gull's way and the whale's way where the
wind's like a whetted knife;
And all I ask is a merry yarn from a laughing fellow-
rover,
And quiet sleep and a sweet dream when the long
trick's over.   *Ib.*

13 Friends and loves we have none, nor wealth nor
blessed abode,
But the hope of the City of God at the other end of
the road.   *The Seekers*

14 It is good to be out on the road, and going one knows
not where.   *Tewkesbury Road*

15 It's a warm wind, the west wind, full of birds' cries;
I never hear the west wind but tears are in my eyes.
For it comes from the west lands, the old brown
hills,
And April's in the west wind, and daffodils.
The West Wind

JACKSON MASON
1833–1889

16 Rise up, My love, My fair one,
Arise and come away.
For lo, 'tis past, the winter,
The winter of thy year;
The rain is past and over,
The flowers on earth appear.
And now the time of singing
Is come for every bird;
And over all the country
The turtle dove is heard.
Suppl. Hymns to Hymns A. and M., 1889.
O Voice of the Beloved

PHILIP MASSINGER
1583–1640

17 Ambition, in a private man a vice,
Is, in a prince, the virtue.   *The Bashful Lover,* I. ii

18 He that would govern others, first should be
The master of himself.   *The Bondman,* I. iii

19   Be wise;
Soar not too high to fall; but stoop to rise.
Duke of Milan, I. ii

20   Greatness, with private men
Esteem'd a blessing, is to me a curse;
And we, whom, for our high births, they conclude
The only freemen, are the only slaves.
Happy the golden mean!
Great Duke of Florence, I. i

21   I am driven
Into a desperate strait and cannot steer
A middle course.   *Ib.* III. i

22 A New Way to Pay Old Debts.   *Title of Play*

23 The devil turned precisian!
A New Way to Pay Old Debts, I. i

24 I write *nil ultra* to my proudest hopes.   *Ib.* IV. i

25 Patience, the beggar's virtue.   *Ib.* V. i

26 Some undone widow sits upon my arm,
And takes away the use of 't; and my sword,
Glued to my scabbard with wrong'd orphans' tears,
Will not be drawn.   *Ib.*

27   View yourselves
In the deceiving mirror of self-love.
Parliament of Love, I. v

28 What pity 'tis, one that can speak so well,
Should in his actions be so ill!   *Ib.* III. iii

1
    All words,
And no performance! *Parliament of Love*, IV. ii

2 There are a thousand doors to let out life. *Ib.*

3
    Serves and fears
The fury of the many-headed monster,
The giddy multitude.
    The Unnatural Combat, III. ii

CHARLES ROBERT MATURIN
1782–1824

4 'Tis well to be merry and wise,
'Tis well to be honest and true;
'Tis well to be off with the old love,
Before you are on with the new. *Bertram. Motto*

SOMERSET MAUGHAM
1874–

5 People ask you for criticism, but they only want praise.
    Of Human Bondage, ch. 50

FREDERICK DENISON MAURICE
1805–1872

6 I knew . . . that I was in danger of attaching myself
to a party which should inscribe 'No Party' on its
flag. Many had fallen into that snare.
 Life . . . chiefly told in his own Letters, ed. F.
 Maurice, 2nd edn. (1884), i. 239

7 Subscription no Bondage.
 Title of pamphlet (1835) against abolishing sub-
 scription to the Thirty-nine Articles.

GEORGE LOUIS PALMELLA BUSSON DU MAURIER
1834–1896

8 Life ain't all beer and skittles, and more's the pity;
but what's the odds, so long as you're happy?
    Trilby, pt. 1

9 The salad, for which, like everybody else I ever met,
he had a special receipt of his own. *Ib.*

10 A little work, a little play
To keep us going—and so, good-day!

A little warmth, a little light
Of love's bestowing—and so, good-night!

A little fun, to match the sorrow
Of each day's growing—and so, good-morrow!

A little trust that when we die
We reap our sowing! and so—good-bye! *Ib.* (end)

TERENTIANUS MAURUS
fl. c. A.D. 200

11 Pro captu lectoris habent sua fata libelli.
 The fate of books depends on the capacity of the
 reader. *De Literis, Syllabis, &c.,* l. 1286

HUGHES MEARNS
1875–

12 As I was going up the stair
I met a man who wasn't there.
He wasn't there again to-day.
I wish, I wish he'd stay away.
    The Psychoed (Antigonish)

WILLIAM LAMB, VISCOUNT MELBOURNE
1779–1848

13 I wish I was as cocksure of anything as Tom Macau-
lay is of everything.
  Earl Cowper's *Preface to Lord Melbourne's*
  Papers, 1889, p. xii

14 [Catholic Emancipation] What all the wise men promised has not happened, and what all the d—d
fools said would happen has come to pass.
   H. Dunckley, *Lord Melbourne* (1890)

15 I like the Garter; there is no damned merit in it.
    On the Order of the Garter

16 Things have come to a pretty pass when religion is
allowed to invade the sphere of private life.
  Remark on hearing an Evangelical Sermon.
  G. W. E. Russell's *Collections and Recollections*,
  ch. 6

17 [At a Cabinet meeting]
Now, is it to lower the price of corn, or isn't it? It is
not much matter which we say, but mind, we must
all say *the same*.
  Attrib. (see Bagehot's *English Constitution*, ch. 1)

18 Damn it all, another Bishop dead,—I verily believe
they die to vex me. *Attrib.*

19 The worst of the present day [1835] is that men hate
one another so damnably. For my part I love
them all. *Attrib.*

20 I don't know, Ma'am, why they make all this fuss
about education; none of the Pagets can read or
write, and they get on well enough. [To the Queen]
    Attrib.

21 While I cannot be regarded as a pillar, I must be
regarded as a buttress of the church, because I
support it from the outside. *Attrib.*

THOMAS MELLOR
1880–1926

22 I wouldn't leave my little wooden hut for you!
I've got one lover and I don't want two.
  I Wouldn't Leave My Little Wooden Hut for You

GEORGE MEREDITH
1828–1909

23 With patient inattention hear him prate.
    Bellerophon, iv

24 Sword of Common Sense!
Our surest gift. *To the Comic Spirit*

25
  And we go,
And we drop like the fruits of the tree,
  Even we,
  Even so. *Dirge in Woods*

26 Keep the young generations in hail,
And bequeath them no tumbled house!
    The Empty Purse

27 The Man of England circled by the sands.
   Epitaph on Gordon of Khartoum

28 Shall man into the mystery of breath
From his quick beating pulse a pathway spy?
Or learn the secret of the shrouded death,
By lifting up the lid of a white eye?
Cleave thou thy way with fathering desire
Of fire to reach to fire. *Hymn to Colour*, v

1 Not forfeiting the beast with which they are crossed,
To stature of the gods they will attain.
Hymn to Colour, xiv

2 The song had ceased; my vision with the song.
Ib. xv

3 Death met I too,
And saw the dawn glow through. *Ib.*

4 Bring the army of the faithful through.
To J[ohn] M[orley]

5 I've studied men from my topsy-turvy
Close, and, I reckon, rather true.
Some are fine fellows: some, right scurvy:
Most, a dash between the two. *Juggling Jerry*, vii

6 I'm the bird dead-struck! *Ib.* xiii

7 Under yonder beech-tree single on the greensward,
Couched with her arms behind her golden head,
Knees and tresses folded to slip and ripple idly,
Lies my young love sleeping in the shade.
Love in the Valley, i

8 She whom I love is hard to catch and conquer,
Hard, but O the glory of the winning were she won!
Ib. ii

9 Lovely are the curves of the white owl sweeping
Wavy in the dusk lit by one large star.
Lone on the fir-branch, his rattle-note unvaried,
Brooding o'er the gloom, spins the brown eve-jar.
Darker grows the valley, more and more forgetting:
So were it with me if forgetting could be willed.
Tell the grassy hollow that holds the bubbling well-spring,
Tell it to forget the source that keeps it filled. *Ib.* v

10 Fain would fling the net, and fain have her free. *Ib.* vi

11 Pure from the night, and splendid for the day. *Ib.* ix

12 In arrowy rain. *Ib.* xii

13 Quaintest, richest carol of all the singing throats!
[Blackbird.] *Ib.* xvii

14 Straight rains and tiger sky. *Ib.* xix

15 Gossips count her faults; they scour a narrow chamber
Where there is no window, read not heaven or her.
Ib. xxii

16 Our souls were in our names. *Ib.* xxiii

17 On a starred night Prince Lucifer uprose.
Tired of his dark dominion swung the fiend . . .
He reached a middle height, and at the stars,
Which are the brain of heaven, he looked, and sank.
Around the ancient track marched, rank on rank,
The army of unalterable law. *Lucifer in Starlight*

18 Each wishing for the sword that severs all.
Modern Love, i

19 He fainted on his vengefulness, and strove
To ape the magnanimity of love, *Ib.* ii

20 Not till the fire is dying in the grate,
Look we for any kinship with the stars. *Ib.* iv

21 With hindward feather, and with forward toe
Her much-adored delightful Fairy Prince! *Ib.* x

22 And if I drink oblivion of a day,
So shorten I the stature of my soul. *Ib.* xii

23 'I play for Seasons; not Eternities!'
Says Nature. *Ib.* xiii

24 It is in truth a most contagious game:
HIDING THE SKELETON, shall be its name. *Ib.* xvii

25 They have the secret of the bull and lamb.
'Tis true that when we trace its source, 'tis beer.
Modern Love, xviii

26 We'll sit contentedly
And eat our pot of honey on the grave. *Ib.* xxix

27 That rarest gift
To Beauty, Common Sense. *Ib.* xxxii

28 O have a care of natures that are mute! *Ib.* xxxv

29 God, what a dancing spectre seems the moon.
Ib. xxxix

30 In tragic life, God wot,
No villain need be! Passions spin the plot:
We are betrayed by what is false within. *Ib.* xliii

31 We saw the swallows gathering in the sky. *Ib.* xlvii

32 The pilgrims of the year waxed very loud
In multitudinous chatterings. *Ib.*

33 Their sense is with their senses all mixed in,
Destroyed by subtleties these women are! *Ib.* xlviii

34 More brain, O Lord, more brain! *Ib.*

35 Thus piteously Love closed what he begat:
The union of this ever diverse pair!
These two were rapid falcons in a snare,
Condemned to do the flitting of a bat. *Ib.* l.

36 Ah, what a dusty answer gets the soul
When hot for certainties in this our life! *Ib.*

37 God! of whom music
And song and blood are pure,
The day is never darkened
That had thee here obscure. *Phoebus with Admetus*

38 You with shelly horns, rams! and, promontory goats,
You whose browsing beards dip in coldest dew!
Bulls, that walk the pastures in kingly-flashing coats!
Laurel, ivy, vine, wreathed for feasts not few! *Ib.*

39 Narrows the world to my neighbour's gate.
Seed Time

40 Through the sermon's dull defile.
The Sage Enamoured, v

41 Into the breast that gives the rose,
Shall I with shuddering fall?
The Spirit of Earth in Autumn

42 Broad as ten thousand beeves
At pasture! *The Spirit of Shakespeare*, i

43 As the birds do, so do we,
Bill our mate, and choose our tree.
The Three Singers to Young Blood, i

44 Lowly, with a broken neck,
The crocus lays her cheek to mire.
The Thrush in February

45 Full lasting is the song, though he,
The singer, passes: lasting too,
For souls not lent in usury,
The rapture of the forward view. *Ib.*

46 We spend our lives in learning pilotage,
And grow good steersmen when the vessel's crank!
The Wisdom of Eld

47 Sweet as Eden is the air,
And Eden-sweet the ray. *Woodland Peace*

48 Enter these enchanted woods,
You who dare. *The Woods of Westermain*

1 Love meet they who do not shove
Cravings in the van of Love. *Woods of Westermain*

2 [*On Carlyle's style*]
A style resembling either early architecture or utter dilapidation, so loose and rough it seemed; a wind-in-the-orchard style, that tumbled down here and there an appreciable fruit with uncouth bluster; sentences without commencements running to abrupt endings and smoke, like waves against a sea-wall, learned dictionary words giving a hand to street-slang, and accents falling on them haphazard, like slant rays from driving clouds; all the pages in a breeze, the whole book producing a kind of electrical agitation in the mind and the joints.
Beauchamp's Career, ch. 2

3 Thoughts of heroes were as good as warming-pans.
Ib. ch. 4

4 'Wilt thou?' said the winged minute. *Ib.* ch. 22

5 They that make of his creed a strait jacket for humanity. *Ib.* ch. 29

6 He had by nature a tarnishing eye that cast discolouration. *Diana of the Crossways*, ch. 1

7 Men may have rounded Seraglio Point: they have not yet doubled Cape Turk. *Ib.*

8 Sentimental people, in her phrase, fiddle harmonics on the strings of sensualism. *Ib.*

9 Rose pink and dirty drab will alike have passed away.
Ib.

10 'Tis Ireland gives England her soldiers, her generals too. *Ib.* ch. 2

11 She did not seduce, she ravished. *Ib.* ch. 7

12 'Hog's my feed,' said Andrew Hedger . . . 'Ah could eat hog a solid hower!' *Ib.* ch. 8

13 She was a lady of incisive features bound in stale parchment. *Ib.* ch. 14

14 Prose can paint evening and moonlight, but poets are needed to sing the dawn. *Ib.* ch. 16

15 'But how divine is utterance!' she said. 'As we to the brutes, poets are to us.' *Ib.*

16 Brittle is foredoomed. *Ib.* ch. 28

17 Between the ascetic rocks and the sensual whirlpools.
Ib. ch. 37

18 He had his nest of wishes piping to him all the time.
Ib. ch. 42

19 There is nothing the body suffers the soul may not profit by. *Ib.* ch. 43

20 You see he has a leg. *The Egoist*, ch. 2

21 A Phoebus Apollo turned fasting friar. *Ib.*

22 A dainty rogue in porcelain. *Ib.* ch. 5

23 Cynicism is intellectual dandyism. *Ib.* ch. 7

24 To plod on and still keep the passion fresh.
Ib. ch. 12

25 In . . . the book of Egoism, it is written, Possession without obligation to the object possessed approaches felicity. *Ib.* ch. 14

26 An aged and a great wine. *Ib.* ch. 20

27 I have but a girl to give! *Ib.*

28 In the middle of the night it rang a little silver bell in my ear. *The Egoist*, ch. 25

29 Are you quite well, Laetitia? *Ib.* ch. 40

30 None of your dam punctilio.
One of Our Conquerors, ch. 1

31 I expect that Woman will be the last thing civilized by Man. *The Ordeal of Richard Feverel*, ch. 1

32 In action Wisdom goes by majorities. *Ib.*

33 Who rises from prayer a better man, his prayer is answered. *Ib.* ch. 12

34 A youth educated by a system. *Ib.* ch. 15

35 Away with Systems! Away with a corrupt world! Let us breathe the air of the Enchanted island.
Golden lie the meadows; golden run the streams; red gold is on the pine-stems. The sun is coming down to earth, and walks the fields and the waters.
The sun is coming down to earth, and the fields and the waters shout to him golden shouts. *Ib.* ch. 19

36 Kissing don't last: cookery do! *Ib.* ch. 28

37 Speech is the small change of silence. *Ib.* ch. 34

38 Italia, Italia shall be free. *Vittoria*, ch. 21

39 Much benevolence of the passive order may be traced to a disinclination to inflict pain upon oneself.
Ib. ch. 42

OWEN MEREDITH
[EDWARD ROBERT BULWER, EARL OF LYTTON]
1831–1891

40 There's nothing certain in man's life but this:
That he must lose it. *Clytemnestra*, pt. xx

41 We may live without poetry, music and art;
We may live without conscience, and live without heart;
We may live without friends; we may live without books;
But civilized man cannot live without cooks.
Lucile, pt. 1, c. 2. xix

42 He may live without books,—what is knowledge but grieving?
He may live without hope,—what is hope but deceiving?
He may live without love,—what is passion but pining?
But where is the man that can live without dining?
Ib. xxiv

43 Genius does what it must, and Talent does what it can.
Poems. Last Words of a Sensitive Second-Rate Poet

DIXON LANIER MERRITT
1879–

44 A wonderful bird is the pelican,
His bill will hold more than his belican.
He can take in his beak
Food enough for a week,
But I'm damned if I see how the helican.
The Pelican

JEAN MESSELIER
eighteenth century

1 Je voudrais, et ce sera le dernier et le plus ardent de mes souhaits, je voudrais que le dernier des rois fût étranglé avec les boyaux du dernier prêtre.

I should like to see, and this will be the last and the most ardent of my desires, I should like to see the last king strangled with the guts of the last priest. *In his Will, 1733, published by Voltaire*

PRINCE METTERNICH
1773–1859

2 Italien ist ein geographischer Begriff.

Italy is a geographical expression.
Letter, 19 Nov. 1849

ALICE MEYNELL
1847–1922

3 Flocks of the memories of the day draw near
The dovecote doors of sleep. *At Night*

4 With this ambiguous earth
His dealings have been told us. These abide:
The signal to a maid, the human birth,
The lesson, and the young Man crucified.
Christ in the Universe

5 I come from nothing; but from where
Come the undying thoughts I bear?
The Modern Poet, or A Song of Derivations

6 I must not think of thee; and, tired yet strong,
I shun the thought that lurks in all delight—
The thought of thee—and in the blue heaven's height,
And in the sweetest passage of a song.
Renouncement (ed. 1923)

7 With the first dream that comes with the first sleep
I run, I run, I am gathered to thy heart. *Ib.*

8 She walks—the lady of my delight—
A shepherdess of sheep. *The Shepherdess*

9 She holds her little thoughts in sight,
Though gay they run and leap.
She is so circumspect and right;
She has her soul to keep. *Ib.*

10 Sudden as sweet
Come the expected feet.
All joy is young, and new all art,
And He too, Whom we have by heart.
Unto us a Son is Given

HUGO MEYNELL
1727–1808

11 The chief advantage of London is, that a man is always so near his burrow.
Boswell's Johnson (ed. 1934), vol. iii, p. 379,
1 Apr. 1779

12 For anything I see, foreigners are fools.
Ib. vol. iv, p. 15, 1780

WILLIAM JULIUS MICKLE
1735–1788

13 The dews of summer night did fall,
The moon, sweet regent of the sky,
Silver'd the walls of Cumnor Hall,
And many an oak that grew thereby.
Cumnor Hall

THOMAS MIDDLETON
1570?–1627

14 I never heard
Of any true affection, but 'twas nipt
With care. *Blurt, Master-Constable*, III. i. 39

15 By many a happy accident.
No Wit, No Help, Like a Woman's, IV. i. 66

16 Though I be poor, I'm honest. *The Witch*, III. ii

17 There's no hate lost between us. *Ib.* IV. iii. 10

18 Black spirits and white, red spirits and gray,
Mingle, mingle, mingle, you that mingle may!
Ib. V. ii. 60

ALBERT MIDLANE
1825–1909

19 There's a Friend for little children
Above the bright blue sky,
A Friend Who never changes,
Whose love will never die.
Good News for the Little Ones

JOHN STUART MILL
1806–1873

20 Ask yourself whether you are happy, and you cease to be so. *Autobiography*, ch. 5

21 No great improvements in the lot of mankind are possible, until a great change takes place in the fundamental constitution of their modes of thought.
Ib. ch. 7

22 As often as a study is cultivated by narrow minds, they will draw from it narrow conclusions.
Auguste Comte and Positivism, 1865, p. 82

23 When society requires to be rebuilt, there is no use in attempting to rebuild it on the old plan.
Dissertations and Discussions, Essay on Coleridge, 1859, vol. i, p. 423

24 Unearned increment. *Ib.* vol. iv, p. 299

25 The sole end for which mankind are warranted, individually or collectively, in interfering with the liberty of action of any of their number, is self-protection. *Liberty*, introduction

26 If all mankind minus one, were of one opinion, and only one person were of the contrary opinion, mankind would be no more justified in silencing that one person, than he, if he had the power, would be justified in silencing mankind. *Ib.* ch. 2

27 We can never be sure that the opinion we are endeavouring to stifle is a false opinion; and if we were sure, stifling it would be an evil still. *Ib.*

28 A party of order or stability, and a party of progress or reform, are both necessary elements of a healthy state of political life. *Ib.*

29 The liberty of the individual must be thus far limited; he must not make himself a nuisance to other people. *Ib.* ch. 3

30 All good things which exist are the fruits of originality. *Ib.*

31 Liberty consists in doing what one desires. *Ib.* ch. 5

32 The worth of a State, in the long run, is the worth of the individuals composing it. *Ib.*

1 A State which dwarfs its men, in order that they may be more docile instruments in its hands even for beneficial purposes—will find that with small men no great thing can really be accomplished.
Liberty, ch. 5

2 When the land is cultivated entirely by the spade and no horses are kept, a cow is kept for every three acres of land.
Political Economy. A Treatise on Flemish Husbandry

3 The great majority of those who speak of perfectibility as a dream, do so because they feel that it is one which would afford them no pleasure if it were realized.
Speech on Perfectibility, 1828

4 If we may be excused the antithesis, we should say that eloquence is *heard*, poetry is *overheard*.
Thoughts on Poetry and its varieties (1859)

EDNA ST. VINCENT MILLAY
1892–

5 Euclid alone has looked on Beauty bare.
The Harp-Weaver, p. IV, sonnet xxii

6 My candle burns at both ends;
It will not last the night;
But oh, my foes, and oh, my friends—
It gives a lovely light.
Poems (1923)

ALICE DUER MILLER
1874–1942

7 I am American bred,
I have seen much to hate here—much to forgive,
But in a world where England is finished and dead,
I do not wish to live.
The White Cliffs (1940)

MRS. EMILY MILLER
1833–1913

8 I love to hear the story
Which angel voices tell.
The Little Corporal. I Love to Hear

WILLIAM MILLER
1810–1872

9 Wee Willie Winkie
Rins through the town,
Upstairs and downstairs
In his nicht-gown,
Tirling at the window,
Crying at the lock,
'Are the weans in their bed,
For it's now ten o'clock?'
Willie Winkie

A. J. MILLS

10 Just like the ivy I'll cling to you.
Title of Song

REV. HENRY HART MILMAN
1791–1868

11 When our heads are bowed with woe,
When our bitter tears o'erflow.
Hymns. When Our Heads

12 Ride on! ride on in majesty!
In lowly pomp ride on to die.
Ib. Ride On!

ALAN ALEXANDER MILNE
1882–

13 There was once an old sailor my grandfather knew,
Who had so many things which he wanted to do
That, whenever he thought it was time to begin,
He couldn't, because of the state he was in.
Now We are Six, The Old Sailor

14 They're changing guard at Buckingham Palace—
Christopher Robin went down with Alice.
When We Were Very Young. Buckingham Palace

15 James James
Morrison Morrison
Weatherby George Dupree
Took great
Care of his Mother
Though he was only three.
Ib. Disobedience

16 You must never go down to the end of the town if you don't go down with me.
Ib.

17 The King asked
The Queen, and
The Queen asked
The Dairymaid:
'Could we have some butter for
The Royal slice of bread?'
Ib. The King's Breakfast

18 I do like a little bit of butter to my bread!
Ib.

19 Little Boy kneels at the foot of the bed,
Droops on the little hands, little gold head;
Hush! Hush! Whisper who dares!
Christopher Robin is saying his prayers.
Ib. Vespers

20 Isn't it funny
How a bear likes honey?
Buzz! Buzz! Buzz!
I wonder why he does?
Winnie-the-Pooh, ch. 1

21 I am a Bear of Very Little Brain, and long words Bother me.
Ib. ch. 4

22 Time for a little something.
Ib. ch. 6

23 'Pathetic', he said. 'That's what it is. Pathetic'.
Ib.

24 On Monday, when the sun is hot,
I wonder to myself a lot:
'Now is it true, or is it not,
'That what is which and which is what?'
Ib. ch. 7

ALFRED, LORD MILNER
1854–1925

25 [*The Peers and the Budget*] If we believe a thing to be bad, and if we have a right to prevent it, it is our duty to try to prevent it and to damn the consequences.
Speech at Glasgow, 26 Nov. 1909

JOHN MILTON
1608–1674

26 Such sweet compulsion doth in music lie.
Arcades, l. 68

27 Before the starry threshold of Jove's Court
My mansion is.
Comus, l. 1

28 Above the smoke and stir of this dim spot,
Which men call Earth.
Ib. l. 5

29 Yet some there be that by due steps aspire
To lay their just hands on that golden key
That opes the palace of Eternity.
Ib. l. 12

1 Rich and various gems inlay
The unadorned bosom of the deep. *Comus*, l. 22

2 An old, and haughty nation proud in arms. *Ib.* l. 33

3 What never yet was heard in tale or song
From old or modern bard in hall or bower. *Ib.* l. 44

4 And the gilded car of day,
His glowing axle doth allay
In the steep Atlantic stream. *Ib.* l. 95

5 What hath night to do with sleep? *Ib.* l. 122

6 Ere the blabbing eastern scout,
The nice Morn on th' Indian steep
From her cabin'd loop-hole peep. *Ib.* l. 138

7 Come, knit hands, and beat the ground,
In a light fantastic round. *Ib.* l. 143

8   When the grey-hooded Even
Like a sad votarist in palmer's weed,
Rose from the hindmost wheels of Phœbus' wain.
Ib. l. 188

9   O thievish Night,
Why shouldst thou, but for some felonious end,
In thy dark lantern thus close up the stars,
That nature hung in heaven, and filled their lamps
With everlasting oil, to give due light
To the misled and lonely traveller? *Ib.* l. 195

10 Calling shapes and beckoning shadows dire,
And airy tongues that syllable men's names
On sands, and shores, and desert wildernesses.
These thoughts may startle well, but not astound
The virtuous mind, that ever walks attended
By a strong siding champion, Conscience. *Ib.* l. 207

11 O welcome pure-ey'd Faith, white-handed Hope,
Thou hovering angel girt with golden wings.
Ib. l. 213

12 Was I deceived, or did a sable cloud
Turn forth her silver lining on the night? *Ib.* l. 221

13 Sweet Echo, sweetest nymph, that liv'st unseen
Within thy airy shell
By slow Meander's margent green,
And in the violet-embroidered vale. *Ib.* l. 230

14 Can any mortal mixture of earth's mould
Breathe such divine enchanting ravishment?
Ib. l. 244

15 How sweetly did they float upon the wings
Of silence, through the empty-vaulted night,
At every fall smoothing the raven down
Of darkness till it smiled! *Ib.* l. 249

16 Such sober certainty of waking bliss
I never heard till now. *Ib.* l. 263

17   Shepherd, I take thy word,
And trust thy honest offer'd courtesy,
Which oft is sooner found in lowly sheds
With smoky rafters, than in tap'stry halls
And courts of princes. *Ib.* l. 321

18 With thy long levell'd rule of streaming light.
Ib. l. 340

19 What need a man forestall his date of grief,
And run to meet what he would most avoid?
Ib. l. 362

20 Virtue could see to do what virtue would
By her own radiant light, though sun and moon
Were in the flat sea sunk. And Wisdom's self
Oft seeks to sweet retired solitude,

Where with her best nurse Contemplation
She plumes her feathers, and lets grow her wings
That in the various bustle of resort
Were all to-ruffled, and sometimes impair'd.
He that has light within his own clear breast
May sit i' th' centre and enjoy bright day;
But he that hides a dark soul and foul thoughts
Benighted walks under the midday sun.
Comus, l. 373

21   The unsunned heaps
Of miser's treasure. *Ib.* l. 398

22 'Tis Chastity, my brother, Chastity:
She that has that, is clad in complete steel. *Ib.* l. 420

23 So dear to Heaven is saintly chastity
That when a soul is found sincerely so
A thousand liveried angels lackey her,
Driving far off each thing of sin and guilt. *Ib.* l. 453

24 How charming is divine philosophy!
Not harsh, and crabbed as dull fools suppose,
But musical as is Apollo's lute,
And a perpetual feast of nectared sweets,
Where no crude surfeit reigns. *Ib.* l. 476

25 What the sage poets taught by th' heavenly Muse,
Storied of old in high immortal verse
Of dire chimeras and enchanted isles
And rifted rocks whose entrance leads to Hell,—
For such there be, but unbelief is blind. *Ib.* l. 515

26 And fill'd the air with barbarous dissonance.
Ib. l. 550

27 A steam of rich distill'd perfumes. *Ib.* l. 556

28   I was all ear,
And took in strains that might create a soul
Under the ribs of Death. *Ib.* l. 560

29   That power
Which erring men call Chance. *Ib.* l. 587

30 Virtue may be assailed, but never hurt,
Surprised by unjust force, but not enthralled.
Ib. l. 589

31   If this fail,
The pillared firmament is rottenness,
And earth's base built on stubble. *Ib.* l. 597

32   The dull swain
Treads on it daily with his clouted shoon. *Ib.* l. 634

33 Hast thou betrayed my credulous innocence
With vizor'd falsehood, and base forgery? *Ib.* l. 697

34   None
But such as are good men can give good things,
And that which is not good, is not delicious
To a well-govern'd and wise appetite. *Ib.* l. 702

35 Budge doctors of the Stoic fur. *Ib.* l. 707

36 Praising the lean and sallow abstinence. *Ib.* l. 709

37 Beauty is Nature's coin, must not be hoarded,
But must be current, and the good thereof
Consists in mutual and partaken bliss. *Ib.* l. 739

38 Beauty is Nature's brag, and must be shown
In courts, at feasts, and high solemnities,
Where most may wonder at the workmanship;
It is for homely features to keep home,
They had their name thence; coarse complexions
And cheeks of sorry grain will serve to ply
The sampler, and to tease the huswife's wool.
What need a vermeil-tinctur'd lip for that,
Love-darting eyes, or tresses like the morn?
Ib. l. 745

1 Obtruding false rules pranked in reason's garb.
Comus, l. 759

2   Through the porch and inlet of each sense
Dropt in ambrosial oils till she reviv'd.   *Ib.* l. 839

3 Sabrina fair,
  Listen where thou art sitting
Under the glassy, cool, translucent wave,
  In twisted braids of lilies knitting
The loose train of thy amber-dropping hair.
Ib. l. 859

4 Thus I set my printless feet
O'er the cowslip's velvet head,
That bends not as I tread.   *Ib.* l. 897

5 Love virtue, she alone is free,
She can teach ye how to climb
Higher than the sphery chime;
Or, if virtue feeble were,
Heaven itself would stoop to her.   *Ib.* l. 1019

6 O fairest flower, no sooner blown but blasted,
Soft silken primrose fading timelessly.
On the Death of a Fair Infant, Dying of a Cough,
l. 1

7 Hence, vain deluding joys,
The brood of Folly without father bred.
Il Penseroso, l. 1

8 Hail divinest Melancholy.   *Ib.* l. 12

9 And looks commercing with the skies,
Thy rapt soul sitting in thine eyes:
There held in holy passion still,
Forget thyself to marble.   *Ib.* l. 39

10 And join with thee calm Peace, and Quiet,
Spare Fast, that oft with gods doth diet.   *Ib.* l. 45

11 And add to these retired Leisure,
That in trim gardens takes his pleasure.   *Ib.* l. 49

12 Him that yon soars on golden wing,
Guiding the fiery-wheeled throne,
The Cherub Contemplation.   *Ib.* l. 52

13 Sweet bird, that shunn'st the noise of folly,
Most musical, most melancholy!   *Ib.* l. 61

14   I walk unseen
On the dry smooth-shaven green,
To behold the wandering moon,
Riding near her highest noon,
Like one that had been led astray
Through the heav'n's wide pathless way;
And oft, as if her head she bow'd,
Stooping through a fleecy cloud.   *Ib.* l. 65

15 Oft, on a plat of rising ground,
I hear the far-off curfew sound
Over some wide-watered shore,
Swinging slow with sullen roar.   *Ib.* l. 73

16 Where glowing embers through the room
Teach light to counterfeit a gloom,
Far from all resort of mirth,
Save the cricket on the hearth.   *Ib.* l. 79

17 Where I may oft outwatch the Bear,
With thrice great Hermes, or unsphere
The spirit of Plato.   *Ib.* l. 87

18 Sometime let gorgeous Tragedy
In sceptred pall come sweeping by,
Presenting Thebes, or Pelops' line,
Or the tale of Troy divine.   *Ib.* l. 97

19 Or bid the soul of Orpheus sing
Such notes as, warbled to the string,
Drew iron tears down Pluto's cheek.
Il Penseroso, l. 105

20 Or call up him that left half told
The story of Cambuscan bold.   *Ib.* l. 109

21 Where more is meant than meets the ear.   *Ib.* l. 120

22 While the bee with honied thigh,
That at her flowery work doth sing,
And the waters murmuring
With such consort as they keep,
Entice the dewy-feather'd sleep.   *Ib.* l. 142

23 But let my due feet never fail
To walk the studious cloister's pale.   *Ib.* l. 155

24 With antique pillars massy proof,
And storied windows richly dight,
Casting a dim religious light.
There let the pealing organ blow,
To the full-voiced quire below,
In service high, and anthems clear
As may, with sweetness, through mine ear,
Dissolve me into ecstasies,
And bring all Heaven before mine eyes.   *Ib.* l. 158

25 Till old experience do attain
To something like prophetic strain.   *Ib.* l. 173

26 Hence, loathed Melancholy,
  Of Cerberus, and blackest Midnight born,
In Stygian cave forlorn,
  'Mongst horrid shapes, and shrieks, and sights un-
    holy.   *L'Allegro*, l. 1

27 So buxom, blithe, and debonair.   *Ib.* l. 24

28 Haste thee Nymph, and bring with thee
Jest and youthful jollity,
Quips and cranks, and wanton wiles,
Nods, and becks, and wreathed smiles.   *Ib.* l. 25

29 Sport that wrinkled Care derides,
And Laughter holding both his sides.
Come, and trip it as ye go
On the light fantastic toe.   *Ib.* l. 31

30 The mountain nymph, sweet Liberty.   *Ib.* l. 36

31 Mirth, admit me of thy crew,
To live with her, and live with thee,
In unreproved pleasures free.
To hear the lark begin his flight,
And singing startle the dull night,
From his watch-tower in the skies,
Till the dappled dawn doth rise;
Then to come in spite of sorrow,
And at my window bid good-morrow.   *Ib.* l. 38

32 While the cock with lively din
Scatters the rear of darkness thin,
And to the stack, or the barn door,
Stoutly struts his dames before.   *Ib.* l. 49

33 Right against the eastern gate,
Where the great Sun begins his state.   *Ib.* l. 59

34   The ploughman near at hand,
Whistles o'er the furrowed land,
And the milkmaid singeth blithe,
And the mower whets his scythe,
And every shepherd tells his tale
Under the hawthorn in the dale.   *Ib.* l. 63

1 Meadows trim with daisies pied,
Shallow brooks and rivers wide.
Towers, and battlements it sees
Bosom'd high in tufted trees,
Where perhaps some beauty lies,
The cynosure of neighbouring eyes. *L'Allegro*, l. 75

2 Of herbs, and other country messes,
Which the neat-handed Phyllis dresses. *Ib.* l. 85

3 To many a youth, and many a maid,
Dancing in the chequered shade.
And young and old come forth to play
On a sunshine holiday. *Ib.* l. 95

4 Then to the spicy nut-brown ale. *Ib.* l. 100

5 Towered cities please us then,
And the busy hum of men. *Ib.* l. 117

6 Store of ladies, whose bright eyes
Rain influence. *Ib.* l. 121

7 And pomp, and feast, and revelry,
With mask, and antique pageantry,
Such sights as youthful poets dream,
On summer eves by haunted stream.
Then to the well-trod stage anon,
If Jonson's learnèd sock be on,
Or sweetest Shakespeare, Fancy's child,
Warble his native wood-notes wild,
And ever against eating cares,
Lap me in soft Lydian airs,
Married to immortal verse
Such as the meeting soul may pierce
In notes, with many a winding bout
Of linked sweetness long drawn out. *Ib.* l. 127

8 The melting voice through mazes running;
Untwisting all the chains that tie
The hidden soul of harmony. *Ib.* l. 142

9 Such strains as would have won the ear
Of Pluto, to have quite set free
His half regain'd Eurydice. *Ib.* l. 148

10 Yet once more, O ye laurels, and once more
Ye myrtles brown, with ivy never sere,
I come to pluck your berries harsh and crude,
And with forc'd fingers rude,
Shatter your leaves before the mellowing year.
Bitter constraint and sad occasion dear
Compels me to disturb your season due,
For Lycidas is dead, dead ere his prime,
Young Lycidas and hath not left his peer.
Who would not sing for Lycidas? he knew
Himself to sing and build the lofty rhyme.
He must not float upon his watery bier
Unwept, and welter to the parching wind
Without the meed of some melodious tear.
Lycidas, l. 1

11 Hence with denial vain, and coy excuse,
So may some gentle Muse
With lucky words favour my destin'd urn,
And as he passes turn,
And bid fair peace be to my sable shroud!
For we were nursed upon the self-same hill.
Ib. l. 18

12 Under the opening eyelids of the morn. *Ib.* l. 26

13 But, O the heavy change, now thou art gone,
Now thou art gone, and never must return! *Ib.* l. 37

14 The gadding vine. *Ib.* l. 40

15 As killing as the canker to the rose. *Lycidas*, l. 45

16 Flowers that their gay wardrobe wear. *Ib.* l. 47

17 Where were ye, Nymphs, when the remorseless deep
Closed o'er the head of your loved Lycidas?
Ib. l. 50

18 Whom universal Nature did lament. *Ib.* l. 60

19 Down the swift Hebrus to the Lesbian shore.
Ib. l. 63

20 Alas! what boots it with uncessant care
To tend the homely, slighted, shepherd's trade,
And strictly meditate the thankless Muse?
Were it not better done, as others use,
To sport with Amaryllis in the shade,
Or with the tangles of Neæra's hair.
Fame is the spur that the clear spirit doth raise
(That last infirmity of noble mind)
To scorn delights, and live laborious days;
But the fair guerdon when we hope to find,
And think to burst out into sudden blaze,
Comes the blind Fury with th' abhorred shears
And slits the thin-spun life. *Ib.* l. 64

21 Touch'd my trembling ears. *Ib.* l. 77

22 Fame is no plant that grows on mortal soil. *Ib.* l. 78

23 As he pronounces lastly on each deed,
Of so much fame in Heaven expect thy meed.
Ib. l. 83

24 That strain I heard was of a higher mood. *Ib.* l. 87

25 It was that fatal and perfidious bark
Built in th' eclipse, and rigged with curses dark,
That sunk so low that sacred head of thine.
Ib. l. 100

26 Last came, and last did go,
The Pilot of the Galilean lake,
Two massy keys he bore of metals twain,
The golden opes, the iron shuts amain. *Ib.* l. 108

27   Such as for their bellies' sake,
Creep and intrude, and climb into the fold.
Of other care they little reckoning make,
Than how to scramble at the shearers' feast,
And shove away the worthy bidden guest. *Ib.* l. 114

28 Blind mouths! that scarce themselves know how to
hold
A sheep-hook, or have learn'd aught else the least
That to the faithful herdman's art belongs!
Ib. l. 119

29   Their lean and flashy songs
Grate on their scrannel pipes of wretched straw,
The hungry sheep look up, and are not fed,
But, swoln with wind and the rank mist they draw,
Rot inwardly and foul contagion spread;
Besides what the grim wolf with privy paw
Daily devours apace, and nothing said.
But that two-handed engine at the door
Stands ready to smite once, and smite no more.
Ib. l. 123

30   Return, Alpheus, the dread voice is past
That shrunk thy streams; return Sicilian Muse.
Ib. l. 132

31 Throw hither all your quaint enamell'd eyes
That on the green turf suck the honied showers,
And purple all the ground with vernal flowers.
Bring the rathe primrose that forsaken dies,

The tufted crow-toe, and pale jessamine,
The white pink, and the pansy freakt with jet,
The glowing violet,
The musk-rose, and the well-attir'd woodbine,
With cowslips wan that hang the pensive head,
And every flower that sad embroidery wears.
Bid amaranthus all his beauty shed,
And daffadillies fill their cups with tears,
To strew the laureate hearse where Lycid lies.
Lycidas, l. 139

1 So to interpose a little ease,
Let our frail thoughts dally with false surmise.
Ib. l. 152

2 Whether beyond the stormy Hebrides,
Where thou perhaps under the whelming tide
Visit'st the bottom of the monstrous world;
Or whether thou, to our moist vows denied,
Sleepst by the fable of Bellerus old,
Where the great Vision of the guarded mount
Looks toward Namancos and Bayona's hold.
Look homeward, Angel, now, and melt with ruth.
Ib. l. 156

3 For Lycidas your sorrow is not dead,
Sunk though he be beneath the watery floor;
So sinks the day-star in the ocean bed,
And yet anon repairs his drooping head,
And tricks his beams, and with new spangled ore,
Flames in the forehead of the morning sky:
So Lycidas sunk low, but mounted high,
Through the dear might of Him that walked the
waves. *Ib.* l. 166

4 In solemn troops, and sweet societies. *Ib.* l. 179

5 Thus sang the uncouth swain. *Ib.* l. 186

6 He touch'd the tender stops of various quills,
With eager thought warbling his Doric lay.
Ib. l. 188

7 At last he rose, and twitch'd his mantle blue;
To-morrow to fresh woods, and pastures new.
Ib. l. 192

8 The bright morning star, day's harbinger.
On May Morning

9 This is the month, and this the happy morn,
Wherein the Son of Heaven's eternal King,
Of wedded maid, and virgin mother born,
Our great redemption from above did bring;
For so the holy sages once did sing,
That He our deadly forfeit should release,
And with His Father work us a perpetual peace.
Hymn. On the Morning of Christ's Nativity, l. 1

10 The star-led wizards haste with odours sweet!
Ib. l. 23

11 It was the winter wild
While the Heav'n-born child
All meanly wrapt in the rude manger lies,
Nature in awe to him
Had doff't her gawdy trim
With her great Master so to sympathize. *Ib.* l. 29

12 Nor war, nor battle's sound
Was heard the world around,
The idle spear and shield were high uphung.
Ib. l. 53

13 Birds of calm sit brooding on the charmèd wave.
Ib. l. 68

14 The stars with deep amaze
Stand fixt in stedfast gaze
Bending one way their precious influence
And will not take their flight
For all the morning light,
Or Lucifer that often warned them thence,
But in their glimmering orbs did glow
Until their Lord himself bespake and bid them go.
Hymn. On the Morning of Christ's Nativity, l. 69

15 Perhaps their loves, or else their sheep,
Was all that did their silly thoughts so busy keep.
Ib. l. 91

16 The helmed Cherubim
And sworded Seraphim,
Are seen in glittering ranks with wings display'd.
Ib. l. 112

17 Ring out ye crystal spheres,
Once bless our human ears
(If ye have power to touch our senses so)
And let your silver chime
Move in melodious time;
And let the base of heav'ns deep organ blow,
And with your ninefold harmony
Make up full consort to th' angelic symphony.
Ib. l. 125

18 Time will run back, and fetch the age of gold.
Ib. l. 135

19 And speckled Vanity
Will sicken soon and die. *Ib.* l. 136

20 Swinges the scaly horror of his folded tail. *Ib.* l. 172

21 The oracles are dumb,
No voice or hideous hum
Runs through the arched roof in words deceiving.
Apollo from his shrine
Can no more divine,
With hollow shriek the steep of Delphos leaving.
No nightly trance or breathèd spell,
Inspires the pale-eyed priest from the prophetic cell.
Ib. l. 173

22 From haunted spring and dale
Edg'd with poplar pale
The parting genius is with sighing sent. *Ib.* l. 184

23 Peor and Baalim
Forsake their temples dim. *Ib.* l. 197

24 So when the sun in bed,
Curtain'd with cloudy red,
Pillows his chin upon an orient wave. *Ib.* l. 229

25 But see the Virgin blest,
Hath laid her Babe to rest,
Time is our tedious song should here have ending,
Heav'n's youngest teemed star,
Hath fixt her polisht car,
Her sleeping lord with handmaid lamp attending:
And all about the courtly stable,
Bright-harnest Angels sit in order serviceable.
Ib. l. 237

26 Rhyme being no necessary adjunct or true ornament
of poem or good verse, in longer works especially,
but the invention of a barbarous age, to set off
wretched matter and lame metre.
The Verse. Preface to Paradise Lost, 1668 ed.

27 The troublesome and modern bondage of Rhyming.
Ib.

1 Of Man's first disobedience, and the fruit
Of that forbidden tree, whose mortal taste
Brought death into the world, and all our woe,
With loss of Eden. *Paradise Lost*, bk. i, l. 1

2 Or if Sion hill
Delight thee more, and Siloa's brook that flow'd
Fast by the oracle of God. *Ib.* l. 10

3 Things unattempted yet in prose or rhyme. *Ib.* l. 16

4 What in me is dark
Illumine, what is low raise and support;
That to the highth of this great argument
I may assert eternal Providence,
And justify the ways of God to Men. *Ib.* l. 22

5 For one restraint, lords of the world besides. *Ib.* l. 32

6 The infernal serpent; he it was, whose guile,
Stirr'd up with envy and revenge, deceived
The mother of mankind. *Ib.* l. 34

7 Him the Almighty Power
Hurled headlong flaming from th' ethereal sky
With hideous ruin and combustion down
To bottomless perdition, there to dwell
In adamantine chains and penal fire
Who durst defy th' Omnipotent to arms. *Ib.* l. 44

8 As far as angels' ken. *Ib.* l. 59

9 A dungeon horrible, on all sides round
As one great furnace flam'd; yet from those flames
No light, but rather darkness visible
Serv'd only to discover sights of woe,
Regions of sorrow, doleful shades, where peace
And rest can never dwell, hope never comes
That comes to all. *Ib.* l. 60

10 As far removed from God and light of heav'n
As from the centre thrice to th' utmost pole.
Ib. l. 73

11 But O how fall'n! how changed
From him who, in the happy realms of light,
Clothed with transcendent brightness didst outshine
Myriads though bright. *Ib.* l. 84

12 United thoughts and counsels, equal hope,
And hazard in the glorious enterprise. *Ib.* l. 88

13 Yet not for those
Nor what the potent victor in his rage
Can else inflict do I repent or change,
Though changed in outward lustre; that fixed mind
And high disdain, from sense of injured merit.
Ib. l. 94

14 What though the field be lost?
All is not lost; th' unconquerable will,
And study of revenge, immortal hate,
And courage never to submit or yield:
And what is else not to be overcome? *Ib.* l. 105

15 Vaunting aloud, but racked with deep despair.
Ib. l. 126

16 Fall'n Cherub, to be weak is miserable
Doing or suffering; but of this be sure,
To do ought good never will be our task,
But ever to do ill our sole delight. *Ib.* l. 157

17 And out of good still to find means of evil. *Ib.* l. 165

18 The seat of desolation, void of light. *Ib.* l. 181

19 What reinforcement we may gain from hope,
If not what resolution from despair. *Ib.* l. 190

20 The will
And high permission of all-ruling Heaven
Left him at large to his own dark designs,
That with reiterated crimes he might
Heap on himself damnation.
Paradise Lost, bk. i, l. 211

21 Is this the region, this the soil, the clime,
Said then the lost Archangel, this the seat
That we must change for Heav'n, this mournful
gloom
For that celestial light? *Ib.* l. 242

22 Farthest from him is best
Whom reason hath equalled, force hath made
supreme
Above his equals. Farewell happy fields
Where joy for ever dwells: Hail horrors, hail
Infernal world, and thou profoundest Hell
Receive thy new possessor: one who brings
A mind not to be changed by place or time.
The mind is its own place, and in it self
Can make a Heav'n of Hell, a Hell of Heav'n.
Ib. l. 247

23 Here we may reign secure, and in my choice
To reign is worth ambition though in hell:
Better to reign in hell, than serve in heav'n.
Ib. l. 261

24 His spear, to equal which the tallest pine
Hewn on Norwegian hills, to be the mast
Of some great ammiral, were but a wand,
He walk'd with to support uneasy steps
Over the burning marle. *Ib.* l. 292

25 Thick as autumnal leaves that strow the brooks
In Vallombrosa, where th' Etrurian shades
High over-arch'd imbower. *Ib.* l. 302

26 Busiris and his Memphian chivalry. *Ib.* l. 307

27 'Awake, arise, or be for ever fall'n!'
They heard, and were abashed, and up they sprung
Upon the wing, as when men wont to watch
On duty, sleeping found by whom they dread,
Rouse and bestir themselves ere well awake.
Ib. l. 330

28 First Moloch, horrid king, besmear'd with blood
Of human sacrifice, and parents' tears. *Ib.* l. 392

29 For spirits when they please
Can either sex assume, or both; so soft
And uncompounded is their essence pure. *Ib.* l. 423

30 Execute their aery purposes. *Ib.* l. 430

31 Astarte, Queen of Heav'n, with crescent horns.
Ib. l. 439

32 Thammuz came next behind,
Whose annual wound in Lebanon allur'd
The Syrian damsels to lament his fate
In amorous ditties all a summer's day,
While smooth Adonis from his native rock
Ran purple to the sea. *Ib.* l. 446

33 A leper once he lost and gain'd a king. *Ib.* l. 471

34 Jehovah, who in one night when he passed
From Egypt marching. *Ib.* l. 487

35 And when night
Darkens the streets, then wander forth the sons
Of Belial, flown with insolence and wine. *Ib.* l. 500

36 Shone like a meteor streaming to the wind. *Ib.* l. 537

1 Sonorous metal blowing martial sounds:
At which the universal host upsent
A shout that tore hell's concave, and beyond
Frighted the reign of Chaos and old Night.
Paradise Lost, bk. i, l. 540

2   Anon they move
In perfect phalanx to the Dorian mood
Of flutes and soft recorders.   *Ib.* l. 549

3   That small infantry
Warred on by cranes.   *Ib.* l. 575

4   What resounds
In fable or romance of Uther's son
Begirt with British and Armoric knights;
And all who since, baptized or infidel
Jousted in Aspramont or Montalban,
Damasco, or Marocco, or Trebisond,
Or whom Biserta sent from Afric shore
When Charlemain with all his peerage fell
By Fontarabbia.   *Ib.* l. 579

5   He above the rest
In shape and gesture proudly eminent
Stood like a tower; his form had yet not lost
All her original brightness, nor appeared
Less than archangel ruined, and th' excess
Of glory obscur'd.   *Ib.* l. 589

6   The sun . . .
In dim eclipse disastrous twilight sheds
On half the nations, and with fear of change
Perplexes monarchs.   *Ib.* l. 594

7   His face
Deep scars of thunder had intrenched, and care
Sat on his faded cheek, but under brows
Of dauntless courage, and considerate pride
Waiting revenge.   *Ib.* l. 600

8   Who overcomes
By force, hath overcome but half his foe. *Ib.* l. 648

9 Mammon led them on,
Mammon, the least erected Spirit that fell
From heav'n, for ev'n in heav'n his looks and thoughts
Were always downward bent, admiring more
The riches of heaven's pavement, trodden gold,
Than aught divine or holy else enjoy'd
In vision beatific.   *Ib.* l. 678

10   Let none admire
That riches grow in hell; that soil may best
Deserve the precious bane.   *Ib.* l. 690

11 Anon out of the earth a fabric huge
Rose like an exhalation.   *Ib.* l. 710

12   From morn
To noon he fell, from noon to dewy eve,
A summer's day; and with the setting sun
Dropt from the zenith like a falling star. *Ib.* l. 742

13   Fairy elves,
Whose midnight revels, by a forest side
Or fountain some belated peasant sees,
Or dreams he sees, while overhead the moon
Sits arbitress.   *Ib.* l. 781

14 High on a throne of royal state, which far
Outshone the wealth of Ormus and of Ind,
Or where the gorgeous East with richest hand
Showers on her kings barbaric pearl and gold,
Satan exalted sat, by merit raised
To that bad eminence; and from despair
Thus high uplifted beyond hope. *Ib.* bk. ii, l. 1

15   The strongest and the fiercest Spirit
That fought in Heav'n; now fiercer by despair.
His trust was with th' Eternal to be deemed
Equal in strength, and rather than be less
Cared not to be at all.   *Paradise Lost*, bk. ii, l. 44

16 My sentence is for open war: of wiles
More unexpert, I boast not.   *Ib.* l. 51

17   When the scourge
Inexorably, and the torturing hour
Calls us to penance.   *Ib.* l. 90

18 Belial, in act more graceful and humane;
A fairer person lost not Heav'n; he seemed
For dignity compos'd and high exploit:
But all was false and hollow; though his tongue
Dropt manna, and could make the worse appear
The better reason.   *Ib.* l. 109

19   For who would lose,
Though full of pain, this intellectual being,
Those thoughts that wander through eternity,
To perish rather, swallowed up and lost
In the wide womb of uncreated night,
Devoid of sense and motion?   *Ib.* l. 146

20 His red right hand.   *Ib.* l. 174

21 Unrespited, unpitied, unreprieved,
Ages of hopeless end.   *Ib.* l. 185

22 Thus Belial with words clothed in reason's garb
Counselled ignoble ease, and peaceful sloth,
Not peace.   *Ib.* l. 226

23 Our torments also may in length of time
Become our elements.   *Ib.* l. 274

24   With grave
Aspect he rose, and in his rising seem'd
A pillar of state; deep on his front engraven
Deliberation sat and public care;
And princely counsel in his face yet shone,
Majestic though in ruin.   *Ib.* l. 300

25   To sit in darkness here
Hatching vain empires.   *Ib.* l. 377

26 Who shall tempt with wand'ring feet
The dark unbottom'd infinite abyss
And through the palpable obscure find out
His uncouth way.   *Ib.* l. 404

27   Long is the way
And hard, that out of hell leads up to light. *Ib.* l. 432

28 O shame to men! devil with devil damn'd
Firm concord holds, men only disagree
Of creatures rational.   *Ib.* l. 496

29   In discourse more sweet
(For eloquence the soul, song charms the sense,)
Others apart sat on a hill retir'd,
In thoughts more elevate, and reason'd high
Of providence, foreknowledge, will, and fate,
Fix'd fate, free will, foreknowledge absolute,
And found no end, in wand'ring mazes lost.
     Ib. l. 555

30 Vain wisdom all, and false philosophy. *Ib.* l. 565

31 A gulf profound as that Serbonian bog
Betwixt Damiata and Mount Casius old,
Where armies whole have sunk: the parching air
Burns frore, and cold performs th' effect of fire.
     Ib. l. 592

1   The bitter change
Of fierce extremes, extremes by change more fierce.
        Paradise Lost, bk. ii, l. 598

2 O'er many a frozen, many a fiery Alp,
Rocks, caves, lakes, fens, bogs, dens, and shades of
death.   *Ib.* l. 620

3   Worse
Than fables yet have feigned, or fear conceived,
Gorgons and Hydras, and Chimæras dire. *Ib.* l. 626

4   The other shape,
If shape it might be call'd that shape had none
Distinguishable in member, joint, or limb,
Or substance might be call'd that shadow seem'd,
For each seem'd either; black it stood as night,
Fierce as ten furies, terrible as hell,
And shook a dreadful dart; what seem'd his head
The likeness of a kingly crown had on.   *Ib.* l. 666

5 Whence and what art thou, execrable shape?
        Ib. l. 681

6 Incens'd with indignation Satan stood
Unterrifi'd, and like a comet burn'd
That fires the length of Ophiucus huge
In th' arctic sky, and from his horrid hair
Shakes pestilence and war.   *Ib.* l. 707

7   Their fatal hands
No second stroke intend.   *Ib.* l. 712

8   I fled, and cry'd out, *Death*;
Hell trembled at the hideous name, and sigh'd
From all her caves, and back resounded, *Death.*
        Ib. l. 787

9   On a sudden open fly
With impetuous recoil and jarring sound
Th' infernal doors, and on their hinges grate
Harsh thunder.   *Ib.* l. 879

10   A dark
Illimitable ocean without bound,
Without dimension, where length, breadth, and
highth,
And time and place are lost.   *Ib.* l. 891

11   Chaos umpire sits,
And by decision more embroils the fray
By which he reigns: next him high arbiter
Chance governs all.   *Ib.* l. 907

12   This wild abyss,
The womb of nature and perhaps her grave.
        Ib. l. 910

13   To compare
Great things with small.   *Ib.* l. 921

14   So eagerly the fiend
O'er bog or steep, through strait, rough, dense, or
rare.
With head, hands, wings, or feet pursues his way,
And swims or sinks, or wades, or creeps, or flies.
        Ib. l. 947

15 Sable-vested Night, eldest of things. *Ib.* l. 962

16 With ruin upon ruin, rout on rout,
Confusion worse confounded.   *Ib.* l. 995

17 So he with difficulty and labour hard
Moved on, with difficulty and labour he. *Ib.* l. 1021

18 Hail, holy light, offspring of Heaven first-born,
Or of th' Eternal co-eternal beam,
May I express thee unblamed? Since God is light,
And never but in unapproached light
Dwelt from eternity.   *Ib.* bk. iii, l. 1

19 So thick a drop serene hath quenched their orbs,
Or dim suffusion veiled. Yet not the more
Cease I to wander where the Muses haunt
Clear spring, or shady grove, or sunny hill.
        Paradise Lost, bk. iii, l. 25

20   Nor sometimes forget
Those other two equall'd with me in fate,
So were I equall'd with them in renown,
Blind Thamyris and blind Mæonides,
And Tiresias and Phineus, prophets old.
Then feed on thoughts, that voluntary move
Harmonious numbers; as the wakeful bird
Sings darkling, and in shadiest covert hid,
Tunes her nocturnal note. Thus with the year
Seasons return, but not to me returns
Day, or the sweet approach of ev'n or morn,
Or sight of vernal bloom, or summer's rose,
Or flocks, or herds, or human face divine;
But cloud instead, and ever-during dark
Surrounds me, from the cheerful ways of men
Cut off, and for the book of knowledge fair
Presented with a universal blank
Of Nature's works to me expung'd and raz'd,
And wisdom at one entrance quite shut out.
So much the rather thou celestial light
Shine inward.   *Ib.* l. 32

21 Freely they stood who stood, and fell who fell.
        Ib. l. 102

22 Dark with excessive bright.   *Ib.* l. 380

23   Sericana, where Chineses drive
With sails and wind their cany waggons light.
        Ib. l. 438

24 Embryos and idiots, eremites and friars,
White, black and grey, with all their trumpery.
        Ib. l. 474

25 Dying put on the weeds of Dominic,
Or in Franciscan think to pass disguised. *Ib.* l. 479

26   Then might ye see
Cowls, hoods, and habits, with their wearers, tost
And fluttered into rags, then relics, beads,
Indulgences, dispenses, pardons, bulls,
The sport of winds.   *Ib.* l. 489

27 Into a Limbo large and broad, since called
The Paradise of Fools, to few unknown. *Ib.* l. 495

28 For neither man nor angel can discern
Hypocrisy, the only evil that walks
Invisible, except to God alone.   *Ib.* l. 682

29   At whose sight all the stars
Hide their diminished heads.   *Ib.* bk. iv, l. 34

30 Warring in Heav'n against Heav'n's matchless King.
        Ib. l. 41

31 And understood not that a grateful mind
By owing owes not, but still pays, at once
Indebted and discharged.   *Ib.* l. 55

32 Me miserable! which way shall I fly
Infinite wrath, and infinite despair?
Which way I fly is Hell; myself am Hell;
And in the lowest deep a lower deep
Still threatening to devour me opens wide,
To which the Hell I suffer seems a Heaven.
        Ib. l. 73

33 So farewell hope, and with hope farewell fear,
Farewell remorse: all good to me is lost;
Evil be thou my Good.   *Ib.* l. 108

1   Off at sea north-east winds blow
Sabæan odours from the spicy shore
Of Araby the blest.   *Paradise Lost*, bk. iv, l. 161

2   Many a league
Cheer'd with the grateful smell old Ocean smiles.
Ib. l. 164

3 So clomb this first grand thief into God's fold:
So since into his church lewd hirelings climb.
Thence up he flew, and on the tree of life,
The middle tree and highest there that grew,
Sat like a cormorant.   *Ib.* l. 192

4 A heaven on earth.   *Ib.* l. 208

5 Groves whose rich trees wept odorous gums and balm,
Others whose fruit burnished with golden rind
Hung amiable, Hesperian fables true,
If true, here only.   *Ib.* l. 248

6 Flowers of all hue, and without thorn the rose.
Ib. l. 256

7 The mantling vine.   *Ib.* l. 258

8   Not that fair field
Of Enna, where Proserpin gathering flowers
Herself a fairer flower by gloomy Dis
Was gathered.   *Ib.* l. 268

9 Nor where Abassin kings their issue guard,
Mount Amara, though this by some supposed
True paradise.   *Ib.* l. 280

10 Two of far nobler shape erect and tall,
Godlike erect, with native honour clad
In naked majesty seemed lords of all.   *Ib.* l. 288

11 For contemplation he and valour formed;
For softness she and sweet attractive grace,
He for God only, she for God in him:
His fair large front and eye sublime declared
Absolute rule.   *Ib.* l. 297

12   Which implied
Subjection, but required with gentle sway
And by her yielded, by him best received;
Yielded with coy submission, modest pride,
And sweet reluctant amorous delay.   *Ib.* l. 307

13 Adam, the goodliest man of men since born
His sons; the fairest of her daughters Eve.   *Ib.* l. 323

14 The savoury pulp they chew, and in the rind
Still as they thirsted scooped the brimming stream.
Ib. l. 335

15 Sporting the lion ramped, and in his paw,
Dandled the kid; bears, tigers, ounces, pards
Gamboll'd before them, th' unwieldy elephant
To make them mirth us'd all his might, and wreathed
His lithe proboscis.   *Ib.* l. 343

16 So spake the Fiend, and with necessity,
The tyrant's plea, excus'd his devilish deeds.
Ib. l. 393

17   With eyes
Of conjugal attraction unreprov'd.   *Ib.* l. 492

18 Imparadised in one another's arms.   *Ib.* l. 506

19 Now came still evening on, and twilight gray
Had in her sober livery all things clad;
Silence accompanied, for beast and bird,
They to their grassy couch, these to their nests,
Were slunk, all but the wakeful nightingale;
She all night long her amorous descant sung;
Silence was pleas'd: now glow'd the firmament

With living sapphires: Hesperus that led
The starry host, rode brightest, till the moon,
Rising in clouded majesty, at length
Apparent queen unveil'd her peerless light,
And o'er the dark her silver mantle threw.
Paradise Lost, bk. iv, l. 598

20 God is thy law, thou mine: to know no more
Is woman's happiest knowledge and her praise.
Ib. l. 637

21 With thee conversing I forget all time.   *Ib.* l. 639

22 Sweet is the breath of morn, her rising sweet,
With charm of earliest birds.   *Ib.* l. 641

23   Sweet the coming on
Of grateful evening mild, then silent night
With this her solemn bird and this fair moon,
And these the gems of Heav'n, her starry train.
Ib. l. 646

24 Millions of spiritual creatures walk the earth
Unseen, both when we wake, and when we sleep.
Ib. l. 677

25   Into their inmost bower
Handed they went; and eas'd the putting off
These troublesome disguises which we wear,
Strait side by side were laid, nor turned I ween
Adam from his fair spouse, nor Eve the rites
Mysterious of connubial love refus'd:
Whatever hypocrites austerely talk
Of purity and place and innocence,
Defaming as impure what God declares
Pure, and commands to some, leaves free to all.
Ib. l. 738

26 Hail wedded love, mysterious law, true source
Of human offspring, sole propriety,
In Paradise of all things common else.   *Ib.* l. 750

27   Sleep on,
Blest pair; and O yet happiest if ye seek
No happier state, and know to know no more.
Ib. l. 773

28   Him there they found
Squat like a toad, close at the ear of Eve.   *Ib.* l. 799

29 Him thus intent Ithuriel with his spear
Touched lightly; for no falsehood can endure
Touch of celestial temper, but returns
Of force to its own likeness; up he starts
Discover'd and surpris'd.   *Ib.* l. 810

30 Not to know me argues yourselves unknown.
Ib. l. 830

31   Abash'd the Devil stood,
And felt how awful goodness is, and saw
Virtue in her shape how lovely.   *Ib.* l. 846

32 Of regal port,
But faded splendour wan.   *Ib.* l. 869

33 But wherefore thou alone? Wherefore with thee
Came not all hell broke loose?   *Ib.* l. 917

34 Then when I am thy captive talk of chains,
Proud limitary Cherub.   *Ib.* l. 970

35 Like Teneriff or Atlas unremov'd.   *Ib.* l. 987

36   Fled
Murmuring, and with him fled the shades of night.
Ib. l. 1014

37   His sleep
Was aery light, from pure digestion bred.
Ib. bk. v, l. 3

MILTON

1 My fairest, my espoused, my latest found,
Heaven's last best gift, my ever new delight.
Paradise Lost, bk. v, l. 18

2 Good, the more
Communicated, more abundant grows. *Ib.* l. 71

3 Best image of myself and dearer half. *Ib.* l. 95

4 These are thy glorious works, Parent of Good,
Almighty, thine this universal frame,
Thus wondrous fair; thyself how wondrous then!
Ib. l. 153

5 Him first, him last, him midst, and without end.
Ib. l. 165

6 A wilderness of sweets. *Ib.* l. 294

7 Another morn
Ris'n on mid-noon. *Ib.* l. 310

8 So saying, with despatchful looks in haste
She turns, on hospitable thoughts intent. *Ib.* l. 331

9 From many a berry, and from sweet kernels press'd
She tempers dulcet creams. *Ib.* l. 346

10 Nor jealousy
Was understood, the injured lover's hell. *Ib.* l. 449

11 Son of Heav'n and Earth,
Attend: that thou art happy, owe to God;
That thou continuest such, owe to thyself,
That is, to thy obedience; therein stand. *Ib.* l. 519

12 Freely we serve,
Because we freely love, as in our will
To love or not; in this we stand or fall. *Ib.* l. 538

13 What if earth
Be but the shadow of Heaven, and things therein
Each to other like, more than on earth is thought?
Ib. l. 574

14 Hear all ye Angels, progeny of light,
Thrones, Dominations, Princedoms, Virtues, Powers.
Ib. l. 600

15 All seemed well pleased, all seemed but were not all.
Ib. l. 617

16 And in their motions harmony divine
So smoothes her charming tones, that God's own ear
Listens delighted. *Ib.* l. 625

17 Satan, so call him now, his former name
Is heard no more in heaven. *Ib.* l. 655

18 So spake the Seraph Abdiel, faithful found
Among the faithless, faithful only he:
Among innumerable false, unmoved,
Unshaken, unseduced, unterrified
His loyalty he kept, his love, his zeal. *Ib.* l. 893

19 All night the dreadless angel unpursued
Through Heaven's wide champain held his way till morn,
Waked by the circling hours, with rosy hand
Unbarred the gates of light. *Ib.* bk. vi, l. 1

20 Servant of God, well done, well hast thou fought
The better fight, who singly hast maintained
Against revolted multitudes the cause
Of truth, in word mightier than they in arms.
Ib. l. 29

21 He onward came; far off his coming shone.
Ib. l. 768

22 Headlong themselves they threw
Down from the verge of Heaven, eternal wrath
Burnt after them to the bottomless pit. *Ib.* l. 864

23 Standing on earth, not rapt above the Pole,
More safe I sing with mortal voice, unchang'd
To hoarse or mute, though fall'n on evil days,
On evil days though fall'n, and evil tongues.
In darkness, and with dangers compass'd round,
And solitude; yet not alone, while thou
Visit'st my slumbers nightly, or when morn
Purples the east: still govern thou my song,
Urania, and fit audience find, though few:
But drive far off the barb'rous dissonance
Of Bacchus and his revellers.
Paradise Lost, bk. vii, l. 23

24 The affable Archangel. *Ib.* l. 41

25 Necessity and chance
Approach not me, and what I will is fate. *Ib.* l. 172

26 There Leviathan
Hugest of living creatures, on the deep
Stretch'd like a promontory sleeps or swims,
And seems a moving land, and at his gills
Draws in, and at his trunk spouts out a sea.
Ib. l. 412

27 Now half appear'd
The tawny lion, pawing to get free
His hinder parts. *Ib.* l. 463

28 The Planets in their stations list'ning stood,
While the bright Pomp ascended jubilant.
Open, ye everlasting gates, they sung,
Open, ye heavens, your living doors; let in
The great Creator from his work return'd
Magnificent, his six days' work, a world. *Ib.* l. 563

29 The Angel ended, and in Adam's ear
So charming left his voice that he a while
Thought him still speaking, still stood fixed to hear.
Ib. bk. viii, l. 1

30 He his fabric of the Heavens
Hath left to their disputes, perhaps to move
His laughter at their quaint opinions wide
Hereafter, when they come to model Heaven
And calculate the stars, how they will wield
The mighty frame, how build, unbuild, contrive
To save appearances, how gird the sphere
With centric and eccentric scribbled o'er,
Cycle and epicycle, orb in orb. *Ib.* l. 76

31 Heaven is for thee too high
To know what passes there; be lowly wise:
Think only what concerns thee and thy being.
Ib. l. 172

32 Liquid lapse of murmuring streams. *Ib.* l. 263

33 And feel that I am happier than I know. *Ib.* l. 282

34 In solitude
What happiness? Who can enjoy alone,
Or all enjoying, what contentment find? *Ib.* l. 364

35 I waked
To find her, or for ever to deplore
Her loss, and other pleasures all abjure. *Ib.* l. 478

36 Grace was in all her steps, heaven in her eye,
In every gesture dignity and love. *Ib.* l. 488

37 Her virtue, and the conscience of her worth,
That would be wooed, and not unsought be won.
Ib. l. 502

38 The amorous bird of night
Sung spousal, and bid haste the evening star
On his hill top, to light the bridal lamp. *Ib.* l. 518

39 The sum of earthly bliss. *Ib.* l. 522

[348]

1   So absolute she seems
And in herself complete, so well to know
Her own, that what she wills to do or say
Seems wisest, virtuousest, discreetest, best.
Paradise Lost, bk. viii, l. 547

2 To whom the Angel with contracted brow.
Accuse not Nature, she hath done her part;
Do thou but thine, and be not diffident
Of wisdom, she deserts thee not, if thou
Dismiss not her.   *Ib.* l. 560

3   Oft-times nothing profits more
Than self-esteem, grounded on just and right
Well manag'd.   *Ib.* l. 571

4   With a smile that glowed
Celestial rosy red, love's proper hue.   *Ib.* l. 618

5   My celestial Patroness, who deigns
Her nightly visitation unimplor'd,
And dictates to me slumb'ring, or inspires
Easy my unpremeditated verse:
Since first this subject for heroic song
Pleas'd me long choosing, and beginning late.
                    Ib. bk. ix, l. 21

6   Unless an age too late, or cold
Climate, or years damp my intended wing. *Ib.* l. 44

7 The serpent subtlest beast of all the field. *Ib.* l. 86

8   For nothing lovelier can be found
In woman, than to study household good,
And good works in her husband to promote.
                    Ib. l. 232

9 For solitude sometimes is best society,
And short retirement urges sweet return. *Ib.* l. 249

10 Wouldst thou approve thy constancy, approve
First thy obedience.   *Ib.* l. 367

11 As one who long in populous city pent,
Where houses thick and sewers annoy the air,
Forth issuing on a summer's morn to breathe
Among the pleasant villages and farms
Adjoin'd, from each thing met conceives delight.
                    Ib. l. 445

12 She fair, divinely fair, fit love for Gods. *Ib.* l. 489

13   Hope elevates, and joy
Brightens his crest.   *Ib.* l. 633

14 God so commanded, and left that command
Sole daughter of his voice; the rest, we live
Law to ourselves, our reason is our law. *Ib.* l. 652

15   Her rash hand in evil hour
Forth reaching to the fruit, she pluck'd, she eat:
Earth felt the wound, and Nature from her seat
Sighing through all her works gave signs of woe
That all was lost.   *Ib.* l. 780

16 Adam shall share with me in bliss or woe:
So dear I love him, that with him all deaths
I could endure, without him live no life. *Ib.* l. 831

17 O fairest of creation! last and best
Of all God's works! creature in whom excell'd
Whatever can to sight or thought be form'd,
Holy, divine, good, amiable, or sweet!
How art thou lost, how on a sudden lost,
Defac'd, deflower'd, and now to Death devote?
                    Ib. l. 896

18   For with thee
Certain my resolution is to die;
How can I live without thee, how forgo
Thy sweet converse and love so dearly joined,
To live again in these wild woods forlorn?
Should God create another Eve, and I
Another rib afford, yet loss of thee
Would never from my heart; no no, I feel
The link of nature draw me: flesh of flesh,
Bone of my bone thou art, and from thy state
Mine never shall be parted, weal or woe.
                    Paradise Lost, bk. ix, l. 906

19   What thou art is mine;
Our state cannot be sever'd, we are one,
One flesh; to lose thee were to lose myself.
                    Ib. l. 957

20   He hears
On all sides, from innumerable tongues,
A dismal universal hiss, the sound
Of public scorn.   *Ib.* bk. x, l. 506

21   Complicated monsters, head and tail,
Scorpion and asp, and Amphisbaena dire,
Cerastes horned, Hydrus, and Ellops drear.
                    Ib. l. 523

22 Chew'd bitter ashes, which th' offended taste
With spattering noise rejected.   *Ib.* l. 566

23   Oh! why did God,
Creator wise, that peopled highest Heaven
With Spirits masculine, create at last
This novelty on Earth, this fair defect
Of Nature?   *Ib.* l. 888

24 Demoniac frenzy, moping melancholy,
And moon-struck madness.   *Ib.* bk. xi, l. 485

25 Nor love thy life, nor hate; but what thou liv'st
Live well, how long or short permit to Heaven.
                    Ib. l. 553

26   The evening star,
Love's harbinger.   *Ib.* l. 588

27 The brazen throat of war had ceased to roar:
All now was turned to jollity and game,
To luxury and riot, feast and dance.   *Ib.* l. 713

28   For now I see
Peace to corrupt no less than war to waste. *Ib.* l. 779

29   Then wilt thou not be loth
To leave this Paradise, but shalt possess
A Paradise within thee, happier far. *Ib.* bk. xii, l. 585

30 In me is no delay; with thee to go,
Is to stay here; without thee here to stay,
Is to go hence unwilling; thou to me
Art all things under Heaven, all places thou,
Who for my wilful crime art banished hence.
                    Ib. l. 615

31 They looking back, all th' eastern side beheld
Of Paradise, so late their happy seat,
Wav'd over by that flaming brand, the Gate
With dreadful faces throng'd and fiery arms.
Some natural tears they dropped, but wiped them soon;
The world was all before them, where to choose
Their place of rest, and Providence their guide:
They hand in hand with wandering steps and slow
Through Eden took their solitary way.   *Ib.* l. 641

32   Satan, bowing low
His gray dissimulation, disappeared.
                    Paradise Regained, bk. i, l. 497

1 Skill'd to retire, and in retiring draw
Hearts after them tangled in amorous nets.
Paradise Regained, bk. ii, l. 161

2   Beauty stands
In the admiration only of weak minds
Led captive.   *Ib.* l. 220

3   And now the herald lark
Left his ground-nest, high tow'ring to descry
The morn's approach, and greet her with his song.
                      Ib. l. 279

4 Ladies of th' Hesperides, that seemed
Fairer than feign'd of old, or fabled since
Of faery damsels met in forest wide
By knights of Logres, or of Lyones,
Lancelot or Pelleas, or Pellenore.   *Ib.* l. 357

5 Of whom to be dispraised were no small praise.
                    Ib. bk. iii, l. 56

6 But on Occasion's forelock watchful wait. *Ib.* l. 173

7 As he who, seeking asses, found a kingdom.
                           Ib. l. 242

8 Elephants endorsed with towers.   *Ib.* l. 329

9 Dusk faces with white silken turbans wreath'd.
                      Ib. bk. iv, l. 76

10   The childhood shows the man,
As morning shows the day. Be famous then
By wisdom; as thy empire must extend,
So let extend thy mind o'er all the world. *Ib.* l. 220

11 Athens, the eye of Greece, mother of arts
And eloquence, native to famous wits
Or hospitable, in her sweet recess,
City or suburban, studious walks and shades;
See there the olive grove of Academe,
Plato's retirement, where the Attic bird
Trills her thick-warbled notes the summer long.
                      Ib. l. 240

12 The first and wisest of them all professed
To know this only, that he nothing knew. *Ib.* l. 293

13 Deep versed in books and shallow in himself.
                      Ib. l. 327

14 In them is plainest taught, and easiest learnt,
What makes a nation happy, and keeps it so.
                    Ib. l. 361

15   Till morning fair
Came forth with pilgrim steps in amice grey.
                    Ib. l. 426

16   Without wing
Of hippogriff.   *Ib.* l. 541

17 And, as that Theban monster that proposed
Her riddle, and him who solved it not devoured;
That once found out and solved, for grief and spite
Cast herself headlong from th' Ismenian steep,
So strook with dread and anguish fell the Fiend;
And to his crew, that sat consulting, brought
Joyless triumphals of his hop't success,
Ruin, and desperation, and dismay,
Who durst so proudly tempt the Son of God.
                    Ib. l. 572

18   He unobserved
Home to his mother's house private returned.
                    Ib. l. 638

19 But headlong joy is ever on the wing.
              The Passion, l. 5

20 A little onward lend thy guiding hand
To these dark steps, a little further on.
          Samson Agonistes, l. 1

21 Eyeless in Gaza, at the mill with slaves.   *Ib.* l. 41

22 O dark, dark, dark, amid the blaze of noon,
Irrecoverably dark, total eclipse
Without all hope of day!   *Ib.* l. 80

23 The sun to me is dark
And silent as the moon,
When she deserts the night
Hid in her vacant interlunar cave.   *Ib.* l. 86

24 To live a life half dead, a living death.   *Ib.* l. 100

25 Ran on embattled armies clad in iron,
And, weaponless himself,
Made arms ridiculous.   *Ib.* l. 129

26   Wisest men
Have erred, and by bad women been deceived;
And shall again, pretend they ne'er so wise.
                    Ib. l. 210

27 Just are the ways of God,
And justifiable to men;
Unless there be who think not God at all. *Ib.* l. 293

28   Of such doctrine never was there school,
But the heart of the fool,
And no man therein doctor but himself.   *Ib.* l. 297

29 What boots it at one gate to make defence,
And at another to let in the foe?   *Ib.* l. 560

30 My race of glory run, and race of shame,
And I shall shortly be with them that rest. *Ib.* l. 597

31 But who is this, what thing of sea or land?
Female of sex it seems,
That so bedeck'd, ornate, and gay,
Comes this way sailing
Like a stately ship
Of Tarsus, bound for th' isles
Of Javan or Gadier,
With all her bravery on, and tackle trim,
Sails fill'd, and streamers waving,
Courted by all the winds that hold them play,
An amber scent of odorous perfume
Her harbinger.   *Ib.* l. 710

32   That grounded maxim
So rife and celebrated in the mouths
Of wisest men; that to the public good
Private respects must yield.   *Ib.* l. 865

33 Yet beauty, though injurious, hath strange power,
After offence returning, to regain
Love once possess'd.   *Ib.* l. 1003

34 Love-quarrels oft in pleasing concord end.
                    Ib. l. 1008

35 Therefore God's universal law
Gave to the man despotic power
Over his female in due awe.   *Ib.* l. 1053

36 O how comely it is, and how reviving
To the spirits of just men long opprest,
When God into the hands of their deliverer
Puts invincible might,
To quell the mighty of the earth, th' oppressor.
                    Ib. l. 1268

37 He's gone, and who knows how he may report
Thy words by adding fuel to the flame? *Ib.* l. 1350

38 Lords are lordliest in their wine.   *Ib.* l. 1418

1 For evil news rides post, while good news baits.
Samson Agonistes, l. 1538

2 And as an ev'ning dragon came,
Assailant on the perched roosts
And nests in order rang'd
Of tame villatic fowl. *Ib.* l. 1692

3 Like that self-begotten bird
In the Arabian woods embost,
That no second knows nor third,
And lay erewhile a holocaust. *Ib.* l. 1699

4 And though her body die, her fame survives,
A secular bird, ages of lives. *Ib.* l. 1706

5 Samson hath quit himself
Like Samson, and heroically hath finish'd
A life heroic. *Ib.* l. 1709

6 Nothing is here for tears, nothing to wail
Or knock the breast; no weakness, no contempt,
Dispraise or blame; nothing but well and fair,
And what may quiet us in a death so noble.
Ib. l. 1721

7 All is best, though we oft doubt,
What th' unsearchable dispose
Of highest wisdom brings about,
And ever best found in the close.
Oft he seems to hide his face,
But unexpectedly returns
And to his faithful champion hath in place
Bore witness gloriously; whence Gaza mourns
And all that band them to resist
His uncontrollable intent,
His servants he with new acquist
Of true experience from this great event
With peace and consolation hath dismiss'd,
And calm of mind all passion spent. *Ib.* l. 1745

8 What needs my Shakespeare for his honour'd bones,
The labour of an age in piled stones,
Or that his hallow'd relics should be hid
Under a star-y-pointing pyramid?
Dear son of memory, great heir of fame,
What need'st thou such weak witness of thy name?
[Epitaph] on Shakespeare

9 Blest pair of Sirens, pledges of Heaven's joy,
Sphere-born harmonious sisters, Voice and Verse.
At a Solemn Music

10 Where the bright Seraphim in burning row
Their loud up-lifted Angel trumpets blow. *Ib.*

11 Till disproportion'd sin
Jarr'd against nature's chime. *Ib.*

12 O nightingale, that on yon bloomy spray
Warbl'st at eve, when all the woods are still.
Sonnet i. To the Nightingale

13 All is, if I have grace to use it so,
As ever in my great Task-Master's eye.
Ib. ii. *On his having arrived at the age of twenty-three*

14 Captain or Colonel, or Knight in arms.
Ib. viii. *When the assault was intended to the city*

15 The great Emathian conqueror bid spare
The house of Pindarus, when temple and tower
Went to the ground. *Ib.*

16 As that dishonest victory
At Chæronea, fatal to liberty,
Killed with report that old man eloquent.
Ib. x. *To the Lady Margaret Ley*

17 Those rugged names to our like mouths grow sleek,
That would have made Quintilian stare and gasp.
Thy age, like ours, O soul of Sir John Cheke,
Hated not learning worse than toad or asp,
When thou taught'st Cambridge, and King Edward
Greek. *Sonnet,* xi. '*A book was writ of late*'

18 I did but prompt the age to quit their clogs,
By the known rules of ancient liberty,
When straight a barbarous noise environs me
Of owls and cuckoos, asses, apes, and dogs.
Ib. xii. *On the Same.* [*the detraction, &c.*]

19 Licence they mean when they cry Liberty;
For who loves that, must first be wise and good. *Ib.*

20 Avenge, O Lord, thy slaughtered saints, whose bones
Lie scattered on the Alpine mountains cold;
Ev'n them who kept thy truth so pure of old,
When all our fathers worshipped stocks and stones,
Forget not. In thy book record their groans
Who were thy sheep, and in their ancient fold
Slain by the bloody Piedmontese, that rolled
Mother with infant down the rocks.
Ib. xv. *On the late Massacre in Piedmont*

21 When I consider how my light is spent,
E're half my days, in this dark world and wide,
And that one Talent which is death to hide,
Lodg'd with me useless, though my Soul more bent
To serve therewith my Maker, and present
My true account, lest He returning chide;
'Doth God exact day-labour, light deny'd?'
I fondly ask; But Patience, to prevent
That murmur, soon replies, 'God doth not need
Either man's work or his own gifts. Who best
Bear his mild yoke, they serve him best, his State
Is Kingly. Thousands at his bidding speed
And post o'er Land and Ocean without rest:
They also serve who only stand and wait.'
Ib. xvi. *On His Blindness*

22 In mirth, that after no repenting draws.
Ib. xviii. *To Cyriac Skinner*

23 To measure life learn thou betimes, and know
Toward solid good what leads the nearest way;
For other things mild Heaven a time ordains,
And disapproves that care, though wise in show,
That with superfluous burden loads the day,
And, when God sends a cheerful hour, refrains. *Ib.*

24 Methought I saw my late espousèd Saint
Brought to me like Alcestis from the grave.
Ib. xix. *On His Deceased Wife*

25 Love, sweetness, goodness, in her person shined. *Ib.*

26 But O as to embrace me she inclined,
I waked, she fled, and day brought back my night. *Ib.*

27 New Presbyter is but old Priest writ large.
*Ib. On the New Forcers of Conscience under the
Long Parliament*

28 For what can war but endless war still breed?
Ib. On the Lord General Fairfax

29 Peace hath her victories
No less renowned than war.
Ib. [*To the Lord General Cromwell, May 1652*]

30 Help us to save free conscience from the paw
Of hireling wolves, whose gospel is their maw. *Ib.*

31 Fly, envious Time, till thou run out thy race:
Call on the lazy leaden-stepping hours. *On Time,* l. 1

1 Beldam Nature.
At a Vacation Exercise in the College, l. 46

2 He who would not be frustrate of his hope to write well hereafter in laudable things ought himself to be a true poem.
Apology for Smectymnuus, introd. to § 1

3 His words . . . like so many nimble and airy servitors trip about him at command. *Ib.* § 12

4 For this is not the liberty which we can hope, that no grievance ever should arise in the Commonwealth, that let no man in this world expect; but when complaints are freely heard, deeply considered, and speedily reformed, then is the utmost bound of civil liberty attained that wise men look for.
Areopagitica

5 Books are not absolutely dead things, but do contain a potency of life in them to be as active as that soul was whose progeny they are; nay they do preserve as in a vial the purest efficacy and extraction of that living intellect that bred them. *Ib.*

6 As good almost kill a man as kill a good book: who kills a man kills a reasonable creature, God's image; but he who destroys a good book, kills reason itself, kills the image of God, as it were in the eye. *Ib.*

7 A good book is the precious life-blood of a master spirit, embalmed and treasured up on purpose to a life beyond life. *Ib.*

8 It was from out the rind of one apple tasted that the knowledge of good and evil as two twins cleaving together leaped forth into the world. *Ib.*

9 He that can apprehend and consider vice with all her baits and seeming pleasures, and yet abstain, and yet distinguish, and yet prefer that which is truly better, he is the true wayfaring Christian. I cannot praise a fugitive and cloistered virtue, unexercised and unbreathed, that never sallies out and sees her adversary, but slinks out of the race, where that immortal garland is to be run for, not without dust and heat. Assuredly we bring not innocence into the world, we bring impurity much rather: that which purifies us is trial, and trial is by what is contrary. *Ib.*

10 Our sage and serious poet Spenser. *Ib.*

11 To be still searching what we know not by what we know, still closing up truth to truth as we find it (for all her body is homogeneal and proportional), this is the golden rule in theology as well as in arithmetic, and makes up the best harmony in a church. *Ib.*

12 God is decreeing to begin some new and great period in His Church, even to the reforming of Reformation itself. What does He then but reveal Himself to His servants, and as His manner is, first to His Englishmen? *Ib.*

13 Behold now this vast city [London]; a city of refuge, the mansion-house of liberty, encompassed and surrounded with His protection. *Ib.*

14 Where there is much desire to learn, there of necessity will be much arguing, much writing, many opinions; for opinion in good men is but knowledge in the making. *Ib.*

15 Methinks I see in my mind a noble and puissant nation rousing herself like a strong man after sleep, and shaking her invincible locks. Methinks I see her as an eagle mewing her mighty youth, and kindling her undazzled eyes at the full midday beam. *Areopagitica*

16 Give me the liberty to know, to utter, and to argue freely according to conscience, above all liberties. *Ib.*

17 Though all the winds of doctrine were let loose to play upon the earth, so Truth be in the field, we do injuriously by licensing and prohibiting to misdoubt her strength. Let her and Falsehood grapple; who ever knew Truth put to the worse, in a free and open encounter. *Ib.*

18 But because about the manner and order of this government, whether it ought to be Presbyterial, or Prelatical, such endless question, or rather uproar is arisen in this land, as may be justly termed, what the fever is to the physicians, the eternal reproach of the divines.
Reason of Church Government, preface

19 This manner of writing [i.e. prose] wherein knowing myself inferior to myself . . . I have the use, as I may account it, but of my left hand.
Ib. bk. ii, introd. to ch. 1

20 A poet soaring in the high region of his fancies with his garland and singing robes about him. *Ib.*

21 By labour and intent study (which I take to be my portion in this life) joined with the strong propensity of nature, I might perhaps leave something so written to after-times, as they should not willingly let it die. *Ib.*

22 Inquisitorious and tyrannical duncery. *Ib.*

23 Beholding the bright countenance of truth in the quiet and still air of delightful studies. *Ib.*

24 Let not England forget her precedence of teaching nations how to live.
The Doctrine and Discipline of Divorce

25 I call therefore a complete and generous education that which fits a man to perform justly, skilfully and magnanimously all the offices both private and public of peace and war. *Of Education*

26 I will point ye out the right path of a virtuous and noble Education; laborious indeed at the first ascent, but else so smooth, so green, so full of goodly prospect, and melodious sounds on every side, that the harp of Orpheus was not more charming. *Ib.*

27 Brave men, and worthy patriots, dear to God, and famous to all ages. *Ib.*

28 Ornate rhetorick taught out of the rule of Plato, . . . To which poetry would be made subsequent, or indeed rather precedent, as being less subtle and fine, but more simple, sensuous and passionate. *Ib.*

29 In those vernal seasons of the year, when the air is calm and pleasant, it were an injury and sullenness against Nature not to go out, and see her riches, and partake in her rejoicing with Heaven and Earth. *Ib.*

30 The Wars of Kites or Crows fighting in the air.
History of Britain, ch. 4

1 For such kind of borrowing as this, if it be not bettered by the borrower, among good authors is accounted plagiary. *Iconoclastes*, ch. 23

2 None can love freedom heartily, but good men; the rest love not freedom, but licence.
Tenure of Kings and Magistrates

3 No man who knows aught, can be so stupid to deny that all men naturally were born free. *Ib.*

COMTE DE MIRABEAU
1749–1791

4 La guerre est l'industrie nationale de la Prusse.
War is the national industry of Prussia.
Attr. to Mirabeau by Albert Sorel, based on his Introduction to his 'Monarchie Prussienne'

MISSAL

5 O felix culpa, quae talem ac tantum meruit habere Redemptorem.
O happy fault, which has deserved to have such and so mighty a Redeemer.
'Exsultet' on Holy Saturday

MARY RUSSELL MITFORD
1787–1855

6 I have discovered that our great favourite, Miss Austen, is my country-woman. . . . with whom mamma before her marriage was acquainted. Mamma says that she was then the prettiest, silliest, most affected, husband-hunting butterfly she ever remembers.
Letter to Sir William Elford, 3 Apr. 1815. Rev. A. G. L'Estrange: Life of Mary Russell Mitford, vol. i, pp. 305–6

EMILIO MOLA
d. 1936

7 La quinta columna.
The fifth column.
Radio Address given when a General in the Spanish Civil War, 1936–1939

JEAN BAPTISTE POQUELIN, *called* MOLIÈRE
1622–1673

8 Vous êtes orfèvre, Monsieur Josse!
You are in the trade, Monsieur Josse!
L'Amour Médecin, I. i

9 Présentez toujours le devant au monde.
Always show your front to the world.
L'Avare, III. ii

10 Il faut manger pour vivre et non pas vivre pour manger.
One should eat to live, not live to eat. *Ib.* v

11 M. JOURDAIN: Quoi? quand je dis: 'Nicole, apportez-moi mes pantoufles, et me donnez mon bonnet de nuit', c'est de la prose?
MAÎTRE DE PHILOSOPHIE: Oui, monsieur.
M. JOURDAIN: Par ma foi! il y a plus de quarante ans que je dis de la prose sans que j'en susse rien.

M. JOURDAIN: What? when I say: 'Nicole, bring me my slippers, and give me my night-cap,' is that prose?

PROFESSOR OF PHILOSOPHY: Yes, Sir.
M. JOURDAIN: Good Heavens! For more than forty years I have been speaking prose without knowing it. *Le Bourgeois Gentilhomme*, II. iv

12 Tout ce qui n'est point prose est vers; et tout ce qui n'est point vers est prose.
All that is not prose is verse; and all that is not verse is prose. *Ib.*

13 Ah, la belle chose que de savoir quelque chose.
Knowledge is a fine thing. *Ib.* vi

14 Je voudrais bien savoir si la grande règle de toutes les règles n'est pas de plaire.
I sometimes wonder whether the greatest rule of all is not—to know how to please.
Critique de L'École des Femmes, vii

15 C'est une étrange entreprise que celle de faire rire les honnêtes gens.
It is an odd calling, to make decent folk laugh. *Ib.*

16 Je vis de bonne soupe et non de beau langage.
It's good food and not fine words that keeps me alive. *Les Femmes Savantes*, II. vii

17 Guenille, si l'on veut: ma guenille m'est chère.
Rags and tatters, maybe: but I am fond of my rags and tatters. *Ib.*

18 Un sot savant est sot plus qu'un sot ignorant.
An erudite fool is a greater fool than an ignorant fool. *Ib.* IV. iii

19 Les livres cadrent mal avec le mariage.
Reading goes ill with the married state. *Ib.* v. iii

20 Qui vit sans tabac n'est pas digne de vivre.
He who lives without tobacco is not worthy to live.
Festin de Pierre, I. i

21 Que diable allait-il faire dans cette galère?
What the devil is he doing in this galley?
Les Fourberies de Scapin, II. vii

22 Vous l'avez voulu, Georges Dandin, vous l'avez voulu.
You asked for it, George Dandin, you asked for it.
Georges Dandin, I. ix

23 L'on a le temps d'avoir les dents longues, lorsqu' on attend pour vivre le trépas de quelqu'un.
He who waits for dead men's leavings may well be sharp set before he gets a meal.
Le Médecin malgré lui, II. ii

24 Oui, cela était autrefois ainsi, mais nous avons changé tout cela.
Yes, it used to be so, but we have changed all that.
Ib. vi. *Said by the pretended doctor to justify his mistake as to the relative positions of heart and liver.*

25 Il faut, parmi le monde, une vertu traitable.
Virtue, in the great world, should be amenable.
Le Misanthrope, I. i

26 C'est une folie à nulle autre seconde,
De vouloir se mêler à corriger le monde.
Of all human follies there's none could be greater Than trying to render our fellow-men better. *Ib.*

1 On doit se regarder soi-même un fort long temps,
Avant que de songer à condamner les gens.

> We should look long and carefully at ourselves
> Before we pass judgement on our fellows.
> *Le Misanthrope*, III. vii

2 Allez-vous-en la voir et me laissez enfin
Dans ce petit coin sombre avec mon noir chagrin.

> Go get you gone—go, seek her out again
> And leave me pent in gloom with my o'er shadow-
> ing pain. *Ib.* v. i

3 C'est un homme expéditif, qui aime à dépêcher ses
malades; et quand on a à mourir, cela se fait avec lui
le plus vite du monde.

> He wastes no time with patients: and if you have
> to die, he will put the business through quicker
> than anybody else.
> *Monsieur de Pourceaugnac*, I. vii

4 Ils commencent ici (Paris) par faire pendre un homme
et puis ils lui font son procès.

> Here, in Paris, they hang a man first, and try him
> afterwards. *Ib.* III. ii

5 Les gens de qualité savent tout sans avoir jamais rien
appris.

> People of quality know everything without ever
> having been taught. *Les Précieuses Ridicules*, x

6 Ah, pour être dévot, je n'en suis pas moins homme.

> I am not the less human for being devout.
> *Tartuffe*, III. iii

7 Le ciel défend, de vrai, certains contentements
Mais on trouve avec lui des accommodements.

> God, it is true, does some delights condemn,
> But 'tis not hard to come to terms with Him.
> *Ib.* IV. v

8 L'homme est, je vous l'avoue, un méchant animal.

> Man, I can assure you, is a nasty creature. *Ib.* v. vi

9 Il m'est permis, disait Molière, de reprendre mon
bien où je le trouve.

> It is permitted me, said Molière, to take good
> fortune where I find it.
> Grimarest, *Vie de Molière* (1704), p. 14

JAMES, DUKE OF MONMOUTH
1649–1685

10 Do not hack me as you did my Lord Russell.
Words to his executioner. Macaulay, *Hist. of
England*, vol. i, ch. 5

JOHN SAMUEL BEWLEY MONSELL
1811–1875

11 Fight the good fight with all thy might,
Christ is thy strength, and Christ thy right;
Lay hold on life, and it shall be
Thy joy and crown eternally.

Run the straight race through God's good grace,
Lift up thine eyes, and seek His Face;
Life with its way before us lies,
Christ is the path, and Christ the prize.
Hymns of Love and Praise. Fight of Faith

12 Faint not nor fear, His arms are near,
He changeth not, and thou art dear;
Only believe, and thou shalt see
That Christ is all in all to thee. *Ib.*

LADY MARY WORTLEY MONTAGU
1689–1762

13 This world consists of men, women, and Herveys.
Letters, vol. i, p. 67

14 But the fruit that can fall without shaking,
Indeed is too mellow for me.
*Letters and Works. Answered, for Lord William
Hamilton*

15 And we meet, with champagne and a chicken, at last.
Ib. The Lover

16 General notions are generally wrong.
Ib. Letter to Mr. Wortley Montagu, 28 Mar. 1710

17 Civility costs nothing and buys everything.
Ib. Letter to the Countess of Bute, 30 May 1756

MICHEL EYQUEM MONTAIGNE
1533–1592

18 Le continuel ouvrage de votre vie, c'est bâtir la mort.

> The ceaseless labour of a man's whole life is to build
> the house of death. *Essais*, I. xx

19 Il faut être toujours botté et prêt à partir.

> One should be ever booted and spurred and ready
> to depart. *Ib.*

20 L'utilité du vivre n'est pas en l'éspace, elle est en
l'usage; tel a vécu longtemps qui a peu vécu . . .
Il gît en votre volonté, non au nombre des ans,
que vous ayez assez vécu.

> The value of life lies not in the length of days, but
> in the use we make of them: a man may live long,
> yet get little from life. Whether you find satis-
> faction in life depends not on your tale of years,
> but on your will. *Ib.*

21 [*Of his friend, Étienne de la Boétie*]
Si l'on me presse de dire pourquoi je l'aimais, je sens
que cela ne se peut exprimer qu'en répondant,
Parce que c'était lui; parce que c'était moi.

> If you press me to say why I loved him, I can say
> no more than it was because he was he and I
> was I. *Ib.* xxviii

22 La gloire et le repos sont choses qui ne peuvent loger
en même gîte.

> Fame and tranquillity can never be bedfellows.
> *Ib.* xxxix

23 Il se faut réserver une arrière boutique, toute notre,
toute franche, en laquelle nous établissons notre
vraie liberté en principale retraicte et solitude.

> A man must keep a little back shop where he can be
> himself without reserve. In solitude alone can he
> know true freedom. *Ib.*

24 La plus grande chose du monde c'est de savoir être
à soi.

> The greatest thing in the world is to know how to be
> sufficient unto oneself. *Ib.*

25 Pour juger des choses grandes et hautes, il faut une
âme de même.

> Only he can judge of matters great and high whose
> soul is likewise. *Ib.* xlii

1 Mon métier et mon art, c'est vivre.

To know how to live is all my calling and all my art.
Essais, II. vi

2 La vertu refuse la facilité pour compagne . . . elle demande un chemin aspre et espineux.

Virtue can have naught to do with ease . . . It craves a steep and thorny path. *Ib.* xi

3 Quand je me joue à ma chatte, qui sait si elle passe son temps de moi, plus que je ne fais d'elle?

When I play with my cat, who knows whether I do not make her more sport than she makes me?
Ib. xii

4 La vie est un songe . . . nous veillons dormants et veillants dormons.

Life is a dream . . . we waking sleep and sleeping wake. *Ib.*

5 Que sais-je?

What do I know? *Ib.*

6 Comme quelqu'un pourrait dire de moi que j'ai seulement fait ici un amas de fleurs étrangères, n'y ayant fourni du mien que le filet à les lier.

And one might therefore say of me that in this book I have only made up a bunch of other people's flowers, and that of my own I have only provided the string that ties them together.
Ib. III. xii

CHARLES DE SECONDAT, BARON DE MONTESQUIEU
1689–1755

7 Les grands seigneurs ont des plaisirs, le peuple a de la joie.

Great lords have their pleasures, but the people have happiness. *Pensées Diverses*

8 Les Anglais sont occupés; ils n'ont pas le temps d'être polis.

The English are busy folk; they have no time in which to be polite. *Ib.*

JAMES MONTGOMERY
1771–1854

9 'For ever with the Lord!'
Amen; so let it be;
Life from the dead is in that word,
'Tis immortality. *At Home in Heaven*

10 Here in the body pent,
Absent from Him I roam,
Yet nightly pitch my moving tent
A day's march nearer home. *Ib.*

11 Prayer is the soul's sincere desire,
Uttered or unexpressed,
The motion of a hidden fire
That trembles in the breast. *What is Prayer?*

12 A day in such serene enjoyment spent
Were worth an age of splendid discontent.
Greenland, canto ii, l. 224

ROBERT MONTGOMERY
1807–1855

13 The solitary monk who shook the world.
Luther. Man's Need and God's Supply, l. 68

14 With fearful gaze, still be it mine to see
How all is fill'd and vivified by Thee;
Upon thy mirror, earth's majestic view,
To paint Thy Presence, and to feel it too.
The Omnipresence of the Deity (ed. 1830), pt. 1,
l. 105

15 And thou, vast ocean! on whose awful face
Time's iron feet can print no ruin-trace. *Ib.* l. 141

16 Ye quenchless stars! so eloquently bright,
Untroubled sentries of the shadowy night. *Ib.* l. 305

17 The soul aspiring pants its source to mount,
As streams meander level with their fount. *Ib.* l. 339

JAMES GRAHAM, MARQUIS OF MONTROSE
1612–1650

18 My dear and only love, I pray
This noble world of thee,
Be govern'd by no other sway
But purest Monarchy.
For if confusion have a part,
Which virtuous souls abhor,
And hold a synod in thy heart,
I'll never love thee more. *My Dear and Only Love*

19 He either fears his fate too much,
Or his deserts are small,
That puts it not unto the touch,
To win or lose it all. *Ib.*

20 But if thou wilt be constant then,
And faithful of thy word,
I'll make thee glorious by my pen,
And famous by my sword. *Ib.*

21 Let them bestow on every airth a limb;
Then open all my veins, that I may swim
To thee, my Maker! in that crimson lake;
Then place my parboiled head upon a stake—
Scatter my ashes—strew them in the air;—
Lord! since thou know'st where all these atoms are,
I'm hopeful thou'lt recover once my dust,
And confident thou'lt raise me with the just.
*Lines Written on the Window of his Jail the Night
before his Execution. Scottish Poetry of the Seven-
teenth Century*

PERCY MONTROSE
nineteenth century

22 In a cavern, in a canyon,
Excavating for a mine,
Dwelt a miner, Forty-niner,
And his daughter, Clementine.
Oh, my darling, oh my darling, oh my darling
Clementine!
Thou art lost and gone for ever, dreadful sorry,
Clementine. *Clementine*

23 Light she was and like a fairy,
And her shoes were number nine;
Herring boxes without topses,
Sandals were for Clementine. *Ib.*

24 But I kissed her little sister,
And forgot my Clementine. *Ib.*

CLEMENT C. MOORE

1779–1863

1 'Twas the night before Christmas, when all through
  the house
  Not a creature was stirring, not even a mouse;
  The stockings were hung by the chimney with care,
  In hopes that St. Nicholas soon would be there.
  The Night before Christmas

EDWARD MOORE

1712–1757

2 This is adding insult to injuries. *The Foundling*, v. ii

3 I am rich beyond the dreams of avarice.
  The Gamester, II. ii

GEORGE MOORE

1852–1933

4 All reformers are bachelors.
  The Bending of the Bough, Act I

5 Art must be parochial in the beginning to become
  cosmopolitan in the end.
  Hail and Farewell! (1925), vol. i, p. 5

6 Acting is therefore the lowest of the arts, if it is an art
  at all. *Mummer-Worship*

THOMAS MOORE

1779–1852

7 For you know, dear—I may, without vanity, hint—
  Though an angel should write, still 'tis *devils* must
  print. *The Fudges in England*, letter iii, l. 64

8 Yet, who can help loving the land that has taught us
  Six hundred and eighty-five ways to dress eggs?
  The Fudge Family in Paris, letter viii. l. 64

9 A Persian's Heaven is easily made;
  'Tis but black eyes and lemonade.
  Intercepted Letters, vi

10 And doth not a meeting like this make amends,
  For all the long years I've been wand'ring away?
  Irish Melodies. And Doth Not a Meeting

11 Believe me, if all those endearing young charms,
  Which I gaze on so fondly to-day.
  Ib. Believe Me, if All

12 And around the dear ruin each wish of my heart
  Would entwine itself verdantly still. *Ib.*

13 No, the heart that has truly lov'd never forgets,
  But as truly loves on to the close,
  As the sun-flower turns on her god, when he sets,
  The same look which she turn'd when he rose. *Ib.*

14 Eyes of most unholy blue! *Ib. By that Lake*

15 Come, rest in this bosom, my own stricken deer,
  Though the herd have fled from thee, thy home is still
  here. *Ib. Come, Rest In This Bosom*

16 I know not, I ask not, if guilt's in that heart,
  But I know that I love thee, whatever thou art. *Ib.*

17 Erin, the tear and the smile in thine eyes,
  Blend like the rainbow that hangs in thy skies!
  Ib. Erin, the Tear

18 You may break, you may shatter the vase, if you will,
  But the scent of the roses will hang round it still.
  Ib. Farewell! But Whenever

19 Go where glory waits thee,
  But, while fame elates thee,
  Oh! still remember me.
  Irish Melodies. Go Where Glory

20 The harp that once through Tara's halls
  The soul of music shed,
  Now hangs as mute on Tara's walls
  As if that soul were fled.—
  So sleeps the pride of former days,
  So glory's thrill is o'er;
  And hearts, that once beat high for praise,
  Now feel that pulse no more.
  Ib. The Harp that Once

21 Thus freedom now so seldom wakes,
  The only throb she gives,
  Is when some heart indignant breaks,
  To show that still she lives. *Ib.*

22 Has sorrow thy young days shaded?
  Ib. Has Sorrow Thy Young

23 And, when once the young heart of a maiden is stolen,
  The maiden herself will steal after it soon.
  Ib. Ill Omens

24 Lesbia hath a beaming eye,
  But no one knows for whom it beameth.
  Ib. Lesbia Hath

25 No, there's nothing half so sweet in life
  As love's young dream. *Ib. Love's Young Dream*

26 There is not in the wide world a valley so sweet
  As that vale in whose bosom the bright waters meet.
  Ib. The Meeting of the Waters

27 The Minstrel Boy to the war is gone,
  In the ranks of death you'll find him;
  His father's sword he has girded on,
  And his wild harp slung behind him.
  Ib. The Minstrel Boy

28 Oh! blame not the bard. *Ib. Oh! Blame Not*

29 Oh! breathe not his name, let it sleep in the shade,
  Where cold and unhonour'd his relics are laid.
  Ib. Oh! Breathe not his Name

30 Rich and rare were the gems she wore,
  And a bright gold ring on her wand she bore.
  Ib. Rich and Rare

31 She is far from the land where her young hero sleeps,
  And lovers are round her, sighing;
  But coldly she turns from their gaze, and weeps,
  For her heart in his grave is lying. *Ib. She is Far*

32 The light, that lies
  In woman's eyes,
  Has been my heart's undoing. *Ib. The Time I've Lost*

33 My only books
  Were woman's looks,
  And folly's all they've taught me. *Ib.*

34 This life is all chequer'd with pleasures and woes.
  Ib. This Life is All Chequered

35 'Tis sweet to think, that, where'er we rove,
  We are sure to find something blissful and dear,
  And that, when we're far from the lips we love,
  We've but to make love to the lips we are near.
  Ib. 'Tis Sweet to Think

36 'Tis the last rose of summer
  Left blooming alone;
  All her lovely companions
  Are faded and gone. *Ib. 'Tis the Last Rose*

1 Then awake! the heavens look bright, my dear;
'Tis never too late for delight, my dear;
And the best of all ways
To lengthen our days
Is to steal a few hours from the night, my dear!
Irish Melodies. The Young May Moon

2 Where I love I must not marry;
Where I marry, cannot love.
Juvenile Poems. Love and Marriage

3 'Twere more than woman to be wise;
'Twere more than man to wish thee so!
Ib. The Ring (ed. 1882)

4 To love you was pleasant enough,
And, oh! 'tis delicious to hate you!
Ib. To—When I Lov'd You

5 Oh! ever thus, from childhood's hour,
I've seen my fondest hopes decay;
I never lov'd a tree or flow'r,
But 'twas the first to fade away.
I never nurs'd a dear gazelle,
To glad me with its soft black eye,
But when it came to know me well,
And love me, it was sure to die!
Lalla Rookh. The Fire-Worshippers, i, l. 279

6 Like Dead Sea fruits, that tempt the eye,
But turn to ashes on the lips! *Ib.* l. 484

7 One Morn a Peri at the gate
Of Eden stood, disconsolate.
Ib. Paradise and the Peri, l. 1

8 Some flow'rets of Eden ye still inherit,
But the trail of the Serpent is over them all!
Ib. l. 206

9 And, when all hope seem'd desp'rate, wildly hurl'd
Himself into the scale, and sav'd a world.
Ib. The Veiled Prophet, iii, l. 211

10 But Faith, fanatic Faith, once wedded fast
To some dear falsehood, hugs it to the last. *Ib.* l. 356

11 'Come, come', said Tom's father, 'at your time of life,
'There's no longer excuse for thus playing the
rake—
'It is time you should think, boy, of taking a wife'—
'Why, so it is, father—whose wife shall I take?'
Miscellaneous Poems. A Joke Versified

12 Disguise our bondage as we will,
'Tis woman, woman, rules us still.
Ib. Sovereign Woman

13 Oft, in the stilly night,
Ere Slumber's chain has bound me,
Fond Memory brings the light
Of other days around me;
The smiles, the tears,
Of boyhood's years,
The words of love then spoken;
The eyes that shone,
Now dimm'd and gone,
The cheerful hearts now broken!
National Airs. Oft in the Stilly Night

14 I feel like one
Who treads alone
Some banquet-hall deserted,
Whose lights are fled,
Whose garlands dead,
And all but he departed! *Ib.*

15 Those evening bells! those evening bells!
How many a tale their music tells,
Of youth, and home, and that sweet time
When last I heard their soothing chime.
National Airs. Those Evening Bells

16 Faintly as tolls the evening chime
Our voices keep tune and our oars keep time.
Soon as the woods on shore look dim,
We'll sing at St. Ann's our parting hymn.
Row, brothers, row, the stream runs fast,
The Rapids are near and the daylight's past.
Poems Relating to America. Canadian Boat Song

17 Sound the loud timbrel o'er Egypt's dark sea!
Jehovah has triumph'd—his people are free.
Sacred Songs. Miriam's Song. Sound the Loud Timbrel

18 There was a little Man, and he had a little Soul,
And he said, 'Little Soul, let us try, try, try'.
Satirical and Humorous Poems. Little Man and Little Soul

19 And one wild Shakespeare, following Nature's lights,
Is worth whole planets, filled with Stagyrites.
The Sceptic

20 Your priests, whate'er their gentle shamming,
Have always had a taste for damning.
Twopenny Post-Bag, letter iv

21 Good at a fight, but better at a play,
Godlike in giving, but—the devil to pay!
On a Cast of Sheridan's Hand. Memoirs of the Life of R. B. Sheridan (1825), p. 712

THOMAS OSBERT MORDAUNT
1730–1809

22 Sound, sound the clarion, fill the fife,
Throughout the sensual world proclaim,
One crowded hour of glorious life
Is worth an age without a name.
The Bee, 12 Oct. 1791. Verses Written During the War, 1756–1763

HANNAH MORE
1745–1833

23 For you'll ne'er mend your fortunes, nor help the just cause,
By breaking of windows, or breaking of laws.
Address to the Meeting in Spa Fields (1817). H. Thompson's *Life* (1838), p. 398

24 A crown! what is it?
It is to bear the miseries of a people!
To hear their murmurs, feel their discontents,
And sink beneath a load of splendid care!
Daniel, pt. vi, l. 72

25 Small habits, well pursued betimes,
May reach the dignity of crimes. *Florio*, l. 77

26 He lik'd those literary cooks
Who skim the cream of others' books;
And ruin half an author's graces
By plucking bon-mots from their places. *Ib.* l. 123

27 Did not God
Sometimes withhold in mercy what we ask,
We should be ruined at our own request.
Moses in the Bulrushes, pt. i, l. 34

1 The sober comfort, all the peace which springs
From the large aggregate of little things;
On these small cares of daughter, wife, or friend,
The almost sacred joys of home depend.
Sensibility, l. 315

SIR THOMAS MORE
1478–1535

2 'In good faith, I rejoiced, son,' quoth he, 'that I had
given the devil a foul fall, and that with those Lords
I had gone so far, as without great shame I could
never go back again.'
Roper, *Life of Sir Thomas More* (1935), p. 69

3 'By god body, master More, *Indignatio principis mors
est.*'
'Is that all, my Lord?' quoth he. 'Then in good faith
is there no more difference between your grace and
me, but that I shall die to-day, and you to-morrow.'
Ib. p. 71

4 Son Roper, I thank our Lord the field is won.
Ib. p. 73

5 Is not this house [the Tower of London] as nigh
heaven as my own? *Ib.* p. 83

6 I pray you, master Lieutenant, see me safe up, and
my coming down let me shift for my self. [On
mounting the scaffold.] *Ib.* p. 103

7 Pluck up thy spirits, man, and be not afraid to do
thine office; my neck is very short; take heed therefore thou strike not awry, for saving of thine
honesty. [To the Executioner.] *Ib.* p. 103

8 This hath not offended the king. [As he drew his
beard aside on placing his head on the block.]
Bacon, *Apophthegms*, 22

9 Yea, marry, now it is somewhat, for now it is rhyme;
before, it was neither rhyme nor reason. [Advising
an author to put his ill-written work into verse.]
A. Cayley's *Memoirs of Sir Thos. More* (1808),
vol. i, p. 247

10 They roll and rumble,
They turn and tumble,
As pigges do in a poke.
Works (1557), ¶ ii. 6. *How a Sergeant would learn
to Play the Frere*

11 This is a fair tale of a tub told us of his elects.
Ib. p. 576. *Confutation of Tyndale's Answers*

12 Your sheep, that were wont to be so meek and tame,
and so small eaters, now, as I hear say, be become
so great devourers, and so wild, that they eat up
and swallow down the very men themselves.
Utopia, bk. 1

THOMAS MORELL
1703–1784

13 See, the conquering hero comes!
Sound the trumpets, beat the drums! *Joshua*, pt. iii

AUGUSTUS DE MORGAN
1806–1871

14 Great fleas have little fleas upon their backs to bite
'em,
And little fleas have lesser fleas, and so *ad infinitum*.
A Budget of Paradoxes (1872), p. 377

ALBERT EDMUND PARKER, EARL OF MORLEY
1843–1905

15 I am always very glad when Lord Salisbury makes a
great speech, . . . It is sure to contain at least one
blazing indiscretion which it is a delight to remember. *Speech, Hull, 25 Nov. 1887*

JOHN, VISCOUNT MORLEY OF BLACKBURN
1838–1923

16 No man can climb out beyond the limitations of his
own character.
Critical Miscellanies (1886), i, *Robespierre*, p. 93

17 [Letter-writing,] that most delightful way of wasting
time. *Ib.* iii. *Life of Geo. Eliot*, p. 96

18 The whole of the golden Gospel of Silence is now
effectively compressed in thirty-five volumes.
Ib. Carlyle, p. 195

CHARLES MORRIS
1745–1838

19 If one must have a villa in summer to dwell,
Oh, give me the sweet shady side of Pall Mall!
The Contrast

20 A house is much more to my taste than a tree,
And for groves, oh! a good grove of chimneys for me.
Ib.

GEORGE POPE MORRIS
1802–1867

21 Woodman, spare that tree!
Touch not a single bough!
In youth it sheltered me,
And I'll protect it now.
Woodman, Spare That Tree

SIR LEWIS MORRIS
1833–1907

22 How far high failure overleaps the bounds of low
success. *The Epic of Hades, Marsyas*

WILLIAM MORRIS
1834–1896

23 One of these cloths is heaven, and one is hell,
Now choose one cloth for ever; which they be,
I will not tell you, you must somehow tell
Of your own strength and mightiness.
Defence of Guenevere

24 And one of these strange choosing cloths was blue,
Wavy and long, and one cut short and red;
No man could tell the better of the two.

After a shivering half-hour you said:
'God help! heaven's colour, the blue;' and he said:
'hell'.
Perhaps you then would roll upon your bed,

And cry to all good men that loved you well,
'Ah Christ! if only I had known, known, known.' *Ib.*

25 The idle singer of an empty day.
The Earthly Paradise. An Apology

1 Dreamer of dreams, born out of my due time,
   Why should I strive to set the crooked straight?
Let it suffice me that my murmuring rhyme
   Beats with light wing against the ivory gate,
   Telling a tale not too importunate
To those who in the sleepy region stay,
Lulled by the singer of an empty day.
       The Earthly Paradise. An Apology

2 Forget six counties overhung with smoke,
Forget the snorting steam and piston stroke,
Forget the spreading of the hideous town;
Think rather of the pack-horse on the down,
And dream of London, small and white and clean,
The clear Thames bordered by its gardens green.
       Ib. Prologue. *The Wanderers*, l. 1

3 Death have we hated, knowing not what it meant;
Life we have loved, through green leaf and through
   sere,
Though still the less we knew of its intent.
       Ib. L'Envoi, xiii

4 Had she come all the way for this,
To part at last without a kiss?
Yea, had she borne the dirt and rain
That her own eyes might see him slain
Beside the haystack in the floods?
       The Haystack in the Floods

5 I know a little garden close
Set thick with lily and red rose,
Where I would wander if I might
From dewy dawn to dewy night,
And have one with me wandering.
       The Life and Death of Jason, l. 577

6 Love is enough: though the world be a-waning,
And the woods have no voice but the voice of complaining.   *Love is Enough*, i

7 But lo, the old inn, and the lights, and the fire,
And the fiddler's old tune and the shuffling of feet;
Soon for us shall be quiet and rest and desire,
And to-morrow's uprising to deeds shall be sweet.
       The Message of the March Winds

8 You must be very old, Sir Giles.   *Old Love*

9 They hammer'd out my basnet point
Into a round salade.   *Ib.*

10 My lady seems of ivory
Forehead, straight nose, and cheeks that be
Hollow'd a little mournfully.
  Beata mea Domina!   *Praise of my Lady*

11 Across the empty garden-beds,
When the Sword went out to sea.
       The Sailing of the Sword

12 There were four of us about that bed;
The mass-priest knelt at the side. *Shameful Death*

13 He did not die in the night,
  He did not die in the day.   *Ib.*

14 It is the longest night in all the year,
Near on the day when the Lord Christ was born;
Six hours ago I came and sat down here,
And ponder'd sadly, wearied and forlorn.
       Sir Galahad, A Christmas Mystery, l. 1

15 O servant of the high God, Galahad!   *Ib.* l. 153

16 Speak but one word to me over the corn,
Over the tender, bow'd locks of the corn.
       Summer Dawn

17 And ever she sung from noon to noon,
'Two red roses across the moon.'
       Two Red Roses Across the Moon

18 Wind, wind! thou art sad, art thou kind? *The Wind*

19 Forsooth, brothers, fellowship is heaven, and lack of
fellowship is hell: fellowship is life, and lack of
fellowship is death: and the deeds that ye do upon
the earth, it is for fellowship's sake that ye do them.
       The Dream of John Ball, ch. 4

THOMAS MORTON
1764?–1838

20 Approbation from Sir Hubert Stanley is praise indeed.
       A Cure for the Heartache, v. ii

21 I eat well, and I drink well, and I sleep well—but
that's all.   *A Roland for an Oliver*, I. ii

22 Always ding, dinging Dame Grundy into my ears—
what will Mrs. Grundy zay? What will Mrs.
Grundy think?   *Speed the Plough*, I. i

JOHN LOTHROP MOTLEY
1814–1877

23 As long as he lived, he was the guiding-star of a whole
brave nation, and when he died the little children
cried in the streets. [William of Orange.]
       Rise of the Dutch Republic, pt. vi, ch. vii

24 Give us the luxuries of life, and we will dispense with
its necessities.
   Remark. O. W. Holmes, *Autocrat of the Breakfast-
Table*, ch. 6

PETER ANTHONY MOTTEUX
1660–1718

25 The devil was sick, the devil a monk wou'd be;
The devil was well, and the devil a monk he'd be.
   Translation of Rabelais. *Gargantua and Panta-
gruel*, bk. iv, ch. 24

HENRY PHIPPS, EARL OF MULGRAVE
1755–1831

26 And toast before each martial tune—
'Howe, and the Glorious First of June!'
       Our Line was Formed

DINAH MARIA MULOCK
see
MRS. DINAH MARIA CRAIK

ANTHONY MUNDAY
1553–1633

27 Beauty sat bathing by a spring
  Where fairest shades did hide her;
The winds blew calm, the birds did sing,
  The cool streams ran beside her.
My wanton thoughts enticed mine eye
  To see what was forbidden:
But better memory said, fie!
  So vain desire was chidden.
      Hey nonny, nonny.
      England's Helicon. To Colin Clout

HECTOR HUGH MUNRO

see

SAKI

C. W. MURPHY

1 We all go the same way home. *Title of Song*

2 Has anybody here seen Kelly?
Kelly from the Isle of Man?
Has Anybody Here seen Kelly?

3 Kelly from the Em'rald Isle. *Ib.*

CHARLES MURRAY

1864–1941

4 Gin danger's there, we'll thole our share,
Gie's but the weapons, we've the will,
Ayont the main, to prove again
Auld Scotland counts for something still. *Hamewith*

FRED MURRAY

5 Carve a little bit off the top for me!
A Little Bit Off The Top

6 Our lodger's such a nice young man. *Title of Song*

ALFRED DE MUSSET

1810–1857

7 Mon verre n'est pas grand mais je bois dans mon verre.
The glass I drink from is not large, but at least it
is my own. *La Coupe et les Lèvres.*

8 Le seul bien qui me reste au monde
Est d'avoir quelquefois pleuré.
The only good thing left to me
Is knowledge that I, too, have wept. *Poèmes*

9 Malgré moi l'infini me tourmente.
I can't help it, the idea of the infinite is a torment to
me. *Premières Poésies, L'Espoir en Dieu*

FREDERICK WILLIAM HENRY MYERS

1843–1901

10 Moses on the mountain
Died of the kisses of the lips of God.
Saint Paul, st. 127

11 Yea, thro' life, death, thro' sorrow and thro' sinning,
He shall suffice me, for he hath sufficed:
Christ is the end, for Christ is the beginning,
Christ the beginning for the end is Christ.
Ib. st. 150

CAROLINA, BARONESS NAIRNE

1766–1845

12 Will ye no come back again?
Better lo'ed ye canna be,
Will ye no come back again?
Life and Songs (1869), *Bonnie Charlie's now awa'*

13 Wha'll buy my caller herrin'?
They're bonnie fish and halesome farin';
Wha'll buy my caller herrin',
New drawn frae the Forth? *Ib. Caller Herrin'*

14 Oh, ye may ca' them vulgar farin',
Wives and mithers maist despairin',
Ca' them lives o' men.
Life and Songs (1869), *Caller Herrin'*

15 Charlie is my darling, my darling, my darling,
Charlie is my darling, the young Chevalier.
Ib. Charlie is My Darling

16 Gude nicht, and joy be wi' you a'. *Ib. Gude Nicht*

17 Wi' a hundred pipers an' a', an' a',
Wi' a hundred pipers an' a', an' a',
We'll up an' gie them a blaw, a blaw,
Wi' a hundred pipers an' a', an' a'.
Ib. The Hundred Pipers

18 A penniless lass wi' a lang pedigree.
Ib. The Laird of Cockpen

19 I'm wearin' awa'
To the land o' the leal. *Ib. The Land o' the Leal*

20 There's nae sorrow there, John,
There's neither cauld nor care, John,
The day is aye fair
In the land o' the leal. *Ib.*

SIR WILLIAM NAPIER

1785–1860

21 Then was seen with what a strength and majesty the
British soldier fights.
History of the War in the Peninsula, bk. xii, ch. 6,
Albuera

NAPOLEON I

1769–1821

22 L'Angleterre est une nation de boutiquiers.
England is a nation of shopkeepers.
*Attr. by B.B.E. O'Meara, Napoleon at St. Helena,
vol. ii. The original is probably 'sono mercanti',
a phrase of Paoli, quoted by Napoleon; see Gourgaud*, Journal Inédit de Ste-Hélène, i. 69.(*See
1:6, 503:11*)

23 Tout soldat français porte dans sa giberne le bâton de
maréchal de France.
Every French soldier carries in his cartridge-pouch
the baton of a marshal of France.
E. Blaze, *La Vie Militaire sous l'Empire*, i. v

24 A la guerre, les trois quarts sont des affaires morales,
la balance des forces réelles n'est que pour un
autre quart.
In war, moral considerations make up three-quar-
ters of the game: the relative balance of man-
power accounts only for the remaining quarter.
Correspondance de Napoléon Ier, xvii, no. 14276
(*Observations sur les affaires d'Espagne, Saint-
Cloud, 27 août 1808*)

25 Quant au courage moral, il avait trouvé fort rare,
disait-il, celui de deux heures après minuit; c'est-
à-dire le courage de l'improviste.
As to moral courage, I have very rarely met with
the two o'clock in the morning courage: I mean
unprepared courage.
Las Cases, *Mémorial de Ste-Hélène*, Dec. 4–5,
1815

26 La carrière ouverte aux talents.
The career open to talents.
O'Meara, *Napoleon in Exile* (1822), vol. i, p. 103

1 Soldats, songez que, du haut de ces pyramides, quarante siècles vous contemplent.

Think of it, soldiers; from the summit of these pyramids, forty centuries look down upon you.
Speech to the Army of Egypt on 21 July 1798, before the Battle of the Pyramids. Gourgaud, *Mémoires, Guerre d'Orient,* i, p. 160

2 Du sublime au ridicule il n'y a qu'un pas.

There is only one step from the sublime to the ridiculous.
To De Pradt, Polish ambassador, after the retreat from Moscow in 1812. De Pradt, *Histoire de l'Ambassade dans le grand-duché de Varsovie en 1812,* ed. 1815, p. 215.

3 Voilà le soleil d'Austerlitz.

There rises the sun of Austerlitz.
To his officers, before Moscow, 7 Sept. 1812

4 Tête d'Armée.   *Last words*

THOMAS NASHE
1567–1601

5 Brightness falls from the air;
Queens have died young and fair;
Dust hath closed Helen's eye.
I am sick, I must die.
Lord have mercy on us.   *In Time of Pestilence*

6 Spring, the sweet spring, is the year's pleasant king;
Then blooms each thing, then maids dance in a ring,
Cold doth not sting, the pretty birds do sing:
Cuckoo, jug-jug, pu-we, to-witta-woo!   *Spring*

JAMES BALL NAYLOR
1860–1945

7 King David and King Solomon
Led merry, merry lives,
With many, many lady friends
And many, many wives;
But when old age crept over them,
With many, many qualms,
King Solomon wrote the Proverbs
And King David wrote the Psalms,
David and Solomon

JAMES MASON NEALE
1818–1866

8 All glory, laud, and honour
To Thee, Redeemer, King,
To whom the lips of children
Made sweet Hosannas ring.
All Glory, Laud, and Honour, trans. from Latin *Gloria, Laus et Honor tibi sit.*

9 Around the throne of God a band
Of glorious Angels always stand.
Around the Throne of God. Hymns for Children, First Series (1842)

10 Art thou weary, art thou languid,
Art thou sore distressed?
Art Thou Weary, trans. from Greek

11 Angels, Martyrs, Prophets, Virgins,
Answer, Yes!   *Ib.*

12 Brief life is here our portion;
Brief sorrow, short-lived care.
Brief Life is Here, trans. from Latin, *Hic breve Vivitur*

13 Christian, dost thou see them
On the holy ground,
How the troops of Midian
Prowl and prowl around?

Christian, up and smite them,
Counting gain but loss;
Smite them by the merit
Of the holy Cross.
Christian, Dost Thou See Them, trans. from Greek

14 Laud and honour to the Father,
Laud and honour to the Son,
Laud and honour to the Spirit,
Ever Three and ever One;
Consubstantial, co-eternal,
While unending ages run.
Come ye Faithful, Raise the Anthem. The Christian Remembrancer, July 1863

15 Loosed from Pharaoh's bitter yoke
Jacob's sons and daughters;
Led them with unmoisten'd foot
Through the Red Sea waters.
Come ye Faithful, Raise the Strain, trans. from Greek

16 Endless noon-day, glorious noon-day.
Light's Abode, Celestial Salem, trans. from Latin, *Hierusalem Luminosa*

17 For thee, O dear, dear Country,
Mine eyes their vigils keep.
For Thee, O Dear, Dear Country, trans. from Latin, *O Bona Patria*

18 Good Christian men, rejoice
With heart, and soul, and voice.
Good Christian Men, Helmore and Neale, *Carols for Christmastide*

19 Good King Wenceslas look'd out,
On the Feast of Stephen;
When the snow lay round about,
Deep and crisp and even.
Good King Wenceslas. Helmore and Neale, *Carols for Christmastide*

20 'Hither, page, and stand by me,
If thou know'st it, telling,
Yonder peasant, who is he?
Where and what his dwelling?'   *Ib.*

21 'Bring me flesh and bring me wine,
Bring me pine-logs hither.'   *Ib.*

22 Page and monarch, forth they went,
Forth they went together.   *Ib.*

23 'Sire, the night is darker now,
And the wind blows stronger,
Fails my heart, I know not how;
I can go no longer.'
'Mark my footsteps, good my page,
Tread thou in them boldly,
Thou shalt find the winter's rage
Freeze thy blood less coldly.'   *Ib.*

24 In his master's steps he trod,
Where the snow lay dinted;
Heat was in the very sod
Which the Saint had printed.
Wherefore, Christian men, be sure,
Wealth or rank possessing,
Ye who now do bless the poor
Shall yourselves find blessing.   *Ib.*

1 Jerusalem the golden,
   With milk and honey blest,
Beneath thy contemplation
   Sink heart and voice opprest.
I know not, oh, I know not,
   What joys await us there,
What radiancy of glory,
   What bliss beyond compare.
      Jerusalem the Golden, trans. from Latin, *Urbs
      Syon Aurea*

2 And bright with many an angel
   And all the martyr throng.   *Ib.*

3 The pastures of the blessèd
   Are deck'd in glorious sheen.   *Ib.*

4 The shout of them that triumph,
   The song of them that feast.   *Ib.*

5 O sweet and blessèd country
   That eager hearts expect!   *Ib.*

6 O come, O come, Emmanuel,
   And ransom captive Israel.
      O Come, O Come, Emmanuel, trans. from Latin,
      Veni, Veni, Emmanuel

7 O happy band of pilgrims,
   If onward ye will tread.
      *O Happy Band of Pilgrims. Hymns of the Eastern
      Church*

8 O happy band of pilgrims,
   Look upward to the skies,
Where such a light affliction
   Shall win you such a prize!   *Ib.*

9 Oh, what the joy and the glory must be,
   Those endless Sabbaths the blessèd ones see.
      Oh, what the Joy, trans. from Latin of Abelard,
      O quanta qualia sunt illa Sabbata

10 Raise the 'Trisagion' ever and aye.
      *Stars of the Morning. Hymns of the Eastern
      Church*

11 Safe home, safe home in port!
   Rent cordage, shatter'd deck,
Torn sails, provisions short,
   And only not a wreck.
      *Safe Home, Safe Home. Hymns of the Eastern
      Church*

12 The prize, the prize secure!
   The athlete nearly fell.   *Ib.*

HORATIO, VISCOUNT NELSON
1758–1805

13 Palmam qui meruit, ferat.
   Let him who merits bear the palm.   *Motto*

14 Sent Admiral Collingwood the Nelson touch.
      Private Diary, 9 Oct. 1805

15 It is my turn now; and if I come back, it is yours.
      *Exercising his privilege, as second lieutenant,
      to board a prize ship before the Master.* Southey's
      Life of Nelson, ch. 1, *Nelson's Memoir of His
      Services.*

16 You must consider every man your enemy who speaks
   ill of your king: and . . . you must hate a Frenchman as you hate the devil.   *Ib.* ch. 3

17 Westminster Abbey or victory!
      At the battle of Cape St. Vincent. Ib. ch. 4

18 Before this time to-morrow I shall have gained a
   peerage, or Westminster Abbey.
      Battle of the Nile. Southey's *Life of Nelson*, ch. 5

19 Victory is not a name strong enough for such a scene.
      At the battle of the Nile. Ib.

20 It is warm work; and this day may be the last to
   any of us at a moment. But mark you! I would
   not be elsewhere for thousands.
      At the battle of Copenhagen. Ib. ch. 7

21 I have only one eye,—I have a right to be blind sometimes: . . . I really do not see the signal!
      At the battle of Copenhagen. Ib.

22 In honour I gained them, and in honour I will die with
   them.
      When asked to cover the stars on his uniform. Ib. ch. 9

23 England expects every man will do his duty.
      At the battle of Trafalgar. Ib.

24 This is too warm work, Hardy, to last long.   *Ib.*

25 Thank God, I have done my duty.   *Ib.*

26 Kiss me, Hardy.   *Ib.*

NERO
A.D. 37–68

27 Qualis artifex pereo!
   What an artist dies with me!
      Suetonius, *Life of Nero*, xlix. 1

EDITH NESBIT
1858–1924

28 Little brown brother, oh! little brown brother,
   Are you awake in the dark?   *Baby Seed Song*

ALLAN NEVINS
1890–

29 The former allies had blundered in the past by offering Germany too little, and offering even that too
   late, until finally Nazi Germany had become a
   menace to all mankind.
      Article in 'Current History', May 1935

SIR HENRY JOHN NEWBOLT
1862–1938

30 Effingham, Grenville, Raleigh, Drake,
   Here's to the bold and free!
Benbow, Collingwood, Byron, Blake,
   Hail to the kings of the sea!   *Admirals All, i*

31 Admirals all, for England's sake,
   Honour be yours, and fame!
And honour, as long as waves shall break,
   To Nelson's peerless name!   *Ib.*

32 He clapped the glass to his sightless eye,
   And 'I'm damned if I see it', he said.   *Ib.*

33 To set the Cause above renown,
   To love the game beyond the prize,
To honour, while you strike him down,
   The foe that comes with fearless eyes:
To count the life of battle good,
   And dear the land that gave you birth,
And dearer yet the brotherhood
   That binds the brave of all the earth.
      The Island Race, Clifton Chapel

1 'Qui procul hinc', the legend's writ,—
  The frontier-grave is far away—
  'Qui ante diem periit:
  Sed miles, sed pro patria.'
  The Island Race, Clifton Chapel

2 'Take my drum to England, hang et by the shore,
  Strike et when your powder's runnin' low;
  If the Dons sight Devon, I'll quit the port o' Heaven,
  An' drum them up the Channel as we drummed them
  long ago.'   *Ib. Drake's Drum*

3 Drake he's in his hammock till the great Armadas
  come.
  (Capten, art tha sleepin' there below?)
  Slung atween the round shot, listenin' for the drum,
  An' dreamin' arl the time o' Plymouth Hoe.
  Call him on the deep sea, call him up the Sound,
  Call him when ye sail to meet the foe;
  Where the old trade's plyin' an' the old flag flyin'
  They shall find him ware an' wakin', as they found
  him long ago!   *Ib.*

4 There's a breathless hush in the Close to-night—
  Ten to make and the match to win—
  A bumping pitch and a blinding light,
  An hour to play and the last man in.
  And it's not for the sake of a ribboned coat,
  Or the selfish hope of a season's fame,
  But his Captain's hand on his shoulder smote—
  'Play up! play up! and play the game!'
      Ib. Vitaï Lampada

5 The voice of the schoolboy rallies the ranks:
  'Play up! play up! and play the game!'   *Ib.*

6 Now the sunset breezes shiver,
  And she's fading down the river,
  But in England's song for ever
  She's the Fighting Téméraire.
      The Fighting Téméraire

7 'Ye have robb'd', said he, 'ye have slaughter'd and
  made an end,
  Take your ill-got plunder, and bury the dead.'
      He Fell Among Thieves

8 But cared greatly to serve God and the King,
  And keep the Nelson touch.   *Minora Sidera*

MARGARET, DUCHESS OF NEWCASTLE
1624?–1673

9 Her name was Margarett Lucas, yongest sister to the
  Lord Lucas of Colchester, a noble familie; for all
  the Brothers were Valiant, and all the Sisters
  virtuous.   *Epitaph, Westminster Abbey*

JOHN HENRY, CARDINAL NEWMAN
1801–1890

10 It is very difficult to get up resentment towards
  persons whom one has never seen.
  Apologia pro Vita Sua (1864). *Mr. Kingsley's
  Method of Disputation*

11 There is such a thing as legitimate warfare: war has
  its laws; there are things which may fairly be done,
  and things which may not be done. . . . He has
  attempted (as I may call it) to *poison the wells. Ib.*

12 I will vanquish, not my Accuser, but my judges.
      Ib. True Mode of meeting Mr. Kingsley

13 I used to wish the Arabian Tales were true.
  Apologia pro Vita Sua (1864). *History of My
  Religious Opinions to the Year 1833*

14 Two and two only supreme and luminously self-
  evident beings, myself and my Creator.   *Ib.*

15 Growth [is] the only evidence of life.   *Ib.*

16 The motto [of *Lyra Apostolica*] shows the feeling of
  both [Hurrell] Froude and myself at the time: we
  borrowed from M. Bunsen a Homer, and Froude
  chose the words in which Achilles, on returning to
  the battle, says, 'You shall know the difference now
  that I am back again'.   *Ib.*

17 It would be a gain to the country were it vastly more
  superstitious, more bigoted, more gloomy, more
  fierce in its religion than at present it shows itself
  to be.
  *Ib. History of My Religious Opinions from
  1833 to 1839*

18 From the age of fifteen, dogma has been the fundamental principle of my religion: I know no other
  religion; I cannot enter into the idea of any other
  sort of religion; religion, as a mere sentiment, is
  to me a dream and a mockery.   *Ib.*

19 This is what the Church is said to want, not party
  men, but sensible, temperate, sober, well-judging
  persons, to guide it through the channel of no-
  meaning, between the Scylla and Charybdis of Aye
  and No.
  *Ib. History of My Religious Opinions from 1839
  to 1841*

20 I recollect an acquaintance saying to me that 'the
  Oriel Common Room stank of Logic'.
  *Ib. History of My Religious Opinions from 1841
  to 1845*

21 Cowards! If I advanced one step, you would run
  away.   *Ib.*

22 Trinity had never been unkind to me. There used
  to be much snap-dragon growing on the walls
  opposite my freshman's rooms there, and I had
  for years taken it as the emblem of my own perpetual residence even unto death in my University.
  On the morning of the 23rd I left the Observa-
  tory. I have never seen Oxford since, excepting its
  spires, as they are seen from the railway.   *Ib.*

23 Ten thousand difficulties do not make one doubt.
      Ib. Position of My Mind since 1845

24 The all-corroding, all-dissolving scepticism of the
  intellect in religious enquiries.   *Ib.*

25 It is almost a definition of a gentleman to say that he
  is one who never inflicts pain.
  *The Idea of a University. Knowledge and Religious
  Duty*

26 Take a mere beggar-woman, lazy, ragged, filthy, and
  not over-scrupulous of truth,—but if she is chaste,
  and sober, and cheerful, and goes to her religious
  duties—she will, in the eyes of the Church, have
  a prospect of heaven, quite closed and refused to
  the State's pattern-man, the just, the upright, the
  generous, the honourable, the conscientious, if he
  be all this, not from a supernatural power,—but
  from mere natural virtue.
      Lectures on Anglican Difficulties. Lecture VIII

1 She [the Catholic Church] holds that it were better for sun and moon to drop from heaven, for the earth to fail, and for all the many millions who are upon it to die of starvation in extremest agony, as far as temporal affliction goes, than that one soul, I will not say, should be lost, but should commit one single venial sin, should tell one wilful untruth, . . . or steal one poor farthing without excuse.
Lectures on Anglican Difficulties. Lecture VIII

2 Ex umbris et imaginibus in veritatem.
From shadows and types to the reality. *Motto*

3 Cor ad cor loquitur.
Heart speaks to heart.
Motto adopted for his coat-of-arms as cardinal. 1879

4 May He support us all the day long, till the shades lengthen, and the evening comes, and the busy world is hushed, and the fever of life is over, and our work is done! Then in His mercy may He give us a safe lodging, and a holy rest, and peace at the last. *Sermon, 1834. Wisdom and Innocence*

5 Firmly I believe and truly
God is Three, and God is One;
And I next acknowledge duly
Manhood taken by the Son.
The Dream of Gerontius

6 Praise to the Holiest in the height,
And in the depth be praise;
In all his words most wonderful,
Most sure in all His ways. *Ib.*

7 A second Adam to the fight
And to the rescue came. *Ib.*

8 O wisest love! that flesh and blood
Which did in Adam fail,
Should strive afresh against their foe,
Should strive and should prevail. *Ib.*

9 Prune thou thy words, the thoughts control
That o'er thee swell and throng;
They will condense within thy soul,
And change to purpose strong.
Flowers Without Fruit. Prune Thou Thy Words

10 Lead, kindly Light, amid the encircling gloom,
Lead thou me on;
They night is dark, and I am far from home,
Lead thou me on.
Keep Thou my feet; I do not ask to see
The distant scene; one step enough for me.
The Pillar of Cloud. Lead Kindly Light

11 I loved the garish day, and, spite of fears,
Pride ruled my will: remember not past years. *Ib.*

12 And with the morn those Angel faces smile,
Which I have loved long since, and lost awhile. *Ib.*

SIR ISAAC NEWTON
1642–1727

13 I do not know what I may appear to the world, but to myself I seem to have been only a boy playing on the sea-shore, and diverting myself in now and then finding a smoother pebble or a prettier shell than ordinary, whilst the great ocean of truth lay all undiscovered before me.
Brewster's *Memoirs of Newton*, vol. ii, ch. 27

14 O Diamond! Diamond! thou little knowest the mischief done!
Remark to a dog who knocked down a candle and so set fire to some papers and 'destroyed the almost finished labours of some years'. Thomas Maude, Wensley-Dale . . . a Poem (1780), p. 28, note

JOHN NEWTON
1725–1807

15 How sweet the name of Jesus sounds
In a believer's ear!
It soothes his sorrows, heals his wounds,
And drives away his fear.
Olney Hymns (1779), How Sweet the Name

16 Glorious things of thee are spoken,
Zion, city of our God. *Ib. Glorious Things of Thee*

NICHOLAS I OF RUSSIA
1796–1855

17 Nous avons sur les bras un homme malade—un homme gravement malade.
We have on our hands a sick man—a very sick man.
[The sick man of Europe, the Turk.]
Parliamentary Papers. Accounts and Papers, vol. lxxi, pt. 5. Eastern Papers, p. 2. Sir G. H. Seymour to Lord John Russell, 11 Jan. 1853

18 Russia has two generals in whom she can confide—Generals Janvier and Février.
Punch, 10 Mar. 1853. Speech of the late Emperor of Russia

NICIAS
c. 470–413 B.C.

19 ἄνδρες γὰρ πόλις, καὶ οὐ τείχη οὐδὲ νῆες ἀνδρῶν κεναί.
It is men who make a city, not walls or ships without crews.
Speech to his army after his defeat by the Syracusans (413 B.C.). Thucydides, vii. 77.

ADELA FLORENCE NICOLSON
see
LAURENCE HOPE

FRIEDRICH WILHELM NIETZSCHE
1844–1900

20 Jenseits von Gut und Böse.
Beyond good and evil. *Title of Book*

21 Herren-Moral und Sklaven-Moral.
Morality of masters and the morality of slaves.
Jenseits von Gut und Böse

22 Ich lehre euch den Übermenschen. Der Mensch ist Etwas, das überwunden werden soll.
I teach you the superman. Man is something to be surpassed. *Thus Spake Zarathustra. Prologue*

23 Blonde Bestie.
Blonde beast. *Zur Genealogie der Moral*

'NIMROD' [CHARLES JAMES APPERLEY]

1779-1843

1 'Who is that under his horse in the brook?'
'Only Dick Christian,' answers Lord Forester, 'and
it's nothing new to him.'
'But he'll be drowned,' exclaims Lord Kinnaird.
'I shouldn't wonder,' observes Mr. William Coke.
'But the pace is too good to inquire.' *The Chase*

2 'Quite the cream of the thing, I suppose,' says Lord
Gardner. *Ib.*

ALBERT JAY NOCK

1873-1945

3 It is an economic axiom as old as the hills that goods
and services can be paid for only with goods and
services. *Memoirs of a Superfluous Man*. iii, ch. 3

RODEN BERKELEY NOEL

1834-1894

4 After battle sleep is best,
After noise, tranquillity. *The Old*

5 Loving, adorable,
Softly to rest,
Here in my crystalline,
Here in my breast! *The Water-Nymph and the Boy*

THOMAS NOEL

1799-1861

6 Rattle his bones over the stones;
He's only a pauper, whom nobody owns!
Rhymes and Roundelays, The Pauper's Drive

REV. JOHN NORRIS

1657-1711

7 Were angels to write, I fancy we should have but few
Folios. *Collections of Miscellanies* (1678), Preface

8 How fading are the joys we doat upon!
Like apparitions seen and gone.
But those which soonest take their flight
Are the most exquisite and strong,—
Like angels' visits, short and bright;
Mortality's too weak to bear them long.
Ib. The Parting

CHRISTOPHER NORTH
[JOHN WILSON]

1785-1854

9 Minds like ours, my dear James, must always be
above national prejudices, and in all companies it
gives me true pleasure to declare, that, as a people,
the English are very little indeed inferior to the
Scotch. *Noctes Ambrosianae*, No. 9 (May 1828)

10 His Majesty's dominions, on which the sun never sets.
Ib. No. 20 (April 1829)

11 Laws were made to be broken.
Ib. No. 24 (May 1830)

12 Insultin the sun, and quarrellin wi' the equawtor.
[*Ettrick Shepherd.*] *Ib.* (May 1830)

13 Animosities are mortal, but the Humanities live for
ever. *Noctes Ambrosianae*, No. 35 (Aug. 1834)

14 I cannot sit still, James, and hear you abuse the
shopocracy. *Ib.* No. 39 (Feb. 1835)

SIR STAFFORD HENRY NORTHCOTE, EARL OF IDDESLEIGH

1818-1887

15 Argue as you please, you are nowhere, that grand old
man, the Prime Minister, insists on the other thing.
Speech at Liverpool, 12 Apr. 1882

CAROLINE ELIZABETH SARAH NORTON

1808-1877

16 My beautiful, my beautiful! that standest meekly by,
With thy proudly-arched and glossy neck, and dark
and fiery eye!
Fret not to roam the desert now, with all thy winged
speed:
I may not mount on thee again!—thou'rt sold, my
Arab steed! *The Arab's Farewell to His Steed*

17 The stranger hath thy bridle-rein, thy master hath his
gold;—
Fleet-limbed and beautiful, farewell; thou'rt sold, my
steed, thou'rt sold. *Ib.*

18 And sitting down by the green well, I'll pause and
sadly think—
"Twas here he bowed his glossy neck when last I saw
him drink.' *Ib.*

19 They tempted me, my beautiful! for hunger's power
is strong—
They tempted me, my beautiful ! but I have loved too
long. *Ib.*

20 'Tis false! 'tis false, my Arab steed! I fling them back
their gold! *Ib.*

21 A soldier of the Legion lay dying in Algiers—
There was lack of woman's nursing, there was
dearth of woman's tears. *Bingen on the Rhine*

22 I do not love thee!—no! I do not love thee!
And yet when thou art absent I am sad.
I Do Not Love Thee

23 For death and life, in ceaseless strife,
Beat wild on this world's shore,
And all our calm is in that balm—
Not lost but gone before. *Not Lost but Gone Before*

NOVALIS [FRIEDRICH VON HARDENBERG]

1772-1801

24 Ein Gott-betrunkener Mensch.
A God-intoxicated man. *Remark about Spinoza*

ALFRED NOYES

1880-

25 Go down to Kew in lilac-time, in lilac-time, in lilac-
time;
Go down to Kew in lilac-time (it isn't far from
London!)
And you shall wander hand in hand with love in
summer's wonderland;
Go down to Kew in lilac-time (it isn't far from
London!) *Barrel Organ*

1 The wind was a torrent of darkness among the gusty
trees,
The moon was a ghostly galleon tossed upon cloudy
seas,
The road was a ribbon of moonlight over the purple
moor,
And the highwayman came riding—
Riding—riding—
The highwayman came riding, up to the old inn-door.
The Highwayman

2 The landlord's black-eyed daughter,
Bess, the landlord's daughter,
Plaiting a dark red love-knot into her long black hair.
Ib.

3 Look for me by moonlight;
Watch for me by moonlight;
I'll come to thee by moonlight, though hell should
bar the way! *Ib.*

4 There's a magic in the distance, where the sea-line
meets the sky. *Forty Singing Seamen*, ix

5 Calling as he used to call, faint and far away,
In Sherwood, in Sherwood, about the break of day.
Sherwood

6 Sherwood in the red dawn, is Robin Hood asleep? *Ib.*

NURSERY RHYMES
(*See* Note to the Second Edition, *p. v*)

7 A was an apple-pie;
B bit it;
C cut it.
Quoted by John Eachard, *Some Observations* (1671)

8 As I was going to St. Ives,
I met a man with seven wives,
Each wife had seven sacks,
Each sack had seven cats,
Each cat had seven kits:
Kits, cats, sacks, and wives,
How many were there going to St. Ives?
Harley MS., 7316 (*c.* 1730)

9 Baa, baa, black sheep,
Have you any wool?
Yes, sir, yes, sir,
Three bags full:
One for the master,
And one for the dame,
And one for the little boy
Who lives down the lane.
Tommy Thumb's Pretty Song Book (*c.* 1744)

10 Boys and girls come out to play,
The moon doth shine as bright as day.
In William King, *Useful Transactions in Philo-
sophy* (1708–9)

11 Bye, baby bunting,
Daddy's gone a-hunting,
Gone to get a rabbit skin
To wrap the baby bunting in.
Gammer Gurton's Garland (1784)

12 Cock a doodle doo!
My dame has lost her shoe;
My master's lost his fiddling-stick,
And knows not what to do.
Quoted in *The Most Cruel And Bloody Murder
Committed by an Innkeepers Wife* (1606)

13 Come, let's to bed, says Sleepy-head;
Tarry a while, says Slow;
Put on the pot, says Greedy-gut,
We'll sup before we go.
Gammer Gurton's Garland (1784)

14 Cross-patch,
Draw the latch,
Sit by the fire and spin:
Take a cup,
And drink it up,
Then call your neighbours in.
Mother Goose's Melody (*c.* 1765)

15 Cry, baby, cry,
Put your finger in your eye,
And tell your mother it wasn't I.
Nursery Rhymes, ed. J. O. Halliwell (1853)

16 Curly locks, Curly locks,
Wilt thou be mine?
Thou shalt not wash dishes
Nor yet feed the swine.
But sit on a cushion
And sew a fine seam,
And feed upon strawberries,
Sugar and cream.
Infant Institutes (1797)

17 Daffy-down-dilly is new come to town,
With a yellow petticoat, and a green gown.
Songs for the Nursery (1805)

18 Ding, dong, bell,
Pussy's in the well.
Who put her in?
Little Johnny Green.
Mother Goose's Melody (*c.* 1765)

19 Four and twenty tailors went to kill a snail,
The best man among them durst not touch her tail.
She put out her horns like a little Kyloe cow,
Run, tailors, run, or she'll kill you all e'en now.
Gammer Gurton's Garland (1784)

20 A fox jumped up one winter's night.
The Opera, ed. James Ballantyne (1832)

21 A frog he would a-wooing go.
'Heigh ho!' says Rowley.
In Thomas Ravenscroft, *Melismata* (1611)

22 Georgie Porgie, pudding and pie,
Kissed the girls and made them cry;
When the boys came out to play
Georgie Porgie ran away.
Nursery Rhymes, ed. J. O. Halliwell (1842)

23 Goosey goosey gander,
Whither shall I wander?
Upstairs and downstairs,
And in my lady's chamber;
There I met an old man
That would not say his prayers;
I took him by the left leg,
And threw him down the stairs.
Gammer Gurton's Garland (1784)

1 Hey diddle diddle,
The cat and the fiddle,
The cow jumped over the moon;
The little dog laughed
To see such sport,
And the dish ran away with the spoon.
Mother Goose's Melody (c. 1765)

2 Hickety, pickety, my black hen,
She lays eggs for gentlemen;
Gentlemen come every day
To see what my black hen doth lay.
Nursery Rhymes, ed. J. O. Halliwell (1853)

3 Hickory, dickory, dock,
The mouse ran up the clock,
The clock struck one,
The mouse ran down;
Hickory, dickory, dock.
Tommy Thumb's Pretty Song Book (c. 1744)

4 How many miles to Babylon?
Threescore miles and ten.
Can I get there by candle-light?
Yes, and back again.
If your heels are nimble and light,
You may get there by candle-light.
Songs for the Nursery (1805)

5 Humpty Dumpty sat on a wall,
Humpty Dumpty had a great fall;
All the king's horses,
And all the king's men,
Couldn't put Humpty together again.
From MS. addition to a copy of *Mother Goose's Melody* (c. 1803)

6 If I'd as much money as I could spend,
I never would cry old chairs to mend;
Cry chairs to mend, old chairs to mend;
I never would cry old chairs to mend.
Gammer Gurton's Garland (1810)

7 I had a little nut tree, nothing would it bear
But a silver nutmeg and a golden pear;
The king of Spain's daughter came to visit me,
And all for the sake of my little nut tree.
Newest Christmas Box (c. 1797)

8 I like little pussy, her coat is so warm,
And if I don't hurt her, she'll do me no harm.
So I'll not pull her tail, nor drive her away,
But pussy and I very gently will play.
Only True Mother Goose Melodies (Boston, c. 1843)

9 Jack and Jill went up the hill
To fetch a pail of water;
Jack fell down and broke his crown,
And Jill came tumbling after.
Mother Goose's Melody (c. 1765)

10 Jack Sprat could eat no fat,
His wife could eat no lean;
And so between them both, you see,
They licked the platter clean.
In John Clarke, *Paroemiologia Anglo-Latina* (1639)

11 The King of France went up the hill,
With forty thousand men;
The King of France came down the hill,
And ne'er went up again.
Quoted by James Howell in a letter to Sir James Crofts, 12 May 1620

12 Ladybird, ladybird, fly away home,
Your house is on fire, and your children all gone.
Tommy Thumb's Pretty Song Book (c. 1744)

13 The lion and the unicorn
Were fighting for the crown;
The lion beat the unicorn
All round about the town.
Some gave them white bread,
And some gave them brown;
Some gave them plum cake,
And sent them out of town.
In William King, *Useful Transactions in Philosophy* (1708–9)

14 Little Bo-Peep has lost her sheep,
And can't tell where to find them;
Leave them alone, and they'll come home,
And bring their tails behind them.
Douce MS. (c. 1805)

15 Little boy blue, come blow up your horn,
The sheep's in the meadow, the cow's in the corn;
But where is the boy that looks after the sheep?
He's under the haycock fast asleep.
Will you wake him? No, not I,
For if I do, he'll be sure to cry.
The Famous Tommy Thumb's Little Story Book (c. 1760)

16 Little Jack Horner sat in the corner,
Eating a Christmas pie:
He put in his thumb, and pulled out a plum,
And said, 'What a good boy am I!'
Quoted by Henry Carey, Namby Pamby (c. 1720)

17 Little Polly Flinders
Sat among the cinders,
Warming her pretty little toes,
Her mother came and caught her,
And whipped her little daughter
For spoiling her nice new clothes.
Original Ditties for the Nursery (c. 1805)

18 Little Tommy Tucker
Sings for his supper;
What shall we give him?
White bread and butter.

How shall he cut it
Without a knife?
How will he be married
Without a wife?
Tommy Thumb's Pretty Song Book (c. 1744)

19 London bridge is broken down,
My fair lady.
Quoted by Henry Carey, Namby Pamby (c. 1720)

20 The man in the wilderness asked me,
How many strawberries grow in the sea?
I answered him, as I thought good,
As many as red herrings grow in the wood.
MS. addition, dated 1744, to the Bath Municipal Library's copy of *The Whole Duty of Man* (1733)

21 Mary, Mary, quite contrary,
How does your garden grow?
With silver bells, and cockle shells,
And pretty maids all in a row.
Tommy Thumb's Pretty Song Book (c. 1744)

1 Monday's child is fair of face,
Tuesday's child is full of grace,
Wednesday's child is full of woe,
Thursday's child has far to go,
Friday's child is loving and giving,
Saturday's child works hard for its living,
And a child that's born on the Sabbath day
Is fair and wise and good and gay.
    Quoted by A. E. Bray, Traditions of Devonshire
    (1838), ii. 288

2 The north wind doth blow,
And we shall have snow,
And what will poor robin do then?
        Poor thing!
He'll sit in a barn,
To keep himself warm,
And hide his head under his wing.
        Poor thing!
            Songs for the Nursery (1805)

3 Old King Cole
Was a merry old soul,
And a merry old soul was he,
He called for his pipe,
And he called for his bowl,
And he called for his fiddlers three.
    *Quoted by William King, Useful Transactions in
    Philosophy* (1708–9)

4 Old Mother Hubbard
Went to the cupboard,
To get her poor dog a bone;
But when she came there
The cupboard was bare,
And so the poor dog had none.
    Sarah Catherine Martin, *The Comic Adventures
    of Old Mother Hubbard* (1805)

5 One a penny, two a penny, hot cross-buns;
If your daughters do not like them, give them to your
    sons.   *Christmas Box* (1797)

6 One, two,
Buckle my shoe;
Three, four,
Knock at the door;
Five, six,
Pick up sticks.
Seven, eight,
Lay them straight;
Nine, ten,
A big fat hen.   *Songs for the Nursery* (1805)

7 Oranges and lemons
Say the bells of St. Clement's.
    Tommy Thumb's Pretty Song Book (c. 1744)

8 When will you pay me?
Say the bells of Old Bailey.
When I grow rich,
Say the bells of Shoreditch.   *Ib.*

9 Here comes a candle to light you to bed,
Here comes a chopper to chop off your head.   *Ib.*

10 Pat-a-cake, pat-a-cake, baker's man,
Bake me a cake as fast as you can;
Pat it and prick it, and mark it with B,
Put it in the oven for baby and me.
    Quoted in Tom D'Urfey, *The Campaigners* (1698)

11 Pease-porridge hot, pease-porridge cold,
Pease-porridge in the pot, nine days old.
            Newest Christmas Box (c. 1797)

12 Peter Piper picked a peck of pickled pepper;
A peck of pickled pepper Peter Piper picked;
If Peter Piper picked a peck of pickled pepper,
Where's the peck of pickled pepper Peter Piper picked?
    *Peter Piper's Practical Principles of Plain and
    Perfect Pronunciation* (1819)

13 Please to remember
The Fifth of November,
    Gunpowder treason and plot;
We know no reason
Why gunpowder treason
    Should ever be forgot.
    Anonymous broadsheet (1826). *See* Wm. Hone,
    The Every-Day Book (1841). *See also 9:11*

14 Pussy cat, pussy cat, where have you been?
I've been up to London to look at the queen.
Pussy cat, pussy cat, what did you there?
I frightened a little mouse under the chair.
            Songs for the Nursery (1805)

15 The Queen of Hearts
She made some tarts,
    All on a summer's day;
The Knave of Hearts
He stole the tarts,
    And took them clean away.
            The European Magazine (April 1782)

16 Rain, rain, go away,
Come again another day.
            In James Howell, *Proverbs* (1659)

17 Ride a cock-horse to Banbury Cross,
To see a fine lady upon a white horse,
Rings on her fingers and bells on her toes,
And she shall have music wherever she goes.
            Gammer Gurton's Garland (1784)

18 See-saw, Margery Daw,
Jacky shall have a new master;
Jacky must have but a penny a day,
Because he can't work any faster.
            Mother Goose's Melody (c. 1765)

19 Simple Simon met a pieman
    Going to the fair:
Says Simple Simon to the pieman,
    'Let me taste your ware.'
    Simple Simon (a chapbook advertisement, 1764)

20 Sing a song of sixpence,
    A pocket full of rye,
Four and twenty blackbirds,
    Baked in a pie;
When the pie was opened,
    The birds began to sing;
Was not that a dainty dish
    To set before the king?

The king was in his counting-house
    Counting out his money;
The queen was in the parlour
    Eating bread and honey;
The maid was in the garden
    Hanging out the clothes,
There came a little blackbird,
    And snapped off her nose.
            Tommy Thumb's Pretty Song Book (c. 1744)

21 Solomon Grundy,
Born on a Monday,
Christened on Tuesday,

Married on Wednesday,
Took ill on Thursday,
Worse on Friday,
Died on Saturday,
Buried on Sunday:
This is the end
Of Solomon Grundy.
Nursery Rhymes, ed. J. O. Halliwell (1842)

1 Taffy was a Welshman, Taffy was a thief;
Taffy came to my house and stole a piece of beef:
I went to Taffy's house, Taffy was not at home;
Taffy came to my house and stole a marrow-bone.
Nancy Cock's Pretty Song Book (c. 1780)

2 Tell tale, tit!
Your tongue shall be split,
And all the dogs in the town
Shall have a little bit.
Nursery Rhymes, ed. J. O. Halliwell (1842)

3 There was a crooked man, and he walked a crooked mile,
He found a crooked sixpence against a crooked stile:
He bought a crooked cat, which caught a crooked
mouse,
And they all lived together in a little crooked house.
Ib.

4 There was an old woman who lived in a shoe,
She had so many children she didn't know what to do;
She gave them some broth without any bread,
She whipped them all soundly and put them to bed.
Gammer Gurton's Garland (1784)

5 Thirty days hath September,
April, June, and November;
All the rest have thirty-one,
Excepting February alone,
And that has twenty-eight days clear
And twenty-nine in each leap year.
Stevins MS. (c. 1555). (*See* 228 : 4)

6 This is the farmer sowing his corn,
That kept the cock that crowed in the morn,
That waked the priest all shaven and shorn,
That married the man all tattered and torn,
That kissed the maiden all forlorn,
That milked the cow with the crumpled horn,
That tossed the dog,
That worried the cat,
That killed the rat,
That ate the malt
That lay in the house that Jack built.
Nurse Truelove's New-Year's-Gift (1755)

7 This little pig went to market;
This little pig stayed at home;
This little pig had roast beef;
And this little pig had none;
And this little pig cried, Wee, wee, wee!
I can't find my way home.
The Famous Tommy Thumb's Little Story Book
(c. 1760)

8 Three blind mice, see how they run!
They all ran after the farmer's wife,
Who cut off their tails with a carving-knife,
Did you ever see such a thing in your life
As three blind mice?
In Thomas Ravenscroft, *Deuteromelia* (1609)

9 Three wise men of Gotham
Went to sea in a bowl:
And if the bowl had been stronger,
My song would have been longer.
Mother Goose's Melody (c. 1765)

10 Tom he was a piper's son,
He learned to play when he was young,
But all the tune that he could play,
Was 'Over the hills and far away.'
Tom, the Piper's Son (c. 1795)

11 Tom, Tom, the piper's son,
Stole a pig, and away he run;
The pig was eat, and Tom was beat,
And Tom went howling down the street. *Ib.*

12 What are little boys made of?
What are little boys made of?
Frogs and snails, and puppy-dogs' tails;
That's what little boys are made of.

What are little girls made of?
What are little girls made of?
Sugar and spice, and all that's nice;
That's what little girls are made of.
Nursery Rhymes, ed. J. O. Halliwell (1844)

13 When I was a little boy, I had but little wit,
'Tis a long time ago, and I have no more yet;
Nor ever ever shall, until that I die,
For the longer I live, the more fool am I.
Wit and Mirth, an Antidote against Melancholy
(1684)

14 Where are you going to, my pretty maid?
Quoted by William Pryce, *Archaeologia Cornu-
Britannica* (1790)

15 'My face is my fortune, sir,' she said. *Ib.*

16 'Nobody asked you, sir,' she said. *Ib.*

17 Who comes here?
A grenadier.
What do you want?
A pot of beer.
Where is your money?
I've forgot.
Get you gone,
You drunken sot!
Henry Carey, *Namby Pamby* (c. 1720)

18 'Who killed Cock Robin?'
'I,' said the Sparrow,
'With my bow and arrow,
I killed Cock Robin.'
All the birds of the air fell a-sighing and a-sobbing
When they heard of the death of poor Cock Robin.
Tommy Thumb's Pretty Song Book (c. 1744)

19 'Who saw him die?'
'I,' said the Fly,
'With my little eye,
I saw him die.' *Ib.*

FREDERICK OAKELEY
1802–1880

20 O come, all ye faithful,
Joyful and triumphant,
O come ye, O come ye to Bethlehem.
O Come, All Ye Faithful, trans. from Latin, *Adeste
Fideles*

SEAN O'CASEY
1884–

1 The whole world is in a state of chassis.
Juno and the Paycock, I. i

ADOLPH S. OCHS
1858–1935

2 All the news that's fit to print.
Motto of the 'New York Times'

WILLIAM DOUGLAS O'CONNOR
1832–1889

3 The Good Gray Poet. [Whitman.] *Title of book*, 1866

JAMES OGILVY, FIRST EARL OF SEAFIELD
1664–1730

4 Now there's ane end of ane old song
As he signed the engrossed exemplification of the Act of Union, 1706. Lockhart Papers (1817), i. 223

JOHN O'KEEFFE
1747–1833

5 Amo, amas, I love a lass,
As a cedar tall and slender;
Sweet cowslip's grace
Is her nom'native case,
And she's of the feminine gender.
  Rorum, corum, sunt Divorum!
  Harum, scarum, Divo!
Tag rag, merry derry, periwig and hatband!
Hic hoc horum Genitivo!
Agreeable Surprise, II. ii. *Song: Amo, Amas*

6 Fat, fair and forty were all the toasts of the young men. *Irish Minnie*, ii

7 You should always except the present company.
London Hermit, I. ii

DENNIS O'KELLY
1720?–1787

8 Eclipse first, the rest nowhere.
Epsom, 3 May 1769. Annals of Sporting, vol. ii, p. 271

JOHN OLDHAM
1653–1683

9 And all your fortune lies beneath your hat.
A Satire addressed to a Friend about to leave the University, l. 25

10 Racks, gibbets, halters, were their arguments.
Satires Upon the Jesuits, Sat. 1, *Garnet's Ghost*, l. 176

WILLIAM OLDYS
1696–1761

11 Busy, curious, thirsty fly.
Busy, Curious, Thirsty Fly, l. 1

JOHN OPIE
1761–1807

12 [When asked with what he mixed his colours.]
I mix them with my brains, sir.
Samuel Smiles, Self-Help, ch. 4

BARONESS ORCZY
[MRS. MONTAGUE BARSTOW]
d. 1947

13 We seek him here, we seek him there,
Those Frenchies seek him everywhere.
Is he in heaven?—Is he in hell?
That demmed, elusive Pimpernel?
The Scarlet Pimpernel, ch. 12

JOHN BOYLE O'REILLY
1844–1890

14 The organized charity, scrimped and iced,
In the name of a cautious, statistical Christ.
Life, Poems, and Speeches (1891), *In Bohemia*, l. 37

META ORRED

15 In the gloaming, O, my darling!
When the lights are dim and low,
And the quiet shadows falling
Softly come and softly go. *In the Gloaming*

GEORGE ORWELL [ERIC BLAIR]
1903–1950

16 All animals are equal, but some animals are more equal than others. *Animal Farm*, ch. 10

DOROTHY OSBORNE [LADY TEMPLE]
1627–1695

17 The heat of the day is spent in reading or working, and about six or seven o'clock I walk out into a common that lies hard by the house, where a great many young wenches keep sheep and cows, and sit in the shade singing of ballads. I go to them and compare their voices and beauties to some ancient shepherdesses I have read of, and find a vast difference there; but, trust me, I think these are as innocent as those could be.
Letter to Sir Wm. Temple, May 1653

18 All letters, methinks, should be as free and easy as one's discourse, not studied as an oration, nor made up of hard words like a charm. *Ib. Oct. 1653*

ARTHUR WILLIAM EDGAR O'SHAUGHNESSY
1844–1881

19 We are the music makers,
We are the dreamers of dreams,
Wandering by lone sea-breakers,
And sitting by desolate streams;—
World-losers and world-forsakers,
On whom the pale moon gleams:
We are the movers and shakers
Of the world for ever, it seems.
Ode: 'We are the Music Makers'

1 One man with a dream, at pleasure,
   Shall go forth and conquer a crown;
   And three with a new song's measure
   Can trample a kingdom down.
                    Ode: 'We are the Music Makers'

2 For each age is a dream that is dying,
   Or one that is coming to birth.   *Ib.*

SIR WILLIAM OSLER
1849–1919

3 The uselessness of men above sixty years of age,
   and the incalculable benefit it would be in commercial, political, and in professional life if, as a
   matter of course, men stopped work at this age.
   Address, Johns Hopkins University, Feb. 1905.
   H. Cushing's *Life of Sir W. Osler* (1925),
   vol. i, p. 667

JOHN O'SULLIVAN
1813–1895

4 Our manifest destiny to overspread the continent
   allotted by Providence for the free development
   of our yearly multiplying millions.
   U.S. Magazine and Democratic Review, vol. xvii,
   p. 5

5 A torchlight procession marching down your throat.
   Description of some whisky. G. W. E. Russell's
   Collections and Recollections, ch. 19

JAMES OTIS
1725–1783

6 Taxation without representation is tyranny.
   Watchword of the American Revolution. Attrib.

THOMAS OTWAY
1652–1685

7 These are rogues that pretend to be of a religion now!
   Well, all I say is, honest atheism for my money.
                    The Atheist, Act III, l. 31

8 Ere man's corruptions made him wretched, he
   Was born most noble that was born most free:
   Each of himself was lord; and unconfin'd
   Obey'd the dictates of his godlike mind.
                    Don Carlos, Act II, l. 3

9 Destructive, damnable, deceitful woman!
                    The Orphan, Act III, l. 586

10 And for an apple damn'd mankind.   *Ib.* l. 594

11 You wags that judge by rote, and damn by rule.
                    Titus and Berenice, prologue, l. 3

12 Oh woman! lovely woman! Nature made thee
   To temper man: we had been brutes without you;
   Angels are painted fair, to look like you;
   There's in you all that we believe of heav'n,
   Amazing brightness, purity, and truth,
   Eternal joy, and everlasting love.
                    Venice Preserved, Act I, l. 337

13 No praying, it spoils business.   *Ib.* Act II, l. 87

SIR THOMAS OVERBURY
1581–1613

14   In part to blame is she,
   Which hath without consent been only tried;
   He comes too near, that comes to be denied.
                    Miscellaneous Works. A Wife, xxvi

15 He disdains all things above his reach, and preferreth
   all countries before his own.
                    Miscellaneous Works. An Affectate Traveller

16 You cannot name any example in any heathen author
   but I will better it in Scripture.
                    Ib. Crumms Fal'n From King James's Table, § 10

OVID
43 B.C.–A.D. 18?

17 Et nulli cessura fides, sine crimine mores,
   Nudaque simplicitas, purpureusque pudor.
      And I have good faith that will yield to none, and
      ways without reproach, and unadorned sim-
      plicity, and blushing modesty.
                    Amores, I. iii. 13. Trans. by Showerman

18 Cetera quis nescit?
   The rest who does not know?   *Ib.* v. 25

19 Procul omen abesto!
   Far from us be the omen!   *Ib.* xiv. 41

20 Vilia miretur vulgus; mihi flavus Apollo
   Pocula Castalia plena ministret aqua.
      Let what is cheap excite the marvel of the crowd;
      for me may golden Apollo minister full cups
      from the Castalian fount.   *Ib.* xv. 35

21 Procul hinc, procul este, severae!
   Away from me, far away, ye austere fair!
                    Ib. II. i. 3

22 Iuppiter ex alto periuria ridet amantum.
   Jupiter from on high laughs at the perjury of lovers.
                    Ars Amatoria, i. 633

23 Forsitan et nostrum nomen miscebitur istis.
   Perhaps too my name will be joined to theirs.
                    Ib. iii. 339

24 Nil mihi rescribas, tu tamen ipse veni!
   Yet write nothing back to me; yourself come!
                    Heroides, I. i. 2. Trans. by Showerman

25 Iam seges est ubi Troia fuit.
   Now are fields of corn where Troy once was.
                    Ib. 53

26 Rudis indigestaque moles.
   An unformed and confused mass.
                    Metamorphoses, i. 7

27 Medio tutissimus ibis.
   You will go most safely in the middle. *Ib.* ii. 137

28 Inopem me copia fecit.
   Plenty makes me poor.   *Ib.* iii. 466

29 Ipse docet quid agam; fas est et ab hoste doceri.
      He himself teaches what I should do; it is right to
      be taught by the enemy.   *Ib.* iv. 428

30   Video meliora, proboque;
   Deteriora sequor.
      I see and approve better things, but follow worse.
                    Ib. vii. 20

31 Tempus edax rerum.
   Time the devourer of all things.   *Ib.* xv. 234

1 Iamque opus exegi, quod nec Iovis ira, nec ignis,
Nec poterit ferrum, nec edax abolere vetustas.

And now I have finished the work, which neither
the wrath of Jove, nor fire, nor the sword, nor
devouring age shall be able to destroy.
Metamorphoses, xv. 871

2 Principiis obsta; sero medicina paratur
Cum mala per longas convaluere moras.

Resist beginnings; too late is the medicine prepared when the disease has gained strength by
long delays.
Remedia Amoris, 91. Trans. by Showerman

3   Qui finem quaeris amoris,
Cedet amor rebus; res age, tutus eris.

You who seek an end of love, love yields to business: be busy, and you will be safe.   *Ib.* 143

4 Tu quoque.
Thou also.   *Tristia*, ii. 39.

5 Teque, rebellatrix, tandem, Germania, magni
Triste caput pedibus supposuisse ducis!

That thou, rebellious Germany, at length hast
lowered thy sorrowing head beneath the foot of
our leader.   *Ib.* III. xii. 47

6 Virgilium vidi tantum.
I had but a glimpse of Virgil.   *Ib.* IV. x. 51

7 Utque solebamus consumere longa loquendo
Tempora, sermonem deficiente die.

As we were wont to pass long hours in converse,
till daylight failed our talk.   *Ib.* v. xiii. 27

8 Nescioqua natale solum dulcedine captos
Ducit et inmemores non sinit esse sui.

By what sweet charm I know not the native land
draws all men nor allows them to forget her.
Epistulae Ex Ponto, i. iii. 35. Trans. by
Wheeler

9 Adde quod ingenuas didicisse fideliter artes
Emollit mores nec sinit esse feros.

Note too that a faithful study of the liberal arts
humanizes character and permits it not to be
cruel.   *Ib.* II. ix. 47

10 Gutta cavat lapidem, consumitur annulus usu.
Drops of water hollow out a stone, a ring is worn
thin by use.   *Ib.* IV. x. 5

11 (Gutta cavat lapidem, non vi sed saepe cadendo.
The drop of rain maketh a hole in the stone, not
by violence, but by oft falling.
Latimer, *7th Sermon before Edw. VI*, 1549)

JOHN OWEN
1560?-1622

12 God and the doctor we alike adore
But only when in danger, not before;
The danger o'er, both are alike requited,
God is forgotten, and the Doctor slighted. *Epigrams*

13 Tempora mutantur nos et mutamur in illis
Quomodo? fit semper tempore pejor homo.

Times change, and we change with them too. How
so?
With time men only the more vicious grow.   *Ib.*

EDWARD OXENFORD
1847-1929

14 I fear no foe in shining armour.   *Song*

COUNT OXENSTIERNA
1583-1654

15 An nescis, mi fili, quantilla prudentia regitur orbis?
Dost thou not know, my son, with how little wis-
dom the world is governed?
Letter to his son, 1648

BARRY PAIN
1864-1928

16 The cosy fire is bright and gay,
The merry kettle boils away
And hums a cheerful song.
I sing the saucer and the cup;
Pray, Mary, fill the teapot up,
And do not make it strong.
The Poets at Tea. Cowper

17 Pour, varlet, pour the water,
The water steaming hot!
A spoonful for each man of us,
Another for the pot!   *Ib. Macaulay*

18 As the sin that was sweet in the sinning
Is foul in the ending thereof,
As the heat of the summer's beginning
Is past in the winter of love:
O purity, painful and pleading!
O coldness, ineffably gray!
O hear us, our handmaid unheeding,
And take it away!   *Ib. Swinburne*

19 I think that I am drawing to an end:
For on a sudden came a gasp for breath,
And stretching of the hands, and blinded eyes,
And a great darkness falling on my soul.
O Hallelujah! . . . Kindly pass the milk.
Ib. Tennyson

20 'Come, little cottage girl, you seem
To want my cup of tea;
And will you take a little cream?
Now tell the truth to me.'

She had a rustic, woodland grin
Her cheek was soft as silk,
And she replied, 'Sir, please put in
A little drop of milk.'   *Ib. Wordsworth*

THOMAS PAINE
1737-1809

21 The sublime and the ridiculous are often so nearly
related, that it is difficult to class them separately.
One step above the sublime, makes the ridiculous;
and one step above the ridiculous, makes the
sublime again.   *Age of Reason* (1795), p. ii, p. 20

22 These are the times that try men's souls.
The American Crisis, No. 1. *Writings* (1894),
vol. 1, p. 170

23 The summer soldier and the sunshine patriot will, in
this crisis, shrink from the service of their country.
Ib. In the *Pennsylvania Journal*, 19 Dec. 1785

1 Government, even in its best state, is but a necessary evil; in its worst state, an intolerable one.
Common Sense, ch. 1

2 The final event to himself [Mr. Burke] has been, that as he rose like a rocket, he fell like the stick.
Letter to the Addressers on the late Proclamation (1792), p. 4

3 [Burke] is not affected by the reality of distress touching his heart, but by the showy resemblance of it striking his imagination. He pities the plumage, but forgets the dying bird.
Rights of Man (1791), p. 26

4 My country is the world, and my religion is to do good. *Ib.* pt. ii, ch. 5

5 The religion of humanity. *Attr. by Edmund Gosse*

REV. WILLIAM PALEY
1743–1805
6 Who can refute a sneer?
Moral Philosophy, bk. v, ch. 9

HENRY JOHN TEMPLE, VISCOUNT PALMERSTON
1784–1865
7 Accidental and fortuitous concurrence of atoms.
Speech, House of Commons, 5 Mar. 1857

8 What is merit? The opinion one man entertains of another.
Quoted by Carlyle in *Critical and Miscellaneous Essays*, viii, 'Shooting Niagara'

9 Die, my dear Doctor, that's the last thing I shall do!
Attr. last words

EDWARD HAZEN PARKER
10 Life's race well run,
Life's work well done,
Life's victory won,
Now cometh rest.
See *Notes and Queries*, 9th Series, vol. iv, p. 167, and vol. vii, p. 406

MARTIN PARKER
d. 1656?
11 Country men of England, who live at home with ease,
And little think what dangers are incident o' th' seas:
Give ear unto the sailor who unto you will show
His case, his case: *How e'er the wind doth blow.*
Sailors for My Money (Roxburghe Ballads, vol. vi, p. 797)

12 You gentlemen of England
Who live at home at ease,
How little do you think
On the dangers of the seas.
The Valiant Sailors (Early Naval Ballads [Percy Society, 1841], p. 34)

13 But all 's to no end, for the times will not mend
Till the king enjoys his own again.
Upon Defacing of Whitehall (The Loyal Garland, 1671). Later title: When the King Enjoys His Own Again. Ritson's *Ancient Songs* (1792), p. 231

14 My skill goes beyond the depths of a pond,
Or rivers, in the greatest rain:
Whereby I can tell, all things will be well,
When the King enjoys his own again. *Ib.*

ROSS PARKER
1914–
and
HUGHIE CHARLES
1907–
15 There'll always be an England
While there's a country lane,
Wherever there's a cottage small
Beside a field of grain.
Song of Second World War, 1939

THEODORE PARKER
1810–1860
16 A democracy, that is, a government of all the people, by all the people, for all the people; of course, a government after the principles of eternal justice, the unchanging law of God; for shortness' sake, I will call it the idea of freedom.
The American Idea. Speech at N. E. Anti-Slavery Convention, Boston, 29 May, 1850. Discourses of Slavery (1863), i

CHARLES STEWART PARNELL
1846–1891
17 No man has a right to fix the boundary of the march of a nation; no man has a right to say to his country —thus far shalt thou go and no further.
Speech at Cork, 21 Jan. 1885

THOMAS PARNELL
1679–1718
18 When thy beauty appears,
In its graces and airs,
All bright as an angel new dropt from the sky;
At distance I gaze, and am aw'd by my fears,
So strangely you dazzle my eye!
Poems (1894). Song, '*When thy Beauty Appears*'

19 Still an angel appear to each lover beside,
But still be a woman to you. *Ib.*

20 We call it only pretty Fanny's way.
Ib. An Elegy, to an Old Beauty, l. 34

BLAISE PASCAL
1623–1662
21 Quand on voit le style naturel, on est tout étonné et ravi, car on s'attendait de voir un auteur, et on trouve un homme.

When we encounter a natural style we are always astonished and delighted, for we expected to see an author, and found a man. *Pensées*, § i. 29

22 Le nez de Cléopâtre: s'il eût été plus court, toute la face de la terre aurait changé.

Had Cleopatra's nose been shorter, the whole history of the world would have been different.
Ib. § ii. 162

1 Le silence éternel de ces espaces infinis m'effraie.

The eternal silence of these infinite spaces [the heavens] terrifies me. *Pensées, § iii. 206*

2 Le dernier acte est sanglant, quelque belle que soit la comédie en tout le reste.

The last act is bloody, however charming the rest of the play may be. *Ib. 210*

3 On mourra seul.

We shall die alone. *Ib. 211*

4 Le cœur a ses raisons que la raison ne connaît point.

The heart has its reasons which reason knows nothing of. *Ib. § iv. 277*

5 L'homme n'est qu'un roseau, le plus faible de la nature; mais c'est un roseau pensant.

Man is only a reed, the weakest thing in nature; but he is a thinking reed. *Ib. § vi. 347*

6 Le moi est haïssable.

The 'self' is hateful. *Ib. § vii. 434*

7 Console-toi, tu ne me chercherais pas si tu ne m'avais trouvé.

Comfort yourself, you would not seek me if you had not found me. *Ib. 553*

8 Je n'ai fait celle-ci plus longue que parceque je n'ai pas eu le loisir de la faire plus courte.

I have made this letter longer than usual, because I lack the time to make it short.
  Lettres Provinciales (1657), xvi

WALTER HORATIO PATER
1839–1894

9 A white bird, she told him once, looking at him gravely, a bird he must carry in his bosom across a crowded public place—his own soul was like that!
  Marius the Epicurean, pt. i, ch. 2

10 The presence that thus rose so strangely beside the waters, is expressive of what in the ways of a thousand years men had come to desire. Hers is the head upon which all 'the ends of the world are come', and the eyelids are a little weary. . . . Set it for a moment beside one of those white Greek goddesses or beautiful women of antiquity, and how would they be troubled by this beauty, into which the soul with all its maladies has passed? [Mona Lisa.]
  The Renaissance. Leonardo da Vinci

11 She is older than the rocks among which she sits; like the vampire, she has been dead many times, and learned the secrets of the grave; and has been a diver in deep seas, and keeps their fallen day about her; and trafficked for strange webs with Eastern merchants: and, as Leda, was the mother of Helen of Troy, and, as Saint Anne, the mother of Mary; and all this has been to her but as the sound of lyres and flutes, and lives only in the delicacy with which it has moulded the changing lineaments, and tinged the eyelids and the hands.
  Ib.

12 All art constantly aspires towards the condition of music. *Ib. The School of Giorgione*

13 For art comes to you, proposing frankly to give nothing but the highest quality to your moments as they pass, and simply for those moments' sake.
  The Renaissance. Conclusion

14 To burn always with this hard, gemlike flame, to maintain this ecstasy, is success in life. *Ib.*

ANDREW PATERSON
1864–1941

15 Once a jolly swagman camped by a billy-bong,
Under the shade of a kulibar tree,
And he sang as he sat and waited for his billy-boil,
'You'll come a-waltzing, Matilda, with me.'
  Waltzing Matilda

COVENTRY PATMORE
1823–1896

16 For dear to maidens are their rivals dead.
  Amelia, l. 135

17 Grant me the power of saying things
Too simple and too sweet for words!
  *The Angel in the House (ed. 1904), bk. 1, c. 1,
Prelude 1, The Impossibility, l. 7*

18 Love, sole mortal thing
Of worth immortal.
  Ib. Prelude 2, Love's Reality, l. 9

19 The fair sum of six thousand years'
Traditions of civility.
  Ib. The Cathedral Close, v, l. 27

20 Ah, wasteful woman, she who may
On her sweet self set her own price,
Knowing man cannot choose but pay,
How has she cheapen'd paradise;
How given for nought her priceless gift,
How spoil'd the bread and spill'd the wine,
Which, spent with due, respective thrift,
Had made brutes men, and men divine.
  Ib. c. iii, Prelude 3, Unthrift

21 Leave us alone! After a while,
This pool of private charity
Shall make its continent an isle,
And roll, a world-embracing sea.
  Ib. c. vi, Prelude 2, Love Justified, l. 9

22 Kind souls, you wonder why, love you,
When you, you wonder why, love none
We love, Fool, for the good we do,
Not that which unto us is done!
  Ib. Prelude 4, A Riddle Solved

23 Love wakes men, once a lifetime each;
They lift their heavy lids, and look;
And, lo, what one sweet page can teach,
They read with joy, then shut the book.
And some give thanks, and some blaspheme,
And most forget; but, either way,
That and the Child's unheeded dream
Is all the light of all their day.
  Ib. c. viii, Prelude 2, The Revelation, l. 5

24 I drew my bride, beneath the moon,
Across my threshold; happy hour!
But, ah, the walk that afternoon
We saw the water-flags in flower!
  Ib. Prelude 3, The Spirit's Epochs, l. 9

1 God's grace is the only grace,
And all grace is the grace of God.
The Angel in the House (ed. 1904), bk. I, c. x,
Prelude 1, *The Joyful Wisdom*

2 'I'll hunt for dangers North and South,
To prove my love, which sloth maligns!'
What seems to say her rosy mouth?
'I'm not convinced by proofs but signs.'
Ib. bk. II, c. iv, Prelude 3, *Valour Misdirected*

3 'I saw you take his kiss!' ''Tis true.'
'O, modesty!' ''Twas strictly kept:
He thought me asleep; at least, I knew
He thought I thought he thought I slept.
Ib. c. viii, Prelude 3, *The Kiss*

4 Why, having won her, do I woo?
Because her spirit's vestal grace
Provokes me always to pursue,
But, spirit-like, eludes embrace.
Ib. c. xii, Prelude 1, *The Married Lover*, l. 1

5 Because, though free of the outer court
I am, this Temple keeps its shrine
Sacred to Heaven; because, in short,
She's not and never can be mine. *Ib.* l. 29

6 Some dish more sharply spiced than this
Milk-soup men call domestic bliss *Olympus*, l. 15

7 Well dost thou, Love, thy solemn Feast to hold
In vestal February.
The Unknown Eros, bk. I. i. *St. Valentine's Day*,
l. 1

8 Fair as the rash oath of virginity
Which is first-love's first cry.
O 'Baby Spring,
That flutter'st sudden 'neath the breast of Earth
A month before the birth. *Ib.* l. 9

9 Thy heart with dead, wing'd innocencies fill'd,
Ev'n as a nest with birds
After the old ones by the hawk are kill'd. *Ib.* l. 51

10 But, in a while,
The immeasurable smile
Is broke by fresher airs to flashes blent
With darkling discontent.
Ib. ii. *Wind and Wave*, l. 15

11 I, singularly moved
To love the lovely that are not beloved,
Of all the Seasons, most
Love Winter. *Ib.* iii. *Winter*, l. 1

12 It *was* the azalea's breath, and she *was* dead!
Ib. vii. *The Azalea*, l. 17

13 So, till to-morrow eve, my Own, adieu!
Parting's well-paid with soon again to meet,
Soon in your arms to feel so small and sweet,
Sweet to myself that am so sweet to you! *Ib.* l. 22

14 It was not like your great and gracious ways!
Do you, that have nought other to lament,
Never, my Love, repent
Of how, that July afternoon,
You went,
With sudden, unintelligible phrase,
And frighten'd eye,
Upon your journey of so many days,
Without a single kiss, or a good-bye?
Ib. viii. *Departure*, l. 1

15 And the only loveless look the look with which you
pass'd. *Ib.* l. 31

16 My little Son, who look'd from thoughtful eyes
And moved and spoke in quiet grown-up wise,
Having my law the seventh time disobey'd,
I struck him, and dismiss'd
With hard words and unkiss'd,
His Mother, who was patient, being dead.
The Unknown Eros, bk. I. x. *The Toys*, l. 1

17 Then, fatherly, not less
Than I whom Thou hast moulded from the clay,
Thou'lt leave Thy wrath, and say,
'I will be sorry for their childishness.' *Ib.*

18 For want of me the world's course will not fail:
When all its work is done, the lie shall rot;
The truth is great, and shall prevail,
When none cares whether it prevail or not.
Ib. xii. *Magna est Veritas*, l. 7

19 In the year of the great crime,
When the false English Nobles and their Jew,
By God demented, slew
The trust they stood twice pledged to keep from
wrong,
One said, Take up thy Song,
That breathes the mild and almost mythic time
Of England's prime! *Ib.* xiii, 1867, l. 1

20 If I were dead, you'd sometimes say, Poor Child!
Ib. xiv. *'If I were dead'*, l. 1

21 With all my will, but much against my heart,
We two now part.
My Very Dear,
Our solace is, the sad road lies so clear.
It needs no art,
With faint, averted feet
And many a tear,
In our opposed paths to persevere.
Ib. xvi. *A Farewell*, l. 1

22 Haply yon wretch, so famous for his falls,
Got them beneath the Devil-defended walls
Of some high Virtue he had vow'd to win.
Ib. xx. *'Let Be'*, l. 17

23 That shaft of slander shot
Miss'd only the right blot.
I see the shame
They cannot see:
'Tis very just they blame
The thing that's not. *Ib.* l. 35

24 Through delicatest ether feathering soft their solitary
beat. *Ib.* bk. II. i. *To the Unknown Eros*, l. 8

25 What in its ruddy orbit lifts the blood,
Like a perturbed moon of Uranus,
Reaching to some great world in ungauged darkness
hid. *Ib.* l. 33

26 Who is this only happy She,
Whom, by a frantic flight of courtesy,
Born of despair
Of better lodging for his Spirit fair,
He adores as Margaret, Maude, or Cecily?
Ib. v. *Sponsa Dei*, l. 30

27 The Jebusite,
That, maugre all God's promises could do,
The chosen People never conquer'd quite;
Who therefore lived with them,
And that by formal truce and as of right,
In metropolitan Jerusalem.
Ib. vii. *To the Body*, l. 32

1 Enoch, Elijah, and the Lady, she
Who left the lilies in her body's lieu.
The Unknown Eros, bk. II. vii. *To the Body*, l. 45

2 Who has thy birth-time's consecrating dew
For death's sweet chrism retain'd,
Quick, tender, virginal, and unprofaned! *Ib.* l. 51

3 There of pure Virgins none
Is fairer seen,
Save One,
Than Mary Magdalene. *Ib.* l. 127

4 Shall I, the gnat which dances in thy ray,
Dare to be reverent?
Ib. xiv. *Psyche's Discontent*, l. 72

5 Maud burst in, while the Earl was there,
With 'Oh, Mama, do be a bear!'
The Victories of Love, bk. II. ii. *From Lady Clitheroe to Mary Churchill*, l. 89

6 No magic of her voice or smile
Suddenly raised a fairy isle,
But fondness for her underwent
An unregarded increment,
Like that which lifts, through centuries,
The coral-reef within the seas,
Till, lo! the land where was the wave,
Alas! 'tis everywhere her grave.
Ib. v. *From Mrs. Graham*, l. 57

7 Faults had she, child of Adam's stem,
But only Heaven knew of them.
Ib. xii. *From Felix to Honoria*, l. 167

8 This is to say, my dear Augusta,
We've had another awful buster:
Ten thousand Frenchmen sent below!
Thank God from whom all blessings flow.
Epigram on King William's dispatch to Queen Augusta reported in The Times, 8 Aug. 1870. B. Champneys, *Coventry Patmore* (1900), i. 286.

JAMES PAYN
1830–1898

9 I had never had a piece of toast
Particularly long and wide,
But fell upon the sanded floor,
And always on the buttered side.
Chambers's Journal, 2 Feb. 1884

JOHN HOWARD PAYNE
1791–1852

10 Mid pleasures and palaces though we may roam,
Be it ever so humble, there's no place like home;
A charm from the sky seems to hallow us there,
Which, seek through the world, is ne'er met with elsewhere.
Home, home, sweet, sweet home!
There's no place like home! there's no place like home!
Clari, the Maid of Milan. Home, Sweet Home

THOMAS LOVE PEACOCK
1785–1866

11 Ancient sculpture is the true school of modesty. But where the Greeks had modesty, we have cant; where they had poetry, we have cant; where they had patriotism, we have cant; where they had anything that exalts, delights, or adorns humanity, we have nothing but cant, cant, cant.
Crotchet Castle, ch. 7

12 A book that furnishes no quotations is, *me judice*, no book—it is a plaything. *Ib.* ch. 9

13 Modern literature having attained the honourable distinction of sharing with blacking and Macassar oil the space which used to be monopolized by razor-strops and the lottery. *Ib.* ch. 15

14 The march of mind—has marched in through my back-parlour shutters, and out again with my silver spoons, in the dead of the night. The policeman, who was sent down to examine, says my house has been broken open on the most scientific principles. *Ib.* ch. 17

15 Nothing can be more obvious than that all animals were created solely and exclusively for the use of man. *Headlong Hall*, ch. 2

16 'Indeed, the loaves and fishes are typical of a mixed diet; and the practice of the Church in all ages shows—'
'That it never loses sight of the loaves and fishes.'
Ib.

17 'I distinguish the picturesque and the beautiful, and I add to them, in the laying out of grounds, a third and distinct character, which I call *unexpectedness*.'
'Pray, sir,' said Mr. Milestone, 'by what name do you distinguish this character, when a person walks round the grounds for the second time?' *Ib.* ch. 4

18 Sir, I have quarrelled with my wife; and a man who has quarrelled with his wife is absolved from all duty to his country. *Nightmare Abbey*, ch. 11

19 He remembered too late on his thorny green bed,
Much that well may be thought cannot wisely be said.
Crotchet Castle (1831): *The Priest and the Mulberry Tree*, st. 5

20 Long night succeeds thy little day
Oh blighted blossom! can it be,
That this gray stone and grassy clay
Have closed our anxious care of thee?
Epitaph on his Daughter. Works of Peacock, ed. Cole (1875), Biographical Notice by E. Nicolls

21 In his last binn Sir Peter lies,
Who knew not what it was to frown:
Death took him mellow by surprise,
And in his cellar stopped him down.
Headlong Hall, ch. 5

22 Hail to the Headlong! the Headlong Ap-Headlong!
All hail to the Headlong, the Headlong Ap-Headlong!
The Headlong Ap-Headlong
Ap-Breakneck Ap-Headlong
Ap-Cataract Ap-Pistyll Ap-Rhaiader Ap-Headlong!
Ib. ch. 13. *Chorus*

23 The mountain sheep are sweeter,
But the valley sheep are fatter;
We therefore deemed it meeter
To carry off the latter.
The Misfortunes of Elphin, ch. 11. *The War-Song of Dinas Vawr*

24 The bowl goes trim. The moon doth shine,
And our ballast is old wine.
Nightmare Abbey, ch. 11

1 In a bowl to sea went wise men three,
　On a brilliant night in June:
They carried a net, and their hearts were set
　On fishing up the moon.
　　The Wise Men of Gotham. Paper Money Lyrics

GEORGE PEELE
1558?–1597?

2 Fair and fair, and twice so fair,
　As fair as any may be;
The fairest shepherd on our green,
　A love for any lady.
　　Works, ed. Bullen, vol. i. *Arraignment of Paris*,
　　I. ii. 55. *Song of Oenone and Paris*

3 What thing is love for (well I wot) love is a thing.
It is a prick, it is a sting,
It is a pretty, pretty thing;
It is a fire, it is a coal
Whose flame creeps in at every hole.
　　Ib. vol. ii. *Miscellaneous Poems. The Hunting of
　　Cupid*, l. 1

4 His golden locks time hath to silver turn'd;
　O time too swift, O swiftness never ceasing!
His youth 'gainst time and age hath ever spurn'd
　But spurn'd in vain; youth waneth by increasing:
Beauty, strength, youth, are flowers but fading seen;
Duty, faith, love, are roots, and ever green.

His helmet now shall make a hive for bees,
　And, lovers' sonnets turn'd to holy psalms,
A man-at-arms must now serve on his knees,
　And feed on prayers, which are age his alms:
But though from court to cottage he depart,
His saint is sure of his unspotted heart.

Goddess, allow this aged man his right,
To be your beadsman now that was your knight.
　　*Ib. Polyhymnia, Sonnet ad finem. A Farewell to
　　Arms*

HENRY HERBERT, EARL OF PEMBROKE
1734–1794

5 My noble friend Lord Pembroke said once to me at
Wilton, with a happy pleasantry and some truth,
that, 'Dr. Johnson's sayings would not appear so
extraordinary, were it not for his *bow-wow way*'.
　　Boswell's *Life of Johnson*, 27 Mar. 1775, note

WILLIAM PENN
1644–1718

6 No Cross, No Crown.　　*Title of Pamphlet*, 1669

7 It is a reproach to religion and government to suffer
so much poverty and excess.
　　Reflexions and Maxims, pt. i, No. 52

8 Men are generally more careful of the breed of their
horses and dogs than of their children.　*Ib.* No. 85

9 The country life is to be preferred, for there we see
the works of God, but in cities little else but the
works of men.　　　　　　　*Ib.* No. 220

SAMUEL PEPYS
1633–1703

10 Strange the difference of men's talk!
　　　　　　　　Diary, 4 Jan. 1659–60

11 And so to bed.　　　　*Diary, 20 Apr. 1660*

12 A silk suit, which cost me much money, and I pray
God to make me able to pay for it. *Ib. 1 July 1660*

13 I . . . sent for Mr. Butler, who was now all full of
his high discourse in praise of Ireland, . . . but so
many lies I never heard in praise of anything as
he told of Ireland.　　　　*Ib. 28 July 1660*

14 I went out to Charing Cross, to see Major-general
Harrison hanged, drawn, and quartered; which
was done there, he looking as cheerful as any man
could do in that condition.　　*Ib. 13 Oct. 1660*

15 Very merry, and the best fritters that ever I eat in
my life.　　*Ib. 26 Feb. 1660–1 (Shrove Tues.)*

16 A good honest and painful sermon.
　　　　　　　　　　Ib. 17 Mar. 1661

17 If ever I was foxed it was now.　*Ib. 23 Apr. 1661*

18 But methought it lessened my esteem of a king, that
he should not be able to command the rain.
　　　　　　　　　　Ib. 19 July 1662

19 I see it is impossible for the King to have things done
as cheap as other men.　　*Ib. 21 July 1662*

20 But Lord! to see the absurd nature of Englishmen,
that cannot forbear laughing and jeering at everything that looks strange.　　*Ib. 27 Nov. 1662*

21 My wife, who, poor wretch, is troubled with her
lonely life.　　　　　　*Ib. 19 Dec. 1662*

22 Went to hear Mrs. Turner's daughter . . . play on
the harpsichon; but, Lord! it was enough to make
any man sick to hear her; yet was I forced to commend her highly.　　　　*Ib. 1 May 1663*

23 Most of their discourse was about hunting, in a
dialect I understand very little.　*Ib. 22 Nov. 1663*

24 While we were talking came by several poor creatures
carried by, by constables, for being at a conven-
ticle. . . . I would to God they would either conform, or be more wise, and not be catched!
　　　　　　　　　　Ib. 7 Aug. 1664

25 Pretty witty Nell. [Nell Gwynne.]　*Ib. 3 Apr. 1665*

26 But Lord! what a sad time it is to see no boats upon
the River; and grass grows all up and down White
Hall Court.　　　　　　*Ib. 20 Sept. 1665*

27 Strange to see how a good dinner and feasting reconciles everybody.　　　　*Ib. 9 Nov. 1665*

28 Strange to say what delight we married people have
to see these poor fools decoyed into our condition.
　　　　　　　　　　Ib. 25 Dec. 1665

29 And mighty proud I am (and ought to be thankful
to God Almighty) that I am able to have a spare
bed for my friends.　　　　*Ib. 8 Aug. 1666*

30 I bless God I do find that I am worth more than
ever I yet was, which is £6,200, for which the
Holy Name of God be praised!　*Ib. 31 Oct. 1666*

31 But it is pretty to see what money will do.
　　　　　　　　　　Ib. 21 Mar. 1667–8

CHARLES PERRAULT
1628–1703

32 'Anne, ma sœur Anne, ne vois-tu rien venir?' Et la
sœur Anne lui répondit, 'Je ne vois rien que le
soleil qui poudroye, et l'herbe qui verdoye.'

'Anne, sister Anne, do you see anybody coming?'
And her sister Anne replied, 'I see nothing but
the sun which makes a dust, and the grass looking
green.'
Perrault, *Histoires ou Contes du Temps Passé*,
1697. Trans. by R. Samber, 1764

PERSIUS
A.D. 34–62

1 Nec te quaesiveris extra.

Nor ask any opinion but your own.
Satires, i. 7. Trans. by Conington

2 At pulchrum est digito monstrari et dicier 'hic est'.

But it is a fine thing for men to point one out and
say 'There he goes'. *Ib.* 28

3 Virtutem videant intabescantque relicta.

Let them look upon virtue, and pine that they have
lost her for ever. *Ib.* iii. 38

4 Venienti occurrite morbo.

Meet the disease at its first stage. *Ib.* 64

5 De nihilo nihilum, in nihilum nil posse reverti.

Nothing can come out of nothing, nothing can go
back to nothing. *Ib.* 84. Trans. by Conington

6 Tecum habita: noris quam sit tibi curta supellex.

Live at home, and learn how slenderly furnished
your apartments are. *Ib.* iv. 52

MARÉCHAL PÉTAIN
1856–1951

7 Ils ne passeront pas.

They shall not pass. *Verdun, Feb. 1916*

PETRONIUS
d. *c.* A.D. 66

8 Cave canem.

Beware of the dog.
Petronii Arbitri Satyricon, 29, 1
Found with picture of a dog on a mosaic floor in Pompeii.

9 Horatii curiosa felicitas.

The exact felicity of Horace. *Ib.* 118

10 Habes confitentem reum.

You have a confessing prisoner. *Ib.* 130

11 Abiit ad plures.

He has joined the great majority.
Cena Trimalchionis, xlii. 5.

EDWARD JOHN PHELPS
1822–1900

12 The man who makes no mistakes does not usually
make anything.
Speech at Mansion House, 24 Jan. 1899

JOHN WOODWARD PHILIP
1840–1900

13 Don't cheer, boys; those poor devils are dying.
At the Battle of Santiago, 4 July 1898

PHILIPPIDES
c. 490 B.C.

14 Χαίρετε, νικῶμεν.

Joy, we win.
*Having run to Athens with the tidings of Mara-
thon. He died upon his message.* Lucian, *Pro Lapsu
in Salutando*, para. iii. Trans. by Fowler

AMBROSE PHILIPS
1675?–1749

15 The flowers anew, returning seasons bring!
But beauty faded has no second spring.
The First Pastoral, Lobbin, l. 55

16 Timely blossom, infant fair,
Fondling of a happy pair,
Every morn, and every night,
Their solicitous delight,
Sleeping, waking, still at ease,
Pleasing without skill to please.
Little gossip, blithe and hale,
Tattling many a broken tale.
To Mistress Charlotte Pulteney, l. 1

JOHN PHILIPS
1676–1709

17 Happy the man, who, void of cares and strife,
In silken or in leathern purse retains
A Splendid Shilling. *The Splendid Shilling*, l. 1

STEPHEN PHILLIPS
1864–1915

18 A man not old, but mellow, like good wine.
Ulysses, III. ii

WENDELL PHILLIPS
1811–1884

19 One, on God's side, is a majority.
Speeches (1880), *Lecture at Brooklyn, N.Y., 1 Nov.
1859*

20 Every man meets his Waterloo at last. *Ib.*

21 We live under a government of men and morning
newspapers. *Address: The Press*

EDEN PHILLPOTTS
1862–

22 His father's sister had bats in the belfry and was put
away. *Peacock House. My First Murder*

PINDAR
c. 522–442 B.C.

23 ἄριστον μὲν ὕδωρ.

Water is best. *Olympian Odes*, I. i

24 φωνᾶντα συνετοῖσιν. ἐς δὲ τὸ πᾶν ἑρμηνέων
χατίζει.

Vocal to the wise; but for the crowd they need
interpreters. *Ib.* ii. 85

SIR ARTHUR WING PINERO

1855–1934

1 What beautiful fruit! I love fruit when it's expensive.
The Second Mrs. Tanqueray, Act I

WILLIAM PITT, EARL OF CHATHAM

1708–1778

2 The atrocious crime of being a young man . . . I shall neither attempt to palliate nor deny.
Speech, House of Commons, 27 Jan. 1741

3 I rejoice that America has resisted. Three millions of people, so dead to all the feelings of liberty, as voluntarily to submit to be slaves, would have been fit instruments to make slaves of the rest.
Ib. 14 Jan. 1766

4 I cannot give them my confidence; pardon me, gentlemen, confidence is a plant of slow growth in an aged bosom: youth is the season of credulity.
Ib.

5 Unlimited power is apt to corrupt the minds of those who possess it.   *Ib. House of Lords, 9 Jan. 1770*

6 There is something behind the throne greater than the King himself.   *Ib. 2 Mar. 1770*

7 We have a Calvinistic creed, a Popish liturgy, and an Arminian clergy.   *Ib. 19 May 1772*

8 If I were an American, as I am an Englishman, while a foreign troop was landed in my country, I never would lay down my arms,—never—never—never!
Ib. 18 Nov. 1777

9 You cannot conquer America.   *Ib.*

10 I invoke the genius of the Constitution!   *Ib.*

11 The poorest man may in his cottage bid defiance to all the forces of the Crown. It may be frail—its roof may shake—the wind may blow through it— the storm may enter—the rain may enter—but the King of England cannot enter—all his force dares not cross the threshold of the ruined tenement!
Ib. Date unknown. Brougham's *Statesmen in the Time of George III*, First Series

12 Our watchword is security.   *Attr.*

13 It was a saying of Lord Chatham, that the parks were the lungs of London.
William Windham, in a Speech in House of Commons, 30 June 1808

WILLIAM PITT

1759–1806

14 Necessity is the plea for every infringement of human freedom. It is the argument of tyrants; it is the creed of slaves.
Speech, House of Commons, 18 Nov. 1783

15 We must recollect . . . what it is we have at stake, what it is we have to contend for. It is for our property, it is for our liberty, it is for our independence, nay, for our existence as a nation; it is for our character, it is for our very name as Englishmen, it is for everything dear and valuable to man on this side of the grave.   *Ib. 22 July 1803*

16 England has saved herself by her exertions, and will, as I trust, save Europe by her example.
Speech. At the Guildhall, 1805

17 Roll up that map; it will not be wanted these ten years.
On a map of Europe, after hearing the news of the Battle of Austerlitz. Stanhope's *Life of the Rt. Hon. William Pitt* (1862), vol. iv, p. 369

18 Oh, my country! how I love my country.
Attr. last words. Ib. p. 382

19 Oh, my country! how I leave my country!
Attr. last words. Ib. (1879), vol. iii, p. 391

20 My country! oh, my country!
Attr. last words. G. Rose, *Diary, 23 Jan. 1806*

21 I think I could eat one of Bellamy's veal pies.
Alternative attributed last words

JAMES ROBINSON PLANCHÉ

1796–1880

22 Ching-a-ring-a-ring-ching! Feast of lanterns!
What a crop of chop-sticks, hongs and gongs!
Hundred thousand Chinese crinkum-crankums,
Hung among the bells and ding-dongs!
The Drama at Home, or An Evening With Puff

23 It would have made a cat laugh.
Extravaganzas (1879), *The Queen of the Frogs*, i. iv

PLATO

c. 429–347 B.C.

24 Σωκράτη φησὶν ἀδικεῖν τούς τε νέους διαφθείροντα καὶ θεοὺς οὓς ἡ πόλις νομίζει οὐ νομίζοντα, ἕτερα δὲ δαιμόνια καινά.
Socrates is charged with corrupting the youth of the city, and with rejecting the gods of Athens and introducing new divinities.
Apologia, 24[b] 9

25 δημοκρατία ἐσχάτη τυραννίς.
Democracy passes into despotism.
Republic, pt. iv, bk. viii. 562. Cornford's translation

PLAUTUS

B.C. 254–184

26 Miles gloriosus.
The boastful soldier.   *Title of Play*

27 GRIPUS: Tum tu mendicus es?
LABRAX: Tetigisti acu.
GRIPUS: Then you are a beggar?
LABRAX: You have touched the point with a needle.
[You have put your finger on the spot.]
Rudens, l. 1305

PLINY

A.D. 23–79

28 Brutum fulmen.
A harmless thunderbolt.
Historia Naturalis, II. xliii

1 **Ex Africa semper aliquid novi.**

There is always something new from Africa. *Proverbial from Pliny:* Unde etiam vulgare Graeciae dictum 'semper aliquid novi Africam adferre'.

Whence it is commonly said among the Greeks that 'Africa always offers something new'.
Historia Naturalis, II. viii. 42

2 **In vino veritas.**

Truth comes out in wine. *Proverbial from Pliny:* Vulgoque veritas iam attributa vino est.

Now truth is commonly said to be in wine.
Ib. xiv. 141

3 **Sal Atticum.**

Attic wit. *Ib.* xxxi. 87

4 **Nulla dies sine linea.**

Not a day without a line. *Proverbial from Pliny:* Apelli fuit alioqui perpetua consuetudo numquam tam occupatam diem agendi, ut non lineam ducendo exerceret artem, quod ab eo in proverbium venit.

It was moreover a regular habit of Apelles never to be so occupied in the business of the day that he could not practise his art by drawing a line, and this gave rise to the proverb.
Ib. xxxv. 36. 12

5 **Ne supra crepidam sutor iudicaret.**

The cobbler should not judge above his last. *Ib.* 85

JOSEPH MARY PLUNKETT
1887–1916

6 I see His blood upon the rose
And in the stars the glory of His eyes.
Poems (1916), *I See His Blood*

EDGAR ALLAN POE
1809–1849

7 This maiden she lived with no other thought
Than to love and be loved by me. *Annabel Lee*

8 I was a child and she was a child,
In this kingdom by the sea;
But we loved with a love which was more than love—
I and my Annabel Lee;
With a love that the wingèd seraphs of heaven
Coveted her and me. *Ib.*

9 The beautiful Annabel Lee. *Ib.*

10 In the sepulchre there by the sea,
In her tomb by the sounding sea. *Ib.*

11 The fever call'd 'Living'
Is conquer'd at last. *For Annie*

12 Keeping time, time, time,
In a sort of Runic rhyme,
To the tintinabulation that so musically wells
From the bells, bells, bells, bells. *The Bells*, l. 9

13 They are neither man nor woman—
They are neither brute nor human,
They are Ghouls. *Ib.* l. 86

14 Vastness! and Age! and Memories of Eld!
Silence! and Desolation! and dim Night!
The Coliseum, l. 10

15 While the angels, all pallid and wan,
Uprising, unveiling, affirm
That the play is the tragedy, 'Man',
And its hero the Conqueror Worm.
The Conqueror Worm, l. 39

16 All that we see or seem
Is but a dream within a dream.
A Dream within a Dream, l. 10

17 Helen, thy beauty is to me
Like those Nicean barks of yore,
That gently, o'er a perfumed sea,
The weary, wayworn wanderer bore
To his own native shore.

On desperate seas long wont to roam,
Thy hyacinth hair, thy classic face,
Thy Naiad airs have brought me home
To the glory that was Greece
And the grandeur that was Rome. *To Helen,* l. 1

18 If I could dwell where Israfel
Hath dwelt, and he where I,—
He might not sing so wildly well
A mortal melody,
While a bolder note than his might swell
From my lyre within the sky. *Israfel*

19 And, Guy de Vere, hast *thou* no tear?—weep now or nevermore!
Lenore, l. 3

20 *Peccavimus;* but rave not thus! and let a Sabbath song
Go up to God so solemnly the dead may feel no wrong. *Ib.* l. 13

21 And all my days are trances,
And all my nightly dreams
Are where thy grey eye glances,
And where thy footstep gleams—
In what ethereal dances,
By what eternal streams. *To One in Paradise,* l. 21

22 Once upon a midnight dreary, while I pondered, weak and weary,
Over many a quaint and curious volume of forgotten lore,
While I nodded, nearly napping, suddenly there came a tapping,
As of some one gently rapping. *The Raven,* i

23 Sorrow for the lost Lenore—
For the rare and radiant maiden whom the angels name Lenore—
Nameless here for evermore. *Ib.* ii

24 Deep into that darkness peering, long I stood there wondering, fearing,
Doubting, dreaming dreams no mortal ever dared to dream before. *Ib.* v

25 Ghastly grim and ancient raven wandering from the nightly shore—
Tell me what thy lordly name is on the Night's Plutonian shore! *Ib.* viii

26 'Prophet!' said I, 'thing of evil—prophet still, if bird or devil!
By that heaven that bends above us—by that God we both adore.' *Ib.* xvi

27 Take thy beak from out my heart, and take thy form from off my door!
Quoth the Raven, 'Nevermore'. *Ib.* xvii

1 The skies they were ashen and sober;
  The leaves they were crisped and sere—
  The leaves they were withering and sere;
It was night in the lonesome October
Of my most immemorial year.   *Ulalume*, l. 1

2 Here once, through an alley Titanic,
  Of cypress, I roamed with my Soul—
  Of cypress, with Psyche, my Soul.   *Ib.* l. 10

JOHN POMFRET
1667–1703

3 We live and learn, but not the wiser grow.
                   Reason, l. 112

MME DE POMPADOUR
1721–1764

4 Après nous le déluge.
  After us the deluge.
    Madame de Hausset, *Mémoires*, p. 19

JOHN POOLE
1786?–1872

5 I hope I don't intrude?   *Paul Pry*, I. ii

ALEXANDER POPE
1688–1744

6 To wake the soul by tender strokes of art,
To raise the genius, and to mend the heart;
To make mankind in conscious virtue bold,
Live o'er each scene, and be what they behold:
For this the Tragic Muse first trod the stage.
   Prologue to Addison's *Cato*, l. 1

7 A brave man struggling in the storms of fate,
And greatly falling, with a falling State.
While Cato gives his little senate laws,
What bosom beats not in his country's cause?
                   Ib. l. 21

8 Ye gods! annihilate but space and time,
And make two lovers happy.
   The Art of Sinking in Poetry, ch. 11

9 And thou Dalhousy, the great God of War,
Lieutenant-Colonel to the Earl of Mar.   *Ib.*

10 A very heathen in the carnal part
Yet still a sad, good Christian at her heart.
   Of the Character of Women

11 Poetic Justice, with her lifted scale,
Where, in nice balance, truth with gold she weighs,
And solid pudding against empty praise.
   The Dunciad, bk. i, l. 52

12 Now night descending, the proud scene was o'er,
But liv'd in Settle's numbers one day more. *Ib.* l. 89

13 Pensive poets painful vigils keep,
Sleepless themselves to give their readers sleep.
                   Ib. l. 93

14 Or where the pictures for the page atone,
And Quarles is sav'd by beauties not his own.
                   Ib. l. 139

15 And gentle dullness ever loves a joke. *Ib.* bk. ii, l. 34

16 Earless on high, stood unabash'd De Foe. *Ib.* l. 147

17 Another, yet the same.   *Ib.* bk. iii, l. 40

18 Lo, where Maeotis sleeps, and hardly flows
The freezing Tanais thro' a waste of snows.
         The Dunciad, bk. iii. l. 87

19 Peel'd, patch'd, and piebald, linsey-wolsey brothers,
Grave mummers! sleeveless some, and shirtless
  others.   *Ib.* l. 115

20 All crowd, who foremost shall be damn'd to fame.
                   Ib. l. 158

21 Some free from rhyme or reason, rule or check,
Break Priscian's head, and Pegasus's neck. *Ib.* l. 161

22 So sweetly mawkish, and so smoothly dull. *Ib.* l. 171

23 And Alma Mater all dissolv'd in port.   *Ib.* l. 338

24 May you, my Cam and Isis, preach it long!
The Right Divine of Kings to govern wrong.
         Ib. bk. iv, l. 187

25 Stretch'd on the rack of a too easy chair. *Ib.* l. 341

26 She comes! she comes! the sable Throne behold
Of Night primæval, and of Chaos old!
Before her, Fancy's gilded clouds decay,
And all its varying rain-bows die away. *Ib.* l. 629

27 See skulking Truth to her old cavern fled,
Mountains of Casuistry heap'd o'er her head!
Philosophy, that lean'd on Heav'n before,
Shrinks to her second cause, and is no more.
Physic of Metaphysic begs defence,
And Metaphysic calls for aid on Sense!
See Mystery to Mathematics fly!
In vain! they gaze, turn giddy, rave, and die.
Religion blushing veils her sacred fires,
And unawares Morality expires.
Nor public flame, nor private, dares to shine;
Nor human spark is left, nor glimpse divine!
Lo! thy dread empire, Chaos! is restor'd;
Light dies before thy uncreating word;
Thy hand, great Anarch! lets the curtain fall,
And universal darkness buries all.   *Ib.* l. 641

28 Vital spark of heav'nly flame!
Quit, oh quit this mortal frame:
Trembling, hoping, ling'ring, flying,
Oh the pain, the bliss of dying!
   The Dying Christian to his Soul

29 Tell me, my soul, can this be death?   *Ib.*

30 What beck'ning ghost, along the moon-light shade
Invites my steps, and points to yonder glade?
   Elegy to the Memory of an Unfortunate Lady, l. 1

31 Is it, in heav'n, a crime to love too well? *Ib.* l. 6

32 Is there no bright reversion in the sky,
For those who greatly think, or bravely die? *Ib.* l. 9

33 Ambition first sprung from your bless'd abodes;
The glorious fault of angels and of gods.   *Ib.* l. 13

34 By foreign hands thy dying eyes were closed,
By foreign hands thy decent limbs composed,
By foreign hands thy humble grave adorned,
By strangers honoured, and by strangers mourned!
                   Ib. l. 51

35 Yet shall thy grave with rising flow'rs be dressed,
And the green turf lie lightly on thy breast. *Ib.* l. 63

36 So peaceful rests, without a stone, a name,
What once had beauty, titles, wealth, and fame.
How loved, how honoured once, avails thee not,
To whom related, or by whom begot;
A heap of dust alone remains of thee;
'Tis all thou art, and all the proud shall be! *Ib.* l. 69

1 Line after line my gushing eyes o'erflow,
Led through a sad variety of woe:
Now warm in love, now with'ring in my bloom,
Lost in a convent's solitary gloom!
Eloisa to Abelard, 1. 35

2 Heav'n first taught letters for some wretch's aid.
Ib. 1. 51

3 No, make me mistress to the man I love
If there be yet another name more free
More fond than mistress, make me that to thee!
Ib. 1. 88

4 Of all affliction taught a lover yet,
'Tis sure the hardest science to forget.
Ib. 1. 189

5 How happy is the blameless vestal's lot!
The world forgetting, by the world forgot.
Ib. 1. 207

6 One thought of thee puts all the pomp to flight,
Priests, tapers, temples, swim before my sight.
Ib. 1. 273

7 See my lips tremble, and my eye-balls roll,
Suck my last breath, and catch my flying soul!
Ib. 1. 323

8 Teach me at once, and learn of me to die. *Ib.* 1. 328

9 You beat your pate, and fancy wit will come:
Knock as you please, there's nobody at home.
Epigrams. An Empty House

10 Has she no faults then (Envy says), Sir?
Yes, she has one, I must aver;
When all the world conspires to praise her,
The woman's deaf, and does not hear.
Ib. On a Certain Lady at Court

11 I am his Highness' dog at Kew;
Pray tell me, sir, whose dog are you?
Ib. On the Collar of a Dog which I gave to his Royal Highness

12 Here rests a woman, good without pretence.
Epitaphs. On Mrs. Corbet

13 Heav'n, as its purest gold, by tortures tried;
The saint sustain'd it, but the woman died. *Ib.*

14 Whether thou choose Cervantes' serious air,
Or laugh and shake in Rab'lais' easy chair,
Or in the graver gown instruct mankind,
Or, silent, let thy morals tell thy mind.
Ib. To Swift. 22 Oct. 1727

15 In wit a man; simplicity a child. *Ib. On Gay*

16 Form'd to delight at once and lash the age. *Ib.* 1. 4

17 Nature and Nature's laws lay hid in night:
God said, *Let Newton be!* and all was light.
Ib. Intended for Sir Isaac Newton

18 Prais'd, wept,
And honour'd by the Muse he lov'd.
Epitaph on James Craggs in Westminster Abbey

19 Ten censure wrong for one who writes amiss;
A fool might once himself alone expose,
Now one in verse makes many more in prose.
'Tis with our judgments as our watches, none
Go just alike, yet each believes his own.
An Essay on Criticism, 1. 6

20 Let such teach others who themselves excel,
And censure freely who have written well. *Ib.* 1. 15

21 Some are bewildered in the maze of schools,
And some made coxcombs nature meant but fools.
An Essay on Criticism, 1. 26

22 A little learning is a dang'rous thing;
Drink deep, or taste not the Pierian spring:
There shallow draughts intoxicate the brain,
And drinking largely sobers us again. *Ib.* 1. 215

23 Hills peep o'er hills, and Alps on Alps arise!
Ib. 1. 232

24 'Tis not a lip, or eye, we beauty call,
But the joint force and full result of all. *Ib.* 1. 245

25 Whoever thinks a faultless piece to see
Thinks what ne'er was, nor is, nor e'er shall be.
Ib. 1. 253

26 Poets, like painters, thus unskilled to trace
The naked nature, and the living grace,
With gold and jewels cover ev'ry part,
And hide with ornaments their want of art.
Ib. 1. 293

27 True wit is nature to advantage dressed,
What oft was thought, but ne'er so well expressed.
Ib. 1. 297

28 Such laboured nothings, in so strange a style,
Amaze th' unlearn'd, and make the learned smile.
Ib. 1. 326

29 Be not the first by whom the new are tried,
Nor yet the last to lay the old aside. *Ib.* 1. 335

30 As some to church repair,
Not for the doctrine, but the music there.
These equal syllables alone require,
Tho' oft the ear the open vowels tire;
While expletives their feeble aid do join;
And ten low words oft creep in one dull line.
Ib. 1. 342

31 Where'er you find 'the cooling western breeze',
In the next line, it 'whispers through the trees':
If crystal streams 'with pleasing murmurs creep',
The reader's threatened, not in vain, with 'sleep':
Then, at the last and only couplet fraught
With some unmeaning thing they call a thought,
A needless Alexandrine ends the song,
That, like a wounded snake, drags its slow length
along. *Ib.* 1. 350

32 True ease in writing comes from art, not chance,
As those move easiest who have learned to dance.
'Tis not enough no harshness gives offence,
The sound must seem an echo to the sense.
Soft is the strain when zephyr gently blows,
And the smooth stream in smoother numbers flows;
But when loud surges lash the sounding shore,
The hoarse, rough verse should like the torrent roar:
When Ajax strives some rock's vast weight to throw,
The line too labours, and the words move slow:
Not so, when swift Camilla scours the plain,
Flies o'er th' unbending corn, and skims along the
main. *Ib.* 1. 362

33 Yet let not each gay turn thy rapture move;
For fools admire, but men of sense approve.
Ib. 1. 390

34 What woeful stuff this madrigal would be,
In some starved hackney sonneteer, or me!
But let a lord once own the happy lines,
How the wit brightens; how the style refines.
Ib. 1. 418

1 Some praise at morning what they blame at night;
But always think the last opinion right.
An Essay on Criticism, l. 430

2 To err is human, to forgive, divine.   *Ib.* l. 525

3 Men must be taught as if you taught them not,
And things unknown proposed as things forgot.
Ib. l. 574

4 The bookful blockhead, ignorantly read,
With loads of learned lumber in his head. *Ib.* l. 612

5 For fools rush in where angels fear to tread.
Ib. l. 625

6 Still pleased to teach, and yet not proud to know.
Ib. l. 632

7 Awake, my St. John! leave all meaner things
To low ambition, and the pride of kings.
Let us, since life can little more supply
Than just to look about us and to die,
Expatiate free o'er all this scene of man;
A mighty maze! but not without a plan.
An Essay on Man. Epistle i, l. 1

8 Eye Nature's walks, shoot folly as it flies,
And catch the manners living as they rise.
Laugh where we must, be candid where we can;
But vindicate the ways of God to man.
Say first, of God above or man below,
What can we reason but from what we know?
Ib. l. 13

9 Observe how system into system runs,
What other planets circle other suns.   *Ib.* l. 25

10 Who sees with equal eye, as God of all,
A hero perish, or a sparrow fall,
Atoms or systems into ruin hurled,
And now a bubble burst, and now a world. *Ib.* l. 87

11 Hope springs eternal in the human breast;
Man never is, but always to be blessed.
The soul, uneasy, and confined from home,
Rests and expatiates in a life to come.
Lo, the poor Indian! whose untutored mind
Sees God in clouds, or hears him in the wind;
His soul proud science never taught to stray
Far as the solar walk or milky way;
Yet simple nature to his hope has giv'n,
Behind the cloud-topped hill, an humbler heav'n.
Ib. l. 95

12 But thinks, admitted to that equal sky,
His faithful dog shall bear him company. *Ib.* l. 111

13 In pride, in reas'ning pride, our error lies;
All quit their sphere and rush into the skies!
Pride still is aiming at the bless'd abodes,
Men would be angels, angels would be gods.
Aspiring to be gods if angels fell,
Aspiring to be angels men rebel.   *Ib.* l. 123

14   The first Almighty Cause
Acts not by partial, but by gen'ral laws. *Ib.* l. 145

15 Why has not man a microscopic eye?
For this plain reason, man is not a fly.   *Ib.* l. 193

16 Die of a rose in aromatic pain?   *Ib.* l. 200

17 The spider's touch how exquisitely fine!
Feels at each thread, and lives along the line.
Ib. l. 217

18 All are but parts of one stupendous whole,
Whose body nature is, and God the soul. *Ib.* l. 267

19 Warms in the sun, refreshes in the breeze,
Glows in the stars, and blossoms in the trees.
An Essay on Man, Ep. i, l. 271

20 As the rapt Seraph that adores and burns. *Ib.* l. 278

21 All nature is but art unknown to thee,
All chance, direction which thou canst not see;
All discord, harmony not understood;
All partial evil, universal good;
And, spite of pride, in erring reason's spite,
One truth is clear, Whatever is, is right.   *Ib.* l. 284

22 Know then thyself, presume not God to scan,
The proper study of mankind is man.
Placed on this isthmus of a middle state,
A being darkly wise, and rudely great:
With too much knowledge for the sceptic side,
With too much weakness for the stoic's pride,
He hangs between; in doubt to act or rest,
In doubt to deem himself a god, or beast;
In doubt his mind or body to prefer;
Born but to die, and reas'ning but to err;
Alike in ignorance, his reason such,
Whether he thinks too little or too much;
Chaos of thought and passion, all confused;
Still by himself abused, or disabused;
Created half to rise, and half to fall;
Great lord of all things, yet a prey to all;
Sole judge of truth, in endless error hurled;
The glory, jest, and riddle of the world!
Ib. Ep. ii, l. 1

23 Go, teach eternal wisdom how to rule—
Then drop into thyself, and be a fool!   *Ib.* l. 29

24 Fix'd like a plant on his peculiar spot,
To draw nutrition, propagate, and rot.   *Ib.* l. 63

25 And hence one master-passion in the breast,
Like Aaron's serpent, swallows up the rest.
Ib. l. 131

26 The young disease, that must subdue at length,
Grows with his growth, and strengthens with his
strength.   *Ib.* l. 135

27 Vice is a monster of so frightful mien,
As to be hated needs but to be seen;
Yet seen too oft, familiar with her face,
We first endure, then pity, then embrace.
But where th' extreme of vice, was ne'er agreed:
Ask where's the North? at York, 'tis on the Tweed;
In Scotland, at the Orcades; and there,
At Greenland, Zembla, or the Lord knows where.
Ib. l. 217

28 Till one man's weakness grows the strength of all.
Ib. l. 252

29 The learn'd is happy nature to explore,
The fool is happy that he knows no more. *Ib.* l. 263

30 Behold the child, by nature's kindly law
Pleased with a rattle, tickled with a straw:
Some livelier plaything gives his youth delight,
A little louder, but as empty quite:
Scarfs, garters, gold, amuse his riper stage,
And beads and pray'r-books are the toys of age:
Pleased with this bauble still, as that before;
Till tired he sleeps, and life's poor play is o'er.
Ib. l. 275

1 For forms of government let fools contest;
Whate'er is best administered is best:
For modes of faith let graceless zealots fight;
His can't be wrong whose life is in the right:
In faith and hope the world will disagree,
But all mankind's concern is charity.
An Essay on Man. Ep. iii, l. 303

2 O Happiness! our being's end and aim,
Good, pleasure, ease, content! whate'er thy name:
That something still which prompts th' eternal sigh,
For which we bear to live, or dare to die.
Ib. Ep. iv. l. 1

3 Order is Heav'n's first law. *Ib.* l. 49

4 Buries madmen in the heaps they raise. *Ib.* l. 76

5 Shall gravitation cease, if you go by?
Or some old temple, nodding to its fall,
For Chartres' head reserve the hanging wall?
Ib. l. 128

6 Go, like the Indian, in another life
Expect thy dog, thy bottle, and thy wife. *Ib.* l. 177

7 Worth makes the man, and want of it the fellow;
The rest is all but leather or prunella. *Ib.* l. 203

8 What can ennoble sots, or slaves, or cowards?
Alas! not all the blood of all the Howards. *Ib.* l. 215

9 A wit's a feather, and a chief a rod;
An honest man's the noblest work of God. *Ib.* l. 247

10 And more true joy Marcellus exil'd feels,
Than Caesar with a senate at his heels. *Ib.* l. 257

11 Truths would you teach, or save a sinking land?
All fear, none aid you, and few understand.
Ib. l. 265

12 If parts allure thee, think how Bacon shined,
The wisest, brightest, meanest of mankind:
Or ravished with the whistling of a name,
See Cromwell, damned to everlasting fame!
Ib. l. 281

13 Know then this truth, enough for man to know,
'Virtue alone is happiness below.' *Ib.* l. 309

14 Slave to no sect, who takes no private road,
But looks through nature up to nature's God.
Ib. l. 331

15 Formed by thy converse, happily to steer
From grave to gay, from lively to severe. *Ib.* l. 379

16 Say, shall my little bark attendant sail,
Pursue the triumph, and partake the gale? *Ib.* l. 385

17 Thou wert my guide, philosopher, and friend.
Ib. l. 390

18 That true self-love and social are the same.
Ib. l. 396

19 All our knowledge is ourselves to know. *Ib.* l. 398

20 Achilles' wrath, to Greece the direful spring
Of woes unnumbered, heavenly goddess, sing.
Iliad, i. 1

21 To observations which ourselves we make,
We grow more partial for th' observer's sake.
Moral Essays, Ep. i, *To Lord Cobham,* l. 11

22 Like following life through creatures you dissect,
You lose it in the moment you detect. *Ib.* l. 29

23 Alas! in truth the man but changed his mind,
Perhaps was sick, in love, or had not dined.
Ib. l. 127

24 'Tis from high life high characters are drawn;
A saint in crape is twice a saint in lawn.
Moral Essays, Ep. i, *To Lord Cobham,* l. 135

25 'Odious! in woollen! 'twould a saint provoke!'
(Were the last words that poor Narcissa spoke:)
Ib. l. 246

26 'One would not, sure, be frightful when one's dead:
And,—Betty,—give this cheek a little red.' *Ib.* l. 250

27 And you, brave Cobham! to the latest breath,
Shall feel your ruling passion strong in death.
Ib. l. 262

28 Most women have no characters at all.
Ib. Ep. ii. *To Mrs. M. Blount,* l. 2

29 Choose a firm cloud, before it fall, and in it
Catch, ere she change, the Cynthia of this minute.
Ib. l. 19

30 Chaste to her husband, frank to all beside,
A teeming mistress, but a barren bride. *Ib.* l. 71

31 Flavia's a wit, has too much sense to pray;
To toast our wants and wishes is her way;
Nor asks of God, but of her stars, to give
The mighty blessing, 'while we live, to live'. *Ib.* l. 87

32 Wise wretch! with pleasures too refined to please;
With too much spirit to be e'er at ease;
With too much quickness ever to be taught;
With too much thinking to have common thought.
Ib. l. 95

33 'With every pleasing, every prudent part,
Say, what can Chloe want?'—She wants a heart.
Ib. l. 159

34 Virtue she finds too painful an endeavour,
Content to dwell in decencies for ever. *Ib.* l. 163

35 In men, we various ruling passions find;
In women, two almost divide the kind;
Those, only fixed, they first or last obey,
The love of pleasure, and the love of sway. *Ib.* l. 207

36 Men, some to business, some to pleasure take;
But every woman is at heart a rake:
Men, some to quiet, some to public strife;
But every lady would be queen for life. *Ib.* l. 215

37 See how the world its veterans rewards!
A youth of frolics, an old age of cards. *Ib.* l. 243

38 She who ne'er answers till a husband cools,
Or, if she rules him, never shows she rules;
Charms by accepting, by submitting, sways,
Yet has her humour most, when she obeys. *Ib.* l. 261

39 And mistress of herself, though china fall. *Ib.* l. 268

40 Woman's at best a contradiction still. *Ib.* l. 270

41 Who shall decide, when doctors disagree,
And soundest casuists doubt, like you and me?
Ib. Ep. iii. *To Lord Bathurst,* l. 1

42 But thousands die, without or this or that,
Die, and endow a college, or a cat. *Ib.* l. 95

43 The ruling passion, be it what it will,
The ruling passion conquers reason still. *Ib.* l. 153

44 Rise, honest Muse! and sing the Man of Ross!
Ib. l. 250

1 In the worst inn's worst room, with mat half-hung,

Great Villiers lies—alas! how changed from him,

Gallant and gay, in Cliveden's proud alcove
The bower of wanton Shrewsbury and love.
    Moral Essays, Ep. iii, *To Lord Bathurst*, ll. 299–308

2 Where London's column, pointing at the skies
Like a tall bully, lifts the head, and lies.   *Ib.* l. 339

3 Grove nods at grove, each alley has a brother,
And half the platform just reflects the other.
    Ib. Ep. iv. *To Lord Burlington*, l. 117.

4 To rest, the cushion and soft dean invite,
Who never mentions hell to ears polite.   *Ib.* l. 149

5 Such were the notes, thy once-loved Poet sung,
Till Death untimely stopped his tuneful tongue.
    Ib. Ep. v. *To the Earl of Oxford and Earl
    Mortimer*, l. 1

6 Statesman, yet friend to truth! of soul sincere,
In action faithful, and in honour clear;
Who broke no promise, served no private end,
Who gained no title, and who lost no friend.
    Ib. Ep. vii. *To Mr. Addison*, l. 67

7 Where'er you walk cool gales shall fan the glade;
Trees, where you sit, shall crowd into a shade;
Where'er you tread, the blushing flow'rs shall rise,
And all things flourish where you turn your eyes.
    Pastorals, Summer, l. 73

8 What dire offence from am'rous causes springs,
What mighty contests rise from trivial things!
    The Rape of the Lock, c. i, l. 1

9 Here files of pins extend their shining rows,
Puffs, powders, patches, bibles, billets-doux.
    Ib. l. 137

10 On her white breast a sparkling cross she wore,
Which Jews might kiss, and infidels adore.
    Ib. c. ii, l. 7

11 Bright as the sun, her eyes the gazers strike,
And, like the sun, they shine on all alike.   *Ib.* l. 13

12 If to her share some female errors fall,
Look on her face, and you'll forget 'em all.   *Ib.* l. 17

13 Fair tresses man's imperial race insnare,
And beauty draws us with a single hair.   *Ib.* l. 27

14 Here thou, great Anna! whom three realms obey,
Dost sometimes counsel take—and sometimes tea.
    Ib. c. iii, l. 7

15 The hungry judges soon the sentence sign,
And wretches hang that jurymen may dine.   *Ib.* l. 21

16 Let spades be trumps! she said, and trumps they
were.   *Ib.* l. 46

17 Not louder shrieks to pitying heav'n are cast,
When husbands, or when lap-dogs breathe their last.
    Ib. l. 157

18 Sir Plume, of amber snuff-box justly vain,
And the nice conduct of a clouded cane.
    Ib. c. iv, l. 123

19 Beauties in vain their pretty eyes may roll;
Charms strike the sight, but merit wins the soul.
    Ib. c. v, l. 33

20 Shut, shut the door, good John! fatigued I said,
Tie up the knocker; say I'm sick, I'm dead.
    *Epistles and Satires of Horace Imitated. Prologue,
    Epistle to Dr. Arbuthnot*, l. 1

21 Is there a parson, much bemused in beer,
A maudlin poetess, a rhyming peer,
A clerk, foredoomed his father's soul to cross,
Who pens a stanza, when he should engross?
    Ib. Epistle to Dr. Arbuthnot, l. 15

22 Fired that the house reject him, "Sdeath I'll print it,
And shame the fools.'   *Ib.* l. 61

23   You think this cruel? take it for a rule,
No creature smarts so little as a fool.
Let peals of laughter, Codrus! round thee break,
Thou unconcern'd canst hear the mighty crack:
Pit, box, and gall'ry in convulsions hurl'd,
Thou stand'st unshook amidst a bursting world.
    Ib. l. 83

24 Destroy his fib or sophistry—in vain!
The creature's at his dirty work again.   *Ib.* l. 91

25 As yet a child, nor yet a fool to fame,
I lisped in numbers, for the numbers came.
    Ib. l. 127

26 This long disease, my life.   *Ib.* l. 132

27 Pretty! in amber to observe the forms
Of hairs, or straws, or dirt, or grubs, or worms!
The things we know are neither rich nor rare,
But wonder how the devil they got there.   *Ib.* l. 169

28 And he, whose fustian's so sublimely bad,
It is not poetry, but prose run mad.   *Ib.* l. 187

29   Were there one whose fires
True genius kindles, and fair fame inspires;
Blest with each talent, and each art to please,
And born to write, converse, and live with ease:
Should such a man, too fond to rule alone,
Bear, like the Turk, no brother near the throne,
View him with scornful, yet with jealous eyes,
And hate for arts that caused himself to rise;
Damn with faint praise, assent with civil leer,
And, without sneering, teach the rest to sneer;
Willing to wound, and yet afraid to strike,
Just hint a fault, and hesitate dislike.
Alike reserved to blame, or to commend,
A timorous foe, and a suspicious friend;
Dreading e'en fools, by flatterers besieged,
And so obliging, that he ne'er obliged;
Like Cato, give his little senate laws,
And sit attentive to his own applause;
While wits and Templars every sentence raise,
And wonder with a foolish face of praise—
Who but must laugh, if such a man there be?
Who would not weep, if Atticus were he!
    [Addison.]   *Ib.* l. 193

30 Let Sporus tremble.—A. What? that thing of silk,
Sporus, that mere white curd of ass's milk?
Satire or sense, alas! can Sporus feel?
Who breaks a butterfly upon a wheel?   *Ib.* l. 305

31 Yet let me flap this bug with gilded wings—
This painted child of dirt, that stinks and stings.
    Ib. l. 309

32 So well-bred spaniels civilly delight
In mumbling of the game they dare not bite.
Eternal smiles his emptiness betray,
As shallow streams run dimpling all the way.
    Ib. l. 313

33 A Cherub's face, a reptile all the rest.   *Ib.* l. 331

34 Wit that can creep, and pride that licks the dust.
    Ib. l. 333

1 That not in fancy's maze he wandered long,
But stooped to truth, and moralised his song.
*Epistles and Satires of Horace Imitated. Prologue,
Epistle to Dr. Arbuthnot*, l. 340

2 The dull, the proud, the wicked and the mad.
Ib. l. 347

3 A knave's a knave to me in every state. *Ib.* l. 361

4 Unlearned, he knew no schoolman's subtle art,
No language, but the language of the heart.
By nature honest, by experience wise,
Healthy by temperance, and by exercise. *Ib.* l. 398

5 There St. John mingles with my friendly bowl
The feast of reason and the flow of soul.
Ib. I. Hor. II, *Sat.* 1. *To Mr. Fortescue*, l. 127

6 For I, who hold sage Homer's rule the best,
Welcome the coming, speed the going guest.
Ib. II. Hor. II, *Sat.* 2. *To Mr. Bethel*, l. 159. (In
Odyssey, xv. 83 with 'parting' for 'going'.)

7 In life's cool evening satiate of applause.
Ib. III. Hor. I, *Ep.* 1. *To Lord Bolingbroke*, l. 9

8 Not to go back, is somewhat to advance,
And men must walk at least before they dance.
Ib. l. 53

9 Get place and wealth—if possible with grace;
If not, by any means, get wealth and place.
Ib. l. 103

10 The worst of madmen is a saint run mad.
Ib. IV. Hor. I, *Ep.* 6. *To Mr. Murray*, l. 27

11 Grac'd as thou art with all the Pow'r of Words,
So known, so honour'd, at the House of Lords.
Ib. l. 48

12 Shakespeare (whom you and every play-house bill
Style the divine, the matchless, what you will)
For gain, not glory, winged his roving flight,
And grew immortal in his own despite.
Ib. V. Hor. II, *Ep.* 1. *To Augustus*, l. 69

13 Who now reads Cowley? if he pleases yet,
His moral pleases, not his pointed wit;
Forgot his epic, nay Pindaric art,
But still I love the language of his heart. *Ib.* l. 75

14 The people's voice is odd,
It is, and it is not, the voice of God. *Ib.* l. 89

15 In quibbles, angel and archangel join,
And God the Father turns a school-divine.
On Paradise Lost. Ib. l. 101

16 The mob of gentlemen who wrote with ease.
Ib. l. 108

17 Waller was smooth; but Dryden taught to join
The varying verse, the full-resounding line,
The long majestic march and energy divine.
Ib. l. 267

18 Ev'n copious Dryden wanted, or forgot,
The last and greatest art, the art to blot. *Ib.* l. 280

19 There still remains to mortify a wit,
The many-headed monster of the pit. *Ib.* l. 304

20 Let humble Allen, with an awkward shame,
Do good by stealth, and blush to find it fame.
Ib. Epilogue, Dial. i, l. 136

21 Argyll, the state's whole thunder born to wield,
And shake alike the senate and the field.
Ib. Dial. ii, l. 86

22 Ask you what provocation I have had?
The strong antipathy of good to bad. *Ib.* l. 197

23 Yes, I am proud; I must be proud to see
Men not afraid of God, afraid of me. *Ib.* l. 208

24 Vain was the chief's, the sage's pride!
They had no poet, and they died.
Imitations of Horace, Odes, IV. IX. iv

25 Bathos, the art of sinking in Poetry.
Miscellanies. Title

26 Happy the man whose wish and care
A few paternal acres bound,
Content to breathe his native air,
In his own ground. *Ode on Solitude*

27 Thus let me live, unseen, unknown,
Thus unlamented let me die,
Steal from the world, and not a stone
Tell where I lie. *Ib.*

28 And the touched needle trembles to the pole.
Temple of Fame, l. 431

29 Father of all! in ev'ry age,
In ev'ry clime adored,
By saint, by savage, and by sage,
Jehovah, Jove, or Lord!

Thou Great First Cause, least understood!
Who all my sense confined
To know but this, that thou art good,
And that myself am blind. *The Universal Prayer*

30 What conscience dictates to be done,
Or warns me not to do,
This teach me more than hell to shun,
That, more than heav'n pursue. *Ib.*

31 Teach me to feel another's woe,
To hide the fault I see;
That mercy I to others show,
That mercy show to me. *Ib.*

32 Oft, as in airy rings they skim the heath,
The clam'rous lapwings feel the leaden death:
Oft, as the mounting larks their notes prepare,
They fall, and leave their little lives in air.
Windsor Forest, l. 131

33 Not to admire, is all the art I know
To make men happy, and to keep them so.
Trans. of Horace, Epistles, I. vi

34 This is the Jew
That Shakspeare drew.
*Of Macklin's performance of Shylock, 14 Feb.
1741*. Baker, Reed, & Jones, *Biographia Drama-
tica* (*1812*), vol. i, pt. ii, p. 469

35 Party-spirit, which at best is but the madness of many
for the gain of a few.
Letters. To E. Blount, 27 Aug. 1714

36 'Blessed is the man who expects nothing, for he shall
never be disappointed', was the ninth beatitude
which a man of wit (who, like a man of wit, was a
long time in gaol) added to the eighth.
Ib. To Fortescue, 23 Sept. 1725

37 How often are we to die before we go quite off this
stage? In every friend we lose a part of ourselves,
and the best part. *Ib. To Swift, 5 Dec. 1732*

38 To endeavour to work upon the vulgar with fine
sense, is like attempting to hew blocks with a razor.
Thoughts on Various Subjects

1 When men grow virtuous in their old age, they only make a sacrifice to God of the devil's leavings.
Thoughts on Various Subjects. (*See 520:48*)

WALTER POPE

1630–1714

2 If I live to be old, for I find I go down,
Let this be my fate in a country town;
May I have a warm house with a stone at the gate,
And a cleanly young girl to rub my bald pate.
May I govern my passion with an absolute sway,
And grow wiser and better as my strength wears away,
Without gout or stone, by a gentle decay.
The Old Man's Wish. H. Playford, *Theater of Musick* (1685), bk. i, p. 50

RICHARD PORSON

1759–1808

3 When Dido found Æneas would not come,
She mourn'd in silence, and was Di-do-dum.
Epigram: On Latin Gerunds. J. S. Watson, *Life of Porson* (1861), p. 418

4 The Germans in Greek
Are sadly to seek:
Not five in five score,
But ninety-five more:
All, save only Herman,
And Herman's a German.
M. L. Clarke, *Life of Porson*, ch. vii

5 Madoc will be read,—when Homer and Virgil are forgotten. [To Southey.]
Rogers, Table Talk, p. 330

6 He sometimes draws out the thread of his verbosity finer than the staple of his argument.
Of Gibbon's *Decline and Fall.* Letters to Travis (1790), preface, p. xxix. (*See 455:24*)

7 I went to Frankfort, and got drunk
With that most learn'd professor, Brunck;
I went to Worts, and got more drunken
With that more learn'd professor, Ruhnken.
Facetiæ Cantabrigienses, 1825

WILLIAM SYDNEY PORTER

see

O. HENRY

BEILBY PORTEUS

1731–1808

8 In sober state,
Through the sequester'd vale of rural life,
The venerable Patriarch guileless held
The tenor of his way.   *Death, l. 108*

9 One murder made a villain,
Millions a hero.   *Ib. l. 155*

10 War its thousands slays, Peace its ten thousands.
Ib. l. 179

11 Teach him how to live,
And, oh! still harder lesson! how to die.   *Ib. l. 319*

FRANCIS POTT

1832–1909

12 The strife is o'er, the battle done;
Now is the Victor's triumph won;
O let the song of praise be sung. Alleluia!
The Strife is O'er. Hymns fitted to the Order of Common Prayer (1861), trans. of Latin, *Finita Iam Sunt Praelia*

HENRY CODMAN POTTER

1835–1908

13 We have exchanged the Washingtonian dignity for the Jeffersonian simplicity, which in due time came to be only another name for the Jacksonian vulgarity.
Address, Washington Centennial, 30 Apr. 1889

SIR JOHN POWELL

1645–1713

14 Let us consider the reason of the case. For nothing is law that is not reason.
Coggs v. Bernard, 2 Lord Raymond, 911

JOHN O'CONNOR POWER

15 The mules of politics: without pride of ancestry, or hope of posterity.
Quoted in H. H. Asquith's *Memories and Reflections*, i. 123

WINTHROP MACKWORTH PRAED

1802–1839

16 I think that nought is worth a thought,
And I'm a fool for thinking.
The Chant of the Brazen Head

17 My own Araminta, say 'No!'   *A Letter of Advice*

18 A happy boy, at Drury's.   *School and Schoolfellows*

19 Just Eton boys grown heavy.   *Ib.*

20 Of science and logic he chatters,
As fine and as fast as he can;
Though I am no judge of such matters,
I'm sure he's a talented man.   *The Talented Man*

21 Whate'er the stranger's caste or creed,
Pundit or Papist, saint or sinner,
He found a stable for his steed,
And welcome for himself, and dinner.   *The Vicar*

22 If he departed as he came,
With no new light on love or liquor,—
Good sooth, the traveller was to blame,
And not the Vicarage, nor the Vicar.   *Ib.*

23 His talk was like a stream, which runs
With rapid change from rocks to roses:
It slipped from politics to puns,
It passed from Mahomet to Moses;
Beginning with the laws which keep
The planets in their radiant courses,
And ending with some precept deep
For dressing eels, or shoeing horses.   *Ib.*

24 The Baptist found him far too deep;
The Deist sighed with saving sorrow;
And the lean Levite went to sleep,
And dreamed of tasting pork to-morrow.   *Ib.*

1 For all who understood admired,
And some who did not understand them. *The Vicar*

CHARLES PRATT, EARL CAMDEN

1714–1794

2 The British Parliament has no right to tax the Americans. . . . Taxation and representation are inseparably united. God hath joined them; no British Parliament can put them asunder. To endeavour to do so is to stab our very vitals.
Speech, House of Lords, 1765

THE BOOK OF COMMON PRAYER

3 The two extremes, of too much stiffness in refusing, and of too much easiness in admitting any variation. *The Preface*

4 There was never any thing by the wit of man so well devised, or so sure established, which in continuance of time hath not been corrupted.
Ib. Concerning the Service of the Church

5 A table of the Moveable Feasts.
Section Heading in Introductory Pages, p. xxxi

6 Dearly beloved brethren, the Scripture moveth us in sundry places to acknowledge and confess our manifold sins and wickedness.
Morning Prayer. Priest's Opening Exhortation

7 We should not dissemble nor cloke them. *Ib.*

8 When we assemble and meet together. *Ib.*

9 Those things which are requisite and necessary, as well for the body as the soul. *Ib.*

10 We have erred, and strayed from thy ways like lost sheep. *Ib. General Confession*

11 We have left undone those things which we ought to have done; And we have done those things which we ought not to have done; And there is no health in us. *Ib.*

12 A godly, righteous, and sober life. *Ib.*

13 And forgive us our trespasses, As we forgive them that trespass against us. *Ib. The Lord's Prayer*

14 As it was in the beginning, is now, and ever shall be: world without end. Amen. *Ib. Gloria*

15 Lord God of Sabaoth. *Ib. Te Deum Laudamus*

16 An infinite Majesty. *Ib.*

17 The sharpness of death. *Ib.*

18 The noble army of martyrs. *Ib.*

19 O Lord, in thee have I trusted: let me never be confounded. *Ib.*

20 O all ye Works of the Lord, bless ye the Lord: praise him, and magnify him for ever. *Ib. Benedicite*

21 O all ye Green Things upon the Earth, bless ye the Lord: praise him, and magnify him for ever. *Ib.*

22 O ye Whales, and all that move in the Waters. *Ib.*

23 O Ananias, Azarias, and Misael, bless ye the Lord: praise him, and magnify him for ever. *Ib.*

24 Give peace in our time, O Lord.
Because there is none other that fighteth for us, but only thou, O God. *Ib. Versicles*

25 The author of peace and lover of concord, in knowledge of whom standeth our eternal life, whose service is perfect freedom.
Morning Prayer. Second Collect, for Peace

26 Neither run into any kind of danger.
Ib. Third Collect, for Grace

27 In Quires and Places where they sing.
Ib. Rubric after Third Collect

28 Grant her in health and wealth long to live.
Ib. A Prayer for the Queen's Majesty

29 The fountain of all goodness.
Ib. Prayer for the Royal Family

30 Almighty and everlasting God, who alone workest great marvels; Send down upon our Bishops, and Curates, and all Congregations committed to their charge, the healthful Spirit of thy grace.
Ib. Prayer for the Clergy and People

31 The continual dew of thy blessing. *Ib.*

32 With one accord to make our common supplications unto thee. *Ib. Prayer of St. Chrysostom*

33 When two or three are gathered together in thy Name thou wilt grant their requests. *Ib.*

34 From whom all holy desires, all good counsels, and all just works do proceed.
Evening Prayer. Second Collect

35 That peace which the world cannot give. *Ib.*

36 Lighten our darkness, we beseech thee, O Lord; and by thy great mercy defend us from all perils and dangers of this night. *Ib. Third Collect*

37 Whosoever will be saved: before all things it is necessary that he hold the Catholick Faith.
Which Faith except every one do keep whole and undefiled: without doubt he shall perish everlastingly. *Athanasian Creed*

38 Neither confounding the Persons: nor dividing the Substance. *Ib.*

39 As also there are not three incomprehensibles, nor three uncreated: but one uncreated, and one incomprehensible. *Ib.*

40 Not three Gods: but one God. *Ib.*

41 Of a reasonable soul and human flesh subsisting. *Ib.*

42 Not by conversion of the Godhead into flesh: but by taking of the Manhood into God. *Ib.*

43 Have mercy upon us miserable sinners. *The Litany*

44 Neither take thou vengeance of our sins. *Ib.*

45 The crafts and assaults of the devil. *Ib.*

46 Envy, hatred, and malice, and all uncharitableness. *Ib.*

47 Deceits of the world, the flesh, and the devil. *Ib.*

48 From battle and murder, and from sudden death. *Ib.*

49 Hardness of heart, and contempt of thy Word and Commandment. *Ib.*

50 Agony and bloody Sweat. *Ib.*

51 In the hour of death, and in the day of judgement. *Ib.*

52 All Bishops, Priests, and Deacons. *Ib.*

53 Unity, peace, and concord. *Ib.*

54 To bring forth the fruits of the Spirit. *Ib.*

1 To strengthen such as do stand; and to comfort and help the weak-hearted; and to raise up them that fall; and finally to beat down Satan under our feet.
The Litany

2 All that are in danger, necessity, and tribulation. *Ib.*

3 All that travel by land or by water, all women labouring of child, all sick persons, and young children; and to shew thy pity upon all prisoners and captives.
Ib.

4 The fatherless children, and widows. *Ib.*

5 Our enemies, persecutors, and slanderers. *Ib.*

6 The kindly fruits of the earth, so as in due time we may enjoy them. *Ib.*

7 Our sins, negligences, and ignorances. *Ib.*

8 The sighing of a contrite heart. *Ib. First Collect*

9 The craft and subtilty of the devil or man. *Ib.*

10 We have heard with our ears, and our fathers have declared unto us, the noble works that thou didst in their days, and in the old time before them.
Ib. Sentences after the First Collect

11 Turn from us all those evils that we most righteously have deserved. *Ib. Second Collect*

12 Tied and bound with the chain of our sins.
Prayers and Thanksgivings, upon Several Occasions. 'O God, whose nature and property'

13 Our Mediator and Advocate. *Ib.*

14 The safety, honour, and welfare of our Sovereign, and her Dominions.
Ib. Prayer for the High Court of Parliament

15 All sorts and conditions of men.
Ib. Prayer for All Conditions of Men

16 All who profess and call themselves Christians. *Ib.*

17 Any ways afflicted, or distressed, in mind, body, or estate. *Ib.*

18 A happy issue out of all their afflictions. *Ib.*

19 Our creation, preservation, and all the blessings of this life. *Ib. Thanksgivings. A General Thanksgiving*

20 For the means of grace, and for the hope of glory. *Ib.*

21 The former and the latter rain. *Ib. For Rain*

22 Cast away the works of darkness, and put upon us the armour of light, now in the time of this mortal life. *Collects. 1st Sunday in Advent*

23 Hear them, read, mark, learn, and inwardly digest them. *Ib. 2nd Sunday in Advent*

24 An acceptable people in thy sight.
Ib. 3rd Sunday in Advent

25 Sore let and hindered in running the race.
Ib. 4th Sunday in Advent

26 Children by adoption and grace. *Ib. Christmas Day*

27 The glory that shall be revealed.
Ib. St. Stephen's Day

28 That they may both perceive and know what things they ought to do, and also may have grace and power faithfully to fulfil the same.
Ib. 1st Sunday after Epiphany

29 Grant us thy peace all the days of our life.
Ib. 2nd Sunday after Epiphany

30 By reason of the frailty of our nature we cannot always stand upright. *Collects. 4th Sunday after Epiphany*

31 That most excellent gift of charity.
Ib. Quinquagesima Sunday

32 All evil thoughts which may assault and hurt the soul.
Ib. 2nd Sunday in Lent

33 Jews, Turks, Infidels, and Hereticks.
Ib. Good Friday. Third Collect

34 Thy special grace preventing us. *Ib. Easter Day*

35 The leaven of malice and wickedness.
Ib. 1st Sunday after Easter

36 Those things that are contrary to their profession.
Ib. 3rd Sunday after Easter

37 The unruly wills and affections of sinful men.
Ib. 4th Sunday after Easter

38 Among the sundry and manifold changes of the world, our hearts may surely there be fixed where true joys are to be found. *Ib.*

39 To have a right judgement in all things.
Ib. Whitsun-day

40 The weakness of our mortal nature.
Ib. 1st Sunday after Trinity

41 We may so pass through things temporal, that we finally lose not the things eternal.
Ib. 4th Sunday after Trinity

42 Such good things as pass man's understanding.
Ib. 6th Sunday after Trinity

43 The author and giver of all good things.
Ib. 7th Sunday after Trinity

44 Running the way of thy commandments.
Ib. 11th Sunday after Trinity

45 Those things whereof our conscience is afraid.
Ib. 12th Sunday after Trinity

46 Increase of faith, hope, and charity.
Ib. 14th Sunday after Trinity

47 Because the frailty of man without thee cannot but fall. *Ib. 15th Sunday after Trinity*

48 Serve thee with a quiet mind.
Ib. 21st Sunday after Trinity

49 Thy household the Church.
Ib. 22nd Sunday after Trinity

50 Stir up, we beseech thee, O Lord, the wills of thy faithful people; that they, plenteously bringing forth the fruit of good works, may of thee be plenteously rewarded.
Ib. 25th Sunday after Trinity

51 Carried away with every blast of vain doctrine.
Ib. St. Mark's Day

52 Whom truly to know is everlasting life.
Ib. St. Philip and St. James's Day

53 Constantly speak the truth, boldly rebuke vice, and patiently suffer for the truth's sake.
Ib. St. John Baptist's Day

54 Ordained and constituted the services of Angels and men in a wonderful order.
Ib. St. Michael and All Angels

55 Who hast knit together thine elect in one communion and fellowship, in the mystical body of thy Son.
Ib. All Saints' Day

1 An open and notorious evil liver.
Holy Communion: Introductory Rubric

2 Truly repented and amended his former naughty life.
Ib.

3 A fair white linen cloth. *Ib.*

4 Unto whom all hearts be open, all desires known, and from whom no secrets are hid.
Ib. Collect for Purity

5 Thou shalt have none other gods but me.
Ib. 1st Commandment

6 Incline our hearts to keep this law.
Ib. Response to Commandments

7 Thou shalt not make to thyself any graven image, nor the likeness of any thing that is in heaven above, or in the earth beneath, or in the water under the earth. Thou shalt not bow down to them, nor worship them: for I the Lord thy God am a jealous God, and visit the sins of the fathers upon the children unto the third and fourth generation.
Ib. 2nd Commandment

8 Thou shalt not take the Name of the Lord thy God in vain. *Ib. 3rd Commandment*

9 Remember that thou keep holy the Sabbath-day. Six days shalt thou labour, and do all that thou hast to do; but the seventh day is the Sabbath of the Lord thy God. *Ib. 4th Commandment*

10 The stranger that is within thy gates. *Ib.*

11 In six days the Lord made heaven and earth, the sea, and all that in them is, and rested the seventh day.
Ib.

12 Honour thy father and thy mother; that thy days may be long in the land which the Lord thy God giveth thee. *Ib. 5th Commandment*

13 Thou shalt do no murder. *Ib. 6th Commandment*

14 Thou shalt not commit adultery.
Ib. 7th Commandment

15 Thou shalt not steal. *Ib. 8th Commandment*

16 Thou shalt not bear false witness against thy neighbour. *Ib. 9th Commandment*

17 Thou shalt not covet thy neighbour's wife, nor his servant, nor his maid, nor his ox, nor his ass, nor any thing that is his. *Ib. 10th Commandment*

18 All things visible and invisible. *Ib. Nicene Creed*

19 Very God of very God. *Ib.*

20 The Lord and giver of life. *Ib.*

21 Who spake by the Prophets. *Ib.*

22 One Catholick and Apostolick Church. *Ib.*

23 In a decent bason to be provided by the Parish.
Ib. Rubric before the Prayer for the Church Militant

24 The whole state of Christ's Church militant here in earth. *Ib. Prayer for the Church Militant*

25 The spirit of truth, unity, and concord. *Ib.*

26 Live in unity and godly love. *Ib.*

27 Truly and indifferently minister justice. *Ib.*

28 Thy true and lively Word. *Ib.*

29 All them, who in this transitory life are in trouble, sorrow, need, sickness, or any other adversity. *Ib.*

30 Departed this life in thy faith and fear.
Holy Communion. Prayer for the Church Militant

31 Discreet and learned Minister of God's Word.
Ib. First Exhortation

32 Ghostly counsel and advice. *Ib.*

33 We eat and drink our own damnation.
Ib. Third Exhortation

34 Ye that do truly and earnestly repent you of your sins, and are in love and charity with your neighbours, and intend to lead a new life. *Ib. The Invitation*

35 Meekly kneeling upon your knees. *Ib.*

36 The burden of them is intolerable.
Ib. General Confession

37 Hear what comfortable words.
Ib. Comfortable Words

38 It is meet and right so to do. *Ib. Versicles*

39 Therefore with Angels and Archangels, and with all the company of heaven. *Ib. Hymn of Praise*

40 Holy, holy, holy, Lord God of hosts, heaven and earth are full of thy glory: Glory be to thee, O Lord most High. *Ib.*

41 By the operation of the Holy Ghost.
Ib. Proper Preface for Christmas Day

42 A full, perfect, and sufficient sacrifice, oblation, and satisfaction. *Ib. Prayer of Consecration*

43 Who, in the same night that he was betrayed. *Ib.*

44 This our bounden duty and service.
Ib. Prayer of Oblation, 1

45 Not weighing our merits, but pardoning our offences
Ib.

46 The mystical body of thy Son, which is the blessed company of all faithful people. *Ib. 2*

47 Heirs through hope of thy everlasting kingdom. *Ib.*

48 The peace of God, which passeth all understanding.
Ib. The Blessing

49 Be amongst you and remain with you always. *Ib.*

50 All the changes and chances of this mortal life.
Ib. Collects after the Offertory, 1

51 Prevent us, O Lord, in all our doings. *Ib. 4*

52 All our works begun, continued, and ended in thee.
Ib.

53 Those things, which for our unworthiness we dare not, and for our blindness we cannot ask. *Ib. 5*

54 For that were Idolatry, to be abhorred of all faithful Christians. *Ib. Black Rubric*

55 In the vulgar tongue.
Publick Baptism of Infants. Introductory Rubric, 1

56 All this I stedfastly believe. *Ib. Vow of Faith*

57 Grant that the old Adam in this Child may be so buried, that the new man may be raised up in him.
Ib. Invocation of Blessing on the Child

58 The faith of Christ crucified.
Ib. Reception and Dedication of the Child

59 Dead unto sin, and living unto righteousness.
Ib. Thanksgiving

60 Crucify the old man. *Ib.*

61 Ministration of Baptism to Such as are of Riper Years. *Title*

1 Put on Christ.
Ministration of Baptism to Such as are of Riper Years. Final Exhortation

2 What is your name?
N. or M.
Who gave you this name?
My Godfathers and Godmothers in my Baptism; wherein I was made a member of Christ, the child of God, and an inheritor of the kingdom of heaven.
What did your Godfathers and Godmothers then for you?
They did promise and vow three things in my name. First, that I should renounce the devil and all his works, the pomps and vanity of this wicked world, and all the sinful lusts of the flesh. Secondly, that I should believe all the Articles of the Christian Faith. And thirdly, that I should keep God's holy will and commandments, and walk in the same all the days of my life. *The Catechism*

3 Yes verily; and by God's help so I will. *Ib.*

4 Rehearse the Articles of thy Belief. *Ib.*

5 My duty towards God, and my duty towards my Neighbour. *Ib.*

6 To love him as myself, and to do to all men, as I would they should do unto me. *Ib.*

7 Governors, teachers, spiritual pastors and masters. *Ib.*

8 To keep my hands from picking and stealing, and my tongue from evil-speaking, lying, and slandering. *Ib.*

9 To learn and labour truly to get mine own living, and to do my duty in that state of life, unto which it shall please God to call me. *Ib.*

10 My good child, know this. *Ib.*

11 Amen, So be it. *Ib.*

12 Two only, as generally necessary to salvation, that is to say, Baptism, and the Supper of the Lord. *Ib.*

13 An outward and visible sign of an inward and spiritual grace. *Ib.*

14 In their Mother Tongue. *Ib. Final Rubric*

15 Confirmation, or laying on of hands. *Title*

16 Being now come to the years of discretion. *Confirmation*

17 Ratify and confirm the same. *Ib.*

18 Our help is in the name of the Lord
Who hath made heaven and earth.
Blessed be the name of the Lord;
Henceforth, world without end.
Lord, hear our prayers;
And let our cry come unto thee. *Ib.*

19 Thy manifold gifts of grace. *Ib.*

20 Defend, O Lord, this thy child [*or* this thy servant] with thy heavenly grace that *he* may continue thine for ever; and daily increase in thy holy Spirit more and more, until *he* come unto thy everlasting kingdom. *Ib.*

21 If any of you know cause, or just impediment, why these two persons should not be joined together in holy Matrimony, ye are to declare it. This is the first time of asking.
Solemnization of Matrimony. The Banns

22 Here in the sight of God, and in the face of this congregation.
Solemnization of Matrimony. Exhortation

23 Brute beasts that have no understanding. *Ib.*

24 First, it was ordained for the procreation of children. *Ib.*

25 A remedy against sin. *Ib.*

26 Such persons as have not the gift of continency. *Ib.*

27 Let him now speak, or else hereafter for ever hold his peace. *Ib.*

28 Wilt thou have this woman to thy wedded wife, to live together after God's ordinance in the holy estate of Matrimony? *Ib. Betrothal*

29 Forsaking all other, keep thee only unto her, so long as ye both shall live. *Ib.*

30 To have and to hold from this day forward, for better for worse, for richer for poorer, in sickness and in health, to love and to cherish, till death us do part, according to God's holy ordinance; and thereto I plight thee my troth. *Ib.*

31 To love, cherish, and to obey. *Ib.*

32 With this Ring I thee wed, with my body I thee worship, and with all my worldly goods I thee endow. *Ib. The Wedding*

33 This Ring given and received. *Ib. The Prayer*

34 Those whom God hath joined together let no man put asunder. *Ib.*

35 Consented together in holy wedlock. *Ib. Priest's Declaration*

36 Peace be to this house. *Visitation of the Sick*

37 Unto God's gracious mercy and protection we commit thee. *Ib.*

38 The inner man. *Ib.*

39 Against the hour of death. *Ib.*

40 Laid violent hands upon themselves.
Burial of the Dead. Introductory Rubric

41 Man that is born of a woman hath but a short time to live, and is full of misery. *Ib. First Anthem*

42 In the midst of life we are in death. *Ib.*

43 Suffer us not, at our last hour, for any pains of death, to fall from thee. *Ib.*

44 We therefore commit *his* body to the ground; earth to earth, ashes to ashes, dust to dust; in sure and certain hope of the Resurrection to eternal life. *Ib.*

45 Sat in the seat of the scornful. *Psalms i. 1*

46 He shall be like a tree planted by the water-side. *Ib. 3*

47 Why do the heathen so furiously rage together: and why do the people imagine a vain thing? *Ib. ii. 1*

48 Let us break their bonds asunder: and cast away their cords from us. *Ib. 3*

49 The Lord shall have them in derision. *Ib. 4*

50 Thou shalt bruise them with a rod of iron: and break them in pieces like a potter's vessel. *Ib. 9*

51 Kiss the Son, lest he be angry, and so ye perish from the right way: if his wrath be kindled, (yea, but a little,) blessed are all they that put their trust in him. *Ib. 12*

52 Stand in awe, and sin not: commune with your own heart, and in your chamber, and be still. *Ib. iv. 4*

1 There be many that say: Who will shew us any good?
Psalms iv. 6

2 Lord, lift thou up the light of thy countenance upon us. *Ib.* 7

3 The Lord will abhor both the bloodthirsty and deceitful man. *Ib.* v. 6

4 Make thy way plain before my face. *Ib.* 8

5 Their throat is an open sepulchre: they flatter with their tongue. *Ib.* 10

6 Let them perish through their own imaginations.
Ib. 11

7 God is a righteous Judge, strong, and patient: and God is provoked every day. *Ib.* vii. 12

8 Out of the mouth of very babes and sucklings hast thou ordained strength, because of thine enemies: that thou mightest still the enemy, and the avenger.
Ib. viii. 2

9 For I will consider thy heavens, even the works of thy fingers: the moon and the stars, which thou hast ordained. *Ib.* 3

10 What is man, that thou art mindful of him: and the son of man, that thou visitest him? *Ib.* 4

11 Thou madest him lower than the angels: to crown him with glory and worship. *Ib.* 5

12 The fowls of the air, and the fishes of the sea: and whatsoever walketh through the paths of the seas.
Ib. 8

13 O thou enemy, destructions are come to a perpetual end. *Ib.* ix. 6

14 Their memorial is perished with them. *Ib.*

15 Up, Lord, and let not man have the upper hand.
Ib. 19

16 That the heathen may know themselves to be but men. *Ib.* 20

17 In the Lord put I my trust: how say ye then to my soul, that she should flee as a bird unto the hill?
Ib. xi. 1

18 That they may privily shoot at them which are true of heart. *Ib.* 2

19 For the foundations will be cast down: and what hath the righteous done? *Ib.* 3

20 They do but flatter with their lips, and dissemble in their double heart. *Ib.* xii. 2

21 The fool hath said in his heart: There is no God.
Ib. xiv. 1

22 There is none that doeth good, no not one. *Ib.* 2

23 They are altogether become abominable. *Ib.* 4

24 Lord, who shall dwell in thy tabernacle: or who shall rest upon thy holy hill?
Even he, that leadeth an uncorrupt life: and doeth the thing which is right, and speaketh the truth from his heart.
He that hath used no deceit in his tongue, nor done evil to his neighbour: and hath not slandered his neighbour.
He that setteth not by himself, but is lowly in his own eyes: and maketh much of them that fear the Lord.
He that sweareth unto his neighbour, and disappointeth him not: though it were to his own hindrance.

He that hath not given his money upon usury: **nor** taken reward against the innocent.
Whoso doeth these things shall never fall. *Psalms* xv

25 Thou shalt maintain my lot. *Ib.* xvi. 6

26 The lot is fallen unto me in a fair ground: yea, I have a goodly heritage. *Ib.* 7

27 For why? thou shalt not leave my soul in hell: neither shalt thou suffer thy Holy One to see corruption.
Thou shalt shew me the path of life; in thy presence is the fulness of joy: and at thy right hand there is pleasure for evermore. *Ib.* 11

28 Keep me as the apple of an eye: hide me under the shadow of thy wings. *Ib.* xvii. 8

29 Thou also shalt light my candle: the Lord my God shalt make my darkness to be light. *Ib.* xviii. 28

30 With the help of my God I shall leap over the wall.
Ib. 29

31 A people whom I have not known: shall serve me.
Ib. 44

32 The heavens declare the glory of God: and the firmament sheweth his handy-work.
One day telleth another: and one night certifieth another.
There is neither speech nor language: but their voices are heard among them.
Their sound is gone out into all lands: and their words into the ends of the world.
In them hath he set a tabernacle for the sun: which cometh forth as a bridegroom out of his chamber, and rejoiceth as a giant to run his course.
It goeth forth from the uttermost part of the heaven, and runneth about unto the end of it again: and there is nothing hid from the heat thereof.
Ib. xix. 1

33 More to be desired are they than gold, yea, than much fine gold: sweeter also than honey, and the honeycomb. *Ib.* 10

34 Who can tell how oft he offendeth: O cleanse thou me from my secret faults.
Keep thy servant also from presumptuous sins, lest they get the dominion over me: so shall I be undefiled, and innocent from the great offence.
Let the words of my mouth, and the meditation of my heart: be alway acceptable in thy sight,
O Lord: my strength, and my redeemer. *Ib.* 12

35 The Lord hear thee in the day of trouble: the Name of the God of Jacob defend thee;
Send thee help from the sanctuary: and strengthen thee out of Sion. *Ib.* xx. 1

36 Grant thee thy heart's desire: and fulfil all thy mind.
Ib. 4

37 Some put their trust in chariots, and some in horses: but we will remember the name of the Lord our God.
They are brought down, and fallen: but we are risen, and stand upright. *Ib.* 7

38 Thou hast given him his heart's desire: and hast not denied him the request of his lips. *Ib.* xxi. 2

39 He asked life of thee, and thou gavest him a long life: even for ever and ever. *Ib.* 4

40 And imagined such a device as they are not able to perform. *Ib.* 11

1 My God, my God, look upon me; why hast thou forsaken me: and art so far from my health, and from the voice of my complaint?

O my God, I cry in the day-time, but thou hearest not: and in the night-season also I take no rest.

And thou continuest holy: O thou worship of Israel. *Psalms* xxii. 1

2 But as for me, I am a worm, and no man. *Ib.* 6

3 All they that see me laugh me to scorn: they shoot out their lips, and shake their heads, saying,

He trusted in God, that he would deliver him: let him deliver him, if he will have him. *Ib.* 7

4 Many oxen are come about me: fat bulls of Basan close me in on every side. *Ib.* 12

5 For many dogs are come about me. *Ib.* 16

6 They pierced my hands and my feet; I may tell all my bones: they stand staring and looking upon me.

They part my garments among them: and cast lots upon my vesture. *Ib.* 17

7 Deliver my soul from the sword: my darling from the power of the dog.

Save me from the lion's mouth: thou hast heard me also from the horns of the unicorns. *Ib.* 20

8 For he hath not despised, nor abhorred, the low estate of the poor. *Ib.* 24

9 All they that go down into the dust shall kneel before him: and no man hath quickened his own soul. *Ib.* 30

10 The Lord is my shepherd: therefore can I lack nothing.

He shall feed me in a green pasture: and lead me forth beside the waters of comfort.

He shall convert my soul: and bring me forth in the paths of righteousness, for his Name's sake.

Yea, though I walk through the valley of the shadow of death, I will fear no evil: for thou art with me; thy rod and thy staff comfort me.

Thou shalt prepare a table before me against them that trouble me: thou hast anointed my head with oil, and my cup shall be full.

But thy loving-kindness and mercy shall follow me all the days of my life: and I will dwell in the house of the Lord for ever. *Ib.* xxiii

11 The earth is the Lord's, and all that therein is: the compass of the world, and they that dwell therein. *Ib.* xxiv. 1

12 Lift up your heads, O ye gates, and be ye lift up, ye everlasting doors: and the King of glory shall come in. *Ib.* 7

13 Who is the King of glory: even the Lord of hosts, he is the King of glory. *Ib.* 10

14 O remember not the sins and offences of my youth. *Ib.* xxv. 6

15 The sorrows of my heart are enlarged. *Ib.* 16

16 Deliver Israel, O God: out of all his troubles. *Ib.* 21

17 Examine me, O Lord, and prove me: try out my reins and my heart. *Ib.* xxvi. 2

18 I will wash my hands in innocency, O Lord: and so will I go to thine altar. *Ib.* 6

19 Lord, I have loved the habitation of thy house: and the place where thine honour dwelleth.

O shut not up my soul with the sinners: nor my life with the blood-thirsty. *Ib.* 8

20 The Lord is my light, and my salvation; whom then shall I fear: the Lord is the strength of my life; of whom then shall I be afraid? *Psalms* xxvii. 1

21 When my father and my mother forsake me: the Lord taketh me up. *Ib.* 12

22 I should utterly have fainted: but that I believe verily to see the goodness of the Lord in the land of the living. *Ib.* 15

23 The voice of the Lord maketh the hinds to bring forth young, and discovereth the thick bushes. *Ib.* xxix. 8

24 The Lord sitteth above the water-flood: and the Lord remaineth a King for ever. *Ib.* 9

25 Give thanks unto him for a remembrance of his holiness.

For his wrath endureth but the twinkling of an eye, and in his pleasure is life: heaviness may endure for a night, but joy cometh in the morning. *Ib.* xxx. 4

26 What profit is there in my blood: when I go down to the pit?

Shall the dust give thanks unto thee; or shall it declare thy truth? *Ib.* 9

27 Into thy hands I commend my spirit. *Ib.* xxxi. 6

28 But hast set my feet in a large room. *Ib.* 9

29 I am clean forgotten, as a dead man out of mind. *Ib.* 14

30 Thanks be to the Lord: for he hath shewed me marvellous great kindness in a strong city. *Ib.* 23

31 For while I held my tongue: my bones consumed away through my daily complaining. *Ib.* xxxii. 3

32 For this shall every one that is godly make his prayer unto thee, in a time when thou mayest be found: but in the great water-floods they shall not come nigh him. *Ib.* 7

33 Thou shalt compass me about with songs of deliverance. *Ib.* 8

34 Be ye not like to horse and mule, which have no understanding: whose mouths must be held with bit and bridle, lest they fall upon thee. *Ib.* 10

35 Rejoice in the Lord, O ye righteous: for it becometh well the just to be thankful.

Praise the Lord with harp: sing praises unto him with the lute, and instrument of ten strings.

Sing unto the Lord a new song: sing praises lustily unto him with a good courage. *Ib.* xxxiii. 1

36 The Lord bringeth the counsel of the heathen to nought: and maketh the devices of the people to be of none effect, and casteth out the counsels of princes. *Ib.* 10

37 There is no king that can be saved by the multitude of an host: neither is any mighty man delivered by much strength.

A horse is counted but a vain thing to save a man: neither shall he deliver any man by his great strength. *Ib.* 15

38 O taste, and see, how gracious the Lord is: blessed is the man that trusteth in him.

O fear the Lord, ye that are his saints: for they that fear him lack nothing.

The lions do lack, and suffer hunger: but they who seek the Lord shall want no manner of thing that is good. *Ib.* xxxiv. 8

1 What man is he that lusteth to live: and would fain see good days? *Psalms* xxxiv. 12

2 Eschew evil, and do good: seek peace, and ensue it. *Ib.* 14

3 Fret not thyself because of the ungodly. *Ib.* xxxvii. 1

4 He shall make thy righteousness as clear as the light: and thy just dealing as the noon-day. *Ib.* 6

5 I have been young, and now am old: and yet saw I never the righteous forsaken, nor his seed begging their bread. *Ib.* 25

6 I myself have seen the ungodly in great power: and flourishing like a green bay-tree.
I went by, and lo, he was gone: I sought him, but his place could no where be found.
Keep innocency, and take heed unto the thing that is right: for that shall bring a man peace at the last. *Ib.* 36

7 Lord, thou knowest all my desire: and my groaning is not hid from thee. *Ib.* xxxviii. 9

8 I held my tongue, and spake nothing: I kept silence, yea, even from good words; but it was pain and grief to me.
My heart was hot within me, and while I was thus musing the fire kindled: and at the last I spake with my tongue;
Lord, let me know mine end, and the number of my days: that I may be certified how long I have to live. *Ib.* xxxix. 3

9 Mine age is even as nothing in respect of thee; and verily every man living is altogether vanity.
For man walketh in a vain shadow, and disquieteth himself in vain: he heapeth up riches, and cannot tell who shall gather them. *Ib.* 6

10 Thou makest his beauty to consume away, like as it were a moth fretting a garment: every man therefore is but vanity. *Ib.* 12

11 For I am a stranger with thee: and a sojourner, as all my fathers were.
O spare me a little, that I may recover my strength: before I go hence, and be no more seen. *Ib.* 14

12 I waited patiently for the Lord: and he inclined unto me, and heard my calling.
He brought me also out of the horrible pit, out of the mire and clay: and set my feet upon the rock, and ordered my goings. *Ib.* xl. 1

13 Burnt-offerings, and sacrifice for sin, hast thou not required: then said I, Lo, I come.
In the volume of the book it is written of me, that I should fulfil thy will, O my God. *Ib.* 9

14 Thou art my helper and redeemer: make no long tarrying, O my God. *Ib.* 21

15 Yea, mine own familiar friend . . . hath lifted up his heel against me. *Ib.* xli. 9 [Bible Version]

16 Like as the hart desireth the water-brooks: so longeth my soul after thee, O God. *Ib.* xlii. 1

17 Why art thou so full of heaviness, O my soul: and why art thou so disquieted within me? *Ib.* 6

18 The little hill of Hermon. *Ib.* 8

19 One deep calleth another, because of the noise of the water-pipes: all thy waves and storms are gone over me. *Ib.* 9

20 While mine enemies that trouble me cast me in the teeth. *Psalms* xlii. 12

21 My heart is inditing of a good matter: I speak of the things which I have made unto the King.
My tongue is the pen of a ready writer. *Ib.* xlv. 1

22 Gird thee with thy sword upon thy thigh, O thou most Mighty: according to thy worship and renown.
Good luck have thou with thine honour: ride on, because of the word of truth, of meekness, and righteousness; and thy right hand shall teach thee terrible things. *Ib.* 4

23 Kings' daughters were among thy honourable women: upon thy right hand did stand the queen in a vesture of gold, wrought about with divers colours.
Hearken, O daughter, and consider, incline thine ear: forget also thine own people, and thy father's house.
So shall the King have pleasure in thy beauty. *Ib.* 10

24 And the daughter of Tyre shall be there with a gift. *Ib.* 13

25 The King's daughter is all glorious within: her clothing is of wrought gold.
She shall be brought unto the King in raiment of needle-work: the virgins that be her fellows shall bear her company, and shall be brought unto thee. *Ib.* 14

26 Instead of thy fathers thou shalt have children: whom thou mayest make princes in all lands. *Ib.* 17

27 God is our hope and strength: a very present help in trouble.
Therefore will we not fear, though the earth be moved: and though the hills be carried into the midst of the sea. *Ib.* xlvi. 1

28 God is in the midst of her, therefore shall she not be removed: God shall help her, and that right early.
The heathen make much ado, and the kingdoms are moved: but God hath shewed his voice, and the earth shall melt away. *Ib.* 5

29 He maketh wars to cease in all the world: he breaketh the bow, and knappeth the spear in sunder, and burneth the chariots in the fire.
Be still then, and know that I am God. *Ib.* 9

30 He shall subdue the people under us: and the nations under our feet. *Ib.* xlvii. 3

31 God is gone up with a merry noise: and the Lord with the sound of the trump. *Ib.* 5

32 For God is the King of all the earth: sing ye praises with understanding. *Ib.* 7

33 For lo, the kings of the earth are gathered, and gone by together.
They marvelled to see such things: they were astonished; and suddenly cast down. *Ib.* xlviii. 3

34 Thou shalt break the ships of the sea, through the east-wind. *Ib.* 6

35 Walk about Sion, and go round about her: and tell the towers thereof.
Mark well her bulwarks, set up her houses: that ye may tell them that come after.
For this God is our God for ever and ever: he shall be our guide unto death. *Ib.* 11

1 And yet they think that their houses shall continue for ever: and that their dwelling-places shall endure from one generation to another; and call the lands after their own names. *Psalms* xlix. 11

2 He shall follow the generation of his fathers: and shall never see light.
Man being in honour hath no understanding: but is compared unto the beasts that perish. *Ib.* 19

3 For all the beasts of the forest are mine: and so are the cattle upon a thousand hills. *Ib.* l. 10

4 Thinkest thou that I will eat bulls' flesh: and drink the blood of goats? *Ib.* 13

5 When thou sawest a thief, thou consentedst unto him: and hast been partaker with the adulterers. *Ib.* 18

6 O consider this, ye that forget God. *Ib.* 22

7 For I acknowledge my faults: and my sin is ever before me.
Against thee only have I sinned, and done this evil in thy sight. *Ib.* li. 3

8 Behold, I was shapen in wickedness: and in sin hath my mother conceived me.
But lo, thou requirest truth in the inward parts: and shalt make me to understand wisdom secretly.
Thou shalt purge me with hyssop, and I shall be clean: thou shalt wash me, and I shall be whiter than snow.
Thou shalt make me hear of joy and gladness: that the bones which thou hast broken may rejoice. *Ib.* 5

9 Make me a clean heart, O God: and renew a right spirit within me.
Cast me not away from thy presence: and take not thy holy Spirit from me.
O give me the comfort of thy help again: and stablish me with thy free Spirit.
Then shall I teach thy ways unto the wicked: and sinners shall be converted unto thee.
Deliver me from blood-guiltiness, O God. *Ib.* 10

10 For thou desirest no sacrifice, else would I give it thee: but thou delightest not in burnt-offerings.
The sacrifice of God is a troubled spirit: a broken and contrite heart, O God, shalt thou not despise.
O be favourable and gracious unto Sion: build thou the walls of Jerusalem. *Ib.* 16

11 Then shall they offer young bullocks upon thine altar. *Ib.* 19

12 My guide, and mine own familar friend.
We took sweet counsel together: and walked in the house of God as friends. *Ib.* lv. 14

13 His words were smoother than oil and yet be they very swords. *Ib.* 22

14 All that they imagine is to do me evil.
They hold all together, and keep themselves close. *Ib.* lvi. 5

15 Thou tellest my flittings; put my tears into thy bottle: are not these things noted in thy book? *Ib.* 8

16 For thou hast delivered my soul from death, and my feet from falling: that I may walk before God in the light of the living. *Ib.* 13

17 Under the shadow of thy wings shall be my refuge, until this tyranny be over-past. *Ib.* lvii. 1

18 God shall send forth his mercy and truth: my soul is among lions.
And I lie even among the children of men, that are set on fire: whose teeth are spears and arrows, and their tongue a sharp sword.
Set up thyself, O God, above the heavens: and thy glory above all the earth.
They have laid a net for my feet, and pressed down my soul: they have digged a pit before me, and are fallen into the midst of it themselves. *Psalms* lvii. 4

19 Awake up, my glory; awake, lute and harp: I myself will awake right early. *Ib.* 9

20 Even like the deaf adder that stoppeth her ears;
Which refuseth to hear the voice of the charmer: charm he never so wisely. *Ib.* lviii. 4

21 Let them consume away like a snail, and be like the untimely fruit of a woman: and let them not see the sun.
Or ever your pots be made hot with thorns: so let indignation vex him, even as a thing that is raw. *Ib.* 7

22 They grin like a dog, and run about through the city. *Ib.* lix. 6

23 God hath spoken in his holiness, I will rejoice, and divide Sichem: and mete out the valley of Succoth.
Gilead is mine, and Manasses is mine: Ephraim also is the strength of my head; Judah is my law-giver.
Moab is my wash-pot; over Edom will I cast out my shoe: Philistia, be thou glad of me.
Who will lead me into the strong city: who will bring me into Edom? *Ib.* lx. 6

24 As for the children of men, they are but vanity: the children of men are deceitful upon the weights, they are altogether lighter than vanity itself.
O trust not in wrong and robbery, give not yourselves unto vanity; if riches increase, set not your heart upon them.
God spake once, and twice I have also heard the same: that power belongeth unto God;
And that thou, Lord, art merciful: for thou rewardest every man according to his work. *Ib.* lxii. 9

25 My soul thirsteth for thee, my flesh also longeth after thee: in a barren and dry land where no water is. *Ib.* lxiii. 2

26 Have I not remembered thee in my bed: and thought upon thee when I was waking? *Ib.* 7

27 Thou that hearest the prayer: unto thee shall all flesh come. *Ib.* lxv. 2

28 Thou that art the hope of all the ends of the earth, and of them that remain in the broad sea.
Who in his strength setteth fast the mountains: and is girded about with power.
Who stilleth the raging of the sea: and the noise of his waves, and the madness of the people. *Ib.* 5

29 Thou that makest the outgoings of the morning and evening to praise thee. *Ib.* 8

30 Thou waterest her furrows, thou sendest rain into the little valleys thereof: thou makest it soft with the drops of rain, and blessest the increase of it.
Thou crownest the year with thy goodness: and thy clouds drop fatness.
They shall drop upon the dwellings of the wilderness: and the little hills shall rejoice on every side.

The folds shall be full of sheep: the valleys also shall stand so thick with corn, that they shall laugh and sing. *Psalms lxv. 11*

1 Who holdeth our soul in life: and suffereth not our feet to slip.
For thou, O God, hast proved us: thou also hast tried us, like as silver is tried. *Ib. lxvi. 8*

2 God be merciful unto us, and bless us: and shew us the light of his countenance, and be merciful unto us.
That thy way may be known upon earth: thy saving health among all nations. *Ib. lxvii. 1*

3 Then shall the earth bring forth her increase: and God, even our own God, shall give us his blessing. *Ib. 6*

4 Let God arise, and let his enemies be scattered: let them also that hate him flee before him.
Like as the smoke vanisheth, so shalt thou drive them away: and like as wax melteth at the fire, so let the ungodly perish at the presence of God. *Ib. lxviii. 1*

5 O sing unto God, and sing praises unto his Name: magnify him that rideth upon the heavens, as it were upon an horse; praise him in his Name JAH, and rejoice before him.
He is a Father of the fatherless, and defendeth the cause of the widows: even God in his holy habitation.
He is the God that maketh men to be of one mind in an house, and bringeth the prisoners out of captivity: but letteth the runagates continue in scarceness.
O God, when thou wentest forth before the people: when thou wentest through the wilderness,
The earth shook, and the heavens dropped at the presence of God. *Ib. 4*

6 Thou, O God, sentest a gracious rain upon thine inheritance: and refreshedst it when it was weary. *Ib. 9*

7 The Lord gave the word: great was the company of the preachers.
Kings with their armies did flee, and were discomfited: and they of the household divided the spoil.
Though ye have lien among the pots, yet shall ye be as the wings of a dove that is covered with silver wings, and her feathers like gold.
When the Almighty scattered kings for their sake: then were they as white as snow in Salmon.
As the hill of Basan, so is God's hill: even an high hill, as the hill of Basan.
Why hop ye so, ye high hills? this is God's hill, in the which it pleaseth him to dwell. *Ib. 11*

8 The chariots of God are twenty thousand, even thousands of angels. *Ib. 17*

9 Thou art gone up on high, thou hast led captivity captive, and received gifts for men. *Ib. 18*

10 God shall wound the head of his enemies: and the hairy scalp of such a one as goeth on still in his wickedness. *Ib. 21*

11 That thy foot may be dipped in the blood of thine enemies: and that the tongue of thy dogs may be red through the same. *Ib. 23*

12 The singers go before, the minstrels follow after: in the midst are the damsels playing with the timbrels. *Psalms lxviii. 25*

13 There is little Benjamin their ruler, and the princes of Judah their counsel. *Ib. 27*

14 When he hath scattered the people that delight in war. *Ib. 30*

15 Lo, he doth send out his voice, yea, and that a mighty voice. *Ib. 33*

16 I paid them the things that I never took: God, thou knowest my simpleness. *Ib. lxix. 5*

17 The zeal of thine house hath even eaten me. *Ib. 9*

18 They that sit in the gate speak against me: and the drunkards make songs upon me. *Ib. 12*

19 I looked for some to have pity on me, but there was no man, neither found I any to comfort me.
They gave me gall to eat: and when I was thirsty they gave me vinegar to drink. *Ib. 21*

20 Let them for their reward be soon brought to shame, that cry over me, There, there. *Ib. lxx. 3*

21 I am become as it were a monster unto many. *Ib. lxxi. 6*

22 Give the King thy judgements, O God: and thy righteousness unto the King's son. *Ib. lxxii. 1*

23 The mountains also shall bring peace: and the little hills righteousness unto the people. *Ib. 3*

24 He shall come down like the rain into a fleece of wool: even as the drops that water the earth. *Ib. 6*

25 His enemies shall lick the dust.
The kings of Tharsis and of the isles shall give presents: the kings of Arabia and Saba shall bring gifts.
All kings shall fall down before him: all nations shall do him service. *Ib. 9*

26 Therefore fall the people unto them: and thereout suck they no small advantage.
Tush, say they, how should God perceive it: is there knowledge in the Most High? *Ib. lxxiii. 10*

27 Then thought I to understand this: but it was too hard for me.
Until I went into the sanctuary of God: then understood I the end of these men. *Ib. 15*

28 O deliver not the soul of thy turtle-dove unto the multitude of the enemies. *Ib. lxxiv. 20*

29 The earth is weak, and all the inhabiters thereof: I bear up the pillars of it. *Ib. lxxv. 4*

30 For promotion cometh neither from the east, nor from the west: nor yet from the south. *Ib. 7*

31 For in the hand of the Lord there is a cup, and the wine is red: it is full mixed, and he poureth out of the same. *Ib. 9*

32 I have considered the days of old: and the years that are past. *Ib. lxxvii. 5*

33 A faithless and stubborn generation. *Ib. lxxviii. 9*

34 Who being harnessed, and carrying bows, turned themselves back in the day of battle. *Ib. 10*

35 So man did eat angels' food. *Ib. 26*

36 Starting aside like a broken bow. *Ib. 58*

1 So the Lord awaked as one out of sleep: and like a giant refreshed with wine.
He smote his enemies in the hinder parts: and put them to a perpetual shame. *Psalms* lxxviii. 66

2 Thou feedest them with the bread of tears. *Ib.* lxxx. 5

3 I proved thee also at the waters of strife. *Ib.* lxxxi. 8

4 They will not be learned nor understand, but walk on still in darkness: all the foundations of the earth are out of course. *Ib.* lxxxii. 5

5 O how amiable are thy dwellings: thou Lord of hosts!
My soul hath a desire and longing to enter into the courts of the Lord: my heart and my flesh rejoice in the living God.
Yea, the sparrow hath found her an house, and the swallow a nest where she may lay her young: even thy altars, O Lord of hosts, my King and my God. *Ib.* lxxxiv. 1

6 Who going through the vale of misery use it for a well: and the pools are filled with water.
They will go from strength to strength. *Ib.* 6

7 For one day in thy courts: is better than a thousand.
I had rather be a door-keeper in the house of my God: than to dwell in the tents of ungodliness. *Ib.* 10

8 Lord, thou art become gracious unto thy land: thou hast turned away the captivity of Jacob. *Ib.* lxxxv. 1

9 Mercy and truth are met together: righteousness and peace have kissed each other.
Truth shall flourish out of the earth: and righteousness hath looked down from heaven. *Ib.* 10

10 Righteousness shall go before him: and he shall direct his going in the way. *Ib.* 13

11 The congregations of naughty men have sought after my soul. *Ib.* lxxxvi. 14

12 Shew some token upon me for good, that they who hate me may see it, and be ashamed. *Ib.* 17

13 Her foundations are upon the holy hills: the Lord loveth the gates of Sion more than all the dwellings of Jacob.
Very excellent things are spoken of thee: thou city of God. *Ib.* lxxxvii. 1

14 The singers also and trumpeters shall he rehearse: All my fresh springs shall be in thee. *Ib.* 7

15 Lord, thou hast been our refuge from one generation to another.
Before the mountains were brought forth, or ever the earth and the world were made: thou art God from everlasting, and world without end.
Thou turnest man to destruction: again thou sayest, Come again, ye children of men.
For a thousand years in thy sight are but as yesterday: seeing that is past as a watch in the night.
As soon as thou scatterest them they are even as a sleep: and fade away suddenly like the grass.
In the morning it is green, and groweth up: but in the evening it is cut down, dried up, and withered. *Ib.* xc. 1

16 For when thou art angry all our days are gone: we bring our years to an end, as it were a tale that is told.
The days of our age are threescore years and ten; and though men be so strong that they come to fourscore years: yet is their strength then but labour and sorrow; so soon passeth it away, and we are gone. *Ib.* 9

17 Prosper thou the work of our hands upon us, O prosper thou our handy-work. *Psalms* xc. 17

18 For he shall deliver thee from the snare of the hunter: and from the noisome pestilence.
He shall defend thee under his wings, and thou shalt be safe under his feathers: his faithfulness and truth shall be thy shield and buckler.
Thou shalt not be afraid for any terror by night: nor for the arrow that flieth by day.
For the pestilence that walketh in darkness: nor for the sickness that destroyeth in the noon-day.
A thousand shall fall beside thee, and ten thousand at thy right hand: but it shall not come nigh thee. *Ib.* xci. 3

19 There shall no evil happen unto thee: neither shall any plague come nigh thy dwelling.
For he shall give his angels charge over thee: to keep thee in all thy ways.
They shall bear thee in their hands: that thou hurt not thy foot against a stone. *Ib.* 10

20 An unwise man doth not well consider this: and a fool doth not understand it. *Ib.* xcii. 6

21 They also shall bring forth more fruit in their age: and shall be fat and well-liking. *Ib.* 13

22 The Lord is King, and hath put on glorious apparel: the Lord hath put on his apparel, and girded himself with strength.
He hath made the round world so sure: that it cannot be moved. *Ib.* xciii. 1

23 The floods are risen, O Lord, the floods have lift up their voice: the floods lift up their waves.
The waves of the sea are mighty, and rage horribly: but yet the Lord, who dwelleth on high, is mightier. *Ib.* 4

24 He that planted the ear, shall he not hear: or he that made the eye, shall he not see? *Ib.* xciv. 9

25 Shew ourselves glad in him with psalms. *Ib.* xcv. 2

26 In his hand are all the corners of the earth: and the strength of the hills is his also.
The sea is his, and he made it: and his hands prepared the dry land. *Ib.* 4

27 O come, let us worship and fall down: and kneel before the Lord our Maker. *Ib.* 6

28 For he is the Lord our God: and we are the people of his pasture, and the sheep of his hand. *Ib.* 7

29 To-day if ye will hear his voice, harden not your hearts: as in the provocation, and as in the day of temptation in the wilderness. *Ib.* 8

30 When your fathers tempted me: proved me, and saw my works. *Ib.* 9

31 The Lord is King, the earth may be glad thereof: yea, the multitude of the isles may be glad thereof. *Ib.* xcvii. 1

32 With trumpets also, and shawms: O shew yourselves joyful before the Lord the King. *Ib.* xcviii. 7

33 The Lord is King, be the people never so impatient: he sitteth between the cherubims, be the earth never so unquiet. *Ib.* xcix. 1

34 Whoso hath also a proud look and high stomach: I will not suffer him. *Ib.* ci. 7

1 I am become like a pelican in the wilderness: and like an owl that is in the desert.

I have watched, and am even as it were a sparrow: that sitteth alone upon the house-top.
Psalms cii. 6

2 They shall perish, but thou shalt endure: they all shall wax old as doth a garment;

And as a vesture shalt thou change them, and they shall be changed: but thou art the same, and thy years shall not fail. *Ib.* 26

3 Praise the Lord, O my soul: and forget not all his benefits. *Ib.* ciii. 2

4 Who satisfieth thy mouth with good things: making thee young and lusty as an eagle. *Ib.* 5

5 He will not alway be chiding: neither keepeth he his anger for ever. *Ib.* 9

6 For look how high the heaven is in comparison of the earth: so great is his mercy also toward them that fear him.

Look how wide also the east is from the west: so far hath he set our sins from us.

Yea, like as a father pitieth his own children: even so is the Lord merciful unto them that fear him.
Ib. 11

7 The days of man are but as grass: for he flourisheth as a flower of the field.

For as soon as the wind goeth over it, it is gone: and the place thereof shall know it no more. *Ib.* 15

8 Who layeth the beams of his chambers in the waters: and maketh the clouds his chariot, and walketh upon the wings of the wind.

He maketh his angels spirits: and his ministers a flaming fire.

He laid the foundations of the earth: that it never should move at any time.

Thou coveredst it with the deep like as with a garment: the waters stand in the hills.

At thy rebuke they flee: at the voice of thy thunder they are afraid.

They go up as high as the hills, and down to the valleys beneath: even unto the place which thou hast appointed for them.

Thou hast set them their bounds which they shall not pass: neither turn again to cover the earth.

He sendeth the springs into the rivers: which run among the hills.

All beasts of the field drink thereof: and the wild asses quench their thirst.

Beside them shall the fowls of the air have their habitation: and sing among the branches.
Ib. civ. 3

9 Wine that maketh glad the heart of man: and oil to make him a cheerful countenance, and bread to strengthen man's heart.

The trees of the Lord also are full of sap: even the cedars of Libanus which he hath planted. *Ib.* 15

10 Wherein the birds make their nests: and the fir-trees are a dwelling for the stork.

The high hills are a refuge for the wild goats: and so are the stony rocks for the conies.

He appointed the moon for certain seasons: and the sun knoweth his going down.

Thou makest darkness that it may be night: wherein all the beasts of the forest do move.

The lions roaring after their prey: do seek their meat from God.

The sun ariseth, and they get them away together: and lay them down in their dens.

Man goeth forth to his work, and to his labour: until the evening. *Psalms* civ. 17

11 So is the great and wide sea also: wherein are things creeping innumerable, both small and great beasts.

There go the ships, and there is that Leviathan: whom thou hast made to take his pastime therein.

These wait all upon thee: that thou mayest give them meat in due season. *Ib.* 25

12 Whose feet they hurt in the stocks: the iron entered into his soul. *Ib.* cv. 18

13 Wonders in the land of Ham. *Ib.* 27

14 Went a whoring with their own inventions.
Ib. cvi. 38

15 Hungry and thirsty: their soul fainted in them.

So they cried unto the Lord in their trouble: and he delivered them from their distress.

He led them forth by the right way: that they might go to the city where they dwelt.

O that men would therefore praise the Lord for his goodness: and declare the wonders that he doeth for the children of men!

For he satisfieth the empty soul: and filleth the hungry soul with goodness.

Such as sit in darkness, and in the shadow of death: being fast bound in misery and iron;

Because they rebelled against the words of the Lord: and lightly regarded the counsel of the most Highest. *Ib.* cvii. 5

16 Their soul abhorred all manner of meat: and they were even hard at death's door. *Ib.* 18

17 They that go down to the sea in ships: and occupy their business in great waters;

These men see the works of the Lord: and his wonders in the deep. *Ib.* 23

18 They reel to and fro, and stagger like a drunken man: and are at their wit's end.

So when they cry unto the Lord in their trouble: he delivereth them out of their distress. *Ib.* 27

19 Then are they glad, because they are at rest: and so he bringeth them unto the haven where they would be. *Ib.* 30

20 Again, he maketh the wilderness a standing water: and water-springs of a dry ground. *Ib.* 35

21 And again, when they are minished, and brought low: through oppression, through any plague, or trouble.
Ib. 39

22 Whoso is wise will ponder these things. *Ib.* 43

23 The Lord said unto my Lord: Sit thou on my right hand, until I make thine enemies thy footstool.
Ib. cx. 1

24 The Lord sware, and will not repent: Thou art a priest for ever after the order of Melchisedech.
Ib. 4

25 The fear of the Lord is the beginning of wisdom: a good understanding have all they that do thereafter; the praise of it endureth for ever. *Ib.* cxi. 10

26 A good man is merciful, and lendeth. *Ib.* cxii. 5

27 He hath dispersed abroad, and given to the poor.
Ib. 9

1 He maketh the barren woman to keep house: and to be a joyful mother of children.   *Psalms* cxiii. 8

2 The sea saw that, and fled: Jordan was driven back.   *Ib.* cxiv. 3

3 The mountains skipped like rams: and the little hills like young sheep.   *Ib.* 4

4 They have mouths, and speak not: eyes have they, and see not.
They have ears, and hear not: noses have they, and smell not.
They have hands, and handle not; feet have they, and walk not: neither speak they through their throat.   *Ib.* cxv. 5

5 The snares of death compassed me round about: and the pains of hell gat hold upon me.   *Ib.* cxvi. 3

6 And why? thou hast delivered my soul from death: mine eyes from tears, and my feet from falling.   *Ib.* 8

7 I said in my haste, All men are liars.   *Ib.* 10

8 The voice of joy and health is in the dwellings of the righteous: the right hand of the Lord bringeth mighty things to pass.   *Ib.* cxviii. 15

9 The right hand of the Lord hath the pre-eminence.   *Ib.* 16

10 I shall not die, but live: and declare the works of the Lord.   *Ib.* 17

11 The same stone which the builders refused: is become the head-stone in the corner.   *Ib.* 22

12 Blessed be he that cometh in the Name of the Lord: we have wished you good luck, ye that are of the house of the Lord.   *Ib.* 26

13 Wherewithal shall a young man cleanse his way: even by ruling himself after thy word.   *Ib.* cxix. 9

14 Make me to go in the path of thy commandments: for therein is my desire.   *Ib.* 35

15 O turn away mine eyes, lest they behold vanity: and quicken thou me in thy law.   *Ib.* 37

16 In the house of my pilgrimage.   *Ib.* 54

17 The law of thy mouth is dearer unto me: than thousands of gold and silver.   *Ib.* 72

18 For I am become like a bottle in the smoke. *Ib.* 83

19 I see that all things come to an end: but thy commandment is exceeding broad.   *Ib.* 96

20 I have more understanding than my teachers: for thy testimonies are my study.
I am wiser than the aged: because I keep thy commandments.   *Ib.* 99

21 Thy word is a lantern unto my feet: and a light unto my paths.
I have sworn, and am stedfastly purposed, to keep thy righteous judgements.   *Ib.* 105

22 O stablish me according to thy word.   *Ib.* 116

23 Princes have persecuted me without a cause. *Ib.* 161

24 What reward shall be given or done unto thee, thou false tongue: even mighty and sharp arrows, with hot burning coals.
Woe is me, that I am constrained to dwell with Mesech: and to have my habitation among th tents of Kedar.   *Ib.* cxx. 3

25 I labour for peace, but when I speak unto them thereof: they make them ready to battle. *Psalms* cxx. 6

26 I will lift up mine eyes unto the hills: from whence cometh my help.   *Ib.* cxxi. 1

27 He will not suffer thy foot to be moved: and he that keepeth thee will not sleep.   *Ib.* 3

28 The Lord himself is thy keeper: the Lord is thy defence upon thy right hand;
So that the sun shall not burn thee by day: neither the moon by night.   *Ib.* 5

29 The Lord shall preserve thy going out, and thy coming in: from this time forth for evermore. *Ib.* 8

30 I was glad when they said unto me: We will go into the house of the Lord.   *Ib.* cxxii. 1

31 O pray for the peace of Jerusalem: they shall prosper that love thee.
Peace be within thy walls: and plenteousness within thy palaces.
For my brethren and companions' sakes: I will wish thee prosperity.
Yea, because of the house of the Lord our God: I will seek to do thee good.   *Ib.* 6

32 Our soul is escaped even as a bird out of the snare of the fowler: the snare is broken, and we are delivered.   *Ib.* cxxiv. 6

33 The hills stand about Jerusalem: even so standeth the Lord round about his people, from this time forth for evermore.
For the rod of the ungodly cometh not into the lot of the righteous: let the righteous put their hand unto wickedness.   *Ib.* cxxv. 2

34 Turn our captivity, O Lord: as the rivers in the south.
They that sow in tears: shall reap in joy.
He that now goeth on his way weeping, and beareth forth good seed: shall doubtless come again with joy, and bring his sheaves with him. *Ib.* cxxvi. 5

35 Except the Lord build the house: their labour is but lost that build it.
Except the Lord keep the city: the watchman waketh but in vain.
It is but lost labour that ye haste to rise up early, and so late take rest, and eat the bread of carefulness: for so he giveth his beloved sleep.
Lo, children and the fruit of the womb are an heritage and gift that cometh of the Lord.
Like as the arrows in the hand of the giant: even so are the young children.
Happy is the man that hath his quiver full of them: they shall not be ashamed when they speak with their enemies in the gate.   *Ib.* cxxvii. 1

36 Thy wife shall be as the fruitful vine upon the walls of thine house.
Thy children like the olive-branches round about thy table.   *Ib.* cxxviii. 3

37 The plowers plowed upon my back: and made long furrows.   *Ib.* cxxix. 3

38 Out of the deep have I called unto thee, O Lord: Lord, hear my voice.   *Ib.* cxxx. 1

39 If thou, Lord, wilt be extreme to mark what is done amiss: O Lord, who may abide it?   *Ib.* 3

40 My soul fleeth unto the Lord: before the morning watch, I say, before the morning watch.   *Ib.* 6

1 Lord, I am not high-minded: I have no proud looks.
I do not exercise myself in great matters: which are too high for me.
But I refrain my soul, and keep it low, like as a child that is weaned from his mother: yea, my soul is even as a weaned child. *Psalms* cxxxi. 1

2 Lord, remember David: and all his trouble.
Ib. cxxxii. 1

3 Behold, how good and joyful a thing it is, brethren, to dwell together in unity!
It is like the precious ointment upon the head that ran down unto the beard: even unto Aaron's beard, and went down to the skirts of his clothing.
Ib. cxxxiii. 1

4 His mercy endureth for ever. *Ib.* cxxxvi. 1

5 By the waters of Babylon we sat down and wept: when we remembered thee, O Sion.
As for our harps, we hanged them up: upon the trees that are therein.
For they that led us away captive required of us then a song, and melody, in our heaviness: Sing us one of the songs of Sion.
How shall we sing the Lord's song in a strange land?
If I forget thee, O Jerusalem: let my right hand forget her cunning.
If I do not remember thee, let my tongue cleave to the roof of my mouth: yea, if I prefer not Jerusalem in my mirth. *Ib.* cxxxvii. 1

6 How they said, Down with it, down with it, even to the ground.
O daughter of Babylon, wasted with misery: yea, happy shall he be that rewardeth thee, as thou hast served us.
Blessed shall he be that taketh thy children: and throweth them against the stones. *Ib.* 7

7 O Lord, thou hast searched me out, and known me: thou knowest my down-sitting, and mine up-rising; thou understandest my thoughts long before. *Ib.* cxxxix. 1

8 Such knowledge is too wonderful and excellent for me: I cannot attain unto it. *Ib.* 5

9 If I take the wings of the morning and remain in the uttermost parts of the sea;
Even there also shall thy hand lead me: and thy right hand shall hold me.
If I say, Peradventure the darkness shall cover me: then shall my night be turned to day.
Yea, the darkness is no darkness with thee, but the night is as clear as the day: the darkness and light to thee are both alike. *Ib.* 8

10 I will give thanks unto thee, for I am fearfully and wonderfully made. *Ib.* 13

11 And in thy book were all my members written.
Ib. 15

12 Thou hast covered my head in the day of battle.
Ib. cxl. 7

13 Let the lifting up of my hands be an evening sacrifice.
Set a watch, O Lord, before my mouth: and keep the door of my lips. *Ib.* cxli. 2

14 Let the righteous rather smite me friendly: and reprove me.
But let not their precious balms break my head.
Ib. 5

15 Let the ungodly fall into their own nets together: and let me ever escape them. *Psalms* cxli. 11

16 That our sons may grow up as the young plants: and that our daughters may be as the polished corners of the temple. *Ib.* cxliv. 12

17 That our oxen may be strong to labour, that there be no decay: no leading into captivity, and no complaining in our streets. *Ib.* 14

18 The Lord is gracious, and merciful: long-suffering, and of great goodness. *Ib.* cxlv. 8

19 O put not your trust in princes, nor in any child of man: for there is no help in them.
For when the breath of man goeth forth he shall turn again to his earth: and then all his thoughts perish.
Ib. cxlvi. 2

20 The Lord careth for the strangers; he defendeth the fatherless and widow: as for the way of the ungodly, he turneth it upside down. *Ib.* 9

21 Yea, a joyful and pleasant thing it is to be thankful.
The Lord doth build up Jerusalem: and gather together the out-casts of Israel.
He healeth those that are broken in heart: and giveth medicine to heal their sickness.
He telleth the number of the stars: and calleth them all by their names. *Ib.* cxlvii. 1

22 He hath no pleasure in the strength of an horse: neither delighteth he in any man's legs. *Ib.* 10

23 He giveth snow like wool: and scattereth the hoar-frost like ashes. *Ib.* 16

24 Praise the Lord upon earth: ye dragons and all deeps;
Fire and hail, snow and vapours: wind and storm, fulfilling his word. *Ib.* cxlviii. 7

25 Young men and maidens, old men and children, praise the Name of the Lord: for his Name only is excellent, and his praise above heaven and earth.
Ib. 12

26 Let the praises of God be in their mouth: and a two-edged sword in their hands. *Ib.* cxiix. 6

27 To bind their kings in chains: and their nobles with links of iron. *Ib.* 8

28 Praise him upon the well-tuned cymbals: praise him upon the loud cymbals.
Let every thing that hath breath: praise the Lord.
Ib. cl. 5

29 Such as pass on the seas upon their lawful occasions.
Forms of Prayer to be Used at Sea. 'O Eternal Lord God'

30 We therefore commit his body to the deep, to be turned into corruption, looking for the resurrection of the body (when the Sea shall give up her dead).
Ib. At the Burial of their Dead at Sea.

31 Come, Holy Ghost, our souls inspire,
And lighten with celestial fire.
Thou the anointing Spirit art,
Who dost thy seven-fold gifts impart.
Ordering of Priests. Veni, Creator Spiritus

32 Enable with perpetual light
The dulness of our blinded sight. *Ib.*

33 Anoint and cheer our soiled face
With the abundance of thy grace,
Keep far our foes, give peace at home:
Where thou art guide, no ill can come. *Ib.*

1 Cheerfully for conscience sake.
Accession Service. Almighty God, who rulest over all the kingdoms

2 We will see there shall be due Execution upon them.
Articles of Religion. His Majesty's Declaration

3 All things necessary to salvation.
Ib. vi. Of the Sufficiency of the Holy Scriptures

4 As the Pelagians do vainly talk.
Ib. Of Original Sin, ix

5 Man is very far gone from original righteousness. *Ib.*

6 Of Works of Supererogation. *Ib. Title of Article xiv*

7 Fond thing vainly invented. *Ib. xxii. Of Purgatory*

8 Understood of the people.
Ib. xxiv. Of Speaking in the Congregation

9 The corrupt following of the Apostles.
Ib. xxv. Of the Sacraments

10 Reserved, carried about, lifted up, or worshipped.
Ib. xxviii. Of the Lord's Supper

11 Blasphemous fables, and dangerous deceits.
Ib. xxxi. Of the One Oblation

12 The Bishop of *Rome* hath no jurisdiction in this Realm of *England.*
Ib. xxxvii. Of the Civil Magistrates

13 It is lawful for Christian men, at the commandment of the Magistrate, to wear weapons, and serve in the wars. *Ib.*

14 As certain Anabaptists do falsely boast.
Ib. xxxviii. Of Christian Men's Goods

15 Table of Kindred and Affinity. *Title*

16 A Man may not marry his Grandmother.
Table of Kindred

ARCHIBALD PHILIP PRIMROSE, EARL OF ROSEBERY

see

ROSEBERY

SIR JAMES PRIOR

1790?–1869

17 Mr. Cruger . . . at the conclusion of one of Mr. Burke's eloquent harangues, finding nothing to add, or perhaps as he thought to add with effect, exclaimed earnestly, in the language of the counting-house, 'I say ditto to Mr. Burke—I say ditto to Mr. Burke.' *Life of Burke*, ch. 5

MATTHEW PRIOR

1664–1721

18 He's half absolv'd who has confess'd.
Alma, c. ii, l. 22

19 Dear Cloe, how blubber'd is that pretty face!
A Better Answer [to Cloe Jealous]

20 Odds life! must one swear to the truth of a song? *Ib.*

21 I court others in verse: but I love thee in prose:
And they have my whimsies, but thou hast my heart.
Ib.

22 Serene yet strong, majestic yet sedate,
Swift without violence, without terror great.
Carmen Seculare, l. 282

23 The song too daring, and the theme too great!
Carmen Seculare, l. 308

24 She may receive and own my flame,
For tho' the strictest prudes should know it,
She'll pass for a most virtuous Dame,
And I for an unhappy poet.
To a Child of Quality Five Years Old

25 That I shall be past making love,
When she begins to comprehend it. *Ib.*

26 Be to her virtues very kind;
Be to her faults a little blind;
Let all her ways be unconfin'd;
And clap your padlock—on her mind.
An English Padlock, l. 79

27 To John I ow'd great obligation;
But John, unhappily, thought fit
To publish it to all the nation:
Sure John and I are more than quit. *Epigram*

28 Nobles and heralds, by your leave,
Here lies what once was Matthew Prior;
The son of Adam and of Eve,
Can Bourbon or Nassau go higher? *Epitaph*

29 Without love, hatred, joy, or fear,
They led—a kind of—as it were:
Nor wish'd, nor car'd, nor laugh'd, nor cried:
And so they liv'd, and so they died.
An Epitaph, l. 59

30 All jargon of the schools.
On Exod. iii. 14. I am that I am. An Ode, l. 65

31 And oft the pangs of absence to remove
By letters, soft interpreters of love.
Henry and Emma, l. 147

32 No longer shall the bodice, aptly lac'd
From thy full bosom to thy slender waist,
That air and harmony of shape express,
Fine by degrees, and beautifully less. *Ib.* l. 427

33 From ignorance our comfort flows,
The only wretched are the wise.
To the Hon. C. Montague, l. 35

34 For the idiom of words very little she heeded,
Provided the matter she drove at succeeded,
She took and gave languages just as she needed.
Jinny the Just

35 Her religion so well with her learning did suit
That in practice sincere, and in controverse mute,
She shewed she knew better to live than dispute. *Ib.*

36 Venus, take my votive glass;
Since I am not what I was,
What from this day I shall be,
Venus, let me never see.
The Lady who Offers her Looking-Glass to Venus

37 My noble, lovely, little Peggy.
A Letter to the Honourable Lady Miss Margaret Cavendish-Holles-Harley

38 The merchant, to secure his treasure,
Conveys it in a borrowed name:
Euphelia serves to grace my measure;
But Chloe is my real flame.
An Ode, 'The Merchant to Secure his Treasure'

39 They never taste who always drink;
They always talk, who never think.
Upon this Passage in the Scaligeriana

1 He rang'd his tropes, and preach'd up patience;
Back'd his opinion with quotations.
Paulo Purganti and his Wife, l. 138

2 Entire and sure the monarch's rule must prove,
Who founds her greatness on her subjects' love.
*Prologue Spoken on Her Majesty's Birthday,
1704*, l. 17

3 Cur'd yesterday of my disease,
I died last night of my physician.
The Remedy Worse than the Disease

4 Abra was ready ere I call'd her name;
And, though I call'd another, Abra came.
Solomon, bk. ii, l. 362

5 What is a King?—a man condemn'd to bear
The public burden of the nation's care.
Ib. bk. iii, l. 275

6 Now fitted the halter, now travers'd the cart;
And often took leave: but was loth to depart.
The Thief and the Cordelier, v.

7 I never strove to rule the roast,
She ne'er refus'd to pledge my toast.
Turtle and Sparrow, l. 334

8 A Rechabite poor Will must live,
And drink of Adam's ale. *The Wandering Pilgrim*, iii

ADELAIDE ANN PROCTER
1825–1864

9 I do not ask, O Lord, that life may be
A pleasant road.
A Chaplet of Verses. Per Pacem ad Lucem

10 Joy is like restless day; but peace divine
Like quiet night:
Lead me, O Lord—till perfect Day shall shine,
Through Peace to Light. *Ib.*

11 Seated one day at the organ,
I was weary and ill at ease,
And my fingers wandered idly
Over the noisy keys.
Legends and Lyrics. A Lost Chord

12 But I struck one chord of music,
Like the sound of a great Amen. *Ib.*

13 It may be that only in Heaven
I shall hear that grand Amen. *Ib.*

14 Rise! for the day is passing,
And you lie dreaming on;
The others have buckled their armour,
And forth to the fight are gone;
A place in the ranks awaits you,
Each man has some part to play;
The Past and the Future are nothing,
In the face of the stern To-day. *Ib. Now*

BRYAN WALLER PROCTER
see
BARRY CORNWALL

PROPERTIUS
b. *c.* 51 B.C.

15 Navita de ventis, de tauris narrat arator,
Enumerat miles vulnera, pastor oves.

The seaman's story is of tempest, the ploughman's
of his team of bulls; the soldier tells his wounds,
the shepherd his tale of sheep.
Elegies, ii. i. 43. Trans. by Phillimore

16 Quodsi deficiant vires, audacia certe
Laus erit: in magnis et voluisse sat est.

And if my strength fail, at least my boldness will
be a title of honour; in great enterprises the
very 'I would' is enough. *Ib.* x. 5

17 Cedite Romani scriptores, cedite Grai!
Nescio quid maius nascitur Iliade.

Give place, you Roman writers, give place, you
Greeks! Here comes to birth something greater
than the Iliad. *Ib.* xxxiv. 65

PROTAGORAS
c. 481–411 B.C.

18 πάντων χρημάτων ἄνθρωπον μέτρον εἶναι.

Man is the measure of all things.
Quoted by Plato in Theaetetus, 160d

PIERRE-JOSEPH PROUDHON
1809–1865

19 La propriété c'est le vol.

Property is theft. *Qu'est-ce que la Propriété?* ch. 1

FATHER PROUT
[FRANCIS SYLVESTER MAHONY]
1804–1866

20 With deep affection,
And recollection,
I often think of
Those Shandon bells. *The Bells of Shandon*

21 'Tis the bells of Shandon,
That sound so grand on
The pleasant waters
Of the River Lee. *Ib.*

WILLIAM JEFFREY PROWSE
1836–1870

22 Though the latitude's rather uncertain,
And the longitude also is vague,
The persons I pity who know not the city,
The beautiful city of Prague. *The City of Prague*

JOHN PUDNEY
1909–

23 You shall inherit hours which are replaced,
The earth won back, the trustier human ways
From history recovered, on them based
An amplitude of noble life. *The Dead*, ii

24 Do not despair
For Johnny head-in-air;
He sleeps as sound
As Johnny underground. *For Johnny*, st. 1

25 Better by far
For Johnny-the-bright-star,
To keep your head
And see his children fed. *Ib.* 3

1 Live and let live.
No matter how it ended,
These lose and, under the sky,
Lie friended.   *Graves—Tobruk*, st. 1

WILLIAM PULTENEY, EARL OF BATH
1684–1764

2 Since twelve honest men have decided the cause,
And were judges of fact, tho' not judges of laws.
The Honest Jury, iii. In *The Craftsman*, 1731,
vol. 5, 337. Refers to Sir Philip Yorke's unsuccessful prosecution of *The Craftsman* (1729)

PUNCH

3 Advice to persons about to marry.—'Don't.'
Punch, vol. viii, p. 1. 1845

4 You pays your money and you takes your choice.
Ib. vol. x, p. 16. 1846

5 The Half-Way House to Rome, Oxford.
Ib. vol. xvi, p. 36. 1849

6 What is better than presence of mind in a railway
accident? Absence of body.
Ib. vol. xvi, p. 231. 1849

7 Never do to-day what you can put off till to-morrow.
Ib. vol. xvii, p. 241. 1849

8 No bread. Then bring me some toast!
Ib. vol. xxii, p. 18. 1852

9 Who's 'im, Bill?
A stranger!
'Eave 'arf a brick at 'im.   *Ib.* vol. xxvi, p. 82. 1854

10 What is Matter?—Never mind.
What is Mind?—No matter.
Ib. vol. xxix, p. 19. 1855

11 '*Peccavi*—I've Scinde' wrote Lord Ellen so proud.
More briefly Dalhousie wrote—'*Vovi*—I've Oude'.
Ib. vol. xxx, p. 141. 1856

12 It ain't the 'unting as 'urts 'un, it's the 'ammer,
'ammer, 'ammer along the 'ard 'igh road.
Ib. vol. xxx, p. 218. 1856

13 Oi'll tak zum o' that in a moog.
Ib. vol. xxxvii, p. 156. 1859

14 I see it's written by a lady, and I want a book that my
daughters may read. Give me something else.
Ib. vol. liii, p. 252. 1867

15 Mun, a had na' been the-erre abune two hours when
—*bang*—went saxpence!!! *Ib.* vol. liv, p. 235. 1868

16 Cats is 'dogs' and rabbits is 'dogs' and so's Parrats,
but this 'ere 'Tortis' is a insect, and there ain't no
charge for it.   *Ib.* vol. lvi, p. 96. 1869

17 Nothink for nothink 'ere, and precious little for sixpence.   *Ib.* vol. lvii, p. 152. 1869

18 Sure, the next train has gone ten minutes ago.
Ib. vol. lx, p. 206. 1871

19 It appears the Americans have taken umbrage.
The deuce they have! Whereabouts is that?
Ib. vol. lxiii, p. 189. 1872

20 Go directly—see what she's doing, and tell her she
mustn't.   *Ib.* vol. lxiii, p. 202. 1872

21 There was one poor tiger that hadn't *got* a Christian.
Ib. vol. lxviii, p. 143. 1875

22 Here was an old owl liv'd in an oak
The more he heard, the less he spoke;
The less he spoke, the more he heard
O, if men were all like that wise bird!
Punch, vol. lxviii, p. **155**. 1875

23 It's worse than wicked, my dear, it's vulgar.
Ib. Almanac. 1876

24 What did you take out of the bag, Mamma? *I* only
got sixpence.   *Ib.* vol. lxx, p. 139. 1876

25 'Is Life worth living?' . . . he suspects it is, in a great
measure, a question of the Liver.
Ib. vol. lxxiii, p. 207. 1877

26 I never read books—I *write* them.
Ib. vol. lxxiv, p. 210. 1878

27 I am not hungry; but thank goodness, I am greedy.
Ib. vol. lxxv, p. 290. 1878

28 BISHOP:
Who is it that sees and hears all we do, and before
whom even I am but as a crushed worm?
PAGE:
The Missus, my Lord.   *Ib.* vol. lxxix, p. 63. 1880

29 Ah whiles hae ma doobts aboot the meenister.
Ib. p. 275. 1880

30 I used your soap two years ago; since then I have used
no other.   *Ib.* vol. lxxxvi, p. 197. 1884

31 What sort of a doctor is he?
Oh, well, I don't know very much about his ability;
but he's got a very good bedside manner!
Ib. p. 121. 1884

32 Don't look at me, Sir, with—ah—in that tone of
voice.   *Ib.* vol. lxxxvii, p. 38. 1884

33 Oh yes! I'm sure he's not so fond of me as at first.
He's away so much, neglects me dreadfully, and
he's so cross when he comes home. What *shall*
I do?
Feed the brute!   *Ib.* vol. lxxxix, p. 206. 1886

34 Hi! James—let loose the Gorgonzola!
Ib. vol. xcvi, p. 82. 1889

35 Nearly all our best men are dead! Carlyle, Tennyson,
Browning, George Eliot!—I'm not feeling very well
myself.   *Ib.* vol. civ, p. 210. 1893

36 Botticelli isn't a wine, you Juggins! Botticelli's a
cheese!   *Ib.* vol. cvi, p. 270. 1894

37 I'm afraid you've got a bad egg, Mr. Jones.
Oh no, my Lord, I assure you! Parts of it are excellent!
Ib. vol. cix, p. 222. 1895

38 Do you know, Carter, that I can actually write my
name in the dust on the table?
Faith, Mum, that's more than I can do. Sure there's
nothing like education, after all.
Ib. vol. cxxii, p. 142. 1902

39 Look here, Steward, if this is coffee, I want tea; but
if this is tea, then I wish for coffee.
Ib. vol. cxxiii, p. 44. 1902

40 We must gie it up, Alfred.
What, gie up gowff?
Nae, nae, mon. Gie up the meenistry.
Ib. vol. cxxvi, p. 117. 1904

ISRAEL PUTNAM

1718–1790

1 Men, you are all marksmen—don't one of you fire until you see the whites of their eyes.
Bunker Hill, 1775. Frothingham, *History of the Siege of Boston* (1873), ch. 5, note. *Also attributed to* William Prescott (1726–95)

ERNIE PYLE

1900–1945

2 The worm's eye point of view.   *Here Is Your War*

FRANCIS QUARLES

1592–1644

3 I wish thee as much pleasure in the reading, as I had in the writing.   *Emblems. To the Reader*

4 The heart is a small thing, but desireth great matters. It is not sufficient for a kite's dinner, yet the whole world is not sufficient for it.
Ib. bk. i, No. 12. *Hugo de Anima*

5 We spend our midday sweat, our midnight oil; We tire the night in thought, the day in toil.
Ib. bk. ii, No. 2, l. 33

6 Be wisely worldly, be not worldly wise.   *Ib.* l. 46

7 Man is Heaven's masterpiece.   *Ib.* No. 6, Epig. 6

8 The road to resolution lies by doubt: The next way home's the farthest way about.
Ib. bk. iv, No. 2, Epig. 2

9 Our God and soldiers we alike adore
Ev'n at the brink of danger; not before:
After deliverance, both alike requited,
Our God's forgotten, and our soldiers slighted.
Epigram

10 My soul, sit thou a patient looker-on;
Judge not the play before the play is done:
Her plot hath many changes; every day
Speaks a new scene; the last act crowns the play.
Epigram. Respice Finem

11 No man is born unto himself alone;
Who lives unto himself, he lives to none.
Esther, Sect. 1, Medit. 1

12 He that had no cross deserves no crown.
Ib. Sect. 9, Medit. 9

13 He teaches to deny that faintly prays.
A Feast for Worms, Sect. 7, Medit. 7, l. 2

14 Man is man's A.B.C. There is none that can Read God aright, unless he first spell Man.
Hieroglyphics, i, l. 1

15 He that begins to live, begins to die.   *Ib.* 1, Epig. 1

16 Physicians of all men are most happy; what good success soever they have, the world proclaimeth, and what faults they commit, the earth covereth.
Ib. iv. *Nicocles*

17 Come then, my brethren, and be glad,
And eke rejoice with me;
Lawn sleeves and rochets shall go down,
And hey! then up go we!
The Shepherd's Oracles. Eclogue xi, *Song of Anarchus*, i

18 We'll cry both arts and learning down,
And hey! then up go we!
The Shepherd's Oracles. Eclogue xi. *Song of Anarchus*, iv

FRANÇOIS QUESNAY

1694–1774

19 Laissez faire, laissez passer.

No interference, and complete freedom of movement.
Of Government interference. Also attributed to Marquis d'Argenson, *Mémoires* (1736)

SIR ARTHUR QUILLER-COUCH

1863–1944

20 Know you her secret none can utter?
Hers of the Book, the tripled Crown?
Poems. Alma Mater

21 Yet if at last, not less her lover,
You in your hansom leave the High;
Down from her towers a ray shall hover—
Touch you, a passer-by!   *Ib.*

22 O pastoral heart of England! like a psalm
Of green days telling with a quiet beat.
Ib. Ode upon Eckington Bridge

23 Turns in her sleep, and murmurs of the Spring. *Ib.*

JOSIAH QUINCY

1772–1864

24 As it will be the right of all, so it will be the duty of some, definitely to prepare for a separation, amicably if they can, violently if they must.
Abridgement of Debates of Congress, 14 Jan. 1811, vol. iv, p. 327

QUINTILIAN

A.D. 40–c. 100

25 Satura quidem tota nostra est.
Satire indeed is entirely our own.
De Institutione Oratoria, x. i. 93

26 [Horatius] et insurgit aliquando et plenus est iucunditatis et gratiae et variis figuris et verbis felicissime audax.
[Horace] soars occasionally, is full of agreeableness and grace, and shows a most happy daring in certain figures and expressions.   *Ib.* 96

FRANÇOIS RABELAIS

1494?–1553

27 L'appétit vient en mangeant.
The appetite grows by eating.   *Gargantua*, i. v

28 Fay ce que vouldras
Do what thou wilt.   *Ib.* 1. lvii

29 Tirez le rideau, la farce est jouée.
Ring down the curtain, the farce is over.
Attr. to Rabelais on his death-bed

30 Je m'en vais chercher un grand peut-être.
I go to seek a great perhaps.   *Ib.*

1 Vogue la galère!
   Let her rip!
   [Literally, the words mean 'loose the galley' or
   'hoist sail'.]
                                        Works, bk. i, ch. 40

JEAN RACINE
1639–1699

2 Elle flotte, elle hésite; en un mot, elle est femme.

   She is all wavering and hesitation: in short, she is a
   woman.   *Athalie*, iii. 3

3 Ce n'est plus une ardeur dans mes veines cachée:
   C'est Vénus toute entière à sa proie attachée.

   It is no longer a passion hidden in my veins: it is
   the goddess Venus herself fastened on her prey.
                                        Phèdre, 1. iii

4 Point d'argent, point de Suisse.
   No money, no Swiss [soldiers].
                                        Les Plaideurs, 1. i.

5 Sans argent l'honneur n'est qu'une maladie.
   Honour, without money, is a mere malady.   *Ib.*

THOMAS RAINBOROWE
d. 1648

6 The poorest he that is in England hath a life to live
   as the greatest he.
      In the Army debates at Putney, 29 Oct. 1647.
      Peacock, *Life of Rainborowe.*

SIR WALTER RALEGH
1552?–1618

7 Go, Soul, the body's guest,
      Upon a thankless arrant:
   Fear not to touch the best;
      The truth shall be thy warrant:
         Go, since I needs must die,
         And give the world the lie.   *The Lie*, i

8 If all the world and love were young,
   And truth in every shepherd's tongue,
   These pretty pleasures might me move
   To live with thee, and be thy love.
      The Nymph's Reply to the [Passionate] Shepherd

9 Give me my scallop-shell of quiet,
   My staff of faith to walk upon,
   My scrip of joy, immortal diet,
   My bottle of salvation,
   My gown of glory, hope's true gage,
   And thus I'll take my pilgrimage.
                        The Passionate Man's Pilgrimage

10 As you came from the holy land
       Of Walsinghame,
   Met you not with my true love
       By the way as you came?

   How shall I know your true love,
       That have met many one
   As I went to the holy land,
       That have come, that have gone?   *Walsinghame*

11 Fain would I climb, yet fear I to fall.
      Line Written on a Window-Pane. Queen Eliza-
      beth wrote under it, 'If thy heart fails thee, climb
      not at all.' Fuller, *Worthies* (1840), i. 419

12 Even such is time, which takes in trust
   Our youth, our joys, and all we have,
   And pays us but with age and dust,
   Who in the dark and silent grave,
   When we have wandered all our ways,
   Shuts up the story of our days.
   And from which earth, and grave, and dust,
   The Lord shall raise me up, I trust.
      Written the night before his death. Found in his
      Bible in the Gate-house at Westminster

13 O eloquent, just, and mighty Death! whom none
   could advise, thou hast persuaded; what none hath
   dared, thou hast done; and whom all the world hath
   flattered, thou only hast cast out of the world and
   despised: thou hast drawn together all the far-
   stretched greatness, all the pride, cruelty, and ambition of man, and covered it all over with these two
   narrow words, *Hic jacet.*
      A History of the World, bk. v, ch. vi, § 12

14 [Feeling the edge of the axe before his execution:]
   'Tis a sharp remedy, but a sure one for all ills.
      Hume, *History of Great Britain* (1754), vol. i,
      ch. iv, p. 72

15 [When asked which way he preferred to lay his head
   on the block:]
   So the heart be right, it is no matter which way the
   head lies.
      W. Stebbing, *Sir Walter Raleigh*, ch. xxx

SIR WALTER A. RALEIGH
1861–1922

16 I wish I loved the Human Race;
   I wish I loved its silly face;
   I wish I liked the way it walks;
   I wish I liked the way it talks;
   And when I'm introduced to one
   I wish I thought *What Jolly Fun!*
      Laughter from a Cloud (1923), p. 228. *Wishes of*
      an Elderly Man

JULIAN RALPH
1853–1903

17 News value.
      Lecture to Brander Matthews's English Class,
      Columbia, 1892. Thomas Beer's *Mauve Decade*

ALLAN RAMSAY
1686–1758

18 Farewell to Lochaber, and farewell my Jean.
      Works (1851), ii, *Lochaber No More*

JAMES RYDER RANDALL
1839–1908

19 The despot's heel is on thy shore,
       Maryland!
   His torch is at thy temple door,
       Maryland!
   Avenge the patriotic gore
   That flecked the streets of Baltimore,
   And be the battle-queen of yore,
       Maryland, my Maryland!
                        Maryland! My Maryland, i

JEREMIAH EAMES RANKIN
1828–1904

1 God be with you, till we meet again,
By His counsels guide, uphold you,
With His sheep securely fold you:
God be with you, till we meet again.   *Hymn*

THOMAS RAVENSCROFT
1592?–1635?

2 We be three poor mariners
Newly come from the seas.
Deuteromelia (1609). *Oxford Song Book*, vol. ii

THOMAS BUCHANAN READ
1822–1872

3 The terrible grumble, and rumble, and roar,
Telling the battle was on once more,
And Sheridan twenty miles away.   *Sheridan's Ride*, i

CHARLES READE
1814–1884

4 Not a day passes over the earth, but men and women
of no note do great deeds, speak great words and
suffer noble sorrows.
The Cloister and the Hearth, ch. 1

5 Courage, mon ami, le diable est mort!
Ib. ch. 24, *and passim*

6 Sow an act, and you reap a habit. Sow a habit, and
you reap a character. Sow a character, and you reap
a destiny.
Attrib. See Notes and Queries, 9th series, vol. 12,
p. 377

ERICH MARIA REMARQUE
1898–

7 Im Westen nichts Neues.
All Quiet on the Western Front.
Title of Novel. Trans. by A. W. Wheen

EBEN REXFORD
1848–1916

8 Darling, I am growing old,
Silver threads among the gold
Shine upon my brow to-day;
Life is fading fast away.
Silver Threads among the Gold

FREDERIC REYNOLDS
1764–1841

9 How goes the enemy? [Said by Mr. Ennui, 'the time-
killer'.]   *The Dramatist*, I. i

SIR JOSHUA REYNOLDS
1723–1792

10 If you have great talents, industry will improve
them: if you have but moderate abilities, industry
will supply their deficiency.
Discourse to Students of the Royal Academy,
11 Dec. 1769

11 A mere copier of nature can never produce anything
great.
Discourse to Students of the Royal Academy,
14 Dec. 1770

12 He who resolves never to ransack any mind but his
own, will be soon reduced, from mere barrenness,
to the poorest of all imitations; he will be obliged
to imitate himself, and to repeat what he has
before often repeated.   *Ib. 10 Dec. 1774*

13 I should desire that the last words which I should
pronounce in this Academy, and from this place,
might be the name of—Michael Angelo.
Ib. 10 Dec. 1790

14 He [Dr. Johnson] has no formal preparation, no
flourishing with his sword; he is through your
body in an instant.
Boswell's Johnson (ed. 1934), vol. ii, p. 365,
18 Apr. 1775

15 He [Johnson] qualified my mind to think justly.
Ib. vol. iii, p. 369, n. 3; *and* Northcote's, *Reynolds*,
vol. ii, p. 282.

ARCHBISHOP WALTER REYNOLDS
[De REYNEL or REGINALD]
d. 1327

16 Vox Populi, vox Dei.
The voice of the people, the voice of God.
*Text of Sermon when Edward III ascended the
throne, 1 Feb. 1327*. Walsingham, *Historia
Anglicana* (ed. 1863), i. 186

CECIL JOHN RHODES
1853–1902

17 So little done, so much to do.
Last words. L. Michell, *Life*, vol. ii, ch. 39

WILLIAM BARNES RHODES
1772–1826

18 'Who dares this pair of boots displace,
Must meet Bombastes face to face.'
Thus do I challenge all the human race.
Bombastes Furioso, sc. iv

19 BOMBASTES:
So have I heard on Afric's burning shore,
A hungry lion give a grievous roar;
The grievous roar echo'd along the shore.
KING:
So have I heard on Afric's burning shore
Another lion give a grievous roar,
And the first lion thought the last a bore.   *Ib.*

GRANTLAND RICE
1880–

20 For when the One Great Scorer comes
To write against your name,
He marks—not that you won or lost—
But how you played the game.   *Alumnus Football*

SIR STEPHEN RICE
1637–1715

21 Sir Stephen Rice . . . having been often heard to
say, before he was a judge, that he will drive a
coach and six horses through the Act of Settlement.
W. King, *State of the Protestants of Ireland*
(1672), ch. 3, § 3, par. 6

JEAN PAUL RICHTER
1763–1825

1 Providence has given to the French the empire of the land, to the English that of the sea, and to the Germans that of the air.
Quoted by Thomas Carlyle, in the Edinburgh Review, *1827*

GEORGE RIDDING, BISHOP OF SOUTHWELL
1828–1904

2 I feel a feeling which I feel you all feel.
Sermon in the London Mission of 1885. G. W. E. Russell's *Collections and Recollections*, ch. 29

JAMES WHITCOMB RILEY
1852–1916

3 An' the gobble-uns 'll git you
Ef you don't watch out!
Poems. Little Orphant Annie

4 It haint no use to grumble and complane
Its jest as cheap and easy to rejoice;
When God sorts out the weather and sends rain,
W'y rain's my choice.   *Ib. Wet-Weather Talk*

ROBERT LEROY RIPLEY
1893–

5 Believe it or not.   *Title of newspaper feature*

ANTOINE DE RIVAROL
1753–1801

6 Ce qui n'est pas clair n'est pas français.
What is not clear is not French.
De l'Universalité de la Langue Française (1784)

SIR BOYLE ROCHE
1743–1807

7 He regretted that he was not a bird, and could not be in two places at once.   *Attr.*

8 Mr. Speaker, I smell a rat; I see him forming in the air and darkening the sky; but I'll nip him in the bud.   *Attr.*

DUC DE LA ROCHEFOUCAULD
1613–1680

9 Nous avons tous assez de force pour supporter les maux d'autrui.
We have all enough strength to bear the misfortunes of others.   *Maximes, 19*

10 On n'est jamais si heureux ni si malheureux qu'on s'imagine.
One is never so happy or so unhappy as one thinks.   *Ib. 49*

11 L'hypocrisie est un hommage que le vice rend à la vertu.
Hypocrisy is homage paid by vice to virtue. *Ib. 218*

12 C'est une grande habileté que de savoir cacher son habileté.

The height of cleverness is to be able to conceal it.
Maximes, 245

13 La reconnaissance de la plupart des hommes n'est qu'une secrète envie de recevoir de plus grands bienfaits.
In most of mankind gratitude is merely a secret hope of further favours.   *Ib. 298*
A saying ascribed to Sir Robert Walpole by Hazlitt in his Wit and Humour: 'The gratitude of place-expectants is a lively sense of future favours' *is obviously derived from La Rochefoucauld.*

14 Dans l'adversité de nos meilleurs amis, nous trouvons quelque chose qui ne nous déplaît pas.
In the misfortune of our best friends, we find something which is not displeasing to us.
Maximes supprimées, 583

DUC DE LA ROCHEFOUCAULD-LIANCOURT
1747–1827

15 LOUIS XVI: C'est une révolte?
LA ROCHEFOUCAULD-LIANCOURT: Non, Sire, c'est une révolution.
LOUIS XVI: Is it a revolt?
LA R.-LIANCOURT: No, Sire, it is a revolution.
When the news arrived at Versailles of the Fall of the Bastille, 1789

JOHN WILMOT, EARL OF ROCHESTER
1647–1680

16 Since 'tis Nature's law to change,
Constancy alone is strange.
Works (1926), A Dialogue between Strephon and Daphne, l. 31

17 The best good man, with the worst-natur'd muse.
To Lord Buckhurst

18 An age in her embraces past,
Would seem a winter's day.   *Ib. The Mistress*

19 Nothing! thou elder brother ev'n to shade.
Ib. Upon Nothing

20 A merry monarch, scandalous and poor.
Ib. A Satire on King Charles II for which he was banished from the Court, l. 19.

21 Reason, an *ignis fatuus* of the mind.
Ib. A Satire Against Mankind, l. 11

22 Then Old Age, and Experience, hand in hand,
Lead him to Death, and make him understand,
After a search so painful, and so long,
That all his life he has been in the wrong.
Huddled in dirt the reasoning engine lies,
Who was so proud, so witty and so wise.   *Ib. l. 25*

23 For all men would be cowards if they durst.
Ib. l. 158

24 Here lies a great and mighty king
Whose promise none relies on;
He never said a foolish thing,
Nor ever did a wise one.
The King's Epitaph. An alternative version of the first line is: 'Here lies our sovereign lord the King.'
For Charles II's answer see 136:4

E. W. ROGERS

1 Ev'ry member of the force
  Has a watch and chain, of course;
  If you want to know the time,
  Ask a P'liceman!   *Ask A P'liceman*

2 Hi-tiddley-hi-ti.   *Title of Song*

JAMES EDWIN THOROLD ROGERS
1823–1890

3 Sir, to be facetious it is not necessary to be indecent.
  *In imitation of Samuel Johnson. Also attributed to
  Birkbeck Hill. Quo. in* John Bailey: *Dr. Johnson
  and his Circle*

4 While ladling butter from alternate tubs
  Stubbs butters Freeman, Freeman butters Stubbs.
  Attrib. in Hutton's *Letters of Bishop Stubbs*

ROBERT CAMERON ROGERS
1862–1912

5 The hours I spent with thee, dear heart,
    Are as a string of pearls to me;
  I count them over, every one apart,
    My rosary.   *The Rosary*

SAMUEL ROGERS
1763–1855

6 Think nothing done while aught remains to do.
                                      Human Life, l. 49

7 But there are moments which he calls his own,
  Then, never less alone than when alone,
  Those whom he loved so long and sees no more,
  Loved and still loves—not dead—but gone before,
  He gathers round him.   *Ib. l. 755*

8 By many a temple half as old as Time.
                                      Italy. A Farewell, ii. 5

9 Go—you may call it madness, folly;
    You shall not chase my gloom away.
  There's such a charm in melancholy,
    I would not, if I could, be gay.   *To —, 1814*

10 Mine be a cot beside the hill;
    A bee-hive's hum shall soothe my ear;
   A willowy brook, that turns a mill,
    With many a fall shall linger near. *A Wish*

11 Sheridan was listened to with such attention that you
   might have heard a pin drop.   *Table Talk*

12 It doesn't much signify whom one marries, for one is
   sure to find next morning that it was someone else.
                                      Ib.

13 Ward has no heart, they say; but I deny it;—
   He has a heart, and gets his speeches by it.
                                      Ib. Epigram upon Lord Dudley

14 When a new book is published, read an old one.
                                      Attr.

MME ROLAND
1754–1793

15 O liberté! O liberté! que de crimes on commet en
   ton nom!

   O liberty! O liberty! what crimes are committed in
     thy name!
     Lamartine, *Histoire des Girondins*, livre li, ch. 8

16 The more I see of men, the better I like dogs. *Attrib.*

JAMES ROLMAZ

17 'Where did you get that hat?
   Where did you get that tile?
   Isn't it a nobby one, and just the proper style?
   I should like to have one just the same as that!'
   Wher'er I go they shout, 'Hello!
   Where did you get that hat?'
                                      Where Did You Get That Hat?

PIERRE RONSARD
1529–1585

18 Quand vous serez bien vieille, au soir, à la chandelle,
   Assise auprès du feu, dévidant et filant,
   Direz, chantant mes vers, en vous émerveillant,
   Ronsard me célébrait du temps que j'étais belle.

     When you are very old, and sit in the candle-light
     at evening spinning by the fire, you will say, as
     you murmur my verses, a wonder in your eyes,
     'Ronsard sang of me in the days when I was fair.'
                                      Sonnets pour Hélène, ii. 43

FRANKLIN DELANO ROOSEVELT
1882–1945

19 I pledge you—I pledge myself—to a new deal for the
   American people.
     Speech at Convention, Chicago, 2 July 1932.
     (*New York Times*, 3 July, sect. 1, p. 8, col. 7.)
     E. K. Lindley, *The Roosevelt Revolution*, ch. 1

20 Let me assert my firm belief that the only thing we
   have to fear is fear itself.
                                      First Inaugural Address, 4 March 1933

21 In the field of world policy; I would dedicate this
   nation to the policy of the good neighbour.   *Ib.*

22 I see one-third of a nation ill-housed, ill-clad, ill-
   nourished.
                                      Second Inaugural Address, 20 Jan. 1937

23 When peace has been broken anywhere, the peace of
   all countries everywhere is in danger.
                                      Fireside Chat, 3 Sept. 1939

24 We must be the great arsenal of democracy.
                                      Ib. 29 Dec. 1940

25 In the future days, which we seek to make secure,
   we look forward to a world founded upon four
   essential freedoms.
   The first is freedom of speech and expression—every-
     where in the world.
   The second is freedom of every person to worship
     God in his own way—everywhere in the world.
   The third is freedom from want. . . .
   The fourth is freedom from fear.
                                      Speech, 6 Jan. 1941

THEODORE ROOSEVELT
1858–1919

26 I wish to preach, not the doctrine of ignoble ease,
   but the doctrine of the strenuous life.
     Speech, Hamilton Club, Chicago, 10 Apr. 1899

27 Speak softly and carry a big stick.
     Ib. Minnesota State Fair, 2 Sept. 1901

1 The first requisite of a good citizen in this Republic of ours is that he shall be able and willing to pull his weight. *Speech, New York, 11 Nov. 1902*

2 A man who is good enough to shed his blood for the country is good enough to be given a square deal afterwards. More than that no man is entitled to, and less than that no man shall have.
Ib. At the Lincoln Monument, Springfield (Illinois), 4 June 1903

3 The men with the muck-rakes are often indispensable to the well-being of society; but only if they know when to stop raking the muck.
Ib. At the laying of the Corner-stone of the Office Building of House of Representatives, 14 Apr. 1906

4 There can be no fifty-fifty Americanism in this country. There is room here for only 100 per cent. Americanism, only for those who are Americans and nothing else. *Ib. Republican Convention, Saratoga*

5 No man is justified in doing evil on the ground of expediency.
The Strenuous Life, Essays. Latitude and Longitude among Reformers

6 We demand that big business give the people a square deal; in return we must insist that when any one engaged in big business honestly endeavors to do right he shall himself be given a square deal. *Autobiography (1913), p. 615*

7 Hyphenated Americans.
Metropolitan Magazine, Oct. 1915, p. 7

ARCHIBALD PHILIP PRIMROSE, EARL OF ROSEBERY
1847–1929

8 Before Irish Home Rule is conceded by the Imperial Parliament, England as the predominant member of the three kingdoms will have to be convinced of its justice and equity.
Speech in the House of Lords, 11 March 1894

9 It is beginning to be hinted that we are a nation of amateurs.
Rectorial Address, Glasgow, 16 Nov. 1900

10 I must plough my furrow alone.
Speech, City of London Liberal Club, 19 July 1901

11 What is the advice I have to offer you? The first is this—that you have to clean your slate. [To the Liberal Party.] *Speech, Chesterfield, 16 Dec. 1901*

12 The fly-blown phylacteries of the Liberal Party. *Ib.*

ALEXANDER ROSS
1699–1784

13 Marri'd an' woo'd an' a',
   Marri'd an' woo'd an' a',
The dandilly toss[1] of the parish,
   Is marri'd and woo'd an' a'.
The Fortunate Shepherdess (1768), p. 139

[1] = toast.

CHRISTINA GEORGINA ROSSETTI
1830–1894

14 My heart is like a singing bird
   Whose nest is in a watered shoot;
My heart is like an apple-tree
   Whose boughs are bent with thickset fruit;
My heart is like a rainbow shell
   That paddles in a halcyon sea;
My heart is gladder than all these
   Because my love is come to me. *A Birthday*

15 Because the birthday of my life
   Is come, my love is come to me. *Ib.*

16 Oh where are you going with your love-locks flowing? *Amor Mundi, i*

17 We shall escape the uphill by never turning back. *Ib.*

18 This downhill path is easy, but there's no turning back. *Ib. v*

19 For there is no friend like a sister
   In calm or stormy weather;
To cheer one on the tedious way,
To fetch one if one goes astray,
To lift one if one totters down,
To strengthen whilst one stands.
Goblin Market (end)

20 In the bleak mid-winter
      Frosty wind made moan,
   Earth stood hard as iron,
      Water like a stone;
Snow had fallen, snow on snow,
      Snow on snow,
In the bleak mid-winter,
      Long ago. *Mid-Winter*

21 In the bleak mid-winter
      A stable-place sufficed
   The Lord God almighty,
      Jesus Christ. *Ib.*

22 A breastful of milk,
   And a mangerful of hay. *Ib.*

23 There was no hurry in her hands,
   No hurry in her feet. *The Prince's Progress, lxxxv*

24 Remember me when I am gone away,
   Gone far away into the silent land. *Remember*

25 Better by far you should forget and smile
   Than that you should remember and be sad. *Ib.*

26 O Earth, lie heavily upon her eyes;
   Seal her sweet eyes weary of watching, Earth. *Rest*

27 Silence more musical than any song. *Ib.*

28 Oh roses for the flush of youth,
   And laurel for the perfect prime;
But pluck an ivy branch for me
   Grown old before my time.
Song: 'Oh Roses for the Flush'

29 When I am dead, my dearest,
   Sing no sad songs for me;
Plant thou no roses at my head,
   Nor shady cypress tree:
Be the green grass above me
   With showers and dewdrops wet;
And if thou wilt, remember,
   And if thou wilt, forget. *Song: 'When I am Dead'*

1 And dreaming through the twilight
   That doth not rise nor set,
Haply I may remember,
   And haply may forget.   *Song: 'When I am Dead'*

2 Does the road wind up-hill all the way?
   Yes, to the very end.
Will the day's journey take the whole long day?
   From morn to night, my friend.   *Up-Hill*

3 They will not keep you standing at that door.   *Ib.*

4 Will there be beds for me and all who seek?
   Yea, beds for all who come.   *Ib.*

DANTE GABRIEL ROSSETTI

1828–1882

5 Mother of the Fair Delight,
Thou handmaid perfect in God's sight.   *Ave*, l. 1

6 Like the sweet apple which reddens upon the topmost bough,
A-top on the topmost twig,—which the pluckers
   forgot, somehow,—
Forgot it not, nay, but got it not, for none could get
   it till now.   *Beauty: A Combination from Sappho*

7 The blessed damozel leaned out
   From the gold bar of Heaven;
Her eyes were deeper than the depth
   Of waters stilled at even;
She had three lilies in her hand,
   And the stars in her hair were seven.
                    The Blessed Damozel, i

8 Her hair that lay along her back
Was yellow like ripe corn.   *Ib.* ii

9 So high, that looking downward thence,
   She scarce could see the sun.   *Ib.* v

10   As low as where this earth
Spins like a fretful midge.   *Ib.* vi

11 And the souls mounting up to God
   Went by her like thin flames.   *Ib.* vii

12 'We two,' she said, 'will seek the groves
   Where the lady Mary is,
With her five handmaidens, whose names
   Are five sweet symphonies,
Cecily, Gertrude, Magdalen,
   Margaret and Rosalys.'   *Ib.* xviii

13   Them
Who are just born, being dead.   *Ib.* xix

14 And laid her face between her hands,
   And wept. (I heard her tears.)   *Ib.* xxiv

15 Still we say as we go,—
   'Strange to think by the way,
Whatever there is to know,
   That shall we know one day.'   *Cloud Confines*

16 Heard through all spheres one song increase,—
   'Even I, even I am Beatrice.'   *Dante at Verona*, xii

17 Where the lean black craft like flies
   Seem well-nigh stagnated,
   Soon to drop off dead.   *Even So*

18 Peace in her chamber, wheresoe'er
   It be, a holy place.   *First Love Remembered*, i

19 'I saw the Sibyl at Cumæ'
   (One said) 'with mine own eye.
She hung in a cage, and read her rune
   To all the passers-by.
Said the boys, "What wouldst thou, Sibyl?"
   She answered, "I would die".'
                    Fragments. The Sibyl

20 Was it a friend or foe that spread these lies?
   Nay, who but infants question in such wise?
'Twas one of my most intimate enemies.   *Fragment*

21 A sonnet is a moment's monument,—
Memorial from the Soul's eternity
To one dead deathless hour.
                    The House of Life, pt. 1. Introd.

22 Love's throne was not with these; but far above
All passionate wind of welcome and farewell
He sat in breathless bowers they dream not of.
                    Ib. i. *Love Enthroned*

23 When do I see thee most, beloved one?
                    Ib. iv. *Lovesight*

24 O love, my love! if I no more should see
Thyself, nor on the earth the shadow of thee,
Nor image of thine eyes in any spring,—
How then should sound upon life's darkening slope
The ground-whirl of the perished leaves of Hope,
The wind of Death's imperishable wing?   *Ib.*

25 Lady, I fain would tell how evermore
Thy soul I know not from thy body, nor
Thee from myself, neither our love from God.
                    Ib. v. *Heart's Hope*

26 I was a child beneath her touch,—a man
When breast to breast we clung, even I and she,—
A spirit when her spirit looked through me,—
A god when all our life-breath met to fan
Our life-blood, till love's emulous ardours ran,
Fire within fire, desire in deity.   *Ib.* vi. *The Kiss*

27 Known for my soul's birth-partner well enough!
                    Ib. xv. *The Birth-Bond*

28 Beauty like hers is genius.   *Ib.* xviii. *Genius in Beauty*

29 'Tis visible silence, still as the hour-glass.
                    Ib. xix. *Silent Noon*

30 Deep in the sun-searched growths the dragon-fly
Hangs like a blue thread loosened from the sky:—
So this wing'd hour is dropt to us from above.
Oh! clasp we to our hearts, for deathless dower,
This close-companioned inarticulate hour
When twofold silence was the song of love.   *Ib.*

31   Shall my sense pierce love,—the last relay
And ultimate outpost of eternity?
                    Ib. xxxiv. *The Dark Glass*

32 Not in thy body is thy life at all,
But in this lady's lips and hands and eyes.
                    Ib. xxxvi. *Life-in-Love*

33 The hour when you too learn that all is vain
   And that Hope sows what Love shall never reap.
                    Ib. xliv. *Cloud and Wind*

34 If to grow old in Heaven is to grow young,
(As the Seer saw and said,) then blest were he
With youth for evermore, whose heaven should be
True Woman, she whom these weak notes have sung.
                    Ib. lviii. *True Woman*, sonnet iii

1 The sunrise blooms and withers on the hill
Like any hillflower; and the noblest troth
Dies here to dust. Yet shall Heaven's promise clothe
Even yet those lovers who have cherished still
This test for love:—in every kiss sealed fast
To feel the first kiss and forebode the last.   *Ib.*

2 Upon the sight of lidless eyes in Hell.
                              Ib. pt. II. lxiii, *Inclusiveness*

3   Thenceforth their incommunicable ways
Follow the desultory feet of Death.
                              Ib. lxv. *Known in Vain*

4 And see the gold air and the silver fade
And the last bird fly into the last night.
                              Ib. lxx. *The Hill Summit*

5 Eat thou and drink; to-morrow thou shalt die.
                              Ib. lxxi. *The Choice*, i

6 They die not,—for their life was death,—but cease;
And round their narrow lips the mould falls close. *Ib.*

7 Think thou and act; to-morrow thou shalt die.
                              Ib. iii

8 Nay, come up hither. From this wave-washed mound
Unto the furthest flood-brim look with me;
Then reach on with thy thought till it be drown'd.
Miles and miles distant though the last line be,
And though thy soul sail leagues and leagues beyond,—
Still, leagues beyond those leagues, there is more sea.
                              Ib.

9 Give honour unto Luke Evangelist;
For he it was (the aged legends say)
Who first taught Art to fold her hands and pray.
                              Ib. lxxiv. *Old and New Art*, i

10 This is that Lady Beauty, in whose praise
Thy voice and hand shake still,—long known to thee
By flying hair and fluttering hem,—the beat
Following her daily of thy heart and feet,
How passionately and irretrievably,
In what fond flight, how many ways and days!
                              Ib. lxxvii. *Soul's Beauty*

11 Lo! as that youth's eyes burned at thine, so went
Thy spell through him, and left his straight neck bent
And round his heart one strangling golden hair.
                              Ib. lxxviii. *Body's Beauty*

12 And in regenerate rapture turns my face
Upon the devious coverts of dismay?
                              Ib. lxxix. *The Monochord*

13 The lost days of my life until to-day,
What were they, could I see them on the street
Lie as they fell?   *Ib.* lxxxvi. *Lost Days*

14 I do not see them here; but after death
God knows I know the faces I shall see,
Each one a murdered self, with low last breath.
'I am thyself,—what hast thou done to me?'
'And I—and I—thyself', (lo! each one saith,)
'And thou thyself to all eternity!'   *Ib.*

15   Even as, heavy-curled,
Stooping against the wind, a charioteer
Is snatched from out his chariot by the hair,
So shall Time be; and as the void car, hurled
Abroad by reinless steeds, even so the world.
                              Ib. xc. '*Retro me, Sathana!*'

16 Thou still, upon the broad vine-sheltered path,
Mayst wait the turning of the phials of wrath
For certain years, for certain months and days. *Ib.*

17 My name is Might-have-been;
I am also called No-more, Too-late, Farewell.
          The House of Life, pt. II. xcvii. *A Superscription*

18 Sleepless with cold commemorative eyes.   *Ib.*

19 When vain desire at last and vain regret
Go hand in hand to death.   *Ib.* ci. *The One Hope*

20 Teach the unforgetful to forget.   *Ib.*

21 The wan soul in that golden air.   *Ib.*

22 Scriptured petals.   *Ib.*

23   The one Hope's one name be there,—
Not less nor more, but even that word alone.   *Ib.*

24 It makes a goblin of the sun.   *Jenny*, l. 205

25 Between the hands, between the brows,
Between the lips of Love-Lily.   *Love-Lily*

26 Whose speech Truth knows not from her thought
Nor Love her body from her soul.   *Ib.*

27 This is that blessed Mary, pre-elect
God's Virgin.   *Mary's Girlhood*

28 Thou fill'st from the winged chalice of the soul
Thy lamp, O Memory, fire-winged to its goal.
                              Mnemosyne

29 Amid the bitterness of things occult.
                              For Our Lady of the Rocks

30 And your own footsteps meeting you,
And all things going as they came.   *The Portrait*, iii

31 Yearned loud the iron-bosomed sea.   *Ib.* x

32   O Mother, Mary Mother,
Three days to-day, between Hell and Heaven!
                              Sister Helen

33 Unto the man of yearning thought
And aspiration, to do nought
Is in itself almost an act.   *Soothsay*, x

34 I have been here before,
   But when or how I cannot tell:
I know the grass beyond the door,
   The sweet keen smell,
The sighing sound, the lights around the shore.
                              Sudden Light, i

35 Heavenborn Helen, Sparta's queen,
          (O Troy Town!)
Had two breasts of heavenly sheen,
The sun and moon of the heart's desire.
                              Troy Town, i

36 The sea hath no king but God alone.
                              The White Ship, l. 6

37 From perfect grief there need not be
Wisdom or even memory:
One thing then learnt remains to me,—
The woodspurge has a cup of three.   *The Woodspurge*

38 Conception, my boy, *fundamental brainwork*, is what
makes the difference in all art.
     Letter to Hall Caine, in Caine's *Recollections of Rossetti* (1882)

39 The Stealthy School of Criticism.   *Title*

ROUGET DE LISLE

1760–1836

1 Allons, enfants de la patrie,
Le jour de gloire est arrivé.

Come, children of our country, the day of glory has
arrived. *La Marseillaise*

JEAN-JACQUES ROUSSEAU

1712–1778

2 L'homme est né libre, et partout il est dans les fers.

Man is born free, and everywhere he is in chains.
Du Contrat Social, ch. 1

3 'Monseigneur, il faut que je vive,' disait un malheureux auteur satirique au ministre qui lui re-
prochait l'infamie de ce métier. 'Je n'en vois pas la
nécessité,' lui repartit froidement l'homme en
place.

'My Lord—I must live'—once said a wretched
author of satire to a minister who had reproached
him for following so degrading a profession.
'I fail to see why,' replied the Great Man coldly.
Émile, iii. (*See 14: 11*)

MARTIN JOSEPH ROUTH

1755–1854

4 You will find it a very good practice always to verify
your references, sir!
Burgon, *Memoir of Dr. Routh. Quarterly Review*,
July 1878, vol. cxlvi

NICHOLAS ROWE

1674–1718

5 That false Lothario!   *The Fair Penitent*, II. i

6 To be good is to be happy.   *Ib.* III. i

7 The evening of my age.   *Ib.* IV. i

8 I feel the pangs of disappointed love.   *Ib.*

9 Is this that haughty, gallant, gay Lothario? *Ib.* V. I

10 Like Helen, in the night when Troy was sack'd,
Spectatress of the mischief which she made.   *Ib.*

11 Death is the privilege of human nature,
And life without it were not worth our taking. *Ib.*

12   Had I but early known
Thy wond'rous worth, thou excellent young man,
We had been happier both.   *Ib.*

13 With rough, majestic force he mov'd the heart,
With strength and nature made amends for art.
[On Shakespeare.]   *Jane Shore*, prologue

14   If I boast of aught,
Be it, to have been Heaven's happy instrument,
The means of good to all my fellow-creatures;
This is a King's best praise.   *Tamerlaine*, II. ii

15   Death is parting,
'Tis the last sad adieu 'twixt soul and body. *Ib.*

16 Think on the sacred dictates of thy faith,
And let that arm thy virtue, to perform
What Cato's daughter durst not,—live Aspasia,
And dare to be unhappy.   *Ib.* IV. i

'RED ROWLEY'

17 Mademoiselle from Armenteers,
Hasn't been kissed in forty years,
Hinky dinky, parley-voo.
Song of the Great War, 1914–18

MATTHEW ROYDON

fl. 1580–1622

18 A sweet attractive kind of grace,
A full assurance given by looks,
Continual comfort in a face,
The lineaments of Gospel books;
I trow that countenance cannot lie,
Whose thoughts are legible in the eye.
An Elegy, or Friend's Passion, for his Astrophill
(i.e. Sir Philip Sidney), xviii

19 Was never eye, did see that face,
Was never ear, did hear that tongue,
Was never mind, did mind his grace,
That ever thought the travel long—
But eyes, and ears, and ev'ry thought,
Were with his sweet perfections caught. *Ib.* xix

JOHN RUSKIN

1819–1900

20 You know there are a great many odd styles of
architecture about; you don't want to do anything
ridiculous; you hear of me, among others, as a
respectable architectural man-milliner; and you
send for me, that I may tell you the leading fashion.
The Crown of Wild Olive, § 53, lecture ii. *Traffic*

21 Thackeray settled like a meat-fly on whatever one had
got for dinner, and made one sick of it.
Fors Clavigera, letter xxxi

22 [On Whistler's 'Nocturne in Black and Gold']
I have seen, and heard, much of Cockney impudence
before now; but never expected to hear a coxcomb
ask two hundred guineas for flinging a pot of paint
in the public's face. *Ib.* letter lxxix, 18 June 1877

23 No person who is not a great sculptor or painter *can*
be an architect. If he is not a sculptor or painter,
he can only be a *builder*.
Lectures on Architecture and Painting, § 61,
Addenda

24 There is nothing in sea-description, detailed, like
Dickens' storm at the death of Ham, in 'David
Copperfield'.
Modern Painters (1888), vol. i, pt. ii, p. 425, note

25 What is poetry? The suggestion, by the imagination,
of noble grounds for the noble emotions.
Ib. vol. iii

26 All violent feelings . . . produce in us a falseness in all
our impressions of external things, which I would
generally characterize as the 'Pathetic Fallacy'. *Ib.*

27 Mountains are the beginning and the end of all
natural scenery.   *Ib.* vol. iv, pt. v, ch. 20, § 1

28 That mysterious forest below London Bridge.
Ib. vol. v, pt. ix, ch. 9, § 7

29 Its symmetry [be] as of thunder answering from two
horizons. [A sentence of Johnson.]
Praeterita, I. xii. *Rosslyn Chapel*, § 251

1 There was a rocky valley between Buxton and Bakewell, ... divine as the vale of Tempe; you might have seen the gods there morning and evening,—Apollo and the sweet Muses of the Light. ... You enterprised a railroad, ... you blasted its rocks away. ... And now, every fool in Buxton can be at Bakewell in half-an-hour, and every fool in Bakewell at Buxton.
Praeterita, III. iv. *Joanna's Cave*, § 84, note

2 All books are divisible into two classes: the books of the hour, and the books of all time.
Sesame and Lilies, Lecture i. *Of Kings' Treasuries*, § 8

3 But whether thus submissively or not, at least be sure that you go to the author to get at *his* meaning, not to find yours. *Ib.* § 13

4 Which of us ... is to do the hard and dirty work for the rest—and for what pay? Who is to do the pleasant and clean work, and for what pay?
Ib. § 30, note

5 What do we, as a nation, care about books? How much do you think we spend altogether on our libraries, public or private, as compared with what we spend on our horses? *Ib.* § 32

6 How long most people would look at the best book before they would give the price of a large turbot for it! *Ib.*

7 We call ourselves a rich nation, and we are filthy and foolish enough to thumb each other's books out of circulating libraries! *Ib.*

8 Will you not covet such power as this, and seek such throne as this, and be no more housewives, but queens? *Ib.* Lecture ii. *Of Queens' Gardens*, § 87

9 There is no putting by that crown; queens you must always be; queens to your lovers; queens to your husbands and your sons; queens of higher mystery to the world beyond. ... But, alas! you are too often idle and careless queens, grasping at majesty in the least things, while you abdicate it in the greatest. *Ib.* § 90

10 I believe the right question to ask, respecting all ornament, is simply this: Was it done with enjoyment—was the carver happy while he was about it?
The Seven Lamps of Architecture, ch. 5. *The Lamp of Life*

11 Better the rudest work that tells a story or records a fact, than the richest without meaning. There should not be a single ornament put upon great civic buildings, without some intellectual intention.
Ib. ch. 6. *The Lamp of Memory*, § 7

12 When we build, let us think that we build for ever.
Ib. § 10

13 Remember that the most beautiful things in the world are the most useless; peacocks and lilies for instance. *The Stones of Venice*, vol. i, ch. 2, § 17

14 The purest and most thoughtful minds are those which love colour the most. *Ib.* vol. ii, ch. 5, § 30

15 All things are literally better, lovelier, and more beloved for the imperfections which have been divinely appointed, that the law of human life may be Effort, and the law of human judgment, Mercy. *Ib.* ch. vi, § 25

16 Fine art is that in which the hand, the head, and the heart of man go together.
The Two Paths, Lecture ii

17 Not only is there but one way of *doing* things rightly, but there is only one way of *seeing* them, and that is, seeing the whole of them. *Ib.*

18 Nobody cares much at heart about Titian; only there is a strange undercurrent of everlasting murmur about his name, which means the deep consent of all great men that he is greater than they. *Ib.*

19 No human being, however great, or powerful, was ever so free as a fish. *Ib.* Lecture v

20 Labour without joy is base. Labour without sorrow is base. Sorrow without labour is base. Joy without labour is base. *Time and Tide*, letter v

21 Your honesty is *not* to be based either on religion or policy. Both your religion and policy must be based on *it*. Your honesty must be based, as the sun is, in vacant heaven; poised, as the lights in the firmament, which have rule over the day and over the night. *Ib.* letter viii

22 To make your children *capable of honesty* is the beginning of education. *Ib.*

23 I hold it for indisputable, that the first duty of a State is to see that every child born therein shall be well housed, clothed, fed, and educated, till it attain years of discretion. But in order to the effecting this the Government must have an authority over the people of which we now do not so much as dream. *Ib.* letter xiii

24 It ought to be quite as natural and straightforward a matter for a labourer to take his pension from his parish, because he has deserved well of his parish, as for a man in higher rank to take his pension from his country, because he has deserved well of his country. *Unto this Last*, preface, § 6 (4)

25 The force of the guinea you have in your pocket depends wholly on the default of a guinea in your neighbour's pocket. If he did not want it, it would be of no use to you. *Ib.* Essay ii, § 27

26 Soldiers of the ploughshare as well as soldiers of the sword. *Ib.* Essay iii, § 54

27 Government and co-operation are in all things the laws of life; anarchy and competition the laws of death. *Ib.*

28 Whereas it has long been known and declared that the poor have no right to the property of the rich, I wish it also to be known and declared that the rich have no right to the property of the poor. *Ib.*

29 There is no wealth but life. *Ib.* Essay iv, § 77

30 There is really no such thing as bad weather, only different kinds of good weather.
Quoted by Lord Avebury

31 Trust thou thy Love: if she be proud, is she not sweet?
Trust thou thy Love: if she be mute, is she not pure?
Lay thou thy soul full in her hands, low at her feet;—
Fail, Sun and Breath!—yet, for thy peace, she shall endure. *Trust Thou Thy Love*

LORD JOHN RUSSELL

1792–1878

1 If peace cannot be maintained with honour, it is no
  longer peace.
    *Speech. Greenock, 19 Sept. 1853. The Times,
    21 Sept. 1853*

2 Among the defects of the Bill, which were numerous,
  one provision was conspicuous by its presence and
  another by its absence.
    *Speech to the electors of the City of London, Apr.
    1859*

3 A proverb is one man's wit and all men's wisdom.
    Ascribed

SIR WILLIAM HOWARD RUSSELL

1820–1907

4 [The Russians] dash on towards that thin red line
  tipped with steel.
    The British Expedition to the Crimea (1877), p. 156

CHARLES SACKVILLE

see

EARL OF DORSET

JOHN L. ST. JOHN

5 Archibald—certainly not!   *Title of Song*

W. ST. LEGER

6 There is a fine stuffed chavender,
  A chavender, or chub,
  That decks the rural pavender,
  The pavender, or pub,
  Wherein I eat my gravender,
  My gravender, or grub.
    The Chavender, or Chub, st. 1

CHARLES-AUGUSTIN SAINTE-BEUVE

1804–1869

7   Et Vigny plus secret,
  Comme en sa tour d'ivoire, avant midi rentrait.
  And Vigny more reserved,
  Returned ere noon, within his ivory tower.
    Quoted in Paléologue's *Vigny, p. 71*

'SAKI'
[HECTOR HUGH MUNRO]

1870–1916

8 'The man is a common murderer.'
  'A common murderer, possibly, but a very uncommon cook.'
    Beasts and Super-Beasts. The Blind Spot

9 When she inveighed eloquently against the evils of
  capitalism at drawing-room meetings and Fabian
  conferences she was conscious of a comfortable
  feeling that the system, with all its inequalities
  and iniquities, would probably last her time. It is
  one of the consolations of middle-aged reformers
  that the good they inculcate must live after them
  if it is to live at all.   *Ib. The Byzantine Omelette*

10 Waldo is one of those people who would be enor-
  mously improved by death.
    Ib. The Feast of Nemesis

11 He's simply got the instinct for being unhappy
  highly developed.
    Chronicles of Clovis. The Match-Maker

12 Oysters are more beautiful than any religion. . . .
  There's nothing in Christianity or Buddhism that
  quite matches the sympathetic unselfishness of an
  oyster.   *Ib.*

13 The cook was a good cook, as cooks go; and as cooks
  go she went.   *Reginald. Reginald on Besetting Sins*

14 Women and elephants never forget an injury.   *Ib.*

15 Addresses are given to us to conceal our whereabouts.
    Reginald in Russia. Cross Currents

16 The Western custom of one wife and hardly any
  mistresses.   *Ib. A Young Turkish Catastrophe*

17 But, good gracious, you've got to educate him first.
  You can't expect a boy to be vicious till he's been
  to a good school.   *Ib. The Baker's Dozen*

18 In baiting a mouse-trap with cheese, always leave
  room for the mouse.
    The Square Egg. The Infernal Parliament

19 Children with Hyacinth's temperament don't know
  better as they grow older; they merely know more.
    The Toys of Peace. Hyacinth

GEORGE AUGUSTUS SALA

1828–1896

20 And now, Sir, we will take a walk down Fleet Street.
    Motto of the Temple Bar *magazine. Ascribed to
    Dr. Johnson.*

JOHN OF SALISBURY

d. 1180

21 Siquidem uita breuis, sensus hebes, negligentiae tor-
  por, inutilis occupatio, nos paucula, scire permit-
  tunt, et eadem iugiter excutit et auellit ab animo
  fraudatrix scientiae, inimica et infida semper
  memoriae nouerca, obliuio.
    The brevity of our life, the dullness of our senses,
    the torpor of our indifference, the futility of our
    occupation, suffer us to know but little: and that
    little is soon shaken and then torn from the mind
    by that traitor to learning, that hostile and faith-
    less stepmother to memory, oblivion.
    *Prologue to the Policraticus. (C. C. J. Webb's
    edition, vol. i, p. 12, ll. 13–16.) Trans. by Helen
    Waddell*

ROBERT CECIL, LORD SALISBURY

1830–1903

22 By office boys for office boys.
    Remark about The Daily Mail. *See H. Hamilton
    Fyfe: Northcliffe, an Intimate Biography, ch. 4*

SALLUST

86–34 B.C.

23 Sed res docuit id verum esse, quod in carminibus
  Appius ait, fabrum esse suae quemque fortunae.
    But the case has proved that to be true which
    Appius says in his songs, that each man is the
    maker of his own fate.   *Ad Caesarem, 1. i. 2*

1 Alieni appetens, sui profusus.

Coveting the property of others, lavish of his own.
Catiline, 5

2 Idem velle atque idem nolle, ea demum firma amicitia est.

Friendship is this—to desire, and to dislike, the same thing. *Ib.* 20

3 Pro patria, pro liberis, pro aris atque focis suis.

On behalf of their country, their children, their altars, and their hearths. *Ib.* 59

4 Urbem venalem et mature perituram, si emptorem invenerit.

The venal city soon to perish, if a buyer can be found. *Jugurtha*, 35

5 Punica fide.

With Carthaginian faith [i.e. treachery]. *Ib.* 108, 3

IRA DAVID SANKEY
1840–1908

6 Light in the darkness, sailor, day is at hand!
See o'er the foaming billows fair Heaven's land.
Drear was the voyage, sailor, now almost o'er;
Safe within the lifeboat, sailor, pull for the shore.
Pull for the shore, sailor, pull for the shore!
Heed not the rolling waves, but bend to the oar.
Sacred Songs. The Life Boat

7 Is there room for Mary there?
Yes, there's room; yes, there's room;
Room in the beautiful heavenly land.
Ib. Room Among the Angels

8 Shall we gather at the river? . . .
Yes, we'll gather at the river,
The beautiful, the beautiful river,
Gather with the saints at the river,
That flows by the throne of God.
Ib. No. 1000. Shall We Gather

9 In the sweet by-and-by,
We shall meet on that beautiful shore.
Ib. Sweet By-and-By

10 That will be glory for me.
Ib. That Will Be Heaven For Me

EPES SARGENT
1813–1880

11 A life on the ocean wave,
A home on the rolling deep.
A Life on the Ocean Wave

SIEGFRIED SASSOON
1886–

12 If I were fierce and bald and short of breath,
I'd live with scarlet Majors at the Base,
And speed glum heroes up the line to death.
Base Details

13 And when the war is done and youth stone dead
I'd toddle safely home and die—in bed. *Ib.*

14 Everyone suddenly burst out singing.
Everyone Sang

15 The song was wordless;
The singing will never be done. *Ib.*

RICHARD SAVAGE
d. 1743

16 No tenth transmitter of a foolish face.
The Bastard, l. 8

17 Perhaps been poorly rich, and meanly great,
The slave of pomp, a cipher in the state. *Ib.* l. 39

18 May see thee now, though late, redeem thy name,
And glorify what else is damn'd to fame.
Character of the Rev. James Foster, l. 45

GEORGE SAVILE, MARQUIS OF HALIFAX
see
HALIFAX

HENRY J. SAYERS
d. 1932

19 Ta-ra-ra-boom-de-ay! *Title of Song* (1891)

FRIEDRICH VON SCHELLING
1775–1854

20 Architecture in general is frozen music.
Philosophie der Kunst

FRIEDRICH VON SCHILLER
1759–1805

21 Freude, schöner Götterfunken,
Tochter aus Elysium,
Wir betreten Feuertrunken,
Himmlische, dein Heiligtum.
Deine Zauber binden wieder,
Was die Mode streng geteilt,
Alle Menschen werden Brüder
Wo dein sanfter Flügel weilt.

Thou radiance sprung from God Himself,
Thou daughter of Elysium, Joy,
Thy shrine we tread, Thou Maid Divine,
Though light's excess our sense destroy,
What harsh world-use has rent apart,
Thy healing spells restore again;
Where'er Thy gentle wings may rest,
Brothers we find our fellow-men. *An die Freude*

22 Die Sonne geht in meinem Staat nicht unter.

The sun does not set in my dominions.
[Philip II.] *Don Carlos*, Act 1, sc. 6

23 Mit der Dummheit kämpfen Götter selbst vergebens.

With stupidity the gods themselves struggle in vain.
Jungfrau von Orleans, III. vi

24 Die Weltgeschichte ist das Weltgericht.

The world's history is the world's judgement.
1st lecture as Prof. of History, Jena. 26 May 1789

25 Ein ruheloser Marsch war unser Leben
Und wie des Windes Sausen, heimatlos,
Durchstürmten wir die kriegbewegte Erde.

Our life was but a battle and a march
And like the wind's blast, never-resting, homeless,
We stormed across the war-convulsèd heath.
Wallenstein's Tod, iii. 15 (Coleridge's translation)

1 Gedanken sind zollfrei.

Thoughts are free from toll.

(*Compare* William Camden, *Remains*, p. 332.)
*Quoted from Luther, Von weltlicher Oberkeit,
wie man ihr Gehorsam schuldig sei*

MAX SCHNECKENBURGER

1819–1849

2 Die Wacht am Rhein.

The watch on the Rhine. *Title of Song*

LOUIS SCHNEIDER

3 O Tannenbaum, O Tannenbaum,
Wie grün sind deine Blätter!

O pine-tree, O pine-tree,
How green are thy leaves!
Der Kurmärker und die Picarde

CHARLES PRESTWICH SCOTT

1846–1932

4 The newspaper is of necessity something of a monopoly, and its first duty is to shun the temptations
of monopoly. Its primary office is the gathering of
news. At the peril of its soul it must see that the
supply is not tainted. Neither in what it gives, nor
in what it does not give, nor in the mode of
presentation, must the unclouded face of truth
suffer wrong. Comment is free but facts are sacred.
In the Manchester Guardian, 6 May 1926

ROBERT FALCON SCOTT

1868–1912

5 Great God! this is an awful place. [The South Pole.]
Journal, 17 Jan. 1912

6 For God's sake look after our people.
Ib. 25 March 1912

7 Had we lived, I should have had a tale to tell of the
hardihood, endurance, and courage of my companions which would have stirred the heart of every
Englishman. These rough notes and our dead
bodies must tell the tale. *Message to the Public*

SIR WALTER SCOTT

1771–1832

8 To the Lords of Convention 'twas Claver'se who
spoke,
'Ere the King's crown shall fall there are crowns to
be broke;
So let each cavalier who loves honour and me,
Come follow the bonnet of Bonny Dundee.
Come fill up my cup, come fill up my can,
Come saddle your horses, and call up your men;
Come open the West Port, and let me gang free,
And it's room for the bonnets of Bonny Dundee!'
Bonny Dundee. (The Doom of Devorgoil, Act II,
sc. ii)

9 But answer came there none.
Bridal of Triermain, c. III. x

10 Here lies that peerless paper peer Lord Peter,
Who broke the laws of God and man and metre.
Epitaph for Patrick ('Peter'), Lord Robertson

11 The stag at eve had drunk his fill,
Where danced the moon on Monan's rill,
And deep his midnight lair had made
In lone Glenartney's hazel shade.
The Lady of the Lake, c. I. i

12 A moment gazed adown the dale,
A moment snuff'd the tainted gale. *Ib.* ii

13 Two dogs of black Saint Hubert's breed,
Unmatch'd for courage, breath, and speed. *Ib.* vii

14 Woe worth the chase, woe worth the day,
That costs thy life, my gallant grey! *Ib.* ix

15 In listening mood, she seem'd to stand,
The guardian Naiad of the strand. *Ib.* xvii

16 And ne'er did Grecian chisel trace
A Nymph, a Naiad, or a Grace
Of finer form, or lovelier face!
What though the sun, with ardent frown,
Had slightly tinged her cheek with brown. *Ib.* xviii

17 The will to do, the soul to dare. *Ib.* xxi

18 His ready speech flow'd fair and free,
In phrase of gentlest courtesy;
Yet seem'd that tone, and gesture bland,
Less used to sue than to command. *Ib.*

19 Soldier, rest! thy warfare o'er,
Sleep the sleep that knows not breaking,
Dream of battled fields no more,
Days of danger, nights of waking. *Ib.* xxxi

20 Huntsman, rest! thy chase is done. *Ib.* xxxii

21 Hail to the Chief who in triumph advances!
Ib. c. II. xix

22 He is gone on the mountain,
He is lost to the forest,
Like a summer-dried fountain,
When our need was the sorest. *Ib.* c. III. xvi

23 Like the dew on the mountain,
Like the foam on the river,
Like the bubble on the fountain,
Thou art gone, and for ever! *Ib.*

24 Which spills the foremost foeman's life,
That party conquers in the strife! *Ib.* c. IV. vi

25 'These are Clan Alpine's warriors true;
And, Saxon,—I am Roderick Dhu!' *Ib.* c. V. ix

26 'Come one, come all! this rock shall fly
From its firm base as soon as I.' *Ib.* x

27 Respect was mingled with surprise,
And the stern joy which warriors feel
In foemen worthy of their steel. *Ib.*

28 Where, where was Roderick then?
One blast upon his bugle-horn
Were worth a thousand men! *Ib.* c. VI. xviii

29 The way was long, the wind was cold,
The Minstrel was infirm and old;
His wither'd cheek and tresses grey,
Seem'd to have known a better day.
The harp, his sole remaining joy,
Was carried by an orphan boy.
The last of all the Bards was he,
Who sung of Border chivalry;
For, welladay! their date was fled,
His tuneful brethren all were dead;
And he, neglected and oppress'd,
Wish'd to be with them, and at rest.
The Lay of the Last Minstrel, introd. l. 1

1 The unpremeditated lay.
The Lay of the Last Minstrel, introd. l. 18

2 Old times were changed, old manners gone;
A stranger fill'd the Stuarts' throne;
The bigots of the iron time
Had call'd his harmless art a crime. *Ib.* l. 19

3 Nine-and-twenty knights of fame
Hung their shields in Branksome Hall;
Nine-and-twenty squires of name
Brought them their steeds to bower from stall;
Nine-and-twenty yeomen tall
Waited, duteous, on them all:
They were all knights of mettle true,
Kinsmen to the bold Buccleuch. *Ib.* c. I. iii

4 They carv'd at the meal
With gloves of steel,
And they drank the red wine through the helmet
barr'd. *Ib.* iv

5 Such is the custom of Branksome Hall. *Ib.* vii

6 Vengeance, deep-brooding o'er the slain,
Had lock'd the source of softer woe;
And burning pride and high disdain
Forbade the rising tear to flow. *Ib.* ix

7 To her bidding she could bow
The viewless forms of air. *Ib.* xii

8 What shall be the maiden's fate?
Who shall be the maiden's mate? *Ib.* xvi

9 Steady of heart, and stout of hand. *Ib.* xxi

10 Sir William of Deloraine, good at need. *Ib.* xxii

11 Yet, through good heart, and Oure Ladye's grace,
At length he gain'd the landing-place. *Ib.* xxix

12 If thou would'st view fair Melrose aright,
Go visit it by the pale moonlight;
For the gay beams of lightsome day
Gild, but to flout, the ruins grey. *Ib.* c. II. i

13 Strange sounds along the chancel pass'd,
The banner wav'd without a blast. *Ib.* xvi

14 Yet somewhat was he chill'd with dread,
And his hair did bristle upon his head. *Ib.*

15 I cannot tell how the truth may be;
I say the tale as 'twas said to me. *Ib.* xxii

16 In peace, Love tunes the shepherd's reed;
In war, he mounts the warrior's steed;
In halls, in gay attire is seen;
In hamlets, dances on the green.
Love rules the court, the camp, the grove,
And men below, and saints above;
For love is heaven, and heaven is love. *Ib.* c. III. ii

17 And laugh'd, and shouted, 'Lost! lost! lost!' *Ib.* xiii

18 Why, when the volleying musket play'd
Against the bloody Highland blade,
Why was not I beside him laid!
Enough, he died the death of fame;
Enough, he died with conquering Graeme. *Ib.* c. IV. ii

19 For ne'er
Was flattery lost on poet's ear:
A simple race! they waste their toil
For the vain tribute of a smile. *Ib.* conclusion

20 Call it not vain; they do not err,
Who say, that when the Poet dies,
Mute Nature mourns her worshipper,
And celebrates his obsequies.
The Lay of the Last Minstrel, c. V. i

21 The secret sympathy,
The silver link, the silken tie,
Which heart to heart, and mind to mind,
In body and in soul can bind. *Ib.* xiii

22 Breathes there the man, with soul so dead,
Who never to himself hath said,
This is my own, my native land!
Whose heart hath ne'er within him burn'd,
As home his footsteps he hath turn'd
From wandering on a foreign strand!
If such there breathe, go, mark him well;
For him no Minstrel raptures swell;
High though his titles, proud his name,
Boundless his wealth as wish can claim;
Despite those titles, power, and pelf,
The wretch, concentred all in self,
Living, shall forfeit fair renown,
And, doubly dying, shall go down
To the vile dust, from whence he sprung,
Unwept, unhonour'd, and unsung.

O Caledonia! stern and wild,
Meet nurse for a poetic child!
Land of brown heath and shaggy wood,
Land of the mountain and the flood,
Land of my sires! what mortal hand
Can e'er untie the filial band
That knits me to thy rugged strand! *Ib.* c. VI. i–ii

23 For Love will still be lord of all. *Ib.* xi

24 The elvish page fell to the ground,
And, shuddering, mutter'd, 'Found! found! found!'
Ib. xxiv

25 That day of wrath, that dreadful day,
When heaven and earth shall pass away. *Ib.* xxxi

26 The dew that on the violet lies
Mocks the dark lustre of thine eyes.
The Lord of the Isles, c. I. iii

27 To show the form it seem'd to hide. *Ib.* v

28 Thus, then, my noble foe I greet;
Health and high fortune till we meet,
And then—what pleases Heaven. *Ib.* c. III. vi

29 Scenes sung by him who sings no more!
His bright and brief career is o'er,
And mute his tuneful strains. *Ib.* c. IV. xi

30 O! many a shaft, at random sent,
Finds mark the archer little meant!
And many a word, at random spoken,
May soothe or wound a heart that's broken.
Ib. c. V. xviii

31 To that dark inn, the grave! *Ib.* c. VI. xxvi

32 O hush thee, my babie, thy sire was a knight,
Thy mother a lady, both lovely and bright.
Lullaby of an Infant Chief

33 Then hush thee, my darling, take rest while you may,
For strife comes with manhood, and waking with day.
Ib.

34 O lovers' eyes are sharp to see,
And lovers' ears in hearing. *The Maid of Neidpath*

35 Till through her wasted hand, at night,
You saw the taper burning. *Ib.*

1 November's sky is chill and drear,
November's leaf is red and sear.
Marmion, c. I, introd. i

2 To him, as to the burning levin,
Short, bright, resistless course was given. *Ib.* vi

3 Had'st thou but liv'd, though stripp'd of power,
A watchman on the lonely tower. [On Pitt.] *Ib.* viii

4 Now is the stately column broke,
The beacon-light is quench'd in smoke,
The trumpet's silver sound is still,
The warder silent on the hill! [On Pitt.] *Ib.*

5 Drop upon Fox's grave the tear,
'Twill trickle to his rival's bier;
O'er Pitt's the mournful requiem sound,
And Fox's shall the notes rebound. *Ib.* xi

6 But search the land of living men,
Where wilt thou find their like agen? *Ib.*

7 Profan'd the God-given strength, and marr'd the
lofty line. *Ib.* xvi

8 His square-turn'd joints, and strength of limb,
Show'd him no carpe knight so trim,
But in close fight a champion grim,
In camps a leader sage. *Ib.* c. I. v

9 Stout heart, and open hand! *Ib.* x

10 And come he slow, or come he fast,
It is but Death who comes at last. *Ib.* c. II. xxx

11 When Prussia hurried to the field,
And snatch'd the spear, but left the shield!
Ib. c. III, introd. l. 63

12 Where shall the lover rest,
Whom the fates sever
From his true maiden's breast,
Parted for ever?
Where, through groves deep and high,
Sounds the far billow,
Where early violets die,
Under the willow. *Ib.* c. III. x

13 In the lost battle,
Borne down by the flying,
Where mingles war's rattle
With groans of the dying. *Ib.* xi

14 Still is thy name in high account,
And still thy verse has charms,
Sir David Lindesay of the Mount,
Lord Lion King-at-arms! *Ib.* c. IV. vii

15 O, young Lochinvar is come out of the west,
Through all the wide Border his steed was the best.
Ib. c. V. xii

16 So faithful in love, and so dauntless in war,
There never was knight like the young Lochinvar.
Ib.

17 For a laggard in love, and a dastard in war.
Was to wed the fair Ellen of brave Lochinvar. *Ib.*

18 'O come ye in peace here, or come ye in war,
Or to dance at our bridal, young Lord Lochinvar?'
Ib.

19 'To lead but one measure, drink one cup of wine.'
Ib.

20 With a smile on her lips, and a tear in her eye. *Ib.*

21 'Now tread we a measure!' said young Lochinvar.
Ib.

22 'She is won! we are gone, over bank, bush, and
scaur;
They'll have fleet steeds that follow' quoth young
Lochinvar. *Marmion*, c. V. xii

23 Heap on more wood!—the wind is chill;
But let it whistle as it will,
We'll keep our Christmas merry still.
Ib. c. VI, introd. i

24 England was merry England, when
Old Christmas brought his sports again.
'Twas Christmas broach'd the mightiest ale;
'Twas Christmas told the merriest tale;
A Christmas gambol oft could cheer
The poor man's heart through half the year. *Ib.* iii

25 What skilful limner e'er would choose
To paint the rainbow's varying hues,
Unless to mortal it were given
To dip his brush in dyes of heaven? *Ib.* v

26 My castles are my King's alone,
From turret to foundation-stone—
The hand of Douglas is his own. *Ib.* xiii

27 'And dar'st thou then
To beard the lion in his den,
The Douglas in his hall?
And hop'st thou thence unscathed to go?
No, by Saint Bride of Bothwell, no!
Up drawbridge, grooms—what, warder, ho!
Let the portcullis fall.' *Ib.* xiv

28 O what a tangled web we weave,
When first we practise to deceive! *Ib.* xvii

29 Scarce could they hear, or see their foes,
Until at weapon-point they close.
They close, in clouds of smoke and dust,
With sword-sway, and with lance's thrust;
And such a yell was there,
Of sudden and portentous birth,
As if men fought upon the earth,
And fiends in upper air. *Ib.* xxv

30 Good-night to Marmion. *Ib.* xxviii

31 O Woman! in our hours of ease,
Uncertain, coy, and hard to please,
And variable as the shade
By the light quivering aspen made;
When pain and anguish wring the brow,
A ministering angel thou! *Ib.* xxx

32 'Charge, Chester, charge! On, Stanley, on!'
Were the last words of Marmion. *Ib.* xxxii

33 Where's now their victor vaward wing,
Where Huntley, and where Home?—
O, for a blast of that dread horn,
On Fontarabian echoes borne! *Ib.* xxxiii

34 The stubborn spear-men still made good
Their dark impenetrable wood,
Each stepping where his comrade stood,
The instant that he fell. *Ib.* xxxiv

35 Still from the sire the son shall hear
Of the stern strife, and carnage drear,
Of Flodden's fatal field,
Where shiver'd was fair Scotland's spear,
And broken was her shield! *Ib.*

36 To all, to each, a fair good-night,
And pleasing dreams, and slumbers light!
Ib. L'envoy

1 But Nora's heart is lost and won,
—She's wedded to the Earlie's son!   *Nora's Vow*

2 Pibroch of Donuil Dhu,
   Pibroch of Donuil,
Wake thy wild voice anew,
   Summon Clan-Conuil.
Come away, come away,
   Hark to the summons!
Come in your war array,
   Gentles and commons.   *Pibroch of Donuil Dhu*

3 Leave untended the herd,
   The flock without shelter;
Leave the corpse uninterr'd,
   The bride at the altar.   *Ib.*

4 Come as the winds come, when
   Forests are rended,
Come as the waves come, when
   Navies are stranded.   *Ib.*

5 Still are the thoughts to memory dear.
          Rokeby, c. I. xxxiii

6 A mother's pride, a father's joy!   *Ib. c. III. xv*

7 O, Brignal banks are wild and fair,
   And Greta woods are green,
And you may gather garlands there
   Would grace a summer queen.   *Ib. xvi*

8 A weary lot is thine, fair maid,
   A weary lot is thine!
To pull the thorn thy brow to braid,
   And press the rue for wine!   *Ib. xxviii*

9 He turn'd his charger as he spake,
   Upon the river shore,
He gave his bridle-reins a shake,
   Said 'Adieu for evermore,
          My love!
   And adieu for evermore.'   *Ib.*

10 Tramp! tramp! along the land they rode,
Splash! splash! along the sea.   *William and Helen*

11 You . . . whirl'd them to the back o' beyont.
          The Antiquary, ch. 2

12 Praetorian here, Praetorian there, I mind the bigging
   o't.   *Ib. ch. 4*

13 It's no fish ye're buying—it's men's lives. *Ib. ch. 11*

14 Widow'd wife, and married maid,
Betrothed, betrayer, and betray'd!
          The Betrothed, ch. 15

15 Woman's faith, and woman's trust—
Write the characters in dust.   *Ib. ch. 20*

16 Look not thou on beauty's charming,—
Sit thou still when kings are arming,—
Taste not when the wine-cup glistens,—
Speak not when the people listens,—
Stop thine ear against the singer,—
From the red gold keep thy finger;—
Vacant heart and hand, and eye,—
Easy live and quiet die.
          The Bride of Lammermoor, ch. 3

17 When the last Laird of Ravenswood to Ravenswood
   shall ride,
And woo a dead maiden to be his bride,
He shall stable his steed in the Kelpie's flow,
And his name shall be lost for evermoe!   *Ib. ch. 18*

18 I live by twa trades, sir, . . . fiddle, sir, and spade;
   filling the world, and emptying of it.   *Ib. ch. 24*

19 Her winding-sheet is up as high as her throat
   already.   *The Bride of Lammermoor, ch. 34*

20 An ower true tale.   *Ib.*

21 Touch not the cat but[1] a glove.
          The Fair Maid of Perth, ch. 34
          [1] without.

22 But no one shall find me rowing against the stream.
   I care not who knows it—I write for the general
   amusement.
          The Fortunes of Nigel, introductory epistle

23 It's ill taking the breeks aff a wild Highlandman.
          Ib. ch. 5

24 For a con-si-de-ra-tion.   *Ib. ch. 22*

25 To be plain, if your lordship does not ken when you
   have a good servant, I ken when I have a kind
   master.   *Ib. ch. 31*

26 O Geordie, Jingling Geordie, it was grand to hear
   Baby Charles laying down the guilt of dissimulation, and Steenie lecturing on the turpitude of
   incontinence.   *Ib.*

27 (He) was ever after designated as a 'stickit minister'.
          Guy Mannering, ch. 2

28 Twist ye, twine[2] ye! even so
   Mingle shades of joy and woe,
   Hope and fear, and peace and strife,
   In the thread of human life.   *Ib. ch. 4*
          [2] divide.

29 'Ride your ways,' said the gipsy, 'ride your ways,
   Laird of Ellangowan—ride your ways, Godfrey
   Bertram!—This day have ye quenched seven
   smoking hearths—see if the fire in your ain parlour
   burn the blither for that. Ye have riven the thack off
   seven cottar houses—look if your ain roof-tree
   stand the faster.—Ye may stable your stirks in the
   shealings at Derncleugh—see that the hare does
   not couch on the hearthstane at Ellangowan.'
          Ib. ch. 8

30 MRS. BERTRAM:
That sounds like nonsense, my dear.
MR. BERTRAM:
May be so, my dear; but it may be very good law
   for all that.   *Ib. ch. 9*

31 Sophia, as you well know, followed me to India. She
   was as innocent as gay; but, unfortunately for us
   both, as gay as innocent.   *Ib. ch. 12*

32 'Pro-di-gi-ous!' exclaimed Dominie Sampson.
          Ib. ch. 14

33 Gin by pailfuls, wine in rivers,
   Dash the window-glass to shivers!
   For three wild lads were we, brave boys,
   And three wild lads were we;
   Thou on the land, and I on the sand,
   And Jack on the gallows-tree!   *Ib. ch. 34*

34 The ancient and now forgotten pastime of high jinks.
          Ib. ch. 36

35 And Bertram's right and Bertram's might
Shall meet on Ellangowan's height.   *Ib. ch. 46*

36 The hour is come, but not the man.
          The Heart of Midlothian, ch. 4, heading

37 The passive resistance of the Tolbooth-gate.
          Ib. ch. 6

1 Jock, when ye hae naething else to do, ye may be ay
sticking in a tree; it will be growing, Jock, when
ye're sleeping. *Guy Mannering*, ch. 8

2 Proud Maisie is in the wood,
Walking so early,
Sweet Robin sits in the bush,
Singing so rarely. *Ib.* ch. 40

3 Come, trowl the brown bowl to me,
Bully boy, bully boy,
Come, trowl the brown bowl to me:
Ho! jolly Jenkin, I spy a knave in drinking,
Come, trowl the brown bowl to me. *Ivanhoe*, ch. 20

4 'Pax vobiscum' will answer all queries. *Ib.* ch. 26

5 When Israel, of the Lord belov'd,
Out of the land of bondage came,
Her fathers' God before her mov'd,
An awful guide in smoke and flame. *Ib.* ch. 39

6 His morning walk was beneath the elms in the
churchyard; 'for death,' he said, 'had been his
next-door neighbour for so many years, that he
had no apology for dropping the acquaintance.'
The Legend of Montrose, introduction

7 But, my lord, there is a Southern proverb,—fine
words butter no parsnips. *Ib.* ch. 3

8 March, march, Ettrick and Teviotdale,
Why the deil dinna ye march forward in order?
March, march, Eskdale and Liddesdale,
All the Blue Bonnets are bound for the Border.
The Monastery, ch. 25

9 Ah! County Guy, the hour is nigh,
The sun has left the lea,
The orange flower perfumes the bower,
The breeze is on the sea. *Quentin Durward*, ch. 4

10 And it's ill speaking between a fou man and a
fasting.
Redgauntlet, Letter 11, *Wandering Willie's Tale*

11 Better a finger off, as ay wagging. *Ib.* ch. 2

12 The ae half of the warld thinks the tither daft.
Ib. ch. 7

13 Over the water, and over the sea,
And over the water to Charlie;
Come weal, come woe, we'll gather and go,
And live or die with Charlie. *Ib.* ch. 11

14 But with the morning cool repentance came.
Rob Roy, ch. 12

15 Come fill up my cup, come fill up my cann,
Come saddle my horses, and call up my man;
Come open your gates, and let me gae free,
I daurna stay langer in bonny Dundee. *Ib.* ch. 23

16 If your honour disna ken when ye hae a gude servant,
I ken when I hae a gude master, and the deil be in
my feet gin I leave ye. *Ib.* ch. 24

17 It's a far cry to Lochow. *Ib.* ch. 29, note

18 There's a gude time coming. *Ib.* ch. 32

19 Speak out, sir, and do not Maister or Campbell me—
my foot is on my native heath, and my name is
MacGregor! *Ib.* ch. 34

20 Fair, fat, and forty. *St. Ronan's Well*, ch. 7

21 'I doubt', said Bruce, 'that I have slain the Red
Comyn.'
'Do you leave such a matter in doubt?' said Kirk-
patrick. 'I will make sicker.'
Tales of a Grandfather, ch. 8

22 The play-bill, which is said to have announced the
tragedy of Hamlet, the character of the Prince of
Denmark being left out.
The Talisman, introduction. *For an earlier report
of this anecdote see* T.L.S. *3 June 1939*

23 Rouse the lion from his lair. *Ib.* ch. 6

24 My heart's in the Highlands, my heart is not here,
My heart's in the Highlands a-chasing the deer;
A-chasing the wild deer, and following the roe,
My heart's in the Highlands wherever I go.
Waverley, ch. 28. *But see* Corrigenda, *p. 587*

25 Bring the bowl which you boast,
Fill it up to the brim;
Here's to him we love most,
And to all who love him.
Brave gallants, stand up,
And avaunt ye, base carles!
Were there death in the cup,
Here's a health to King Charles!
Woodstock, ch. 20

26 But I must say to the Muse of fiction, as the Earl of
Pembroke said to the ejected nun of Wilton, 'Go
spin, you jade, go spin!' *Journal, 9 Feb. 1826*

27 I . . . have arrived at a *flocci-pauci-nihili-pili-fication*
of money, and I thank Shenstone for inventing that
long word. *Ib. 8 March 1826*

28 The Big Bow-Wow strain I can do myself like any
now going; but the exquisite touch, which renders
ordinary commonplace things and characters
interesting, from the truth of the description and
the sentiment, is denied to me. [On Jane Austen.]
Ib. 14 Mar. 1826

29 I would like to be there, were it but to see how the
cat jumps. *Ib. 7 Oct. 1826*

30 The blockheads talk of my being like Shakespeare—
not fit to tie his brogues. *Ib. 11 Dec. 1826*

31 From the lone shieling of the misty island
Mountains divide us, and the waste of seas—
Yet still the blood is strong, the heart is Highland,
And we in dreams behold the Hebrides!
Fair these broad meads, these hoary woods are grand;
But we are exiles from our fathers' land.
Canadian Boat Song. Of disputed authorship.
See *Times Literary Supplement*, 23 Dec. 1904,
G. M. Fraser's *article.*

WILLIAM SCOTT, LORD STOWELL

1745–1836

32 The elegant simplicity of the three per cents.
Campbell's *Chancellors* (1857), vol. x, ch. 212,
p. 218

33 A precedent embalms a principle.
*An Opinion, while Advocate-General, 1788.
Attrib.*

SCOTTISH METRICAL PSALMS

1650

1 The Lord's my shepherd, I'll not want.
   He makes me down to lie
In pastures green: he leadeth me
   the quiet waters by.
My soul he doth restore again;
   and me to walk doth make
Within the paths of righteousness,
   ev'n for his own name's sake.

Yea, though I walk in death's dark vale,
   yet will I fear none ill:
For thou art with me; and thy rod
   and staff me comfort still.
My table thou hast furnished
   in presence of my foes;
My head thou dost with oil anoint,
   and my cup overflows.   *Psalm* xxiii. 1

2 Ye gates, lift up your heads on high;
   ye doors that last for aye,
Be lifted up, that so the King
   of glory enter may.
But who of glory is the King?
   The mighty Lord is this;
Ev'n that same Lord, that great in might
   and strong in battle is.

Ye gates, lift up your heads; ye doors,
   doors that do last for aye,
Be lifted up, that so the King
   of glory enter may.
But who is he that is the King
   of glory? who is this?
The Lord of hosts, and none but he,
   The King of glory is.   *Ib.* xxiv. 7

3 How lovely is thy dwelling-place,
   O Lord of hosts, to me!
The tabernacles of thy grace
   how pleasant, Lord, they be!
My thirsty soul longs veh'mently,
   yea faints, thy courts to see:
My very heart and flesh cry out,
   O living God, for thee.   *Ib.* lxxxiv. 1

4 I to the hills will lift mine eyes,
   from whence doth come mine aid.
My safety cometh from the Lord,
   who heav'n and earth hath made. *Ib.* cxxi. 1

5 Pray that Jerusalem may have
   peace and felicity:
Let them that love thee and thy peace
   have still prosperity.   *Ib.* cxxii. 1

6 The race that long in darkness pin'd
   have seen a glorious light.
        Paraphrase 19. *Isaiah* ix. 2–8

SIR OWEN SEAMAN

1861–1936

7 New Art would better Nature's best,
   But Nature knows a thing or two.
        Battle of the Bays. Ars Postera, v

8 She must know all the needs of a rational being,
   Be skilled to keep counsel, to comfort, to coax;
And, above all things else, be accomplished at seeing
        My jokes.   *A Plea for Trigamy*

EDMUND HAMILTON SEARS

1810–1876

9 Calm on the listening ear of night
   Came Heaven's melodious strains,
Where wild Judea stretches far
   Her silver-mantled plains.
        Boston Observer, 1834. *Christmas Hymn: Calm on the Listening Ear*

10 It came upon the midnight clear,
   That glorious song of old,
From Angels bending near the earth
   To touch their harps of gold;
'Peace on the earth, good will to man
   From Heaven's all gracious King.'
The world in solemn stillness lay
   To hear the angels sing.
        The Christian Register (1850). *That Glorious Song of Old*

SIR CHARLES SEDLEY

1639?–1701

11 Ah, Chloris! that I now could sit
   As unconcerned as when
Your infant beauty could beget
   No pleasure, nor no pain!   *Child and Maiden*

12 Love still has something of the sea
   From whence his mother rose.
        Love still has Something

13 Phyllis is my only joy,
   Faithless as the winds or seas;
Sometimes coming, sometimes coy,
   Yet she never fails to please.
        Song. Phyllis is my Only Joy

14   She deceiving,
         I believing;
What need lovers wish for more?   *Ib.*

15 Phyllis, without frown or smile,
   Sat and knotted all the while.
        Song [*Phyllis Knotting*]. *Hears not my Phyllis*

16 Not, Celia, that I juster am
   Or better than the rest,
For I would change each hour like them,
   Were not my heart at rest.
        Song [*To Celia*]. *Not, Celia, that I juster am*

17 Why then should I seek farther store,
   And still make love anew;
When change itself can give no more,
   'Tis easy to be true.   *Ib.*

ALAN SEEGER

1888–1916

18 I have a rendezvous with Death
   At some disputed barricade.
        I Have a Rendezvous with Death

SIR JOHN ROBERT SEELEY

1834–1895

19 We [the English] seem, as it were, to have conquered
   and peopled half the world in a fit of absence of
   mind.   *The Expansion of England,* Lecture I

20 History is past politics, and politics present history.
        Growth of British Policy

JOHN SELDEN

1584–1654

scripturas. These two words have undone
   ...orld.
   Table Talk (1892), p. 10. *Bible, Scripture*

2 Old friends are best. King James used to call for his old shoes; they were easiest for his feet.
   Ib. p. 71, *Friends*

3 'Tis not the drinking that is to be blamed, but the excess. *Ib.* p. 78. *Humility*

4 Ignorance of the law excuses no man; not that all men know the law, but because 'tis an excuse every man will plead, and no man can tell how to confute him. *Ib.* p. 99. *Law*

5 Take a straw and throw it up into the air, you shall see by that which way the wind is. *Ib.* p. 105. *Libels*

6 Marriage is nothing but a civil contract.
   Ib. p. 109. *Marriage*

7 There never was a merry world since the fairies left off dancing, and the Parson left conjuring.
   Ib. p. 130. *Parson*

8 There is not anything in the world so much abused as this sentence, *Salus populi suprema lex esto.*
   Ib. p. 131. *People*

9 Philosophy is nothing but discretion.
   Ib. p. 132. *Philosophy*

10 Pleasure is nothing else but the intermission of pain.
   Ib. Pleasure

11 Preachers say, Do as I say, not as I do.
   Ib. p. 147. *Preaching*

WALTER CARRUTHERS SELLAR

1898–
and
ROBERT JULIAN YEATMAN

contemporary

12 1066 and all that. *Title of Book*

13 The Roman Conquest was, however, a *Good Thing.*
   1066, And All That, ch. 1

14 James I slobbered at the mouth and had favourites; he was thus a Bad King. *Ib.* ch. 34

15 The National Debt is a very Good Thing and it would be dangerous to pay it off for fear of Political Economy. *Ib.* ch. 38

16 Napoleon's armies always used to march on their stomachs, shouting: 'Vive l'Intérieur!' *Ib.* ch. 48

17 A Bad Thing: America was thus clearly top nation, and History came to a . *Ib.* ch. 62

SENECA

d. A.D. 65

18 Contra bonum morem.
   Against good custom. *Dialogues*, VI. i. 2

19 Illi mors gravis incubat
   Qui notus nimis omnibus
   Ignotus moritur sibi.
      On him does death lie heavily who, but too well known to all, dies to himself unknown.
   Thyestes, ii, *chorus.* Trans. by Miller

ROBERT WILLIAM SERVICE

1874–

20 This is the Law of the Yukon, that only the Strong shall thrive;
   That surely the Weak shall perish, and only the Fit survive.
   Dissolute, damned, and despairful, crippled and palsied and slain,
   This is the Will of the Yukon,—Lo! how she makes it plain!
      Songs of a Sourdough. The Law of the Yukon

21 The lady that's known as Lou.
   Ib. The Shooting of Dan McGrew

22 The summer—no sweeter was ever;
   The sunshiny woods all athrill;
   The greyling aleap in the river,
   The bighorn asleep on the hill.
   The strong life that never knows harness;
   The wilds where the caribou call;
   The freshness, the freedom, the farness—
   O God! how I'm stuck on it all.
      Ib. The Spell of the Yukon

WILLIAM HENRY SEWARD

1801–1872

23 The Constitution devotes the domain to union, to justice, to defence, to welfare, and to liberty. But there is a higher law than the Constitution.
   Speech in U.S. Senate, 11 March 1850

24 I know, and all the world knows, that revolutions never go backward.
   Ib. At Rochester on the Irrepressible Conflict, Oct. 1858

EDWARD SEXBY

d. 1658

25 Killing no Murder Briefly Discourst in Three Questions. *Title of Pamphlet, 1657*

RICHARD SHACKLOCK

c. 1575

26 Proud as peacocks. *Hatchet of Heresies* (1565), p. 26*b*

THOMAS SHADWELL

1642?–1692

27 Words may be false and full of art,
   Sighs are the natural language of the heart.
      Psyche, Act III

28 'Tis the way of all flesh. *The Sullen Lovers*, V. ii

29 And wit's the noblest frailty of the mind.
   A True Widow, II. i

30 The haste of a fool is the slowest thing in the world.
   Ib. III. i

31 I am, out of the ladies' company, like a fish out of the water. *Ib.*

32 Every man loves what he is good at. *Ib.* V. i

33 Instantly, in the twinkling of a bed-staff.
   Virtuoso, I. i

ANTHONY ASHLEY COOPER, EARL OF SHAFTESBURY

1621–1683

1 'People differ in their discourse and profession about these matters, but men of sense are really but of one religion.' . . . 'Pray, my lord, what religion is that which men of sense agree in?' 'Madam,' says the earl immediately, 'men of sense never tell it.'
Burnet, *History of My Own Time*, vol. 1, bk. ii, ch. 1, note by Onslow

WILLIAM SHAKESPEARE

1564–1616

In the references the line number is given without brackets where the scene is all verse up to the quotation and the line number is certain. It is given in square brackets where prose makes it variable, and the references are to the Oxford Standard Authors Shakespeare in one volume.

2   It were all one
That I should love a bright particular star
And think to wed it, he is so above me.
All's Well That Ends Well, I. i. [97]

3 My friends were poor but honest. *Ib.* iii. [203]

4 They say miracles are past. *Ib.* II. iii. [1]

5 A young man married is a man that's marred.
Ib. [315]

6 I know a man that had this trick of melancholy sold a goodly manor for a song. *Ib.* III. ii. [8]

7 The web of our life is of a mingled yarn, good and ill together: our virtues would be proud if our faults whipped them not; and our crimes would despair if they were not cherished by our own virtues.
Ib. IV. iii. [83]

8 There's place and means for every man alive.
Ib. [379]

9 The flowery way that leads to the broad gate and the great fire. *Ib.* v. [58]

10   Praising what is lost
Makes the remembrance dear. *Ib.* v. iii. 19

11 The triple pillar of the world transform'd
Into a strumpet's fool. *Antony and Cleopatra*, I. i. 12

12 CLEOPATRA:
If it be love indeed, tell me how much.
ANTONY:
There's beggary in the love that can be reckoned.
CLEOPATRA:
I'll set a bourn how far to be belov'd.
ANTONY:
Then must thou needs find out new heaven, new earth. *Ib.* 14

13 The scarce-bearded Cæsar. *Ib.* 21

14 Let Rome in Tiber melt, and the wide arch
Of the rang'd empire fall! Here is my space.
Kingdoms are clay; our dungy earth alike
Feeds beast as man; the nobleness of life
Is to do thus; when such a mutual pair
And such a twain can do't. *Ib.* 33

15 Whom everything becomes, to chide, to laugh,
To weep; whose every passion fully strives
To make itself, in thee, fair and admir'd. *Ib.* 49

16 In Nature's infinite book of secrecy
A little I can read. *Ib.* ii. [11]

17 You shall be yet far fairer than you are. *Ib.* [18]

18 You shall be more beloving than belov'd.
Antony and Cleopatra, I. ii. [24]

19 O excellent! I love long life better than figs. *Ib.* [34]

20 Mine, and most of our fortunes, to-night, shall be,—drunk to bed. *Ib.* [47]

21 But a worky-day fortune. *Ib.* [57]

22   On the sudden
A Roman thought hath struck him. *Ib.* [90]

23 The nature of bad news infects the teller. *Ib.* [103]

24 These strong Egyptian fetters I must break,
Or lose myself in dotage. *Ib.* [125]

25 I have seen her die twenty times upon far poorer moment. I do think there is mettle in death which commits some loving act upon her, she hath such a celerity in dying. *Ib.* [150]

26 We cannot call her winds and waters sighs and tears; they are greater storms and tempests than almanacs can report. *Ib.* [157]

27 O sir! you had then left unseen a wonderful piece of work which not to have been blessed withal would have discredited your travel. *Ib.* [164]

28 Indeed the tears live in an onion that should water this sorrow. *Ib.* [181]

29   If you find him sad,
Say I am dancing; if in mirth, report
That I am sudden sick. *Ib.* iii. 3

30 CHARMIAN:
In each thing give him way, cross him in nothing.
CLEOPATRA:
Thou teachest like a fool; the way to lose him. *Ib.* 9

31 In time we hate that which we often fear. *Ib.* 12

32 It cannot thus be long, the sides of nature
Will not sustain it. *Ib.* 16

33 Eternity was in our lips and eyes,
Bliss in our brows bent. *Ib.* 35

34 Quietness, grown sick of rest, would purge
By any desperate change. *Ib.* 53

35 Though age from folly could not give me freedom,
It does from childishness. *Ib.* 57

36 At the last, best. *Ib.* 61

37 O! my oblivion is a very Antony,
And I am all forgotten. *Ib.* 90

38   'Tis sweating labour
To bear such idleness so near the heart
As Cleopatra this. *Ib.* 93

39   This common body,
Like to a vagabond flag upon the stream,
Goes to and back, lackeying the varying tide,
To rot itself with motion. *Ib.* iv. 44

40   On the Alps
It is reported thou didst eat strange flesh,
Which some did die to look on. *Ib.* 66

41 Give me to drink mandragora. . . .
That I might sleep out this great gap of time
My Antony is away. *Ib.* v. 4

42 The demi-Atlas of this earth, the arm
And burgonet of men. *Ib.* 23

43 Where's my serpent of old Nile? *Ib.* 25

1
 Think on me,
That am with Phœbus' amorous pinches black,
And wrinkled deep in time? Broad-fronted Cæsar,
When thou wast here above the ground I was
A morsel for a monarch, and great Pompey
Would stand and make his eyes grow in my brow;
There would he anchor his aspect and die
With looking on his life.
Antony and Cleopatra, I. v. 27

2
 My salad days,
When I was green in judgment. *Ib.* 73

3
 We, ignorant of ourselves,
Beg often our own harms, which the wise powers
Deny us for our good; so find we profit
By losing of our prayers. *Ib.* II. i. 5

4 I do not much dislike the matter, but
The manner of his speech. *Ib.* ii. 117

5 No worse a husband than the best of men. *Ib.* 135

6 The barge she sat in, like a burnish'd throne,
Burn'd on the water; the poop was beaten gold,
Purple the sails, and so perfumed, that
The winds were love-sick with them, the oars were
 silver,
Which to the tune of flutes kept stroke, and made
The water which they beat to follow faster,
As amorous of their strokes. For her own person,
It beggar'd all description; she did lie
In her pavilion,—cloth-of-gold of tissue,—
O'er-picturing that Venus where we see
The fancy outwork nature; on each side her
Stood pretty-dimpled boys, like smiling Cupids,
With divers-colour'd fans, whose wind did seem
To glow the delicate cheeks which they did cool,
And what they undid did. *Ib.* [199]

7 Her gentlewomen, like the Nereides,
So many mermaids, tended her i' the eyes,
And made their bends adornings; at the helm
A seeming mermaid steers; the silken tackle
Swell with the touches of those flower-soft hands,
That yarely frame the office. From the barge
A strange invisible perfume hits the sense
Of the adjacent wharfs. The city cast
Her people out upon her, and Antony,
Enthron'd i' the market-place, did sit alone,
Whistling to the air; which, but for vacancy,
Had gone to gaze on Cleopatra too
And made a gap in nature. *Ib.* [214]

8
 I saw her once
Hop forty paces through the public street;
And having lost her breath, she spoke, and panted
That she did make defect perfection,
And, breathless, power breathe forth. *Ib.* [236]

9 Age cannot wither her, nor custom stale
Her infinite variety; other women cloy
The appetites they feed, but she makes hungry
Where most she satisfies; for vilest things
Become themselves in her, that the holy priests
Bless her when she is riggish. *Ib.* [243]

10 Read not my blemishes in the world's report;
I have not kept the square, but that to come
Shall all be done by the rule. *Ib.* iii. 5

11
 Music, moody food
Of us that trade in love. *Ib.* v. 1

12 I laugh'd him out of patience; and that night
I laugh'd him into patience: and next morn,
Ere the ninth hour, I drunk him to his bed. *Ib.* 19

13
 There is gold, and here
My bluest veins to kiss; a hand that kings
Have lipp'd, and trembled kissing.
Antony and Cleopatra, II. v. 28

14 Pour out the pack of matter to mine ear,
The good and bad together. *Ib.* 54

15 Though it be honest, it is never good
To bring bad news; give to a gracious message
A host of tongues, but let ill tidings tell
Themselves when they be felt. *Ib.* 85

16 I will praise any man that will praise me. *Ib.* vi. [88]

17 LEPIDUS:
What manner o' thing is your crocodile?
ANTONY:
It is shaped, sir, like itself, and it is as broad as it
 hath breadth; it is just so high as it is, and moves
 with its own organs; it lives by that which nourish-
 eth it; and the elements once out of it, it trans-
 migrates.
LEPIDUS:
What colour is it of?
ANTONY:
Of its own colour too.
LEPIDUS:
'Tis a strange serpent.
ANTONY:
'Tis so; and the tears of it are wet. *Ib.* vii. [47]

18
 Ah! this thou shouldst have done,
And not have spoken on't. In me 'tis villany;
In thee't had been good service. *Ib.* [80]

19 Come, thou monarch of the vine,
Plumpy Bacchus with pink eyne!
In thy fats our cares be drown'd,
With thy grapes our hairs be crown'd:
 Cup us, till the world go round,
 Cup us, till the world go round! *Ib.* [119]

20
 Ambition,
The soldier's virtue. *Ib.* III. i. 22

21
 The swan's down-feather,
That stands upon the swell at full of tide,
And neither way inclines. *Ib.* ii. 48

22 The ostentation of our love, which, left unshown,
Is often left unlov'd. *Ib.* vi. 52

23 But let determin'd things to destiny
Hold unbewail'd their way. *Ib.* 84

24
 We have kiss'd away
Kingdoms and provinces. *Ib.* viii. 17

25
 Fortune knows
We scorn her most when most she offers blows.
Ib. ix. 73

26 Which had superfluous kings for messengers
Not many moons gone by. *Ib.* x. 5

27
 He wears the rose
Of youth upon him. *Ib.* xi. 20

28
 Men's judgments are
A parcel of their fortunes, and things outward
Do draw the inward quality after them,
To suffer all alike. *Ib.* 31

29 Against the blown rose may they stop their nose,
That kneel'd unto the buds. *Ib.* 39

30
 Yet he that can endure
To follow with allegiance a fall'n lord,
Does conquer him that did his master conquer,
And earns a place i' the story. *Ib.* 43

1   Your Cæsar's father oft,
When he hath mus'd of taking kingdoms in,
Bestow'd his lips on that unworthy place,
As it rain'd kisses.
                    Antony and Cleopatra, III. xi. 82

2 But when we in our viciousness grow hard,—
O misery on't!—the wise gods seel our eyes;
In our own filth drop our clear judgments; make us
Adore our errors; laugh at's while we strut
To our confusion.   *Ib.* 111

3 I found you as a morsel, cold upon
Dead Cæsar's trencher.   *Ib.* 116

4 My playfellow, your hand; this kingly seal
And plighter of high hearts.   *Ib.* 125

5   Henceforth,
The white hand of a lady fever thee,
Shake thou to look on 't.   *Ib.* 137

6 Let's have one other gaudy night.   *Ib.* 182

7   Since my lord
Is Antony again, I will be Cleopatra.   *Ib.* 185

8 Know that to-morrow the last of many battles
We mean to fight.   *Ib.* IV. i. 11

9 To business that we love we rise betime,
And go to 't with delight.   *Ib.* iv. 20

10   O! my fortunes have
Corrupted honest men.   *Ib.* v. 16

11 I am alone the villain of the earth,
And feel I am so most.   *Ib.* vi. 30

12   Leap thou, attire and all,
Through proof of harness to my heart, and there
Ride on the pants triumphing.   *Ib.* viii. 14

13 O infinite virtue! com'st thou smiling from
The world's great snare uncaught?   *Ib.* 17

14   My nightingale,
We have beat them to their beds.   *Ib.* 18

15 O sovereign mistress of true melancholy.   *Ib.* ix. 12

16   Swallows have built
In Cleopatra's sails their nests; the augurers
Say they know not, they cannot tell.   *Ib.* x. 16

17   The hearts
That spaniel'd me at heels, to whom I gave
Their wishes, do discandy, melt their sweets
On blossoming Cæsar.   *Ib.* 33

18 The soul and body rive not more in parting
Than greatness going off.   *Ib.* xi. 5

19 Sometimes we see a cloud that's dragonish;
A vapour sometime like a bear or lion,
A tower'd citadel, a pendant rock,
A forked mountain, or blue promontory
With trees upon 't, that nod unto the world
And mock our eyes with air: thou hast seen these
    signs;
They are black vesper's pageants.   *Ib.* xii. 2

20 That which is now a horse, even with a thought
The rack dislimns, and makes it indistinct,
As water is in water.   *Ib.* 9

21 Unarm, Eros; the long day's task is done,
And we must sleep.   *Ib.* 35

22 I will o'ertake thee, Cleopatra, and
Weep for my pardon. So it must be, for now
All length is torture; since the torch is out,
Lie down, and stray no further. Now all labour
Mars what it does; yea, very force entangles

Itself with strength; seal then, and all is done.
Eros!—I come, my queen.—Eros!—Stay for me:
Where souls do couch on flowers, we'll hand in hand,
And with our sprightly port make the ghosts gaze;
Dido and her Æneas shall want troops,
And all the haunt be ours.
                    Antony and Cleopatra, IV. xii. 44

23   Since Cleopatra died,
I have liv'd in such dishonour, that the gods
Detest my baseness.   *Ib.* 55

24   But I will be
A bridegroom in my death, and run into 't
As to a lover's bed.   *Ib.* 99

25 All strange and terrible events are welcome,
But comforts we despise.   *Ib.* xiii. 3

26 ANTONY:
Not Cæsar's valour hath o'erthrown Antony
But Antony's hath triumphed on itself.
CLEOPATRA:
So it should be, that none but Antony
Should conquer Antony.   *Ib.* 14

27 I am dying, Egypt, dying; only
I here importune death awhile, until
Of many thousand kisses the poor last
I lay upon thy lips.   *Ib.* 18

28 The miserable change now at my end
Lament nor sorrow at; but please your thoughts
In feeding them with those my former fortunes
Wherein I liv'd, the greatest prince o' the world,
The noblest; and do now not basely die,
Not cowardly put off my helmet to
My countryman; a Roman by a Roman
Valiantly vanquished.   *Ib.* 51

29 Hast thou no care of me? shall I abide
In this dull world, which in thy absence is
No better than a sty? O! see my women,
The crown o' the earth doth melt. My lord!
O! wither'd is the garland of the war,
The soldier's pole is fall'n; young boys and girls
Are level now with men; the odds is gone,
And there is nothing left remarkable
Beneath the visiting moon.   *Ib.* 60

30 No more, but e'en a woman and commanded
By such poor passion as the maid that milks
And does the meanest chares.   *Ib.* 73

31   What's brave, what's noble,
Let's do it after the high Roman fashion,
And make death proud to take us.   *Ib.* 86

32   A rarer spirit never
Did steer humanity; but you, gods, will give us
Some faults to make us men.   *Ib.* v. i. 31

33 My desolation does begin to make
A better life. 'Tis paltry to be Cæsar;
Not being Fortune, he's but Fortune's knave,
A minister of her will; and it is great
To do that thing that ends all other deeds,
Which shackles accidents, and bolts up change,
Which sleeps, and never palates more the dug,
The beggar's nurse and Cæsar's.   *Ib.* ii. 1

34 Nor once be chastis'd with the sober eye
Of dull Octavia. Shall they hoist me up
And show me to the shouting varletry
Of censuring Rome? Rather a ditch in Egypt
Be gentle grave unto me! rather on Nilus' mud
Lay me stark naked, and let the water-flies
Blow me into abhorring!   *Ib.* 54

B 3806   [425]   P*

1 His legs bestrid the ocean; his rear'd arm
Crested the world; his voice was propertied
As all the tuned spheres, and that to friends;
But when he meant to quail and shake the orb,
He was as rattling thunder. For his bounty,
There was no winter in't; an autumn was
That grew the more by reaping; his delights
Were dolphin-like, they show'd his back above
The element they liv'd in; in his livery
Walk'd crowns and crownets, realms and islands were
As plates dropp'd from his pocket.
Antony and Cleopatra, v. ii. 82

2 He words me, girls, he words me, that I should not
Be noble to myself. *Ib.* 190

3 Finish, good lady; the bright day is done,
And we are for the dark. *Ib.* 192

4   Antony
Shall be brought drunken forth, and I shall see
Some squeaking Cleopatra boy my greatness
I' the posture of a whore. *Ib.* 217

5   I am again for Cydnus,
To meet Mark Antony. *Ib.* 227

6 His biting is immortal; those that do die of it do
seldom or never recover. *Ib.* [246]

7 A very honest woman, but something given to lie.
Ib. [251]

8 I know that a woman is a dish for the gods, if the
devil dress her not. *Ib.* [274]

9   I have
Immortal longings in me. *Ib.* [282]

10   Husband, I come:
Now to that name my courage prove my title!
I am fire and air; my other elements
I give to baser life. *Ib.* [289]

11 If thou and nature can so gently part,
The stroke of death is as a lover's pinch,
Which hurts, and is desir'd. *Ib.* [296]

12 If thus thou vanishest, thou tell'st the world
It is not worth leave-taking. *Ib.* [299]

13 CLEOPATRA:
If she first meet the curled Antony,
He'll make demand of her, and spend that kiss
Which is my heaven to have. Come, thou mortal
wretch,
With thy sharp teeth this knot intrinsicate
Of life at once untie; poor venomous fool,
Be angry, and dispatch. O! couldst thou speak,
That I might hear thee call great Cæsar ass
Unpolicied.
CHARMIAN:
         O eastern star!
CLEOPATRA: Peace! peace!
Dost thou not see my baby at my breast,
That sucks the nurse asleep? *Ib.* [303]

14 Now boast thee, death, in thy possession lies
A lass unparallel'd. *Ib.* [317]

15 It is well done, and fitting for a princess
Descended of so many royal kings. *Ib.* [328]

16 As she would catch another Antony
In her strong toil of grace. *Ib.* [348]

17 She hath pursu'd conclusions infinite
Of easy ways to die. *Ib.* [356]

18 Let us sit and mock the good housewife Fortune
from her wheel, that her gifts may henceforth be
bestowed equally. *As You Like It*, I. ii. [35]

19 How now, wit! whither wander you? *Ib.* [60]

20 Well said: that was laid on with a trowel. *Ib.* [113]

21 Your heart's desires be with you! *Ib.* [214]

22 One out of suits with fortune. *Ib.* [263]

23 My pride fell with my fortunes. *Ib.* [269]

24 Sir, you have wrestled well, and overthrown
More than your enemies. *Ib.* [271]

25 Hereafter, in a better world than this,
I shall desire more love and knowledge of you.
Ib. [301]

26 Thus must I from the smoke into the smother;
From tyrant duke unto a tyrant brother. *Ib.* [304]

27 O, how full of briers is this working-day world!
Ib. iii. [12]

28 We'll have a swashing and a martial outside,
As many other mannish cowards have
That do outface it with their semblances. *Ib.* [123]

29 Hath not old custom made this life more sweet
Than that of painted pomp? Are not these woods
More free from peril than the envious court?
Here feel we but the penalty of Adam,
The seasons' difference; as, the icy fang
And churlish chiding of the winter's wind,
Which, when it bites and blows upon my body,
Even till I shrink with cold, I smile and say,
'This is no flattery.' *Ib.* II. i. 2

30 Sweet are the uses of adversity,
Which like the toad, ugly and venomous,
Wears yet a precious jewel in his head;
And this our life, exempt from public haunt,
Finds tongues in trees, books in the running brooks,
Sermons in stones, and good in everything. *Ib.* 12

31   The big round tears
Cours'd one another down his innocent nose,
In piteous chase. *Ib.* 38

32 'Poor deer,' quoth he, 'thou mak'st a testament
As worldlings do, giving thy sum of more
To that which had too much.' *Ib.* 47

33 Sweep on, you fat and greasy citizens! *Ib.* 55

34 I love to cope him in these sullen fits,
For then he's full of matter. *Ib.* 67

35 Unregarded age in corners thrown. *Ib.* iii. 42

36   Though I look old, yet I am strong and lusty;
For in my youth I never did apply
Hot and rebellious liquors in my blood. *Ib.* 47

37 Therefore my age is as a lusty winter,
Frosty, but kindly. *Ib.* 52

38 O good old man! how well in thee appears
The constant service of the antique world,
When service sweat for duty, not for meed!
Thou art not for the fashion of these times,
Where none will sweat but for promotion,
And having that, do choke their service up
Even with the having. *Ib.* 56

39 Ay, now am I in Arden; the more fool I. When I
was at home I was in a better place; but travellers
must be content. *Ib.* iv. [16]

1   As true a lover
As ever sigh'd upon a midnight pillow.
                    As You Like It, II. iv. [26]

2 If thou remember'st not the slightest folly
That ever love did make thee run into,
Thou hast not lov'd.   *Ib.* [34]

3 We that are true lovers run into strange capers.
                    Ib. [53]

4 Thou speakest wiser than thou art ware of. *Ib.* [57]

5 I shall ne'er be ware of mine own wit till I break my
shins against it.   *Ib.* [59]

6 My master is of churlish disposition
And little recks to find the way to heaven
By doing deeds of hospitality.   *Ib.* [81]

7 Under the greenwood tree
Who loves to lie with me,
And turn his merry note
Unto the sweet bird's throat,
Come hither, come hither, come hither:
      Here shall he see
      No enemy
But winter and rough weather.   *Ib.* v. 1

8 I can suck melancholy out of a song as a weasel sucks
eggs.   *Ib.* [12]

9 Who doth ambition shun
And loves to live i' the sun,
Seeking the food he eats,
And pleas'd with what he gets.   *Ib.* [38]

10 I'll rail against all the first-born in Egypt.   *Ib.* [60]

11 A fool, a fool! I met a fool i' the forest,
A motley fool.   *Ib.* vii. 12

12 And rail'd on Lady Fortune in good terms,
In good set terms.   *Ib.* 16

13 'Call me not fool till heaven hath sent me fortune.'
And then he drew a dial from his poke,
And, looking on it with lack-lustre eye,
Says very wisely, 'It is ten o'clock;
Thus may we see,' quoth he, 'how the world wags.'
                    Ib. 19

14 And so, from hour to hour, we ripe and ripe,
And then from hour to hour, we rot and rot:
And thereby hangs a tale.   *Ib.* 26

15 My lungs began to crow like chanticleer,
That fools should be so deep-contemplative,
And I did laugh sans intermission
An hour by his dial. O noble fool!
A worthy fool! Motley's the only wear.   *Ib.* 30

16 And says, if ladies be but young and fair,
They have the gift to know it: and in his brain,—
Which is as dry as the remainder biscuit
After a voyage,—he hath strange places cramm'd
With observation, the which he vents
In mangled forms.   *Ib.* 37

17   I must have liberty
Withal, as large a charter as the wind,
To blow on whom I please.   *Ib.* 47

18 The 'why' is plain as way to parish church. *Ib.* 52

19   But whate'er you are
That in this desert inaccessible,
Under the shade of melancholy boughs,
Lose and neglect the creeping hours of time;
If ever you have look'd on better days,
If ever been where bells have knoll'd to church,

If ever sat at any good man's feast,
If ever from your eyelids wip'd a tear,
And know what 'tis to pity, and be pitied,
Let gentleness my strong enforcement be.
                    As You Like It, II. vii. 109

20 There is an old poor man,
      .   .   .
Oppress'd with two weak evils, age and hunger.
                    Ib. 129

21   All the world's a stage,
And all the men and women merely players:
They have their exits and their entrances;
And one man in his time plays many parts,
His acts being seven ages. At first the infant,
Mewling and puking in the nurse's arms.
And then the whining schoolboy, with his satchel,
And shining morning face, creeping like snail
Unwillingly to school. And then the lover,
Sighing like furnace, with a woful ballad
Made to his mistress' eyebrow. Then a soldier,
Full of strange oaths, and bearded like the pard,
Jealous in honour, sudden and quick in quarrel,
Seeking the bubble reputation
Even in the cannon's mouth. And then the justice,
In fair round belly with good capon lin'd,
With eyes severe, and beard of formal cut,
Full of wise saws and modern instances;
And so he plays his part. The sixth age shifts
Into the lean and slipper'd pantaloon,
With spectacles on nose and pouch on side,
His youthful hose well sav'd a world too wide
For his shrunk shank; and his big manly voice,
Turning again towards childish treble, pipes
And whistles in his sound. Last scene of all,
That ends this strange eventful history,
Is second childishness, and mere oblivion,
Sans teeth, sans eyes, sans taste, sans everything.
                    Ib. 139

22 Blow, blow, thou winter wind,
Thou art not so unkind
      As man's ingratitude:
Thy tooth is not so keen,
Because thou art not seen,
      Although thy breath be rude.
Heigh-ho! sing, heigh-ho! unto the green holly:
Most friendship is feigning, most loving mere folly.
      Then heigh-ho! the holly!
      This life is most jolly.

Freeze, freeze, thou bitter sky,
That dost not bite so nigh
      As benefits forgot:
Though thou the waters warp,
Thy sting is not so sharp
      As friend remember'd not.   *Ib.* 174

23 Run, run, Orlando: carve on every tree
The fair, the chaste, and unexpressive she.
                    Ib. III. ii. 9

24 Hast any philosophy in thee, shepherd?   *Ib.* [22]

25 He that wants money, means, and content is without
three good friends.   *Ib.* [25]

26 Thou art in a parlous state.   *Ib.* [46]

27 I earn that I eat, get that I wear, owe no man hate,
envy no man's happiness, glad of other men's
good, content with my harm.   *Ib.* [78]

28 From the east to western Ind,
No jewel is like Rosalind.   *Ib.* [94]

1 This is the very false gallop of verses.
As You Like It, III. ii. [120]

2 Let us make an honourable retreat; though not with bag and baggage, yet with scrip and scrippage.
Ib. [170]

3 O wonderful, wonderful, and most wonderful wonderful! and yet again wonderful, and after that, out of all whooping!
Ib. [202]

4 It is as easy to count atomies as to resolve the propositions of a lover.
Ib. [246]

5 Do you not know I am a woman? when I think, I must speak.
Ib. [265]

6 I do desire we may be better strangers.
Ib. [276]

7 You have a nimble wit; I think 'twas made of Atalanta's heels.
Ib. [294]

8 I will chide no breather in the world but myself, against whom I know most faults.
Ib. [298]

9 Time travels in divers paces with divers persons. I'll tell you who Time ambles withal, who Time trots withal, who Time gallops withal, and who he stands still withal.
Ib. [328]

10 Every one fault seeming monstrous till his fellow fault came to match it.
Ib. [377]

11 Truly, I would the gods had made thee poetical.
Ib. iii. [16]

12 I am not a slut, though I thank the gods I am foul.
Ib. [40]

13 ROSALIND:
His hair is of a good colour.
CELIA:
An excellent colour; your chestnut was ever the only colour.
Ib. iv. [10]

14   Down on your knees,
And thank heaven, fasting, for a good man's love.
Ib. v. 57

15 Dead shepherd, now I find thy saw of might:
'Who ever lov'd that lov'd not at first sight?' *Ib.* 81

16 It is a melancholy of mine own, compounded of many simples, extracted from many objects, and indeed the sundry contemplation of my travels, which, by often rumination, wraps me in a most humorous sadness.
Ib. IV. i. [16]

17 Farewell, Monsieur Traveller: look you lisp and wear strange suits, disable all the benefits of your own country, be out of love with your nativity, and almost chide God for making you that countenance you are, or I will scarce think you have swam in a gondola.
Ib. [35]

18 Break an hour's promise in love! He that will divide a minute into a thousand parts, and break but a part of the thousandth part of a minute in the affairs of love, it may be said of him that Cupid hath clapped him o' the shoulder, but I'll warrant him heart-whole.
Ib. [46]

19 For now I am in a holiday humour.
Ib. [70]

20 When you were gravelled for lack of matter.
Ib. [76]

21 Men have died from time to time, and worms have eaten them, but not for love.
Ib. [110]

22 Men are April when they woo, December when they wed: maids are May when they are maids, but the sky changes when they are wives.
Ib. [153]

23 The horn, the horn, the lusty horn
Is not a thing to laugh to scorn.
As You Like It, IV. ii. [17]

24 Chewing the food of sweet and bitter fancy.
Ib. iii. [103]

25 Cæsar's thrasonical brag of 'I came, saw, and overcame'.
Ib. v. ii. [35]

26 No sooner met, but they looked; no sooner looked but they loved; no sooner loved but they sighed; no sooner sighed but they asked one another the reason; no sooner knew the reason but they sought the remedy.
Ib. [37]

27 Oh! how bitter a thing it is to look into happiness through another man's eyes.
Ib. [48]

28 PHEBE:
Good shepherd, tell this youth what 'tis to love.
SILVIUS:
It is to be all made of sighs and tears;—

It is to be all made of faith and service;—

It is to be all made of fantasy,
All made of passion, and all made of wishes;
All adoration, duty, and observance;
All humbleness, all patience, and impatience;
All purity, all trial, all obeisance.
Ib. [90]

29 'Tis like the howling of Irish wolves against the moon.
Ib. [120]

30 It was a lover and his lass,
With a hey, and a ho, and a hey nonino,
That o'er the green cornfield did pass,
    In the spring time, the only pretty ring time,
When birds do sing, hey ding a ding, ding;
Sweet lovers love the spring.
Ib. iii. [18]

31 Between the acres of the rye,
With a hey, and a ho, and a hey nonino,
These pretty country folks would lie,
    In the spring time, &c.
Ib. [24]

32 This carol they began that hour,
With a hey, and a ho, and a hey nonino,
How that a life was but a flower,
    In the spring time, &c.
Ib. [28]

33 And therefore take the present time,
With a hey, and a ho, and a hey nonino;
For love is crowned with the prime
    In the spring time, &c.
Ib. [32]

34 Here comes a pair of very strange beasts, which in all tongues are called fools.
Ib. iv. [36]

35 An ill-favoured thing, sir, but mine own.
Ib. [60]

36 Rich honesty dwells like a miser, sir, in a poor house; as your pearl in your foul oyster.
Ib. [62]

37 The retort courteous . . . the quip modest . . . the reply churlish . . . the reproof valiant . . . the coun, check quarrelsome . . . the lie circumstantial . . . the lie direct.
Ib. [96]

38 Your 'if' is the only peace-maker; much virtue in 'if'.
Ib. [108]

39 He uses his folly like a stalking-horse, and under the presentation of that he shoots his wit. *Ib.* [112]

40 If it be true that 'good wine needs no bush', 'tis true that a good play needs no epilogue.
Ib. Epilogue [3]

1 They brought one Pinch, a hungry, lean-fac'd
villain,
A mere anatomy, a mountebank,
A threadbare juggler, and a fortune-teller,
A needy, hollow-ey'd, sharp-looking wretch,
A living-dead man. *The Comedy of Errors*, v. i. 238

2 He's a very dog to the commonalty.
Coriolanus, I. i. [29]

3 The kingly crowned head, the vigilant eye,
The counsellor heart, the arm our soldier,
Our steed the leg, the tongue our trumpeter.
Ib. [121]

4 What's the matter, you dissentious rogues,
That, rubbing the poor itch of your opinion,
Make yourselves scabs? *Ib.* [170]

5 They threw their caps
As they would hang them on the horns o' the moon,
Shouting their emulation. *Ib.* [218]

6 Oh! I warrant, how he mammocked it! *Ib.* iii. [71]

7 My gracious silence, hail! *Ib.* II. i. [194]

8 Such eyes the widows in Corioli wear,
And mothers that lack sons. *Ib.* [197]

9 Custom calls me to 't:
What custom wills, in all things should we do't,
The dust on antique time would lie unswept,
And mountainous error be too highly heap'd
For truth to o'erpeer. *Ib.* II. iii. [124]

10 I thank you for your voices, thank you,
Your most sweet voices. *Ib.* [179]

11 The mutable, rank-scented many. *Ib.* III. i. 65

12 Hear you this Triton of the minnows? mark you
His absolute 'shall'? *Ib.* 88

13 His nature is too noble for the world:
He would not flatter Neptune for his trident,
Or Jove for's power to thunder. His heart's his
mouth:
What his breast forges, that his tongue must vent.
Ib. 254

14 You common cry of curs! whose breath I hate
As reek o' the rotten fens, whose loves I prize
As the dead carcases of unburied men
That do corrupt my air,—I banish you. *Ib.* iii. 118

15 The beast
With many heads butts me away. *Ib.* IV. i. 1

16 Under the canopy . . . I' the city of kites and crows.
Ib. v. [41]

17 I'll never
Be such a gosling to obey instinct, but stand
As if a man were author of himself
And knew no other kin. *Ib.* v. iii. 34

18 Like a dull actor now,
I have forgot my part, and I am out,
Even to a full disgrace. *Ib.* 40

19 O! a kiss
Long as my exile, sweet as my revenge!
Now, by the jealous queen of heaven, that kiss
I carried from thee, dear, and my true lip
Hath virgin'd it e'er since. *Ib.* 44

20 Chaste as the icicle
That's curdied by the frost from purest snow,
And hangs on Dian's temple. *Ib.* 65

21 Like a great sea-mark, standing every flaw.
Coriolanus, v. iii. 74

22 Thou hast never in thy life
Show'd thy dear mother any courtesy;
When she—poor hen! fond of no second brood—
Has cluck'd thee to the wars, and safely home,
Loaden with honour. *Ib.* 160

23 If you have writ your annals true, 'tis there,
That, like an eagle in a dove-cote, I
Flutter'd your Volscians in Corioli:
Alone I did it. *Ib.* v. 114

24 On her left breast
A mole cinque-spotted, like the crimson drops
I' the bottom of a cowslip. *Cymbeline*, II. ii. 37

25 Hark! hark! the lark at heaven's gate sings,
And Phœbus 'gins arise,
His steeds to water at those springs
On chalic'd flowers that lies;
And winking Mary-buds begin
To ope their golden eyes:
With everything that pretty is,
My lady sweet, arise! *Ib.* iii. [22]

26 Is there no way for men to be, but women
Must be half-workers? *Ib.* v. 1

27 As chaste as unsunn'd snow. *Ib.* 13

28 There be many Cæsars
Ere such another Julius. Britain is
A world by itself, and we will nothing pay
For wearing our own noses. *Ib.* III. i. 11

29 The natural bravery of your isle, which stands
As Neptune's park, ribbed and paled in
With rocks unscalable, and roaring waters. *Ib.* 18
Ib. ii. [49]

30 O, for a horse with wings!

31 What should we speak of
When we are old as you? when we shall hear
The rain and wind beat dark December, how,
In this our pinching cave, shall we discourse
The freezing hours away? *Ib.* iii. 35

32 Some jay of Italy,
Whose mother was her painting, hath betray'd him:
Poor I am stale, a garment out of fashion.
Ib. iv. [51]

33 I have not slept one wink. *Ib.* [103]

34 Hath Britain all the sun that shines? *Ib.* [139]

35 To lapse in fulness
Is sorer than to lie for need, and falsehood
Is worse in kings than beggars. *Ib.* vi. 12

36 Weariness
Can snore upon the flint when resty sloth
Finds the down pillow hard. *Ib.* 33

37 Thou shalt not lack
The flower that's like thy face, pale primrose, nor
The azur'd harebell, like thy veins. *Ib.* IV. ii. 220

38 Great griefs, I see, medicine the less. *Ib.* 243

39 Though mean and mighty rotting
Together, have one dust, yet reverence—
That angel of the world—doth make distinction
Of place 'tween high and low. *Ib.* 246

40 Thersites' body is as good as Ajax'
When neither are alive. *Ib.* 252

[429]

1 Fear no more the heat o' the sun,
  Nor the furious winter's rages;
Thou thy worldly task hast done,
  Home art gone and ta'en thy wages:
Golden lads and girls all must,
As chimney-sweepers, come to dust.

Fear no more the frown o' the great,
  Thou art past the tyrant's stroke:
Care no more to clothe and eat;
  To thee the reed is as the oak:
The sceptre, learning, physic, must
All follow this, and come to dust.

Fear no more the lightning flash,
  Nor the all-dreaded thunder-stone;
Fear not slander, censure rash;
  Thou hast finish'd joy and moan:
All lovers young, all lovers must
Consign to thee, and come to dust.

No exorciser harm thee!
  Nor no witchcraft charm thee!
Ghost unlaid forbear thee!
  Nothing ill come near thee!
Quiet consummation have:
  And renowned be thy grave!   *Cymbeline*, IV. ii. 258

2 Every good servant does not all commands.
                                          Ib. v. i. 6

3 He that sleeps feels not the toothache.   *Ib.* iv. [176]

4 He spake of her as Dian had hot dreams,
And she alone were cold.   *Ib.* v. 181

5 IMOGEN:
Why did you throw your wedded lady from you?
Think that you are upon a rock; and now
Throw me again.
POSTHUMUS:
                    Hang there like fruit, my soul,
Till the tree die!   *Ib.* 262

6 Pardon's the word to all.   *Ib.* 423

7 You come most carefully upon your hour.
                                  Hamlet, I. i. 6

8 For this relief much thanks; 'tis bitter cold,
And I am sick at heart.   *Ib.* 8

9 BERNARDO:
What! is Horatio there?
HORATIO:
                    A piece of him.   *Ib.* 19

10 What! has this thing appear'd again to-night? *Ib.* 21

11 Look, where it comes again!   *Ib.* 40

12 But in the gross and scope of my opinion,
This bodes some strange eruption to our state.
                                         Ib. 68

13   This sweaty haste
Doth make the night joint-labourer with the day.
                                         Ib. 77

14 In the most high and palmy state of Rome,
A little ere the mightiest Julius fell,
The graves stood tenantless and the sheeted dead
Did squeak and gibber in the Roman streets.
                                         Ib. 113

15   The moist star
Upon whose influence Neptune's empire stands
Was sick almost to doomsday with eclipse. *Ib.* 118

16 I'll cross it, though it blast me.   *Ib.* 127

17 We do it wrong, being so majestical,
To offer it the show of violence;
For it is, as the air, invulnerable,
And our vain blows malicious mockery. *Hamlet*, I. i. 143

18 And then it started like a guilty thing
Upon a fearful summons.   *Ib.* 148

19 Whether in sea or fire, in earth or air,
The extravagant and erring spirit hies
To his confine.   *Ib.* 153

20 It faded on the crowing of the cock.
Some say that ever 'gainst that season comes
Wherein our Saviour's birth is celebrated,
The bird of dawning singeth all night long;
And then, they say, no spirit can walk abroad;
The nights are wholesome; then no planets strike,
No fairy takes, nor witch hath power to charm,
So hallow'd and so gracious is the time.   *Ib.* 157

21 But, look, the morn, in russet mantle clad,
Walks o'er the dew of yon high eastern hill.
                                            Ib. 166

22 The memory be green.   *Ib.* ii. 2

23 Therefore our sometime sister, now our queen. *Ib.* 8

24 With one auspicious and one dropping eye,
With mirth in funeral and with dirge in marriage,
In equal scale weighing delight and dole.   *Ib.* 11

25 The head is not more native to the heart.   *Ib.* 47

26 A little more than kin, and less than kind. *Ib.* 65

27 Not so, my lord; I am too much i' the sun.   *Ib.* 67

28 Good Hamlet, cast thy nighted colour off,
And let thine eye look like a friend on Denmark.
                                            Ib. 68

29 QUEEN:
Thou know'st 'tis common; all that live must die,
Passing through nature to eternity.
HAMLET:
Ay, madam, it is common.   *Ib.* 72

30 Seems, madam! Nay, it is; I know not 'seems'.
'Tis not alone my inky cloak, good mother,
Nor customary suits of solemn black,
Nor windy suspiration of forc'd breath,
No, nor the fruitful river in the eye,
Nor the dejected 'haviour of the visage,
Together with all forms, modes, shows of grief,
That can denote me truly; these indeed seem,
For they are actions that a man might play:
But I have that within which passeth show;
These but the trappings and the suits of woe. *Ib.* 76

31   But to persever
In obstinate condolement is a course
Of impious stubbornness; 'tis unmanly grief;
It shows a will most incorrect to heaven,
A heart unfortified, a mind impatient.   *Ib.* 92

32 HAMLET:
I shall in all my best obey you, madam.
KING:
Why, 'tis a loving and a fair reply.   *Ib.* 120

33 O! that this too too solid flesh would melt,
Thaw, and resolve itself into a dew;
Or that the Everlasting had not fix'd
His canon 'gainst self-slaughter! O God! O God!
How weary, stale, flat, and unprofitable
Seem to me all the uses of this world.
Fie on't! O fie! 'tis an unweeded garden,

That grows to seed; things rank and gross in nature
Possess it merely. That it should come to this!
But two months dead: nay, not so much, not two:
So excellent a king; that was, to this,
Hyperion to a satyr: so loving to my mother,
That he might not beteem the winds of heaven
Visit her face too roughly. Heaven and earth!
Must I remember? Why, she would hang on him,
As if increase of appetite had grown
By what it fed on; and yet, within a month,
Let me not think on't: Frailty, thy name is woman!
A little month; or ere those shoes were old
With which she follow'd my poor father's body,
Like Niobe, all tears; why she, even she,——
O God! a beast, that wants discourse of reason,
Would have mourn'd longer,—married with mine
  uncle,
My father's brother, but no more like my father
Than I to Hercules.   *Hamlet*, I. ii. 129

1 It is not, nor it cannot come to good;
But break, my heart, for I must hold my tongue!
                                        Ib. 158

2 A truant disposition, good my lord.   *Ib.* 169

3 We'll teach you to drink deep ere you depart. *Ib.* 175

4 Thrift, thrift, Horatio! the funeral bak'd meats
Did coldly furnish forth the marriage tables.
Would I had met my dearest foe in heaven
Ere I had ever seen that day, Horatio!   *Ib.* 180

5 In my mind's eye, Horatio.   *Ib.* 185

6 He was a man, take him for all in all,
I shall not look upon his like again.   *Ib.* 187

7 Season your admiration for a while.   *Ib.* 192

8 In the dead vast and middle of the night. *Ib.* 198

9 Armed at points exactly, cap-a-pe.   *Ib.* 200

10   Distill'd
Almost to jelly with the act of fear.   *Ib.* 204

11 These hands are not more like.   *Ib.* 212

12 But answer made it none.   *Ib.* 215

13 A countenance more in sorrow than in anger.
                                        Ib. 231

14 While one with moderate haste might tell a hundred.
                                        Ib. 237

15 HAMLET:
His beard was grizzled, no?
HORATIO:
It was, as I have seen it in his life,
A sable silver'd.   *Ib.* 239

16 Give it an understanding, but no tongue. *Ib.* 249

17 Upon the platform, 'twixt eleven and twelve.
                                        Ib. 251

18   All is not well;
I doubt some foul play.   *Ib.* 254

19   Foul deeds will rise,
Though all the earth o'erwhelm them, to men's eyes.
                                        Ib. 256

20 A violet in the youth of primy nature,
Forward, not permanent, sweet, not lasting.
The perfume and suppliance of a minute. *Ib.* iii. 7

21 His greatness weigh'd, his will is not his own,
For he himself is subject to his birth;
He may not, as unvalu'd persons do,
Carve for himself, for on his choice depends
The safety and the health of the whole state.
                                    Hamlet, I. iii. 17

22 And keep you in the rear of your affection. *Ib.* 34

23 Do not, as some ungracious pastors do,
Show me the steep and thorny way to heaven,
Whiles, like a puff'd and reckless libertine,
Himself the primrose path of dalliance treads,
And recks not his own rede.   *Ib.* 47

24 A double blessing is a double grace;
Occasion smiles upon a second leave.   *Ib.* 53

25 And these few precepts in thy memory
Look thou character. Give thy thoughts no tongue,
Nor any unproportion'd thought his act.
Be thou familiar, but by no means vulgar;
The friends thou hast, and their adoption tried,
Grapple them to thy soul with hoops of steel;
But do not dull thy palm with entertainment
Of each new-hatch'd, unfledg'd comrade. Beware
Of entrance to a quarrel; but, being in,
Bear't that th' opposed may beware of thee.
Give every man thine ear, but few thy voice;
Take each man's censure, but reserve thy judgment.
Costly thy habit as thy purse can buy,
But not express'd in fancy; rich, not gaudy;
For the apparel oft proclaims the man,
And they in France of the best rank and station
Are most select and generous, chief in that.
Neither a borrower, nor a lender be;
For loan oft loses both itself and friend,
And borrowing dulls the edge of husbandry,
This above all: to thine own self be true,
And it must follow, as the night the day,
Thou canst not then be false to any man.
Farewell; my blessing season this in thee! *Ib.* 58

26   You speak like a green girl,
Unsifted in such perilous circumstance.   *Ib.* 101

27 Ay, springes to catch woodcocks. I do know,
When the blood burns, how prodigal the soul
Lends the tongue vows.   *Ib.* 115

28 Be somewhat scanter of your maiden presence.
                                        Ib. 121

29 I would not, in plain terms, from this time forth,
Have you so slander any moment's leisure. *Ib.* 132

30 HAMLET:
The air bites shrewdly; it is very cold.
HORATIO:
It is a nipping and an eager air.   *Ib.* iv. 1

31 But to my mind,—though I am native here,
And to the manner born,—it is a custom
More honour'd in the breach than the observance.
                                        Ib. 14

32 Angels and ministers of grace defend us!
Be thou a spirit of health or goblin damn'd,
Bring with thee airs from heaven or blasts from hell,
Be thy intents wicked or charitable,
Thou com'st in such a questionable shape
That I will speak to thee: I'll call thee Hamlet,
King, father; royal Dane, O! answer me:
Let me not burst in ignorance; but tell
Why thy canoniz'd bones, hearsed in death,
Have burst their cerements; why the sepulchre,

Wherein we saw thee quietly inurn'd,
Hath op'd his ponderous and marble jaws,
To cast thee up again. What may this mean,
That thou, dead corse, again in complete steel
Revisit'st thus the glimpses of the moon,
Making night hideous; and we fools of nature
So horridly to shake our disposition
With thoughts beyond the reaches of our souls?
Hamlet I. iv. 39

1   Look, with what courteous action
It waves you to a more removed ground.   *Ib.* 60

2 I do not set my life at a pin's fee;
And for my soul, what can it do to that,
Being a thing immortal as itself?   *Ib.* 65

3   My fate cries out,
And makes each petty artery in this body
As hardy as the Nemean lion's nerve.   *Ib.* 81

4   Unhand me, gentlemen,
By heaven! I'll make a ghost of him that lets me.
    Ib. 84

5 Something is rotten in the state of Denmark. *Ib.* 90

6 Whither wilt thou lead me? speak; I'll go no further.
    Ib. v. 1

7 Alas! poor ghost.   *Ib.* 4

8 I am thy father's spirit;
Doom'd for a certain term to walk the night. *Ib.* 9

9   But that I am forbid
To tell the secrets of my prison-house,
I could a tale unfold whose lightest word
Would harrow up thy soul, freeze thy young blood,
Make thy two eyes, like stars, start from their spheres,
Thy knotted and combined locks to part,
And each particular hair to stand an end,
Like quills upon the fretful porpentine:
But this eternal blazon must not be
To ears of flesh and blood. List, list, O, list! *Ib.* 13

10 Revenge his foul and most unnatural murder. *Ib.* 25

11 Murder most foul, as in the best it is;
But this most foul, strange, and unnatural. *Ib.* 27

12 And duller shouldst thou be than the fat weed
That rots itself in ease on Lethe wharf. *Ib.* 32

13   O my prophetic soul!
My uncle!   *Ib.* 40

14 That it went hand in hand even with the vow
I made to her in marriage.   *Ib.* 49

15 But, soft! methinks I scent the morning air. *Ib.* 58

16 In the porches of mine ears.   *Ib.* 63

17 Cut off even in the blossoms of my sin,
Unhousel'd, disappointed, unanel'd,
No reckoning made, but sent to my account
With all my imperfections on my head:
O, horrible! O, horrible! most horrible!
If thou hast nature in thee, bear it not. *Ib.* 76

18   Leave her to heaven,
And to those thorns that in her bosom lodge,
To prick and sting her.   *Ib.* 86

19 The glow-worm shows the matin to be near,
And 'gins to pale his uneffectual fire. *Ib.* 89

20   While memory holds a seat
In this distracted globe. Remember thee!
Yea, from the table of my memory

I'll wipe away all trivial fond records,
All saws of books, all forms, all pressures past,
That youth and observation copied there.
Hamlet, I. v. 96

21 O most pernicious woman!
O villain, villain, smiling, damned villain!
My tables,—meet it is I set it down,
That one may smile, and smile, and be a villain;
At least I'm sure it may be so in Denmark. *Ib.* 105

22 HAMLET:
There's ne'er a villain dwelling in all Denmark,
But he's an arrant knave.
HORATIO:
There needs no ghost, my lord, come from the grave,
To tell us this.   *Ib.* 123

23   And, for mine own poor part,
Look you, I'll go pray.   *Ib.* 131

24 It is an honest ghost, that let me tell you. *Ib.* 138

25   Art thou there, true-penny?
Come on,—you hear this fellow in the cellarage.
    Ib. 150

26 Hic et ubique? then we'll shift our ground. *Ib.* 156

27 Well said, old mole! canst work i' the earth so fast?
    Ib. 162

28 O day and night, but this is wondrous strange!
    Ib. 164

29 There are more things in heaven and earth, Horatio,
Than are dreamt of in your philosophy. *Ib.* 166

30 To put an antic disposition on.   *Ib.* 172

31 Rest, rest, perturbed spirit!   *Ib.* 182

32 The time is out of joint; O cursed spite,
That ever I was born to set it right! *Ib.* 188

33 Your bait of falsehood takes this carp of truth.
    Ib. II. i. 63

34 By indirections find directions out.   *Ib.* 66

35 Lord Hamlet, with his doublet all unbrac'd;
No hat upon his head; his stockings foul'd,
Ungarter'd, and down-gyved to his ankle. *Ib.* 78

36   Such thanks
As fits a king's remembrance.   *Ib.* ii. 25

37 Thou still hast been the father of good news. *Ib.* 42

38 Brevity is the soul of wit.   *Ib.* 90

39 More matter with less art.   *Ib.* 95

40 That he is mad, 'tis true; 'tis true 'tis pity;
And pity 'tis 'tis true: a foolish figure;
But farewell it, for I will use no art. *Ib.* 97

41 That's an ill phrase, a vile phrase; 'beautified' is a
vile phrase.   *Ib.* [110]

42 Doubt thou the stars are fire;
Doubt that the sun doth move;
Doubt truth to be a liar;
But never doubt I love.   *Ib.* [115]

43 Lord Hamlet is a prince, out of thy star. *Ib.* [141]

44 If circumstances lead me, I will find
Where truth is hid, though it were hid indeed
Within the centre.   *Ib.* [157]

45 Let me be no assistant for a state,
But keep a farm, and carters.   *Ib.* [166]

1 POLONIUS:
Do you know me, my lord?

HAMLET:
Excellent well; you are a fishmonger. *Hamlet*,II.ii.[173]

2 Ay, sir; to be honest, as this world goes, is to be one man picked out of ten thousand. *Ib.* [179]

3 Still harping on my daughter. *Ib.* [190]

4 POLONIUS:
What do you read, my lord?

HAMLET:
Words, words, words. *Ib.* [195]

5 All which, sir, though I most powerfully and potently believe, yet I hold it not honesty to have it thus set down. *Ib.* [206]

6 Though this be madness, yet there is method in it. *Ib.* [211]

7 Except my life, except my life, except my life. *Ib.* [225]

8 These tedious old fools! *Ib.* [227]

9 As the indifferent children of the earth. *Ib.* [235]

10 HAMLET:
Then you live about her waist, or in the middle of her favours?

GUILDENSTERN:
Faith, her privates we.

HAMLET:
In the secret parts of Fortune? O! most true; she is a strumpet. What news?

ROSENCRANTZ:
None, my lord, but that the world's grown honest.

HAMLET:
Then is doomsday near. *Ib.* [240]

11 There is nothing either good or bad, but thinking makes it so. *Ib.* [259]

12 O God! I could be bounded in a nut-shell, and count myself a king of infinite space, were it not that I have bad dreams. *Ib.* [263]

13 GUILDENSTERN:
The very substance of the ambitious is merely the shadow of a dream.

HAMLET:
A dream itself is but a shadow.

ROSENCRANTZ:
Truly, and I hold ambition of so airy and light a quality that it is but a shadow's shadow. *Ib.* [268]

14 Beggar that I am, I am poor even in thanks. *Ib.* [286]

15 It goes so heavily with my disposition that this goodly frame, the earth, seems to me a sterile promontory; this most excellent canopy, the air, look you, this brave o'erhanging firmament, this majestical roof fretted with golden fire, why, it appears no other thing to me but a foul and pestilent congregation of vapours. What a piece of work is a man! How noble in reason! how infinite in faculty! in form, in moving, how express and admirable! in action how like an angel! in apprehension how like a god! the beauty of the world! the paragon of animals! And yet, to me, what is this quintessence of dust? man delights not me; no, nor woman neither, though, by your smiling, you seem to say so. *Ib.* [316]

16 There was no such stuff in my thoughts. *Ib.* [332]

17 What lenten entertainment the players shall receive from you. *Hamlet*, II. ii. [337]

18 Make those laugh whose lungs are tickle o' the sere. *Ib.* [346]

19 There is something in this more than natural, if philosophy could find it out. *Ib.* [392]

20 I am but mad north-north-west; when the wind is southerly, I know a hawk from a handsaw.[1] *Ib.* [405]

[1] = heron-shaw, or heron.

21 That great baby you see there is not yet out of his swaddling-clouts. *Ib.* [410]

22 Seneca cannot be too heavy, nor Plautus too light. *Ib.* [428]

23 One fair daughter and no more,
The which he loved passing well. *Ib.* [435]

24 Come, give us a taste of your quality. *Ib.* [460]

25 The play, I remember, pleased not the million; 'twas caviare to the general. *Ib.* [465]

26 The rugged Pyrrhus, like the Hyrcanian beast. *Ib.* [481]

27 Head to foot
Now is he total gules. *Ib.* [487]

28 The mobled queen. *Ib.* [533]

29 Good my lord, will you see the players well bestowed? Do you hear, let them be well used; for they are the abstracts and brief chronicles of the time: after your death you were better have a bad epitaph than their ill report while you live. *Ib.* [553]

30 Use every man after his desert, and who should 'scape whipping? *Ib.* [561]

31 O, what a rogue and peasant slave am I:
Is it not monstrous that this player here,
But in a fiction, in a dream of passion,
Could force his soul so to his own conceit
That from her working all his visage wann'd,
Tears in his eyes, distraction in 's aspect,
A broken voice, and his whole function suiting
With forms to his conceit? and all for nothing!
For Hecuba!
What's Hecuba to him or he to Hecuba
That he should weep for her? *Ib.* [584]

32 He would drown the stage with tears,
And cleave the general ear with horrid speech,
Make mad the guilty, and appal the free,
Confound the ignorant, and amaze, indeed,
The very faculties of eyes and ears. *Ib.* [596]

33 A dull and muddy-mettled rascal. *Ib.* [602]

34 But I am pigeon-livered, and lack gall
To make oppression bitter. *Ib.* [613]

35 I should have fatted all the region kites
With this slave's offal. *Ib.* [615]

36 I have heard,
That guilty creatures sitting at a play
Have by the very cunning of the scene
Been struck so to the soul that presently
They have proclaim'd their malefactions;
For murder, though it have no tongue, will speak
With most miraculous organ. *Ib.* [625]

37 Abuses me to damn me. *Ib.* [640]

1   The play's the thing
Wherein I'll catch the conscience of the king.
Hamlet, II. ii. [641]

2 Nor do we find him forward to be sounded,
But, with a crafty madness, keeps aloof,
When we would bring him on to some confession
Of his true state. *Ib.* III. i. 7

3 'Tis too much prov'd—that with devotion's visage
And pious action, we do sugar o'er
The devil himself. *Ib.* 47

4 To be, or not to be: that is the question:
Whether 'tis nobler in the mind to suffer
The slings and arrows of outrageous fortune,
Or to take arms against a sea of troubles,
And by opposing end them? To die: to sleep;
No more; and, by a sleep to say we end
The heart-ache and the thousand natural shocks
That flesh is heir to, 'tis a consummation
Devoutly to be wish'd. To die, to sleep;
To sleep: perchance to dream: ay, there's the rub;
For in that sleep of death what dreams may come
When we have shuffled off this mortal coil,
Must give us pause. There's the respect
That makes calamity of so long life;
For who would bear the whips and scorns of time,
The oppressor's wrong, the proud man's contumely,
The pangs of dispriz'd love, the law's delay,
The insolence of office, and the spurns
That patient merit of the unworthy takes,
When he himself might his quietus make
With a bare bodkin? Who would fardels bear,
To grunt and sweat under a weary life,
But that the dread of something after death,
The undiscover'd country from whose bourn
No traveller returns, puzzles the will,
And makes us rather bear those ills we have,
Than fly to others that we know not of?
Thus conscience doth make cowards of us all;
And thus the native hue of resolution
Is sicklied o'er with the pale cast of thought,
And enterprises of great pith and moment
With this regard their currents turn awry,
And lose the name of action. *Ib.* 56

5   Nymph, in thy orisons
Be all my sins remember'd *Ib.* 89

6   For, to the noble mind,
Rich gifts wax poor when givers prove unkind.
Ib. 100

7 Get thee to a nunnery. *Ib.* [124]

8 I am myself indifferent honest. *Ib.* [125]

9 I am very proud, revengeful, ambitious; with more
offences at my beck, than I have thoughts to put
them in, imagination to give them shape, or time
to act them in. What should such fellows as I do
crawling between heaven and earth? *Ib.* [128]

10 Let the doors be shut upon him, that he may play
the fool nowhere but in 's own house. *Ib.* [137]

11 Be thou as chaste as ice, as pure as snow, thou shalt
not escape calumny. *Ib.* [142]

12 I have heard of your paintings too, well enough. God
hath given you one face, and you make yourselves
another. *Ib.* [150]

13 I say, we will have no more marriages. *Ib.* [156]

14 O! what a noble mind is here o'erthrown:
The courtier's, soldier's, scholar's, eye, tongue, sword;
The expectancy and rose of the fair state,
The glass of fashion, and the mould of form,
The observed of all observers, quite, quite, down!
And I, of ladies most deject and wretched,
That suck'd the honey of his music vows,
Now see that noble and most sovereign reason,
Like sweet bells jangled, out of tune and harsh;
That unmatch'd form and figure of blown youth,
Blasted with ecstasy: O! woe is me,
To have seen what I have seen, see what I see!
Hamlet, III. i. [159]

15 Speak the speech, I pray you, as I pronounced it to
you, trippingly on the tongue; but if you mouth
it, as many of your players do, I had as lief the
town-crier spoke my lines. Nor do not saw the
air too much with your hand, thus; but use all
gently: for in the very torrent, tempest, and—as
I may say—whirlwind of passion, you must
acquire and beget a temperance, that may give it
smoothness. O! it offends me to the soul to hear
a robustious periwig-pated fellow tear a passion to
tatters, to very rags, to split the ears of the ground-
lings, who for the most part are capable of nothing
but inexplicable dumb-shows and noise: I would
have such a fellow whipped for o'erdoing Terma-
gant; it out-herods Herod: pray you, avoid it.
Ib. ii. 1

16 Be not too tame neither, but let your own discretion
be your tutor: suit the action to the word, the word
to the action; with this special observance, that
you o'erstep not the modesty of nature. *Ib.* [19]

17 The purpose of playing, whose end, both at the first
and now, was and is, to hold, as 'twere, the mirror
up to nature. *Ib.* [24]

18 To show . . . the very age and body of the time his
form and pressure. *Ib.* [26]

19 Neither having the accent of Christians nor the gait
of Christian, pagan, nor man. *Ib.* [35]

20 I have thought some of nature's journeymen had
made men, and not made them well, they imitated
humanity so abominably. *Ib.* [38]

21 FIRST PLAYER:
I hope we have reformed that indifferently with us.
HAMLET:
O, reform it altogether. *Ib.* [41]

22 That's villanous, and shows a most pitiful ambition
in the fool that uses it. *Ib.* [49]

23 Horatio, thou art e'en as just a man
As e'er my conversation cop'd withal. *Ib.* [59]

24   Nay, do not think I flatter:
For what advancement may I hope from thee,
That no revenue hast, but thy good spirits? *Ib.* [61]

25 Since my dear soul was mistress of her choice
And could of men distinguish, her election
Hath seal'd thee for herself. *Ib.* [68]

26 A man that fortune's buffets and rewards
Hast ta'en with equal thanks; and bless'd are those
Whose blood and judgment are so well co-mingled
That they are not a pipe for Fortune's finger
To sound what stop she please. Give me that man
That is not passion's slave, and I will wear him
In my heart's core, ay, in my heart of heart,
As I do thee. Something too much of this. *Ib.* [72]

1 And my imaginations are as foul
As Vulcan's stithy.   *Hamlet*, III. ii. [88]

2 The chameleon's dish: I eat the air, promise-crammed.   *Ib.* [98]

3 Here's metal more attractive.   *Ib.* [117]

4 That's a fair thought to lie between maids' legs.
                                            Ib. [126]

5 Die two months ago, and not forgotten yet? Then
there's hope a great man's memory may outlive
his life half a year; but, by'r lady, he must build
churches then.   *Ib.* [140]

6 For, O! for, O! the hobby-horse is forgot. *Ib.* [145]

7 Marry, this is miching mallecho.   *Ib.* [148]

8 OPHELIA:
'Tis brief, my lord.
HAMLET:
As woman's love.   *Ib.* [165]

9 Where love is great, the littlest doubts are fear;
When little fears grow great, great love grows there.
                                            Ib. [183]

10 What to ourselves in passion we propose,
The passion ending, doth the purpose lose. *Ib.* [206]

11 This world is not for aye, nor 'tis not strange
That even our love should with our fortunes change.
                                            Ib. [212]

12 The great man down, you mark his favourite flies;
The poor advanc'd makes friends of enemies.
                                            Ib. [216]

13 Our wills and fates do so contrary run
That our devices still are overthrown.   *Ib.* [223]

14   Sleep rock thy brain;
And never come mischance between us twain!
                                            Ib. [239]

15 The lady doth protest too much, methinks. *Ib.* [242]

16 We that have free souls, it touches us not: let the
galled jade wince, our withers are unwrung.
                                            Ib. [255]

17 The story is extant, and writ in very choice Italian.
                                            Ib. [277]

18 What! frighted with false fire?   *Ib.* [282]

19 So runs the world away.   *Ib.* [289]

20 Put your discourse into some frame, and start not so
wildly from my affair.   *Ib.* [325]

21 O wonderful son, that can so astonish a mother!
                                            Ib. [347]

22 The proverb is something musty.   *Ib.* [366]

23 It will discourse most eloquent music.   *Ib.* [381]

24 You would play upon me; you would seem to know
my stops; you would pluck out the heart of my
mystery; you would sound me from my lowest
note to the top of my compass.   *Ib.* [387]

25 Do you think I am easier to be played on than a pipe?
Call me what instrument you will, though you can
fret me, you cannot play upon me.   *Ib.* [393]

26 HAMLET:
Do you see yonder cloud that's almost in shape of a
camel?
POLONIUS:
By the mass, and 'tis like a camel, indeed.

HAMLET:
Methinks it is like a weasel.
POLONIUS:
It is backed like a weasel.
HAMLET:
Or like a whale?
POLONIUS:
Very like a whale.   *Hamlet*, III. ii. [400]

27 They fool me to the top of my bent.   *Ib.* [408]

28 By and by is easily said.   *Ib.* [411]

29 'Tis now the very witching time of night. *Ib.* [413]

30 Let me be cruel, not unnatural;
I will speak daggers to her, but use none. *Ib.* [420]

31 O! my offence is rank, it smells to heaven. *Ib.* iii. 36

32 My stronger guilt defeats my strong intent;
And, like a man to double business bound,
I stand in pause where I shall first begin,
And both neglect.   *Ib.* 40

33   Whereto serves mercy
But to confront the visage of offence?   *Ib.* 46

34 May one be pardon'd and retain the offence? *Ib.* 56

35   'Tis not so above;
There is no shuffling, there the action lies
In his true nature, and we ourselves compell'd,
Even to the teeth and forehead of our faults
To give in evidence.   *Ib.* 60

36 Now might I do it pat, now he is praying. *Ib.* 73

37 He took my father grossly, full of bread,
With all his crimes broad blown, as flush as May;
And how his audit stands who knows save heaven?
                                            Ib. 80

38 Tell him his pranks have been too broad to bear
with.   *Ib.* iv. 2

39 You go not, till I set you up a glass
Where you may see the inmost part of you. *Ib.* 19

40 How now! a rat? Dead, for a ducat, dead! *Ib.* 23

41 A bloody deed! almost as bad, good mother,
As kill a king, and marry with his brother. *Ib.* 28

42 As false as dicers' oaths.   *Ib.* 45

43 A rhapsody of words.   *Ib.* 48

44   Ay me! what act,
That roars so loud, and thunders in the index?
                                            Ib. 51

45 Look here, upon this picture, and on this. *Ib.* 53

46 Could you on this fair mountain leave to feed,
And batten on this moor?   *Ib.* 66

47 You cannot call it love, for at your age
The hey-day in the blood is tame, it's humble,
And waits upon the judgment.   *Ib.* 68

48   Speak no more;
Thou turn'st mine eyes into my very soul. *Ib.* 88

49 A cut-purse of the empire and the rule,
That from a shelf the precious diadem stole,
And put it in his pocket!   *Ib.* 99

50 A king of shreds and patches.   *Ib.* 102

51 Do you not come your tardy son to chide? *Ib.* 106

52 Conceit in weakest bodies strongest works. *Ib.* 113

1   Bring me to the test,
And I the matter will re-word, which madness
Would gambol from. Mother, for love of grace,
Lay not that flattering unction to your soul.
         Hamlet, III. iv. 142

2   Confess yourself to heaven;
Repent what's past; avoid what is to come. *Ib.* 149

3 For in the fatness of these pursy times,
Virtue itself of vice must pardon beg.   *Ib.* 153

4 QUEEN:
O Hamlet! thou hast cleft my heart in twain.
HAMLET:
O! throw away the worser part of it,
And live the purer with the other half.   *Ib.* 156

5 Assume a virtue, if you have it not.
That monster, custom, who all sense doth eat,
Of habits devil, is angel yet in this.   *Ib.* 160

6 And when you are desirous to be bless'd,
I'll blessing beg of you.   *Ib.* 171

7 I must be cruel, only to be kind.   *Ib.* 178

8 For 'tis the sport to have the enginer
Hoist with his own petar: and it shall go hard
But I will delve one yard below their mines,
And blow them at the moon.   *Ib.* 206

9 He keeps them, like an ape doth nuts, in the corner
of his jaw; first mouthed, to be last swallowed.
       Ib. IV. ii. [19]

10 A knavish speech sleeps in a foolish ear. *Ib.* [25]

11   Diseases desperate grown,
By desperate appliances are reliev'd,
Or not at all.   *Ib.* iii. 9

12 A certain convocation of politic worms are e'en at
him. Your worm is your only emperor for diet.
       Ib. [21]

13 A man may fish with the worm that hath eat of a
king, and eat of the fish that hath fed of that worm.
       Ib. [29]

14 We go to gain a little patch of ground,
That hath in it no profit but the name. *Ib.* iv. 18

15 How all occasions do inform against me,
And spur my dull revenge! What is a man,
If his chief good and market of his time
Be but to sleep and feed? a beast, no more.
Sure he that made us with such large discourse,
Looking before and after, gave us not
That capability and god-like reason
To fust in us unus'd.   *Ib.* 32

16   Some craven scruple
Of thinking too precisely on the event.   *Ib.* 40

17   Rightly to be great
Is not to stir without great argument,
But greatly to find quarrel in a straw
When honour's at the stake.   *Ib.* 53

18 So full of artless jealousy is guilt,
It spills itself in fearing to be spilt.   *Ib.* v. 19

19 How should I your true love know
  From another one?
By his cockle hat and staff,
  And his sandal shoon.   *Ib.* [23]

20 He is dead and gone, lady,
  He is dead and gone,
At his head a grass-green turf;
  At his heels a stone.   *Hamlet*, IV. v. [29]

21 White his shroud as the mountain snow. *Ib.* [36]

22   Larded with sweet flowers;
Which bewept to the grave did go
  With true-love showers.   *Ib.* [38]

23 Then up he rose, and donn'd his clothes. *Ib.* [53]

24 Come, my coach! Good-night, ladies; good-night,
  sweet ladies; good night, good-night. *Ib.* [72]

25 When sorrows come, they come not single spies,
But in battalions.   *Ib.* [78]

26   We have done but greenly
In hugger-mugger to inter him.   *Ib.* [83]

27 There's such divinity doth hedge a king,
That treason can but peep to what it would. *Ib.* [123]

28 To hell, allegiance! vows, to the blackest devil!
Conscience and grace, to the profoundest pit!
I dare damnation.   *Ib.* [130]

29 Nature is fine in love, and where 'tis fine
It sends some precious instance of itself
After the thing it loves.   *Ib.* [160]

30 They bore him barefac'd on the bier;
  Hey non nonny, nonny, hey nonny;
And in his grave rain'd many a tear.   *Ib.* [163]

31 There's rosemary, that's for remembrance; pray,
  love, remember: and there is pansies, that's for
  thoughts.   *Ib.* [174]

32 You must wear your rue with a difference. There's
  a daisy; I would give you some violets, but they
  withered all when my father died.   *Ib.* [181]

33 They say he made a good end.   *Ib.* [184]

34 For bonny sweet Robin is all my joy.   *Ib.* [186]

35 No, no, he is dead;
  Go to thy death-bed,
He never will come again.   *Ib.* [191]

36 He is gone, he is gone,
  And we cast away moan,
God ha' mercy on his soul!   *Ib.* [196]

37 His means of death, his obscure burial,
No trophy, sword, nor hatchment o'er his bones,
No noble rite nor formal ostentation.   *Ib.* [213]

38 And where the offence is let the great axe fall.
       Ib. [218]

39   You must not think
That we are made of stuff so fat and dull
That we can let our beard be shook with danger
And think it pastime.   *Ib.* vii. 30

40 It warms the very sickness in my heart,
That I shall live and tell him to his teeth,
'Thus diddest thou.'   *Ib.* 55

41 A very riband in the cap of youth.   *Ib.* 77

42   He grew into his seat,
And to such wondrous doing brought his horse,
As he had been incorps'd and demi-natur'd
With the brave beast.   *Ib.* 85

43 No place, indeed, should murder sanctuarize. *Ib.* 127

1 There is a willow grows aslant a brook,
That shows his hoar leaves in the glassy stream;
There with fantastic garlands did she come,
Of crow-flowers, nettles, daisies, and long purples,
That liberal shepherds give a grosser name,
But our cold maids do dead men's fingers call them:
There, on the pendent boughs her coronet weeds
Clambering to hang, an envious sliver broke,
When down her weedy trophies and herself
Fell in the weeping brook. Her clothes spread wide,
And, mermaid-like, awhile they bore her up;
Which time she chanted snatches of old tunes,
As one incapable of her own distress.
Hamlet, IV. vii. 167

2 Too much of water hast thou, poor Ophelia,
And therefore I forbid my tears; but yet
It is our trick, nature her custom holds,
Let shame say what it will. *Ib.* 186

3 Is she to be buried in Christian burial that wilfully
seeks her own salvation? *Ib.* v. i. 1

4 Ay, marry, is't; crowner's quest law. *Ib.* [23]

5 There is no ancient gentlemen but gardeners, ditchers
and grave-makers; they hold up Adam's profession.
Ib. [32]

6 The gallows-maker; for that frame outlives a thousand
tenants. *Ib.* [47]

7 Cudgel thy brains no more about it, for your dull ass
will not mend his pace with beating. *Ib.* [61]

8 The houses that he makes last till doomsday.
Ib. [64]

9 Has this fellow no feeling of his business? *Ib.* [71]

10 The hand of little employment hath the daintier
sense. *Ib.* [75]

11 The pate of a politician, . . . one that would circum-
vent God. *Ib.* [84]

12 How absolute the knave is! we must speak by the
card, or equivocation will undo us. *Ib.* [147]

13 The age is grown so picked that the toe of the peasant
comes so near the heel of the courtier, he galls his
kibe. *Ib.* [150]

14 FIRST CLOWN:
He that is mad, and sent into England.
HAMLET:
Ay, marry; why was he sent into England?
FIRST CLOWN:
Why, because he was mad; he shall recover his wits
there; or, if he do not, 'tis no great matter there.
HAMLET:
Why?
FIRST CLOWN:
'Twill not be seen in him there; there the men are
as mad as he. *Ib.* [160]

15 Alas! poor Yorick. I knew him, Horatio; a fellow of
infinite jest, of most excellent fancy; he hath
borne me on his back a thousand times; and now,
how abhorred in my imagination it is! my gorge
rises at it. Here hung those lips that I have kissed
I know not how oft. Where be your gibes now?
your gambols? your songs? your flashes of merriment, that were wont to set the table on a roar?
Not one now, to mock your own grinning? quite
chap-fallen? Now get you to my lady's chamber,
and tell her, let her paint an inch thick, to this
favour she must come. *Ib.* [201]

16 To what base uses we may return, Horatio!
Hamlet, v. i. [222]

17 'Twere to consider too curiously to consider so.
Ib. [226]

18 Imperious Cæsar, dead, and turn'd to clay,
Might stop a hole to keep the wind away. *Ib.* [235]

19 We should profane the service of the dead,
To sing a requiem, and such rest to her
As to peace-parted souls. *Ib.* [258]

20 　　　　　Lay her i' the earth;
And from her fair and unpolluted flesh
May violets spring! I tell thee, churlish priest,
A ministering angel shall my sister be,
When thou liest howling. *Ib.* [260]

21 Sweets to the sweet: farewell! *Ib.* [265]

22 I thought thy bride-bed to have deck'd, sweet maid,
And not have strewed thy grave. *Ib.* [267]

23 For, though I am not splenetive and rash
Yet have I in me something dangerous. *Ib.* [283]

24 I lov'd Ophelia: forty thousand brothers
Could not, with all their quantity of love,
Make up my sum. *Ib.* [291]

25 And thus a while the fit will work on him;
Anon, as patient as the female dove,
When that her golden couplets are disclos'd,
His silence will sit drooping. *Ib.* [307]

26 This grave shall have a living monument. *Ib.* [319]

27 There's a divinity that shapes our ends,
Rough-hew them how we will. *Ib.* ii. 10

28 It did me yeoman's service. *Ib.* 36

29 HAMLET:
Dost know this water-fly?
HORATIO:
　　　　　　　　No, my good lord.
HAMLET:
Thy state is the more gracious; for 'tis a vice to
know him. *Ib.* [84]

30 What imports the nomination of this gentleman?
Ib. [134]

31 The phrase would be more german to the matter, if
we could carry cannon by our sides. *Ib.* [165]

32 'Tis the breathing time of day with me. *Ib.* [181]

33 But thou wouldst not think how ill all's here about
my heart. *Ib.* [222]

34 Not a whit, we defy augury; there's a special providence in the fall of a sparrow. If it be now, 'tis
not to come; if it be not to come, it will be now;
if it be not now, yet it will come: the readiness is
all. *Ib.* [232]

35 I have shot mine arrow o'er the house,
And hurt my brother. *Ib.* [257]

36 Now the king drinks to Hamlet! *Ib.* [292]

37 A hit, a very palpable hit. *Ib.* [295]

38 Why, as a woodcock to mine own springe, Osric;
I am justly kill'd with my own treachery. *Ib.* [320]

39 O villany! Ho! let the door be lock'd:
Treachery! seek it out. *Ib.* [325]

40 The point envenom'd too!—
Then, venom, to thy work. *Ib.* [335].

1   This fell sergeant, death,
Is strict in his arrest.   *Hamlet*, v. ii. [350]

2 Report me and my cause aright.   *Ib.* [353]

3 I am more an antique Roman than a Dane. *Ib.* [355]

4   Horatio, what a wounded name,
Things standing thus unknown, shall live behind me.
If thou didst ever hold me in thy heart,
Absent thee from felicity awhile,
And in this harsh world draw thy breath in pain,
To tell my story.   *Ib.* [358]

5 The potent poison quite o'ercrows my spirit.
        Ib. [367]

6 The rest is silence.   *Ib.* [372]

7 Now cracks a noble heart. Good-night, sweet prince,
And flights of angels sing thee to thy rest! *Ib.* [373]

8   O proud death!
What feast is toward in thine eternal cell? *Ib.* [378]

9   Purposes mistook
Fall'n on the inventors' heads.   *Ib.* [398]

10 For he was likely, had he been put on,
To have prov'd most royally.   *Ib.* [411]

11 So shaken as we are, so wan with care.
      King Henry IV, Part I, I. i. 1

12   In those holy fields
Over whose acres walk'd those blessed feet,
Which fourteen hundred years ago were nail'd
For our advantage, on the bitter cross. *Ib.* 24

13 The blessed sun himself a fair hot wench in flame-
colour'd taffeta.   *Ib.* ii. [10]

14 I see no reason why thou shouldst be so superfluous
to demand the time of the day.   *Ib.* [11]

15 Phœbus, he 'that wandering knight so fair'. *Ib.* [16]

16 Let us be Diana's foresters, gentlemen of the shade,
minions of the moon.   *Ib.* [28]

17 FALSTAFF:
And is not my hostess of the tavern a most sweet
wench?
PRINCE:
As the honey of Hybla, my old lad of the castle.
        Ib. [44]

18 What, in thy quips and thy quiddities? *Ib.* [50]

19 Shall there be gallows standing in England when
thou art king, and resolution thus fobbed as it is
with the rusty curb of old father antick, the law?
        Ib. [66]

20 Thou hast the most unsavoury similes. *Ib.* [89]

21 I would to God thou and I knew where a commodity
of good names were to be bought.   *Ib.* [92]

22 O! thou hast damnable iteration, and art, indeed,
able to corrupt a saint.   *Ib.* [101]

23 Now am I, if a man should speak truly, little better
than one of the wicked.   *Ib.* [105]

24 I'll be damned for never a king's son in Christendom.
        Ib. [108]

25 Why, Hal, 'tis my vocation, Hal; 'tis no sin for a
man to labour in his vocation.   *Ib.* [116]

26 How agrees the devil and thee about thy soul, that
thou soldest him on Good Friday last for a cup
of Madeira and a cold capon's leg? *Ib.* [126]

27 There's neither honesty, manhood, nor good fellowship in thee.   *King Henry IV, Part I*, I. ii. [154]

28 Farewell, thou latter spring! Farewell, All-hallown
summer!   *Ib.* [176]

29 If he fight longer than he sees reason, I'll forswear
arms.   *Ib.* [206]

30 I know you all, and will awhile uphold
The unyok'd humour of your idleness. *Ib.* [217]

31 If all the year were playing holidays,
To sport would be as tedious as to work;
But when they seldom come, they wish'd for come.
        Ib. [226]

32   A certain lord, neat, and trimly dress'd,
Fresh as a bridegroom; and his chin, new-reap'd,
Show'd like a stubble-land at harvest home:
He was perfumed like a milliner,
And 'twixt his finger and his thumb he held
A pouncet-box, which ever and anon
He gave his nose and took't away again. *Ib.* iii. 33

33 And as the soldiers bore dead bodies by,
He call'd them untaught knaves, unmannerly,
To bring a slovenly, unhandsome corpse
Betwixt the wind and his nobility.
With many holiday and lady terms
He question'd me.   *Ib.* 42

34 So pester'd with a popinjay.   *Ib.* 50

35   He made me mad
To see him shine so brisk, and smell so sweet
And talk so like a waiting-gentlewoman
Of guns, and drums, and wounds,—God save the
mark!—
And telling me the sovereign'st thing on earth
Was parmaceti for an inward bruise;
And that it was great pity, so it was,
This villainous saltpetre should be digg'd
Out of the bowels of the harmless earth,
Which many a good tall fellow had destroy'd
So cowardly; and but for these vile guns,
He would himself have been a soldier. *Ib.* 53

36 To put down Richard, that sweet lovely rose,
And plant this thorn, this canker, Bolingbroke.
        Ib. 175

37 WORCESTER:
As to o'er-walk a current roaring loud,
On the unsteadfast footing of a spear.
HOTSPUR:
If he fall in, good-night! or sink or swim:
Send danger from the east unto the west,
So honour cross it from the north to south,
And let them grapple: O! the blood more stirs
To rouse a lion than to start a hare. *Ib.* 192

38 By heaven methinks it were an easy leap
To pluck bright honour from the pale-fac'd moon,
Or dive into the bottom of the deep,
Where fathom-line could never touch the ground,
And pluck up drowned honour by the locks;
So he that doth redeem her thence might wear
Without corrival all her dignities:
But out upon this half-fac'd fellowship! *Ib.* 201

39 Why, what a candy deal of courtesy
This fawning greyhound then did proffer me! *Ib.* 251

40 I know a trick worth two of that.   *Ib.* II. i. [40]

41 At hand, quoth pick-purse.   *Ib.* [53]

1 We have the receipt of fern-seed, we walk invisible.
King Henry IV, Part I, II. i. [95]

2 I am bewitched with the rogue's company. If the rascal have not given me medicines to make me love him, I'll be hanged. *Ib.* ii. [19]

3 Go hang thyself in thine own heir-apparent garters!
Ib. [49]

4 Farewell, and stand fast. *Ib.* [78]

5 Happy man be his dole. *Ib.* [84]

6 On, bacons, on! *Ib.* [99]

7 It would be argument for a week, laughter for a month, and a good jest for ever. *Ib.* [104]

8   Falstaff sweats to death
And lards the lean earth as he walks along. *Ib.* [119]

9 Out of this nettle, danger, we pluck this flower, safety. *Ib.* iii. [11]

10 A good plot, good friends, and full of expectation; an excellent plot, very good friends. *Ib.* [21]

11   Constant you are,
But yet a woman: and for secrecy,
No lady closer; for I well believe
Thou wilt not utter what thou dost not know.
Ib. [113]

12 Show it a fair pair of heels. *Ib.* iv. [52]

13 I am not yet of Percy's mind, the Hotspur of the North; he that kills me some six or seven dozen of Scots at a breakfast, washes his hands, and says to his wife, 'Fie upon this quiet life! I want work.'
Ib. [116]

14 Didst thou never see Titan kiss a dish of butter—pitiful-hearted Titan, that melted at the sweet tale of the sun? *Ib.* [135]

15 There live not three good men unhanged in England, and one of them is fat and grows old. *Ib.* [146]

16 Call you that backing of your friends? A plague upon such backing! give me them that will face me.
Ib. [168]

17 A plague of all cowards, still say I. *Ib.* [175]

18 I am a Jew else; an Ebrew Jew. *Ib.* [201]

19 All! I know not what ye call all. *Ib.* [208]

20 Nay that's past praying for: I have peppered two of them: two I am sure I have paid, two rogues in buckram suits. I tell thee what, Hal, if I tell thee a lie, spit in my face, call me horse. Thou knowest my old ward; here I lay, and thus I bore my point. Four rogues in buckram let drive at me— *Ib.* [214]

21 O monstrous! eleven buckram men grown out of two.
Ib. [247]

22 Three misbegotten knaves in Kendal-green.
Ib. [249]

23 These lies are like the father that begets them; gross as a mountain, open, palpable. *Ib.* [253]

24 Give you a reason on compulsion! if reasons were as plentiful as blackberries I would give no man a reason upon compulsion, I. *Ib.* [267]

25 Mark now, how a plain tale shall put you down.
Ib. [285]

26 What a slave art thou, to hack thy sword as thou hast done, and then say it was in fight! *Ib.* [292]

27 Instinct is a great matter, I was a coward on instinct.
King Henry IV, Part I, II. iv. [304]

28 Ah! No more of that, Hal, an thou lovest me.
Ib. [316]

29 What doth gravity out of his bed at midnight?
Ib. [328]

30 A plague of sighing and grief! It blows a man up like a bladder. *Ib.* [370]

31 I will do it in King Cambyses' vein. *Ib.* [430]

32 QUICKLY:
O Jesu! he doth it as like one of these harlotry players as ever I see!
FALSTAFF:
Peace, good pint-pot! *Ib.* [441]

33 Shall the blessed sun of heaven prove a micher and eat blackberries? A question not to be asked.
Ib. [454]

34 There is a devil haunts thee in the likeness of a fat old man; a tun of man is thy companion.
Ib. [498]

35 That roasted Manningtree ox with the pudding in his belly, that reverend vice, that grey iniquity, that father ruffian, that vanity in years. *Ib.* [504]

36 If sack and sugar be a fault, God help the wicked!
Ib. [524]

37 No, my good lord; banish Peto, banish Bardolph, banish Poins; but for sweet Jack Falstaff, kind Jack Falstaff, true Jack Falstaff, valiant Jack Falstaff, and therefore more valiant, being, as he is, old Jack Falstaff, banish not him thy Harry's company: banish not him thy Harry's company: banish plump Jack and banish all the world. *Ib.* [528]

38 Play out the play. *Ib.* [539]

39 O monstrous! but one half-pennyworth of bread to this intolerable deal of sack! *Ib.* [598]

40 GLENDOWER: At my nativity
The front of heaven was full of fiery shapes,
Of burning cressets; and at my birth
The frame and huge foundation of the earth
Shak'd like a coward.
HOTSPUR:
Why, so it would have done at the same season, if your mother's cat had but kittened. *Ib.* III. i. 13

41 And all the courses of my life do show
I am not in the roll of common men. *Ib.* [42]

42 GLENDOWER:
I can call spirits from the vasty deep.
HOTSPUR:
Why, so can I, or so can any man;
But will they come when you do call for them?
Ib. [53]

43 O! while you live, tell truth, and shame the devil!
Ib. [62]

44 See how this river comes me cranking in,
And cuts me from the best of all my land
A huge half-moon, a monstrous cantle out. *Ib.* [99]

45 I had rather be a kitten and cry mew
Than one of these same metre ballad-mongers.
Ib. [128]

46 Mincing poetry. *Ib.* [133]

1 And such a deal of skimble-skamble stuff
  As puts me from my faith.
               King Henry IV, Part I, III. i. [153]

2   O! he's as tedious
  As a tired horse, a railing wife;
  Worse than a smoky house. I had rather live
  With cheese and garlic in a windmill, far,
  Than feed on cates and have him talk to me
  In any summer-house in Christendom.   *Ib.* [158]

3 I understand thy kisses, and thou mine,
  And that's a feeling disputation.   *Ib.* [204]

4 Makes Welsh as sweet as ditties highly penn'd,
  Sung by a fair queen in a summer's bower,
  With ravishing division, to her lute.   *Ib.* [208]

5 Now I perceive the devil understands Welsh.
                           Ib. [233]

6 You swear like a comfit-maker's wife.   *Ib.* [252]

7 Swear me, Kate, like a lady as thou art,
  A good mouth-filling oath.   *Ib.* [257]

8 The skipping king, he ambled up and down
  With shallow jesters and rash bavin wits. *Ib.* ii. 60

9   Being daily swallow'd by men's eyes,
  They surfeited with honey and began
  To loathe the taste of sweetness, whereof a little
  More than a little is by much too much.
  So, when he had occasion to be seen,
  He was but as the cuckoo is in June,
  Heard, not regarded.   *Ib.* 70

10 My near'st and dearest enemy.   *Ib.* 123

11 Well, I'll repent, and that suddenly, while I am in
  some liking; I shall be out of heart shortly, and
  then I shall have no strength to repent. *Ib.* iii. [5]

12 Company, villanous company, hath been the spoil of
  me.   *Ib.* [10]

13 Come, sing me a bawdy song; make me merry.
                           Ib. [15]

14 Shall I not take mine ease in mine inn?   *Ib.* [91]

15 I have more flesh than another man, and therefore
  more frailty.   *Ib.* [187]

16   That daff'd the world aside,
  And bid it pass.   *Ib.* IV. i. 96

17 All plum'd like estridges that wing the wind,
  Baited like eagles having lately bath'd.   *Ib.* 98

18 I saw young Harry, with his beaver on,
  His cushes on his thighs, gallantly arm'd,
  Rise from the ground like feather'd Mercury,
  And vaulted with such ease into his seat,
  As if an angel dropp'd down from the clouds,
  To turn and wind a fiery Pegasus,
  And witch the world with noble horsemanship.
                            Ib. 104

19 Doomsday is near; die all, die merrily.   *Ib.* 134

20 I have misus'd the king's press damnably. *Ib.* ii. [13]

21 The cankers of a calm world and a long peace.
                           Ib. [32]

22 I am as vigilant as a cat to steal cream.   *Ib.* [64]

23 Tut, tut; good enough to toss; food for powder, food
  for powder; they'll fill a pit as well as better:
  tush, man, mortal men, mortal men.   *Ib.* [72]

24 To the latter end of a fray and the beginning of a
  feast
  Fits a dull fighter and a keen guest.
                King Henry IV, Part I, IV. ii. [86]

25 Greatness knows itself.   *Ib.* iii. 74

26 For mine own part, I could be well content
  To entertain the lag-end of my life
  With quiet hours.   *Ib.* v. i. 23

27 Rebellion lay in his way, and he found it.   *Ib.* 28

28 I do not think a braver gentleman,
  More active-valiant or more valiant-young,
  More daring or more bold, is now alive
  To grace this latter age with noble deeds.
  For my part, I may speak it to my shame,
  I have a truant been to chivalry.   *Ib.* 89

29 FALSTAFF:
  I would it were bed-time, Hal, and all well.
  PRINCE:
  Why, thou owest God a death.   *Ib.* [125]

30 Honour pricks me on. Yea, but how if honour prick
  me off when I come on? how then? Can honour
  set-to a leg? No. Or an arm? No. Or take away
  the grief of a wound? No. Honour hath no skill
  in surgery, then? No. What is honour? A word.
  What is that word, honour? Air. A trim reckoning! Who hath it? He that died o' Wednesday.
  Doth he feel it? No. Doth he hear it? No. It is
  insensible then? Yea, to the dead. But will it not
  live with the living? No. Why? Detraction will
  not suffer it. Therefore I'll none of it: honour is
  a mere scutcheon: and so ends my catechism.
                            Ib. [131]

31 Suspicion all our lives shall be stuck full of eyes;
  For treason is but trusted like the fox,
  Who, ne'er so tame, so cherish'd, and lock'd up,
  Will have a wild trick of his ancestors.   *Ib.* ii. 8

32 O gentlemen! the time of life is short;
  To spend that shortness basely were too long,
  If life did ride upon a dial's point,
  Still ending at the arrival of an hour.
  An if we live, we live to tread on kings;
  If die, brave death, when princes die with us!
  Now, for our consciences, the arms are fair,
  When the intent of bearing them is just.   *Ib.* 81

33 Now, *Esperance*! Percy! and set on.   *Ib.* 96

34 I have led my ragamuffins where they are peppered:
  there's not three of my hundred and fifty left
  alive, and they are for the town's end, to beg
  during life.   *Ib.* iii. [36]

35 I like not such grinning honour as Sir Walter hath:
  give me life; which if I can save, so; if not, honour
  comes unlooked for, and there's an end. *Ib.* [61]

36 Two stars keep not their motion in one sphere.
                            Ib. iv. 65

37 But thought's the slave of life, and life time's fool;
  And time, that takes survey of all the world,
  Must have a stop.   *Ib.* [81]

38   Fare thee well, great heart!
  Ill-weav'd ambition, how much art thou shrunk!
  When that this body did contain a spirit,
  A kingdom for it was too small a bound;
  But now two paces of the vilest earth
  Is room enough: this earth, that bears thee dead,
  Bears not alive so stout a gentleman.   *Ib.* [87]

1 Thy ignominy sleep with thee in the grave,
But not remember'd in thy epitaph!
What! old acquaintance! could not all this flesh
Keep in a little life? Poor Jack, farewell!
I could have better spar'd a better man.
King Henry IV, Part I, v. iv. [100]

2 The better part of valour is discretion. *Ib.* [120]

3   Full bravely hast thou flesh'd
Thy maiden sword. *Ib.* [132]

4 Lord, Lord, how this world is given to lying! I grant
you I was down and out of breath; and so was he;
but we rose both at an instant, and fought a long
hour by Shrewsbury clock. *Ib.* [148]

5 For my part, if a lie may do thee grace,
I'll gild it with the happiest terms I have. *Ib.* [161]

6 I'll purge, and leave sack, and live cleanly, as a
nobleman should do. *Ib.* [168]

7 I speak of peace, while covert enmity
Under the smile of safety wounds the world.
King Henry IV, Part II, Induction, 9

8   Rumour is a pipe
Blown by surmises, jealousies, conjectures,
And of so easy and so plain a stop
That the blunt monster with uncounted heads,
The still-discordant wavering multitude,
Can play upon it. *Ib.* 15

9 Even such a man, so faint, so spiritless,
So dull, so dead in look, so woe-begone,
Drew Priam's curtain in the dead of night,
And would have told him, half his Troy was burn'd.
Ib. I. i. 70

10 Yet the first bringer of unwelcome news
Hath but a losing office, and his tongue
Sounds ever after as a sullen bell,
Remember'd knolling a departed friend. *Ib.* 100

11 The brain of this foolish-compounded clay, man, is
not able to invent anything that tends to laughter,
more than I invent or is invented on me: I am
not only witty in myself, but the cause that wit is
in other men. I do here walk before thee like a sow
that hath overwhelmed all her litter but one. *Ib.* ii. [7]

12 A rascally yea-forsooth knave. *Ib.* [40]

13 Your lordship, though not clean past your youth,
hath yet some smack of age in you, some relish of
the saltness of time. *Ib.* [111]

14 This apoplexy is, as I take it, a kind of lethargy, an't
please your lordship; a kind of sleeping in the
blood, a whoreson tingling. *Ib.* [127]

15 It is the disease of not listening, the malady of not
marking, that I am troubled withal. *Ib.* [139]

16 I am as poor as Job, my lord, but not so patient.
Ib. [145]

17 Well, I am loath to gall a new-healed wound.
Ib. [169]

18 You that are old consider not the capacities of us
that are young; you measure the heat of our livers
with the bitterness of your galls; and we that are
in the vaward of our youth, I must confess, are
wags too. *Ib.* [198]

19 Have you not a moist eye, a dry hand, a yellow cheek,
a white beard, a decreasing leg, an increasing
belly? *Ib.* [206]

20 Every part about you blasted with antiquity.
King Henry IV, Part II, I. ii. [210]

21 My lord, I was born about three of the clock in the
afternoon, with a white head, and something of a
round belly. For my voice, I have lost it with
hollaing, and singing of anthems. *Ib.* [213]

22 CHIEF JUSTICE:
God send the prince a better companion!
FALSTAFF:
God send the companion a better prince! I cannot
rid my hands of him. *Ib.* [227]

23 All you that kiss our lady Peace at home. *Ib.* [236]

24 It was always yet the trick of our English nation, if
they have a good thing, to make it too common.
Ib. [244]

25 I would to God my name were not so terrible to the
enemy as it is: I were better to be eaten to death
with rust than to be scoured to nothing with perpetual motion. *Ib.* [247]

26 I can get no remedy against this consumption of the
purse: borrowing only lingers and lingers it out,
but the disease is incurable. *Ib.* [268]

27   O, thoughts of men accurst!
Past and to come seem best; things present, worst.
Ib. iii. 107

28 A poor lone woman. *Ib.* II. i. [37]

29 Away, you scullion! you rampallion! you fustilarian!
I'll tickle your catastrophe. *Ib.* [67]

30 He hath eaten me out of house and home. *Ib.* [82]

31 Thou didst swear to me upon a parcel-gilt goblet,
sitting in my Dolphin-chamber, at the round
table, by a sea-coal fire, upon Wednesday in
Wheeson week. *Ib.* [97]

32 Doth it not show vilely in me to desire small beer?
Ib. ii. [7]

33 I do now remember the poor creature, small beer.
Ib. [12]

34 Let the end try the man. *Ib.* [52]

35 Never a man's thought in the world keeps the roadway better than thine. *Ib.* [64]

36   He was indeed the glass
Wherein the noble youth did dress themselves.
Ib. iii. 21

37 Hollow pamper'd jades of Asia. *Ib.* iv [177]

38 By my troth, captain, these are very bitter words.
Ib. [183]

39 Thou whoreson little tidy Bartholomew boar-pig.
Ib. [249]

40 Patch up thine old body for heaven. *Ib.* [251]

41   O sleep! O gentle sleep!
Nature's soft nurse, how have I frighted thee,
That thou no more wilt weigh mine eyelids down
And steep my senses in forgetfulness?
Why rather, sleep, liest thou in smoky cribs,
Upon uneasy pallets stretching thee,
And hush'd with buzzing night-flies to thy slumber,
Than in the perfum'd chambers of the great,
Under the canopies of costly state,
And lull'd with sound of sweetest melody?
Ib. III. i. 5

1 Wilt thou upon the high and giddy mast
Seel up the ship-boy's eyes, and rock his brains
In cradle of the rude imperious surge,
And in the visitation of the winds,
Who take the ruffian billows by the top,
Curling their monstrous heads, and hanging them
With deaf'ning clamour in the slippery clouds,
That with the hurly death itself awakes?
       King Henry IV, Part II, III. i. 18

2 With all appliances and means to boot.   *Ib.* 29

3   Then, happy low, lie down!
Uneasy lies the head that wears a crown.   *Ib.* 30

4 O God! that one might read the book of fate. *Ib.* 45

5   O! if this were seen,
The happiest youth, viewing his progress through,
What perils past, what crosses to ensue,
Would shut the book, and sit him down and die.
                       Ib. 54

6 There is a history in all men's lives,
Figuring the nature of the times deceas'd,
The which observ'd, a man may prophesy,
With a near aim, of the main chance of things
As yet not come to life, which in their seeds
And weak beginnings lie intreasured.   *Ib.* 80

7 Death, as the Psalmist saith, is certain to all; all shall
die. How a good yoke of bullocks at Stamford
fair?   *Ib.* ii. [41]

8 And is old Double dead?   *Ib.* [58]

9 A soldier is better accommodated than with a wife.
                       Ib. [73]

10 Most forcible Feeble.   *Ib.* [181]

11 We have heard the chimes at midnight. *Ib.* [231]

12 I care not; a man can die but once; we owe God a
death.   *Ib.* [253]

13 He that dies this year is quit for the next. *Ib.* [257]

14 Lord, Lord, how subject we old men are to this vice
of lying!   *Ib.* [329]

15 Like a man made after supper of a cheese-paring:
when a' was naked, he was, for all the world, like
a forked radish, with a head fantastically carved
upon it with a knife.   *Ib.* [335]

16 Talks as familiarly of John a Gaunt as if he had been
sworn brother to him.   *Ib.* [348]

17 Against ill chances men are ever merry,
But heaviness foreruns the good event. *Ib.* IV. ii. 81

18 A peace is of the nature of a conquest;
For then both parties nobly are subdu'd,
And neither party loser.   *Ib.* 89

19 That I may justly say with the hook-nosed fellow of
Rome, 'I came, saw, and overcame.' *Ib.* iii. [44]

20 A man cannot make him laugh; but that's no marvel;
he drinks no wine.   *Ib.* [95]

21 A good sherris-sack hath a two-fold operation in it.
It ascends me into the brain; dries me there all the
foolish and dull and crudy vapours which environ
it; makes it apprehensive, quick, forgetive, full of
nimble fiery and delectable shapes; which, deliver'd o'er to the voice, the tongue, which is the
birth, becomes excellent wit. The second property
of your excellent sherris is, the warming of the
blood; which, before cold and settled, left the liver

white and pale, which is the badge of pusillanimity
and cowardice: but the sherris warms it and makes
it course from the inwards to the parts extreme.
It illumineth the face, which, as a beacon, gives
warning to all the rest of this little kingdom, man,
to arm; and then the vital commoners and inland
petty spirits muster me all to their captain, the
heart, who, great and puffed up with this retinue,
doth any deed of courage; and this valour comes
of sherris. So that skill in the weapon is nothing
without sack, for that sets it a-work; and learning,
a mere hoard of gold kept by a devil till sack
commences it and sets it in act and use.
       King Henry IV, Part II, IV. iii. [103]

22 If I had a thousand sons, the first human principle
I would teach them should be, to forswear thin
potations.   *Ib.* [133]

23 Most subject is the fattest soil to weeds. *Ib.* iv. 54

24   Thou art a summer bird,
Which ever in the haunch of winter sings
The lifting up of day.   *Ib.* [91]

25 O polish'd perturbation! golden care!
That keep'st the ports of slumber open wide
To many a watchful night! Sleep with it now!
Yet not so sound, and half so deeply sweet
As he whose brow with homely biggin bound
Snores out the watch of night.   *Ib.* v. 22

26 This sleep is sound indeed; this is a sleep
That from this golden rigol hath divorc'd
So many English kings.   *Ib.* 34

27 Thy wish was father, Harry, to that thought. *Ib.* 91

28   Commit
The oldest sins the newest kind of ways. *Ib.* 124

29 It hath been prophesied to me many years
I should not die but in Jerusalem,
Which vainly I suppos'd the Holy Land.
But bear me to that chamber; there I'll lie:
In that Jerusalem shall Harry die.   *Ib.* 235

30 Any pretty little tiny kickshaws, tell William cook.
                     Ib. v. i. [29]

31 Not Amurath an Amurath succeeds,
But Harry, Harry.   *Ib.* ii. 48

32 Sorrow so royally in you appears,
That I will deeply put the fashion on.   *Ib.* 51

33 'Tis merry in hall when beards wag all. *Ib.* iii. [35]

34 A foutra for the world, and worldlings base!
I speak of Africa and golden joys.   *Ib.* [100]

35 Under which king, Bezonian? speak, or die!
                       Ib. [116]

36 Let us take any man's horses; the laws of England
are at my commandment.   *Ib.* [139]

37 I know thee not, old man: fall to thy prayers;
How ill white hairs become a fool and jester!
I have long dream'd of such a kind of man,
So surfeit-swell'd, so old, and so profane. *Ib.* v. [52]

38 Make less thy body hence, and more thy grace;
Leave gormandising; know the grave doth gape
For thee thrice wider than for other men. *Ib.* [57]

39 Presume not that I am the thing I was.   *Ib.* [61]

40 Master Shallow, I owe you a thousand pound.
                        Ib. [78]

1 Where, for anything I know, Falstaff shall die of a sweat, unless already a' be killed with your hard opinions; for Oldcastle died a martyr, and this is not the man.
King Henry IV, Part II. Epilogue, [32]

2 O! for a Muse of fire, that would ascend
The brightest heaven of invention.
King Henry V, Chorus, 1

3 The flat unraised spirits. *Ib.* 9

4   Can this cockpit hold
The vasty fields of France? or may we cram
Within this wooden O the very casques
That did affright the air at Agincourt? *Ib.* 11

5 Consideration like an angel came,
And whipp'd the offending Adam out of him.
Ib. I. i. 28

6 Never came reformation in a flood,
With such a heady currance, scouring faults. *Ib.* 33

7   When he speaks,
The air, a charter'd libertine, is still. *Ib.* 47

8 O noble English! that could entertain
With half their forces the full pride of France,
And let another half stand laughing by,
All out of work, and cold for action. *Ib.* ii. 111

9 And make your chronicle as rich with praise
As is the owse and bottom of the sea
With sunken wrack and sumless treasuries. *Ib.* 163

10   For so work the honey-bees,
Creatures that by a rule in nature teach
The act of order to a peopled kingdom.
They have a king and officers of sorts;
Where some, like magistrates, correct at home,
Others, like merchants, venture trade abroad,
Others, like soldiers, armed in their stings,
Make boot upon the summer's velvet buds;
Which pillage they with merry march bring home
To the tent-royal of their emperor:
Who, busied in his majesty, surveys
The singing masons building roofs of gold,
The civil citizens kneading up the honey,
The poor mechanic porters crowding in
Their heavy burdens at his narrow gate,
The sad-ey'd justice, with his surly hum,
Delivering o'er to executors pale
The lazy yawning drone. *Ib.* 187

11 His present and your pains we thank you for:
When we have match'd our rackets to these balls,
We will in France, by God's grace, play a set
Shall strike his father's crown into the hazard.
Ib. 260

12 Now all the youth of England are on fire,
And silken dalliance in the wardrobe lies;
Now thrive the armourers, and honour's thought
Reigns solely in the breast of every man:
They sell the pasture now to buy the horse,
Following the mirror of all Christian kings,
With winged heels, as English Mercuries.
For now sits Expectation in the air
And hides a sword from hilts unto the point
With crowns imperial, crowns and coronets,
Promis'd to Harry and his followers.
Ib. II. Chorus, 1

13 O England! model to thy inward greatness,
Like little body with a mighty heart,
What might'st thou do, that honour would thee do,
Were all thy children kind and natural!
But see thy fault! *King Henry V*, II. Chorus, 16

14 I dare not fight; but I will wink and hold out mine iron. *Ib.* i. [7]

15 That's the humour of it. *Ib.* [63]

16 Base is the slave that pays. *Ib.* [100]

17 For, lambkins, we will live. *Ib.* [134]

18 Would I were with him, wheresome'er he is, either in heaven or in hell. *Ib.* iii. [7]

19 He's in Arthur's bosom, if ever man went to Arthur's bosom. A' made a finer end, and went away an it had been any christom child; a' parted even just between twelve and one, even at the turning o' the tide: for after I saw him fumble with the sheets and play with flowers and smile upon his fingers' ends, I knew there was but one way; for his nose was as sharp as a pen, and a' babbled of green fields. [Theobald's emendation of the Folio's reading: 'A table of green fields'.] *Ib.* [9]

20 So a' cried out 'God, God, God!' three or four times: now I, to comfort him, bid him a' should not think of God, I hoped there was no need to trouble himself with any such thoughts yet. *Ib.* [19]

21 As cold as any stone. *Ib.* [25]

22 BOY:
Yes, that a' did; and said they were devils incarnate.
HOSTESS:
A' never could abide carnation; 'twas a colour he never liked.
BOY:
A' said once, the devil would have him about women.
Ib. [33]

23   Trust none;
For oaths are straws, men's faiths are wafer-cakes,
And hold-fast is the only dog, my duck. *Ib.* [53]

24 Once more unto the breach, dear friends, once more;
Or close the wall up with our English dead!
In peace there's nothing so becomes a man
As modest stillness and humility:
But when the blast of war blows in our ears,
Then imitate the action of the tiger;
Stiffen the sinews, summon up the blood,
Disguise fair nature with hard-favour'd rage;
Then lend the eye a terrible aspect. *Ib.* III. i. 1

25   On, on you noblest English!
Whose blood is fet from fathers of war-proof;
Fathers that, like so many Alexanders,
Have in these parts from morn till even fought,
And sheath'd their swords for lack of argument. *Ib.* 17

26   And you, good yeomen,
Whose limbs were made in England, show us here
The mettle of your pasture. *Ib.* 25

27 I see you stand like greyhounds in the slips,
Straining upon the start. The game's afoot:
Follow your spirit; and, upon this charge
Cry 'God for Harry! England and Saint George!'
Ib. 31

28 I would give all my fame for a pot of ale, and safety. *Ib.* ii. [14]

29 Men of few words are the best men. *Ib.* [40]

1 A' never broke any man's head but his own, and that was against a post when he was drunk.

King Henry V, III. ii. [43]

2 He will maintain his argument as well as any military man in the world, in the disciplines of the pristine wars of the Romans. *Ib.* [89]

3 One Bardolph, if your majesty know the man: his face is all bubukles, and whelks, and knobs, and flames o' fire. *Ib.* vi. [110]

4 I thought upon one pair of English legs
Did march three Frenchmen. *Ib.* [161]

5 Give them great meals of beef and iron and steel, they will eat like wolves and fight like devils.

Ib. vii. [166]

6 Now entertain conjecture of a time
When creeping murmur and the poring dark
Fills the wide vessel of the universe.
From camp to camp, through the foul womb of night,
The hum of either army stilly sounds,
That the fix'd sentinels almost receive
The secret whispers of each other's watch.
Fire answers fire, and through their paly flames
Each battle sees the other's umber'd face:
Steed threatens steed, in high and boastful neighs
Piercing the night's dull ear; and from the tents
The armourers, accomplishing the knights,
With busy hammers closing rivets up,
Give dreadful note of preparation. *Ib.* IV. Chorus, 1

7 The royal captain of this ruin'd band. *Ib.* 29

8 A largess universal, like the sun
His liberal eye doth give to every one,
Thawing cold fear. *Ib.* 43

9 A little touch of Harry in the night. *Ib.* 47

10 O for pity,—we shall much disgrace,
With four or five most vile and ragged foils,
Right ill dispos'd in brawl ridiculous,
The name of Agincourt. *Ib.* 49

11 Gloucester, 'tis true that we are in great danger;
The greater therefore should our courage be.

Ib. IV. i. 1

12 There is some soul of goodness in things evil,
Would men observingly distil it out. *Ib.* 4

13 Thus may we gather honey from the weed,
And make a moral of the devil himself. *Ib.* 11

14 Art thou base, common and popular? *Ib.* 37

15 Trail'st thou the puissant pike? *Ib.* 40

16 If you would take the pains but to examine the wars of Pompey the Great, you shall find, I warrant you, that there is no tiddle-taddle nor pibble-pabble in Pompey's camp. *Ib.* [69]

17 There is much care and valour in this Welshman.

Ib. [85]

18 I think the king is but a man, as I am: the violet smells to him as it doth to me. *Ib.* [106]

19 I am afeard there are few die well that die in a battle; for how can they charitably dispose of any thing when blood is their argument? *Ib.* [149]

20 Every subject's duty is the king's; but every subject's soul is his own. *Ib.* [189]

21 Upon the king! let us our lives, our souls,
Our debts, our careful wives,
Our children, and our sins lay on the king!
We must bear all. O hard condition!

King Henry V, IV. ii. [250]

22 What infinite heart's ease
Must kings neglect, that private men enjoy!
And what have kings that privates have not too,
Save ceremony, save general ceremony? *Ib.* [256]

23 'Tis not the balm, the sceptre and the ball,
The sword, the mace, the crown imperial,
The intertissued robe of gold and pearl,
The farced title running 'fore the king,
The throne he sits on, nor the tide of pomp
That beats upon the high shore of this world,
No, not all these, thrice-gorgeous ceremony,
Not all these, laid in bed majestical,
Can sleep so soundly as the wretched slave,
Who with a body fill'd and vacant mind
Gets him to rest, cramm'd with distressful bread;
Never sees horrid night, the child of hell,
But, like a lackey, from the rise to set
Sweats in the eye of Phœbus, and all night
Sleeps in Elysium; next day after dawn,
Doth rise and help Hyperion to his horse,
And follows so the ever-running year
With profitable labour to his grave:
And, but for ceremony, such a wretch,
Winding up days with toil and nights with sleep,
Hath the forehand and vantage of a king. *Ib.* [280]

24 O God of battles! steel my soldiers' hearts;
Possess them not with fear; take from them now
The sense of reckoning, if the opposed numbers
Pluck their hearts from them. *Ib.* [309]

25 O! that we now had here
But one ten thousand of those men in England
That do no work to-day. *Ib.* iii. 16

26 If we are mark'd to die, we are enow
To do our country loss; and if to live,
The fewer men, the greater share of honour. *Ib.* 20

27 I am not covetous for gold,
. . . . .
But if it be a sin to covet honour
I am the most offending soul alive. *Ib.* 24

28 He which hath no stomach to this fight,
Let him depart; his passport shall be made,
And crowns for convoy put into his purse:
We would not die in that man's company
That fears his fellowship to die with us.
This day is called the feast of Crispian:
He that outlives this day and comes safe home,
Will stand a tip-toe when this day is nam'd,
And rouse him at the name of Crispian.
He that shall live this day, and see old age,
Will yearly on the vigil feast his neighbours,
And say, 'To-morrow is Saint Crispian:'
Then will he strip his sleeve and show his scars,
And say, 'These wounds I had on Crispin's day.'
Old men forget: yet all shall be forgot,
But he'll remember with advantages
What feats he did that day. Then shall our names,
Familiar in his mouth as household words,
Harry the King, Bedford and Exeter,
Warwick and Talbot, Salisbury and Gloucester,
Be in their flowing cups freshly remember'd.
This story shall the good man teach his son;
And Crispin Crispian shall ne'er go by,

From this day to the ending of the world,
But we in it shall be remembered;
We few, we happy few, we band of brothers;
For he to-day that sheds his blood with me
Shall be my brother; be he ne'er so vile
This day shall gentle his condition:
And gentlemen in England, now a-bed
Shall think themselves accurs'd they were not here,
And hold their manhoods cheap whiles any speaks
That fought with us upon Saint Crispin's day.
King Henry V, IV. iii. 35

1 Thou damned and luxurious mountain goat.
Ib. iv. [20]

2 I'll fer him, and firk him, and ferret him. *Ib.* [29]

3 And all my mother came into mine eyes
And gave me up to tears. *Ib.* vi. 31

4 There is a river in Macedon, and there is also moreover a river at Monmouth: . . . and there is salmons
in both. *Ib.* vii. [28]

5 But now behold,
In the quick forge and working-house of thought,
How London doth pour out her citizens.
Ib. v. Chorus, 22

6 Were now the general of our gracious empress,—
As in good time he may,—from Ireland coming,
Bringing rebellion broached on his sword. *Ib.* 30

7 There is occasions and causes why and wherefore in
all things. *Ib.* v. i. [3]

8 Not for Cadwallader and all his goats. *Ib.* [29]

9 By this leek, I will most horribly revenge. *Ib.* [49]

10 Why that the naked, poor, and mangled Peace,
Dear nurse of arts, plenties, and joyful births.
Ib. ii. 34

11 The even mead, that erst brought sweetly forth
The freckled cowslip, burnet, and green clover,
.   .   .   .   .
Conceives by idleness, and nothing teems
But hateful docks, rough thistles, kecksies, burs.
Ib. 48

12 If not, to say to thee that I shall die, is true; but for
thy love, by the Lord, no; yet I love thee too.
Ib. [157]

13 For these fellows of infinite tongue, that can rhyme
themselves into ladies' favours, they do always
reason themselves out again. *Ib.* [162]

14 Shall not thou and I, between Saint Denis and Saint
George, compound a boy, half-French, half-
English, that shall go to Constantinople and take
the Turk by the beard? *Ib.* [218]

15 It is not a fashion for the maids in France to kiss
before they are married. *Ib.* [287]

16 God, the best maker of all marriages,
Combine your hearts in one. *Ib.* [387]

17 Hung be the heavens with black, yield day to night!
King Henry VI, Part I, I. i. 1

18 Expect Saint Martin's summer, halcyon days.
Ib. ii. 131

19 Unbidden guests
Are often welcomest when they are gone.
Ib. II. ii. 55

20 But in these nice sharp quillets of the law,
Good faith, I am no wiser than a daw. *Ib.* iv. 17

21 From off this brier pluck a white rose with me.
King Henry VI, Part I, II. iv. 30

22 Pluck a red rose from off this thorn with me. *Ib.* 33

23 PLANTAGENET:
Hath not thy rose a canker, Somerset?
SOMERSET:
Hath not thy rose a thorn, Plantagenet? *Ib.* 68

24 Delays have dangerous ends. *Ib.* III. ii. 33

25 I owe him little duty and less love. *Ib.* IV. iv. 34

26 So doth the swan her downy cygnets save,
Keeping them prisoners underneath her wings.
Ib. v. iii. 56

27 She's beautiful and therefore to be woo'd;
She is a woman, therefore to be won; *Ib.* 78

28 She bears a duke's revenues on her back,
And in her heart she scorns our poverty.
King Henry VI, Part II, I. iii. [83]

29 Could I come near your beauty with my nails
I'd set my ten commandments in your face. *Ib.* [144]

30 What stronger breastplate than a heart untainted!
Thrice is he arm'd that hath his quarrel just,
And he but naked, though lock'd up in steel,
Whose conscience with injustice is corrupted.
Ib. III. ii. 232

31 He dies, and makes no sign. *Ib.* iii. 29

32 Forbear to judge, for we are sinners all.
Close up his eyes, and draw the curtain close;
And let us all to meditation. *Ib.* 31

33 The gaudy, blabbing, and remorseful day
Is crept into the bosom of the sea. *Ib.* IV. i. 1

34 True nobility is exempt from fear. *Ib.* 129

35 I say it was never merry world in England since
gentlemen came up. *Ib.* ii. [10]

36 There shall be in England seven halfpenny loaves
sold for a penny; the three-hooped pot shall have
ten hoops; and I will make it felony to drink small
beer. *Ib.* [73]

37 The first thing we do, let's kill all the lawyers.
Ib. [86]

38 Is not this a lamentable thing, that of the skin of an
innocent lamb should be made parchment? that
parchment, being scribbled o'er, should undo a
man? *Ib.* [88]

39 And Adam was a gardener. *Ib.* [146]

40 Thou hast most traitorously corrupted the youth of
the realm in erecting a grammar school: and
whereas, before, our forefathers had no other
books but the score and the tally, thou hast
caused printing to be used; and, contrary to the
king, his crown and dignity, thou hast built a
paper-mill. *Ib.* vii. [35]

41 Away with him! away with him! he speaks Latin.
Ib. [62]

42 Lord, who would live turmoiled in the court,
And may enjoy such quiet walks as these? *Ib.* x. [18]

43 O tiger's heart wrapp'd in a woman's hide!
King Henry VI, Part III, I. iv. 137

44 This battle fares like to the morning's war,
When dying clouds contend with growing light,
What time the shepherd, blowing of his nails,
Can neither call it perfect day nor night. *Ib.* II. v. 1

1 O God! methinks it were a happy life,
To be no better than a homely swain;
To sit upon a hill, as I do now,
To carve out dials, quaintly, point by point,
Thereby to see the minutes how they run,
How many make the hour full complete;
How many hours bring about the day;
How many days will finish up the year;
How many years a mortal man may live.
King Henry VI, Part III, II. v. 21

2 Gives not the hawthorn bush a sweeter shade
To shepherds, looking on their silly sheep,
Than doth a rich embroider'd canopy
To kings that fear their subjects' treachery? *Ib.* 42

3　　　　　See, see! what showers arise,
Blown with the windy tempest of my heart. *Ib.* 85

4　　　　　Warwick, peace;
Proud setter up and puller down of kings.
Ib. III. iii. 156

5 A little fire is quickly trodden out,
Which, being suffer'd, rivers cannot quench.
Ib. IV. viii. 7

6 Live we how we can, yet die we must. *Ib.* V. ii. 28

7 Suspicion always haunts the guilty mind;
The thief doth fear each bush an officer. *Ib.* vi. 11

8 Down, down to hell; and say I sent thee thither.
Ib. 67

9　　　　　They
Made Britain India: every man that stood
Show'd like a mine. *King Henry VIII*, I. i. 20

10 Heat not a furnace for your foe so hot
That it do singe yourself. *Ib.* 140

11 If I chance to talk a little wild, forgive me;
I had it from my father. *Ib.* iv. 26

12 The mirror of all courtesy. *Ib.* II. i. 53

13 Go with me, like good angels, to my end;
And, as the long divorce of steel falls on me,
Make of your prayers one sweet sacrifice,
And lift my soul to heaven. *Ib.* 75

14 CHAMBERLAIN:
It seems the marriage with his brother's wife
Has crept too near his conscience.
SUFFOLK:
　　　　　No; his conscience
Has crept too near another lady. *Ib.* ii. [17]

15 This bold bad man. *Ib.* [44]

16　　　　　Verily,
I swear, 'tis better to be lowly born,
And range with humble livers in content,
Than to be perk'd up, in a glist'ring grief,
And wear a golden sorrow. *Ib.* iii. 18

17　　　　　I would not be a queen
For all the world. *Ib.* 45

18 Orpheus with his lute made trees,
And the mountain-tops that freeze,
　Bow themselves when he did sing:
To his music plants and flowers
Ever sprung; as sun and showers
　There had made a lasting spring.

Everything that heard him play,
Even the billows of the sea,
　Hung their heads, and then lay by.

In sweet music is such art,
Killing care and grief of heart
　Fall asleep, or hearing die. *King Henry VIII*, III. i. 3

19 Heaven is above all yet; there sits a judge,
That no king can corrupt. *Ib.* 99

20 A spleeny Lutheran. *Ib.* ii. 100

21　　　　　'Tis well said again;
And 'tis a kind of good deed to say well:
And yet words are no deeds. *Ib.* 153

22　　　　　And then to breakfast, with
What appetite you have. *Ib.* 203

23　　　　　That in all you writ to Rome, or else
To foreign princes, '*Ego et Rex meus*'
Was still inscrib'd. *Ib.* 314

24 Farewell! a long farewell, to all my greatness!
This is the state of man: to-day he puts forth
The tender leaves of hope; to-morrow blossoms,
And bears his blushing honours thick upon him;
The third day comes a frost, a killing frost;
And, when he thinks, good easy man, full surely
His greatness is a-ripening, nips his root,
And then he falls, as I do. I have ventur'd,
Like little wanton boys that swim on bladders,
This many summers in a sea of glory,
But far beyond my depth: my high-blown pride
At length broke under me, and now has left me
Weary and old with service, to the mercy
Of a rude stream that must for ever hide me.
Vain pomp and glory of this world, I hate ye:
I feel my heart new open'd. O how wretched
Is that poor man that hangs on princes' favours!
There is, betwixt that smile we would aspire to,
That sweet aspect of princes, and their ruin,
More pangs and fears than wars or women have;
And when he falls, he falls like Lucifer,
Never to hope again. *Ib.* 352

25 A peace above all earthly dignities,
A still and quiet conscience. *Ib.* 380

26 A load would sink a navy. *Ib.* 384

27 There was the weight that pull'd me down. O
Cromwell!
The king has gone beyond me: all my glories
In that one woman I have lost for ever. *Ib.* 408

28 Cromwell, I did not think to shed a tear
In all my miseries; but thou hast forc'd me,
Out of thy honest truth, to play the woman. *Ib.* 429

29 Let's dry our eyes: and thus far hear me, Cromwell;
And, when I am forgotten, as I shall be,
And sleep in dull cold marble, where no mention
Of me more must be heard of, say, I taught thee,
Say, Wolsey, that once trod the ways of glory,
And sounded all the depths and shoals of honour,
Found thee a way, out of his wrack, to rise in;
A sure and safe one, though thy master miss'd it.
Ib. 432

30 Cromwell, I charge thee, fling away ambition:
By that sin fell the angels. *Ib.* 441

31 Love thyself last: cherish those hearts that hate thee;
Corruption wins not more than honesty.
Still in thy right hand carry gentle peace,
To silence envious tongues: be just, and fear not.
Let all the ends thou aim'st at be thy country's,
Thy God's, and truth's: then if thou fall'st, O Cromwell!
Thou fall'st a blessed martyr. *Ib.* 444

1 Had I but serv'd my God with half the zeal
I serv'd my king, he would not in mine age
Have left me naked to mine enemies.
King Henry VIII, III. ii. 456

2 She had all the royal makings of a queen. *Ib.* IV. i. 87

3 An old man, broken with the storms of state
Is come to lay his weary bones among ye;
Give him a little earth for charity. *Ib.* ii. 21

4 He gave his honours to the world again,
His blessed part to Heaven, and slept in peace.
Ib. 29

5 So may he rest; his faults lie gently on him! *Ib.* 31

6   He was a man
Of an unbounded stomach. *Ib.* 33

7 His promises were, as he then was, mighty;
But his performance, as he is now, nothing. *Ib.* 41

8 Men's evil manners live in brass; their virtues
We write in water. *Ib.* 45

9 He was a scholar, and a ripe and good one;
Exceeding wise, fair-spoken, and persuading:
Lofty and sour to them that lov'd him not;
But, to those men that sought him, sweet as summer.
Ib. 51

10 Those twins of learning that he rais'd in you,
Ipswich and Oxford! *Ib.* 58

11 After my death I wish no other herald,
No other speaker of my living actions,
To keep mine honour from corruption,
Than such an honest chronicler as Griffith. *Ib.* 69

12 To dance attendance on their lordships' pleasures.
Ib. v. ii. 30

13   'Tis a cruelty
To load a falling man. *Ib.* 76

14 In her days every man shall eat in safety
Under his own vine what he plants; and sing
The merry songs of peace to all his neighbours.
Ib. v. 34

15   Those about her
From her shall read the perfect ways of honour.
Ib. 37

16 Nor shall this peace sleep with her; but as when
The bird of wonder dies, the maiden phœnix,
Her ashes new-create another heir
As great in admiration as herself. *Ib.* 40

17   Some come to take their ease
And sleep an act or two. *Ib.* Epilogue, 2

18 Lord of thy presence and no land beside.
King John, I. i. 137

19 For new-made honour doth forget men's names.
Ib. 186

20 Sweet, sweet, sweet poison for the age's tooth.
Ib. 213

21 Bearing their birthrights proudly on their backs.
Ib. II. i. 70

22 For courage mounteth with occasion. *Ib.* 82

23 Saint George, that swinged the dragon, and e'er since
Sits on his horse back at mine hostess' door. *Ib.* 288

24 Mad world! Mad kings! Mad composition! *Ib.* 561

25 That smooth-fac'd gentleman, tickling Commodity,
Commodity, the bias of the world. *Ib.* 573

26 Well, whiles I am a beggar, I will rail,
And say there is no sin, but to be rich;
And, being rich, my virtue then shall be,
To say there is no vice, but beggary.
King John, II. i. 593

27   Here I and sorrows sit;
Here is my throne, bid kings come bow to it.
Ib. III. i. 73

28 Thou wear a lion's hide! doff it for shame,
And hang a calf's-skin on those recreant limbs!
Ib. 128

29   No Italian priest
Shall tithe or toll in our dominions. *Ib.* 153

30 Old Time the clock-setter, that bald sexton, Time.
Ib. 324

31 Bell, book, and candle shall not drive me back,
When gold and silver becks me to come on.
Ib. iii. 12

32 KING JOHN:
Death.
HUBERT:
          My lord?
KING JOHN:
          A grave.
HUBERT:
          He shall not live.
KING JOHN:
          Enough.
I could be merry now. *Ib.* 66

33 Look, who comes here! a grave unto a soul;
Holding the eternal spirit, against her will,
In the vile prison of afflicted breath. *Ib.* iv. 17

34 Grief fills the room up of my absent child,
Lies in his bed, walks up and down with me,
Puts on his pretty looks, repeats his words,
Remembers me of all his gracious parts,
Stuffs out his vacant garments with his form. *Ib.* 93

35 Life is as tedious as a twice-told tale,
Vexing the dull ear of a drowsy man. *Ib.* 108

36 Heat me these irons hot. *Ib.* IV. i. 1

37 Methinks nobody should be sad but I:
Yet I remember, when I was in France,
Young gentlemen would be as sad as night,
Only for wantonness. *Ib.* 13

38 I knit my handkercher about your brows,—
The best I had, a princess wrought it me. *Ib.* 41

39 To gild refined gold, to paint the lily,
To throw a perfume on the violet,
To smooth the ice, or add another hue
Unto the rainbow, or with taper light
To seek the beauteous eye of heaven to garnish,
Is wasteful and ridiculous excess. *Ib.* ii. 11

40 The spirit of the time shall teach me speed. *Ib.* 176

41 Another lean unwash'd artificer. *Ib.* 201

42 It is the curse of kings to be attended
By slaves that take their humours for a warrant
To break within the bloody house of life. *Ib.* 208

43 How oft the sight of means to do ill deeds
Makes ill deeds done! *Ib.* 219

44 Whate'er you think, good words, I think, were best.
Ib. iii. 28

45 Unthread the rude eye of rebellion,
And welcome home again discarded faith. *Ib.* v. iv. 11

1 I beg cold comfort. *King John*, v. vii. 42

2 This England never did, nor never shall,
Lie at the proud foot of a conqueror,
But when it first did help to wound itself.
Now these her princes are come home again,
Come the three corners of the world in arms,
And we shall shock them: nought shall make us rue,
If England to itself do rest but true. *Ib.* 112

3 Hence! home, you idle creatures, get you home:
Is this a holiday? *Julius Cæsar*, I. i. 1

4 What trade, thou knave? thou naughty knave, what
trade? *Ib.* [15]

5 FLAVIUS:
Thou art a cobbler, art thou?
2ND COMMONER:
Truly, sir, all that I live by is with the awl: ... I am
indeed, sir, a surgeon to old shoes. *Ib.* [22]

6 As proper men as ever trod upon neat's-leather.
Ib. [27]

7 Wherefore rejoice? What conquest brings he home?
Ib. [36]

8 You blocks, you stones, you worse than senseless
things!
O you hard hearts, you cruel men of Rome,
Knew you not Pompey? *Ib.* [39]

9 Have you not made a universal shout,
That Tiber trembled underneath her banks,
To hear the replication of your sounds
Made in her concave shores? *Ib.* [48]

10 Speak; Cæsar is turn'd to hear. *Ib.* ii. 17

11 Beware the ides of March. *Ib.* 18

12 He is a dreamer; let us leave him: pass. *Ib.* 24

13 I am not gamesome: I do lack some part
Of that quick spirit that is in Antony. *Ib.* 28

14 Brutus, I do observe you now of late:
I have not from your eyes that gentleness
And show of love as I was wont to have:
You bear too stubborn and too strange a hand
Over your friend that loves you. *Ib.* 32

15 Poor Brutus, with himself at war,
Forgets the shows of love to other men. *Ib.* 46

16 Set honour in one eye and death i' the other,
And I will look on both indifferently. *Ib.* 86

17 Well, honour is the subject of my story.
I cannot tell what you and other men
Think of this life: but, for my single self,
I had as lief not be as live to be
In awe of such a thing as I myself. *Ib.* 92

18 'Dar'st thou, Cassius, now,
Leap in with me into this angry flood,
And swim to yonder point?' Upon the word,
Accoutred as I was, I plunged in,
And bade him follow. *Ib.* 102

19 Stemming it with hearts of controversy. *Ib.* 109

20 His coward lips did from their colour fly,
And that same eye whose bend doth awe the world
Did lose his lustre. *Ib.* 122

21 Ye gods, it doth amaze me,
A man of such a feeble temper should
So get the start of the majestic world,
And bear the palm alone. *Ib.* 128

22 Why, man, he doth bestride the narrow world
Like a Colossus; and we petty men
Walk under his huge legs, and peep about
To find ourselves dishonourable graves.
Men at some time are masters of their fates:
The fault, dear Brutus, is not in our stars,
But in ourselves, that we are underlings.
Julius Cæsar, I. ii.134

23 'Brutus' will start a spirit as soon as 'Cæsar'.
Now in the names of all the gods at once,
Upon what meat doth this our Cæsar feed,
That he is grown so great? *Ib.* 146

24 Now is it Rome indeed and room enough. *Ib.* 155

25 But, look you, Cassius,
The angry spot doth glow on Cæsar's brow. *Ib.* 181

26 Let me have men about me that are fat;
Sleek-headed men and such as sleep o' nights;
Yond' Cassius has a lean and hungry look;
He thinks too much: such men are dangerous.
Ib. 191

27 Would he were fatter! but I fear him not:
Yet if my name were liable to fear,
I do not know the man I should avoid
So soon as that spare Cassius. He reads much;
He is a great observer, and he looks
Quite through the deeds of men; he loves no plays,
As thou dost, Antony; he hears no music;
Seldom he smiles, and smiles in such a sort
As if he mock'd himself, and scorn'd his spirit,
That could be mov'd to smile at anything.
Such men as he be never at heart's ease,
Whiles they behold a greater than themselves,
And therefore are they very dangerous.
I rather tell thee what is to be fear'd
Than what I fear, for always I am Cæsar. *Ib.* 197

28 'Tis very like: he hath the falling sickness. *Ib.* [255]

29 If Cæsar had stabbed their mothers, they would have
done no less. *Ib.* [277]

30 For mine own part, it was Greek to me. *Ib.* [288]

31 Therefore 'tis meet
That noble minds keep ever with their likes;
For who so firm that cannot be seduc'd? *Ib.* [315]

32 Besides—I have not since put up my sword,—
Against the Capitol I met a lion,
Who glar'd upon me, and went surly by,
Without annoying me. *Ib.* iii. 19

33 Yesterday the bird of night did sit,
Even at noon-day, upon the market-place,
Hooting and shrieking. *Ib.* 26

34 But men may construe things after their own fashion,
Clean from the purpose of the things themselves.
Ib. 34

35 Cassius from bondage will deliver Cassius. *Ib.* 90

36 Nor stony tower, nor walls of beaten brass,
Nor airless dungeon, nor strong links of iron,
Can be retentive to the strength of spirit;
But life, being weary of these worldly bars,
Never lacks power to dismiss itself. *Ib.* 93

37 So every bondman in his own hand bears
The power to cancel his captivity. *Ib.* 101

38 I will set this foot of mine as far
As who goes furthest. *Ib.* 118

1 O! he sits high in all the people's hearts:
And that which would appear offence in us,
His countenance, like richest alchemy,
Will change to virtue and to worthiness.
Julius Cæsar, I. iii. 157

2 It is the bright day that brings forth the adder;
And that craves wary walking. *Ib.* II. i. 14

3   'Tis a common proof,
That lowliness is young ambition's ladder,
Whereto the climber-upward turns his face;
But when he once attains the upmost round,
He then unto the ladder turns his back,
Looks in the clouds, scorning the base degrees
By which he did ascend. *Ib.* 21

4   Therefore think him as a serpent's egg
Which, hatch'd, would, as his kind, grow mischievous,
And kill him in the shell. *Ib.* 32

5 Between the acting of a dreadful thing
And the first motion, all the interim is
Like a phantasma, or a hideous dream:
The genius and the mortal instruments
Are then in council; and the state of man,
Like to a little kingdom, suffers then
The nature of an insurrection. *Ib.* 63

6   O conspiracy!
Sham'st thou to show thy dangerous brow by night,
When evils are most free? *Ib.* 77

7 For if thou path, thy native semblance on,
Not Erebus itself were dim enough
To hide thee from prevention. *Ib.* 83

8 For he will never follow anything
That other men begin. *Ib.* 151

9 Let us be sacrificers, but not butchers, Caius.
Ib. 166

10 Let's carve him as a dish fit for the gods,
Not hew him as a carcass fit for hounds. *Ib.* 173

11 For he is superstitious grown of late,
Quite from the main opinion he held once
Of fantasy, of dreams, and ceremonies. *Ib.* 195

12 But when I tell him he hates flatterers,
He says he does, being then most flattered. *Ib.* 207

13 Enjoy the honey-heavy dew of slumber. *Ib.* 230

14 With an angry wafture of your hand,
Gave sign for me to leave you. *Ib.* 246

15   What! is Brutus sick,
And will he steal out of his wholesome bed
To dare the vile contagion of the night? *Ib.* 263

16   That great vow
Which did incorporate and make us one. *Ib.* 272

17 PORTIA:
      Dwell I but in the suburbs
Of your good pleasure? If it be no more,
Portia is Brutus' harlot, not his wife.
BRUTUS:
You are my true and honourable wife,
As dear to me as are the ruddy drops
That visit my sad heart. *Ib.* 285

18 I grant I am a woman, but, withal,
A woman that Lord Brutus took to wife;
I grant I am a woman, but, withal,
A woman well-reputed, Cato's daughter.
Think you I am no stronger than my sex,
Being so fathered and so husbanded? *Ib.* 292

19 *Enter Cæsar, in his night-gown.*
     Julius Cæsar, II. ii. *Stage Direction*

20 Nor heaven nor earth have been at peace to-night.
Ib. 1

21 CALPHURNIA:
     These things are beyond all use,
And I do fear them.
CÆSAR:
      What can be avoided
Whose end is purpos'd by the mighty gods? *Ib.* 25

22 CALPHURNIA:
When beggars die, there are no comets seen;
The heavens themselves blaze forth the death of
    princes.
CÆSAR:
Cowards die many times before their deaths;
The valiant never taste of death but once.
Of all the wonders that I yet have heard,
It seems to me most strange that men should fear;
Seeing that death, a necessary end,
Will come when it will come. *Ib.* 30

23   Danger knows full well
That Cæsar is more dangerous than he:
We are two lions litter'd in one day,
And I the elder and more terrible:
And Cæsar shall go forth. *Ib.* 44

24 The cause is in my will: I will not come. *Ib.* 71

25 See! Antony, that revels long o' nights,
Is notwithstanding up. *Ib.* 116

26 My heart laments that virtue cannot live
Out of the teeth of emulation. *Ib.* iii. [13]

27 O constancy! be strong upon my side;
Set a huge mountain 'tween my heart and tongue;
I have a man's mind, but a woman's might.
How hard it is for women to keep counsel! *Ib.* iv. 6

28 CÆSAR:
The ides of March are come.
SOOTHSAYER:
Ay, Cæsar; but not gone. *Ib.* III. i. 1

29   Sweet words,
Low-crooked curtsies, and base spaniel fawning.
Ib. 42

30 If I could pray to move, prayers would move me;
But I am constant as the northern star,
Of whose true-fix'd and resting quality
There is no fellow in the firmament.
The skies are painted with unnumber'd sparks,
They are all fire and every one doth shine,
But there's but one in all doth hold his place:
So, in the world; 'tis furnish'd well with men,
And men are flesh and blood, and apprehensive;
Yet in the number I do know but one
That unassailable holds on his rank,
Unshak'd of motion: and that I am he,
Let me a little show it, even in this,
That I was constant Cimber should be banish'd,
And constant do remain to keep him so. *Ib.* 59

31 Et tu, Brute! *Ib.* 77

32 Ambition's debt is paid. *Ib.* 83

33 That we shall die, we know; 'tis but the time
And drawing days out, that men stand upon. *Ib.* 99

34 He that cuts off twenty years of life
Cuts off so many years of fearing death. *Ib.* 101

1 CASSIUS:
                                    How many ages hence
Shall this our lofty scene be acted o'er,
In states unborn, and accents yet unknown!
BRUTUS:
How many times shall Cæsar bleed in sport.
                                    Julius Cæsar, III. i. 111

2 O mighty Cæsar! dost thou lie so low?
Are all thy conquests, glories, triumphs, spoils,
Shrunk to this little measure?   *Ib.* 148

3   Your swords, made rich
With the most noble blood of all this world. *Ib.* 155

4   Live a thousand years,
I shall not find myself so apt to die.   *Ib.* 159

5 The choice and master spirits of this age.   *Ib.* 163

6 Let each man render me his bloody hand
First, Marcus Brutus, will I shake with you. *Ib.* 184

7 Though last, not least in love.   *Ib.* 189

8 My credit now stands on such slippery ground,
That one of two bad ways you must conceit me,
Either a coward or a flatterer.   *Ib.* 191

9   Here wast thou bay'd, brave hart;
Here didst thou fall; and here thy hunters stand,
Sign'd in thy spoil, and crimson'd in thy leth.
O world! thou wast the forest to this hart;
And this, indeed, O world! the heart of thee. *Ib.* 204

10 The enemies of Cæsar shall say this;
Then, in a friend, it is cold modesty.   *Ib.* 212

11 O! pardon me, thou bleeding piece of earth,
That I am meek and gentle with these butchers;
Thou art the ruins of the noblest man
That ever lived in the tide of times.   *Ib.* 254

12   Cæsar's spirit, ranging for revenge,
With Ate by his side, come hot from hell,
Shall in these confines, with a monarch's voice
Cry, 'Havoc!' and let slip the dogs of war.   *Ib.* 270

13 Passion, I see, is catching.   *Ib.* 283

14 Not that I loved Cæsar less, but that I loved Rome
more.   *Ib.* ii. [22]

15 As he was valiant, I honour him: but, as he was
ambitious, I slew him.   *Ib.* [27]

16 Who is here so base that would be a bondman? If
any, speak; for him have I offended. Who is here
so rude that would not be a Roman? If any,
speak; for him have I offended. Who is here so
vile that will not love his country? If any, speak;
for him have I offended. I pause for a reply.
                                                                    Ib. [31]

17 Friends, Romans, countrymen, lend me your ears;
I come to bury Cæsar, not to praise him.
The evil that men do lives after them,
The good is oft interred with their bones;
So let it be with Cæsar. The noble Brutus
Hath told you Cæsar was ambitious;
If it were so, it was a grievous fault;
And grievously hath Cæsar answer'd it.   *Ib.* [79]

18 For Brutus is an honourable man;
So are they all, all honourable men.   *Ib.* [88]

19 He was my friend, faithful and just to me:
But Brutus says he was ambitious;
And Brutus is an honourable man.   *Ib.* [91]

20 When that the poor have cried, Cæsar hath wept;
Ambition should be made of sterner stuff.
                                    Julius Cæsar, III. ii. [97]

21 You all did love him once, not without cause.
                                                                    Ib. [108]

22 O judgment! thou art fled to brutish beasts,
And men have lost their reason.   *Ib.* [110]

23 But yesterday the word of Cæsar might
Have stood against the world; now lies he there,
And none so poor to do him reverence.   *Ib.* [124]

24 Let but the commons hear this testament—
Which, pardon me, I do not mean to read—
And they would go and kiss dead Cæsar's wounds
And dip their napkins in his sacred blood,
Yea, beg a hair of him for memory,
And, dying, mention it within their wills,
Bequeathing it as a rich legacy
Unto their issue.   *Ib.* [136]

25 The will, the will! we will hear Cæsar's will.
                                                                    Ib. [145]

26 You are not wood, you are not stones, but men.
                                                                    Ib. [148]

27 If you have tears, prepare to shed them now.
You all do know this mantle: I remember
The first time ever Cæsar put it on;
'Twas on a summer's evening, in his tent,
That day he overcame the Nervii.   *Ib.* [174]

28 See what a rent the envious Casca made.   *Ib.* [180]

29 For Brutus, as you know, was Cæsar's angel.
                                                                    Ib. [186]

30 This was the most unkindest cut of all.   *Ib.* [188]

31 Ingratitude, more strong than traitors' arms,
Quite vanquish'd him: then burst his mighty heart;
And, in his mantle muffling up his face,
Even at the base of Pompey's statua,
Which all the while ran blood, great Cæsar fell.
O! what a fall was there, my countrymen;
Then I, and you, and all of us fell down,
Whilst bloody treason flourish'd over us.
O! now you weep, and I perceive you feel
The dint of pity; these are gracious drops. *Ib.* [190]

32 Good friends, sweet friends, let me not stir you up
To such a sudden flood of mutiny.
They that have done this deed are honourable:
What private griefs they have, alas! I know not,
That made them do it; they are wise and honourable,
And will no doubt with reasons answer you.
I come not, friends, to steal away your hearts:
I am no orator, as Brutus is;
But, as you know me all, a plain, blunt man,
That love my friend.   *Ib.* [214]

33 For I have neither wit, nor words, nor worth,
Action, nor utterance, nor power of speech,
To stir men's blood; I only speak right on;
I tell you that which you yourselves do know.
                                                                    Ib. [225]

34   But were I Brutus,
And Brutus Antony, there were an Antony
Would ruffle up your spirits, and put a tongue
In every wound of Cæsar, that should move
The stones of Rome to rise and mutiny.   *Ib.* [230]

35 Here was a Cæsar! when comes such another?
                                                                    Ib. [257]

1 Now let it work; mischief, thou art afoot,
Take thou what course thou wilt!
Julius Cæsar, III. ii. [265]

2   Fortune is merry,
And in this mood will give us anything. *Ib.* [271]

3 Tear him for his bad verses, tear him for his bad
verses.   *Ib.* iii. [34]

4 He shall not live; look, with a spot I damn him.
    Ib. IV. i. 6

5 This is a slight unmeritable man,
Meet to be sent on errands.   *Ib.* 12

6 OCTAVIUS:
He's a tried and valiant soldier.
ANTONY:
So is my horse, Octavius; and for that
I do appoint him store of provender. *Ib.* 28

7   We are at the stake,
And bay'd about with many enemies;
And some that smile have in their hearts, I fear,
Millions of mischiefs.   *Ib.* 48

8 Not with such familiar instances,
Nor with such free and friendly conference,
As he hath us'd of old.   *Ib.* ii. 16

9 When love begins to sicken and decay,
It useth an enforced ceremony.
There are no tricks in plain and simple faith. *Ib.* 20

10 CASSIUS:
In such a time as this it is not meet
That every nice offence should bear his comment.
BRUTUS:
Let me tell you, Cassius, you yourself
Are much condemn'd to have an itching palm.
    Ib. iii. 7

11 Remember March, the ides of March remember.
    Ib. 18

12   Shall we now
Contaminate our fingers with base bribes? *Ib.* 23

13 I had rather be a dog, and bay the moon,
Than such a Roman.   *Ib.* 27

14 Away, slight man!   *Ib.* 37

15 I'll use you for my mirth, yea, for my laughter,
When you are waspish.   *Ib.* 49

16   For mine own part,
I shall be glad to learn of noble men. *Ib.* 53

17 You wrong me every way; you wrong me, Brutus;
I said an elder soldier, not a better:
Did I say 'better'?   *Ib.* 55

18 Do not presume too much upon my love;
I may do that I shall be sorry for. *Ib.* 63

19 There is no terror, Cassius, in your threats;
For I am arm'd so strong in honesty
That they pass by me as the idle wind,
Which I respect not.   *Ib.* 66

20 By heaven, I had rather coin my heart,
And drop my blood for drachmas, than to wring
From the hard hands of peasants their vile trash
By any indirection.   *Ib.* 72

21 Should I have answer'd Caius Cassius so?
When Marcus Brutus grows so covetous,
To lock such rascal counters from his friends,
Be ready, gods, with all your thunderbolts;
Dash him to pieces!   *Ib.* 78

22 A friend should bear his friend's infirmities,
But Brutus makes mine greater than they are.
Julius Cæsar, IV. iii. 85

23 A friendly eye could never see such faults. *Ib.* 89

24   All his faults observ'd,
Set in a note-book, learn'd, and conn'd by rote,
To cast into my teeth.   *Ib.* 96

25 O Cassius! you are yoked with a lamb
That carries anger as the flint bears fire;
Who, much enforced, shows a hasty spark,
And straight is cold again.   *Ib.* 109

26 O Cassius! I am sick of many griefs. *Ib.* 143

27 I have as much of this in art as you,
But yet my nature could not bear it so. *Ib.* 193

28 Good reasons must, of force, give place to better.
    Ib. 202

29 There is a tide in the affairs of men,
Which, taken at the flood, leads on to fortune;
Omitted, all the voyage of their life
Is bound in shallows and in miseries.
On such a full sea are we now afloat,
And we must take the current when it serves,
Or lose our ventures.   *Ib.* 217

30 The deep of night is crept upon our talk,
And nature must obey necessity. *Ib.* 225

31 This was an ill beginning of the night:
Never come such division 'tween our souls! *Ib.* 233

32 BRUTUS:
Then I shall see thee again?
GHOST:
Ay, at Philippi.
BRUTUS:
Why, I will see thee at Philippi, then. *Ib.* 283

33 But for your words, they rob the Hybla bees,
And leave them honeyless. *Ib.* v. i. 34

34 You know that I held Epicurus strong,
And his opinion; now I change my mind,
And partly credit things that do presage. *Ib.* 77

35 The gods to-day stand friendly, that we may,
Lovers in peace, lead on our days to age! *Ib.* 94

36   I know not how,
But I do find it cowardly and vile,
For fear of what might fall, so to prevent
The time of life.   *Ib.* 103

37   Think not, thou noble Roman,
That ever Brutus will go bound to Rome;
He bears too great a mind: but this same day
Must end that work the ides of March begun;
And whether we shall meet again, I know not.
Therefore our everlasting farewell take:
For ever, and for ever, farewell, Cassius!
If we do meet again, why, we shall smile!
If not, why then, this parting was well made. *Ib.* 111

38   O! that a man might know
The end of this day's business, ere it come;
But it sufficeth that the day will end,
And then the end is known.   *Ib.* 123

39 This day I breathed first: time is come round,
And where I did begin, there shall I end;
My life is run his compass.   *Ib.* iii. 23

40 O hateful error, melancholy's child!
Why dost thou show, to the apt thoughts of men,
The things that are not?   *Ib.* 67

1 O Julius Cæsar! thou art mighty yet!
Thy spirit walks abroad, and turns our swords
In our own proper entrails.   *Julius Cæsar*, v. iii. 94

2 Are yet two Romans living such as these?
The last of all the Romans, fare thee well!
It is impossible that ever Rome
Should breed thy fellow. Friends, I owe more tears
To this dead man than you shall see me pay.—
I shall find time, Cassius, I shall find time.   *Ib.* 98

3 When you do find him, or alive or dead,
He will be found like Brutus, like himself. *Ib.* iv. 24

4   I had rather have
Such men my friends than enemies.   *Ib.* 28

5 Thou seest the world, Volumnius, how it goes;
Our enemies have beat us to the pit:
It is more worthy to leap in ourselves,
Than tarry till they push us.   *Ib.* v. 22

6 Thou art a fellow of a good respect;
Thy life hath had some smatch of honour in it.
                                              Ib. 45

7   Cæsar, now be still;
I kill'd not thee with half so good a will.   *Ib.* 50

8 This was the noblest Roman of them all.   *Ib.* 68

9 He, only, in a general honest thought
And common good to all, made one of them.
His life was gentle, and the elements
So mix'd in him that Nature might stand up
And·say to all the world, 'This was a man!'   *Ib.* 71

10 LEAR:
So young, and so untender?
CORDELIA:
So young, my lord, and true.   *King Lear*, I. i. [108]

11 A still-soliciting eye.   *Ib.* [234]

12   Love is not love
When it is mingled with regards that stand
Aloof from the entire point.   *Ib.* [241]

13 Fairest Cordelia, that art most rich, being poor;
Most choice, forsaken; and most lov'd, despis'd!
                                              Ib. [253]

14 Who in the lusty stealth of nature take
More composition and fierce quality
Than doth, within a dull, stale, tired bed,
Go to the creating a whole tribe of fops.   *Ib.* ii. 11

15 These late eclipses in the sun and moon portend no
good to us.   *Ib.* [115]

16 We have seen the best of our time: machinations,
hollowness, treachery, and all ruinous disorders,
follow us disquietly to our graves.   *Ib.* [125]

17 This is the excellent foppery of the world. *Ib.* [132]

18 We make guilty of our disasters the sun, the moon,
and the stars; as if we were villains by necessity,
fools by heavenly compulsion.   *Ib.* [134]

19 An admirable evasion of whoremaster man, to lay
his goatish disposition to the charge of a star!
                                              Ib. [141]

20 My nativity was under Ursa Major; so that it follows
I am rough and lecherous.   *Ib.* [145]

21 Pat he comes, like the catastrophe of the old comedy;
my cue is villanous melancholy, with a sigh like
Tom o' Bedlam.   *Ib.* [150]

22 KENT:
You have that in your countenance which I would
fain call master.
LEAR:
What's that?
KENT:
Authority.   *King Lear*, I. iv. [29]

23 Not so young, sir, to love a woman for singing, nor
so old to dote on her for any thing.   *Ib.* [40]

24 Lady the brach may stand by the fire and stink.
                                              Ib. [125]

25 Have more than thou showest,
Speak less than thou knowest,
Lend less than thou owest.   *Ib.* [132]

26 LEAR:
Dost thou call me fool, boy?
FOOL:
All thy other titles thou hast given away; that thou
wast born with.   *Ib.* [163]

27 The hedge-sparrow fed the cuckoo so long,
That it had it head bit off by it young.   *Ib.* [238]

28 Ingratitude, thou marble-hearted fiend,
More hideous, when thou show'st thee in a child,
Than the sea-monster.   *Ib.* [283]

29 Into her womb convey sterility!
Dry up in her the organs of increase.   *Ib.* [302]

30 How sharper than a serpent's tooth it is
To have a thankless child!   *Ib.* [312]

31 How far your eyes may pierce I cannot tell;
Striving to better, oft we mar what's well.   *Ib.* [370]

32 A knave; a rascal; an eater of broken meats.
                                              Ib. II. ii. [15]

33 Thou whoreson zed! thou unnecessary letter!
                                              Ib. [68]

34 I'd drive ye cackling home to Camelot.   *Ib.* [89]

35 I have seen better faces in my time
Than stands on any shoulder that I see
Before me at this instant.   *Ib.* [99]

36 Winter's not gone yet, if the wild-geese fly that way.
                                              Ib. iv. [46]

37   Down, thou climbing sorrow!
Thy element's below.   *Ib.* [57]

38 That sir which serves and seeks for gain,
    And follows but for form,
Will pack when it begins to rain,
    And leave thee in the storm.   *Ib.* [79]

39   O, sir! you are old;
Nature in you stands on the very verge
Of her confine.   *Ib.* [148]

40   But I'll not chide thee;
Let shame come when it will, I do not call it:
I do not bid the thunder-bearer shoot,
Nor tell tales of thee to high-judging Jove. *Ib.* [228]

41   Our basest beggars
Are in the poorest thing superfluous:
Allow not nature more than nature needs,
Man's life is cheap as beast's.   *Ib.* [267]

42 You see me here, you gods, a poor old man,
As full of grief as age; wretched in both! *Ib.* [275]

1 I will have such revenges on you both
That all the world shall—I will do such things,—
What they are yet I know not,—but they shall be
The terrors of the earth.   *King Lear*, II. iv. [282]

2   To wilful men,
The injuries that they themselves procure
Must be their schoolmasters.   *Ib.* [305]

3 Contending with the fretful elements;
Bids the wind blow the earth into the sea,
Or swell the curled waters 'bove the main.
                                    Ib. III. i. 4

4 Strives in his little world of man to out-scorn
The to-and-fro conflicting wind and rain.
This night, wherein the cub-drawn bear would couch,
The lion and the belly-pinched wolf
Keep their fur dry.   *Ib.* 10

5 Blow, winds, and crack your cheeks! rage! blow!
You cataracts and hurricanoes, spout
Till you have drench'd our steeples, drown'd the
    cocks!
You sulphurous and thought-executing fires,
Vaunt-couriers to oak-cleaving thunderbolts,
Singe my white head! And thou, all-shaking thunder,
Strike flat the thick rotundity o' the world!
Crack nature's moulds, all germens spill at once
That make ingrateful man!   *Ib.* ii. 1

6 I tax not you, you elements, with unkindness;
I never gave you kingdom, call'd you children,
You owe me no subscription: then, let fall
Your horrible pleasure; here I stand, your slave,
A poor, infirm, weak, and despis'd old man.
But yet I call you servile ministers,
That have with two pernicious daughters join'd
Your high-engender'd battles 'gainst a head
So old and white as this.   *Ib.* [16]

7 There was never yet fair woman but she made mouths
    in a glass.   *Ib.* [35]

8   Things that love night
Love not such nights as these.   *Ib.* [42]

9   Let the great gods,
That keep this dreadful pother o'er our heads,
Find out their enemies now. Tremble, thou wretch,
That hast within thee undivulged crimes,
Unwhipp'd of justice.   *Ib.* [49]

10   Close pent-up guilts,
Rive your concealing continents, and cry
These dreadful summoners grace. I am a man
More sinned against than sinning.   *Ib.* [57]

11 The art of our necessities is strange,
That can make vile things precious.   *Ib.* [70]

12   When the mind's free,
The body's delicate.   *Ib.* iv. 11

13 O! that way madness lies; let me shun that.   *Ib.* 21

14 Poor naked wretches, wheresoe'er you are,
That bide the pelting of this pitiless storm,
How shall your houseless heads and unfed sides,
Your looped and window'd raggedness, defend you
From seasons such as these?   *Ib.* 28

15   Take physic, pomp;
Expose thyself to feel what wretches feel.   *Ib.* 33

16 Tom's a-cold.   *Ib.* [57]

17 Pillicock sat on Pillicock-hill:
Halloo, halloo, loo, loo!   *Ib.* [75]

18 Take heed o' the foul fiend!   *King Lear*, III. iv. [79]

19 A serving-man, proud in heart and mind: that curled
my hair, wore gloves in my cap, served the lust of
my mistress's heart, and did the act of darkness
with her; swore as many oaths as I spake words,
and broke them in the sweet face of heaven; one
that slept in the contriving of lust, and waked to
do it.   *Ib.* [84]

20 Keep thy foot out of brothels, thy hand out of
plackets, thy pen from lenders' books, and defy
the foul fiend.   *Ib.* [96]

21 Thou art the thing itself; unaccommodated man is
no more but such a poor, bare, forked animal as
thou art.   *Ib.* [109]

22 'Tis a naughty night to swim in.   *Ib.* [113]

23 Drinks the green mantle of the standing pool.
                                    Ib. [136]

24 But mice and rats and such small deer
Have been Tom's food for seven long year.   *Ib.* [142]

25 The prince of darkness is a gentleman.   *Ib.* [148]

26 I'll talk a word with this same learned Theban.
                                    Ib. [161]

27 Child Roland to the dark tower came,
His word was still, Fie, foh, and fum,
I smell the blood of a British man.   *Ib.* [185]

28 Nero is an angler in the lake of darkness.   *Ib.* vi. [8]

29   The little dogs and all,
Tray, Blanch, and Sweet-heart, see, they bark at me.
                                    Ib. [65]

30 Mastiff, greyhound, mongrel grim,
Hound or spaniel, brach or lym,
Or bobtail tike, or trundle-tail.   *Ib.* [71]

31 You, sir, I entertain for one of my hundred; only I
do not like the fashion of your garments: you will
say, they are Persian attire; but let them be
changed.   *Ib.* [83]

32   'Tis most ignobly done
To pluck me by the beard.   *Ib.* vii. [35]

33 I am tied to the stake, and I must stand the course.
                                    Ib. [54]

34 The sea, with such a storm as his bare head
In hell-black night endur'd, would have buoy'd up,
And quench'd the stelled fires.   *Ib.* [59]

35 Out, vile jelly!   *Ib.* [83]

36 The lowest and most dejected thing of fortune.
                                    Ib. IV. i. 3

37 The lamentable change is from the best;
The worst returns to laughter.   *Ib.* 5

38 I have no way, and therefore want no eyes;
I stumbled when I saw.   *Ib.* 18

39   The worst is not,
So long as we can say, 'This is the worst.'   *Ib.* 27

40 As flies to wanton boys, are we to the gods;
They kill us for their sport.   *Ib.* 36

41 You are not worth the dust which the rude wind
Blows in your face.   *Ib.* ii. 30

42 She that herself will sliver and disbranch
From her material sap, perforce must wither
And come to deadly use.   *Ib.* 34

1 Wisdom and goodness to the vile seem vile;
Filths savour but themselves. *King Lear*, IV. ii. 38

2 Crown'd with rank fumiter and furrow weeds,
With burdocks, hemlock, nettles, cuckoo-flowers,
Darnel, and all the idle weeds that grow
In our sustaining corn. *Ib. iv. 3*

3 How fearful
And dizzy 'tis to cast one's eyes so low!
The crows and choughs that wing the midway air
Show scarce so gross as beetles; half-way down
Hangs one that gathers samphire, dreadful trade!
Methinks he seems no bigger than his head.
The fishermen that walk upon the beach
Appear like mice, and yond tall anchoring bark
Diminish'd to her cock, her cock a buoy
Almost too small for sight. The murmuring surge,
That on the unnumber'd idle pebbles chafes,
Cannot be heard so high. *Ib. vi. 12*

4 The shrill-gorg'd lark so far
Cannot be seen or heard. *Ib. 59*

5 Think that the clearest gods, who make them honours
Of men's impossibilities, have preserv'd thee. *Ib. 74*

6 They told me I was every thing; 'tis a lie, I am not
ague-proof. *Ib. [107]*

7 GLOUCESTER:
Is't not the king?
LEAR:
Ay, every inch a king. *Ib. [110]*

8 The wren goes to 't, and the small gilded fly
Does lecher in my sight. *Ib. [115]*

9 Give me an ounce of civet, good apothecary, to
sweeten my imagination. *Ib. [133]*

10 A man may see how this world goes with no eyes.
Look with thine ears: see how yond justice rails
upon yond simple thief. Hark, in thine ear: change
places; and, handy-dandy, which is the justice,
which is the thief? *Ib. [154]*

11 Get thee glass eyes;
And, like a scurvy politician, seem
To see the things thou dost not. *Ib. [175]*

12 When we are born we cry that we are come
To this great stage of fools. *Ib. [187]*

13 Mine enemy's dog,
Though he had bit me, should have stood that night
Against my fire. *Ib. vii. 36*

14 Thou art a soul in bliss; but I am bound
Upon a wheel of fire, that mine own tears
Do scald like molten lead. *Ib. 46*

15 I am a very foolish, fond old man,
Fourscore and upward, not an hour more or less;
And, to deal plainly,
I fear I am not in my perfect mind. *Ib. 60*

16 For, as I am a man, I think this lady
To be my child Cordelia. *Ib. 69*

17 Pray you now, forget and forgive. *Ib. [85]*

18 Men must endure
Their going hence, even as their coming hither:
Ripeness is all. *Ib. v. ii. 9*

19 Come, let's away to prison;
We two alone will sing like birds i' the cage:
When thou dost ask me blessing, I'll kneel down,
And ask of thee forgiveness: and we'll live,

And pray, and sing, and tell old tales, and laugh
At gilded butterflies, and hear poor rogues
Talk of court news; and we'll talk with them too,
Who loses, and who wins; who's in, who's out;
And take upon 's the mystery of things,
As if we were God's spies; and we'll wear out,
In a wall'd prison, packs and sets of great ones
That ebb and flow by the moon. *King Lear*, v. iii. 8

20 Upon such sacrifices, my Cordelia,
The gods themselves throw incense. *Ib. 20*

21 The gods are just, and of our pleasant vices
Make instruments to plague us. *Ib. [172]*

22 The wheel is come full circle. *Ib. [176]*

23 His flaw'd heart,—
Alack! too weak the conflict to support;
'Twixt two extremes of passion, joy and grief,
Burst smilingly. *Ib. [198]*

24 Her voice was ever soft,
Gentle and low, an excellent thing in woman.
Ib. [274]

25 I have seen the day, with my good biting falchion
I would have made them skip. *Ib. [278]*

26 And my poor fool is hang'd! No, no, no life!
Why should a dog, a horse, a rat, have life,
And thou no breath at all? Thou'lt come no more,
Never, never, never, never, never!
Pray you, undo this button. *Ib. [307]*

27 Vex not his ghost: O! let him pass; he hates him
That would upon the rack of this tough world
Stretch him out longer. *Ib. [314]*

28 The weight of this sad time we must obey,
Speak what we feel; not what we ought to say.
The oldest hath borne most: we that are young,
Shall never see so much, nor live so long. *Ib. [325]*

29 Let fame, that all hunt after in their lives,
Live register'd upon our brazen tombs.
Love's Labour's Lost, I. i. 1

30 Spite of cormorant devouring Time. *Ib. 4*

31 Why, all delights are vain; but that most vain,
Which, with pain purchas'd, doth inherit pain.
Ib. 72

32 Study is like the heaven's glorious sun,
That will not be deep-search'd with saucy looks;
Small have continual plodders ever won,
Save base authority from others' books.
These earthly godfathers of Heaven's lights
That give a name to every fixed star,
Have no more profit of their shining nights
Than those that walk and wot not what they are.
Ib. 84

33 At Christmas I no more desire a rose
Than wish a snow in May's new-fangled mirth;
But like of each thing that in season grows. *Ib. 105*

34 So study evermore is overshot. *Ib. [141]*

35 If I break faith, this word shall speak for me,—
I am forsworn 'on mere necessity'. *Ib. [152]*

36 A child of our grandmother Eve, a female; or, for
thy more sweet understanding, a woman. *Ib. [263]*

37 The world was very guilty of such a ballad some three
ages since; but, I think, now 'tis not to be found.
Ib. ii. [117]

1 Devise, wit! write, pen! for I am for whole volumes in folio! *Love's Labour's Lost*, I. ii. [194]

2 Beauty is bought by judgment of the eye,
Not utter'd by base sale of chapmen's tongues.
Ib. II. i. 15

3   A merrier man,
Within the limit of becoming mirth,
I never spent an hour's talk withal. *Ib.* 66

4 Your wit's too hot, it speeds too fast, 'twill tire.
Ib. [119]

5 Thy own wish wish I thee in every place! *Ib.* [178]

6 Warble, child; make passionate my sense of hearing.
Ib. III. i. 1

7 A very beadle to a humorous sigh. *Ib.* [185]

8 This wimpled, whining, purblind, wayward boy,
This senior-junior, giant-dwarf, Dan Cupid;
Regent of love rhymes, lord of folded arms,
The anointed sovereign of sighs and groans,
Liege of all loiterers and malcontents. *Ib.* [189]

9 With two pitch balls stuck in her face for eyes.
Ib. [207]

10 Some men must love my lady, and some Joan.
Ib. [215]

11 He hath not fed of the dainties that are bred in a book; he hath not eat paper, as it were; he hath not drunk ink. *Ib.* IV. ii. [25]

12 These are begot in the ventricle of memory, nourished in the womb of pia mater, and delivered upon the mellowing of occasion. *Ib.* [70]

13 Old Mantuan! old Mantuan! Who understandeth thee not, loves thee not. *Ib.* [102]

14 The elegancy, facility, and golden cadence of poesy.
Ib. [126]

15 By heaven, I do love, and it hath taught me to rhyme, and to be melancholy. *Ib.* iii. [13]

16 The heavenly rhetoric of thine eye. *Ib.* [60]

17 Love, whose month is ever May,
Spied a blossom passing fair,
Playing in the wanton air;
Through the velvet leaves the wind,
All unseen, 'gan passage find;
That the lover, sick to death,
Wish'd himself the heaven's breath. *Ib.* [102]

18 Thou for whom e'en Jove would swear
Juno but an Ethiop were;
And deny himself for Jove,
Turning mortal for thy love. *Ib.* [117]

19 Now step I forth to whip hypocrisy. *Ib.* [151]

20 From women's eyes this doctrine I derive:
They are the ground, the books, the academes,
From whence doth spring the true Promethean fire.
Ib. [302]

21 For where is any author in the world
Teaches such beauty as a woman's eye?
Learning is but an adjunct to ourself. *Ib.* [312]

22 But love, first learned in a lady's eyes,
Lives not alone immured in the brain,
But, with the motion of all elements,
Courses as swift as thought in every power,
And gives to every power a double power,
Above their functions and their offices.

It adds a precious seeing to the eye;
A lover's eyes will gaze an eagle blind;
A lover's ears will hear the lowest sound,
When the suspicious head of theft is stopp'd:
Love's feeling is more soft and sensible
Than are the tender horns of cockled snails:
Love's tongue proves dainty Bacchus gross in taste.
For valour, is not love a Hercules,
Still climbing trees in the Hesperides?
Subtle as Sphinx; as sweet and musical
As bright Apollo's lute, strung with his hair;
And when Love speaks, the voice of all the gods
Makes heaven drowsy with the harmony.
Never durst poet touch a pen to write
Until his ink were temper'd with Love's sighs.
Love's Labour's Lost, IV. iii. [327]

23 From women's eyes this doctrine I derive:
They sparkle still the right Promethean fire;
They are the books, the arts, the academes,
That show, contain, and nourish all the world.
Ib. [350]

24 He draweth out the thread of his verbosity finer than the staple of his argument. *Ib.* V. i. [18]

25 Priscian a little scratched; 'twill serve. *Ib.* [31]

26 MOTH:
They have been at a great feast of languages, and stolen the scraps.
COSTARD:
O! they have lived long on the alms-basket of words. I marvel thy master hath not eaten thee for a word; for thou art not so long by the head as honorificabilitudinitatibus: thou art easier swallowed than a flap-dragon. *Ib.* [39]

27 In the posteriors of this day; which the rude multitude call the afternoon. *Ib.* [96]

28   Had she been light, like you,
Of such a merry, nimble, stirring spirit,
She might ha' been a grandam ere she died;
And so may you; for a light heart lives long.
Ib. ii. 15

29 Taffeta phrases, silken terms precise,
Three-pil'd hyperboles, spruce affectation,
Figures pedantical. *Ib.* 407

30 In russet yeas and honest kersey noes. *Ib.* 414

31 When in the world I liv'd, I was the world's commander;
By east, west, north, and south, I spread my conquering might:
My scutcheon plain declares that I am Alisander.
Ib. [563]

32 Let me take you a button-hole lower. *Ib.* [705]

33 A world-without-end bargain. *Ib.* [797]

34 A jest's prosperity lies in the ear
Of him that hears it, never in the tongue
Of him that makes it. *Ib.* [869]

35 When daisies pied and violets blue
    And lady-smocks all silver-white
And cuckoo-buds of yellow hue
    Do paint the meadows with delight,
The cuckoo then, on every tree,
Mocks married men; for thus sings he,
              Cuckoo;
Cuckoo, cuckoo; O, word of fear,
Unpleasing to a married ear! *Ib.* [902]

1 When icicles hang by the wall,
   And Dick, the shepherd, blows his nail,
And Tom bears logs into the hall,
   And milk comes frozen home in pail,
When blood is nipp'd and ways be foul,
Then nightly sings the staring owl,
             Tu-who;
Tu-whit, tu-who—a merry note,
While greasy Joan doth keel the pot.

When all aloud the wind doth blow,
   And coughing drowns the parson's saw;
And birds sit brooding in the snow,
   And Marion's nose looks red and raw,
When roasted crabs hiss in the bowl.
       Love's Labour's Lost, v. ii. [920]

2 The words of Mercury are harsh after the songs of
   Apollo.   *Ib.* [938]

3 FIRST WITCH:
When shall we three meet again
In thunder, lightning, or in rain?
SECOND WITCH:
When the hurly-burly's done,
When the battle's lost and won.
THIRD WITCH:
That will be ere the set of sun.
FIRST WITCH:
Where the place?
SECOND WITCH:
         Upon the heath.
THIRD WITCH:
There to meet with Macbeth.
FIRST WITCH:
I come, Graymalkin!
SECOND WITCH:
         Paddock calls.
THIRD WITCH:
Anon!
ALL:
Fair is foul, and foul is fair:
Hover through the fog and filthy air.
        Macbeth, I. i. 1

4 DUNCAN:
What bloody man is that? . . .
MALCOLM:
      This is the sergeant. *Ib.* ii. 1

5 Disdaining fortune, with his brandish'd steel,
Which smok'd with bloody execution,
Like valour's minion carv'd out his passage. *Ib.* 17

6 Memorize another Golgotha.   *Ib.* 41

7 So well thy words become thee as thy wounds;
They smack of honour both.   *Ib.* 44

8 Banners flout the sky.   *Ib.* 50

9 Till that Bellona's bridegroom, lapp'd in proof,
Confronted him with self-comparisons,
Point against point, rebellious arm 'gainst arm,
Curbing his lavish spirit.   *Ib.* 55

10 A sailor's wife had chestnuts in her lap,
And munch'd, and munch'd, and munch'd: 'Give
   me,' quoth I:
'Aroint thee, witch!' the rump-fed ronyon cries.
Her husband's to Aleppo gone, master o' the Tiger:
But in a sieve I'll thither sail,
And, like a rat without a tail,
I'll do, I'll do, and I'll do.   *Ib.* iii. 4

11 Sleep shall neither night nor day
Hang upon his pent-house lid.
He shall live a man forbid.
Weary se'nnights nine times nine
Shall he dwindle, peak, and pine:
Though his bark cannot be lost,
Yet it shall be tempest-tost.   *Macbeth*, I. iii. 19

12 So foul and fair a day I have not seen.   *Ib.* 38

13   What are these,
So withered, and so wild in their attire,
That look not like th' inhabitants o' the earth,
And yet are on 't?   *Ib.* 39

14   You should be women,
And yet your beards forbid me to interpret
That you are so.   *Ib.* 45

15 If you can look into the seeds of time,
And say which grain will grow and which will not.
               Ib. 58

16 Stay, you imperfect speakers, tell me more. *Ib.* 70

17   The Thane of Cawdor lives,
A prosperous gentleman; and to be king
Stands not within the prospect of belief;
No more than to be Cawdor. Say, from whence
You owe this strange intelligence? or why
Upon this blasted heath you stop our way
With such prophetic greeting?   *Ib.* 72

18 The earth hath bubbles, as the water has,
And these are of them.   *Ib.* 79

19 Were such things here as we do speak about?
Or have we eaten on the insane root
That takes the reason prisoner?   *Ib.* 83

20 Strange images of death.   *Ib.* 97

21 What! can the devil speak true?   *Ib.* 107

22 And oftentimes, to win us to our harm,
The instruments of darkness tell us truths;
Win us with honest trifles, to betray 's
In deepest consequence.   *Ib.* 123

23   Two truths are told,
As happy prologues to the swelling act
Of the imperial theme.   *Ib.* 127

24 This supernatural soliciting
Cannot be ill, cannot be good; if ill,
Why hath it given me earnest of success,
Commencing in a truth? I am Thane of Cawdor:
If good, why do I yield to that suggestion
Whose horrid image doth unfix my hair
And make my seated heart knock at my ribs,
Against the use of nature? Present fears
Are less than horrible imaginings;
My thought, whose murder yet is but fantastical,
Shakes so my single state of man that function
Is smother'd in surmise, and nothing is
But what is not.   *Ib.* 130

25 If chance will have me king, why, chance may crown
   me.   *Ib.* 143

26   Come what come may,
Time and the hour runs through the roughest day.
               Ib. 146

27 MALCOLM:
        Nothing in his life
Became him like the leaving it; he died
As one that had been studied in his death
To throw away the dearest thing he owed
As 'twere a careless trifle.

DUNCAN:

               There's no art
To find the mind's construction in the face;
He was a gentleman on whom I built
An absolute trust.   *Macbeth*, I. iv. 7

1 Glamis thou art, and Cawdor; and shalt be
What thou art promis'd. Yet do I fear thy nature;
It is too full o' the milk of human kindness
To catch the nearest way; thou wouldst be great,
Art not without ambition; but without
The illness should attend it; what thou wouldst
    highly,
That thou wouldst holily; wouldst not play false,
And yet wouldst wrongly win; thou'dst have, great
    Glamis,
That which cries, 'Thus thou must do, if thou have
    it';
And that which rather thou dost fear to do
Than wishest should be undone.   *Ib.* v. [16]

2   The golden round,
Which fate and metaphysical aid doth seem
To have thee crown'd withal.   *Ib.* [29]

3   The raven himself is hoarse
That croaks the fatal entrance of Duncan
Under my battlements. Come, you spirits
That tend on mortal thoughts! unsex me here,
And fill me from the crown to the toe top full
Of direst cruelty; make thick my blood,
Stop up the access and passage to remorse,
That no compunctious visitings of nature
Shake my fell purpose, nor keep peace between
The effect and it! Come to my woman's breasts,
And take my milk for gall, you murdering ministers,
Wherever in your sightless substances
You wait on nature's mischief! Come, thick night,
And pall thee in the dunnest smoke of hell,
That my keen knife see not the wound it makes,
Nor heaven peep through the blanket of the dark,
To cry 'Hold, hold!'   *Ib.* [38]

4 Greater than both, by the all-hail hereafter! *Ib.* [56]

5 Your face, my thane, is as a book where men
May read strange matters. To beguile the time,
Look like the time; bear welcome in your eye,
Your hand, your tongue: look like the innocent
    flower,
But be the serpent under't.   *Ib.* [63]

6 DUNCAN:
This castle hath a pleasant seat; the air
Nimbly and sweetly recommends itself
Unto our gentle senses.

BANQUO:

             This guest of summer,
The temple-haunting martlet, does approve
By his lov'd mansionry that the heaven's breath
Smells wooingly here: no jutty, frieze,
Buttress, nor coign of vantage, but this bird
Hath made his pendent bed and procreant cradle:
Where they most breed and haunt, I have observ'd,
The air is delicate.   *Ib.* vi. 1

7 If it were done when 'tis done, then 'twere well
It were done quickly: if the assassination
Could trammel up the consequence, and catch
With his surcease success; that but this blow
Might be the be-all and the end-all here,
But here, upon this bank and shoal of time,
We'd jump the life to come.   *Ib.* vii. 1

8 This even-handed justice.   *Macbeth*, I. vii. 10

9   Besides, this Duncan
Hath borne his faculties so meek, hath been
So clear in his great office, that his virtues
Will plead like angels trumpet-tongu'd, against
The deep damnation of his taking-off;
And pity, like a naked new-born babe,
Striding the blast, or heaven's cherubim, hors'd
Upon the sightless couriers of the air,
Shall blow the horrid deed in every eye,
That tears shall drown the wind. I have no spur
To prick the sides of my intent, but only
Vaulting ambition, which o'erleaps itself,
And falls on the other.   *Ib.* 16

10 We will proceed no further in this business:
He hath honour'd me of late; and I have bought
Golden opinions from all sorts of people. *Ib.* 31

11   Was the hope drunk,
Wherein you dress'd yourself? hath it slept since,
And wakes it now, to look so green and pale
At what it did so freely? From this time
Such I account thy love. Art thou afeard
To be the same in thine own act and valour
As thou art in desire? Wouldst thou have that
Which thou esteem'st the ornament of life,
And live a coward in thine own esteem,
Letting 'I dare not' wait upon 'I would,'
Like the poor cat i' the adage.   *Ib.* 35

12 I dare do all that may become a man;
Who dares do more is none.   *Ib.* 46

13 LADY MACBETH:

           I have given suck, and know
How tender 'tis to love the babe that milks me:
I would, while it was smiling in my face,
Have pluck'd my nipple from his boneless gums,
And dash'd the brains out, had I so sworn as you
Have done to this.

MACBETH:

           If we should fail,—

LADY MACBETH:

               We fail!
But screw your courage to the sticking-place,
And we'll not fail.   *Ib.* 54

14 That memory, the warder of the brain,
Shall be a fume.   *Ib.* 65

15   Bring forth men-children only;
For thy undaunted mettle should compose
Nothing but males.   *Ib.* 72

16 Away, and mock the time with fairest show:
False face must hide what the false heart doth know.
    Ib. 81

17   There's husbandry in heaven;
Their candles are all out.   *Ib.* II. i. 4

18   Merciful powers!
Restrain in me the cursed thoughts that nature
Gives way to in repose.   *Ib.* 7

19   Shut up
In measureless content.   *Ib.* 16

20 Is this a dagger which I see before me,
The handle toward my hand? Come, let me clutch
    thee:
I have thee not, and yet I see thee still.
Art thou not, fatal vision, sensible
To feeling as to sight? or art thou but
A dagger of the mind, a false creation,
Proceeding from the heat-oppressèd brain? *Ib.* 33

1　　　　　Now o'er the one half-world
Nature seems dead, and wicked dreams abuse
The curtain'd sleep; witchcraft celebrates
Pale Hecate's offerings; and wither'd murder,
Alarum'd by his sentinel, the wolf,
Whose howl's his watch, thus with his stealthy pace,
With Tarquin's ravishing strides, toward his design
Moves like a ghost. Thou sure and firm-set earth,
Hear not my steps, which way they walk, for fear
The very stones prate of my whereabout,
And take the present horror from the time,
Which now suits with it. Whiles I threat he lives:
Words to the heat of deeds too cold breath gives.
I go, and it is done; the bell invites me.
Hear it not, Duncan; for it is a knell
That summons thee to heaven or to hell.
　　　　　　　　　　Macbeth, II. i. 49

2 That which hath made them drunk hath made me
　　bold,
What hath quench'd them hath given me fire.
　　　　　　　　　　　　　　　　Ib. ii. 1

3 It was the owl that shriek'd, the fatal bellman,
Which gives the stern'st good-night.　　*Ib.* 4

4　　　　　The attempt and not the deed,
Confounds us.　　　　　　　　　　*Ib.* 12

5　　　　　Had he not resembled
My father as he slept I had done 't.　　*Ib.* 14

6 I have done the deed. Didst thou not hear a noise?
　　　　　　　　　　　　　　　　Ib. 16

7 As they had seen me with these hangman's hands.
　　　　　　　　　　　　　　　　Ib. 29

8 Consider it not so deeply.　　　　　*Ib.* 31

9 I had most need of blessing, and 'Amen'
Stuck in my throat.　　　　　　　　*Ib.* 33

10 These deeds must not be thought
After these ways; so, it will make us mad.　*Ib.* 34

11 Methought I heard a voice cry, 'Sleep no more!
Macbeth does murder sleep,' the innocent sleep,
Sleep that knits up the ravell'd sleave of care,
The death of each day's life, sore labour's bath,
Balm of hurt minds, great nature's second course,
Chief nourisher in life's feast.　　　　*Ib.* 36

12 Glamis hath murder'd sleep, and therefore Cawdor
Shall sleep no more, Macbeth shall sleep no more!
　　　　　　　　　　　　　　　　Ib. 43

13 You do unbend your noble strength to think
So brainsickly of things.　　　　　　*Ib.* 46

14 MACBETH:
I am afraid to think what I have done;
Look on't again I dare not.
LADY MACBETH:
　　　　　　　　　Infirm of purpose!
Give me the daggers. The sleeping and the dead
Are but as pictures; 'tis the eye of childhood
That fears a painted devil.　　　　　*Ib.* 52

15 Will all great Neptune's ocean wash this blood
Clean from my hand? No, this my hand will rather
The multitudinous seas incarnadine,
Making the green one red.　　　　　*Ib.* 61

16 A little water clears us of this deed.　*Ib.* 68

17 Here's a farmer that hanged himself on the expectation of plenty.　　　　　　　　　*Ib.* iii. [5]

18 Faith, here's an equivocator.　　　*Ib.* [9]

19 The primrose way to the everlasting bonfire.
　　　　　　　　　　Macbeth, II. iii. [22]

20 The labour we delight in physics pain.　*Ib.* [56]

21 The night has been unruly: where we lay
Our chimneys were blown down; and, as they say,
Lamentings heard i' the air; strange screams of
　　death,
And prophesying with accents terrible
Of dire combustion and confus'd events
New-hatch'd to the woeful time. The obscure bird
Clamour'd the live-long night: some say the earth
Was feverous and did shake.　　　　*Ib.* [60]

22 Confusion now hath made his masterpiece!
Most sacrilegious murder hath broke ope
The Lord's anointed temple, and stole thence
The life o' the building!　　　　　*Ib.* [72]

23 Shake off this downy sleep, death's counterfeit,
And look on death itself! up, up, and see
The great doom's image!　　　　　*Ib.* [83]

24 Had I but died an hour before this chance,
I had liv'd a blessed time; for, from this instant,
There's nothing serious in mortality:
All is but toys; renown and grace is dead,
The wine of life is drawn, and the mere lees
Is left this vault to brag of.　　　　*Ib.* [98]

25 Who can be wise, amazed, temperate, and furious,
Loyal and neutral, in a moment? No man. *Ib.* [115]

26 In the great hand of God I stand, and thence
Against the undivulg'd pretence I fight
Of treasonous malice.　　　　　　*Ib.* [137]

27 There's daggers in men's smiles.　*Ib.* [147]

28 A falcon, towering in her pride of place,
Was by a mousing owl hawk'd at and kill'd.
　　　　　　　　　　　　　　　　Ib. iv. 12

29 Thriftless ambition, that wilt ravin up
Thine own life's means!　　　　　*Ib.* 28

30 Thou hast it now: King, Cawdor, Glamis, all,
As the weird women promis'd; and, I fear,
Thou play'dst most foully for 't; yet it was said
It should not stand in thy posterity,
But that myself should be the root and father
Of many kings.　　　　　　*Ib.* III. i. 1

31 I must become a borrower of the night
For a dark hour or twain.　　　　　*Ib.* 27

32　　　　　　　　　　To be thus is nothing;
But to be safely thus.　　　　　　*Ib.* 48

33　　　　　　　　There is none but he
Whose being I do fear; and, under him
My genius is rebuk'd: as, it is said,
Mark Antony's was by Cæsar.　　　*Ib.* 54

34　　　　　　　Mine eternal jewel
Given to the common enemy of man.　*Ib.* 68

35 FIRST MURDERER:
　　　　　　We are men, my liege.
MACBETH:
Ay, in the catalogue ye go for men.　*Ib.* 91

36 SECOND MURDERER:
　　　　　　　　　I am one, my liege,
Whom the vile blows and buffets of the world
Have so incens'd, that I am reckless what
I do to spite the world.

FIRST MURDERER:

     I another,
So weary with disasters, tugg'd with fortune,
That I would set my life on any chance,
To mend it or be rid on 't. *Macbeth*, III. i. 108

1 Leave no rubs nor botches in the work. *Ib.* 134

2   Thy soul's flight,
If it find heaven, must find it out to-night. *Ib.* 141

3   Nought's had, all's spent,
Where our desire is got without content:
'Tis safer to be that which we destroy,
Than, by destruction, dwell in doubtful joy. *Ib.* ii. 4

4 LADY MACBETH:

    Things without all remedy
Should be without regard: what's done is done.

MACBETH:

We have scotch'd the snake, not killed it:
She'll close and be herself, whilst our poor malice
Remains in danger of her former tooth
But let the frame of things disjoint, both the worlds
 suffer,
Ere we will eat our meal in fear, and sleep
In the affliction of these terrible dreams
That shake us nightly. Better be with the dead,
Whom we, to gain our peace, have sent to peace,
Than on the torture of the mind to lie
In restless ecstasy. Duncan is in his grave;
After life's fitful fever he sleeps well;
Treason has done his worst: nor steel, nor poison,
Malice domestic, foreign levy, nothing,
Can touch him further.   *Ib.* 11

5 Make our faces vizards to our hearts,
Disguising what they are.   *Ib.* 34

6 But in them nature's copy's not eterne. *Ib.* 38

7 A deed of dreadful note.   *Ib.* 44

8 Be innocent of the knowledge, dearest chuck,
Till thou applaud the deed. Come, seeling night,
Scarf up the tender eye of pitiful day,
And with thy bloody and invisible hand,
Cancel and tear to pieces that great bond
Which keeps me pale! Light thickens, and the crow
Makes wing to the rooky wood;
Good things of day begin to droop and drowse,
Whiles night's black agents to their preys do rouse.
         Ib. 45

9 Things bad begun make strong themselves by ill.
         Ib. 55

10 Now spurs the lated traveller apace
To gain the timely inn.   *Ib.* iii. 6

11 Ourself will mingle with society
And play the humble host.   *Ib.* iv. 3

12 But now I am cabin'd, cribb'd, confin'd, bound in
To saucy doubts and fears.   *Ib.* 24

13 Now good digestion wait on appetite,
And health on both!   *Ib.* 38

14 Which of you have done this? *Ib.* 49

15 Thou canst not say I did it: never shake
Thy gory locks at me.   *Ib.* 50

16 The air-drawn dagger.   *Ib.* 62

17   The times have been,
That, when the brains were out, the man would die,
And there an end; but now they rise again,
With twenty mortal murders on their crowns,
And push us from our stools: this is more strange
Than such a murder is. *Macbeth*, III. iv. 78

18 I drink to the general joy of the whole table. *Ib.* 89

19 Thy bones are marrowless, thy blood is cold;
Thou hast no speculation in those eyes
Which thou dost glare with.   *Ib.* 94

20 What man dare, I dare;
Approach thou like the rugged Russian bear,
The arm'd rhinoceros or the Hyrcan tiger,
Take any shape but that, and my firm nerves
Shall never tremble.   *Ib.* 99

21   Hence, horrible shadow!
Unreal mockery, hence!   *Ib.* 106

22 LADY MACBETH:
You have displaced the mirth, broke the good
 meeting,
With most admir'd disorder.

MACBETH:

      Can such things be,
And overcome us like a summer's cloud,
Without our special wonder? *Ib.* 109

23 Stand not upon the order of your going,
But go at once.   *Ib.* 119

24 MACBETH:
It will have blood, they say; blood will have blood:
Stones have been known to move and trees to speak;
Augurs and understood relations have
By maggot-pies and choughs and rooks brought forth
The secret'st man of blood. What is the night?

LADY MACBETH:
Almost at odds with morning, which is which.
         Ib. 122

25   I am in blood
Stepp'd in so far that, should I wade no more,
Returning were as tedious as go o'er. *Ib.* 136

26 You lack the season of all natures, sleep. *Ib.* 141

27 Upon the corner of the moon
There hangs a vaporous drop profound;
I'll catch it ere it come to ground. *Ib.* v. 23

28 And you all know, security
Is mortals' chiefest enemy.   *Ib.* 32

29 Round about the cauldron go;
In the poison'd entrails throw. *Ib.* IV. i. 4

30 Double, double toil and trouble;
Fire burn, and cauldron bubble. *Ib.* 10

31 Eye of newt and toe of frog,
Wool of bat and tongue of dog. *Ib.* 14

32   Slips of yew
Sliver'd in the moon's eclipse. *Ib.* 27

33 Finger of birth-strangled babe,
Ditch-deliver'd by a drab,
Make the gruel thick and slab. *Ib.* 30

34 *Black spirits and white,*
 Red spirits and grey,
Mingle, mingle, mingle,
 You that mingle may.
 Ib. 44. *Stage direction. Davenant's version of*
 Macbeth

[459]

1 By the pricking of my thumbs,
Something wicked this way comes.
   Open, locks,
   Whoever knocks.   *Macbeth*, IV. i. 44

2 How now, you secret, black, and midnight hags!
             Ib. 48

3 A deed without a name.   *Ib.* 49

4 Though you untie the winds and let them fight
Against the churches; though the yesty waves
Confound and swallow navigation up. *Ib.* 52

5 Be bloody, bold, and resolute; laugh to scorn
The power of man, for none of woman born
Shall harm Macbeth.   *Ib.* 79

6 But yet I'll make assurance double sure,
And take a bond of fate.   *Ib.* 83

7 That I may tell pale-hearted fear it lies,
And sleep in spite of thunder.   *Ib.* 85

8   Wears upon his baby brow the round
And top of sovereignty.   *Ib.* 88

9   Take no care
Who chafes, who frets, or where conspirers are:
Macbeth shall never vanquish'd be until
Great Birnam wood to high Dunsinane hill
Shall come against him.   *Ib.* 90

10 Show his eyes, and grieve his heart;
Come like shadows, so depart!   *Ib.* 110

11 What! will the line stretch out to the crack of doom?
           Ib. 117

12 For the blood-bolter'd Banquo smiles upon me.
           Ib. 123

13 The weird sisters.   *Ib.* 136

14 The flighty purpose never is o'ertook,
Unless the deed go with it.   *Ib.* 145

15 The very firstlings of my heart shall be
The firstlings of my hand.   *Ib.* 147

16 His flight was madness: when our actions do not,
Our fears do make us traitors.   *Ib.* ii. 3

17 He wants the natural touch; for the poor wren,
The most diminutive of birds, will fight—
Her young ones in her nest—against the owl. *Ib.* 9

18 Angels are bright still, though the brightest fell.
           Ib. iii. 22

19 MACDUFF:
Stands Scotland where it did?
 ROSS:
      Alas! poor country;
Almost afraid to know itself. It cannot
Be call'd our mother, but our grave. *Ib.* 164

20 What! man; ne'er pull your hat upon your brows;
Give sorrow words: the grief that does not speak
Whispers the o'er-fraught heart, and bids it break.
           Ib. 208

21   All my pretty ones?
Did you say all? O hell-kite! All?
What! all my pretty chickens and their dam,
At one fell swoop?   *Ib.* 216

22 MALCOLM:
Dispute it like a man.
 MACDUFF:
     I shall do so;
But I must also feel it as a man;

I cannot but remember such things were,
That were most precious to me. *Macbeth*, IV. iii. 219

23 DOCTOR:
You see her eyes are open.
 GENTLEWOMAN:
Ay, but their sense is shut.   *Ib.* v. i. [27]

24 Out, damned spot! out, I say! One; two: why then,
'tis time to do't. Hell is murky! Fie, my lord, fie!
a soldier, and afeard? What need we fear who
knows it, when none can call our power to account?
Yet who would have thought the old man to have
had so much blood in him?   *Ib.* [38]

25 The Thane of Fife had a wife: where is she now?
What! will these hands ne'er be clean? *Ib.* [46]

26 She has spoke what she should not, I am sure of
that: Heaven knows what she has known. *Ib.* [52]

27 All the perfumes of Arabia will not sweeten this
little hand.   *Ib.* [56]

28 I would not have such a heart in my bosom for the
dignity of the whole body.   *Ib.* [60]

29 Foul whisperings are abroad.   *Ib.* [78]

30 More needs she the divine than the physician.
           Ib. [81]

31 Those he commands move only in command,
Nothing in love; now does he feel his title
Hang loose about him, like a giant's robe
Upon a dwarfish thief.   *Ib.* ii. 19

32   All that is within him does condemn
Itself for being there.   *Ib.* 24

33 Bring me no more reports; let them fly all:
Till Birnam wood remove to Dunsinane
I cannot taint with fear.   *Ib.* iii. 1

34   The spirits that know
All mortal consequences have pronounc'd me thus.
           Ib. 4

35 The devil damn thee black, thou cream-faced loon!
Where gott'st thou that goose look? *Ib.* 11

36   This push
Will cheer me ever or disseat me now.
I have lived long enough: my way of life
Is fall'n into the sear, the yellow leaf;
And that which should accompany old age,
As honour, love, obedience, troops of friends,
I must not look to have; but, in their stead,
Curses, not loud but deep, mouth-honour, breath,
Which the poor heart would fain deny, and dare not.
           Ib. 20

37 DOCTOR:
      Not so sick, my lord,
As she is troubled with thick-coming fancies,
That keep her from her rest.
 MACBETH:
       Cure her of that:
Canst thou not minister to a mind diseas'd,
Pluck from the memory a rooted sorrow,
Raze out the written troubles of the brain,
And with some sweet oblivious antidote
Cleanse the stuff'd bosom of that perilous stuff
Which weighs upon the heart?
 DOCTOR:
       Therein the patient
Must minister to himself.
 MACBETH:
Throw physic to the dogs; I'll none of it. *Ib.* 37

1   If thou couldst, doctor, cast
The water of my land, find her disease,
And purge it to a sound and pristine health,
I would applaud thee to the very echo,
That should applaud again.   *Macbeth*, v. iii. 50

2 Hang out our banners on the outward walls;
The cry is still, 'They come;' our castle's strength
Will laugh a siege to scorn.   *Ib.* v. 1

3 I have almost forgot the taste of fears.
The time has been my senses would have cool'd
To hear a night-shriek, and my fell of hair
Would at a dismal treatise rouse and stir
As life were in't. I have supp'd full with horrors;
Direness, familiar to my slaughterous thoughts,
Cannot once start me.   *Ib.* 9

4 SEYTON:
The queen, my lord, is dead.
MACBETH:
She should have died hereafter;
There would have been a time for such a word.
To-morrow, and to-morrow, and to-morrow,
Creeps in this petty pace from day to day,
To the last syllable of recorded time;
And all our yesterdays have lighted fools
The way to dusty death. Out, out, brief candle!
Life's but a walking shadow, a poor player,
That struts and frets his hour upon the stage,
And then is heard no more; it is a tale
Told by an idiot, full of sound and fury,
Signifying nothing.   *Ib.* 16

5 I pull in resolution, and begin
To doubt the equivocation of the fiend
That lies like truth: 'Fear not, till Birnam wood
Do come to Dunsinane.'   *Ib.* 42

6 I 'gin to be aweary of the sun,
And wish the estate o' the world were now undone.
   Ib. 49

7   Blow, wind! come, wrack!
At least we'll die with harness on our back.   *Ib.* 51

8 They have tied me to a stake; I cannot fly.
But bear-like I must fight the course.   *Ib.* vii. 1

9 Why should I play the Roman fool, and die
On mine own sword?   *Ib.* 30

10 I bear a charmed life.   *Ib.* 41

11 And let the angel whom thou still hast served
Tell thee, Macduff was from his mother's womb
Untimely ripp'd.   *Ib.* 43

12 And be these juggling fiends no more believ'd,
That palter with us in a double sense;
That keep the word of promise to our ear,
And break it to our hope.   *Ib.* 48

13 Live to be the show and gaze o' the time.   *Ib.* 53

14   Lay on, Macduff;
And damn'd be him that first cries, 'Hold, enough!'
   Ib. 62

15 SIWARD:
    Had he his hurts before?
ROSS:
Ay, on the front.
SIWARD:
    Why, then, God's soldier be he!
Had I as many sons as I have hairs,
I would not wish them to a fairer death.   *Ib.* 75

16   For if our virtues
Did not go forth of us, 'twere all alike
As if we had them not. Spirits are not finely touch'd
But to fine issues.   *Measure for Measure*, I. i. 33

17 The sanctimonious pirate, that went to sea with the
Ten Commandments, but scraped one out of the
table.   *Ib.* ii. [7]

18 And liberty plucks justice by the nose.   *Ib.* iii. 29

19 I hold you as a thing ensky'd and sainted. *Ib.* iv. 34

20   A man whose blood
Is very snow-broth; one who never feels
The wanton stings and motions of the sense. *Ib.* 57

21   Our doubts are traitors,
And make us lose the good we oft might win,
By fearing to attempt.   *Ib.* 77

22 We must not make a scarecrow of the law,
Setting it up to fear the birds of prey,
And let it keep one shape, till custom make it
Their perch and not their terror.   *Ib.* II. i. 1

23 'Tis one thing to be tempted, Escalus,
Another thing to fall. I not deny,
The jury, passing on the prisoner's life,
May in the sworn twelve have a thief or two
Guiltier than him they try.   *Ib.* 17

24 Some rise by sin, and some by virtue fall. *Ib.* 38

25 This will last out a night in Russia,
When nights are longest there.   *Ib.* [144]

26   I am
At war 'twixt will and will not.   *Ib.* ii. 32

27 Condemn the fault and not the actor of it? *Ib.* 37

28 No ceremony that to great ones 'longs,
Not the king's crown, nor the deputed sword,
The marshal's truncheon, nor the judge's robe,
Become them with one half so good a grace
As mercy does.   *Ib.* 59

29 Why, all the souls that were were forfeit once;
And He that might the vantage best have took,
Found out the remedy. How would you be,
If He, which is the top of judgment, should
But judge you as you are?   *Ib.* 73

30   O! it is excellent
To have a giant's strength, but it is tyrannous
To use it like a giant.   *Ib.* 107

31 Merciful Heaven!
Thou rather with thy sharp and sulphurous bolt
Split'st the unwedgeable and gnarled oak
Than the soft myrtle; but man, proud man,
Drest in a little brief authority,
Most ignorant of what he's most assur'd,
His glassy essence, like an angry ape,
Plays such fantastic tricks before high heaven,
As make the angels weep.   *Ib.* 114

32 Great men may jest with saints; 'tis wit in them,
But, in the less foul profanation.   *Ib.* 127

33 That in the captain's but a choleric word,
Which in the soldier is flat blasphemy.   *Ib.* 130

34   I am that way going to temptation,
Where prayers cross.   *Ib.* 158

35 Having waste ground enough,
Shall we desire to raze the sanctuary
And pitch our evils there?   *Ib.* 170

1 O cunning enemy, that, to catch a saint,
With saints dost bait thy hook! Most dangerous
Is that temptation that doth goad us on
To sin in loving virtue. *Measure for Measure*, II. ii. 180

2 When I would pray and think, I think and pray
To several subjects: Heaven hath my empty words.
Ib. iv. 1

3 CLAUDIO:
The miserable have no other medicine
But only hope:
I have hope to live, and am prepar'd to die.
DUKE:
Be absolute for death; either death or life
Shall thereby be the sweeter. Reason thus with life:
If I do lose thee, I do lose a thing
That none but fools would keep: a breath thou art
Servile to all the skyey influences. *Ib.* III. i. 2

4   If thou art rich, thou'rt poor;
For, like an ass whose back with ingots bows,
Thou bear'st thy heavy riches but a journey,
And death unloads thee. *Ib.* 25

5 Thou hast nor youth nor age;
But, as it were, an after-dinner's sleep,
Dreaming on both. *Ib.* 32

6 Palsied eld. *Ib.* 35

7   Dar'st thou die?
The sense of death is most in apprehension,
And the poor beetle, that we tread upon,
In corporal sufferance finds a pang as great
As when a giant dies. *Ib.* 75

8   If I must die,
I will encounter darkness as a bride,
And hug it in mine arms. *Ib.* 81

9 CLAUDIO:
                  Death is a fearful thing.
ISABELLA:
And shamed life a hateful.
CLAUDIO:
Ay, but to die, and go we know not where;
To lie in cold obstruction and to rot;
This sensible warm motion to become
A kneaded clod; and the delighted spirit
To bathe in fiery floods, or to reside
In thrilling region of thick-ribbèd ice;
To be imprisoned in the viewless winds,
And blown with restless violence round about
The pendant world! *Ib.* 114

10 The weariest and most loathèd worldly life
That age, ache, penury, and imprisonment
Can lay on nature, is a paradise
To what we fear of death. *Ib.* 127

11   O, fie, fie, fie!
Thy sin's not accidental, but a trade. *Ib.* 146

12 The hand that hath made you fair hath made you good.
Ib. [182]

13 Virtue is bold, and goodness never fearful. *Ib.* [214]

14 There, at the moated grange, resides this dejected
Mariana. *Ib.* [279]

15 A very superficial, ignorant, unweighing fellow.
Ib. ii. [151]

16 Take, O take those lips away,
     That so sweetly were forsworn;
And those eyes, the break of day,
     Lights that do mislead the morn:

But my kisses bring again, bring again;
Seals of love, but seal'd in vain, seal'd in vain.
Measure for Measure, IV. i. 1

17   Though music oft hath such a charm
To make bad good, and good provoke to harm. *Ib.* 16

18 He will discredit our mystery. *Ib.* ii. [29]

19 Every true man's apparel fits your thief. *Ib.* [46]

20 Look, here's the warrant, Claudio, for thy death:
'Tis now dead midnight, and by eight to-morrow
Thou must be made immortal. *Ib.* [66]

21 A man that apprehends death no more dreadfully
but as a drunken sleep. *Ib.* [148]

22 Look, the unfolding star calls up the shepherd.
Ib. [219]

23 I am a kind of burr; I shall stick. *Ib.* iii. [193]

24 A forted residence 'gainst the tooth of time,
And razure of oblivion. *Ib.* v. i. 12

25   Let the devil
Be sometime honour'd for his burning throne.
Ib. [289]

26 Haste still pays haste, and leisure answers leisure;
Like doth quit like, and Measure still for Measure.
Ib. [411]

27 They say best men are moulded out of faults,
And, for the most, become much more the better
For being a little bad. *Ib.* [440]

28 In sooth I know not why I am so sad:
It wearies me; you say it wearies you;
But how I caught it, found it, or came by it,
What stuff 'tis made of, whereof it is born,
I am to learn. *The Merchant of Venice*, I. i. 1

29 There, where your argosies with portly sail,—
Like signiors and rich burghers on the flood,
Or, as it were, the pageants of the sea,—
Do overpeer the petty traffickers. *Ib.* 9

30 Nature hath fram'd strange fellows in her time:
Some that will evermore peep through their eyes
And laugh like parrots at a bagpiper:
And other of such vinegar aspect
That they'll not show their teeth in way of smile,
Though Nestor swear the jest be laughable. *Ib.* 51

31 I hold the world but as the world, Gratiano;
A stage where every man must play a part,
And mine a sad one. *Ib.* 77

32 Why should a man, whose blood is warm within,
Sit like his grandsire cut in alabaster? *Ib.* 83

33 There are a sort of men whose visages
Do cream and mantle like a standing pond. *Ib.* 88

34 As who should say, 'I am Sir Oracle,
And when I ope my lips let no dog bark!'
O, my Antonio, I do know of these,
That therefore only are reputed wise,
For saying nothing. *Ib.* 93

35   Fish not, with this melancholy bait,
For this fool gudgeon, this opinion. *Ib.* 101

36   Silence is only commendable
In a neat's tongue dried and a maid not vendible.
Ib. 111

1 Gratiano speaks an infinite deal of nothing, more than any man in all Venice. His reasons are as two grains of wheat, hid in two bushels of chaff: you shall seek all day ere you find them; and, when you have them, they are not worth the search.
The Merchant of Venice, I. i. 114

2 My purse, my person, my extremest means
Lie all unlock'd to your occasions. *Ib.* [139]

3   Sometimes from her eyes
I did receive fair speechless messages. *Ib.* [164]

4 By my troth, Nerissa, my little body is aweary of this great world. *Ib.* ii. 1

5 They are as sick that surfeit with too much, as they that starve with nothing. *Ib.* [5]

6 Superfluity comes sooner by white hairs, but competency lives longer. *Ib.* [9]

7 If to do were as easy as to know what were good to do, chapels had been churches, and poor men's cottages princes' palaces. *Ib.* [13]

8 It is a good divine that follows his own instructions; I can easier teach twenty what were good to be done, than be one of the twenty to follow mine own teaching. *Ib.* [15]

9 He doth nothing but talk of his horse. *Ib.* [43]

10 God made him, and therefore let him pass for a man.
Ib. [59]

11 If I should marry him, I should marry twenty husbands. *Ib.* [66]

12 I think he bought his doublet in Italy, his round hose in France, his bonnet in Germany, and his behaviour everywhere. *Ib.* [78]

13 I will do anything, Nerissa, ere I will be married to a sponge. *Ib.* [105]

14 I dote on his very absence. *Ib.* [118]

15 Ships are but boards, sailors but men; there be land-rats and water-rats, land-thieves and water-thieves.
Ib. iii. [22]

16 I will buy with you, sell with you, talk with you, walk with you, and so following; but I will not eat with you, drink with you, nor pray with you. What news on the Rialto? *Ib.* [36]

17 How like a fawning publican he looks!
I hate him for he is a Christian;
But more for that in low simplicity
He lends out money gratis, and brings down
The rate of usance here with us in Venice.
If I can catch him once upon the hip,
I will feed fat the ancient grudge I bear him.
He hates our sacred nation, and he rails,
Even there where merchants most do congregate,
On me, my bargains, and my well-won thrift.
Ib. [42]

18 The devil can cite Scripture for his purpose.
Ib. [99]

19 A goodly apple rotten at the heart.
O, what a goodly outside falsehood hath! *Ib.* [102]

20 Signior Antonio, many a time and oft
In the Rialto you have rated me. *Ib.* [107]

21 For sufferance is the badge of all our tribe. *Ib.* [111]

22 'Hath a dog money? Is it possible
A cur can lend three thousand ducats?' or
Shall I bend low, and in a bondman's key,
With bated breath, and whispering humbleness,
Say this:—
'Fair sir, you spet on me on Wednesday last;
You spurn'd me such a day; another time
You call'd me dog; and for these courtesies
I'll lend you thus much moneys?'
The Merchant of Venice, I. iii. [122]

23   For when did friendship take
A breed for barren metal of his friend? *Ib.* [134]

24 O father Abram! what these Christians are,
Whose own hard dealing teaches them suspect
The thoughts of others! *Ib.* [161]

25 I like not fair terms and a villain's mind. *Ib.* [180]

26 Mislike me not for my complexion,
The shadow'd livery of the burnished sun.
Ib. II. i. 1

27 An honest man's son,—or rather an honest woman's son;—for, indeed, my father did something smack, something grow to, he had a kind of taste;—well, my conscience says, 'Launcelot, budge not.' 'Budge,' says the fiend. 'Budge not,' says my conscience. 'Conscience,' say I, 'you counsel well;' 'fiend,' say I, 'you counsel well.' *Ib.* ii. [16]

28 O heavens! this is my true-begotten father. *Ib.* [36]

29 An honest exceeding poor man. *Ib.* [54]

30 The very staff of my age, my very prop. *Ib.* [71]

31 It is a wise father that knows his own child. *Ib.* [83]

32 Truth will come to light; murder cannot be hid long.
Ib. [86]

33 Lord worshipped might he be! What a beard hast thou got! *Ib.* [101]

34 There is some ill a-brewing towards my rest,
For I did dream of money-bags to-night. *Ib.* v. 17

35 Then it was not for nothing that my nose fell a-bleeding on Black Monday. *Ib.* [24]

36 And the vile squealing of the wry-neck'd fife. *Ib.* [30]

37 But love is blind, and lovers cannot see
The pretty follies that themselves commit. *Ib.* vi. 36

38 What! must I hold a candle to my shames? *Ib.* 41

39   Men that hazard all
Do it in hope of fair advantages:
A golden mind stoops not to shows of dross.
Ib. vii. 18

40 Pause there, Morocco. *Ib.* 24

41 Young in limbs, in judgment old. *Ib.* 71

42 My daughter! O my ducats! O my daughter!
Fled with a Christian! O my Christian ducats!
Ib. viii. 15

43 The fool multitude, that choose by show. *Ib.* ix. 26

44   Like the martlet,
Builds in the weather on the outward wall,
Even in the force and road of casualty.
I will not choose what many men desire,
Because I will not jump with common spirits
And rank me with the barbarous multitude. *Ib.* 28

1   Let none presume
To wear an undeserved dignity.
O! that estates, degrees, and offices
Were not deriv'd corruptly, and that clear honour
Were purchased by the merit of the wearer!
         The Merchant of Venice, II. ix. 39

2 The portrait of a blinking idiot.   *Ib.* 54

3 The fire seven times tried this:
Seven times tried that judgment is
That did never choose amiss.
Some there be that shadows kiss;
Such have but a shadow's bliss.   *Ib.* 63

4 Thus hath the candle sing'd the moth.
O, these deliberate fools!   *Ib.* 79

5 The ancient saying is no heresy:
'Hanging and wiving goes by destiny.'   *Ib.* 82

6 The Goodwins, I think they call the place; a very dangerous flat, and fatal, where the carcasses of many a tall ship lie buried, as they say, if my gossip Report be an honest woman of her word.
    Ib. III. i. [4]

7 Let him look to his bond.   *Ib.* [51, 52, 54]

8 Hath not a Jew eyes? hath not a Jew hands, organs, dimensions, senses, affections, passions? fed with the same food, hurt with the same weapons, subject to the same diseases, healed by the same means, warmed and cooled by the same winter and summer, as a Christian is? If you prick us, do we not bleed? if you tickle us, do we not laugh? if you poison us, do we not die? and if you wrong us, shall we not revenge?   *Ib.* [63]

9 The villany you teach me I will execute, and it shall go hard but I will better the instruction.
    Ib. [76]

10 Thou stick'st a dagger in me.   *Ib.* [118]

11 TUBAL:
One of them showed me a ring that he had of your daughter for a monkey.
SHYLOCK:
I would not have given it for a wilderness of monkeys.
    Ib. [126]

12   He makes a swan-like end
Fading in music.   *Ib.* ii. 44

13   Tell me where is fancy bred,
      Or in the heart or in the head?
    How begot, how nourished?
      Reply, reply.

It is engender'd in the eyes,
With gazing fed; and fancy dies
In the cradle where it lies.
    Let us all ring fancy's knell:
      I'll begin it,—Ding, dong, bell.
    Ib. 63

14 So may the outward shows be least themselves:
The world is still deceived with ornament.
In law, what plea so tainted and corrupt
But, being season'd with a gracious voice,
Obscures the show of evil? In religion,
What damned error, but some sober brow
Will bless it and approve it with a text,
Hiding the grossness with fair ornament?   *Ib.* 73

15   Ornament is but the guiled shore
To a most dangerous sea; the beauteous scarf
Veiling an Indian beauty; in a word,
The seeming truth which cunning times put on
To entrap the wisest.
    The Merchant of Venice, III. ii. 97

16   Thou pale and common drudge
'Tween man and man.   *Ib.* 103

17   Rash-embrac'd despair,
And shuddering fear, and green-ey'd jealousy.
    Ib. 109

18   What demi-god
Hath come so near creation?   *Ib.* 115

19 An unlesson'd girl, unschool'd, unpractis'd;
Happy in this, she is not yet so old
But she may learn; happier than this,
She is not bred so dull but she can learn. *Ib.* 160

20 I wish you all the joy that you can wish. *Ib.* 191

21 My eyes, my lord, can look as swift as yours:
You saw the mistress, I beheld the maid. *Ib.* 198

22 Here are a few of the unpleasant'st words
That ever blotted paper!   *Ib.* 252

23 I will have my bond.   *Ib.* iii. 17

24 This comes too near the praising of myself. *Ib.* iv. 22

25 How every fool can play upon the word! *Ib.* v. [48]

26 Wilt thou show the whole wealth of thy wit in an instant? I pray thee, understand a plain man in his plain meaning.   *Ib.* [62]

27   I'll not answer that:
But say it is my humour.   *Ib.* IV. i. 42

28 A harmless necessary cat.   *Ib.* 55

29 I am not bound to please thee with my answer.
    Ib. 65

30 What judgment shall I dread, doing no wrong?
    Ib. 89

31 I am a tainted wether of the flock,
Meetest for death: the weakest kind of fruit
Drops earliest to the ground.   *Ib.* 114

32 I never knew so young a body with so old a head.
    Ib. [163]

33 PORTIA:
    Then must the Jew be merciful.
SHYLOCK:
On what compulsion must I? tell me that.
PORTIA:
The quality of mercy is not strain'd,
It droppeth as the gentle rain from heaven
Upon the place beneath: it is twice bless'd;
It blesseth him that gives and him that takes:
'Tis mightiest in the mightiest: it becomes
The throned monarch better than his crown;
His sceptre shows the force of temporal power,
The attribute to awe and majesty,
Wherein doth sit the dread and fear of kings;
But mercy is above this sceptred sway,
It is enthroned in the hearts of kings,
It is an attribute to God himself,
And earthly power doth then show likest God's
When mercy seasons justice. Therefore, Jew,
Though justice be thy plea, consider this,
That in the course of justice none of us
Should see salvation: we do pray for mercy,
And that same prayer doth teach us all to render
The deeds of mercy.   *Ib.* [182]

1 My deeds upon my head! I crave the law.
The Merchant of Venice, IV. i. [206]

2 Wrest once the law to your authority:
To do a great right, do a little wrong. *Ib.* [215]

3 'Twill be recorded for a precedent,
And many an error by the same example
Will rush into the state. *Ib.* [220]

4 A Daniel come to judgment! yea, a Daniel!
O wise young judge, how I do honour thee!
Ib. [223]

5 An oath, an oath, I have an oath in heaven:
Shall I lay perjury upon my soul?
No, not for Venice. *Ib.* [228]

6   I charge you by the law,
Whereof you are a well-deserving pillar,
Proceed to judgment. *Ib.* [238]

7 Is it so nominated in the bond? *Ib.* [260]

8 'Tis not in the bond. *Ib.* [263]

9 For herein Fortune shows herself more kind
Than is her custom: it is still her use
To let the wretched man outlive his wealth,
To view with hollow eye and wrinkled brow
An age of poverty. *Ib.* [268]

10 The court awards it, and the law doth give it.
Ib. [301]

11   Thyself shalt see the act;
For, as thou urgest justice, be assur'd
Thou shalt have justice, more than thou desir'st.
Ib. [315]

12 A second Daniel, a Daniel, Jew!
Now, infidel, I have thee on the hip. *Ib.* [334]

13 I thank thee, Jew, for teaching me that word.
Ib. [342]

14 You take my house when you do take the prop
That doth sustain my house; you take my life
When you do take the means whereby I live. *Ib.* [376]

15 He is well paid that is well satisfied. *Ib.* [416]

16 You taught me first to beg, and now methinks
You teach me how a beggar should be answer'd.
Ib. [440]

17 LORENZO:
        In such a night
Troilus methinks mounted the Troyan walls,
And sigh'd his soul toward the Grecian tents,
Where Cressid lay that night.
JESSICA:
        In such a night
Did Thisbe fearfully o'ertrip the dew,
And saw the lion's shadow ere himself,
And ran dismay'd away.
LORENZO:
        In such a night
Stood Dido with a willow in her hand
Upon the wild sea-banks, and waft her love
To come again to Carthage.
JESSICA:
        In such a night
Medea gather'd the enchanted herbs
That did renew old Æson. *Ib.* v. i. 3

18 How sweet the moonlight sleeps upon this bank!
Here will we sit, and let the sounds of music
Creep in our ears: soft stillness and the night
Become the touches of sweet harmony.
Sit, Jessica: look, how the floor of heaven

Is thick inlaid with patines of bright gold:
There's not the smallest orb which thou behold'st
But in his motion like an angel sings,
Still quiring to the young-eyed cherubins;
Such harmony is in immortal souls;
But, whilst this muddy vesture of decay
Doth grossly close it in, we cannot hear it.
The Merchant of Venice, v. i. 54

19 I am never merry when I hear sweet music. *Ib.* 69

20   Therefore the poet
Did feign that Orpheus drew trees, stones, and floods;
Since nought so stockish, hard, and full of rage,
But music for the time doth change his nature.
The man that hath no music in himself,
Nor is not mov'd with concord of sweet sounds,
Is fit for treasons, stratagems, and spoils;
The motions of his spirit are dull as night,
And his affections dark as Erebus:
Let no such man be trusted. *Ib.* 79

21 PORTIA:
How far that little candle throws his beams!
So shines a good deed in a naughty world.
NERISSA:
When the moon shone, we did not see the candle.
PORTIA:
So doth the greater glory dim the less:
A substitute shines brightly as a king
Until a king be by, and then his state
Empties itself, as doth an inland brook
Into the main of waters. *Ib.* 90

22 The crow doth sing as sweetly as the lark
When neither is attended, and I think
The nightingale, if she should sing by day,
When every goose is cackling, would be thought
No better a musician than the wren.
How many things by season season'd are
To their right praise and true perfection!
Peace, ho! the moon sleeps with Endymion,
And would not be awak'd! *Ib.* 102

23 This night methinks is but the daylight sick. *Ib.* 124

24 For a light wife doth make a heavy husband. *Ib.* 130

25 These blessed candles of the night. *Ib.* 220

26 I will make a Star-Chamber matter of it.
The Merry Wives of Windsor, I. i. 1

27 She has brown hair, and speaks small like a woman.
Ib. [48]

28 Pribbles and prabbles. *Ib.* [56]

29 Drink down all unkindness. *Ib.* [203]

30 I had rather than forty shillings I had my Book of
Songs and Sonnets here. *Ib.* [205]

31 I will make an end of my dinner; there's pippins and
seese to come. *Ib.* ii. [12]

32 'Convey,' the wise it call. 'Steal!' foh! a fico for the
phrase! *Ib.* iii. [30]

33 Here will be an old abusing of God's patience, and
the king's English. *Ib.* iv. [5]

34 We burn daylight. *Ib.* II. i. [54]

35 There's the humour of it. *Ib.* [139]

36 Faith, thou hast some crotchets in thy head now.
Ib. [158]

37 Why, then the world's mine oyster,
Which I with sword will open. *Ib.* ii. 2

1 Marry, this is the short and the long of it.
The Merry Wives of Windsor, II. ii. [62]

2 Like a fair house built upon another man's ground.
Ib. [229]

3 Ah, sweet Anne Page! *Ib.* III. i. [40]

4 I cannot tell what the dickens his name is.
Ib. ii. [20]

5 He capers, he dances, he has eyes of youth, he writes
verses, he speaks holiday, he smells April and May.
Ib. [71]

6 O, what a world of vile ill-favour'd faults
Looks handsome in three hundred pounds a year!
Ib. iv. [32]

7 If it be my luck, so; if not, happy man be his dole!
Ib. [67]

8 If I be served such another trick, I'll have my brains
ta'en out, and buttered, and give them to a dog
for a new year's gift. *Ib.* v. [7]

9 I have a kind of alacrity in sinking. *Ib.* [13]

10 As good luck would have it. *Ib.* [86]

11 A man of my kidney. *Ib.* [119]

12 Vengeance of Jenny's case! *Ib.* IV. i. [65]

13 So curses all Eve's daughters, of what complexion
soever. *Ib.* ii. [24]

14 This is the third time; I hope good luck lies in odd
numbers. . . . There is divinity in odd numbers,
either in nativity, chance or death. *Ib.* v. i. 2

15 Fairies, black, grey, green, and white,
You moonshine revellers, and shades of night.
Ib. v. [43]

16 To live a barren sister all your life,
Chanting faint hymns to the cold fruitless moon.
A Midsummer Night's Dream, I. i. 72

17 But earthlier happy is the rose distill'd,
Than that which withering on the virgin thorn
Grows, lives, and dies, in single blessedness. *Ib.* 76

18 Ay me! for aught that ever I could read,
Could ever hear by tale or history,
The course of true love never did run smooth.
Ib. 132

19 O hell! to choose love by another's eye. *Ib.* 140

20   If there were a sympathy in choice,
War, death, or sickness did lay siege to it,
Making it momentany as a sound,
Swift as a shadow, short as any dream,
Brief as the lightning in the collied night,
That, in a spleen, unfolds both heaven and earth,
And ere a man hath power to say, 'Behold!'
The jaws of darkness do devour it up:
So quick bright things come to confusion. *Ib.* 141

21   Your tongue's sweet air
More tuneable than lark to shepherd's ear,
When wheat is green, when hawthorn buds appear.
Ib. 183

22 Love looks not with the eyes, but with the mind,
And therefore is wing'd Cupid painted blind.
Ib. 234

23 The most lamentable comedy, and most cruel death
of Pyramus and Thisby. *Ib.* ii. [11]

24 Masters, spread yourselves. *Ib.* [16]

25 A part to tear a cat in, to make all split.
A Midsummer Night's Dream, I. ii. [32]

26 This is Ercles' vein. *Ib.* [43]

27 I'll speak in a monstrous little voice. *Ib.* [55]

28 I am slow of study. *Ib.* [70]

29 I will roar, that I will do any man's heart good to
hear me. *Ib.* [73]

30 I will aggravate my voice so that I will roar you as
gently as any sucking dove; I will roar you as
'twere any nightingale. *Ib.* [84]

31 A proper man, as one shall see in a summer's day.
Ib. [89]

32 Hold, or cut bow-strings. *Ib.* [115]

33 Over hill, over dale,
Thorough bush, thorough brier,
Over park, over pale,
Thorough flood, thorough fire. *Ib.* II. i. 2

34 The cowslips tall her pensioners be;
In their gold coats spots you see;
Those be rubies, fairy favours,
In those freckles live their savours. *Ib.* 10

35 I must go seek some dew-drops here,
And hang a pearl in every cowslip's ear. *Ib.* 14

36 The middle summer's spring. *Ib.* 82

37 Therefore the moon, the governess of floods,
Pale in her anger, washes all the air,
That rheumatic diseases do abound:
And thorough this distemperature we see
The seasons alter: hoary-headed frosts
Fall in the fresh lap of the crimson rose. *Ib.* 103

38 Since once I sat upon a promontory,
And heard a mermaid on a dolphin's back
Uttering such dulcet and harmonious breath,
That the rude sea grew civil at her song,
And certain stars shot madly from their spheres,
To hear the sea-maid's music. *Ib.* 149

39 But I might see young Cupid's fiery shaft
Quench'd in the chaste beams of the wat'ry moon,
And the imperial votaress passed on,
In maiden meditation, fancy-free.
Yet mark'd I where the bolt of Cupid fell:
It fell upon a little western flower,
Before milk-white, now purple with love's wound,
And maidens call it, Love-in-idleness. *Ib.* 161

40 I'll put a girdle round about the earth
In forty minutes. *Ib.* 175

41 I know a bank whereon the wild thyme blows,
Where oxlips and the nodding violet grows
Quite over-canopied with luscious woodbine,
With sweet musk-roses, and with eglantine:
There sleeps Titania some time of the night,
Lull'd in these flowers with dances and delight;
And there the snake throws her enamell'd skin,
Weed wide enough to wrap a fairy in. *Ib.* 249

42 Some to kill cankers in the musk-rose buds,
Some war with rere-mice for their leathern wings,
To make my small elves coats. *Ib.* ii. 3

43 The clamorous owl, that nightly hoots, and wonders
At our quaint spirits. *Ib.* 6

44 You spotted snakes with double tongue,
Thorny hedge-hogs, be not seen;
Newts, and blind-worms, do no wrong;
Come not near our fairy queen. *Ib.* 9

1 Weaving spiders come not here;
Hence, you long-legg'd spinners, hence!
Beetles black, approach not near;
Worm nor snail, do no offence.
A Midsummer Night's Dream, II. ii. 20

2 This green plot shall be our stage, this hawthorn-brake our tiring-house. *Ib.* III. i. [3]

3 God shield us!—a lion among ladies, is a most dreadful thing; for there is not a more fearful wild-fowl than your lion living. *Ib.* [32]

4 What hempen home-spuns have we swaggering here, So near the cradle of the fairy queen? *Ib.* [82]

5 Bless thee, Bottom! bless thee! thou art translated.
Ib. [124]

6 The throstle with his note so true,
The wren with little quill. *Ib.* [133]

7 As wild geese that the creeping fowler eye,
Or russet-pated choughs, many in sort,
Rising and cawing at the gun's report,
Sever themselves, and madly sweep the sky.
Ib. ii. 20

8 Lord, what fools these mortals be! *Ib.* 115

9 So we grew together,
Like to a double cherry, seeming parted,
But yet an union in partition;
Two lovely berries moulded on one stem. *Ib.* 208

10 For night's swift dragons cut the clouds full fast,
And yonder shines Aurora's harbinger;
At whose approach, ghosts, wandering here and there,
Troop home to churchyards. *Ib.* 379

11 Cupid is a knavish lad,
Thus to make poor females mad. *Ib.* 440

12 Jack shall have Jill;
Nought shall go ill;
The man shall have his mare again,
And all shall be well. *Ib.* 461

13 I must to the barber's, mounsieur, for methinks I am marvellous hairy about the face. *Ib.* IV. i. [25]

14 I have a reasonable good ear in music: let us have the tongs and the bones. *Ib.* [32]

15 Methinks I have a great desire to a bottle of hay: good hay, sweet hay, hath no fellow. *Ib.* [37]

16 But, I pray you, let none of your people stir me: I have an exposition of sleep come upon me.
Ib. [43]

17 But as the fierce vexation of a dream. *Ib.* [75]

18 My Oberon! what visions have I seen!
Methought I was enamour'd of an ass. *Ib.* [82]

19 Then, my queen, in silence sad,
Trip we after the night's shade;
We the globe can compass soon,
Swifter than the wandering moon. *Ib.* [101]

20 HIPPOLYTA:
I was with Hercules and Cadmus once,
When in a wood of Crete they bay'd the bear
With hounds of Sparta: never did I hear ...
So musical a discord, such sweet thunder.
THESEUS:
My hounds are bred out of the Spartan kind,
So flew'd, so sanded; and their heads are hung
With ears that sweep away the morning dew;
Crook-knee'd, and dew-lapp'd like Thessalian bulls;
Slow in pursuit, but match'd in mouth like bells.
Ib. [118]

21 Saint Valentine is past:
Begin these wood-birds but to couple now?
A Midsummer Night's Dream, IV. i. [145]

22 I have had a dream, past the wit of man to say what dream it was. *Ib.* [211]

23 The eye of man hath not heard, the ear of man hath not seen, man's hand is not able to taste, his tongue to conceive, nor his heart to report, what my dream was. *Ib.* [218]

24 The lunatic, the lover, and the poet,
Are of imagination all compact:
One sees more devils than vast hell can hold,
That is, the madman; the lover, all as frantic,
Sees Helen's beauty in a brow of Egypt:
The poet's eye, in a fine frenzy rolling,
Doth glance from heaven to earth, from earth to heaven;
And, as imagination bodies forth
The forms of things unknown, the poet's pen
Turns them to shapes, and gives to airy nothing
A local habitation and a name.
Such tricks hath strong imagination,
That, if it would but apprehend some joy,
It comprehends some bringer of that joy;
Or in the night, imagining some fear,
How easy is a bush suppos'd a bear! *Ib.* V. i. 7

25 What revels are in hand? Is there no play,
To ease the anguish of a torturing hour? *Ib.* 36

26 Very tragical mirth. *Ib.* [57]

27 For never anything can be amiss,
When simpleness and duty tender it. *Ib.* [82]

28 That is the true beginning of our end.
Consider then we come but in despite.
We do not come as minding to content you,
Our true intent is. All for your delight,
We are not here. *Ib.* [111]

29 Whereat, with blade, with bloody blameful blade,
He bravely broach'd his boiling bloody breast.
Ib. [148]

30 The best in this kind are but shadows, and the worst are no worse, if imagination amend them.
Ib. [215]

31 A very gentle beast, and of a good conscience.
Ib. [233]

32 Well roared, Lion. *Ib.* [272]

33 This passion, and the death of a dear friend, would go near to make a man look sad. *Ib.* [295]

34 The iron tongue of midnight hath told twelve;
Lovers, to bed; 'tis almost fairy time. *Ib.* [372]

35 Now the hungry lion roars,
And the wolf behowls the moon;
Whilst the heavy ploughman snores,
All with weary task fordone. *Ib.* ii. 1

36 Not a mouse
Shall disturb this hallow'd house:
I am sent with broom before,
To sweep the dust behind the door. *Ib.* 17

37 A victory is twice itself when the achiever brings home full numbers.
Much Ado About Nothing, I. i. [8]

38 He hath indeed better bettered expectation than you must expect of me to tell you how. *Ib.* [15]

39 He is a very valiant trencher-man. *Ib.* [52]

1 I see, lady, the gentleman is not in your books.
Much Ado About Nothing, I. i. [79]

2 BEATRICE:
I wonder that you will still be talking, Signior Benedick: nobody marks you.
BENEDICK:
What! my dear Lady Disdain, are you yet living?
Ib. [121]

3 Shall I never see a bachelor of three-score again?
Ib. [209]

4 BENEDICK:
I will live a bachelor.
DON PEDRO:
I shall see thee, ere I die, look pale with love.
BENEDICK:
With anger, with sickness, or with hunger, my lord; not with love. *Ib.* [256]

5 In time the savage bull doth bear the yoke. *Ib.* [271]

6 Benedick the married man. *Ib.* [278]

7 What need the bridge much broader than the flood?
Ib. [326]

8 Would it not grieve a woman to be over-mastered with a piece of valiant dust? to make an account of her life to a clod of wayward marl? *Ib.* II. i. [64]

9 Wooing, wedding, and repenting, is as a Scotch jig, a measure, and a cinque-pace. *Ib.* [77]

10 I have a good eye, uncle: I can see a church by daylight. *Ib.* [86]

11 Speak low, if you speak love. *Ib.* [104]

12 Friendship is constant in all other things
Save in the office and affairs of love. *Ib.* [184]

13 She speaks poniards, and every word stabs: if her breath were as terrible as her terminations, there were no living near her; she would infect to the north star. *Ib.* [257]

14 Silence is the perfectest herald of joy: I were but little happy, if I could say how much. *Ib.* [319]

15 Speak, cousin, or, if you cannot, stop his mouth with a kiss. *Ib.* [322]

16 There was a star danced, and under that was I born.
Ib. [351]

17 Lie ten nights awake, carving the fashion of a new doublet. *Ib.* iii. [18]

18 Note this before my notes;
There's not a note of mine that's worth the noting.
Ib. [57]

19 Is it not strange that sheep's guts should hale souls out of men's bodies? *Ib.* [62]

20 Sigh no more, ladies, sigh no more,
Men were deceivers ever;
One foot in sea, and one on shore,
To one thing constant never.
    Then sigh not so,
    But let them go,
And be you blithe and bonny,
Converting all your sounds of woe
Into Hey nonny, nonny.

Sing no more ditties, sing no mo
Of dumps so dull and heavy;
The fraud of men was ever so,
Since summer first was leavy. *Ib.* [65]

21 Sits the wind in that corner? *Much Ado*, II. iii. [108]

22 Doth not the appetite alter? A man loves the meat in his youth that he cannot endure in his age.
Ib. [258]

23 Paper bullets of the brain. *Ib.* [261]

24 The world must be peopled. When I said I would die a bachelor, I did not think I should live till I were married. *Ib.* [262]

25 Disdain and scorn ride sparkling in her eyes.
Ib. III. i. 51

26 One doth not know
How much an ill word may empoison liking. *Ib.* 85

27 Contempt, farewell! and maiden pride, adieu!
No glory lives behind the back of such.
And, Benedick, love on; I will requite thee,
Taming my wild heart to thy loving hand. *Ib.* 109

28 He hath a heart as sound as a bell, and his tongue is the clapper; for what his heart thinks his tongue speaks. *Ib.* ii. [12]

29 BENEDICK:
I have the toothache.
    .   .   .
DON PEDRO:
What! sigh for the toothache? *Ib.* [21]

30 Well, every one can master a grief but he that has it.
Ib. [28]

31 A' brushes his hat a mornings; what should that bode? *Ib.* [41]

32 The barber's man hath been seen with him; and the old ornament of his cheek hath already stuffed tennis-balls. *Ib.* [45]

33 Are you good men and true? *Ib.* iii. 1

34 To be a well-favoured man is the gift of fortune; but to write and read comes by nature. *Ib.* [14]

35 Well, for your favour, sir, why, give God thanks, and make no boast of it; and for your writing and reading, let that appear when there is no need of such vanity. You are thought here to be the most senseless and fit man for the constable of the watch.
Ib. [19]

36 You shall comprehend all vagrom men. *Ib.* [25]

37 SECOND WATCH:
How, if a' will not stand?
DOGBERRY:
Why, then, take no note of him, but let him go; and presently call the rest of the watch together, and thank God you are rid of a knave. *Ib.* [28]

38 For the watch to babble and to talk is most tolerable and not to be endured. *Ib.* [36]

39 If they make you not then the better answer, you may say they are not the men you took them for.
Ib. [49]

40 The most peaceable way for you, if you do take a thief, is, to let him show himself what he is and steal out of your company. *Ib.* [61]

41 I know that Deformed. *Ib.* [132]

42 I thank God, I am as honest as any man living, that is an old man and no honester than I. *Ib.* v. [15]

43 Comparisons are odorous. *Ib.* [18]

1 If I were as tedious as a king, I could find in my heart to bestow it all of your worship.
Much Ado About Nothing, III. v. [23]

2 A good old man, sir; he will be talking: as they say, 'when the age is in, the wit is out.' *Ib.* [36]

3 Well, God's a good man. *Ib.* [39]

4 O! what men dare do! what men may do! what men daily do, not knowing what they do! *Ib.* IV. i. [19]

5   For it so falls out
That what we have we prize not to the worth
Whiles we enjoy it, but being lack'd and lost,
Why, then we rack the value, then we find
The virtue that possession would not show us
Whiles it was ours. *Ib.* [219]

6 The idea of her life shall sweetly creep
Into his study of imagination,
And every lovely organ of her life
Shall come apparell'd in more precious habit,
More moving-delicate, and full of life
Into the eye and prospect of his soul. *Ib.* [226]

7 Write down that they hope they serve God: and write God first; for God defend but God should go before such villains! Masters, it is proved already that you are little better than false knaves, and it will go near to be thought so shortly. *Ib.* ii. [21]

8 Yea, marry, that's the eftest way. *Ib.* [39]

9 Flat burglary as ever was committed. *Ib.* [54]

10 O that he were here to write me down an ass! but, masters, remember that I am an ass; though it be not written down, yet forget not that I am an ass. *Ib.* [80]

11 A fellow that hath had losses; and one that hath two gowns, and everything handsome about him. *Ib.* [90]

12 Patch grief with proverbs. *Ib.* v. i. 17

13 For there was never yet philosopher
That could endure the toothache patiently. *Ib.* 35

14 In a false quarrel there is no true valour. *Ib.* [121]

15 What though care killed a cat, thou hast mettle enough in thee to kill care. *Ib.* [135]

16 No, I was not born under a riming planet. *Ib.* ii. [40]

17 The trumpet of his own virtues. *Ib.* [91]

18 Done to death by slanderous tongues. *Ib.* iii. 3

19 The wolves have prey'd; and look, the gentle day,
Before the wheels of Phœbus, round about
Dapples the drowsy east with spots of grey. *Ib.* 25

20 Horribly stuff'd with epithets of war.
Othello, I. i. 14

21 A fellow almost damn'd in a fair wife. *Ib.* 21

22 The bookish theoric. *Ib.* 24

23 This counter-caster. *Ib.* 31

24   'Tis the curse of the service,
Preferment goes by letter and affection,
Not by the old gradation, where each second
Stood heir to the first. *Ib.* 35

25 I follow him to serve my turn upon him;
We cannot all be masters, nor all masters
Cannot be truly follow'd. *Ib.* 42

26 Wears out his time, much like his master's ass,
For nought but provender, and when he's old, cashier'd;
Whip me such honest knaves. *Othello*, I. i. 47

27 In following him, I follow but myself. *Ib.* 58

28 But I will wear my heart upon my sleeve
For daws to peck at: I am not what I am. *Ib.* 64

29   An old black ram
Is tupping your white ewe. *Ib.* 88

30 'Zounds! sir, you are one of those that will not serve God if the devil bid you. *Ib.* 108

31 Your daughter and the Moor are now making the beast with two backs. *Ib.* [117]

32 The gross clasps of a lascivious Moor. *Ib.* [127]

33 An extravagant and wheeling stranger
Of here and every where. *Ib.* [137]

34 I do hate him as I do hell-pains. *Ib.* [155]

35 I must show out a flag and sign of love,
Which is indeed but sign. *Ib.* [157]

36 Though in the trade of war I have slain men,
Yet do I hold it very stuff o' the conscience
To do no contriv'd murder: I lack iniquity
Sometimes to do me service. *Ib.* ii. 1

37   I fetch my life and being
From men of royal siege. *Ib.* 21

38 I would not my unhoused free condition
Put into circumscription and confine
For the sea's worth. *Ib.* 26

39 My parts, my title, and my perfect soul
Shall manifest me rightly. *Ib.* 31

40 Keep up your bright swords, for the dew will rust them. *Ib.* 59

41 The wealthy curled darlings of our nation. *Ib.* 68

42   The sooty bosom
Of such a thing as thou. *Ib.* 70

43   My particular grief
Is of so flood-gate and o'erbearing nature
That it engluts and swallows other sorrows
And it is still itself. *Ib.* iii. 55

44   The bloody book of law
You shall yourself read in the bitter letter
After your own sense. *Ib.* 67

45 Most potent, grave, and reverend signiors,
My very noble and approv'd good masters,
That I have ta'en away this old man's daughter,
It is most true; true, I have married her:
The very head and front of my offending
Hath this extent, no more. Rude am I in my speech,
And little bless'd with the soft phrase of peace;
For since these arms of mine had seven years' pith,
Till now some nine moons wasted, they have us'd
Their dearest action in the tented field;
And little of this great world can I speak,
More than pertains to feats of broil and battle;
And therefore little shall I grace my cause
In speaking for myself. Yet, by your gracious patience,
I will a round unvarnish'd tale deliver
Of my whole course of love; what drugs, what charms,
What conjuration, and what mighty magic,
For such proceeding I am charg'd withal,
I won his daughter. *Ib.* 76

1   A maiden never bold;
Of spirit so still and quiet, that her motion
Blush'd at herself.   *Othello*, I. iii. 94

2 Her father lov'd me; oft invited me;
Still question'd me the story of my life
From year to year, the battles, sieges, fortunes
That I have pass'd.
I ran it through, even from my boyish days
To the very moment that he bade me tell it;
Wherein I spake of most disastrous chances,
Of moving accidents by flood and field,
Of hair-breadth 'scapes i' the imminent deadly breach,
Of being taken by the insolent foe
And sold to slavery, of my redemption thence
And portance in my travel's history:
Wherein of antres vast and desarts idle,
Rough quarries, rocks and hills whose heads touch
     heaven,
It was my hint to speak, such was the process;
And of the Cannibals that each other eat,
The Anthropophagi, and men whose heads
Do grow beneath their shoulders. This to hear
Would Desdemona seriously incline.   *Ib.* 128

3 And often did beguile her of her tears,
When I did speak of some distressful stroke
That my youth suffer'd. My story being done,
She gave me for my pains a world of sighs:
She swore, in faith, 'twas strange, 'twas passing
     strange;
'Twas pitiful, 'twas wondrous pitiful:
She wish'd she had not heard it, yet she wish'd
That heaven had made her such a man; she thank'd
     me,
And bade me, if I had a friend that lov'd her,
I should but teach him how to tell my story,
And that would woo her. Upon this hint I spake:
She lov'd me for the dangers I had pass'd,
And I lov'd her that she did pity them.
This only is the witchcraft I have us'd.   *Ib.* 156

4 I do perceive here a divided duty.   *Ib.* 181

5 To mourn a mischief that is past and gone
Is the next way to draw new mischief on.   *Ib.* 204

6 The robb'd that smiles steals something from the
     thief.   *Ib.* 208

7 But words are words; I never yet did hear
That the bruis'd heart was pierced through the ear.
                                    Ib. 218

8 The tyrant custom, most grave senators,
Hath made the flinty and steel couch of war
My thrice-driven bed of down.   *Ib.* [230]

9   My heart's subdu'd
Even to the very quality of my lord.   *Ib.* [252]

10 I saw Othello's visage in his mind.   *Ib.* [254]

11 A moth of peace.   *Ib.* [258]

12 BRABANTIO:
She has deceiv'd her father, and may thee.
OTHELLO:
My life upon her faith!   *Ib.* [295]

13 I will incontinently drown myself.   *Ib.* [307]

14 It is silliness to live when to live is torment; and then
     have we a prescription to die when death is our
     physician.   *Ib.* [310]

15 Virtue! a fig! 'tis in ourselves that we are thus, or thus.
     Our bodies are our gardens, to the which our wills
     are gardeners.   *Othello*, I. iii. [323]

16 Put money in thy purse.   *Ib.* [345]

17 The food that to him now is as luscious as locusts,
     shall be to him shortly as bitter as coloquintida.
                                     Ib. [354]

18 There are many events in the womb of time which
     will be delivered.   *Ib.* [377]

19 Thus do I ever make my fool my purse.   *Ib.* [389]

20   He holds me well;
The better shall my purpose work on him.   *Ib.* [396]

21 Framed to make women false.   *Ib.* [404]

22 The Moor is of a free and open nature,
That thinks men honest that but seem to be so.
                                     Ib. [405]

23 I have 't; it is engender'd; hell and night
Must bring this monstrous birth to the world's light.
                                     Ib. [409]

24 Our great captain's captain.   *Ib.* II. i. 74

25   You are pictures out of doors,
Bells in your parlours, wild cats in your kitchens,
Saints in your injuries, devils being offended,
Players in your housewifery, and housewives in your
     beds.   *Ib.* 109

26   Do not put me to 't,
For I am nothing if not critical.   *Ib.* 118

27 I am not merry, but I do beguile
The thing I am by seeming otherwise.   *Ib.* 122

28 IAGO:
She never yet was foolish that was fair,
For even her folly help'd her to an heir.
DESDEMONA:
These are old fond paradoxes to make fools laugh i'
     the alehouse.   *Ib.* 136

29 IAGO
She that was ever fair and never proud,
Had tongue at will and yet was never loud,
Never lack'd gold and yet went never gay,
Fled from her wish and yet said 'Now I may,'
She that being anger'd, her revenge being nigh,
Bade her wrong stay and her displeasure fly,
She that in wisdom never was so frail
To change the cod's head for the salmon's tail,
She that could think and ne'er disclose her mind,
See suitors following and not look behind,
She was a wight, if ever such wight were,—
DESDEMONA:
To do what?
IAGO:
To suckle fools and chronicle small beer.
DESDEMONA:
O most lame and impotent conclusion!   *Ib.* 148

30 With as little a web as this will I ensnare as great a fly
     as Cassio.   *Ib.* [169]

31 OTHELLO:
           If it were now to die,
'Twere now to be most happy, for I fear
My soul hath her content so absolute
That not another comfort like to this
Succeeds in unknown fate.

DESDEMONA:
　　　　　　　The heavens forbid
But that our loves and comforts should increase
Even as our days do grow!　　*Othello,* II. i. [192]

1 A slipper and subtle knave, a finder-out of occasions.
　　　　　　　　　　　　　　　　　　　Ib. [247]

2 A pestilent complete knave! and the woman hath
　found him already.　　　　　　　　*Ib.* [253]

3 This poor trash of Venice.　　　　　　*Ib.* [315]

4 Make the Moor thank me, love me, and reward me
　For making him egregiously an ass.　　*Ib.* [320]

5 Let's teach ourselves that honourable stop,
　Not to outsport discretion.　　　　　　*Ib.* iii. 2

6 She is sport for Jove.　　　　　　　　*Ib.* [17]

7 I have very poor and unhappy brains for drinking:
　I could well wish courtesy would invent some other
　custom of entertainment.　　　　　　*Ib.* [34]

8 My boat sails freely, both with wind and stream.
　　　　　　　　　　　　　　　　　　　Ib. [66]

9 And let me the canakin clink:
　　A soldier's a man;
　　A life's but a span;
　Why then let a soldier drink.　　　　　*Ib.* [73]

10 England, where indeed they are most potent in pot-
　ting.　　　　　　　　　　　　　　　*Ib.* [79]

11 King Stephen was a worthy peer,
　　His breeches cost him but a crown;
　He held them sixpence all too dear,
　　With that he call'd the tailor lown.　*Ib.* [93]

12 'Tis pride that pulls the country down.　*Ib.* [99]

13 Well, God's above all; and there be souls must be
　saved, and there be souls must not be saved.
　　　　　　　　　　　　　　　　　　Ib. [106]

14 The lieutenant is to be saved before the ancient.
　　　　　　　　　　　　　　　　　　Ib. [115]

15 He is a soldier fit to stand by Cæsar
　And give direction.　　　　　　　　*Ib.* [128]

16 Silence that dreadful bell! it frights the isle
　From her propriety.　　　　　　　　*Ib.* [177]

17 But men are men; the best sometimes forget. *Ib.* [243]

18 Thy honesty and love doth mince this matter.
　　　　　　　　　　　　　　　　　　Ib. [249]

19 　　　　　　Cassio, I love thee;
　But never more be officer of mine.　　*Ib.* [250]

20 Reputation, reputation, reputation! O! I have lost
　my reputation. I have lost the immortal part of
　myself, and what remains is bestial. My reputation,
　Iago, my reputation!　　　　　　　*Ib.* [264]

21 O thou invisible spirit of wine! if thou hast no name
　to be known by, let us call thee devil!　*Ib.* [285]

22 O God! that men should put an enemy in their
　mouths to steal away their brains; that we should,
　with joy, pleasance, revel, and applause, transform
　ourselves into beasts.　　　　　　　*Ib.* [293]

23 CASSIO:
　Every inordinate cup is unblessed, and the ingredient
　is a devil.
　IAGO:
　Come, come; good wine is a good familiar creature if
　it be well used; exclaim no more against it.
　　　　　　　　　　　　　　　　　　Ib. [312]

24 How poor are they that have not patience!
　What wound did ever heal but by degrees?
　　　　　　　　　　　　Othello, II. iii. [379]

25 O! thereby hangs a tail.　　　　*Ib.* III. i. [8]

26 Talk him out of patience.　　　　*Ib.* iii. 23

27 Excellent wretch! Perdition catch my soul
　But I do love thee! and when I love thee not,
　Chaos is come again.　　　　　　　*Ib.* 90

28 By heaven, he echoes me,
　As if there were some monster in his thought
　Too hideous to be shown.　　　　　*Ib.* 106

29 　Men should be what they seem;
　Or those that be not, would they might seem none!
　　　　　　　　　　　　　　　　　Ib. 126

30 Good name in man and woman, dear my lord,
　Is the immediate jewel of their souls;
　Who steals my purse steals trash; 'tis something,
　　nothing;
　'Twas mine, 'tis his, and has been slave to thousands;
　But he that filches from me my good name
　Robs me of that which not enriches him,
　And makes me poor indeed.　　　　*Ib.* 155

31 　O! beware, my lord, of jealousy;
　It is the green-ey'd monster which doth mock
　The meat it feeds on.　　　　　　*Ib.* 165

32 But, O! what damned minutes tells he o'er
　Who dotes, yet doubts; suspects, yet soundly loves!
　　　　　　　　　　　　　　　　　Ib. 169

33 Poor and content is rich, and rich enough.　*Ib.* 172

34 Think'st thou I'd make a life of jealousy,
　To follow still the changes of the moon
　With fresh suspicions? No; to be once in doubt
　Is once to be resolved.　　　　　　*Ib.* 177

35 In Venice they do let heaven see the pranks
　They dare not show their husbands; their best
　　conscience
　Is not to leave 't undone, but keep 't unknown.
　　　　　　　　　　　　　　　　　Ib. 202

36 I humbly do beseech you of your pardon
　For too much loving you.　　　　　*Ib.* 212

37 This fellow's of exceeding honesty.　*Ib.* 258

38 　　　　　If I do prove her haggard,
　Though that her jesses were my dear heart-strings,
　I'd whistle her off and let her down the wind,
　To prey at fortune.　　　　　　　*Ib.* 260

39 　　　　　For I am declin'd
　Into the vale of years.　　　　　　*Ib.* 265

40 　　　　　O curse of marriage!
　That we can call these delicate creatures ours,
　And not their appetites. I had rather be a toad,
　And live upon the vapour of a dungeon,
　Than keep a corner in the thing I love
　For others' uses.　　　　　　　　*Ib.* 268

41 If she be false, O! then heaven mocks itself.
　I'll not believe it.　　　　　　　　*Ib.* 278

42 　　　　　Trifles light as air
　Are to the jealous confirmations strong
　As proofs of holy writ.　　　　　　*Ib.* 323

43 　　　　　Not poppy, nor mandragora,
　Nor all the drowsy syrups of the world,
　Shall ever medicine thee to that sweet sleep
　Which thou ow'dst yesterday.　　　*Ib.* 331

1 Avaunt! be gone! thou hast set me on the rack;
I swear 'tis better to be much abus'd
Than but to know 't a little.　　*Othello*, III. iii. 336

2 He that is robb'd, not wanting what is stol'n,
Let him not know 't and he's not robb'd at all.
　　　　　　　　　　　　　　　　Ib. 343

3 I had been happy, if the general camp,
Pioners and all, had tasted her sweet body,
So I had nothing known. O! now, for ever
Farewell the tranquil mind; farewell content!
Farewell the plumed troop and the big wars
That make ambition virtue! O, farewell!
Farewell the neighing steed and the shrill trump,
The spirit-stirring drum, the ear-piercing fife,
The royal banner, and all quality,
Pride, pomp, and circumstance of glorious war!
And, O you mortal engines, whose rude throats
The immortal Jove's dread clamours counterfeit,
Farewell! Othello's occupation's gone!　　*Ib.* 346

4 Be sure of it; give me the ocular proof.　　*Ib.* 361

5 Never pray more; abandon all remorse;
On horror's head horrors accumulate.　　*Ib.* 370

6 　　　　　　　O wretched fool!
That liv'st to make thine honesty a vice.
O monstrous world! Take note, take note, O world!
To be direct and honest is not safe.　　*Ib.* 376

7 　　　　　　By the world,
I think my wife be honest and think she is not;
I think that thou art just and think thou art not.
　　　　　　　　　　　　　　　　Ib. 384

8 There are a kind of men so loose of soul
That in their sleeps will mutter their affairs. *Ib.* 417

9 But this denoted a foregone conclusion.　　*Ib.* 429

10 　　　　Swell, bosom, with thy fraught,
For 'tis of aspics' tongues!　　　　　　*Ib.* 450

11 O! blood, blood, blood!　　　　　　　*Ib.* 452

12 　　　　　Like to the Pontick sea,
Whose icy current and compulsive course
Ne'er feels retiring ebb, but keeps due on
To the Propontic and the Hellespont,
Even so my bloody thoughts, with violent pace,
Shall ne'er look back, ne'er ebb to humble love,
Till that a capable and wide revenge
Swallow them up.　　　　　　　　　*Ib.* 454

13 For here's a young and sweating devil here,
That commonly rebels.　　　　*Ib.* iv. 43

14 　　　The hearts of old gave hands,
But our new heraldry is hands not hearts.　*Ib.* 47

15 That handkerchief
Did an Egyptian to my mother give.　　*Ib.* 56

16 'Tis true; there's magic in the web of it;
A sibyl, that had number'd in the world
The sun to course two hundred compasses,
In her prophetic fury sew'd the work;
The worms were hallow'd that did breed the silk,
And it was dy'd in mummy which the skilful
Conserv'd of maidens' hearts.　　　*Ib.* 70

17 But jealous souls will not be answer'd so;
They are not ever jealous for the cause,
But jealous for they are jealous.　　*Ib.* 158

18 What! keep a week away? seven days and nights?
Eight score eight hours? and lovers' absent hours,
More tedious than the dial eight score times?
O, weary reckoning!　　　*Othello*, III. iv. 172

19 I do attend here on the general,
And think it no addition nor my wish
To have him see me woman'd.　　　*Ib.* 192

20 　　　　O! it comes o'er my memory,
As doth the raven o'er the infected house,
Boding to all.　　　　　　　*Ib.* IV. i. 20

21 　Many worthy and chaste dames even thus,
All guiltless, meet reproach.　　　*Ib.* 47

22 To beguile many and be beguil'd by one.　*Ib.* 98

23 They laugh that win.　　　　　*Ib.* [123]

24 I would have him nine years a-killing.　*Ib.* [186]

25 My heart is turned to stone; I strike it, and it hurts
my hand.　　　　　　　　　*Ib.* [190]

26 O! the world hath not a sweeter creature; she might
lie by an emperor's side and command him tasks.
　　　　　　　　　　　　　　Ib. [192]

27 O, she will sing the savageness out of a bear.
　　　　　　　　　　　　　　Ib. [198]

28 But yet the pity of it, Iago! O! Iago, the pity of it,
Iago!　　　　　　　　　　　*Ib.* [205]

29 The justice of it pleases.　　　　*Ib.* [221]

30 O well-painted passion!　　　　*Ib.* [268]

31 Goats and monkeys!　　　　　*Ib.* [274]

32 　　　　　Whose solid virtue
The shot of accident nor dart of chance
Could neither graze nor pierce?　　*Ib.* [277]

33 Your mystery, your mystery; nay, dispatch.
　　　　　　　　　　　　　　Ib. ii. 29

34 　　　　　Had it pleas'd heaven
To try me with affliction, had he rain'd
All kinds of sores, and shames, on my bare head,
Steep'd me in poverty to the very lips,
Given to captivity me and my utmost hopes,
I should have found in some part of my soul
A drop of patience; but, alas! to make me
The fixed figure for the time of scorn
To point his slow and moving finger at;
Yet could I bear that too; well, very well.
But there, where I have garner'd up my heart,
Where either I must live or bear no life,
The fountain from the which my current runs
Or else dries up; to be discarded thence!
Or keep it as a cistern for foul toads
To knot and gender in! Turn thy complexion there,
Patience, thou young and rose-lipp'd cherubin;
Ay, there, look grim as hell!　　　*Ib.* 46

35 　　　　　O thou weed!
Who art so lovely fair and smell'st so sweet
That the sense aches at thee, would thou hadst ne'er
been born!　　　　　　　　　*Ib.* 66

36 Heaven stops the nose at it and the moon winks.
　　　　　　　　　　　　　　Ib. 76

37 I took you for that cunning whore of Venice
That married with Othello. You, mistress,
That have the office opposite to Saint Peter,
And keep the gate of hell!　　　　*Ib.* 88

1 I will be hang'd, if some eternal villain,
Some busy and insinuating rogue,
Some cogging cozening slave, to get some office,
Have not devis'd this slander.   *Othello*, IV. ii. 130

2 O heaven! that such companions thou'dst unfold,
And put in every honest hand a whip
To lash the rascals naked through the world,
Even from the east to the west!   *Ib.* 141

3   Unkindness may do much;
And his unkindness may defeat my life,
But never taint my love.   *Ib.* 159

4 Why, now I see there's mettle in thee, and even from
this instant do build on thee a better opinion than
ever before.   *Ib.* [207]

5 EMILIA:
I would you had never seen him.
DESDEMONA:
So would not I; my love doth so approve him.
    Ib. iii. 18

6 The poor soul sat sighing by a sycamore tree,
Sing all a green willow;
Her hand on her bosom, her head on her knee,
Sing willow, willow, willow:
The fresh streams ran by her, and murmur'd her
    moans;
Sing willow, willow, willow:
Her salt tears fell from her, and soften'd the stones;—
Sing willow, willow, willow:
Sing all a green willow must be my garland.   *Ib.* [41]

7 DESDEMONA:
        Mine eyes do itch;
Doth that bode weeping?
EMILIA:
'Tis neither here nor there.   *Ib.* [59]

8 Who would not make her husband a cuckold to make
him a monarch?   *Ib.* [76]

9 He hath a daily beauty in his life
That makes me ugly.   *Ib.* v. i. 19

10   This is the night
That either makes me or fordoes me quite.   *Ib.* 128

11 It is the cause, it is the cause, my soul;
Let me not name it to you, you chaste stars!
It is the cause. Yet I'll not shed her blood,
Nor scar that whiter skin of hers than snow,
And smooth as monumental alabaster.
Yet she must die, else she'll betray more men.
Put out the light, and then put out the light:
If I quench thee, thou flaming minister,
I can again thy former light restore,
Should I repent me; but once put out thy light,
Thou cunning'st pattern of excelling nature,
I know not where is that Promethean heat
That can thy light relume. When I have pluck'd the
    rose,
I cannot give it vital growth again,
It needs must wither: I'll smell it on the tree.
O balmy breath, that dost almost persuade
Justice to break her sword! One more, one more.
Be thus when thou art dead, and I will kill thee,
And love thee after. One more, and this the last:
So sweet was ne'er so fatal. I must weep,
But they are cruel tears; this sorrow's heavenly,
It strikes where it doth love.   *Ib.* ii. 1

12 If you bethink yourself of any crime
Unreconcil'd as yet to heaven and grace,
Solicit for it straight.   *Othello*, v. ii. 26

13 Alas! why gnaw you so your nether lip?
Some bloody passion shakes your very frame;
These are portents, but yet, I hope, I hope
They do not point on me.   *Ib.* 43

14 For to deny each article with oath
Cannot remove nor choke the strong conception
That I do groan withal.   *Ib.* 54

15 Had all his hairs been lives, my great revenge
Had stomach for them all.   *Ib.* 74

16 It is the very error of the moon;
She comes more near the earth than she was wont,
And makes men mad.   *Ib.* 107

17 Not Cassio kill'd! then murder's out of tune,
And sweet revenge grows harsh.   *Ib.* 113

18 A guiltless death I die.   *Ib.* 120

19 Nobody; I myself; farewell.   *Ib.* 122

20 OTHELLO:
She's like a liar gone to burning hell;
'Twas I that kill'd her.
EMILIA:
        O! the more angel she,
And you the blacker devil.   *Ib.* 127

21   Nay, had she been true,
If heaven would make me such another world
Of one entire and perfect chrysolite,
I'd not have sold her for it.   *Ib.* 141

22 She was too fond of her most filthy bargain.   *Ib.* 155

23 Thou hast not half the power to do me harm
As I have to be hurt.   *Ib.* 160

24 You told a lie, an odious damned lie;
Upon my soul, a lie, a wicked lie.   *Ib.* 178

25 Curse his better angel from his side,
And fall to reprobation.   *Ib.* 206

26 With that recognizance and pledge of love.   *Ib.* 212

27   Are there no stones in heaven
But what serve for the thunder?   *Ib.* 232

28 Every puny whipster gets my sword.   *Ib.* 242

29   I will play the swan,
And die in music.   *Ib.* 245

30 Who can control his fate?   *Ib.* 264

31 Here is my journey's end, here is my butt,
And very sea-mark of my utmost sail.   *Ib.* 266

32   O ill-starr'd wench!
Pale as thy smock! when we shall meet at compt,
This look of thine will hurl my soul from heaven,
And fiends will snatch at it. Cold, cold, my girl!
Even like thy chastity.
O! cursed, cursed slave. Whip me, ye devils,
From the possession of this heavenly sight!
Blow me about in winds! roast me in sulphur!
Wash me in steep-down gulfs of liquid fire!
O Desdemona! Desdemona! dead!   *Ib.* 271

33 I look down towards his feet; but that's a fable.
If that thou be'st a devil, I cannot kill thee.   *Ib.* 285

34 An honourable murderer, if you will;
For nought did I in hate, but all in honour.   *Ib.* 293

1 OTHELLO:
Will you, I pray, demand that demi-devil
Why he hath thus ensnar'd my soul and body?
IAGO:
Demand me nothing: what you know, you know:
From this time forth I never will speak word.
Othello, v. ii. 300

2 I have done the state some service, and they know 't;
No more of that. I pray you, in your letters,
When you shall these unlucky deeds relate,
Speak of me as I am; nothing extenuate,
Nor set down aught in malice: then, must you speak
Of one that lov'd not wisely but too well;
Of one not easily jealous, but, being wrought,
Perplex'd in the extreme; of one whose hand,
Like the base Indian, threw a pearl away
Richer than all his tribe; of one whose subdu'd eyes
Albeit unused to the melting mood,
Drop tears as fast as the Arabian trees
Their med'cinable gum. Set you down this;
And say besides, that in Aleppo once,
Where a malignant and a turban'd Turk
Beat a Venetian and traduc'd the state,
I took by the throat the circumcised dog,
And smote him thus. *Ib.* 338

3 All that 's spoke is marred. *Ib.* 356

4 I kiss'd thee ere I kill'd thee. *Ib.* 357

5 See, where she comes apparell'd like the spring.
Pericles, I. i. 12

6 Few love to hear the sins they love to act. *Ib.* 92

7 O you gods!
Why do you make us love your goodly gifts,
And snatch them straight away? *Ib.* III. i. 22

8 Old John of Gaunt, time-honour'd Lancaster.
King Richard II, I. i. 1

9 Let's purge this choler without letting blood. *Ib.* 153

10 The purest treasure mortal times afford
Is spotless reputation; that away,
Men are but gilded loam or painted clay.
A jewel in a ten-times-barr'd-up chest
Is a bold spirit in a loyal breast.
Mine honour is my life; both grow in one;
Take honour from me, and my life is done. *Ib.* 177

11 We were not born to sue, but to command. *Ib.* 196

12 Stay, stay, the king hath thrown his warder down.
Ib. iii. 118

13 This must my comfort be,
That sun that warms you here shall shine on me.
Ib. 144

14 The language I have learn'd these forty years,
My native English, now I must forego;
And now my tongue's use is to me no more
Than an unstringed viol or a harp. *Ib.* 159

15 I am too old to fawn upon a nurse,
Too far in years to be a pupil now. *Ib.* 170

16 How long a time lies in one little word!
Four lagging winters and four wanton springs
End in a word; such is the breath of kings. *Ib.* 213

17 Things sweet to taste prove in digestion sour. *Ib.* 236

18 Boast of nothing else
But that I was a journeyman to grief? *Ib.* 273

19 All places that the eye of heaven visits
Are to a wise man ports and happy havens.
Teach thy necessity to reason thus;
There is no virtue like necessity.
King Richard II, I. iii. 275

20 O! who can hold a fire in his hand
By thinking on the frosty Caucasus?
Or cloy the hungry edge of appetite,
By bare imagination of a feast?
Or wallow naked in December snow
By thinking on fantastic summer's heat?
O, no! the apprehension of the good
Gives but the greater feeling to the worse. *Ib.* 294

21 Methinks I am a prophet new inspir'd,
And thus expiring do foretell of him:
His rash fierce blaze of riot cannot last,
For violent fires soon burn out themselves;
Small showers last long, but sudden storms are short;
He tires betimes that spurs too fast betimes.
Ib. II. i. 31

22 This royal throne of kings, this scepter'd isle,
This earth of majesty, this seat of Mars,
This other Eden, demi-paradise,
This fortress built by Nature for herself
Against infection and the hand of war,
This happy breed of men, this little world,
This precious stone set in the silver sea,
Which serves it in the office of a wall,
Or as a moat defensive to a house,
Against the envy of less happier lands,
This blessed plot, this earth, this realm, this England,
This nurse, this teeming womb of royal kings,
Fear'd by their breed and famous by their birth,
Renowned for their deeds as far from home,—
For Christian service and true chivalry,—
As is the sepulchre in stubborn Jewry
Of the world's ransom, blessed Mary's Son:
This land of such dear souls, this dear, dear land.
Ib. 40

23 England, bound in with the triumphant sea. *Ib.* 61

24 That England, that was wont to conquer others,
Hath made a shameful conquest of itself. *Ib.* 65

25 Can sick men play so nicely with their names?
Ib. 84

26 Lay aside life-harming heaviness,
And entertain a cheerful disposition. *Ib.* ii. 3

27 Believe me, noble lord,
I am a stranger here in Gloucestershire:
These high wild hills and rough uneven ways
Draw out our miles and make them wearisome.
Ib. iii. 2

28 I count myself in nothing else so happy
As in a soul remembering my good friends. *Ib.* 46

29 Bloody with spurring, fiery-red with haste. *Ib.* 58

30 Grace me no grace, nor uncle me no uncle. *Ib.* 87

31 The caterpillars of the commonwealth. *Ib.* 166

32 Things past redress are now with me past care.
Ib. 171

33 Eating the bitter bread of banishment. *Ib.* III. i. 21

34 I weep for joy
To stand upon my kingdom once again.
Dear earth, I do salute thee with my hand,
Though rebels wound thee with their horses' hoofs.
Ib. ii. 4

1 Not all the water in the rough rude sea
Can wash the balm from an anointed king;
The breath of worldly men cannot depose
The deputy elected by the Lord.
For every man that Bolingbroke hath press'd
To lift shrewd steel against our golden crown,
God for his Richard hath in heavenly pay
A glorious angel; then, if angels fight,
Weak men must fall, for heaven still guards the
right.   *King Richard II*, III. ii. 54

2 O! call back yesterday, bid time return.   *Ib.* 69

3 Is not the king's name twenty thousand names?
Arm, arm, my name! A puny subject strikes
At thy great glory.   *Ib.* 85

4 The worst is death, and death will have his day.
                                             Ib. 103

5 Sweet love, I see, changing his property,
Turns to the sourest and most deadly hate. *Ib.* 135

6   Of comfort no man speak:
Let's talk of graves, of worms, and epitaphs;
Make dust our paper, and with rainy eyes
Write sorrow on the bosom of the earth.
Let's choose executors, and talk of wills.   *Ib.* 144

7 For God's sake, let us sit upon the ground
And tell sad stories of the death of kings:
How some have been depos'd, some slain in war,
Some haunted by the ghosts they have depos'd,
Some poison'd by their wives, some sleeping kill'd;
All murder'd: for within the hollow crown
That rounds the mortal temples of a king
Keeps Death his court, and there the antick sits,
Scoffing his state and grinning at his pomp;
Allowing him a breath, a little scene,
To monarchize, be fear'd, and kill with looks,
Infusing him with self and vain conceit
As if this flesh which walls about our life
Were brass impregnable; and humour'd thus
Comes at the last, and with a little pin
Bores through his castle wall, and farewell king!
                                             Ib. 155

8 See, see, King Richard doth himself appear,
As doth the blushing discontented sun
From out the fiery portal of the east.   *Ib.* iii. 62

9   O! that I were as great
As is my grief, or lesser than my name,
Or that I could forget what I have been,
Or not remember what I must be now.   *Ib.* 136

10 What must the king do now? Must he submit?
The king shall do it: must he be depos'd?
The king shall be contented: must he lose
The name of king? o' God's name, let it go.
I'll give my jewels for a set of beads,
My gorgeous palace for a hermitage,
My gay apparel for an almsman's gown,
My figur'd goblets for a dish of wood,
My sceptre for a palmer's walking staff,
My subjects for a pair of carved saints,
And my large kingdom for a little grave,
A little little grave, an obscure grave;
Or I'll be buried in the king's highway,
Some way of common trade, where subjects' feet
May hourly trample on their sovereign's head;
For on my heart they tread now whilst I live;
And buried once, why not upon my head?   *Ib.* 143

11 You make a leg.   *Ib.* 175

12 Go, bind thou up yon dangling apricocks,
Which, like unruly children, make their sire
Stoop with oppression of their prodigal weight.
                        King Richard II, III. iv. 29

13 Old Adam's likeness, set to dress this garden. *Ib.* 73

14 Here did she fall a tear; here, in this place,
I'll set a bank of rue, sour herb of grace;
Rue, even for ruth, here shortly shall be seen,
In the remembrance of a weeping queen.   *Ib.* 104

15 If I dare eat, or drink, or breathe, or live,
I dare meet Surrey in a wilderness,
And spit upon him, whilst I say he lies,
And lies, and lies.   *Ib.* IV. i. 73

16   And there at Venice gave
His body to that pleasant country's earth,
And his pure soul unto his captain Christ,
Under whose colours he had fought so long. *Ib.* 97

17 Peace shall go sleep with Turks and infidels.
                                             Ib. 139

18 God save the king! Will no man say, amen?
Am I both priest and clerk? Well then, amen.
                                             Ib. 172

19 Give me the crown. Here, cousin, seize the crown;
Here cousin,
On this side my hand and on that side thine.
Now is this golden crown like a deep well
That owes two buckets filling one another;
The emptier ever dancing in the air,
The other down, unseen, and full of water:
That bucket down and full of tears am I,
Drinking my griefs, whilst you mount up on high.
                                             Ib. 181

20 You may my glories and my state depose,
But not my griefs; still am I king of those. *Ib.* 192

21 Now mark me how I will undo myself.   *Ib.* 203

22 With mine own tears I wash away my balm,
With mine own hands I give away my crown.
                                             Ib. 207

23 God pardon all oaths that are broke to me!
God keep all vows unbroke are made to thee! *Ib.* 214

24 A mockery king of snow.   *Ib.* 260

25 An if my word be sterling yet in England. *Ib.* 264

26 Julius Cæsar's ill-erected tower.   *Ib.* v. i. 2

27   I am sworn brother, sweet,
To grim Necessity, and he and I
Will keep a league till death.   *Ib.* 20

28 That were some love but little policy.   *Ib.* 84

29 As in a theatre, the eyes of men,
After a well-grac'd actor leaves the stage,
Are idly bent on him that enters next,
Thinking his prattle to be tedious.   *Ib.* ii. 23

30   Who are the violets now
That strew the green lap of the new come spring?
                                             Ib. 46

31 Give me my boots I say.   *Ib.* 77 and 87

32 He prays but faintly and would be denied. *Ib.* iii. 103

33 I have been studying how I may compare
This prison where I live unto the world. *Ib.* v. 1

34   How sour sweet music is,
When time is broke, and no proportion kept!
So is it in the music of men's lives.   *Ib.* 42

1 Mount, mount, my soul! thy seat is up on high,
Whilst my gross flesh sinks downwards, here to die.
King Richard II, v. v. 112

2 Now is the winter of our discontent
Made glorious summer by this sun of York.
King Richard III, I. i. 1

3 Our stern alarums changed to merry meetings;
Our dreadful marches to delightful measures. *Ib.* 7

4 He capers nimbly in a lady's chamber
To the lascivious pleasing of a lute. *Ib.* 12

5 This weak piping time of peace. *Ib.* 24

6 And therefore, since I cannot prove a lover, . . .
I am determined to prove a villain. *Ib.* 28

7 No beast so fierce but knows some touch of pity.
Ib. ii. 71

8 Was ever woman in this humour woo'd?
Was ever woman in this humour won? *Ib.* 229

9 Fram'd in the prodigality of Nature. *Ib.* 245

10 By silken, sly, insinuating Jacks. *Ib.* iii. 53

11 Since every Jack became a gentleman
There's many a gentle person made a Jack. *Ib.* 72

12 And thus I clothe my naked villany
With odd old ends stol'n forth of holy writ,
And seem a saint when most I play the devil.
Ib. 336

13 O, I have pass'd a miserable night,
So full of ugly sights, of ghastly dreams,
That, as I am a Christian faithful man,
I would not spend another such a night,
Though 'twere to buy a world of happy days,
So full of dismal terror was the time! *Ib.* iv. 2

14 Lord, Lord! methought what pain it was to drown:
What dreadful noise of water in mine ears!
What sights of ugly death within mine eyes!
Methought I saw a thousand fearful wracks;
A thousand men that fishes gnaw'd upon;
Wedges of gold, great anchors, heaps of pearl,
Inestimable stones, unvalu'd jewels,
All scatter'd in the bottom of the sea.
Some lay in dead men's skulls; and in those holes
Where eyes did once inhabit, there were crept
As 'twere in scorn of eyes, reflecting gems,
That woo'd the slimy bottom of the deep,
And mock'd the dead bones that lay scatter'd by.
Ib. 21

15 The empty, vast, and wandering air. *Ib.* 39

16 Clarence is come,—false, fleeting, perjur'd Clarence.
Ib. 55

17 As snow in harvest. *Ib.* [252]

18 Woe to the land that's govern'd by a child!
Ib. II. iii. 11

19 So wise so young, they say, do never live long.
Ib. III. i. 79

20 I moralize two meanings in one word. *Ib.* 83

21 My Lord of Ely, when I was last in Holborn,
I saw good strawberries in your garden there.
Ib. iv. 31

22 Talk'st thou to me of 'ifs'? Thou art a traitor.
Off with his head! *Ib.* 74

23 High-reaching Buckingham grows circumspect.
Ib. IV. ii. 31

24 I am not in the giving vein to-day.
King Richard III, IV. ii. 115

25 The sons of Edward sleep in Abraham's bosom.
Ib. iii. 38

26 Let not the heavens hear these tell-tale women
Rail on the Lord's anointed. *Ib.* iv. 150

27 A grievous burthen was thy birth to me;
Tetchy and wayward was thy infancy. *Ib.* 168

28 An honest tale speeds best being plainly told.
Ib. 359

29 Harp not on that string. *Ib.* 365

30 Relenting fool, and shallow, changing woman!
Ib. 432

31 Is the chair empty? is the sword unsway'd?
Is the king dead? the empire unpossess'd? *Ib.* 470

32 Thus far into the bowels of the land
Have we march'd on without impediment.
Ib. v. ii. 3

33 True hope is swift, and flies with swallow's wings;
Kings it makes gods, and meaner creatures kings.
Ib. 23

34 The king's name is a tower of strength. *Ib.* iii. 12

35 Give me another horse! bind up my wounds!
Have mercy, Jesu! Soft! I did but dream.
O coward conscience, how dost thou afflict me!
Ib. 178

36 My conscience hath a thousand several tongues,
And every tongue brings in a several tale,
And every tale condemns me for a villain. *Ib.* 194

37 I shall despair. There is no creature loves me;
And if I die, no soul will pity me:
Nay, wherefore should they, since that I myself
Find in myself no pity to myself? *Ib.* 201

38 By the apostle Paul, shadows to-night
Have struck more terror to the soul of Richard
Than can the substance of ten thousand soldiers.
Ib. 217

39 Jockey of Norfolk, be not too bold,
For Dickon thy master is bought and sold. *Ib.* 305

40 A thing devised by the enemy. *Ib.* 307

41 Conscience is but a word that cowards use,
Devis'd at first to keep the strong in awe. *Ib.* 310

42 A horse! a horse! my kingdom for a horse! *Ib.* iv. 7

43 Slave! I have set my life upon a cast,
And I will stand the hazard of the die.
I think there be six Richmonds in the field. *Ib.* 9

44 A pair of star-cross'd lovers.
Romeo and Juliet, Prologue, 6

45 The two hours' traffic of our stage. *Ib.* 12

46 ABRAHAM:
Do you bite your thumb at us, sir?
SAMPSON:
Is the law of our side if I say ay?
GREGORY:
No.
SAMPSON:
No, sir, I do not bite my thumb at you, sir; but I bite
my thumb, sir. *Ib.* I. i. [52]

47 Gregory, remember thy swashing blow. *Ib.* [68]

48 Saint-seducing gold. *Ib.* [220]

1   And 'tis not hard, I think,
For men so old as we to keep the peace.
                   Romeo and Juliet, I. ii. 2

2 PARIS:
Younger than she are happy mothers made.
CAPULET:
And too soon marr'd are those so early made. *Ib.* 12

3 And then my husband—God be with his soul!
A' was a merry man—took up the child:
'Yea,' quoth he, 'dost thou fall upon thy face?
Thou wilt fall backward when thou hast more wit;
Wilt thou not, Jule?' and, by my halidom,
The pretty wretch left crying, and said 'Ay.'
                           Ib. iii. 39

4 Pretty fool, it stinted and said 'Ay'.   *Ib.* 48

5 I am proverb'd with a grandsire phrase;
I'll be a candle-holder, and look on.   *Ib.* iv. 37

6 Come, we burn daylight, ho!   *Ib.* 43

7 O! then, I see, Queen Mab hath been with you. . . .
She is the fairies' midwife, and she comes
In shape no bigger than an agate-stone
On the forefinger of an alderman,
Drawn with a team of little atomies
Athwart men's noses as they lie asleep;
Her waggon-spokes made of long spinners' legs;
The cover, of the wings of grasshoppers;
The traces, of the smallest spider's web;
The collars, of the moonshine's watery beams;
Her whip, of cricket's bone; the lash, of film;
Her waggoner, a small grey-coated gnat,
Not half so big as a round little worm
Prick'd from the lazy finger of a maid;
Her chariot is an empty hazel-nut,
Made by the joiner squirrel or old grub,
Time out o' mind the fairies' coach-makers.
And in this state she gallops night by night
Through lovers' brains, and then they dream of love;
O'er courtiers' knees, that dream on curtsies straight;
O'er lawyers' fingers, who straight dream on fees;
O'er ladies' lips, who straight on kisses dream;
Which oft the angry Mab with blisters plagues,
Because their breaths with sweetmeats tainted are.
Sometimes she gallops o'er a courtier's nose,
And then dreams he of smelling out a suit;
And sometimes comes she with a tithe-pig's tail,
Tickling a parson's nose as a' lies asleep,
Then dreams he of another benefice;
Sometimes she driveth o'er a soldier's neck,
And then dreams he of cutting foreign throats,
Of breaches, ambuscadoes, Spanish blades,
Of healths five fathom deep; and then anon
Drums in his ear, at which he starts and wakes;
And, being thus frighted, swears a prayer or two,
And sleeps again. This is that very Mab
That plats the manes of horses in the night;
And bakes the elf-locks in foul sluttish hairs,
Which once untangled much misfortune bodes;
This is the hag, when maids lie on their backs,
That presses them and learns them first to bear,
Making them women of good carriage.   *Ib.* 53

8 For you and I are past our dancing days. *Ib.* v. [35]

9 O! she doth teach the torches to burn bright.
It seems she hangs upon the cheek of night
Like a rich jewel in an Ethiop's ear;
Beauty too rich for use, for earth too dear. *Ib.* [48]

10 We have a trifling foolish banquet towards. *Ib.* [126]

11 My only love sprung from my only hate!
               Romeo and Juliet, I. v. [142]

12 Young Adam Cupid, he that shot so trim
When King Cophetua lov'd the beggar-maid.
                        Ib. II. i. 13

13 He jests at scars, that never felt a wound.
But, soft! what light through yonder window breaks?
It is the east, and Juliet is the sun.   *Ib.* ii. 1

14 See! how she leans her cheek upon her hand:
O! that I were a glove upon that hand,
That I might touch that cheek.   *Ib.* 23

15 O Romeo, Romeo! wherefore art thou Romeo?
                                Ib. 33

16 What's in a name? that which we call a rose
By any other name would smell as sweet. *Ib.* 43

17 For stony limits cannot hold love out.   *Ib.* 67

18 Thou know'st the mask of night is on my face,
Else would a maiden blush bepaint my cheek.
                                Ib. 85

19 Fain would I dwell on form, fain, fain deny
What I have spoke: but farewell compliment! *Ib.* 88

20   At lovers' perjuries,
They say, Jove laughs. O gentle Romeo!
If thou dost love, pronounce it faithfully:
Or if thou think'st I am too quickly won,
I'll frown and be perverse and say thee nay,
So thou wilt woo; but else, not for the world.
In truth, fair Montague, I am too fond.   *Ib.* 92

21   I'll prove more true
Than those that have more cunning to be strange.
                              Ib. 100

22 ROMEO:
Lady, by yonder blessed moon I swear
That tips with silver all these fruit-tree tops,—
JULIET:
O! swear not by the moon, the inconstant moon,
That monthly changes in her circled orb,
Lest that thy love prove likewise variable. *Ib.* 107

23   Do not swear at all;
Or, if thou wilt, swear by thy gracious self,
Which is the god of my idolatry.   *Ib.* 112

24 It is too rash, too unadvis'd, too sudden;
Too like the lightning, which doth cease to be
Ere one can say it lightens. Sweet, good-night!
This bud of love, by summer's ripening breath,
May prove a beauteous flower when next we meet.
                                Ib. 118

25 Love goes toward love, as schoolboys from their
    books;
But love from love, toward school with heavy looks.
                              Ib. 156

26   O! for a falconer's voice,
To lure this tassel-gentle back again.
Bondage is hoarse, and may not speak aloud,
Else would I tear the cave where Echo lies. *Ib.* 158

27 It is my soul that calls upon my name:
How silver-sweet sound lovers' tongues by night,
Like softest music to attending ears! *Ib.* 164

28 'Tis almost morning; I would have thee gone;
And yet no further than a wanton's bird,
Who lets it hop a little from her hand,
Like a poor prisoner in his twisted gyves,
And with a silk thread plucks it back again,
So loving-jealous of his liberty.   *Ib.* 176

1 JULIET:
Yet I should kill thee with much cherishing.
Good-night, good-night! parting is such sweet sorrow
That I shall say good-night till it be morrow.
ROMEO:
Sleep dwell upon thine eyes, peace in thy breast!
Would I were sleep and peace, so sweet to rest!
Romeo and Juliet, II. ii. 183

2 Wisely and slow; they stumble that run fast.
Ib. iii. 94

3 One, two, and the third in your bosom. *Ib.* iv. [24]

4 O flesh, flesh, how art thou fishified! *Ib.* [41]

5 I am the very pink of courtesy. *Ib.* [63]

6 A gentleman, nurse, that loves to hear himself talk,
and will speak more in a minute than he will stand
to in a month. *Ib.* [156]

7 Two may keep counsel, putting one away. *Ib.* [211]

8 These violent delights have violent ends,
And in their triumph die. *Ib.* vi. 9

9 Therefore love moderately; long love doth so;
Too swift arrives as tardy as too slow. *Ib.* 14

10   O! so light a foot
Will ne'er wear out the everlasting flint. *Ib.* 16

11 Thy head is as full of quarrels as an egg is full of
meat. *Ib.* III. i. [23]

12 A word and a blow. *Ib.* [43]

13 Men's eyes were made to look, and let them gaze;
I will not budge for no man's pleasure, I. *Ib.* [59]

14 No, 'tis not so deep as a well, nor so wide as a church
door; but 'tis enough, 'twill serve: ask for me to-
morrow, and you shall find me a grave man. I am
peppered, I warrant, for this world. *Ib.* [100]

15   A plague o' both your houses!
They have made worms' meat of me. *Ib.* [112]

16 O! I am Fortune's fool. *Ib.* [142]

17 Gallop apace, you fiery-footed steeds,
Towards Phœbus' lodging. *Ib.* ii. 1

18   Come, civil night,
Thou sober-suited matron, all in black. *Ib.* 10

19 For thou wilt lie upon the wings of night,
Whiter than new snow on a raven's back. *Ib.* 18

20 Give me my Romeo: and, when he shall die,
Take him and cut him out in little stars,
And he will make the face of heaven so fine
That all the world will be in love with night,
And pay no worship to the garish sun. *Ib.* 21

21   He was not born to shame:
Upon his brow shame is ashamed to sit. *Ib.* 91

22 Romeo, come forth; come forth, thou fearful man:
Affliction is enamour'd of thy parts,
And thou art wedded to calamity. *Ib.* iii. 1

23 Thou cutt'st my head off with a golden axe. *Ib.* 22

24 Adversity's sweet milk, philosophy. *Ib.* 54

25   Hang up philosophy!
Unless philosophy can make a Juliet. *Ib.* 56

26 Wilt thou be gone? it is not yet near day:
It was the nightingale, and not the lark,
That pierc'd the fearful hollow of thine ear;
Nightly she sings on yon pomegranate tree:
Believe me, love, it was the nightingale. *Ib.* v. 1

27 Night's candles are burnt out, and jocund day
Stands tiptoe on the misty mountain tops.
Romeo and Juliet, III. v. 9

28 Villain and he be many miles asunder. *Ib.* 82

29 Thank me no thankings, nor proud me no prouds.
Ib. 153

30 Is there no pity sitting in the clouds,
That sees into the bottom of my grief? *Ib.* 198

31 Romeo's a dishclout to him. *Ib.* 221

32 'Tis an ill cook that cannot lick his own fingers.
Ib. IV. ii. [6]

33 All things that we ordained festival,
Turn from their office to black funeral;
Our instruments to melancholy bells,
Our wedding cheer to a sad burial feast,
Our solemn hymns to sullen dirges change,
Our bridal flowers serve for a buried corse,
And all things change them to the contrary. *Ib.* v. 84

34 My bosom's lord sits lightly in his throne. *Ib.* v. i. 3

35 I do remember an apothecary,
And hereabouts he dwells. *Ib.* 37

36 Being holiday, the beggar's shop is shut. *Ib.* 56

37 The world is not thy friend, nor the world's law.
Ib. 72

38 APOTHECARY:
My poverty, but not my will, consents.
ROMEO:
I pay thy poverty, and not thy will. *Ib.* 75

39 The time and my intents are savage-wild,
More fierce and more inexorable far
Than empty tigers or the roaring sea. *Ib.* iii. 37

40 Tempt not a desperate man. *Ib.* 59

41 One writ with me in sour misfortune's book. *Ib.* 82

42 How oft when men are at the point of death
Have they been merry! which their keepers call
A lightning before death. *Ib.* 88

43   Beauty's ensign yet
Is crimson in thy lips and in thy cheeks,
And death's pale flag is not advanced there. *Ib.* 94

44   Shall I believe
That unsubstantial Death is amorous,
And that the lean abhorred monster keeps
Thee here in dark to be his paramour?
For fear of that I still will stay with thee,
And never from this palace of dim night
Depart again: here, here will I remain
With worms that are thy chambermaids; O! here
Will I set up my everlasting rest,
And shake the yoke of inauspicious stars
From this world-wearied flesh. Eyes, look your last!
Arms, take your last embrace! and, lips, O you
The doors of breath, seal with a righteous kiss
A dateless bargain to engrossing death! *Ib.* 102

45 Look in the chronicles; we came in with Richard
Conqueror. *The Taming of the Shrew*, Induction i. [4]

46 As Stephen Sly, and old John Naps of Greece,
And Peter Turf, and Henry Pimpernell,
And twenty more such names and men as these,
Which never were nor no man ever saw. *Ib.* ii. [95]

47 No profit grows where is no pleasure ta'en;
In brief, sir, study what you most affect. *Ib.* I. i. 39

48 There's small choice in rotten apples. *Ib.* [137]

1 Nothing comes amiss, so money comes withal.
The Taming of the Shrew, I. ii. [82]

2 O! this learning, what a thing it is. *Ib.* [163]

3 She is your treasure, she must have a husband;
I must dance bare-foot on her wedding day,
And, for your love to her, lead apes in hell.
Ib. II. i. 32

4 Say that she rail; why then I'll tell her plain
She sings as sweetly as a nightingale:
Say that she frown; I'll say she looks as clear
As morning roses newly wash'd with dew:
Say she be mute and will not speak a word;
Then I'll commend her volubility,
And say she uttereth piercing eloquence. *Ib.* 171

5 And thereby hangs a tale. *Ib.* IV. i. [59]

6 He kills her in her own humour. *Ib.* [183]

7 She shall watch all night:
And if she chance to nod I'll rail and brawl,
And with the clamour keep her still awake.
This is the way to kill a wife with kindness. *Ib.* [208]

8 What say you to a piece of beef and mustard?
Ib. iii. [23]

9 And as the sun breaks through the darkest clouds,
So honour peereth in the meanest habit. *Ib.* [175]

10 PETRUCHIO:
It shall be what o'clock I say it is.
HORTENSIO:
Why, so this gallant will command the sun. *Ib.* [197]

11 O vile,
Intolerable, not to be endur'd! *Ib.* v. ii. 93

12 A woman mov'd is like a fountain troubled,
Muddy, ill-seeming, thick, bereft of beauty. *Ib.* 143

13 Such duty as the subject owes the prince,
Even such a woman oweth to her husband. *Ib.* 156

14 I am asham'd that women are so simple
To offer war where they should kneel for peace.
Ib. 162

15 What cares these roarers for the name of king?
The Tempest, I. i. [18]

16 He hath no drowning mark upon him; his complexion is perfect gallows. *Ib.* [33]

17 Now would I give a thousand furlongs of sea for an acre of barren ground. *Ib.* [70]

18 The wills above be done! but I would fain die a dry death. *Ib.* [72]

19 O! I have suffer'd
With those that I saw suffer: a brave vessel,
Who had, no doubt, some noble creatures in her,
Dash'd all to pieces. O! the cry did knock
Against my very heart. Poor souls, they perish'd.
Ib. ii. 5

20 What seest thou else
In the dark backward and abysm of time? *Ib.* 49

21 Your tale, sir, would cure deafness. *Ib.* 106

22 My library
Was dukedom large enough. *Ib.* 109

23 Knowing I lov'd my books, he furnish'd me,
From mine own library with volumes that
I prize above my dukedom. *Ib.* 166

24 From the still-vexed Bermoothes. *Ib.* 229

25 I will be correspondent to command
And do my spiriting gently. *The Tempest*, I. ii. 297

26 You taught me language; and my profit on't
Is, I know how to curse: the red plague rid you,
For learning me your language! *Ib.* 363

27 Fill all thy bones with aches. *Ib.* 370

28 Come unto these yellow sands,
And then take hands:
Curtsied when you have, and kiss'd,—
The wild waves whist,—
Foot it featly here and there;
And, sweet sprites, the burden bear.
Hark, hark!
Bow, wow,
The watch-dogs bark:
Bow, wow,
Hark, hark! I hear
The strain of strutting Chanticleer
Cock-a-diddle-dow. *Ib.* 375

29 This music crept by me upon the waters,
Allaying both their fury, and my passion,
With its sweet air. *Ib.* 389

30 Full fathom five thy father lies;
Of his bones are coral made:
Those are pearls that were his eyes:
Nothing of him that doth fade,
But doth suffer a sea-change
Into something rich and strange.
Sea-nymphs hourly ring his knell:
Ding-dong.
Hark! now I hear them,—ding-dong, bell. *Ib.* 394

31 The fringed curtains of thine eye advance,
And say what thou seest yond. *Ib.* 405

32 At the first sight
They have changed eyes. *Ib.* 437

33 There's nothing ill can dwell in such a temple:
If the ill spirit have so fair a house,
Good things will strive to dwell with 't. *Ib.* 454

34 Look, he's winding up the watch of his wit, by and by it will strike. *Ib.* II. i. [12]

35 What's past is prologue. *Ib.* [261]

36 They'll take suggestion as a cat laps milk. *Ib.* [296]

37 Open-ey'd conspiracy
His time doth take. *Ib.* [309]

38 A very ancient and fish-like smell. *Ib.* ii. [27]

39 When they will not give a doit to relieve a lame beggar, they will lay out ten to see a dead Indian.
Ib. [33]

40 Misery acquaints a man with strange bedfellows.
Ib. [42]

41 Well, here's my comfort. [*Drinks.*] *Ib.* [48]

42 For she had a tongue with a tang. *Ib.* [53]

43 'Ban, 'Ban, Ca-Caliban,
Has a new master—Get a new man. *Ib.* [197]

44 For several virtues
Have I lik'd several women; never any
With so full soul but some defect in her
Did quarrel with the noblest grace she ow'd,
And put it to the foil. *Ib.* III. i. 42

1 FERDINAND:
Here's my hand.
MIRANDA:
And mine, with my heart in 't. *The Tempest*, III. i. 89

2 Thou deboshed fish thou. *Ib*. ii. [30]

3 Flout 'em, and scout 'em; and scout 'em, and flout 'em;
Thought is free. *Ib*. [133]

4 He that dies pays all debts. *Ib*. [143]

5   The isle is full of noises,
Sounds and sweet airs, that give delight, and hurt not. *Ib*. [147]

6 Spongy April. *Ib*. IV. i. 65

7 You sun-burn'd sicklemen, of August weary. *Ib*. 134

8 Our revels now are ended. These our actors,
As I foretold you, were all spirits and
Are melted into air, into thin air:
And, like the baseless fabric of this vision,
The cloud-capp'd towers, the gorgeous palaces,
The solemn temples, the great globe itself,
Yea, all which it inherit, shall dissolve
And, like this insubstantial pageant faded,
Leave not a rack behind. We are such stuff
As dreams are made on, and our little life
Is rounded with a sleep. *Ib*. 148

9 I do begin to have bloody thoughts. *Ib*. [221]

10 With foreheads villanous low. *Ib*. [252]

11 Now does my project gather to a head. *Ib*. v. i. 1

12   Demi-puppets, that
By moonshine do the green sour ringlets make
Whereof the ewe not bites. *Ib*. 36

13 Deeper than did ever plummet sound,
I'll drown my book. *Ib*. 56

14 Where the bee sucks, there suck I
In a cowslip's bell I lie;
There I couch when owls do cry.
On the bat's back I do fly
After summer merrily:
Merrily, merrily shall I live now
Under the blossom that hangs on the bough. *Ib*. 88

15   O brave new world,
That has such people in 't. *Ib*. 183

16   Retire me to my Milan, where
Every third thought shall be my grave. *Ib*. [310]

17 'Tis not enough to help the feeble up,
But to support him after. *Timon of Athens*, I. i. 108

18 He that loves to be flattered is worthy o' the flatterer. *Ib*. [233]

19   The strain of man's bred out
Into baboon and monkey. *Ib*. [260]

20 I wonder men dare trust themselves with men. *Ib*. ii. [45]

21 Immortal gods, I crave no pelf;
I pray for no man but myself. *Ib*. [64]

22 Like madness is the glory of this life. *Ib*. [141]

23 Men shut their doors against a setting sun *Ib*. [152]

24 Nothing emboldens sin so much as mercy. *Ib*. III. v. 3

25 Uncover, dogs, and lap. *Ib*. vi. [96]

26 You fools of fortune, trencher-friends time's flies. *Timon of Athens*, III. vi. [107]

27 We have seen better days. *Ib*. IV. ii. 27

28 O! the fierce wretchedness that glory brings us. *Ib*. 30

29 He has almost charmed me from my profession, by persuading me to it. *Ib*. iii. [457]

30   My long sickness
Of health and living now begins to mend,
And nothing brings me all things. *Ib*. v. i. [191]

31 Life's uncertain voyage. *Ib*. [207]

32 Timon hath made his everlasting mansion
Upon the beached verge of the salt flood;
Who once a day with his embossed froth
The turbulent surge shall cover. *Ib*. [220]

33 She is a woman, therefore may be woo'd;
She is a woman, therefore may be won;
She is Lavinia, therefore must be lov'd.
What, man! more water glideth by the mill
Than wots the miller of; and easy it is
Of a cut loaf to steal a shive, we know. *Titus Andronicus*, II. i. 82

34 Come, and take choice of all my library,
And so beguile thy sorrow. *Ib*. IV. i. 34

35 The eagle suffers little birds to sing,
And is not careful what they mean thereby. *Ib*. iv. [82]

36 If one good deed in all my life I did,
I do repent it from my very soul. *Ib*. v. iii. [189]

37 The ravish'd Helen, Menelaus' queen,
With wanton Paris sleeps. *Troilus and Cressida*, Prologue, 9

38 PANDARUS:
He that will have a cake out of the wheat must tarry the grinding.
TROILUS:
Have I not tarried?
PANDARUS:
Ay, the grinding; but you must tarry the bolting.
TROILUS:
Have I not tarried?
PANDARUS:
Ay, the bolting; but you must tarry the leavening.
TROILUS:
Still have I tarried.
PANDARUS:
Ay, to the leavening; but here's yet in the word 'hereafter' the kneading, the making of the cake, the heating of the oven, and the baking; nay, you must stay the cooling too, or you may chance to burn your lips. *Ib*. I. i. [15]

39   O! that her hand,
In whose comparison all whites are ink,
Writing their own reproach; to whose soft seizure
The cygnet's down is harsh, and spirit of sense
Hard as the palm of ploughman. *Ib*. [57]

40 I have had my labour for my travail. *Ib*. [73]

41   Women are angels, wooing:
Things won are done; joy's soul lies in the doing:
That she belov'd knows nought that knows not this:
Men prize the thing ungain'd more than it is. *Ib*. ii. [310]

1   The sea being smooth
How many shallow bauble boats dare sail
Upon her patient breast.
           Troilus and Cressida, I. iii. 34

2 The heavens themselves, the planets, and this centre
Observe degree, priority, and place,
Insisture, course, proportion, season, form,
Office, and custom, in all line of order.   *Ib.* 85

3   O! when degree is shak'd,
Which is the ladder to all high designs,
The enterprise is sick.   *Ib.* 101

4 Take but degree away, untune that string,
And, hark! what discord follows; each thing meets
In mere oppugnancy.   *Ib.* 109

5   The general's disdain'd
By him one step below, he by the next,
That next by him beneath; so every step,
Exampled by the first pace that is sick
Of his superior, grows to an envious fever
Of pale and bloodless emulation.   *Ib.* 129

6   Like a strutting player, whose conceit
Lies in his hamstring, and doth think it rich
To hear the wooden dialogue and sound
'Twixt his stretch'd footing and the scaffoldage.
             Ib. 153

7   But we are soldiers;
And may that soldier a mere recreant prove,
That means not, hath not, or is not in love! *Ib.* 286

8 And in such indexes, although small pricks
To their subsequent volumes, there is seen
The baby figure of the giant mass
Of things to come at large.   *Ib.* 343

9 Mongrel beef-witted lord.   *Ib.* II. i. [14]

10 Who wears his wit in his belly, and his guts in his
head.   *Ib.* [78]

11 The wound of peace is surety,
Surety secure.   *Ib.* ii. 14

12 TROILUS:
What is aught, but as 'tis valued?
HECTOR:
But value dwells not in particular will;
It holds his estimate and dignity
As well wherein 'tis precious of itself
As in the prizer. 'Tis mad idolatry
To make the service greater than the god.   *Ib.* 52

13   Young men, whom Aristotle thought
Unfit to hear moral philosophy.   *Ib.* 166

14   Thus to persist
In doing wrong extenuates not wrong,
But makes it much more heavy.   *Ib.* 186

15 I am giddy, expectation whirls me round.
The imaginary relish is so sweet
That it enchants my sense.   *Ib.* III. ii. [17]

16   To be wise, and love,
Exceeds man's might.   *Ib.* [163]

17 Time hath, my lord, a wallet at his back,
Wherein he puts alms for oblivion,
A great-siz'd monster of ingratitudes:
Those scraps are good deeds past; which are devour'd
As fast as they are made, forgot as soon
As done.   *Ib.* iii. 145

18   Perseverance, dear my lord,
Keeps honour bright: to have done, is to hang
Quite out of fashion, like a rusty mail
In monumental mockery.
         Troilus and Cressida, III. iii. 150

19 For honour travels in a strait so narrow
Where one but goes abreast.   *Ib.* 154

20   Time is like a fashionable host
That slightly shakes his parting guest by the hand,
And with his arms outstretch'd, as he would fly,
Grasps in the comer: welcome ever smiles,
And farewell goes out sighing.   *Ib.* 165

21   Beauty, wit,
High birth, vigour of bone, desert in service,
Love, friendship, charity, are subjects all
To envious and calumniating time.
One touch of nature makes the whole world kin,
That all with one consent praise new-born gawds.
             Ib. 171

22 And give to dust that is a little gilt
More laud than gilt o'er-dusted.   *Ib.* 178

23 A plague of opinion! a man may wear it on both
sides, like a leather jerkin.   *Ib.* [267]

24 How my achievements mock me!   *Ib.* IV. ii. [72]

25   Sometimes we are devils to ourselves
When we will tempt the frailty of our powers,
Presuming on their changeful potency. *Ib.* iv. [95]

26   Fie, fie upon her!
There's language in her eye, her cheek, her lip,
Nay, her foot speaks; her wanton spirits look out
At every joint and motive of her body.   *Ib.* v. 54

27 What's past, and what's to come, is strew'd with
husks
And formless ruin of oblivion.   *Ib.* 165

28   The end crowns all,
And that old common arbitrator, Time,
Will one day end it.   *Ib.* 223

29 Words, words, mere words, no matter from the heart.
            Ib. v. iii. [109]

30 If music be the food of love, play on;
Give me excess of it, that, surfeiting,
The appetite may sicken, and so die.
That strain again! it had a dying fall:
O! it came o'er my ear like the sweet sound
That breathes upon a bank of violets,
Stealing and giving odour! Enough! no more:
'Tis not so sweet now as it was before.
O spirit of love! how quick and fresh art thou,
That notwithstanding thy capacity
Receiveth as the sea, nought enters there,
Of what validity and pitch soe'er,
But falls into abatement and low price,
Even in a minute: so full of shapes is fancy,
That it alone is high fantastical. *Twelfth Night*, I. i. 1

31 O! when mine eyes did see Olivia first,
Methought she purg'd the air of pestilence.
That instant was I turn'd into a hart,
And my desires, like fell and cruel hounds,
E'er since pursue me.   *Ib.* 19

32 The element itself, till seven years' heat,
Shall not behold her face at ample view;
But, like a cloistress, she will veiled walk,
And water once a day her chamber round
With eye-offending brine.   *Ib.* 26

1 Away before me to sweet beds of flowers;
Love-thoughts lie rich when canopied with bowers.
Twelfth Night, I. i. 40

2 And what should I do in Illyria?
My brother he is in Elysium. *Ib.* ii. 2

3 O my poor brother! *Ib.* 6

4 He's as tall a man as any's in Illyria. *Ib.* iii. [21]

5 Speaks three or four languages word for word without
book. *Ib.* [28]

6 Methinks sometimes I have no more wit than a
Christian or an ordinary man has; but I am a great
eater of beef, and I believe that does harm to my
wit. *Ib.* [90]

7 SIR ANDREW:
I would I had bestowed that time in the tongues that
I have in fencing, dancing, and bear-baiting. O!
had I but followed the arts!
SIR TOBY:
Then hadst thou had an excellent head of hair.
Ib. [99]

8 Wherefore are these things hid? wherefore have
these gifts a curtain before 'em? are they like to
take dust, like Mistress Mall's picture? why dost
thou not go to church in a galliard, and come home
in a coranto? My very walk should be a jig.
Ib. [135]

9 Is it a world to hide virtues in? *Ib.* [142]

10   Diana's lip
Is not more smooth and rubious; thy small pipe
Is as the maiden's organ, shrill and sound;
And all is semblative a woman's part. *Ib.* iv. 31

11 Many a good hanging prevents a bad marriage.
Ib. v. [20]

12 What says Quinapalus? 'Better a witty fool than a
foolish wit.' *Ib.* [37]

13 Virtue that transgresses is but patched with sin; and
sin that amends is but patched with virtue.
Ib. [52]

14 Good my mouse of virtue, answer me. *Ib.* [68]

15 O! you are sick of self-love, Malvolio. *Ib.* [96]

16 A plague o' these pickle herring! *Ib.* [127]

17 Not yet old enough for a man, nor young enough for
a boy; as a squash is before 'tis a peascod, or a
codling when 'tis almost an apple: 'tis with him in
standing water, between boy and man. He is very
well-favoured, and he speaks very shrewishly: one
would think his mother's milk were scarce out of
him. *Ib.* [166]

18 I would be loath to cast away my speech, for besides
that it is excellently well penned, I have taken
great pains to con it. *Ib.* [184]

19 I can say little more than I have studied, and that
question's out of my part. *Ib.* [191]

20 OLIVIA:
'Tis in grain, sir; 'twill endure wind and weather.
VIOLA:
'Tis beauty truly blent, whose red and white
Nature's own sweet and cunning hand laid on:
Lady, you are the cruell'st she alive
If you will lead these graces to the grave
And leave the world no copy. *Ib.* [257]

21 Item, Two lips, indifferent red; Item, Two grey eyes
with lids to them; Item, One neck, one chin, and
so forth. *Twelfth Night*, I. v. [268]

22 Make me a willow cabin at your gate,
And call upon my soul within the house;
Write loyal cantons of contemnèd love,
And sing them loud even in the dead of night;
Halloo your name to the reverberate hills,
And make the babbling gossip of the air
Cry out, 'Olivia'. *Ib.* [289]

23 Farewell, fair cruelty. *Ib.* [309]

24   'What is your parentage?'
'Above my fortune, yet my state is well:
I am a gentleman.' *Ib.* [310]

25 She is drowned already, sir, with salt water, though
I seem to drown her remembrance again with
more. *Ib.* II. i. [31]

26 I am yet so near the manners of my mother, that upon
the least occasion more mine eyes will tell tales of
me. *Ib.* [42]

27 Not to be a-bed after midnight is to be up betimes.
... To be up after midnight and to go to bed then,
is early; so that to go to bed after midnight is to
go to bed betimes. *Ib.* iii. [1 and 7]

28 O mistress mine! where are you roaming?
O! stay and hear; your true love's coming,
    That can sing both high and low.
Trip no further, pretty sweeting;
Journeys end in lovers meeting,
    Every wise man's son doth know.

    .   .   .

What is love? 'tis not hereafter;
Present mirth hath present laughter;
    What's to come is still unsure:
In delay there lies no plenty;
Then come kiss me, sweet and twenty,
    Youth's stuff will not endure. *Ib.* [42]

29 Am not I consanguineous? am I not of her blood?
Tillyvally, lady! *Ib.* [85]

30 He does it with a better grace, but I do it more
natural. *Ib.* [91]

31 Is there no respect of place, persons, nor time, in
you? *Ib.* [100]

32 SIR TOBY:
Dost thou think, because thou art virtuous, there
shall be no more cakes and ale?
CLOWN:
Yes, by Saint Anne, and ginger shall be hot i' the
mouth too. *Ib.* [124]

33 MARIA:
Marry, sir, sometimes he is a kind of puritan.
SIR ANDREW:
O, if I thought that, I'd beat him like a dog!
Ib. [153]

34 I will drop in his way some obscure epistles of love;
wherein by the colour of his beard, the shape of
his leg, the manner of his gait, the expressure of
his eye, forehead, and complexion, he shall find
himself most feelingly personated. *Ib.* [171]

35 My purpose is, indeed, a horse of that colour.
Ib. [184]

1 Now, good Cesario, but that piece of song,
That old and antique song we heard last night;
Methought it did relieve my passion much,
More than light airs and recollected terms
Of these most brisk and giddy-paced times:
Come, but one verse. *Twelfth Night*, II. iv. 2

2 DUKE:
　　　　　If ever thou shalt love,
In the sweet pangs of it remember me;
For such as I am all true lovers are:
Unstaid and skittish in all motions else,
Save in the constant image of the creature
That is belov'd. How dost thou like this tune?
VIOLA:
It gives a very echo to the seat
Where love is enthron'd. *Ib.* 15

3 　　　　　Let still the woman take
An elder than herself, so wears she to him,
So sways she level in her husband's heart:
For, boy, however we do praise ourselves,
Our fancies are more giddy and unfirm,
More longing, wavering, sooner lost and worn,
Than women's are. *Ib.* 29

4 Then let thy love be younger than thyself,
Or thy affection cannot hold the bent. *Ib.* 36

5 Mark it, Cesario; it is old and plain.
The spinsters and the knitters in the sun
And the free maids that weave their thread with bones
Do use to chant it: it is silly sooth,
And dallies with the innocence of love,
Like the old age. *Ib.* 43

6 Come away, come away, death,
　　And in sad cypress let me be laid;
Fly away, fly away, breath:
　　I am slain by a fair cruel maid.
My shroud of white, stuck all with yew,
　　O! prepare it.
My part of death no one so true
　　Did share it.

Not a flower, not a flower sweet,
　　On my black coffin let there be strown;
Not a friend, not a friend greet
　　My poor corse, where my bones shall be thrown.
A thousand thousand sighs to save,
　　Lay me, O! where
Sad true lover never find my grave,
　　To weep there. *Ib.* 51

7 Now, the melancholy god protect thee, and the tailor
make thy doublet of changeable taffeta, for thy
mind is a very opal. *Ib.* [74]

8 Get thee to yond same sovereign cruelty:
Tell her, my love, more noble than the world,
Prizes not quantity of dirty lands. *Ib.* [82]

9 　　　　　There is no woman's sides
Can bide the beating of so strong a passion
As love doth give my heart; no woman's heart
So big, to hold so much; they lack retention.
Alas! their love may be call'd appetite,
No motion of the liver, but the palate,
That suffer surfeit, cloyment, and revolt;
But mine is all as hungry as the sea,
And can digest so much. *Ib.* [95]

10 DUKE:
And what's her history?

VIOLA:
A blank, my lord. She never told her love,
But let concealment, like a worm i' the bud,
Feed on her damask cheek: she pin'd in thought;
And with a green and yellow melancholy,
She sat like patience on a monument,
Smiling at grief. Was not this love indeed?
We men may say more, swear more; but, indeed,
Our shows are more than will; for still we prove
Much in our vows, but little in our love.
Twelfth Night, II. iv. [111]

11 I am all the daughters of my father's house,
And all the brothers too. *Ib.* [122]

12 How now, my metal of India! *Ib.* v. [17]

13 Here comes the trout that must be caught with
tickling. *Ib.* [25]

14 Contemplation makes a rare turkey-cock of him:
how he jets under his advanced plumes! *Ib.* [35]

15 In my branched velvet gown. *Ib.* [54]

16 Now is the woodcock near the gin. *Ib.* [93]

17 I may command where I adore. *Ib.* [116]

18 But be not afraid of greatness: some men are born
great, some achieve greatness, and some have greatness thrust upon them. *Ib.* [158]

19 Let thy tongue tang arguments of state; put thyself
into the trick of singularity. She thus advises thee
that sighs for thee. Remember who commended
thy yellow stockings, and wished to see thee ever
cross-gartered. *Ib.* [165]

20 Jove and my stars be praised! Here is yet a postscript.
Ib. [189]

21 He will come to her in yellow stockings, and 'tis a
colour she abhors; and cross-gartered, a fashion
she detests. *Ib.* [220]

22 Now Jove, in his next commodity of hair, send thee
a beard. *Ib.* III. i. [51]

23 This fellow's wise enough to play the fool,
And to do that well craves a kind of wit. *Ib.* [68]

24 Taste your legs, sir; put them to motion. *Ib.* [88]

25 Most excellent accomplished lady, the heavens rain
odours on you! *Ib.* [96]

26 　　　　　'Twas never merry world
Since lowly feigning was called compliment.
Ib. [110]

27 O world! how apt the poor are to be proud.
Ib. [141]

28 O! what a deal of scorn looks beautiful
In the contempt and anger of his lip. *Ib.* [159]

29 Love sought is good, but giv'n unsought is better.
Ib. [170]

30 They have been grand-jurymen since before Noah
was a sailor. *Ib.* ii. [18]

31 You should then have accosted her, and with some
excellent jests, fire-new from the mint, you should
have banged the youth into dumbness. *Ib.* [23]

32 Where you will hang like an icicle on a Dutchman's
beard. *Ib.* [30]

33 I had as lief be a Brownist as a politician. *Ib.* [35]

34 Although the sheet were big enough for the bed of
Ware in England. *Ib.* [52]

1 Let there be gall enough in thy ink, though thou write with a goose-pen, no matter.
Twelfth Night, III. ii. [54]

2 If he were opened, and you find so much blood in his liver as will clog the foot of a flea, I'll eat the rest of the anatomy. *Ib*. [68]

3 Look, where the youngest wren of nine comes.
Ib. [73]

4 More lines than are in the new map with the augmentation of the Indies. *Ib*. [87]

5 In the south suburbs, at the Elephant. *Ib*. iii. 39

6 I think we do know the sweet Roman hand.
Ib. iv. [31]

7 Why, this is very midsummer madness. *Ib*. [62]

8 What, man! defy the devil: consider, he's an enemy to mankind. *Ib*. [109]

9 Go, hang yourselves all! you are idle shallow things: I am not of your element. *Ib*. [138]

10 If this were played upon a stage now, I could condemn it as an improbable fiction. *Ib*. [142]

11 More matter for a May morning. *Ib*. [158]

12 Still you keep o' the windy side of the law. *Ib*. [183]

13 Fare thee well; and God have mercy upon one of our souls! He may have mercy upon mine, but my hope is better; and so look to thyself. *Ib*. [185]

14 Nay, let me alone for swearing. *Ib*. [204]

15 He is knight dubbed with unhatched rapier, and on carpet consideration. *Ib*. [260]

16 I am one that had rather go with sir priest than sir knight; I care not who knows so much of my mettle. *Ib*. [300]

17 Out of my lean and low ability
I'll lend you something. *Ib*. [380]

18 I hate ingratitude more in a man
Than lying, vainness, babbling drunkenness,
Or any taint of vice whose strong corruption
Inhabits our frail blood. *Ib*. [390]

19 In nature there's no blemish but the mind;
None can be call'd deform'd but the unkind.
Ib. [403]

20 Out, hyperbolical fiend! *Ib*. IV. ii. [29]

21 For I am one of those gentle ones that will use the devil himself with courtesy. *Ib*. [37]

22 CLOWN:
What is the opinion of Pythagoras concerning wild fowl?
MALVOLIO:
That the soul of our grandam might haply inhabit a bird.
CLOWN:
What thinkest thou of his opinion?
MALVOLIO:
I think nobly of the soul, and no way approve his opinion. *Ib*. [55]

23 Leave thy vain bibble-babble. *Ib*. [106]

24 We took him for a coward, but he's the very devil incardinate. *Ib*. v. i. [185]

25 And made the most notorious geck and gull
That e'er invention play'd. *Ib*. [355]

26 And thus the whirligig of time brings in his revenges.
Twelfth Night, v. i. [388]

27 When that I was and a little tiny boy,
With hey, ho, the wind and the rain;
A foolish thing was but a toy,
For the rain it raineth every day.

But when I came to man's estate,
With hey, ho, the wind and the rain;
'Gainst knaves and thieves men shut their gates,
For the rain it raineth every day.

But when I came, alas! to wive,
With hey, ho, the wind and the rain;
By swaggering could I never thrive,
For the rain it raineth every day.

But when I came unto my beds,
With hey, ho, the wind and the rain;
With toss-pots still had drunken heads,
For the rain it raineth every day.

A great while ago the world begun,
With hey, ho, the wind and the rain;
But that's all one, our play is done,
And we'll strive to please you every day. *Ib*. [401]

28 Home-keeping youth have ever homely wits.
The Two Gentlemen of Verona, I. i. 2

29 For he was more than over shoes in love. *Ib*. 24

30 I have no other but a woman's reason:
I think him so, because I think him so. *Ib*. ii. 23

31 Fie, fie! how wayward is this foolish love
That, like a testy babe, will scratch the nurse
And presently all humbled kiss the rod! *Ib*. 55

32 Poor wounded name! my bosom, as a bed
Shall lodge thee till thy wound be throughly heal'd.
Ib. 111

33 O! how this spring of love resembleth
The uncertain glory of an April day. *Ib*. iii. 84

34 Or as one nail by strength drives out another,
So the remembrance of my former love
Is by a newer object quite forgotten. *Ib*. II. iv. 194

35 He makes sweet music with th' enamell'd stones,
Giving a gentle kiss to every sedge
He overtaketh in his pilgrimage;
And so by many winding nooks he strays
With willing sport, to the wild ocean. *Ib*. vii. 28

36 Except I be by Silvia in the night,
There is no music in the nightingale;
Unless I look on Silvia in the day,
There is no day for me to look upon. *Ib*. III. i. 178

37 Ay,
Much is the force of heaven-bred poesy. *Ib*. ii. 71

38 A man I am cross'd with adversity. *Ib*. IV. i. 12

39 You know that love
Will creep in service where it cannot go. *Ib*. ii. 19

40 Who is Sylvia? what is she,
That all our swains commend her?
Holy, fair, and wise is she;
The heaven such grace did lend her,
That she might admired be.

Is she kind as she is fair?
For beauty lives with kindness:
Love doth to her eyes repair,
To help him of his blindness;
And, being help'd, inhabits there.

Then to Silvia let us sing,
  That Silvia is excelling;
She excels each mortal thing
  Upon the dull earth dwelling;
To her let us garlands bring.
                    Two Gentlemen of Verona, IV. ii. 40

1 How use doth breed a habit in a man!   *Ib.* v. iv. 1

2   O heaven! were man
But constant, he were perfect.   *Ib.* 110

3 Two lads that thought there was no more behind
But such a day to-morrow as to-day,
And to be boy eternal.   *The Winter's Tale*, I. ii. 63

4 We were as twinn'd lambs that did frisk i' the sun,
And bleat the one at the other: what we chang'd
Was innocence for innocence; we knew not
The doctrine of ill-doing, no, nor dream'd
That any did.   *Ib.* 67

5 Three crabbed months had sour'd themselves to death,
Ere I could make thee open thy white hand
And clap thyself my love.   *Ib.* 102

6 Paddling palms and pinching fingers.   *Ib.* 116

7   Still virginalling
Upon his palm.   *Ib.* 126

8 Affection! thy intention stabs the centre:
Thou dost make possible things not so held,
Communicat'st with dreams.   *Ib.* 139

9 How like, methought, I then was to this kernel,
This squash, this gentleman.   *Ib.* 160

10   A sad tale's best for winter.
I have one of sprites and goblins.   *Ib.* II. i. 24

11 It is a heretic that makes the fire,
Not she which burns in 't.   *Ib.* iii. 114

12   What's gone, and what's past help
Should be past grief.   *Ib.* III. ii. [223]

13 *Bohemia. A desert Country near the Sea.*
                    Ib. iii. *Stage Direction*

14   Our ship hath touch'd upon
The desarts of Bohemia.   *Ib.* 1

15 *Exit, pursued by a bear.*   *Ib. Stage Direction*

16 When daffodils begin to peer,
  With heigh! the doxy, over the dale,
Why, then comes in the sweet o' the year;
  For the red blood reigns in the winter's pale.

The white sheet bleaching on the hedge,
  With heigh! the sweet birds, O, how they sing!
Doth set my pugging tooth on edge;
  For a quart of ale is a dish for a king.

The lark, that tirra-lirra chants,
  With, heigh! with, heigh! the thrush and the jay,
Are summer songs for me and my aunts,
  While we lie tumbling in the hay.   *Ib.* IV. ii. 1

17 But shall I go mourn for that, my dear?   *Ib.* [15]

18 A snapper-up of unconsidered trifles.   *Ib.* [26]

19 For the life to come, I sleep out the thought of it.
                    Ib. [30]

20 Prig, for my life, prig; he haunts wakes, fairs, and bear-baitings.   *Ib.* [109]

21 Jog on, jog on the foot-path way,
  And merrily hent the stile-a:
A merry heart goes all the day,
  Your sad tires in a mile-a.   *Ib.* [133]

22 For you there's rosemary and rue; these keep
Seeming and savour all the winter long.
                    The Winter's Tale, IV. iii. 74

23   The fairest flowers o' the season
Are our carnations and streak'd gillyvors,
Which some call nature's bastards.   *Ib.* 81

24 Yet nature is made better by no mean
But nature makes that mean.   *Ib.* 89

25   Here's flowers for you;
Hot lavender, mints, savory, marjoram;
The marigold, that goes to bed wi' the sun,
And with him rises weeping.   *Ib.* 103

26   O Proserpina!
For the flowers now that frighted thou let'st fall
From Dis's waggon! daffodils,
That come before the swallow dares, and take
The winds of March with beauty; violets dim,
But sweeter than the lids of Juno's eyes
Or Cytherea's breath; pale prime-roses,
That die unmarried, ere they can behold
Bright Phœbus in his strength,—a malady
Most incident to maids; bold oxlips and
The crown imperial; lilies of all kinds,
The flower-de-luce being one.   *Ib.* 116

27 PERDITA: Sure this robe of mine
Doth change my disposition.
FLORIZEL: What you do
Still betters what is done. When you speak, sweet,
I'd have you do it ever: when you sing,
I'd have you buy and sell so; so give alms;
Pray so; and, for the ordering your affairs,
To sing them too: when you do dance, I wish you
A wave o' the sea, that you might ever do
Nothing but that; move still, still so,
And own no other function: each your doing,
So singular in each particular,
Crowns what you are doing in the present deed,
That all your acts are queens.   *Ib.* 134

28   Good sooth, she is
The queen of curds and cream.   *Ib.* 160

29 Lawn as white as driven snow.   *Ib.* [220]

30 I love a ballad in print, a-life, for then we are sure
they are true.   *Ib.* [262]

31 The self-same sun that shines upon his court
Hides not his visage from our cottage, but
Looks on alike.   *Ib.* [457]

32 Being now awake, I'll queen it no inch further,
But milk my ewes and weep.   *Ib.* [462]

33 Prosperity's the very bond of love,
Whose fresh complexion and whose heart together
Affliction alters.   *Ib.* [586]

34 Ha, ha! what a fool Honesty is! and Trust his sworn
brother, a very simple gentleman!   *Ib.* [608]

35 Though I am not naturally honest, I am so sometimes by chance.   *Ib.* [734]

36 That rare Italian master, Julio Romano.
                    Ib. v. ii. [108]

37 Thou art a tall fellow of thy hands.   *Ib.* [185]

38 'Tis time; descend; be stone no more; approach.
                    Ib. iii. 99

1   O! she's warm.
If this be magic, let it be an art
Lawful as eating.   *The Winter's Tale*, v. iii. 109

2 Crabbed age and youth cannot live together:
Youth is full of pleasance, age is full of care.
    The Passionate Pilgrim, xii

3 Age, I do abhor thee, youth, I do adore thee. *Ib.*

4 What I have done is yours; what I have to do is
yours; being part in all I have, devoted yours.
    The Rape of Lucrece, Preface

5 Beauty itself doth of itself persuade
The eyes of men without an orator.   *Ib.* l. 29

6 Or sells eternity to get a toy.   *Ib.* l. 214

7 Time's glory is to calm contending kings,
To unmask falsehood, and bring truth to light.
    Ib. l. 939

8 Cloud-kissing Ilion.   *Ib.* l. 1370

9 From fairest creatures we desire increase,
That thereby beauty's rose might never die.
    Sonnets, 1

10 When forty winters shall besiege thy brow,
And dig deep trenches in thy beauty's field. *Ib.* 2

11 Thou art thy mother's glass, and she in thee
Calls back the lovely April of her prime.   *Ib.* 3

12 Lo! in the orient when the gracious light
Lifts up his burning head, each under eye
Doth homage to his new-appearing sight.   *Ib.* 7

13 Music to hear, why hear'st thou music sadly?
Sweets with sweets war not, joy delights in joy:
Why lov'st thou that which thou receiv'st not gladly,
Or else receiv'st with pleasure thine annoy? *Ib.* 8

14 True concord of well-tuned sounds.   *Ib.*

15 When lofty trees I see barren of leaves,
Which erst from heat did canopy the herd,
And summer's green all girded up in sheaves,
Borne on the bier with white and bristly beard.
    Ib. 12

16 If I could write the beauty of your eyes
And in fresh numbers number all your graces,
The age to come would say, 'This poet lies;
Such heavenly touches ne'er touch'd earthly faces.'
    Ib. 17

17 And stretched metre of an antique song.   *Ib.*

18 Shall I compare thee to a summer's day?
Thou art more lovely and more temperate:
Rough winds do shake the darling buds of May,
And summer's lease hath all too short a date:
Sometimes too hot the eye of heaven shines,
And often is his gold complexion dimm'd;
And every fair from fair sometime declines,
By chance, or nature's changing course untrimm'd;
But thy eternal summer shall not fade,
Nor lose possession of that fair thou ow'st,
Nor shall death brag thou wander'st in his shade,
When in eternal lines to time thou grow'st;
So long as men can breathe, or eyes can see,
So long lives this, and this gives life to thee. *Ib.* 18

19 My glass shall not persuade me I am old,
So long as youth and thou are of one date;
But when in thee time's furrows I behold,
Then look I death my days should expiate.   *Ib.* 22

20 As an unperfect actor on the stage,
Who with his fear is put besides his part. *Sonnets*, 23

21 O! let my books be then the eloquence
And dumb presagers of my speaking breast. *Ib.*

22 The painful warrior famoused for fight,
After a thousand victories once foil'd,
Is from the book of honour razed quite,
And all the rest forgot for which he toil'd. *Ib.* 25

23 Weary with toil, I haste me to my bed. *Ib.* 27

24 When in disgrace with fortune and men's eyes
I all alone beweep my outcast state,
And trouble deaf heaven with my bootless cries,
And look upon myself and curse my fate,
Wishing me like to one more rich in hope,
Featur'd like him, like him with friends possess'd,
Desiring this man's art, and that man's scope,
With what I most enjoy contented least;
Yet in these thoughts myself almost despising,
Haply I think on thee,—and then my state,
Like to the lark at break of day arising
From sullen earth, sings hymns at heaven's gate;
For thy sweet love remember'd such wealth brings
That then I scorn to change my state with kings.
    Ib. 29

25 When to the sessions of sweet silent thought
I summon up remembrance of things past,
I sigh the lack of many a thing I sought,
And with old woes new wail my dear times' waste:
Then can I drown an eye, unus'd to flow,
For precious friends hid in death's dateless night,
And weep afresh love's long since cancell'd woe,
And moan the expense of many a vanish'd sight:
Then can I grieve at grievances foregone,
And heavily from woe to woe tell o'er
The sad account of fore-bemoaned moan,
Which I new pay as if not paid before.
But if the while I think on thee, dear friend,
All losses are restor'd and sorrows end. *Ib.* 30

26 But since he died, and poets better prove,
Theirs for their style I'll read, his for his love.
    Ib. 32

27 Full many a glorious morning have I seen
Flatter the mountain-tops with sovereign eye,
Kissing with golden face the meadows green,
Gilding pale streams with heavenly alchemy. *Ib.* 33

28 But, out! alack! he was but one hour mine,
The region cloud hath mask'd him from me now. *Ib.*

29 Suns of the world may stain when heaven's sun
    staineth.   *Ib.*

30 Why didst thou promise such a beauteous day,
And make me travel forth without my cloak? *Ib.* 34

31 Roses have thorns, and silver fountains mud;
Clouds and eclipses stain both moon and sun,
And loathsome canker lives in sweetest bud.
All men make faults.   *Ib.* 35

32 As a decrepit father takes delight
To see his active child do deeds of youth,
So I, made lame by fortune's dearest spite,
Take all my comfort of thy worth and truth. *Ib.* 37

33 Against that time when thou shalt strangely pass,
And scarcely greet me with that sun, thine eye,
When love, converted from the thing it was,
Shall reasons find of settled gravity.   *Ib.* 49

1 Like stones of worth they thinly placed are,
Or captain jewels in the carconet.   *Sonnets*, 52

2 What is your substance, whereof are you made,
That millions of strange shadows on you tend?
                                            Ib. 53

3 You in Grecian tires are painted new.   *Ib.*

4 The spring and foison of the year.   *Ib.*

5 O! how much more doth beauty beauteous seem
By that sweet ornament which truth doth give!
                                            Ib. 54

6 Not marble, nor the gilded monuments
Of princes, shall outlive this powerful rhyme. *Ib.* 55

7 Being your slave, what should I do but tend
Upon the hours and times of your desire?
I have no precious time at all to spend,
Nor services to do, till you require.
Nor dare I chide the world-without-end hour
Whilst I, my sovereign, watch the clock for you,
Nor think the bitterness of absence sour
When you have bid your servant once adieu;
Nor dare I question with my jealous thought
Where you may be, or your affairs suppose,
But like a sad slave, stay and think of nought
Save, where you are, how happy you make those.
So true a fool is love that in your will,
Though you do anything, he thinks no ill.   *Ib.* 57

8 Like as the waves make towards the pebbled shore,
So do our minutes hasten to their end.   *Ib.* 60

9 Time doth transfix the flourish set on youth
And delves the parallels in beauty's brow.   *Ib.*

10 Sin of self-love possesseth all mine eye.   *Ib.* 62

11 When I have seen by Time's fell hand defac'd
The rich-proud cost of outworn buried age.   *Ib.* 64

12 When I have seen the hungry ocean gain
Advantage on the kingdom of the shore.   *Ib.*

13 Since brass, nor stone, nor earth, nor boundless sea,
But sad mortality o'ersways their power,
How with this rage shall beauty hold a plea,
Whose action is no stronger than a flower?   *Ib.* 65

14 Tir'd with all these, for restful death I cry,
As to behold desert a beggar born,
And needy nothing trimm'd in jollity,
And purest faith unhappily forsworn,
And gilded honour shamefully misplac'd,
And maiden virtue rudely strumpeted,
And right perfection wrongfully disgrac'd,
And strength by limping sway disabled,
And art made tongue-tied by authority,
And folly—doctor-like—controlling skill,
And simple truth miscall'd simplicity,
And captive good attending captain ill:
Tir'd with all these, from these I would be gone,
Save that, to die, I leave my love alone.   *Ib.* 66

15 No longer mourn for me when I am dead
Than you shall hear the surly sullen bell
Give warning to the world that I am fled
From this vile world, with vilest worms to dwell.
                                            Ib. 71

16 That time of year thou mayst in me behold
When yellow leaves, or none, or few, do hang
Upon those boughs which shake against the cold,
Bare ruin'd choirs, where late the sweet birds sang.

In me thou see'st the twilight of such day
As after sunset fadeth in the west;
Which by and by black night doth take away,
Death's second self, that seals up all in rest.
                                            Sonnets, 73

17 This thou perceiv'st, which makes thy love more
        strong,
To love that well which thou must leave ere long.
                                            Ib.

18 So all my best is dressing old words new.   *Ib.* 76

19 Like unletter'd clerk, still cry 'Amen'.   *Ib.* 85

20 Was it the proud full sail of his great verse,
Bound for the prize of all too precious you,
That did my ripe thoughts in my brain inhearse,
Making their tomb the womb wherein they grew?
                                            Ib. 86

21   That affable familiar ghost
Which nightly gulls him with intelligence.   *Ib.*

22 Farewell! thou art too dear for my possessing,
And like enough thou know'st thy estimate:
The charter of thy worth gives thee releasing;
My bonds in thee are all determinate.
For how do I hold thee but by thy granting?
And for that riches where is my deserving?
The cause of this fair gift in me is wanting,
And so my patent back again is swerving.
Thyself thou gav'st, thy own worth then not
        knowing,
Or me, to whom thou gav'st it, else mistaking;
So thy great gift, upon misprision growing,
Comes home again, on better judgment making.
Thus have I had thee, as a dream doth flatter,
In sleep a king, but, waking, no such matter. *Ib.* 87

23 Ah, do not, when my heart hath 'scap'd this sorrow,
Come in the rearward of a conquer'd woe;
Give not a windy night a rainy morrow,
To linger out a purpos'd overthrow.   *Ib.* 90

24 They that have power to hurt and will do none,
That do not do the thing they most do show,
Who, moving others, are themselves as stone,
Unmoved, cold, and to temptation slow.   *Ib.* 94

25 They are the lords and owners of their faces,
Others but stewards of their excellence.
The summer's flower is to the summer sweet,
Though to itself it only live and die.   *Ib.*

26 Lilies that fester smell far worse than weeds.   *Ib.*

27 How like a winter hath my absence been
From thee, the pleasure of the fleeting year!
What freezings have I felt, what dark days seen!
What old December's bareness every where! *Ib.* 97

28 From you have I been absent in the spring,
When proud-pied April, dress'd in all his trim,
Hath put a spirit of youth in every thing.   *Ib.* 98

29 To me, fair friend, you never can be old,
For as you were when first your eye I ey'd,
Such seems your beauty still. Three winters cold
Have from the forests shook three summers' pride,
Three beauteous springs to yellow autumn turn'd
In process of the seasons have I seen,
Three April perfumes in three hot Junes burn'd,
Since first I saw you fresh, which yet are green.
Ah! yet doth beauty, like a dial-hand,
Steal from his figure, and no pace perceiv'd;
So your sweet hue, which methinks still doth stand,

Hath motion, and mine eye may be deceiv'd:
For fear of which, hear this, thou age unbred:
Ere you were born was beauty's summer dead.
Sonnets, 104

1 And beauty, making beautiful old rhyme. *Ib.* 106

2 Not mine own fears, nor the prophetic soul
Of the wide world dreaming on things to come,
Can yet the lease of my true love control,
Suppos'd as forfeit to a confin'd doom.
The mortal moon hath her eclipse endur'd,
And the sad augurs mock their own presage. *Ib.* 107

3 And thou in this shalt find thy monument,
When tyrants' crests and tombs of brass are spent. *Ib.*

4 O! never say that I was false of heart,
Though absence seem'd my flame to qualify. *Ib.* 109

5 Alas! 'tis true I have gone here and there,
And made myself a motley to the view,
Gor'd mine own thoughts, sold cheap what is most dear,
Made old offences of affections new;
Most true it is that I have look'd on truth
Askance and strangely; but, by all above,
These blenches gave my heart another youth,
And worse essays prov'd thee my best of love.
Ib. 110

6 My nature is subdu'd
To what it works in, like the dyer's hand;
Pity me, then, and wish I were renew'd. *Ib.* 111

7 Let me not to the marriage of true minds
Admit impediments. Love is not love
Which alters when it alteration finds,
Or bends with the remover to remove:
O, no! it is an ever-fixed mark,
That looks on tempests and is never shaken;
It is the star to every wandering bark,
Whose worth's unknown, although his height be taken.
Love's not Time's fool, though rosy lips and cheeks
Within his bending sickle's compass come;
Love alters not with his brief hours and weeks,
But bears it out even to the edge of doom.
If this be error, and upon me prov'd,
I never writ, nor no man ever lov'd. *Ib.* 116

8 What potions have I drunk of Siren tears,
Distill'd from limbecks foul as hell within. *Ib.* 119

9 O benefit of ill! now I find true
That better is by evil still made better. *Ib.*

10 'Tis better to be vile than vile esteem'd,
When not to be receives reproach of being. *Ib.* 121

11 The expense of spirit in a waste of shame
Is lust in action; and till action, lust
Is perjur'd, murderous, bloody, full of blame,
Savage, extreme, rude, cruel, not to trust. *Ib.* 129

12 Mad in pursuit, and in possession so;
Had, having, and in quest to have, extreme;
A bliss in proof,—and prov'd, a very woe;
Before, a joy propos'd; behind, a dream.
All this the world well knows; yet none knows well:
To shun the heaven that leads men to this hell. *Ib.*

13 My mistress' eyes are nothing like the sun;
Coral is far more red than her lips' red:
If snow be white, why then her breasts are dun;
If hairs be wires, black wires grow on her head.
Ib. 130

14 And yet, by heaven, I think my love as rare
As any she belied with false compare. *Sonnets*, 130

15 Whoever hath her wish, thou hast thy *Will*,
And *Will* to boot, and *Will* in over-plus. *Ib.* 135

16 When my love swears that she is made of truth,
I do believe her, though I know she lies. *Ib.* 138

17 Lo, as a careful housewife runs to catch
One of her feather'd creatures broke away. *Ib.* 143

18 Two loves I have of comfort and despair,
Which like two spirits do suggest me still:
The better angel is a man right fair,
The worser spirit a woman colour'd ill. *Ib.* 144

19 Yet this shall I ne'er know, but live in doubt,
Till my bad angel fire my good one out. *Ib.*

20 Poor soul, the centre of my sinful earth,
[Fool'd by] these rebel powers that thee array,
Why dost thou pine within and suffer dearth,
Painting thy outward walls so costly gay?
Why so large cost, having so short a lease,
Dost thou upon thy fading mansion spend? *Ib.* 146

21 So shalt thou feed on Death, that feeds on men,
And Death once dead, there's no more dying then.
Ib.

22 For I have sworn thee fair, and thought thee bright,
Who art as black as hell, as dark as night. *Ib.* 147

23 Love is too young to know what conscience is;
Yet who knows not conscience is born of love?
Ib. 151

24 The first heir of my invention.
Venus and Adonis, Preface.

25 Hunting he lov'd, but love he laugh'd to scorn.
Ib. l. 4

26 Bid me discourse, I will enchant thine ear,
Or like a fairy trip upon the green,
Or, like a nymph, with long dishevell'd hair,
Dance on the sands, and yet no footing seen:
Love is a spirit all compact of fire,
Not gross to sink, but light, and will aspire.
Ib. l. 145

27 Round-hoof'd, short-jointed, fetlocks shag and long,
Broad breast, full eye, small head and nostril wide,
High crest, short ears, straight legs and passing strong,
Thin mane, thick tail, broad buttock, tender hide:
Look, what a horse should have he did not lack,
Save a proud rider on so proud a back. *Ib.* l. 295

28 By this, poor Wat, far off upon a hill,
Stands on his hinder legs with listening ear,
To hearken if his foes pursue him still. *Ib.* l. 697

29 Good friend, for Jesu's sake forbear
To dig the dust enclosed here.
Blest be the man that spares these stones,
And curst be he that moves my bones.
Shakespeare's Epitaph (chosen by himself for his tomb at Stratford-on-Avon)

30 Item, I give unto my wife my second best bed, with the furniture. *Will*, 1616

DAVID TAYLOR SHAW
1813–1890

1 O Britannia, the pride of the ocean,
　The home of the brave and the free,
The shrine of the sailor's devotion,
　No land can compare unto thee!
　　The Red, White, and Blue. First line changed to
　　'Columbia, the gem of the ocean', *when sung by*
　　Shaw in America. Attrib. also to Thomas à Becket,
　　1850

GEORGE BERNARD SHAW
1856–1950

2 All great truths begin as blasphemies.
　　　　　　　Annajanska (1919), p. 262

3 One man that has a mind and knows it, can always
　beat ten men who havnt and dont.
　　　　　　　The Apple Cart (1930), Act I

4 What Englishman will give his mind to politics as
　long as he can afford to keep a motor car?　*Ib.*

5 I never resist temptation, because I have found that
　things that are bad for me do not tempt me.
　　　　　　　　　　　Ib. Act II

6 You can always tell an old soldier by the inside of his
　holsters and cartridge boxes. The young ones carry
　pistols and cartridges: the old ones, grub.
　　　　　　　Arms and the Man, Act I

7 I never apologize.　　　　　　·　*Ib.* Act III

8 You're not a man, you're a machine.　　*Ib.*

9 When a stupid man is doing something he is ashamed
　of, he always declares that it is his duty.
　　　　　　　Cæsar and Cleopatra, Act III

10 He who has never hoped can never despair.
　　　　　　　　　　　Ib. Act IV

11 A man of great common sense and good taste,—mean-
　ing thereby a man without originality or moral
　courage.　　　*Ib. Notes. Julius Cæsar*

12 We have no more right to consume happiness without
　producing it than to consume wealth without pro-
　ducing it.　　　　　*Candida*, Act I

13 Do you think that the things people make fools of
　themselves about are any less real and true than
　the things they behave sensibly about?　*Ib.*

14 It is easy—terribly easy—to shake a man's faith in
　himself. To take advantage of that to break a
　man's spirit is devil's work.　　　*Ib.*

15 I'm only a beer teetotaller, not a champagne tee-
　totaller.　　　　　　　*Ib.* Act III

16 The worst sin towards our fellow creatures is not to
　hate them, but to be indifferent to them: that's the
　essence of inhumanity.　*The Devil's Disciple*, Act II

17 I never expect a soldier to think.　　*Ib.* Act III

18 The British soldier can stand up to anything except
　the British War Office.　　　　*Ib.*

19 Stimulate the phagocytes.
　　　　　The Doctor's Dilemma (1906), Act I

20 All professions are conspiracies against the laity.　*Ib.*

21 I believe in Michael Angelo, Velasquez, and Rem-
　brandt; in the might of design, the mystery of color,
　the redemption of all things by Beauty everlasting,
　and the message of Art that has made these hands
　blessed.　　*The Doctor's Dilemma* (1906), Act IV

22 With the single exception of Homer, there is no
　eminent writer, not even Sir Walter Scott, whom
　I can despise so entirely as I despise Shakespeare
　when I measure my mind against his. . . . It would
　positively be a relief to me to dig him up and
　throw stones at him.
　　　Dramatic Opinions and Essays (1907), vol. II,
　　　p. 52

23 Parentage is a very important profession; but no test
　of fitness for it is ever imposed in the interest of the
　children.
　　　Everybody's Political What's What, ch. ix, p. 74

24 It's all that the young can do for the old, to shock
　them and keep them up to date.
　　　　　Fanny's First Play (1911), Induction

25 You don't expect me to know what to say about a
　play when I don't know who the author is, do you?
　. . . If it's by a good author, it's a good play, naturally.
　That stands to reason.　　　*Ib.* Epilogue

26 What God hath joined together no man shall ever
　put asunder: God will take care of that.
　　　　　　Getting Married (1911), p. 216

27 When you loved me I gave you the whole sun and
　stars to play with. I gave you eternity in a single
　moment, strength of the mountains in one clasp
　of your arms, and the volume of all the seas in one
　impulse of your soul.　　　*Ib.* p. 278

28 We possessed all the universe together; and you ask
　me to give you my scanty wages as well. I have
　given you the greatest of all things; and you ask
　me to give you little things. I gave you your own
　soul: you ask me for my body as a plaything. Was
　it not enough? Was it not enough?　　*Ib.*

29 I cannot bear men and women.
　　　　　Heartbreak House (1919), Act II

30 Go anywhere in England, where there are natural,
　wholesome, contented, and really nice English
　people; and what do you always find? That the
　stables are the real centre of the household.
　　　　　　　　　　　Ib. Act III

31 The captain is in his bunk, drinking bottled ditch-
　water; and the crew is gambling in the forecastle.
　She will strike and sink and split. Do you think
　the laws of God will be suspended in favour of
　England because you were born in it?　　*Ib.*

32 Money is indeed the most important thing in the
　world; and all sound and successful personal and
　national morality should have this fact for its basis.
　　　　The Irrational Knot (1905), Preface, p. xiv

33 Though the Life Force supplies us with its own
　purpose, it has no other brains to work with than
　those it has painfully and imperfectly evolved in
　our heads.　　　　　　　*Ib.* p. xxv

34 Reminiscences make one feel so deliciously aged and
　sad.　　　　　　　　　*Ib.* ch. 14

35 A man who has no office to go to—I don't care who
　he is—is a trial of which you can have no con-
　ception.　　　　　　　　*Ib.* ch. 18

1 What really flatters a man is that you think him worth flattering.   *John Bull's Other Island* (1907), Act IV

2 There are only two qualities in the world: efficiency and inefficiency; and only two sorts of people: the efficient and the inefficient.   *Ib.*

3 The greatest of evils and the worst of crimes is poverty.   *Major Barbara* (1907), Preface

4 Nobody can say a word against Greek: it stamps a man at once as an educated gentleman.   *Ib.* Act I

5 Wot prawce Selvytion nah?   *Ib.* Act II

6 I am a Millionaire. That is my religion.   *Ib.*

7 I am a sort of collector of religions: and the curious thing is that I find I can believe in them all.   *Ib.*

8 I cant talk religion to a man with bodily hunger in his eyes.   *Ib.*

9 Nothing is ever done in this world until men are prepared to kill one another if it is not done.   *Ib.* Act III

10 Our political experiment of democracy, the last refuge of cheap misgovernment.   *Man and Superman* (1903), Epistle Dedicatory, p. xxi.

11 He who has nothing to assert has no style and can have none: he who has something to assert will go as far in power of style as its momentousness and his conviction will carry him.   *Ib.* p. xxxv

12 A lifetime of happiness: no man alive could bear it: it would be hell on earth.   *Ib.* Act I

13 The more things a man is ashamed of, the more respectable he is.   *Ib.*

14 Vitality in a woman is a blind fury of creation.   *Ib.*

15 The true artist will let his wife starve, his children go barefoot, his mother drudge for his living at seventy, sooner than work at anything but his art.   *Ib.*

16 Is the devil to have all the passions as well as all the good tunes?   *Ib.*

17 Never mind her; go on talking.   *Ib.*

18 You think that you are Ann's suitor; that you are the pursuer and she the pursued; that it is your part to woo, to persuade, to prevail, to overcome. Fool: it is you who are the pursued, the marked-down quarry, the destined prey.   *Ib.* Act II

19 Marry Ann; and at the end of a week you'll find no more inspiration in her than in a plate of muffins.   *Ib.*

20 Hell is full of musical amateurs: music is the brandy of the damned.   *Ib.* Act III

21 An Englishman thinks he is moral when he is only uncomfortable.   *Ib.*

22 As an old soldier I admit the cowardice: it's as universal as seasickness, and matters just as little.   *Ib.*

23 When the military man approaches, the world locks up its spoons and packs off its womankind.   *Ib.*

24 What is virtue but the Trade Unionism of the married?   *Ib.*

25 Those who talk most about the blessings of marriage and the constancy of its vows are the very people who declare that if the chain were broken and the prisoners left free to choose, the whole social fabric would fly asunder. You cannot have the argument both ways. If the prisoner is happy, why lock him in? If he is not, why pretend that he is?   *Man and Superman* (1903), Act III

26 There are two tragedies in life. One is not to get your heart's desire. The other is to get it.   *Ib.* Act IV

27 Do not do unto others as you would they should do unto you. Their tastes may not be the same.   *Ib. Maxims for Revolutionists*, p. 227

28 The golden rule is that there are no golden rules. *Ib.*

29 Democracy substitutes election by the incompetent many for appointment by the corrupt few.   *Ib.* p. 228

30 Liberty means responsibility. That is why most men dread it.   *Ib.* p. 229

31 He who can, does. He who cannot, teaches.   *Ib.* p. 230

32 Marriage is popular because it combines the maximum of temptation with the maximum of opportunity.   *Ib.* p. 231

33 If you strike a child, take care that you strike it in anger, even at the risk of maiming it for life. A blow in cold blood neither can nor should be forgiven.   *Ib.* p. 234

34 The reasonable man adapts himself to the world: the unreasonable one persists in trying to adapt the world to himself. Therefore all progress depends on the unreasonable man.   *Ib.* p. 238

35 The man who listens to Reason is lost: Reason enslaves all whose minds are not strong enough to master her.   *Ib.*

36 Home is the girl's prison and the woman's workhouse.   *Ib.* p. 240

37 Every man over forty is a scoundrel.   *Ib.* p. 242

38 There is nothing so bad or so good that you will not find Englishmen doing it; but you will never find an Englishman in the wrong. He does everything on principle. He fights you on patriotic principles; he robs you on business principles; he enslaves you on imperial principles.   *The Man of Destiny*

39 An English army led by an Irish general: that might be a match for a French army led by an Italian general.   *Ib.*

40 A great devotee of the Gospel of Getting On.   *Mrs. Warren's Profession* (1893), Act IV

41 The fickleness of the women I love is only equalled by the infernal constancy of the women who love me.   *The Philanderer* (1893), Act II

42 It is clear that a novel cannot be too bad to be worth publishing. . . . It certainly is possible for a novel to be too good to be worth publishing.   *Plays Pleasant and Unpleasant* (1898), vol. 1, Preface, p. vi

43 There is only one religion, though there are a hundred versions of it.   *Ib.* vol. 2, Preface, p. vii

44 The English have no respect for their language, and will not teach their children to speak it. . . . It is impossible for an Englishman to open his mouth, without making some other Englishman despise him.   *Pygmalion* (1912), Preface

1 Not bloody likely.   *Pygmalion* (1912), Act II

2 Assassination is the extreme form of censorship.
        The Rejected Statement, Pt. 1

3 If ever I utter an oath again may my soul be blasted
to eternal damnation!   *St. Joan* (1924), Sc. ii

4 How can what an Englishman believes be heresy?
It is a contradiction in terms.   *Ib.* Sc. iv

5 Must then a Christ perish in torment in every age to
save those that have no imagination? *Ib.* Epilogue

6 They tell me that So-and-So, who does not write
prefaces, is no charlatan. Well, I am. I first caught
the ear of the British public on a cart in Hyde Park,
to the blaring of brass bands, and this . . . because
. . . I am a natural-born mountebank.
        Three Plays for Puritans (1901), Preface

7 Well, sir, you never can tell. That's a principle in
life with me, sir, if you'll excuse my having such
a thing.   *You Never Can Tell* (1898), Act II

8 People must not be forced to adopt me as their
favourite author, even for their own good.
        Letter to Alma Murray, 20 Oct. 1886

HENRY WHEELER SHAW
['JOSH BILLINGS']
1818–1885

9 Thrice is he armed that hath his quarrel just,
But four times he who gets his blow in fust.
        Josh Billings, his Sayings (1865)

10 The trouble with people is not that they don't know
but that they know so much that ain't so.
        Josh Billings' Encyclopedia of Wit and Wisdom
        (1874)

RICHARD SHEALE
sixteenth century

11 For Witherington needs must I wail,
        As one in doleful dumps;
For when his legs were smitten off,
        He fought upon his stumps.
        Ballad of Chevy Chase, Pt. II, x

JOHN SHEFFIELD, DUKE OF BUCKINGHAM
see
BUCKINGHAM

MARY WOLLSTONECRAFT SHELLEY
1797–1851

12 Mrs. Shelley was choosing a school for her son, and
asked the advice of this lady, who gave for advice—
to use her own words to me—'Just the sort of
banality, you know, one does come out with: "Oh,
send him somewhere where they will teach him
to think for himself!"' . . . Mrs. Shelley answered:
'Teach him to think for himself? Oh, my God,
teach him rather to think like other people!'
        Matthew Arnold, *Essays in Criticism, Second
        Series; Shelley*

PERCY BYSSHE SHELLEY
1792–1822

13 It might make one in love with death, to think that
one should be buried in so sweet a place.
        Adonais. Preface

14 I weep for Adonais—he is dead!
O, weep for Adonais! though our tears
Thaw not the frost which binds so dear a head!
        Ib. I

15 Most musical of mourners, weep again!
Lament anew, Urania!—He died,
Who was the Sire of an immortal strain,
Blind, old, and lonely, when his country's pride,
The priest, the slave, and the liberticide,
Trampled and mocked with many a loathed rite
Of lust and blood; he went, unterrified,
Into the gulf of death; but his clear Sprite
Yet reigns o'er earth; the third among the sons of
        light.   *Ib.* IV

16 But now, thy youngest, dearest one, has perished—
The nursling of thy widowhood.   *Ib.* VI

17 To that high Capital, where kingly Death
Keeps his pale court in beauty and decay,
He came.   *Ib.* VII

18 He will awake no more, oh, never more!   *Ib.* VIII

19   The quick Dreams,
The passion-winged Ministers of thought.   *Ib.* IX

20 Lost Angel of a ruin'd Paradise!
She knew not 'twas her own; as with no stain
She faded, like a cloud which had outwept its rain.
        Ib. X

21   Desires and Adorations,
Wingèd Persuasions and veiled Destinies,
Splendours, and Glooms, and glimmering Incarna-
        tions
Of hopes and fears, and twilight Phantasies;
And Sorrow, with her family of Sighs,
And Pleasure, blind with tears, led by the gleam
Of her own dying smile instead of eyes,
Came in slow pomp.   *Ib.* XIII

22 Ah, woe is me! Winter is come and gone,
But grief returns with the revolving year. *Ib.* XVIII

23 The great morning of the world when first
God dawned on Chaos.   *Ib.* XIX

24 Alas! that all we loved of him should be,
But for our grief, as if it had not been,
And grief itself be mortal!   *Ib.* XXI

25 Whence are we, and why are we? Of what scene
The actors or spectators?   *Ib.*

26 As long as skies are blue, and fields are green,
Evening must usher night, night urge the morrow,
Month follow month with woe, and year wake year
to sorrow.   *Ib.*

27 Why didst thou leave the trodden paths of men
Too soon, and with weak hands though mighty heart
Dare the unpastured dragon in his den?
Defenceless as thou wert, oh, where was then
Wisdom the mirrored shield, or scorn the spear?
        Ib. XXVII

28 The herded wolves, bold only to pursue;
The obscene ravens, clamorous o'er the dead.
        Ib. XXVIII

1 The Pilgrim of Eternity, whose fame
Over his living head like Heaven is bent,
An early but enduring monument,
Came, veiling all the lightnings of his song
In sorrow. *Adonais*, xxx

2 A pard-like Spirit, beautiful and swift—
A Love in desolation masked;—a Power
Girt round with weakness;—it can scarce uplift
The weight of the superincumbent hour;
It is a dying lamp, a falling shower,
A breaking billow;—even whilst we speak
Is it not broken? *Ib.* xxxii

3 A herd-abandoned deer struck by the hunter's dart.
Ib. xxxiii

4 Our Adonais has drunk poison—oh!
What deaf and viperous murderer could crown
Life's early cup with such a draught of woe?
Ib. xxxvi

5 He wakes or sleeps with the enduring dead;
Thou canst not soar where he is sitting now—
Dust to the dust! but the pure spirit shall flow
Back to the burning fountain whence it came,
A portion of the Eternal. *Ib.* xxxviii

6 He hath awakened from the dream of life—
'Tis we, who lost in stormy visions, keep
With phantoms an unprofitable strife,
And in mad trance, strike with our spirit's knife
Invulnerable nothings *Ib.* xxxix

7 He has out-soared the shadow of our night;
Envy and calumny and hate and pain,
And that unrest which men miscall delight,
Can touch him not and torture not again;
From the contagion of the world's slow stain
He is secure, and now can never mourn
A heart grown cold, a head grown grey in vain.
Ib. xl

8 He lives, he wakes,—'tis Death is dead, not he.
Ib. xli

9 He is made one with Nature: there is heard
His voice in all her music, from the moan
Of thunder, to the song of night's sweet bird. *Ib.* xlii

10 He is a portion of the loveliness
Which once he made more lovely. *Ib.* xliii

11 The inheritors of unfulfilled renown
Rose from their thrones, built beyond mortal thought,
Far in the Unapparent. *Ib.* xlv

12 Sublimely mild, a Spirit without spot. [Sidney.] *Ib.*

13 Oblivion as they rose shrank like a thing reproved.
Ib.

14 What Adonais is, why fear we to become? *Ib.* li

15 The One remains, the many change and pass;
Heaven's light forever shines, Earth's shadows fly;
Life, like a dome of many-coloured glass,
Stains the white radiance of Eternity.
Ib. lii

16 The soul of Adonais, like a star,
Beacons from the abode where the Eternal are.
Ib. lv

17 The lone Chorasmian shore. *Alastor*, l. 272

18 But thou art fled
Like some frail exhalation. *Ib.* l. 686

19 Pale despair and cold tranquillity,
Nature's vast frame, the web of human things,
Birth and the grave, that are not as they were.
Alastor, l. 718

20 Arethusa arose
From her couch of snows
In the Acroceraunian mountains,—
From cloud and from crag,
With many a jag,
Shepherding her bright fountains. *Arethusa*

21 Like friends once parted
Grown single-hearted. *Ib.*

22 'Do you not hear the Aziola cry?
Methinks she must be nigh,'
Said Mary as we sate
In dusk, ere stars were lit, or candles brought;
And I, who thought
This Aziola was some tedious woman,
Asked, 'Who is Aziola?' *The Aziola*

23 Give yourself no unnecessary pain,
My dear Lord Cardinal. Here, Mother, tie
My girdle for me, and bind up this hair
In any simple knot; ay, that does well.
And yours I see is coming down. How often
Have we done this for one another; now
We shall not do it any more. My Lord,
We are quite ready. Well, 'tis very well.
The Cenci, v. iv. 158

24 A widow bird sate mourning for her love
Upon a wintry bough;
The frozen wind crept on above,
The freezing stream below.

There was no leaf upon the forest bare,
No flower upon the ground,
And little motion in the air
Except the mill-wheel's sound.
Charles the First, sc. v, l. 10

25 I bring fresh showers for the thirsting flowers,
From the seas and the streams;
I bear light shade for the leaves when laid
In their noonday dreams. *The Cloud*

26 I wield the flail of the lashing hail,
And whiten the green plains under,
And then again I dissolve it in rain,
And laugh as I pass in thunder. *Ib.*

27 I sift the snow on the mountains below,
And their great pines groan aghast;
And all the night 'tis my pillow white,
While I sleep in the arms of the blast.
Sublime on the towers of my skiey bowers,
Lightning my pilot sits;
In a cavern under is fettered the thunder,
It struggles and howls at fits. *Ib.*

28 And I all the while bask in Heaven's blue smile,
Whilst he is dissolving in rains. *Ib.*

29 That orbèd maiden, with white fire laden,
Whom mortals call the Moon,
Glides glimmering o'er my fleece-like floor,
By the midnight breezes strewn;
And wherever the beat of her unseen feet,
Which only the angels hear,
May have broken the woof of my tent's thin roof,
The stars peep behind her and peer;
And I laugh to see them whirl and flee
Like a swarm of golden bees,

When I widen the rent in my wind-built tent,
  Till the calm rivers, lakes, and seas,
Like strips of the sky fallen through me on high,
  Are each paved with the moon and these.
                                        The Cloud

1 I am the daughter of Earth and Water,
    And the nursling of the Sky;
  I pass through the pores of the ocean and shores;
    I change, but I cannot die.
  For after the rain when with never a stain
    The pavilion of Heaven is bare,
  And the winds and sunbeams with their convex
      gleams
    Build up the blue dome of air,
  I silently laugh at my own cenotaph,
    And out of the caverns of rain,
  Like a child from the womb, like a ghost from the
      tomb,
    I arise and unbuild it again.   *Ib.*

2   How wonderful is Death,
      Death and his brother Sleep!
  One pale as yonder wan and horned moon,
      With lips of lurid blue,
  The other glowing like the vital morn,
      When throned on ocean's wave
      It breathes over the world:
  Yet both so passing strange and wonderful!
            The Daemon of the World, Part 1, l. 1

3 My Song, I fear that thou wilt find but few
  Who fitly shall conceive thy reasoning,
  Of such hard matter dost thou entertain.
            Epipsychidion. Advertisement

4 My last delight! tell them that they are dull,
  And bid them own that thou art beautiful.   *Ib.*

5   Sweet as stops
  Of planetary music heard in trance.   *Ib.* l. 85

6 The spirit of the worm beneath the sod
  In love and worship, blends itself with God.
                                    Ib. l. 128

7 The fields of Immortality.   *Ib.* l. 133

8   Are we not formed, as notes of music are,
  For one another, though dissimilar.   *Ib.* l. 142

9 I never was attached to that great sect,
  Whose doctrine is, that each one should select
  Out of the crowd a mistress or a friend,
  And all the rest, though fair and wise, commend
  To cold oblivion.   *Ib.* l. 149

10 Who travel to their home among the dead
  By the broad highway of the world, and so
  With one chained friend, perhaps a jealous foe,
  The dreariest and the longest journey go.   *Ib.* l. 156

11 True Love in this differs from gold and clay,
  That to divide is not to take away.   *Ib.* l. 160

12 A ship is floating in the harbour now,
  A wind is hovering o'er the mountain's brow;
  There is a path on the sea's azure floor,
  No keel has ever ploughed that path before.
                                    Ib. l. 408

13   An isle under Ionian skies,
  Beautiful as a wreck of Paradise.   *Ib.* l. 422

14   Day and night, aloof, from the high towers
  And terraces, the Earth and Ocean seem
  To sleep in one another's arms, and dream
  Of waves, flowers, clouds, woods, rocks, and all that we
  Read in their smiles, and call reality.   *Ib.* l. 508

15 I pant, I sink, I tremble, I expire!
                              Epipsychidion, l. 591

16 Chameleons feed on light and air:
  Poets' food is love and fame.   *An Exhortation*

17 And bloody Faith the foulest birth of time.
                        Feelings of a Republican

18   Time's printless torrent grew
  A scroll of crystal, blazoning the name
  Of Adonais!   *Fragment on Keats*

19 My head is wild with weeping.
                      Fragment: My head is wild

20 My spirit like a charmed bark doth swim
  Upon the liquid waves of thy sweet singing.
                      Fragment: To One Singing

21 Good-night? ah! no; the hour is ill
    Which severs those it should unite;
  Let us remain together still,
    Then it will be *good* night.   *Good Night*

22 To hearts which near each other move
    From evening close to morning light,
  The night is good; because, my love,
    They never *say* good-night.   *Ib.*

23 Life may change, but it may fly not;
  Hope may vanish, but can die not;
  Truth be veiled, but still it burneth;
  Love repulsed,—but it returneth!   *Hellas*, l. 34

24 Let there be light! said Liberty,
  And like sunrise from the sea,
  Athens arose!   *Ib.* l. 682

25 The world's great age begins anew,
    The golden years return,
    The earth doth like a snake renew
      Her winter weeds outworn;
  Heaven smiles, and faiths and empires gleam,
  Like wrecks of a dissolving dream.

  A brighter Hellas rears its mountains
    From waves serener far;
  A new Peneus rolls his fountains
    Against the morning star.
  Where fairer Tempes bloom, there sleep
  Young Cyclads on a sunnier deep.

  A loftier Argo cleaves the main,
    Fraught with a later prize;
  Another Orpheus sings again,
    And loves, and weeps, and dies.
  A new Ulysses leaves once more
  Calypso for his native shore.   *Ib.* l. 1060

26 Riddles of death Thebes never knew.   *Ib.* l. 1083

27 Another Athens shall arise,
    And to remoter time
  Bequeath, like sunset to the skies,
    The splendour of its prime;
  And leave, if nought so bright may live,
  All earth can take or Heaven can give.

  Saturn and Love their long repose
  Shall burst, more bright and good
  Than all who fell, than One who rose,
    Than many unsubdued:
  Not gold, not blood, their altar dowers,
  But votive tears and symbol flowers.

[493]

Oh cease! must hate and death return?
Cease! must men kill and die?
Cease! drain not to its dregs the urn
Of bitter prophecy.
The world is weary of the past,
Oh, might it die or rest at last!
Hellas, l. 1090

1 I am the eye with which the Universe
Beholds itself and knows itself divine;
All harmony of instrument or verse,
All prophecy, all medicine is mine,
All light of art or nature;—to my song
Victory and praise in its own right belong.
Hymn of Apollo

2 I pursued a maiden and clasped a reed.
Gods and men, we are all deluded thus!
It breaks in our bosom and then we bleed.
Hymn of Pan

3 The awful shadow of some unseen Power
Floats though unseen among us,—visiting
This various world with as inconstant wing
As summer winds that creep from flower to flower.
Hymn to Intellectual Beauty

4 Spirit of Beauty, that dost consecrate
With thine own hues all thou dost shine upon
Of human thought or form.   *Ib.*

5 While yet a boy I sought for ghosts, and sped
Through many a listening chamber, cave and ruin,
And starlight wood, with fearful steps pursuing
Hopes of high talk with the departed dead.
I called on poisonous names with which our youth
is fed.   *Ib.*

6 The day becomes more solemn and serene
When noon is past—there is a harmony
In autumn, and a lustre in its sky,
Which through the summer is not heard or seen,
As if it could not be, as if it had not been! *Ib.*

7 I arise from dreams of thee
In the first sweet sleep of night,
When the winds are breathing low,
And the stars are shining bright:
I arise from dreams of thee,
And a spirit in my feet
Hath led me—who knows how?
To thy chamber window, Sweet!

The wandering airs they faint
On the dark, the silent stream—
The Champak odours fail
Like sweet thoughts in a dream;
The nightingale's complaint,
It dies upon her heart;—
As I must on thine,
Oh, beloved as thou art!

Oh lift me from the grass!
I die! I faint! I fail!
Let thy love in kisses rain
On my lips and eyelids pale.
My cheek is cold and white, alas!
My heart beats loud and fast;—
Oh! press it to thine own again,
Where it will break at last.   *The Indian Serenade*

8 Best and brightest, come away!
Fairer far than this fair day. *To Jane: The Invitation*

9 I am gone into the fields
To take what this sweet hour yields;—
Reflection, you may come to-morrow,
Sit by the fireside with Sorrow.—
You with the unpaid bill, Despair,—
You, tiresome verse-reciter, Care,—
I will pay you in the grave,—
Death will listen to your stave.
To Jane: The Invitation

10 The daisy-star that never sets,
And wind-flowers, and violets,
Which yet join not scent to hue.   *Ib.*

11 Soothed by every azure breath
That under Heaven is blown.
To Jane: The Recollection

12 Less oft is peace in Shelley's mind,
Than calm in waters, seen.   *Ib.*

13 I love all waste
And solitary places; where we taste
The pleasure of believing what we see
Is boundless, as we wish our souls to be.
Julian and Maddalo, l. 14

14 Thou Paradise of exiles, Italy!   *Ib.* l. 57

15 It is our will
That thus enchains us to permitted ill—
We might be otherwise—we might be all
We dream of happy, high, majestical.   *Ib.* l. 170

16 Me—who am as a nerve o'er which do creep
The else unfelt oppressions of this earth. *Ib.* l. 449

17 Most wretched men
Are cradled into poetry by wrong:
They learn in suffering what they teach in song.
Ib. l. 543

18 O world! O life! O time!
On whose last steps I climb,
Trembling at that where I had stood before;
When will return the glory of your prime?
No more—Oh, never more!   *A Lament*

19 Fresh spring, and summer, and winter hoar,
Move my faint heart with grief, but with delight
No more—Oh, never more!   *Ib.*

20 When the lamp is shattered
The light in the dust lies dead—
When the cloud is scattered
The rainbow's glory is shed.
When the lute is broken,
Sweet tones are remembered not;
When the lips have spoken,
Loved accents are soon forgot.
Lines: When the Lamp

21 When hearts have once mingled
Love first leaves the well-built nest;
The weak one is singled
To endure what it once possessed.
O Love! who bewailest
The frailty of all things here,
Why choose you the frailest
For your cradle, your home, and your bier? *Ib.*

22 Many a green isle needs must be
In the deep wide sea of misery,
Or the mariner, worn and wan,
Never thus could voyage on.
Lines written amongst the Euganean Hills, l. 1

23 Ay, many flowering islands lie
In the waters of wide Agony.   *Ib.* l. 66

1 Beneath is spread like a green sea
The waveless plain of Lombardy,
Bounded by the vaporous air,
Islanded by cities fair;
Underneath Day's azure eyes
Ocean's nursling, Venice lies,
A peopled labyrinth of walls,
Amphitrite's destined halls.
Lines written amongst the Euganean Hills, l. 90

2 Sun-girt city, thou hast been
Ocean's child, and then his queen;
Now is come a darker day,
And thou soon must be his prey. *Ib.* l. 115

3 My spirit which so long
Darkened this swift stream of song. *Ib.* l. 311

4 Peopling the lone universe. *Ib.* l. 319

5 Other flowering isles must be
In the sea of Life and Agony. *Ib.* l. 335

6 What! alive, and so bold, O earth?
*Lines written on hearing the News of the Death of
Napoleon*

7 The fountains mingle with the river,
And the rivers with the ocean;
The winds of heaven mix for ever
With a sweet emotion;
Nothing in the world is single;
All things, by a law divine,
In one another's being mingle.
Why not I with thine?—

See the mountains kiss high Heaven
And the waves clasp one another;
No sister-flower would be forgiven
If it disdained its brother;
And the sunlight clasps the earth
And the moonbeams kiss the sea:
What are all these kissings worth
If thou kiss not me? *Love's Philosophy*

8 Under the roof of blue Italian weather.
Letter to Maria Gisborne, l. 147

9 London, that great sea, whose ebb and flow
At once is deaf and loud, and on the shore
Vomits its wrecks, and still howls on for more.
Ib. l. 193

10 You will see Coleridge—he who sits obscure
In the exceeding lustre and the pure
Intense irradiation of a mind,
Which, through its own internal lightning blind,
Flags wearily through darkness and despair—
A cloud-encircled meteor of the air,
A hooded eagle among blinking owls.
You will see Hunt—one of those happy souls
Which are the salt of the earth, and without whom
This world would smell like what it is—a tomb.
Ib. l. 202

11 Have you not heard
When a man marries, dies, or turns Hindoo,
His best friends hear no more of him? *Ib.* l. 235

12 The milk-white Snowdonian antelope
Matched with this cameleopard. *Ib.* l. 239

13 His fine wit
Makes such a wound, the knife is lost in it.
[T. L. Peacock.] *Ib.* l. 240

14 Wit and sense,
Virtue and human knowledge; all that might
Make this dull world a business of delight,
Are all combined in Horace Smith.
Letter to Maria Gisborne, l. 247

15 I met Murder in the way—
He had a mask like Castlereagh.
The Mask of Anarchy, II

16 Ye are many—they are few. *Ib.* XXXVIII

17 Its horror and its beauty are divine.
The 'Medusa' of Leonardo da Vinci

18 Some say that gleams of a remoter world
Visit the soul in sleep,—that death is slumber,
And that its shapes the busy thoughts outnumber
Of those who wake and live. *Mont Blanc*, l. 49

19 Art thou pale for weariness
Of climbing heaven, and gazing on the earth,
Wandering companionless
Among the stars that have a different birth,—
And ever changing, like a joyless eye
That finds no object worth its constancy?
To the Moon

20 Nought may endure but Mutability. *Mutability*

21 Swiftly walk over the western wave,
Spirit of Night!
Out of the misty eastern cave,
Where, all the long and lone daylight,
Thou wovest dreams of joy and fear,
Which make thee terrible and dear,—
Swift be thy flight! *To Night*

22 Wrap thy form in a mantle gray,
Star-inwrought!
Blind with thine hair the eyes of Day;
Kiss her until she be wearied out,
Then wander o'er city, and sea, and land,
Touching all with thine opiate wand—
Come, long-sought! *Ib.*

23 Thy brother Death came, and cried,
Wouldst thou me?
Thy sweet child Sleep, the filmy-eyed,
Murmured like a noontide bee,
Shall I nestle near thy side?
Wouldst thou me? *Ib.*

24 Death will come when thou art dead,
Soon, too soon—
Sleep will come when thou art fled;
Of neither would I ask the boon
I ask of thee, beloved Night—
Swift be thine approaching flight,
Come soon, soon! *Ib.*

25 A glorious people vibrated again
The lightning of the nations. *Ode to Liberty*, l. 1

26 My soul spurned the chains of its dismay,
And in the rapid plumes of song
Clothed itself, sublime and strong,
(As a young eagle soars the morning clouds among.)
Ib. l. 5

27 When o'er the Aegean main
Athens arose: a city such as vision
Builds from the purple crags and silver towers
Of battlemented cloud, as in derision
Of kingliest masonry: the ocean-floors
Pave it; the evening sky pavilions it;
Its portals are inhabited
By thunder-zoned winds. *Ib.* l. 60

1 Within the surface of Time's fleeting river
  Its wrinkled image lies, as then it lay
Immovably unquiet, and for ever
  It trembles, but it cannot pass away!
                    Ode to Liberty, l. 76

2 I stood within the City disinterred;
And heard the autumnal leaves like light footfalls
Of spirits passing through the streets; and heard
The Mountain's slumbrous voice at intervals
Thrill through those roofless halls.
                    Ode to Naples, l. 1

3 Long lost, late won, and yet but half-regained.
                    Ib. l. 58

4 O wild West Wind, thou breath of Autumn's being,
Thou, from whose unseen presence the leaves dead
Are driven, like ghosts from an enchanter fleeing,

Yellow, and black, and pale, and hectic red,
Pestilence-stricken multitudes: O thou,
Who chariotest to their dark wintry bed

The winged seeds, where they lie cold and low,
Each like a corpse within its grave, until
Thine azure sister of the spring shall blow

Her clarion o'er the dreaming earth, and fill
(Driving sweet buds like flocks to feed in air)
With living hues and odours plain and hill:

Wild Spirit, which art moving everywhere;
Destroyer and preserver; hear, oh, hear!
                    Ode to the West Wind, l. 1

5 Shook from the tangled boughs of Heaven and Ocean,
Angels of rain and lightning.   *Ib.* l. 17

6 Like the bright hair uplifted from the head
Of some fierce Maenad.   *Ib.* l. 20

7   Thou dirge
Of the dying year, to which this closing night
Will be the dome of a vast sepulchre.   *Ib.* l. 23

8 Thou who didst waken from his summer dreams
  The blue Mediterranean, where he lay,
Lulled by the coil of his crystalline streams

  Beside a pumice isle in Baiae's bay,
And saw in sleep old palaces and towers
  Quivering within the wave's intenser day,

All overgrown with azure moss and flowers
So sweet, the sense faints picturing them. *Ib.* l. 29

9   Far below
The sea-blooms and the oozy woods which wear
The sapless foliage of the ocean, know
Thy voice, and suddenly grow gray with fear,
And tremble and despoil themselves.   *Ib.* l. 38

10 If I were a dead leaf thou mightest bear;
If I were a swift cloud to fly with thee;
A wave to pant beneath thy power, and share

The impulse of thy strength, only less free
Than thou, O uncontrollable! If even
I were as in my boyhood, and could be

The comrade of thy wanderings over Heaven,
As then, when to outstrip thy skiey speed
Scarce seemed a vision; I would ne'er have striven

As thus with thee in prayer in my sore need,
Oh, lift me as a wave, a leaf, a cloud!
I fall upon the thorns of life! I bleed!   *Ib.* l. 43

11 Make me thy lyre, even as the forest is:
What if my leaves are falling like its own?
The tumult of thy mighty harmonies

Will take from both a deep, autumnal tone,
Sweet though in sadness. Be thou, Spirit fierce,
My spirit! Be thou me, impetuous one!

Drive my dead thoughts over the universe
Like withered leaves to quicken a new birth!
And, by the incantation of this verse,

Scatter, as from an unextinguished hearth
Ashes and sparks, my words among mankind!
Be through my lips to unawakened earth

The trumpet of a prophecy! O, Wind,
If Winter comes, can Spring be far behind?
                    Ode to the West Wind, 57

12 Or *anything*, as the learned Boar observed.
                    Oedipus Tyrannus, ii. i. 105

13 I met a traveller from an antique land
Who said: Two vast and trunkless legs of stone
Stand in the desert.   *Ozymandias*

14 My name is Ozymandias, king of kings:
Look on my works, ye Mighty, and despair!   *Ib.*

15 Nothing beside remains. Round the decay
Of that colossal wreck, boundless and bare
The lone and level sands stretch far away.   *Ib.*

16 Hell is a city much like London—
A populous and smoky city.
                    Peter Bell the Third, pt. 3. *Hell*, i

17 But from the first 'twas Peter's drift
  To be a kind of moral eunuch,
He touched the hem of Nature's shift,
  Felt faint—and never dared uplift
  The closest, all-concealing tunic. *Ib.* pt. 4. *Sin*, xi

18   Ere Babylon was dust,
The Magus Zoroaster, my dead child,
Met his own image walking in the garden,
That apparition, sole of men, he saw.
                    Prometheus Unbound, i, l. 191

19 Dreams and the light imaginings of men,
And all that faith creates or love desires,
Terrible, strange, sublime and beauteous shapes.
                    Ib. 200

20 Cruel he looks, but calm and strong,
Like one who does, not suffers wrong.   *Ib.* 238

21 It doth repent me: words are quick and vain;
Grief for awhile is blind, and so was mine.
I wish no living thing to suffer pain.   *Ib.* 303

22 Kingly conclaves stern and cold
Where blood with guilt is bought and sold.   *Ib.* 530

23 See a disenchanted nation
Springs like day from desolation;
To Truth its state is dedicate,
And Freedom leads it forth, her mate.   *Ib.* 567

24 The good want power, but to weep barren tears.
The powerful goodness want: worse need for them.
The wise want love; and those who love want wisdom.
                    Ib. 625

25 Thy words are like a cloud of winged snakes;
And yet I pity those they torture not.   *Ib.* 632

26   Peace is in the grave.
The grave hides all things beautiful and good:
I am a God and cannot find it there.   *Ib.* 638

1 The dust of creeds outworn.
Prometheus Unbound, i. 697

2 On a poet's lips I slept
Dreaming like a love-adept
In the sound his breathing kept;
Nor seeks nor finds he mortal blisses,
But feeds on the aërial kisses
Of shapes that haunt thought's wildernesses.
He will watch from dawn to gloom
The lake-reflected sun illume
The yellow bees in the ivy-bloom,
Nor heed, nor see, what things they be;
But from these create he can
Forms more real than living man,
Nurslings of immortality! *Ib.* 737

3   That sense, which when the winds of Spring
In rarest visitation, or the voice
Of one beloved heard in youth alone,
Fills the faint eyes with falling tears which dim
The radiant looks of unbewailing flowers,
And leaves this peopled earth a solitude
When it returns no more. *Ib.* ii. iv. 12

4   To be
Omnipotent but friendless is to reign. *Ib.* 47

5 He gave man speech, and speech created thought,
Which is the measure of the universe. *Ib.* 73

6 All spirits are enslaved which serve things evil.
Ib. 110

7 Fate, Time, Occasion, Chance, and Change? To these
All things are subject but eternal Love. *Ib.* 119

8 My coursers are fed with the lightning,
They drink of the whirlwind's stream,
And when the red morning is bright'ning
They bathe in the fresh sunbeam. *Ib.* 163

9 Life of Life! thy lips enkindle
With their love the breath between them;
And thy smiles before they dwindle
Make the cold air fire; then screen them
In those looks, where whoso gazes
Faints, entangled in their mazes.
Child of Light! thy limbs are burning
Through the vest which seems to hide them;
As the radiant lines of morning
Through the clouds ere they divide them;
And this atmosphere divinest
Shrouds thee wheresoe'er thou shinest. *Ib.* v. 48

10 My soul is an enchanted boat,
Which, like a sleeping swan, doth float
Upon the silver waves of thy sweet singing. *Ib.* 72

11 Death is the veil which those who live call life:
They sleep, and it is lifted. *Ib.* iii. iii. 113

12 The loathsome mask has fallen, the man remains
Sceptreless, free, uncircumscribed, but man
Equal, unclassed, tribeless, and nationless,
Exempt from awe, worship, degree, the king
Over himself; just, gentle, wise: but man
Passionless?—no, yet free from guilt or pain,
Which were, for his will made or suffered them,
Nor yet exempt, though ruling them like slaves,
From chance, and death, and mutability,
The clogs of that which else might oversoar
The loftiest star of unascended heaven,
Pinnacled dim in the intense inane. *Ib.* 193

13 Familiar acts are beautiful through love. *Ib.* iv. 403

14 Language is a perpetual Orphic song,
Which rules with Daedal harmony a throng
Of thoughts and forms, which else senseless and
shapeless were. *Prometheus Unbound*, iv. 415

15 Elysian, windless, fortunate abodes
Beyond Heaven's constellated wilderness. *Ib.* 531

16 A traveller from the cradle to the grave
Through the dim night of this immortal day.
Ib. 551

17 To suffer woes which Hope thinks infinite;
To forgive wrongs darker than death or night;
To defy Power, which seems omnipotent;
To love, and bear; to hope till Hope creates
From its own wreck the thing it contemplates;
Neither to change, nor falter, nor repent;
This, like thy glory, Titan, is to be
Good, great and joyous, beautiful and free;
This is alone Life, Joy, Empire and Victory.
Ib. 570

18 How wonderful is Death,
Death and his brother Sleep! *Queen Mab*, c. 1, l. 1

19 That sweet bondage which is freedom's self.
Ib. c. 9, l. 76

20 I dreamed that, as I wandered by the way,
Bare Winter suddenly was changed to Spring,
And gentle odours led my steps astray,
Mixed with a sound of water's murmuring
Along a shelving bank of turf, which lay
Under a copse, and hardly dared to fling
Its green arms round the bosom of the stream,
But kissed it and then fled, as thou mightst in
dream. *The Question*

21 There grew pied wind-flowers and violets,
Daisies, those pearled Arcturi of the earth,
The constellated flower that never sets. *Ib.*

22 And in the warm hedge grew lush eglantine,
Green cowbind and the moonlight-coloured may,
And cherry-blossoms, and white cups, whose wine
Was the bright dew, yet drained not by the day;
And wild roses, and ivy serpentine,
With its dark buds and leaves, wandering astray;
And flowers azure, black, and streaked with gold,
Fairer than any wakened eyes behold. *Ib.*

23 And nearer to the river's trembling edge
There grew broad flag-flowers, purple, pranked
with white,
And starry river buds among the sedge,
And floating water-lilies, broad and bright. *Ib.*

24 With hue like that when some great painter dips
His pencil in the gloom of earthquake and eclipse.
The Revolt of Islam, c. 5. xxiii

25 A Sensitive Plant in a garden grew.
The Sensitive Plant, pt. 1, l. 1

26 And the rose like a nymph to the bath addressed,
Which unveiled the depth of her glowing breast,
Till, fold after fold, to the fainting air
The soul of her beauty and love lay bare. *Ib.* 1. 29

27 And the jessamine faint, and the sweet tuberose,
The sweetest flower for scent that blows. *Ib.* l. 37

28 It is a modest creed, and yet
Pleasant if one considers it,
To own that death itself must be
Like all the rest, a mockery. *Ib. Conclusion*

1 Hail to thee, blithe Spirit!
  Bird thou never wert,
That from Heaven, or near it,
  Pourest thy full heart
In profuse strains of unpremeditated art.
                    To a Skylark

2 And singing still dost soar, and soaring ever singest.
                    Ib.

3 Like an unbodied joy whose race is just begun. *Ib.*

4 Thou art unseen, but yet I hear thy shrill delight.
                    Ib.

5 Keen as are the arrows
  Of that silver sphere,
Whose intense lamp narrows
  In the white dawn clear
Until we hardly see,—we feel that it is there. *Ib.*

6 Like a Poet hidden
  In the light of thought,
Singing hymns unbidden,
  Till the world is wrought
To sympathy with hopes and fears it heeded not:

Like a high-born maiden
  In a palace-tower,
Soothing her love-laden
  Soul in secret hour
With music sweet as love, which overflows her bower.
                    Ib.

7 Chorus Hymeneal,
  Or triumphal chant,
Matched with thine would be all
  But an empty vaunt,
A thing wherein we feel there is some hidden want.
                    Ib.

8 What objects are the fountains
  Of thy happy strain?
What fields, or waves, or mountains?
  What shapes of sky or plain?
What love of thine own kind? what ignorance of
  pain?   *Ib.*

9 With thy clear keen joyance
  Languor cannot be:
Shadow of annoyance
  Never came near thee:
Thou lovest—but ne'er knew love's sad satiety.

Waking or asleep,
  Thou of death must deem
Things more true and deep
  Than we mortals dream,
Or how could thy notes flow in such a crystal stream?

We look before and after;
  We pine for what is not;
Our sincerest laughter
  With some pain is fraught;
Our sweetest songs are those that tell of saddest
  thought.   *Ib.*

10 Better than all measures
  Of delightful sound,
Better than all treasures
  That in books are found,
Thy skill to poet were, thou scorner of the ground!

Teach me half the gladness
  That thy brain must know,
Such harmonious madness
  From my lips would flow
The world should listen then—as I am listening now.
                    Ib.

11 Rarely, rarely, comest thou,
  Spirit of Delight! *Song: Rarely, Rarely, Comest Thou*

12 I love all that thou lovest,
  Spirit of Delight:
The fresh Earth in new leaves dressed,
  And the starry night;
Autumn evening, and the morn
When the golden mists are born.   *Ib.*

13 I love snow, and all the forms
  Of the radiant frost.   *Ib.*

14   Everything almost
Which is Nature's, and may be
Untainted by man's misery.   *Ib.*

15 I love tranquil solitude,
  And such society
As is quiet, wise, and good;
  Between thee and me
What difference? but thou dost possess
The things I seek, not love them less.   *Ib.*

16 I love Love—though he has wings,
  And like light can flee,
But above all other things,
  Spirit, I love thee—
Thou art love and life! Oh, come,
Make once more my heart thy home.   *Ib.*

17 Men of England, wherefore plough
  For the lords who lay you low?
                    Song to the Men of England

18 An old, mad, blind, despised, and dying king.
                    Sonnet: England in 1819

19 Lift not the painted veil which those who live
  Call Life.   *Sonnet: Lift not the Painted Veil*

20   He sought,
For his lost heart was tender, things to love,
But found them not, alas! nor was there aught
The world contains, the which he could approve.
Through the unheeding many he did move,
A splendour among shadows, a bright blot
Upon this gloomy scene, a Spirit that strove
For truth, and like the Preacher found it not.   *Ib.*

21 The City's voice itself is soft like Solitude's.
                    Stanzas Written in Dejection, near Naples

22 I see the waves upon the shore,
Like light dissolved in star-showers, thrown.   *Ib.*

23 How sweet! did any heart now share in my emotion.
                    Ib.

24 Alas! I have nor hope nor health,
  Nor peace within nor calm around,
Nor that content surpassing wealth
  The sage in meditation found,
And walked with inward glory crowned.   *Ib.*

25 I could lie down like a tired child,
  And weep away the life of care
Which I have borne and yet must bear,
  Till death like sleep might steal on me.   *Ib.*

26 Away! the moor is dark beneath the moon,
Rapid clouds have drank the last pale beam of even:
Away! the gathering winds will call the darkness soon,
And profoundest midnight shroud the serene lights of
  heaven.

Stanzas.—April 1814: Away! the Moor is Dark

1 Music, when soft voices die,
Vibrates in the memory—
Odours, when sweet violets sicken,
Live within the sense they quicken.

Rose leaves, when the rose is dead,
Are heaped for the beloved's bed;
And so thy thoughts, when thou art gone,
Love itself shall slumber on.
To——. Music, When Soft Voices

2 I fear thy kisses, gentle maiden,
Thou needest not fear mine;
My spirit is too deeply laden
Ever to burthen thine.

I fear thy mien, thy tones, thy motion,
Thou needest not fear mine;
Innocent is the heart's devotion
With which I worship thine.
To——. I Fear thy Kisses

3 One word is too often profaned
For me to profane it,
One feeling too falsely disdained
For thee to disdain it.
To——. One Word is too often Profaned

4 The desire of the moth for the star,
Of the night for the morrow,
The devotion to something afar
From the sphere of our sorrow. *Ib.*

5 And like a dying lady, lean and pale,
Who totters forth, wrapped in a gauzy veil.
The Waning Moon

6 A lovely lady, garmented in light
From her own beauty. *The Witch of Atlas, v*

7 For she was beautiful—her beauty made
The bright world dim, and everything beside
Seemed like the fleeting image of a shade. *Ib.* xii

8 The rapid, blind
And fleeting generations of mankind. *Ib.* lxxi

9 In honoured poverty thy voice did weave
Songs consecrate to truth and liberty,—
Deserting these, thou leavest me to grieve,
Thus having been, that thou shouldst cease to be.
To Wordsworth

10 Poets are the unacknowledged legislators of the world.
A Defence of Poetry

11 The rich have become richer, and the poor have
become poorer; and the vessel of the state is driven
between the Scylla and Charybdis of anarchy and
despotism. *Ib.*

12 Poetry is the record of the best and happiest moments
of the happiest and best minds. *Ib.*

WILLIAM SHENSTONE
1714–1763

13 Whoe'er has travell'd life's dull round,
Where'er his stages may have been,
May sigh to think he still has found
The warmest welcome, at an inn.
At an Inn at Henley

14 My banks they are furnish'd with bees,
Whose murmur invites one to sleep;
My grottoes are shaded with trees,
And my hills are white over with sheep.
A Pastoral Ballad. Pt. II, Hope, i

15 I have found out a gift for my fair;
I have found where the wood-pigeons **breed**;
But let me that plunder forbear,
She will say 'twas a barbarous deed.
A Pastoral Ballad. Pt. II, Hope, v

16 A little bench of heedless bishops here,
And there a chancellor in embryo,
Or bard sublime, if bard may e'er be so.
The Schoolmistress, xxviii

17 I loved him for nothing so much as his f-p-n-p-fica-
tion of money. *Letters. xxii. 1777*

18 Laws are generally found to be nets of such a texture,
as the little creep through, the great break through,
and the middle-sized are alone entangled in.
Essays on Men and Manners. On Politics

19 A fool and his words are soon parted; a man of genius
and his money. *Ib. On Reserve*

ROBERT LOWE, VISCOUNT SHERBROOKE
1811–1892

20 I believe it will be absolutely necessary that you
should prevail on our future masters to learn their
letters.
*Speech in House of Commons (on the passing of
the Reform Bill), 15 July 1867. Popularized as
'We must educate our masters'*

PHILIP HENRY SHERIDAN
1831–1888

21 The only good Indian is a dead Indian.
Attr., at Fort Cobb, Jan. 1869

RICHARD BRINSLEY SHERIDAN
1751–1816

22 Not a translation—only *taken from the French*.
The Critic, I.

23 Steal! to be sure they may; and egad, serve your best
thoughts as gypsies do stolen children,—disfigure
them to make them pass for their own. *Ib.*

24 The newspapers! Sir, they are the most villainous—
licentious—abominable—infernal—Not that I ever
read them—no—I make it a rule never to look
into a newspaper. *Ib.*

25 If it is abuse—why one is always sure to hear of it
from one damned good-natured friend or other!
Ib.

26 Egad, I think the interpreter is the hardest to be
understood of the two! *Ib.* ii

27 Yes, sir, puffing is of various sorts; the principal are,
the puff direct, the puff preliminary, the puff col-
lateral, the puff collusive, and the puff oblique, or
puff by implication. *Ib.*

28 No scandal about Queen Elizabeth, I hope? *Ib.* II. i

29 I open with a clock striking, to beget an awful
attention in the audience: it also marks the time,
which is four o'clock in the morning, and saves a
description of the rising sun, and a great deal
about gilding the eastern hemisphere. *Ib.* ii

30 Where they do agree on the stage, their unanimity is
wonderful! *Ib.*

31 Inconsolable to the minuet in Ariadne! *Ib.*

1 The Spanish fleet thou canst not see because—
It is not yet in sight! *The Critic*, II. ii

2 All that can be said is, that two people happened to
hit on the same thought—and Shakespeare made
use of it first, that's all. *Ib.* III. i

3 *Burleigh comes forward, shakes his head, and exit.*
SNEER: He is very perfect indeed. Now pray, what
did he mean by that?

. . . . .

PUFF: Why, by that shake of the head, he gave you to
understand that even though they had more justice
in their cause and wisdom in their measures, yet,
if there was not a greater spirit shown on the part
of the people, the country would at last fall a sacrifice to the hostile ambition of the Spanish
monarchy.
SNEER: The devil!—did he mean all that by shaking
his head?
PUFF: Every word of it. If he shook his head as I
taught him. *Ib.*

4 WHISKERANDOS: And Whiskerandos quits this bust-
ling scene
For all eter——
BEEFEATER: —nity—he would have added, but stern
death
Cut short his being, and the noun at once! *Ib.*

5 I wish sir, you would practise this without me.
I can't stay dying here all night. *Ib.*

6 O Lord, sir, when a heroine goes mad she always goes
into white satin. *Ib.*

7 An oyster may be crossed in love. *Ib.*

8 I ne'er could any lustre see
In eyes that would not look on me.
The Duenna, I. ii. Air

9 I loved him for himself alone. *Ib.* iii

10 Had I a heart for falsehood framed,
I ne'er could injure you. *Ib.* v

11 I was struck all of a heap. *Ib.* II. ii

12 Conscience has no more to do with gallantry than it
has with politics. *Ib.* iv

13 The throne *we* honour is the *people's choice.*
Pizarro, II. i

14 Illiterate him, I say, quite from your memory.
The Rivals, I. ii

15 'Tis safest in matrimony to begin with a little aversion.
Ib.

16 Madam, a circulating library in a town is as an ever-
green tree of diabolical knowledge! It blossoms
through the year! And depend on it, Mrs. Mala-
prop, that they who are so fond of handling the
leaves, will long for the fruit at last. *Ib.*

17 You gentlemen's gentlemen are so hasty. *Ib.* II. ii

18 He is the very pine-apple of politeness! *Ib.* III. iii

19 An aspersion upon my parts of speech! *Ib.*

20 If I reprehend any thing in this world, it is the use
of my oracular tongue, and a nice derangement of
epitaphs! *Ib.*

21 She's as headstrong as an allegory on the banks of the
Nile. *Ib.*

22 Too civil by half. *Ib.* iv

23 Our ancestors are very good kind of folks; but they
are the last people I should choose to have a
visiting acquaintance with. *The Rivals*, IV. i

24 No caparisons, miss, if you please. Caparisons don't
become a young woman. *Ib.* ii

25 You are not like Cerberus, three gentlemen at once,
are you? *Ib.*

26 The quarrel is a very pretty quarrel as it stands; we
should only spoil it by trying to explain it. *Ib.* iii

27 Very pretty small-sword light. *Ib.*

28 There's nothing like being used to a thing. *Ib.* v. iii

29 My valour is certainly going!—it is sneaking off! I
feel it oozing out as it were at the palms of my
hands! *Ib.*

30 I own the soft impeachment. *Ib.*

31 Thro' all the drama—whether damned or not—
Love gilds the scene, and women guide the plot.
Ib. Epilogue

32 Tale-bearers are as bad as the tale-makers.
The School for Scandal, I. i

33 You shall see them on a beautiful quarto page, where
a neat rivulet of text shall meander through a
meadow of margin. *Ib.*

34 You had no taste when you married me. *Ib.* ii

35 MRS. CANDOUR:
I'll swear her colour is natural: I have seen it come
and go.
LADY TEAZLE:
I dare swear you have ma'am: it goes off at night,
and comes again in the morning. *Ib.* II. ii

36 Here is the whole set! a character dead at every word.
Ib.

37 I'm called away by particular business. But I leave
my character behind me. *Ib.*

38 Oh! plague of his sentiments! *Ib.* iii

39 Here's to the maiden of bashful fifteen;
Here's to the widow of fifty;
Here's to the flaunting, extravagant quean;
And here's to the housewife that's thrifty.
Let the toast pass,—
Drink to the lass,
I'll warrant she'll prove an excuse for the glass.
Ib. III. iii. Song

40 Here's to the charmer whose dimples we prize;
Now to the maid who has none, sir;
Here's to the girl with a pair of blue eyes,
And here's to the nymph with but one, sir. *Ib.*

41 Damned disinheriting countenance. *Ib.* IV. i

42 CHARLES SURFACE:
Lady Teazle, by all that's wonderful!
SIR PETER TEAZLE:
Lady Teazle, by all that's damnable! *Ib.* iii

43 It was an amiable weakness. *Ib.* v. i

44 ROWLEY:
I believe there is no sentiment he has such faith in
as that 'charity begins at home'.
SIR OLIVER SURFACE:
And his, I presume, is of that domestic sort which
never stirs abroad at all. *Ib.*

45 There is no trusting appearances. *Ib.* ii

1 The Right Honourable gentleman is indebted to his memory for his jests, and to his imagination for his facts.
Speech in Reply to Mr. Dundas. T. Moore, *Life of Sheridan* (1825), II. 471

2 You write with ease, to show your breeding,
But easy writing's vile hard reading.
Clio's Protest. See Moore's *Life of Sheridan,* I. 55

3 Won't you come into the garden? I would like my roses to see you.
To a young lady. Attrib. in *The Perfect Hostess*

WILLIAM TECUMSEH SHERMAN
1820–1891

4 There is many a boy here to-day who looks on war as all glory, but, boys, it is all hell.
Speech, Columbus, Ohio, 11 Aug. 1880. Lewis's *Sherman, Fighting Prophet*

JAMES SHIRLEY
1596–1666

5 The glories of our blood and state
Are shadows, not substantial things;
There is no armour against fate;
Death lays his icy hand on kings:
    Sceptre and crown
    Must tumble down,
And in the dust be equal made
With the poor crooked scythe and spade.
The Contention of Ajax and Ulysses, I. iii

6 Only the actions of the just
Smell sweet, and blossom in their dust. *Ib.*

7 I presume you're mortal, and may err.
The Lady of Pleasure, II. ii

8   How little room
Do we take up in death, that, living know
No bounds?   *The Wedding,* IV. iv

THE SHORTER CATECHISM

9 'What is the chief end of man?'
'To glorify God and to enjoy him for ever.'

JOSEPH HENRY SHORTHOUSE
1834–1903

10 'The Church of England,' I said, seeing that Mr. Inglesant paused, 'is no doubt a compromise.'
John Inglesant (1880), ch. 40

11 In all probability 'Wordsworth's standard of intoxication was miserably low'.
Remark to some Wordsworthians who were deploring W.'s confession that he got drunk at Cambridge. G. W. E. Russell's *Collections and Recollections,* ch. 8

HENRY SIDGWICK
1838–1900

12 We think so because other people all think so,
Or because—or because—after all we do think so,
Or because we were told so, and think we must think so,

Or because we once thought so, and think we still think so,
Or because having thought so, we think we *will* think so.   *Memoir* (1906), end of ch. 11

ALGERNON SIDNEY
1622–1683

13 Liars ought to have good memories.
Discourses on Government, ch. 2, § xv

14 Men lived like fishes; the great ones devour'd the small.   *Ib.* § xviii

15 'Tis not necessary to light a candle to the sun.
Ib. § xxiii

SIR PHILIP SIDNEY
1554–1586

16 High erected thoughts seated in the heart of courtesy.
The Arcadia, bk. i, ch. 2

17 Shallow brooks murmur most, deep silent slide away.
Ib. First Eclogues, Lalus and Dorus, st. ii

18 Who shoots at the mid-day sun, though he be sure he shall never hit the mark; yet as sure he is he shall shoot higher than who aims but at a bush.
Ib. bk. ii, ch. 6

19 My true love hath my heart and I have his,
By just exchange one for the other giv'n;
I hold his dear, and mine he cannot miss,
There never was a better bargain driv'n.
Ib. bk. iii, *ad fin.*

20 Doubt you to whom my Muse these notes intendeth,
Which now my breast o'ercharged to music lendeth?
To you, to you, all song of praise is due;
Only in you my song begins and endeth.
Astrophel and Stella, Song I: Doubt You to Whom

21 Have I caught my heav'nly jewel.
Ib. Song II: Have I Caught

22 Thy fair hair my heart enchained.
Ib. Certain Sonnets, To the tune of a Neapolitan Villanelle

23 'Fool!' said my Muse, to me, 'look in thy heart, and write.'   *Ib. Sonnet I*

24 With how sad steps, O Moon, thou climb'st the skies!
How silently, and with how wan a face!
What! may it be that even in heavenly place
That busy archer his sharp arrows tries?
Ib. Sonnet XXXI

25 Do they call virtue there ungratefulness?   *Ib.*

26 Come, Sleep! O Sleep, the certain knot of peace,
The baiting-place of wit, the balm of woe,
The poor man's wealth, the prisoner's release,
Th' indifferent judge between the high and low.
Ib. Sonnet XXXIX

27 Take thou of me smooth pillows, sweetest bed,
A chamber deaf to noise and blind to light,
A rosy garland and a weary head.   *Ib.*

28 That sweet enemy, France.   *Ib. Sonnet XLI*

29 They love indeed who quake to say they love.
Ib. Sonnet LIV

1 Oh heav'nly fool, thy most kiss-worthy face
  Anger invests with such a lovely grace,
  That Anger's self I needs must kiss again.
  Astrophel and Stella, Sonnet LXXIII

2 I never drank of Aganippe well,
  Nor ever did in shade of Tempe sit,
  And Muses scorn with vulgar brains to dwell;
  Poor layman I, for sacred rites unfit.
  Ib. Sonnet LXXIV

3 Highway, since you my chief Parnassus be,
  And that my Muse, to some ears not unsweet,
  Tempers her words to trampling horses' feet
  More oft than to a chamber melody,
  Now blessed you, bear onward blessed me
  To her, where I my heart, safe-left, shall meet.
  Ib. Sonnet LXXXIV

4 Hundreds of years you Stella's feet may kiss.   *Ib.*

5 Leave me, O Love, which reacheth but to dust;
  And thou, my mind, aspire to higher things;
  Grow rich in that which never taketh rust;
  Whatever fades, but fading pleasure brings.
  Ib. Sonnet CX: Splendidis Longum Valedico Nugis

6 Never love was so abused.
  Pansies from Penshurst and Wilton. V. Love

7 O fair! O sweet! When I do look on thee,
  In whom all joys so well agree,
  Heart and soul do sing in me,
  Just accord all music makes.
  Ib. VIII. Verses, To the Tune of a Spanish Song

8 With a tale forsooth he cometh unto you, with a tale
  which holdeth children from play, and old men
  from the chimney corner.
  The Defence of Poesy (1595)

9 Certainly I must confess mine own barbarousness, I
  never heard the old song of Percy and Douglas,
  that I found not my heart moved more than with
  a trumpet.   *Ib. p. 24*

10 Philip of Macedon reckoned a horse-race won at
   Olympus among his three fearful felicities.   *Ib.*

11 To be rhymed to death as is said to be done in Ireland.
   Ib.

12 Thy necessity is yet greater than mine.
   *On giving his water-bottle to a dying soldier on
   the battle-field of Zutphen, 1586.* Sir Fulke
   Greville's *Life* (1907), ch. 12. *The word 'necessity'
   is more often quoted as 'need'*

EMMANUEL JOSEPH SIEYÈS
1748–1836

13 La mort, sans phrases.
   Death, without phrases.
   *Attributed to Sieyès on voting in the French Con-
   vention for the death of Louis XVI, 19 Jan. 1793.
   Afterwards repudiated by him*

SIMONIDES
556–468 B.C.

14 ὦ ξεῖν', ἀγγειλον Λακεδαιμονίοις ὅτι τῇδε
   κείμεθα, τοῖς κείνων ῥήμασι πειθόμενοι.

   Go, tell the Spartans, thou who passest by,
   That here obedient to their laws we lie.
   Select Epigrams (ed. Mackail), iii. 4

GEORGE R. SIMS

15 It was Christmas Day in the workhouse.   *Song*

SIR OSBERT SITWELL
1892–

16 The British Bourgeoisie
   Is not born,
   And does not die,
   But, if it is ill,
   It has a frightened look in its eyes.
   At the House of Mrs. Kinfoot

JOHN SKELTON
1460?–1529

17 As patient and as still
   And as full of goodwill,
   As the fair Isyphill,
   Coliander,
   Sweet pomander,
   Good Cassander;
   Steadfast of thought,
   Well made, well wrought.
   Far may be sought
   Erst ye can find
   So courteous, so kind,
   As Merry Margaret, the midsummer flower,
   Gentle as falcon or hawk of the tower.
   To Mistress Margaret Hussey

18 With solace and gladness,
   Much mirth and no madness,
   All good and no badness;
   So joyously,
   So maidenly,
   So womanly,
   Her demeaning.   *Ib.*

19 She is the violet,
   The daisy delectable,
   The columbine commendable,
   The jelofer amiable;
   For this most goodly flower,
   This blossom of fresh colour,
   So Jupiter me succour,
   She flourisheth new and new
   In beauty and virtue.
   The Commendations of Mistress Jane Scrope

20 For the soul of Philip Sparrow,
   That was late slain at Carrow
   Among the Nunnes Black,
   For that sweet soul's sake
   And for all sparrows' souls
   Set in our bead-rolls,
   Pater noster qui
   With an *Ave Mari*.   *The Sparrow's Dirge*

21 The Tunning of Elynour Rumming.
   Title of poem

JOHN SKINNER
1721–1807

22 Let Whig and Tory a' agree,
   Whig and Tory, Whig and Tory,
   Whig and Tory a' agree,
   To drop their Whigmigmorum;

Let Whig and Tory a' agree
To spend the night in mirth and glee,
And cheerfu' sing alang wi' me
    The reel o' Tullochgorum.
    Tullochgorum, st. i. *The Songs of Scotland,* ed.
    G. F. Graham. *A version of 1776 gives line 4 as*
    'To drop their whimpegorum'

ADAM SKIRVING

1719–1803

1 Hey, Johnnie Cope, are ye wauking yet?
    Or are your drums a-beating yet?

CHRISTOPHER SMART

1722–1771

2 He sung of God—the mighty source
Of all things—the stupendous force
    On which all strength depends;
From whose right arm, beneath whose eyes,
All period, pow'r, and enterprize
    Commences, reigns, and ends.
    Song to David, st. 18

3 Tell them I am, Jehova said
To Moses; while earth heard in dread,
    And smitten to the heart,
At once above, beneath, around,
All nature, without voice or sound,
    Replied, O Lord, Thou art.   *Ib.* st. 40

4 For Adoration all the ranks
Of angels yield eternal thanks,
    And David in the midst.   *Ib.* st. 51

5 Strong is the horse upon his speed;
Strong in pursuit the rapid glede,
    Which makes at once his game:
Strong the tall ostrich on the ground;
Strong thro' the turbulent profound
    Shoots xiphias to his aim.

Strong is the lion—like a coal
His eye-ball—like a bastion's mole
    His chest against his foes:
Strong, the gier-eagle on his sail,
Strong against tide, th' enormous whale
    Emerges as he goes.

Where ask is have, where seek is find,
    Where knock is open wide.   *Ib.* st. 75–77

6 Glorious the sun in mid-career;
Glorious th' assembled fires appear;
    Glorious the comet's train:
Glorious the trumpet and alarm;
Glorious th' almighty stretch'd-out arm;
    Glorious th' enraptur'd main.

Glorious the northern lights astream;
Glorious the song, when God's the theme;
    Glorious the thunder's roar:
Glorious hosanna from the den;
Glorious the catholic amen;
    Glorious the martyr's gore.

Glorious—more glorious is the crown
Of Him that brought salvation down
    By meekness, call'd thy Son;
Thou that stupendous truth believ'd,
And now the matchless deed's achiev'd,
    Determined, dared, and done.   *Ib.* st. 84–86

FRANCIS EDWARD SMEDLEY

1818–1864

7 You are looking as fresh as paint.
    Frank Fairlegh, ch. 41

SAMUEL SMILES

1812–1904

8 A place for everything, and everything in its place.
    Thrift, ch. 5

9 Cecil's despatch of business was extraordinary, his
maxim being, 'The shortest way to do many things
is to do only one thing at once.'   *Self-Help,* ch. 9

10 His [Dr. Priestley's] appointment [to act as astronomer to Captain Cook's expedition to the southern
seas] had been cancelled, as the Board of Longitude objected to his theology.
    Men of Invention and Industry, ch. 3

ADAM SMITH

1723–1790

11 To found a great empire for the sole purpose of
raising up a people of customers, may at first
sight appear a project fit only for a nation of shopkeepers. It is, however, a project altogether unfit
for a nation of shopkeepers; but extremely fit for
a nation that is governed by shopkeepers.
    Wealth of Nations, vol. ii, bk. iv, ch. **7, pt. iii.**
    (*See 1:6, 360:22*)

ALEXANDER SMITH

1830–1867

12 Like a pale martyr in his shirt of fire.
    A Life of Drama, ii

13 In winter, when the dismal rain
    Came down in slanting lines,
And Wind, that grand old harper, smote
    His thunder-harp of pines.   *Ib.*

ALFRED EMANUEL SMITH

1873–1944

14 Nothing doing. That's just boloney. Everybody
knows I can't lay bricks.
    *Remark at the laying of the corner-stone of the
    New York State Office Building*

ERNEST BRAMAH SMITH

1868–1942

15 It is a mark of insincerity of purpose to spend one's
time in looking for the sacred Emperor in the low-
class tea-shops.
    The Wallet of Kai Lung. Transmutation of Ling

16 An expression of no-encouragement.
    Ib. Confession of Kai Lung

17 The whole narrative is permeated with the odour of
joss-sticks and honourable high-mindedness.
    Ib. Kin Yen

18 However entrancing it is to wander unchecked
through a garden of bright images, are we not enticing your mind from another subject of almost
equal importance?
    Kai Lung's Golden Hours. Story of Hien

FREDERICK EDWIN SMITH, EARL OF BIRKENHEAD

see

BIRKENHEAD

JAMES SMITH

1775–1839

and

'HORACE' [HORATIO] SMITH

1779–1849

1 And hast thou walk'd about (how strange a story!)
   In Thebes's streets three thousand years ago,
   When the Memnonium was in all its glory.
                              Address to a Mummy

2 In Craven-street, Strand, ten attorneys find place,
   And ten dark coal-barges are moor'd at its base.
   Fly, Honesty, fly! seek some safer retreat;
   For there's craft in the river, and craft in the street.
                              Craven Street, Strand

3 And when that donkey look'd me in the face,
   His face was sad! and you are sad, my Public!
                              Playhouse Musings, l. 4

4 Hail, glorious edifice, stupendous work!
   God bless the Regent and the Duke of York!
                    Rejected Addresses. No. 1. *Loyal Effusion*, l. 1

5 Who makes the quartern loaf and Luddites rise?
   Who fills the butchers' shops with large blue flies?
                              Ib. l. 48

6 I saw them go: one horse was blind,
   The tails of both hung down behind,
     Their shoes were on their feet.
        Ib. No. 2. *The Baby's Début*, vi. (Parody of
        Wordsworth)

7 What stately vision mocks my waking sense?
   Hence, dear delusion, sweet enchantment, hence!
        Ib. No. 3. *An Address Without a Phoenix*

8 I am a blessed Glendoveer:
   'Tis mine to speak, and yours to hear.
        Ib. No. 7. *The Rebuilding*

9 Thinking is but an idle waste of thought,
   And nought is every thing, and every thing is nought.
        Ib. No. 8. *Cui bono?*

10 'Why are you in such doleful dumps?
   A fireman, and afraid of bumps!—
   What are they fear'd on? fools! 'od rot 'em!'
   Were the last words of Higginbottom.
        Ib. No. 9. *Drury Lane*. (Parody of Scott)

11 In the name of the Prophet—figs!
        Ib. No. 10. *Johnson's Ghost*

12 John Richard William Alexander Dwyer
   Was footman to Justinian Stubbs, Esquire.
        The Theatre. (Parody of Crabbe)

LANGDON SMITH

1858–1918

13 When you were a tadpole, and I was a fish,
     In the Palaeozoic time,
   And side by side in the ebbing tide
     We sprawled through the ooze and slime.
        A Toast to a Lady. (*The Scrap-Book*, April
        1906)

LOGAN PEARSALL SMITH

1865–1946

14 There are two things to aim at in life: first, to get
   what you want; and, after that, to enjoy it. Only
   the wisest of mankind achieve the second.
                              Afterthoughts (1931), p. 4

15 There are few sorrows, however poignant, in which
   a good income is of no avail.   *Ib.* p. 12

16 People say that life is the thing, but I prefer reading.
                              Ib. p. 71

17 The old know what they want; the young are sad and
   bewildered.   *All Trivia*, Last Words

18 Thank heavens, the sun has gone in, and I don't have
   to go out and enjoy it.   *Ib.*

SAMUEL FRANCIS SMITH

1808–1895

19 My country, 'tis of thee,
   Sweet land of liberty,
     Of thee I sing:
   Land where my fathers died,
   Land of the pilgrims' pride,
   From every mountain-side
     Let freedom ring.   *America*

REV. SYDNEY SMITH

1771–1845

20 It requires a surgical operation to get a joke well into
   a Scotch understanding. Their only idea of wit
   . . . is laughing immoderately at stated intervals.
        Lady Holland, *Memoir* (1st ed. 1855), vol. 1, ch.
        2, p. 15.

21 I heard him [Jeffrey] speak disrespectfully of the
   Equator!   *Ib.* p. 17

22 That knuckle-end of England—that land of Calvin,
   oat-cakes, and sulphur.   *Ib.*

23 Take short views, hope for the best, and trust in God.
                              Ib. ch. 6, p. 48

24 Looked as if she had walked straight out of the Ark.
                              Ib. ch. 7, p. 157

25 No furniture so charming as books. *Ib.* ch. 9, p. 240

26 Madam, I have been looking for a person who disliked gravy all my life; let us swear eternal friendship.   *Ib.* p. 257

27 How can a bishop marry? How can he flirt? The
   most he can say is, 'I will see you in the vestry
   after service.'   *Ib.* p. 258

28 Not body enough to cover his mind decently with;
   his intellect is improperly exposed.   *Ib.*

29 I have, alas, only one illusion left, and that is the
   Archbishop of Canterbury.   *Ib.* p. 259

30 You find people ready enough to do the Samaritan,
   without the oil and twopence.   *Ib.* p. 261

31 As the French say, there are three sexes—men,
   women, and clergymen.   *Ib.* p. 262

32 Praise is the best diet for us, after all. *Ib.* p. 265

33 Daniel Webster struck me much like a steam-engine
   in trousers.   *Ib.* p. 267

1 He [Macaulay] is like a book in breeches.
Lady Holland, *Memoir*, vol. I, ch. 11, p. 363

2 He [Macaulay] has occasional flashes of silence, that make his conversation perfectly delightful. *Ib.*

3 Let onion atoms lurk within the bowl,
And, scarce-suspected, animate the whole.
Recipe for Salad, Ib. p. 373

4 Serenely full, the epicure would say,
Fate cannot harm me, I have dined to-day. *Ib.*

5 You remember Thurlow's answer . . . you never expected justice from a company, did you? They have neither a soul to lose, nor a body to kick.
Ib. p. 376

6 Deserves to be preached to death by wild curates.
Ib. p. 384

7 I never read a book before reviewing it; it prejudices a man so.
H. Pearson, *The Smith of Smiths* (1934), ch. iii, p. 54

8 It is a place with only one post a day. . . . In the country I always fear that creation will expire before tea-time. *Ib.* ch. 5, p. 92

9 Minorities . . . are almost always in the right.
Ib. ch. 9, p. 220

10 ——'s idea of heaven is, eating *pâtés de foie gras* to the sound of trumpets. *Ib.* ch. 10, p. 236

11 What a pity it is that we have no amusements in England but vice and religion! *Ib.*

12 Let the Dean and Canons lay their heads together and the thing will be done. *It being proposed to surround St. Paul's with a wooden pavement Ib.* p. 237

13 Death must be distinguished from dying, with which it is often confused. *Ib.* ch. 11, p. 271

14 The only way to deal with such a man as O'Connell is to hang him up and erect a statue to him under the gallows. *Ib.* p. 272

15 What two ideas are more inseparable than Beer and Britannia? *Ib.*

16 I am just going to pray for you at St. Paul's, but with no very lively hope of success.
Ib. ch. 13, p. 308

17 Poverty is no disgrace to a man, but it is confoundedly inconvenient. *His Wit and Wisdom* (1900), p. 89

18 One of the greatest pleasures of life is conversation.
Essays (1877). *Female Education*, p. 103

19 This great spectacle of human happiness.
Ib. Waterton's Wanderings, p. 465

20 The moment the very name of Ireland is mentioned, the English seem to bid adieu to common feeling, common prudence, and common sense, and to act with the barbarity of tyrants, and the fatuity of idiots. *Peter Plymley's Letters* (1929), p. 9

21 A Curate—there is something which excites compassion in the very name of a Curate!!!
Ib. p. 127. *Persecuting Bishops*

22 Dame Partington . . . was seen . . . with mop and pattens . . . vigorously pushing away the Atlantic Ocean. The Atlantic Ocean beat Mrs. Partington.
Ib. p. 228

23 Bishop Berkeley destroyed this world in one volume octavo; and nothing remained, after his time, but mind; which experienced a similar fate from the hand of Mr. Hume in 1739.
Sketches of Moral Philosophy. Introd.

24 We shall generally find that the triangular person has got into the square hole, the oblong into the triangular, and a square person has squeezed himself into the round hole. The officer and the office, the doer and the thing done, seldom fit so exactly that we can say they were almost made for each other. *Ib.* Lect. ix

25 I never could find any man who could think for two minutes together. *Ib.* Lect. xix

26 The motto I proposed for the [*Edinburgh*] *Review* was: *Tenui musam meditamur avena*—'We cultivate literature upon a little oatmeal.'
Works (1859), vol. i, Preface, p. v

27 We can inform Jonathan what are the inevitable consequences of being too fond of glory;—Taxes upon every article which enters into the mouth, or covers the back, or is placed under the foot . . . taxes on everything on earth, and the waters under the earth.
Ib. vol. i. *Review of Seybert's Statistical Annals of the United States*, p. 291

28 The schoolboy whips his taxed top—the beardless youth manages his taxed horse, with a taxed bridle, on a taxed road;—and the dying Englishman, pouring his medicine, which has paid seven per cent., into a spoon that has paid fifteen per cent.—flings himself back upon his chintz bed, which has paid twenty-two per cent.—and expires in the arms of an apothecary who has paid a licence of a hundred pounds for the privilege of putting him to death. *Ib.*

29 What bishops like best in their clergy is a dropping-down-deadness of manner.
Ib. vol. ii, *First Letter to Archdeacon Singleton*, p. 271. *Note*

30 I like, my dear Lord, the road you are travelling, but I don't like the pace you are driving; too similar to that of the son of Nimshi. I always feel myself inclined to cry out, Gently, John, gently down hill. Put on the drag.
Ib. vol. ii, *Letter to Lord John Russell*, p. 300

31 I look upon Switzerland as an inferior sort of Scotland.
Letters. Lady Holland, *Memoir*, vol. ii. *To Lord Holland, 1815*

32 Tory and Whig in turns shall be my host,
I taste no politics in boil'd and roast.
Ib. To John Murray. Nov. 1834

33 What would life be without arithmetic, but a scene of horrors? *Ib. To Miss ——, 22 July 1835*

34 I am convinced digestion is the great secret of life.
Ib. To Arthur Kinglake, 30 Sept. 1837

35 I have no relish for the country; it is a kind of healthy grave. *Ib. To Miss G. Harcourt, 1838*

36 I have seen nobody since I saw you, but persons in orders. My only varieties are vicars, rectors, curates, and every now and then (by way of turbot) an archdeacon. *Ib. To Miss Berry, 28 Jan. 1843*

1 One very hot evening in summer, Lady Holland and
a large party of friends were suffering from the
stifling atmosphere, and a general dulness had crept
over the company. Then Milnes was seen to enter.
'Ah! here comes the cool of the evening,' cried
Sydney Smith, and immediately everybody grew
brighter. [Milnes resented this and other nicknames, and Sydney Smith wrote to him: 'The
names of "Cool of the evening", "London Assurance", and "In-I-go Jones", are, I give you my
word, not mine.']
T. Wemyss Reid, *Life of Lord Houghton* (1890),
vol. i, p. 213

2 [William Whewell.] Science is his forte, and omniscience his foible.
In Isaac Todhunter, *William Whewell* (1876),
i. 410

TOBIAS GEORGE SMOLLETT
1721–1771

3 Mourn, hapless Caledonia, mourn
Thy banish'd peace, thy laurels torn!
The Tears of Scotland

4 I think for my part one half of the nation is mad—
and the other not very sound.
The Adventures of Sir Launcelot Greaves, ch. 6

5 He was formed for the ruin of our sex.
Roderick Random, ch. 22

6 That great Cham of literature, Samuel Johnson.
Letter to John Wilkes, 16 Mar. 1759. Boswell's
Johnson (1934), vol. i, p. 348

GEORGE HUNT SMYTTAN
1822–1870
and
FRANCIS POTT
1832–1909

7 Forty days and forty nights
Thou wast fasting in the wild,
Forty days and forty nights
Tempted, and yet undefiled.
*Hymn: Forty Days and Forty Nights. The Penny
Post*, 1856

8 Prowling beasts about Thy way;
Stones Thy pillow, earth Thy bed. *Ib.*

SOCRATES
469–399 B.C.

9 ἀλλὰ γὰρ ἤδη ὥρα ἀπιέναι, ἐμοὶ μὲν ἀποθανουμένῳ, ὑμῖν δὲ
βιωσομένοις. ὁπότεροι δὲ ἡμῶν ἔρχονται ἐπὶ ἄμεινον
πρᾶγμα ἄδηλον παντὶ πλὴν ἢ τῷ θεῷ.

The hour of departure has arrived, and we go our
ways—I to die, and you to live. Which is the
better, God only knows.
Plato, Apologia, Last words

10 ὦ Κρίτων, τῷ Ἀσκληπιῷ ὀφείλομεν ἀλεκτρυόνα. ἀλλὰ
ἀπόδοτε καὶ μὴ ἀμελήσητε.

Crito, we owe a cock to Aesculapius; pay it, therefore, and do not neglect it.
Last words, 399 B.C. Plato, *Phaedo,* 118a

SOLON
c. 640–c. 558 B.C.

11 γηράσκω δ' αἰεὶ πολλὰ διδασκόμενος.
I grow old ever learning many things.
Poetae Lyrici Graeci (ed. Bergk), *Solon,* 18

12 πρὶν δ' ἂν τελευτήσῃ, ἐπισχεῖν μηδὲ καλέειν κω ὄλβιον, ἀλλ'
εὐτυχέα.
Call no man happy till he dies, he is at best but
fortunate. *Herodotus, Histories,* i. 32

WILLIAM SOMERVILLE
1675–1742

13 My hoarse-sounding horn
Invites thee to the chase, the sport of kings;
Image of war, without its guilt.
The Chase, bk. i, l. 13

14 Hail, happy Britain! highly favoured isle,
And Heaven's peculiar care! *Ib.* l. 84

15 If this pale rose offend your sight,
It in your bosom wear;
'Twill blush to find itself less white,
And turn Lancastrian there.
*Presenting to a Lady a White Rose and a Red on
the Tenth of June*

SOPHOCLES
495–406 B.C.

16 πολλὰ τὰ δεινὰ κοὐδὲν ἀνθρώπου δεινότερον πέλει.
Wonders are many, and none is more wonderful
than man. *Antigone,* 332. Trans. by Jebb

17 ὦ παῖ, γένοιο πατρὸς εὐτυχέστερος.
Ah, boy, may'st thou prove happier than thy sire.
Ajax, 550. Trans. by Jebb

18 μὴ φῦναι τὸν ἅπαντα νικᾷ λόγον.
Not to be born is best. *Oedipus Coloneus,* 1225

CHARLES HAMILTON SORLEY
1895–1915

19 We have the evil spirits too
That shake our soul with battle-din.
But we have an eviller spirit than you,
We have a dumb spirit within:
The exceeding bitter agony
But not the exceeding bitter cry. *To Poets*

20 We swing ungirded hips,
And lightened are our eyes,
The rain is on our lips,
We do not run for prize. *Song of the Ungirt Runners*

21 We run because we like it
Through the broad bright land. *Ib.*

JOHN BABSONE LANE SOULE
1815–1891

22 Go west, young man.
Article in the Terre Haute, Indiana, *Express*
(1851) .

REV. ROBERT SOUTH
1634–1716

1 An Aristotle was but the rubbish of an Adam, and
   Athens but the rudiments of Paradise.
                     Sermons, vol. I. ii

THOMAS SOUTHERNE
1660–1746

2   And when we're worn,
Hack'd, hewn with constant service, thrown aside
To rust in peace, or rot in hospitals.
                     Loyal Brother, Act 1

ROBERT SOUTHEY
1774–1843

3 It was a summer evening,
   Old Kaspar's work was done,
And he before his cottage door
   Was sitting in the sun,
And by him sported on the green
His little grandchild Wilhelmine.
              The Battle of Blenheim

4 He came to ask what he had found,
That was so large, and smooth, and round.   *Ib.*

5 Now tell us all about the war,
And what they fought each other for.   *Ib.*

6 But what they fought each other for,
   I could not well make out.   *Ib.*

7 But things like that, you know, must be
   At every famous victory.   *Ib.*

8 Great praise the Duke of Marlbro' won,
   And our good Prince Eugene.   *Ib.*

9 'And everybody praised the Duke,
   Who this great fight did win.'
'But what good came of it at last?'
   Quoth little Peterkin.
'Why that I cannot tell,' said he,
'But 'twas a famous victory.'   *Ib.*

10 My name is Death: the last best friend am I.
   *Carmen Nuptiale. The Lay of the Laureate. The
   Dream*, lxxxvii

11 How does the water
   Come down at Lodore?   *The Cataract of Lodore*

12 And this way the water comes down at Lodore.   *Ib.*

13 Curses are like young chickens, they always come
   home to roost.   *The Curse of Kehama. Motto*

14   Water shall hear me,
And know thee and fly thee.   *Ib.* II. 14

15 And Sleep shall obey me,
   And visit thee never,
And the Curse shall be on thee
   For ever and ever.   *Ib.*

16 Hark! at the Golden Palaces
   The Brahmin strikes the hour.   *Ib.* v. 1

17 They sin who tell us love can die.
   With life all other passions fly,
   All others are but vanity.   *Ib.* x. 10

18 Thou hast been call'd, O Sleep! the friend of Woe,
But 'tis the happy who have called thee so.
                  Ib. xv. 12

19 From his brimstone bed, at break of day
   A walking the Devil is gone,
To look at his little snug farm of the World,
   And see how his stock went on.
       The Devil's Walk, i. (*See 151:7–12*)

20 His coat was red and his breeches were blue,
And there was a hole where his tail came through.
                       Ib. iii

21 He passed a cottage with a double coach-house,
   A cottage of gentility!
And he owned with a grin
That his favourite sin
   Is pride that apes humility.   *Ib.* viii

22 As he passed through Cold Bath fields, he looked
   At a solitary cell;
And he was well-pleased, for it gave him a hint
   For improving the prisons of Hell.   *Ib.* xv

23 And all at once to the Bishop they go.
        God's Judgment on a Wicked Bishop

24 No stir in the air, no stir in the sea,
The ship was still as she could be.
                The Inchcape Rock

25 And then they knew the perilous rock,
   And blest the Abbot of Aberbrothok.   *Ib.*

26 O Christ! It is the Inchcape Rock!   *Ib.*

27 Sir Ralph the Rover tore his hair;
   He curst himself in his despair.   *Ib.*

28 Day after day, day after day the same—
   A weary waste of waters!
     Madoc: Pt. I, Madoc in Wales. IV, The Voyage,
     l. 32

29 Blue, darkly, deeply, beautifully blue.
            Ib. V, *Lincoya*, l. 102

30 We wage no war with women nor with priests.
      Ib. XV, *The Excommunication*, l. 65

31 What will not woman, gentle woman dare,
When strong affection stirs her spirit up?
    Ib. Pt. II, *Madoc in Aztlan*. II, *The Tidings*,
    l. 125

32 Yet leaving here a name, I trust,
That will not perish in the dust.
           My Days Among the Dead

33 You are old, Father William, the young man cried,
   The few locks which are left you are grey;
You are hale, Father William, a hearty old man,
   Now tell me the reason, I pray.
    *The Old Man's Comforts, and how he Gained
    them*

34 You are old, Father William, the young man cried
   And pleasures with youth pass away,
And yet you lament not the days that are gone,
   Now tell me the reason, I pray.   *Ib.*

35 In the days of my youth I remembered my God!
   And He hath not forgotten my age.   *Ib.*

36 The Monk my son, and my daughter the Nun.
          The Old Woman of Berkeley

37 Their wintry garment of unsullied snow
The mountains have put on.
    *The Poet's Pilgrimage. Pt. I, The Journey. II,
    Flanders, 23*

1 He ran against a shooting star,
So fast for fear did he sail,
And he singed the beard of the Bishop
Against a comet's tail;
And he passed between the horns of the moon,
With Antidius on his back;
And there was an eclipse that night,
Which was not in the Almanac.
St. Antidius, the Pope and the Devil

2 How beautiful is night!
A dewy freshness fills the silent air;
No mist obscures, nor cloud, nor speck, nor stain,
Breaks the serene of heaven.
Thalaba the Destroyer, bk. I, i

3 A vague, a dizzy, a tumultuous joy. *Ib.* bk. III. xix

4 'I had a home once—I had once a husband—
I am a widow, poor and broken-hearted!'
Loud blew the wind, unheard was her complaining,
On drove the chariot. *The Widow*, v

5 Stern to inflict and stubborn to endure,
That laughed in death.
Poetical address to the author. In Amos Cottle,
Icelandic Poetry (1797)

6 The arts babblative and scribblative.
*Colloquies on the Progress and Prospects of
Society.* Coll. x. Pt. ii

7 The march of intellect. *Ib.* Coll. xiv

8 Your true lover of literature is never fastidious.
The Doctor, ch. 17

9 Show me a man who cares no more for one place
than another, and I will show you in that same
person one who loves nothing but himself. Beware
of those who are homeless by choice. *Ib.* ch. 34

10 Live as long as you may, the first twenty years are
the longest half of your life. *Ib.* ch. 130

11 The death of Nelson was felt in England as something
more than a public calamity; men started at the
intelligence, and turned pale, as if they had heard
of the loss of a dear friend.
The Life of Nelson, ch. 9

12 The Satanic School. *The Vision of Judgment.* Preface

13 The pander of posterity. *Ib.*

ROBERT SOUTHWELL

1561?–1595

14 As I in hoary winter's night stood shivering in the
snow,
Surprised I was with sudden heat which made my
heart to glow;
And lifting up a fearful eye to view what fire was near,
A pretty Babe all burning bright did in the air appear.
The Burning Babe

15 'The fuel justice layeth on, and mercy blows the
coals;
The metal in this furnace wrought are men's defiled
souls:
For which, as now on fire I am to work them to their
good,
So will I melt into a bath to wash them in my blood.'
With this he vanished out of sight and swiftly shrunk
away,
And straight I called unto mind that it was Christmas
Day. *Ib.*

16 Come, Raphael, this Babe must eat,
Provide our little Toby meat.
New Heaven, New War

17 Behold, a silly tender Babe
In freezing winter night
In homely manger trembling lies,
Alas, a piteous sight! *New Prince, New Pomp*

18 With joy approach, O Christian wight,
Do homage to thy King;
And highly praise his humble pomp,
Which he from heaven doth bring. *Ib.*

19 Times go by turns, and chances change by course,
From foul to fair, from better hap to worse.
Times go by Turns

HERBERT SPENCER

1820–1903

20 Time: That which man is always trying to kill, but
which ends in killing him. *Definitions*

21 Science is organized knowledge. *Education*, ch. 2

22 Absolute morality is the regulation of conduct in such
a way that pain shall not be inflicted.
Essays (1891), vol. iii, p. 152. *Prison Ethics*

23 The ultimate result of shielding men from the effects
of folly, is to fill the world with fools.
Ib. p. 354. *State Tamperings with Money and
Banks*

24 The Republican form of Government is the highest
form of government; but because of this it requires
the highest type of human nature—a type nowhere
at present existing. *Ib.* p. 478. *The Americans*

25 Evolution . . . is—a change from an indefinite, inco-
herent homogeneity, to a definite coherent hetero-
geneity. *First Principles*, ch. 16, § 138

26 This survival of the fittest.
Principles of Biology, pt. iii, ch. 12, *Indirect
Equilibration*, § 165

27 Progress, therefore, is not an accident, but a necessity.
. . . It is a part of nature.
Social Statics, pt. i, ch. 2, § 4

28 Education has for its object the formation of character. *Ib.* pt. ii, ch. 17, § 4

29 Opinion is ultimately determined by the feelings, and
not by the intellect. *Ib.* pt. iv, ch. 30, § 8

30 No one can be perfectly free till all are free; no one
can be perfectly moral till all are moral; no one
can be perfectly happy till all are happy. *Ib.* 16

31 It was remarked to me by the late Mr. Charles
Roupell . . . that to play billiards well was a sign of
an ill-spent youth.
Remark. Duncan, *Life and Letters of Spencer*
(1908), ch. 20, p. 298

WILLIAM ROBERT SPENCER

1769–1834

32 In fancy's ear he oft would hear
Poor Gêlert's dying yell. *Beth-Gêlert*, xxiii

STEPHEN SPENDER

1909–

1 I think continually of those who were truly great—
The names of those who in their lives fought for life,
Who wore at their hearts the fire's centre.
I Think Continually of Those

2 Born of the sun they travelled a short while towards
the sun,
And left the vivid air signed with their honour. *Ib.*

EDMUND SPENSER

1552?–1599

3 The merry cuckoo, messenger of Spring,
His trumpet shrill hath thrice already sounded.
Amoretti. Sonnet xix

4 Most glorious Lord of life, that on this day
Didst make thy triumph over death and sin:
And, having harrow'd hell, didst bring away
Captivity thence captive, us to win. *Ib.* lxviii

5 So let us love, dear Love, like as we ought,
—Love is the lesson which the Lord us taught. *Ib.*

6 Fresh spring the herald of love's mighty king,
In whose coat armour richly are display'd
All sorts of flowers the which on earth do spring
In goodly colours gloriously array'd. *Ib.* lxx

7 One day I wrote her name upon the strand,
But came the waves and washed it away:
Again I wrote it with a second hand,
But came the tide, and made my pains his prey.
Vain man, said she, that dost in vain assay,
A mortal thing so to immortalize,
For I myself shall like to this decay,
And eke my name be wiped out likewise.
Not so, quoth I, let baser things devise
To die in dust, but you shall live by fame:
My verse your virtues rare shall eternize,
And in the heavens write your glorious name,
Where when as death shall all the world subdue,
Our love shall live, and later life renew *Ib.* lxxv

8 Triton blowing loud his wreathed horn.
Colin Clout's Come Home Again, l. 245

9 The Shepherd of the Ocean (quoth he)
Unto that Goddess' grace me first enhanc'd,
And to mine oaten pipe inclin'd her ear. *Ib.* l. 358

10 So love is Lord of all the world by right. *Ib.* l. 883

11 The woods shall to me answer and my echo ring.
Epithalamion, l. 18

12 Open the temple gates unto my love,
Open them wide that she may enter in. *Ib.* l. 204

13 Behold whiles she before the altar stands
Hearing the holy priest that to her speaks
And blesseth her with his two happy hands.
Ib. l. 223

14 Ah! when will this long weary day have end,
And lend me leave to come unto my love? *Ib.* l. 278

15 Song made in lieu of many ornaments,
With which my love should duly have been deck'd.
Ib. l. 427

16 Fierce wars and faithful loves shall moralize my song.
The Faerie Queene, bk. I, introd. i. 1

17 A gentle knight was pricking on the plain. *Ib.* c. 1. i

18 But on his breast a bloody cross he bore,
The dear remembrance of his dying Lord.
The Faerie Queene, bk. I. c. 1. ii

19 But of his cheer did seem too solemn sad;
Yet nothing did he dread, but ever was ydrad. *Ib.*

20 A bold bad man. *Ib.* xxxvii

21 Her angel's face
As the great eye of heaven shined bright,
And made a sunshine in the shady place;
Did never mortal eye behold such heavenly grace.
Ib. c. III. vi

22 And all the hinder parts, that few could spy,
Were ruinous and old, but painted cunningly.
Ib. c. IV. v

23 The Noble heart, that harbours virtuous thought,
And is with child of glorious great intent,
Can never rest, until it forth have brought
Th' eternal brood of glory excellent. *Ib.* c. v. i

24 A cruel crafty Crocodile,
Which in false grief hiding his harmful guile,
Doth weep full sore, and sheddeth tender tears.
Ib. xviii

25 As when that devilish iron engine, wrought
In deepest hell, and fram'd by furies' skill,
With windy nitre and quick sulphur fraught,
And ramm'd with bullet round, ordain'd to kill,
Conceiveth fire. *Ib.* c. VII. xiii

26 Still as he fled, his eye was backward cast,
As if his fear still followed him behind. *Ib.* c. IX. xxi

27 That darksome cave they enter, where they find
That cursed man, low sitting on the ground,
Musing full sadly in his sullen mind. *Ib.* xxxv

28 Sleep after toil, port after stormy seas,
Ease after war, death after life does greatly please.
Ib. xl

29 Death is the end of woes: die soon, O fairy's son.
Ib. xlvii

30 So double was his pains, so double be his praise.
Ib. bk. II, c. II. xxv

31 Upon her eyelids many Graces sate,
Under the shadow of her even brows. *Ib.* c. III. xxv

32 And all for love, and nothing for reward.
Ib. c. VIII. ii

33 So passeth, in the passing of a day,
Of mortal life the leaf, the bud, the flower,
No more doth flourish after first decay,
That erst was sought to deck both bed and bower,
Of many a Lady, and many a Paramour:
Gather therefore the Rose, whilst yet is prime,
For soon comes age, that will her pride deflower:
Gather the Rose of love, whilst yet is time,
Whilst loving thou mayst loved be with equal crime.
Ib. c. XII. lxxv

34 Let Grill be Grill, and have his hoggish mind.
Ib. lxxxvii

35 O goodly usage of those antique times,
In which the sword was servant unto right;
When not for malice and contentious crimes,
But all for praise, and proof of manly might,
The martial brood accustomed to fight:
Then honour was the meed of victory,
And yet the vanquished had no despite.
Ib. bk. III, c. I. xiii

[509]

1 Divine tobacco. *The Faerie Queene*, bk. III, c. v. xxxii

2 Hard is to teach an old horse amble true.
Ib. c. VIII. xxvi

3 And painful pleasure turns to pleasing pain.
Ib. c. X. lx

4 And as she look'd about, she did behold,
How over that same door was likewise writ,
Be bold, be bold, and everywhere Be bold.
. . . .
At last she spied at that room's upper end
Another iron door, on which was writ
Be not too bold. *Ib.* c. XI. liv

5 Dan Chaucer, well of English undefiled,
On Fame's eternal beadroll worthy to be filed.
Ib. bk. IV, c. II. xxxii

6 For all that nature by her mother wit
Could frame in earth. *Ib.* c. X. xxi

7 O sacred hunger of ambitious minds.
Ib. bk. V, c. XII. i

8 A monster, which the Blatant beast men call,
A dreadful fiend of gods and men ydrad. *Ib.* xxxvii

9 The gentle mind by gentle deeds is known.
For a man by nothing is so well bewray'd,
As by his manners. *Ib.* bk. VI, c. III. i

10 What man that sees the ever-whirling wheel
Of Change, the which all mortal things doth sway,
But that thereby doth find, and plainly feel,
How Mutability in them doth play
Her cruel sports, to many men's decay?
Ib. bk. VII, c. VI. i

11 For all that moveth doth in Change delight:
But thenceforth all shall rest eternally
With Him that is the God of Sabbaoth hight:
O that great Sabbaoth God, grant me that Sabbaoth's
sight. *Ib.* c. VIII. ii

12 That beauty is not, as fond men misdeem,
An outward show of things, that only seem.
An Hymn in Honour of Beauty, l. 90

13 For of the soul the body form doth take;
For soul is form, and doth the body make. *Ib.* l. 132

14 The hearts of men, which fondly here admire
Fair seeming shows, and feed on vain delight,
Transported with celestial desire
Of those fair forms, may lift themselves up higher,
And learn to love with zealous humble duty
Th' eternal fountain of that heavenly beauty.
Hymn of Heavenly Beauty, l. 16

15 Of such deep learning little had he need,
Ne yet of Latin, ne of Greek, that breed
Doubts 'mongst Divines, and difference of texts,
From whence arise diversity of sects,
And hateful heresies.
Complaints. Mother Hubbard's Tale, l. 385

16 Full little knowest thou that hast not tried,
What hell it is, in suing long to bide:
To lose good days, that might be better spent;
To waste long nights in pensive discontent;
To speed to-day, to be put back to-morrow;
To feed on hope, to pine with fear and sorrow;
To have thy Prince's grace, yet want her Peers';
To have thy asking, yet wait many years;
To fret thy soul with crosses and with cares;
To eat thy heart through comfortless despairs;

To fawn, to crouch, to wait, to ride, to run,
To spend, to give, to want, to be undone,
Unhappy wight, born to disastrous end,
That doth his life in so long tendance spend.
Complaints. Mother Hubbard's Tale, l. 895

17 What more felicity can fall to creature,
Than to enjoy delight with liberty.
Muiopotmos, l. 209

18 I was promis'd on a time,
To have reason for my rhyme;
From that time unto this season,
I received nor rhyme nor reason.
Lines on his Pension. (Traditional)

19 Calm was the day, and through the trembling air,
Sweet breathing Zephyrus did softly play.
Prothalamion, l. 1

20 With that, I saw two Swans of goodly hue,
Come softly swimming down along the Lee;
Two fairer Birds I yet did never see:
The Snow which doth the top of Pindus strew,
Did never whiter show,
Nor Jove himself when he a Swan would be
For love of Leda, whiter did appear:
Yet Leda was they say as white as he,
Yet not so white as these, nor nothing near;
So purely white they were,
That even the gentle stream, the which them bare,
Seem'd foul to them, and bade his billows spare
To wet their silken feathers, lest they might
Soil their fair plumes with water not so fair
And mar their beauties bright,
That shone as Heaven's light,
Against their Bridal day, which was not long:
Sweet Thames, run softly, till I end my Song.
Ib. l. 37

21 At length they all to merry London came,
To merry London, my most kindly nurse,
That to me gave this life's first native source:
Though from another place I take my name,
An house of ancient fame.
There when they came, whereas those bricky towers,
The which on Thames' broad aged back do ride,
Where now the studious Lawyers have their bowers
There whilom wont the Templar Knights to bide,
Till they decay'd through pride. *Ib.* l. 127

22 To be wise and eke to love,
Is granted scarce to God above.
The Shepherd's Calendar. March. Willy's Emblem

23 Bring hither the Pink and purple Columbine,
  With Gillyflowers:
Bring Coronation, and Sops in wine,
  Worn of paramours.
Strew me the ground with Daffadowndillies,
And Cowslips, and Kingcups, and loved Lilies:
  The pretty Pawnce,
  And the Chevisaunce,
Shall match with the fair flower Delice.
Ib. April, l. 136

24 And he that strives to touch the stars,
  Oft stumbles at a straw. *Ib. July*, l. 99

25 The rugged brow of careful Policy.
Dedicatory Sonnets. To Sir Christopher Hatton

26 Uncouth unkist, said the old famous Poet Chaucer.
The Shepherd's Calendar. Letter to Gabriel Harvey

1 So now they have made our English tongue a galli-
maufry or hodgepodge of all other speeches.
The Shepherd's Calendar. Letter to Gabriel Harvey

REV. WILLIAM ARCHIBALD SPOONER
1844–1930

2 Kinquering Congs their titles take.
*Announcing the hymn in New College Chapel,
1879. (See 135:12)*

3 You have deliberately tasted two worms and you can
leave Oxford by the town drain.
Dismissing a student. Attributed

SIR CECIL ARTHUR SPRING-RICE
1858–1918

4 I vow to thee, my country—all earthly things above—
Entire and whole and perfect, the service of my love.
Last Poem

5 I am the Dean of Christ Church, Sir:
There's my wife; look well at her.
She's the Broad and I'm the High;
We are the University.
*The Masque of Balliol, composed by and current
among members of Balliol College, Oxford, in the
late 1870s. This first couplet (identified as by
C. A. Spring-Rice) was unofficially altered to:*

6 I am the Dean, and this is Mrs. Liddell;
She is the first and I the second fiddle.
(See also 8:15, 39:5.)

CHARLES HADDON SPURGEON
1834–1892

7 The Lord gets his best soldiers out of the highlands
of affliction.
*Gleanings among the Sheaves (1864), p. 132,
Sorrow's Discipline*

SIR JOHN COLLINGS SQUIRE
1884–

8 It did not last: the Devil howling 'Ho!
Let Einstein be!' restored the status quo.
Answer to Pope's epitaph for Sir Isaac Newton

MME DE STAËL
1766–1817

9 Tout comprendre rend très indulgent.
To know all makes one tolerant.
Corinne (1807), lib. iv, ch. 3

REV. ARTHUR PENRHYN STANLEY
1815–1881

10 They claim no thrones, they only ask to share
The common liberty of earth and air. *The Gipsies*

EDWARD STANLEY, EARL OF DERBY
1799–1869

11 When I first came into Parliament, Mr. Tierney, a
great Whig authority, used always to say that
the duty of an Opposition was very simple—it
was, to oppose everything, and propose nothing.
*House of Commons, 4 June 1841. Hansard, 3rd
Ser. lviii. 1188*

12 Don't you see that we have dished the Whigs?
With reference to the Reform Bill of 1867.
Monypenny and Buckle, *Life of Disraeli*, ii. 285

SIR HENRY MORTON STANLEY
1841–1904

13 Dr. Livingstone, I presume?
How I found Livingstone, ch. 11

FRANK LEBBY STANTON
1857–1927

14 Sweetest li'l feller, everybody knows;
Dunno what to call him, but he's mighty lak' a rose;
Lookin' at his mammy wid eyes so shiny blue
Mek' you think that Heav'n is comin' clost ter you.
Mighty Lak' a Rose

JOHN STARK
1728–1822

15 We beat them to-day or Molly Stark's a widow.
*Before Battle of Bennington, 16 Aug. 1777.
Appleton's Cyclopaedia of American Biography,
vol. v*

SIR RICHARD STEELE
1672–1729

16 I have often thought that a story-teller is born, as
well as a poet. *The Guardian, No. 24*

17 Gained universal applause by explaining a passage in
the game-act. *The Spectator, No. 2*

18 I have heard Will Honeycomb say, A Woman seldom
Writes her Mind but in her Postscript. *Ib. No. 79*

19 We were in some little time fixed in our seats, and
sat with that dislike which people not too good-
natured usually conceive of each other at first sight.
Ib. No. 132

20 The noblest motive is the public good.
Ib. No. 200. Motto in Ed. 1744

21 There are so few who can grow old with a good grace.
Ib. No. 263

22 Will Honeycomb calls these over-offended ladies the
outrageously virtuous. *Ib. No. 266*

23 Fashion, the arbiter, and rule of right.
Ib. No. 478. Motto in Ed. 1744

24 It is to be noted that when any part of this paper appears dull, there is a design in it.
The Tatler, No. 38

25 Though her mien carries much more invitation than
command, to behold her is an immediate check to
loose behaviour; to love her is a liberal education.
Ib. No. 49

26 Every man is the maker of his own fortune.
Ib. No. 52

27 The insupportable labour of doing nothing.
Ib. No. 54

28 Reading is to the mind what exercise is to the body.
Ib. No. 147

29 The truth of it is, the first rudiments of education
are given very indiscreetly by most parents.
Ib. No. 173

1 Let your precept be, Be easy. *The Tatler,* No. 196

2 The pink of courtesy. *Ib.* No. 204

3 These ladies of irresistible modesty are those who make virtue unamiable. *Ib.* No. 217

4 I fared like a distressed Prince who calls in a powerful Neighbour to his Aid; I was undone by my Auxiliary; when I had once called him in, I could not subsist without Dependance on him.
Ib. Preface to vol. iv (*1711*). On his co-editorship, with Addison, of *The Spectator*

GEORGE STEEVENS
1736–1800

5 And when the Pye was open'd
The birds began to sing,
And was not this a dainty dish
To set before the King!
*Recorded in Lamb's Letter to Miss Sarah James,
? April, 1829. A parody on 368:20*

JAMES KENNETH STEPHEN
1859–1892

6 Two voices are there: one is of the deep;
. . . .
And one is of an old half-witted sheep
Which bleats articulate monotony,
. . . .
And Wordsworth, both are thine.
Lapsus Calami. Sonnet

7 Good Lord! I'd rather be
Quite unacquainted with the A.B.C.
Than write such hopeless rubbish as thy worst. *Ib.*

8 When the Rudyards cease from kipling
And the Haggards ride no more. *Ib. To R. K.*

9 Ah! Matt.: old age has brought to me
Thy wisdom, less thy certainty:
The world's a jest, and joy's a trinket:
I knew that once: but now—I think it.
Ib. Senex to Matt. Prior

JAMES STEPHENS
1882–1950

10 I heard a bird at dawn
Singing sweetly on a tree,
That the dew was on the lawn,
And the wind was on the lea;
But I didn't listen to him,
For he didn't sing to me. *The Rivals,* st. 1

11 I was singing all the time,
Just as prettily as he. *Ib.* 3

12 I heard a sudden cry of pain!
There is a rabbit in a snare. *The Snare*

13 Little One! Oh, Little One!
I am searching everywhere! *Ib.*

ISABELLA S. STEPHENSON
1843–1890

14 Holy Father, in Thy mercy,
Hear our anxious prayer,
Keep our loved ones, now far absent,
'Neath Thy care.
Holy Father, in Thy Mercy. Hymns A. and M.,
Supplement to Revised Edition, 1889

15 When in sorrow, when in danger,
When in loneliness,
In Thy love look down and comfort
Their distress. *Holy Father, in Thy Mercy*

LAURENCE STERNE
1713–1768

16 They order, said I, this matter better in France.
A Sentimental Journey, l. 1

17 I had had an affair with the moon, in which there was neither sin nor shame. *Ib. The Monk. Calais*

18 The Sentimental Traveller (meaning thereby myself) who have travell'd, and of which I am now sitting down to give an account—as much out of necessity, and the *besoin de voyager,* as any one in the class.
Ib. Preface. In the Desobligeant

19 As an English man does not travel to see English men, I retired to my room. *Ib.*

20 I pity the man who can travel from Dan to Beersheba, and cry, 'tis all barren. *Ib. In the Street. Calais*

21 Having been in love with one princess or another, almost all my life, and I hope I shall go on so, till I die, being firmly persuaded, that if I ever do a mean action, it must be in some interval betwixt one passion and another. *Ib. Montriul*

22 Vive l'amour! et vive la bagatelle! *Ib. The letter*

23 Hail ye small sweet courtesies of life.
Ib. The Pulse. Paris

24 There are worse occupations in this world than feeling a woman's pulse. *Ib.*

25 'I can't get out,—I can't get out,' said the starling.
Ib. The Passport. The Hotel at Paris

26 He gave a deep sigh—I saw the iron enter into his soul! *Ib. The Captive. Paris*

27 I think there is a fatality in it—I seldom go to the place I set out for. *Ib. The Address. Versailles*

28 God tempers the wind, said Maria, to the shorn lamb.
Ib. Maria. From a French proverb, but familiar in Sterne's form of words

29 Dear sensibility! source inexhausted of all that's precious in our joys, or costly in our sorrows!
Ib. The Bourbonnois

30 If the supper was to my taste—the grace which followed it was much more so. *Ib. The Supper*

31 But the fille de chambre hearing there were words between us, and fearing that hostilities would ensue in due course, had crept silently out of her closet, and it being totally dark, had stolen so close to our beds, that she had got herself into the narrow passage which separated them, and had advanced so far up as to be in a line betwixt her mistress and me—
So that when I stretched out my hand, I caught hold of the fille de chambre's.
Ib. The Case of Delicacy

32 I live in a constant endeavour to fence against the infirmities of ill health, and other evils of life, by mirth; being firmly persuaded that every time a man smiles,—but much more so, when he laughs, that it adds something to this Fragment of Life.
Tristram Shandy. Dedication

1 'Pray, my dear,' quoth my mother, 'have you not forgot to wind up the clock?'—'Good G——!' cried my father, making an exclamation, but taking care to moderate his voice at the same time,—'Did ever woman, since the creation of the world, interrupt a man with such a silly question?'
Tristram Shandy, bk. i, ch. 1

2 As we jog on, either laugh with me, or at me, or in short do anything,—only keep your temper.
Ib. ch. 6

3 He was within a few hours of giving his enemies the slip for ever.
Ib. ch. 12

4 'Tis known by the name of perseverance in a good cause,—and of obstinacy in a bad one.
Ib. ch. 17

5 Persuasion hung upon his lips.
Ib. ch. 19

6 What is the character of a family to an hypothesis? my father would reply.
Ib. ch. 21

7 My uncle Toby would never offer to answer this by any other kind of argument, than that of whistling half a dozen bars of Lillabullero.
Ib.

8 Digressions, incontestably, are the sunshine;—they are the life, the soul of reading;—take them out of this book for instance,—you might as well take the book along with them.
Ib. ch. 22

9 I should have no objection to this method, but that I think it must smell too strong of the lamp.
Ib. ch. 23

10 'I'll not hurt thee,' says my uncle Toby, rising from his chair, and going across the room, with the fly in his hand,—'I'll not hurt a hair of thy head:— Go,' says he, lifting up the sash, and opening his hand as he spoke, to let it escape;—'go, poor devil, get thee gone, why should I hurt thee?—This world surely is wide enough to hold both thee and me.'
Ib. bk. ii, ch. 12

11 Whenever a man talks loudly against religion,— always suspect that it is not his reason, but his passions which have got the better of his creed.
Ib. ch. 17

12 'Sir,' replied Dr. Slop, 'it would astonish you to know what improvements we have made of late years in all branches of obstetrical knowledge, but particularly in that one single point of the safe and expeditious extraction of the foetus,—which has received such lights, that, for my part (holding up his hands) I declare I wonder how the world has——.'
'I wish,' quoth my uncle Toby, 'you had seen what prodigious armies we had in Flanders.' *Ib.* ch. 18

13 That's another story.
Ib.

14 'Our armies swore terribly in Flanders,' cried my uncle Toby,—'but nothing to this.' *Ib.* bk. iii, ch. 11

15 The corregiescity of Corregio. *Ib.* ch. 12. (*See* **126:10**)

16 Of all the cants which are canted in this canting world,—though the cant of hypocrites may be the worst,—the cant of criticism is the most tormenting!
Ib.

17 Is this a fit time, said my father to himself, to talk of Pensions and Grenadiers? *Ib.* bk. iv, ch. 5

18 The nonsense of the old women (of both sexes).
Ib. ch. 16

19 There is a North-west passage to the intellectual World.
Ib. ch. 42.

20 'The poor soul will die:—'
'He shall not die, by G——', cried my uncle Toby.— The Accusing Spirit, which flew up to heaven's chancery with the oath, blush'd as he gave it in;— and the Recording Angel, as he wrote it down, dropp'd a tear upon the word, and blotted it out for ever.
Tristram Shandy, bk. vi, ch. 8

21 An eye full of gentle salutations—and soft responses —...whispering soft—like the last low accents of an expiring saint. ... It did my uncle Toby's business.
Ib. bk. viii, ch. 25

22 'I am half distracted, Captain Shandy,' said Mrs. Wadman, ... 'a mote—or sand—or something—I know not what, has got into this eye of mine—do look into it.' ... In saying which, Mrs. Wadman edged herself close in beside my uncle Toby, ... 'Do look into it'—said she. ...
If thou lookest, uncle Toby, ... thou art undone.
Ib.

23 That eternal separation which we are shortly to make.
Ib. bk. ix, ch. 8

24 Said my mother, 'what is all this story about?'— 'A Cock and a Bull,' said Yorick.
Ib. ch. 33

25 This sad vicissitude of things.
Sermon xv

ROBERT LOUIS STEVENSON

1850–1894

26 The harmless art of knucklebones has seen the fall of the Roman empire and the rise of the United States.
Across the Plains. VII. *The Lantern-Bearers,*

27 All the while, deep down in the privacy of your fool's heart, to know you had a bull's-eye at your belt, and to exult and sing over the knowledge.
Ib.

28 The bright face of danger.
Ib. iv

29 Every one lives by selling something.
Ib. IX. *Beggars,* iii

30 Our frailties are invincible, our virtues barren; the battle goes sore against us to the going down of the sun.
Ib. XI. *Pulvis et Umbra*

31 Surely we should find it both touching and inspiriting, that in a field from which success is banished, our race should not cease to labour.
Ib. ii

32 Still obscurely fighting the lost fight of virtue, still clinging, in the brothel or on the scaffold, to some rag of honour, the poor jewel of their souls!
Ib.

33 To make our idea of morality centre on forbidden acts is to defile the imagination and to introduce into our judgments of our fellow-men a secret element of gusto.
Ib. XII. *A Christmas Sermon,* i

34 A mortified appetite is never a wise companion.
Ib.

35 To be honest, to be kind—to earn a little and to spend a little less, to make upon the whole a family happier for his presence, to renounce when that shall be necessary and not be embittered, to keep a few friends, but these without capitulation— above all, on the same grim condition, to keep friends with himself—here is a task for all that a man has of fortitude and delicacy.
Ib.

36 Here lies one who meant well, tried a little, failed much:—surely that may be his epitaph, of which he need not be ashamed.
Ib. iv

1 There goes another Faithful Failure!
Across the Plains. XII. *A Christmas Sermon*, iv

2 Lamplough was genteel, Eno was omnipresent; Lamplough was trite, Eno original and abominably vulgar. . . . Am I, then, to sink with Lamplough, or to soar with Eno?
The Dynamiter. The Superfluous Mansion

3 He who was prepared to help the escaping murderer or to embrace the impenitent thief, found, to the overthrow of all his logic, that he objected to the use of dynamite. *Ib.*

4 'Or Opulent Rotunda Strike the Sky,' said the shopman to himself, in the tone of one considering a verse. 'I suppose it would be too much to say "orotunda", and yet how noble it were! "Or Opulent Orotunda Strike the Sky." But that is the bitterness of arts; you see a good effect, and some nonsense about sense continually intervenes.'
Ib. Epilogue of the Cigar Divan

5 These are my politics: to change what we can; to better what we can; but still to bear in mind that man is but a devil weakly fettered by some generous beliefs and impositions; and for no word however sounding, and no cause however just and pious, to relax the stricture of these bonds. *Ib.*

6 Politics is perhaps the only profession for which no preparation is thought necessary.
Familiar Studies of Men and Books. 'Yoshida-Torajiro'

7 Am I no a bonny fighter? [*Alan Breck.*]
Kidnapped, ch. 10

8 I've a grand memory for forgetting, David. [*Alan Breck.*] *Ib.* ch. 18

9 I have thus played the sedulous ape to Hazlitt, to Lamb, to Wordsworth, to Sir Thomas Browne, to Defoe, to Hawthorne, to Montaigne, to Baudelaire and to Obermann.
Memories and Portraits, ch. 4

10 Each has his own tree of ancestors, but at the top of all sits Probably Arboreal. *Ib.* ch. 6, *Pastoral*

11 The devil, depend upon it, can sometimes do a very gentlemanly thing.
New Arabian Nights. The Suicide Club. Story of the Young Man with the Cream Tarts

12 Is there anything in life so disenchanting as attainment? *Ib. The Adventure of the Hansom Cab*

13 I regard you with an indifference closely bordering on aversion.
Ib. The Rajah's Diamond. Story of the Bandbox

14 For my part, I travel not to go anywhere, but to go. I travel for travel's sake. The great affair is to move.
Travels with a Donkey. Cheylard and Luc

15 I own I like definite form in what my eyes are to rest upon; and if landscapes were sold, like the sheets of characters of my boyhood, one penny plain and twopence coloured, I should go the length of twopence every day of my life. *Ib. Father Apollinaris*

16 A faddling hedonist. *Ib. The Boarders*

17 The true Babel is a divergence upon morals.
Ib. Florac

18 Fifteen men on the dead man's chest
Yo-ho-ho, and a bottle of rum!
Drink and the devil had done for the rest—
Yo-ho-ho, and a bottle of rum!
Treasure Island, ch. 1

19 Tip me the black spot. *Ib.* ch. 3

20 Pieces of eight! *Ib.* ch. 10

21 Many's the long night I've dreamed of cheese—toasted, mostly. [*Ben Gunn.*] *Ib.* ch. 15

22 In marriage, a man becomes slack and selfish, and undergoes a fatty degeneration of his moral being.
Virginibus Puerisque, I. i

23 Acidulous vestals. *Ib.*

24 They have never been in love, or in hate. *Ib.*

25 Even if we take matrimony at its lowest, even if we regard it as no more than a sort of friendship recognised by the police. *Ib.*

26 A little amateur painting in water-colour shows the innocent and quiet mind. *Ib.*

27 Lastly (and this is, perhaps, the golden rule), no woman should marry a teetotaller, or a man who does not smoke. *Ib.*

28 Marriage is a step so grave and decisive that it attracts light-headed, variable men by its very awfulness. *Ib.*

29 Marriage is like life in this—that it is a field of battle, and not a bed of roses. *Ib.*

30 Times are changed with him who marries; there are no more by-path meadows, where you may innocently linger, but the road lies long and straight and dusty to the grave. *Ib.* ii

31 To marry is to domesticate the Recording Angel. Once you are married, there is nothing left for you, not even suicide, but to be good. *Ib.*

32 Man is a creature who lives not upon bread alone, but principally by catchwords. *Ib.*

33 The cruellest lies are often told in silence.
Ib. iv. *Truth of Intercourse*

34 Old and young, we are all on our last cruise.
Ib. Crabbed Age and Youth

35 Youth is the time to go flashing from one end of the world to the other both in mind and body; to try the manners of different nations; to hear the chimes at midnight; to see sunrise in town and country; to be converted at a revival; to circumnavigate the metaphysics, write halting verses, run a mile to see a fire, and wait all day long in the theatre to applaud 'Hernani'. *Ib.*

36 The weak brother is the worst of mankind. *Ib.*

37 It is better to be a fool than to be dead. *Ib.*

38 To love playthings well as a child, to lead an adventurous and honourable youth, and to settle when the time arrives, into a green and smiling age, is to be a good artist in life and deserve well of yourself and your neighbour. *Ib.*

39 I still remember that Emphyteusis is not a disease, nor Stillicide a crime.
Ib. III. *An Apology for Idlers*

40 There is no duty we so much underrate as the duty of being happy. *Ib.*

1 He sows hurry and reaps indigestion.
Virginibus Puerisque, III. *An Apology for Idlers*

2 By the time a man gets well into the seventies his continued existence is a mere miracle.
Ib. v. *Æs Triplex*

3 Into what great waters, not to be crossed by any swimmer, God's pale Prætorian throws us over in the end! *Ib.*

4 Philosophy, in its more rigid sense, has been at the same work for ages; and . . . has the honour of laying before us . . . her contribution towards the subject: that life is a Permanent Possibility of Sensation. *Ib.*

5 Even if the doctor does not give you a year, even if he hesitates about a month, make one brave push and see what can be accomplished in a week. *Ib.*

6 To travel hopefully is a better thing than to arrive, and the true success is to labour.
Ib. VI. *El Dorado*

7 The great barons of the mind. *Ib.* x. *Walking Tours*

8 Though we are mighty fine fellows nowadays, we cannot write like Hazlitt. *Ib.*

9 You must not fancy I am sick, only over-driven and under the weather. *The Wrecker*, ch. 4

10 'HEBDOMADARY . . . well, you're a boss word', I said. 'Before you're very much older, I'll have you in type as long as yourself.' *Ib.* ch. 7

11 Nothing like a little judicious levity.
[*Michael Finsbury.*] *The Wrong Box*, ch. 7

12 'The "Athæneum", that was the name! Golly, what a paper!' ' "Athenæum", you mean,' said Morris.
Ib. ch. 15

13 I believe in an ultimate decency of things.
Letter, 23 August 1893

14 In winter I get up at night
And dress by yellow candle-light.
In summer, quite the other way,—
I have to go to bed by day.

I have to go to bed and see
The birds still hopping on the tree,
Or hear the grown-up people's feet
Still going past me in the street.

And does it not seem hard to you,
When all the sky is clear and blue,
And I should like so much to play,
To have to go to bed by day?
A Child's Garden of Verses. I. *Bed in Summer*

15 It is very nice to think
The world is full of meat and drink,
With little children saying grace
In every Christian kind of place. *Ib.* II. *A Thought*

16 A child should always say what's true,
And speak when he is spoken to,
And behave mannerly at table:
At least as far as he is able.
Ib. v. *Whole Duty of Children*

17 Fairy land,
Where all the children dine at five,
And all the playthings come alive.
Ib. VIII. *Foreign Lands*

18 When I am grown to man's estate
I shall be very proud and great,
And tell the other girls and boys
Not to meddle with my toys.
A Child's Garden of Verses, XII. *Looking Forward*

19 The pleasant land of counterpane.
Ib. XVI. *The Land of Counterpane*

20 The child that is not clean and neat,
With lots of toys and things to eat,
He is a naughty child, I'm sure—
Or else his dear papa is poor. *Ib.* XIX. *System*

21 The friendly cow, all red and white,
I love with all my heart:
She gives me cream with all her might,
To eat with apple-tart. *Ib.* XXIII. *The Cow*

22 The world is so full of a number of things,
I'm sure we should all be as happy as kings.
Ib. XXIV. *Happy Thought*

23 Children, you are very little,
And your bones are very brittle;
If you would grow great and stately,
You must try to walk sedately.
Ib. XXVII. *Good and Bad Children*

24 But the unkind and the unruly,
And the sort who eat unduly,
They must never hope for glory—
Theirs is quite a different story!

Cruel children, crying babies,
All grow up as geese and gabies,
Hated, as their age increases,
By their nephews and their nieces. *Ib.*

25 A birdie with a yellow bill
Hopped upon the window-sill,
Cocked his shining eye and said:
'Ain't you 'shamed, you sleepy-head?'
Ib. XXXIV. *Time to Rise*

26 Must we to bed indeed? Well then,
Let us arise and go like men,
And face with an undaunted tread
The long black passage up to bed.
Ib. XLI. *North-West Passage.* I. *Good-Night*

27 Give to me the life I love,
Let the lave go by me,
Give the jolly heaven above
And the byway nigh me.
Bed in the bush with stars to see,
Bread I dip in the river—
There's the life for a man like me,
There's the life for ever.
Songs of Travel. I. *The Vagabond*

28 Let the blow fall soon or late,
Let what will be o'er me;
Give the face of earth around
And the road before me.
Wealth I seek not, hope nor love,
Nor a friend to know me;
All I seek, the heaven above
And the road below me. *Ib.*

29 The untented Kosmos my abode,
I pass, a wilful stranger;
My mistress still the open road
And the bright eyes of danger.
Ib. II. *Youth and Love*

1 Here, lady, lo! that servant stands
   You picked from passing men,
And should you need nor heart nor hands
   He bows and goes again.
                 Songs of Travel. VII

2 I will make you brooches and toys for your delight
Of bird-song at morning and star-shine at night.
I will make a palace fit for you and me
Of green days in forests and blue days at sea.
I will make my kitchen, and you shall keep your room,
Where white flows the river and bright blows the broom,
And you shall wash your linen and keep your body white
In rainfall at morning and dewfall at night.   *Ib.* XI

3 Bright is the ring of words
   When the right man rings them,
Fair the fall of songs
   When the singer sings them.
Still they are carolled and said—
   On wings they are carried—
After the singer is dead
   And the maker buried.   *Ib.* XIV

4 Low as the singer lies
   In the field of heather,
Songs of his fashion bring
   The swains together.
And when the west is red
   With the sunset embers,
The lover lingers and sings
   And the maid remembers.   *Ib.*

5 In the highlands, in the country places,
Where the old plain men have rosy faces,
And the young fair maidens
   Quiet eyes.   *Ib.* XV

6 Trusty, dusky, vivid, true,
With eyes of gold and bramble-dew,
Steel-true and blade-straight,
The great artificer
Made my mate.   *Ib.* XXV. *My Wife*

7 Sing me a song of a lad that is gone,
   Say, could that lad be I?
Merry of soul he sailed on a day
   Over the sea to Skye.   *Ib.* XLII

8 Mull was a-stern, Rum on the port,
   Eigg on the starboard bow;
Glory of youth glowed in his soul,
   Where is that glory now?   *Ib.*

9 Blows the wind to-day, and the sun and the rain are flying,
Blows the wind on the moors to-day and now,
Where about the graves of the martyrs the whaups are crying,
   My heart remembers how!
          Ib. XLV. *To S. R. Crockett*

10 Be it granted to me to behold you again in dying,
   Hills of home! and to hear again the call;
Hear about the graves of the martyrs the peewees crying,
   And hear no more at all.   *Ib.*

11 Of all my verse, like not a single line;
But like my title, for it is not mine.
That title from a better man I stole;
Ah, how much better, had I stol'n the whole!
            Underwoods. Foreword

12 Go, little book, and wish to all
Flowers in the garden, meat in the hall,
A bin of wine, a spice of wit,
A house with lawns enclosing it,
A living river by the door,
A nightingale in the sycamore!
       Underwoods, bk. I. i. *Envoy*

13 The gauger walked with willing foot,
And aye the gauger played the flute;
And what should Master Gauger play
But 'Over the hills and far away'?
       Ib. ii. *A Song of the Road*

14 There's nothing under Heav'n so blue
That's fairly worth the travelling to.   *Ib.* iv

15 Under the wide and starry sky
   Dig the grave and let me lie.
Glad did I live and gladly die,
   And I laid me down with a will.
This be the verse you grave for me:
   'Here he lies where he longed to be;
Home is the sailor, home from sea,
   And the hunter home from the hill.'
         Ib. xxi. *Requiem*

16 If I have faltered more or less
In my great task of happiness;
If I have moved among my race
And shown no glorious morning face;
If beams from happy human eyes
Have moved me not; if morning skies,
Books, and my food, and summer rain
Knocked on my sullen heart in vain:—
Lord, thy most pointed pleasure take
And stab my spirit broad awake;
Or, Lord, if too obdurate I,
Choose thou, before that spirit die,
A piercing pain, a killing sin,
And to my dead heart run them in!
     Ib. xxii. *The Celestial Surgeon*

17 Unfrowning caryatides.
     Ib. xxiii. *Our Lady of the Snows*

18 I am a kind of farthing dip,
   Unfriendly to the nose and eyes;
A blue-behinded ape, I skip
   Upon the trees of Paradise.   *Ib.* xxx. *A Portrait*

19   In the afternoon of time
A strenuous family dusted from its hands
The sand of granite, and beholding far
Along the sounding coast its pyramids
And tall memorials catch the dying sun,
Smiled well content, and to this childish task
Around the fire addressed its evening hours.
  Ib. xxxviii. *Say not of me that weakly I declined*

20 A mile an' a bittock, a mile or twa,
Abüne the burn, ayont the law,
Davie an' Donal' an' Cherlie an' a',
An' the müne was shinin' clearly!
   Ib. bk. ii. iv. *A mile an' a bittock*, 1

WILLIAM STEVENSON
1530?–1575

21 I can not eat but little meat,
   My stomach is not good;
But sure I think, that I can drink
   With him that wears a hood.
Though I go bare, take ye no care,
   I am nothing acold:

I stuff my skin, so full within,
  Of jolly good ale and old,
Back and side go bare, go bare,
  Both foot and hand go cold:
But belly God send thee good ale enough,
  Whether it be new or old.
          Gammer Gurton's Needle, Act II, *Song*

SAMUEL JOHN STONE
1839–1901

1 The Church's one foundation
    Is Jesus Christ her Lord;
  She is His new creation
    By water and the Word.
          Lyra Fidelium (1866). *The Church's One Foundation*

2 Yet Saints their watch are keeping,
    Their cry goes up, 'How long?'
  And soon the night of weeping
    Shall be the morn of song.   *Ib.*

3 'Mid toil and tribulation,
    And tumult of her war,
  She waits the consummation
    Of peace for evermore;
  Till with the vision glorious
    Her longing eyes are blest,
  And the great Church victorious
    Shall be the Church at rest.   *Ib.*

4 Weary of earth and laden with my sin.
          Ib. Weary of Earth and Laden

HARRIET BEECHER STOWE
1811–1896

5 'Who was your mother?' 'Never had none!' said the
  child, with another grin. 'Never had any mother?
  What do you mean? Where were you born?'
  'Never was born!' persisted Topsy.
          Uncle Tom's Cabin, ch. 20

6 'Do you know who made you?' 'Nobody, as I knows
  on,' said the child, with a short laugh. . . . 'I 'spect
  I grow'd.'   *Ib.*

7 'Cause I's wicked—I is. I's mighty wicked, any
  how. I can't help it.   *Ib.*

BISHOP WILLIAM STUBBS
1825–1901

8 Froude informs the Scottish youth
  That parsons do not care for truth.
  The Reverend Canon Kingsley cries
  History is a pack of lies.
  What cause for judgments so malign?
  A brief reflection solves the mystery—
  Froude believes Kingsley a divine,
  And Kingsley goes to Froude for history.
          In Stubbs's Letter to J. R. Green, 17 Dec. 1871.
          Letters of Stubbs (1904), p. 162

GEOFFREY ANKETELL STUDDERT-KENNEDY
1883–1929

9 When in the darkest depths the miner striving,
  Feels in his arms the vigour of the Lord,
  Strikes for a Kingdom and his King's arriving,
  Holding his pick more splendid than the sword.
          Songs of Faith and Doubt (1922), p. 7. *Then Will*
          He Come: 'When Through the Whirl'

SIR JOHN SUCKLING
1609–1642

10 Why so pale and wan, fond lover?
     Prithee, why so pale?
   Will, when looking well can't move her,
     Looking ill prevail?
   Prithee, why so pale?   *Aglaura*, IV. i. *Song*

11 Quit, quit, for shame, this will not move:
     This cannot take her.
   If of herself she will not love,
     Nothing can make her:
     The devil take her!   *Ib.*

12 Her feet beneath her petticoat,
   Like little mice, stole in and out,
     As if they fear'd the light.
          Ballad. Upon a Wedding, viii

13 For streaks of red were mingled there,
   Such as are on a Catherine pear
     (The side that's next the sun).   *Ib.*

14 Her lips were red, and one was thin,
   Compar'd to that was next her chin
     (Some bee had stung it newly).   *Ib.* xi

15 The Prince of Darkness is a gentleman.
          The Goblins. Act III, *A Catch.* (*See* 453:25)

16 I prithee send me back my heart,
     Since I cannot have thine:
   For if from yours you will not part,
     Why then shouldst thou have mine?
          Song. I Prithee Send me Back

17 But love is such a mystery,
     I cannot find it out:
   For when I think I'm best resolv'd,
     I then am in most doubt.   *Ib.*

18 Out upon it, I have loved
     Three whole days together;
   And am like to love three more,
     If it prove fair weather.

   Time shall moult away his wings,
     Ere he shall discover
   In the whole wide world again
     Such a constant lover.   *A Poem with the Answer*

19 Had it any been but she,
     And that very face,
   There had been at least ere this
     A dozen dozen in her place.   *Ib.*

SUETONIUS
fl. c. A.D. 120

20 Ita feri ut se mori sentiat.
     Strike him so that he can feel that he is dying.
          Caligula, xxx

21 Festina lente. [Σπεῦδε βραδέως.]
     Hasten slowly.   *Divus Augustus*, 25

22 Ave, Imperator, morituri te salutant.
     Hail, Emperor, those about to die salute thee.
          Life of Claudius, 21

MAXIMILIAN DE BETHUNE, DUC DE SULLY
1559–1641

23 Les anglais s'amusent tristement selon l'usage de leur
   pays.
     The English take their pleasures sadly after the
     fashion of their country.   *Memoirs, c.* 1630

HENRY HOWARD, EARL OF SURREY
1517?–1547

1 My friend, the things that do attain
    The happy life be these, I find:
The riches left, not got with pain;
    The fruitful ground, the quiet mind;

The equal friend; no grudge, no strife;
    No charge of rule, nor governance;
Without disease the healthy life;
    The household of continuance.
Martial's Quiet Life, st. i, ii

2 The faithful wife, without debate;
    Such sleeps as may beguile the night:
Content thyself with thine estate;
    Neither wish death nor fear his might.   *Ib.* st. iv

3 The soote season, that bud and bloom forth brings.
Spring

ROBERT SMITH SURTEES
1803–1864

4 More people are flattered into virtue than bullied out
of vice.
The Analysis of the Hunting Field (1846), ch. 1

5 The only infallible rule we know is, that the man who
is always talking about being a gentleman never is
one.   *Ask Mamma* (1858), ch. 1

6 Major Yammerton was rather a peculiar man, inasmuch as he was an ass, without being a fool.
Ib. ch. 25

7 'Unting is all that's worth living for—all time is lost
wot is not spent in 'unting—it is like the hair we
breathe—if we have it not we die—it's the sport
of kings, the image of war without its guilt, and
only five-and-twenty per cent. of its danger.
Handley Cross (1843), ch. 7

8 'Unting fills my thoughts by day, and many a good
run I have in my sleep. Many a dig in the ribs I
gives Mrs. J. when I think they're running into
the warmint (renewed cheers). No man is fit to be
called a sportsman wot doesn't kick his wife out of
bed on a haverage once in three weeks! *Ib.* ch. 11

9 Tell me a man's a fox-hunter, and I loves him at
once.   *Ib.*

10 Come Hup! I say, you hugly beast!   *Ib.* ch. 13

11 He will bring his nightcap with him, for where the
M.F.H. dines he sleeps, and where the M.F.H.
sleeps he breakfasts.   *Ib.* ch. 15

12 I'll fill hup the chinks wi' cheese.   *Ib.*

13 Well did that great man, I think it was Sir Walter
Scott, but if it warn't, 'twas little Bartley, the boot-
maker, say, that there was no young man wot
would not rather have a himputation on his
morality than on his 'ossmanship.   *Ib.* ch. 16

14 It ar'n't that I loves the fox less, but that I loves the
'ound more.   *Ib.*

15 The 'oss loves the 'ound, and I loves both.   *Ib.*

16 Dinner lost! 'ounds lost, self lost—all lost together!
Ib. ch. 21

17 I can stand a wast of praise.   *Ib.* ch. 24

18 From the bonded warehouse of my knowledge.
Ib. ch. 27

19 Bishops' boots Mr. Radcliffe also condemned, and
spoke highly in favour of tops cleaned with champagne and abricot jam.   *Handley Cross*, ch. 27

20 Unless a man has a good many servants, he had
better have them cleanin' his 'oss than cleanin' his
breeches.   *Ib.*

21 Full o' beans and benevolence!   *Ib.*

22 Paid for catching my 'oss, 6*d.*   *Ib.* ch. 29

23 Letting in the Latchfords.   *Ib.* ch. 31

24 Con-found all presents wot eat!   *Ib.* ch. 37

25 Hellish dark, and smells of cheese!   *Ib.* ch. 50

26 I feels all over tremmulation and fear, like a maid that
thinks she's not a-goin' to be married. *Ib.* ch. 52

27 'Hurrah! blister my kidneys!' exclaimed he in delight, 'it is a frost!—the dahlias are dead!'
Ib. ch. 59

28 Howsomever, never mind—the country has its
charms—cheapness for one.
Hillingdon Hall (1845), ch. 5

29 Three things I never lends—my 'oss, my wife, and
my name.   *Ib.* ch. 33

30 Every man shouting in proportion to the amount of
his subscription.
Jorrocks's Jaunts and Jollities (1838). No. 1. *Swell
and the Surrey*

31 Jorrocks, who is not afraid of 'the pace' so long as
there is no leaping.   *Ib.*

32 And a nod or a wink for every pretty maid that
showed at the windows; for . . . , as he says, 'there
is no harm in looking'.
Ib. No. 4. *Surrey Stag-Hounds*

33 Champagne certainly gives one werry gentlemanly
ideas, but for a continuance, I don't know but I
should prefer mild hale.
Ib. No. 9. *Mr. Jorrocks in Paris*

34 No one knows how ungentlemanly he can look, until
he has seen himself in a shocking bad hat.
Mr. Facey Romford's Hounds (1865), ch. 9

35 Bob Short, who had replied to Facey's advertisement
for a 'strong persevering man, to clean horses'.
Ib. ch. 19

36 Better be killed than frightened to death. *Ib.* ch. 32

37 Thinking that life would be very pleasant if it were
not for its enjoyments.   *Ib.*

38 These sort of boobies think that people come to balls
to do nothing but dance; whereas everyone knows
that the real business of a ball is either to look out
for a wife, to look after a wife, or to look after
somebody else's wife.   *Ib.* ch. 56

39 The young ladies entered the drawing-room in the
full fervour of sisterly animosity.
Mr. Sponge's Sporting Tour (1853), ch. 17

40 Women never look so well as when one comes in wet
and dirty from hunting.   *Ib.* ch. 21

41 He was a gentleman who was generally spoken of as
having nothing a-year, paid quarterly. *Ib.* ch. 24

42 There is no secret so close as that between a rider
and his horse.   *Ib.* ch. 31

43 He had a tremendous determination of words to the
mouth.   *Ib.* ch. 34

1 When at length they rose to go to bed, it struck each man as he followed his neighbour upstairs that the one before him walked very crookedly.
Mr. Sponge's Sporting Tour (1853), ch. 35

CHARLES SWAIN

1801–1874

2 Time to me this truth has taught
('Tis a treasure worth revealing),
More offend from want of thought,
Than from any want of feeling.   *Want of Thought*

JONATHAN SWIFT

1667–1745

3 I conceive some scattered notions about a superior power to be of singular use for the common people, as furnishing excellent materials to keep children quiet when they grow peevish, and providing topics of amusement in a tedious winter-night.
An Argument Against Abolishing Christianity

4 Satire is a sort of glass, wherein beholders do generally discover everybody's face but their own.
The Battle of the Books, preface

5 Instead of dirt and poison we have rather chosen to fill our hives with honey and wax; thus furnishing mankind with the two noblest of things, which are sweetness and light.   *Ib.*

6 I have heard of a man who had a mind to sell his house, and therefore carried a piece of brick in his pocket, which he shewed as a pattern to encourage purchasers.
The Drapier's Letters, No. 2 (4 Aug. 1724)

7 Laws are like cobwebs, which may catch small flies, but let wasps and hornets break through.
A Tritical Essay upon the Faculties of the Mind

8 There is nothing in this world constant, but inconstancy.   *Ib.*

9 He [the emperor] is taller by almost the breadth of my nail than any of his court, which alone is enough to strike an awe into the beholders.
Gulliver's Travels. Voyage to Lilliput, ch. 2

10 The colonel and his officers were in much pain, especially when they saw me take out my penknife.
Ib.

11 He put this engine [a watch] to our ears, which made an incessant noise like that of a water-mill; and we conjecture it is either some unknown animal, or the god that he worships; but we are more inclined to the latter opinion.   *Ib.*

12 Flimnap, the Treasurer, is allowed to cut a caper on the straight rope, at least an inch higher than any other lord in the whole empire. I have seen him do the summerset several times together. *Ib.* ch. 3

13 It is alleged indeed, that the high heels are most agreeable to our ancient constitution: but however this be, his Majesty hath determined to make use of only low heels in the administration of the government.   *Ib.* ch. 4

14 He could not forbear taking me up in his right hand, and stroking me gently with the other, after an hearty fit of laughing, asked me whether I were a Whig or a Tory. *Ib. Voyage to Brobdingnag*, ch. 3

15 I cannot but conclude the bulk of your natives to be the most pernicious race of little odious vermin that nature ever suffered to crawl upon the surface of the earth.
Gulliver's Travels. Voyage to Brobdingnag, ch. 6

16 He was amazed how so impotent and grovelling an insect as I (these were his expressions) could entertain such inhuman ideas.   *Ib.* ch. 7

17 And he gave it for his opinion, that whoever could make two ears of corn or two blades of grass to grow upon a spot of ground where only one grew before, would deserve better of mankind, and do more essential service to his country than the whole race of politicians put together.   *Ib.*

18 He had been eight years upon a project for extracting sun-beams out of cucumbers, which were to be put into vials hermetically sealed, and let out to warm the air in raw inclement summers.
Ib. Voyage to Laputa, etc., ch. 5

19 I said the thing which was not.
Ib. A Voyage to the Houyhnhnms, ch. 3

20 I told him . . . that we ate when we were not hungry, and drank without the provocation of thirst.
Ib. ch. 6

21 Plaguy twelvepenny weather.
Journal to Stella, 26 Oct. 1710

22 'Tis very warm weather when one's in bed.
Ib. 8 Nov. 1710

23 With my own fair hands.   *Ib. 4 Jan. 1711*

24 We are so fond of one another, because our ailments are the same.   *Ib. 1 Feb. 1711*

25 Will she pass in a crowd? Will she make a figure in a country church?   *Ib. 9 Feb. 1711*

26 I love good creditable acquaintance; I love to be the worst of the company.   *Ib. 17 May 1711*

27 He was a fiddler, and consequently a rogue.
Ib. 25 July 1711

28 He showed me his bill of fare to tempt me to dine with him; poh, said I, I value not your bill of fare, give me your bill of company.   *Ib. 2 Sept. 1711*

29 We were to do more business after dinner; but after dinner is after dinner—an old saying and a true, 'much drinking, little thinking'. *Ib. 26 Feb. 1712*

30 Monday is parson's holiday.   *Ib. 3 Mar. 1712*

31 Not die here in a rage, like a poisoned rat in a hole.
Letter to Bolingbroke, 21 Mar. 1729

32 I have ever hated all nations, professions and communities, and all my love is towards individuals. . . . But principally I hate and detest that animal called man; although I heartily love John, Peter, Thomas, and so forth.   *Letter to Pope, 29 Sept. 1725*

33 If Heaven had looked upon riches to be a valuable thing, it would not have given them to such a scoundrel.
Letter to Miss Vanhomrigh, 12–13 Aug. 1720

34 You have but a very few years to be young and handsome in the eyes of the world; and as few months to be so in the eyes of a husband, who is not a fool.
Letter to a Young Lady on her Marriage (1723)

35 What they call 'running a man down'.   *Ib.*

1 **Proper words in proper places, make the true definition of a style.**
Letter to a Young Clergyman, 9 Jan. 1720

2 Surely man is a broomstick!
A Meditation upon a Broomstick

3 I have been assured by a very knowing American of
my acquaintance in London, that a young healthy
child well nursed is at a year old a most delicious,
nourishing, and wholesome food, whether stewed,
roasted, baked, or boiled, and I make no doubt
that it will equally serve in a fricassee, or a ragout.
*A Modest Proposal for Preventing the Children
of Ireland from being a Burden to their Parents
or Country*

4 Promises and pie-crust are made to be broken.
Polite Conversation. Dialogue 1

5 Bachelor's fare; bread and cheese, and kisses. *Ib.*

6 Like an owl in an ivy-bush. *Ib.*

7 I mean, you lie—under a mistake. *Ib.*

8 Why every one as they like; as the good woman said
when she kissed her cow. *Ib.*

9 Why, madam, Queen Elizabeth's dead. *Ib.*

10 The sight of you is good for sore eyes. *Ib.*

11 'Tis as cheap sitting as standing. *Ib.*

12 Prythee, Tom, sit a little farther: I believe your
father was no glazier. *Ib.*

13 You were half seas over. *Ib.*

14 I won't quarrel with my bread and butter. *Ib.*

15 I swear, she's no chicken; she's on the wrong side of
thirty, if she be a day. *Ib.*

16 If it had been a bear, it would have bit you. *Ib.*

17 She wears her clothes, as if they were thrown on her
with a pitchfork. *Ib.*

18 Faith, that's as well said, as if I had said it myself.
Ib. Dialogue 2

19 You must take the will for the deed. *Ib.*

20 She has more goodness in her little finger, than he has
in his whole body. *Ib.*

21 Lord, I wonder what fool it was that first invented
kissing! *Ib.*

22 I'll give you leave to call me anything, if you don't call
me spade. *Ib.*

23 The best doctors in the world are Doctor Diet,
Doctor Quiet, and Doctor Merryman. *Ib.*

24 I always love to begin a journey on Sundays, because
I shall have the prayers of the church, to preserve
all that travel by land, or by water. *Ib.*

25 I know Sir John will go, though he was sure it would
rain cats and dogs. *Ib.*

26 'Tis happy for him, that his father was before him.
Ib. Dialogue 3

27 There's none so blind as they that won't see. *Ib.*

28 She watches him, as a cat would watch a mouse. *Ib.*

29 She pays him in his own coin. *Ib.*

30 All the world and his wife. *Ib.*

31 Damn your cards, said he, they are the devil's books.
Ib.

32 There's two words to that bargain.
Polite Conversation. Dialogue 3

33 It is a maxim, that those to whom everybody allows
the second place, have an undoubted title to the
first. *A Tale of a Tub.* Dedication

34 Books, like men their authors, have no more than one
way of coming into the world, but there are ten
thousand to go out of it, and return no more. *Ib.*

35 Satire, being levelled at all, is never resented for an
offence by any. *Ib.* Preface

36 What though his head be empty, provided his
commonplace book be full.
Ib. Digression in Praise of Digression

37 I never saw, heard, nor read, that the clergy were beloved in any nation where Christianity was the
religion of the country. Nothing can render them
popular but some degree of persecution.
Thoughts on Religion

38 We have just enough religion to make us hate, but
not enough to make us love one another.
Thoughts on Various Subjects

39 What they do in heaven we are ignorant of; what
they do *not* we are told expressly, that they neither
marry, nor are given in marriage. *Ib.*

40 The reasons why so few marriages are happy, is,
because young ladies spend their time in making
nets, not in making cages. *Ib.*

41 Few are qualified to shine in company; but it is in
most men's power to be agreeable. *Ib.*

42 Every man desires to live long; but no man would
be old. *Ib.*

43 A nice man is a man of nasty ideas. *Ib.*

44 Old men and comets have been reverenced for the
same reason; their long beards, and pretences to
foretell events. *Ib.*

45 I never wonder to see men wicked, but I often
wonder to see them not ashamed. *Ib.*

46 A man should never be ashamed to own he has been
in the wrong, which is but saying, in other words,
that he is wiser to-day than he was yesterday. *Ib.*

47 Party is the madness of many, for the gain of a few.
Ib.

48 When men grow virtuous in their old age, they only
make a sacrifice to God of the devil's leavings.
Ib. (See 387:1)

49 The most positive men are the most credulous. *Ib.*

50 [Of *The Tale of a Tub.*]
Good God! what a genius I had when I wrote that book.
Sir Walter Scott's *Life of Swift. Works of Swift*
(1824), vol. i, p. 89

51 I shall be like that tree, I shall die at the top.
Sir Walter Scott, *Memoirs of Swift*

52 Only a woman's hair. *Ib.* ch. 5

53 How haughtily he cocks his nose,
To tell what every schoolboy knows.
The Country Life, l. 81

54 Lose no time to contradict her,
Nor endeavour to convict her. *Daphne,* l. 29

55 Only take this rule along,
Always to advise her wrong;
And reprove her when she's right;
She may then grow wise for spite. *Ib.* l. 35

1 In all distresses of our friends,
  We first consult our private ends;
  While nature, kindly bent to ease us,
  Points out some circumstance to please us.
  On the Death of Dr. Swift, l. 7

2 Poor Pope will grieve a month, and Gay
  A week, and Arbuthnot a day.
  St. John himself will scarce forbear
  To bite his pen, and drop a tear.
  The rest will give a shrug, and cry,
  'I'm sorry—but we all must die!'
  Ib. l. 207

3 Yet malice never was his aim;
  He lash'd the vice, but spared the name;
  No individual could resent,
  Where thousands equally were meant.
  Ib. l. 512

4 He gave the little wealth he had
  To build a house for fools and mad;
  And show'd, by one satiric touch,
  No nation wanted it so much.
  Ib. l. 538

5 A coming shower your shooting corns presage.
  Description of a City Shower, l. 9

6 They never would hear,
  But turn the deaf ear,
  As a matter they had no concern in.
  Dingley and Brent, ii

7 I often wish'd that I had clear,
  For life, six hundred pounds a-year,
  A handsome house to lodge a friend,
  A river at my garden's end,
  A terrace walk, and half a rood
  Of land, set out to plant a wood.
  Imitation of Horace, bk. **11**, sat. vi, l. 1

8 Removed from kind Arbuthnot's aid,
  Who knows his art, but not the trade.
  Preferring his regard for me
  Before his credit, or his fee.
  In Sickness, l. 9

9 Convey a libel in a frown,
  And wink a reputation down.
  Journal of a Modern Lady, l. 192

10 'Libertas et natale solum':
  Fine words! I wonder where you stole 'em.
  *Lines written in 1724 on Chief Justice Whitshed's
  motto on his coach, after the trial of Drapier*

11 Hail, fellow, well met,
  All dirty and wet:
  Find out, if you can,
  Who's master, who's man.
  My Lady's Lamentation, l. 171

12 Th' artillery of words   *Ode to Sancroft*, i

13 Philosophy, the lumber of the schools.
  Ode to Sir W. Temple, ii

14 Walls have tongues, and hedges ears.
  Pastoral Dialogue, l. 8

15 Say, Britain, could you ever boast,—
  Three poets in an age at most?
  Our chilling climate hardly bears
  A sprig of bays in fifty years.   *On Poetry*, l. 5

16 Then, rising with Aurora's light,
  The Muse invoked, sit down to write;
  Blot out, correct, insert, refine,
  Enlarge, diminish, interline.
  Ib. l. 85

17 As learned commentators view
  In Homer more than Homer knew.   *Ib.* l. 103

18 So geographers, in Afric-maps,
  With savage-pictures fill their gaps;
  And o'er unhabitable downs
  Place elephants for want of towns.   *On Poetry*, l. 177

19 Read all the prefaces of Dryden,
  For these our critics much confide in,
  ('Tho' merely writ at first for filling
  To raise the volume's price, a shilling.)   *Ib.* l. 251

20 He gives directions to the town,
  To cry it up, or run it down.   *Ib.* l. 269

21 Hobbes clearly proves, that every creature
  Lives in a state of war by nature.   *Ib.* l. 319

22 So, naturalists observe, a flea
  Hath smaller fleas that on him prey;
  And these have smaller fleas to bite 'em,
  And so proceed *ad infinitum.*
  Thus every poet, in his kind,
  Is bit by him that comes behind.   *Ib.* l. 337

23 To guide his steps afford your kindest aid,
  And gently pity whom ye can't persuade;
  Leave to avenging Heaven his stubborn will,
  For, O, remember, he's your brother still.
  Swan Tripe Club in Dublin, l. 489

24 Humour is odd, grotesque, and wild,
  Only by affectation spoil'd;
  'Tis never by invention got,
  Men have it when they know it not.
  To Mr. Delany, 10 Oct. 1718, l. 25

25 Hated by fools, and fools to hate,
  Be that my motto and my fate.   *Ib.* l. 171

26 A beggarly people!
  A church and no steeple! [Of St. Ann's Church,
  Dublin]
  Attrib. to Swift by Malone. See Prior's *Life of
  Malone* (1860), p. 381

27 Ubi saeva indignatio ulterius cor lacerare nequit.
  Where fierce indignation can no longer tear his
  heart.   *Swift's Epitaph*

ALGERNON CHARLES SWINBURNE
1837–1909

28 Superflux of pain.   *Anactoria*, l. 27

29 Maiden, and mistress of the months and stars
  Now folded in the flowerless fields of heaven.
  Atalanta in Calydon. Collected Poetical Works
  (1924), vol. ii, p. 247, l. 1

30 When the hounds of spring are on winter's traces,
  The mother of months in meadow or plain
  Fills the shadows and windy places
  With lisp of leaves and ripple of rain;
  And the brown bright nightingale amorous
  Is half assuaged for Itylus,
  For the Thracian ships and the foreign faces,
  The tongueless vigil and all the pain.

  Come with bows bent and with emptying of quivers,
  Maiden most perfect, lady of light,
  With a noise of winds and many rivers,
  With a clamour of waters, and with might;
  Bind on thy sandals, O thou most fleet,
  Over the splendour and speed of thy feet;
  For the faint east quickens, the wan west shivers,
  Round the feet of the day and the feet of the night.

Where shall we find her, how shall we sing to her,
Fold our hands round her knees, and cling?
O that man's heart were as fire and could spring to her,
Fire, or the strength of the streams that spring!
For the stars and the winds are unto her
As raiment, as songs of the harp-player;
For the risen stars and the fallen cling to her,
And the southwest-wind and west-wind sing.

For winter's rains and ruins are over,
And all the season of snows and sins;
The days dividing lover and lover,
The light that loses, the night that wins;
And time remembered is grief forgotten,
And frosts are slain and flowers begotten,
And in green underwood and cover
Blossom by blossom the spring begins.
Atalanta in Calydon, Chorus, p. 249

1 And the hoofed heel of a satyr crushes
The chestnut-husk at the chestnut-root. *Ib.* p. 250

2 And Pan by noon and Bacchus by night,
Fleeter of foot than the fleet-foot kid,
Follows with dancing and fills with delight
The Maenad and the Bassarid;
And soft as lips that laugh and hide
The laughing leaves of the tree divide,
And screen from seeing and leave in sight
The god pursuing, the maiden hid. *Ib.*

3 The ivy falls with the Bacchanal's hair
Over her eyebrows hiding her eyes;
The wild vine slipping down leaves bare
Her bright breast shortening into sighs. *Ib.*

4 The wolf that follows, the fawn that flies. *Ib.*

5 Before the beginning of years
There came to the making of man
Time with a gift of tears,
Grief with a glass that ran.
Pleasure with pain for leaven,
Summer with flowers that fell,
Remembrance fallen from heaven,
And Madness risen from hell,
Strength without hands to smite,
Love that endures for a breath;
Night, the shadow of light,
And Life, the shadow of death. *Ib.* p. 258

6 For a day and a night and a morrow,
That his strength might endure for a span
With travail and heavy sorrow,
The holy spirit of man. *Ib.* p. 259

7 Eyesight and speech they wrought
For the veil of the soul therein,
A time for labour and thought,
A time to serve and to sin;
They gave him light in his ways,
And love, and a space for delight,
And beauty and length of days,
And night, and sleep in the night.
His speech is a burning fire;
With his lips he travaileth;
In his heart is a blind desire,
In his eyes foreknowledge of death;
He weaves, and is clothed with derision;
Sows, and he shall not reap;
His life is a watch or a vision
Between a sleep and a sleep. *Ib.*

8 We have seen thee, O love, thou art fair; thou art goodly, O Love.
Atalanta in Calydon, Chorus, p. 273

9 For words divide and rend;
But silence is most noble till the end. *Ib.* p. 299

10 Where the narrowing Symplegades whitened the straits of Propontis with spray. *Ib.* p. 327

11 Shall I strew on thee rose or rue or laurel,
Brother, on this that was the veil of thee?
Or quiet sea-flower moulded by the sea,
Or simplest growth of meadow-sweet or sorrel?
Ave atque Vale, i

12 Now all strange hours and all strange loves are over,
Dreams and desires and sombre songs and sweet,
Hast thou found place at the great knees and feet
Of some pale Titan-woman like a lover,
Such as thy vision here solicited,
Under the shadow of her fair vast head,
The deep division of prodigious breasts,
The solemn slope of mighty limbs asleep? *Ib.* vi

13 Sleep; and if life was bitter to thee, pardon,
If sweet, give thanks; thou hast no more to live;
And to give thanks is good, and to forgive.
Ib. xvii

14 For thee, O now a silent soul, my brother,
Take at my hands this garland and farewell.
Thin is the leaf, and chill the wintry smell,
And chill the solemn earth, a fatal mother,
With sadder than the Niobean womb
And in the hollow of her breasts a tomb. *Ib.* xviii

15 There lies not any troublous thing before,
Nor sight nor sound to war against thee more,
For whom all winds are quiet as the sun,
All waters as the shore. *Ib.*

16 This is the end of every man's desire.
A Ballad of Burdens

17 Poor splendid wings so frayed and soiled and torn!
Poor kind wild eyes so dashed with light quick tears!
Ballad of François Villon

18 Villon, our sad bad glad mad brother's name. *Ib.*

19 Strung with subtle-coloured hair
Of some dead lute-player. *A Ballad of Life*

20 O slain and spent and sacrificed
People, the grey-grown speechless Christ.
Before a Crucifix. Poetical Works (1924), vol. i, p. 744

21 No soul that lived, loved, wrought and died,
Is this their carrion crucified. *Ib.* p. 747

22 We shift and bedeck and bedrape us,
Thou art noble and nude and antique. *Dolores*, vii

23 Change in a trice
The lilies and languors of virtue
For the raptures and roses of vice. *Ib.* ix

24 O splendid and sterile Dolores,
Our Lady of Pain. *Ib.*

25 Ah beautiful passionate body
That never has ached with a heart! *Ib.* xi

26 But sweet as the rind was the core is;
We are fain of thee still, we are fain,
O sanguine and subtle Dolores,
Our Lady of Pain. *Ib.* xiii

27 The delight that consumes the desire,
The desire that outruns the delight. *Ib.* xiv

1 For the crown of our life as it closes
   Is darkness, the fruit thereof dust;
No thorns go as deep as a rose's,
   And love is more cruel than lust.
Time turns the old days to derision,
   Our loves into corpses or wives;
And marriage and death and division
   Make barren our lives.   *Dolores*, xx

2 Ringed round with a flame of fair faces,
   And splendid with swords.   *Ib.* xxx

3 What ailed us, O gods, to desert you
   For creeds that refuse and restrain?
Come down and redeem us from virtue,
   Our Lady of Pain.   *Ib.* xxxv

4 On thy bosom though many a kiss be,
   There are none such as knew it of old.
Was it Alciphron once or Arisbe,
   Male ringlets or feminine gold,
That thy lips met with under the statue,
   Whence a look shot out sharp after thieves
From the eyes of the garden-god at you
   Across the fig-leaves?   *Ib.* xxxviii

5 Old poets outsing and outlove us,
   And Catullus makes mouths at our speech. *Ib.* xliii

6 Where are they, Cotytto or Venus,
   Astarte or Ashtaroth, where?
Do their hands as we touch come between us?
   Is the breath of them hot in thy hair?
From their lips have thy lips taken fever,
   With the blood of their bodies grown red?
Hast thou left upon earth a believer
   If these men are dead?   *Ib.* lii

7 O daughter of Death and Priapus,
   Our Lady of Pain.   *Ib.* liii

8 I shall remember while the light lives yet
And in the night time I shall not forget.   *Erotion*

9 There was a poor poet named Clough,
Whom his friends all united to puff,
   But the public, though dull,
   Had not such a skull
As belonged to believers in Clough.
Essays and Studies (1875), *Matthew Arnold*
(printed as prose)

10 Bright with names that men remember, loud with
   names that men forget.   *Eton: An Ode*

11 What adders came to shed their coats?
   What coiled obscene
Small serpents with soft stretching throats
   Caressed Faustine?   *Faustine*

12 Those eyes the greenest of things blue,
   The bluest of things grey.   *Félise*

13 In a coign of the cliff between lowland and highland,
At the sea-down's edge between windward and lee,
Walled round with rocks as an inland island,
   The ghost of a garden fronts the sea.
      A Forsaken Garden

14 The fields fall southward, abrupt and broken,
   To the low last edge of the long lone land.
If a step should sound or a word be spoken,
   Would a ghost not rise at the strange guest's hand?
So long have the grey bare walls lain guestless,
Through branches and briars if a man make way,
He shall find no life but the sea-wind's, restless
      Night and day.   *Ib.*

15 Heart handfast in heart as they stood, 'Look thither,'
   Did he whisper? 'look forth from the flowers to the
      sea;
For the foam-flowers endure when the rose-blossoms
      wither
   And men that love lightly may die—but we?'
And the same wind sang and the same waves
      whitened,
And or ever the garden's last petals were shed,
In the lips that had whispered, the eyes that had
      lightened,
      Love was dead.   *A Forsaken Garden*

16 Stretched out on the spoils that his own hand spread.
As a god self-slain on his own strange altar,
      Death lies dead.   *Ib.*

17 Here, where the world is quiet;
   Here, where all trouble seems
Dead winds' and spent waves' riot
   In doubtful dreams of dreams.
      The Garden of Proserpine

18 I am tired of tears and laughter,
   And men that laugh and weep;
Of what may come hereafter
   For men that sow and reap:
I am weary of days and hours,
   Blown buds of barren flowers,
Desires and dreams and powers
   And everything but sleep.   *Ib.*

19 Here life has death for neighbour,
   And far from eye or ear
Wan waves and wet winds labour,
   Weak ships and spirits steer.   *Ib.*

20 Pale, beyond porch and portal,
   Crowned with calm leaves, she stands
Who gathers all things mortal
   With cold immortal hands.   *Ib.*

21 Dead dreams of days forsaken,
   Blind buds that snows have shaken,
Wild leaves that winds have taken,
   Red strays of ruined springs.   *Ib.*

22 We are not sure of sorrow,
   And joy was never sure.   *Ib.*

23 From too much love of living,
   From hope and fear set free,
We thank with brief thanksgiving
   Whatever gods may be
That no man lives forever,
That dead men rise up never;
That even the weariest river
   Winds somewhere safe to sea.   *Ib.*

24 Then star nor sun shall waken,
   Nor any change of light:
Nor sound of waters shaken,
   Nor any sound or sight:
Nor wintry leaves nor vernal,
Nor days nor things diurnal;
Only the sleep eternal
   In an eternal night.   *Ib.*

25 Calling a crowned man royal
That was no more than a king. *The Halt before Rome*

26 Fiddle, we know, is diddle: and diddle, we take it,
   is dee.
   *The Heptalogia. The Higher Pantheism in a Nut-
   shell*

1 I am that which began;
　Out of me the years roll;
　Out of me God and man;
　I am equal and whole;
God changes, and man, and the form of them bodily;
　I am the soul. *Hertha*

2 But what thing dost thou now,
　Looking Godward, to cry
　'I am I, thou art thou,
　I am low, thou art high'?
I am thou, whom thou seekest to find him; find thou
　but thyself, thou art I. *Ib.*

3 A creed is a rod,
　And a crown is of night;
　But this thing is God.
　To be man with thy might,
To grow straight in the strength of thy spirit, and live
　out thy life as the light. *Ib.*

4 Green leaves of thy labour, white flowers of thy
　thought, and red fruit of thy death. *Ib.*

5 Man, equal and one with me, man that is made of me,
　man that is I. *Ib.*

6 Hope thou not much, and fear thou not at all.
　Hope and Fear

7 In the fair days when God
　By man as godlike trod,
And each alike was Greek, alike was free.
　To Victor Hugo

8 And a bird overhead sang *Follow*,
　And a bird to the right sang *Here*;
And the arch of the leaves was hollow,
　And the meaning of May was clear. *An Interlude*

9 I remember the way we parted,
　The day and the way we met;
You hoped we were both broken-hearted,
　And knew we should both forget. *Ib.*

10 And the best and the worst of this is
　That neither is most to blame,
If you have forgotten my kisses
　And I have forgotten your name. *Ib.*

11 Swallow, my sister, O sister swallow,
　How can thine heart be full of the spring?
A thousand summers are over and dead.
　What hast thou found in the spring to follow?
What hast thou found in thine heart to sing?
　What wilt thou do when the summer is shed?
　Itylus

12 Hast thou forgotten ere I forget? *Ib.*

13 Sister, my sister, O fleet sweet swallow,
　Thy way is long to the sun and the south;
But I, fulfilled of my heart's desire,
　Shedding my song upon height, upon hollow,
From tawny body and sweet small mouth
　Feed the heart of the night with fire.

I the nightingale all spring through,
　O swallow, sister, O changing swallow,
All spring through till the spring be done,
　Clothed with the light of the night on the dew,
Sing, while the hours and the wild birds follow,
　Take flight and follow and find the sun. *Ib.*

14 Till life forget and death remember,
　Till thou remember and I forget. *Ib.*

15 Thy lord the summer is good to follow,
　And fair the feet of thy lover the spring:
But what wilt thou say to the spring thy lover?
　Itylus

16 But mine goes forth among sea-gulfs hollow
　To the place of the slaying of Itylus,
The feast of Daulis, the Thracian sea. *Ib.*

17 The small slain body, the flower-like face,
　Can I remember if thou forget? *Ib.*

18 Thou hast forgotten, O summer swallow,
　But the world shall end when I forget. *Ib.*

19 Apples of gold for the king's daughter.
　The King's Daughter

20 I came as one whose thoughts half linger,
　Half run before;
The youngest to the oldest singer
　That England bore.
　In Memory of Walter Savage Landor

21 O father of all of us, Paian, Apollo,
　Destroyer and healer, hear! *The Last Oracle*

22 God by God goes out, discrowned and disanointed,
　But the soul stands fast that gave them shape and
　speech. *Ib.*

23 Ah, yet would God this flesh of mine might be
Where air might wash and long leaves cover me;
Where tides of grass break into foam of flowers,
Or where the wind's feet shine along the sea.
　Laus Veneris

24 Until God loosen over sea and land
The thunder of the trumpets of the night. *Ib.*

25 Let us go hence, my songs; she will not hear.
Let us go hence together without fear.
　A Leave-taking

26 But God, if a God there be, is the substance of men
　which is man. *Hymn of Man*

27 Glory to Man in the highest! for Man is the master
　of things. *Ib.*

28 If love were what the rose is,
　And I were like the leaf,
Our lives would grow together
　In sad or singing weather,
Blown fields or flowerful closes,
　Green pleasure or grey grief. *A Match*

29 If you were thrall to sorrow,
　And I were page to joy. *Ib.*

30 If you were April's lady,
　And I were lord in May. *Ib.*

31 If you were queen of pleasure,
　And I were king of pain. *Ib.*

32 But you would have felt my soul in a kiss,
　And known that once if I loved you well;
And I would have given my soul for this
　To burn for ever in burning hell. *Les Noyades*

33 Ask nothing more of me, sweet;
　All I can give you I give.
Heart of my heart, were it more,
　More would be laid at your feet:
Love that should help you to live,
　Song that should spur you to soar. *The Oblation*

[524]

1 I turn to thee as some green afternoon
Turns toward sunset, and is loth to die;
Ah God, ah God, that day should be so soon!
In the Orchard

2 For a day and a night Love sang to us, played with us,
Folded us round from the dark and the light;
And our hearts were fulfilled with the music he made
with us,
Made with our hands and our lips while he stayed
with us,
Stayed in mid passage his pinions from flight
For a day and a night. *At Parting*

3 The world has no such flowers in any land,
And no such pearl in any gulf the sea,
As any babe on any mother's knee. *Pelagius*

4 I have lived long enough, having seen one thing, that
love hath an end;
Goddess and maiden and queen, be near me now and
befriend. *Hymn to Proserpine*

5 Yea, is not even Apollo, with hair and harpstring of
gold,
A bitter God to follow, a beautiful God to behold?
I am sick of singing: the bays burn deep and chafe:
I am fain
To rest a little from praise and grievous pleasure and
pain. *Ib.*

6 Wilt thou yet take all, Galilean? but these thou shalt
not take,
The laurel, the palms and the paean, the breasts of
the nymphs in the brake;
Breasts more soft than a dove's, that tremble with
tenderer breath;
And all the wings of the Loves, and all the joy before
death. *Ib.*

7 For no man under the sky lives twice, outliving his
day. *Ib.*

8 Thou hast conquered, O pale Galilean; the world has
grown grey from Thy breath;
We have drunken of things Lethean, and fed on the
fullness of death.
Laurel is green for a season, and love is sweet for a
day;
But love grows bitter with treason, and laurel outlives
not May. *Ib.*

9 For the old faiths loosen and fall, the new years ruin
and rend. *Ib.*

10 O ghastly glories of saints, dead limbs of gibbeted
Gods! *Ib.*

11 Impelled of invisible tides, and fulfilled of unspeakable things. *Ib.*

12 All ye as a wind shall go by, as a fire shall ye pass and
be past;
Ye are Gods, and behold, ye shall die, and the waves
be upon you at last. *Ib.*

13 Though the feet of thine high priests tread where thy
lords and our forefathers trod,
Though these that were Gods are dead, and thou
being dead art a God,
Though before thee the throned Cytherean be fallen,
and hidden her head,
Yet thy kingdom shall pass, Galilean, thy dead shall
go down to thee dead. *Ib.*

14 As the deep dim soul of a star. *Ib.*

15 A little soul for a little bears up this corpse which is
man. *Hymn to Proserpine*

16 Love alone, with yearning
Heart for astrolabe,
Takes the star's height, burning
O'er the babe. *A Rhyme*

17 Say, was not this thy Passion, to foreknow
In death's worst hour the works of Christian men?
On the Russian Persecution of the Jews

18 In the heart is the prey for gods,
Who crucify hearts, not hands. *Satia te Sanguine*

19 Good hap to the fresh fierce weather,
The quiver and beat of the sea!
While three men hold together,
The kingdoms are less by three.
A Song in Time of Order 1852

20 They have tied the world in a tether,
They have bought over God with a fee. *Ib.*

21 When the devil's riddle is mastered
And the galley-bench creaks with a Pope,
We shall see Buonaparte the bastard
Kick heels with his throat in a rope. *Ib.*

22 Had you loved me once, as you have not loved;
Had the chance been with us that has not been.
The Triumph of Time

23 I have put my days and dreams out of mind,
Days that are over, dreams that are done. *Ib.*

24 The strong sea-daisies feast on the sun. *Ib.*

25 Who swims in sight of the great third wave
That never a swimmer shall cross or climb. *Ib.*

26 A broken blossom, a ruined rhyme. *Ib.*

27 I had wrung life dry for your lips to drink,
Broken it up for your daily bread. *Ib.*

28 Content you;
The gate is strait; I shall not be there. *Ib.*

29 I will go back to the great sweet mother,
Mother and lover of men, the sea.
I will go down to her, I and no other,
Close with her, kiss her and mix her with me. *Ib.*

30 I shall sleep, and move with the moving ships,
Change as the winds change, veer in the tide. *Ib.*

31 There lived a singer in France of old
By the tideless dolorous midland sea.
In a land of sand and ruin and gold
There shone one woman, and none but she. *Ib*

32 In heaven,
If I cry to you then, will you hear or know? *Ib*

33 One the last flower of Catholic love, that grows
Amid bare thorns their only thornless rose.
Two Leaders

34 Sweet red splendid kissing mouth.
*Translations from Villon. Complaint of the fair
Amouress*

35 There's no good girl's lip out of Paris.
Ib. Ballad of the Women of Paris

JOSHUA SYLVESTER
1563–1618

36 Were I as base as is the lowly plain,
And you (my Love) as high as Heaven above.
Sonnet. (Attrib.) Oxford Book of 16th Cent. Verse

JOHN ADDINGTON SYMONDS
1840–1893

1 These things shall be! A loftier race
Than e'er the world hath known shall rise,
With flame of freedom in their souls,
And light of knowledge in their eyes. *Hymn*

PUBLILIUS SYRUS
fl. 1st cent. B.C.

2 Bis dat qui cito dat.
He gives twice who gives soon.
Proverbial, attrib. to Syrus

3 Beneficium inopi bis dat, qui dat celeriter.
He doubly benefits the needy who gives quickly.
Sententiæ, 6

4 Iudex damnatur ubi nocens absolvitur.
The judge is condemned when the criminal is
acquitted. *Ib. 247*

5 Necessitas dat legem non ipsa accipit.
Necessity gives the law and does not itself receive
it. *Ib. 399*

6 Necessitas non habet legem.
Necessity has no law. *Proverbial, attrib. to Syrus*

JOSEPH TABRAR
nineteenth century

7 In over a year and a half,
I've only sung it once,
And I don't suppose I shall sing it again
For months and months and months.
For Months and Months and Months

TACITUS
c. A.D. 55–*c.* 117

8 Atque omne ignotum pro magnifico est; sed nunc
terminus Britanniae patet.
For wonder grows where knowledge fails. But now
the very bounds of Britain are laid bare.
Agricola, 30. Trans. by Fyfe

9 Ubi solitudinem faciunt, pacem appellant.
When they make a wilderness they call it peace.
Ib.

10 Proprium humani ingenii est odisse quem laeseris.
It is human nature to hate the man whom you
have hurt. *Ib. 42*

11 Felix . . . opportunitate mortis.
Fortune favoured him . . . in the opportune moment
of his death. *Ib. 45*

12 Editis annalibus laudatoque M. Bruto C. Cassium
Romanorum ultimum dixisset.
In his history he had praised Brutus and had called
Cassius the last of the Romans. *Annals, iv. 34*

13 Elegantiae arbiter. [Petronius.]
Judge of taste. *Ib. xvi. 18*

14 Rara temporum felicitate ubi sentire quae velis et
quae sentias dicere licet.
It is the rare fortune of these days that a man may
think what he likes and say what he thinks.
Histories, 1. i. Trans. by Fyfe

15 Maior privato visus dum privatus fuit, et omnium
consensu capax imperii nisi imperasset
When he was a commoner he seemed too big for
his station, and had he never been emperor, no
one would have doubted his ability to reign.
[Servius Galba] *Histories, 1. xlix*

16 Etiam sapientibus cupido gloriae novissima exuitur.
For even with philosophers the passion for fame
is often their last rag of infirmity. *Ib. IV. vi*

CHARLES-MAURICE DE TALLEYRAND
1754–1838

17 Ils n'ont rien appris, ni rien oublié.
They have learnt nothing, and forgotten nothing.
*Attributed to Talleyrand by the Chevalier de Panat
in a letter to Mallet du Pan, Jan. 1796*, 'Personne
n'est corrigé, personne n'a su ni rien oublier ni rien
apprendre.' (*Mémoires et correspondance de Mallet
du Pan* (1851), II. 196.) *See also 195:1*

18 N'ayez pas de zèle.
Not too much zeal.
*Sainte-Beuve, Portraits de femmes, Madame de
Staël, p. 131*

19 Voilà le commencement de la fin.
This is the beginning of the end.
*On the announcement of Napoleon's defeat at
Borodino, 1812*

20 War is much too serious a thing to be left to military
men.
*Quoted by Briand to Lloyd George during the First
World War*

ROBERT TANNAHILL
1774–1810

21 When gloamin' treads the heels o' day,
And birds sit courin' on the spray,
Alang the flow'ry hedge I stray,
To meet mine ain dear somebody.
Songs and Poems (1911), *Mine ain dear Somebody*

NAHUM TATE
1652–1715
and
NICHOLAS BRADY
1659–1726

22 To the hills and the vales,
To the rocks and the mountains,
To the musical groves
And the cool shady fountains,
Let the triumphs of Love,
And of Beauty be shown!
Go revel, ye Cupids,
The day is your own.
Dido and Æneas, Act I (By Nahum Tate)

23 Take a bowsey short leave of your nymphs on the
shore,
And silence their mourning
With vows of returning,
Though never intending to visit them more.
Ib. Act III

1 As pants the hart for cooling streams
   When heated in the chase.
     New Version of the Psalms (1696). *As Pants the
     Hart*

2 Through all the changing scenes of life.
     Ib. Through all the Changing

3 Fear Him, ye saints, and you will then
   Have nothing else to fear.   *Ib.*

4 While shepherds watch'd their flocks by night,
   All seated on the ground,
   The Angel of the Lord came down,
   And glory shone around.

   'Fear not,' said he, for mighty dread
   Had seized their troubled mind;
   'Glad tidings of great joy I bring
   To you and all mankind.'
     *Supplement to the New Version of the Psalms
     (1700). While Shepherds Watched*

ANN TAYLOR
1782–1866
and
JANE TAYLOR
1783–1827

5 I thank the goodness and the grace
   Which on my birth have smiled,
   And made me, in these Christian days,
   A happy English child.
     Hymns for Infant Minds, 1. *A Child's Hymn of
     Praise*

6 O that it were my chief delight
   To do the things I ought!
   Then let me try with all my might
   To mind what I am taught.
     Ib. 18. For a Very Little Child

7 'Tis a *credit* to any good girl to be neat,
   But quite a *disgrace* to be fine.
     Hymns for Sunday Schools. The Folly of Finery

8 Who ran to help me when I fell,
   And would some pretty story tell,
   Or kiss the place to make it well?
     My Mother.
     Original Poems. My Mother. (*By Ann Taylor*)

9 How pleasant it is, at the end of the day,
   No follies to have to repent;
   But reflect on the past, and be able to say,
   That my time has been properly spent.
     Rhymes for the Nursery. The Way to be Happy.
     (*By Jane Taylor*)

10 Twinkle, twinkle, little star,
   How I wonder what you are!
   Up above the world so high,
   Like a diamond in the sky!
     Ib. The Star. (*By Jane Taylor*)

BAYARD TAYLOR
1825–1878

11 Till the sun grows cold,
   And the stars are old,
   And the leaves of the Judgment Book unfold.
     Bedouin Song. Refrain

SIR HENRY TAYLOR
1800–1886

12 Quoth tongue of neither maid nor wife
   To heart of neither wife nor maid—
   Lead we not here a jolly life
   Betwixt the shine and shade?

   Quoth heart of neither maid nor wife
   To tongue of neither wife nor maid—
   Thou wagg'st, but I am worn with strife,
   And feel like flowers that fade.
     Philip Van Artevelde, Pt. II. v. i. 2

BISHOP JEREMY TAYLOR
1613–1667

13 Too quick a sense of a constant infelicity.
     Holy Dying, ch. I, § v

14 Every school-boy knows it.
     On the Real Presence, § v, par. 1

15 The union of hands and hearts.
     Sermons. The Marriage Ring, pt. i

JOHN TAYLOR
1580–1653

16 'Tis a mad world, my masters. *Western Voyage*, l. 1

ARCHBISHOP FREDERICK TEMPLE
1821–1902

17 There is a certain class of clergyman whose mendicity
   is only equalled by their mendacity.
     *Remark at a meeting of the Ecclesiastical Com-
     missioners quoted by Sir George Leveson Gower:
     Years of Endeavour, 1942*

SIR WILLIAM TEMPLE
1628–1699

18 When all is done, human life is, at the greatest and
   the best, but like a froward child, that must be
   play'd with and humoured a little to keep it quiet
   till it falls asleep, and then the care is over.
     Essay on Poetry, ad fin.

ARCHBISHOP WILLIAM TEMPLE
1881–1944

19 'Are you not,' a Rugby master had asked him in discussing one of his [schoolboy] essays, 'a little out of
   your depth here?' 'Perhaps, Sir,' was the confident
   reply, 'but I can swim.'
     F. A. Iremonger, William Temple

ALFRED, LORD TENNYSON
1809–1892

20 The noblest answer unto such,
   Is kindly silence when they brawl.
     After-Thought, v

21 For nothing worthy proving can be proven,
   Nor yet disproven.   *The Ancient Sage*, l. 66

22 Cleave ever to the sunnier side of doubt. *Ib.* l. 68

23 The rabbit fondles his own harmless face.
     Aylmer's Field, l. 851

1 Her arms across her breast she laid;
 She was more fair than words can say:
Bare-footed came the beggar maid
 Before the king Cophetua.
In robe and crown the king stept down,
 To meet and greet her on her way;
'It is no wonder,' said the lords,
 'She is more beautiful than day.'
      The Beggar Maid

2 As shines the moon in clouded skies,
 She in her poor attire was seen:
One praised her ankles, one her eyes,
 One her dark hair and lovesome mien.
So sweet a face, such angel grace,
 In all that land had never been:
Cophetua sware a royal oath:
 'This beggar maid shall be my queen!' *Ib.*

3 Break, break, break,
 On thy cold gray stones, O Sea!
And I would that my tongue could utter
 The thoughts that arise in me.

O well for the fisherman's boy,
 That he shouts with his sister at play!
O well for the sailor lad,
 That he sings in his boat on the bay!

And the stately ships go on
 To their haven under the hill;
But O for the touch of a vanish'd hand,
 And the sound of a voice that is still!

Break, break, break,
 At the foot of thy crags, O Sea!
But the tender grace of a day that is dead
 Will never come back to me. *Break, Break, Break*

4 A happy bridesmaid makes a happy bride.
      The Bridesmaid, l. 4

5 I come from haunts of coot and hern,
 I make a sudden sally
And sparkle out among the fern,
 To bicker down a valley. *The Brook*, l. 23

6 For men may come and men may go,
 But I go on for ever.   *Ib.* l. 33

7 Here and there a lusty trout,
 And here and there a grayling.   *Ib.* l. 57

8 That petitionary grace
 Of Sweet Seventeen.   *Ib.* l. 112

9 The Lord let the house of a brute to the soul of a man,
 And the man said, 'Am I your debtor?'
And the Lord—'Not yet: but make it as clean as you
 can,
And then I will let you a better.' *By an Evolutionist*

10 He that only rules by terror
 Doeth grievous wrong.   *The Captain*, l. 1

11 Slav, Teuton, Kelt, I count them all
 My friends and brother souls,
With all the peoples, great and small,
 That wheel between the poles.
 Epilogue to The Charge of the Heavy Brigade, l. 18

12 The song that nerves a nation's heart,
 Is in itself a deed.   *Ib.* l. 81

13 Half a league, half a league,
 Half a league onward.
    The Charge of the Light Brigade

14 'Forward, the Light Brigade!'
 Was there a man dismay'd?
    The Charge of the Light Brigade

15 Some one had blunder'd.   *Ib.*

16 Their's not to make reply,
 Their's not to reason why,
 Their's but to do and die:
Into the valley of Death
 Rode the six hundred.   *Ib.*

17 Cannon to right of them
 Cannon to left of them,
 Cannon in front of them
  Volley'd and thunder'd.   *Ib.*

18 Into the jaws of Death,
 Into the mouth of Hell.   *Ib.*

19 When can their glory fade?
 O the wild charge they made!
 All the world wonder'd.   *Ib.*

20   The golden guess
Is morning-star to the full round of truth.
     Columbus, l. 42

21 Come not, when I am dead,
 To drop thy foolish tears upon my grave,
To trample round my fallen head,
 And vex the unhappy dust thou wouldst not save.
    Come Not, When I Am Dead, i

22 Sunset and evening star,
 And one clear call for me!
And may there be no moaning of the bar,
 When I put out to sea,

But such a tide as moving seems asleep,
 Too full for sound and foam,
When that which drew from out the boundless deep
 Turns again home.

Twilight and evening bell,
 And after that the dark!
And may there be no sadness of farewell,
 When I embark;

For tho' from out our bourne of Time and Place
 The flood may bear me far,
I hope to see my Pilot face to face
 When I have crost the bar. *Crossing the Bar*

23 O Love what hours were thine and mine,
 In lands of palm and southern pine;
 In lands of palm, of orange-blossom,
Of olive, aloe, and maize and vine. *The Daisy*, i

24 A mount of marble, a hundred spires! *Ib.* xv

25 Gray metropolis of the North. [Edinburgh.] *Ib.* xxvi

26 This proverb flashes thro' his head,
 'The many fail: the one succeeds.'
   The Day-dream. The Arrival, ii

27 But dallied with his golden chain,
 And, smiling, put the question by.
     Ib. The Revival

28 And on her lover's arm she leant,
 And round her waist she felt it fold,
And far across the hills they went
 In that new world which is the old.
     Ib. The Departure, i

29 And o'er the hills, and far away
 Beyond their utmost purple rim,
Beyond the night, across the day,
 Thro' all the world she follow'd him. *Ib.* iv

1 And is there any moral shut
　　Within the bosom of the rose?
　　　　　　　　　The Day-dream. Moral, i

2 But any man that walks the mead,
　　In bud or blade, or bloom, may find,
　　According as his humours lead,
　　A meaning suited to his mind.　　*Ib.* ii

3 Wearing his wisdom lightly, like the fruit
　　Which in our winter woodland looks a flower.
　　　　　　　　　A Dedication

4 And ever upon the topmost roof our banner of Eng-
　　land blew.　　　*The Defence of Lucknow*

5 Out of the deep, my child, out of the deep.
　　　　　　　　　De Profundis, i, l. 1

6 I read, before my eyelids dropt their shade,
　　'The Legend of Good Women', long ago
　　Sung by the morning star of song, who made
　　　His music heard below.
　　　　　　　　　A Dream of Fair Women, l. i

7 The spacious times of great Elizabeth.　　*Ib.* l. 7

8 A daughter of the gods, divinely tall
　　And most divinely fair.　　　*Ib.* l. 87

9 A queen, with swarthy cheeks and bold black eyes,
　　Brow-bound with burning gold.　　*Ib.* l. 127

10 He clasps the crag with crooked hands;
　　Close to the sun in lonely lands,
　　Ring'd with the azure world, he stands.
　　The wrinkled sea beneath him crawls;
　　He watches from his mountain walls,
　　And like a thunderbolt he falls.　　*The Eagle*

11 Once more the Heavenly Power
　　Makes all things new,
　　And domes the red-plow'd hills
　　With loving blue;
　　The blackbirds have their wills,
　　The throstles too.　　　*Early Spring*, i

12 The curate; he was fatter than his cure.
　　　　　　　　　Edwin Morris, l. 15

13 God made the woman for the man,
　　And for the good and increase of the world. *Ib.* l. 50

14 　Slight Sir Robert with his watery smile
　　And educated whisker.　　　*Ib.* l. 128

15 And when they buried him the little port
　　Had seldom seen a costlier funeral.　*Enoch Arden*

16 Barbarous experiment, barbarous hexameters.
　　*Experiments. In quantity. On Translation of
　　Homer*

17 O mighty-mouth'd inventor of harmonies,
　　O skill'd to sing of Time or Eternity,
　　God-gifted organ-voice of England,
　　Milton, a name to resound for ages.
　　　　　　　　　Ib. Milton. Alcaics

18 　All that bowery loneliness,
　　The brooks of Eden mazily murmuring.　　*Ib.*

19 O you chorus of indolent reviewers.
　　　　　　　Ib. Milton. Hendecasyllabics

20 　　　　A tiny poem
　　All composed in a metre of Catullus,
　　All in quantity, careful of my motion,
　　Like the skater on ice that hardly bears him.　*Ib.*

21 The mellow lin-lan-lone of evening bells.
　　　　　　　　　Far-Far-Away

22 O Love, O fire! once he drew
　　With one long kiss my whole soul thro'
　　My lips, as sunlight drinketh dew.　　*Fatima*, iii

23 Read my little fable:
　　He that runs may read.
　　Most can raise the flowers now,
　　For all have got the seed.　　　*The Flower*, v

24 Flower in the crannied wall,
　　I pluck you out of the crannies,
　　I hold you here, root and all, in my hand,
　　Little flower—but *if* I could understand
　　What you are, root and all, and all in all,
　　I should know what God and man is.
　　　　　　　　　Flower in the Crannied Wall

25 More black than ashbuds in the front of March.
　　　　　　　　　The Gardener's Daughter, l. 28

26 A sight to make an old man young.　　*Ib.* l. 140

27 Then she rode forth, clothed on with chastity.
　　　　　　　　　Godiva, l. 53

28 With twelve great shocks of sound, the shameless
　　noon
　　Was clash'd and hammer'd from a hundred towers.
　　　　　　　　　Ib. l. 74

29 Move onward, leading up the golden year.
　　　　　　　　　The Golden Year, l. 26

30 　Ah! when shall all men's good
　　Be each man's rule, and universal Peace
　　Lie like a shaft of light across the land?　*Ib.* l. 47

31 Thro' all the circle of the golden year.　　*Ib.* l. 51

32 That a lie which is all a lie may be met and fought
　　with outright,
　　But a lie which is part a truth is a harder matter to
　　fight.　　　*The Grandmother*, viii

33 That man's the true Conservative
　　Who lops the moulder'd branch away.
　　　　　　　　　Hands All Round, i

34 Pray God our greatness may not fail
　　Thro' craven fears of being great.　　　*Ib.* iii

35 Gigantic daughter of the West,
　　We drink to thee across the flood . . .
　　For art thou not of British blood?
　　　Ib. iv. In original version, published in *The
　　Examiner*, 7 Feb. 1852

36 Senlac! Sanguelac,
　　The lake of Blood!　　　*Harold*, III. i

37 Sanguelac! Sanguelac! the arrow! the arrow!　*Ib.*

38 Speak to Him thou for He hears, and Spirit with
　　Spirit can meet—
　　Closer is He than breathing, and nearer than hands
　　and feet.　　　*The Higher Pantheism*, vi

39 Wearing the white flower of a blameless life,
　　Before a thousand peering littlenesses,
　　In that fierce light which beats upon a throne,
　　And blackens every blot.
　　　　　The Idylls of the King, Dedication, l. 24

40 Man's word is God in man.
　　　　　　Ib. The Coming of Arthur, l. 132

41 A doubtful throne is ice on summer seas.　*Ib.* l. 247

42 Clothed in white samite, mystic, wonderful.
　　Ib. l. 284, and *The Passing of Arthur*, l. 199

1 Rain, rain, and sun! a rainbow in the sky!
A young man will be wiser by and by;
An old man's wit may wander ere he die.
The Idylls of the King, The Coming of Arthur, l. 402

2 From the great deep to the great deep he goes.
Ib. l. 410

3 Blow trumpet, for the world is white with May.
Ib. l. 481

4 Live pure, speak true, right wrong, follow the King—
Else, wherefore born? *Ib. Gareth and Lynette*, l. 117

5   The city is built
To music, therefore never built at all,
And therefore built for ever. *Ib.* l. 272

6 Lightly was her slender nose
Tip-tilted like the petal of a flower. *Ib.* l. 576

7 Lead, and I follow. *Ib.* l. 726

8 O purblind race of miserable men,
How many among us at this very hour
Do forge a lifelong trouble for ourselves,
By taking true for false, or false for true!
Ib. Geraint and Enid, l. 1

9 But o'er her meek eyes came a happy mist
Like that which kept the heart of Eden green
Before the useful trouble of the rain. *Ib.* l. 769

10 Too late, too late! ye cannot enter now.
Ib. Guinevere, l. 168

11 For manners are not idle, but the fruit
Of loyal nature, and of noble mind. *Ib.* l. 333

12 The children born of thee are sword and fire,
Red ruin, and the breaking up of laws. *Ib.* l. 422

13 To reverence the King, as if he were
Their conscience, and their conscience as their King,
To break the heathen and uphold the Christ,
To ride abroad redressing human wrongs,
To speak no slander, no, nor listen to it,
To honour his own word as if his God's. *Ib.* l. 465

14 To love one maiden only, cleave to her,
And worship her by years of noble deeds,
Until they won her; for indeed I knew
Of no more subtle master under heaven
Than is the maiden passion for a maid,
Not only to keep down the base in man,
But teach high thought, and amiable words
And courtliness, and the desire of fame,
And love of truth, and all that makes a man.
Ib. l. 472

15 Our fair father Christ. *Ib.* l. 559

16 Hereafter in that world where all are pure
We two may meet before high God, and thou
Wilt spring to me, and claim me thine, and know
I am thine husband—not a smaller soul,
Nor Lancelot, nor another. *Ib.* l. 560

17   He never mocks,
For mockery is the fume of little hearts. *Ib.* l. 627

18 I thought I could not breathe in that fine air
That pure severity of perfect light—
I yearn'd for warmth and colour which I found
In Lancelot. *Ib.* l. 640

19 It was my duty to have loved the highest:
It surely was my profit had I known:
It would have been my pleasure had I seen.
We needs must love the highest when we see it,
Not Lancelot, nor another. *Ib.* l. 652

20 To where beyond these voices there is peace.
The Idylls of the King. Guinevere, l. 692

21 For good ye are and bad, and like to coins,
Some true, some light, but every one of you
Stamp'd with the image of the King.
Ib. The Holy Grail, l. 25

22 The cup, the cup itself, from which our Lord
Drank at the last sad supper with his own. *Ib.* l. 46

23 God make thee good as thou art beautiful. *Ib.* l. 136

24 For when was Lancelot wanderingly lewd? *Ib.* l. 148

25 I, maiden, round thee, maiden, bind my belt.
Ib. l. 159

26   Ye follow wandering fires
Lost in the quagmire! *Ib.* l. 319

27 This madness has come on us for our sins. *Ib.* l. 356

28 And lifting up mine eyes, I found myself
Alone, and in a land of sand and thorns. *Ib.* l. 374

29 I saw the fiery face as of a child
That smote itself into the bread, and went. *Ib.* l. 473

30 And in the strength of this I rode,
Shattering all evil customs everywhere. *Ib.* l. 483

31 I will be deafer than the blue-eyed cat,
And thrice as blind as any noon-tide owl,
To holy virgins in their ecstasies,
Henceforward. *Ib.* l. 865

32 So spake the King: I knew not all he meant.
Ib. l. 919

33 Elaine the fair, Elaine the loveable,
Elaine, the lily maid of Astolat.
Ib. Lancelot and Elaine, l. 1

34   To me
He is all fault who hath no fault at all:
For who loves me must have a touch of earth.
Ib. l. 131

35   In me there dwells
No greatness, save it be some far-off touch
Of greatness to know well I am not great. *Ib.* l. 447

36 I know not if I know what true love is,
But if I know, then, if I love not him,
I know there is none other I can love. *Ib.* l. 672

37 The shackles of an old love straiten'd him,
His honour rooted in dishonour stood,
And faith unfaithful kept him falsely true. *Ib.* l. 870

38 Sweet is true love tho' given in vain, in vain;
And sweet is death who puts an end to pain.
Ib. l. 1000

39   Never yet
Was noble man but made ignoble talk.
He makes no friend who never made a foe.
Ib. l. 1080

40 Our bond is not the bond of man and wife.
Ib. l. 1199

41 'Forgive me; mine was jealousy in love.'
He answer'd with his eyes upon the ground,
'That is love's curse; pass on, my Queen, forgiven.'
Ib. l. 1340

42 Free love—free field—we love but while we may.
Ib. The Last Tournament, l. 281

43 The dirty nurse, Experience, in her kind
Hath foul'd me. *Ib.* l. 317

1 The greater man, the greater courtesy.
The Idylls of the King. The Last Tournament, l. 628

2 The ptarmigan that whitens ere his hour
Woos his own end. *Ib.* l. 692

3 Our hoard is little, but our hearts are great.
Ib. The Marriage of Geraint, l. 352

4 For man is man and master of his fate. *Ib.* l. 355

5 Hark, by the bird's song ye may learn the nest.
Ib. l. 359

6 They take the rustic murmur of their bourg
For the great wave that echoes round the world.
Ib. l. 419

7 Mother, a maiden is a tender thing,
And best by her that bore her understood. *Ib.* l. 510

8 Brave hearts and clean! and yet—God guide them—
young. *Ib. Merlin and Vivien*, l. 29

9 As, on a dull day in an ocean-cave,
The blind wave, feeling round his long sea-hall
In silence. *Ib.* l. 229

10 Unfaith in aught is want of faith in all. *Ib.* l. 387

11 It is the little rift within the lute,
That by and by will make the music mute,
And ever widening slowly silence all. *Ib.* l. 388

12 And trust me not at all or all in all. *Ib.* l. 396

13 Lo now, what hearts have men! they never mount
As high as woman in her selfless mood. *Ib.* l. 440

14 Man dreams of fame while woman wakes to love.
Ib. l. 458

15 With this for motto, 'Rather use than fame'.
Ib. l. 478

16 Where blind and naked Ignorance
Delivers brawling judgments, unashamed,
On all things all day long. *Ib.* l. 662

17 But every page having an ample marge,
And every marge enclosing in the midst
A square of text that looks a little blot. *Ib.* l. 667

18 And none can read the text, not even I;
And none can read the comment but myself.
Ib. l. 679

19 Or some black wether of St. Satan's fold. *Ib.* l. 748

20 O selfless man and stainless gentleman! *Ib.* l. 790

21 Defaming and defacing, till she left
Not even Lancelot brave, nor Galahad clean.
Ib. l. 802

22 For men at most differ as Heaven and Earth,
But women, worst and best, as Heaven and Hell.
Ib. l. 812

23 Face-flatterer and backbiter are the same. *Ib.* l. 822

24 And the thicket closed
Behind her, and the forest echo'd 'fool'. *Ib.* l. 971

25 O great and sane and simple race of brutes
That own no lust because they have no law!
Ib. Pelleas and Ettarre, l. 471

26 I found Him in the shining of the stars,
I mark'd Him in the flowering of His fields,
But in His ways with men I find Him not.
Ib. The Passing of Arthur, l. 9

27 Why is all around us here
As if some lesser god had made the world,
But had not force to shape it as he would? *Ib.* l.

28 This way and that dividing the swift mind.
The Idylls of the King. The Passing of Arthur, l. 60

29 So all day long the noise of battle roll'd
Among the mountains by the winter sea. *Ib.* l. 170

30 On one side lay the Ocean, and on one
Lay a great water, and the moon was full. *Ib.* l 179

31 Authority forgets a dying king. *Ib.* l. 289

32 Clothed with his breath, and looking, as he walk'd,
Larger than human on the frozen hills.
He heard the deep behind him, and a cry
Before. *Ib.* l. 350

33 When every morning brought a noble chance,
And every chance brought out a noble knight.
Ib. l. 398

34 Among new men, strange faces, other minds.
Ib. l. 406

35 And slowly answer'd Arthur from the barge:
'The old order changeth, yielding place to new,
And God fulfils himself in many ways,
Lest one good custom should corrupt the world.'
Ib. l. 407

36 If thou shouldst never see my face again,
Pray for my soul. More things are wrought by prayer
Than this world dreams of. Wherefore, let thy voice
Rise like a fountain for me night and day.
For what are men better than sheep or goats
That nourish a blind life within the brain,
If, knowing God, they lift not hands of prayer
Both for themselves and those who call them friend?
For so the whole round earth is every way
Bound by gold chains about the feet of God.
Ib. l. 414

37 I am going a long way
With these thou seest—if indeed I go
(For all my mind is clouded with a doubt)—
To the island-valley of Avilion;
Where falls not hail, or rain, or any snow,
Nor ever wind blows loudly; but it lies
Deep-meadow'd, happy, fair with orchard lawns
And bowery hollows crown'd with summer sea,
Where I will heal me of my grievous wound.
Ib. l. 424

38 Like some full-breasted swan
That, fluting a wild carol ere her death,
Ruffles her pure cold plume, and takes the flood
With swarthy webs. *Ib.* l. 434

39 Believing where we cannot prove.
In Memoriam, prologue. (*The numbering of the
Cantos follows that of the latest edition, and includes the additional Canto No. xxxix, first
published in 1869*)

40 Thou madest man, he knows not why,
He thinks he was not made to die;
And thou hast made him: thou art just. *Ib.*

41 Our little systems have their day;
They have their day and cease to be:
They are but broken lights of thee,
And thou, O Lord, art more than they. *Ib.*

42 Let knowledge grow from more to more,
But more of reverence in us dwell;
That mind and soul, according well,
May make one music as before. *Ib.*

[531]

1   I held it truth, with him who sings
     To one clear harp in divers tones,
     That men may rise on stepping-stones
  Of their dead selves to higher things.
                  In Memoriam, i

2   Who changest not in any gale,
     Nor branding summer suns avail
  To touch thy thousand years of gloom.
                  Ib. ii

3   For words, like Nature, half reveal
  And half conceal the Soul within.
                  Ib. v

4   But, for the unquiet heart and brain,
     A use in measured language lies;
     The sad mechanic exercise,
  Like dull narcotics, numbing pain.
                  Ib.

5   And common is the commonplace,
  And vacant chaff well meant for grain.
                  Ib. vi

6   Never morning wore
  To evening, but some heart did break.
                  Ib.

7   His heavy-shotted hammock-shroud
  Drops in his vast and wandering grave.
                  Ib.

8 Dark house, by which once more I stand
     Here in the long unlovely street,
     Doors, where my heart was used to beat
  So quickly, waiting for a hand.
                  Ib. vii

9   And ghastly thro' the drizzling rain
  On the bald streets breaks the blank day.
                  Ib.

10 More than my brothers are to me.   *Ib.* ix

11   Or where the kneeling hamlet drains
  The chalice of the grapes of God.
                  Ib. x

12   The last red leaf is whirl'd away,
  The rooks are blown about the skies.
                  Ib. xv

13   Thou comest, much wept for: such a breeze
     Compell'd thy canvas.
                  Ib. xvii

14   And from his ashes may be made
  The violet of his native land.
                  Ib. xviii

15   There twice a day the Severn fills;
     The salt sea-water passes by,
     And hushes half the babbling Wye,
  And makes a silence in the hills.
                  Ib. xix

16   I do but sing because I must,
  And pipe but as the linnets sing.
                  Ib. xxi

17   The Shadow cloak'd from head to foot,
  Who keeps the keys of all the creeds.
                  Ib. xxiii

18   And Thought leapt out to wed with Thought
  Ere Thought could wed itself with Speech.
                  Ib.

19   I envy not in any moods
     The captive void of noble rage,
     The linnet born within the cage,
  That never knew the summer woods.
                  Ib. xxvii

20   'Tis better to have loved and lost
  Than never to have loved at all.
                  Ib.

21 The time draws near the birth of Christ. *Ib.* xxviii

22   'Where wert thou, brother, those four days?'
     There lives no record of reply,
     Which telling what it is to die
  Had surely added praise to praise.

  From every house the neighbours met,
     The streets were fill'd with joyful sound,
     A solemn gladness even crown'd
  The purple brows of Olivet.

  Behold a man raised up by Christ!
     The rest remaineth unreveal'd;
     He told it not; or something seal'd
  The lips of that Evangelist.   *In Memoriam*, xxxi

23 Her eyes are homes of silent prayer.   *Ib.* xxxii

24 Leave thou thy sister when she prays,
     Her early Heaven, her happy views;
     Nor thou with shadow'd hint confuse
  A life that leads melodious days.

  Her faith thro' form is pure as thine,
     Her hands are quicker unto good:
     Oh, sacred be the flesh and blood
  To which she links a truth divine!   *Ib.* xxxiii

25 And so the Word had breath, and wrought
     With human hands the creed of creeds
     In loveliness of perfect deeds,
  More strong than all poetic thought.   *Ib.* xxxvi

26   Short swallow-flights of song, that dip
     Their wings in tears, and skim away.   *Ib.* xlviii

27   And Time, a maniac scattering dust,
  And Life, a Fury slinging flame.   *Ib.* l

28   Do we indeed desire the dead
     Should still be near us at our side?
     Is there no baseness we would hide?
  No inner vileness that we dread?   *Ib.* li

29   How many a father have I seen,
     A sober man, among his boys,
     Whose youth was full of foolish noise. *Ib.* liii

30   Hold thou the good: define it well:
     For fear divine Philosophy
     Should push beyond her mark, and be
  Procuress to the Lords of Hell.   *Ib.*

31   Oh yet we trust that somehow good
  Will be the final goal of ill.   *Ib.* liv

32   That nothing walks with aimless feet;
     That not one life shall be destroy'd,
     Or cast as rubbish to the void,
  When God hath made the pile complete;   *Ib.*

33   That not a worm is cloven in vain;
     That not a moth with vain desire
     Is shrivell'd in a fruitless fire,
  Or but subserves another's gain.   *Ib.*

34   But what am I?
     An infant crying in the night:
     An infant crying for the light:
  And with no language but a cry.   *Ib.*

35   So careful of the type she seems,
  So careless of the single life.   *Ib.* lv

36   The great world's altar-stairs
  That slope thro' darkness up to God.   *Ib.*

37 Nature, red in tooth and claw.   *Ib.* lvi

38   Dragons of the prime,
  That tare each other in their slime,
  Were mellow music match'd with him.   *Ib.*

39   Peace; come away: the song of woe
     Is after all an earthly song:
     Peace; come away: we do him wrong
  To sing so wildly: let us go.   *Ib.* lvii

40   The passing of the sweetest soul
  That ever look'd with human eyes.   *Ib.*

41   O Sorrow, wilt thou live with me
  No casual mistress, but a wife.   *Ib.* lix

1 As some divinely gifted man,
   Whose life in low estate began
And on a simple village green;

Who breaks his birth's invidious bar,
   And grasps the skirts of happy chance,
   And breasts the blows of circumstance,
And grapples with his evil star.   *In Memoriam*, lxiv

2 Yet feels, as in a pensive dream,
   When all his active powers are still,
   A distant dearness in the hill,
A secret sweetness in the stream.   *Ib.*

3 So many worlds, so much to do,
   So little done, such things to be.   *Ib.* lxxiii

4   Death has made
His darkness beautiful with thee.   *Ib.* lxxiv

5   And round thee with the breeze of song
To stir a little dust of praise.   *Ib.* lxxv

6 O last regret, regret can die!   *Ib.* lxxviii

7 Laburnums, dropping-wells of fire.   *Ib.* lxxxiii

8 God's finger touch'd him, and he slept. *Ib.* lxxxv

9 I, the divided half of such
A friendship as had master'd Time.   *Ib.*

10 Dusty purlieus of the law.   *Ib.* lxxxix

11 The hard heir strides about their lands,
And will not yield them for a day.   *Ib.* xc

12 When rosy plumelets tuft the larch,
   And rarely pipes the mounted thrush;
   Or underneath the barren bush
Flits by the sea-blue bird of March.   *Ib.* xci

13 You tell me, doubt is Devil-born.   *Ib.* xcvi

14 There lives more faith in honest doubt,
Believe me, than in half the creeds.   *Ib.*

15 Their meetings made December June,
Their every parting was to die.   *Ib.* xcvii

16 He seems so near and yet so far.   *Ib.*

17 Ring out, wild bells, to the wild sky.   *Ib.* cvi

18 Ring out the old, ring in the new,
   Ring, happy bells, across the snow:
   The year is going, let him go;
Ring out the false, ring in the true.   *Ib.*

19 Ring out the feud of rich and poor.   *Ib.*

20 Ring out a slowly dying cause,
   And ancient forms of party strife;
   Ring in the nobler modes of life,
With sweeter manners, purer laws.

Ring out the want, the care, the sin,
   The faithless coldness of the times;
   Ring out, ring out my mournful rhymes,
But ring the fuller minstrel in.

Ring out false pride in place and blood,
   The civic slander and the spite;
   Ring in the love of truth and right,
Ring in the common love of good.

Ring out old shapes of foul disease;
   Ring out the narrowing lust of gold;
   Ring out the thousand wars of old,
Ring in the thousand years of peace.

Ring in the valiant man and free,
   The larger heart, the kindlier hand;
   Ring out the darkness of the land;
Ring in the Christ that is to be.   *Ib.*

21 'Tis held that sorrow makes us wise,
Whatever wisdom sleep with thee.   *In Memoriam*, cviii

22   Not the schoolboy hear,
The blind hysterics of the Celt.   *Ib.* cix

23 And thus he bore without abuse
   The grand old name of gentleman,
   Defamed by every charlatan,
And soil'd with all ignoble use.   *Ib.* cxi

24 Now fades the last long streak of snow
   Now burgeons every maze of quick
   About the flowering squares and thick
By ashen roots the violets blow.   *Ib.* cxv

25 And drown'd in yonder living blue
The lark becomes a sightless song.   *Ib.*

26 But trust that those we call the dead
   Are breathers of an ampler day
For ever nobler ends.   *Ib.* cxviii

27 There, where the long street roars, hath been
The stillness of the central sea.   *Ib.* cxxiii

28 And all is well, tho' faith and form
   Be sunder'd in the night of fear.   *Ib.* cxxvii

29 The red fool-fury of the Seine.   *Ib.*

30 Wearing all that weight
Of learning lightly like a flower. *Ib. Conclusion*, st. x

31 One God, one law, one element,
   And one far-off divine event,
To which the whole creation moves.   *Ib.* st. xxxvi

32 All along the valley, stream that flashest white.
           In the Valley of Cauteretz

33 The voice of the dead was a living voice to me. *Ib.*

34 God gives us love. Something to love
   He lends us; but, when love is grown
To ripeness, that on which it throve
   Falls off, and love is left alone.   *To J. S.*, iv

35 At me you smiled, but unbeguiled
   I saw the snare, and I retired:
The daughter of a hundred Earls,
   You are not one to be desired.
         Lady Clara Vere de Vere, i

36 A simple maiden in her flower
   Is worth a hundred coats-of-arms.   *Ib.* ii

37 Her manners had not that repose
   Which stamps the caste of Vere de Vere. *Ib.* v

38 From yon blue heavens above us bent
   The gardener Adam and his wife
   Smile at the claims of long descent.
Howe'er it be, it seems to me,
   'Tis only noble to be good.
Kind hearts are more than coronets,
   And simple faith than Norman blood.   *Ib.* vi

39 Oh! teach the orphan-boy to read,
   Or teach the orphan-girl to sew.   *Ib.*

40 On either side the river lie
   Long fields of barley and of rye.
          The Lady of Shalott, pt. i

41 Willows whiten, aspens quiver.
   Little breezes dusk and shiver.   *Ib.*

42 But who hath seen her wave her hand?
   Or at the casement seen her stand?
   Or is she known in all the land,
   The Lady of Shalott?   *Ib.*

1 Only reapers, reaping early
In among the bearded barley,
Hear a song that echoes cheerly
From the river winding clearly
Down to tower'd Camelot.
The Lady of Shalott, pt. i

2 She hath no loyal knight and true,
The Lady of Shalott.　　　　*Ib*. pt. ii

3 Or when the moon was overhead,
Came two young lovers lately wed;
'I am half sick of shadows,' said
The Lady of Shalott.　　　　　　*Ib*.

4 A bow-shot from her bower-eaves,
He rode between the barley-sheaves,
The sun came dazzling thro' the leaves,
And flamed upon the brazen greaves
Of bold Sir Lancelot.
A red-cross knight for ever kneel'd
To a lady in his shield,
That sparkled on the yellow field,
Beside remote Shalott.　　　*Ib*. pt. iii

5 All in the blue unclouded weather.　　*Ib*.

6 'Tirra lirra,' by the river
Sang Sir Lancelot.　　　　　　　*Ib*.

7 She left the web, she left the loom,
She made three paces thro' the room,
She saw the water-lily bloom,
She saw the helmet and the plume,
She look'd down to Camelot.
Out flew the web and floated wide;
The mirror crack'd from side to side;
'The curse is come upon me,' cried
The Lady of Shalott.　　　　　　*Ib*.

8 Like some bold seër in a trance,
Seeing all his own mischance—
With a glassy countenance
Did she look to Camelot.　　*Ib*. pt. iv

9 Heard a carol, mournful, holy,
Chanted loudly, chanted lowly,
Till her blood was frozen slowly,
And her eyes were darken'd wholly,
Turn'd to tower'd Camelot.　　　　*Ib*.

10 Who is this? and what is here?
And in the lighted palace near
Died the sound of royal cheer;
And they cross'd themselves for fear,
All the knights at Camelot:
But Lancelot mused a little space;
He said, 'She has a lovely face;
God in his mercy lend her grace,
The Lady of Shalott.'　　　　　　*Ib*.

11 Slander, meanest spawn of Hell.　　*The Letters*

12 Airy, fairy Lilian.　　　　　　*Lilian*

13 Comrades, leave me here a little, while as yet 'tis
early morn:
Leave me here, and when you want me, sound upon
the bugle-horn.　　　　*Locksley Hall*, l. i

14 The fairy tales of science, and the long result of Time.
Ib. l. 12

15 In the Spring a livelier iris changes on the burnish'd
dove;
In the Spring a young man's fancy lightly turns to
thoughts of love.　　　　　　*Ib*. l. 19

16 Love took up the glass of Time, and turn'd it in his
glowing hands;
Every moment, lightly shaken, ran itself in golden
sands.
Love took up the harp of Life, and smote on all the
chords with might;
Smote the chord of Self, that, trembling, pass'd in
music out of sight.　　　　*Locksley Hall*, l. 31

17 And our spirits rush'd together at the touching of the
lips.　　　　　　　　　　*Ib*. l. 38

18 As the husband is, the wife is.　　*Ib*. l. 47

19 He will hold thee, when his passion shall have spent
its novel force.
Something better than his dog, a little dearer than his
horse.　　　　　　　　　　*Ib*. l. 49

20 The many-winter'd crow that leads the clanging
rookery home.　　　　　　*Ib*. l. 68

21 This is truth the poet sings,
That a sorrow's crown of sorrow is remembering
happier things.　　　　　　*Ib*. l. 75

22 Like a dog, he hunts in dreams.　　*Ib*. l. 79

23 With a little hoard of maxims preaching down a
daughter's heart.　　　　　　*Ib*. l. 94

24 But the jingling of the guinea helps the hurt that
Honour feels.　　　　　　　*Ib*. l. 105

25 Men, my brothers, men the workers, ever reaping
something new:
That which they have done but earnest of the things
that they shall do:
For I dipt into the future, far as human eye could see,
Saw the Vision of the world, and all the wonder that
would be.　　　　　　　　*Ib*. l. 117

26 Heard the heavens fill with shouting, and there rain'd
a ghastly dew
From the nations' airy navies grappling in the central
blue.　　　　　　　　　　*Ib*. l. 123

27 In the Parliament of man, the Federation of the
world.　　　　　　　　　　*Ib*. l. 128

28 Science moves, but slowly slowly, creeping on from
point to point.　　　　　　*Ib*. l. 134

29 Yet I doubt not thro' the ages one increasing purpose
runs,
And the thoughts of men are widen'd with the process
of the suns.　　　　　　　*Ib*. l. 137

30 Knowledge comes, but wisdom lingers.　*Ib*. l. 143

31 I am shamed thro' all my nature to have loved so
slight a thing.　　　　　　*Ib*. l. 148

32 Woman is the lesser man, and all thy passions,
match'd with mine,
Are as moonlight unto sunlight, and as water unto
wine.　　　　　　　　　　*Ib*. l. 151

33 I will take some savage woman, she shall rear my
dusky race.　　　　　　　*Ib*. l. 168

34 Not with blinded eyesight poring over miserable
books.　　　　　　　　　　*Ib*. l. 172

35 I the heir of all the ages, in the foremost files of time.
Ib. l. 178

36 　　　　　Forward, forward let us range,
Let the great world spin for ever down the ringing
grooves of change.　　　　　*Ib*. l. 181

1 Better fifty years of Europe than a cycle of Cathay.
Locksley Hall, l. 184

2 He is but a landscape-painter,
And a village maiden she.
The Lord of Burleigh, l. 7

3 Let us see these handsome houses
Where the wealthy nobles dwell. *Ib.* l. 23

4 Many a gallant gay domestic
Bows before him at the door. *Ib.* l. 47

5 But he clasp'd her like a lover,
And he cheer'd her soul with love.
So she strove against her weakness,
Tho' at times her spirit sank. *Ib.* l. 67

6 And the people loved her much. *Ib.* l. 76

7 But a trouble weigh'd upon her,
And perplex'd her, night and morn,
With the burthen of an honour
Unto which she was not born. *Ib.* l. 77

8   'Oh, that he
Were once more that landscape-painter,
Which did win my heart from me!' *Ib.* l. 82

9 Three fair children first she bore him,
Then before her time she died. *Ib.* l. 87

10 Weeping, weeping late and early,
Walking up and pacing down,
Deeply mourn'd the Lord of Burleigh,
Burleigh-house by Stamford-town. *Ib.* l. 89

11 'Bring the dress and put it on her,
That she wore when she was wed.' *Ib.* l. 95

12 'Courage!' he said, and pointed toward the land.
The Lotos-Eaters

13   A land
In which it seemed always afternoon. *Ib.*

14 Music that gentlier on the spirit lies,
Than tir'd eyelids upon tir'd eyes. *Ib. Choric Song*, i

15 There is no joy but calm! *Ib.* ii

16   Ah, why
Should life all labour be? *Ib.* iv

17 Let us alone. Time driveth onward fast,
And in a little while our lips are dumb.
Let us alone. What is it that will last?
All things are taken from us, and become
Portions and parcels of the dreadful Past. *Ib.*

18 The Lotos blooms below the barren peak:
The Lotos blows by every winding creek:
All day the wind breathes low with mellower tone:
Thro' every hollow cave and alley lone,
Round and round the spicy downs the yellow Lotos-
dust is blown. *Ib.* viii

19   Live and lie reclined
On the hills like Gods together, careless of mankind.
For they lie beside their nectar, and the bolts are
hurl'd
Far below them in the valleys, and the clouds are
lightly curl'd
Round their golden houses, girdled with the gleaming
world. *Ib.*

20 Surely, surely, slumber is more sweet than toil, the
shore
Than labour in the deep mid-ocean, wind and wave
and oar;
Oh rest ye, brother mariners, we will not wander
more. *Ib.*

21 Of love that never found his earthly close,
What sequel? Streaming eyes and breaking hearts?
Or all the same as if he had not been?
Love and Duty, l. 1

22 The long mechanic pacings to and fro,
The set gray life, and apathetic end. *Ib.* l. 17

23 Raw Haste, half-sister to Delay.
Love thou thy Land, xxiv

24 Ruining along the illimitable inane. *Lucretius*, l. 40

25   Nor at all can tell
Whether I mean this day to end myself,
Or lend an ear to Plato where he says,
That men like soldiers may not quit the post
Allotted by the Gods. *Ib.* l. 145

26 That stays the rolling Ixionian wheel,
And numbs the Fury's ringlet-snake, and plucks
The mortal soul from out immortal hell. *Ib.* l. 260

27 Passionless bride, divine Tranquillity. *Ib.* l. 265

28 Without one pleasure and without one pain.
Ib. l. 268

29 The lonely moated grange. *Mariana*

30 She only said, 'My life is dreary,
He cometh not,' she said;
She said, 'I am aweary, aweary.
I would that I were dead!' *Ib.*

31 Her tears fell with the dews at even;
Her tears fell ere the dews were dried. *Ib.*

32 She wept, 'I am aweary, aweary,
O God, that I were dead!' *Ib.*

33 I hate the dreadful hollow behind the little wood.
Maud, Pt. I. i. i

34 The smooth-faced snubnosed rogue. *Ib.* xiii

35 Faultily faultless, icily regular, splendidly null. *Ib.* II

36 A monstrous eft was of old the Lord and Master of
Earth. *Ib.* IV. vi

37 The passionate heart of the poet is whirl'd into folly
and vice. *Ib.* vii

38 And most of all would I flee from the cruel madness
of love—
The honey of poison-flowers and all the measureless
ill. *Ib.* x

39 Maud with her exquisite face,
And wild voice pealing up to the sunny sky,
And feet like sunny gems on an English green.
Ib. v. ii

40 That jewell'd mass of millinery,
That oil'd and curl'd Assyrian Bull. *Ib.* VI. vi

41 She came to the village church,
And sat by a pillar alone;
An angel watching an urn
Wept over her, carved in stone. *Ib.* VIII

42 The snowy-banded, dilettante,
Delicate-handed priest intone. *Ib.*

43 Ah God, for a man with heart, head, hand,
Like some of the simple great ones gone
For ever and ever by,
One still strong man in a blatant land,
Whatever they call him, what care I,
Aristocrat, democrat, autocrat—one
Who can rule and dare not lie.

And ah for a man to arise in me,
That the man I am may cease to be!
Maud, Pt. I. x. v–vi

1 O let the solid ground
Not fail beneath my feet
Before my life has found
What some have found so sweet.
Ib. XI. i

2 Birds in the high Hall-garden
When twilight was falling,
Maud, Maud, Maud, Maud,
They were crying and calling.
Ib. XII. i

3 I kiss'd her slender hand,
She took the kiss sedately;
Maud is not seventeen,
But she is tall and stately.
Ib. iv

4 I know the way she went
Home with her maiden posy,
For her feet have touch'd the meadows
And left the daisies rosy.
Ib. vi

5 Gorgonised me from head to foot
With a stony British stare.
Ib. XIII. ii

6 Go not, happy day,
From the shining fields,
Go not, happy day,
Till the maiden yields.
Rosy is the West,
Rosy is the South,
Roses are her cheeks,
And a rose her mouth.
Ib. XVII

7 Blush from West to East,
Blush from East to West,
Till the West is East,
Blush it thro' the West.
Ib.

8 A livelier emerald twinkles in the grass,
A purer sapphire melts into the sea.
Ib. XVIII. vi

9 Come into the garden, Maud,
For the black bat, night, has flown;
Come into the garden, Maud,
I am here at the gate alone;
And the woodbine spices are wafted abroad,
And the musk of the rose is blown.

10 For a breeze of morning moves,
And the planet of Love is on high,
Beginning to faint in the light that she loves
On a bed of daffodil sky.
Ib. XXII. i–ii

11 All night have the roses heard
The flute, violin, bassoon;
All night has the casement jessamine stirr'd
To the dancers dancing in tune;
Till a silence fell with the waking bird,
And a hush with the setting moon.
Ib. iii

12 Whenever a March-wind sighs
He sets the jewel-print of your feet
In violets blue as your eyes.
Ib. vii

13 The slender acacia would not shake
One long milk-bloom on the tree;
The white lake-blossom fell into the lake
As the pimpernel dozed on the lea;
But the rose was awake all night for your sake,
Knowing your promise to me;
The lilies and roses were all awake,
They sigh'd for the dawn and thee.
Ib. viii

14 Queen rose of the rosebud garden of girls.
Ib. ix

15 There has fallen a splendid tear
From the passion-flower at the gate.
She is coming, my dove, my dear;
She is coming, my life, my fate;
The red rose cries, 'She is near, she is near;'
And the white rose weeps, 'She is late;'
The larkspur listens, 'I hear, I hear;'
And the lily whispers, 'I wait.'

She is coming, my own, my sweet;
Were it ever so airy a tread,
My heart would hear her and beat,
Were it earth in an earthy bed;
My dust would hear her and beat,
Had I lain for a century dead;
Would start and tremble under her feet,
And blossom in purple and red.
Maud, Pt. I. XXII. x–xi

16 The Christless code,
That must have life for a blow.
Ib. Pt. II. I. i

17 O that 'twere possible
After long grief and pain
To find the arms of my true love
Round me once again!
Ib. IV.

18 Ah Christ, that it were possible
For one short hour to see
The souls we loved, that they might tell us
What and where they be.
Ib. iii

19 But the churchmen fain would kill their church,
As the churches have kill'd their Christ.
Ib. v. ii

20 O me, why have they not buried me deep enough?
Is it kind to have made me a grave so rough,
Me, that was never a quiet sleeper?
Ib. xi

21 Bury me, bury me
Deeper, ever so little deeper.
Ib.

22 My life has crept so long on a broken wing
Thro' cells of madness, haunts of horror and fear,
That I come to be grateful at last for a little thing.
Ib. Pt. III. VI. i

23 When the face of night is fair on the dewy downs,
And the shining daffodil dies.
Ib.

24 The blood-red blossom of war with a heart of fire.
Ib. iv

25 It is better to fight for the good, than to rail at the ill;
I have felt with my native land, I am one with my kind,
I embrace the purpose of God, and the doom assign'd.
Ib. v

26 You must wake and call me early, call me early,
mother dear;
To-morrow 'ill be the happiest time of all the glad
New-year;
Of all the glad New-year, mother, the maddest
merriest day;
For I'm to be Queen o' the May, mother, I'm to be
Queen o' the May.
The May Queen

27 It seem'd so hard at first, mother, to leave the blessed
sun,
And now it seems as hard to stay, and yet His will be
done!
But still I think it can't be long before I find release;
And that good man, the clergyman, has told me
words of peace.
Ib. Conclusion

1 All in the wild March-morning I heard the angels
   call;
   It was when the moon was setting, and the dark was
   over all;
   The trees began to whisper, and the wind began to
   roll,
   And in the wild March-morning I heard them call
   my soul.   *The May Queen.* Conclusion

2 Follow the Gleam.   *Merlin and the Gleam*

3   In after-dinner talk,
   Across the walnuts and the wine.
                             The Miller's Daughter

4   What, it's you,
   The padded man—that wears the stays.
                        The New Timon and the Poets

5 What profits now to understand
   The merits of a spotless shirt—
   A dapper boot—a little hand—
   If half the little soul is dirt?   *Ib.*

6 Doesn't thou 'ear my 'erse's legs, as they canters
   awaäy?
   Proputty, proputty, proputty—that's what I 'ears 'em
   saäy.   *Northern Farmer. New Style*

7 But I knaw'd a Quaäker feller as often 'as towd me
   this:
   'Doänt thou marry for munny, but goä wheer munny
   is!'   *Ib.*

8 Taake my word for it, Sammy, the poor in a loomp
   is bad.   *Ib.*

9 An' I thowt a said whot a owt to 'a said an' I coom'd
   awaäy.   *Northern Farmer. Old Style*

10 Do godamoighty knaw what a's doing a-taäkin' o'
   meä?

11 Bury the Great Duke
   With an empire's lamentation,
   Let us bury the Great Duke
   To the noise of the mourning of a mighty nation.
        Ode on the Death of the Duke of Wellington, i

12 Let the sound of those he wrought for,
   And the feet of those he fought for,
   Echo round his bones for evermore.   *Ib.* ii

13 The last great Englishman is low.   *Ib.* iii

14 Foremost captain of his time,
   Rich in saving common-sense,
   And, as the greatest only are,
   In his simplicity sublime.
   O good grey head which all men knew!   *Ib.* iv

15 O fall'n at length that tower of strength
   Which stood four-square to all the winds that blew!
                                              Ib.

16 Under the cross of gold
   That shines over city and river.   *Ib.* v

17 Mighty Seaman, this is he
   Was great by land as thou by sea.   *Ib.* vi

18 For this is England's greatest son,
   He that gain'd a hundred fights,
   Nor ever lost an English gun.   *Ib.*

19 Clash'd with his fiery few and won.   *Ib.*

20 In that world-earthquake, Waterloo!   *Ib.*

21 Thank Him who isled us here, and roughly set
   His Briton in blown seas and storming showers.
                                              Ib. vii

22 That sober freedom out of which there springs
   Our loyal passion for our temperate kings.
        Ode on the Death of the Duke of Wellington, vii

23 Who never sold the truth to serve the hour,
   Nor palter'd with Eternal God for power. *Ib.*

24 Truth-teller was our England's Alfred named.   *Ib.*

25 Not once or twice in our rough island-story,
   The path of duty was the way to glory.   *Ib.* viii

26 He shall find the stubborn thistle bursting
   Into glossy purples, which outredden
   All voluptuous garden-roses.   *Ib.*

27   The shining table-lands
   To which our God Himself is moon and sun. *Ib.*

28 Speak no more of his renown,
   Lay your earthly fancies down,
   And in the vast cathedral leave him,
   God accept him, Christ receive him.   *Ib.* ix

29 There lies a vale in Ida, lovelier
   Than all the valleys of Ionian hills.   *Œnone*, l. 1

30 O mother Ida, many-fountain'd Ida.   *Ib.* l. 22

31 Dear mother Ida, harken ere I die.
   It was the deep midnoon: one silvery cloud
   Had lost his way between the piney sides
   Of this long glen. Then to the bower they came,
   Naked they came to that smooth-swarded bower,
   And at their feet the crocus brake like fire,
   Violet, amaracus, and asphodel,
   Lotos and lilies.   *Ib.* l. 89

32 Self-reverence, self-knowledge, self-control,
   These three alone lead life to sovereign power.
                                              Ib. l. 142

33   Because right is right, to follow right
   Were wisdom in the scorn of consequence. *Ib.* l. 147

34 I built my soul a lordly pleasure-house,
   Wherein at ease for aye to dwell.
                                 The Palace of Art, i

35 Still as, while Saturn whirls, his stedfast shade
   Sleeps on his luminous ring.   *Ib.* iv

36 A haunt of ancient Peace.   *Ib.* xxii

37 Plato the wise, and large-brow'd Verulam,
   The first of those who know.   *Ib.* xli

38 On corpses three-months-old at noon she came,
   That stood against the wall.   *Ib.* lxi

39 Act first, this Earth, a stage so gloom'd with woe
   You all but sicken at the shifting scenes.
   And yet be patient. Our Playwright may show
   In some fifth Act what this wild Drama means.
                                              The Play

40 Dower'd with the hate of hate, the scorn of scorn,
   The love of love.   *The Poet*

41 And Freedom rear'd in that august sunrise
   Her beautiful bold brow.   *Ib.*

42 Vex not thou the poet's mind
   With thy shallow wit:
   Vex not thou the poet's mind;
   For thou canst not fathom it.
   Clear and bright it should be ever,
   Flowing like a crystal river;
   Bright as light, and clear as wind. *The Poet's Mind*

43 Dark-brow'd sophist, come not anear:
   All the place is holy ground.   *Ib.*

1 And he sat him down in a lonely place,
  And chanted a melody loud and sweet,
  That made the wild-swan pause in her cloud,
  And the lark drop down at his feet. *The Poet's Song*

2 The swallow stopt as he hunted the fly,
  The snake slipt under a spray,
  The wild hawk stood with the down on his beak,
  And stared, with his foot on the prey. *Ib.*

3 For some cry 'Quick' and some cry 'Slow',
  But, while the hills remain,
  Up hill 'Too-slow' will need the whip,
  Down hill 'Too-quick', the chain. *Politics*

4 The cuckoo of a joyless June
  Is calling out of doors.
  Prefatory Poem to my Brother's Sonnets

5 The cuckoo of a worse July
  Is calling thro' the dark. *Ib.*

6 Here, in this roaring moon of daffodil
  And crocus.
  Prefatory Sonnet to the 'Nineteenth Century'

7 With prudes for proctors, dowagers for deans,
  And sweet girl-graduates in their golden hair.
  The Princess, prologue, l. 141

8 A rosebud set with little wilful thorns,
  And sweet as English air could make her, she.
  Ib. l. 153

9 As thro' the land at eve we went,
  And pluck'd the ripen'd ears,
  We fell out, my wife and I,
  O we fell out I know not why,
  And kiss'd again with tears.
  And blessings on the falling out
  That all the more endears,
  When we fall out with those we love
  And kiss again with tears! *Ib.* ii. *Introd. Song*

10 O hard, when love and duty clash! *Ib.* ii. l. 273

11 And quoted odes, and jewels five-words long,
  That on the stretch'd forefinger of all Time
  Sparkle for ever. *Ib.* l. 355

12 Sweet and low, sweet and low,
  Wind of the western sea,
  Low, low, breathe and blow,
  Wind of the western sea!
  Over the rolling waters go,
  Come from the dying moon, and blow,
  Blow him again to me;
  While my little one, while my pretty one, sleeps.
  Ib. iii. *Introd. Song*

13 A Memnon smitten with the morning Sun.
  Ib. l. 100

14 The splendour falls on castle walls
  And snowy summits old in story:
  The long light shakes across the lakes,
  And the wild cataract leaps in glory.
  Blow, bugle, blow, set the wild echoes flying,
  Blow, bugle; answer, echoes, dying, dying, dying.
  Ib. iv. *Introd. Song*

15 O hark, O hear! how thin and clear,
  And thinner, clearer, farther going!
  O sweet and far from cliff and scar
  The horns of Elfland faintly blowing! *Ib.*

16 O love, they die in yon rich sky,
  They faint on hill or field or river:
  Our echoes roll from soul to soul,
  And grow for ever and for ever.
  The Princess, iv. *Introd. Song*

17 Tears, idle tears, I know not what they mean,
  Tears from the depth of some divine despair
  Rise in the heart, and gather to the eyes,
  In looking on the happy Autumn-fields,
  And thinking of the days that are no more. *Ib.* l. 21

18 So sad, so fresh, the days that are no more. *Ib.* l. 30

19 Ah, sad and strange as in dark summer dawns
  The earliest pipe of half-awaken'd birds
  To dying ears, when unto dying eyes
  The casement slowly grows a glimmering square;
  So sad, so strange, the days that are no more.

  Dear as remembered kisses after death,
  And sweet as those by hopeless fancy feign'd
  On lips that are for others: deep as love,
  Deep as first love, and wild with all regret;
  O Death in Life, the days that are no more. *Ib.* l. 31

20 O Swallow, Swallow, flying, flying South,
  Fly to her, and fall upon her gilded eaves,
  And tell her, tell her, what I tell to thee.

  O tell her, Swallow, thou that knowest each,
  That bright and fierce and fickle is the South,
  And dark and true and tender is the North. *Ib.* l. 75

21 O tell her, Swallow, that thy brood is flown:
  Say to her, I do but wanton in the South,
  But in the North long since my nest is made.

  O tell her, brief is life but love is long,
  And brief the sun of summer in the North,
  And brief the moon of beauty in the South.

  O Swallow, flying from the golden woods,
  Fly to her, and pipe and woo her, and make her mine,
  And tell her, tell her, that I follow thee. *Ib.* l. 90

22 Thy voice is heard thro' rolling drums,
  That beat to battle where he stands;
  Thy face across his fancy comes,
  And gives the battle to his hands:
  A moment, while the trumpets blow,
  He sees his brood about thy knee;
  The next, like fire he meets the foe,
  And strikes him dead for thine and thee.
  Ib. l. 552

23 Man is the hunter; woman is his game. *Ib.* v, l. 147

24 Man for the field and woman for the hearth:
  Man for the sword and for the needle she:
  Man with the head and woman with the heart:
  Man to command and woman to obey;
  All else confusion. *Ib.* l. 427

25 Home they brought her warrior dead.
  She nor swoon'd, nor utter'd cry:
  All her maidens, watching, said,
  'She must weep or she will die.' *Ib.* vi. *Introd. Song*

26 Home they brought him slain with spears,
  They brought him home at even-fall.
  Ib. Version reprinted in Poems (1912), p. 870

27 Rose a nurse of ninety years,
  Set his child upon her knee—
  Like summer tempest came her tears—
  'Sweet my child, I live for thee.' *Ib.*

28   The woman is so hard
  Upon the woman. *Ib.* l. 205

1 Ask me no more: the moon may draw the sea;
The cloud may stoop from heaven and take the shape
With fold to fold, of mountain or of cape;
But O too fond, when have I answer'd thee?
                        Ask me no more.

Ask me no more: what answer should I give?
I love not hollow cheek or faded eye:
Yet, O my friend, I will not have thee die!
Ask me no more, lest I should bid thee live;
                        Ask me no more.

Ask me no more: thy fate and mine are seal'd:
I strove against the stream and all in vain:
Let the great river take me to the main:
No more, dear love, for at a touch I yield;
                        Ask me no more.
          The Princess, vii. *Introd. Song*

2 Now sleeps the crimson petal, now the white;
Nor waves the cypress in the palace walk;
Nor winks the gold fin in the porphyry font:
The fire-fly wakens: waken thou with me.

Now droops the milk-white peacock like a ghost,
And like a ghost she glimmers on to me.

Now lies the Earth all Danaë to the stars,
And all thy heart lies open unto me.
Now slides the silent meteor on, and leaves
A shining furrow, as thy thoughts in me.

Now folds the lily all her sweetness up,
And slips into the bosom of the lake:
So fold thyself, my dearest, thou, and slip
Into my bosom and be lost in me.   *Ib.* l. 161

3 Come down, O maid, from yonder mountain height:
What pleasure lives in height?   *Ib.* l. 177

4 For Love is of the valley, come thou down
And find him; by the happy threshold, he,
Or hand in hand with Plenty in the maize,
Or red with spirted purple of the vats,
Or foxlike in the vine; nor cares to walk
With Death and Morning on the silver horns.
                        Ib. l. 184

5   Sweet is every sound,
Sweeter thy voice, but every sound is sweet;
Myriads of rivulets hurrying thro' the lawn,
The moan of doves in immemorial elms,
And murmuring of innumerable bees.   *Ib.* l. 203

6 The woman's cause is man's: they rise or sink
Together.   *Ib.* l. 243

7 Like perfect music unto noble words.   *Ib.* l. 270

8   Happy he
With such a mother! faith in womankind
Beats with his blood, and trust in all things high
Comes easy to him, and tho' he trip and fall
He shall not blind his soul with clay.   *Ib.* l. 308

9 No little lily-handed Baronet he,
A great broad-shoulder'd genial Englishman.
              Ib. Conclusion, l. 84

10 A pamphleteer on guano and on grain.   *Ib.* l. 89

11 This laurel greener from the brows
Of him that utter'd nothing base.
     To the Queen (1851), '*Revered, beloved*'

12 Her court was pure; her life serene;
  God gave her peace; her land reposed;
  A thousand claims to reverence closed
In her as Mother, Wife, and Queen;

And statesmen at her council met
  Who knew the seasons when to take
  Occasion by the hand, and make
The bounds of freedom wider yet.   *To the Queen*

13 Broad-based upon her people's will,
And compass'd by the inviolate sea.   *Ib.*

14   Our slowly-grown
And crown'd Republic's crowning common-sense.
    Ib. '*O loyal to the royal in thyself*', l. 59

15 For it was in the golden prime
  Of good Haroun Alraschid.
     Recollections of the Arabian Nights, i

16   At Flores in the Azores Sir Richard Grenville lay,
And a pinnace, like a fluttered bird, came flying from
  far away:
'Spanish ships of war at sea! we have sighted fifty-
  three!'   *The Revenge*, i

17 Then sware Lord Thomas Howard: "'Fore God I am
  no coward;
But I cannot meet them here, for my ships are out of
  gear,
And the half my men are sick. I must fly, but follow
  quick.
We are six ships of the line; can we fight with fifty-
  three?'   *Ib.*

18 Then spake Sir Richard Grenville: 'I know you are
  no coward;
You fly them for a moment to fight with them again.
But I've ninety men and more that are lying sick
  ashore.
I should count myself the coward if I left them, my
  Lord Howard,
To these Inquisition dogs and the devildoms of
  Spain.'   *Ib.* ii

19 So Lord Howard past away with five ships of war
  that day,
Till he melted like a cloud in the silent summer
  heaven;
But Sir Richard bore in hand all his sick men from
  the land
Very carefully and slow,
Men of Bideford in Devon,
And we laid them on the ballast down below;
For we brought them all aboard,
And they blest him in their pain, that they were not
  left to Spain,
To the thumbscrew and the stake, for the glory of
  the Lord.   *Ib.* iii

20 'Shall we fight or shall we fly?
Good Sir Richard, tell us now,
For to fight is but to die!
There'll be little of us left by the time this sun be set.'
And Sir Richard said again: 'We be all good English
  men.
Let us bang these dogs of Seville, the children of the
  devil,
For I never turn'd my back upon Don or devil yet.'
                        Ib. iv

21 And the sun went down, and the stars came out far
  over the summer sea,
But never a moment ceased the fight of the one and
  the fifty-three.
Ship after ship, the whole night long, their high-built
  galleons came,
Ship after ship, the whole night long, with her battle-
  thunder and flame;

Ship after ship, the whole night long, drew back with
her dead and her shame.

For some were sunk and many were shatter'd, and so
could fight us no more—

God of battles, was ever a battle like this in the world
before? *The Revenge*, ix

1 'Sink me the ship, Master Gunner—sink her, split her
in twain!

Fall into the hands of God, not into the hands of
Spain!' *Ib.* xi

2 And the gunner said 'Ay, ay', but the seamen made
reply:

'We have children, we have wives,
And the Lord hath spared our lives.' *Ib.* x·i

3 And they praised him to his face with their courtly
foreign grace;

But he rose upon their decks, and he cried:

'I have fought for Queen and Faith like a valiant man
and true;

I have only done my duty as a man is bound to do:
With a joyful spirit I Sir Richard Grenville die!'

And he fell upon their decks, and he died. *Ib.* xiii

4 And the little Revenge herself went down by the
island crags

To be lost evermore in the main. *Ib.* xiv

5 Form, Form, Riflemen Form! *Riflemen Form!*

6 Make thou my spirit pure and clear
As are the frosty skies,
Or the first snowdrop of the year
That in my bosom lies. *St. Agnes' Eve*

7 The sabbaths of Eternity,
One sabbath deep and wide—
A light upon the shining sea—
The Bridegroom with his bride! *Ib.*

8 Battering the gates of heaven with storms of prayer.
St. Simeon Stylites, l. 7

9 What does little birdie say
In her nest at peep of day? *Sea Dreams*, l. 281

10 Birdie, rest a little longer,
Till the little wings are stronger.
So she rests a little longer,
Then she flies away. *Ib.* l. 285

11 My strength is as the strength of ten,
Because my heart is pure. *Sir Galahad*

12 So pass I hostel, hall, and grange;
By bridge and ford, by park and pale,
All-arm'd I ride, whate'er betide,
Until I find the holy Grail. *Ib.*

13 A man had given all other bliss,
And all his worldly worth for this,
To waste his whole heart in one kiss
Upon her perfect lips.
Sir Launcelot and Queen Guinevere

14 Alone and warming his five wits,
The white owl in the belfry sits. *Song. The Owl*

15 Thou art no sabbath-drawler of old saws,
Distill'd from some worm-canker'd homily.
Sonnet. To J. M. K.

16 Thou from a throne
Mounted in heaven wilt shoot into the dark
Arrows of lightnings. I will stand and mark. *Ib.*

17 Oh teach me yet
Somewhat before the heavy clod
Weighs on me, and the busy fret
Of that sharp-headed worm begins
In the gross blackness underneath.
*Supposed Confessions of a Second-Rate Sensitive
Mind*

18 In tea-cup times of hood and hoop,
Or while the patch was worn.
The Talking Oak, xvi

19 And far below the Roundhead rode,
And humm'd a surly hymn. *Ib.* lxxv

20 The woods decay, the woods decay and fall,
The vapours weep their burthen to the ground,
Man comes and tills the field and lies beneath,
And after many a summer dies the swan.
Tithonus, l. 1

21 Here at the quiet limit of the world. *Ib.* l. 7

22 Why wilt thou ever scare me with thy tears,
And make me tremble lest a saying learnt,
In days far-off, on that dark earth, be true?
'The gods themselves cannot recall their gifts.'
Ib. l. 46

23 Of happy men that have the power to die,
And grassy barrows of the happier dead. *Ib.* l. 70

24 A still small voice spake unto me,
'Thou art so full of misery,
Were it not better not to be?' *The Two Voices*, i

25 This truth within thy mind rehearse,
That in a boundless universe
Is boundless better, boundless worse. *Ib.* ix

26 'Consider well,' the voice replied,
'His face, that two hours since hath died;
Wilt thou find passion, pain, or pride?' *Ib.* lxxxi

27 No life that breathes with human breath
Has ever truly long'd for death. *Ib.* cxxxii

28 For, being of that honest few,
Who give the Fiend himself his due,
Should eighty-thousand college-councils
Thunder 'Anathema', friend, at you.
To the Rev. F. D. Maurice, ii

29 A careless-order'd garden
Close to the ridge of a noble down. *Ib.* iv

30 You'll have no scandal while you dine,
But honest talk and wholesome wine. *Ib.* v

31 It little profits that an idle king,
By this still hearth, among these barren crags,
Match'd with an aged wife, I mete and dole
Unequal laws unto a savage race. *Ulysses*, l. 1

32 I will drink
Life to the lees: all times I have enjoy'd
Greatly, have suffer'd greatly, both with those
That loved me, and alone; on shore, and when
Thro' scudding drifts the rainy Hyades
Vext the dim sea: I am become a name;
For always roaming with a hungry heart
Much have I seen and known; cities of men
And manners, climates, councils, governments,
Myself not least, but honour'd of them all;
And drunk delight of battle with my peers,
Far on the ringing plains of windy Troy.
I am a part of all that I have met;
Yet all experience is an arch wherethro'

Gleams that untravell'd world, whose margin fades
For ever and for ever when I move.
How dull it is to pause, to make an end,
To rust unburnish'd, not to shine in use!
As tho' to breathe were life. Life piled on life
Were all too little, and of one to me
Little remains: but every hour is saved
From that eternal silence, something more,
A bringer of new things.   *Ulysses*, l. 6

1   This gray spirit yearning in desire
To follow knowledge like a sinking star,
Beyond the utmost bound of human thought.
                                    Ib. l. 30

2 This is my son, mine own Telemachus.   *Ib.* l. 33

3 There lies the port; the vessel puffs her sail:
There gloom the dark broad seas. My mariners,
Souls that have toil'd, and wrought, and thought
    with me—
That ever with a frolic welcome took
The thunder and the sunshine, and opposed
Free hearts, free foreheads—you and I are old;
Old age hath yet his honour and his toil;
Death closes all: but something ere the end,
Some work of noble note, may yet be done,
Not unbecoming men that strove with gods.
The lights begin to twinkle from the rocks:
The long day wanes: the slow moon climbs: the deep
Moans round with many voices. Come, my friends,
'Tis not too late to seek a newer world.
Push off, and sitting well in order smite
The sounding furrows; for my purpose holds
To sail beyond the sunset, and the baths
Of all the western stars, until I die.
It may be that the gulfs will wash us down:
It may be we shall touch the Happy Isles,
And see the great Achilles, whom we knew.
Tho' much is taken, much abides; and tho'
We are not now that strength which in old days
Moved earth and heaven; that which we are, we are;
One equal temper of heroic hearts,
Made weak by time and fate, but strong in will
To strive, to seek, to find, and not to yield. *Ib.* l. 44

4 What is it all but a trouble of ants in the gleam of a
    million million of suns?   *Vastness*

5 Household happiness, gracious children, debtless
    competence, golden mean.   *Ib.*

6 An' I thowt 'twur the will o' the Lord, but Miss Annie
    she said it wur draäins.   *The Village Wife*, ii

7 All the charm of all the Muses often flowering in a
    lonely word.   *To Virgil*, iii

8   I salute thee, Mantovano,
I that loved thee since my day began,
Wielder of the stateliest measure ever moulded by
    the lips of man.   *Ib.* x

9 As 'twere a hundred-throated nightingale.
                            The Vision of Sin, II

10 God made Himself an awful rose of dawn.   *Ib.* III

11 Bitter barmaid, waning fast!   *Ib.* IV. ii

12 Let us have a quiet hour,
Let us hob-and-nob with Death.   *Ib.* iii

13 Every moment dies a man,
Every moment one is born.   *Ib.* ix

14 Fill the can, and fill the cup:
    All the windy ways of men
Are but dust that rises up,
    And is lightly laid again.
                        The Vision of Sin, IV. xviii

15 Drink to heavy Ignorance!
    Hob-and-nob with brother Death!   *Ib.* xxxiii

16 We knew the merry world was round,
And we might sail for evermore.   *The Voyage*, i

17 Give her the wages of going on, and not to die.
                                        Wages, ii

18 Sea-King's daughter from over the sea, Alexandra!
Saxon and Norman and Dane are we,
But all of us Danes in our welcome of thee, Alexandra!
                        A Welcome to Alexandra

19 Oh well for him whose will is strong!
He suffers, but he will not suffer long;
He suffers, but he cannot suffer wrong.   *Will*

20 O plump head-waiter at the Cock
To which I most resort.
                Will Waterproof's Lyrical Monologue, i

21 Or that eternal want of pence,
    Which vexes public men.   *Ib.* vi

22 High over roaring Temple-bar,
    And set in Heaven's third story,
I look at all things as they are,
    But thro' a kind of glory.   *Ib.* ix

23 Right down by smoky Paul's they bore,
    Till, where the street grows straiter,
One fix'd for ever at the door,
    And one became head-waiter.   *Ib.* xviii

24 A land of settled government,
    A land of just and old renown,
Where Freedom slowly broadens down
From precedent to precedent. '*You ask me, why*,' iii

25 While I live, the Owls!
When I die, the GHOULS!!!
    *Written by the side of an epigram on a poet's fate
    by Thomas Hood.* H. Tennyson's *Alfred, Lord
    Tennyson* (1898), ii. 96

26 A louse in the locks of literature.
    Said to Churton Collins to Edmund Gosse. Evan
    Charteris's *Life and Letters of Sir Edmund Gosse*,
    ch. xiv

TERENCE

c. 190–159 B.C.

27   Id arbitror
Adprime in vita esse utile, ut nequid nimis.
    My view is that the most important thing in life
    is never to have too much of anything.
                                    Andria, 61

28 Davos sum, non Oedipus.
    I am Davos, not Oedipus.   *Ib.* 194

29 Amantium irae amoris integratio est.
    The quarrels of lovers are the renewal of love.
                                        Ib. 555

30 Homo sum; humani nil a me alienum puto.
    I am a man, I count nothing human indifferent to
    me.   *Heauton Timorumenos*, I. i. 25

31 Fortis fortuna adiuvat.
    Fortune aids the brave.   *Phormio*, 203

1 Quot homines tot sententiae: suo quoque mos.

So many men, so many opinions; his own a law to
each.   *Phormio*, 454

TERTULLIAN

A.D. *c.* 160–*c.* 225

2 O testimonium animae naturaliter Christianae.

O witness of the soul naturally Christian.
                                         Apol. xvii

3 Plures efficimus quoties metimur a vobis, semen est
sanguis Christianorum.

The more ye mow us down, the more we grow, the
seed is the blood of Christians. (*Traditionally
rendered as* 'The blood of the martyrs is the seed
of the Church'.)   *Ib.* l. *ad fin.*

4 Certum est quia impossibile est.

It is certain because it is impossible.
                            De Carne Christi, 5

EDWARD TESCHEMACHER

nineteenth century

5 There is a garden that I dream of.
                      The Garden of Your Heart

6 Where my caravan has rested,
Flowers I leave you on the grass.
              Where My Caravan Has Rested

WILLIAM MAKEPEACE THACKERAY

1811–1863

7 He who meanly admires mean things is a Snob.
                      The Book of Snobs, ch. 2

8 It is impossible, in our condition of Society, not to be
sometimes a Snob.   *Ib.* ch. 3

9 'Tis not the dying for a faith that's so hard, Master
Harry—every man of every nation has done that—
'tis the living up to it that is difficult.
                            Esmond, bk. i, ch. 6

10 'Tis strange what a man may do, and a woman yet
think him an angel.   *Ib.* ch. 7

11 We love being in love, that's the truth on't.
                            Ib. bk. ii, ch. 15

12 Why do they always put mud into coffee on board
steamers? Why does the tea generally taste of
boiled boots?   *The Kickleburys on the Rhine*

13 What woman, however old, has not the bridal-favours
and raiment stowed away, and packed in lavender,
in the inmost cupboards of her heart?
                      Lovel the Widower, ch. 28

14 When I say that I know women, I mean I know that
I don't know them. Every single woman I ever
knew is a puzzle to me, as, I have no doubt, she is
to herself.   *Mr. Brown's Letters*

15 A military gent I see—and while his face I scan,
I think you'll all agree with me—He came from
Hindostan.   *The Newcomes*, bk. i, ch. 1

16 Kind, cheerful, merry Dr. Brighton.   *Ib.* ch. 9

17 What money is better bestowed than that of a schoolboy's tip?   *Ib.* ch. 16

18 As the last bell struck, a peculiar sweet smile shone
over his face, and he lifted up his head a little, and
quickly said, 'Adsum!' and fell back. It was the
word we used at school, when names were called;
and lo, he, whose heart was as that of a little child,
had answered to his name, and stood in the presence of The Master.
                      The Newcomes, bk. i. ch. 80

19 Rake's progress.
Pendennis, title of ch. 19.   *Used earlier by Hogarth*

20 Yes, I am a fatal man, Madame Fribsbi. To inspire
hopeless passion is my destiny. [*Mirobolant.*]
                                         Ib. ch. 23

21 Remember, it is as easy to marry a rich woman as a
poor woman.   *Ib.* ch. 28

22 For a slashing article, sir, there's nobody like the
Capting.   *Ib.* ch. 32

23 The *Pall Mall Gazette* is written by gentlemen for
gentlemen.   *Ib.*

24 Now Valoroso is a man again! [*Valoroso.*]
                      The Rose and the Ring, ch. 1

25 Business first; pleasure afterwards. [*Queen of
Paflagonia.*]   *Ib.*

26 Runs not a river by my palace wall? Have I not sacks
to sew up wives withal? [*Valoroso.*]   *Ib.* ch. 9

27 'No business before breakfast, Glum!' says the King.
'Breakfast first, business next.' [*Valoroso.*]
                                         Ib. ch. 11

28 My bold, my beautiful, my Bulbo! [*Angelica.*] *Ib.*

29 Thorns in the Cushion.   *Roundabout Papers*

30 [Quoting a newspaper:] 'Written, strange to say, on
club note-paper.'   *Ib.*

31 Illuminated with the Author's own candles.
                      Vanity Fair. Before the Curtain

32 This I set down as a positive truth. A woman with
fair opportunities and without a positive hump,
may marry whom she likes.   *Ib.* ch. 4

33 [Miss Crawley] had been in France—and loved, ever
after, French novels, French cookery, and French
wines.   *Ib.* ch. 10

34 Whenever he met a great man he grovelled before
him, and my-lorded him as only a free-born Briton
can do.   *Ib.* ch. 13

35 Arms and Hatchments, Resurgam.—Here is an
opportunity for moralizing!   *Ib.* ch. 14

36 Them's my sentiments! [*Fred Bullock.*]   *Ib.* ch. 21

37 Darkness came down on the field and city: and
Amelia was praying for George, who was lying on
his face, dead, with a bullet through his heart.
                                         Ib. ch. 32

38 Nothing like blood, sir, in hosses, dawgs, and men.
[*James Crawley.*]   *Ib.* ch. 35

39 How to live well on nothing a year.
                                Ib. Title of ch. 36

40 Ah! *Vanitas Vanitatum!* Which of us is happy in this
world? Which of us has his desire? or, having it,
is satisfied?—Come, children, let us shut up the
box and the puppets, for our play is played out.
                                         Ib. ch. 67

41 There's no sweeter tobacco comes from Virginia,
and no better brand than the Three Castles.
                            The Virginians, ch. 1

1 Fashnable fax and polite annygoats.
The Yellowplush Papers, pt. i, title

2 My ma wrapped up my buth in a mistry.
Ib. pt. ii, *Miss Shum's Husband*, ch. 1

3 Ho, pretty page, with the dimpled chin
That never has known the barber's shear,
All your wish is woman to win,
This is the way that boys begin.
Wait till you come to Forty Year.
The Age of Wisdom

4 Although I enter not,
Yet round about the spot
Ofttimes I hover;
And near the sacred gate,
With longing eyes I wait,
Expectant of her.
At the Church Gate

5 Then sing as Martin Luther sang,
As Doctor Martin Luther sang,
'Who loves not wine, woman and song,
He is a fool his whole life long.'
A Credo

6 The play is done; the curtain drops,
Slow falling to the prompter's bell:
A moment yet the actor stops,
And looks around, to say farewell.
It is an irksome word and task:
And, when he's laughed and said his say,
He shows, as he removes the mask,
A face that's anything but gay.
The End of the Play

7 There were three sailors of Bristol City
Who took a boat and went to sea.
But first with beef and captain's biscuits
And pickled pork they loaded she.
There was gorging Jack and guzzling Jimmy,
And the youngest he was little Billee.
Now when they got as far as the Equator
They'd nothing left but one split pea. *Little Billee*

8 Says gorging Jim to guzzling Jacky,
We have no wittles, so we must eat *we*. *Ib.*

9 There's little Bill as is young and tender,
We're old and tough—so let's eat *he*. *Ib.*

10 He scarce had said his Cathechism,
When up he jumps: 'There's land I see!
There's Jerusalem and Madagascar,
And North and South Ameri*key*.
There's the British Fleet a-riding at anchor,
With Admiral Napier, K.C.B.' *Ib.*

11 Christmas is here:
Winds whistle shrill,
Icy and chill.
Little care we;
Little we fear
Weather without,
Sheltered about
The Mahogany Tree. *The Mahogany Tree*

12 Werther had a love for Charlotte
Such as words could never utter;
Would you know how first he met her?
She was cutting bread and butter.

Charlotte was a married lady,
And a moral man was Werther,
And for all the wealth of Indies,
Would do nothing for to hurt her.

So he sighed and pined and ogled,
And his passion boiled and bubbled,
Till he blew his silly brains out
And no more was by it troubled.

Charlotte, having seen his body
Borne before her on a shutter,
Like a well-conducted person,
Went on cutting bread and butter.
Sorrows of Werther

13 Oh, Vanity of vanities!
How wayward the decrees of Fate are;
How very weak the very wise,
How very small the very great are!
Vanitas Vanitatum

WILLIAM MAKEPEACE THAYER

14 Log-cabin to White House.
*Title of a biography (1910) of James Garfield
(1831–1881)*

FRANCIS THOMPSON
1859–1907

15 Pontifical Death, that doth the crevasse bridge
To the steep and trifid God. *Anthem of Earth*

16 Here I shake off
The bur o' the world, man's congregation shun,
And to the antique order of the dead
I take the tongueless vows: my cell is set
Here in thy bosom; my little trouble is ended
In a little peace. *Ib.*

17 And thou—what needest with thy tribe's black tents
Who hast the red pavilion of my heart?
Arab Love Song

18 He the Anteros and Eros,
I the body, He the Cross;
He upbeareth me, *Ischyros*,
Agios Athanatos! *Assumpta Maria*

19 Lo! He standeth, Spouse and Brother,
I to Him, and He to me,
Who upraised me where my mother
Fell beneath the apple-tree. *Ib.*

20 Life is a coquetry
Of Death, which wearies me,
Too sure
Of the amour.
To the Dead Cardinal of Westminster

21 I have no angels left
Now, Sweet, to pray to. *A Carrier Song*

22 The hills look over on the South,
And Southward dreams the sea;
And with the sea-breeze hand in hand,
Came innocence and she. *Daisy*

23 Where 'mid the gorse the raspberry
Red for the gatherer springs,
Two children did we stray and talk
Wise, idle, childish things. *Ib.*

24 The fairest things have fleetest end,
Their scent survives their close:
But the rose's scent is bitterness
To him that loved the rose. *Ib.*

1 She went her unremembering way,
　　She went and left in me
　The pang of all the partings gone,
　　And partings yet to be.

　She left me marvelling why my soul
　　Was sad that she was glad;
　At all the sadness in the sweet,
　　The sweetness in the sad.　　*Daisy*

2 Nothing begins and nothing ends
　　That is not paid with moan;
　For we are born in other's pain,
　　And perish in our own.　　*Ib.*

3 Ah, for a heart less native to high Heaven,
　A hooded eye, for jesses and restraint,
　Or for a will accipitrine to pursue!
　　The Dread of Height

4 Go, songs, for ended is our brief sweet play;
　　Go, children of swift joy and tardy sorrow:
　And some are sung, and that was yesterday,
　　And some unsung, and that may be to-morrow
　　　　　　Envoy

5 Little Jesus, wast Thou shy
　Once, and just so small as I?
　And what did it feel to be
　Out of Heaven and just like me?　*Ex Ore Infantium*

6 　　　　Did the things
　Play 'Can you see me?' through their wings?　*Ib.*

7 Cast wide the folding doorways of the East,
　For now is light increased!
　And the wind-besomed chambers of the air,
　See they be garnished fair.
　　From the Night of Forebeing. Ode to Easter

8 Spring is come home with her world-wandering feet.
　And all things are made young with young desires.
　　　　　　Ib.

9 Let even the slug-abed snail upon the thorn
　Put forth a conscious horn!　　*Ib.*

10 Look for me in the nurseries of Heaven.
　　　　To My Godchild

11 O nothing, in this corporal earth of man,
　That to the imminent heaven of his high soul
　Responds with colour and with shadow, can
　Lack correlated greatness.　　*The Heart*, ii

12 And all man's Babylons strive but to impart
　The grandeurs of his Babylonian heart.　*Ib.*

13 I fled Him, down the nights and down the days;
　　I fled Him, down the arches of the years;
　I fled Him, down the labyrinthine ways
　　Of my own mind; and in the mist of tears
　I hid from Him, and under running laughter.
　　　　The Hound of Heaven

14 But with unhurrying chase,
　And unperturbèd pace,
　Deliberate speed, majestic instancy,
　They beat—and a Voice beat
　More instant than the Feet—
　'All things betray thee, who betrayest Me.'　*Ib.*

15 (For, though I knew His love Who followed,
　　Yet was I sore adread
　Lest, having Him, I must have naught beside.)　*Ib.*

16 Fear wist not to evade, as Love wist to pursue.　*Ib.*

17 I said to Dawn: Be sudden—to Eve: Be soon.　*Ib.*

18 To all swift things for swiftness did I sue;
　Clung to the whistling mane of every wind.
　　　　The Hound of Heaven

19 Came on the following Feet,
　And a Voice above their beat—
　'Naught shelters thee, who wilt not shelter Me.'　*Ib.*

20 I sought no more that after which I strayed
　　In face of man or maid;
　But still within the little children's eyes
　　Seems something, something that replies,
　They at least are for me, surely for me!
　I turned me to them very wistfully;
　But just as their young eyes grew sudden fair
　　With dawning answers there,
　Their angel plucked them from me by the hair.　*Ib.*

21 I was heavy with the even
　When she lit her glimmering tapers
　Round the day's dead sanctities.　　*Ib.*

22 My harness piece by piece Thou hast hewn from me
　And smitten me to my knee.　　*Ib.*

23 Yea, faileth now even dream
　The dreamer, and the lute the lutanist;
　Even the linked fantasies, in whose blossomy twist
　I swung the earth a trinket at my wrist.　*Ib.*

24 　　　　Ah! must—
　　Designer infinite!—
　Ah! must Thou char the wood ere Thou canst limn
　with it?　　*Ib.*

25 　　Such is; what is to be?
　The pulp so bitter, how shall taste the rind?　*Ib.*

26 Yet ever and anon a trumpet sounds
　From the hid battlements of Eternity;
　Those shaken mists a space unsettle, then
　Round the half-glimpsèd turrets slowly wash again.
　　　　　　Ib.

27 Whether man's heart or life it be which yields
　　Thee harvest, must Thy harvest-fields
　　Be dunged with rotten death?　　*Ib.*

28 　Now of that long pursuit
　　Comes on at hand the bruit;
　That Voice is round me like a bursting sea:
　　'And is thy earth so marred,
　　Shattered in shard on shard?
　Lo, all things fly thee, for thou fliest Me!'　*Ib.*

29 And human love needs human meriting:
　　How hast thou merited—
　Of all man's clotted clay the dingiest clot?
　　Alack, thou knowest not
　How little worthy of any love thou art.　*Ib.*

30 All which I took from thee I did but take,
　　Not for thy harms,
　But just that thou might'st seek it in My arms.　*Ib.*

31 　Halts by me that footfall:
　　Is my gloom, after all,
　Shade of His hand, outstretched caressingly?
　　'Ah, fondest, blindest, weakest,
　　I am He whom thou seekest!
　Thou dravest love from thee, who dravest Me.'　*Ib.*

32 There is no expeditious road
　To pack and label men for God,
　And save them by the barrel-load.
　　Epilogue to 'A Judgment in Heaven'

1 O world invisible, we view thee,
O world intangible, we touch thee,
O world unknowable, we know thee,
Inapprehensible, we clutch thee!

Does the fish soar to find the ocean,
The eagle plunge to find the air—
That we ask of the stars in motion
If they have rumour of thee there?

Not where the wheeling systems darken,
And our benumbed conceiving soars!—
The drift of pinions, would we hearken,
Beats at our own clay-shuttered doors.

The angels keep their ancient places;—
Turn but a stone, and start a wing!
'Tis ye, 'tis your estrangèd faces,
That miss the many-splendoured thing.

But (when so sad thou canst not sadder)
Cry;—and upon thy so sore loss
Shall shine the traffic of Jacob's ladder
Pitched betwixt Heaven and Charing Cross.

Yea, in the night, my Soul, my daughter,
Cry,—clinging Heaven by the hems;
And lo, Christ walking on the water
Not of Gennesareth, but Thames!
                    The Kingdom of God

2 It is little I repair to the matches of the Southron
    folk,
Though my own red roses there may blow;
It is little I repair to the matches of the Southron
    folk,
Though the red roses crest the caps I know.
For the field is full of shades as I near the shadowy
    coast,
And a ghostly batsman plays to the bowling of a
    ghost,
And I look through my tears on a soundless-clapping
    host
    As the run-stealers flicker to and fro,
        To and fro:—
O my Hornby and my Barlow long ago! *At Lord's*

3 Secret was the garden,
Set i' the pathless awe.   *The Mistress of Vision*

4 East, ah, east of Himalay,
Dwell the nations underground.   *Ib.*

5 Where is the land of Luthany,
And where the region Elenore?
I do faint therefor.

When to the new eyes of thee
All things by immortal power,
Near or far,
Hiddenly
To each other linked are,
That thou canst not stir a flower
Without troubling of a star.   *Ib.*

6 Lo, in the sanctuaried East,
Day, a dedicated priest,
In all his robes pontifical exprest,
Lifteth slowly, lifteth sweetly,
From out its Orient tabernacle drawn,
Yon orbed sacrament confest
Which sprinkles benediction through the dawn.
                    Orient Ode

7 Ah! let the sweet birds of the Lord
With earth's waters make accord;

Teach how the crucifix may be
Carven from the laurel-tree,
Fruit of the Hesperides
Burnish take on Eden-trees,
The Muses' sacred grove be wet
With the red dew of Olivet,
And Sappho lay her burning brows
In white Cecilia's lap of snows!
                To a Poet Breaking Silence

8 Summer set lip to earth's bosom bare,
And left the flushed print in a poppy there.
                    The Poppy

9 The sleep-flower sways in the wheat its head,
Heavy with dreams, as that with bread:
The goodly grain and the sun-flushed sleeper
The reaper reaps, and Time the reaper.

I hang 'mid men my needless head,
And my fruit is dreams, as theirs is bread:
The goodly men and the sun-hazed sleeper
Time shall reap, but after the reaper
The world shall glean of me, me the sleeper.   *Ib.*

10 I had endured through watches of the dark
The abashless inquisition of each star.
                    Sister Songs, i

11 The innocent moon, which nothing does but shine,
Moves all the labouring surges of the world.   *Ib.*

12 What heart could have thought you?—
Past our devisal
(O filigree petal!)
Fashioned so purely,
Fragilely, surely,
From what Paradisal
Imagineless metal,
Too costly for cost?   *To a Snowflake*

13 His hammer of wind,
And His graver of frost.   *Ib.*

14 And, while she feels the heavens lie bare,
She only talks about her hair.   *The Way of a Maid*

HAROLD WILLIAM THOMPSON
1891–

15 What shall we do—or go fishing?
        Body, Boots and Britches (1940), p. 504

WILLIAM HEPWORTH THOMPSON
1810–1886

16 I did not think we should miss poor Kingsley so soon.
        On Seeley's inaugural lecture as Professor of History, following Charles Kingsley

17 We are none of us infallible—not even the youngest
    of us.
        Remark referring to G. W. Balfour, then Junior Fellow of Trinity. G. W. E. Russell's *Collections and Recollections*, ch. 18

JAMES THOMSON
1700–1748

18 When Britain first, at heaven's command,
Arose from out the azure main,
This was the charter of the land,
And guardian angels sung this strain:
'Rule, Britannia, rule the waves;
Britons never will be slaves.'
        Alfred: a Masque (1740), Act II, Scene the last

1 The world of waters wild. *Britannia*, l. 27

2 A pleasing land of drowsyhead it was.
The Castle of Indolence, c. 1. vi

3 As when a shepherd of the Hebrid Isles,
Placed far amid the melancholy main. *Ib.* xxx

4 A bard here dwelt, more fat than bard beseems.
Ib. lxviii

5 Poured forth his unpremeditated strain. *Ib.*

6 A little, round, fat, oily man of God. *Ib.* lxix

7 For ever, Fortune, wilt thou prove
An unrelenting foe to love,
And, when we meet a mutual heart,
Come in between and bid us part? *To Fortune*

8 Come then, expressive Silence, muse His praise.
A Hymn on the Seasons, l. 118

9 How the heart listened while he pleading spoke!
While on the enlightened mind, with winning art,
His gentle reason so persuasive stole
That the charmed hearer thought it was his own.
To the Memory of the Lord Talbot, l. 103

10 Come, gentle Spring! ethereal mildness, come.
The Seasons, Spring, l. 1

11 The stately-sailing swan
Gives out his snowy plumage to the gale,
And, arching proud his neck, with oary feet
Bears forward fierce, and guards his osier-isle,
Protective of his young. *Ib.* l. 778

12 Delightful task! to rear the tender thought,
To teach the young idea how to shoot. *Ib.* l. 1152

13 An elegant sufficiency, content,
Retirement, rural quiet, friendship, books.
Ib. l. 1161

14 The sober-suited songstress. [The nightingale.]
Ib. Summer, l. 746

15 Ships, dim-discovered, dropping from the clouds.
Ib. l. 946

16 Or sighed and looked unutterable things. *Ib.* l. 1188

17 While Autumn nodding o'er the yellow plain
Comes jovial on. *Ib. Autumn*, l. 2

18 While listening senates hang upon thy tongue.
Ib. l. 15

19 For loveliness
Needs not the foreign aid of ornament,
But is when unadorned adorned the most. *Ib.* l. 204

20 Poor is the triumph o'er the timid hare! *Ib.* l. 401

21 The big round tears run down his dappled face.
Ib. l. 454

22 The Atlantic surge
Pours in among the stormy Hebrides. *Ib.* l. 864

23 Find other lands beneath another sun. *Ib.* l. 1286

24 See, Winter comes to rule the varied year,
Sullen and sad. *Ib. Winter*, l. 1

25 Welcome, kindred glooms!
Congenial horrors, hail! *Ib.* l. 5

26 The redbreast, sacred to the household gods,
Wisely regardful of the embroiling sky,
In joyless fields and thorny thickets leaves
His shivering mates, and pays to trusted man
His annual visit. Half afraid, he first

Against the window beats; then brisk alights
On the warm hearth; then hopping o'er the floor,
Eyes all the smiling family askance,
And pecks, and starts, and wonders where he is—
Till, more familiar grown, the table-crumbs
Attract his slender feet. *The Seasons, Winter*, l. 246

27 Studious let me sit,
And hold high converse with the mighty dead.
Ib. l. 431

28 Oh! Sophonisba! Sophonisba! oh! *Sophonisba*, III. ii

JAMES THOMSON
1834–1882

29 The City is of Night; perchance of Death,
But certainly of Night. *The City of Dreadful Night*

30 As we rush, as we rush in the train,
The trees and the houses go wheeling back,
But the starry heavens above that plain
Come flying on our track. *Sunday at Hampstead*, x

31 Give a man a horse he can ride,
Give a man a boat he can sail.
Sunday up the River, xv

HENRY DAVID THOREAU
1817–1862

32 The mass of men lead lives of quiet desperation.
Walden. Economy

33 It is a characteristic of wisdom not to do desperate
things. *Ib.*

34 I have lived some thirty years on this planet, and I
have yet to hear the first syllable of valuable or
even earnest advice from my seniors. *Ib.*

35 I long ago lost a hound, a bay horse, and a turtle-
dove, and am still on their trail. *Ib.*

36 It is true, I never assisted the sun materially in his
rising, but, doubt not, it was of the last importance
only to be present at it. *Ib.*

37 Tall arrowy white pines. *Ib.*

38 The owner of the axe, as he released his hold on it,
said that it was the apple of his eye; but I returned
it sharper than I received it. *Ib.*

39 For more than five years I maintained myself thus
solely by the labor of my hands, and I found, that
by working about six weeks in a year, I could meet
all the expenses of living. *Ib.*

40 As for Doing-good, that is one of the professions
which are full. Moreover, I have tried it fairly,
and, strange as it may seem, am satisfied that it
does not agree with my constitution. *Ib.*

41 The government of the world I live in was not
framed, like that of Britain, in after-dinner conversations over the wine. *Ib.* conclusion

42 Simplify, simplify.
Ib. Where I Lived, and What I Lived For

43 The three-o'-clock in the morning courage, which
Bonaparte thought was the rarest. *Ib. Sounds*

44 Wherever a man goes, men will pursue him and paw
him with their dirty institutions, and, if they can,
constrain him to belong to their desperate odd-
fellow society. *Ib. The Village*

1 I frequently tramped eight or ten miles through the deepest snow to keep an appointment with a beech-tree, or a yellow birch, or an old acquaintance among the pines. *Walden. Winter Visitors*

2 I once had a sparrow alight upon my shoulder for a moment while I was hoeing in a village garden, and I felt that I was more distinguished by that circumstance than I should have been by any epaulet I could have worn. *Ib.*

3 It takes two to speak the truth,—one to speak, and another to hear.
A Week on the Concord and Merrimack Rivers, Wednesday

4 Some circumstantial evidence is very strong, as when you find a trout in the milk.
Unpublished MSS. in Miscellanies, Biographical Sketch (1918), vol. x, p. 30

5 Not that the story need be long, but it will take a long while to make it short.
Letter to Mr. B., 16 Nov. 1857. (See 374:8)

ROSE HARTWICK THORPE
1850–1939

6 Curfew must not ring to-night. *Title of poem*

REV. GODFREY THRING
1823–1903

7 Fierce raged the tempest o'er the deep,
Watch did thine anxious servants keep,
But thou wast wrapp'd in guileless sleep,
   Calm and still.
Chope's Hymnal (1862). Fierce Raged The Tempest

THUCYDIDES
b. c. 471 B.C.

8 κτῆμα ἐς ἀεί.
A possession for ever. *Thucydides, i. 22*

9 φιλοκαλοῦμέν τε γὰρ μετ' εὐτελείας καὶ φιλοσοφοῦμεν ἄνευ μαλακίας.
For we are lovers of the beautiful, yet simple in our tastes, and we cultivate the mind without loss of manliness. *Ib. ii. 40, § 1. Trans. by Jowett*

10 ἀνδρῶν γὰρ ἐπιφανῶν πᾶσα γῆ τάφος.
The whole earth is the sepulchre of famous men.
Ib. 43, § 3

11 τῆς τε γὰρ ὑπαρχούσης φύσεως μὴ χείροσι γενέσθαι ὑμῖν μεγάλη ἡ δόξα, καὶ ἧς ἂν ἐπ' ἐλάχιστον ἀρετῆς πέρι ἢ ψόγου ἐν τοῖς ἄρσεσι κλέος ᾖ.
To a woman not to show more weakness than is natural to her sex is great glory, and not to be talked of for good or evil among men.
Ib. 45, § 2

JAMES THURBER
1894–

12 The War Between Men and Women.
Title of series of cartoons

EDWARD, FIRST BARON THURLOW
1731–1806

13 As guardian of his Majesty's conscience.
Speech in the House of Lords, 1779. C. Butler, *Reminiscences*, vol. 1, p. 200

14 His debt of gratitude also to his Majesty was ample . . .; and which, when he forgot, might God forget him!
Speech in the House of Lords, 15 Dec. 1778. Parl. Hist. (1814), vol. xxvii, col. 680

15 Did you ever expect a corporation to have a conscience, when it has no soul to be damned, and no body to be kicked?
Attrib. Wilberforce, *Life of Thurlow*, vol. iii, Appendix

EDWARD, SECOND BARON THURLOW
1781–1829

16 Nature is always wise in every part.
Select Poems. Sonnet. To a Bird, that haunted the Waters of Lacken, in the Winter

PAUL W. TIBBET
contemporary

17 A mushroom of boiling dust up to 20,000 feet.
Description of atomic bomb explosion

TIBULLUS
54?–18? B.C.

18 Te spectem, suprema mihi cum venerit hora,
Te teneam moriens deficiente manu.
Let me behold thee when my last hour is come,
thee let me hold with my dying hand. *I. i. 59*

19 Iuppiter pluvius.
Jupiter the rain-bringer. *Ib. vii. 26*

CHIDIOCK TICHBORNE
1558?–1586

20 My prime of youth is but a frost of cares;
My feast of joy is but a dish of pain;
My crop of corn is but a field of tares;
And all my good is but vain hope of gain.
The day is past, and yet I saw no sun;
And now I live, and now my life is done.
Verses of Praise and Joy. Elegy. (Written in the Tower before his execution)

THOMAS TICKELL
1686–1740

21 I hear a voice you cannot hear,
 Which says I must not stay;
I see a hand you cannot see,
 Which beckons me away. *Colin and Lucy, v. 4*

22 There taught us how to live; and (oh! too high
The price for knowledge) taught us how to die.
Epitaph. On the Death of Mr. Addison, l. 81.
Addison's *Works (1721)*, preface, p. xx

HARRY TILZER

1 Come, Come, Come and have a drink with me
Down at the old 'Bull and Bush'.
Song sung by Florrie Ford

2 Come, Come, Come and make eyes at me. *Ib.*

MATTHEW TINDAL

1657–1733

3 Matters of fact, which as Mr. Budgell somewhere observes, are very stubborn things.
Will of Matthew Tindal (1733), p. 23

TITUS VESPASIANUS

A.D. 40 or 41–81

4 Amici, diem perdidi.
Friends, I have lost a day.
Suetonius, Titus, ch. 8, i

JOHN TOBIN

1770–1804

5 The man that lays his hand upon a woman,
Save in the way of kindness, is a wretch
Whom 't were gross flattery to name a coward.
The Honeymoon, II. i

JACOPONE DA TODI

d. 1306

6 Stabat mater dolorosa
Iuxta crucem lacrimosa.

At the cross her station keeping
Stood the mournful mother weeping.
Pachen, Jacopone da Todi. Trans. in English Hymnal. Also ascribed to Innocent III

LEO TOLSTOY

1828–1910

7 All happy families resemble each other, each unhappy family is unhappy in its own way.
Anna Karenina, pt. i, ch. 1. *Trans. by Maude*

8 Pure and complete sorrow is as impossible as pure and complete joy.
War and Peace, bk. xv, ch. 1. *Trans. by Maude*

9 Art is not a handicraft, it is the transmission of feeling the artist has experienced.
What is Art? ch. 19. *Trans. by Maude*

10 I sit on a man's back, choking him and making him carry me, and yet assure myself and others that I am very sorry for him and wish to ease his lot by all possible means—except by getting off his back.
What Then Must We Do? ch. 16. *Trans. by Maude*

AUGUSTUS MONTAGUE TOPLADY

1740–1778

11 Rock of ages, cleft for me,
Let me hide myself in thee.
The Gospel Magazine, Oct. 1775. *Rock of Ages*

12 Nothing in my hand I bring,
Simply to thy Cross I cling;
Naked, come to thee for dress;
Helpless, look to thee for grace;
Foul, I to the Fountain fly;
Wash me, Saviour, or I die. *Rock of Ages*

THOMAS TRAHERNE

1637?–1674

13 You never enjoy the world aright, till the sea itself floweth in your veins, till you are clothed with the heavens, and crowned with the stars: and perceive yourself to be the sole heir of the whole world, and more than so, because men are in it who are every one sole heirs as well as you. Till you can sing and rejoice and delight in God, as misers do in gold, and kings in sceptres, you never enjoy the world.
Centuries of Meditations. Cent. i, § 29

14 The corn was orient and immortal wheat, which never should be reaped, nor was ever sown. I thought it had stood from everlasting to everlasting.
Ib. Cent. iii, § 3

15 The Men! O what venerable and reverend creatures did the aged seem! Immortal Cherubims! And young men glittering and sparkling Angels, and maids strange seraphic pieces of life and beauty! Boys and girls tumbling in the street, and playing, were moving jewels. I knew not that they were born or should die; but all things abided eternally as they were in their proper places. *Ib.*

16 Contentment is a sleepy thing
If it in death alone must die;
A quiet mind is worse than poverty,
Unless it from enjoyment spring!
That's blessedness alone that makes a King!
Of Contentment

17 O yonder is the moon
Newly come after me to town,
That shin'd at Lugwardin but yesternight,
Where I enjoy'd the self-same light.
On Leaping over the Moon, viii

18 I within did flow
With seas of life, like wine. *Wonder*, iii

HENRY DUFF TRAILL

1842–1900

19 Look in my face. My name is Used-to-was;
I am also called Played-out and Done-to-death,
And It-will-wash-no-more.
After Dilettante Concetti [*i.e. Dante Gabriel Rossetti, see 411:17*], viii

JOSEPH TRAPP

1679–1747

20 The King, observing with judicious eyes
The state of both his universities,
To Oxford sent a troop of horse, and why?
That learned body wanted loyalty;
To Cambridge books, as very well discerning
How much that loyal body wanted learning.
On George I's Donation of the Bishop of Ely's Library to Cambridge University. Nichols's *Literary Anecdotes*, vol. iii, p. 330. *For the reply see 87:26*

1 Our royal master saw, with heedful eyes,
The wants of his two universities:
Troops he to Oxford sent, as knowing why
That learned body wanted loyalty:
But books to Cambridge gave, as well discerning
That that right loyal body wanted learning.
Alternative version recited by Dr. Johnson.
Johnsonian Miscellanies (1897), vol. i, p. 171

HERBERT TRENCH
1865–1923

2 But when Night is on the hills, and the great Voices
Roll in from Sea,
By starlight and by candlelight and dreamlight
She comes to me.
She Comes Not When Noon is on the Roses

3 Come, let us make love deathless, thou and I.
To Arolilia, No. 2. *'Come, let us make love death-less'*

4 O dreamy, gloomy, friendly Trees. *Title of poem*

RICHARD TRENCH, ARCHBISHOP OF DUBLIN
1807–1886

5 England, we love thee better than we know.
Gibraltar

6 I say to thee, do thou repeat
To the first man thou mayest meet
In lane, highway, or open street—
That he and we and all men move
Under a canopy of love,
As broad as the blue sky above. *The Kingdom of God*

7 This *is* blessing, this *is* life. *Ib.*

GEORGE MACAULAY TREVELYAN
1876–

8 Disinterested intellectual curiosity is the life blood of real civilisation.
English Social History (1942), preface, viii

9 Education . . . has produced a vast population able to read but unable to distinguish what is worth reading. *Ib.* ch. 18

ANTHONY TROLLOPE
1815–1882

10 He must have known me had he seen me as he was wont to see me, for he was in the habit of flogging me constantly. Perhaps he did not recognize me by my face. *Autobiography*, ch. 1

11 Take away from English authors their copyrights, and you would very soon take away from England her authors. *Ib.* ch. 6

12 Three hours a day will produce as much as a man ought to write. *Ib.* ch. 15

13 I think that Plantagenet Palliser, Duke of Omnium, is a perfect gentleman. If he be not, then am I unable to describe a gentleman. *Ib.* ch. 20

14 She [Mrs. Stanhope] was rich in apparel, but not bedizened with finery . . . she well knew the great architectural secret of decorating her constructions, and never descended to construct a decoration.
Barchester Towers, ch. 9

15 'Unhand it, sir!' said Mrs. Proudie. From what scrap of dramatic poetry she had extracted the word cannot be said; but it must have rested on her memory, and now seemed opportunely dignified for the occasion. *Barchester Towers*, ch. 11

16 It's dogged as does it. It ain't thinking about it.
Last Chronicle of Barset, ch. 61

17 We know that power does corrupt. [*Duke of Omnium.*]
The Prime Minister, ch. 68

18 The tenth Muse, who now governs the periodical press. *The Warden*, ch. 14

ST. VINCENT TROUBRIDGE
1895–

19 There is an iron curtain across Europe.
Sunday Empire News, 21 Oct. 1945

MARTIN FARQUHAR TUPPER
1810–1889

20 A good book is the best of friends, the same to-day and for ever.
Proverbial Philosophy, Series 1. *Of Reading*

WALTER JAMES REDFERN TURNER
1889–1946

21 Chimborazo, Cotopaxi,
They had stolen my soul away! *Romance*, vii

THOMAS TUSSER
1524?–1580

22 Make hunger thy sauce, as a medicine for health.
Five Hundred Points of Good Husbandry, **ch.**
10. *Good Husbandry Lessons*

23 At Christmas play and make good cheer,
For Christmas comes but once a year.
Ib. ch. 12. *The Farmer's **daily** Diet*

24 Yet true it is, as cow chaws cud,
And trees at spring do yield forth bud,
Except wind stands as never it stood,
It is an ill wind turns none to good.
Ib. ch. 13. *Description of the Properties of Winds*

25 Who goeth a borrowing
Goeth a sorrowing.
Few lend (but fools)
Their working tools. *Ib.* ch. 15. *September's Abstract*

26 In doing of either, let wit bear a stroke,
For buying or selling of pig in a poke.
Ib. September's Husbandry

27 Naught venture, naught have.
Ib. ch. 16. *October's Abstract*

28 To dog in the manger some liken I could.
Ib. ch. 28. *Against Fantastical Scrupleness*

29 Feb, fill the dyke
With what thou dost like.
Ib. ch. 34. *February's Husbandry*

30 March dust to be sold
Worth ransom of gold.
Ib. ch. 36. *March's Husbandry*

31 Sweet April showers
Do spring May flowers.
Ib. ch. 38. *April's Husbandry*

1 **Cold** May and windy,
Barn filleth up finely.
Five Hundred Points of Good Husbandry, ch. 40.
May's Husbandry

2 Dry August and warm
Doth harvest no harm.
Ib. ch. 46. *August's Husbandry*

3 Look ere thou leap, see ere thou go.
Ib. ch. 56. *Dialogue of Wiving and Thriving*

4 Some respite to husbands the weather may send,
But housewives' affairs have never an end.
Ib. Preface to the Book of Housewifery

5 The stone that is rolling can gather no moss,
For master and servant, oft changing is loss.
Ib. Housewifely Admonitions

6 Dry sun, dry wind;
Safe bind, safe find.
Ib. Washing

LAWRENCE TUTTIETT
1825–1897

7 Father, let me dedicate
All this year to thee.
Gems of Thought (1864), *Father, Let Me Dedicate*

MARK TWAIN [SAMUEL LANGHORNE CLEMENS]
1835–1910

8 There was things which he stretched, but mainly he
told the truth.
The Adventures of Huckleberry Finn, ch. 1

9 The statements was interesting, but tough.
Ib. ch. 17

10 All kings is mostly rapscallions. *Ib.* ch. 23

11 If there was two birds sitting on a fence, he would bet
you which one would fly first.
The Celebrated Jumping Frog, p. 17

12 I don't see no p'ints about that frog that's any
better'n any other frog. *Ib.* p. 20

13 Soap and education are not as sudden as a massacre,
but they are more deadly in the long run.
The Facts concerning the Recent Resignation.
Sketches New & Old (1900), p. 350

14 They spell it Vinci and pronounce it Vinchy;
foreigners always spell better than they pronounce.
Innocents Abroad, ch. 19

15 I do not want Michael Angelo for breakfast—for
luncheon—for dinner—for tea—for supper—for
between meals. *Ib.* ch. 27

16 Lump the whole thing! say that the Creator made
Italy from designs by Michael Angelo! *Ib.*

17 Guides cannot master the subtleties of the American
joke. *Ib.*

18 If you've got a nice *fresh* corpse, fetch him out! *Ib.*

19 Are you going to hang him *anyhow*—and try him
afterward? *Innocents at Home*, ch. 5

20 When I'm playful I use the meridians of longitude
and parallels of latitude for a seine, and drag the
Atlantic Ocean for whales! I scratch my head with
the lightning and purr myself to sleep with the
thunder! *Life on the Mississippi*, ch. 3

21 At bottom he was probably fond of them, but he was
always able to conceal it. [On Thomas Carlyle and
Americans.] *My First Lie*

22 An experienced, industrious, ambitious, and often
quite picturesque liar.
Private History of a Campaign that Failed

23 Adam was but human—this explains it all. He did
not want the apple for the apple's sake, he wanted
it only because it was forbidden.
Pudd'nhead Wilson, heading of ch. 2

24 Whoever has lived long enough to find out what life
is, knows how deep a debt of gratitude we owe to
Adam, the first great benefactor of our race. He
brought death into the world. *Ib.* heading of ch. 3

25 There's plenty of boys that will come hankering and
gruvvelling around when you've got an apple, and
beg the core off you; but when *they've* got one, and
you beg for the core and remind them how you
give them a core one time, they make a mouth at
you and say thank you 'most to death, but there
ain't-a-going to *be* no core.
Tom Sawyer Abroad, ch. 1

26 There ain't no way to find out why a snorer can't hear
himself snore. *Ib.* ch. 10

27 They inwardly resolved that so long as they remained
in the business, their piracies should not again be
sullied with the crime of stealing. *Ib.* ch. 13

28 The cross of the Legion of Honour has been con-
ferred upon me. However, few escape that distinction. *A Tramp Abroad*, ch. 8

29 This poor little one-horse town.
The Undertaker's Chat

30 The report of my death was an exaggeration.
Cable from Europe to the Associated Press

31 There is a sumptuous variety about the New England
weather that compels the stranger's admiration—
and regret. The weather is always doing something there; always attending strictly to business;
always getting up new designs and trying them on
the people to see how they will go. But it gets
through more business in spring than in any other
season. In the spring I have counted one hundred
and thirty-six different kinds of weather inside of
four-and-twenty hours.
*The Weather. Speech at dinner of New England
Society, New York, 22 Dec. 1876. Speeches*
(1910), p. 59

HENRY TWELLS
1823–1900

32 At even ere the sun was set,
The sick, O Lord, around thee lay.
Hymns Ancient and Modern (1868), Appendix.
At Even Ere the Sun Was Set

EDWARD SMITH UFFORD
1851–1929

33 Throw out the life-line across the dark wave,
There is a brother whom someone should save,
Throw out the life-line, throw out the life-line,
Someone is sinking to-day. *Revivalist Hymn* (1884)

MIGUEL DE UNAMUNO
1864–1937

1 Fe que no duda es fe muerta.
Faith which does not doubt is dead faith.
La Agonía del Cristianismo, p. 34

2 Cúrate de la afección de preocuparte cómo aparezcas a los demás. Cuídate sólo . . . de la idea que de ti Dios tenga.
Cure yourself of the inclination to bother about how you look to other people. Be concerned only . . . with the idea God has of you.
Vida de D. Quijote y Sancho, p. 27

MRS. C. UNWIN

3 The Hungry Forties. *Title of book* (1905)

RALPH R. UPTON

4 Stop; look; listen.
Slogan devised in 1912 to replace the old U.S. railway-crossing signs of 'Look out for the locomotive'

W. UPTON

5 This lass so neat, with smile so sweet,
Has won my right good will,
I'd crowns resign to call thee mine,
Sweet lass of Richmond Hill.
The Lass of Richmond Hill. Oxford Song Book.
(*See* 327:5)

SIR JOHN VANBRUGH
1664–1726

6 The want of a thing is perplexing enough, but the possession of it is intolerable.
The Confederacy, I. ii

7 Much of a muchness. *The Provok'd Husband,* I. i

8 BELINDA:
Ay, but you know we must return good for evil.
LADY BRUTE:
That may be a mistake in the translation.
The Provok'd Wife, I. i

9 Britons, strike home. *Ib.* IV. i

10 Thinking is to me the greatest fatigue in the world.
The Relapse, II. i

11 No man worth having is true to his wife, or can be true to his wife, or ever was, or ever will be so.
Ib. III. ii

WILLIAM HENRY VANDERBILT
1821–1885

12 The public be damned!
Reply to a question whether the public should be consulted about luxury trains. A. W. Cole's *Letter, New York Times,* 25 August 1918.

BARTOLOMEO VANZETTI
1888–1927

13 I found myself compelled to fight back from my eyes the tears, and quanch my heart trobling to my throat to not weep before him. But Sacco's name will live in the hearts of the people, when your name, your laws, institutions, and your false god are but a dim remomoring of a cursed past in which man was wolf to the man.
Last speech to the Massachusetts court, which was trying him and Nicolo Sacco on charges of murder and robbery. Both were self-confessed anarchists and labour agitators. Both were convicted, and were executed 23 Aug. 1927

CHARLES JOHN VAUGHAN
1816–1897

14 Must you go? Can't you stay?
Remark with which he broke up awkward breakfast parties of schoolboys who were too shy to go. Story retold with the words transposed, 'Can't you go? Must you stay?' G. W. E. Russell's *Collections and Recollections,* ch. 24

HENRY VAUGHAN
1622–1695

15 Man is the shuttle, to whose winding quest
And passage through these looms
God order'd motion, but ordain'd no rest.
Silex Scintillans. Man.

16 Father of lights! what sunny seed,
What glance of day hast Thou confin'd
Into this bird? To all the breed
This busy ray Thou hast assign'd;
Their magnetism works all night,
And dreams of Paradise and light.
Ib. Cock-Crowing

17 I cannot reach it; and my striving eye
Dazzles at it, as at eternity. *Ib. Childhood*

18 Through that pure virgin shrine,
That sacred veil drawn o'er Thy glorious noon,
That men might look and live, as glow-worms shine,
And face the moon;
Wise Nicodemus saw such light
As made him know his God by night.
Ib. The Night, l. 1

19 Most blest believer he!
Who in that land of darkness and blind eyes
Thy long expected healing wings could see
When Thou didst rise!
And, what can never more be done,
Did at midnight speak with the Sun! *Ib.* l. 7

20 Dear Night! this world's defeat;
The stop to busy fools; care's check and curb;
The day of spirits; my soul's calm retreat
Which none disturb!
Christ's progress, and His prayer-time;
The hours to which high Heaven doth chime.
Ib. l. 25

21 There is in God—some say—
A deep, but dazzling darkness; as men here
Say it is late and dusky, because they
See not all clear.
O for that Night! where I in Him
Might live invisible and dim! *Ib.* l. 49

1 My soul, there is a country
   Far beyond the stars,
Where stands a wingèd sentry
   All skilful in the wars:
There, above noise and danger,
   Sweet Peace is crown'd with smiles,
And One born in a manger
   Commands the beauteous files.
                 Silex Scintillans. Peace

2 If thou canst get but thither,
   There grows the flower of Peace,
The Rose that cannot wither,
   Thy fortress, and thy ease.
Leave then thy foolish ranges;
   For none can thee secure,
But One, who never changes,
   Thy God, thy life, thy cure.   *Ib.*

3 Happy those early days, when I
Shin'd in my angel-infancy.
Before I understood this place
Appointed for my second race,
Or taught my soul to fancy aught
But a white, celestial thought;
When yet I had not walked above
A mile or two from my first love,
And looking back—at that short space—
Could see a glimpse of His bright face.
              Ib. The Retreat, l. 1

4 And in those weaker glories spy
Some shadows of eternity.   *Ib.* l. 13

5 But felt through all this fleshly dress
Bright shoots of everlastingness.   *Ib.* l. 19

6 O how I long to travel back,
And tread again that ancient track!
That I might once more reach that plain,
Where first I left my glorious train;
From whence th' enlighten'd spirit sees
The shady City of palm-trees.   *Ib.* l. 21

7 Some men a forward motion love,
But I by backward steps would move,
And when this dust falls to the urn,
In that state I came, return.   *Ib.* l. 29

8 They are all gone into the world of light,
   And I alone sit lingering here;
Their very memory is fair and bright,
   And my sad thoughts doth clear.
              Ib. They Are All Gone

9 I see them walking in an air of glory,
   Whose light doth trample on my days:
My days, which are at best but dull and hoary,
   Mere glimmering and decays.   *Ib.*

10 Dear, beauteous death! the jewel of the just,
   Shining nowhere but in the dark;
What mysteries do lie beyond thy dust,
   Could man outlook that mark!   *Ib.*

11 He that hath found some fledg'd bird's nest, may
   know
   At first sight, if the bird be flown;
But what fair well or grove he sings in now,
   That is to him unknown.   *Ib.*

12 And yet, as angels in some brighter dreams
   Call to the soul when man doth sleep,
So some strange thoughts transcend our wonted
   themes,
   And into glory peep.   *Ib.*

13 I saw Eternity the other night,
Like a great ring of pure and endless light,
   All calm, as it was bright;
And round beneath it, Time in hours, days, years,
   Driv'n by the spheres
Like a vast shadow mov'd; in which the world
   And all her train were hurl'd.
              Silex Scintillans. The World

LUC DE CLAPIER, MARQUIS DE VAUVENARGUES

1715-1747

14 Les grandes pensées viennent du cœur.
   Great thoughts come from the heart.
              Réflexions et Maximes

THOMAS, LORD VAUX

1510-1556

15 For Age, with stealing steps,
   Hath clawed me with his clutch.
      Poems (1872), p. 42. *The Aged Lover Renounceth*
      Love. A Ditty . . . Representing the Image of
      Death

VEGETIUS

4th cent. A.D.

16 Qui desiderat pacem, praeparet bellum.
   Let him who desires peace, prepare for war.
              De Re Mil. 3, prol.

PIERRE VERGNIAUD

1753-1793

17 Il a été permis de craindre que la Révolution, comme
   Saturne, dévorât successivement tous ses enfants.
   There was reason to fear that the Revolution, like
   Saturn, might devour in turn each one of her
   children.
      Lamartine, *Histoire des Girondins*, bk. xxxviii,
      ch. 20

PAUL VERLAINE

1844-1896

18 Et tout le reste est littérature.
   All the rest is mere fine writing. *Jadis et Naguère*

QUEEN VICTORIA

1819-1901

19 I will be good.
   Letter from the Baroness Lehzen to Her Majesty,
   2 Dec. 1867. Martin's *The Prince Consort* (1875),
   vol. i, p. 13

20 We are not amused.
       Notebooks of a Spinster Lady, 2 *Jan.* 1900

21 We are not interested in the possibilities of defeat.
      To A. J. Balfour, in 'Black Week', Dec. 1899

22 He [Mr. Gladstone] speaks to Me as if I was a public
   meeting.
      G. W. E. Russell's *Collections and Recollections*,
      ch. 14

ALFRED DE VIGNY

1797–1863

1 J'aime la majesté des souffrances humaines.

I love the majesty of human suffering.
La Maison du Berger

2 Seul le silence est grand; tout le reste est faiblesse …
Fais énergiquement ta longue et lourde tâche …
Puis, après, comme moi, souffre et meurs sans parler.

Silence alone is great; all else is feebleness …
Perform with all your heart your long and heavy task. …
Then as do I, say naught, but suffer and die.
La Mort du Loup

FRANÇOIS VILLON

b. 1431

3 Mais où sont les neiges d'antan?

But where are the snows of yesteryear?
Le Grand Testament, Ballade des Dames du Temps Jadis. Trans. by D. G. Rossetti

ST. VINCENT OF LERINS

d. c. A.D. 450

4 Quod semper, quod ubique, quod ab omnibus creditum est.

What is always, what is everywhere, what is by all people believed. *Commonitorium*, ii

VIRGIL

70–19 B.C.

5 Arma virumque cano, Troiae qui primus ab oris
Italiam fato profugus Lavinaque venit
Litora—multum ille et terris iactatus et alto
Vi superum, saevae memorem Iunonis ob iram.

Arms I sing, and the man, who first from the shores of Troy came, Fate-exiled, to Italy and her Lavinian strand—much buffeted he on flood and field by constraint of Heaven and fell Juno's unslumbering ire. *Aeneid*, i. 1. *Trans. by Jackson*

6 Quo numine laeso.

Wherein was her godhead affronted. *Ib*. 8

7 Tantaene animis caelestibus irae?

Can heavenly spirits cherish resentment so dire?
Ib. 11

8 Necdum etiam causae irarum saevique dolores
Exciderant animo; manet alta mente repostum
Iudicium Paridis spretaeque iniuria formae.

Nor yet had the causes of her wrath, nor her hot resentment, faded from her soul. Deep-written in her heart the judgement of Paris remained, and the outrage to her slighted beauty. *Ib*. 25

9 Tantae molis erat Romanam condere gentem.

So vast was the struggle to found the Roman state.
Ib. 33

10 Apparent rari nantes in gurgite vasto.

Here and there in the wastes of ocean a swimmer was seen. *Ib*. 118

11 Furor arma ministrat.

Fury ministers arms. *Ib*. 150

12 Fidus quae tela gerebat Achates.

Loyal Achates bore the weapons. *Aeneid*, i. 188

13 O passi graviora, dabit deus his quoque finem.

Friends, that have endured yet heavier blows, God will grant an ending even to this. *Ib*. 199

14 Forsan et haec olim meminisse iuvabit.

The day may dawn when this plight shall be sweet to remember. *Ib*. 203

15 Durate, et vosmet rebus servate secundis.

Then endure for a while, and live for a happier day! *Ib*. 207

16 Dux femina facti.

A woman the head of their emprize. *Ib*. 364

17 Vera incessu patuit dea.

The goddess indubitable was revealed in her step.
Ib. 405

18 'En Priamus. Sunt hic etiam sua praemia laudi;
Sunt lacrimae rerum et mentem mortalia tangunt.
Solve metus; feret haec aliquam tibi fama salutem.'
Sic ait atque animum pictura pascit inani.

'Lo, here is Priam! Even here, virtue hath her rewards, and mortality her tears: even here, the woes of man touch the heart of man! Dispel thy fears; this fame of ours is herald to some salvation.' He said, and sated his soul with the barren portraiture. *Ib*. 461

19 Impar congressus Achilli.

Fronted Achilles with unequal arm. *Ib*. 475

20 Mens sibi conscia recti.

A mind conscious of the right. *Ib*. 604

21 In freta dum fluvii current, dum montibus umbrae
Lustrabunt convexa, polus dum sidera pascet,
Semper honos nomenque tuum laudesque manebunt.

While the rivers shall run to ocean, while the shadows shall move in the mountain valleys, while the sky shall feed the stars, always shall thy honour, and thy name, and thy glory abide.
Ib. 607

22 Non ignara mali miseris succurrere disco.

Not unschooled in woe do I learn to succour unhappiness! *Ib*. 630

23 Conticuere omnes intentique ora tenebant.

Every tongue was still, every face turned rapt upon him. *Ib*. ii. 1

24 Infandum, regina, iubes renovare dolorem.

Too deep for words, O queen, lies the sorrow thou bidst me renew. *Ib*. 3

25   Quaeque ipse miserrima vidi
Et quorum pars magna fui.

All the deeds of woe mine eyes have beheld, and those whereof I was no small part. *Ib*. 5

26   Et iam nox umida caelo
Praecipitat suadentque cadentia sidera somnos.

And now dewy Night falls precipitate from heaven, and the setting stars counsel sleep! *Ib*. 8

27   Equo ne credite, Teucri.
Quidquid id est, timeo Danaos et dona ferentis.

Men of Troy, trust not the horse! Be it what it may, I fear the Danaans, though their hands proffer gifts. *Ib*. 48

1   In utrumque paratus,
Seu versare dolos seu certae occumbere morti.

> Nerved to either event, whether to spin his toils, or
> to fall under death inevitable.   *Aeneid*, ii. 61

2   Crimine ab uno
Disce omnes.

> From a single crime know the nation.   *Ib.* 65

3 Horresco referens.

> I shudder at the word.   *Ib.* 204

4 Tacitae per amica silentia lunae.

> Through the friendly silence of the mute moon.
>   *Ib.* 255

5 Tempus erat quo prima quies mortalibus aegris
Incipit et dono divum gratissima serpit.

> It was the hour when the first sleep of suffering
> mortality begins, and, by the grace of Heaven,
> steals on its sweetest errand of mercy. *Ib.* 268

6   Quantum mutatus ab illo
Hectore qui redit exuvias indutus Achilli.

> How was he changed from that Hector, who
> wended homeward, clad in the spoils of Achilles.
>   *Ib.* 274

7   Iam proximus ardet
Ucalegon.

> Already neighbour Ucalegon burns.   *Ib.* 311

8   Fuimus Troes, fuit Ilium et ingens
Gloria Teucrorum.

> Trojans we are no more, Ilium is no more, and
> the great glory of the Teucrians is departed!
>   *Ib.* 325

9 Una salus victis nullam sperare salutem.

> There is but one safety to the vanquished—to hope
> not safety!   *Ib.* 354

10 Dis aliter visum.

> Heaven's thought was otherwise.   *Ib.* 428

11 Non tali auxilio nec defensoribus istis
Tempus eget.

> The hour calls not for such succour, nor such
> defenders.   *Ib.* 521

12 Sequiturque patrem non passibus aequis.

> Follows his father with unmatched step. *Ib.* 724

13   Quid non mortalia pectora cogis,
Auri sacra fames!

> O cursed lust of gold, to what canst thou not com-
> pel the heart of man!   *Ib.* iii. 56

14 Monstrum horrendum, informe, ingens, cui lumen
ademptum.

> A monster fearful and hideous, vast and eyeless.
>   *Ib.* 658

15 Agnosco veteris vestigia flammae.

> I feel again a spark of that ancient flame.
>   *Ib.* iv. 23

16 Virisque adquirit eundo.

> At every step she [Fame] gathers strength. *Ib.* 175

17   Sese interea . . .
Temptaturum aditus et quae mollissima fandi
Tempora.

> Himself meanwhile . . . would assay to find access
> and watch what hour might be the smoothest
> for his tale.   *Ib.* 291

18 Quis fallere possit amantem?

> Who shall deceive a lover's thought?
>   *Aeneid*, iv. 296

19   Nec me meminisse pigebit Elissae
Dum memor ipse mei, dum spiritus hos regit artus.

> Nor ever shall the thought of Elissa be bitter to
> me, while yet I have remembrance of myself
> and the breath governs these limbs.   *Ib.* 335

20   Varium et mutabile semper
Femina.

> A fickle thing and changeful is woman always!
>   *Ib.* 569

21 Exoriare aliquis nostris ex ossibus ultor.

> Arise, thou avenger to come, out of my ashes.
>   *Ib.* 625

22 Hos successus alit: possunt, quia posse videntur.

> To those success was good, and the semblance
> of power gave power indeed.   *Ib.* v. 231

23   Facilis descensus Averni:
Noctes atque dies patet atri ianua Ditis;
Sed revocare gradum superasque evadere ad auras,
Hoc opus, hic labor est.

> Light is the descent to Avernus! Night and day
> the portals of gloomy Dis stand wide: but to
> recall thy step and issue to the upper air—there is
> the toil and there the task!   *Ib.* vi. 126

24   Primo avulso non deficit alter
Aureus, et simili frondescit virga metallo.

> When the first is rent away a second, golden no
> less, succeeds, and the bough blossoms with ore
> as precious.   *Ib.* 143

25 Procul, o procul este, profani.

> Hence, O hence, . . . ye that are uninitiated. *Ib.* 258

26 Nunc animis opus, Aenea, nunc pectore firmo.

> Now is the hour, Aeneas, for the dauntless spirit
> —now for the stout heart.   *Ib.* 261

27 Vestibulum ante ipsum primis in faucibus Orci
Luctus et ultrices posuere cubilia Curae;
Pallentesque habitant Morbi tristisque Senectus,
Et Metus et malesuada Fames ac turpis Egestas.

> Hard before the portal, in the opening jaws of
> Hell, Grief and avenging Cares have made their
> couch; and with them dwell wan Disease and
> sorrowful Age, and Fear, and Hunger, temptress
> to Sin, and loathly Want.   *Ib.* 273

28 Tendebantque manus ripae ulterioris amore.

> Their hands outstretched in yearning for the
> farther shore.   *Ib.* 314

29 Inventas aut qui vitam excoluere per artis,
Quique sui memores alios fecere merendo.

> Or who ennobled life by arts discovered; with
> all whose service to their kind won them remem-
> brance among men.   *Ib.* 663

30 Spiritus intus alit, totamque infusa per artus
Mens agitat molem et magno se corpore miscet.

> An indwelling spirit sustains, and a mind fused
> throughout the limbs sways the whole mass and
> mingles with the giant frame.   *Ib.* 726

31 Igneus est ollis vigor et caelestis origo
Seminibus.

> To these seeds a flame-like vigour pertains and an
> origin celestial.   *Ib.* 730

1 Tu regere imperio populos, Romane, memento
(Hae tibi erunt artes), pacisque imponere morem,
Parcere subiectis et debellare superbos.

> Roman, be this thy care—these thine arts—to bear
> dominion over the nations and to impose the law
> of peace, to spare the humbled and to war down
> the proud! *Aeneid*, vi. 851

2 Sunt geminae Somni portae, quarum altera fertur
Cornea, qua veris facilis datur exitus umbris,
Altera candenti perfecta nitens elephanto,
Sed falsa ad caelum mittunt insomnia manes.

> There are two gates of Sleep:—of horn, fame tells,
> the one, through which the spirits of truth find
> an easy passage; the other, wrought smooth-
> gleaming with sheen of ivory, but false the
> visions that the nether powers speed therefrom
> to the heaven above. *Ib.* 893

3 Geniumque loci . . .
          precatur.
Implored the Genius of the place. *Ib.* vii. 136

4 Flectere si nequeo superos, Acheronta movebo.

> And if Heaven be inflexible, Hell shall be un-
> leashed! *Ib.* 312

5 O mihi praeteritos referat si Iuppiter annos.

> O, would Jupiter restore me the years that are fled!
> *Ib.* viii. 560

6 Quadripedante putrem sonitu quatit ungula campum.

> The sound of galloping hooves shook the crumb-
> ling plain. *Ib.* 596

7 Me, me, adsum qui feci, in me convertite ferrum.

> On me,—here I stand who did the deed,—on me
> turn your steel. *Ib.* ix. 427

8 Dum domus Aeneae Capitoli immobile saxum
Accolet imperiumque pater Romanus habebit.

> So long as the house of Aeneas shall dwell by the
> Capitol's unmoved rock and the Father of Rome
> bear sceptre! *Ib.* 448

9 Macte nova virtute, puer, sic itur ad astra.

> Good speed to thy youthful valour, child! So
> shalt thou scale the stars! *Ib.* 641

10 Audentis Fortuna iuvat.

> Fortune is ally to the brave. *Ib.* x. 284

11 Experto credite.

> Credit one who has proved. *Ib.* xi. 283

12 Audiit et voti Phoebus succedere partem
Mente dedit, partem volucris dispersit in auras.

> Phoebus heard, and in thought vouchsafed that
> half his vow should prosper: half he scattered to
> the fleet winds. *Ib.* 794

13 Di me terrent et Iuppiter hostis.

> The gods dismay me, and Jove my foe! *Ib.* xii. 895

14 Tityre, tu patulae recubans sub tegmine fagi
Silvestrem tenui musam meditaris avena.

> Tityrus, thou liest canopied beneath thy spreading
> beech and wooing the silvan Muse on thy slender
> oat. *Eclogue*, i. 1. *Trans. by Jackson*

15 Formosam resonare doces Amaryllida silvas.

> Thou teachest the responsive woods to call
> Amaryllis fair! *Ib.* 5

16 O Meliboee, deus nobis haec otia fecit.

> O Meliboeus, it was a god gave us this peace.
> *Eclogue*, i. 6

17 Non equidem invideo, miror magis.

> As for me I grudge thee not—rather I marvel!
> *Ib.* 11

18   Sic parvis componere magna solebam
Verum haec tantum alias inter caput extulit urbes
Quantum lenta solent inter viburna cupressi.

> I only measured great by small but, above all other
> cities, this so far exalts her head as the cypress
> above the lissom osiers! *Ib.* 23

19 Et penitus toto divisos orbe Britannos.

> Or where the Briton dwells utterly estranged from
> all the world! *Ib.* 66

20 Formosum pastor Corydon ardebat Alexim.

> Shepherd Corydon was all aflame for fair Alexis.
> *Ib.* ii. 1

21 O formose puer, nimium ne crede colori!

> Sweet boy, trust not over much to thy hue!
> *Ib.* 17

22 Quem fugis, a, demens? Habitarunt di quoque silvas.

> Ah, madman, whom dost thou flee? Even gods
> have dwelt in woods. *Ib.* 60

23 Trahit sua quemque voluptas.

> Each draws to his best-loved. *Ib.* 65

24 Nunc frondent silvae, nunc formosissimus annus.

> Now the woods are green, and the year is love-
> liest. *Ib.* iii. 57

25 Ab Iove principium musae: Iovis omnia plena.

> From Jove my lay begins: Jove filleth all. *Ib.* 60

26 Malo me Galatea petit, lasciva puella,
Et fugit ad salices et se cupit ante videri.

> Galatea, wayward girl, pelts me with apples, then
> runs behind the willows—and hopes I saw her
> first! *Ib.* 64

27 Latet anguis in herba.

> A snake lurks in the grass! *Ib.* 93

28 Non nostrum inter vos tantas componere lites.

> Not ours to decide such high dispute! *Ib.* 108

29 Claudite iam rivos, pueri; sat prata biberunt.

> Swains, close now the springs. The meadows have
> drunk enough! *Ib.* 111

30 Sicelides Musae, paulo maiora canamus!
Non omnis arbusta iuvant humilisque myrica.
Si canimus silvas, silvae sint consule dignae.
Ultima Cumaei venit iam carminis aetas;
Magnus ab integro saeclorum nascitur ordo.
Iam redit et virgo, redeunt Saturnia regna
Iam nova progenies caelo demittitur alto.

> Sicilian Muses, let us raise a somewhat loftier
> strain. Not all do orchards and the lowly tamarisk
> delight. If the woodland be our theme, let our
> woods be worthy of a consul's ear! The last age,
> heralded in Cumean song, is come, and the great
> march of the centuries, begins anew. Now the
> Virgin returns: now Saturn is king again, and a
> new and better race descends from on high.
> *Ib.* iv. 1

1 Incipe, parve puer, risu cognoscere matrem.

> Begin, baby boy, to know thy mother with a smile.
> *Eclogue*, iv. 60

2 Incipe, parve puer: qui non risere parenti,
Nec deus hunc mensa, dea nec dignata cubili est.

> Begin, baby boy! Him who had never a smile for
> a parent, no god honours with his board, no god-
> dess with her bed!   *Ib.* 62

3   Arcades ambo,
Et cantare pares et respondere parati.

> Both Arcadians, both ready to sing in even con-
> test, both ready to make reply!   *Ib.* vii. 4

4 Saepibus in nostris parvam te roscida mala
(Dux ego vester eram) vidi cum matre legentem.
Alter ab undecimo tum me iam acceperat annus,
Iam fragilis poteram a terra contingere ramos:
Ut vidi, ut perii, ut me malus abstulit error!

> Within our orchard's walls I saw thee—for I was
> there to point the way—a little maid gathering
> dewy apples with my mother! Eleven years I
> had numbered, and the twelfth already claimed
> me; from the ground already I could reach the
> frail boughs. Ah, how I saw! How I fell! How
> that fatal blindness swept me away!   *Ib.* viii. 37

5 Nunc scio quid sit Amor.

> Now do I know what Love is!   *Ib.* 43

6 Non omnia possumus omnes.

> All power is not to all.   *Ib.* 63

7   Et me fecere poetam
Pierides, sunt et mihi carmina, me quoque dicunt
Vatem pastores; sed non ego credulus illis.
Nam neque adhuc Vario videor nec dicere Cinna
Digna, sed argutos inter strepere anser olores.

> Me, too, the Pierian sisters have made a singer; I,
> too, have songs: ay, and the shepherds dub me
> *poet*, but I trust them not! For as yet, methinks,
> my strains befit not a Varius, nor a Cinna, but,
> gooselike, I cackle amid quiring swans!
>   *Ib.* ix. 32

8 Omnia vincit Amor: et nos cedamus Amori.

> Love is lord of all: yield we, too, to Love!
>   *Ib.* x. 69

9 Ite domum saturae, venit Hesperus, ite capellae.

> Get ye home, my full-fed goats, get ye home—the
> Evening-star draws on!   *Ib.* 77

10 Ultima Thule.

> Farthest Thule. *Georgics*, i. 30. *Trans. by Jackson*

11   Labor omnia vicit
Improbus et duris urgens in rebus egestas.

> Never-flinching labour proved lord of all, and the
> stress of need in a life of struggles! *Ib.* 145

12   Imponere Pelio Ossam
Scilicet, atque Ossae frondosum involvere Olympum.

> In sooth . . . to pile Ossa on Pelion and roll leaf-
> crowned Olympus on Ossa.   *Ib.* 281

13 Miscueruntque herbas et non innoxia verba.

> Mingled herbs and charms of bale.   *Ib.* ii. 129

14 Salve, magna parens frugum, Saturnia tellus,
Magna virum.

> Hail, Saturn's land, great mother of the harvest,
> great mother of men!   *Ib.* 173

15 O fortunatos nimium, sua si bona norint,
Agricolas! Quibus ipsa procul discordibus armis
Fundit humo facilem victum iustissima tellus.

> Ah, blest beyond all bliss the husbandmen, did
> they but know their happiness! On whom, far
> from the clash of arms, the most just Earth
> showers from her bosom a toilless sustenance.
>   *Georgics*, ii. 458

16 Felix qui potuit rerum cognoscere causas.

> Happy he, who has availed to read the causes of
> things.   *Ib.* 490

17 Strepitumque Acherontis avari.

> The roaring of the hungry stream of Death. *Ib.* 492

18 Fortunatus et ille deos qui novit agrestis.

> And happy he, who has knowledge of the wood-
> land gods.   *Ib.* 493

19   Temptanda via est, qua me quoque possim
Tollere humo victorque virum volitare per ora.

> I must assay a path, whereby I may raise me from
> earth and flit conqueror through the mouths of
> men!   *Ib.* iii. 8

20 Optima quaeque dies miseris mortalibus aevi
Prima fugit: subeunt morbi tristisque senectus
Et labor, et durae rapit inclementia mortis.

> It is ever the brightest day of life that is first to
> bid adieu to our hapless mortality: disease and
> gloomy eld steal upon us, and anon suffering,
> and the ruthless tyranny of Death, sweep us
> away.   *Ib.* 66

21 Sed fugit interea, fugit inreparabile tempus.

> Meanwhile, Time is flying—flying, never to return.
>   *Ib.* 284

22 Hi motus animorum atque haec certamina tanta
Pulveris exigui iactu compressa quiescent.

> Yet all this tumult of soul and all this savagery
> of conflict may be quelled and laid to rest by
> the scattering of a little dust.   *Ib.* iv. 86

23   Agmine facto
Ignavum fucos pecus a praesepibus arcent.

> They form in array and cast out the drones and
> their idle bands from the homestead. *Ib.* 167

24 Si parva licet componere magnis.

> If it be meet to measure small by great. *Ib.* 176

25 At genus immortale manet, multosque per annos
Stat fortuna domus, et avi numerantur avorum.

> Yet the race abides immortal, the star of their
> house sets not through many years, and grand-
> sire's grandsire is numbered in the roll. *Ib.* 208

26   Victorque volentis
Per populos dat iura viamque adfectat Olympo.

> Assigning in victorious march, laws to the will-
> ing nations, and assaying on earth the path to
> Heaven!   *Ib.* 561

27 Sic vos non vobis mellificatis apes.
Sic vos non vobis nidificatis aves.
Sic vos non vobis vellera fertis oves.

> So you bees make your honey, not for yourselves.
> So you birds make nests, not for yourselves.
> So you sheep bear fleeces, not for yourselves.
> *Attrib. On Bathyllus' claiming the authorship
> of certain lines by Virgil*

VOLTAIRE
1694–1778

1 Dans ce pays-ci il est bon de tuer de temps en temps un amiral pour encourager les autres.

In this country [England] it is thought well to kill an admiral from time to time to encourage the others. *Candide, ch. 23*

2 Tout est pour le mieux dans le meilleur des mondes possibles.

All is for the best in the best of possible worlds. *Ib. 30*

3 Cela est bien dit, répondit Candide, mais il faut cultiver notre jardin.

'That is well said,' replied Candide, 'but we must cultivate our garden.' (We must attend to our own affairs.) *Ib.*

4 Ils ne se servent de la pensée que pour autoriser leurs injustices, et n'emploient les paroles que pour déguiser leurs pensées.

[Men] use thought only to justify their wrongdoings, and speech only to conceal their thoughts. *Dialogue xiv. Le Chapon et la Poularde*

5 Le mieux est l'ennemi du bien.

The best is the enemy of the good. *Dict. Philosophique, art. Art Dramatique*

6 Tous les genres sont bons hors le genre ennuyeux.

All styles are good save the tiresome kind. *L'Enfant Prodigue, preface*

7 Si Dieu n'existait pas, il faudrait l'inventer.

If God did not exist, it would be necessary to invent him. *Épîtres, xcvi. A l'Auteur du Livre des Trois Imposteurs*

8 Ce corps qui s'appelait et qui s'appelle encore le saint empire romain n'était en aucune manière ni saint, ni romain, ni empire.

This agglomeration which was called and which still calls itself the Holy Roman Empire was neither holy, nor Roman, nor an empire. *Essai sur les Mœurs et l'Esprit des Nations, lxx*

9 Quoi que vous fassiez, écrasez l'infâme, et aimez qui vous aime.

Whatever you do, trample down abuses, and love those who love you. *Lettres. A. M. d'Alembert, 28 Nov. 1762*

10 On dit que Dieu est toujours pour les gros bataillons.

It is said that God is always for the big battalions. *Ib. A. M. Le Riche, 6 Feb. 1770*

11 Le superflu, chose très nécessaire.

The superfluous is very necessary. *Le Mondain, v. 22*

12 La foi consiste à croire ce que la raison ne croit pas. ... Il ne suffit pas qu'une chose soit possible pour la croire.

Faith consists in believing when it is beyond the power of reason to believe. It is not enough that a thing be possible for it to be believed. *Questions sur l'Encyclopédie*

13 Le secret d'ennuyer est ... de tout dire.

The way to be a bore [for an author] is to say everything. *Sept Discours en vers sur l'Homme, VI. Sur la Nature de l'Homme. v. 174–5*

14 Habacuc était capable de tout.

Habakkuk was capable of anything. *Attrib. see Notes and Queries, clxxxi. 46*

15 I disapprove of what you say, but I will defend to the death your right to say it. *Attrib. in S. G. Tallentyre, The Friends of Voltaire (1907), p. 199*

JOSEPH AUGUSTINE WADE
1796?–1845

16 Meet me by moonlight alone. *Meet Me by Moonlight*

HENRY WALLACE
1888–

17 The century on which we are entering can be and must be the century of the common man. *Address: The Price of Free World Victory, 8 May 1942*

LEW WALLACE
1827–1905

18 Beauty is altogether in the eye of the beholder. *The Prince of India, III. vi. 78. (See 265:14)*

WILLIAM ROSS WALLACE
d. 1881

19 The hand that rocks the cradle
Is the hand that rules the world. *John o' London's Treasure Trove*

GRAHAM WALLAS
1858–1932

20 The little girl had the making of a poet in her who, being told to be sure of her meaning before she spoke, said: 'How can I know what I think till I see what I say?' *The Art of Thought*

EDMUND WALLER
1606–1687

21 So was the huntsman by the bear oppress'd,
Whose hide he sold—before he caught the beast! *Battle of the Summer Islands, ii, l. 111*

22 Poets that lasting marble seek
Must carve in Latin or in Greek. *Of English Verse*

23 Others may use the ocean as their road,
Only the English make it their abode. *Of a War with Spain, l. 25*

24 The seas are quiet when the winds give o'er;
So, calm are we when passions are no more! *On the Foregoing Divine Poems, l. 7*

25 The soul's dark cottage, batter'd and decay'd
Lets in new light through chinks that time has made;
Stronger by weakness, wiser men become,
As they draw near to their eternal home.

Leaving the old, both worlds at once they view,
That stand upon the threshold of the new.
On the Foregoing Divine Poems, l. 18

1 That which her slender waist confin'd
Shall now my joyful temples bind;
No monarch but would give his crown
His arms might do what this has done.

It was my heaven's extremest sphere,
The pale which held that lovely deer:
My joy, my grief, my hope, my love,
Did all within this circle move.

A narrow compass! and yet there
Dwelt all that's good, and all that's fair:
Give me but what this riband bound,
Take all the rest the sun goes round.   *On a Girdle*

2 Rome, though her eagle through the world had flown,
Could never make this island all her own.
Panegyric to My Lord Protector, xvii

3 Illustrious acts high raptures do infuse,
And every conqueror creates a Muse.   *Ib*. xlvi

4   Go, lovely Rose!
Tell her, that wastes her time and me,
That now she knows,
When I resemble her to thee,
How sweet and fair she seems to be.
Song: 'Go Lovely Rose!'

5 Small is the worth
Of beauty from the light retir'd;
Bid her come forth,
Suffer'd herself to be desir'd,
And not blush so to be admir'd.   *Ib*.

6 Why came I so untimely forth
Into a world which, wanting thee,
Could entertain us with no worth,
Or shadow of felicity?
To My Young Lady Lucy Sidney

7   So all we know
Of what they do above,
Is that they happy are, and that they love.
Upon the Death of My Lady Rich, l. 75

8 Under the tropic is our language spoke,
And part of Flanders hath receiv'd our yoke.
Upon the Death of the Lord Protector, l. 21

HORACE WALPOLE, FOURTH EARL OF ORFORD
1717-1797

9 Alexander at the head of the world never tasted the
true pleasure that boys of his own age have enjoyed at the head of a school.
Letters, To Montagu, 6 May 1736

10 Our supreme governors, the mob.
Ib. To Horace Mann, 7 Sept. 1743

11 [Strawberry Hill] is a little plaything-house that I got
out of Mrs. Chenevix's shop, and is the prettiest
bauble you ever saw. It is set in enamelled
meadows, with filigree hedges.
To Conway, 8 June 1747

12 But, thank God! the Thames is between me and the
Duchess of Queensberry.   *Ib*.

13 Every drop of ink in my pen ran cold.
Ib. To Montagu, 3 July 1752

14 It has the true rust of the Barons' Wars.
Ib. To Bentley, Sept. 1753

15 At present, nothing is talked of, nothing admired, but
what I cannot help calling a very insipid and
tedious performance: it is a kind of novel, called
The Life and Opinions of Tristram Shandy; the
great humour of which consists in the whole narra-
tion always going backwards.
To Dalrymple, 4 Apr. 1760

16 One of the greatest geniuses that ever existed,
Shakespeare, undoubtedly wanted taste.
Ib. To Wren, 9 Aug. 1764

17 The works of Richardson . . . which are pictures of
high life as conceived by a bookseller, and romances
as they would be spiritualized by a Methodist
preacher.   *Ib. To Mann, 20 Dec. 1764*

18 At Madame du Deffand's, an old blind *débauchée* of
wit.   *Ib. To Conway, 6 Oct. 1765*

19 It is charming to totter into vogue.
Ib. To Selwyn, 2 Dec. 1765

20 Yes, like Queen Eleanor in the ballad, I sunk at
Charing Cross, and have risen in the Faubourg St.
Germain.   *Ib. To Gray, 25 Jan. 1766*

21 The best sun we have is made of Newcastle coal.
Ib. To Montagu, 15 June 1768

22 Everybody talks of the constitution, but all sides
forget that the constitution is extremely well, and
would do very well, if they would but let it alone.
Ib. To Sir Horace Mann, 18-19 Jan. 1770

23 It was easier to conquer it [the East] than to know
what to do with it.   *Ib. To Mann, 27 Mar. 1772*

24 The way to ensure summer in England is to have it
framed and glazed in a comfortable room.
Ib. To Cole, 28 May 1774

25 The next Augustan age will dawn on the other side
of the Atlantic. There will, perhaps, be a Thucydides at Boston, a Xenophon at New York, and,
in time, a Virgil at Mexico, and a Newton at
Peru. At last, some curious traveller from Lima
will visit England and give a description of the
ruins of St. Paul's, like the editions of Balbec and
Palmyra.   *Ib. To Mann, 24 Nov. 1774*

26 By the waters of Babylon we sit down and weep, when
we think of thee, O America!
Ib. To Mason, 12 June 1775

27 This world is a comedy to those that think, a tragedy
to those that feel.
*Ib. To the Countess of Upper Ossory, 16 Aug.
1776*

28 Prognostics do not always prove prophecies,—at least
the wisest prophets make sure of the event first.
Ib. To Thos. Walpole, 19 Feb. 1785

29 All his [Sir Joshua Reynolds's] own geese are swans,
as the swans of others are geese.
Ib. To the Countess of Upper Ossory, 1 Dec. 1786

SIR ROBERT WALPOLE, FIRST EARL OF ORFORD
1676-1745

30 They now *ring* the bells, but they will soon *wring*
their hands.
*Remark on the declaration of war with Spain,
1739. W. Coxe, Memoirs of Sir Robert Walpole
(1798), vol. i, p. 618*

31 All those men have their price.   *Ib. p. 757*

1 Madam, there are fifty thousand men slain this year in Europe, and not one Englishman.
Remark to Queen Caroline, 1734. Hervey, *Memoirs* (1848), vol. i, p. 398

2 My Lord Bath, you and I are now two as insignificant men as any in England.
To Pulteney, Earl of Bath, on their promotion to the House of Lords. W. King, *Political & Literary Anecdotes* (1819), p. 43

3 The balance of power.
Speech in the House of Commons, 13 Feb. 1741

4 Sir Robert Walpole's definition of the gratitude of place-expectants, 'That it is a lively sense of *future* favours'.
W. Hazlitt, *Lectures on the English Comic Writers, Wit and Humour*, p. 27. (*See 407:13*)

WILLIAM WALSH
1663–1708

5 And sadly reflecting,
That a lover forsaken
A new love may get,
But a neck when once broken
Can never be set.   *The Despairing Lover, l. 17*

6 Of all the torments, all the cares,
With which our lives are curst;
Of all the plagues a lover bears,
Sure rivals are the worst!
By partners, in each other kind,
Afflictions easier grow;
In love alone we hate to find
Companions of our woe. *Song, Of All the Torments*

7 I can endure my own despair,
But not another's hope.   *Ib.*

IZAAK WALTON
1593–1683

8 Angling may be said to be so like the mathematics, that it can never be fully learnt.
Compleat Angler. Epistle to the Reader

9 And for winter fly-fishing it is as useful as an almanac out of date.   *Ib.*

10 As no man is born an artist, so no man is born an angler.   *Ib.*

11 I shall stay him no longer than to wish him a rainy evening to read this following discourse; and that if he be an honest angler, the east wind may never blow when he goes a-fishing.   *Ib.*

12 I am, Sir, a Brother of the Angle.   *Ib. pt. i, ch. 1*

13 It [angling] deserves commendations; . . . it is an art, and an art worthy the knowledge and practice of a wise man.   *Ib.*

14 Angling is somewhat like poetry, men are to be born so.   *Ib.*

15 Sir Henry Wotton . . . was also a most dear lover, and a frequent practiser of the art of angling; of which he would say, 'it was an employment for his idle time, which was then not idly spent . . . a rest to his mind, a cheerer of his spirits, a diverter of sadness, a calmer of unquiet thoughts, a moderator of passions, a procurer of contentedness; and that it begat habits of peace and patience in those that professed and practised it.'   *Ib.*

16 I remember that a wise friend of mine did usually say, 'that which is everybody's business is nobody's business.'   *Compleat Angler, pt. i, ch. 2*

17 Good company and good discourse are the very sinews of virtue.   *Ib.*

18 An excellent angler, and now with God.   *Ib. ch. 4*

19 When I was last this way a-fishing.   *Ib.*

20 I love such mirth as does not make friends ashamed to look upon one another next morning.   *Ib. ch. 5*

21 A good, honest, wholesome, hungry breakfast.   *Ib.*

22 No man can lose what he never had.   *Ib.*

23 Thus use your frog. . . . Put your hook, I mean the arming-wire, through his mouth, and out at his gills; and then with a fine needle and silk sew the upper part of his leg, with only one stitch, to the arming-wire of your hook; or tie the frog's leg, above the upper joint, to the armed-wire; and, in so doing, use him as though you loved him.   *Ib. ch. 8*

24 This dish of meat is too good for any but anglers, or very honest men.   *Ib.*

25 I love any discourse of rivers, and fish and fishing.   *Ib. ch. 18*

26 Look to your health; and if you have it, praise God, and value it next to a good conscience; for health is the second blessing that we mortals are capable of; a blessing that money cannot buy.   *Ib. ch. 21*

27 Let the blessing of St. Peter's Master be . . . upon all that are lovers of virtue; and dare trust in His providence; and be quiet; and go a-Angling.   *Ib.*

28 But God, who is able to prevail, wrestled with him, as the Angel did with Jacob, and marked him; marked him for his own.   *Life of Donne*

29 The great Secretary of Nature and all learning, Sir Francis Bacon.   *Life of Herbert*

30 Of this blest man, let his just praise be given,
Heaven was in him, before he was in heaven.
Written in Dr. Richard Sibbes's Returning Backslider, now preserved in Salisbury Cathedral Library

BISHOP WILLIAM WARBURTON
1698–1779

31 Orthodoxy is my doxy; heterodoxy is another man's doxy.
Remark to Lord Sandwich. Priestley, *Memoirs* (1807), vol. i, p. 372

ARTEMUS WARD [CHARLES FARRAR BROWNE]
1834–1867

32 I now bid you a welcome adoo.
Artemus Ward His Book. The Shakers

33 'Mister Ward, don't yur blud bile at the thawt that three million and a half of your culled brethren air a clanking their chains in the South?' Sez I, 'not a bile! Let 'em clank!'   *Ib. Oberlin*

34 The College has konfired upon me the honery title of T.K., of which I'm suffishuntly prowd.   *Ib.*

35 'I wish thar was winders to my Sole,' sed I, 'so that you could see some of my feelins.'
Ib. The Showman's Courtship

1 If you mean gettin hitched, I'M IN!
Artemus Ward His Book. The Showman's Courtship

2 My pollertics, like my religion, bein of a exceedin accommodatin character. *Ib. The Crisis*

3 Shall we sell our birthrite for a mess of potash? *Ib.*

4 N.B. This is rote Sarcasticul.
Ib. A Visit to Brigham Young

5 I girdid up my Lions & fled the Seen. *Ib.*

6 Did you ever hav the measels, and if so how many?
Ib. The Census

7 'Fair youth, do you know what I'd do with you if you was my sun?' 'No,' sez he. 'Wall,' sez I, 'I'd appint your funeral to-morrow arternoon & the *korps should be ready!* You're too smart to live on this yearth.' *Ib. Edwin Forrest as Othello*

8 Before he retired to his virtuous couch. *Ib.*

9 The female woman is one of the greatest institooshuns of which this land can boste. *Ib. Woman's Rights*

10 Do me eyes deceive me earsight? Is it some dreams?
Ib. Moses, the Sassy

11 By a sudden and adroit movement I placed my left eye agin the Secesher's fist.
Ib. Thrilling Scenes in Dixie

12 The ground flew up and hit me in the hed. *Ib.*

13 I presunted myself at Betty's bedside late at nite, with considerbul licker koncealed about my persun.
Ib. Betsy-Jain Re-orgunised

14 The happy marrid man dies in good stile at home, surrounded by his weeping wife and children. The old batchelor don't die at all—he sort of rots away, like a polly-wog's tail. *Ib. Draft in Baldinsville*

15 It is a pity that Chawcer, who had geneyus, was so unedicated. He's the wuss speller I know of.
Artemus Ward in London, ch. 4. At the Tomb of Shakespeare

16 Why these weeps? *Artemus Ward's Lecture*

17 One of the principal features of my Entertainment is that it contains so many things that don't have anything to do with it. *Ib.*

18 I can't sing. As a singist I am not a success. I am saddest when I sing. So are those who hear me. They are sadder even than I am. *Ib.*

19 He [Brigham Young] is dreadfully married. He's the most married man I ever saw in my life. *Ib.*

20 Why is this thus? What is the reason of this thusness? *Ib.*

21 I am happiest when I am idle. I could live for months without performing any kind of labour, and at the expiration of that time I should feel fresh and vigorous enough to go right on in the same way for numerous more months.
Pyrotechny. III. *Pettingill*

22 Why care for grammar as long as we are good?
Ib. v

23 Let us all be happy, and live within our means, even if we have to borrer the money to do it with.
Science and Natural History

MRS. HUMPHRY WARD
1851–1920

24 'Propinquity does it'—as Mrs. Thornburgh is always reminding us. *Robert Elsmere, bk. i, ch. 2*

REV. NATHANIEL WARD
1578–1652

25 The world is full of care, much like unto a bubble; Women and care, and care and women, and women and care and trouble.
Epigram. Attributed by Ward to a lady at the Court of the Queen of Bohemia. Simple Cobler's Boy (1648), p. 25

SUSAN WARNER
1819–1885

26 Jesus loves me—this I know,
For the Bible tells me so. *The Love of Jesus*

HENRY STEVENSON WASHBURN
1813–1903

27 We shall meet, but we shall miss him,
There will be one vacant chair:
We shall linger to caress him,
When we breathe our evening prayer.
The Vacant Chair, chorus

GEORGE WASHINGTON
1732–1799

28 Father, I cannot tell a lie, I did it with my little hatchet.
Attrib. remark. Mark Twain's *Mark Twain as George Washington. Another version is:* I can't tell a lie, Pa; you know I can't tell a lie. I did cut it with my hatchet.
Weems, *Washington, 1800* (Fifth edition, 1806)

29 It is our true policy to steer clear of permanent alliance with any portion of the foreign world.
His Farewell Address to the People of the United States, 17 Sept. 1796

30 Labour to keep alive in your breast that little spark of celestial fire, called conscience.
Rules of Civility and Decent Behaviour. Sparks's *Life of Washington* (1839), vol. ii, p. 109

31 We must consult Brother Jonathan.
Said to have been a frequent remark of his during the American Revolution, referring to Jonathan Trumbull, 1710–85, Governor of Connecticut. Norwich Evening Courier, 12 Nov. 1846, No. 797, p. 2. (Publications of the Colonial Society of Massachusetts (1905), vol. vii, p. 94)

32 Put none but Americans on guard to-night.
Attrib. remark, based on his circular letter to regimental commanders, 30 April 1777

ROWLAND WATKYNS
fl. 1662

33 I love him not, but shew no reason can
Wherefore, but this, *I do not love* the man.
Flamma sine fumo. Antipathy

1 For every marriage then is best in tune,
When that the wife is May, the husband June.
*Flamma sine fumo. To the most Courteous and Fair
Gentlewoman, Mrs. Elinor Williams*

WILLIAM WATSON
1559?–1603

2 Fiat justitia et ruant coeli.
Let justice be done though the heavens fall.
Quodlibets of Religion and State (1602). (*See 203:38*)

SIR WILLIAM WATSON
1858–1936

3 April, April,
Laugh thy girlish laughter;
Then, the moment after,
Weep thy girlish tears!   *April*

4 O be less beautiful, or be less brief.   *Autumn*

5 Slight not the songsmith.   *England my Mother*

6 Plucked by his hand, the basest weed that grows
Towers to a lily, reddens to a rose.   *Epigram*

7 How all her care was but to be fair,
And all her task to be sweet. *The Heart of the Rose*

8 When, upon orchard and lane, breaks the white foam
of the Spring.   *Hymn to the Sea, Pt. III, 12*

9 Who never negligently yet
Fashioned an April violet,
Nor would forgive, did June disclose
Unceremoniously the rose.   *Nature's Way*

10 Time and the ocean, and some fostering star,
In high cabal have made us what we are.
Ode on the Coronation of Edward VII, l. 8

11 Forget not, brother singer, that though Prose
Can never be too truthful or too wise,
Song is not Truth, not Wisdom, but the rose
Upon Truth's lips, the light in Wisdom's eyes.
Ode to J. C. Collins

12 We are children of splendour and flame,
Of shuddering, also, and tears;
Magnificent out of the dust we came,
And abject from the spheres.   *Ode in May*

13 The staid, conservative, Came-over-with-the-Con-
queror type of mind. *A Study in Contrasts, i, 1. 42*

14 The thirst to know and understand,
A large and liberal discontent;
These are the goods in life's rich hand,
The things that are more excellent.
Things That Are More Excellent, viii

15 And not uncrowned with honours ran
My days, and not without a boast shall end!
For I was Shakespeare's countryman;
And wert not thou my friend?   *To R. H. Hutton*

16 Another bruising of the hapless head
Of a wronged people yearning to be free.
Ver Tenebrosum. 2. Hasheen

17 In this house with starry dome,
Floored with gemlike plains and seas,
Shall I never feel at home,
Never wholly be at ease?   *World-Strangeness*

18 On from room to room I stray,
Yet mine Host can ne'er espy,
And I know not to this day
Whether guest or captive I.   *World-Strangeness*

ISAAC WATTS
1674–1748

19 Whene'er I take my walks abroad,
How many poor I see!
What shall I render to my God
For all his gifts to me?
Divine Songs for Children, iv. Praise for Mercies

20 Lord, I ascribe it to Thy grace,
And not to chance, as others do,
That I was born of Christian race,
And not a Heathen, or a Jew.
Ib. vi. Praise for the Gospel

21 There's no repentance in the grave.
Ib. x. Solemn Thoughts of God and Death

22 There is a dreadful Hell,
And everlasting pains;
There sinners must with devils dwell
In darkness, fire, and chains.
Ib. xi. Heaven and Hell

23 But liars we can never trust,
Though they should speak the thing that's true;
And he that does one fault at first,
And lies to hide it, makes it two.
Ib. xv. Against Lying

24 Let dogs delight to bark and bite,
For God hath made them so;
Let bears and lions growl and fight,
For 'tis their nature too.
Ib. xvi. Against Quarrelling

25 But, children, you should never let
Such angry passions rise;
Your little hands were never made
To tear each other's eyes.   *Ib.*

26 Whatever brawls disturb the street,
There should be peace at home.
Ib. xvii. Love between Brothers and Sisters

27 Birds in their little nests agree
And 'tis a shameful sight,
When children of one family
Fall out, and chide, and fight.   *Ib.*

28 How doth the little busy bee
Improve each shining hour,
And gather honey all the day
From every opening flower!
Ib. xx. Against Idleness and Mischief

29 In works of labour, or of skill,
I would be busy too;
For Satan finds some mischief still
For idle hands to do.   *Ib.*

30 One sickly sheep infects the flock,
And poisons all the rest.
Ib. xxi. Against Evil Company

31 Let me be dress'd fine as I will,
Flies, worms, and flowers, exceed me still.
Ib. xxii. Against Pride in Clothes

32 I have been there, and still would go;
'Tis like a little Heaven below.
Ib. xxviii. Lord's Day. Evening

1 Hush! my dear, lie still and slumber,
  Holy angels guard thy bed!
Heavenly blessings without number
  Gently falling on thy head.
      Divine Songs for Children, xxxv. Cradle Hymn

2 Were I so tall to reach the Pole,
  Or grasp the ocean in my span,
I must be measured by my soul;
  The mind 's the standard of the man.
                            Ib. False Greatness

3 'Tis the voice of the sluggard; I heard him complain,
'You have wak'd me too soon, I must slumber again'.
As the door on its hinges, so he on his bed,
Turns his sides and his shoulders and his heavy head.
                            Moral Songs, i. The Sluggard

4 Abroad in the meadows to see the young lambs
Run sporting about by the side of their dams,
With fleeces so clean and so white.
                            Ib. ii. Innocent Play

5 How rude are the boys that throw pebbles and mire!
                                                Ib.

6 I'll not willingly offend,
  Nor be easily offended;
What's amiss I'll strive to mend,
  And endure what can't be mended.
                            Ib. vi. Good Resolution

7 Lord, in the morning thou shalt hear
  My voice ascending high.   *Psalms, v*

8 Jesus shall reign where e'er the sun
  Does his successive journeys run;
His kingdom stretch from shore to shore
Till moons shall wax and wane no more. *Ib. lxxii*

9 Our God, our help in ages past
  Our hope for years to come,
Our shelter from the stormy blast,
  And our eternal home.

Beneath the shadow of Thy Throne
  Thy saints have dwelt secure;
Sufficient is Thine Arm alone,
  And our defence is sure.

Before the hills in order stood,
  Or earth received her frame,
From everlasting Thou art God,
  To endless years the same.

A thousand ages in Thy sight
  Are like an evening gone;
Short as the watch that ends the night
  Before the rising sun.

Time, like an ever-rolling stream,
  Bears all its sons away;
They fly forgotten, as a dream
  Dies at the opening day.
      *Ib. xc. First line altered by John Wesley to
      'O God...'*

10 How bright these glorious spirits shine!
  Whence all their white array?
How came they to the blissful seats
  Of everlasting day?
      *Hymns and Spiritual Songs, bk. i, No. 41, How
      Bright These Glorious Spirits. First line altered
      from Watts's original: 'These glorious minds
      how bright they shine'*

11 Hark! from the tombs a doleful sound.
      Ib. bk. ii, No. 63. Hark! from the Tombs

12 When I can read my title clear
  To mansions in the skies,
I bid farewell to every fear,
  And wipe my weeping eyes.
      Hymns and Spiritual Songs, bk. ii, No. 65

13 There is a land of pure delight,
  Where saints immortal reign;
Infinite day excludes the night,
  And pleasures banish pain.
      Ib. No. 66. There is a Land of Pure Delight

14 Death, like a narrow sea, divides
  That heavenly land from ours.   *Ib.*

15 So to the Jews old Canaan stood,
  While Jordan rolled between.   *Ib.*

16 But timorous mortals start and shrink
  To cross the narrow sea,
And linger shivering on the brink,
  And fear to launch away.   *Ib.*

17 Could we but climb where Moses stood,
  And view the landscape o'er;
Not Jordan's stream, nor death's cold flood,
  Should fright us from the shore.   *Ib.*

18 When I survey the wondrous Cross,
  On which the Prince of glory died,
My richest gain I count but loss
  And pour contempt on all my pride.
      *Ib. bk. iii, No. 7. When I Survey the Wondrous
      Cross*

19 Were the whole realm of nature mine,
  That were a present far too small;
Love so amazing, so Divine,
  Demands my soul, my life, my all.   *Ib.*

FREDERIC EDWARD WEATHERLY
1848–1929

20 Where are the boys of the Old Brigade?
                            The Old Brigade

21 Not in the Abbey proudly laid
    Find they a place or part;
The gallant boys of the old brigade,
    They sleep in old England's heart.   *Ib.*

22 Why, Jack's the king of all,
  For they all love Jack!   *They All Love Jack*

SIDNEY WEBB, LORD PASSFIELD
1859–1947

23 The inevitability of gradualness.
      *Presidential address to the annual conference of the
      Labour Party, 1920*

WILLIAM WEBB
fl. 1839

24 His throat they cut from ear to ear,
  His brains they punched in,
His name was Mr. William Weare,
  Wot lived in Lyon's Inn.
      *Ballad. See Lord William Lennox in The
      Sporting Review, July 1839, vol. ii, p. 42. Also
      attrib. to Theodore Hook (1788–1841). See C.
      Hindley's Life and Times of James Catnach
      (1878), p. 145*

DANIEL WEBSTER
1782–1852

1 There is always room at the top.
When advised not to become a lawyer as the profession was overcrowded

2 The gentleman has not seen how to reply to this, otherwise than by supposing me to have advanced the doctrine that a national debt is a national blessing.
Second Speech in the Senate on Foot's Resolution, 26 Jan. 1830

3 The people's government, made for the people, made by the people, and answerable to the people.   *Ib.*

4 He [Alexander Hamilton] smote the rock of the national resources, and abundant streams of revenue gushed forth. He touched the dead corpse of the Public Credit, and it sprung upon its feet.
Speech at a Public Dinner at New York, 10 March 1831

5 On this question of principle, while actual suffering was yet afar off, they [the Colonies] raised their flag against a power, to which, for purposes of foreign conquest and subjugation, Rome, in the height of her glory, is not to be compared; a power which has dotted over the surface of the whole globe with her possessions and military posts, whose morning drum-beat, following the sun, and keeping company with the hours, circles the earth with one continuous and unbroken strain of the martial airs of England.
Speech in the Senate on the President's Protest, 7 May 1834

6 Thank God, I—I also—am an American!
Speech on the Completion of Bunker Hill Monument, 17 June 1843

7 The Law: It has honoured us, may we honour it.
Ib.

8 I was born an American; I will live an American; I shall die an American.
Speech in the Senate on 'The Compromise Bill', 17 July 1850

9 Fearful concatenation of circumstances.
Argument on the Murder of Captain Joseph White

JOHN WEBSTER
1580?–1625?

10 She's loose i' th' hilts.   *The Duchess of Malfi,* II. v

11 Rais'd by that curious engine, your white hand.
Ib. III. ii. 297

12 I am acquainted with sad misery
As the tann'd galley-slave is with his oar.
Ib. IV. ii. 25

13 I have made a soap-boiler costive.   *Ib.* l. 117

14 I am Duchess of Malfi still.   *Ib.* l. 146

15 Glories, like glow-worms, afar off shine bright.
But looked to near, have neither heat nor light.
Ib. l. 148

16 I know death hath ten thousand several doors
For men to take their exits.   *Ib.* l. 222

17 So I were out of your whispering.   *Ib.* l. 226

18 FERDINAND:
Cover her face; mine eyes dazzle: she died young.
BOSOLA:
I think not so; her infelicity
Seem'd to have years too many.
The Duchess of Malfi, IV. ii, l. 267

19 Physicians are like kings,—
They brook no contradiction.   *Ib.* v. ii. 72

20 We are merely the stars' tennis-balls, struck and bandied
Which way please them.   *Ib.* iv. 52

21 When I look into the fish-ponds in my garden,
Methinks I see a thing arm'd with a rake,
That seems to strike at me.   *Ib.* v. 5

22 Is not old wine wholesomest, old pippins toothsomest, old wood burn brightest, old linen wash whitest? Old soldiers, sweethearts, are surest, and old lovers are soundest.   *Westward Hoe,* II. ii

23 I saw him even now going the way of all flesh.   *Ib.*

24 Fortune's a right whore:
If she give ought, she deals it in small parcels,
That she may take away all at one swoop.
The White Devil, I. i. 4

25 'Tis just like a summer bird-cage in a garden: the birds that are without despair to get in, and the birds that are within despair and are in a consumption for fear they shall never get out.
Ib. ii. 47

26 A mere tale of a tub, my words are idle.   *Ib.* II. i. 92

27 Cowardly dogs bark loudest.   *Ib.* III. i. 163

28 A rape! a rape! . . , Yes, you have ravish'd justice;
Forced her to do your pleasure.   *Ib.* l. 271

29 There's nothing sooner dry than women's tears.
Ib. v. iii. 192

30 Call for the robin redbreast and the wren,
Since o'er shady groves they hover,
And with leaves and flowers do cover
The friendless bodies of unburied men.   *Ib.* iv. 100

31 And of all axioms this shall win the prize,—
'Tis better to be fortunate than wise.   *Ib.* vi. 183

32 I am i' th' way to study a long silence.   *Ib.* l. 204

33 There's nothing of so infinite vexation
As man's own thoughts.   *Ib.* l. 206

34 My soul, like to a ship in a black storm,
Is driven, I know not whither.   *Ib.* l. 248

35 Prosperity doth bewitch men, seeming clear;
But seas do laugh, show white, when rocks are near.
Ib. l. 250

36 I have caught
An everlasting cold; I have lost my voice
Most irrecoverably.   *Ib.* l. 270

THOMAS EARLE WELBY
1881–1933

37 'Turbot, Sir,' said the waiter, placing before me two fishbones, two eyeballs, and a bit of black mackintosh.   *The Dinner Knell*

ARTHUR WELLESLEY, DUKE OF WELLINGTON
1769–1852

1 Not upon a man from the colonel to the private in a regiment—both inclusive. We may pick up a marshal or two perhaps; but not worth a damn.
   On being asked whether he calculated upon any desertion in Buonaparte's army. Creevey Papers, ch. x, p. 228

2 It has been a damned serious business—Blücher and I have lost 30,000 men. It has been a damned nice thing—the nearest run thing you ever saw in your life.... By God! I don't think it would have done if I had not been there.   *Ib.* p. 236

3 All the business of war, and indeed all the business of life, is to endeavour to find out what you don't know by what you do; that's what I called 'guessing what was at the other side of the hill'.
   Croker Papers (1885), vol. iii, p. 276

4 Nothing except a battle lost can be half so melancholy as a battle won.
   Dispatch from the field of Waterloo, June 1815

5 I never saw so many shocking bad hats in my life.
   On seeing the first Reformed Parliament. Sir William Fraser, *Words on Wellington* (1889), p. 12

6 The battle of Waterloo was won in the playing fields of Eton.
   Montalembert, *De l'Avenir Politique de l'Angleterre* (1855). *The attribution has been refuted by the present Duke.*

7 By God, I never saw so many whores
   In all my life before.
   Hardy, *The Dynasts*, Pt. III. ii. iii

8 UXBRIDGE:
   I have lost my leg, by God!
   WELLINGTON:
   By God, and have you!   *Ib.* vii. viii

9 The next greatest misfortune to losing a battle is to gain such a victory as this.
   S. Rogers, *Recollections* (1859), p. 215

10 'What a glorious thing must be a victory, Sir.' 'The greatest tragedy in the world, Madam, except a defeat.'   *Ib.* footnote

11 The Government was contemplating the dispatch of an expedition to Burma, with a view to taking Rangoon, and a question arose as to who would be the fittest general to be sent in command of the expedition. The Cabinet sent for the Duke of Wellington, and asked his advice. He instantly replied, 'Send Lord Combermere.'
   'But we have always understood that your Grace thought Lord Combermere a fool.'
   'So he is a fool, and a d—d fool; but he can take Rangoon.'
   G. W. E. Russell's *Collections and Recollections,* ch. 2

12 In refusing the dedication of a song (the Duke of Wellington) informed Mrs. Norton that he had been obliged to make a rule of refusing dedications, 'because, in his situation as Chancellor of the University of Oxford, he had been much exposed to authors.'   *Ib.*

13 [*To Mrs. Arbuthnot, who asked:* 'Is it true you were surprised at Waterloo, Duke?']
   Not half so surprised as I am now, Mum!   *Ib.*

14 I have no small talk and Peel has no manners.
   G. W. E. Russell's *Collections and Recollections,* ch. 14

15 F.M. the Duke of Wellington presents his compliments to Mr. —— and declines to interfere in circumstances over which he has no control.
   G. A. Sala, *Echoes of the Week* in *London Illustrated News,* 23 Aug. 1884. Vol. lxxxv, p. 171, col. 1

16 Hard pounding this, gentlemen; let's see who will pound longest.
   At Waterloo. Sir W. Scott, *Paul's Letters* (1815)

17 I used to say of him [Napoleon] that his presence on the field made the difference of forty thousand men.
   Stanhope, *Notes of Conversations with the Duke of Wellington,* 2 Nov. 1831

18 Ours [our army] is composed of the scum of the earth—the mere scum of the earth. *Ib.* 4 Nov. 1831

19 My rule always was to do the business of the day in the day.   *Ib.* 2 Nov. 1835

20 What is the best to be done for the country? How can the Government be carried on?
            Ib. 18 May 1839
   ('The Queen's Government must be carried on'— *and variants—was used by him on several occasions.*)

21 I don't know what effect these men will have upon the enemy, but, by God, they terrify me.
   On a draft of troops sent to him in Spain, 1809. (*Also attributed to George III*)

22 [*To a gentleman who accosted him in the street saying,* 'Mr. Jones, I believe?']
   If you believe that you will believe anything. *Attrib.*

23 There is no mistake; there has been no mistake; and there shall be no mistake.
            Wellingtoniana (1852), p. 78

24 Up Guards and at them again!
   Attrib. to Wellington during the Battle of Waterloo. Capt. Batty's letter, 22 June 1815, in Booth's Battle of Waterloo. J. W. Croker, in a letter to A. Greville, 14 Mar. 1852, wrote 'Perhaps I might also venture to ask his Grace whether he did say, "Up Guards and at them".' *Wellington replied in an undated letter to Croker which is in Croker Correspondence and Diaries (1884), vol. iii, p. 280:* 'What I must have said and possibly did say was, Stand up, Guards! and then gave the commanding officers the order to attack'

25 I don't care a twopenny damn what becomes of the ashes of Napoleon Buonaparte.
   Attrib. Farmer and Henley, *Slang and its Analogues*

26 Publish and be damned.   *Attrib.*

HERBERT GEORGE WELLS
1866–1946

27 'I'm a Norfan, both sides,' he would explain, with the air of one who had seen trouble.
   Kipps, bk. i, ch. 6, § 1

28 'I expect,' he said, 'I was thinking jest what a Rum Go everything is. I expect it was something like that.'   *Ib.* bk. iii, ch. 3, § 8

29 Human history becomes more and more a race between education and catastrophe.
   The Outline of History, ch. 15

1 The Shape of Things to Come. *Title of book* (1933)

2 The Time-Machine. *Title of novel* (1895)

3 The War that will end War. *Title of book* (1914)

CHARLES WESLEY
1707–1788

4 'Christ, the Lord, is risen to-day,'
Sons of men and angels say,
Raise your joys and triumphs high,
Sing, ye heavens, and earth reply.
Hymns and Sacred Poems (1739). *Christ, the Lord, is Risen To-day*

5 Jesu, Lover of my soul,
Let me to Thy Bosom fly,
While the nearer waters roll,
While the tempest still is high;
Hide me, O my Saviour, hide,
Till the storm of life is past;
Safe into the haven guide,
O receive my soul at last.
Ib. (1740), *Jesu, Lover of My Soul*

6 Other refuge have I none;
Hangs my helpless soul on Thee. *Ib.*

7 Cover my defenceless head
With the shadow of Thy wing. *Ib.*

8 Thou of Life the Fountain art;
Freely let me take of Thee;
Spring Thou up within my heart,
Rise to all eternity. *Ib.*

9 Gentle Jesus, meek and mild,
Look upon a little child;
Pity my simplicity,
Suffer me to come to thee.
Ib. (1742), *Gentle Jesus, Meek and Mild*

10 Soldiers of Christ, arise,
And put your armour on.
Ib. (1749), *Soldiers of Christ, Arise*

11 Lift up your heart, lift up your voice;
Rejoice, again I say, rejoice.
Hymns for Our Lord's Resurrection (1746):
Rejoice, the Lord is King

12 Hark! the herald-angels sing
Glory to the new-born King:
Peace on earth, and mercy mild,
God and sinners reconciled.
*Ib. Christmas Hymn: Hark! the Herald Angels
Sing. First two lines altered by George Whitefield
in 1753 from Wesley's original*

Hark, how all the welkin rings,
'Glory to the King of kings'.

13 Lo! He comes with clouds descending.
Hymns of Intercession for all Mankind (1758):
*Lo! He Comes with Clouds. New Version of John
Cennick's 'Lo! He cometh, countless trumpets',
in Collection of Sacred Hymns, 1752*

14 Those who set at naught and sold Him,
Pierced and nail'd Him to the Tree,
Deeply wailing,
Shall the true Messiah see. *Ib.*

15 Let saints on earth in concert sing.
Funeral Hymns (1759): *Let saints on earth.*
Altered by F. H. Murray in his *Hymnal for
Use in the English Church* (1852), from 'Let all
the saints terrestrial sing'

JOHN WESLEY
1703–1791

16 I look upon all the world as my parish.
Journal, 11 June 1739

17 Once in seven years I burn all my sermons; for it is
a shame if I cannot write better sermons now than
I did seven years ago. *Ib. 1 Sept. 1778*

18 Though I am always in haste, I am never in a hurry.
Select Letters (1837). *Letter to a member of the
Society. 10 Dec. 1777*

19 Do all the good you can,
By all the means you can,
In all the ways you can,
In all the places you can,
At all the times you can,
To all the people you can,
As long as ever you can.
Letters (1915). *Rule of Conduct*

20 Let it be observed, that slovenliness is no part of
religion; that neither this, nor any text of Scripture,
condemns neatness of apparel. Certainly this is a
duty, not a sin. 'Cleanliness is, indeed, next to
godliness.' *Sermons*, No. xciii. *On Dress*

REV. SAMUEL WESLEY
1662–1735

21 Style is the dress of thought; a modest dress,
Neat, but not gaudy, will true critics please.
An Epistle to a Friend concerning Poetry (1700)

MAE WEST
1893–

22 Come up and see me sometime. *Diamond Lil* (1932)

EDWARD NOYES WESTCOTT
1846–1898

23 They say a reasonable amount o' fleas is good fer a
dog—keeps him from broodin' over bein' a dog,
mebbe. *David Harum, ch. 32*

EDITH WHARTON
1862–1937

24 Mrs. Ballinger is one of the ladies who pursue Culture in bands, as though it were dangerous to meet
it alone. *Xingu, ch. 1*

RICHARD WHATELY, ARCHBISHOP OF DUBLIN
1787–1863

25 Preach not because you have to say something, but
because you have something to say. *Apophthegms*

26 Happiness is no laughing matter. *Ib.* p. 218

27 It is a folly to expect men to do all that they may
reasonably be expected to do. *Ib.* p. 219

28 Honesty is the best policy; but he who is governed
by that maxim is not an honest man. *Ib.*

WILLIAM WHEWELL
1794–1866

1 And so no force, however great,
Can stretch a cord, however fine,
Into a horizontal line
That shall be absolutely straight.
Quoted as an example of accidental metre and rhyme. Printed in prose in Whewell's Elementary Treatise on Mechanics, *1819*

JAMES ABBOTT McNEILL WHISTLER
1834–1903

2 I am not arguing with you—I am telling you.
Gentle Art of Making Enemies

3 Art is upon the Town! 'Ten O'Clock'

4 Listen! There never was an artistic period. There never was an Art-loving nation. *Ib.*

5 Nature is usually wrong. *Ib.*

6 'I only know of two painters in the world,' said a newly introduced feminine enthusiast to Whistler, 'yourself and Velasquez.' 'Why,' answered Whistler in dulcet tones, 'why drag in Velasquez?'
D. C. Seitz, *Whistler Stories* (1913), p. 27

7 [*In answer to a lady who said that a landscape reminded her of his work*]
Yes madam, Nature is creeping up. *Ib.*, p. 9

8 [*In answer to the question* 'For two days' labour, you ask two hundred guineas?']
No, I ask it for the knowledge of a lifetime. *Ib.*, p. 40

9 You shouldn't say it is not good. You should say you do not like it; and then, you know, you're perfectly safe. *Ib.*, p. 35

10 [*Answering Oscar Wilde's* 'I wish I had said that']
You will, Oscar, you will.
L. C. Ingleby, *Oscar Wilde*, p. 67

HENRY KIRKE WHITE
1785–1806

11 Oft in danger, oft in woe,
Onward, Christians, onward go.
W. J. Hall's *Mitre Hymn Book*, 1836. *Adapted by Dr. W. B. Collyer from White's original* 'Much in sorrow, oft in woe'

JOSEPH BLANCO WHITE
1775–1841

12 Mysterious Night! when our first parent knew
Thee from report divine, and heard thy name,
Did he not tremble for this lovely frame,
This glorious canopy of light and blue?
To Night, l. 1

13 Hesperus with the host of heaven came,
And lo! Creation widened in man's view. *Ib.* l. 8

14 If Light can thus deceive, wherefore not Life?
Ib. l. 14

WILLIAM ALLEN WHITE
1868–1944

15 All dressed up, with nowhere to go.
On the Progressive Party in the U.S.A. in 1916, after Theodore Roosevelt had retired from the Presidential campaign

WILLIAM LINDSAY WHITE
1900–

16 They Were Expendable. *Title of book* (1942)

GEORGE WHITEFIELD
1714–1770

17 I had rather wear out than rust out.
Attrib. by Robert Southey

WILLIAM WHITEHEAD
1715–1785

18 Yes, I'm in love, I feel it now,
And Caelia has undone me;
And yet I'll swear I can't tell how
The pleasing plague stole on me.
The Je ne sçay quoi, st. i. Song

19 Her voice, her touch, might give th' alarm—
'Twas both perhaps, or neither;
In short, 'twas that provoking charm
Of Caelia altogether. *Ib.*

WILLIAM WHITING
1825–1878

20 O hear us when we cry to Thee
For those in peril on the sea.
Hymn: Eternal Father Strong to Save

WALT WHITMAN
?1819–1892

21 Silent and amazed even when a little boy,
I remember I heard the preacher every Sunday put God in his statements,
As contending against some being or influence.
A Child's Amaze

22 Give me the splendid silent sun with all his beams full-dazzling! *Give Me the Splendid Silent Sun*

23 I dream'd in a dream I saw a city invincible to the attacks of the whole of the rest of the earth,
I dream'd that was the new city of Friends.
I Dream'd in a Dream

24 The institution of the dear love of comrades.
I Hear it was Charged against Me

25 Joy, shipmate, joy!
(Pleas'd to my soul at death I cry,)
Our life is closed, our life begins,
The long, long anchorage we leave,
The ship is clear at last, she leaps!
She swiftly courses from the shore,
Joy, shipmate, joy. *Joy, Shipmate, Joy*

26 Me imperturbe, standing at ease in Nature.
Me Imperturbe

27 O Captain! my Captain! our fearful trip is done,
The ship has weather'd every rack, the prize we sought is won,
The port is near, the bells I hear, the people all exulting. *O Captain! My Captain!* i

28 The ship is anchor'd safe and sound, its voyage closed and done.
From fearful trip the victor ship comes in with object won;

Exult O shores, and ring O bells! But I with mournful tread
Walk the deck my Captain lies, Fallen cold and dead.
O Captain! My Captain! iii

1 Out of the cradle endlessly rocking,
Out of the mocking-bird's throat, the musical shuttle,
. . . . .
A reminiscence sing.
Out of the Cradle endlessly Rocking

2 O we can wait no longer,
We too take ship O soul,
Joyous we too launch out on trackless seas,
Fearless for unknown shores on waves of ecstasy to sail,
Amid the wafting winds (thou pressing me to thee, I thee to me, O soul,)
Caroling free, singing our song of God,
Chanting our chant of pleasant exploration.
Passage to India, 8

3 O my brave soul!
O farther, farther, sail!
O daring joy, but safe; are they not all the seas of God?
O farther, farther, farther sail! *Ib.* 9

4 Come my tan-faced children,
Follow well in order, get your weapons ready,
Have you your pistols? have you your sharp-edged axes?
Pioneers! O pioneers! *Pioneers! O Pioneers!*

5 Beautiful that war and all its deeds of carnage must in time be utterly lost,
That the hands of the sisters Death and Night incessantly softly wash again, and ever again, this soil'd world;
For my enemy is dead, a man as divine as myself is dead,
I look where he lies white-faced and still in the coffin—I draw near,
Bend down and touch lightly with my lips the white face in the coffin. *Reconciliation*

6 Camerado, this is no book,
Who touches this touches a man. *So Long!*

7 Where the populace rise at once against the never-ending audacity of elected persons.
Song of the Broad Axe, 5, l. 12

8 Where women walk in public processions in the streets the same as the men,
Where they enter the public assembly and take places the same as the men;
Where the city of the faithfullest friends stands,
Where the city of the cleanliness of the sexes stands,
Where the city of the healthiest fathers stands,
Where the city of the best-bodied mothers stands,
There the great city stands. *Ib.* l. 20

9 I celebrate myself, and sing myself.
Song of Myself, 1

10 I loafe and invite my soul. *Ib.*

11 Urge and urge and urge,
Always the procreant urge of the world. *Ib.* 3

12 A child said *What is the grass?* fetching it to one with full hands;
. . . . .
Or I guess it is the handkerchief of the Lord,
A scented gift and remembrancer designedly dropt,

Bearing the owner's name someway in the corners, that we may see and remark, and say *Whose?*
. . . . .
And now it seems to me the beautiful uncut hair of graves. *Song of Myself*, 6

13 Has any one supposed it lucky to be born?
I hasten to inform him or her, it is just as lucky to die, and I know it. *Ib.* 7

14 The look of the bay mare shames silliness out of me.
Ib. 13

15 I also say it is good to fall, battles are lost in the same spirit in which they are won. *Ib.* 18

16 I am he that walks with the tender and growing night,
I call to the earth and sea half-held by the night.
Press close bare-bosom'd night—press close magnetic nourishing night!
Night of south winds—night of the large few stars!
Still nodding night—mad naked summer night.
Ib. 21

17 Earth of the vitreous pour of the full moon just tinged with blue! *Ib.*

18 Far-swooping elbow'd earth—rich apple-blossom'd earth!
Smile, for your lover comes. *Ib.*

19 I believe a leaf of grass is no less than the journey-work of the stars,
And the pismire is equally perfect, and a grain of sand, and the egg of the wren,
And the tree toad is a chef-d'oeuvre for the highest,
And the running blackberry would adorn the parlors of heaven. *Ib.* 31

20 I think I could turn and live with animals, they are so placid and self-contain'd,
I stand and look at them long and long.
They do not sweat and whine about their condition,
They do not lie awake in the dark and weep for their sins,
They do not make me sick discussing their duty to God,
Not one is dissatisfied, not one is demented with the mania of owning things,
Not one kneels to another, nor to his kind that lived thousands of years ago,
Not one is respectable or unhappy over the whole earth. *Ib.* 32

21 Behold, I do not give lectures or a little charity,
When I give I give myself. *Ib.* 39

22 My rendezvous is appointed, it is certain,
The Lord will be there and wait till I come on perfect terms,
The great Camerado, the lover true for whom I pine will be there. *Ib.* 44

23 I have said that the soul is not more than the body,
And I have said that the body is not more than the soul,
And nothing, not God, is greater to one than one's self is. *Ib.* 47

24 In the faces of men and women I see God, and in my own face in the glass,
I find letters from God dropt in the street, and every one is sign'd by God's name,
And I leave them where they are, for I know that wheresoe'er I go,
Others will punctually come for ever and ever. *Ib.*

1 Do I contradict myself?
Very well then I contradict myself,
(I am large, I contain multitudes.)
Song of Myself, 50

2 I sound my barbaric yawp over the roofs of the world.
Ib. 51

3 Afoot and light-hearted I take to the open road,
Healthy, free, the world before me,
The long brown path before me leading wherever I
choose. *Song of the Open Road*, 1, l. 1

4 The earth, that is sufficient,
I do not want the constellations any nearer,
I know they are very well where they are,
I know they suffice for those who belong to them.
Ib. l. 8

5 I am larger, better than I thought,
I did not know I held so much goodness. *Ib.* 5, l. 1

6 I will put in my poems that with you is heroism upon
land and sea,
And I will report all heroism from an American point
of view. *Starting from Paumanok*, 6

7 This dust was once the man,
Gentle, plain, just and resolute, under whose cautious
hand,
Against the foulest crime in history known in any
land or age,
Was saved the Union of these States.
This Dust was Once the Man

8 When lilacs last in the dooryard bloom'd,
And the great star early droop'd in the western sky in
the night,
I mourn'd, and yet shall mourn with ever-returning
spring.
When Lilacs Last in the Dooryard Bloom'd, 1

9 Come lovely and soothing death,
Undulate round the world, serenely arriving, arriving,
In the day, in the night, to all, to each,
Sooner or later, delicate death.
Prais'd be the fathomless universe,
For life and joy, and for objects and knowledge
curious,
And for love, sweet love—but praise! praise! praise!
For the sure-enwinding arms of cool-enfolding death.
Ib. 14

10 These United States.
A Backward Glance O'er Travell'd Roads. 'These
States' *is* passim *throughout Whitman's verse*

JOHN GREENLEAF WHITTIER
1807–1892

11 Up from the meadows rich with corn,
Clear in the cool September morn,
The clustered spires of Frederick stand
Green-walled by the hills of Maryland.
Barbara Frietchie, l. 1

12 Bravest of all in Frederick town,
She took up the flag the men hauled down. *Ib.* l. 17

13 Up the street came the rebel tread,
Stonewall Jackson riding ahead. *Ib.* l. 23

14 'Shoot, if you must, this old gray head,
But spare your country's flag,' she said. *Ib.* l. 35

15 'Who touches a hair of yon gray head
Dies like a dog! March on!' he said.
Barbara Frietchie, l. 41

16 I know not where His islands lift
Their fronded palms in air;
I only know I cannot drift
Beyond His love and care.
The Eternal Goodness, xx

17 For all sad words of tongue or pen,
The saddest are these: 'It might have been!'
Maud Muller, l. 105

18 The Indian Summer of the heart! *Memories*, ix

19 Dinna ye hear it?—Dinna ye hear it?
The pipes o' Havelock sound! *Pipes at Lucknow*, iv

20 O brother man! fold to thy heart thy brother.
Worship, l. 49

CORNELIUS WHURR
c. 1845

21 What lasting joys the man attend
Who has a polished female friend.
The Accomplished Female Friend

GEORGE JOHN WHYTE-MELVILLE
1821–1878

22 Then drink, puppy, drink, and let ev'ry puppy drink,
That is old enough to lap and to swallow;
For he'll grow into a hound, so we'll pass the bottle
round,
And merrily we'll whoop and we'll holloa.
Drink, Puppy, Drink, chorus

23 The swallows are making them ready to fly,
Wheeling out on a windy sky:
Goodbye, Summer, goodbye, goodbye.
Goodbye, Summer

24 Wrap me up in my tarpaulin jacket,
And say a poor buffer lies low,
And six stalwart lancers shall carry me,
With steps solemn, mournful, and slow.
The Tarpaulin Jacket

BISHOP SAMUEL WILBERFORCE
1805–1873

25 If I were a cassowary
On the plains of Timbuctoo,
I would eat a missionary,
Cassock, band, and hymn-book too.
Impromptu verse, Ascribed

ELLA WHEELER WILCOX
1855–1919

26 Laugh and the world laughs with you;
Weep, and you weep alone;
For the sad old earth must borrow its mirth,
But has trouble enough of its own. *Solitude*

27 So many gods, so many creeds,
So many paths that wind and wind,
While just the art of being kind
Is all the sad world needs. *The World's Need*

OSCAR WILDE
1856–1900

1 He did not wear his scarlet coat,
    For blood and wine are red,
And blood and wine were on his hands
    When they found him with the dead.
        The Ballad of Reading Gaol (1898), pt. 1. i

2 I never saw a man who looked
    With such a wistful eye
Upon that little tent of blue
    Which prisoners call the sky.   *Ib.* iii

3 When a voice behind me whispered low,
    'That fellow's got to swing.'   *Ib.* iv

4 Yet each man kills the thing he loves,
    By each let this be heard,
Some do it with a bitter look,
    Some with a flattering word.
The coward does it with a kiss,
    The brave man with a sword!   *Ib.* vii

5 It is sweet to dance to violins
    When Love and Life are fair:
To dance to flutes, to dance to lutes
    Is delicate and rare:
But it is not sweet with nimble feet
    To dance upon the air!   *Ib.* II. ix

6 Like two doomed ships that pass in storm
    We had crossed each other's way:
But we made no sign, we said no word,
    We had no word to say.   *Ib.* xii

7 The Governor was strong upon
    The Regulations Act:
The Doctor said that Death was but
    A scientific fact:
And twice a day the Chaplain called,
    And left a little tract.   *Ib.* III. iii

8 And once, or twice, to throw the dice
    Is a gentlemanly game,
But he does not win who plays with Sin
    In the secret House of Shame.   *Ib.* xxiii

9 Something was dead in each of us,
    And what was dead was Hope.   *Ib.* xxxi

10 And the wild regrets, and the bloody sweats,
    None knew so well as I:
For he who lives more lives than one
    More deaths than one must die.   *Ib.* xxxvii

11 I know not whether Laws be right,
    Or whether Laws be wrong;
All that we know who lie in gaol
    Is that the wall is strong;
And that each day is like a year,
    A year whose days are long.   *Ib.* v. i

12 How else but through a broken heart
    May Lord Christ enter in?   *Ib.* xiv

13 Surely there was a time I might have trod
The sunlit heights, and from life's dissonance
Struck one clear chord to reach the ears of God.
    Hélas! (*Lines prefixed to his Poems, Paris edition,*
    1903)

14   And yet, and yet,
These Christs that die upon the barricades,
God knows it I am with them, in some ways.
    Sonnet to Liberty: Not that I Love Thy Children

15 All her bright golden hair
    Tarnished with rust,
She that was young and fair
    Fallen to dust.   *Requiescat*

16 O Singer of Persephone!
In the dim meadows desolate
Dost thou remember Sicily?   *Theocritus*

17 Art never expresses anything but itself.
    The Decay of Lying (1891), p. 43

18 Really, if the lower orders don't set us a good example,
    what on earth is the use of them?
    The Importance of Being Earnest (1895), Act 1

19 It is very vulgar to talk like a dentist when one isn't
    a dentist. It produces a false impression.   *Ib.*

20 Truth is never pure, and rarely simple.   *Ib.*

21 In married life three is company and two none.   *Ib.*

22 I have invented an invaluable permanent invalid
    called Bunbury, in order that I may be able to go
    down into the country whenever I choose.   *Ib.*

23 To lose one parent, Mr. Worthing, may be regarded
    as a misfortune; to lose both looks like carelessness.
    Ib.

24 All women become like their mothers. That is their
    tragedy. No man does. That's his.   *Ib.*

25 The good ended happily, and the bad unhappily.
    That is what Fiction means. [*Miss Prism on her novel.*]
    Ib. Act II

26 The chapter on the Fall of the Rupee you may omit.
    It is somewhat too sensational.   *Ib.*

27 Charity, dear Miss Prism, charity! None of us are
    perfect. I myself am peculiarly susceptible to
    draughts.   *Ib.*

28 On an occasion of this kind it becomes more than a
    moral duty to speak one's mind. It becomes a
    pleasure.   *Ib.*

29 Please do not shoot the pianist. He is doing his best.
    Impressions of America. Leadville

30 Meredith is a prose Browning, and so is Browning.
    He used poetry as a medium for writing in prose.
    The Critic as Artist. Part 1. *Intentions*

31 A little sincerity is a dangerous thing, and a great deal
    of it is absolutely fatal.   *Ib.* 2

32 Ah! don't say that you agree with me. When people
    agree with me I always feel that I must be wrong.
    Ib.

33 As long as war is regarded as wicked, it will always
    have its fascination. When it is looked upon as
    vulgar, it will cease to be popular.   *Ib.*

34 There is no sin except stupidity.   *Ib.*

35 I couldn't help it. I can resist everything except
    temptation. *Lady Windermere's Fan* (1891), Act 1

36 Many a woman has a past, but I am told that she has
    at least a dozen, and that they all fit.   *Ib.*

37 We are all in the gutter, but some of us are looking
    at the stars.   *Ib.* Act III

38 There is nothing in the whole world so unbecoming
    to a woman as a Nonconformist conscience.   *Ib.*

1 CECIL GRAHAM:
What is a cynic?
LORD DARLINGTON:
A man who knows the price of everything and the value of nothing. *Lady Windermere's Fan*, Act III

2 DUMBY:
Experience is the name every one gives to their mistakes.
CECIL GRAHAM:
One shouldn't commit any.
DUMBY:
Life would be very dull without them. *Ib.*

3 There is no such thing as a moral or an immoral book. Books are well written, or badly written.
Picture of Dorian Gray (1891), preface

4 The moral life of man forms part of the subject-matter of the artist, but the morality of art consists in the perfect use of an imperfect medium. *Ib.*

5 There is only one thing in the world worse than being talked about, and that is not being talked about.
Ib. ch. 1

6 A man cannot be too careful in the choice of his enemies. *Ib.*

7 The only way to get rid of a temptation is to yield to it. *Ib. ch. 2*

8 A cigarette is the perfect type of a perfect pleasure. It is exquisite, and it leaves one unsatisfied. What more can one want? *Ib. ch. 6*

9 It is better to be beautiful than to be good. But . . . it is better to be good than to be ugly. *Ib. ch. 17*

10 Anybody can be good in the country. *Ib. ch. 19*

11 As for the virtuous poor, one can pity them, of course, but one cannot possibly admire them.
Soul of Man under Socialism

12 Democracy means simply the bludgeoning of the people by the people for the people. *Ib.*

13 MRS. ALLONBY:
They say, Lady Hunstanton, that when good Americans die they go to Paris.
LADY HUNSTANTON:
Indeed? And when bad Americans die, where do they go to?
LORD ILLINGWORTH:
Oh, they go to America.
A Woman of No Importance (1893), Act I. (*See* 14:1)

14 The youth of America is their oldest tradition. It has been going on now for three hundred years. *Ib.*

15 The English country gentleman galloping after a fox —the unspeakable in full pursuit of the uneatable.
Ib.

16 One should never trust a woman who tells one her real age. A woman who would tell one that, would tell one anything. *Ib.*

17 LORD ILLINGWORTH:
The Book of Life begins with a man and a woman in a garden.
MRS. ALLONBY:
It ends with Revelations. *Ib.*

18 Children begin by loving their parents; after a time they judge them; rarely, if ever, do they forgive them. *Ib.*

19 GERALD:
I suppose society is wonderfully delightful!
LORD ILLINGWORTH:
To be in it is merely a bore. But to be out of it simply a tragedy. *A Woman of No Importance*, Act III

20 You should study the Peerage, Gerald. . . . It is the best thing in fiction the English have ever done.
Ib.

21 A thing is not necessarily true because a man dies for it.
Sebastian Melmoth (1904), p. 12. *Oscariana* (1910), p. 8

22 [*At the New York Custom House*]
I have nothing to declare except my genius.
F. Harris, *Oscar Wilde* (1918), p. 75

23 He [Bernard Shaw] hasn't an enemy in the world, and none of his friends like him.
Quoted in Shaw: *Sixteen Self Sketches*, ch. 17

24 [*A huge fee for an operation was mentioned*]
'Ah, well, then,' said Oscar, 'I suppose that I shall have to die beyond my means'.
R. H. Sherard, *Life of Oscar Wilde* (1906), p. 421

JOHN WILKES
1727–1797

25 The chapter of accidents is the longest chapter in the book.
Attributed to John Wilkes by Southey in The Doctor (1837), vol. iv, p. 166

WILLIAM WILKIE
1721–1772

26 [His] labour for his pains.
Fables. The Boy and the Rainbow, ad fin.

EMMA HART WILLARD
1787–1876

27 Rocked in the cradle of the deep. *Song*

WILLIAM III OF GREAT BRITAIN
1650–1702

28 I will die in the last ditch.
Hume, *History of Great Britain*, vol. ii (1757), p. 226. *Charles II*, ch. 3

29 Every bullet has its billet.
John Wesley, *Journal*, 6 *June 1765*

SIR CHARLES HANBURY WILLIAMS
1708–1759

30 Dear Betty, come, give me sweet kisses,
For sweeter no girl ever gave:
But why in the midst of our blisses,
Do you ask me how many I'd have?
I'm not to be stinted in pleasure,
Then prithee, dear Betty, be kind;
For as I love thee beyond measure,
To numbers I'll not be confin'd.
A Ballad in Imitation of Martial, Lib. 6, Ep. 34.
Works (1822), vol. i, p. 111

HARRY WILLIAMS
and
JACK JUDGE

1 It's a long way to Tipperary, it's a long way to go;
It's a long way to Tipperary, to the sweetest girl I
know!
Good-bye Piccadilly, Farewell Leicester Square;
It's a long, long way to Tipperary, but my heart's
right there!
*It's a Long Way to Tipperary. Chorus claimed by
Alice Smythe B. Jay. Written in 1908. See New
York Times, 20 Sept. 1907*

2 In the shade of the old apple tree. *Title of song*

3 I'm afraid to come home in the dark. *Title of song*

ISAAC WILLIAMS
1802–1865

4 Disposer Supreme,
And Judge of the earth.
*Hymns translated from the Parisian Breviary
(1839), p. 271*

NATHANIEL PARKER WILLIS
1806–1867

5 At present there is no distinction among the upper
ten thousand of the city.
Necessity for a Promenade Drive

W. G. WILLS
nineteenth century

6 I'll sing thee songs of Araby,
And tales of wild Cashmere,
Wild tales to cheat thee of a sigh,
Or charm thee to a tear. *Lalla Rookh*

D. EARDLEY WILMOT
contemporary

7 It's a corner of heaven itself,
Though it's only a tumble-down nest,
But with love brooding there, why, no place can
compare,
With my little grey home in the west.
My Little Grey Home

HARRIETTE WILSON
1789–1846

8 I shall not say why and how I became, at the age of
fifteen, the mistress of the Earl of Craven.
Memoirs, First sentence

JOHN WILSON
1785–1854
see
CHRISTOPHER NORTH

JOHN WILSON
d. 1889

9 Oh for a book and a shady nook,
Either in door or out;
With the green leaves whispering overhead,
Or the street cries all about.

Where I may read all at my ease,
Both of the new and old;
For a jolly good book whereon to look,
Is better to me than gold.
*Lines written as a motto to a second-hand books
catalogue.* Lubbock, *Pleasures of Life* (ed. 1887),
p. 48

THOMAS WOODROW WILSON
1856–1924

10 There is such a thing as a man being too proud to
fight. *Address at Philadelphia, 10 May 1915*

11 We have stood apart, studiously neutral.
Message to Congress, 7 Dec. 1915

12 Armed neutrality. *Ib. 26 Feb. 1917*

13 A little group of wilful men reflecting no opinion but
their own have rendered the great Government of
the United States helpless and contemptible.
*Statement made on 4 March 1917 after a successful
filibuster against his bill to arm American merchant
ships against German submarine attacks*

14 The world must be made safe for democracy.
Address to Congress, 2 Apr. 1917

15 It is indispensable that the governments associated
against Germany should know beyond a peradventure with whom they are dealing.
Note to Germany, 14 Oct. 1918

16 Sometimes people call me an idealist. Well, that is the
way I know I am an American. America is the only
idealistic nation in the world.
Address at Sioux Falls, 8 Sept. 1919

ARTHUR WIMPERIS
1874–

17 Gilbert, the Filbert,
The Colonel of the Knuts. *Gilbert the Filbert*

ANNE FINCH, LADY WINCHILSEA
d. 1720

18 Nor will in fading silks compose
Faintly the inimitable rose. *The Spleen*

19 Now the Jonquille o'ercomes the feeble brain;
We faint beneath the aromatic pain. *Ib.*

WILLIAM WINDHAM
1750–1810

20 Those entrusted with arms . . . should be persons of
some substance and stake in the country.
Speech in the House of Commons, 22 July 1807

CATHERINE WINKWORTH
1829–1878

21 Now thank we all our God,
With heart and hands and voices
Who wondrous things hath done
In whom His world rejoices.
Trans. of Martin Rinkart: Nun danket alle Gott

ROBERT CHARLES WINTHROP
1809–1894

1 A Star for every State, and a State for every Star.
Speech on Boston Common, 27 Aug. 1862

GEORGE WITHER
1588–1667

2 Shall I, wasting in despair,
　Die because a woman's fair?
Or make pale my cheeks with care,
　'Cause another's rosy are?
Be she fairer than the day,
　Or the flow'ry meads in May;
If she think not well of me,
　What care I how fair she be?　*Sonnet*

3 I loved a lass, a fair one,
　As fair as e'er was seen;
She was indeed a rare one,
　Another Sheba queen. *I Loved a Lass, a Fair One*

4 But, fool as then I was,
　I thought she loved me too:
But now, alas! she's left me,
　Falero, lero, loo!　*Ib.*

PELHAM GRENVILLE WODEHOUSE
1881–

5 He spoke with a certain what-is-it in his voice, and
I could see that, if not actually disgruntled, he was
far from being gruntled. *The Code of the Woosters*

6 Slice him where you like, a hellhound is always a
hellhound.　*Ib.*

7 Donning the soup-and-fish in preparation for the
evening meal.　*Jeeves and the Impending Doom*

8 Excellent browsing and sluicing.
Jeeves and the Unbidden Guest

9 There was another ring at the front door. Jeeves
shimmered out and came back with a telegram.
Jeeves Takes Charge

CHARLES WOLFE
1791–1823

10 Not a drum was heard, not a funeral note,
　As his corse to the rampart we hurried.
The Burial of Sir John Moore at Corunna, i

11 We buried him darkly at dead of night,
　The sods with our bayonets turning.　*Ib.* ii

12 But he lay like a warrior taking his rest,
　With his martial cloak around him.　*Ib.* iii

13 Few and short were the prayers we said,
　And we spoke not a word of sorrow;
But we steadfastly gazed on the face that was dead,
　And we bitterly thought of the morrow.　*Ib.* iv

14 We carved not a line, and we raised not a stone—
　But we left him alone with his glory.　*Ib.* viii

JAMES WOLFE
1727–1759

15 The General . . . repeated nearly the whole of Gray's
Elegy . . . adding, as he concluded, that he would
prefer being the author of that poem to the glory
of beating the French to-morrow.
J. Playfair, *Biogr. Acc. of J. Robinson* in *Transactions R. Soc. Edinb. 1814,* vii. 499

16 Now God be praised, I will die in peace.
Dying words. J. Knox, *Historical Journal of
Campaigns, 1757–60.* Published 1769. Ed. 1914,
vol. ii, p. 114

THOMAS, CARDINAL WOLSEY
1475?–1530

17 Father Abbot, I am come to lay my bones amongst
you.
Cavendish, *Negotiations of Thomas Woolsey*
(1641), p. 108

18 Had I but served God as diligently as I have served
the King, he would not have given me over in my
gray hairs.　*Ib.* p. 113

MRS. HENRY WOOD
1814–1887

19 Dead! and . . . never called me mother.
*East Lynne (dramatized version by T. A. Palmer,
1874). These words do not occur in the novel*

J. T. WOOD

20 Wait till the clouds roll by, Jenny,
Wait till the clouds roll by;
Jenny, my own true loved one,
Wait till the clouds roll by.
Wait Till the Clouds Roll By

REV. SAMUEL WOODFORD
1636–1700

21 To his very Worthy Friend Mr. Izaak Walton, upon
his Writing and Publishing the Life of the Venerable and Judicious Mr. Richard Hooker.
Title of verses prefixed to the Life, 1670

VIRGINIA WOOLF
1882–1941

22 A Room of One's Own.　*Title of book*

ELIZABETH WORDSWORTH
1840–1932

23 If all the good people were clever,
　And all clever people were good,
The world would be nicer than ever
　We thought that it possibly could.

But somehow, 'tis seldom or never
　The two hit it off as they should;
The good are so harsh to the clever,
　The clever so rude to the good!
*St. Christopher and Other Poems: Good and
Clever*

WILLIAM WORDSWORTH
1770–1850

24 Where art thou, my beloved Son,
　Where art thou, worse to me than dead?
The Affliction of Margaret

25 　　　　To keep
An incommunicable sleep.　*Ib.*

1 My apprehensions come in crowds;
   I dread the rustling of the grass;
   The very shadows of the clouds
   Have power to shake me as they pass.
                    The Affliction of Margaret

2   Lady of the Mere,
   Sole-sitting by the shores of old romance.
                    A Narrow Girdle of Rough Stones and Crags

3 And three times to the child I said,
   'Why, Edward, tell me why?'   *Anecdote for Fathers*

4 At Kilve there was no weather-cock;
   And that's the reason why.   *Ib.*

5 A Poet!—He hath put his heart to school.
                    Miscellaneous Sonnets, pt. III, xxvii. *A Poet!—He Hath Put*

6 A slumber did my spirit seal;
   I had no human fears:
   She seemed a thing that could not **feel**
   The touch of earthly years.

   No motion has she now, no force;
   She neither hears nor sees;
   Rolled round in earth's diurnal course,
   With rocks, and stones, and trees.
                    A Slumber did My Spirit Seal

7 Action is transitory,—a step, a blow,
   The motion of a muscle, this way or that—
   'Tis done, and in the after-vacancy
   We wonder at ourselves like men betrayed:
   Suffering is permanent, obscure and dark,
   And shares the nature of infinity.
                    The Borderers, III. 1539

8 Love had he found in huts where poor men lie;
   His daily teachers had been woods and rills,
   The silence that is in the starry sky,
   The sleep that is among the lonely hills.
                    Song at the Feast of Brougham Castle

9 But ne'er to a seductive lay
   Let faith be given;
   Nor deem that 'light which leads astray
   Is light from Heaven.'   *To the Sons of Burns*

10 The best of what we do and are
   Just God, forgive!
                    Memorials of a Tour in Scotland, 1803. iii.
                    Thoughts near Burns's Residence

11 Sweet childish days, that were as long
   As twenty days are now.
                    To a Butterfly: I've Watched You Now

12   I, with many a fear
   For my dear country, many heartfelt sighs,
   'Mongst men who do not love her, linger here.
                    Poems Dedicated to National Independence. pt. I,
                    i. *Near Calais, Aug. 1802: Fair Star of Evening*

13 Jones! as from Calais southward you and I
   Went pacing side by side.
                    Ib. iii. *Composed near Calais, on the Road to
                    Ardres.*

14 Isis and Cam, to patient science dear!
                    Ecclesiastical Sonnets, pt. III, xlii. *Cathedrals, &c.
                    Open your Gates, ye Everlasting Piles!*

15 To be a Prodigal's favourite,—then, worse **truth**,
   A Miser's Pensioner,—behold our lot!
   O Man, that from thy fair and shining youth
   Age might but take the things Youth needed not!
                    The Small Celandine: There is a Flower

16 There's a flower that shall be mine,
   'Tis the little celandine.
                    To the Small Celandine: Pansies, Lilies

17 Pleasures newly found are sweet
   When they lie about our feet:
   February last, my heart
   First at sight of thee was glad;
   All unheard of as thou art,
   Thou must needs, I think have had,
   Celandine! and long ago,
   Praise of which I nothing know.
                    To the Same Flower: Pleasures Newly Found

18 Small service is true service while it lasts:
   Of humblest friends, bright creature! scorn not one:
   The daisy, by the shadow that it casts,
   Protects the lingering dewdrop from the sun.
                    To a Child. Written in her Album

19 O blithe new-comer! I have heard,
   I hear thee and rejoice.
   O Cuckoo! Shall I call thee bird,
   Or but a wandering voice?
                    To the Cuckoo: O Blithe New-comer!

20 Thrice welcome, darling of the Spring!   *Ib.*

21 'Tis the still hour of thinking, feeling, loving.
                    On a High Part of the Coast of Cumberland

22 Thou unassuming common-place
   Of Nature, with that homely face,
   And yet with something of a grace
   Which love makes for thee.
                    *To the Same Flower [Daisy]. With Little Here
                    To Do*

23 Oft on the dappled turf at ease
   I sit, and play with similes,
   Loose types of things through all degrees.   *Ib.*

24 Degenerate Douglas! Oh, the unworthy lord!
                    Memorials of a Tour in Scotland, 1803. xii.
                    Sonnet: Degenerate Douglas!

25 A brotherhood of venerable trees.   *Ib.*

26 I thought of Thee, my partner and my guide,
   As being past away—Vain sympathies!
   For, backward, Duddon! as I cast my eyes,
   I see what was, and is, and will abide;
   Still glides the Stream, and shall for ever glide;
   The Form remains, the Function never dies.
                    The River Duddon, xxxiv. *After-Thought*

27 Enough, if something from our hands have power
   To live, and act, and serve the future hour;
   And if, as toward the silent tomb we go,
   Through love, through hope, and faith's transcen-
        dent dower,
   We feel that we are greater than we know.   *Ib.*

28 Stern daughter of the voice of God!
   O Duty! if that name thou love
   Who art a light to guide, a rod
   To check the erring and reprove.   *Ode to Duty*

29 But thee I now will serve more strictly, if I may. *Ib.*

30 Me this unchartered freedom tires;
   I feel the weight of chance-desires:
   My hopes no more must change their name,
   I long for a repose that ever is the same.   *Ib.*

31 Thou dost preserve the stars from wrong;
   And the most ancient heavens, through Thee, are
   fresh and strong.   *Ib.*

1 Give unto me, made lowly wise,
The spirit of self-sacrifice;
The confidence of reason give;
And in the light of truth thy Bondman let me live!
Ode to Duty

2 Thine is the tranquil hour, purpureal Eve!
But long as god-like wish, or hope divine,
Informs my spirit, ne'er can I believe
That this magnificence is wholly thine!
—From worlds not quickened by the sun
A portion of the gift is won;
An intermingling of Heaven's pomp is spread
On ground which British shepherds tread.
Composed upon an Evening of Extraordinary Splendour

3 Not in the lucid intervals of life
That come but as a curse to party strife.
Evening Voluntaries, iv. *Not in the Lucid Intervals*

4 By grace divine,
Not otherwise, O Nature, we are thine. *Ib.*

5 On Man, on Nature, and on Human Life,
Musing in solitude. *The Excursion*, preface, 1. i

6 Joy in widest commonalty spread. *Ib.* l. 18

7 The Mind of Man—
My haunt, and the main region of my song. *Ib.* l. 40

8 The discerning intellect of Man,
When wedded to this goodly universe
In love and holy passion, shall find these
A simple produce of the common day. *Ib.* l. 52

9 A metropolitan temple in the hearts
Of mighty Poets. *Ib.* l. 86

10 Oh! many are the Poets that are sown
By Nature; men endowed with highest gifts,
The vision and the faculty divine;
Yet wanting the accomplishment of verse.
Ib. bk. i, l. 77

11 What soul was his, when, from the naked top
Of some bold headland, he beheld the sun
Rise up, and bathe the world in light! *Ib.* l. 198

12 The imperfect offices of prayer and praise. *Ib.* l. 216

13 That mighty orb of song,
The divine Milton. *Ib.* l. 249

14 The good die first,
And they whose hearts are dry as summer dust
Burn to the socket. *Ib.* l. 500

15 The intellectual power, through words and things,
Went sounding on, a dim and perilous way!
Ib. bk. iii, l. 700

16 Society became my glittering bride,
And airy hopes my children. *Ib.* l. 735

17 'Tis a thing impossible, to frame
Conceptions equal to the soul's desires;
And the most difficult of tasks to *keep*
Heights which the soul is competent to gain.
Ib. bk. iv, l. 136

18 As fast as a musician scatters sounds
Out of an instrument. *Ib.* l. 524

19 We live by admiration, hope, and love;
And even as these are well and wisely fixed,
In dignity of being we ascend. *Ib.* l. 763

20 I have seen
A curious child, who dwelt upon a tract
Of inland ground, applying to his ear
The convolutions of a smooth-lipped shell;
To which, in silence hushed, his very soul
Listened intensely; and his countenance soon
Brightened with joy; for from within were heard
Murmurings, whereby the monitor expressed
Mysterious union with its native sea.
The Excursion, bk. iv, l. 1132

21 Spires whose 'silent fingers point to heaven.'
Ib. bk. vi, l. 19. Quoting Coleridge, *The Friend*,
sec. i, No. 14

22 The head and mighty paramount of truths,—
Immortal life, in never-fading worlds,
For mortal creatures, conquered and secured.
Ib. l. 85

23 Amid the groves, under the shadowy hills,
The generations are prepared; the pangs,
The internal pangs, are ready; the dread strife
Of poor humanity's afflicted will
Struggling in vain with ruthless destiny. *Ib.* l. 553

24 A man of hope and forward-looking mind
Even to the last! *Ib.* bk. vii, l. 276

25 'To every Form of being is assigned',
Thus calmly spoke the venerable Sage,
'An *active* Principle.' *Ib.* bk. ix, l. 1

26 Spirit that knows no insulated spot,
No chasm, no solitude; from link to link
It circulates, the Soul of all the worlds. *Ib.* l. 13

27 And hear the mighty stream of tendency
Uttering, for elevation of our thought,
A clear sonorous voice, inaudible
To the vast multitude. *Ib.* l. 87. (*See* 20:13)

28 The primal duties shine aloft like stars;
The charities that soothe, and heal, and bless,
Are scattered at the feet of man, like flowers.
Ib. l. 238

29 Nor less I deem that there are Powers
Which of themselves our minds impress;
That we can feed this mind of ours
In a wise passiveness. *Expostulation and Reply*

30 Think you mid all this mighty sum
Of things for ever speaking,
That nothing of itself will come,
But we must still be seeking? *Ib.*

31 How nourished there through that long time
He knows who gave that love sublime. *Fidelity*

32 'What is good for a bootless bene?'
With these dark words begins my tale;
And their meaning is, whence can comfort spring
When prayer is of no avail? *The Force of Prayer*

33 My eyes are dim with childish tears,
My heart is idly stirred,
For the same sound is in my ears
Which in those days I heard. *The Fountain*

34 The wiser mind
Mourns less for what age takes away
Than what it leaves behind *Ib.*

35 And often, glad no more,
We wear a face of joy because
We have been glad of yore. *Ib.*

1 A power is passing from the earth
To breathless Nature's dark abyss;
But when the great and good depart,
What is it more than this—

That Man who is from God sent forth,
Doth yet again to God return?—
Such ebb and flow must ever be,
Then wherefore should we mourn?
  Lines on the Expected Dissolution of Mr. Fox

2 Bliss was it in that dawn to be alive,
But to be young was very heaven!
  French Revolution, as it Appeared to Enthusiasts,
  and *The Prelude*, bk. xi, l. 108

3   Sets . . .
The budding rose above the rose full blown.
  Ib. and *The Prelude*, bk. xi, l. 121

4 And homeless near a thousand homes I stood,
And near a thousand tables pined and wanted food.
  Guilt and Sorrow, xli

5 Who is the happy Warrior? Who is he
That every man in arms should wish to be?
It is the generous spirit, who, when brought
Among the tasks of real life, hath wrought
Upon the plan that pleased his childish thought:
Whose high endeavours are an inward light
That makes the path before him always bright:
Who, with a natural instinct to discern
What knowledge can perform, is diligent to learn.
  Character of the Happy Warrior

6 Who, doomed to go in company with Pain,
And Fear, and Bloodshed, miserable train!
Turns his necessity to glorious gain;
In face of these doth exercise a power
Which is our human nature's highest dower;
Controls them, and subdues, transmutes, bereaves
Of their bad influence, and their good receives. *Ib.*

7 More skilful in self-knowledge, even more pure,
As tempted more; more able to endure,
As more exposed to suffering and distress;
Thence also, more alive to tenderness. *Ib.*

8 And in himself possess his own desire. *Ib.*

9 And therefore does not stoop, nor lie in wait
For wealth, or honours, or for worldly state. *Ib.*

10 Whose powers shed round him in the common strife
Or mild concerns of ordinary life,
A constant influence, a peculiar grace;
But who if he be called upon to face
Some awful moment to which Heaven has joined
Great issues, good or bad for human kind,
Is happy as a lover; and attired
With sudden brightness, like a man inspired;
And, through the heat of conflict, keeps the law
In calmness made, and sees what he foresaw. *Ib.*

11 'Tis, finally, the Man, who, lifted high,
Conspicuous object in a Nation's eye,
Or left unthought of in obscurity,—
Who, with a toward or untoward lot,
Prosperous or adverse, to his wish or not—
Plays, in the many games of life, that one
Where what he most doth value must be won:
Whom neither shape of danger can dismay,
Nor thought of tender happiness betray. *Ib.*

12 The moving accident is not my trade;
To freeze the blood I have no ready arts:
'Tis my delight, alone in summer shade,
To pipe a simple song for thinking hearts.
  Hart-leap Well, p. 2, l. 1

13 The Being that is in the clouds and air,
That is in the green leaves among the groves,
Maintains a deep and reverential care
For the unoffending creatures whom he loves.
  Ib. l. 165

14 Never to blend our pleasure or our pride
With sorrow of the meanest thing that feels.
  Ib. l. 179

15 High is our calling, friend! Creative Art
(Whether the instrument of words she use,
Or pencil pregnant with ethereal hues,)
Demands the service of a mind and heart,
Though sensitive, yet, in their weakest part,
Heroically fashioned.
  Miscellaneous Sonnets, pt. ii, iii. *To B. R. Haydon: High is our Calling, Friend!*

16 Sweet Highland Girl, a very shower
Of beauty is thy earthly dower.
  Memorials of a Tour in Scotland, 1803. vi. *To a Highland Girl*

17 The rapt one, of the godlike forehead,
The heaven-eyed creature sleeps in earth:
And Lamb, the frolic and the gentle,
Has vanished from his lonely hearth.
  Extempore Effusion upon the Death of James Hogg

18 How fast has brother followed brother,
From sunshine to the sunless land! *Ib.*

19 Him whom you love, your Idiot Boy. *The Idiot Boy*

20 And as her mind grew worse and worse,
Her body—it grew better. *Ib.*

21 Wisdom and Spirit of the Universe!
Thou Soul that art the Eternity of thought!
And giv'st to forms and images a breath
And everlasting motion!
  Influence of Natural Objects, and *The Prelude*,
  bk. i, l. 401

22 A grandeur in the beatings of the heart. *Ib.*

23   All shod with steel
We hissed along the polished ice, in games
Confederate.
  Ib. and *The Prelude*, bk. i, l. 414

24   With the din
Smitten, the precipices rang aloud;
The leafless trees and every icy crag
Tinkled like iron; while far-distant hills
Into the tumult sent an alien sound
Of melancholy. *Ib.*

25   Leaving the tumultuous throng
To cut across the reflex of a star;
Image, that flying still before me, gleamed
Upon the glassy plain. *Ib.*

26   Yet still the solitary cliffs
Wheeled by me—even as if the earth had rolled
With visible motion her diurnal round!
  Ib. and *The Prelude*. bk. i, l. 458

1 There was a time when meadow, grove, and stream,
  The earth, and every common sight,
    To me did seem
    Apparelled in celestial light,
  The glory and the freshness of a dream.
  It is not now as it hath been of yore;—
    Turn wheresoe'er I may,
      By night or day,
  The things which I have seen I now can see no more.
                    Ode. Intimations of Immortality, i

2   The rainbow comes and goes,
      And lovely is the rose,
      The moon doth with delight
  Look round her when the heavens are bare,
      Waters on a starry night
      Are beautiful and fair;
    The sunshine is a glorious birth:
  But yet I know, where'er I go,
  That there hath passed away a glory from the earth.
                    Ib. ii

3 And while the young lambs bound
    As to the tabor's sound.   *Ib*. iii

4 A timely utterance gave that thought relief,
  And I again am strong.   *Ib*.

5 The winds come to me from the fields of sleep. *Ib*.

6 Shout round me, let me hear thy shouts, thou happy
    Shepherd-boy.   *Ib*.

7 And the babe leaps up on his mother's arm. *Ib*. iv

8 —But there's a tree, of many, one
  A single field which I have looked upon,
  Both of them speak of something that is gone:
    The pansy at my feet
    Doth the same tale repeat:
  Whither is fled the visionary gleam?
  Where is it now, the glory and the dream? *Ib*.

9 Our birth is but a sleep and a forgetting:
    The Soul that rises with us, our life's Star,
    Hath had elsewhere its setting,
      And cometh from afar:
  Not in entire forgetfulness,
  And not in utter nakedness,
  But trailing clouds of glory do we come
    From God, who is our home:
  Heaven lies about us in our infancy!
  Shades of the prison-house begin to close
    Upon the growing boy,
  But he beholds the light, and whence it flows,
    He sees it in his joy;
  The youth, who daily farther from the east
    Must travel, still is Nature's priest,
    And by the vision splendid
    Is on his way attended;
  At length the man perceives it die away,
  And fade into the light of common day. *Ib*. v

10 Behold the child among his new-born blisses,
  A six years' darling of a pigmy size!
  See, where 'mid work of his own hand he lies,
  Fretted by sallies of his mother's kisses,
  With light upon him from his father's eyes! *Ib*. vii

11 As if his whole vocation
    Were endless imitation.   *Ib*.

12 Thou, whose exterior semblance doth belie
    Thy soul's immensity.   *Ib*. viii

13   Thou Eye among the blind,
  That, deaf and silent, read'st the eternal deep
  Haunted for ever by the eternal mind.
                Ode. Intimations of Immortality, viii

14 Thou, over whom thy immortality
  Broods like the day, a master o'er a slave. *Ib*.

15   Provoke
  The years to bring the inevitable yoke. *Ib*.

16 And custom lie upon thee with a weight,
  Heavy as frost, and deep almost as life! *Ib*.

17   O joy! that in our embers
    Is something that doth live,
    That nature yet remembers
    What was so fugitive!
  The thought of our past years in me doth breed
  Perpetual benediction.   *Ib*. ix

18 Not for these I raise
  The song of thanks and praise;
    But for those obstinate questionings
    Of sense and outward things,
    Fallings from us, vanishings;
    Blank misgivings of a creature
  Moving about in worlds not realised,
  High instincts before which our mortal nature
  Did tremble like a guilty thing surprised:
    But for those first affections,
    Those shadowy recollections,
  Which, be they what they may,
  Are yet the fountain-light of all our day,
  Are yet a master-light of all our seeing. *Ib*.

19 Our noisy years seem moments in the being
  Of the eternal Silence: truths that wake,
    To perish never:
  Which neither listlessness, nor mad endeavour,
    Nor Man nor Boy,
  Nor all that is at enmity with joy,
  Can utterly abolish or destroy!

  Hence in a season of calm weather
    Though inland far we be,
  Our souls have sight of that immortal sea
    Which brought us hither,
    Can in a moment travel thither,
  And see the children sport upon the shore,
  And hear the mighty waters rolling evermore. *Ib*.

20 Though nothing can bring back the hour
  Of splendour in the grass, of glory in the flower;
  We will grieve not, rather find
  Strength in what remains behind;
  In the primal sympathy
  Which having been must ever be;
  In the soothing thoughts that spring
  Out of human suffering,
  In the faith that looks through death,
  In years that bring the philosophic mind. *Ib*.

21 And O, ye fountains, meadows, hills and groves,
  Forbode not any severing of our loves!
  Yet in my heart of hearts I feel your might;
  I only have relinquished one delight
  To live beneath your more habitual sway. *Ib*. xi

22 The innocent brightness of a new-born day
    Is lovely yet;
  The clouds that gather round the setting sun
  Do take a sober colouring from an eye
  That hath kept watch o'er man's mortality;

[576]

Another race hath been, and other palms are won.
Thanks to the human heart by which we live,
Thanks to its tenderness, its joys, and fears,
To me the meanest flower that blows can give
Thoughts that do often lie too deep for tears.
Ode. Intimations of Immortality, xi

1 It is a beauteous evening, calm and free,
The holy time is quiet as a nun,
Breathless with adoration; the broad sun
Is sinking down in its tranquillity;
The gentleness of heaven broods o'er the Sea;
Listen! the mighty Being is awake,
And doth with his eternal motion make
A sound like thunder—everlastingly.
Dear Child! dear Girl! that walkest with me here
If thou appear untouched by solemn thought,
Thy nature is not therefore less divine.
Thou liest in Abraham's bosom all the year;
And worshipp'st at the temple's inner shrine,
God being with thee when we know it not.
Miscellaneous Sonnets, pt. I, xxx. *It is a Beauteous Evening*

2 It is not not to be thought of that the Flood
Of British freedom, which, to the open sea
Of the world's praise, from dark antiquity
Hath flowed, 'with pomp of waters, unwithstood' . . .
Should perish.
National Independence and Liberty. xvi. *It is not to be thought of*

3 In our halls is hung
Armoury of the invincible Knights of old:
We must be free or die, who speak the tongue
That Shakespeare spake; the faith and morals hold
Which Milton held.—In everything we are sprung
Of Earth's first blood, have titles manifold. *Ib.*

4 I travelled among unknown men
In lands beyond the sea;
Nor, England! did I know till then
What love I bore to thee.
I Travelled among Unknown Men

5 I wandered lonely as a cloud
That floats on high o'er vales and hills,
When all at once I saw a crowd,
A host, of golden daffodils;
Beside the lake, beneath the trees,
Fluttering and dancing in the breeze.
I Wandered Lonely as a Cloud

6 Continuous as the stars that shine
And twinkle on the milky way. *Ib.*

7 A poet could not but be gay,
In such a jocund company:
I gazed—and gazed—but little thought
What wealth to me the show had brought:
For oft, when on my couch I lie
In vacant or in pensive mood,
They flash upon that inward eye
Which is the bliss of solitude;
And then my heart with pleasure fills,
And dances with the daffodils. *Ib.*

8 Vanguard of Liberty, ye men of Kent.
National Independence and Liberty, pt. I, xxiii.
To the Men of Kent: Vanguard of Liberty

9 Give all thou canst; high Heaven rejects the lore
Of nicely-calculated less or more.
Ecclesiastical Sonnets, pt. III, xliii. *King's College Chapel. Tax not the Royal Saint*

10 Where light and shade repose, where music dwells
Lingering—and wandering on as loth to die;
Like thoughts whose very sweetness yieldeth proof
That they were born for immortality. *Ib.*

11 They dreamt not of a perishable home
Who thus could build.
Ib. xlv. *Continued. They Dreamt not of a Perishable Home*

12 The gods approve
The depth, and not the tumult, of the soul.
Laodamia, l. 74

13 Of all that is most beauteous—imaged there
In happier beauty; more pellucid streams,
An ampler ether, a diviner air,
And fields invested with purpureal gleams. *Ib.* l. 103

14 Milton! thou shouldst be living at this hour:
England hath need of thee; she is a fen
Of stagnant waters.
National Independence and Liberty, pt. I, xiv.
London. Milton! thou shouldst

15 Thy soul was like a star, and dwelt apart;
Thou hadst a voice whose sound was like the sea:
Pure as the naked heavens, majestic, free,
So didst thou travel on life's common way
In cheerful godliness; and yet thy heart
The lowliest duties on herself did lay. *Ib.*

16 Plain living and high thinking are no more:
The homely beauty of the good old cause
Is gone; our peace, our fearful innocence,
And pure religion breathing household laws.
Ib. xiii. *Written in London. O Friend! I Know Not*

17 I chanced to see at break of day
The solitary child. *Lucy Gray*

18 No mate, no comrade Lucy knew;
She dwelt on a wild moor,
The sweetest thing that ever grew
Beside a human door! *Ib.*

19 And sings a solitary song
That whistles in the wind. *Ib.*

20 The cattle are grazing,
Their heads never raising;
There are forty feeding like one! *Written in March*

21 Like an army defeated
The snow hath retreated. *Ib.*

22 Meantime Luke began
To slacken in his duty; and at length,
He in the dissolute city gave himself
To evil courses. *Michael*, l. 442

23 Many and many a day he thither went,
And never lifted up a single stone. *Ib.* l. 465

24 Most sweet it is with unuplifted eyes
To pace the ground, if path there be or none,
While a fair region round the traveller lies,
Which he forbears again to look upon.
Most Sweet It Is

25 My heart leaps up when I behold
A rainbow in the sky:
So was it when my life began;
So is it now I am a man;
So be it when I shall grow old,
Or let me die!
The Child is father of the Man;
And I could wish my days to be
Bound each to each by natural piety.
My Heart Leaps Up

1 From low to high doth dissolution climb.
Ecclesiastical Sonnets, pt. III, xxxiv. *Mutability. From Low to High*

2 The unimaginable touch of time. *Ib.*

3 Soft is the music that would charm for ever;
The flower of sweetest smell is shy and lowly.
Miscellaneous Sonnets, pt. II, ix. *Not Love, not War*

4 Another year!—another deadly blow!
Another mighty Empire overthrown!
And we are left, or shall be left, alone.
National Independence and Liberty, pt. I, xxvii. *November. Another Year!*

5 We shall exult, if they who rule the land
Be men who hold its many blessings dear,
Wise, upright, valiant; not a servile band,
Who are to judge of danger which they fear,
And honour which they do not understand. *Ib.*

6 Nuns fret not at their convent's narrow room;
And hermits are contented with their cells.
Miscellaneous Sonnets, pt. I, i. *Nuns Fret Not*

7 The weight of too much liberty. *Ib.*

8 There is a spirit in the woods. *Nutting*

9 But Thy most dreaded instrument
In working out a pure intent,
Is man,—arrayed for mutual slaughter,
Yea, Carnage is Thy daughter.
National Independence and Liberty, pt. II, xlv. *Ode* (1815), l. 106. *Imagination Ne'er Before Content*

10 O dearer far than light and life are dear.
To ——: O Dearer Far than Light

11 I heard a Stock-dove sing or say
His homely tale, this very day;
His voice was buried among trees,
Yet to be come-at by the breeze:
He did not cease; but cooed—and cooed;
And somewhat pensively he wooed;
He sang of love, with quiet blending,
Slow to begin, and never ending;
Of serious faith, and inward glee;
That was the song,—the song for me!
O Nightingale! Thou Surely Art

12 Ye sacred Nurseries of blooming Youth!
Miscellaneous Sonnets, pt. III, ii. *Oxford: Ye Sacred Nurseries*

13 A genial hearth, a hospitable board,
And a refined rusticity.
Ecclesiastical Sonnets, pt. III, xviii. *Pastoral Character. A Genial Hearth*

14 The light that never was, on sea or land,
The consecration, and the poet's dream.
Elegiac Stanzas Suggested by a Picture of Peele Castle in a Storm

15 A deep distress hath humanized my soul. *Ib.*

16 Farewell, farewell the heart that lives alone,
Housed in a dream, at distance from the Kind! *Ib.*

17 But welcome fortitude, and patient cheer,
And frequent sights of what is to be borne!
Such sights, or worse, as are before me here.—
Not without hope we suffer and we mourn. *Ib.*

18 I am not one who much or oft delight
To season my fireside with personal talk.
Personal Talk, i

19   Sweetest melodies
Are those that are by distance made more sweet.
Ib. ii

20 Dreams, books, are each a world; and books, we know,
Are a substantial world, both pure and good.
Round these, with tendrils strong as flesh and blood,
Our pastime and our happiness will grow. *Ib.* iii

21 The gentle lady married to the Moor;
And heavenly Una with her milk-white lamb. *Ib.*

22 Oh! might my name be numbered among theirs.
Ib. iv

23 There's something in a flying horse,
There's something in a huge balloon.
Peter Bell, prologue, l. 1

24 Full twenty times was Peter feared
For once that Peter was respected. *Ib.* pt. i, l. 204

25 A primrose by a river's brim
A yellow primrose was to him,
And it was nothing more. *Ib.* l. 249

26 He gave a groan, and then another,
Of that which went before the brother,
And then he gave a third. *Ib.* l. 443

27 Is it a party in a parlour?
Cramm'd just as they on earth were cramm'd—
Some sipping punch, some sipping tea,
But, as you by their faces see,
All silent and all damned! *Ib.* pt. ii, l. 516

28 The dew was falling fast, the stars began to blink;
I heard a voice; it said, 'Drink, pretty creature, drink!'
The Pet Lamb

29 Art thou a Man of purple cheer?
A rosy Man, right plump to see? *A Poet's Epitaph*

30 A fingering slave,
One that would peep and botanize
Upon his mother's grave?
A reasoning, self-sufficing thing,
An intellectual All-in-all! *Ib.*

31 But who is He, with modest looks,
And clad in homely russet brown?
He murmurs near the running brooks
A music sweeter than their own. *Ib.*

32 He is retired as noontide dew,
Or fountain in a noon-day grove;
And you must love him, ere to you
He will seem worthy of your love. *Ib.*

33 Impulses of deeper birth
Have come to him in solitude. *Ib.*

34 In common things that round us lie
Some random truths he can impart,—
The harvest of a quiet eye,
That broods and sleeps on his own heart.

But he is weak; both Man and Boy,
Hath been an idler in the land;
Contented if he might enjoy
The things which others understand. *Ib*

35 Weak as is a breaking wave. *Ib.*

1   My soul
Once more made trial of her strength, nor lacked
Aeolian visitations.   *The Prelude*, bk. i, l. 94

2 Feels immediately some hollow thought
Hang like an interdict upon her hopes.   *Ib.* l. 259

3 Unprofitably travelling towards the grave. *Ib.* l. 267

4 Made one long bathing of a summer's day. *Ib.* l. 290

5 Fair seed-time had my soul, and I grew up
Fostered alike by beauty and by fear.   *Ib.* l. 301

6   When the deed was done
I heard among the solitary hills
Low breathings coming after me, and sounds
Of undistinguishable motion, steps
Almost as silent as the turf they trod.   *Ib.* l. 321

7   Though mean
Our object and inglorious, yet the end
Was not ignoble.   *Ib.* l. 328

8 With what strange utterance did the loud dry wind
Blow through my ear! the sky seemed not a sky
Of earth—and with what motion moved the clouds!
                         Ib. l. 337

9 Dust as we are, the immortal spirit grows
Like harmony in music; there is a dark
Inscrutable workmanship that reconciles
Discordant elements, makes them cling together
In one society.   *Ib.* l. 340

10   The grim shape
Towered up between me and the stars, and still,
For so it seemed, with purpose of its own
And measured motion like a living thing,
Strode after me.   *Ib.* l. 382

11 Unknown modes of being.   *Ib.* l. 393

12   Huge and mighty forms that do not live
Like living men, moved slowly through the mind
By day, and were a trouble to my dreams. *Ib.* l. 398

13 Not with the mean and vulgar works of man,
But with high objects, with enduring things.
                         Ib. l. 408

14 Strife too humble to be named in verse. *Ib.* l. 513

15 The self-sufficing power of Solitude. *Ib.* bk. ii, l. 77

16   A prop
To our infirmity.   *Ib.* l. 214

17 Thence did I drink the visionary power;
And deem not profitless those fleeting moods
Of shadowy exultation.   *Ib.* l. 311

18   The soul,
Remembering how she felt, but what she felt
Remembering not, retains an obscure sense
Of possible sublimity.   *Ib.* l. 315

19   Where the statue stood
Of Newton, with his prism and silent face,
The marble index of a mind for ever
Voyaging through strange seas of thought alone.
               Ib. bk. iii, l. 61

20 Sweet Spenser, moving through his clouded heaven
With the moon's beauty and the moon's soft pace,
I called him Brother, Englishman, and Friend!
                       Ib. l. 280

21   Here and there
Slight shocks of young love-liking interspersed.
               Ib. bk. iv. l. 316

22   Bond unknown to me
Was given, that I should be, else sinning greatly,
A dedicated spirit.   *The Prelude*, bk. iv, l. 335

23   A day
Spent in a round of strenuous idleness. *Ib.* l. 377

24   That uncertain heaven, received
Into the bosom of the steady lake. *Ib.* bk. v, l. 387

25   Visionary power
Attends the motions of the viewless winds,
Embodied in the mystery of words.   *Ib.* l. 595

26 Present themselves as objects recognized,
In flashes, and with glory not their own. *Ib.* l. 604

27   Whether we be young or old,
Our destiny, our being's heart and home,
Is with infinitude, and only there;
With hope it is, hope that can never die,
Effort, and expectation, and desire,
And something evermore about to be.
               Ib. bk. vi, l. 603

28   We were brothers all
In honour, as in one community,
Scholars and gentlemen.   *Ib.* bk. ix, l. 227

29   In the People was my trust,
And in the virtues which mine eyes had seen.
               Ib. bk. x, l. 11

30 Not in Utopia—subterranean fields,—
Or some secreted island, Heaven knows where!
But in the very world, which is the world
Of all of us,—the place where, in the end
We find our happiness, or not at all!   *Ib.* l. 140

31 The dupe of folly, or the slave of crime. *Ib.* l. 320

32   There is
One great society alone on earth:
The noble living and the noble dead.   *Ib.* l. 393

33 A sensitive being, a *creative* soul. *Ib.* bk. xii, l. 207

34 Oh! mystery of man, from what a depth
Proceed thy honours. I am lost, but see
In simple childhood something of the base
On which thy greatness stands.   *Ib.* l. 272

35 Animate an hour of vacant ease.   *Ib.* l. 335

36 Sorrow, that is not sorrow, but delight;
And miserable love, that is not pain
To hear of, for the glory that redounds
Therefrom to human kind, and what we are.
              Ib. bk. xiii, l. 246

37   Imagination, which, in truth,
Is but another name for absolute power
And clearest insight, amplitude of mind,
And Reason in her most exalted mood.
               Ib. bk. xiv, l. 190

38 Prophets of Nature, we to them will speak
A lasting inspiration, sanctified
By reason, blest by faith: what we have loved,
Others will love, and we will teach them how;
Instruct them how the mind of man becomes
A thousand times more beautiful than the earth
On which he dwells, above this frame of things
(Which, 'mid all revolution in the hopes
And fears of men, doth still remain unchanged)
In beauty exalted, as it is itself
Of quality and fabric more divine.   *Ib.* l. 444

1 Art thou the bird whom man loves best,
The pious bird with the scarlet breast,
   Our little English robin?
               The Redbreast Chasing the Butterfly

2 Love him, or leave him alone!   *Ib.*

3 Habit rules the unreflecting herd.
   Ecclesiastical Sonnets, pt. II, xxviii. *Reflections.
   Grant that by this Unsparing Hurricane*

4 There was a roaring in the wind all night.
               Resolution and Independence, i

5 As high as we have mounted in delight
In our dejection do we sink as low.   *Ib.* iv

6 But how can he expect that others should
Build for him, sow for him, and at his call
Love him, who for himself will take no heed at all?
                                       Ib. vi

7 I thought of Chatterton, the marvellous boy,
The sleepless soul, that perished in his pride;
Of him who walked in glory and in joy,
Following his plough, along the mountain side:
By our own spirits are we deified:
We poets in our youth begin in gladness;
But thereof comes in the end despondency and mad-
   ness.   *Ib.* vii

8 The oldest man he seemed that ever wore grey hairs.
                                       Ib. viii

9 As a huge stone is sometimes seen to lie
Couched on the bald top of an eminence. *Ib.* ix

10 Like a sea-beast crawled forth, that on a shelf
Of rock or sand reposeth, there to sun itself. *Ib.*

11 That heareth not the loud winds when they call,
And moveth all together, if it moves at all. *Ib.* xi

12 Choice words, and measured phrase, above the reach
Of ordinary men; a stately speech;
Such as grave livers do in Scotland use. *Ib.* xiv

13 And mighty poets in their misery dead. *Ib.* xvii

14 'How is it that you live, and what is it you do?' *Ib.*

15   The good old rule
Sufficeth them, the simple plan,
That they should take, who have the power,
   And they should keep who can.
   Memorials of a Tour in Scotland, 1803. xi. *Rob
   Roy's Grave*

16 Scorn not the Sonnet; Critic, you have frowned,
Mindless of its just honours; with this key
Shakespeare unlocked his heart.
   Miscellaneous Sonnets, pt. II, i. *Scorn Not the
   Sonnet*

17   And when a damp
Fell round the path of Milton, in his hand
The Thing became a trumpet; whence he blew
Soul-animating strains,—alas! too few. *Ib.*

18 She dwelt among the untrodden ways
   Beside the springs of Dove,
A maid whom there were none to praise
   And very few to love:

A violet by a mossy stone
   Half hidden from the eye!
Fair as a star, when only one
   Is shining in the sky.

She lived unknown, and few could know
   When Lucy ceased to be;
But she is in her grave, and, oh,
   The difference to me!
               She Dwelt Among the Untrodden Ways

19 She was a phantom of delight
When first she gleamed upon my sight;
A lovely apparition, sent
To be a moment's ornament;
Her eyes as stars of twilight fair;
Like twilight's, too, her dusky hair;
But all things else about her drawn
From May-time and the cheerful dawn;
A dancing shape, an image gay,
To haunt, to startle, and waylay.
               She was a Phantom of Delight

20 I saw her upon nearer view,
A spirit, yet a woman too!
Her household motions light and free,
And steps of virgin liberty;
A countenance in which did meet
Sweet records, promises as sweet;
A creature not too bright or good
For human nature's daily food;
For transient sorrows, simple wiles,
Praise, blame, love, kisses, tears, and smiles. *Ib.*

21 And now I see with eye serene,
The very pulse of the machine;
A being breathing thoughtful breath,
A traveller betwixt life and death;
The reason firm, the temperate will,
Endurance, foresight, strength, and skill;
A perfect woman, nobly planned,
To warn, to comfort, and command;
And yet a spirit still, and bright
With something of angelic light. *Ib.*

22 For still, the more he works, the more
Do his weak ankles swell.   *Simon Lee*

23 O reader! had you in your mind
Such stores as silent thought can bring,
O gentle reader! you would find
A tale in every thing.   *Ib.*

24 I've heard of hearts unkind, kind deeds
With coldness still returning;
Alas! the gratitude of men
Hath oftener left me mourning.   *Ib.*

25 Characters of the great Apocalypse,
The types and symbols of Eternity,
Of first, and last, and midst, and without end.
   The Simplon Pass: Brook and Road, and *The
   Prelude*, bk. vi, l. 636

26 Ethereal minstrel! pilgrim of the sky!
Dost thou despise the earth where cares abound?
Or, while the wings aspire, are heart and eye
Both with thy nest upon the dewy ground?
Thy nest which thou canst drop into at will,
Those quivering wings composed, that music still!
               To a Skylark

27 Type of the wise who soar, but never roam;
True to the kindred points of heaven and home! *Ib.*

28 Behold her, single in the field,
   Yon solitary Highland lass!
   Memorials of a Tour in Scotland, 1803, ix. *The
   Solitary Reaper*

1 A voice so thrilling ne'er was heard
In spring-time from the Cuckoo-bird,
Breaking the silence of the seas
Among the farthest Hebrides.   *The Solitary Reaper*

2 Will no one tell me what she sings?—
Perhaps the plaintive numbers flow
For old, unhappy, far-off things,
And battles long ago.   *Ib.*

3 Some natural sorrow, loss, or pain
That has been, and may be again.   *Ib.*

4 The music in my heart I bore,
Long after it was heard no more.   *Ib.*

5 Spade! with which Wilkinson hath tilled his lands.
    To the Spade of a Friend

6 She gave me eyes, she gave me ears;
And humble cares, and delicate fears;
A heart, the fountain of sweet tears;
And love, and thought, and joy.
    The Sparrow's Nest

7 In that sweet mood when pleasant thoughts
Bring sad thoughts to the mind.
    Lines Written in Early Spring

8 And much it grieved my heart to think
What man has made of man.   *Ib.*

9 And 'tis my faith that every flower
Enjoys the air it breathes.   *Ib.*

10 Have I not reason to lament
What man has made of man?   *Ib.*

11 Strange fits of passion I have known.
    Strange Fits of Passion

12 What fond and wayward thoughts will slide
Into a Lover's head!
'O mercy!' to myself I cried,
'If Lucy should be dead!'   *Ib.*

13 Two Voices are there; one is of the sea,
One of the mountains; each a mighty Voice,
In both from age to age thou didst rejoice,
They were thy chosen music, Liberty!
    National Independence and Liberty, xii. *Thought
    of a Briton on the Subjugation of Switzerland: Two
    Voices are There*

14 Up! up! my friend, and quit your books;
Or surely you'll grow double:
Up! up! my friend, and clear your looks;
Why all this toil and trouble?   *The Tables Turned*

15 Books! 'tis a dull and endless strife:
Come, hear the woodland linnet,
How sweet his music! on my life,
There's more of wisdom in it.

And hark! how blithe the throstle sings!
He, too, is no mean preacher:
Come forth into the light of things,
Let Nature be your teacher.   *Ib.*

16 Spontaneous wisdom breathed by health,
Truth breathed by cheerfulness.

One impulse from a vernal wood
May teach you more of man,
Of moral evil and of good,
Than all the sages can.

Sweet is the lore which Nature brings;
Our meddling intellect
Misshapes the beauteous forms of things:—
We murder to dissect.

Enough of science and of art;
Close up these barren leaves;
Come forth, and bring with you a heart
That watches and receives.   *The Tables Turned*

17   Every gift of noble origin
Is breathed upon by Hope's perpetual breath.
    National Independence and Liberty, pt. 1, xx.
    These Times Strike Monied Worldlings

18 The power of Armies is a visible thing,
Formal, and circumscribed in time and place.
    Ib. pt. 11, xxxii. *The Power of Armies*

19 A noticeable man with large grey eyes
And a pale face. [Coleridge.]
    *Stanzas written in my pocket copy of Thomson's
    'Castle of Indolence'*

20 I've measured it from side to side:
'Tis three feet long, and two feet wide.
    The Thorn, iii [early reading]

21 Then nature said, 'A lovelier flower
On earth was never sown;
This child I to myself will take;
She shall be mine, and I will make
A lady of my own.'   *Three Years She Grew*

22 The stars of midnight shall be dear
To her; and she shall lean her ear
In many a secret place
Where rivulets dance their wayward round,
And beauty born of murmuring sound
Shall pass into her face.   *Ib.*

23   Sensations sweet,
Felt in the blood, and felt along the heart.
    Lines composed a few miles above Tintern Abbey,
    l. 27

24   That best portion of a good man's life,
His little, nameless, unremembered acts
Of kindness and of love.   *Ib.* l. 33

25   That blessed mood,
In which the burthen of the mystery,
In which the heavy and the weary weight
Of all this unintelligible world,
Is lightened:—that serene and blessed mood,
In which the affections gently lead us on,—
Until, the breath of this corporeal frame
And even the motion of our human blood
Almost suspended, we are laid asleep
In body, and become a living soul:
While with an eye made quiet by the power
Of harmony, and the deep power of joy,
We see into the life of things.   *Ib.* l. 37

26   For nature then
(The coarser pleasures of my boyish days,
And their glad animal movements all gone by)
To me was all in all.—I cannot paint
What then I was. The sounding cataract
Haunted me like a passion: the tall rock,
The mountain, and the deep and gloomy wood,
Their colours and their forms, were then to me
An appetite; a feeling and a love,
That had no need of a remoter charm,
By thought supplied, nor any interest
Unborrowed from the eye.   *Ib.* l. 72

1   I have learned
To look on nature, not as in the hour
Of thoughtless youth; but hearing often-times
The still, sad music of humanity,
Nor harsh nor grating, though of ample power
To chasten and subdue. And I have felt
A presence that disturbs me with the joy
Of elevated thoughts; a sense sublime
Of something far more deeply interfused,
Whose dwelling is the light of setting suns,
And the round ocean and the living air,
And the blue sky, and in the mind of man.
     Lines composed a few miles above Tintern Abbey,
     l. 88

2   All the mighty world
Of eye, and ear,—both what they half create,
And what perceive.   *Ib.* l. 105

3   Oh! yet a little while
May I behold in thee what I was once,
My dear, dear Sister! and this prayer I make,
Knowing that Nature never did betray
The heart that loved her; 'tis her privilege,
Through all the years of this our life, to lead
From joy to joy: for she can so inform
The mind that is within us, so impress
With quietness and beauty, and so feed
With lofty thoughts, that neither evil tongues,
Rash judgments, nor the sneers of selfish men,
Nor greetings where no kindness is, nor all
The dreary intercourse of daily life,
Shall e'er prevail against us, or disturb
Our cheerful faith, that all which we behold
Is full of blessings.   *Ib.* l. 121

4   Thou hast left behind
Powers that will work for thee; air, earth, and skies;
There's not a breathing of the common wind
That will forget thee; thou hast great allies;
Thy friends are exultations, agonies,
And love, and man's unconquerable mind.
     National Independence and Liberty, pt. I, viii. *To
     Toussaint L'Ouverture: Toussaint, the Most
     Unhappy*

5 Once did she hold the gorgeous East in fee,
And was the safeguard of the West.
     Ib. vi. *On the Extinction of the Venetian Republic:
     Once Did She Hold*

6 Venice, the eldest Child of Liberty.
She was a maiden City, bright and free.   *Ib.*

7 And when she took unto herself a Mate,
She must espouse the everlasting Sea.   *Ib.*

8 Men are we, and must grieve when even the shade
Of that which once was great is passed away.   *Ib.*

9 Our tainted nature's solitary boast.
     Ecclesiastical Sonnets, pt. ii, No. xxv. *The Virgin*

10   A shy spirit in my heart,
That comes and goes—will sometimes leap
From hiding-places ten years deep.
     The Waggoner, iv, l. 210

11   A simple child, dear brother Jim
That lightly draws its breath,
And feels its life in every limb,
What should it know of death?
     *We are Seven. The words 'dear brother Jim'
     were omitted in the 1815 edition of his poems.*

12 I take my little porringer
And eat my supper there.   *We are Seven*

13 'But they are dead; those two are dead!
Their spirits are in Heaven!'
'Twas throwing words away; for still
The little Maid would have her will,
And said, 'Nay, we are seven!'   *Ib.*

14 Earth has not anything to show more fair:
Dull would he be of soul who could pass by
A sight so touching in its majesty:
This City now doth, like a garment, wear
The beauty of the morning; silent, bare,
Ships, towers, domes, theatres, and temples lie
Open unto the fields, and to the sky;
All bright and glittering in the smokeless air.
Never did sun more beautifully steep
In his first splendour, valley, rock, or hill;
Ne'er saw I, never felt, a calm so deep!
The river glideth at his own sweet will:
Dear God! the very houses seem asleep;
And all that mighty heart is lying still!
     Miscellaneous Sonnets, pt. II, xxxvi. *Composed
     upon Westminster Bridge*

15 What wonder if a Poet now and then,
Among the many movements of his mind,
Felt for thee as a lover or a child! [England]
     National Independence and Liberty, pt. I, xvii.
     When I Have Borne in Memory.

16 Where lies the Land to which yon Ship must go?
     Miscellaneous Sonnets, pt. I, xxxi. *Where Lies the
     Land*

17 With Ships the sea was sprinkled far and nigh.
     Ib. xxxii. *With Ships the Sea was Sprinkled*

18 The world is too much with us; late and soon,
Getting and spending, we lay waste our powers:
Little we see in Nature that is ours;
We have given our hearts away, a sordid boon!
This Sea that bares her bosom to the moon;
The winds that will be howling at all hours,
And are up-gathered now like sleeping flowers;
For this, for everything, we are out of tune;
It moves us not; Great God! I'd rather be
A Pagan suckled in a creed outworn,
So might I, standing on this pleasant lea,
Have glimpses that would make me less forlorn;
Have sight of Proteus rising from the sea,
Or hear old Triton blow his wreathed horn.
     Ib. xxxiii. *The World is Too Much with Us.*

19 Let . . .
The swan on still St. Mary's Lake
Float double, swan and shadow!
     Memorials of a Tour in Scotland, 1803. xiii.
     Yarrow Unvisited

20 But thou, that didst appear so fair
To fond imagination,
Dost rival in the light of day
Her delicate creation.
     *Memorials of a Tour in Scotland, 1814. Yarrow
     Visited*

21 Like,—but oh how different!
       Yes, it was the Mountain Echo

22   Fear and trembling Hope,
Silence and Foresight; Death the Skeleton
And Time the Shadow.   *Yew Trees*

1 Thou, while thy babes around thee cling,
Shalt show us how divine a thing
A woman may be made. *To a Young Lady*

2 But an old age, serene and bright,
And lovely as a Lapland night,
Shall lead thee to thy grave. *Ib.*

3 Poetry is the breath and finer spirit of all knowledge;
it is the impassioned expression which is in the
countenance of all science.
Lyrical Ballads, preface

4 Poetry is the spontaneous overflow of powerful feelings: it takes its origin from emotion recollected in
tranquillity. *Ib.*

5 Every great and original writer, in proportion as he
is great and original, must himself create the taste
by which he is to be relished.
Letter to Lady Beaumont

HENRY CLAY WORK
1832–1884

6 Bring the good old bugle, boys, we'll sing another
song;
Sing it with a spirit that will start the world along,
Sing it as we used to sing it—fifty thousand strong,
As we were marching through Georgia.
Marching Through Georgia

7 'Hurrah! hurrah! we bring the Jubilee!
Hurrah! hurrah! the flag that makes you free!'
So we sang the chorus from Atlanta to the sea,
As we were marching through Georgia. *Ib. Chorus*

8 Father, dear father, come home with me now,
The clock in the belfry strikes one.
Temperance song, 1864

SIR HENRY WOTTON
1568–1639

9 How happy is he born and taught
That serveth not another's will;
Whose armour is his honest thought,
And simple truth his utmost skill!
Character of a Happy Life, i

10 Who God doth late and early pray
More of his grace than gifts to lend;
And entertains the harmless day
With a religious book, or friend. *Ib.* v

11 This man is freed from servile bands,
Of hope to rise, or fear to fall:—
Lord of himself, though not of lands,
And having nothing, yet hath all. *Ib.* vi

12 He first deceas'd; she for a little tri'd
To live without him: lik'd it not, and di'd.
Death of Sir Albertus Moreton's Wife

13 You meaner beauties of the night,
That poorly satisfy our eyes,
More by your number, than your light;
You common people of the skies,
What are you when the moon shall rise?
On His Mistress, the Queen of Bohemia

14 At my departure toward Rome . . . I had won confidence enough to beg his advice [Alberto Scipioni's]
how I might carry myself securely there without
offence of others, or of mine own conscience.

'*Signor Arrigo mio*', says he, '*I pensieri stretti ed il
viso sciolto* will go safely over the whole world.'
['Sir Henry . . . the thoughts secret and the coun-
tenance open.']
Letter to Milton, 13 Apr. 1638, prefixed to
Comus

15 An ambassador is an honest man sent to lie abroad for
the good of his country.
Written in the Album of Christopher Fleckmore
(1604)

SIR CHRISTOPHER WREN
1632–1723

16 Si monumentum requiris, circumspice.
If you would see his monument look around.
*Inscription over the interior of the North Door in
St. Paul's Cathedral, London. Written by Wren's
son*

SIR THOMAS WYATT
1503?–1542

17 Blame not my lute! for he must sound
Of this and that as liketh me. *The Lute Obeys*, i

18 And wilt thou leave me thus?
Say nay, say nay, for shame! *An Appeal*

19 Forget not yet the tried intent
Of such a truth as I have meant;
My great travail so gladly spent
Forget not yet! *Steadfastness*

20 They flee from me, that sometime did me seek.
Remembrance

21 My lute, awake! perform the last
Labour that thou and I shall waste,
The end that I have now begun;
For when this song is sung and past,
My lute, be still, for I have done. *To His Lute*

WILLIAM WYCHERLEY
1640?–1716

22 Go to your business, I say, pleasure, whilst I go to
my pleasure, business. *Country Wife*, Act II

23 Nay, you had both felt his desperate deadly daunting
dagger:—there are your d's for you!
Gentleman Dancing-Master, Act V

24 Fy! madam, do you think me so ill bred as to love a
husband? *Love in a Wood*, III. iv

25 QUAINT:
With sharp invectives—
WIDOW:
Alias, Billingsgate. *Plain Dealer*, Act III

WYNTOUN'S CHRONICLE

26 Quhen Alysander oure kyng wes dede,
That Scotland led in luve and le,
Away wes sons of ale and brede,
Of wyne and wax, of gamyn and gle:
Oure gold wes changyd into lede,
Cryst, borne into virgynyte,
Succour Scotland, and remede,
That stad is in perplexyte.
From Andrew Wyntoun's *Cronykill*, vol. i,
p. 401, ed. 1795 *(the edition used by Scott) and
in the edition of 1872, vol. ii, p. 266*

XENOPHON
b. *c.* 430 B.C.

1 θάλαττα θάλαττα.

The sea! the sea!   *Anabasis*, iv. vii. 24

WILLIAM BUTLER YEATS
1865–1939

2   A line will take us hours may be;
Yet if it does not seem a moment's thought,
Our stitching and unstitching has been naught.
    Adam's Curse

3 O heart, be at peace, because
  Nor knave nor dolt can break
What's not for their applause,
  Being for a woman's sake. *Against Unworthy Praise*

4   When I was young,
I had not given a penny for a song
Did not the poet sing it with such airs
That one believed he had a sword upstairs.
    All Things Can Tempt Me

5 The phantom, Beauty, in a mist of tears.
    Anashuya and Vijaya

6 The old priest Peter Gilligan
Was weary night and day;
For half his flock were in their beds,
Or under green sods lay. *Ballad of Father Gilligan*

7 He Who is wrapped in purple robes,
With planets in His care,
Had pity on the least of things
Asleep upon a chair.   *Ib.*

8 The years like great black oxen tread the world,
And God the herdsman goads them on behind,
And I am broken by their passing feet.
    The Countess Cathleen, Act IV

9   The Light of Lights
Looks always on the motive, not the deed,
The Shadow of Shadows on the deed alone.   *Ib.*

10 God's laughing in Heaven
To see you so good.   *A Cradle Song*

11 Down by the salley gardens my love and I did meet;
She passed the salley gardens with little snow-white feet.
She bid me take love easy, as the leaves grow on the tree;
But I, being young and foolish, with her would not agree.

In a field by the river my love and I did stand,
And on my leaning shoulder she laid her snow-white hand.
She bid me take life easy, as the grass grows on the weirs;
But I was young and foolish, and now am full of tears.
    Down by the Salley Gardens

12 She was more beautiful than thy first love,
This lady by the trees.   *A Dream of Death*

13 He found the unpersuadable justice.
    Ego Dominus Tuus

14 The coarse-bred son of a livery stable keeper. [Keats.]
    Ib.

15 We who are old, old and gay
O so old!
Thousands of years, thousands of years,
If all were told.   *A Faery Song*

16 But weigh this song with the great and their pride;
I made it out of a mouthful of air,
Their children's children shall say they have lied.
    He Thinks of Those who have Spoken Evil of his Beloved

17 Had I the heavens' embroidered cloths,
Enwrought with golden and silver light,
The blue and the dim and the dark cloths
Of night and light and the half-light,
I would spread the cloths under your feet:
But I, being poor, have only my dreams;
I have spread my dreams under your feet;
Tread softly, because you tread on my dreams.
    He Wishes for the Cloths of Heaven

18 I mourn for that most lovely thing; and yet God's will be done:
I knew a phoenix in my youth, so let them have their day.   *His Phoenix*

19 Out-worn heart, in a time out-worn,
Come clear of the nets of wrong and right;
Laugh, heart, again in the grey twilight,
Sigh, heart, again in the dew of the morn.
    Into the Twilight

20 And God stands winding His lonely horn,
And time and the world are ever in flight;
And love is less kind than the grey twilight,
And hope is less dear than the dew of the morn. *Ib.*

21 Nor law, nor duty bade me fight,
Nor public men, nor cheering crowds,
A lonely impulse of delight
Drove to this tumult in the clouds;
I balanced all, brought all to mind,
The years to come seemed waste of breath,
A waste of breath the years behind
In balance with this life, this death.
    An Irish Airman Foresees His Death

22 All the wild witches, those most noble ladies,
For all their broom-sticks and their tears,
Their angry tears, are gone.
    Lines Written in Dejection

23 What were all the world's alarms
To mighty Paris when he found
Sleep upon a golden bed,
That first dawn in Helen's arms.   *Lullaby*, st. 1

24 Never give all the heart, for love
Will hardly seem worth thinking of
To passionate women if it seem
Certain, and they never dream
That it fades out from kiss to kiss.
    Never Give All the Heart

25 Why, what could she have done, being what she is?
Was there another Troy for her to burn?
    No Second Troy

26 To shake their wicked sides at youth
Restraining reckless middle-age?
    On hearing that the Students of our new University have joined the Agitation against Immoral Literature

27 Was it for this the wild geese spread
The grey wing upon every tide;
For this that all that blood was shed,
For this Edward Fitzgerald died,
And Robert Emmet and Wolfe Tone,
All that delirium of the brave?
Romantic Ireland's dead and gone,
It's with O'Leary in the grave.   *September 1913*

1 For the good are always the merry,
Save by an evil chance,
And the merry love the fiddle,
And the merry love to dance. *The Fiddler of Dooney*

2 When I play on my fiddle in Dooney
Folk dance like a wave of the sea. *Ib.*

3 One that is ever kind said yesterday
'Your well-beloved's hair has threads of grey,
And little shadows come about her eyes.'
The Folly of Being Comforted

4 Time can but make her beauty over again:
Because of that great nobleness of hers.
The fire that stirs about her, when she stirs,
Burns but more clearly. O she had not these ways
When all the wild summer was in her gaze. *Ib.*

5 O heart! O heart! if she'd but turn her head,
You'd know the folly of being comforted. *Ib.*

6 The little fox murmured,
'O what of the world's bane?'
The sun was laughing sweetly,
The moon plucked at my rein;
But the little red fox murmured,
'O do not pluck at his rein,
He is riding to the townland
That is the world's bane.' *The Happy Townland*

7 The host is riding from Knocknarea
And over the grave of Clooth-na-Bare;
Caoilte tossing his burning hair,
And Niamh calling Away, come away.
The Hosting of the Sidhe

8 Who holds the world between His bill and made us
strong or weak
Is an undying moorfowl, and He lives beyond the
sky.
The rains are from His dripping wings, the moonbeams from His eye. *The Indian upon God*

9 Who made the world and ruleth it, He hangeth on
a stalk,
For I am in His image made, and all this tinkling
tide
Is but a sliding drop of rain between His petals wide. *Ib.*

10 The Stamper of the Skies,
He is a gentle roebuck; for how else, I pray, could He
Conceive a thing so sad and soft, a gentle thing like
me? *Ib.*

11 Who made the grass and made the worms and made
my feathers gay,
He is a monstrous peacock, and He waveth all the
night
His languid tail above us, lit with myriad spots of
light. *Ib.*

12 I will arise and go now, and go to Innisfree,
And a small cabin build there, of clay and wattles
made:
Nine bean-rows will I have there, a hive for the
honey-bee,
And live alone in the bee-loud glade.

And I shall have some peace there, for peace comes
dropping slow,
Dropping from the veils of the morning to where the
cricket sings;
There midnight's all a-glimmer, and noon a purple
glow,
And evening full of the linnet's wings.

I will arise and go now, for always night and day
I hear lake water lapping with low sounds by the
shore;
While I stand on the roadway, or on the pavements
gray
I hear it in the deep heart's core.
The Lake Isle of Innisfree

13 The wind blows out of the gates of the day,
The wind blows over the lonely of heart,
And the lonely of heart is withered away.
The Land of Heart's Desire

14 The land of faery,
Where nobody gets old and godly and grave,
Where nobody gets old and crafty and wise,
Where nobody gets old and bitter of tongue. *Ib.*

15 Of a land where even the old are fair,
And even the wise are merry of tongue. *Ib.*

16 Land of Heart's Desire,
Where beauty has no ebb, decay no flood,
But joy is wisdom, Time an endless song. *Ib.*

17 All things uncomely and broken, all things worn out
and old,
The cry of a child by the roadway, the creak of a
lumbering cart,
The heavy steps of the ploughman, splashing the
wintry mould,
Are wronging your image that blossoms a rose in
the deeps of my heart.
The wrong of unshapely things is a wrong too great to
be told;
I hunger to build them anew and sit on a green knoll
apart,
With the earth and the sky and the water, re-made,
like a casket of gold;
For my dreams of your image that blossoms a rose in
the deeps of my heart.
The Lover Tells of the Rose in his Heart

18 When I was a boy with never a crack in my heart.
The Meditation of the Old Fisherman

19 I heard the old, old men say,
'All that's beautiful drifts away
Like the waters.'
The Old Men Admiring Themselves in the Water

20 A pity beyond all telling
Is hid in the heart of love. *The Pity of Love*

21 Rose of all Roses, Rose of all the World!
The Rose of Battle

22 Who dreamed that beauty passes like a dream?
For these red lips, with all their mournful pride,
Mournful that no new wonder may betide,
Troy passed away in one high funeral gleam,
And Usna's children died.

We and the labouring world are passing by:
Amid men's souls, that waver and give place
Like the pale waters in their wintry race,
Under the passing stars, foam of the sky,
Lives on this lonely face.
Bow down, archangels, in your dim abode;
Before you were, or any hearts to beat,
Weary and kind one linger'd by His seat;
He made the world to be a grassy road
Before her wandering feet. *The Rose of the World*

23 Far off, most secret, and inviolate Rose,
Enfold me in my hour of hours. *The Secret Rose*

1 **A** woman of so shining loveliness
That men threshed corn at midnight by a tress.
The Secret Rose.

2 When shall the stars be blown about the sky,
Like the sparks blown out of a smithy, and die?
Surely thine hour has come, thy great wind blows,
Far-off, most secret, and inviolate Rose? *Ib.*

3 It is love that I am seeking for,
But of a beautiful, unheard-of kind
That is not in the world. *The Shadowy Waters*

4 Do you not know
How great a wrong it is to let one's thought
Wander a moment when one is in love? *Ib.*

5 Bend lower, O king, that I may crown you with it.
O flower of the branch, O bird among the leaves,
O silver fish that my two hands have taken
Out of the running stream, O morning star,
Trembling in the blue heavens like a white fawn
Upon the misty border of the wood,
Bend lower, that I may cover you with my hair,
For we will gaze upon this world no longer. *Ib.*

6 And pluck till time and times are done
The silver apples of the moon
The golden apples of the sun.
The Song of Wandering Ængus

7 The brawling of a sparrow in the eaves,
The brilliant moon and all the milky sky,
And all that famous harmony of leaves,
Had blotted out man's image and his cry.

A girl arose that had red mournful lips
And seemed the greatness of the world in tears,
Doomed like Odysseus and the labouring ships
And proud as Priam murdered with his peers;

Arose, and on the instant clamorous eaves,
A climbing moon upon an empty sky,
And all that lamentation of the leaves,
Could but compose man's image and his cry.
The Sorrow of Love

8 And the loud chaunting of the unquiet leaves
Are shaken with earth's old and weary cry.
The Sorrow of Love (1893 version)

9 Come away, O human child!
To the waters and the wild
With a faery, hand in hand,
For the world's more full of weeping than you can
understand. *The Stolen Child*

10 Nor know that what disturbs our blood
Is but its longing for the tomb. *The Wheel*

11 I would that we were, my beloved, white birds on the
foam of the sea! *The White Birds*

12 But was there ever dog that praised his fleas?
*To a Poet, who would have me praise certain bad
Poets, Imitators of his and mine*

13 I know what wages beauty gives,
How hard a life her servant lives,
Yet praise the winters gone:
There is not a fool can call me friend,
And I may dine at journey's end
With Landor and with Donne. *To a Young Beauty*

14 Know, that I would accounted be
True brother of a company
That sang, to sweeten Ireland's wrong,
Ballad and story, rann and song;

Nor be I any less of them,
Because the red-rose-bordered hem
Of her, whose history began
Before God made the angelic clan,
Trails all about the written page.
To Ireland in the Coming Times

15 For the elemental creatures go
About my table to and fro. *Ib.*

16 Ah, faeries, dancing under the moon,
A Druid land, a Druid tune! *Ib.*

17 Red Rose, Proud Rose, sad Rose of all my days!
To the Rose upon the Rood of Time

18 Eternal beauty wandering on her way. *Ib.*

19 All changed, changed utterly:
A terrible beauty is born. *Under Saturn*

20 Dwell in the house of the Fenians, be they in flames
or at feast. *The Wanderings of Oisin*, bk. iii

21 When you are old and gray and full of sleep,
And nodding by the fire, take down this book,
And slowly read, and dream of the soft look
Your eyes had once, and of their shadows deep;
How many loved your moments of glad grace,
And loved your beauty with love false or true,
But one man loved the pilgrim soul in you,
And loved the sorrows of your changing face.
And bending down beside the glowing bars,
Murmur, a little sadly, how Love fled
And paced upon the mountains overhead
And hid his face amid a crowd of stars.
When you are Old

ANDREW YOUNG
1807–1889

22 There is a happy land,
Far, far away,
Where Saints in glory stand,
Bright, bright as day.
Hymn: There is a Happy Land. C. H. Bate-
man's *Sacred Song Book*, 1843

EDWARD YOUNG
1683–1765

23 Be wise with speed;
A fool at forty is a fool indeed.
Love of Fame, Sat. ii, l. 281

24 For who does nothing with a better grace?
Ib. Sat. iv, l. 86

25 For ever most divinely in the wrong.
Ib. Sat. vi, l. 106

26 For her own breakfast she'll project a scheme,
Nor take her tea without a stratagem. *Ib.* l. 187

27 One to destroy, is murder by the law;
And gibbets keep the lifted hand in awe;
To murder thousands, takes a specious name,
War's glorious art, and gives immortal fame.
Ib. Sat. vii, l. 55

28 How commentators each dark passage shun,
And hold their farthing candle to the sun. *Ib.* l. 97

29 Tir'd Nature's sweet restorer, balmy sleep!
He, like the world, his ready visit pays
Where fortune smiles; the wretched he forsakes.
The Complaint: Night Thoughts, Night i, l. 1

1 Night, sable goddess! from her ebon throne
In rayless majesty, now stretches forth
Her leaden sceptre o'er a slumb'ring world.
The Complaint: Night Thoughts, Night i, l. 18

2   We take no note of Time
But from its Loss.   *Ib*. l. 55

3 Be wise to-day; 'tis madness to defer.   *Ib*. l. 390

4 Procrastination is the thief of time.   *Ib*. l. 393

5 Of man's miraculous mistakes, this bears
The palm, 'That all men are about to live'.
Ib. l. 399

6 At thirty man suspects himself a fool;
Knows it at forty, and reforms his plan;
At fifty chides his infamous delay,
Pushes his prudent purpose to resolve;
In all the magnanimity of thought
Resolves; and re-resolves; then dies the same.
Ib. l. 417

7 All men think all men mortal, but themselves.
Ib. l. 424

8   Beautiful as sweet!
And young as beautiful! and soft as young!
And gay as soft! and innocent as gay.
Ib. Night iii, l. 81

9 Man wants but little; nor that little, long.
Ib. Night iv, l. 118

10 A God all mercy, is a God unjust.   *Ib*. l. 233

11 By night an atheist half believes a God.
Ib. Night v, l. 176

12 To know the world, not love her, is thy point;
She gives but little, nor that little, long.
Ib. Night viii, l. 1276

13 Devotion! daughter of astronomy!
An undevout astronomer is mad.
The Complaint: Night Thoughts, Night ix, l. 769

14 Life is the desert, life the solitude;
Death joins us to the great majority.
The Revenge, Act IV

15 Accept a miracle, instead of wit,
See two dull lines, with Stanhope's pencil writ.
Written with Lord Chesterfield's Diamond Pencil.
Spence, *Anecdotes* (1820), p. 378

16 You are so witty, profligate, and thin,
At once we think thee Milton, Death, and Sin.
Epigram on Voltaire

ISRAEL ZANGWILL
1864–1926

17 Scratch the Christian and you find the pagan—
spoiled.   *Children of the Ghetto*, bk. ii, ch. 6

18 America is God's Crucible, the great Melting-Pot
where all the races of Europe are melting and reforming! . . . God is making the American.
The Melting Pot, Act I

ÉMILE ZOLA
1840–1902

19 J'accuse.
I accuse.
Title of an open letter to the President of the Republic, in connexion with the Dreyfus case, published in L'Aurore, 13 Jan. 1898

CORRIGENDA

6:13, 125:15, 250:14   *A detailed history of this song, which has appeared in many versions, is given in Percy A. Scholes*, God Save the Queen! (*1954*).

7:18   *A more precise source is given at 254:2.*

73:14   *For an earlier history of this rhyme see* The Oxford Dictionary of Nursery Rhymes (*1951*).

210:5   *An earlier source for these words is given at 10:20.*

277:19   *This occurs in Boswell's* Life, *vol. ii, p. 13. 15 February 1766*:
So far is it from being true that men are naturally equal, that no two people can be half an hour together, but one shall acquire an evident superiority over the other.

420:24   *These lines are quoted by Scott. They form the burden of an old song to which Burns wrote additional verses.*

INDEX

NOTE

The index references show the page number followed by the numerical position of the quotation on the page (e.g. 163:15 = the fifteenth quotation on page 163).

The order of the index both in the keywords and in the entries under the keywords is strictly alphabetical.

To save space the keyword is replaced by its initial letter in the individual entries.

Foreign quotations have been included in the general alphabetical scheme and for greater clarity are printed in italic in this index. A separate Greek index follows the general one.

Irregular spellings (such as occur in Dickens,

Artemus Ward, &c.), early English words, and dialect words are indexed under their normal modern equivalents except where there is no exact equivalent. Some words are given in both their original and their normal forms.

The definite and indefinite article have been dropped from the beginnings of most entries, and the alphabetical order is therefore decided by more significant words: thus—under 'Face'—'a garden in her face' and 'the garden of your face' follow each other instead of being separated by over a hundred other 'face' entries.

A

A was an apple-pie	366:7
Aaron: A.'s rod	45:42
even unto A.'s beard	400:3
like A.'s serpent	383:25
Abana and Pharpar	48:22
Abandon: a. all remorse	472:5
a. his mind to it	275:8
a. yourselves to your..appetites	85:8
all hope a.	168:17
Abandoned: what God a.	264:4
Abased: whosoever exalteth himself ..a.	62:4
whosoever shall exalt himself..a.	60:16
Abashed: a. the Devil stood	347:31
heard, and were a.	344:27
newe a. nightingale	138:34
Abashless inquisition of each star	545:10
Abassin kings their issue guard	347:9
Abate—Cardinal,—Christ	96:17
Abated: the agony is a.	326:10
Abatement: a. and low price	481:30
earth's a.	94:1
Abba, Father	65:53
Abbey: his name on the A.-stones	92:38
not in the A. proudly laid	562:21
Abbot: A. of Aberbrothok	507:25
Bishop, and a., and prior	34:8
Abby-nay: all along of a.	295:22
A.B.C.: man is man's A.	404:14
unacquainted with the A.	512:7
Abdicate it in the greatest	413:9
Abdiel: Seraph A., faithful found	348:18
Abed-nego: Meshach and A.	55:41
Abel: Cain and his brother, A.	151:10
Aberbrothok: Abbot of A.	507:25
Aberdeen: the Quaker (Lord A.)	28:25
Aberdour: half-owre to A.	32:2
Aberglaube: der A. is die Poesie	224:3
Abhor: a. the makers	192:32
age, I do a. thee	486:3
Abhorred: a. all manner of meat	398:16
hath not ..a...the poor	393:8
how a. in my imagination	437:15
Idolatry, to be a.	390:54
lean a. monster	478:44
Abhorrence: my heart's a.!	96:38
Abhorring: blow me into a.	425:34
Abide: a. in this dull world	425:29
a. with me	322:1
a. with me from morn till eve	291:10
I a. by my Mother's House	300:11
no where did a.	149:23
there he would a.	165:10
was, and is, and will a.	573:26
who may a. it?	399:39

Abide (*cont.*)	
with me and mine a.	324:11
Abided: all things a. eternally	548:15
Abides: in mystery our soul a.	16:29
much is taken, much a.	541:3
Abideth: a. not in words	296:31
now a. faith, hope, charity	66:46(-67)
where my Love a.	94:24
Abi-Ezer: vintage of A.	46:53
Abiit: a. ad plures	125:34, 378:11
a., excessit, evasit, erupit	145:13
Abilities: according to his a.	333:12
God has given you good a.	54:13
Ability: according to his several a.	60:28
furnished with a.	57:16
my lean and low a.	484:17
studies serve..for a.	27:13
3rdly, intellectual a.	20:21
Abire: tempus a. tibi est	257:21
Abject: a. from the spheres	561:12
doubting in his a. spirit	320:12
I'll be this a. thing no more	229:5
so a.—yet alive!	118:19
Abjure: a. the Scriptures	329:25
other pleasures all a.	348:35
Ablaze: Britain set the world a.	219:7
Able: a. to do..abundantly	67:55
let me see if he is a.	249:23
tempted above that ye are a.	66:38
Ablution: priest-like task of pure a.	288:17
Aboard: Donkey wint a.	298:21
once a. the lugger	279:16
we brought them all a.	539:19
Abode: a. his destin'd Hour	205:30
a. his Hour or two	205:29
a. where the Eternal are	492:16
archangels, in your dim a.	585:22
English make it their a.	557:23
his frailties from their dread a.	230:13
nor wealth nor blessed a.	334:13
we live in a numble a.	174:26
Abodes: aiming at the bless'd a.	383:13
Elysian, windless, fortunate a.	497:15
remembers its august a.	308:28
sprung from your bless'd a.	381:33
Abolish: utterly a. or destroy	576:19
Abominable: altogether become a.	392:23
Abomination: a. of desolation	60:24
an a. unto the Lord, but	5:6
incense is an a.	52:29
Abominations: the mother of harlots and a.	71:32
Aboon: a. the burn, ayont the law	516:20
a heart a. them a!	108:15
Abora: singing of Mount A.	151:33(-152)
Abou Ben Adhem (may his tribe increase!)	265:16

Abound: grace did much more a.	65:42
that grace may a.	65:43
where beauties most a.	116:43
About: a., a., in reel and rout	149:6
a. it and a.	206:10
a. must, and a. must go	186:10
all men are a. to live	587:5
something evermore a. to be	579:27
what are you a.?	87:27
Above: a. himself..erect himself	168:5
around, beneath, a.	81:10
at once a., beneath, around	503:3
every good gift..from a.	69:29
far a. the great	231:16
he is so a. me	423:2
set your affection on things a.	68:30
some descending from a.	24:17
square, and a. the board	234:11
this wisdom..not from a.	69:39
thy glory a. all the earth	395:18
'tis not so a.	435:35
unseen things a.	235:10
what they do a.	558:7
Abra was ready..Abra came	402:4
Abraham: are they the seed of A.?	67:33
carried..into A.'s bosom	62:25
God of Isaac,..of Jacob	45:38
in A.'s bosom all the year	577:1
sleep in A.'s bosom	476:25
Abreast: keep a. of Truth	320:13
one but goes a.	481:19
Abridgement of all that was pleasant	225:30
Abroad: come to starve a.	192:28
Cupid a. was lated	231:33
for the good of my country..a.	203:12
I will a.	244:10
ships shall go a.	298:17
when he next doth ride a.	160:11
you are ordered a.	305:1
Absalom, my son, my son	47:37
Absence: a. doth join	262:5
a. from whom we love	160:20
a., hear thou my protestation	262:5
a. makes the heart grow fonder	5:3, 36:28
a. of body	403:6
a...of educated..opinion	19:16
a. of the planet Venus	177:22
a. seemed my flame to qualify	488:4
by a. this good means	262:6
cannot admit a.	186:25
conquered..in a fit of a. of mind	421:19
conspicuous..by its a.	414:2
how like a winter..my a.	487:27
I dote on his very a.	463:14
in thy a. is..a sty	425:29

[589]

INDEX

INDEX

INDEX

INDEX

INDEX

INDEX

[614]

INDEX

Bellies: for their b.' sake 342:27
Bellman: B., perplexed and distressed 128:9
fatal b. 458:3
Bellona's bridegroom 456:9
Bellow: the bleat, the bark, b., and roar 73:26
Bellows: my b. have quite lost their wind 8:13
Bell-rope: swam to the b. 39:11
Bells: air broke into a mist with b. 94:29
all the b. on earth did ring 7:14
at last the b. ringeth to even-songe 239:6
b. I hear 566:27
b. in your parlours 470:25
b. of hell go ting-a-ling-a-ling 8:19
b. on her toes 368:17
b. they sound on Bredon 263:2
b. they sound so clear 262:21
b. were ringing the Old Year out 288:8
buds, and b., and stars 288:8
chime of full, sad b. 269:25
church-b. chimed 334:6
dear b.! 253:15
deep in the b. and grass 249:7
from the b., b., b., b., 380:12
hung among the b. and ding-dongs 379:22
instruments to melancholy b. 478:33
lin-lan-lone of evening b. 529:21
match'd in mouth like b. 467:20
Oh, noisy b., be dumb 263:2
ring O b. 566:28(-567)
ring out, wild b. 533:17
say the b. of St. Clement's 368:7
silver b., and cockle shells 367:21
sweet b. jangled 434:14
they now ring the b. 558:30
those evening b.! 357:15
those Shandon b. 402:20
'twould ring the b. of heaven 249:5
where b. have knoll'd to church 427:19
with a tower and b. 164:29
Bell-swarmed: cuckoo-echoing, b. 254:22
Bellum: praeparet b. 552:16
Belly: B. God send thee good ale 516:21(-517)
best fits a little b. 245:19
filled his b. with the husks 62:14
he who does not mind his b. 271:17
his b. is as bright ivory 52:14
his wit in his b. 481:10
increasing b. 441:19
in fair round b. 427:21
in the b. of the fish 56:5
I wish it was in Jonadge's b. 176:27
more than his b. can 337:44
my b. was bitter 71:14
noise in the beast's b. 328:4
pudding in his b. 439:35
something of a round b. 441:21
thy b. is like an heap of wheat 52:18
whose God is their b. 68:24
Belly-ache: no compensation for a b. 304:24
Belly-pinched wolf 453:4
Belong: aught that wad b. thee 104:26
secret things b. unto the Lord 46:29
Beloved: b. as thou art 494:7
b. from pole to pole 149:27
b., it is morn 248:7
b. of their dams 156:19
b. over all 302:13
b. till life can charm no more 153:22
Daniel, a man greatly b. 55:44
escape me? never—b.! 92:41
forget the Suspenders, Best B. 304:11
giveth his b. sleep 88:25, 399:35
heaped for the b.'s bed 499:1
how far to be b. 423:12
if ye find my b. 52:12
image of the creature .. b. 483:2
I opened to my b. 52:11
leaning upon her b. 52:22
Leda, the b. of Jupiter 309:12
let us stay rather on earth, B. 88:20
lovely that are not b. 375:11
more beloving than b. 423:18
my b. had withdrawn 52:11
my b. is mine 52:3

Beloved (cont.)
my b. is white and ruddy 52:13
names of things b. are dear 80:23
never be b. by men 73:22
only b., and loving me 158:13
that she b. knows nought 480:41
this is my b. 52:14
this is my b. Son 57:33
thy power .. of being b. 96:24
voice of my b. that knocketh 52:9
voice of one b. 497:3
what is thy b. more than another b. 52:12
Beloving: more b. than beloved 423:18
Below: at peace with all b. 119:2
b. the kirk, the hill, the lighthouse-top 148:21
down and away b. 15:22
faithful b., he did his duty 173:11
fall b. Demosthenes or Cicero 202:16
Heaven itself lies here b. 166:4
land-lubbers lying down b. 9:3
man wants but little drink b. 251:1
man wants but little here b. 112:10, 225:13
thy element's b. 452:37
Belt: my leathern b. likewise 159:39
round thee, maiden, bind my b. 530:25
Belted you an' flayed you 297:6
Belvoir's lordly terraces 322:23
Bemused: much b. in beer 385:21
Ben: B. Adhem's name led 265:18
B. Battle was a soldier bold 252:29
'Next Poet'—(Manners, B.!) 93:27
O rare B. Jonson 282:9
Sweet Alice, B. Bolt 201:24
Benbow, Collingwood, Byron 362:30
Bench: drowsy B. protect 165:20
little b. of heedless bishops 499:16
Benches: rub not clean their b. 281:6
Bend: b. all the three 308:13
b. down and touch lightly 567:5
b. lower, O king 586:5
b. on me .. thy tender eyes 322:8
b. to the oar 415:6
shall I b. low 463:22
whose b. doth awe the world 448:20
Bending: Angels b. near the earth 421:10
b. down beside the glowing bars 586:21
b. one way their influence 343:14
my head is b. low 210:17
Bends: b. not as I tread 341:4
the gallant mast 167:20
b. with the remover 488:7
blue sky b. over all 150:23
he who b. to himself a joy 74:27
made their b. adornings 424:7
though she b. him 317:27
Bene: good for a bootless b. 574:32
Bene: de quoquam quicquam b. velle mereri 133:12
Beneath: around, b. above 81:10
at once above, b., around 503:3
b. the good how far 231:16
b. the tartan plaid 23:17
b. whose awful Hand 300:24
prayer for all who lie b. 295:5
some springing from b. 24:17
Benedicamus Domino 41:30
Benedick the married man 468:6
Benediction: perpetual b. 576:17
sprinkles b. through the dawn 545:6
Benedictions: over-bowed by many b. 92:33
Benefacta: recordanti b. priora voluptas 133:13
Benefactor: Adam, the first great b. 550:24
Benefice: dreams he of another b. 477:7
Beneficent: zealous, b., firm 17:17
Benefices twinkl'd from afar 192:28
Benefit: o b. of ill 488:9
without the b. o' the Clergy 155:10
Benefits: all the b. of your own country 428:17
b. forgot 427:22
forget not all his b. 398:3
Benevolence: b. of the passive order 337:39
full o' beans and b. 518:21
lazy glow of b. 90:31

Benevolence (cont.)
whether the b. .. does most good or harm 29:7
Benevolent: heart b. and kind 108:35
Benight: ourselves b. our happiest day 184:28
Benighted: b. walks under the midday sun 340:20
pore b. 'eathen 296:23
Benison: b. of hot water 83:22
for a b. to fall 247:15
Benjamin: B.'s mess was five times so much 45:22
little B. their ruler 396:13
Bent: b. head and beseeching hand 95:37
fool must follow his .. b. 303:13
they are not our b. 221:38
thy affection cannot hold the b. 483:4
to the top of my b. 435:27
Benumbed: our b. conceiving soars 545:1
we feel b. 118:24
Benumbs: a pen .. b. all his faculties 270:8
Bequeath them no tumbled house 335:26
Bereaves of their bad influence 575:6
Bereft: b. of wet and of wildness 254:30
of friends, of hope, of all b. 159:1
thick, b. of beauty 479:12
Berenice's ever-burning hair 135:15
Berkeley: Bishop B. destroyed this world 505:23
Bishop B. said '.. no matter' 116:30
Coxcombs vanquish B. by a grin 85:4
Berkeley Square: faith that ye share with B. 302:26
not in B. 302:22
Bermudas: from the still-vexed B. 479:24
remote B. ride 332:1
Berries: b. and plums to eat 249:7
two lovely b. 467:9
your b. harsh and crude 342:10
Berry: from many a b. 348:9
God could have made a better b. 112:21
redder b. on the thorn 248:7
sweeter than the b. 214:8
Berth: happen'd in his b. 252:32
Bertie: Burlington B. 237:28
Bertram's right and B.'s might 419:35
Beruffled: blast-b. plume 235:17
Beryl: eighth b. 72:1
gold rings set with the b. 52:14
Beschränken: sich zu b. 223:14
Beseeching: bent head and b. hand 95:37
Beseems: none b. him half so well 23:24
Beset: sin which doth so easily b. us 69:18
who so b. him round 99:36
Beside: b. him laid 417:18
B. the Seaside 223:6
Paul, thou art b. thyself 65:23
Besieged: by battery b. Belgrade 5:7
like bread in a b. town 272:31
Besmeared: b. with blood and dust 119:16
with blood of human sacrifice 344:28
Besoin: travell'd .. out of .. the b. de voyager 512:18
Besom of destruction 53:23
Besotted myriads of people 109:12
Bespake: the Lord himself b. 343:14
Bespangling: dew b. herb and tree 245:25
Bespeak her to my blisses 166:18
Besprent with April dew 282:2
Bess, the landlord's daughter 366:2
Best: about the b. thing God invents 91:31
acts the b. 29:9
afflict the b. 230:15
all is b. 351:7
all is for the b. 557:2
all my b. is dressing old words 487:18
all that's b. of dark and bright 119:1
any other person's b. 239:13
at the last, b. 423:36
bad's the b. of us 37:17
beauty being the b. of all we know 80:26
b. and brightest, come away 494:8
b. and happiest moments 499:12
b. and the last 95:10
b. and the worst of this is 524:10
b. .. are but shadows 467:30

INDEX

[619]

INDEX

INDEX

[635]

INDEX

INDEX

INDEX

INDEX

G

INDEX

Gay (cont.)

always g.!	11:24
bedeck'd, ornate, and g.	350:31
each g. turn	382:33
face that's anything but g.	543:6
from grave to g.	384:15
g. as soft!	587:8
G. a week	521:2
g. gilded scenes	2:2
g. in the mazy	146:23
g. Robin is seen no more	80:20
g., the g. and festive scene	178:12
g. without frivolity	16:9
gild and make them g.	189:10
I'm a g. deceiver	154:12
impiously g.	164:40
innocent as g.	419:31, 587:8
life on the whole is far from g.	312:11
though g. they run	338:9
thy outward walls so costly g.	488:20
went never g.	470:29
wise and good and g.	368:1
would not, if I could, be g.	408:9

Gaza: eyeless in G. | 350:21
whence G. mourns | 351:7

Gaze: coldly she turns from their

g.	356:31
fix thy firm g. on virtue	324:17
fixt in stedfast g.	343:14
g. an eagle blind	455:22
g. on so fondly to-day	356:11
g. upon this world no longer	586:5
gone to g. on Cleopatra too	424:7
let them g.	478:13
show and g. o' the time	401:13
they g., turn giddy	381:27
thou art gone from my g.	314:20
wild summer.. in her g.	585:4
with fearful g.	355:14

Gazed: g. adown the dale | 416:12
g. on the face that was dead | 572:13
I g.—and g. | 577:7
too much g. at | 285:39

Gazelle: never nursed a dear G.
177:33, 357:5

Gazer: rash g. wipe his eye | 245:13

Gazes: g. on the ground | 329:19
whoso g. faints | 497:9

Gazing: every evening found him

g.	311:20
g. on the earth	495:19
why stand ye g. up?	64:22
with g. fed	464:13

Gear: tho' poor in g. | 108:1

Gebet: das vollkommenste G. | 313:17

Geck: notorious g. and gull | 484:25

Gedanke: ein einziger dankbarer G.
313:17
ein G. | 234:17

Gedanken sind zollfrei | 416:1

Geese: all his own g. are swans | 558:29
g. are getting fat | 5:23
g. are swans | 16:19
grow up as g. and gabies | 515:24
wild g. spread the grey wing | 584:27
wild g...the creeping fowler eye | 467:7

Gehazi: whence comest thou, G.? | 64:22

Gehenna: down to G. | 304:2

Geist: der G. der stets verneint | 223:17

Gêlert's dying yell | 508:32

Gem: consider'd a perfect g. | 120:22
g. of all joy | 195:5
many a g. of purest ray | 230:5

Gems: brilliant.. with thousand g. | 82:9
feet like sunny g. | 535:39
g. she wore | 356:30
..n scorn of eyes, reflecting g. | 476:14
rich and various g. | 340:1
these the g. of Heav'n | 347:23

Gender: for foul toads to knot and
g. in | 472:34
of the feminine g. | 370:5

Genealogies: fables and endless g. | 68:41

General: attend here on the g. | 472:19
by g. laws | 383:14
caviare to the g. | 433:25
English army led by an Irish
g...French army led by an
Italian g. | 490:39
g.'s disdain'd | 481:5
G. Good is the plea of the
scoundrel | 75:7

General (cont.)

g. notions are generally wrong	354:16
g. of our gracious empress	445:6
mind of large g. powers	278:2
not local prejudices.. but the g. good	100:14
so useless as a g. maxim	325:7
worthy G...'immoral man'	295:13

Generalities: glittering and sound-
ing g. | 142:25
glittering g.!.. blazing ubiqui-
ties | 201:21

Generally: so g. civil | 273:24

Generals: bite some other of my g. | 216:12
despite of all your g. ye prevail | 308:21
G. Janvier and Février | 364:18
Ireland gives England her g. | 337:10

Generate: spirituality..typewriter
does not g. | 188:9

Generation: evil and adulterous g. | 59:16
faithless and stubborn g. | 396:33
follow the g. of his fathers | 395:2
had it been the whole g. | 6:20
O g. of vipers | 57:30
one g. passeth.. another g. cometh | 50:59
to every g. these come.. down
unto the third and fourth g. | 200:46
ye are a chosen g. | 390:7
| 69:48 |

Generations: all g...call me
blessed | 61:13
fleeting g. of mankind | 499:8
g. are prepared | 574:23
no hungry g. | 288:1
soothed the griefs of forty g. | 325:36
ten g. failed to alter | 236:42
young g. in hail | 335:26

Generous: bane of the most g.
souls | 229:9
booksellers are g...men | 270:30
g. aspirings.. in vain | 307:12
g. nature..her own way | 100:25
it is the g. spirit | 575:5
just, the upright, the g. | 363:26
like g. wine | 111:24
most select and g. | 431:25
most vain, most g. | 241:29

Genesis: square with G. again | 89:37

Geneva: grim G. ministers | 24:7
open onto the Lake of G. | 290:16

Genevieve: G., sweet G. | 157:1

Genial: froze the g. current | 230:5
great..g. Englishman | 539:9

Génie: le g...aptitude à la patience | 98:18
vous vous croyez un grand g. | 37:11

Genitivo: hic hoc horum G. | 370:5

Geniumque loci..precatur | 555:3

Genius: beauty like hers is g. | 410:28
creates a g. to do it | 201:8
eccentricities of g. | 179:1
Edmund, whose g. was such | 225:27
g. and the mortal instruments | 449:5
g...aptitude for patience | 98:18
'g'...capacity of taking trouble
111:40, 126:9
G. does what it must | 337:43
g. found respectable | 87:33
g...getting its possessors into
trouble | 111:40
g. is of no country | 143:18
g...ninety-nine per cent. per-
spiration | 195:22
g. of the Constitution | 379:10
gives g. a better discerning | 226:2
good G. presiding | 289:13
great and hardy g. | 226:27
if Shakespeare's g. had been
cultivated | 139:21
man of g. and his money | 499:19
many a g...slow of growth | 313:22
most singular g. | 78:20
nothing to declare except my g. | 570:22
parting g. | 343:22
Philistine of g. | 20:19
ramp up my g. | 281:3
right sphere for Shelley's g. | 19:13
rules and models destroy g. | 240:4
talent instantly recognizes g. | 188:28
taste is the feminine of g. | 207:34
thine own g. gave the..blow | 117:25
tho' g. bless | 153:28
three fifths of him g. | 320:4

Genius (cont.)

to believe your own thought..g.	200:36
to raise the g.	381:6
under him my g. is rebuk'd	458:33
what a g. I had	520:50
whom g. gave to shine	231:3
whose fires true g. kindles	385:29
with want of g. curst	192:10
works of g...the first things	289:23

Gennesareth: not of G., but
Thames | 545:1

Genteel: Lamplough was g. | 514:2
no dancing bear was so g. | 160:13
to the truly g. | 237:6

Genteelly: debauch his friend's
wife g. | 272:26

Genterye: of his g. him deyneth
nat | 138:20

Gentes: augescunt aliae g. | 321:1
multas per g. | 133:20

Gentile: might of the G. | 118:39

Gentiles: boastings as the G. use | 300:26

Gentility: cottage of g. | 151:11, 507:21

Gentle: brave notions and g. ex-
pressions | 280:1
each g. and each dreadful scene | 37:6
g. and virtuous deeds | 328:1
g. as falcon | 502:17
g. Jesus, meek and mild | 565:9
g. kind of the lioun | 138:20
g. lady married to the Moor | 578:21
g. mind by g. deeds is known | 510:9
g., plain, just | 568:7
g. shepherd, tell me where | 264:14
g. thing like me | 585:10
he is g. that doth g. dedis | 138:12
her voice..g. and low | 454:24
his life was g. | 452:9
his manners were g. | 225:34
I knew a g. maid | 232:19
just, g., wise | 497:12
many a g. person..a Jack | 476:11
one of those g. ones | 484:21
pitee..in g. herte | 137:31
Sleep! it is a g. thing | 149:27
some g. Muse | 342:11
this day..g. his condition | 444:28(–445)
though g., yet not dull | 172:10
very g. beast | 467:31
very parfit g. knight | 136:24

Gentle-hearted: my g. Charles | 152:2

Gentleman: as a g. switches his
cane | 151:8
be a little g. | 249:23
cannot make a g. | 103:27
fat g. in such a passion | 202:17
fine old English g. | 8:5
fine puss-g. | 159:19
finish'd g. | 116:42
first true g. | 170:18
g. and scholar | 108:18
g...never go beyond a song | 202:3
g...never inflicts pain | 363:25
g. on whom..absolute trust
456:27(–457)
g. said to the fi' pun' note | 178:41
g., though spoiled i' the breeding | 82:26
g. to haul..with the mariner | 189:1
G. who held the patent for his
honours | 105:16
grand old name of g. | 533:23
'I am a g.' | 482:24
'no g.'s library..without' | 306:26
not..a braver g. | 440:28
not quite a g. | 20:27
old worshipful g. | 5:10
once a g., and always a g. | 176:3
Prince of Darkness is a g.
453:25, 517:15
prosperous g. | 456:17
since every Jack..a g. | 476:11
so stout a g. | 440:38
stainless g. | 531:20
stamps a man..as an educated g. | 490:4
St. Patrick was a g. | 42:19
talking about being a g. | 518:5
tea..is a g. | 142:9
this knight..a valiant g. | 202:12
true breeding of a g. | 115:41
unable to describe a g. | 549:13
very gallant g. | 21:8

B 3806

B b

INDEX

Grave (*cont.*)

g. is not its goal	317:5
g. man. . Adam	146:16
g.'s a fine and private place	333:9
g.'s one violet	94:45
g. so rough	536:20
g. unto a soul	447:33
g. where English oak	238:26
g., where is thy victory?	67:18
her heart in his g.	356:31
in cold g. she was lain	32:16
in his g. rain'd many a tear	436:30
in his vast and wandering g.	532:7
in love with the g.	203:28
in the cold g.	253:28
in the dark and silent g.	405:12
jealousy is cruel as the g.	52:22
keep a dream or g. apart	89:3
kind of healthy g.	505:35
lead but to the g.	230:1
lead thee to thy g.	583:2
lead these graces to the g.	482:20
learned the secrets of the g.	374:11
lies a mould'ring in the g.	234:7
little little g., an obscure g.	475:10
marriage is a step so g.	514:28
meteor on the g.	118:8
mild o'er her g.	18:19
moral, g.	27:19
most. . have sunk into the g.	270:28
mourn all at her g.	32:16
my g., as now my bed	87:1
never find my g.	483:6
no repentance in the g.	561:21
not have strewed thy g.	437:22
not rest in an English g.	119:33
now in his colde g.	137:34
no work. . in the g.	51:21
O G., thy victoree?	8:19
old and godly and g.	585:14
on his g. . . the Syrian stars	17:9
our mother, but our g.	460:19
over the g. of Clooth-na-Bare	585:7
pay you in the g.	494:9
peace is in the g.	496:26
perhaps her g.	346:12
pompous in the g.	87:20
potent, g., and reverend signiors	469:45
precedence in the g.	292:20
renowned be thy g.	430:1
she is in her g.	580:18
sitting crowned upon the g.	248:23
soldier. . a quiet, g. man	29:6
soldier's g.	118:27
straight and dusty to the g.	514:30
temple of fame. . upon the g.	239:20
that ayont the g.	108:17
that dark inn, the g.	417:31
there lies a lonely g.	3:16
this g. . . a living monument	437:26
thy g. with rising flow'rs	381:35
thy humble g. adorned	381:34
thy root is ever in its g.	245:13
to glory, or the g.	122:19
tongue. . silent in the g.	161:8
travelling towards the g.	579:3
twice at the grip of the G.	302:29
untimely g.	125:3
upon his mother's g.	578:30
when my g. is broke up	186:8
where, G., thy victory?	322:2
without a g.	114:28
with profitable labour to his g.	444:23
with sorrow to the g.	45:21

Grave-digger: if I were a g. 269:14
Gravel: grubbing weeds from g. paths 296:32
I 'eard the feet on the g. 294:25
Gravelled for lack of matter 428:20
Grave-makers: gardeners, ditchers, and g. 437:5
Graven: not make. . any g. image 390:7
Gravender: my g., or grub 414:6
Graver: g. had a strife 281:9
His g. of frost 545:13
Graves: about the g. of the martyrs 516:9
arise from their g. and aspire 76:7
emblem of untimely g. 163:29
find ourselves dishonourable g. 448:22
follow us disquietly to our g. 452:16
g. have learnt 186:8

Graves (*cont.*)

g. of deceased languages	175:6
g. stood tenantless	430:14
have no g. as yet	140:24
have their g. at home	140:24
let's talk of g.	475:6
their g. are sever'd	241:8
they watch from their g.	93:4
uncut hair of g.	567:12

Gravitation: shall g. cease? 384:5
Gravity: g. out of his bed 439:29
reasons find of settled g. 486:33
Gravy: person who disliked g. 504:26
Gray: Auld Robin G. . . came a-courting 35:8
G.'s poetry. . above the common mark 273:12
Grayling: g. aleap in the river 422:22
here and there a g. 528:7
Graymalkin: I come, G. 456:3
Graze: g. him as he passes 38:24
neither g. nor pierce 472:32
Grazed: g the common of literature 271:7
Grazing: satyrs g. on the lawns 329:20
Greasy: fat and g. citizens 426:33
g. Joan 456:1
grey-green, g. Limpopo River 304:17
Great: aim not to be g. 322:4
all creatures g. and small 3:14
all g. men make mistakes 143:33
applause so g. as thine 158:4
as g. as is my grief 475:9
because his soul was g. 188:33
between the small and g. 164:12
biography of g. men 126:24
both g. and small 150:16
compare g. things with small 346:13
consent of all g. men 413:18
darkly wise, and rudely g. 383:22
disbelief in g. men 126:23
do this g. thing 48:25
Dr. Busby, a g. man 2:17
dull. . made many people think him g. 272:23
even g. men have. . poor relations 174:2
everything that is g. . . done by youth 181:36
far above the g. 231:16
fears of being g. 529:34
from the ashes of g. men 239:20
frown o' the g. 430:1
good, g. and joyous 497:17
g. and hardy genius 226:27
g. as a king 173:9
g. break through 499:18
g. by land 537:17
g. empire and little minds 101:14
g., ere fortune made him so 192:2
g. grey-green, greasy 304:17
g. is Diana of the Ephesians 65:8
g. is Truth 56:17
g., just, good God 96:6
g. man down 435:12
g. man helped the poor 323:21
g. man's memory. . outlive his life 435:5
g. Marlbro's mighty soul 1:9
g. men are not always wise 49:12
g. men are the guide-posts 100:10
g. men contending with adversity 109:16
g. men. . inspired texts 127:16
g. men may jest with saints 461:32
g. men. . not. . g. scholars 251:18
g. men. . see. . that thoughts rule 201:4
g. no heart 97:33
g. ones devour'd the small 501:14
g. right of an excessive wrong 96:3
g. to do that thing that ends 425:33
g. to little man 226:6
g. was the fall of it 58:28
g. without a foe 114:24
he bears too g. a mind 451:37
heights by g. men reached 316:31
he is always g. 194:6
how g. should be 319:7
how indigent the g. 231:7
how very small the very g. 543:13
if you would grow g. 515:23
in man. . nothing g. but mind 235:4

Great (*cont.*)

instinct of all g. souls	100:11
I shall be very proud and g.	515:18
just as he really promised something g.	116:35
know well I am not g.	530:35
Life of Johnson. . a very g. work	325:26
lives of g. men	317:8
men in g. place	26:22
nearer the g. white throne	131:32
no g. and no small	199:1
no g. man lives in vain	126:24
not exercise myself in g. matters	400:1
nothing g. . . without enthusiasm	200:9
not ignorant. . in a g. matter	56:35
on earth. . nothing g. but man	235:4
only know it shall be g.	264:7
only truly g. . . from the passions	181:42
only truly g. who are truly good	135:23
packs and sets of g. ones	454:19
poetry. . g. and unobtrusive	289:25
poorly rich, and meanly g.	415:17
rightly to be g.	436:17
rising to g. place	26:28
rule of men entirely g.	322:11
seekest thou g. things for thyself?	55:22
silence alone is g.	553:2
simple g. ones	535:43
smallest. . ever set in a g. place	29:5
some men are born g.	483:29
streets where the g. men go	208:5
that Caesar might be g.	122:36
that he is grown so g.	448:23
that which once was g.	582:8
these are g. days	144:7
those who were truly g.	509:1
though fallen, g.	113:19
thou wouldst be g.	457:1
to be g. is to be misunderstood	200:41
to do a g. right	465:2
to g. ones 'longs	461:28
to grow g. in fame	173:4
too humble nor too g.	327:14
weigh this song with the g.	584:22
what did you do in the G. War?	11:15
whatever was little seemed. . g.	325:22
whenever he met a g. man	542:34
when the g. and good depart	575:1
while the g. and wise decay	312:24
with a g. thing to pursue	91:41
with consistency a g. soul	200:40
without terror g.	401:22
with small men no g. thing	339:1
worship of the g. of old	118:10
your g. and gracious ways	375:1

Great-coat: shaggy white g. 175:12
Greater: Brutus makes mine g. 451:22
consent. . that he is g. than they 413:18
four things g. than all things 294:29
g. are none 303:5
g. glory dim the less 405:21
g. man, the g. courtesy 531:1
g. prey upon the less 231:26
g. than both 457:4
g. than Solomon 59:17
g. than their knowing 302:4
g. than the King 379:6
g. than themselves 448:27
g. than we know 573:27
there's something g. 128:3
thy necessity. . g. than mine 502:12
Greatest: as the g. he 405:6
given you the g. of all things 489:28
g. as not exempted 253:36
g. happiness for the g. numbers 266:11
g., nor the worst of men 113:40
g. of these is charity 66:46(-67)
how much the g. event 210:20
not be among the g. 290:8
one of the g. . . poems 194:11
standing with the g. man 276:24
Great-heart: one G. 99:30
Great-hearted gentlemen 90:16
Greatly: come into port g. 200:18
Greatness: all g. . . not. . exact 100:6
all the far-stretched g. 405:13
base on which thy g. stands 579:34
be not afraid of g. 483:18
boy my g. 426:4
farewell to all my g. 446:24

INDEX

INDEX

INDEX

INDEX

INDEX

INDEX

Ridiculous (cont.)
sublime to the r.	228:8, 361:2
wasteful and r. excess	447:39

Riding: highwayman came r. — 366:1
my r. is better — 92:38
r. down by the Eildon Tree — 32:6
r. near her highest noon — 341:14
r. o'er land — 114:39
r. o'er the azure realm — 229:23
r.'s a joy — 92:39
r. to the townland — 585:6

Rife: blessings are plentiful and r. 245:8
Riff-raff .. to what is respectable 254:8
Rifiuto: il gran r. — 168:19
Rifle: r. all the breathing Spring 153:21
roll to your r. — 304:4
your r. an' yourself jus' so — 295:22
Riflemen Form! — 540:5
Rift: little r. within the lute — 531:11
load every r...with ore — 291:1
Riga: young lady of R. — 11:2
Rigdum-Funnidos: gentle R. 125:14
Rigged with curses dark — 342:25
Riggish: bless her when she is r. 424:9
Right: all is r. as r. can be — 219:18
all's r. with the world — 94:40
always in the r. — 159:14
and I am r., and you are r. — 219:18
as God gives us to see the r. 314:13
as men strive for R. — 88:24
as much r...as pigs have to fly 129:19
attains to think r. — 278:8
at thy r. hand..pleasure — 392:27
aye upheld the r. — 324:6
because not all was r. — 165:11
because r. is r., to follow r. 537:33
Bertram's r. — 419:35
born to set it r. — 432:32
by the r. way — 398:15
Christ thy r. — 354:11
circles and r. lines — 87:13
dare not be in the r. with two
  or three — 320:15
dawn on my r. — 41:20
did not write it r. — 248:12
do the R. — 327:3
do what is r. — 266:21
earl by r. — 23:13
every single one..is r. — 297:9
firmness in the r. — 314:13
generalities of natural r. 142:25
great r. of an excessive wrong 96:3
heaven still guards the r. 475:1
he's all r. — 233:12
his conduct still r. — 225:29
his life..was in the r. — 158:5
his r. hand doth embrace me 51:45
in his r. mind — 60:58
in thy r. hand..peace — 446:31
it must be r. — 164:32
Judge of all the earth do r. 44:52
length of days is in her r. hand 49:40
little from the r. — 165:16
makes us r. or wrang — 105:22
meet and r. so to do — 390:38
minorities..always in the r. 505:9
my r. good-will — 327:5
my r. hand forget her cunning 400:5
my r. there is none to dispute 164:22
of r. and wrong he taught 14:26
on the r. went down — 148:21
our country, r. or wrong 169:28
publish, r. or wrong — 117:9
quite lawful nor quite r. 111:35
rage to set things r. — 89:25
rather be r. than be President 140:2
reading is r. — 278:25
Real R. Thing — 268:10
renew a r. spirit — 395:9
reprove her when she's r. 520:55
r. against the eastern gate 341:13
r. and round about — 106:18
r. as a Ribstone Pippin — 41:25
r., by chance — 159:12
r. deed for the wrong reason 197:25
R. Divine..to govern wrong 381:24
r. good captain too — 221:10
r. hand of the Lord — 399:8, 9
r. hands of fellowship — 67:40
r. it should be so — 73:24
r. little, tight little Island 173:15

Right (cont.)
r. makes might — 314:8
r. man in the r. place — 268:29
r. man to fill the r. place 310:25
r. of an earlier creation — 325:4
r. of election — 282:17
r. of governing — 210:21
r. of the ignorant — 126:5
r. part wrote Liddell — 11:7
r. was r. — 165:10
secure of private r. — 190:28
servant unto r. — 509:35
serve it r. for being so dear 177:2
set thee r. — 161:10
sit thou on my r. hand — 398:23
smite thee on thy r. cheek 57:50
sometimes in the r. — 194:9
speak true, r. wrong — 530:4
talks about justice and r. 300:7
ten thousand at thy r. hand 397:18
that which is lawful and r. 55:30
thing that is r. — 394:6
thing which is r. — 392:24
think, at your age, it is r.? 128:28
think it only r. — 221:12
though r. were worsted — 97:4
thy r. hand shall hold me 400:9
thy r. hand shall teach thee 394:22
to do a great r. — 465:2
too fond of the r. — 225:28
to set me r. — 308:24
Ulster will be r. — 143:29
upon thy r. hand..the queen 394:23
whatever is, is r. — 383:21
what's r. and fair — 265:1
what thy r. hand doeth — 58:2
when all goes r. — 222:1
when the r. man rings them 516:3
where r. is wrong — 218:6
who'll do him r. now? — 90:17
whose life is in the r. — 384:1
without so much labour appear
  to be r. — 278:25
your judgement..probably .. r. 329:11
your r. to say it — 557:15
Right-doing: relinquish r., even in
  dreams — 120:17
Right-down regular Royal Queen 218:21
Righteous: armor of a r. cause 98:1
be not r. over much — 51:14
death of the r. — 46:18
dwellings of the r. — 399:8
fervent prayer of a r. man 69:44
God is a r. Judge — 392:7
godly, r. and sober — 388:12
let the r. rather smite me 400:14
not come to call the r. — 58:40
O ye r. — 393:35
r. are bold as a lion — 50:49
r., let him be r. still — 72:8
r. man regardeth..his beast 50:2
r. minds of inn-keepers 142:1
r. put their hand unto wickedness 399:33
r. work..not be forgiven 140:4
saw I never the r. forsaken 394:5
souls of the r. — 56:23
what hath the r. done? — 392:19
when the r. man turneth away 111:35
Righteousness: from original r. 401:5
fulfil all r. — 57:32
he looked for..r — 53:2
little hills r. — 396:23
living unto r. — 390:59
makes for r. — 20:14, 17
paths of r. — 393:10, 421:1
r. and peace have kissed 397:9
r. exalteth a nation — 50:9
r. hath looked down — 397:9
r. shall go before him — 397:10
Sun of r. arise — 56:15
thirst after r. — 57:39
thy r. as clear — 394:4
thy r. as the waves — 54:20
thy r. unto the King's son 396:22
what r. really is — 20:18
word of..r. — 394:22
worketh not the r. of God 69:30
your r...exceed the r. of the
  scribes — 57:44
Righteousnesses: our r...as filthy
  rags — 55:8

Rightful: for our r. King — 106:16
Right-hand foot — 131:25
Righting: good for r. wrongs 315:12
Right-lined: mortal r. circle 87:13
Rightly done! — 265:20
Rights: its duties as well as its r. 189:24
lies in his r. of a man — 89:13
r. inherent and inalienable 268:19
r. of an Englishman — 282:16
unalienable r. — 11:11
whose r. he has trodden 101:27
Rigid: very r. and exact — 293:2
Rigida: pallidula r. nudula 233:19
Rigol: this golden r. — 442:26
Rigour: my r. relents — 100:25
Riled: no sense in gittin' r. 238:28
Riles: Christian r. — 300:6
Rill: Siloam's shady r. — 240:16
Rills: bright with sinuous r. 151:32
r. fashion..their nursling 309:5
Rim: over the mountain's r. 94:27
Sun's r. dips — 149:14
utmost purple r. — 528:29
Rime-ringed: to the r. sun 298:28
Rimini: Francesca di R. — 221:6
Rimmon: in the house of R. 48:23
Rind: burnished with golden r. 347:5
from out the r. of one apple 352:8
how shall taste the r.? — 544:25
in the r...scooped — 347:14
sweet as the r. was — 522:26
Ring: bright gold r. — 356:30
curfew must not r. to-night 547:6
draw the chalky r. — 164:8
for one shilling your r. — 312:2
for you alone I ride the r. 228:13
he rid at the r. — 30:9
maids dance in a r. — 361:6
more than gold was in a r. 140:26
only pretty r. time — 428:30
rare gold r. of verse — 96:17
r. at the end of his nose 312:1
r. from their marble caves 190:3
r. O bells — 566:28(-567)
r. of pure and endless light 552:13
r. of words — 516:3
r. out..r. in — 533:18, 19, 20
r. out, wild bells — 533:17
r. out ye crystal spheres 343:17
r. so worn — 105:21
r. that he had of your daughter 464:11
r. the bells of Heaven 249:5
round both the shires they r. 262:21
sleeps on his luminous r. 537:35
they now r. the bells — 558:30
this R. given and received 391:33
unconquered in a r. — 141:30
what shall we do for a r.? 312:1
with this R. I thee wed 391:32
Ringdove's neck — 123:5
Ringed: r. round with a flame 523:2
r. with the azure world 529:10
Ringing down the street — 23:22
Ringlets: green sour r. — 480:12
male r. — 523:4
Ringlet-snake: Fury's r. 535:20
Rings: as in airy r. — 386:32
chain of countless r. — 199:17
his hands are as gold r. 52:14
right man r. them — 516:3
r. on her fingers — 368:17
wearers of r. and chains 308:24
Rinsed with wine — 254:27
Rio: rolling down to R. — 297:24
Riot: luxury and r. — 349:27
rash fierce blaze of r. — 474:21
Riotous living — 62:13
Ripae ulterioris amore — 554:28
Ripe: cherry r. — 4:14, 124:5, 245:21
r. and good one — 447:9
we r. and r. — 427:14
what shelter to grow r. — 17:4
Ripeness: certain r. in intellect 289:26
r. is all — 454:18
when love is grown to r. 533:34
Ripening: his greatness is a-r. 446:24
Riper: of R. Years — 390:61
Ripes: ventiferous r. — 251:19
Ripped: from his mother's womb
  untimely r. — 461:11
Ripple: slip and r. idly — 336:7

INDEX

INDEX

Sheep (cont.)

like a flock of s.	52:5
like lost s.	388:10
like s. have gone astray	54:26
little hills like young s.	399:3
looking on their silly s.	446:2
lost her s.	307:14
lost s. of the house of Israel	58:46
mountain s...valley s.	376:23
noble ensample to his s.	137:17
old half-witted s.	512:6
one sickly s.	501:30
or else their s.	343:15
other s. I have	63:39
plunge the struggling s.	323:12
s. before her shearers	54:26
s. of his hand	397:28
s.'s guts..hale souls	468:19
s.'s in the meadow	367:15
s. that have not a shepherd	48:13
s. which was lost	62:11
when the s. are in the fauld	35:7
white over with s.	499:14
who were thy s.	351:20
with His s. securely fold you	406:1
your s...wont to be so meek	358:12
Sheep-bells and the ship-bells	302:10
Sheep-hook: how to hold a s.	342:28
Sheep-worry of Europe	82:14
Sheer: bare, s., penetrating power	19:19
down a furlong s.	301:27
Sheet: float that standard s.	234:13
great s. knit	64:46
s. were big enough	483:34
wet s. and a flowing sea	167:20
white s. bleaching	485:16
Sheets: cool kindliness of s.	83:21
fumble with the s.	443:19
whitest s. of snow	166:3
Sheffield: Brooks of S.	174:12
Shelf: from a s. the..diadem	435:49
occupy one s.	89:29
on a s. of rock or sand	580:10
upper s.	325:1
Shell: kill him in the s.	449:4
like a rainbow s.	409:14
shaved with a s.	309:28
smooth-lipped s.	574:20
thine outgrown s.	251:15
within thy airy s.	340:13
Shelley: Burns, S., were with us	93:4
peace in S.'s mind	494:12
see S. plain	93:23
S., whom envy never touched	309:20
sphere for S.'s genius	19:13
there S. dream'd	269:24
to us arose S.	80:24
Shellover: 'Come!' said old S.	171:23
Shells: silver bells and cockle s.	367:21
sinuous s., of pearly hue	308:26
Shelly horns	336:38
Shelter: I'd s. thee	107:24
our s. from the stormy blast	562:9
s. me from the cold	42:7
what s. to grow ripe is ours?	17:4
Sheltered: in youth it s. me	358:21
s. about the Mahogany Tree	543:11
Shelters: naught s. thee	544:19
Shelves: spoilers of the symmetry of s.	306:21
Shem: it might be S.	303:9
S., Ham and Japheth	44:36
Tents of S.	298:27
Shenandoah, I long to hear you	8:21
Shepherd: calls up the s.	462:22
dead s.	428:15
Dick the s.	456:1
equals the s. with the king	134:18
every s.'s tongue	405:8
every s. tells his tale	341:34
fairest s. on our green	377:2
faithful s.l to come	17:19
feed his flock like a s.	54:11
gentle S., tell me where	264:14
God of love my S. is	245:10
good s. giveth his life	63:37
King of Love my S. is	29:12
lark to s.'s ear	466:21
Love tunes the s.'s reed	417:16
not love a s. swain	232:5
philosophy in thee, s.?	427:24

Shepherd (cont.)

sheep that have not a s.	48:13
S. and Bishop of your souls	69:52
s., blowing of his nails	445:44
s. in Virgil	270:17
s., I take thy word	340:17
s.—of his love	33:13
s. of the Hebrid Isles	546:3
s. of the Ocean	509:9
S.'s care	2:21
S.'s sweet lot	76:11
slighted, s.'s trade	342:20
sweet unto a s.	232:5
the Lord is my s.	393:10
the Lord's my s.	421:1
they call you, S.	18:5
weather the s. shuns	236:32
Shepherd-boy: happy S.	576:6
Shepherdess of sheep	338:8
Shepherdesses: ancient s. I have read of	370:17
Shepherding her bright fountains	492:20
Shepherds: British s.	574:2
liberal s. give a grosser name	437:1
s., looking on their silly sheep	446:2
warmth of s.' flames	331:2
while s. watch'd	527:4
Sheridan: S. twenty miles away	406:3
S. was listened to	408:11
Sheriffmuir: at S.	327:1
Sherris: this valour comes of s.	442:21
Sherris-sack: good s.	442:21
Sherry: S. is dull	271:14
with ham and s.	84:5
Sherwood: in S., in S.	366:5
S. in the red dawn	366:6
Sheugh: nor yet in any s.	33:2
She-wolf: eats the s.'s young	150:9
Shield: broken s. was hung	140:18
broken was her s.!	418:35
courteout knight that ever bare s.	328:24
left the s.	418:11
s. of faith	68:13
s. of the mighty..cast away	47:29
sword, a horse, a s.	319:10
thy s. and buckler	397:18
wisdom the mirrored s.	491:27
Shielding men from the effects of folly	508:23
Shields: s. in Branksome Hall	417:3
s. of mighty men	52:5
Shieling: from the lone s.	420:31
Shift: coming down..s. for myself	358:6
s. one's position	267:24
we'll s. our ground	432:26
we s. and bedeck	522:22
Shifted his trumpet	225:35
Shifting his sail	161:38
Shifts her passions	215:14
Shilling: Philip and Mary on a s.	111:8
raise the volume's price a s.	521:19
sell for one s. your ring	312:2
s. a day	301:12
Splendid S.	378:17
Shillings: payment of half twenty s.	100:5
reduced the answer to s. and pence	129:28
Shimmered: Jeeves s. out	572:9
Shine: afar off s. bright	563:15
anxious for to s.	220:25
arise, s.	54:39
betwixt the s. and shade	527:12
coin of silvery s.	131:24
every one doth s.	449:30
fair days will s.	221:30
few are qualified to s.	520:41
his face s. upon thee	46:10
if the moon s. at full or no	111:4
I'll s. on ye yet	167:24
let your light so s. before men	57:42
no shade, no s.	253:12
nothing does but s.	545:11
not to s. in use	540:32(-541)
scatteringly doth s.	332:8
see him s. so brisk	438:35
s., and seek to mend	185:18
s. as it shines now	185:24
s. forth upon our clouded hills	75:16
s. in my arms	231:38

Shine (cont.)

s. inward	346:20
s. no more	160:22
s. on all alike	385:11
s. the traffic of Jacob's ladder	545:1
s. through the gloom	322:2
s. upon the road	161:1
s. with Pye	117:14
singing as they s.	2:28
that sun..shall s. on me	474:13
they shall s...like sparks	56:24
wit will s.	193:11
Shined: how Bacon s.	384:12
in her person s.	351:25
s. at Lugwardin	548:17
s. in my angel-infancy	552:3
Shines: how s. your tower	77:30
more it's shook it s.	235:3
she s. sae bright	108:31
s. brightly as a king	465:21
s. over city and river	537:16
Shinest: wheresoe'er thou s.	497:9
Shineth: light s. in darkness	62:60
s. more and more	49:43
Shingles: naked s. of the world	15:7
Shining: calculation s. out of the other	176:10
I see it s. plain	263:14
once a s. store	160:22
profit of their s. nights	454:32
quietly s. to the quiet moon	151:25
season of clear s.	161:21
s. morning face	427:21
s. nowhere but in the dark	552:10
s. still	19:1
s. with all his might	130:9
somewhere the sun is s.	238:6
through the dark cloud s.	210:4
transient, s. trouble	228:18
Shins: break my s. against it	427:5
Ship: all I ask is a tall s.	334:10
brake that gallant s.	30:19
carcasses of many a tall s.	464:6
ever scuttled s.	115:41
gart build a bonny s.	31:8
he was born in a s.	16:3
idle as a painted s.	149:5
in a s...in a jail	270:32
into our s.'s side	31:25(-32)
it reached the s.	150:10
land to which the s. would go	147:13
like a stately s.	350:31
one leak will sink a s.	99:28
O S. of State!	316:1
our s. hath touch'd..Bohemia	485:14
our s. not far from land	9:3
rapt s. run on her side	135:19
s. after s., the whole night long	539:21
s., an isle, a sickle moon	208:19
s. has weather'd every rack	566:27
s. I have got	30:23
s. in a black storm	503:34
s. is anchor'd	566:28
s. is clear at last, she leaps	566:25
s. is floating in the harbour	493:12
s. me somewheres east of Suez	299:15
s.'s huge shadow	149:25
s. that goes	173:8
s. was cheered	148:21
s. was still	507:24
s. went down like lead	150:10
s. would not travel due West!	128:9
sink me the s.	540:1
so old a s.	208:16
stately s. is seen no more	312:24
there was a s.	148:20
to which yon S. must go	582:16
undergirding the s.	65:28
victor s. comes in	566:28
way of a s.	50:56
we too take s. O soul	567:2
what is a s. but a prison?	109:19
when you go on board s.	39:1
whither, O splendid s.	81:26
Ship-bells: sheep-bells and the s.	302:10
Ship-boy: seel up the s.'s eyes	442:1
Shipman: a S. was ther	137:11
Shipmate: joy, s., joy!	566:25
Shipping: fishes first to s.	191:29
sink all the s. there	281:19
Ships: break the s. of the sea	394:34

T